THE BATTLE OF BRITAIN
THEN AND NOW

Edited by Winston G. Ramsey

AN

PUBLICATION

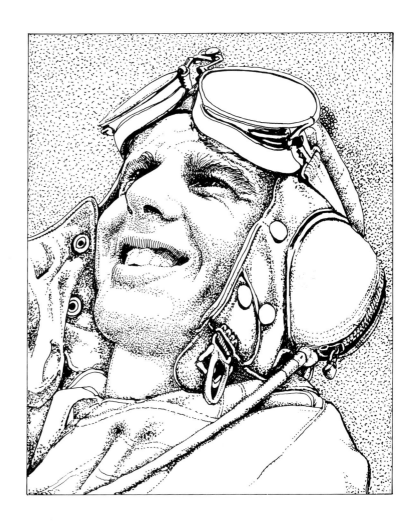

© After the Battle Magazine, 1980

ISBN 0-9009 13-19-3

Printed in Great Britain.

Designed and edited by
Winston G. Ramsey
Editor *After the Battle* magazine.

PUBLISHERS
Battle of Britain Prints International Limited,
3 New Plaistow Road,
London, E15 3JA
England.

PRINTERS
Plaistow Press Limited,
3 New Plaistow Road,
London, E15 3JA
England.

PHOTOGRAPHS
Copyright is indicated on all wartime photographs where known. All present-day photographs (including aerial photographs) copyright *After the Battle* magazine unless stated otherwise.

EXTRACTS
Extract from *The Second World War Volume II Their Finest Hour* by Winston S. Churchill by permission of Cassell Limited.

FRONT COVER
Reproduced from a painting by George A. Campbell of nineteen-year-old Pilot Officer Keith Gillman of No. 32 Squadron missing over the Channel on August 25, 1940.

BACK COVER
The seldom recognised but equally important part of the summer air battles of 1940 — the skilled, diligent work of the ground crews. Here armourers from No. 312 (Czech) Squadron re-arm L1926 at Duxford in September 1940. In the eight-gun fighters, a typical loading would consist of De Wilde in one gun (an incendiary ammunition without a tracer effect but in short supply during the battle); armour piercing in two guns; the old-type of incendiary in another two (which gave a smoke-tracer effect) and ball in the remaining three (Imperial War Museum).

FRONT ENDPAPER
'A' Flight dispersal at North Weald during the battle. Squadron Leader G. A. L. Manton, CO of No. 56 Squadron, on the telephone with Flight Lieutenant Percy Weaver on the left, killed in action on August 31, 1940, and Flying Officer R. E. B. Brooker killed later in the war.

REAR ENDPAPER
Clip from a cine film taken during the battle. A Hurricane, R4197, from No. 56 Squadron at the forward base of Rochford.

THEN AND NOW FOOTNOTE
The price of the book (£24.95) if reflected in 1940 prices would have been £1 14s 2d (£1.71). The purchasing power of £1 in 1980 is now only 6.87p in 'Battle of Britain' money. Put another way, one would now need £14.55 to purchase what £1 would have bought during the battle.

Editor's Acknowledgement

With a book as complex as this, a complete acknowledgement list would be formidable. There are our authors and contributors; the relatives of all those that were killed in 1940, and who have co-operated in every way; the countless individuals who helped and guided us during our travels all over the United Kingdom taking the photographs, and the many other people and official bodies who gave invaluable help. The book could not have been produced without the considerable assistance provided by the Commonwealth War Graves Commission, and the Editor is indebted to Hazel Kissoon for putting up with regular Monday morning telephone calls over several months. Likewise Patricia Elderfield of the Ministry of Defence AR9 casualty branch was most understanding and always willing to help, as was Dennis Bateman of the Air Historical Branch.

Although it has been a routine printing job for Plaistow Press, the size of the project has meant a considerable effort by all members of the staff, many of whom worked long hours to complete their role on time. Everyone really gave of their best and they should be very proud of the result.

On a more personal level, Wilf Nicoll has been a pillar of enthusiasm and support from the very first conception of the idea of presenting the Battle of Britain in a 'then and now' format. My mother and her husband, George Campbell, came to my assistance in visiting and photographing a great proportion of the graves of 'The Few' and became totally committed to the task which lasted many weeks. My long suffering but extremely tolerant wife Jennifer has accepted without complaint late hours and working weekends for too long to remember, and my son has helped with many duties during the eighteen months it has taken us to bring this project to fruition. Without you I could not have completed the task — thank you all very much.

OPENING CHAPTER PHOTOGRAPHS

The Few
Page 6
The Battle of Britain is recreated over Kent in 1952 during the filming of *Angels One Five* using Hurricanes from the Portuguese Air Force.

The Way it was . . .
Pages 8-9
Pilots of No. 32 Squadron at 'A' Flight dispersal at Hawkinge, July 1940 - see page 110 (Fox Photos).
Pages 10-11
Possibly taken at Hornchurch, Spitfires scramble for a patrol over London. A machine from No. 610 Squadron is parked in the foreground but the other squadron codes are too indistinct to be positively identified.

The Aerodromes
Page 29
Tangmere in October 1979 with its satellite Westhampnett in the background.

The Casualties
Pages 250-251
Funeral of Flight Lieutenant Hugh Beresford at Brookwood Military Cemetery, November 16, 1979.

The Aircraft Losses
Pages 314-315
A Spitfire triumphantly circles the burning wreck of Heinkel He 111, serial 5680, of I/KG26 at Burmarsh, Kent shot down by British fighters and anti-aircraft fire on September 11, 1940 (Fox Photos).

The Royal Air Force
Page 319
Hurricane V6799 of No. 501 Squadron which forced-landed outside Folkestone after Pilot Officer K. W. MacKenzie hit a Messerschmitt Bf 109 with his starboard wing on October 7, 1940 (Fox Photos).

The Luftwaffe
Pages 534-535
Heinkel He 111, serial 3305, brought down on Haxted Farm, Lingfield, near Oxted on August 30, 1940 (Fox Photos).

Tribute to The Few
Pages 716-717
Winston Churchill visits the crash site of Messerschmitt Bf 109E-4, serial 941, of Stab I/JG3 at Church Whitfield, near Dover on August 28, 1940 (Imperial War Museum).

Contents

INTRODUCTION 4

ULTRA AND THE BATTLE OF BRITAIN 5

FOREWORD *Gwen Black* 7

THE WAY IT WAS . . . *Wilf Nicoll* 8

THE COMMANDERS 12

THE OPERATION ROOMS 14

THE AERODROMES 29

For convenience, the aerodromes are grouped geographically according to the map on pages 16-17. These are not necessarily the Sectors under which they were controlled in the battle.

SECTOR A
Tangmere Sector Station *Jim Beedle* 30
Westhampnett *Wilf Nicoll* 42

SECTOR B
Kenley Sector Station *Peter Corbell* 46
Croydon *Wilf Nicoll* 52

SECTOR C
Biggin Hill Sector Station *Peter Halliday* 62
West Malling *Robin J. Brooks* 70

SECTOR D
Hornchurch Sector Station *Group Captain H. T. Sutton* 76
Hawkinge *Roy Humphreys* 88
Gravesend *Ray Munday* 136
Manston *The Late Flying Officer W. Fraser* 143
Rochford *Bill Gent* 154

SECTOR E
North Weald Sector Station *Wilf Nicoll* 160
Martlesham Heath *Wilf Nicoll* 176
Stapleford Tawney *Peter Norris* 184

SECTOR F
Debden Sector Station *Keith Braybrooke* 190

SECTOR G
Duxford/Fowlmere Sector Station *Alister Raby* 198

SECTOR W
Exeter *Michael Payne* 212

SECTOR Y
Middle Wallop Sector Station *Norman Parker* 218
Warmwell *Ivan Mason* 230

SECTOR Z
Northolt Sector Station *Peter Norris* 236

THE CASUALTIES 250

THE RUNNYMEDE MEMORIAL 298

THE POLISH MEMORIAL 302

THE BATTLE OF BRITAIN VC *Andy Saunders* 306

THE AIRCRAFT LOSSES *Peter D. Cornwell* 314

AVIATION ARCHAEOLOGY AND THE BATTLE OF BRITAIN 317

THE ROYAL AIR FORCE 319
July 320
August 337
September 404
October 491

THE LUFTWAFFE 534
July 537
August 552
September 614
October 671

THE BALANCE SHEET 706

THE SURVIVORS *Gordon Riley* 708

THE BATTLE OF BRITAIN MEMORIAL FLIGHT 714

TRIBUTE TO THE FEW 716

ADDENDA 718

Many excellent accounts have been written about the Battle of Britain since the summer of 1940 when the existence of the free world hung in the balance. This book is in no way intended to compete with what has gone before but to be complementary and to bring a new dimension to the battle through the 'then and now' comparison photographs which are the theme of all *After the Battle* publications.

With the passage of forty years the countryside of England has seen varied changes. In some parts, such as at Gravesend and Hornchurch, development has meant a complete obliteration of the former aerodromes and our comparison photographs provide a fascinating contrast between these and other parts of the 'battleground' where little has changed over the intervening years. In most cases, the present day comparison picture has been taken during the same season as the original battle thus retaining the atmosphere of that fine summer in 1940.

It has been the editor's deliberate intention to present the battle from the defenders' — the British — angle. There are several reasons for this.

Firstly, by accepting to limit the coverage of the book to the events which took place between July and October 1940, one is acceding to the official British 'dating' of the battle. A publication orientated from the German point of view would begin shortly after the capture of Dunkirk and continue throughout the Blitz until the attack on Russia in May 1941 — all this period being considered by the Luftwaffe to be the 'Luftschlacht um England' or the air attack on England. To the Germans, the 'Battle of Britain' never existed in the traditional British sense.

Secondly, over seven years' experience of producing *After the Battle* magazine has made the difficulty of photographing in or around Continental military establishments or aerodromes abundantly clear. It would not have been possible to include comparison photographs, either on the ground or in the air, of all the bases used by the Luftwaffe which are now utilised by the air forces of Belgium, France, Holland or Norway. Also, as the temporary airstrips laid down by the Luftwaffe along the Channel coast have now reverted to farmland, 'then and now' photographs of these would have been extremely disappointing.

The problem of finding suitable photographs for comparison of the Royal Air Force aerodromes has been difficult to surmount as few pictures with a recognisable background were taken during the period of the battle. Private photography was forbidden by the authorities at the time and official contemporary coverage of some aerodromes is non-existent. This is partly the reason for the omission of some stations which would otherwise have been included. In addition those aerodromes in the far north saw little of the real fighting or bombing and others were used as rest or re-forming bases. We have therefore presented profiles of twenty of the most famous aerodromes associated with the battle, each one authored by an expert who has made a detailed study of 'his' aerodrome, together with an in-depth account of one typical Battle of Britain front line station.

Hawkinge was in the forefront of the battle from beginning to end and it is one of the few 'grass field' aerodromes of the period which has retained its former character. We are most fortunate to have as our author one who has lovingly studied Hawkinge from every angle during the past thirty years and it is solely due to Roy Humphreys' efforts that a memorial to all the aircrew who lost their lives flying from Hawkinge was erected on the perimeter in 1978.

Likewise Peter Cornwell has spent many years in research and study to perfect his record of every RAF and Luftwaffe crash throughout the period of the battle. Working with every form of reference including eye-

Introduction by the Editor

witness accounts, his listing can be considered the most accurate available today. However, Peter admits that the records made at the time leave much to be desired and it is by publication of this work that further information may come to light.

While not in any way decrying the efforts of those well-known personalities who survived the battle, it has been the editor's deliberate intention to give emphasis to the five hundred and thirty-seven pilots and aircrew who were killed — the true unsung heroes of the conflict. Some lasted only a matter of days; some hours. Some failed to score against the enemy and some died accidentally but all are included for, without their presence while fighting a numerically-superior foe, the battle would have surely been lost. That is why we have chosen to feature on our cover the face of one of the young men who died — that of nineteen-year-old Pilot Officer Keith Gillman of No. 32 Squadron who failed to return from a sortie over the Channel on August 25 — as the epitome of all those that were lost.

It is for a similar reason that we invited the widow of one of the pilots who was lost to write our foreword. It seems the done thing these days to introduce a book with a few well chosen words by some titled personality. However we feel it is more in keeping with the spirit which has guided this production to give that honour to one who can truly represent those that were lost.

The editorial staff have also visited the graves of every pilot and aircrew serving with Fighter Command who died during the battle. There is not a corner of England, Scotland, Ireland or Wales that does not have its local Battle of Britain hero. Some share the simple yet impressive Commonwealth War Graves Commission headstones while others, perhaps buried with mum or dad or brothers killed in other battles, have memorials as varied as they are numerous. Sadly, we found some overgrown and abandoned but we hope that publication of this book will help to rectify such cases and lead to the 'adoption' of those graves for whom there is no longer anyone to maintain them.

No expense or effort has been spared to bring this project to a conclusion. If in some way it helps to repay the debt we all owe to those that fought for us four decades ago, we can ask for no finer reward.

Ultra and the Battle of Britain

In 1974, publication of Group Captain F. W. Winterbotham's book *The Ultra Secret* threw doubts on every previously written account recording the history of the Second World War. The fact that the Allied commanders were provided with detailed advance knowledge of the enemy's plans and intentions through the remarkable British success of cryptanalysis (codenamed ULTRA), meant that many of our history books would have to be rewritten. The conduct of every battle was brought into question and not least that of the Battle of Britain.

The AOC-in-C Fighter Command, Air Chief-Marshal Sir Hugh Dowding, was naturally privy to the closely-guarded secret of Ultra. How detailed was his prior knowledge of the Luftwaffe's plans is not yet known as none of Fighter Command's Ultra decodes have been made public. However, hindsight enables us to re-read contemporary accounts looking for a new meaning in what would otherwise be innocuous statements, e.g. paragraph 118 of Dowding's despatch on the Battle of Britain published by the Air Ministry in September 1946: 'Although Secret Intelligence sources supplemented the information available, it is possible that on days of heavy fighting complete formations may have escaped recorded observation altogether.' Nevertheless what we do know is that, out of the three German services, the Luftwaffe in 1940 were the most prolific users of radio for sending messages enabling British listening stations to intercept and later decode them.

The few copies of Ultra messages which have been released are filed at the Public Record Office at Kew and, in the main, comprise naval with some military intelligence copies. An illustration of these is given with the fascimile reproduction of one which does concern Fighter Command in the chapter on Warmwell aerodrome. Therefore, one of the reasons why readers will not find the usual day-to-day account of the battle repeated in this book is that until the Fighter Command Ultra files are available, little can be added to what is already known.

However, the controversial 'Big Wing' argument can now be looked at afresh and it is certain that Dowding (and through him his No. 11 Group AOC Air Vice-Marshal Keith Park) operated their aircraft in the most suitable way *in the light of the knowledge that they knew in advance what the Luftwaffe was planning to do*. One considerable problem for Dowding must have been the difficulty of warning his own stations without giving away the top secret that he had advance warning of impending attacks. Only the most senior commanders were in on Ultra on a strict 'need to know' basis. Consequently, our author Ray Munday in his chapter on Gravesend raises an interesting theory that the formation of the Fighter Interception Unit by Air Vice-Marshal Park could have been specifically to enable Dowding to seem to act on information provided by its reconnaissance but that, in reality, he was only sending the unit out to where he knew the Luftwaffe would be found. When he warned his aerodromes of impending attacks, it would then seem to the controllers that their chief was acting on information from the FIU alone.

To Dowding's great credit, even when his conduct of the battle was brought into question at the meeting which eventually led to his dismissal, he refused to divulge in his defence one of the best kept secrets of the Second World War. On October 17, 1940, when the battle had virtually been won, Dowding's 'Big Wing' critics furthered their arguments at a high-level conference held at the Air Ministry in King Charles Street. Air Vice-Marshal Leigh-Mallory, AOC No. 10 Group, saw fit to bring along one of his young pilots (Squadron Leader Douglas Bader) to help argue the case against Keith Park, whose No. 11 Group had borne the brunt of the battle. Sir John Slessor, who was present at that meeting, comments in his foreword to *The Ultra Secret* that, 'I know that in his place, I should have been sorely tempted to use my knowledge of it (Ultra) to confute his more junior critics who, unfortunately but quite rightly had, for security reasons, not been admitted to this priceless secret.'

The Few

And most of them are gone, the gay, the bright ones,
  Whose laughter was too spiral for the earth;
  Who sought above the clouds a swifter mirth,
And found a strange peace there, the winged, the fleet ones.

Dawn with its gradual bugles found them soaring,
  And sunset made of earth a kindly toy,
  A place of sleep and warmth to eke their joy,
And bring them love's release from their exploring.

And all of them were young, their lustihood
  Full-set for zenith, vibrant as a flute;
  They knew hope's blossom, not its bitter fruit,
Nor aught of life except that life was good.

We knew them not; they lived with us; we loved them;
  We knew their tricks of gesture; how they smiled;
  What foods and books they liked; but not the wild
Meridians of the heart that fired and proved them.

But now, behind the stars, beyond all sweetness,
  Hid in the heart of music, voiced in song,
  They are ours. The fall of evening finds us strong,
And kind words bring to us their rich completeness.

Foreword

I was deeply aware of the honour bestowed upon me when I was invited to write the Foreword to this book, representing as I do the relatives of those members of the team, who fought in the Battle of Britain, and who were called to 'Higher Service', but without whom the team would not have possessed the solidarity that it did.

'Forty years on' is a time when one can see more clearly the events, and the aftermath of those critical days, and can appreciate to the full the sacrifice of that gallant 'Few'. I found this book to be compulsive reading; having begun I sat well into the night to complete the task. The jacket with its picture of the youthful airman's face so truly depicting the qualities of a fighter pilot, the very generous supply of pictures linking the past with the present, the enthusiasm, devotion, and singlemindedness of purpose the writers so sensitively portray, all cleverly recapture the spirit of the airmen of 1940. This spirit was infectious to those who lived closely with these men.

As I read of their exploits I became very conscious once again of the great privilege I was granted, — denied to so many wives and parents — that of speaking with my husband in hospital after his last sortie, and hearing from his own lips of the wonderful fellowship which existed between the men of a squadron. Although he was far too badly wounded, and burned, and shocked, to speak much he was able to express his gratitude to the pilots who covered his retreat. He spoke of that horrific moment when, badly wounded from gun-fire, his Hurricane burning fiercely, he discovered himself trapped in the cockpit. After a superlative struggle and moments that seemed like hours, he managed to free himself and escape by parachute, and saw to his delight two British planes circling him and warding off a further attack from the enemy. It was with deep feeling he said — 'They followed me down' — words I could not forget. I was reminded of them when present at the unveiling of the Battle of Britain Memorial Chapel in Westminster Abbey by His Majesty King George VI as I read beneath the Memorial Window the quotation from Shakespeare 'We few, we happy few, we band of brothers'.

The painstaking research which has been undertaken so lovingly in the compilation of this book presents a worthy tribute to those it commemorates.

The format of the book, with sections for the stations, the diary of events, and the alphabetical list of graves makes it a book one can easily consult and browse with and I am confident it will be treasured in many homes of our land. I have re-read again extracts from the now famous airman's letter to his mother published in *The Times* on 18th June 1940. One passage can well be quoted: 'My death,' he writes to his mother, 'would not mean that your struggle has been in vain. Far from it, it means that your sacrifice is as great as mine. Those who serve England must expect nothing from her; we debase ourselves if we regard our country as merely a place in which to eat and sleep'. On behalf of the relatives of the airmen commemorated in this book I say, 'We have a right to share these words.'

'Teach us, Good Lord
To serve Thee as Thou deservest
To give and not to count the cost'

Gwen Black.

A fighter pilot's day began at the far from finest hour between three and four o'clock in the morning. Shaken out of his exhaustion after a meagre night's sleep, eyes half open, by the light of a torch he was required to sign against his name in a grubby Stationery Office notebook to show that he had received this early morning call. To soften the blow — if he was well looked after — a mug of steaming tea or cocoa would soon materialise. Dragging himself from his iron-framed bed, he washed, shaved and dressed and made his way to where the other pilots were gathering in small groups beside whatever transport would convey them to their dispersal.

As the first streaks of dawn broke through the darkness, the fitters were completing the warming up of the engines and their pre-flight inspections; when the noise died away only the chug of the petrol bowsers topping up the fuel tanks disturbed the stillness across the aerodrome. Over at the pilots' flight dispersal area, the Flight Commander telephoned Operations from the readiness hut or tent to state that they were ready for action. If a standing patrol had to be flown, the pilots rummaged through their flying clothing lockers, extracting helmets, gauntlets, Mae Wests (the inflatable life jackets named after the ample-bosomed American actress of the 1930s) and parachutes. Insulated from the early morning chill in their fleece-lined Irvine jackets, as the mist began to clear they walked through the dew-soaked grass towards the outlines of their aircraft. The fitters and riggers greeted their pilot, reported on the state of his machine and helped him into his parachute pack. Carefully climbing on to the wing root (a slip on a moist wing could play havoc with the shins), he would lower himself into the constricted space of the cockpit, settle in, and then carry out his pre-flight checks.

One by one the Merlins roared into life; the exhausts, sounding like six simultaneously-fired shotguns, sending back a blast of heat past the edge of the cockpit and belching clouds of blue gases . . . immediately blown into nothingness as the engine caught, spinning the big three-blade propellor. Rising in note as the throttles were opened the chorus of Merlins, amplified by the walls of the station buildings and hangars, rent the air. With his checks completed, each pilot throttled back and awaited the order for take-off. When it came he taxied towards the take-off position, fish-tailing his fighter as he went and moving his head from one side of the cockpit to the other to ensure the way ahead was clear; for even with the canopy locked back and the seat raised to its limit the forward view was restricted by the long nose of the fighter. Reaching the end of the grass runway he turned his aircraft to face across the aerodrome. Lined up for take-off in a loose vic of three behind the Flight Commander and with one section closely following the other, another quick check satisfied him that everything was functioning as it should. A deep breath of oxygen to clear the last remnants of sleep from the brain — and then it was his turn. Holding the aircraft on its brakes he advanced the throttles smoothly until the fighter shuddered and bucked against being held in check, then released the brake lever on the control column and the aircraft bounded forward. Lurching and bobbing across the rough grass surface, the fighters picked up speed until one by one the tails rose. At full take-off power they thundered across the field to lift, bounce, and lift again, climbing after the fast dwindling tails of the previous section. Mere feet above the aerodrome's surface they retracted the undercarriages (a quick flick of the brake lever stopped the spinning wheels before they entered the wells on the underside of the wings), lowered their seats and closed their canopies. As the straggling formation climbed towards the upper layers of the sky, and the earth below receded in the last shreds of darkness, the stragglers began to catch up and the formation tightened into a broad arrowhead — with the solitary exception of tail-end Charlie who positioned himself above and behind the squadron to guard them from surprise attacks from the rear, and who was usually the first to be shot down.

Arriving at their patrol line they would proceed to fly up and down their allocated patch of sky until it was time to return to base, when they would normally be relieved by another squadron. Sometimes they would be vectored on to a single, high-flying enemy weather reconnaissance

The way it was...

machine which they would endeavour to intercept and engage. If they were lucky enough to do so, these encounters provided a useful baptism of fire for young replacement pilots fresh from Operational Training Units who would be led through the attack by one of the veteran pilots.

Their return to base was eagerly watched by their faithful ground crews looking for the tell-tale signs that their guns had been fired. If the canvas gun-port patches were missing it was a sure indication that the aircraft had been in action. Back at dispersal, before the propellor had given its last convulsive jerk, they would be up on the wing roots enquiring how their pilot had fared.

As the pilots adjourned to the readiness hut to make their reports to the Intelligence Officer and, if necessary, complete any combat reports, the bowsers trundled from one group of aircraft to another replenishing the nearly empty fuel tanks. Fitters, riggers and armourers

by Wilf Nicoll

swarmed around the fighter in their care, beavering to keep the aircraft at its peak. Now the waiting game began for every member of the squadron. As the sun rose higher, the pilots whiled away the time until the next call to action or until they left the dispersal for breakfast, which they did in sections, one section at a time for a period of about twenty minutes, with the same arrangements for lunch and dinner. Meals, however,

were very much a hit and miss affair and had to be taken if or when the opportunity arose — sometimes just a mug of tea, cocoa or soup and a sandwich eaten beside the aircraft or in the shade of its wing. Then there were those who were so affected by nerves and tension that they found it virtually impossible to take any sustenance or, having taken it, found it impossible to keep it down. Beneath the blazing hot summer sky time ticked inexorably away; the atmosphere at the dispersals became electric and the tension built up until it was almost tangible. The ball games, darts and shove ha'penny continued to be played or the latest well-thumbed copy of 'Lilliput' or 'Men Only' diligently studied from cover to cover; but it only required the resonant click of the microphone switch through the 'Tannoy' loudspeakers or the jangling of a telephone bell to send someone hurrying behind a hut or tent or the tail of an aircraft to retch and heave helplessly until he was rendered breathless, even if only the most innocuous of messages followed. Combat psychology was a science yet to be appreciated.

When the real thing came, the ground crews would be alerted with the shout of 'Start 'em up!' and the sight of pilots sprinting furiously for their aircraft. In seconds the parachutes would be off the leading edge of the wings or tailplanes and clipped on to the backs of the pilots; the engines would be running as they climbed into the cockpit and, as the ground crews dodged clear, the fighters would be rolling fast across the field. Screaming over the sun-baked ground, the squadron were airborne in about two minutes, the leading section curving away from the aerodrome to allow the following sections to cut across the arc of flight and catch them up. Tightening up the formation, they climbed at full throttle to gain the all-important height advantage they would need when they encountered the enemy. After the heart-pounding excitement of the 'scramble' they concentrated every faculty and nerve in their search of the hostile sky. Their deft fingers moved around the cockpit automatically making adjustments and settings, leaving their minds free to assess anything that might happen. Then the sudden surge of adrenalin as the enemy was spotted by one of the formation and their position called over the radio-telephone when the leader would form them into the attacking formation they had developed and practised to perfection. With throttles advanced to the limit the squadron headed for the enemy, each pilot making his last checks: oxygen fully on, reflector sight turned to the bright or daylight position and the gun button on 'fire'.

To the watchers below, the vapour trails could be viewed as possessing the subtle rhythms of a phantom ballet or as having the sinuous beauty of gothic tracery; to the pilots above, the whirling patterns depicted a maniacal dance of life or death, with little grace or splendour. The ability to wrench an aircraft into a vicious, stressful manoeuvre was paramount to survival. The smooth evolutions of peace-time aerobatics, entertaining for air display crowds, were useless in aerial combat and pilots hurled their fighters into manoeuvres that would have made the designer close his eyes and swallow hard before rushing back to his slide rule. Cocooned in his fighter, each man was subjected to the colossal stresses and strains imposed on the human frame by gravity, high altitude flight, centrifugal and other forces. The hellish din of combat incessantly battered his senses; the twelve-cylindered Rolls-Royce Merlin, three feet in front of him, screaming at full power; the muffled roar of his battery of eight Browning machine guns when he thumbed the button; the mush and crackle in his earphones punctuated by warning shouts from other pilots and the dry rasping of his own breath into the microphone. The smell in the cockpit was a mixture of high octane petrol, hot metal and rubber, aircraft dope, cordite and vomit. His empty stomach heaved and revolted against the violent gyrations to which it was subjected, the gases expanding with the lowered pressures of altitude causing him to belch frequently into his face mask. His right arm, after a few minutes of fighting, felt like a ton weight as it strained to maintain control of the aircraft against the massive elemental forces acting on the control surfaces. Amidst all this he needed — if he wanted to live — cool, clear thinking, the ability to anticipate his opponent's next move, sharp eyesight, intrinsic flying skill, good marksmanship . . . and luck. A minor irritation was 'fighter pilot's rash' — caused by the neck chafing against a sweat-soaked shirt or roll-neck jersey as the pilot maintained a constant all round look-out.

After the battle, back at the aerodrome, the head count began, followed by the interminable wait for stragglers to return or for the telephone to ring with news of their whereabouts. Sometimes the hours would pass until all hope sank slowly with the sun and the realisation that the missing would never return. In desperate but usually forlorn attempts to locate a missing pilot, patrols would be hurriedly despatched to conduct a search of the area of sea over which the battle had been fought, with each pilot straining his eyes to pick out the yellow pin-point of a Mae West in the vast expanse of water.

Cockpit readiness was all that the words implied. The pilots in full flying equipment were harnessed into their cramped cockpits, sometimes with the engines of their fighters idling, awaiting the order from the controller that would send them streaking across the aerodrome into action. Their degree of physical comfort then depended on the weather and the time of day. At high noon on an August day it was an ordeal to be confined in a metal box with the sun beating down and with hot exhaust gases streaming past either side of an open cockpit and engine temperatures mounting by the minute. The increase in nervous tension while awaiting release from the stifling wait tended to fray already overwrought nerves, and tempers would flare causing hasty exchanges between pilots and controller. Invariably, when the order came through their earphones, it was followed by a scramble take-off with the fighters roaring across the aerodrome at full power, climbing away over the boundary, their wings rocking in the rising thermals from the sun-baked earth as they strove for precious height.

And so the morning passed in uncertainty, tension and fear. At the sun's zenith there were still another nine or ten hours before the order came through to stand down; weariness overtook them, and between sorties the banter and the games died. They fell asleep in their cockpits directly they switched off their engines at dispersal, and

another more insidious enemy began to take its toll — exhaustion. Taxi-ing accidents took place which caused damage on the ground to much-needed equipment; such mishaps were a source of annoyance but could usually be put right, whereas in the air an error of judgement, impaired vision, lapse in concentration, a delayed or mistaken decision could not always be so easily rectified and was often fatal. There were also the hazards of returning to a crater-pocked aerodrome exhausted, perhaps wounded, with a severely damaged aircraft which perversely wanted to fall out of the sky with every little adjustment of the controls. Many did arrive back safely at their aerodromes with their fighters literally hanging together by the control cables, after courageously and skilfully flying the wreck home across miles of merciless sky and sea, only to die in a twisted tangle of metal during a landing they had made uneventfully many times in the past.

Death when it came was not always clean and swift. Many died trapped in the narrow confines of the cockpit while the fighter plunged thousands of feet before burying itself in the earth; conscious every second of the fall, struggling to release a trapped limb or jammed hood, coolly and clinically at first until realisation came that there was no release and that time and height had slipped away; then, before the final impact with the earth, the final indignity of befouling themselves. Others watched the sea close over them, or suffered the agonies of being cremated alive. Men died burnt or wounded, helpless and alone, drifting down on the end of a parachute at the whim of the wind; or were victims of the cold-blooded fury of an enemy pilot who had seen a close friend shot down, and for the simple reason that they were combatants who must not survive to fight again. Sometimes, after baling out and pulling the parachute release handle, nothing happened — a moment of mounting horror, then an eternity of terror before life was smashed out. Ironically, death also stalked at the end of a safe descent as parachutes delivered pilots into buildings, trees and overhead hazards. The 'lucky' ones were killed outright in combat by enemy gunfire; of the injured who survived, many were to linger in hospital perhaps for weeks or months before succumbing to their wounds. Others pulled through only to live out their lives mentally and physically broken.

At last — at about half past nine in the evening — their day ended and the survivors were able to take stock of eighteen hours' duty. It was time to unwind, to laugh and perhaps (without ever referring directly to it) to be thankful for being alive. Time to do nothing but sleep, or for a 'thrash' at the pub or a drink in the mess. For these men there was no time for discussion of grand strategy, the overall picture or the issues at stake: that was for later years . . . for those who came through.

The Commanders

AOC-in-C FIGHTER COMMAND

SIR HUGH DOWDING

Air Chief-Marshal Sir Hugh Dowding, GCB, GCVO, CMG, died at his home in Tunbridge Wells, Kent, last Sunday, February 15, 1970. He was 87. 'Stuffy' Dowding, as he became known, was AOC-in-C Fighter Command during the Battle of Britain in 1940. Thanks to his foresight and leadership the RAF defeated the full strength of the German Air Force and prevented the invasion of Britain.

Hugh Caswell Tremenheere, First Baron Dowding of Bentley Priory, was born on April 24, 1882. He was educated at Winchester and joined the Army in 1900 from the Royal Military Academy, Woolwich. He served in Gibraltar, Colombo and Hong Kong before transferring to the Mountain Artillery for a six-year spell in India. At the Military Staff College, Camberley (to which he was sent in 1912 after a number of unsuccessful applications), Dowding was struck by the widespread ignorance of aviation shown in Army circles. He became attracted to aviation and learned to fly, gaining his licence on the same day as he passed out from Camberley.

On the outbreak of war in 1914, Dowding went with the Royal Flying Corps to Belgium. After serving for some time in France he returned to Britain and commanded No. 16 Squadron. In 1916 he served at Farnborough and later went back to front-line duties at the Somme. It was at this time that he first encountered Trenchard, with whom he had a misunderstanding over the advisability of patrolling well-defended enemy lines. As a result of this he was relieved of his command and came back to Britain.

With the formation of the Royal Air Force in April 1918, Dowding was appointed Group Commander at Henley and later Director of Training at the Air Ministry. He served on the Air Council between 1930 and 1936 as Air Member for supply, research and development where his practical understanding of the role of the Royal Air Force proved invaluable, particularly in a time of recession. It was during this period that many of the technical advances which were to give Britain the margin of technical superiority during the early war battles were made. In particular the Air Staff were gradually convinced of the superiority of the monoplane, while radar was in the course of development.

It was in 1936 that Dowding was elected to the post which gained for him the gratitude of the country and the indifference of the Government: he was appointed as Air Officer Commander-in-Chief, Fighter Command. In May 1940 the Government was being pressed by France to supply aircraft in a hopeless attempt to ward off the German onslaught. Dowding spoke out strongly against depleting RAF stocks of aircraft, which he could see would become crucial as soon as the German invasion of France had been completed. His outspoken criticism of Government policy to support crumbling French forces did as much to ensure the success of the RAF during the crucial months of 1940 as his handling of the Battle itself.

A criticism which was made of him (albeit in later years) was his philosophy of using aircraft in 'penny packets' towards the end of the Battle; his argument was that individual night fighters aimed by radar could do a better job in overcoming the night bomber menace. Much controversy has been generated by his removal from office in November 1940 (although he had held this post for a longer time than would have been usual). He retired in 1942 without attaining the rank of Marshal of the Royal Air Force, which title was reserved for those officers who had been appointed Chiefs of the Air Staff.

Group Captain Douglas Bader, who achieved distinction during the Battle of Britain, has recorded the following tribute to this former head of Fighter Command: 'Lord Dowding is probably unknown to most of the younger generation. Yet it was because of him as much as any other man that they have been brought up in the English way of life, speaking the English language. They might have been speaking German. Without his vision, his planning, his singleness of purpose, and his complete disregard for personal aggrandizement, Fighter Command might have been unable to win the Battle of Britain in the summer of 1940. What rankled most with the fighter pilots of 1940 was that he was never made Marshal of the Royal Air Force. Seldom in our history has a man deserved so much of his fellow countrymen and wanted and received so little. He surely earned his place alongside Nelson and Wellington and other great military names in our history.'

Flight International. February 19. 1970

COMMANDER, No. 10 GROUP

SIR QUINTIN BRAND

Air Vice-Marshal Sir Quintin Brand, KBE, DSO, MC, DFC, died at Umtali, Rhodesia, on March 7, 1968, at the age of 74.

Brand, who was born at Beaconsfield, near Kimberley, on May 25, 1893 and educated at the Marist Brothers, Johannesburg, had an extremely distinguished career in the 1914-18 War in the RFC and RAF, winning the DSO, MC and DFC, and being mentioned in despatches. He shot down a German Gotha in the last raid of the war on England.

With General Sir Pierre van Ryneveld he made the first flight from England to the Cape in 1920. They set out from Brooklands on February 4, 1920 and reached Wynberg on March 20. The actual flying time was about 109 hours, but the pioneers encountered some tricky weather and had several mishaps.

Silver Queen I (a Vickers Vimy bomber), the aircraft in which they set out, crashed at Wadi Haifa and was wrecked. The engines were salvaged, however, and fitted to Silver Queen II, which crashed near Bulawayo when the fliers were setting out from Pretoria. They finally reached the Cape in 'Voortrekker' which the Union Government had supplied.

They received a telegram from King George V and were both knighted. In May, they were honoured at a banquet at the Savoy Hotel, London, and their health proposed by the Secretary of State for Air, Winston Churchill.

Air Vice-Marshal Brand was Director General of Aviation, Egypt, from 1932 to 1936, Director of Repair and Maintenance, Air Ministry, from 1937 to 1939 and from 1939 to 1941 Commander No. 10 Fighter Group, RAF. He retired in 1943.

The Times, March 9, 1968

COMMANDER, No. 11 GROUP

SIR KEITH PARK

Air Chief-Marshal Sir Keith Rodney Park, who died on February 6, 1975 in Auckland, New Zealand aged 82, commanded the Fighter Command Group which bore the brunt of the Nazi onslaught when the Battle of Britain began.

It has been said of him by one of the greatest fighter leaders of the war, Air Vice-Marshal 'Johnnie' Johnson, that 'he was the only man who could have lost the war in a day or even an afternoon'.

A New Zealander, and son of Professor James Park, he came to Britain to serve in the 1914-18 war as a gunner. In 1917 he transferred to the Royal Flying Corps and went on to receive a permanent commission in the RAF.

He was given his first command of a squadron in 1920, passed through the RAF Staff College and was appointed air attache at Buenos Aires. By 1938 he had become Lord Dowding's right hand man as senior Staff Officer in Fighter Command, and then commander of 11 Group.

But the sequel to his activities was remarkable. Immediately after the Battle he was released to the command of a Flying Training Group. At the same time Lord Dowding, head of Fighter Command, was sent on a mission to the United States.

'Dropping the pilot,' so far as the comparison related to Sir Keith Park, was the outcome of pointed criticism of his tactics by Air Chief-Marshal Sir Trafford Leigh-Mallory. Each commanded a Group in Fighter Command, and their areas adjoined one another.

He was at Air HQ in Egypt in 1942, when he was appointed AOC Malta. This was during the anxious period in which the defence of the island was being conducted with such grim determination. His fighter force consisted of only a few obsolescent Hurricanes until, with the arrival of Spitfires and other substantial aid, the Mediterranean was cleared and the garrison saved.

In January, 1944, he became AOC-in-C Middle East, and a year later Allied Air C-in-C of the South-East Asia Command.

The Daily Telegraph, February 6, 1975

COMMANDER, No. 12 GROUP

SIR TRAFFORD LEIGH-MALLORY

It was officially announced last night that the aircraft in which Air Chief-Marshal Sir Trafford Leigh-Mallory and Lady Leigh-Mallory were travelling to South-East Asia, and which left this country on November 14, 1944 did not arrive at its destination. The Air Chief-Marshal was on his way to take up his new appointment as Air Commander-in-Chief, South-East Asia Command.

Born on November 7, 1892, at Mobberley, Cheshire, he joined a Territorial battalion of The King's (Liverpool) Regiment on the outbreak of war in 1914, and shortly afterwards received a commission in The Lancashire Fusiliers. Seconded to the RFC in July, 1916, he was graded as major in the RAF on the formation of the separate force on April 1, 1918. For services in France he was mentioned in dispatches and awarded the DSO.

Having been granted a permanent RAF commission with the rank of squadron leader, in 1921 he joined the School of Army Co-operation, which he was later to command for three years. Further experience of air-land co-operation was gained through courses at the Army Senior Officers' School at Woking and as an instructor at the Army Staff College,

Camberley. After service at the Air Ministry and overseas, in 1937 he was given command of No. 12 Group Fighter Command and while occupying this post during the early stages of the war he played a part in fighting the Battle of Britain. In 1942 he became AOC, No. 11 Group, which had taken an even bigger share in the Battle of Britain, and four months later, having been promoted air marshal, was appointed AOC-in-C Fighter Command.

Almost throughout his Air Force career Sir Trafford Leigh-Mallory has been closely concerned with air co-operation with the Army, so that it came as no surprise when, in December of last year, he was appointed to command the Allied air forces placed at the disposal of General Eisenhower for the assault on the continent of Europe. Having accomplished that task with great distinction and success he was released last October in order that he might prepare for the bringing of a similar weight of air support to the Allied armies engaged against the Japanese.

Lady Leigh-Mallory was accompanying her husband in order to carry out in South-East Asia similar social work to that undertaken in the Middle East and European theatres of war by Lady Tedder.

The Times, November 18, 1944

The Operation Rooms

Above: **Bentley Priory in 1928 shortly after its purchase by the Air Ministry.** *Below:* **Photographed in 1966, the conservatory is a prominent ommission (Aerofilms).**

In 1936, as part of the major re-organisation and expansion programme of the Royal Air Force, the Air Ministry split the former Air Defence of Great Britain into two separate formations, each with its own Commander-in-Chief, covering the fighting and bombing roles. On July 14 RAF Fighter Command came into being with its headquarters at Bentley Priory with Air Chief-Marshal Sir Hugh Dowding as its first Air Officer Commanding-in-Chief.

Bentley Priory at Stanmore in Middlesex was designed by Sir John Soane in 1788 and built to the order of John James Hamilton, the Ninth Earl and First Marquis of Abercorn. It became a mansion of great distinction and a rendezvous for many of the political and literary celebrities and statesmen of the day. On the death of the First Marquis in 1818, the Priory passed into the hands of his grandson and, later, the Duke of Abercorn who lived there intermittently from 1832-1840. The widow of William IV, the Dowager Queen Adelaide, leased the Priory in 1846 and died there three years later.

In 1863, the Hamilton family sold the house and estate to Sir John Kelk — the railway engineer who had built the Albert Memorial in Hyde Park free for the nation. It was during Sir John's ownership that the clock tower, terrace and ornamental lake were added.

The Priory passed into the hands of a Mr.

Frederick Gordon in 1882 who intended turning the building into a private residential hotel and it was due to his enterprise that the railway was extended from Wealdstone to Stanmore in 1890, with the proviso that no trains should run on a Sunday — a restriction which was faithfully obeyed by the London and North-Western Railway Company until 1935.

The hotel was not a financial success and, on the death of Mr. Gordon, the Priory changed hands again — this time to become a girls' school. In front of the main entrance some twelve grass tennis courts were laid out while inside alterations provided sound-proofed music rooms sufficient for twenty

pianos to cater for the seventy boarders. However, in the post-First World War depression, the school lost money and was finally closed at the end of the winter term in 1924.

After standing empty for some months, the estate was split into two lots of forty and 240 acres. The latter was sold to a syndicate and split up into building plots, with ninety acres going to the Middlesex County Council which they retained as parkland. The smaller plot including the Priory itself was purchased by the Air Ministry for a sum believed to be £25,000 and, on May 26, 1926, the Inland Area Headquarters moved into the Priory from Uxbridge.

On the formation of Fighter Command in 1936, its headquarters were installed in the mansion and work began to convert the building for its command role. Most important was the adaption of two of the largest rooms to form temporary Filter and Operation Rooms in order to gain experience of their operation while a permanent underground structure was being designed.

As the inevitability of war came closer, the more important offices were protected with sandbags to give protection against bomb blast, trenches were dug, trees cut down to give an all round field of fire (including a beautiful Occidental Plane in front of the terrace) and the whole, white stucco building was sprayed green and brown. The face of the clock tower was painted black as were many of the windows and the conservatory was pulled down to make way for temporary office accommodation for the operations staff.

Meanwhile the excavation of a huge hole just to the east of the Priory was begun in January 1939 for the installation of the underground command centre. One humorous story is told about an unwary workman who slipped into the quagmire of sticky mud which had formed in the bottom of the hole. This came up to his waist and, unable to climb out, a crane was brought up to lift him to safety. He grabbed hold of the hook and, as he slurped out of the mud, much to his embarrassment, the suction neatly removed his trousers!

The average depth of the excavation was forty-two feet and some 58,000 tons of earth were dug out to be replaced over and round the underground rooms. Over 17,000 tons of reinforced concrete went into their construction, the whole complex having its own services, filtration and gas-tight doors. It was completed by March 9, 1940.

However the creation of what was to become the nerve centre of Fighter Command during the Battle of Britain was only one part of the overall plan; more important were the actual methods, devised by Air Chief-Marshal Dowding, to command and control his squadrons in action.

Fighter Command was, by July 1940, composed of four Groups — Nos. 10, 11, 12 and 13 — covering the south-west, south-east, central and northern parts of Britain respectively. The first three Groups had, in turn, been sub-divided into sectors — two for No. 10 Group, seven for No. 11 Group and six for No. 12 Group. Both Groups and Sectors had individual Operation Rooms with control limited to their own defined area.

Information was received by the Filter Rooms attached to each Operations Room, primarily from radio-location posts and the Observer Corps. The Filter Room was basically a telephone exchange or series of switchboards which collated, cross-checked and simplified the intelligence before passing it to the adjoining Operations Room where it would be displayed visually on maps, blackboards and the 'ops table'. Each table consisted of a simple outline map, centered on the area of responsibility, squared off using the British Modified Grid system (which differed from both the military Cassini and the National Grid). All enemy raids were plotted by WAAFS receiving instructions through telephone headsets plugged into jack sockets in the edge of the table. By means of magnetic 'rakes', they positioned counters of three different colours, either yellow, red or blue, to represent enemy formations. The colour to be used was changed every five minutes according to a colour-coded clock. This enabled the controller to see the 'age' of a plot and facilitated its removal or update so that all information on the table could be guaranteed to be no older than fifteen minutes.

Air Chief-Marshal Dowding accepted that tactical control of the battle could not be centralised at Bentley Priory and that even Group commanders would be too busy during hectic periods of fighting to get involved with

The colour-coded Operations Room clock from Biggin Hill now on display at the Battle of Britain Museum at Chilham Castle in Kent.

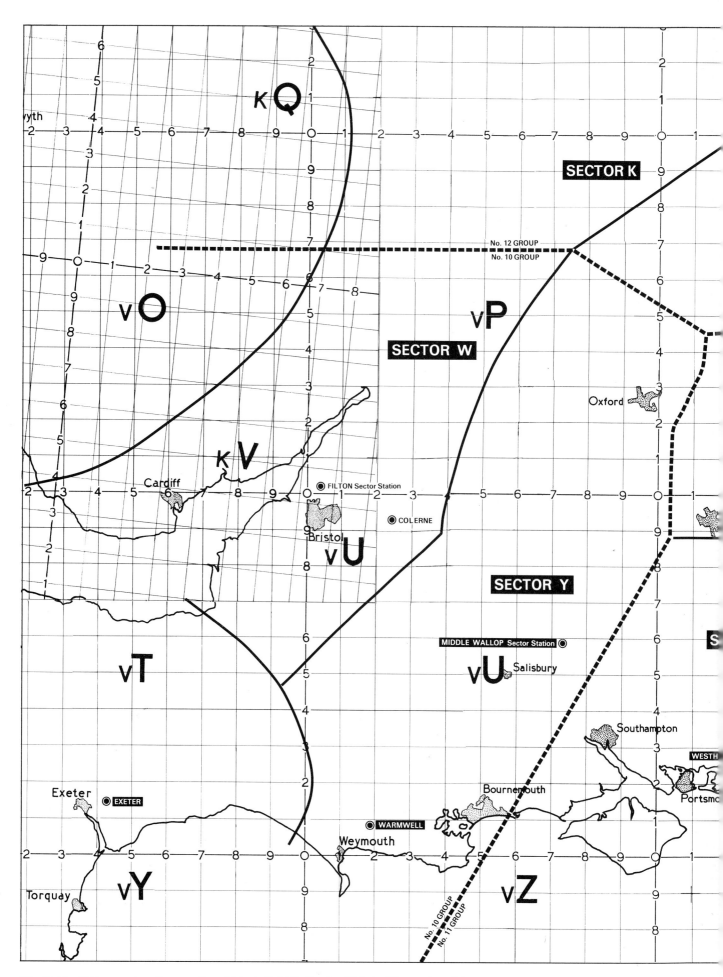

The Fighter Grid as used on the operations tables to fight the Battle of Britain. The overlap of the Irish Military Grid is shown in the west

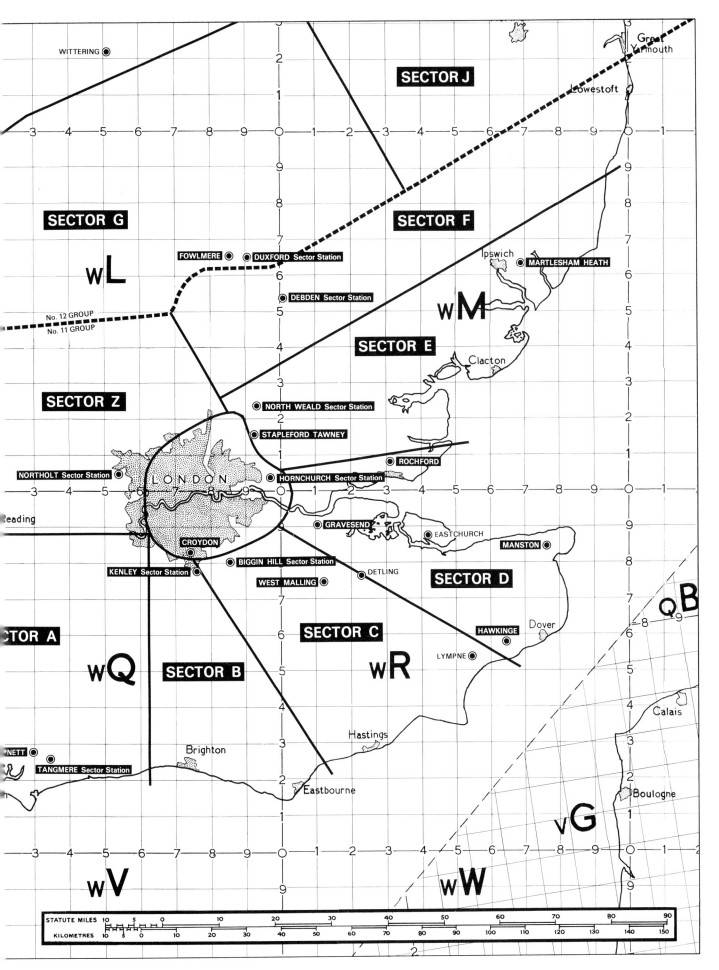

and the French Military Grid to the east. Aerodromes visited and included in this book are printed in black squares (Crown Copyright).

17

actual interceptions. Thus he determined that the Fighter Command Operations Room would be responsible for the identification of approaching formations and for the allotment of enemy raids to Groups where any doubt existed. Command would also order the reinforcement of a hard pressed Group by their neighbouring Group.

As far as Bentley Priory was concerned, radio location plots were received direct and, after surplus information had been eliminated, were passed down the chain of command to Groups and Sectors. Observer Group sightings, on the other hand, came in the opposite direction: first to the local Observer Corps control centre, then to the Sectors and Groups before arriving at Fighter Command. Additional intelligence was provided direct to the Command by the 'Y' Service wireless listening posts and the top secret 'Ultra' decoding centre at Bletchley Park, Buckinghamshire.

One important feature, unique to Bentley Priory, was the operation of the national Air-Raid Warning System. This covered the whole country (except the Orkneys and Shetlands) which had been divided into 130 'Warning Districts' determined by the layout of the telephone network. Three Bentley Priory telephone operators were in constant communication with the 'Trunk' exchanges in London, Liverpool and Glasgow. 'Yellow' warnings were issued when a raid was within twenty minutes flying time of a district and served to warn the local services, fire stations and police. If the raid continued to approach a specific target, a 'Red' warning would be issued five minutes later. This was the signal for the public air-raid sirens to be sounded. A 'Green' signal indicated 'Raiders Passed' and the sirens sounded the 'all clear'. (A fourth 'Purple' warning was later introduced which was the signal to extinguish exposed lights but which did not denote a public warning.) Liaison officers from Bomber and Coastal

command endeavoured to ensure that friendly formations were correctly identified to avoid false air-raid warnings being given. Later, a device carried by each aircraft modified the radar echo received in Britain and so 'identified friend or foe' (IFF).

The Germans paid scant attention to the Priory during the battle and, indeed, it suffered little damage throughout the entire war. Two small bombs destroyed a wooden hut near the married quarters; in 1944 blast from a V1 broke some windows and in

Above: **The underground Fighter Command Operations Room which gave Sir Hugh Dowding an overall picture of the battle (Imperial War Museum).** *Below:* **Exactly the same view in February 1980. The room, which now controls the air defence of the UK, had been specially 'prepared' for our visit.**

February 1945 glass in the Officers' Mess ante-room was shattered by a V2.

After the war, Bentley Priory continued its

role as the headquarters of Fighter Command until its merger with Bomber Command in April 1968. The new Strike Command HQ was located in a purpose-built operations centre at High Wycombe (although administration remained at Stanmore) whereupon Bentley Priory became the headquarters of No. 11 Group. Although the present-day No. 11 Group has no historical ties of descent with the No. 11 Group of 1940, its role within Strike Command is exactly that of Bentley Priory during the battle — the air defence of the United Kingdom.

The Priory itself was used by the AOC and SASO (Senior Air Staff Officer) for their office accommodation and it also accommodated the Officers' Mess. However, the building was badly in need of restoration and it ceased to be used in 1974. In February 1979, a £1 million programme was put in hand with Cubitts, a firm still retaining the specialist craftsmen with the ability to restore the internal decorations and intricate plasterwork. All the floors and the roof were to be strengthened by replacing rotting timbers with steel beams. Wood from the flooring from the pre-war Operations Room was removed for making up into plaques for sale on behalf of the RAF Battle of Britain Museum. It was during the early stages of reconstruction, when the interior had been gutted, that the building caught fire. The alarm was raised shortly after 8.30 p.m. on June 21 but it was three-and-a-half hours before the fire could be brought under control despite the attendance of twenty-three fire appliances from Wembley, Harrow, Northolt, Hayes, Hillingdon, Southall and Stanmore as well as from as far afield as Finchley, Euston and Hertford. The fire completely destroyed the roof and three floors in the west wing and the stairway, hall and clock tower were also badly damaged but, fortunately, all the contents and furnishings were in store at RAF Quedgeley, Gloucestershire at the time. After the damage had been assessed it was decided that the building could still be saved and when the work has been completed in two years time, the Priory will serve as accommodation and as the No. 11 Group Officers' Mess. Lord Dowding's office at the rear of the building with its balcony view over London will be restored as it was in 1940 and will be used by the RAF as a historical tribute to 'The Few'.

When we visited Bentley Priory on February 1, 1980, rebuilding work was in full swing on the Priory itself and as it was still fenced off it was not possible to examine the interior. However, we were privileged to be allowed to visit and photograph the Fighter Command Operations Room — still one of the top security areas in the United Kingdom and in full use twenty-four hours of the day. Today

The 'Tote' board has now been replaced by electronic display screens.

one enters the two-storey underground complex via a covered walkway from the modern Station HQ building. After descending several flights of stairs, past the electrical and air purifying equipment, the Operations Room itself is reached, the simple '24' on its door belieing its continuing historic role in the air defence of the country.

For security reasons, the room had been 'prepared' for our visit and the operations table itself (now centred on Europe, Scandinavia and the western part of the Soviet Union) was completely bare. No attack was imminent. Likewise the huge 'Tote' board which would portray, as in 1940, squadrons at readiness, stand-by and reserve, etc., was blank except for the glowing orange and yellow lines and headings. The 'Tote' board is now electronically controlled, almost like a twenty-foot-square television screen, and could obviously be 'wiped' clean from the control panels in the observation box. Here two duty controllers sat in subdued light and flanked a battered, but no doubt original, leather club armchair where the AOC will sit when controlling our destiny in any future war. Other swivel chairs around the ops table below were also empty as if the whole scenario was awaiting the players of a huge electronic TV game.

After our memorable visit, for which the editor is indebted to the Ministry of Defence especially for giving us permission to take photographs for this book, we walked around to the rear of the Priory to match up the pictures of the visit of HM King George VI and Queen Elizabeth to the very same room on September 6, 1940.

Following our sortie to Stanmore, in the afternoon of February 1, 1980 we visited the equally historic No. 11 Group Operations Room in the grounds of the Royal Air Force station at Uxbridge. It was from here that Air Vice-Marshal Keith Park controlled his squadrons which bore the brunt of the battle. On September 7, for example, Air Vice-Marshal Park had twenty-three squadrons in the group whereas No. 10 to the west had nine-and-a-half and No. 12 to the north fifteen with a further twelve-and-a-half in No. 13 Group in the far north of Britain. No. 11 Group played the key role protecting 'Hell-fire corner', as it became known during the war, and the underground Operations Room completed in 1939 in the south-eastern corner of the camp, became its nerve centre.

Because the task of the Group Operation Rooms was the tactical control of the battle, the workings of the room differed somewhat to that at Command. The Senior Controller and

Left: On September 6, 1940 King George VI and Queen Elizabeth visited Fighter Command HQ and are seen here ascending the westernmost steps to the terrace with Sir Hugh Dowding.

Right: Just over thirty-nine years later, Mrs Audrey Hurran, Flying Officer David Morris and Squadron Leader Warwick Bayley sportingly re-enacted the visit for our comparison.

his assistants were positioned in the central box overlooking the plotting table and tote board but screened and sound-proofed from the 'theatre' below by glass. On either side two smaller boxes contained naval, Observer Corps and anti-aircraft command liaison officers. Within the room itself, supervisory personnel controlled the operations on the bottom dais and the plotters around the table itself. The whole room could be viewed from a VIP box behind glass in the right-hand wall.

Rather more by chance than by design, Winston Churchill was present on September 15 and witnessed first hand the climax of the battle:

'It was one of the decisive battles of the war', wrote Churchill later in his memoirs, 'and, like the Battle of Waterloo, it was on a Sunday. I was at Chequers. I had already on several occasions visited the headquarters of No. 11 Fighter Group in order to witness the conduct of an air battle, when not much had

Above: **The Operations Room (seen here on November 11, 1942) at Uxbridge where Air Vice-Marshal Keith Park controlled No. 11 Group (Imperial War Museum).** *Below:* **In 1975 the room was restored to its 1940 configuration and is now preserved as at 11.30 a.m. on September 15 when Winston Churchill watched the action from the glass-fronted box — now a rest room for WRAF telephone operators for the underground exchange.**

The No. 11 Group ops room was restored by No. 9 Signals Unit, RAF, commanded by Flight Lieutenant Michael Cooke.

happened. However, the weather on this day seemed suitable to the enemy, and accordingly I drove over to Uxbridge and arrived at the Group Headquarters. No. 11 Group comprised no fewer than twenty-five squadrons covering the whole of Essex, Kent, Sussex and Hampshire, and all the approaches across them to London. Air Vice-Marshal Park had for six months commanded this group, on which our fate largely depended. From the beginning of Dunkirk all the daylight actions in the south of England had already been conducted by him, and all his arrangements and apparatus had been brought to the highest perfection. My wife and I were taken down to the bomb-proof Operations Room, fifty feet below ground. . . .

'The Group Operations Room was like a small theatre, about sixty feet across, and with two storeys. We took our seats in the Dress Circle. Below us was the large-scale map table, around which perhaps twenty highly-trained young men and women with their telephone assistants, were assembled. Opposite to us, covering the entire wall, where the theatre curtain would be, was a gigantic blackboard divided into six columns with electric bulbs, for the six fighter stations, each of their squadrons having a sub-column of its own, and also divided by lateral lines. Thus the lowest row of bulbs showed as they were lighted the squadrons which were "Standing By" at two minutes' notice, the next row those at "Readiness", five minutes, then at "Available", twenty minutes, then those which had taken off, the next row those which had reported having seen the enemy, the next — with red lights — those which were in action, and the top row those which were returning home. On the left-hand side, in a kind of glass stage-box, were the four or five officers whose duty it was to weigh and measure the information received from our Observer Corps, which at this time numbered upwards of fifty thousand men, women, and youths. Radar was still in its infancy, but it gave warning of raids approaching our coast, and the observers, with field-glasses and portable telephones, were our main source of information about raiders flying overland.

Thousands of messages were therefore received during an action. Several roomfuls of experienced people in other parts of the underground headquarters sifted them with great rapidity, and transmitted the results from minute to minute directly to the plotters seated around the table on the floor and to the officer supervising from the glass stage-box.

'On the right hand was another glass stage-box containing Army officers who reported the action of our anti-aircraft batteries, of which at this time in the Command there were two hundred. At night it was of vital importance to stop these batteries firing over certain areas in which our fighters would be closing with the enemy. I was not unacquainted with the general outlines of this system, having had it explained to me a year before the war by Dowding when I visited him at Stanmore. It had been shaped and refined in constant action, and all was now fused together into a most elaborate instrument of war, the like of which existed nowhere in the world.

'"I don't know," said Park, as we went down, "whether anything will happen today. At present all is quiet." However, after a quarter of an hour the raid-plotters began to move about. An attack of "40 plus" was reported to be coming from the German stations in the Dieppe area. The bulbs along the bottom of the wall display-panel began to glow as various squadrons came to "Stand By". Then in quick succession "20 plus", "40 plus" signals were received, and in another ten minutes it was evident that a serious battle impended. On both sides the air began to fill.

'One after another signals came in, "40 plus", "60 plus"; there was even an "80 plus". On the floor-table below us the movement of all the waves of attack was marked by pushing discs forward from minute to minute along different lines of approach, while on the blackboard facing us the rising lights showed our fighter squadrons getting into the air, till there were only four or five left

"At Readiness". These air battles, on which so much depended, lasted little more than an hour from the first encounter. The enemy had ample strength to send out new waves of attack, and our squadrons, having gone all out to gain the upper air, would have to refuel after seventy or eighty minutes, or land to rearm after a five-minute engagement. If at this moment of refuelling or rearming the enemy were able to arrive with fresh un-challenged squadrons some of our fighters could be destroyed on the ground. It was therefore one of our principal objects to direct our squadrons so as not to have too many on the ground refuelling or rearming simultaneously during daylight.

'Presently the red bulbs showed that the majority of our squadrons were engaged. A subdued hum arose from the floor, where the busy plotters pushed their discs to and fro in accordance with the swiftly-changing situation. Air Vice-Marshal Park gave general directions for the disposition of his fighter force, which were translated into detailed orders to each Fighter Station by a youngish officer in the centre of the Dress Circle, at whose side I sat. Some years after I asked his name. He was Lord Willoughby de Broke. (I met him next in 1947, when the Jockey Club, of which he was a Steward, invited me to see the Derby. He was surprised that I remembered the occasion.) He now gave the orders for the individual squadrons to ascend and patrol as the result of the final information which appeared on the map table. The Air Marshal himself walked up and down behind, watching with vigilant eye every move in the game, supervising his junior executive hand, and only occasionally intervening with some decisive order, usually to reinforce a threatened area. In a little while all our squadrons were fighting, and some had already begun to return for fuel. All were in the air. The lower line of bulbs was out. There was not one squadron left in reserve. At this moment Park spoke to Dowding at Stanmore, asking for three squadrons from No. 12 Group

Air Chief-Marshal Lord Dowding (right) unveils the memorial stone on April 22, 1958 erected directly above the Operations Room (Crown Copyright).

to be put at his disposal in case of another major attack while his squadrons were rearming and refuelling. This was done. They were specially needed to cover London and our fighter aerodromes, because No. 11 Group had already shot their bolt.

'The young officer, to whom this seemed a matter of routine, continued to give his orders, in accordance with the general directions of his Group Commander, in a calm, low monotone, and the three reinforcing squadrons were soon absorbed. I became conscious of the anxiety of the Commander, who now stood still behind his subordinate's chair. Hitherto I had watched in silence. I now asked: "What other reserves have we?" "There are none," said Air Vice-Marshal Park. In an account which he wrote about it afterwards he said that at this I "looked grave". Well I might. What losses should we not suffer if our refuelling planes were caught on the ground by further raids of "40 plus" or "50 plus"! The odds were great; our margins small; the stakes infinite.

'Another five minutes passed, and most of our squadrons had now descended to refuel. In many cases our resources could not give them overhead protection. Then it appeared that the enemy were going home. The shifting of the discs on the table below showed a continuous eastward movement of German bombers and fighters. No new attack appeared. In another ten minutes the action was ended. We climbed again the stairways which led to the surface, and almost as we emerged the "All Clear" sounded.'

Today RAF Uxbridge is the base of No. 219 Communications Squadron and also the home of The Queen's Colour Squadron. Although the underground Operations Block continued to be used after the war as a military telephone exchange based on the Filter Room communications network, the Operations Room itself fell into disuse, the controllers box becoming the tea room for the WRAF personnel manning the exchange.

A memorial obelisk was unveiled by Lord Dowding on his visit to Uxbridge on April 22, 1958 but it was due to the interest and dedication of Flight Lieutenant Michael Cooke and his No. 9 Signals Unit that the room itself was restored, the tote board rebuilt to its 1940 pattern and the map table renovated during 1975. On September 15 it was officially re-opened as a museum piece but with restricted access by prior appointment only. The counters on the table and

As the ops room at Uxbridge is within the perimeter of the RAF station, it can only be visited by prior appointment. However, an exact replica has been constructed in the RAF Battle of Britain Museum at Hendon where one can view the room from the controller's position (RAF Museum).

Above: **No. 10 Group Operations Room at Rudloe Manor, Box in Wiltshire (Imperial War Museum). Still a top security area, we were kindly supplied the comparison photograph** *below* **by the Ministry of Defence (Crown Copyright).**

bulbs on the tote display the state of the battle at 11.30 a.m. on the morning of September 15, 1940. (An exact copy of the room can be seen at the RAF Museum at Hendon.)

The two other Group operations centres covered in our survey were No. 10 Group at Rudloe Manor at Box in Wiltshire and No. 12 Group at Watnall. The former Group covered south-west England and southern Wales and it had Air Vice-Marshal Sir Christopher Brand as its AOC. Air Vice-Marshal Brand had served in the Royal Flying Corps in the Great War as a Major and was one of the earliest successful night fighter pilots having a personal score of six victories. Rudloe Manor has continued in Ministry ownership becoming the HQ of the Royal Observer Corps Southern Area in 1953. The old No. 10 Group Operations Room has now been sub-divided into smaller offices which are part of the HQ of the Provost and Security Service for the UK. Although it was not possible to visit the room, the Ministry were most obliging in providing present-day comparison photographs.

No. 12 Group, commanded by Air Vice-Marshal Trafford Leigh-Mallory, had its headquarters in a camp site straddling the B600 at Watnall, north-west of Nottingham, and within a mile of Hucknall aerodrome. The underground operations block lay on the eastern side of the road beside the headquarters building to which it was connected. After the war, this also became a Royal Observer Corps HQ until 1953 when the Midland Area of that organisation was disbanded. The Royal Air Force retained the site until 1967 when a meteorological office was built on the southern corner of the former camp on the eastern side of the road. The No. 12 headquarters building was demolished to make way for a heavy goods vehicle testing centre and the underground block, then full of water, was sealed off. Today virtually the whole camp has disappeared, all the barrack blocks on the western side of the B600 having been replaced by a new housing estate.

The Sector Operation Rooms, as their name implies, controlled the sub-divisions within the Groups and were initially located on the master aerodrome in each sector. We visited all those in No. 11 Group; Exeter in No. 10 Group and Duxford in No. 13 Group and the description of each is covered within the chapter on the aerodrome concerned.

There were two basic styles of Sector Operation Rooms in use during the Battle of Britain. The pre-war, single storey, pitched roof-type building had been used as control rooms during the inter-war period of the old scheme of Air Defence of Great Britain. They were not bomb proof and only had a blast wall comprising a bank of earth surrounding them to the height of the eaves. Their vulnerability in time of war was appreciated and a new building programme put in hand for more substantial operation blocks to be built as replacements. The aerodromes built during the period of the expansion of the RAF automatically had the new 'Mk II' design and an example of the latter can be seen at Debden. New L-shaped blocks were built at Tangmere, Hornchurch and North Weald and that at Middle Wallop (originally planned as a bomber station) was completed during the battle. Kenley, Duxford, Northolt and Biggin Hill had to make do with the old style buildings. Nevertheless it was appreciated that the only really safe method of protection for this vital aspect of control of the squadrons would be to disperse the Operation Rooms away from the aerodromes which were natural targets although this would mean some loss of efficiency.

Such a contingency had already been planned for in No. 11 Group during the first eight-months of phoney war by the then-commander Air Vice-Marshal E. L. Gossage and buildings were earmarked two to three miles from each sector aerodrome for the

All that can be seen today of Air Vice-Marshal Trafford Leigh Mallory's No. 12 Group underground operations block at Watnall.

siting of emergency Operation Rooms should the need arise. These were of a makeshift nature, being situated in shops, schools or halls and some had to be moved again into more adequate accommodation.

At the end of August, the attacks on Fighter Command aerodromes reached a peak and two ops blocks received direct hits. That at North Weald — the Mk II bomb-proof version — survived but the old style building at Biggin Hill was completely destroyed with heavy casualties. The dispersal plans were then immediately put into effect.

Typical of the old-style Sector Operation Rooms on the aerodromes themselves was that at Hornchurch described here by Group Captain H. T. Sutton:

The inside of the Operations Room was more impressive than its exterior suggested. During the period of the Battle of Britain an army sentry with fixed bayonet would be stationed outside whilst an RAF sentry with a revolver guarded the inner door. The entrance to the Operations Room itself was at the top of a short flight of stairs which gave access to a built-up timber platform running right down the side of the room. Spreading into a wide platform at the left of the entrance, the built-up floor thus formed a raised area which looked down from a height of about four feet on to the centre of the room.

The wide part of the platform to the left of the entrance was known as the dais, and along it sat, first and nearest the door, the Ops. B officer, who was assistant to the controller. On the left of Ops. B was a leading aircraftsman, and to the left again an aircraftsman wearing a head-and-breast telephone set. In the centre of the dais, a section of the floor was raised by another six inches, and here sat the Senior Controller, in the beginning a Flight Lieutenant, but later a Squadron Leader. Further again to the left, against the windows, sat an Army officer, whose duty was to keep liaison between the AA guns and the RAF, with two army signallers to assist him.

Along the full length of the dais was a built-in desk containing numerous telephone keys, labelled clearly as to their separate function,

and which supplied each place on the dais with communications to the squadrons, aircraft in the air and all the many other units and headquarters to which messages passed. Behind this, three windows gave access to wireless cabinets in which, sound-proofed to preserve the quiet of the Operations Room, wireless operators maintained contact with the fighters in the air and switched the radio-telephone (R/T) through to the controller or his assistants in obedience to a pressed switch on the control desk.

The part of the platform facing the entrance ran the full length of the room and led into an extension to the original building. This contained a plotting table manned by a sergeant and a team of plotters. Here the radio cross-bearings of the Sector fighter aircraft were plotted on the plotting table and the results passed by telephone to the main Operations Room.

Sitting centrally, the controllers had a clear view below them of the main plotting table,

central and to the right, which displayed the plots of hostile raids, and alongside it to the left, a smaller table on which the movements of the Hornchurch fighters were plotted in coloured chalk. The bigger plotting table was covered with an outline map of south-east England drawn as a black outline on a white ground, and the other was a blackboard with the Sector outlined by a white line.

In the far corner on the left there was another large blackboard on which was chalked the weather situation at Hornchurch and at adjoining aerodromes. Above the board, high up on the wall, were long panels of coloured glass behind which electric bulbs were lighted to indicate the state of readiness of the squadrons. Each squadron, flight and section was represented by these panels, and the controller could see at once exactly how many aircraft were available to him 'at readiness,' which meant ready to take off within a minute or two, at 'available,' which meant a less immediate state of preparedness,

The Sector C Operations Room at Biggin Hill was the only pre-war style ops block to receive a direct hit — see page 65 (Air Vice-Marshal J. Worrall).

Above: The Sector G Operations Room at Duxford. Note the Squadron radio call signs for Nos. 242, 302 and 310 Squadrons on the wall (see page 255). In the cubicles behind the controller are the R/T operators in direct touch with the aircraft (Imperial War Museum). *Below:* The author of our chapter on Duxford and Fowlmere, Alister Raby, contemplates the former glories of the same room now used by the Imperial War Museum for school lectures.

The best example of the inter-war style of RAF Sector control rooms used by the Royal Air Force during the Battle of Britain is that at Duxford, preserved by the Imperial War Museum (Clive Norman).

or 'stand down.' The panels also indicated how long aircraft on sorties had been in flight, so that the controller could keep a check on the petrol and oxygen endurance left to the pilots.

A twenty-four-hour watch was kept in the Operations Room, in four watches: from 8.00 a.m. to 2.00 p.m., from 2.00 p.m. to 8.00 p.m., from 8.00 p.m. to 2.00 a.m. and from 2.00 a.m. to 8.00 a.m. Instructions were given to the pilots over the R/T by means of a simple code which was easily memorized. For example 'scramble' meant take-off, 'orbit' meant circle, 'vector 230 degrees' meant fly on a course of 230 degrees, 'pancake' meant leave patrol line and land, and the 1915 word 'bandit' was used again to signify hostile aircraft. 'Angels' followed by a number meant fly at that height in thousands of feet. When German pilots began to listen in to RAF control communications and began to try to act on the information, Air Chief-Marshal Dowding introduced false commands to mislead the enemy. i.e. 'Angels 18' would mean instead fly at 21,000 feet, thus German fighter formations often found themselves unexpectedly below their intended quarry. Pilots told the controller that they were about to engage the enemy by the cry of 'Tally-ho!'

Before the war began it was appreciated that the range of the TR9 high-frequency (HF) radio-telephone set was too short and the overall performance too variable to give efficient air to ground communication for the new interception systems being evolved. Its limitations had been recognised as early as January 1937 when the requirements for an R/T range of 100 miles had been formally stated. A high-frequency set to extend to this range could not be produced without an increase in weight and electrical power. Furthermore, the number of civil, military and foreign stations using the HF band had increased enormously since it had been adopted by the Royal Air Force. Also the number of channels were limited and the HF band was vulnerable to jamming by stations situated 200 to 300 miles away (i.e. the potential enemy to the east - Germany). It was therefore essential that the RAF's next R/T equipment worked on a higher frequency band.

Radio-telephony development on very high frequencies (VHF) had been carried out at the Royal Aircraft Establishment since 1935. By July 1938, the development was still four years from successful completion although the Dutch Air Force already had the higher frequency sets in use. Dismayed at the prospect of waiting until 1941/42 for a new set, the Air Staff decided that there was no alternative but to go ahead and order an interim VHF set based on the research already

undertaken. However, the RAE, through an unexpected degree of success and accelerated progress, managed to produce an improved apparatus which enabled an earlier changeover to VHF. With provisional approval and action, it was planned to fully equip eight Sectors with ground transmitters and receivers including D/F (Direction-Finding) stations plus 200 to 300 aircraft with VHF sets by September 1939.

The new sets, operating in the 100 to 120 megacycles per second frequency band, were little different from the old TR9 and squadron signals personnel were able to change to VHF or back to HF in about an hour-and-a-half once the new wiring, generating and voltage controls were installed in the aircraft.

Of the eight Sector stations earmarked for VHF, four were in No. 11 Group (Debden, Biggin Hill, Hornchurch and North Weald) and four in No. 12 Group (Duxford, Wittering, Catterick and Digby). Debden, Hornchurch and North Weald worked on HF and VHF simultaneously. Service trials of the new TR1133 VHF set took place at Duxford on October 30, 1939 with six Spitfires of No. 66 Squadron. The results exceeded all expectations. An air-ground range of 140 miles was obtained at 20,000 feet and an air-to-air range of 100 miles. Speech was clearer, the set controls simpler to operate and the sharpness of the D/F facility improved considerably.

The improved TR1143 set (embodying crystal control in both receiver and transmitter to overcome frequency drift) planned for issue in May 1940, did not materialise until late summer. During the Dunkirk evacuation, the shortage of VHF equipment

made itself keenly felt and Air Chief-Marshal Dowding despatched the following signal to Group Commanders in Fighter Command:

'To Nos. 11, 12, 13 Groups repeated Air Ministry. In view necessity for maintaining flexibility in operation of all Fighter Squadrons at present time and limited wireless apparatus available, all VHF equipment in aircraft is to be replaced by HF TR9D sets forthwith. VHF equipment is to be retained in reserve by VHF sector stations. Squadrons concerned to report as change over completed. VHF ground personnel to remain in their sectors but employed to best advantage pending return to VHF.'

On June 1, 1940 he explained his actions and motives in a letter to the Air Ministry, deploring the inadequacy of supplies of VHF sets and defending his decision to prevent the loss of valuable VHF equipment over Belgium and the Channel in order to harbour it against the time of greater need.

Another most important, yet hitherto unsung, part played in winning the Battle of Britain was provided by the telephone engineers of the General Post Office. Air Commodore David Roberts, commander of the Middle Wallop Sector during the battle, has said that without the dedication of these engineers who worked all hours repairing communications, installing completely new facilities in the emergency centres, and keeping the vital nervous system of Fighter Command functioning, the fight could not have been won. We therefore feel that a technical description of the systems provided by the Post Office (reproduced here from the

---

TYPICAL DIMENSIONS OF THE PRE-WAR TYPE OF SECTOR OPERATIONS BLOCKS

Single Storey: Slate roof, red facing brick, centrally heated. Floors mainly boarded. Surrounded by earthen blast protection.

Main lecture room, 31ft by 25ft	775 sq ft
Lecture room, 28ft 9in by 20ft. Part solid, part boarded floor	575 sq ft
Reading room, 20ft by 12ft 6in	250 sq ft
Office, 15ft by 14ft 9in. Wood block floor	220 sq ft
Store, 15ft by 10ft	150 sq ft
Ancillary accommodation	
Basement	
Total Net Area	**1,970 sq ft**

Post Office Electrical Engineers Journal by Mr. A. M. Hanna) is worthy of inclusion:

During the Battle of Britain, a vast and intricate network of communications was necessary to keep Fighter Command furnished with up-to-date information derived from a multiplicity of sources. The main sources of raid information were the Observer Corps centres and radar stations which maintained a constant watch over land and sea areas respectively. When the approach of aircraft was recorded on the detecting apparatus at these stations, the information was passed by tellers over direct speech circuits to Group Filter Rooms where it was plotted on the tables. Here the information was speedily co-ordinated and was retold in detail by observers on the balcony via speech broadcast circuits to the Group Operations Room and to Sector Operations Rooms within the Group area. Other observers relayed the information in lesser detail (that is, the highlights) to adjacent Groups and to headquarters Fighter Command. Similarly observers in the Sector Operations Room passed all relevant information obtained from the plotting table to anti-aircraft and searchlight Operations Rooms and to Balloon Command. Speech circuits also existed between the Sector Operations Room and such points as the watch office located at each aerodrome to the radio telephone transmitting and receiving stations. Liaison and intelligence circuits connected with the plotting organisation existed between all the stations mentioned.

The majority of plotting circuits in use by Fighter Command were of the undirectional, point-to-point type. Within a station they were routed via a floor supervisor's keyboard (for monitoring purposes) and a patching panel, to predetermined plotting positions. Point-to-point circuits were necessary by virtue of the continuous nature of the information passed and because the shortest of switchboard operating delays could not be tolerated.

The patching panel provided a large measure of flexibility inasmuch as any particular plotting circuit could be connected to any desired plotting position at the table. This facility was especially useful when the map, which was often composed of removable sections, was moved up or down or across the table.

As may quite easily occur where unidirectional circuits are employed, a

A programme to replace the vulnerable, single storey Sector operation blocks was begun in 1938-39. However, the new L-shaped constructions, supposedly bomb proof, were still sited on the aerodromes. This is the one at Tangmere for Sector A.

TYPICAL DIMENSIONS OF THE Mk II 1939 VERSION OF SECTOR OPERATION BLOCKS

Single Storey: Flat roof, brick built walls, solid floors. Centrally heated. Surrounded by blast walls.

Main Operations Room, 49ft by 37ft 6in. Double level floor	1,460 sq ft
Four offices, each 7ft 9in by 6ft 9in	210 sq ft
Signals office, 14ft by 9ft 9in. Wood strip floor	135 sq ft
Signals office, 18ft by 19ft 9in. Wood strip floor	355 sq ft
Office, 16ft by 7ft 9in. Wood strip floor	125 sq ft
Office, 16ft by 12ft. Wood strip floor	190 sq ft
Workroom, 16ft by 8ft. Deep sink	130 sq ft
Exchange room, 12ft 9in by 8ft. Wood strip floor	100 sq ft
Office, 12ft 9in by 7ft 6in. Wood strip floor	95 sq ft
Ancillary accommodation	
Toilet A: Lavatory basin, WC	
Toilet B: Lavatory basin, WC	
Air conditioning plant room	
Boiler room with solid fuel boiler	
Total Net Area	**2,800 sq ft**

The new blocks were constructed with dead space between the building and the surrounding earth bank to absorb the shock of a near miss. The whole block was still above ground with the 'well' of the ops room itself sunk some three feet. The entrance through the blast wall was angled as a further protection against blast. This is the Sector F block at Debden.

Above: **An added refinement at Debden was this extremely cramped observation position on the roof. Because the aerodrome has never been out of Ministry hands since 1940, its ops block is the best preserved of the later type that we visited.** *Below:* **The code room with its twin safes . . . still locked.**

disconnection may exist unnoticed during slack periods. To avoid this possibility an 800 c/s pip-tone of 100/150ms duration was transmitted from the telling end at half-minute intervals, its absence at the plotting position being indicative of the existence of a fault condition.

The plotter's position comprised a standard CB operator's telephone circuit using a double headgear receiver and transmitter. The raid information, which was plotted on the table, was interspersed periodically by tote or ancillary information. This information was preceded, however, by the work 'Tote' followed by a brief pause, during which the plotter extended the plotting line to the tote position by operating a key conveniently fitted at the edge of the table. Keeping the key depressed, the plotter monitored the message passed and at its conclusion released the connection. The reverse action of the key connected the plotter's transmitter to the tote position so that any inaccuracy in the information subsequently displayed on the tote panel could be rectified.

Approximately one thousand head and breast sets were constantly in use for plotting purposes in Fighter Command.

The operations officers occupying positions on the balconies were each provided with an operations keyboard. Access to remote stations with which the officer's particular duty was concerned was available from the keyboard. Inter-keyboard circuits for communication between officers within the Operations Room and circuits to the operations PBX were also provided.

The keyboards were designed, manufactured and installed, in common with all other line telecommunications equipment, by the Post Office. They were of the lamp-signalling ancillary type and were produced in five sizes accommodating 1, 5, 10, 20 and 30 lines respectively.

The opportunities of performing maintenance work in Operations Rooms were few and far between and for this reason all auxiliary signalling equipment, speaking sets, etc., were accommodated in the apparatus room, the bare essentials only being fitted in the keyboard.

Two speaking positions were provided on each keyboard, access to any line being effected by operating the line key to the appropriate speaking position. Signalling was effected by the operation of a common signal key which extended 17 c/s to line, the 17 c/s being converted if necessary to any other desired method of signalling by signal conversion units located in the apparatus room. A calling and an engaged lamp in respect of each line were located above the line key. Limited switchboard facilities were provided for use in exceptional circumstances.

The 20 and 30 line keyboards were provided with broadcast facilities in addition to those already mentioned. When these facilities were required, a multiphone amplifier located in the apparatus was associated with the keyboard and could be connected to either speaking position by the operation of the appropriate amplifier key. For fitting and maintenance reasons the connection strips were not fitted inside the keyboard but were attached to 30in tails from which point they were cabled to the apparatus room distribution frame. Normally the keyboards were let into the table top but could be installed in the upright position if desired.

Communication between aircraft in flight and the Sector controller was maintained by radio-telephone, each Sector station being allotted a certain number of frequencies on which to operate. The R/T transmitting and receiving stations were divided into two classes, referred to as 'local stations' and

'forward relay' stations. The former were usually about three miles distant from the Sector Operations Room and the latter approximately 100 miles away. Usually the local stations operated on twelve frequencies and the forward relays on eight. The frequencies in use at the forward relays were duplicates of a corresponding number of frequencies at the local station, thus affording greater radio coverage on those frequencies.

The land line connections between the R/T stations and the Sector Operations Room were referred to as channels and consisted of 4-wire circuits.

In the Operations Room, the local and forward relay channels were terminated on a twenty-three-line R/T keyboard at the controller's position and were ancillaried to eight other deputy-controller's positions. Each channel was also connected to a separate R/T monitor's position where it was permanently monitored. When a signal from an aircraft was heard by the monitor (and if the monitor was unable to deal with the situation), a controller was called into circuit by the operation of a signalling key which caused the calling lamp associated with the particular channel to glow on each of the controller's keyboards.

The facilities provided by the keyboards may be summarised as follows:

Controller's position.
(i) Access to any of twenty R/T channels for monitoring and transmitting purposes.
(ii) Both-way signalling and intercommunication facilities to any monitor's position.
(iii) Remote switching of the R/T transmitter and automatic attenuation of the R/T receiver during sending.
(iv) Access to D/F stations.

Monitor's positions.
(i) Permanent connection to the receiver half of one channel only.
(ii) Both-way signalling and intercommunication facilities to all controller's positions.
(iii) Remote switching of the R/T transmitter and automatic attenuation of the R/T receiver during sending.

By virtue of the vital nature of the messages passed over them, the majority of circuits terminated on the operations keyboards were of the point-to-point type. Access to the lesser important circuits was made via the operations PBX. The operations PBX consisted normally of a four-position PMBX No. 1A switchboard, on which were terminated lines to satellite, aircraft dispersal points, flying control offices, etc.

The standard Post Office 65-line PBX switchboard served many important functions in the Fighter Command organisation. Prominent among these were the administrative services at all stations, the flying control arrangements at aerodrome and the movement liaison service at Group headquarters.

The flying control PBX situated in the watch office provided intercommunication between the flying control officer and such points as the ambulance service, crash tender, and dispersal points. Communication was also available through this PBX to the parent Sector and Group headquarters.

In the end, however, in spite of all the Operations Rooms, controls, guidance methods and communications, results from the system depended on one man — the pilot — and Air Chief-Marshal Dowding simplified this in his report on the 114-day battle published in 1946:

'The indomitable courage of the fighter pilots and the skill of their leaders brought us through the crisis, and the morale of the Germans eventually cracked because of the stupendous losses which they sustained.'

The Aerodromes

SECTOR A
Tangmere

BY JIM BEEDLE

On November 16, 1916, while on a flight from Gosport in a F.E.2b, Geoffrey Dorman force-landed at Bayleys Farm near the village of Tangmere, three miles east of Chichester. His report on the incident included a suggestion that the site would be eminently suitable for an aerodrome and, in spite of local opposition, construction began in 1917, German POW labour being drafted in to assist in October.

Although first used for training, the aerodrome saw the arrival of three operational Squadrons, Nos. 91, 92 and 93 in March 1918. These all left for France early in July

and, during the last months before the Armistice, Tangmere was loaned to the American forces for flying training. Early in 1919 the aerodrome was closed but retained by the Air Ministry.

It was re-opened in June 1925 but saw no aircraft until No. 43 Squadron arrived from Henlow in December 1926. They were joined in February 1927 by the newly re-formed No. 1 Squadron, both squadrons being equipped with Gloster Gamecocks. Apart from their replacement, first with Armstrong Whitworth Siskins and, in 1931, the 200 mph Hawker Fury, Tangmere changed little over the next eleven years. It was unique among RAF Home Stations in operating a 'Summer Routine' from May to August which meant com-

pressing all flying into the morning period and virtually closing down from 1.00 p.m.

The aerodrome was originally grass measuring 775 yards SE-NW; 800 yards N-S; 1,000 yards from E-W and 1,500 yards from NE-SW. However from 1937 Tangmere grew with the expansion of the RAF. New station workshops, MT buildings and barracks were started and the following year saw the beginnings of blast-protection pens around a newly-laid perimeter track. Two runways running N-S and NE-SW (each of 1,600 x 50 yards) were also begun though these were not completed until the autumn of 1939.

In the last week of August 1939, No. 217 Squadron, which had arrived with Avro Ansons in 1937, left for Cornwall and No. 1

Top: **Their spinners raised in salute, the Hurricanes of No. 1 Squadron silently acknowledge the aerial mastery of their kin as a fellow member beats-up the aerodrome at Tangmere. The codes, markings and camouflage are all post-Munich, 1938 (Andy Saunders).** *Below:* **There were none to salute the** *After the Battle* **Land-Rover as it carried out its solitary 'beat-up' of the Tangmere apron on November 13, 1979.**

Above: **In an age when aeroplanes and elegance went hand in glove, the Fury was supreme. Hawker Fury Is of Nos. 43 and 1 Squadrons in front of Tangmere's hangars in 1938.** *Right:* **Tangmere, November 1979 and the stark utilitarian design of the post-war hangars which replaced those destroyed during the battle stamps them as products of a mass production age.**

went to France. No. 92 Squadron formed at the station with Blenheim fighters and No. 43 moved to Acklington in November. The first winter of the war passed quietly with Nos. 501 and 605 Squadrons in residence.

Tangmere was not greatly involved during the fighting in France in May 1940 but became busier during the Dunkirk evacuation and in June when a number of Mohawks flew in after the French armed forces collapsed.

During July 1940 the Tangmere Squadrons, variously Nos. 1, 43, 145 and 601, were engaged on many occasions in the preliminary skirmishing over the Channel which occurred prior to the all-out attacks which the Luftwaffe launched on 'Adlertag'. On August 8, No. 145 Squadron especially (and Nos. 43 and 601 to a lesser extent) achieved many successes during a day-long battle over a westbound convoy.

That same day the satellite aerodrome at Westhampnett was brought into operation and No. 145 Squadron transferred there from the parent station.

Below: **The brand-new Officers' Mess seen from the camp main gate about 1930 (Jim Beedle).** *Right:* **In the autumn of 1979, we photographed the neglected, weed-ravaged tennis courts in front of the boarded-up Mess. Early in 1979, Royal Engineers carried out an anti-terrorist exercise in the building, blowing holes through many of the interior walls.**

Above: July 1940, renowned aviation photographer Charles E. Brown visited Tangmere. His complete sequence of photographs is shown here. No. 601 Squadron crewroom. Flight Lieutenant Willie Rhodes-Moorhouse (killed on September 6) concentrates his skill on the shove-halfpenny board while Flying Officer Billy Clyde keeps his aiming eye in on the dartboard. *Below:* The result of too hard a throw! The site of the old crew rooms on November 13, 1979. Large patches of Air Ministry issue brown linoleum, although badly weathered, still adhere to the concrete base. In the little grove of trees, an original Nissen hut still stands.

Above: **Squadron Leader Max Aitken (extreme right) with Flight Lieutenant Rhodes-Moorhouse (in white overalls) awaits the completion of refuelling and re-arming of three No. 601 Squadron machines. The fitter is about to replace the radio access panel on Hurricane WF-B.** *Below:* **We took our photograph from the balcony of the watch office — due for demolition in 1980. The ladder gave us the same height to that of the petrol bowser for the final two comparison photographs** *(bottom).* **The house on the skyline is the reference point.**

At 1.00 p.m. on Friday, August 16, Tangmere was the target for a large force of Junkers Ju 87 dive-bombers. Many of the attackers were intercepted before reaching the aerodrome but those that got through caused immense damage and destruction in the space of the few minutes that the raid actually lasted.

Two hangars were totally destroyed, one of them by fire, and the other three damaged. The station workshops and the fire-hydrant pump house received direct hits as did a nearby air-raid shelter. Stores, sick quarters, the Y-service hut, Officers' Mess and a Salvation Army hut were also severely damaged. Six Blenheims, seven Hurricanes and one Magister were either destroyed or damaged together with nearly forty motor vehicles. The Station Operations Record states that: 'The depressing situation was dealt with in an orderly manner and it is considered that the traditions of the RAF were upheld by all ranks.'

The entry finishes with the dubious conclusion: 'It must be considered that the major attack launched on this station by the enemy was a victory for the RAF!'

While the attack was in progress, Pilot Officer Billy Fiske of No. 601 Squadron crash-landed his burning Hurricane on the aerodrome. He died of his wounds the next day, possibly the first American airman to die in the Battle of Britain.

In spite of considerable cratering of the aerodrome, all the airborne Hurricanes of Nos. 43 and 601 landed back safely and Tangmere was never at any time non-operational for a single hour. Inspections and repairs previously carried out in the hangars were switched to dispersals and the Tangmere squadrons, which apart from those already mentioned included at differing times Nos. 17, 213, 602 and 607, continued to give a good account of themselves until the Battle of Britain finally petered out as winter approached.

From early 1941 various Spitfire Squadrons comprising the 'Tangmere Wing' took their share of the 'sweeps' across the Channel which were a feature of those times. No. 1 Squadron came back with their Hurricanes painted black and most nights flew off across the Channel to intrude upon and upset the night-flying activities of the Luftwaffe in northern France. The Germans retaliated in kind on a night early in 1941 when Tangmere, as one of the few fog-free spots in the UK, was receiving returning aircraft of Bomber Command and a number of bombs were dropped, one of which destroyed a barrack block.

Other all-black aeroplanes to be seen at Tangmere from 1941 onwards were the Westland Lysanders of the Special Duty Squadrons. They would land and refuel during the afternoon and disappear into the night, carrying agents of the SOE who, while awaiting air passage, were kept in Tangmere Cottage, a small house across the road from

Above: **Panorama of the camp and blazing hangars after the German bombing raid on August 16, 1940. All the Belfast hangars were hit or damaged and all were demolished by the war's end. The bases were then used for the erection of three T2 hangars which were converted in 1979 with the addition of air conditioning and humidity controls for the storage of part of the European Economic Community's food surplus** *photo below.*

Above: Tangmere's technical site in 1930. The old-style Operations Block then in use (building 33) is marked and also the site for the replacement block constructed in 1939. The long 'garage' hangar is prominent in the foreground. *Right:* Interior of the Operations Room in the new building 113 which was used during the major part of the Battle of Britain — a few regulation-issue drawing pins and a solitary table is all that have survived.

Above: St. James' School in St. James' Road, Chichester was requisitioned as Sector A Operations Centre after the intensive and accurate air attack on Tangmere on August 16, 1940.

Contemporary drawing by war artist Felix Topolski of the Operations Room which was set up in the school hall, photographed for us today by the present headmaster Mr. D. L. Pay

during rehearsals for the Christmas play 1979 — the 'Wizard of Oz'. Evidence of cable runs and other alterations are still visible in parts of the school including a three-phase electricity supply.

Tangmere and its satellites of Westhampnett and Merston photographed by the Luftwaffe at 4.53 p.m. on September 4, 1940. All are well camouflaged with painted tar lines on the aerodrome surfaces to represent fields although the unmistakable 'T' of the two Tangmere runways is evident. Also visible is the cratering caused by the recent bombing (US National Archives).

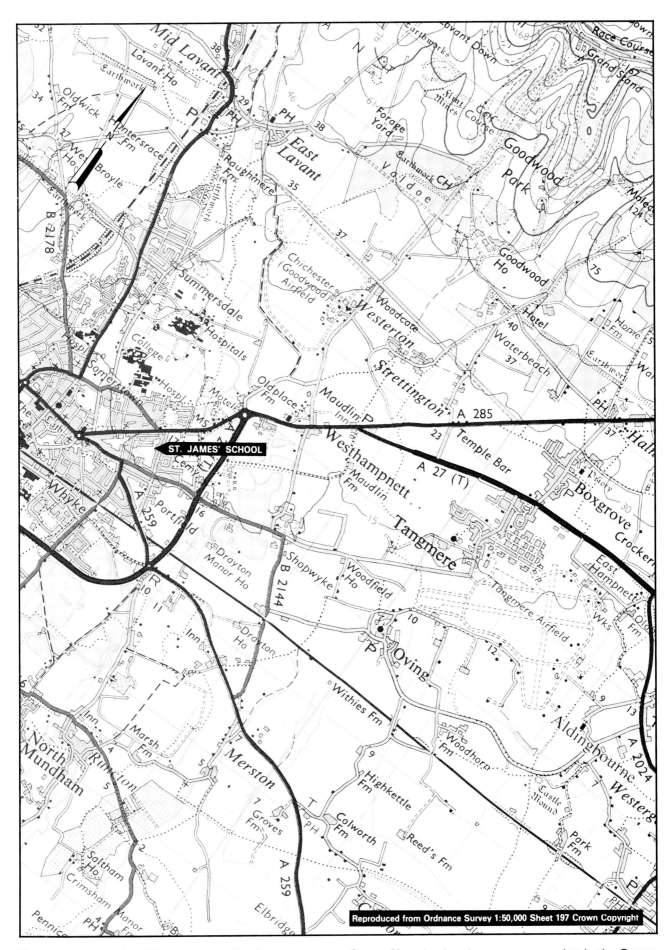

ST. JAMES' SCHOOL

Reproduced from Ordnance Survey 1:50,000 Sheet 197 Crown Copyright

The post-war expansion of Tangmere as well as the construction of the Goodwood motor-racing circuit on Westhampnett aerodrome are graphically illustrated on this current Ordnance Survey Map showing the same area as that in the German reconnaissance photo. St. James' Primary School, the new location for the Tangmere Operations Room, is indicated.

the main entrance to the camp. A second satellite aerodrome to the south at Merston came under Tangmere control in 1941.

On August 19, 1942, the day of the raid on Dieppe, no fewer than ten squadrons of Spitfires and Hurricanes flew more than 400 sorties from Tangmere.

In 1943 the low-level daylight raids by Focke-Wulf Fw 190 fighter-bombers brought two squadrons of Hawker Typhoons to Tangmere as a counter measure.

The build up of air power prior to the Normandy landings in June 1944 saw six Canadian Spitfire IX squadrons of Nos. 126 and 127 Wings in residence and further satellites at Funtingdon, Bognor and Selsey were brought into use.

Following the successful landings in France, Tangmere became a comparatively quiet backwater but, soon after the war was concluded, the Fighter Leaders' School was established there and remained throughout 1945.

In 1946 Meteor jets of the RAF High Speed Flight arrived to set up a new world air speed record of 616 mph. Seven years later Squadron Leader Neville Duke flew in a Hawker Hunter from Tangmere to reclaim the record from a US North American F-86D Sabre (715.67 mph) at 727.6 mph.

A photograph often used to depict the Battle of Britain — taken in fact in 1941! *Above:* **Pilots of No. 601 'County of London' Squadron sprint towards their aircraft on their dispersal at the south-east corner of the drome on January 9 (Fox Photos).** *Below:* **The perimeter tracks of Tangmere are now used for training purposes by the Sussex Police Driving School. Police Constables Cooper, Burns and Flescher with their instructor PC Robins prepare to mount up on the same spot. The huge concrete baffles were erected after the war for the jet era.**

In the post-war period the aerodrome was extended southward and westward, the main runway, NE-SW, being lengthened to 1,800 yards — an operation that necessitated the demolition of the 'Tangmere Arms', the only pub in the village! Three T2 hangars were erected on the bases of those that had been bombed and all traces of those existing prior to 1939, except the remains of the western-most 'garage' hangar, disappeared.

From 1945 to 1958, when Tangmere severed its connections with Fighter Command, the squadrons based there, variously Nos. 1, 25, 29, 43, 85, 164 and 266, flew the usual fighter aircraft of the time — Spitfire LF 16s, 22s, Mosquito NF 36s later Meteor 3s, Meteor 4s, Meteor 8s, Meteor NF 11s and finally the Hawker Hunter. Also, as had been the case prior to 1939, Tangmere was a popular and much visited site for the summer training camps of the Royal Auxiliary Air Force.

From 1958 to 1970 Tangmere was occupied by different Signals Units and also, for the last six years of its active life, by No. 38 Group Support Unit, the aerodrome being used extensively as a dropping zone for training tactical transport aircraft crews.

The final closure parade took place on October 16, 1970 when the Scroll, presented to Tangmere when the station was granted the Honorary Freedom of the City of Chichester in May 1960, was handed back to the Mayor and in 1974 the Ministry of Defence transferred the entire complex of buildings and aerodrome to the Property Services Agency for disposal.

Like many disused airfields, Tangmere has its own band of dedicated devotees who are establishing a Tangmere Aerodrome Memorial Museum. In December 1976, the Tangmere Village Community Centre was instrumental in erecting a memorial stone on the small green adjoining St. Andrews Church.

Above: The end of a morning sortie. Spitfires of No. 92 'East India' Squadron roll across Tangmere's turf towards their dispersals in 1941. Aircraft P7753 apparently displays reversed colours on the fuselage roundel and fin flash indicating that it is flown by a Free French pilot (Jim Beedle). *Below:* The view across the aerodrome in November 1979 from the top of the blast pen which sheltered Spitfire II, QJ-X and which still remains.

'Krautlax for relief!'. The inner wall of the men's toilet which absorbed some of the punishment in the Luftwaffe's guaranteed laxative action.

Cannon shell and machine gun bullet strikes from a strafing attack by a Bf 109F in 1941 still visible on the rear of one of the barrack blocks at Tangmere in November 1979.

Overleaf: Tangmere in October 1979.

PRE-WAR LANDING CIRCLE

NEW OPERATIONS BLOCK

TANGMERE looking south in October 1979

41

NEW ROAD

T2

RUNWAY EXTENSION ACROSS ROAD

Westhampnett

BY WILF NICOLL

Westhampnett began its existence as an emergency landing ground for the fighter squadrons based at Tangmere. In the beginning it was little more than a level meadow but during the month of July 1940 it gradually assumed the status of a satellite landing ground and, as the Battle of Britain progressed, became in turn a satellite aerodrome of Tangmere with its own resident fighter squadron. Later in the war it housed more than one squadron.

Situated approximately one-and-a-half miles north of Chichester, Sussex and just north of the A27 Southampton-Brighton road, it was established in open countryside within the huge estate of Frederick Charles Gordon-Lennox, the Duke of Richmond and Gordon. In time four grass runways were marked out: the longest of 1,500 yards running SE-NW, one of 1,130 yards from NE-SW and another of 1,030 yards extended N-S while the shortest of 920 yards (later extended to 1,100 yards) ran E-W. Later development provided a thirty-five-foot wide tarmacadam surfaced perimeter track encompassing the aerodrome for a total distance of 4,076 yards. Twenty-four thousand gallons of aviation fuel were stored and refuelling was carried out by means of a bowser and trailer tankers. MT petrol supplies amounted to 2,000 gallons.

Aircraft were dispersed and serviced in seven over blister and one extra-over blister hangars and a tin-fronted watch office was built in the north-eastern corner. Early accommodation for pilots and ground crews was, at its best, primitive consisting initially of canvas bell tents until the later erection of barrack and nissen huts. The Officers' Mess was installed in the nearby manor house of Shopwhyke Hall while ORs took their meals 'al fresco'.

The first unit to be accorded the dubious honour of operating from the infant Westhampnett was No. 145 Squadron which took up residence in July 1940. Their tenancy was still in its early stages when Pilot Officer J. E. Storrar more or less unofficially christened the aerodrome when he crashed on take-off on Wednesday, July 24 in Hurricane P3516. Both aircraft and occupant survived to fly another day.

Three days later, the oppressive heat which had been building up over the southern counties broke in a series of colossal thunderstorms which deluged and flooded a number of operational aerodromes to such an extent that all sorties from them were brought to an abrupt halt. Westhampnett was no exception and, until the field dried out, No. 145 returned to the somewhat better drained surfaces of Tangmere.

Operating as it was from one of the most forward of the southern aerodromes, No. 145 Squadron was required to fly virtually every single day of the convoy battles which took place during the month of July.

Westhampnett photographed one year after the end of the war. An extension to the NE-SW runway runs across the perimeter track to Sidengreen Lane (Crown Copyright).

In the late afternoon of August 1, after a relatively quiet morning, David Lloyd, the Tangmere controller scrambled two sections of Hurricanes to investigate two separate plots approaching the south coast. One made indeterminate contact with a Ju 88 while the other caught up with a Henschel Hs 126 of 4(H)/31 about ten miles south of Hastings. It was despatched into the Channel but not before the gunner hit Hurricane P3155 with an accurate burst of machine gun fire which sent it plummeting into the sea, taking the pilot, Sub-Lieutenant I. H. Kestin, to his death.

The squadron's greatest day of combat came on August 8, 1940. During the course of three separate actions south of the Isle of Wight, No. 145 Squadron destroyed seven Ju 87s and four Bf 109s, damaging another five Ju 87s and two Bf 110s. None of this was achieved without cost — and it was high. Five pilots and their aircraft fell into the Channel none of whose bodies have ever been found. At the end of the gruelling day when the shattered survivors had returned to Westhampnett the congratulatory telegrams began flooding in. It is not recorded what effect the high-sounding phrases had on the exhausted pilots although the Secretary of State for Air, the Chief of the Air Staff and the AOC No. 11

Group were all sincere in their praise as was HRH the Duke of Gloucester when he visited Westhampnett later on in the day and personally thanked the airmen for their efforts.

Three days later the squadron was engaged in another life or death struggle over the wide sweep of Weymouth Bay. On August 11 at 10.06 a.m., David Lloyd despatched twelve Hurricanes to reinforce other units heading for Portland and the threat of a '100-plus hostiles' approaching the naval base. In the savage, drifting melee, the squadron lost four Hurricanes, the pilots of two escaping by parachute. Flying Officer A. Ostowicz, either trapped or dead in his stricken aircraft, was carried to an unknown grave. Flying Officer Guy Branch was seen to bale out and land in the sea within sight of the Swanage shore. The Poole lifeboat nearly tore its engine out in a desperate attempt to save him but when they reached the area he had disappeared. His body was eventually washed ashore in France where the Germans buried him with military honours in Quiberville Churchyard.

The following day saw the squadron again committed to action when the Ju 88s of the 'Edelweiss' Geschwader, KG51 attacked the town and dockyards of Portsmouth. Escorted by the Bf 110s of ZGs 2 and 76 and the Bf 109s of JG53, a total of nearly 150 enemy aircraft filled the mid-day sky over the Royal Naval base. In the high whirling dog-fight with the escorts, the squadron lost three pilots and their aircraft. Another was attacked and set on fire by a Spitfire over the Isle of Wight, but was nursed back to Westhampnett by Flight Lieutenant A. H. McN. Boyd who survived the subsequent crash landing. The waters of the Channel had claimed Pilot Officer J. H. Harrison, Sergeant J. Kweicinski and Flight Lieutenant W. Pankratz.

On August 14, No. 602 'City of Glasgow' Auxiliary Squadron flew south from Drem aerodrome in East Lothian to relieve the remnants of No. 145. The story goes that one of the pilots from the new squadron, when about to introduce a colleague to the members of the departing unit, said: 'Come and meet 145. They're nice chaps — all four of them'.

Westhampnett's new tenants wasted no time in making their presence felt. At 6.50 a.m. on the day following their arrival, six Spitfires rose through the early morning mist to take up patrol along the Sussex coastline. At 8.00 a.m. they surprised a solitary reconnaissance Dornier 17 near Portsmouth and, after a wild chase across the Isle of Wight, sent it spinning with all its crew into the Channel.

On August 16, Tangmere's 'Black Friday', when the station was heavily bombed by a large and aggressive force of Ju 87s, No. 602, in defence of their parent station, attacked the escorting Bf 109s of JG2, successfully diverting them from their protective role while Nos. 1, 43 and 601 Squadrons fell upon the Stukas. Two of the units Spitfires returned to

Above: **Squadron Leader A. V. R. Johnstone of No. 602 Squadron lets down over the north-eastern corner at Westhampnett in September 1940 (Crown Copyright).** *Below:* **With the old Goodwood pits in the background, another high-performance machine enjoys the freedom of an empty perimeter track.**

base badly damaged, one of them, P9463, crash-landing in flames. Both pilots were unhurt and the aircraft were ultimately repaired. Approximately three hours later a coastal patrol from Westhampnett downed two Bf 110s of ZG76 without loss.

Two days after the Tangmere attack the Luftwaffe attempted similar raids on the naval aerodromes at Ford and Gosport and the Coastal Command base at Thorney Island. A fourth formation headed for the Chain Home radar station at Poling. Having been alerted in plenty of time and fearing a repetition of the previous Friday's dive-bombing attack, David Lloyd had scrambled his squadrons with orders to patrol their bases. Just after 2.00 p.m. the enemy force, composed of eighty-five Ju 87s from three Gruppen of StG 77 and twenty-five Ju 88s of KG54 escorted by two Gruppen of Bf 109s from JG27, crossed the Sussex coast and headed for their allotted targets. The Ju 88s carried out a successful and unopposed attack on Gosport before escaping back to France and it was left to the Ju 87s to weather the storm of fire that was about to fall upon them. With their escort fully engaged by the attentions of No. 234 Squadron's Spitfires, the Stukas suffered heavily at the hands of Nos. 152, 601 and 602 Squadrons. Eighteen Ju 87s were lost or had to be written off including the leader of the raid, Hauptmann Meisel, and his gunner,

Obergefreiter Jakob. It was to be the last appearance of the Stuka in force over Britain. Out of the impressive total, No. 602 claimed four destroyed and four damaged for the loss of one Spitfire whose pilot Sergeant B. E. P. Whall ditched it at Elmer Sands, Middleton to emerge unscathed. Four other Spitfires were damaged, two pilots being wounded.

One of the most remarkable escapes of the day was that of Flying Officer P. J. Ferguson whose Spitfire K9969 was hit by Bf 109 machine gun fire in the port wing and petrol tank. Wounded and in shock he was returning to base when he collided with the Poling RDF mast causing further damage to his aircraft which necessitated an immediate crash-landing. This he successfully accomplished at Norway Farm, Rustington after flying through a line of high tension electricity cables!

On August 23, Pilot Officer T. G. F. Ritchie returned to base with a badly-bent Spitfire after miraculously surviving a high-speed collision with an unidentified RAF fighter during a furious chase through broken cloud after three Ju 88s which had made a hit and run attack on Thorney Island.

Three days later Flying Officer C. H. McLean in an agony of pain from wounds received in a skirmish with Bf 109s of JG53, belly-landed his battle-torn aircraft at Tangmere. In the crash-landing, the officer's right foot was amputated. The Spitfire,

WOODCOTE CORNER

LAVANT STRAIGHT

LAVANT CORNER

ST. MARY'S

X4187, was later repaired and flown again in battle.

From August 24, the Luftwaffe introduced a new tactic into the battle — one which had worked well during the German conquests from Poland to France. In an all out effort to decimate Fighter Command, the new phase brought attacks in strength against the southern aerodromes. For the RAF's fighter pilots, it meant greater pressures and even less respite than they had had before. Later, a retaliatory bombing raid carried out on Berlin by Bomber Command on the night of August 25/26 was to result in the introduction of the third phase of the battle.

On the day of London's martyrdom, September 7, No. 602 Squadron lost two pilots. Twenty-three-year-old Pilot Officer W. H. Coverley, trapped in his blazing Spitfire high over Tonbridge, eventually succeeded in abandoning it. While many witnessed the fiery end of his aircraft at Fosters Farm, no one it seems saw him drift to earth. He died of grievous burns where he landed, his body remaining undiscovered for nine days. No trace was ever found of the other casualty, Pilot Officer H. W. Moody.

Elements of the squadron undertook night-flying training from Tangmere on September 10 in their eagerness to get to grips with the German bombers now pounding the capital nightly. The only thing that they succeeded in proving was the unsuitability of the Spitfire for the night-fighting role. Three aircraft were damaged in the exercise, two of them trying to land back at Tangmere the other crashing on Felpham Golf Course. Fortunately none of the pilots was injured.

The following day, No. 602 tangled with enemy fighters over Selsey Bill. Sergeant Cyril Babbage and Pilot Officer S. N. Rose reached Westhampnett with damaged aircraft, the latter being slightly wounded but Sergeant M. H. Sprague failed to return. One month later the sea gave up its dead when his body was washed ashore at Brighton.

With the advent of October came the Jabos. The late autumn weather with its low, broken cloud and rain squalls made it ideal sport for the low-flying, bomb-carrying Bf 109s which were rarely picked up on the radio location screens. In an effort to counteract the new menace, squadrons were forced to maintain standing patrols. In was now two months since No. 602 had arrived at Westhampnett and the pressures and strain of continuous combat flying from a front line aerodrome began to take their toll of the weary pilots.

On October 5, Sergeant B. E. P. Whall, DFM, his Spitfire badly damaged by the return fire from a Ju 88 off Beachy Head, attempted to force-land at Willington but spun in and exploded on impact. An experienced fighter pilot at the age of twenty-two, he died as the ambulance reached hospital. Towards the end of the battle Sergeant D. W. Elcome, who had survived the night crash on Felpham Golf Course, lifted his Spitfire from Westhampnett and set course for his patrol line. Soon he was lost to sight in the haze over the Channel. Just another routine patrol but not for this twenty-one-year-old pilot as neither he nor his aircraft were ever found.

On October 30, three of the squadron's Spitfires were surprised by Bf 109s in a classic 'bounce' over Dungeness. One returned to base with wing tip damage and one forced-landed near Dymchurch both pilots being unhurt. The third was crash-landed on the foreshore at Lydd by its wounded pilot, Sergeant W. B. Smith.

No. 602 Squadron remained at Westhampnett until December, 1940 when they were replaced by another Spitfire-equipped Auxiliary unit, No. 610 'County of Chester' Squadron. Meanwhile, in November, No. 302, the first of the Polish fighter squadrons to have been formed, arrived from Northolt with their Hurricane Is to take up residence.

Early in May 1941, No. 616 'South Yorkshire' Squadron joined Westhampnett's other tenants, bringing with it pilots whose

TANGMERE

MADGEWICK CORNER

names are recorded in the annals of the Royal Air Force. Men such as Flying Officer H. S. L. 'Cocky' Dundas, Pilot Officer J. E. 'Johnny' Johnson and the living legend of the service — Wing Commander D. R. S. Bader.

During this time, the commissioned pilots still continued to use Shopwhyke Hall as the Officers' Mess but were accommodated in the large rambling house called 'Rushmans' in the village of Oving due, in the main, to the regular nocturnal visits by the Luftwaffe to Tangmere. Off-duty hours were frequently spent sampling the local brew in the Unicorn public house at Chichester and occasionally, when their slender means permitted, dining at 'The Old Ship' Club at Bosham.

All the south-east coast aerodromes were now given over to the business of carrying the war to the enemy in the form of offensive sweeps of various kinds. Code names such as 'Rhubarb', 'Circus', 'Rodeo' and 'Ramrod' became part of the English language and the British, Allied and Commonwealth exponents of the art filtered through Westhampnett at irregular intervals, adding its name to their log books in passing.

During the build-up to the invasion of Europe, Westhampnett played its part by providing fighter aircraft as escorts for the great daylight bombing raids planned to disrupt the rail and road transport systems in

German-occupied Europe, and later as fighter cover for the D-Day landings and for anti-'Diver' patrols during the V1 flying bomb campaign.

However, as the Allied armies thrust their way into Europe and fighter units took up bases on landing grounds carved out of French, Belgian and Dutch fields so the aerodromes in the United Kingdom were left high and dry by the receding tide of battle. After September 1944, combat operations ceased from Westhampnett and the fighting units departed.

With the cessation of hostilities in May 1945, Westhampnett looked like suffering the same fate as hundreds of other aerodromes spawned in the turmoil of war. However, the Duke of Richmond and Gordon a noted patron of motor-racing and himself a skilled racing driver, recognised the potential of the two-and-a-half miles of tarmacadam perimeter track which had been constructed on his land and, on Saturday, September 18, 1948, the circuit, renamed Goodwood, was officially opened. The winner of the first race was Reg Parnell driving at an average of 80.56 mph and he was awarded the Goodwood Trophy. Thereafter the name of Goodwood became a byword in post-war motor-racing.

Although some alterations were carried out in 1952, the increasing speed and develop-

Note the close proximity of Tangmere, just two miles to the south-east, in this oblique taken on October 18, 1979.

ment of cars, together with several tricky corners on the relatively narrow track, made the course increasingly dangerous. Stirling Moss suffered a particularly nasty accident and the lack of crash barriers around the majority of the circuit did little to ensure the safety of drivers or spectators. In the end, the cost of the necessary improvements were deemed to be too great and the British Automobile Racing Circuit closed in 1965. However, Goodwood continues to be used by manufacturers and teams for practise and testing of racing cars.

The resurrection of Westhampnett/ Goodwood as an active airfield came in 1958 when planning permission was received for the provision of two landing strips and a form of flying control. Developed by the Goodwood Terrena Company, the aerodrome now covers 265 acres and provides three grass runways, the longest being 1,458 with two of 1,013 yards and 980 yards respectively.

Today the aerodrome sees over 50,000 aircraft movements per year and a new hangar and flying club offices have been erected although many of the RAF buildings still remain.

SECTOR B
Kenley

BY PETER CORBELL

Above: **Pilots, ground crews, pets and Hurricane Is of No. 3 Squadron assemble in front of the signals square at Kenley on May 23, 1938. In the background a camouflaged Demon taxies towards the watch office (Flight).** *Below:* **Looking north-west across the aerodrome from the watch office site on October 23, 1979. The only activity in sight once more centres around dogs. These belong to the Surrey Police and with their handlers find the old aerodrome an ideal place for training.**

Kenley was originally established in the summer of 1917 as No. 7 Acceptance Park, RFC. In April 1919, No. 1 (Communication) Squadron arrived from Hendon and, until September of the same year, operated a regular service between London and Paris for the convenience of members of the Government attending the Peace Conference at Versailles.

The aerodrome was reconstructed in the early twenties and Station Headquarters was formed there on September 22, 1924, the original squadrons being No. 24 (Communications), equipped with Avro 504s, DH9s and F2Bs, and No. 32 Squadron equipped with Snipes.

In September 1932, the squadrons moved to Biggin Hill whilst Kenley was closed for further rebuilding. By 1934, the construction work had been completed and in May Station HQ and Nos. 3 and 17 Squadrons arrived from Upavon. Between the wars, squadrons from Kenley took part in the annual air display at Hendon and, due to its proximity to London, received many important visitors.

The aerodrome at that time had an irregularly-shaped grass landing area measuring 775 yards N-S; 843 yards NE-SW; 629 yards from E-W and SE-NW.

At the beginning of 1939, squadrons present were No. 3 (Hurricanes), No. 17 (Gauntlets) and No. 615 (Tutors and Hectors). 'F' Maintenance Unit was also there. Both the regular squadrons moved away in May 1939 and by August the aerodrome was mainly out of commission due to the laying of runways and perimeter tracks. The site was handed to the contractors, Constable, Hart & Co., on July 12. Demolition of the old hangars took place and, by the end of the year, the establishment of the new concrete runways and taxitracks was completed.

The perimeter track was 50ft wide whilst the two runways running NW-SE and NE-SW measured 1,000 and 1,200 yards respectively.

Fuel storage totalled 35,000 gallons of aviation spirit, 8,000 gallons of motor fuel and 2,500 gallons of oil. One-and-a-quarter million rounds of small arms ammunition was kept immediately available on the station.

Aerodrome defence consisted of four 40mm Bofors guns manned by the 31st Light Anti-Aircraft Battery (the 'Rough Riders'), two 3-inch guns operated by the 148th Light AA Battery and twenty or so Lewis guns in a dual ground-air role. Kenley also had a secret weapon in the form of a parachute and cable installation along the northern perimeter track. This device fired a cable suspended by a parachute some 600 feet into the air and was to be launched in salvoes in the path of low-flying aircraft. If an aircraft hit the cable, a second parachute opened at the lower end to counterbalance the whole contraption and, hopefully, drag the entangled aircraft down.

Soon Croydon became available as a wartime satellite and the two regular squadrons, now equipped with Hurricanes, were posted there to be joined later by No. 615 Squadron. Kenley was established as Sector HQ of 'B' Sector in No. 11 Group, Fighter Command. Redhill became an alternative airfield for Croydon and the satellite at Gatwick was to be used if Kenley had to be evacuated.

No. 56 Elementary and Reserve Flying Training School, which had formed on August 24, 1939, was closed the following month after only six Tiger Moths and three Harts had been received. In January 1940, No. 3 Squadron returned to Kenley to be joined by No. 253 Squadron from Northolt. No. 3 was despatched to the Continent on May 10, 1940 and one Ensign, one Bombay and one Harrow with ground crews and equipment accompanied the Hurricanes.

Seven days later, 'B' Flight of No. 111 Squadron arrived to form a composite squadron with 'A' Flight from No. 253

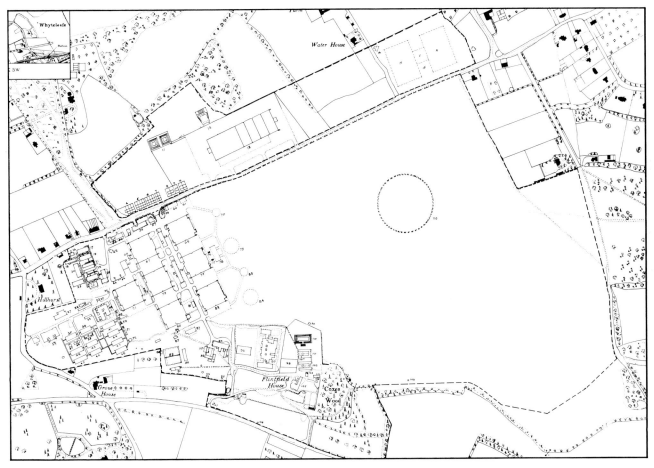

The expansion of Kenley in 1939. *Above:* An extract from a 1932 drawing showing the old hangars and small grass field (RAF Museum) *Below:* Sketch in the station ORB showing the diversion of Hayes Lane and new runways (Crown Copyright).

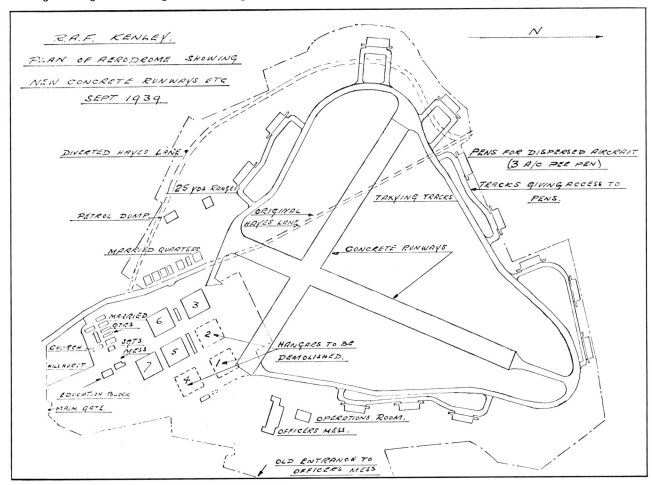

R.A.F. KENLEY.
PLAN OF AERODROME SHOWING
NEW CONCRETE RUNWAYS ETC
SEPT 1939

DIVERTED HAYES LANE

25 YDS RANGE

PETROL DUMP

MARRIED QUARTERS

ORIGINAL HAYES LANE

PENS FOR DISPERSED AIRCRAFT
(3 A/C PER PEN)

TRACKS GIVING ACCESS TO PENS.

TAXYING TRACKS

CONCRETE RUNWAYS

MARRIED QTRS

SGTS MESS

CHURCH

HILLHURST

EDUCATION BLOCK

MAIN GATE

HANGARS TO BE DEMOLISHED.

OPERATIONS ROOM.

OFFICERS MESS.

OLD ENTRANCE TO OFFICERS MESS

N

The walls and main entrance to the boarded-up Officers' Mess still retain the scars of battle. The building may shortly be converted for use as a radio research centre.

Squadron and on the 18th this unit flew over France on a Cambrai/Le Cateau patrol shooting down five enemy aircraft for the loss of one. Two aircraft returned to Kenley direct but the rest landed in France at Vitry-en-Artois. They were preparing to take off to return to Kenley when the aerodrome was bombed and only three Hurricanes survived to return home. During the rest of May, aircraft of Nos. 3 and 615 Squadrons returned from France and a flight from No. 229 Squadron arrived to form a squadron with No. 253. On July 12 Prime Minister Winston Churchill inspected No. 615 (County of Surrey) Squadron at Kenley.

Right: Kenley photographed in October 1979 looking towards the direction from where the German raiders attacked the aerodrome on August 18. *Below:* Picture taken by German war photographer Rolf von Pebal in one of the low-flying Dorniers crossing the drome. The diverted Hayes Lane can be seen top left. (The original track of the road can still be seen crossing the aerodrome in the modern oblique.)

OPERATIONS BLOCK

PRE-WAR LANDING CIRCLE

An airman sadly contemplates the wrecks of cars in the burnt out remains of the MT hangar at Kenley after the raid of August 18, 1940.

Another picture of the wrecked hangar — or is it? A remarkably similar photograph of the last remaining hangar after it was burnt down on October 23, 1978!

'We best teach
Bloody instructions, which being taught, return
To plague the inventor.'

William Shakespeare, Macbeth.

Left: Pilots of No. 253 Squadron with their commanding officer, Squadron Leader P. R. 'Johnny' Walker (with pipe) at an impromptu aircraft recognition lecture held by the squadron intelligence officer in December 1940 in one of the eastern perimeter aircraft blast pens (Popperfoto). *Right:* The inexorable advance of nature is apparent everywhere at Kenley as it is on other deserted aerodromes. The blast pen where the lessons of identification were taught is crumbling away year by year.

On August 18 at 1.22 p.m., between thirty and fifty enemy bombers attacked the aerodrome at medium level whilst a Staffel of Do 17s escorted by Bf 109s came in low from the east. Despite a barrage from the parachute and cable installation which brought down one Dornier which crashed just outside the aerodrome, the station suffered considerable damage from about 100 HE bombs of which twenty-four were delayed action. All told, three hangars, equipment stores, four Hurricanes on the ground and a Blenheim were destroyed and four other aircraft damaged. All communications were cut as were water and gas mains. There were nineteen casualties including nine deaths.

A further attack occurred on September 1 when eight bombers flew in at 2.30 p.m. in a combined high-level and dive-bombing attack. However only one bomb fell on RAF property, two near the main gates and the rest further afield. Three bombs fell in Buxton Lane causing serious damage to living quarters.

On September 4, No. 253 Squadron shot down six Bf 110s without loss and five days later destroyed a further five Ju 88s in the Leatherhead/Brooklands area. On October 17 there was a further attack in which nine aircraft on the ground were hit and seven craters made in the landing ground. The following month a night-bombing attack damaged a hangar, living quarters and offices and killed two. By now, Shoreham and Redhill were also satellites and, at the latter, No. 219 Squadron were receiving their first Beaufighters.

In 1941, the Kenley Wing took to the offensive with 'rhubarbs' and 'circuses' escorting Blenheims and, in July, Stirlings. In September the Station HQ at High House, Whyteleafe Road moved to Peterswood in Torwood Lane. An unusual operation in November was to provide an escort for three Tomahawks covering a recce on Cap Gris Nez for the Dover guns.

At the beginning of 1942, Group Captain F. V. Beamish became Officer Commanding. An officer at the time stated that to serve under Beamish was an inspiration. There was not a job on the ground or in the air that he could not do and not a man or woman on the station that he did not know by name in a very short time. He frequently flew with the Wing and was the first to spot the German battleships steaming up the Channel in February 1942. On March 28 the Kenley Wing engaged enemy fighters about to dive on the Biggin Hill Wing and Group Captain Beamish and three others were lost. Eleven aircraft were claimed shot down.

In August, No. 308 FS, USAAF with Spitfires arrived and took part in a 'rodeo' on the 5th. On the 19th, in Operation Jubilee, the Wing Commander (Flying) flew four sorties over Dieppe, Nos. 611 and 402 Squadrons five sorties each and Nos. 111, 350 and 308 (US) Squadrons four sorties each.

No. 308 (US) Squadron then departed to be replaced by No. 4 FS, 52nd FG, also with Spitfires. In September, Nos. 401, 412 and 416 Squadrons, all of the Royal Canadian Air Force, arrived to form a Canadian Spitfire Wing and, for a number of months, Canadian squadrons operated from Kenley, led by Wing Commander J. E. Johnson from March 1943.

As at June 1, 1943, the Kenley Sector consisted of forward aerodromes at Croydon and Redhill and satellites at Friston, Penshurst and Shoreham. 'Ramrods' were now the chief operations of the No. 11 Group squadrons. No. 127 (RCAF) Airfield formed on July 12, moving out to summer quarters at Lashenden in August and arriving back in mid-October. In the meantime, RAF fighter squadrons returned to Kenley to escort B-26s and B-17s over France.

The Kenley sector was absorbed by Biggin Hill on March 4, 1944 and, nine days later, the last operation from Kenley was carried out. This consisted of 'Ramrod 730' when Nos. 416 and 421 Squadrons escorted bombers to Namur in Belgium. On the 15th, No. 127 Airfield moved out to Tangmere and Kenley was thereafter administered by a

Above: Fifteen years after the Battle of Britain, Kenley relived some of the great moments of its past when the station became the location for the making of the film 'Reach for the Sky'. Kenneth More played the part of Douglas Bader in the biographical film and here, on September 10, 1955, he gets a few pointers on tactics from Group Captain Harry 'Wings' Day (Radio Times).

holding party. In all, the Sector had destroyed 603 enemy aircraft with 231 probably destroyed.

By June 1944, the anti-V1 balloon barrage had closed Kenley to flying altogether and, on the 28th of that month, a flying bomb fell among requisitioned properties just south of the camp doing considerable damage to houses and the camp cinema.

No. 11 Group lost control of Kenley on July 1, 1945 when it was transferred to No. 46 Group, Transport Command. In October the following year, the aerodrome became the HQ of No. 61 Group, Reserve Command.

During 1946-7, Kenley was used as a store for captured German and Japanese equipment and, amongst the varied specialist weapons and vehicles V1s and V2s were readily available for examination by the Air Ministry technicians. Also during this period Westminster Airways operated a passenger service from the aerodrome and shared the only available hangar with No. 61 Group Communications Flight. The Air Officer Commanding, Air Commodore Harry Broadhurst, would often land his personal steed, a captured Fieseler Storch painted bright blue, on the width of the runway!

A POW compound was maintained on the Group HQ side of the aerodrome and some seventy-three Germans helped in redecorating the buildings including the station church.

Flying was mainly carried out by the Auxiliary Air Observation Post Flights Nos. 1957 and 1960 (661 Squadron) with Austers and Tiger Moths. No. 143 Gliding School and London University Air Squadron were also present for shorter periods. RAF Kenley was eventually disbanded on May 1, 1959 to become Air Ministry Unit, No. 615 (Air Cadets) Gliding School, with Sedbergh and Cadet gliders continued to use the airfield. Various Reserve Flights occupied the station from late 1959 until 1964 when the sole occupants were No. 605 Mobile Signals Unit which had arrived on September 26, 1963. They, in turn, were posted on February 21, 1966 leaving the station to a 'care and maintenance' party.

Today the whole of the technical site is under Army control and the RAF married quarters are now occupied by the families of men serving with the 2nd Battalion, The Coldstream Guards, based at Caterham. The aerodrome however is still under the management of RAF Biggin Hill and is officially designated an emergency landing airfield and is used by the Air Training Corps for gliding instruction.

In October 1978, the destruction of the hangars, begun by the Germans in 1940, was completed when a glow was seen in the storeroom of the sole remaining Belfast. The hangar was soon ablaze and nothing could be done by the fire brigade to save the building

Above: **The standard pre-war RAF Operations Block. The only protection to the ordinary single-storey brick building was a six-foot earth bank. This one at Kenley still survives.**

The nerve centre of Sector B — the Operations Room. Although now derelict and vandalised, it still retains the raised walkway although the controller's platform on the right has gone. The only old-style Sector ops room to have survived more or less as it was is at Duxford. At 8.30 p.m. on September 3, operations were moved according to the pre-arranged dispersal plans formulated by Air Vice-Marshal E. L. Gossage, who commanded No. 11 Group during the first eight months of war. 'Camp B', as the new Kenley Operations Block was code-named, was in fact a butcher's shop!

from being gutted. Photographs taken afterwards showed a remarkable similarity to those taken in 1940 following the bombing attack of August 18 which had destroyed the other hangars. By September 1979 the walls had been demolished and the rubble cleared prior to the erection in wood and canvas of a temporary hangar for the Air Cadets.

Old Caterham, 1902. No.11 Godstone Road, the butcher's shop owned by Messrs. Spice and Wallis, is arrowed.

Demolished in 1970, the site was replaced by a new building now occupied by the Dalgety freezer centre.

51

Croydon

BY WILF NICOLL

Situated fourteen miles south of London on the southern edge of the town of Croydon, the old aerodrome is bounded on the north by the B271, on the east by the A23 and on the west by the B272. Its name stands out like a beacon in the annals of civil aviation history and is synonymous with the development and expansion of British air transport. Although Croydon's connections with military aviation are brief its short history is nonetheless a distinguished one.

In 1915, the War Office established an aerodrome on land purchased from a local farmer to house No. 17 Reserve Air Squadron, Royal Flying Corps. It was then known as Waddon aerodrome and was made up of three wooden hangars and a collection of huts situated on the west side of Plough Lane.

On the night of April 2/3, 1916, Croydon was one of the four aerodromes from which seven aircraft took off to intercept a German Army airship which had dropped its entire bomb load on Waltham Abbey, Essex. Although the raider was seen, the pilots found it impossible to overhaul the enemy and engage him and the gas-filled leviathan was last seen ascending rapidly eastwards towards the coast. Three of the aircraft were damaged on return to their bases without injury to their pilots.

With the advent of the Armistice came the disbandment of many of the Royal Air Force's squadrons. Two of the most famous, Nos. 32 and 41, both formed in 1916, were briefly based at Croydon in October 1919 before disbanding. No. 32 Squadron ceased to exist on December 29, 1919 and No. 41 Squadron on December 31. However, both units were reformed on April 1, 1923 and were to acquit themselves nobly during the Battle of Britain.

An important announcement made by the Government on May 1, 1919 had a direct bearing on Croydon's future prosperity. This took the form of official permission for civil flying to recommence. It was from this date that Croydon's role as a major civil airport was assured although it did not become London's main airport until April 1, 1920.

A new landing area had now been established on the east side of Plough Lane and, in consequence, a man was employed to stop road traffic with a red flag when aircraft were taxi-ing across. Later a level crossing was constructed to facilitate the passage of aircraft from the hangars to the landing area.

The following year saw the opening of two routes to the Continent: between London and Paris on March 19 and from London to Amsterdam on April 14. The terminal area at this time was situated adjacent to Plough Lane and it was said that pilots of the early, open cockpit passenger aircraft could fly into the aerodrome on the smell wafted from Croydon's municipal gasworks!

In mid-1921, the Air Ministry erected a wooden tower, similar in appearance to an oil derrick and 140 feet high, on the old wartime aerodrome in preparation for the arrival of the dirigible R33 in July. This visited Croydon on two consecutive days as an experiment and, with the aid of a fairground style traction engine, was coupled to the mooring line and successfully hauled down and anchored to the nose cone atop the masthead. It later transpired that the tower had been erected without the landowner's permission and the Ministry were obliged to dismantle it, thereafter abandoning the project.

On April 1, 1924, one of the most important events in the history of the airport took place with the merger of Instone Air Line Ltd., Daimler Airways Ltd., Handley Page Transport Ltd. and The British Marine Air Navigation Co. Ltd. into the new company of Imperial Airways Ltd. — a name inseparable from that of Croydon itself. Almost immediately the infant company was hit by industrial strife in the form of a strike by pilots and staff — the tourists had their problems even then. This however was settled on May 2 and Imperial Airways went on to become one of the most famous trail-blazing companies in civil aviation. Between 1924 and 1931 air routes from Croydon to every country in the Commonwealth and Europe were opened and developed. Meanwhile the airport itself was growing to meet the demands of heavier air traffic.

What was described in contemporary news accounts as the worst disaster in British aviation occurred on Wednesday, December 24, 1924, when an Imperial Airways' DH 34 suffered engine failure just after take-off. The pilot attempted to turn back for a landing on the aerodrome but stalled, spun-in and crashed on the outskirts of Purley killing himself and his seven passengers.

'Blessed be the man that spares these stones' — Shakespeare. The facade of Croydon's terminal building in the winter of 1937-38. A member of the aerodrome control staff scrutinizes the photographer through binoculars from the control tower (Fox Photos).

During the 1920s and '30s, Croydon was the departure and arrival point for many of the record-breaking flights and such was the intensity of the competition that records set one week were invariably broken the next. Many household names of the period such as Cobham, Johnson, Mollison, Chichester and Kingsford-Smith found their way into the newspaper headlines and the record books via Croydon.

It was during this period that the centre of Plough Lane disappeared from the road maps when the original RFC site was fully incorporated within the landing field area.

In May 1927, the airport was thronged with over 100,000 people waiting to greet their hero of the hour, Captain Charles Lindbergh, who flew his Ryan NYA Monoplane *Spirit of St. Louis* into Croydon a few days after his arrival in Paris at the end of his epic solo Atlantic flight. He was followed by two of his countrymen on August 28 when Schlee and Brock landed during their round the world flight.

May 2, 1928 saw the inaugural opening of the still-existing terminal building by Lady Maude Hoare, wife of the then-Air Minister. Later the same year, on September 18, a new flight form was witnessed at Croydon when

Left: **Croydon just prior to the outbreak of war looking east with the terminal building on the far boundary (Aerofilms).** *Above:* **October 1979, just twenty years after its closure, a factory estate, offices and a school gradually encroach on the aerodrome.**

Senor Don Juan de la Cierva, the Spanish pioneer of VTOL aircraft, flew his autogiro from the airport to Paris. Tragically, and ironically, he was killed in an airliner crash at Croydon on December 9, 1936.

The form of markings then employed at the aerodrome conformed to Air Ministry practice as described in Annex F, Section II of the Convention Relating to the Regulation of Air Navigation. Displayed on the centre of the airfield surface was a large white landing circle, approximately 150 feet in diameter, with the name of the airport painted alongside in letters twenty feet high, sixteen feet wide and spaced a similar distance apart. A long, straight white line ran across the aerodrome for the guidance of pilots taking off in fog and, close to the landing circle, a wind direction indicator emitted white smoke. An illuminated T-shaped wind indicator, the arms of which were twenty feet long and two feet wide, was installed near the hangars on the north-east side of the aerodrome. Boundary lights, spaced 100 yards apart

marked the confines of the landing ground in orange coloured lamps and a morse code flashing 'Pundit' beacon identified the aerodrome at night.

Croydon's control tower was situated some sixty feet above ground on the operational side of the terminal building. Divided by a glass partition, one part housed the duty controller's watch office and the other the radio communications office and equipment. The watch office was about thirty feet square, glazed on all sides and surrounded by an observation balcony. Immediately in front and extending to right and left was a tarmac apron for the parking of aircraft and the embarking and setting down of passengers. To the right of the terminal building lay the Aerodrome Hotel.

The signal for an aircraft to taxi across the aerodrome prior to departure was given by the display of a large green panel on the side of the control tower parapet with the international letter of the aircraft displayed upon it in white. Having reached the take-off position, the pilot turned his machine into wind and watched the tower for the take-off signal. This took the form of a white light which was beamed through a swivel telescope aligned on the aircraft. At night a hand-held Aldis lamp was used to transmit the aircraft's call sign in Morse code — in green if clear to take-off or land and red if not. Red Very lights were also used. In foggy weather only one aircraft at a time was allowed to leave the tarmac to taxi across the aerodrome.

To commemorate the 20th Anniversary of his cross-channel flight, Monsieur Bleriot flew into Croydon on July 27, 1929. (His original feat took place on July 25, 1909.)

With the arrival of the thirties came the era of the air taxi and 'joy flights'. Private charter aircraft were readily available from any one of a dozen companies. Used in the main by punters attending the various race meetings, business men and commercial travellers, they were a boon to anyone to whom speed was essential. Eloping couples and honeymooners were among the first to grasp the benefits and the romance then attached to flying no doubt added piquancy to the occasion.

Charges for private charter ranged from one shilling (5 pence) per mile for a two-passenger Leopard Moth, one shilling and fourpence (7

Airport House, August 1979. Like a retired diplomat behind sandwich boards, the venerable old building is obscured by a modern self-service petrol station. The telephone kiosk has also survived, albeit in a more up to date form.

pence) for a three-passenger Vega Gull, two shillings (10 pence) for a six-passenger Dragon Rapide and three shillings and six-pence (17½ pence) per mile for a ten-passenger, four-engined De Havilland 86B Express airliner! On one occasion an aircraft was chartered from Birkett Air Services Ltd. to fly two men to Tangier for the purpose of enlisting in the French Foreign Legion. However both had to return to that which they were trying to forget when they were rejected by the recruiting officer!

It had been realized for some time that Croydon was becoming increasingly un-suitable for the position of London's main airport in view of the volume of traffic using the aerodrome. Added to this was the frequency of fog, low-lying cloud, the congestion of radio aids and the en-croachment of housing development with urban expansion. In 1938 air traffic movements exceeded a 100 per day with more than 100,000 visitors to the airport being recorded annually plus a further 70,000 admissions to the public enclosure. At this time, although the Government were spending over £40,000 annually on its upkeep, Croydon operated at an annual loss of nearly £2,000.

On August 29, 1939, the evacuation plans for Croydon were put into effect. All civil aircraft were dispersed to Coventry, Exeter and Whitchurch and the airport became Royal Air Force Station, Croydon. The air-field was chosen to be a semi-permanent base within No. 11 Group Fighter Command to which squadrons could be withdrawn for short periods from the sector and forward aerodromes for tactical or logistical reasons. Its parent station was Kenley and squadrons from there used it on a rotational basis or when that aerodrome became unusable for any reason whatever. Officially it had ac-commodation for two fighter squadrons. Four landing areas had been specifically laid out on the grass surface of the aerodrome, the two longest, each of 1,200 yards running N-S and NE-SW. The E-W runway had a length of 1,120 yards and that from SE-NW a total distance of only 966 yards. The terminal building had now become the administration block and the thirty-bedroom Aerodrome Hotel was taken over for pilots ac-commodation and messing. Storage was available for 46,000 gallons of aviation fuel, 2,000 gallons of MT fuel and 2,000 gallons of oil. Two ammunition stores had been built in

Above: **An example of the camouflage expert's art. A D-type hangar at Croydon displays the subtlety of its disguise in early 1939. Lining the aerodrome's northern boundary are the houses in Stafford Road (Imperial War Museum).** *Below:* **The site of the camouflaged hangar in August 1979 now occupied by Brown Brothers Ltd.**

the extreme south-east corner of the station and these now housed 1,500,000 rounds of small arms ammunition. Later in the war a concrete perimeter track 35 feet 6 inches wide was constructed around the grass together with a number of fighter pens and hard-standings, all of which were situated on the west side of the aerodrome.

The last grains of peace were trickling inexorably through the time glass when pilots of No. 3 Squadron flew their Hurricanes from Biggin Hill on Saturday September 2, to take up station at Croydon. They were joined by No. 615 'County of Surrey' Auxiliary Air Force Squadron from Kenley equipped with Gladiators.

On Monday, September 4, No. 3 Squadron were sent on their first scramble of the war. No enemy was encountered and the pilots returned with the fabric patches still intact over their gun ports.

October 10 saw the re-forming of No. 145 Squadron at Croydon as a day and night fighter unit.

During December No. 3 Squadron left for the forward 'drome at Hawkinge while into Croydon came another Blenheim-equipped fighter unit. This was No. 92 Squadron which had reformed on October 10 at Tangmere. During its stay at Croydon, the squadron supplied a detachment of aircraft to Gatwick, the Sussex airport completed in 1936 but now absorbed into the air defence system.

With the coming of spring the squadron converted to Spitfire 1As, much to the relief and undisguised delight of its pilots. Amongst the pilots of No. 145 Squadron there was a feeling of envy tinged with a modicum of anticipation as it was rumoured that they would soon follow suit. When the changeover came in March, it materialised in the hump-backed form of Hawker Hurricanes. From then on there was no holding back for either unit. In the spirit of friendly rivalry that existed between squadrons in the Royal Air Force, the race to be the first to reach operational perfection with their new mounts was on. Night flying training under the im-posed black-out conditions of the time was full of terrifying hazards for inexperienced pilots. On one night alone at Croydon, four accidents

involving Hurricanes took place. Two aircraft collided with each other while taxi-ing to the take-off point while another taxied into a searchlight position. A fourth having got airborne made three unsuccessful attempts to land, suffered engine failure on the fourth circuit and crashed into the grounds of Purley Hospital.

On May 10, 1940, the German 'Blitzkrieg' in the west began. All the RAF units in France took heavy losses from the first day until June 18 when the last squadron was withdrawn. Many were decimated. During May, No. 145 Squadron left Croydon for the Bristol Aircraft Company's aerodrome at Filton where it ferried Hurricanes to France and participated in the fighting. Towards the end of May the survivors began arriving back in Britain. On May 22, 1940, the tattered exhausted rem-nants of No. 607 Squadron returned to Croydon. However, what was left of the unit had to be despatched to its home base at Usworth, near Gateshead, County Durham, to re-equip and remuster.

In June No. 111 Squadron flew in to Croydon from North Weald. It had been heavily engaged in patrols and the subsequent air battles over the beaches and evacuation ports of France and Belgium and now needed a quiet backwater to recover its strength. On the 21st they were joined by No. 501 Squadron which moved west to Middle Wallop on July 3 after refitting. Later that month No. 1 Royal Canadian Air Force Squadron moved in to Croydon on a non-operational basis while modifications were carried out on its Canadian-built Hurricanes.

Thus far, Croydon itself had experienced little to suggest that it was now a station within the battleground. This was soon to change. Thursday, August 15, was fine and warm and the squadrons of No. 11 Group had been activated on scrambles and patrols since early morning. Shortly before noon a reconnaissance Dornier flew on a sortie taking in Shoreham, Kenley, Croydon and Northolt, successfully avoiding the attentions of three squadrons patrolling as a deterrent against such activity.

About 6.20 p.m. fifteen bomb-laden Bf 110s and eight similarly-armed Bf 109s

raced over the threshold of Kent near Dungeness. These were the aircraft of the precision attack specialists, Erprobungsgruppe 210, led by their Swiss-born commander, Hauptmann Walter Rubensdorffer. Just beyond Sevenoaks, the twenty-three aircraft swung as a single entity to the north-west on a course which would bring them north of their target. This would position them for a fast, strafing run across their objective before flying hell-for-leather for the south coast and home. Below them the ground was lost in the summer evening haze but soon the leader spotted a group of aerodrome buildings through the gauzy air. Like swimmers diving into a pond the formation tilted and plunged earthwards.

At 6.30 p.m., the station siren reverberated across Croydon and all personnel not actively engaged on aerodrome defence or essential duties hurried for shelter. Led by their C.O. Squadron Leader 'Tommy' Thompson, No. 111 Squadron scrambled nine Hurricanes with instructions to orbit the base. With throttles wide open they clawed for precious height and, at ten thousand feet, levelled out, circled and waited. Twenty-nine interminable minutes later the aircraft of Gruppe 210 exploded out of the haze two thousand feet below, diving on the 'drome. The Hurricanes winged over and fell upon them.

With cannons and machine guns blazing, Rubensdorffer planted the first bombs on the aerodrome while his cohort fanned out to select their targets. Before they could orientate themselves fully, the Hurricanes were amongst them, their wing leading edges ablaze as the British pilots endeavoured to interrupt the enemy's bombing runs. Squadron Leader Thompson attacked a Bf 110 in a near vertical climb as it zoomed up from its strafing run, blowing large chunks from the port engine and wing before breaking away in time to avoid colliding. The Luftwaffe pilot pulled off a masterly landing in a nearby field. Shaken by the sudden counter attack, many of the bombs fell wide around the aerodrome boundaries causing casualties among the civilian population. With the element of surprise gone the Bf 110s took up their standard defensive tactic — the 'circle of death'. Around this time reinforcements arrived in the shape of nine Hurricanes of No. 32 Squadron led by Squadron Leader John Worrall, who engaged the Bf 109s of 3 Staffel which, having unshackled their bombs, were now free to follow the fighter role. But time and fuel were running out for the Germans, and as if on sudden command, they broke the circle and streaked southwards in three groups. There followed a running battle between Hurricanes and their selected victims which, at times, took the combatants below tree-top level. Thompson, in a low-level chase, saw his tracers send tiles scattering from a roof-top before he realised the danger and broke away. Rubensdorffer's Zerstorer, hugging the contours of the land, sped south-east pursued by a solitary Hurricane in a dogged, no-quarter hunt. Turning and twisting, at times only feet above the ground the Swiss found he could not shake off his pursuer. The end came near Rothersfield, Sussex when the Bf 110 rose trailing flame and smoke, staggered, then fell to earth and exploded. The gallant, debonair Rubensdorffer and his gunner, Feldwebel Richard Ehekercher, were dead. Seven aircraft of Erprobungsgruppe 210 fell that day, six Bf 110s and one Bf 109. It was a terrible price to pay for a navigational error — the scheduled target was Kenley.

The raid had lasted between five and ten minutes. Curiously, the air raid warning did not sound in the town of Croydon itself until 7.16 p.m. by which time the old airport was virtually hidden under a pall of grey dust. A pillar of dense black smoke pinpointed the blazing armoury which had taken a direct hit, eventually burning itself out. The venerable

old terminal building was badly damaged on its south wing while the control tower exhibited evidence of accurate machine-gunning. 'D' hangar, damaged by blast, had also been heavily raked by cannon and machine gun fire. 'C' hangar, used by Rollason Aircraft Services Ltd., had been set alight by incendiary bombs turning it into a melting pot for the forty-odd training aircraft stored inside. At the rear of this building, Rollason's factory and a components workshop were badly hit and a large number of civilian casualties occurred. 'A' hangar escaped virtually unscathed with only a few windows broken. The officers' mess was reduced to a shambles from blast which was sufficiently strong to damage a concrete blockhouse nearby. Seven 250kg bombs, two 50kg bombs and a number of incendiaries were accounted for on the aerodrome. The grass field resembled a miniature lunar landscape dotted with curiously ridged craters twenty-eight feet in diameter and ten feet deep. A fuel pipe to the MT fuel installation had also been severed. Six airmen died in the attack, five from No. 111 Squadron and one from Station Headquarters. There were sixty-two civilian deaths from incidents in areas fringing the aerodrome. Four No. 111 Squadron airmen, one officer from No. 1 (RCAF) Squadron and two civilian telephone operators were injured and 185 civilians.

Following the attack, No. 111 Squadron was diverted to Hawkinge while repairs were carried out at Croydon and within two days the craters had been filled and the aerodrome was again proclaimed operational.

The pressure on Fighter Command's pilots was building up rapidly with unbroken periods of fine and sunny weather and mounting numbers of sorties to be flown daily. The pace told in increasing losses of pilots and aircraft. By mid-August, the squadron's effective strength was reduced to nine pilots. A unique feature of 111's combat tactics had been the head-on attack with the whole of the formation flying in line abreast, a manoeuvre guaranteed to break up any bomber group however courageous and disciplined. With the loss of experienced pilots, however, this opening gambit was abandoned.

Replacements came, fresh from Operational Training Units with a minimum of experience on Hurricanes and Spitfires. Almost immediately they were thrown into combat to survive as best they could. There was simply no time to give them the simulated battle experience which they should have had.

'It wasn't all Brylcreem and cushy billets' — Former WWII RAF erk. *Above:* A Blenheim IF of No. 92 Squadron runs up its engines at Croydon in January 1940. Erks muffled to the eyebrows against the near Arctic cold of that first severe winter of the war, clear part of the apron to facilitate taxi-ing (Imperial War Museum). *Below:* Prolific verdure hides the former wintry scene in August 1979. The hangar on the left is now occupied by the freight terminal of Whiteheads storage and the three-bay hangar by Industrolite Ltd. Photo taken from the first floor of the terminal building.

On one day in August, two very young, fresh-faced sergeant pilots, exuberant with enthusiasm over their first posting to an operational unit, drove into Croydon as replacements for No. 111 Squadron. Apologetically, Squadron Leader John Thompson told them that he had no alternative but to commit them to action that same afternoon. A few hours later, one was dead and the other in hospital seriously wounded, shocked into a state of amnesia whereby he

Above: **A funeral pyre towers into the early evening sky above Croydon aerodrome after the raid on August 15, 1940. Homegoing workers line the boundary fence in Stafford Road while a harassed looking air-raid warden hurries past two indifferent private soldiers in the roadway whose apparent task is to keep traffic moving. More important for two cyclists is the repair of a rear wheel puncture (Radio Times).** *Below:* **The excitement has gone from Stafford Road in August 1979. On the site of the old airport buildings now stands the GPO Service Centre. In the prosperity of a four-decade interval, the Rolls-Royce has replaced the 'Baby' Austin.**

could not remember his own name. It is doubtful if anyone else on the squadron remembered their passing. All that remained as evidence of their presence at Croydon was their old car parked on the apron with their baggage still inside.

On Sunday, August 18, 1940, fine weather brought out the early Luftwaffe aircraft to report on the state of No. 11 Group's aerodromes. Then, about 12.50 p.m., a massive formation of bombers crossed over the Kentish coastline between Dungeness and Dover heading for the fighter aerodromes south of London. They were harried along their route by four squadrons of RAF fighters who could do little to divert the stream in the face of intense opposition by a large and aggressive escort. Whilst this melee was drifting high across the hop fields and orchards of Kent, nine Dornier Do 17Zs of 9/KG76 roared over the coast between Seaford and Beachy Head 'on the deck', making for the sector station at Kenley. Wave-clipping their way across the channel they had escaped the probing fingers of the coastal radar but were spotted by the Observer Corps post on Beachy Head. News of their passage was passed by telephone to the Observer Group HQ at Horsham, thence to No. 11 Group HQ at Uxbridge from where the Sector Operations Room at Kenley was informed.

From the high-level group of raiders about fifty Do 17s splintered from the main stream and also headed for Kenley where the Sector Controller, Squadron Leader Anthony Norman, scrambled Nos. 64 and 615 Squadrons to meet the threat. At Croydon, No. 111 Squadron, under the leadership of Flight Lieutenant S. D. P. Connors, was at cockpit readiness, impatiently awaiting the scramble order from Group when Squadron Leader Norman ordered them off with instructions to orbit Kenley at three thousand feet.

With all the serviceable aircraft engaged elsewhere, Croydon now lay undefended before the high-flying Dorniers which proceeded to disgorge their bomb loads on to the aerodrome. In the duration of five minutes they succeeded in dropping nineteen bombs

on target, eleven high explosive and eight delayed-action. 'A' hangar was seriously damaged when a 50kg HE and an incendiary penetrated the roof and exploded inside. Two HEs fell on the edge of the tarmac apron close by the main building producing the typical lunar craters while another bomb landed in the middle of the main building itself. A fifth struck the roadway between the guardroom and the airmen's cookhouse adjacent to Purley Way. The others fell around the aerodrome boundary. There were no service casualties arising from this raid.

The dust had hardly begun to settle when a Hurricane, KW-Z of 615 Squadron flown by Pilot Officer D. J. Looker, approached the field for an emergency landing after sustaining severe battle damage in combat

with a Bf 109. With his canopy locked back and his seat raised, Pilot Officer Looker anxiously peered into the pall of dust hanging in the air, trying to find an unbroken strip of ground on which to set down his machine. Suddenly from out of the murk tracer bullets were hosing up at him from all directions. The gunners of Croydon's ground defences had a severe case of the 'twitch' after Rubens-dorffer's strafing of the airfield three days previously. Miraculously, both pilot and aircraft survived only to find that a complaint had been filed by an over-zealous official against the unannounced use of the landing facilities! (Today, Hurricane L1592, KW-Z, is preserved in the Science Museum, South Kensington.)

On Monday, August 19, eighteen

Hurricanes of No. 85 Squadron arrived from Debden led by their CO, Squadron Leader Peter Townsend. After a brief exchange of news and pleasantries, Squadron Leader John Thompson led what was left of No. 111 Squadron north to Debden for a respite from the battle. As the nine Hurricanes climbed away from Croydon no one could foresee that they were to return in less than two weeks, fewer still in number. Their ground crew remained to service the new squadron's aircraft as their counterparts on the Essex airfield would provide a reciprocal service.

After two air raids the necessity of aircraft dispersal had been well and truly learned. No. 85 Squadron's dispersal area was close to Plough Lane North, on the western side of the aerodrome where advantage had been taken of a row of vacant villas for use as rest rooms for pilots and ground crews. Five days of bad weather followed the squadron's arrival at Croydon giving everyone on the station a much needed break.

On August 25, the squadron returned from a scramble, to discover that His Royal Highness the Duke of Kent had chosen this particular day for a visit to the old airport but had missed the take-off. On their return the pilots were introduced to the Duke by Peter Townsend — complete with toothbrush sticking out of his top pocket, such had been the rapidity of the scramble. The following day a less welcome visitor put in an appearance.

On Monday, August 26, at 1.32 a.m., a solitary aircraft throbbed its way around the station for about three minutes at a great height. Eventually it made three gliding attacks, dropping a number of small bombs each time. On the first, three bombs fell: one west of Foresters Drive, one to the east of Foresters Drive close to a public shelter and the third on the west side of the aerodrome near Round Shaw. During the second attack a number of bombs fell between Nos. 1 and 7 gun posts, while the third group of bombs fell in the vicinity of Waddon. There were no casualties but one Hurricane was destroyed by fire resulting from a bomb splinter in the petrol tank. Two more Hurricanes were damaged but repairable. The raider left on a sweet note however as for days afterwards the air of Croydon was redolent with the scent of 'Evening in Paris'. The bombs dropped at Waddon had hit the Bourjois scent factory! It was reported afterwards that the door of a lighted room had been seen opening and shutting at erratic intervals, although whether or not as a signal was never established despite intensive enquiries by the Special Investigation Branch and the local CID.

In mid-August, No. 1 (RCAF) Squadron, now considered fully operational, transferred to Northolt.

On the morning of Saturday, August 31, No. 85 Squadron were assembled at cockpit readiness, engines ticking over waiting for the Group Controller to unleash them. Just before 12.55 p.m. the order came and with a wild surge of power twelve Hurricanes roared across the grass, the bellowing of their engines drowning the sound of the approaching Dorniers. Between fifteen and twenty thousand feet over Croydon, the escort of Bf 110s and 109s turned sedately to watch the bombers race across the target at two thousand feet planting their bombs accurately across the face of the aerodrome. Mere yards ahead of the deluge, the Hurricanes laboured heavenwards as the huge earth fountains strode across the grass towards their climbing tails. So close run had it been that the engine of Peter Townsend's aircraft faltered when struck by a blast wave as he rose. By the time the squadron had climbed to two thousand feet, the Dorniers were well on their way home but the escorting Messerschmitts were intercepted by the squadron at nine thousand feet over Tunbridge Wells. In the ensuing battle the squadron destroyed two 109s and

Above: **In the dawn light of August 26, 1940, the Bourjois scent factory at Waddon still burns after being bombed in the early hours by a single German raider, who: 'being demanded, whether a good spirit or bad, returned no answer but disappeared with a curious perfume and most melodious twang' — John Aubrey, antiquary 1626-1697 (Popperfoto).** *Below:* **In August 1979 a different aroma emanates from the factory site which now houses, along with other companies, that of Coburg Coffee.**

one 110 for the loss of three Hurricanes, one pilot force-landing unhurt and two baling out wounded. One of the wounded pilots was Peter Townsend.

The attack on the aerodrome lasted six minutes and bombs were dropped ranging from 50 up to 500 kilograms. The inevitable strafing by machine guns took place aimed largely at the airmen's cookhouse. It was thereafter rumoured that a serving airman had a relation in the Luftwaffe! The hangar of the Redwing Aircraft Co. on the south-east corner was demolished by a direct hit from a 500kg bomb. Another fell directly on to the company's shelter although no casualties were sustained. Two 100kg and one 50kg bombs penetrated the landing ground, while another 100kg. fell to the south of 'B' hangar causing splinter damage to the walls and broken windows. Two 500kgs. dropped on the south side of No. 2 Hispano gun post.

Outside the periphery of the aerodrome, a 250kg. bomb landed in the centre of Purley Way opposite the main gates whilst the bulk of the missiles, thirteen in all, fell on the recreation ground on the east side of Purley Way opposite the main buildings. Two of these weighed 50kgs. and the rest were estimated at between 200 and 500kgs. One new Dennis 30cwt lorry was also destroyed. Surprisingly, the only injury reported was to a soldier of the Royal Artillery engaged on aerodrome defence.

On Monday, September 2, 1940, the remnants of No. 85 Squadron withdrew to Debden. Of the eighteen pilots who had flown in to Croydon thirteen days before, fourteen had been shot down, a few of them twice. Three had been killed and five wounded or burned. One of those wounded was Sergeant G. B. Booth who was shot down by Bf 109s

near Purley on the squadron's last day of action from Croydon. He baled out with his parachute ablaze, crashed to the ground and broke his back, an arm and leg. After enduring months of agony, he died on February 7, 1941. Glendon Booth had joined the squadron on July 15, 1940 — he was 20 years old.

Still seriously understrength, No. 111 Squadron returned to Croydon after sustaining further losses of pilots and aircraft whilst operating from Debden and Martlesham Heath. Also at Croydon, where they had arrived on the first of the month, were the pilots and Spitfires of No. 72 Squadron, led by Squadron Leader A. R. Collins. In their first two days of engagements with the enemy, Squadron Leader Collins was twice wounded and compelled to relinquish leadership of the squadron to Wing Commander R. Lees, who in turn was badly wounded while leading his first sortie with the squadron.

On Saturday, September 7, the Luftwaffe attempted to smash the whole of London's dockland into submission with the biggest daylight raid to date. On this day the Battle of Britain virtually became the Battle of London. Launching 300 bombers with 600 plus single and twin-engined fighters as escorts, the Luftwaffe hoped to deliver a double punch which would strike at the administrative and commercial heart of the Kingdom while, at the same time, drawing the RAF's depleted Fighter Command into a mass aerial battle. By 4.30 p.m., virtually every squadron within sixty miles of London had despatched all its serviceable aircraft to meet the aerial armada droning high above the Thames towards the capital. What followed was a battle, on a Homeric scale, which reduced the British fighter force still further but, more important, delivered a severe jolt to the German feeling of invincibility.

While the attack on London was at its height, part of the Bf 110 escort withdrew to the south and formed a defensive circle over Croydon awaiting the retreat of the bombers who would then return to their French bases by way of Maidstone and Dymchurch. Boosting their engines to full power, the pilots of No. 111 Squadron, who had been scrambled late, now climbed desperately towards the Zerstorers which were flaunting themselves within sight of the RAF base. With suicidal fury the nine Hurricanes tore into the 'circle of death' breaking the formation, only to find themselves in a whirling, drifting dogfight that took them across the county of Kent. It was their last engagement in the south during the 'battle'; next day they took their seven remaining Hurricanes north to the Scottish aerodrome at Drem in East Lothian.

Into Croydon as replacements came the Hurricanes of No. 605 'County of Warwick' Squadron from the same northern aerodrome to which the former had just flown. Led by Squadron Leader W. M. Churchill, the squadron from the first day of their tenure found that they had entered a maelstrom of mounting intensity and savagery which reached its peak on the 'great day' of September 15.

During the night of September 11/12, 1940, intermittent high-level bombing attacks were made on Croydon throughout the hours of darkness. Two oil bombs, dropped in the vicinity of the Trojan Sports Ground pavilion, burned out sections of the wooden fence. One 100kg high explosive bomb exploded about thirty yards south of No. 2 Hispano gun post leaving a fifteen-foot crater which was filled in later the same day and one delayed-action bomb landed near No. 1 machine gun post at Plough Lane North. There were neither casualties nor damage. It is doubtful if the exhausted pilots were even aware of the disturbance, for by this stage of the battle they were lucky to realize five hours sleep a night. No station warning had been sounded.

During the month, No. 72 Squadron returned to the sector station at Biggin Hill, while No. 605, now under the leadership of Squadron Leader Archibald McKellar, quickly became an adroit, battle-hardened unit. One of the Auxiliary Air Force's elite, McKellar was insistent that his pilots always be presentably turned out. Immaculately would have been preferable but one had to make allowances for the times!

On Sunday, September 15 at about 11.25 a.m., the Hurricanes of No. 605 roared at fifteen thousand feet across London in a head-on attack on a formation of Dorniers. The bomber force split up in panic and scattered, dropping their bomb loads at random. In a running battle across Surrey and Kent, one 605 Squadron pilot, Pilot Officer T. P. M. Cooper-Slipper, was attacked by a Bf 109 and his aircraft set on fire. As he prepared to abandon his Hurricane he discovered three Dorniers approaching him head on and instead decided to ram them. At an impact speed of over 600 miles per hour he struck the centre bomber and, as he said later, 'things became a bit confused then'. Miraculously he found himself swinging on the end of his parachute which had somehow opened and was undamaged. After numerous adventures, which included near lynching by hop pickers, he was returned to Croydon in an Army vehicle via a children's party and numerous pubs — he found on his arrival back at base that he had somehow acquired a rubber dinghy and two Luftwaffe Schwimmwesten!

The German Air Force dropped in for one more visit during the month when intermittent raids were carried out by two or three aircraft bombing from a high altitude during the night of September 23/24. During the course of the raids, nine one-kilogramme incendiary bombs were scattered along the aerodrome bound-

Still showing evidence of all the wartime dispersals, this was how Croydon looked in April 1947 (Crown Copyright).

aries by Stafford Road and Plough Lane North. Several of these fell on the south-west corner of the Redwing Building in Stafford Road on quarters occupied by 'F' Company, 12th Queens Royal Regiment, causing damage to the roof from fire and water. In later attacks, two 500kg high explosive bombs fell on the south-west corner of the aerodrome, one fifteen yards from a Bofors gun post and the other eight yards further on in the direction of 'D' hangar. One delayed-action bomb fell in the south-east corner. There were no casualties but one Hurricane was badly damaged and two more to a lesser degree. The landing ground was unaffected.

The first day of October dawned fair but with a gusting north-easterly wind. Minutes had ticked away since reveille and airmen were contemplating their wartime breakfast with varying degrees of enthusiasm when, at 6.47 a.m., a lone twin-engined aircraft approached the aerodrome from the east. Dropping two high explosive bombs on the playing field close to the Bofors gun emplacement, it then crossed over the main terminal block at about four thousand feet in a dive towards 'B' hangar, machine gunning as it went. Banking in the direction of Plough Lane North it passed over No. 2 Bofors gun pit, round the dispersal point and made off to the south. There was no station warning, the guns of the airfield defence did not engage . . . and breakfast was late that morning.

At 3.15 p.m. Air Marshall H. R. Nicholls, CB, CBE paid a flying visit to the station while, on the following day, Squadron Leader John Thompson dropped in to look up old acquaintances.

October 3, brought four days of rain, poor visibility and another enemy to contend with — fog. Ideal weather conditions for the Jabos, the bomb-carrying Bf 109s, which could slip in over the coast low and fast, unseen by both radar and Observer Corps, plant a quick bomb on any target that took their fancy and be on their way out again before their presence was noted.

On Friday, October 4, No. 605 tangled with the Junkers Ju 88s of II/LG1 over the Folkestone area, claiming one destroyed. Later in the day Pilot Officer C. E. English forced-landed his Hurricane near Westerham owing to atrocious weather conditions, walking away unhurt. On Monday, October 7 about 1.30 p.m., Squadron Leader McKellar downed a brace of Bf 109s in the short space of three minutes but in the same skirmish Pilot Officer English was shot down and killed not far from the spot where he had successfully forced-landed three days before.

With the onset of winter, the strain normally imposed by combat flying in near perfect conditions was increased tenfold by the additional hazards of deteriorating weather. It became almost a daily feature of life to enter Croydon's messes and find some familiar face missing. Monday, October 7: Pilot Officer C. E. English. Saturday, October 12: Sergeant P. R. C. McIntosh. Monday, October 14: Flying Officer R. Hope (who chased a Heinkel 111 into the Inner Defence Zone and struck a balloon cable). Tuesday, October 15: Pilot Officer I. J. Muirhead who had successfully baled out of his Hurricane eight days before.

During the night of October 15, a lone German raider flew over the aerodrome and unleashed a solitary HE bomb which landed on the Trojan playing fields on the south-east corner. Four nights later (at 8.20 p.m. on October 19), the exercise was repeated. On this occasion the bomb-aimer excelled himself by planting one HE bomb smack in the centre of the landing ground. If it was the same crew that visited the aerodrome on the 15th they must have put in some hard practice on the two intervening nights! The following night, not to be outdone, the Royal Artillery had a go at Croydon and did considerably better. Two anti-aircraft shells landed in the vicinity of the main block, exploded and wrecked the Link Trainer building. Unfortunately, silhouettes of Link Trainers could not be painted as victory tallies on gunshields! (One wonders if

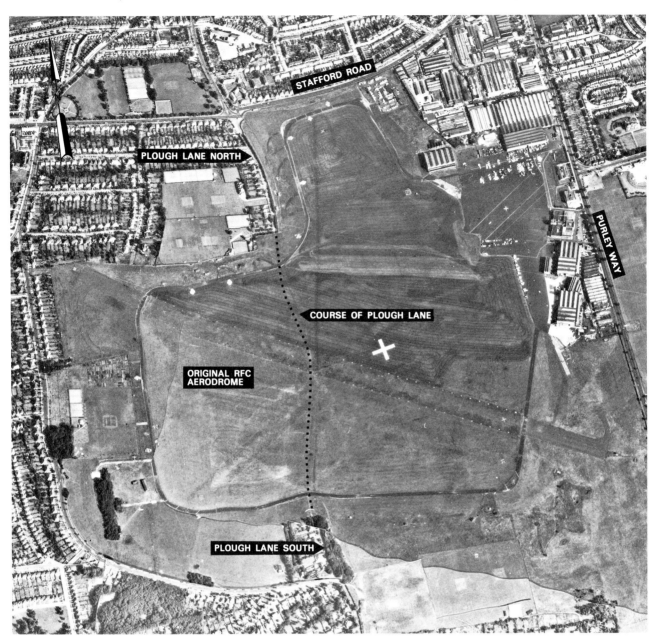

The aerodrome photographed on August 16, 1961 two years after its closure denoted by the white X (Crown Copyright).

the incident inspired the visit at 4.30 p.m. the following day by Squadron Leader E. V. N. Bell from No. 11 Group HQ at Uxbridge.)

The tenacity of purpose of the Luftwaffe was astounding. In the early hours of October 23, a solitary high-flying bomber, the crew of which had possibly not heard of the prowess of the local gun batteries, circled the aerodrome and dropped one HE bomb in the grounds of Woodcote House. No. 23 Ridge Park was severely damaged and one UXB fell on the sports ground eighty yards from the junction of Foresters Drive and Plough Lane South.

The weather continued cloudy with rain, drizzle and fog but once again on October 24, the inevitable nocturnal visitor arrived and dropped a stick of five HE bombs. Only one of these landed on the aerodrome in the north-west corner. This was to be the last enemy tilt at Croydon during the Battle of Britain period.

On the day after the Battle officially ended (October 31), the redoubtable Archie McKellar was shot down and killed in combat.

During November, No. 605 Squadron began to re-equip with the Hawker Hurricane IIA which retained the eight Browning machine guns in the wings but was fitted with the Rolls-Royce Merlin XX two-stage supercharged engine. With its new machines it commenced working-up exercises to prepare for the fighter offensive which was being planned for the coming spring. Once it had reached full operational status it moved to Martlesham in February 1941. In its place came the Mk.IIA Hurricanes of No. 17 Squadron on their first visit to Croydon since their brief stay in that distant September of 1939. This time their tenancy lasted for slightly longer but in March they too flew north to Martlesham.

From Kenley in April came another Hurricane unit, this time No. 1 Squadron, also equipped with Mk.IIAs. Like its predecessors it was actively engaged on 'Rhubarb' and 'Circus' operations but with the emphasis on its activities shifting towards the role of night fighting. Later, with the four cannon-armed Mk.IIC Hurricane, the squadron was to be in the van of the Intruders carrying terror and destruction to returning Luftwaffe bomber crews over the illusory sanctuary of their own bases. The following month No. 1 moved to Redhill. With the Royal Air Force now fully geared for an offensive war, many of the squadrons of Fighter Command now operated from aerodromes closer to the Channel and the enemy coast. Consequently, Croydon's importance as a front line station began to dwindle although it was still utilized for short periods as a quasi resting base for squadrons engaged on offensive sweeps.

On August 12, 1941, the station saw the emergence of a new unit, when No. 414 Squadron RCAF was formed for fighter-reconnaissance equipped with Westland Lysander IIs. Later came issues of the Mk.IIIA but from June 1942 conversion to Curtiss Tomahawk Is took place, these in turn being replaced by North American Mustangs.

In June 1942 two of the Polish Air Force's eight fighter squadrons moved into Croydon. No. 302 'Poznan' Squadron and No. 317 'Wilno' Squadron were both equipped with Spitfire VBs and took the war and their intense hatred to the Germans on 'Ramrod' and similar offensive operations. Their stay was short and the following month of July saw the departure of both, No. 302 for Heston and No. 317 for Northolt.

An increasingly important aspect of the war was the ability of any combatant to transfer men and supplies to any theatre as rapidly and efficiently as possible. It was to this end that Transport Command was formed on March

In the former booking and waiting hall of Croydon's main building, Air Marshal The Honourable Sir Ralph Cochrane KBE, CB, AFC, addresses officers, men and WAAF members of No. 110 Wing, Transport Command on February 6, 1946 when certain air services were transferred to BEA (Charles E. Brown).

Where lies the dignity of history? Statesmen and actors courtesans and duchesses have all passed this way in Croydon's distinguished past. Now occupied by Allied Carpets, it is used as a warehouse and lies littered with the remnants of the trade.

25, 1943 with headquarters at Harrow, Middlesex. This new structure absorbed the earlier Ferry Command and assumed responsibility for the despatch and transport of aircraft, materiel and personnel within the RAF's spheres of operations. An integral part of the new Command was No. 110 Wing which settled in at the old terminal building at Croydon where, as the war moved across the Channel with the 'D-Day' landings and as the Allied armies progressed into Europe, they built up a network of air routes and services to the liberated countries. Thus Croydon's tale had come full circle and once more it was engaged in the business of transportation. On November 13, 1944, the first civil air service to operate since before the war was inaugurated by the Railway Air Services between London and Belfast via Liverpool. Later companies using Croydon included Scottish Airways, Jersey Airways and Morton Air Services who all moved into the aerodrome at the end of the war.

By September 23, 1945, No. 110 Wing had carried its 100,000th passenger. The following year, on February 6, in the old booking and waiting hall of the former terminal building, there took place the ceremony of transfer of responsibility for certain air services from No. 110 Wing to British European Airways, a corporate airline operating out of Northolt. Officers, airmen and WAAF members of the Wing were addressed by Air Marshall, The Honourable Sir Ralph A. Cochrane K.B.E., C.B., A.F.C., one of Bomber Command's most famous and respected AOCs. Nine days later the Wing was formally disbanded.

A detachment of No. 435 Squadron, RCAF, which had arrived at Croydon the previous October remained there until the end of March — one of their more unusual loads being over 212,000 hatching eggs from Washington en route for Prague.

The last RAF unit left Croydon on September 15, 1946 and on November 12, RAF Croydon was closed down.

Croydon was just getting back into the routine of a civil airport when there occurred one of the most horrendous accidents in its long history. On January 25, 1947 a Douglas C-47A Dakota, VP-YFE of Spencer's Airways, Southern Rhodesia had just become airborne from the snow-encrusted grass in appalling visibility. Climbing in a semi-stalled condition, the inevitable happened and the heavily-loaded aircraft crashed on to another parked Dakota, bursting into flames. The pilot and airline owner, Captain E. H. Spencer and twelve people aboard were killed with another four persons seriously injured.

Four months later on May 23, a Vickers Viking I, G-AHPJ of Hunting Air Travel Ltd., arriving from Verona, Italy, landed heavily on the aerodrome causing complete under-carriage collapse, fortunately without serious consequences.

Less than a month later on June 14, a Miles Aerovan IV, G-AISG, piloted by Mr. Malcom Oliver Kerr and laden with 604 racing pigeons, stalled while attempting a steep climb on take-off. In the subsequent crash the pilot was killed and the radio operator and one passenger were injured. As a result of an investigation the aircraft was found to have been overloaded by 446lbs.

At 4.00 p.m. on Saturday, November 1, 1947, a De Havilland D.H.89A Dragon Rapide, G-AGIF of BEAC took off from Croydon for Guernsey on the last scheduled flight from the airfield. Thereafter regular air services from Croydon ceased although charter companies, both British and European continued to use it. Part of the glamour attached to international airports returned to Croydon during the early 1950s when many famous (and infamous) personalities used it as an entry and exit point to the United Kingdom. Internationally known VIPs arrived and left in psuedo-anonymity knowing there would be less competition for the newsmen's attention than at Heathrow or Gatwick.

Nevertheless, charter, club and private flying continued to flourish, more than 76,000 movements being recorded in 1957, a total exceeded that year only by Heathrow and Southend. However Croydon's days were numbered and moves were made to close the airport on the grounds of noise, cost and air traffic control problems due to the proximity

to Heathrow, Gatwick and Biggin Hill. Flying club activities were ordered to cease on December 31, 1958 with a few extra months given for the run down of charter companies.

Meetings were held with the Ministry of Transport and Civil Aviation to prevent the closure and a protest flight by twenty-five light aircraft was planned (but later cancelled) along the Thames. However all attempts to avert the will of the Ministry were to no avail and the last aircraft, a Miles Gemini, left the deserted airfield at 7.45 p.m. on September 30, 1959. As the senior Air Traffic Control officer, Eric Brewerton, switched off the airport lights for the last time, an effigy of the Minister of Transport and Civil Aviation was burned on the tarmac.

Today the terminal building and control tower remain, converted into offices. The historic Aerodrome Hotel also still stands. Industrial buildings are creeping across the landing area and two hangars are used for storage. The former National Aircraft Factory hangar, subsequently used after the airfield's closure as a paper store, burned down in the

1960s. Another near Stafford Road known as the Flight Shed has been completely dismantled. A new housing estate now occupies the site of the original Waddon aerodrome although the roads have been given suitable aviation names as a last link with the past.

On December 7, 1978, a public meeting was held in the Aerodrome Hotel to discuss the formation of the Croydon Airport Society. Some sixty persons were present and they heard Sir Peter Masefield strongly support the formation of the association to promote and encourage public interest in the airport. The constitution of the Society allows for Individual, Associate, Senior Individual (for those over sixty-five years of age) and Junior membership. Regular newsletters are published and the eventual aim of the society is to see the setting up of a permanent civil aviation museum and exhibition in a building on the aerodrome. Already the terminal buildings have been added to the Department of the Environment's list of buildings of architectural or historic interest.

SECTOR C
Biggin Hill

BY PETER HALLIDAY

On Tuesday, August 8, 1939, when the RAF played at war, the pilots of No. 79 Squadron scramble to their Hurricanes at the start of the Air Defence Exercises. The following year they would be less encumbered and the erk on the bicycle would be in imminent danger of being unseated (Keystone). *Below:* Only the lazy drone of a light aircraft disturbs the serenity of the same scene in August 1979. Although it has been announced that the station is to close, the Royal Air Force still occupy North Camp, albeit in a non-flying role. South Camp is now used by civilian pilots.

The site for Biggin Hill aerodrome really owes its existence to a Lieutenant Hansard who remembered the site when the RFC were looking for an alternative location for Joyce Green camp near Woolwich at the beginning of 1916.

The site selected was a large meadow of some eighty acres, approximately one-and-a-half miles north of the village of Aperfield or Biggin Hill as it became known. To the west of the landing area and running roughly SE-NW a large, deep valley put the proposed aerodrome above any fog or mist that formed locally, a fortunate asset for many pilots — then as now.

Although the Earl of Standhope, at that time on active service in France, did not oppose the idea of an aerodrome on his land his tenant, Mr. J. Westacot, needed to be persuaded that it was in the national interest to give up some of his acreage.

The first aircraft to land on the new aerodrome was an RE7, piloted by Lieutenant

Forty years separate these two photographs. This is a pre-war photograph taken by the German airline Lufthansa en route for Croydon, some six miles to the north-west.

Dickie with his mechanic Chadwick, on February 2, 1917 and Biggin Hill was officially opened twelve days later as an RFC Radio Signals unit.

The first fatality of the many pilots who were to lose their lives whilst flying from Biggin occured in 1917 when Lieutenant Pownell crashed his BE2 into a wood near Norheads Farm on the opposite side of the valley.

Later that year, No. 141 Squadron, RFC, arrived and, equipped with Bristol Fighters, formed part of the Inner Patrol Zone of the London Air Defence Area. During this time, most of the activity centred around what was known as the South Camp but, in an extensive building programme begun in 1929, the RAF constructed a new technical site on the northern perimeter. Hangars, workshops, barrack blocks and administration offices were built together with the innumerable little buildings that make up an active station. The

only building that did not need erecting was the Officers' Mess — a large house which stood on the opposite side of the Bromley-Westerham Road to the main camp and which had been acquired by the RFC in the early days.

Two hundred yards south of the Officers' Mess stood a little house which had a rather strange history. The story generally believed by the locals was that the owner had refused point-blank to sell or move when the station was built and, subsequently, had hung himself. Truth or not, the tiny house stayed inside the aerodrome perimeter at the top of Salt Box Hill and was reckoned to be the 'salt box' after which the hill was named.

Reputedly haunted, it stood derelict until it was finally pulled down in the mid-fifties.

The first squadrons to occupy the reconstructed aerodrome in 1930 were Nos. 23 and 32 and thereafter the airfield settled down to being one of the capital's most-important Fighter Command stations. Further expansion took place in 1938 and sixteen married quarters and a radio receiving building were among the new additions.

After the Munich crisis in 1938, the buildings were camouflaged, air raid shelters were dug and a large number of trees planted to help disguise the aerodrome. Nos. 32 and 79, the resident Squadrons, began to exchange their biplanes for the new Hurricane

Almost the same view looking north in October 1979. Note the absence of the South Camp Belfast hangar, destroyed in the battle.

fighters and, by April 1939, the change-over was complete and pilots were busy familiarising themselves with the complexities of retractable undercarriages and closed canopies. During that period, more than one pilot found that the sinking rate on landing was more than that of the old biplanes and several aircraft finished up in various fields adjacent to the aerodrome. One just missed the club house of the Down Golf Club and ended up in the hedge between the club and the aerodrome. The pilot, uninjured, walked back to the station no doubt feeling very embarrassed.

On September 1, 1939, families in the married quarters were given two hours to leave. Transport was provided to convey them to the main London railway stations for dispersal to addresses all over England, accommodation having been pre-arranged by the RAF six months earlier. On the outbreak of war, the station HQ was under the command of Wing Commander R. Grice.

The aerodrome then consisted of an oddly-shaped landing field 710 yards from E-W and 2,000 yards on the longest SW-NW dimension. Landings were also possible N-S (1,666 yards) and NE-SW (1,333 yards). The main tarmac runway was constructed in the autumn of 1939 on a bearing of 26°T and measured 1,600 x 50 yards. Later two other runways were added, each 790 x 50 yards, fanning out on 45°T and 108°T.

Above: **Hurricane Is of 'B' Flight of No. 79 Squadron in front of the North Camp triple-bay Belfast hangar, air exercising in 1939.** *Below:* **Now completely transformed with the aircrew selection Reception and Control building occupying the site of the hangar, only the physical training building on the left remains as a reference point.**

In the first year of the war, Biggin Hill was only troubled by the occasional German high-flying photographic aircraft. Most of the time the squadrons were kept busy by patrols, the Battle of France and the sorties to protect the channel convoys.

The first time the personnel of Biggin caught sight of enemy planes in any number was on Thursday evening August 15, when a formation of Bf 110s passed to the west, one being brought down some two miles away within sight of the aerodrome.

The first attack on Biggin occured on August 18, at about 1.30 p.m. The raid lasted just over an hour with most of the bombs falling on the adjacent golf course. A few fell within the perimeter but caused only slight damage.

Left: **Biggin Hill investiture held in front of the same hangar on June 25, 1940. HM King George VI chats to Flight Lieutenant Michael N. Crossley of No. 32 Squadron after conferring upon him the DFC. Waiting for awards are Pilot Officer V. G. Daw, DFC and Douglas H. Grice, DFC, both of No. 32 Squadron; Pilot** Officer D. W. A. Stones, DFC, Sergeant H. Cartwright, DFM and Sergeant A. W. Whitby DFM, all of No. 79 Squadron. *Right:* **Thirty-nine years later, the hangar has gone although the single storey battery charging room remains. The rear of the memorial chapel is on the extreme left.**

Above: **Wing Commander J. R. Myers, Station CO, on the site of the Sector Operations Block, which received a direct hit in the raid on Saturday, August 31. It is now the Officers' Mess car park. The following day the station was dispersed and a temporary ops room was set up in an empty shop in The Pantiles, half-a-mile south of the drome — now the Biggin Hill Hire Centre,** *photo below.*

Top: **Towerfield near the Keston crossroads was selected as the permanent location for the new 'C' Sector Operations Room. The sentiments expressed at the end of the war were that this Victorian mansion, then shabby and deserted, should 'become a national monument as a visible reminder of Britain's finest hour and of the imperishable glory of the RAF' (Drawing by Captain Bryan de Grineau, Illustrated London News).** *Above:* **Still shabby but not deserted. The tower was demolished only recently when a new private housing estate was constructed in the grounds.**

Left: **Originally the lounge of Towerfield, this was converted into the Operations Room itself. On September 15, 1945, BBC commentator Richard Dimbleby broadcast from the room on the fifth anniversary of the battle and declared, 'It is one room in** which you could say: ''That is where they won the war'' ' (Illustrated London News). *Right:* **Today, sub-divided into self-contained flats, No. 6 was up for sale when we photographed it. Price of a unique piece of history: £25,000.**

Biggin's heroines. Sergeant Joan E. Mortimer, MM (seen in action with LAC Bill Brooker in Salt Box Gun Post *photo left*),

Flight Officer Elspeth C. Henderson, MM and Sergeant Helen E. Turner, MM, at Biggin in October 1940 (Imperial War Museum).

Throughout the next two weeks, the aerodrome suffered almost daily air raids. On some occasions attacks came in twice a day, the buildings being knocked out one by one, consequently reducing the efficiency of the station. Although morale was high, weariness was beginning to show in the eyes of the pilots and ground crews. All available men were fully occupied keeping the aerodrome operational and filling craters. Clearing rubble was an everyday job to be fitted around their normal duties.

Friday, August 30, 1940 was the day Biggin was nearly knocked out of the battle altogether. The day dawned fair with about four-tenths cloud cover and a visibility of five to ten miles. The first raid hit the aerodrome from high level at mid-day, cratering the landing area and hitting also Biggin Hill and Keston villages. Then at 6.00 p.m. came the big one. Nine Ju 88s swept in across the aerodrome from the south, at less than a thousand feet. No air-raid warning was given and the suddenness of the attack caught many personnel at tea in the cook house. The raid lasted only half-an-hour but, in that time, most of the buildings were destroyed or so badly damaged they were too unsafe to be used. The raiders dropped sixteen HE bombs (estimated as 1,000 pounders), of which six scored direct hits on the technical site. The transport yard, stores, barrack stores, armoury, guardroom and meteorological office, the Station Institute and other workshops were all hit. One of the hangars in the North Camp was also badly damaged. All power, gas and water mains were severed and the telephone lines running north of the camp were cut in three places.

The worst blow was a WAAF shelter which received a direct hit, killing many of the girls inside. The terrible task of having to dig them out went on all through that night and the following day. Altogether casualties totalled thirty-nine killed and twenty-six wounded.

The following day, Biggin was hit twice, at 1.00 p.m. and again at 5.30 p.m. Hangars in the South Camp were badly damaged together with the triple-bay hangar on the northern side. The Operations Block received a direct hit, the bomb exploding on the concrete roof, collapsing it on to the ops table. The warrant officers' quarters were hit by blast and rendered unsafe and windows in the Officers' Mess broken. The temporary lash-up of telephone lines, improvised after the previous evening's raid, was completely destroyed.

Biggin was given no respite. At 1.30 p.m.

Mrs. A. W. Green, MM, formerly Corporal Henderson, and Miss J. Mortimer, MM, return to Biggin on July 26, 1974 when roads on the station were re-named in their honour (Central Press).

On October 9, 1979 the editor took this photograph of pretty Flying Officer Judith Buchanan, Station Catering Officer, leaving her Ration Store which stands by the site of the WAAF shelter which received a direct hit on August 30, killing many of the girls sheltering inside. Tragically, ten weeks later she was dead, killed on December 22 in an unexplained car accident while motoring to Yorkshire for her Christmas leave.

the next day, September 1, more bombs were dropped from a high level although by now there were few buildings left in the camp to destroy. Three WAAF teleprinter operators received the Military Medal for continuing to work the defence lines while under attack during the second raid. The aerodrome was now only capable of operating a single squadron and after this raid it was decided to disperse sections to Keston because of the danger from collapsing buildings and all equipment which was undamaged was salvaged. Practically no buildings remained in a habitable condition and the main road running through the camp was blocked by two large craters. All services and communications were out of action and the Operations Room was temporarily moved to a shop a quarter-of-a-mile away in the Pantiles. Later a permanent location, used for the remainder of the war, was found in the old requisitioned Victorian house 'Towerfield' beside the Keston crossroad some two miles from the aerodrome.

Five days later the Germans launched another attack although this time most of the bombs fell wide along the Westerham Road. By now, Biggin Hill shared with Hornchurch the distinction of being the most bombed aerodrome in Fighter Command — almost a compliment from the Luftwaffe as to its operational value. Group Captain Grice was of the opinion that as long as the wreckage of the hangars remained standing the Germans would try to knock it down so he authorised their demolition by having them blown up. (Subsequently he was court-martialled for his action but was exonerated!)

In 1942 the British squadrons operating from Biggin Hill were joined by No. 133 'Eagle' Squadron and additional American visitors in August were Nos. 2 and 307 Pursuit

Above: **Bathed in the pale light of a wintry sun, four Spitfire IXs of No. 611 'West Lancs' Squadron fly low over Salt Box House towards West Wickham on December 9, 1942. The walls are all that remain of the triple-bay hangar finally blown up by Group Captain Grice (Radio Times).** *Below:* **One corner of the hangar still survives today.** *Bottom:* **Otherwise everything has changed — the Salt Box has gone and the replacement T2 hangars are on a completely different alignment.**

Squadrons which came for a month's experience. By July the station's score of enemy aircraft destroyed reached 900, the 1000th victim being downed the following year on May 15, 1943, establishing a sector record which remained unequalled to the end of the war.

After a long interval the Germans returned on January 20, 1943, coming in low and fast over the coast. Reaching the aerodrome, they first flew around the perimeter giving the resident aircraft ample time to scramble. In the ensuing fight, six German machines were downed for no loss to the RAF.

On September 19, 1943, St. George's

Chapel of Remembrance was dedicated, Group Captain Malan unveiling the altar during the service. The idea for the chapel had originated with Squadron Leader The Reverend Cecil King (Biggin's chaplain throughout the war) who wrote to the next-of-kin of airmen who had been killed flying from the aerodrome suggesting they contribute whatever they could afford; the result was the chapel constructed in a wood and asbestos building on the southern side of the 'drome. The dedication ceremony was timed shortly after the destruction of the 1,000th enemy aircraft, this honour being jointly held by Squadron Leader E. F. J. 'Jack' Charles,

The wartime chaplain of Biggin Hill, The Reverend Cecil King, was the guiding influence behind the construction of the first chapel which was to be a memorial to all those airmen who had been killed flying from the aerodrome.

Above: Dedication Service conducted by The Reverend M. H. Edwards of the first St. George's Chapel at Biggin in a hut in the South Camp, September 19, 1943 (Crown Copyright). *Below:* A skeleton of charred girders and debris is all that remained after the fire in 1946.

After considerable investigation, we pinpointed the site of the old chapel — now in the centre of a new warehousing construction site.

Below: Reproduction of the Remembrance Card sent to all the next-of-kin.

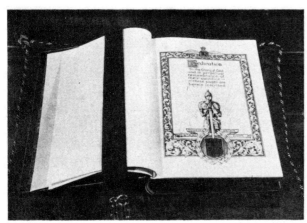

THE BOOK OF REMEMBRANCE IN ST. GEORGE'S CHAPEL

We will remember, with proud thanksgiving, the name of

Sergeant Eric Thomas George Frith, No. 92 Squadron

on the anniversary of his last operational flight

17th October, 1940

"AS STRONG STARS AT MIDNIGHT, HIS LAMP THEY UPLIFTED,
And strode to their task like tall ships running free.

· · · · · · · · · ·

We are debtors to them, who with lamps ever burning,
Forgather this instant, in heed to his call.
Reunion they bought us by never returning,
And, homeless, they builded a house for us all."

(from P. B. Clayton's hymn)

DFC, the Canadian CO of No. 611 Squadron and Commandant Rene Mouchotte, DFC, commanding the Free French Squadron No. 341 (Alsace).

Late in 1943, the Americans brought their P-47 Thunderbolts to Biggin and during a visit by a high-ranking American officer, the P-47s put on a low-level display. During the fly past one aircraft came too low and struck a tree, crashing onto a bungalow in Jail Lane, near the Old Tye Avenue junction, killing the pilot.

During the flying bomb period, the station was taken over by Balloon Command and Biggin Hill lay in the centre of the biggest balloon barrage ever known. The aerodrome was also right in the middle of 'Bomb Alley' and no less than six V1s crashed inside the aerodrome boundary.

At the end of 1944, Balloon Command moved out and the Squadrons returned, this time being joined by aircraft of Transport Command.

In June 1945, Biggin was transferred completely from Fighter Command to No. 46 Group Transport Command and, in addition, No. 168 Squadron, RCAF and No. 314 Squadron, USAAF operated from the aerodrome with Dakotas.

Early one morning in December 1946, fire broke out in the small St. George's Chapel. Although an airman raised the alarm, despite every effort, the building was totally gutted. Gone was the beautiful reredos with the polished panels recording the names of those that had died and also the oil lamp given by the local Air Training Corps which had burned continuously for the past three years. A charred visitors' book alone was saved and, out of a total of 6,000 names, one of the few still legible was that of Winston Churchill. In March 1947 it was announced by the Air Council Committee on War Memorials that they had decided that the old Operations Room, blitzed and vacated on August 31, 1940 and which was still standing near the Officers' Mess, should be redesigned and converted into the new St. George's Chapel of Remembrance. Mr W. Wylton Todd, ARIBA, who designed the original chapel and who was stationed at Biggin Hill for a time, offered his services free to design the new building. It was stated that there would be no national appeal and that funds would again be requested from relatives and friends of pilots killed while operating with the Biggin Hill sector of No. 11 Group. It was announced that the gallery of the Operations Room would be included in the new chapel although all these plans were later changed and a new site chosen on the base of one of the old bombed hangars. The new chapel was opened by the

Lord Bishop of Rochester on November 10, 1951.

In August 1946 Biggin Hill had been given to Reserve Command and Auxiliary Squadrons were the sole occupants until 1951. The station had also been switched back to Fighter Command in November 1949, operating first Spitfires and later Meteors. Late in June 1951 a tragic accident claimed the lives of three pilots when their aircraft crashed on take-off for a fly-past for Winston Churchill who was visiting the airfield.

In 1957 the main runway was extended for the safer operation of newer, faster jet aircraft and No. 41 Squadron joined the Auxiliaries that same year.

With the increasingly crowded airspace around Biggin, the RAF ceased flying operations from the station on February 7, 1959. They did however retain the North Camp to house the Officers' Selection Centre which opened in April that year followed by the Aircrew Selection Centre three years later.

Surrey Aviation leased the South Camp two years later for private flying and, with the closing of Croydon, many other operators chose Biggin as their base which had already been used by many entrants in the London to Paris Air race in July 1959. Under the management of ex-Squadron Leader J. R. Maitland (who was formerly stationed at the

aerodrome during the war and one of the first pilots to break the sound barrier), Biggin Hill was given a new lease of life as a thriving civilian airport, being the venue for an annual Air Fair.

Late in 1979, the Government confirmed its earlier decision to close the RAF camp at Biggin Hill with the intention of demolishing all the buildings except the Officers' Mess (which is to house the RAF Chaplains' School, presently at Amport House, Hampshire) and the Chapel. The RAF Selection Centre will then be moved to Bentley Priory. Possibly the last major event to be held on the historic aerodrome concerning the Battle of Britain will be the mammoth reunion for former aircrew who served at Biggin Hill during the battle planned by Wing Commander J. R. Myers and his staff which is to be held on Sunday, September 21, 1980.

Part of the morning Church Service will be taken from the last St. George's Festival Order of Service held before the original Chapel burnt down in 1946, a copy of which was provided by the sister-in-law of one of the pilots that died — Sergeant E. T. G. Frith of No. 92 Squadron. The coming together of hundreds of former Biggin servicemen at their former camp during its last months of existence will be a unique event and a fitting finale for the 40th Anniversary of the battle.

West Malling

BY ROBIN J. BROOKS

West Malling aerodrome began its long career as a private landing ground in 1930 housing the Maidstone School of Flying. With the erection of a marquee in the southern part of the parish, some four-and-a-half miles north-west of Maidstone to house an aeroplane, it was named Maidstone Airport. It was also known as Kingshill due to the many gliding activities there led by Mr. C. H. Lowe-Wylde, often called the father of gliding in Kent.

In 1931, a company called Kent Aeronautical Services operated from the aerodrome using modified SE5As called Dudley Watt DW1s and a Sopwith Dove which was owned by Mr. Lowe-Wylde. (The latter aircraft was abandoned at Malling after the owner's death, in a powered glider that he had designed and built himself, and this aircraft was rebuilt as a Pup in 1937/8 by R. O. Shuttleworth and still survives today in the Shuttleworth Collection.)

Maidstone Airport was registered as a company in 1932. In December of that year it appeared in the Aerodrome Directory of Great Britain and Northern Ireland as a civil aerodrome five miles west of Maidstone and one-and-a-half miles from West Malling on the B228 road.

In 1934 a new company called Malling Aviation arrived at Maidstone Airport. They owned a varied collection of aircraft including several De Havilland DH60s and at least one Hawker Tomtit — G-AALL — which was an ex-Prince of Wales King's Cup entrant. They also owned a De Havilland Gypsy Moth which was impressed with No. 41 Group in 1939 and used as a decoy dummy in 1941.

In 1935 Malling Aviation became proprietors of the airport and renamed it Malling Aero Club. With the change, the aerodrome became well known and many displays were held. Alan Cobham and Amy Johnson flew into Malling as did the 'Flying Flea', a very lethal do-it-yourself enthusiast aircraft.

With the clouds of war looming, the aerodrome began to change from peace into war. An RAF station headquarters was formed at West Malling at the beginning of June 1940 under the administration of Fighter Command. No. 26 (Army Co-Operation) Squadron and No. 51 Wing moved in on June 8. The former, flying the Westland Lysander, was employed to carry out reconnaissance and photographic sorties in co-operation with anti-aircraft and searchlight units.

The grass-surfaced aerodrome at this time measured some 1,100 yards NE-SW; 1,300 yards SE-NW; 1,200 yards from N-S and 1,400 yards from E-W. Somerfeld track had to be laid to give the aerodrome all-weather serviceability as the grass became very wet in winter. The N-S landing direction was later extended to 1,666 yards and the main E-W by an additional 760 yards. One J-type hangar and sixteen blister hangars were in existence by 1941. Petrol storage totalled 72,000 gallons of aviation spirit and 5,000 gallons of MT fuel.

On July 12, No. 141 Squadron, equipped with the Boulton Paul Defiant, arrived at Malling and undertook its first engagement with the enemy on the 21st. This was an interception patrol over the channel. A superior number of Bf 109s, whose pilots knew the Defiant to be vulnerable from below, attacked from that position and, in the ensuing battle, shot down six aircraft — virtually wiping out No. 141 Squadron. The remainder of the unit was immediately posted back to Prestwick.

Following their departure, No. 26 Squadron remained the sole occupants at Malling which was designated a satellite for Kenley and to be

One of West Malling's bomb-damaged buildings now occupied by the Kent County Council. In October 1979 it still showed signs of extensive repair work.

used as an advanced aerodrome for both Kenley and Biggin Hill.

August saw the beginning of a series of bombing attacks which were to render the aerodrome unserviceable for the major part of the battle. The station diary, recalled forty years after the event, describes the raids in impassionate terms as these extracts disclose:

10.8.40: Station attacked by one twin-engined enemy aircraft at 0730 hours. No warning of attack; aircraft emerged from thick cloud base of 800 feet and did two runs entering cloud between each attack. 14 bombs dropped altogether on landing surface, among buildings of new station at requisitioned premises known as Workhouse and in surrounding fields. Two Lysander aircraft damaged by machine gun fire and bomb splinters on aerodrome. Bombs dropped among buildings of new station caused superficial damage and many windows in buildings near completion were shattered. 17 workmen injured by splinters and machine gun fire; one of the workmen died later. One bomb fell on block of workhouse, injuring three R.E. sappers. Block extensively damaged by splinters and machine gun fire. Enemy

Maidstone aerodrome in 1936 looking north towards the clubhouse. By 1940 it had been renamed RAF West Malling, the grass landing area extended and construction of an extensive technical site begun on the western boundary (Aerofilms).

A toilet block still bears the scars of the 1940 battle.

71

aircraft attacked by Ground Defence Lewis Guns, 175 rounds fired from 4 posts but accuracy of fire doubtful. Bofor Guns were slow in getting into action and only fired a few rounds. Attack only lasted three minutes when aircraft re-entered clouds after a final look round and proceeded in an easterly direction.

15.8.40 Bombing attack high altitude made on station today at 1900 hours. Two airmen killed and considerable damage to new station particularly wooden structures. One ambulance badly damaged and written off.

16.8.40 Further high altitude enemy bombing attack on aerodrome. No casualties. Three aircraft of 26 Squadron badly damaged and further damage to new station. Hangar roof hit and badly damaged.

18.8.40 Medium dive bombing attack on station today at 1320 hours. Further damage to new hangars and three Lysanders written off. No casualties. At least two enemy aircraft hit.

24.8.40 Unexploded bombs reported on boundary of aerodrome 400 yards off northern boundary of aerodrome and to north thereof.

28.8.40 Several bombs dropped by single aircraft in district during night.

3.9.40 From four to six enemy aircraft attacked Station at 1512 hours, came in unseen from South-East and dropped about 30 bombs. Kenley Operations had reported "All Clear" at the time of raid which lasted about two minutes. One civilian wounded. 20 craters on aerodrome and several unexploded bombs dispersed among buildings of New Station; parachute section slightly damaged.

7.9.40 Resident Engineer reported this morning that his employees would not be at work to-day as someone had spread an alarmist report to the effect that West Malling would be raided to-day. This is an example of what effect rumours produce.

8.9.40 System of Alerts introduced by Air Ministry. Alert 3 "Invasion likely but improbable during next three days"; alert 2 "Invasion probable within next three days"; alert 1 "Invasion imminent and likely to occur within next 12 hours". On instructions from 11 Group, Alert No. 1 in force from 2000 hours. Sporadic bomb raids during day and night. Several bombs dropped on main London Road near West Malling. West Malling Telephone Service out of action. Established communication with Kenley by W/T and eventually communication established with Maidstone. West Malling and District likely to be out of communication for next 48 hours.

9.9.40 Alert 1 continues. Strangely quiet morning. Landline communications re-established with Kenley Operations and Kenley main exchange. Rail communication with London interrupted owing to bomb damage on line. No morning mail or papers. Recalled all personnel from leave.

10.9.40 Rail communication with London re-established and telephone services restored. Alert 1 continues. Surprise attack on aerodrome by a single enemy aircraft at 1720 hours, probably a Dornier 17. Made one run over aerodrome and dropped six anti-personnel bombs. One bomb scored a direct hit on a post of Army Details (Queens Regt.), killing six soldiers and wounding three, one airman injured through falling down a trench. Two temporary buildings on New Station gutted by fire and three bombs dropped on aerodrome but craters quickly filled in. Enemy aircraft came through cloud and covered by sun at about 5,000 feet.

15.9.40 One enemy aircraft Heinkel 111 forced down on aerodrome at 1500 hours. Heavy firing from eight or nine attacking Hurricanes and Spitfires made aerodrome unhealthy. Machine badly damaged. Of

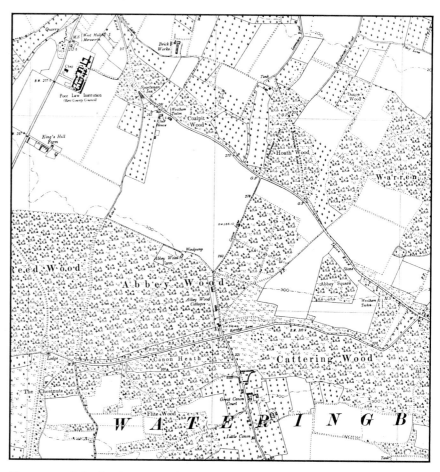

The extent of the development of West Malling which had taken place by the Battle of Britain is graphically demonstrated by the plan *above* taken from the 1936-37 revision of the Ordnance Survey and the German reconnaissance photograph *below* taken on September 7, 1940 (US National Archives).

crew, one was dead, two seriously wounded and admitted to Preston Hall Hospital, one slightly wounded and one unhurt. The dead airman, Gefreiter Lange, placed in Station Mortuary.

(Discrepancy with entry in Luftwaffe losses is probably explained by mis-identity. Ed.)

16.9.40 One enemy aircraft dropped three bombs near billets, no material damage.

17.9.40 Four H.E. bombs were dropped in vicinity of Army Control post, no damage to personnel or buildings.

18.9.40 Three anti-personnel bombs dropped at 0950 hours. One fell near Station Headquarters damaging hangars and blowing out a number of windows in Station Headquarters. No damage to personnel and damage to buildings moderate. Alert No. 1 reduced to Alert No. 2 by broadcast signal from Air Ministry.

28.9.40 Enemy aircraft dropped several anti-personnel bombs and numerous incendiary bombs in vicinity of Station at 0040 hours. Three tents destroyed in Orchard Camp Site and an Army Lorry wrecked. One airman wounded and two soldiers slightly wounded. Several incendiary bombs fell on aerodrome and one tent burnt out.

4.10.40 One enemy aircraft dropped 12 bombs just off aerodrome at 1315 hours. No damage done.

7.10.40 6 Bombs dropped by high flying enemy aircraft probably M.E. 109s at approximately 1615 hours. One landed on landing surface, and between Institution and Aerodrome and others off the Station. No damage to Aerodrome or Equipment.

13.10.40 Four bombs dropped from high flying M.E. 109 aircraft at 1345 hours. All burst clear of landing surface. No damage to Equipment or personnel. Two bombs burst in air about 200-300 feet up near landing surface. Probably new type of bomb known as "Goering Bomb Basket". Big blast effect but no damage or splinters found.

14.10.40 One enemy aircraft dropped 4 bombs at 2030 hours by moonlight, 3 heavy H.E. Bombs fell on landing surface and one oil bomb near boundary of Aerodrome. No damage to personnel or equipment.

18.10.40 One aircraft dived through low clouds and mist at 1630 hours dropped one bomb off Aerodrome and machine gunned landing surfaces no casualties or damage.

The bombing forced No. 26 Squadron to leave the aerodrome and it was not until October 30, 1940, at the end of the Battle of Britain, that the station was ready to receive any units. No. 66 flew in with Spitfires and the posting to Malling gave them a brief respite from the ordeal of constant battle. With No. 66 came No. 421 Flight.

However, it was not until April 14, 1941 that the station was ready to accept a full squadron. Together with a Cierva autogiro conscripted for radar calibration tests, No. 264 arrived with Defiants — this time flying in the night-fighter role. Again as, with No. 141 Squadron before them, No. 264 were also decimated and were withdrawn to a quieter area.

On April 30 No. 29 Squadron, flying the new Beaufighter night interceptor, came to Malling and immediately began to notch up many kills with the help of airborne radar. Serving with the squadron at this time were two bomber pilots, Guy Gibson and Don Parker. Their knowledge of evading the Luftwaffe's night-fighters was invaluable to the British pilots when attacking the German bombers at night. It is no secret that Gibson regarded his time at Malling as a very happy period and he often came back to the base until his untimely death in 1944.

To keep the squadron company came No. 33 flying Hurricanes to undertake offensive fighter sweeps over France and with No. 253 and the Fighter Interception Unit, West

Clock and lectern Bible from the station church now on display at the Lashenden Air Warfare Museum at Headcorn Aerodrome, Ashford, Kent,

Malling again became a front line aerodrome. No. 1428 (Enemy Aircraft) Squadron also arrived to give the personnel a closer inspection of the He 111, Bf 109 and 110 and to enable the pilots to fly against them in mock battle.

Between August 16-20, 1943, day fighters flew in to the station from Nos. 411, 485 and 610 Squadrons which were attached for combined operations on the Dieppe raid.

On the night of April 16, 1943 came one of Malling's strangest incidents when a single-engined aircraft was heard approaching the aerodrome. After circling twice it landed and, assuming it to be a Defiant that was short on fuel, the fire tender and crash crew drove from the watch office to intercept and inform the pilot where he was. On approaching the aircraft, the crash crew saw a large Balkan-kreuz on the fuselage and realized it was a

A direct descendant of the beacon and martello towers is West Malling's unique observation tower. Standing on a hill in Teston Road on the northern fringe of the aerodrome, it was manned day and night until late September 1944 by both the RAF Regiment and the Home Guard whose duties were to warn of approaching enemy aircraft. It was connected by telephone to the West Malling control tower and local anti-aircraft units. Our author, Robin Brooks, has appealed for its preservation.

Focke Wulf 190. Then a second aircraft came into land, this also being German. The first pilot gave himself up but the second attempted to swing back onto the runway and take off. Some shots from the fire tender hit the oxygen bottles in the pilot's cockpit which exploded blowing the cockpit apart. A third enemy plane undershot and landed in the orchard at the lower end of the runway and a fourth crashed at Staplehurst. Later it transpired that fifteen FW 190s had been sent over on intruder operations and had got hopelessly lost.

On May 13, 1943, No. 29 Squadron left to be replaced by No. 85 with Wing Commander John 'Cats Eyes' Cunningham. No. 3 Squadron also flew in with 'Bombphoons' (Typhoons fitted with bombs) and No. 486 to fly by day.

In July 1943, Malling began to accept the heavy bombers of the RAF and USAAF and, to supplement the day squadrons, Thunderbolts of the Eighth Air Force arrived to escort the American bombers.

On June 12, 1944, No. 85 Squadron having left, Malling entered a new stage when No. 91 Squadron arrived to mount 'Diver' operations against the German pilotless aircraft or V1s. The Tempests that they flew were ideal for this purpose and together with No. 274 and 157, these squadrons made Malling the main base for tipping and crashing doodle-bugs.

However on August 30 war activities ceased at the base when workmen arrived to carry out extensive improvements including the construction of a new concrete runway. These alterations took until June 1945.

In September, No. 29 Squadron came back now equipped with Mosquitos and No. 287 with Tempests. Shortly afterwards No. 29 changed their Mosquitos for the new Meteor jet and No. 500 Squadron of the Royal Auxiliary Air Force, also flying Meteors, arrived to give support to the regular RAF. When this organization disbanded in 1957, Malling was left to No. 29 Squadron then flying Javelins.

With the post-war reductions in defence, the field was placed under care and maintenance on August 17, 1964 and the sound of Meteors, Vampires and Javelins left for good. A year later the base was re-opened when a United States Navy facility flight flew in with communications and transport aircraft. The Americans had originally been based at Hendon but when this closed Malling was chosen as a replacement.

Super DC 3s and Convair 340s now flew into the aerodrome, the force using the base for nearly two years before transferring to Blackbushe.

When they left, no further flying took place. During its existence as a military aerodrome, it had accounted for the destruction of 165 enemy aircraft with thirty-four probably destroyed and fifty-nine damaged.

While the fate of the aerodrome was being decided, No. 618 Gliding School arrived to give air cadets instruction and Short Brothers, the commercial aero firm, moved a maintenance section from Rochester to Malling for the purpose of servicing Varsity and Chipmunk aircraft for the RAF.

In 1970, Kent County Council bought the aerodrome and converted many of the brick buildings into offices and, in 1972, it was used as a reception centre for many of the Asians who arrived in Britain from Uganda.

Today the airfield is still in a good state of preservation and, although Shorts have now left the aerodrome, Kent County Council have a plan to lease the airfield to operators for passenger and freight traffic. Although there is much local opposition to the scheme, it is hoped to commence some regular traffic in 1980.

The aerodrome looking east down the single 1,760-yard runway in October 1979. The observation tower is arrowed.

SECTOR D
Hornchurch

BY GROUP CAPTAIN H. T. SUTTON, OBE, DFC.

The aerodrome at Hornchurch was originally established in 1915 in an effort to combat the incursions of German airships over Britain. A site on Sutton's Farm, then worked by Mr. Tom Crawford, seemed ideally placed to guard the eastern approach to the capital and, by October that year, two canvas RE5 hangars had been erected just to the west of the farmhouse on the edge of a landing area some 500 yards square.

The first aircraft to use the new aerodrome was a BE 2c flown by Second Lieutenant H. MacD. O'Malley of No. 13 Squadron, RFC, who arrived on Sunday, October 3, 1915. Facilities were very simple and a primitive petrol tin flare path 300 yards long enabled flying to be undertaken at night.

By the following year, Sutton's Farm (as the aerodrome was then called) was one of the nine landing grounds which ringed London as part of the 18th Wing which included all the air defences of London. At first, each station was allocated two aircraft but, by March 1916, those at Hornchurch became part of No. 39 Home Defence Squadron with its HQ at Woodford in Essex and the aircraft were to be concentrated in larger flights on three aerodromes to the east of London. Sutton's Farm was selected to be one of these and plans were drawn up for the permanent construction of wooden hangars, workshops and living accommodation.

On September 2, 1916, the little aerodrome received its first spectacular victory when one of its pilots, Lieutenant W. Leefe-Robinson attacked Schutte-Lanz SL 11 and brought it down at Cuffley. This was the first real success against the German airships and the demise of the SL 11, in full view of thousands of cheering Londoners, brought Lieutenant Leefe-Robinson overnight fame and a Victoria Cross. Three weeks later, on the night of September 23/24, two more Sutton's Farm

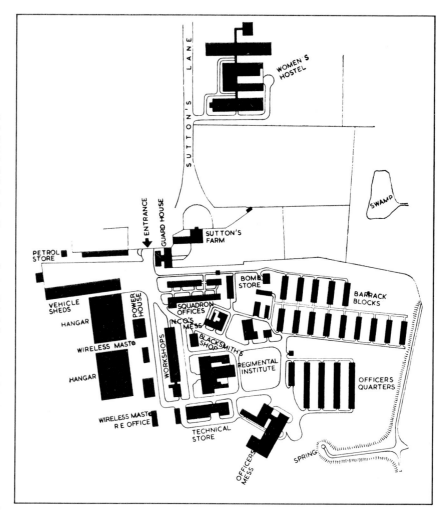

It is important to appreciate that the technical site of Sutton's Farm landing ground during the Great War lay almost in the middle of the Second World War Hornchurch aerodrome. Careful reference to the plan *above* of the site in 1918 and the 1935 plan *below* show the comparative location of the old with the new technical area built beside South End Road (Crown Copyright).

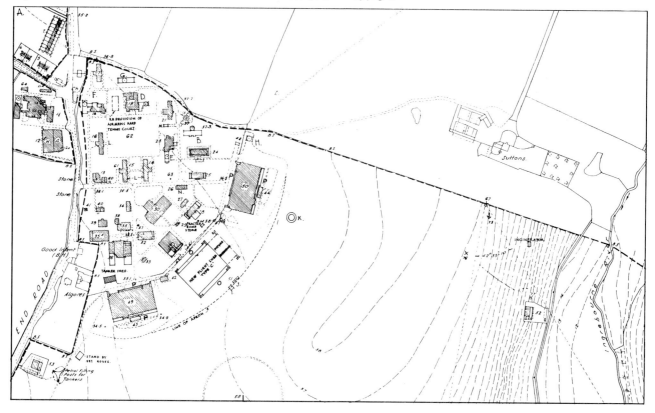

Hornchurch as it was at the end of the Second World War. A northern extension of dispersals stretches far beyond the Sutton's Farm site while, to the west, an E-W extension crosses the line of South End Road (Crown Copyright).

pilots, Second Lieutenants A de B Brandon and Sowrey made it a hat-trick by downing the super Zeppelins L.33 and L.32.

Although this action routed the attacks on London by the German Airship Service, new bombing operations were begun by twin-engined Gotha G.11 aircraft. To counter this new threat, No. 46 Squadron was recalled from France to be based at Sutton's Farm as part of the London Air Defence Area formed in July 1917. One of the pilots on the strength of the squadron at the time was Major J. T. B. McCudden, VC. No. 48 Squadron was later replaced, on a permanent basis, by No. 78 who were joined in April 1918 by No. 189 Night Training Squadron.

By the time the Armistice was signed in November, the permanent buildings were nearly all completed but barely a year later the Air Ministry informed Mr. Crawford that they had no further use for the aerodrome and that his land would be returned to him as near as possible to its condition when first requisitioned. This entailed demolishing all the recently-constructed buildings and hangars, removing drains and reinstating the farmland.

Nevertheless, within four years of the end of the war, the wisdom of the complete post-war run-down of the Royal Air Force was being

questioned and a decision was made to re-form fifteen new squadrons immediately. On November 24, 1922, just two years after most of the wartime buildings at Sutton's Farm had been demolished, an inspection was made of the area to establish its suitability as a permanent aerodrome. The report on the site stated that the former landing ground was now under cultivation and had been divided into three separate fields of potatoes, turnips and clover. A few buildings from the former camp still existed, one being the transport shed, which was in use by the farmer as a corn store, and the women's quarters which had become an extension for the Romford workhouse. The blacksmith's shop and old guardroom stood empty and derelict and work was still proceeding on the final stages of lifting the old foundations and roads.

Although a survey of other possible aerodrome sites in the area was carried out the following month, the conclusion was that Sutton's Farm was by far the best for the purpose. However, having only recently recovered his land from the Government, Mr. Crawford was in no mood to give it back and

firmly told the Air Ministry there was nothing doing.

However Sutton's Farm had already proved itself indispensable to the defences of London and its recovery as an aerodrome was not to be abandoned too easily. Air Marshal Sir Hugh Trenchard, in a minute to the Deputy Chief of the Air Staff, said: 'It is decided that Sutton's Farm or an aerodrome in the vicinity is a necessity for the defensive measures of England.' A further search was made in the area for an alternative to Sutton's Farm but to no avail. The Deputy Director of Organization wrote in a minute to the Chief of Air Staff: 'It will be seen that careful reconnaissance of the area had been made and only two possible sites have been discovered. Neither of them are in any way as desirable as Sutton's Farm and either would be equally costly to acquire as we shall only be able to obtain them by exercising compulsory powers. There is therefore nothing to be gained by proceeding with any alternative proposals to Sutton's Farm.'

On June 14, 1923, the Chief of Air Staff gave orders for the Director of Organization to

'proceed with the necessary action to get Sutton's Farm,' and on July 11, compulsory powers were sought in a letter to the Secretary of the Treasury.

The title deeds of Sutton's Farm proved to be very ancient. The farmhouse stood on the site of the old manor house of the Manor of Sutton. This Manor, together with the Manor of Hornchurch Hall, was acquired by William of Wykeham in the year 1392 from the Monks of St. Bernard. It was presented to New College, Oxford, which Wykeham had founded and endowed in close association with his College in Winchester.

New College, Oxford, agreed to sell 120 acres of their land, but insisted that the northern boundary of the landing ground should be 300 yards south of the farmhouse. It could not be denied that this was a reasonable enough arrangement. During the war, Mr. Crawford had undergone an inconvenience no greater than any citizen could expect in war time, in having an aerodrome built on his very doorstep, but in peace time such an encroachment would be intolerable. The Air Ministry therefore agreed to this and, in the plan for the new aerodrome, the area set aside for the technical site was on the opposite side of the landing ground from Sutton's Farm, thus leaving Mr. Crawford as undisturbed as possible. This, however, did involve the purchase of more land on the western side of the area and it delayed the building for several months. The sale of the land belonging to New College was completed in May 1924 and, by the end of that month, building of the aerodrome was put in hand.

In 1926 the bye-laws for Sutton's Farm Aerodrome were published above the signature of Sir Samuel Hoare as President of the Air Council and H. B. Ayres and William C. Allen, representing the Urban District Council of Hornchurch. Some of the clauses have the authentic ring of fantasy which is characteristic of all genuine bye-laws as illustrated by Provision 2:

'2. No costermonger, hawker, pedlar, huckster, marine store dealer or other dealer, or rag and bone and bottle gatherer, or bookmaker or racing or betting tout or vendor of

Above: **The last rehearsal before the curtain went up. Hornchurch prepares for the Air Defence Exercises of August 1939. No. 54 Squadron Spitfires lined up facing No. 2 Hangar with four Blenheims of No. 25 Squadron on attachment from Tangmere and the Spitfires of No. 74 Squadron beyond. To the right are the Spitfires of No. 65 Squadron while five Avro Ansons of an unidentified unit are parked to the left of the 100ft-tall chimney stack of St. George's Hospital (Keystone).**

In November 1979 the old aerodrome presented a scene of waterlogged misery. Like a miniature Offa's Dyke, an earthen rampart effectively separates the former RAF camp from the mangled remains of the flying field.

newspapers or any kind of literature or photographer or person engaged in any similar traffic or occupation to one of those specified, unless in possession of a Pass issued under the authority of the Officer Commanding, Royal Air Force Station, Sutton's Farm, shall intrude or enter or be upon the said land for the purpose of selling, buying or trafficking or otherwise carrying on his or her or any like business at Sutton's Farm.'

The building programme continued over the next two years and, on April 1, 1928, the new Royal Air Force station was opened. Its first squadron was No. 111 (F) commanded by Squadron Leader Keith Park who, twelve years later, would fight the Battle of Britain at No. 11 Group Headquarters.

Renamed RAF Hornchurch in January

1929, the new base had the dubious honour to receive a formation from a future enemy when Generale Italo Balbo, Chief of the Regia Aeronautica, landed with eleven aircraft at the end of a non-stop flight from Rome.

The following year Hornchurch became a two-squadron station with the re-forming of No. 54 (F) at the aerodrome. Air displays and participation in Air Defence of Great Britain exercises occupied the 1930s, developing new techniques and equipment for air fighting. No. 111 Squadron moved out in July 1934 to be replaced by another famous squadron reformed during the pre-World War II expansion period, No. 65. Two years later, Hornchurch added a third squadron with the arrival of No. 74 Squadron.

Its closeness to London made the

aerodrome a centre of great interest for Londoners and fine Sunday afternoons saw streams of visitors hoping to get the chance of seeing aircraft taking off. Empire Air Days held at the station helped to foster interest in flying as well as adding to the finances of the RAF Benevolent Fund.

In 1936, Hornchurch became part of No. 11 Group in the newly formed Fighter Command when the RAF Home Defence Force was reorganised and, in December, Air Marshal Sir Hugh Dowding arrived at the station to discuss the layout of the new Operations Room. Hornchurch was to be a Sector Headquarters and the new organisation was given its first real test in the Home Defence Exercises held in August 1938 between 'Eastland' and 'Westland'. Many lessons were learned from the conduct of the 'battle' in which the new radio-location (radar) stations had participated and one outcome was the transmission of a signal by friendly aircraft which could be recognised by the radar operators. This became known throughout the Second World War as IFF or Identification Friend or Foe.

Above: **Swing low sweet chariot! Two Blenheims IFs of No. 25 Squadron ease down over the Ingrebourne River to land at Hornchurch on August 11, 1939 during the last big air exercises before the outbreak of war (Charles E. Brown).** *Below:* **Rainclouds scud over the Ingrebourne on a bleak November day in 1979. The river, not to be confused with the ditch in the foreground, cuts across the middle distance. The aspect looks different as the height of the aerodrome on the eastern perimeter has been raised by some twenty feet by the extraction of gravel and rubbish infilling.**

Left: **Buffeted by the slipstream, two erks ballast the bouncing tail of one of the Blenheims while the engines are test run. The rifle butts in the background were situated in the centre of the eastern** perimeter, opposite the main camp (Charles E. Brown). *Right:* **November 1979. An indication of the new ground level can be seen by the almost complete burial of one of the E-pens.**

Left: **Outside their mobile HQ, the pilots and crews enter the days activities in the flying log. Even with the outbreak of war only twenty-four days distant, the atmosphere is that of a summer** picnic (Charles E. Brown). *Right:* **Where the flying men played at war forty years ago. The Hornchurch savannah of 1979 is the result of seventeen years of disuse.**

Above: **Before the award of decorations on June 27, 1940, HM King George VI chats with officer pilots on the station (Imperial War Museum).** *Below:* **How many residents of Tangmere Crescent, Hornchurch are aware that the King once stood virtually on their doorstep? The scene of the 'hollow square' in November 1979 computed by overlaying a plan of the camp on a present-day street map.**

Above: **The aerodrome looking north in April 1941 and right thirty-eight years later.**

In August 1939 orders were issued to camouflage all buildings and, from September 1, the Operations Room was manned continuously. However, the appointment of Group Captain C. A. Bouchier on December 20 helped to mellow the stark, impersonal face wrought on the station by the coming of war as the entry in the station record book for April 30, 1940 records:

'During the last month a determined drive has been made by the Station Commander to make the Station a pleasanter and more attractive place. Roads and paths were cleared up and edges whitewashed, grass verges trimmed and lawns cut. A large number of bulbs, plants and rose trees were planted and every squadron and section were given tools to cultivate their own part of the camp. In consequence, the main road to Headquarters and the ground around the hangars and workshops are gay with spring flowers and should be gayer still when summer comes.'

The first offensive patrol from Hornchurch was mounted by twelve Spitfires from each of Nos. 74 and 54 Squadrons on May 21 but the first station victory fell to the guns of Spitfires from No. 65 Squadron the following day when a Ju 88 was shot down over Flushing. By June 1, eight various squadrons had flown from Hornchurch and had a confirmed total of 122

victories having lost 26 of their own aircraft. Two days later, Marshal of the Royal Air Force Lord Trenchard (father of the RAF and Hornchurch itself) visited the station to compliment the airmen and officers. Then, on June 27, Hornchurch was honoured by the visit of HM King George VI, accompanied by Air Chief-Marshal Sir Hugh Dowding, to present decorations to five officers. Squadron Leader J. A. Leathart of No. 54 Squadron received the Distinguished Service Order and Distinguished Flying Crosses were awarded to Flight Lieutenants R. R. Stanford Tuck (No. 65 Squadron); A. G. 'Sailor' Malan (No. 74 Squadron); A. C. 'Al' Deere (No. 54 Squadron) and Pilot Officer J. R. Allen also of No. 54 Squadron.

By now, the whole Station was surrounded by barbed wire and pill boxes were sited at strategic points around the perimeter. The slight ridge which overlooked the aerodrome on the far side of the Ingrebourne River was guarded day and night by a strong detachment of the Glasgow Highlanders. Armoured cars manned by Army personnel and two armoured motor vehicles (in reality large steel boxes mounted on lorry chassis armed with Bren guns) were put at the disposal of RAF personnel. A searchlight was erected on the west side of the aerodrome to illuminate any

German forces which might attempt to land at night. Four Bofors guns, each protected by a series of trenches, were manned by a detachment from the 33rd 'Rough Riders' Regiment. Other trenches guarded vital positions and Royal Engineers had completed plans for the demolition of the petrol dump and stores in the event of the evacuation of the station. Emergency billeting had been provided for a thousand 'bodies' in Hornchurch and Sutton's Institute and roads had been earmarked by a newly-appointed RAF transport liaison officer to be used if the aerodrome was abandoned.

No runways existed at Hornchurch, the grass aerodrome allowing for a 1,200 yard run from N-S; 1,130 yards from NE-SW; 850 yards from SE-NW and 830 yards from E-W (a Spitfire usually needed about 150 yards to become airborne). A perimeter track 18ft wide circled the landing area and covered accommodation was provided by three C-type hangars. Petrol storage amounted to 72,000 gallons with 4,000 gallons of oil. One-and-a-half million rounds of .303 ammunition were available from stores.

Flying obstructions were created by a factory chimney 100ft high on the north-eastern boundary and the nearby London balloon barrage. Ford's car factory with three chimneys lay three miles to the south.

Squadrons based at Hornchurch during the Battle of Britain were No. 54 with Spitfires from August 8-September 3; No. 65 with Spitfires from June 5-August 27; No. 74, also with Spitfires, from June 26-August 14; No. 600 from August 24-September 19 with

Blenheims; No. 41 from July 26-August 8 with Spitfires; No. 222 from August 29-November 10 with Spitfires; No. 266 from August 14-21 with Spitfires; No. 264 with Defiants from August 21-29 and No. 603 August 10 to late in October.

Hornchurch suffered at least twenty separate bombing attacks during the Battle of Britain, the most serious occurring on August 31 at lunchtime as described in the war diary of No. 54 Squadron:

'1315. A large formation of enemy bombers — a most impressive sight in vic formation at 15,000 feet — reached the aerodrome and dropped their bombs (probably sixty in all) in a line from the other side of our dispersal pens to the petrol dump and beyond into Elm Park. Perimeter track, dispersals and barrack block windows suffered but no other damage to buildings was caused and the aerodrome, in spite of its ploughed-up condition, remained serviceable. The squadron was ordered off just as the first bombs were beginning to fall and eight of our machines safely cleared the ground. The remaining section, however, just became airborne as the bombs exploded. All the machines were wholly wrecked in the air. The survival of the pilots is a complete miracle. Sergeant Davis, taking-off across the airfield towards the hangars, was thrown back to the other side of the River Ingrebourne, two fields away, and scrambled out of his machine unharmed.

'Flight Lieutenant Deere had one wing and his prop torn off; climbing to about a hundred feet he turned over and, coming down, slid along the aerodrome for a hundred yards, upside down. He was rescued from this unenviable position by Pilot Officer Edsall, the third member of the Section, who had suffered a similar fate, except that he had landed the right way up. Rushing across the aerodrome, with bombs still dropping, he extricated Flight Lieutenant Deere from his machine. "The first and last time — I hope," was the verdict of these truly amazing pilots — all of whom were ready for battle again by next morning.'

Above: **The blast-mangled shape of a Spitfire of No. 222 Squadron which received a direct hit during the bombing of Hornchurch on August 31. This aircraft can be seen lying behind Hillary's Spitfire in the picture at the top of the page.** *Below:* **Photographed by 'Joe' Crawshaw surreptitiously from the top of a fuel bowser, an Anson arrives, believed to have been carrying staff officers to inspect the damage to the station caused by the extensive bombing.**

Flight Lieutenant Deere later described his incredible escape:

'My Section was nearly airborne when the first bomb fell. The next second, a one-thousand-pounder dropped plumb in front of my nose. The blast blew my Number Three two fields away, my Number Two had his wing blown off and slithered along the ground on his belly. I seemed to be flung miles into the air, then my machine flicked on to its back and crashed on to the aerodrome to career upside down for some 250 yards. My head was scraping along the ground and slowly but surely I was being squeezed into a ball in the cockpit. At last the aircraft stopped. Everything was pitch black. The earth shook with the explosion of bombs. My mouth was full of blood and grit; my head rested in a pool of petrol from the burst tank.

'It was frightening, balancing there on my head, realizing that with one spark I would be enveloped in flaming petrol. Then a voice called, ''Are you all right, Al?'' Spitting out mouthfuls of earth, I bawled, ''Yes, but for hell's sake get me out of here.'' A rending and tearing from the outside broke open the cockpit door, through which, after releasing my harness and parachute, I managed to crawl. My rescuer was my section Number Two, Pilot Officer Edsall. Supporting each other (Edsall was injured too), we made a dash for the shelter of the hangars. Our bright yellow 'Mae Wests' had attracted the attention of a Hun fighter pilot who was diving down to machine gun us. Somehow we managed to reach the safety of the hangars just in time to miss a stream of hot lead which spattered on the iron girders.

'Afterwards I had a good look at my machine and wondered: ''How did I get out of that alive?'' The engine had been blown off — this explains the absence of fire — the port wing was nowhere to be seen, and the complete tail unit rested in a huge bomb-crater which marked the spot at which I had been hit.'

Whilst these very noisy events were taking place in and around the aerodrome, No. 603 Squadron and No. 222 Squadron were doing great execution at a distance. For No. 603, the Edinburgh Auxiliary Squadron, it was to be an immensely successful day with no less than fourteen enemy aircraft falling to their guns for the loss of only one pilot and two Spitfires.

A second attack that day came at precisely 6.00 p.m. when, despite strong fighter opposition and heavy AA fire, German bombers penetrated the defences. However their aim was inaccurate and the sticks of bombs ran out towards the edge of the 'drome. Two parked Spitfires were written off and one airman was killed. However, apart from damage to the dispersal pens, perimeter track and aerodrome surface, Hornchurch remained serviceable.

A remarkable set of photographs taken on September 1 by one of the No. 222 Squadron airframe mechanics 'Joe' Crawshaw (pictured *below* in the cockpit of his personal charge P9323). Using a 35mm Agfa Karat, he was able to capture the aftermath of the bombing raids of the previous day. *Left:* Of the three No. 222 Squadron Spitfires in the foreground, ZD-D, X4278 was shot down over Maidstone three days later, carrying to his death Flying Officer J. W. Cutts. The No. 603 Squadron Spitfire XT-M, X4277 was that flown by Pilot Officer Richard Hillary when he was shot down off Margate and badly burned on September 3. *Above:* Hornchurch in November 1979 badly needs tidying up after the attentions of the gravel extractors. It would take more than the solitary 1940 steam roller to level this lot!

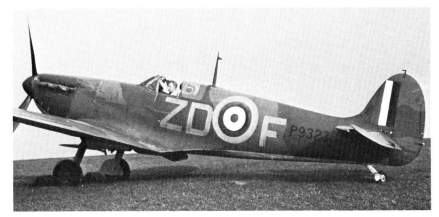

Flight mechanics of 'Natal' Squadron take a breather during the battle.

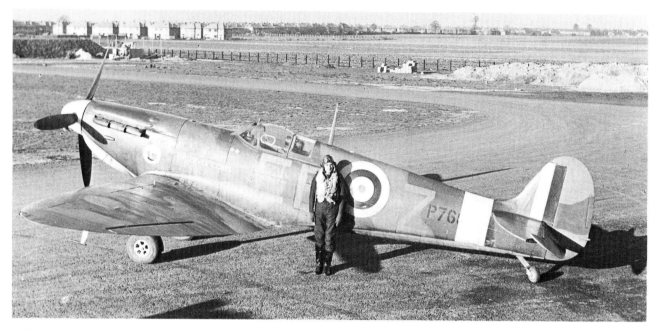

On September 20 two land mines were dropped on the aerodrome, one of which landed on the perimeter track in the south-western corner just beyond the stop butts and failed to explode. The following day a naval demolition squad under Lieutenant-Commander Ryan came to defuse the mine. This was carried out successfully and, after staying for lunch, the team went off to deal with two other mines which had dropped in Dagenham. At 4.30 p.m. personnel on the station heard a loud explosion and news came later that Ryan and his Petty Officer had both been killed.

On October 15 the Operations Room on the station, which had suffered a near miss on September 9, was moved to more spacious accommodation at Lamborne Hall, Romford where it remained for the duration of the war.

After the 'Battle' had been won, the RAF turned its attention to attacking enemy barges being assembled at the invasion ports along the Channel coast. On January 7, 1941, the Hornchurch Wing — consisting of three Spitfire squadrons, Nos. 41, 64 and 611 — made the first offensive operation from Hornchurch since the Battle, escorting a 'Circus' formation of Blenheim bombers to attack Luftwaffe objectives in the Foret de Guines on what proved to be a completely successful raid, accomplished without any loss whatsoever.

The aerodrome itself was still heavily guarded against invasion which was, at that time, still considered a strong possibility. Six platoons of E Company of the 70th Essex Regiment, comprising a total of 258 men, manned the defences. The road between south Hornchurch and Elm Park which passed the main entrance had been closed much earlier in the war to enable the aerodrome to be extended to the south-west. The entrance gate across the road to the south was manned by RAF personnel although a 31-man Home Guard unit were responsible for local defence. The northern road barrier was the responsibility of the men of the Essex Regiment. A heavy 4.5-in AA detachment of the Royal Artillery was stationed on the western side of the boundary.

The aerodrome was well-defended against low-flying aircraft with eight Bofors being manned by the 109th Canadian Light AA Battery and an RAF ground defence section with Hispano and Vickers guns. Three light tanks from the 48th RCT and four RAF-manned 'Armadillos' formed a mobile back-up force while 680 officers and men of the 10th Essex Regiment were camped in reserve a mile to the east at Hacton House.

Early one morning in February 1941, Squadron Leader D. O. Finlay of No. 41 Squadron stands beside his Spitfire IIA, EB-Z, P7666 on the extreme north-east perimeter at Hornchurch. Later in the month P7666 was transferred to No. 54 Squadron and as KL-Z was shot down in flames over the Channel on April 20, 1941 (Imperial War Museum).

A good indication of the problems matching up photographs taken forty years later. Squadron Leader Finlay was standing on the corner of the first loop of the northern dispersal — the shadow was cast by the blast pen itself. A new housing estate and Scotts School cover the site.

Sadly the historic Sutton's Farm, on the north-eastern side where the old WWI station had been located, had by now been demolished to make way for additional Spitfire dispersals.

On August 19, 1941 an unusual mission was carried out from Hornchurch when an artificial leg was dropped over France for Wing Commander D. R. S. Bader who had been shot down and captured, minus his false leg, earlier that month. This operation was carried out in the course of a normal fighter sweep in which six German aircraft were destroyed.

With the build-up and integration of Allied resources, pilots from Europe and the Commonwealth moved into Hornchurch. No. 313 (Czech) Squadron arrived in December, 1941; No. 411 (Canadian) Squadron came in to replace No. 54, and No. 64 remained as the third squadron of the Wing. All flew the Spitfire Mk. VB armed with two 20mm cannons and four .303 machine guns and achieved a mounting score of victories over Messerschmitts and Focke-Wulfs. Wing Commander B. E. 'Paddy' Finucane, one of the many outstanding pilots who had flown from Hornchurch, came back as Wing Commander, Flying in June, 1942. In that month No. 340 (Free French) Squadron replaced the Czech unit and the Canadian squadron also departed. In due course No. 453 (Australian) Squadron superseded the Free French unit and a New Zealand squadron — No. 485 — arrived in October 1942. Early in 1943, the Hornchurch Wing consisted of Nos. 453, 222 and 137 Squadrons, and Wing Commander W. V. Crawford-Compton had become Wing Commander, Flying. He subsequently became the most decorated New Zealand pilot.

In December, 1943, No. 350 (Belgian) Squadron moved into Hornchurch and beside escort duties and cross-Channel sweeps, the Spitfires were called on to combat spasmodic German raids against the United Kingdom. Another type of fighter — the Mustang — was seen at the station when No. 239 Squadron arrived in August, 1943.

Throughout 1943 the RAF continued its attacks on the Continent leading up to the Normandy landings of June 1944. At the end of 1943, with the reduced threat of attack in the south-east, the Hornchurch Operations Room was stood down and the squadrons flew out to other bases. The last to go was No. 504 which left on February 18, 1944. At that time the Wing, according to contemporary records, had accounted for 906 enemy aircraft

Above: **On the outbreak of war, Sector D Operations Room was still in the old-style ops building constructed in 1926. This is the exact location of Building 24 demolished in the late 1960s.**

Above: **Although construction of one of the more substantial 'Mk II' Operations Blocks had begun in 1939, it was not ready for occupation by the time the Battle of Britain started. Numbered 97, it lay some fifty yards north-east of Building 24, now ignominiously occupied by a pair of garages.** *Below:* **When the decision was made to disperse the sector operations, it moved to Lambourne Hall in Romford in October 1940. This also has now disappeared to make way for a huge shopping centre. Our photograph shows the site of the hall demolished in the 1960s.**

Virtually alongside the main gate, the landlord of The Good Intent keeps a visitor's book for returning servicemen and also a more potent reminder of the war. The sharp end of a Hermann bomb dug up by REs from the aerodrome and given to the pub in March 1976.

providing aircrews for them. An Aircrew Selection Centre was established there on April 1, 1952, with the introduction of the scheme whereby boys of sixteen could be tested for training. For ten years Hornchurch operated in this capacity until, on April 9, 1962, the ASC moved to RAF Biggin Hill, Kent, and was renamed the Officers and Aircrew Selection Centre.

Although Hornchurch had been given an extended lease of life it was only to be temporary and, like the predecessor aerodrome of WWI, it was finally closed with the disbandment of the holding party on July 1, 1962. The following year it was to be the venue for its own funeral when the auctioneers, Kemsleys, put the aerodrome under the hammer on February 27 at 3.30 p.m. on behalf of the Air Ministry.

The airfield itself became the East London quarry of Hoveringham Gravels (Southern) Ltd whilst the technical site was purchased by a property company for development. Today all the buildings have been demolished to be replaced by a trim housing estate, the only concession to its former use being that all the roads have aviation connections. When the gravel on the landing area itself was exhausted, the resulting quarry was used as a rubbish tip. By 1979 this was completely filled and 'dozed over, raising the level of the aerodrome at the eastern side by some twenty to thirty feet. However two lengths of the old perimeter track still remain together with E-type dispersals and the odd pillbox, the area providing a convenient course for weekend motorcyclists improving their cross-country skills.

destroyed, plus 440 probably destroyed; 481 Allied pilots had been lost.

Soon after D-Day the V1 flying-bombs began their destructive attacks on London and south-east England, and Hornchurch, which had become a forward station of the North Weald Sector, became the home of a repair unit engaged on restoring vital buildings in London which had been damaged. A great many V1s landed in the vicinity. In November 1944, Hornchurch became a marshalling area, handling personnel in transit to and from the battle front.

By VE-Day there was little to remind one of the glorious days of the famous fighter station, and in June 1945 it was transferred to Technical Training Command. The transit unit and Personnel Despatch Centre were closed down in 1947 and the aerodrome was put on a 'care and maintenance' basis.

But the station was not dead. Although not suitable for the jet-engined aircraft which were coming into the RAF in increasing numbers, it could still contribute towards

Hawkinge

BY ROY HUMPHREYS

Aviation first began at Hawkinge with the appearance of a flimsy contraption built of spruce, welded tube and covered with mutton cloth. Its barking engine reverberated loudly from the surrounding trees as it hopped across the turf in a frantic effort to become airborne. These sounds announced the beginning of an era that was to remain for over half a century.

A Dutchman named W. B. Megone, but referred to by all and sundry as 'that damn foreigner', arrived about 1910, and set about designing and building a flying machine. He chose to work in comparative secrecy rejecting any kind of publicity, tucked away in a corner of a field in virtual seclusion to invent a flying machine which he hoped could eventually be used for military purposes.

The landing field like others around was part of Lord Radnor's estate and was leased to a local farmer. Although the others were reasonably rich pastures, that used by

Megone, by comparison was of poor quality. In one corner Megone erected a large corrugated metal shed which contained the brazing lamps, vices and tools needed for some of the complex workmanship. Even the massive wooden propellors, ten feet in diameter, were made there.

The first machine constructed of light metal tube, the kind used by cycle makers, was an ugly design, and in that respect was no different from other early flying machines. The engine was housed in a large box-like arrangement built between wing sections upon which the pilot sat completely open to the elements. The wings and tail assembly were covered with mutton cloth stretched and glued over a spruce framework.

Megone, reluctant to pilot his brainchild, bestowed this honour, such as it was, upon his helper, Victor Hunt who, with the aspirations and fearless spontaneity of a true pioneer, tackled the beast with enthusiasm. After several modifications, more a compromise with nature than anything else, the contraption did finally leave the ground in a series of hops and skips like some pre-historic winged kangaroo.

However, one Sunday afternoon in September 1914, Victor found the shed padlocked. Megone had gone. Quite naturally the Dutchman's sudden disappearance gave vent to speculation among the villagers. His jaunts into the countryside with his blue Schneider motor car had not gone unnoticed. His knowledge of photography was remembered. Everything about the man took on sinister implications, especially after the Great War started, and more so when German Gothas bombed Folkestone in 1917.

Those stories had persisted throughout the war, and the pioneering spirit which had prevailed for four years had come to an end. Soon a completely new era in aviation was to begin at this tiny aerodrome which was eventually to lead to Hawkinge becoming linked to the defence system of the British Isles.

By 1915, the War Office was looking for suitable fields in the county of Kent to be used to ferry war planes to the Western Front. Realising that sites were badly needed, the village sub-postmaster at Hawkinge wrote suggesting Megone's field as a possible location. By September of that year, Royal

'Fierce fiery warriors fought upon the clouds,
In ranks and squadrons and right form of war.'
Julius Caesar, William Shakespeare.

The Spitfires of No. 610 'County of Chester' Squadron waiting to be unleashed after refuelling at 'A' Flight dispersal at Hawkinge in early July 1940. Spitfire DW-T, P9452 was shot down into the Channel north of Calais on July 18, carrying Pilot Officer Peter Litchfield to his death (Fox Photos).

Flying Corps personnel arrived and within a week, unfamiliar canvas structures appeared on the skyline in the shape of three Bessoneau hangars.

Three weeks later, Corporal Perrott, Very pistol in hand, strode out onto the grass to receive the first military aeroplanes to the newest RFC aerodrome. Perrott's green Very light spluttered and curved into the sky as Major Newall brought his dozen or so BE2cs of No. 12 Squadron over the pocket-size field. They landed to the cheers of villagers who had turned out in force and, in no time at all, the sound of castor-oiled machinery ticked and whirred from all corners of the field. The business of ferrying aircraft across the Channel was to be the only function of the aerodrome throughout the Great War period.

Roy Humphreys surveys the same scene in October 1979. The old watch office stands in the centre background — censored with a black line in the 1940 photograph.

89

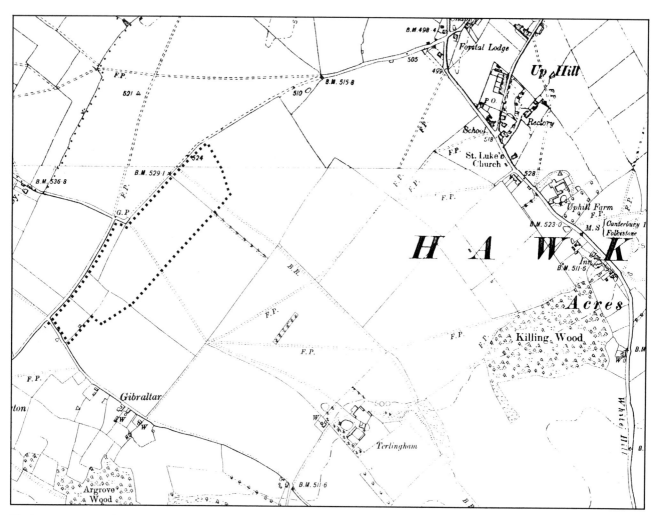

The beginnings of Hawkinge. Megone's landing ground outlined on a 1906 Ordnance Survey of the area (Crown Copyright).

This gradually increased from mid-1916 and, by the spring of the following year, building began with a marked degree of permanency. The fading Bessoneau hangars, which had blown down on numerous occasions during the past two years, were finally replaced by brick Belfast types. Single-storey barrack blocks replaced the tented accommodation, materials arriving daily from Folkestone harbour and railway station transported by large traction engines pulling wooden-sided trucks.

The new aerodrome came into its own from the onset by being the only emergency landing ground which had two large white circles cut into the turf. From these pilots could take a compass bearing, between Cap Griz Nez and Cap Blanc Nez, and on to St. Omer.

From January 1917, the Headquarters of 21st Wing, Royal Flying Corps, had issued a directive to the effect that all RFC aerodromes were to be known by their actual locality. Up to this time the Hawkinge flying field had been known as Folkestone. No one it seems, had heard of 'Hawkinge' outside the county — but now it was going on the map as the 'Aeroplane Despatch Section Hawkinge'.

The unification of the two air arms on April 1, 1918, brought about the birth of the Royal Air Force which was by far the largest air force in the world. Nevertheless when the First World War ended eight months later it was reduced to a fraction of its former strength and most home-based units began to unwind. A number of non-operational squadrons returned to the United Kingdom and a few of these arrived at Hawkinge where, after some months of inactivity, they were either re-numbered by amalgamating two or more squadrons or disbanded without any kind of ceremony.

The Despatch Section, Hawkinge 1916 (L. K. Kettle).

An SE5a, Avro 504 and a Spad outside the Bessoneau hangar in June 1917 (Bass).

90

Private and commercial experiments in aviation were now a new feature and the skills and rapid developments experienced during the war now lent themselves easily to all kinds of projects. One of the most interesting developments concerned an air transport service established between England and Belgium, organised at the request of the Belgian Government and operated by a company called Air Transport and Travel Ltd. One of the first airlifts, it used a number of converted DH9 aircraft with RAF pilots and flew between Hawkinge and an aerodrome near Ghent, carrying clothing, food and other urgent necessities.

Following the Armistice, a decision was made to provide British troops in Germany with an aerial mail service. As a result, No. 120 Squadron moved to Hawkinge from nearby Lympne and, on March 1, 1919, four DH9s, specially modified to take freight, carried twenty-three bags of mail to Marquise in France. In just two months, the aircraft at Hawkinge handled 1,634 bags of mail (over ninety tons) in 289 flights with only ten recorded as non-operational due to bad weather. In July the squadron moved back to Lympne and the following month the mail service ceased.

At the dawn of the new decade, the Royal Air Force had been cut back drastically both in personnel and equipment and, at one stage, it was so thinly spread that the defence of the Realm rested squarely on the shoulders of one fighter squadron. That squadron, the first to use Hawkinge in its new peacetime role, assembled its dispersed equipment to reform in April 1920, as No. 25 (F) squadron.

Above: The recently-completed No. 3 hangar photographed around 1924. The aircraft is a Little Whippet folding-wing, sporting biplane which could be purchased for £275 from the Austin Motor Company. An Avro 504K of No. 17 Squadron stands in the hangar. *Below:* All that remains of No. 3 hangar today is the overgrown concrete base. It was destroyed during the bombing attack on August 12, 1940.

In 1923, under the direction of Lord Salisbury, a committee recommended the creation of a Home Defence Force and from this emerged the new command called the 'Air Defence of Great Britain'. RAF Hawkinge, just twenty-five miles from the French coast, became a vital link in the new system, such as it was. Not unnaturally, the all important factor was that our defending fighters should reach comparable heights with enemy formations before their arrival but, even after years of painstaking experiments, the acoustic warning devices of that time were totally inadequate.

Water tanks on stilts, new fences and iron railings were now a more permanent feature of Hawkinge. Trees disappeared and telephone poles went up. The largest buildings completed before the end of the Great War were the hangars. With the exception of the Handley Page sheds, which stood at right angles to the road on the eastern boundary, they were of the Belfast bow-strut type.

The well-established pattern of peacetime training included air firing, camera-gun practice, pin-pointing, wireless practice and

Above: **The interior of No. 2 hangar with the silver and black Gloster Grebe IIs of No. 25 Squadron ready for the 1928 Hendon Air Pageant. Pilot Officer W. K. Beisiegal took these photographs, the one** *below* **showing his immaculate personal mount 'The Bicycle'. No. 1 hangar on the left, No. 2 on the right.** *Bottom:* **Surrounded by a cat's cradle of rusting wire and old fence posts, this is the site of No. 2 hangar destroyed in August 1940.**

of course aerobatics. Recovery from spins and simulated forced landings were other equally important sessions. Air-to-air firing practice was naturally as close to real aerial combat as could be reasonably obtained in peacetime using the camera-gun. When developed the film indicated the skill of the pilot in his deflection shots. Air-to-ground firing was usually carried out at Lydd ranges, near the Camber Sands, although later, the ranges at the Hythe School of Musketry were also used.

During air to ground practice firing, No. 25 squadron lost one of their pilots in a fatal accident on December 9, 1926. A section of Gloster Grebes had been diving towards a target which in this case was a series of circles cut into the turf near the centre of the aerodrome. (These circles were the same ones which had been used by the ferrying pilots in 1917, as a navigational aid.) Flying Officer Purvis however, lost control and his Grebe dived into a small hollow near Terlingham Manor Farm where it burst into flames. The farmer, Albert Daniels, dragged Purvis clear of the wreckage but he was already dead. For this act of bravery Daniels was given a gold watch. Purvis was a nephew of Sir John Gilmour, the then Secretary of State for Scotland, and news of his death reached the House of Commons during a debate on the growing number of fatalities in the Royal Air Force. It was during this debate that Sir Samuel Hoare as Air Minister, remarked that they had not yet discovered a remedy against flying accidents!

Fields adjacent and to the north of the aerodrome, which had been used during the Great War for troop training, were sold to Folkestone Corporation in 1927. Almost immediately the land was used for the establishment of a cemetery. Never an encouraging sight from the air it did however, by its very presence, instill in certain individuals whose flying was considered somewhat flamboyant, a sense of quiet caution and in the long history of the aerodrome, no record exists of there ever having been an accident or landing within the cemetery boundary.

Wandering airmen were, it seems, a special breed of their own. Either walking or riding cycles they seemed oblivious to aircraft landing and taking off. Without thinking of the hazards they appeared to wander everywhere and always at the wrong moment. Special notices were put up to discourage this trend but the most effective method was to chase them with low-flying aircraft!

Operating from Hawkinge, if a pilot was unfamiliar with it, was sometimes difficult. It had a slight dip in the centre with a gradual slope to the east. Almost a saucer shape, although it looked flat from the air, one could

These Hawker Audax from No. 2 (Army Co-operation) Squadron were photographed by Rex Puttee taxi-ing down the field from No. 5 hangar which stood on the eastern side of the aerodrome. Also called the Handley Page shed, having been originally intended for the 0/400s, it was bombed on August 12 and partially demolished. Later on, it was completely dismantled and absolutely nothing remains to mark its position today.

stand near the eastern boundary and watch an aircraft almost disappear as it taxied away to the west. At night with a strong cross-wind blowing it could be quite unhealthy for the unwary pilot.

One night fatality was a detached Pilot Officer called Vaughan-Fowler from No. 41 Squadron who had volunteered to fly over the annual searchlight tattoo at Folkestone held on August 10, 1931. The crowds were enthralled with his performance not least because his Armstrong Whitworth Siskin was lit up with dozens of electric light bulbs. However fate took a hand in the proceedings when the Jaguar engine developed a fault just as he was about to make his landing approach. It was a pitch dark night. Building obstruction lights were switched on and glim lamps had been set out to indicate a flare path. (Gone were the days when primitive flarepath equipment consisted of a dozen or so oil drums cut in half and stuffed with oil-soaked rags.) Vaughan-Fowler's Siskin failed to make the aerodrome and was seen to drop like a stone on the edge of the field. His aircraft cartwheeled and burst into flames, killing the pilot instantly.

Another accident in September 1931 involved an officer from one of the foreign air forces who, from time to time, were attached to RAF squadrons. Two in particular were Siamese, Lieutenants Sujiritkul and Rasanandar. Tragedy struck when Sujiritkul, after completing a camera-gun attack on ground targets, pulled out of his dive to find he was on

a collision course with his brother officer. A pall of black smoke curled above Caesars Camp hill, close to the aerodrome, where the Siskin had stalled and spun in.

With considerable insight into the needs of a fast growing service, in 1931 the Air Ministry launched a two-year building programme at the aerodrome. Two barrack blocks were the first to be constructed around the original drill square, designed to replace the single storey huts put up in 1917 but, nevertheless, the latter remained for another forty years. A mortuary was also built, incredibly small by any standards, and one wonders if the planners ever envisaged that it would in years to come house briefly before interment, the bodies of airmen slain during some of the greatest air battles.

In charge of the rebuilding programme was an officer seconded from the Royal Engineers, Major Arnold, who witnessed with some displeasure the burning down of No. 4 hangar. It all came about when the special reserve squadron, No. 504 (County of Nottingham) based at Hucknall, brought their Hawker Horsley bombers to the aerodrome for their summer camp in 1933. About a dozen arrived followed by over one hundred airmen and at least two dozen officers. Their rather intensive training programme included at least twenty-five hours flying for every gunner on unit strength. They flew their air-to-ground gunnery practice at Lydd and used the Leysdown ranges near Sheppey for bombing practice.

SCALE OF FEET.

0   100 200 300 400 500   1000   1500   2000 FEET.

Elvington

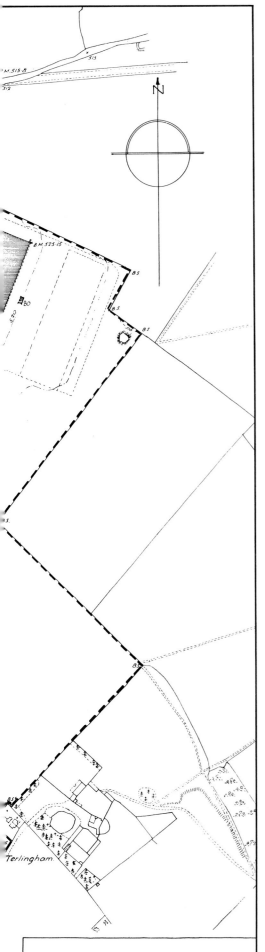

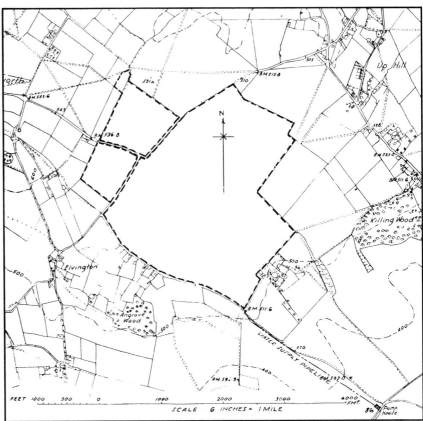

Nº	BUILDING	Nº	BUILDING
78	ABLUTION. (SUMMER CAMP)	34	MORTUARY
46	AIRCRAFT SHED	50	OFFICES STATION
54	" "	28	OFFICERS MESS & QUARTERS
56	" " DESTROYED BY FIRE.	52	OPERATIONS BLOCK
69	" "	74	PARAFFIN TANK (BULK)
40Z	" REPAIR SHED	35	PETROL INSTALLATION AVIATION (BULK)
51	ARMOURY	36	" " "
30	BARRACK BLOCK	37	" " " M.T.
31	DO. DO	7	PIGGERIES
32	DO. DO AIRMEN PILOTS!	29	POWER HOUSE
9	BARRACK BLOCK & EDUCATIONAL ACCOM.	86	PUMP " (Outside Stn Boundary)
72	BOMBING TARGET	22	RESERVOIR (100,000 Gallons)
73	" ARROW	57	RUNNING SHED (FOR DISPOSAL)
24	BOOSTER HOUSE	59	" (")
45	BOWSER SHED		RECREATIONAL FACILITIES
60	COMPASS PLATFORM	11	CHILDRENS PLAYGROUND
13	DINING ROOM & COOKHOUSE	64	CRICKET NET SITE
9	EDUCATIONAL BUILDING AND BARRACK BLOCK	68B	" PITCH
38	ENGINE TEST HOUSE	68C	FOOTBALL
26	FIRE PARTY & GUARD HOUSE	68A	HOCKEY "
41	FLAG STAFF	67	SPORTS PAVILION
80	GAS CHAMBER	27	SQUASH RACQUETS COURT
26	GUARDHOUSE & FIRE PARTY	10	TENNIS COURT - AIRMEN - (HARD)
62	GYMNASIUM	25	SERGEANTS MESS
6	INCINERATOR	5	SEWAGE DISPOSAL WORKS.
14	INSTITUTE	12	SICK QUARTERS
71	LANDING CIRCLE	50	STATION OFFICES
79	LATRINES (SUMMER CAMP)		STORES.
47	" TECHNICAL	66	DETONATOR & SPECIAL AMMUNITION STRS
77	LUBRICATING OIL INSTALLATION (BULK)	55	FUEL STORE
63	MACHINE GUN RANGE	75	"
58	" TEST BUTT	77	LUBRICATING OIL INSTALLATION (BULK)
1	MARRIED QUARTERS - OFFICERS - GROUP IV	49	MAIN STORES
2	" " " GROUP V	42	OIL STORE
3	" " " GROUP V	43	"
17	" " WARRANT OFFICERS Nº 3	48	PARACHUTE STORE
19	" " " Nºs 1&2	74	PARAFFIN TANK
15	" " AIRMEN Nºs 13 to 16	53	PYROTECHNIC STORE OLD
16	" " " 1 to 4	65	"
18	" " " 5 to 8	21	RATION STORE
20	" " " 9 to 12	33	WATER TANK
44	" " " Bijou Cottage	23	WT & R.T. BUILDING
40X	MECHANICAL TRANSPORT SHED	8	WT & R.T. BUILDING
40Y	" CIVILIANS.	61	W & B OFFICE & CONTRACTORS YARD
		39	WORKSHOPS - SMITHS & WELDERS.

Hawkinge site plan April 18, 1935. Crown Copyright/ RAF Museum.

Early on August 7, 1933, a flight of Horsleys had left for the bombing ranges and some two hours later Flight Lieutenant Hartridge made his landing approach from over the village roof tops. Suddenly the Rolls Royce Condor engine died on him and two-and-a-half tons of aeroplane made an almost perfect three-pointer on the single-bay roof of No. 4 hangar, rolling miraculously to a stop at the brick parapet above the doors at the far end. Fuel escaping from the punctured tanks trickled down inside the walls and ignited. Inside the building were six Blackburn Darts in storage. While the pilot and his navigator scrambled to safety down a hastily-placed ladder, airmen dragged clear a brimming petrol bowser, its paint blistering in the searing heat and likely to explode at any minute. It was a timely escape before the whole hangar was gutted.

Squadron Leader W. F. Dickson, CO of No. 25 Squadron since January 1935 became station commander when Hawkinge was made a Station HQ in November. The aerodrome was then typical of most RAF stations in that peaceful era, being laid out in orderly fashion with each building served by a well-kept path along which had been planted shrubs and flowers. At one stage, the solid looking hangars were whitewashed and could easily be seen from the French coast. The whole aerodrome became a magnificent fragrant landscape where the perfume of flowers mingled with the pungent aroma of petrol and oil. The grass was cut with meticulous care, each mowing made with guardsman-like precision. It was a sight which would have delighted the crowds at Wembley Stadium. This was no coincidence either, for Mr. King, an ex-Grenadier guardsman who had seen action in France in the Great War, took pride in his work.

Later the same year — lunch time on November 3 to be precise — a convoy of heavily-laden lorries turned into the gate between the hangars and stopped outside No. 3. Within the hour fifteen silver Hawker Audax biplanes of No. 2 (Army Co-operation) Squadron had landed from Manston. The precise function of army co-operation squadrons was to work in close liaison with ground units of infantry, artillery and tanks.

The first casualty suffered by No. 2 Squadron since arriving at Hawkinge occurred the following year at the Empire Air

Above: **August 7, 1933 and No. 4 hangar blazes fiercely after a Hawker Horsley of No. 504 'City of Nottingham' Squadron landed on its roof (Group Captain F. W. Wiseman-Clarke).** *Below:* **After the fire, the hangar was demolished and never rebuilt. Today the base is almost completely lost under the grass.**

Day held on May 23. The afternoon's flying always culminated with the traditional attack on the canvas fort. Announcing the event, the Tannoy system broke into the hubbub emanating from over 3,000 people enjoying the display: ' . . . the three aeroplanes now taking off you will observe are carrying what we call anti-personnel bombs and they will be making a low level attack upon the tribal fort which you can see situated in the centre of the aerodrome. This attack is being led by Flight Lieutenant Geddes of No. 2 Squadron . . . ' Airmen, suitably dressed in flowing white sheets ran about shooting off blank cartridges from disguised service rifles as the three Audax aircraft made their first attack. Flour-packed canisters hit the ground and burst into a white cascade. It was realistic and great fun. Heavily concealed anti-aircraft guns on the perimeter let fly with blank shells at near point-blank range as the aeroplanes noisily made their hurried exit. However, it was, perhaps, a little too realistic. As Flight Lieutenant Geddes left the perimeter bombarded with cardboard particles from the blank shells, closely followed by the second machine, the third, piloted by Flying Officer

Ashton with LAC Simpson in the rear cockpit, touched a 33,000-volt electric cable at Holywell. Both were killed instantly. It was a disaster all the more significant because of the mood of the audience. Now the atmosphere changed and the stunned crowd quietly left the aerodrome.

The following year's Empire Air Day saw another incident although rather more amusing. Members of the public were encouraged to give flying directions to a single machine by wireless. Not many people availed themselves of this once-in-a-lifetime opportunity, but one over-zealous chap thought it great fun. Such phrases as ' . . . will you turn left please . . . ' and ' . . . would you be good enough to dive please . . . ', not only sent the signals section into hysterics, but caused the pilot innumerable difficulties. Participation in public relations could prove costly as the squadron were about to find out. The Hawker Fury had changed direction so many times in the few minutes allowed that the pilot was seriously thinking of turning the radio receiver off. As it was, he found himself gradually descending closer to the ground and, even worse, in the general direction of the solid

Above: The eagle-eyed gunner in K3057 spots the cameraman as these Hawker Audaxes of No. 2 (Army Co-operation) Squadron sweep over the aviation fuel dump in impeccable formation at Hawkinge in 1937 (Rex Puttee).

Below: By the end of the war No. 1 hangar in the foreground was the only one still standing. This was demolished in 1964 although the fire tender building still remains beside the skeletal pipes of the fuel pumps.

Above: **Photograph taken by Sergeant Pilot D. A. Upton just before No. 4 hangar (on the right) was burnt down in 1933.** *Below:* **Editor W. G. Ramsey's picture taken on October 21, 1979. We deliberately delayed taking all our aerial photographs for this book until ploughing had taken place as we knew that this would** bring out latent images in the soil. Even so, we were very surprised to see the aerodrome identification circle and the word 'HAWKINGE' clearly visible. More amazing, the compass rose, cut in the turf during the First World War, showed up clearer today than it did in 1933!

looking hangars. He took the only action open to him in the interests of safety and landed. However, his speed was far in excess of normal and the aircraft bounced like a demented kangaroo coming to rest on its nose with an expensive sounding crack. A very red-faced member of the public walked away from the microphone muttering to his spouse, '. . . but I didn't tell him to do that dear . . . !'

On September 29, 1938 all ranks were recalled from leave. The Station Defence scheme was immediately put into action and all buildings 'darkened' in a first attempt to camouflage the station. Re-equipping began although the pilots of No. 25 viewed with horror the first Bristol Blenheim that landed at Hawkinge on December 10. Conversion flying began almost at once but it proved a lengthy process to adapt the fighter pilots to a twin-engined fighter-bomber.

The Blenheims had a formidable thirst which caused four new 12,000 gallon fuel tanks to be installed. Filling them was completed one Friday afternoon and a hastily-convened Court of Enquiry the following Monday failed to find the chap who had left the controlling valves open. Remarkably no-one had thrown a match onto the flooded aerodrome!

Above: **The Blenheims arrive. With Mercurys throttled back to a grumble, L1440 of No. 25 Squadron crosses Gibraltar Lane which formed the western boundary of the aerodrome.** *Below:* **The fired stubble of the 1979 harvest leaves its serpentine trails over Hawkinge's hallowed ground. The foundations of the house still remain.**

Left: **The same aircraft on the taxi-track beyond the site of No. 4 hangar looking towards Hawkinge village (Rex Puttee).**

Right: **The perimeter track still remains although now liberally coated with a mixture of mud and muck.**

Then whilst No. 25 Squadron were away at Sutton Bridge completing their training programme they were instructed to take up new quarters at Northolt. One of the reasons given was that the Blenheims required hard-based runways and not slippery grass, but whatever the reason for their departure, it proved a kind of death knell for Hawkinge. The aerodrome had been the squadron's home for nineteen years. Now there began a colder, harsher era in its history. Looking back to flying in peaceful years it had been for most a great adventure. Young men eager for excitement were now to find it all a more serious affair. Had they absorbed the knowledge imparted by their instructors? If they had then they were confident men. But even confident men, flying unfamiliar patterns in a hostile sky, would find it hard to survive the terrors of warfare.

Inevitably mobilisation of the three Services was the natural outcome when Great Britain declared war on Germany on September 3, 1939. What was not so obvious, and seen by many as a surprise move, was that RAF Hawkinge became No. 3 Recruit Training Pool. Everyone from the Station CO, downwards could not understand how a front-line station of vital importance could possibly be anything else other than a fighter station. Nevertheless, over 300 raw recruits arrived for their initial training, most of which was done in torrential rain, flooding and mud.

No. 2 (Army Co-operation) Squadron suddenly received a signal to pack their bags and move to France within twenty-four hours. The squadron silver was hastily sent to a bank in Folkestone and the road party left for Dover. So as not to reveal their port of embarkation the convoy headed for Folkestone.

Above: **No. 25 Squadron's MT section parked outside the western end of No. 1 hangar in 1934. L-R: Leyland 3-tonner, Crossley 30cwt, the Commanding Officer's Morris, Morris six-wheel fire tender, Crossley ambulance, Trojan light van, Model 'T' Ford Hucks Starter, Morris six-wheel 30cwt and a Leyland 3-tonner (R. Marwood).** *Below:* **Looking eastwards at the site of No. 1 hangar in September 1979.**

Unfortunately some of the heavily-loaded vehicles were unable to pass under the railway bridge near Folkestone Junction Station and there were a few red faces before the convoy got under way again. A week later, the Squadron's eighteen Lysanders left the aerodrome for Abbeville and Drucat.

Almost every week during November and December, Army Officers arrived to discuss airfield defences with station personnel. On November 20 things really began to heat up when an enemy aircraft was reported flying over the area. This violation of British air space occurred again the next day by an aircraft flying at about 3,000 feet. The Dover guns fired a few rounds but there was no air raid warning given. The 5th Buffs Territorial Regiment were manning the machine guns strategically placed around the aerodrome but they did not open fire. No one had, as yet, decided whether light AA guns should be installed.

A decision was then made to re-camouflage the aerodrome. This had first been done just after the Munich crisis but this time they were to make a better job of it. Every building, post, road and path, even the grass was sprayed in kaleidoscopic greens, browns and deep yellows. From the air the whole 'drome resembled a patchwork quilt but unfortunately the village stood out in complete contrast. Nature fought against this treatment however and, within a month, it was more or less back to its former hue. Sheep, which had

been used to crop the grass, were given to fits of sneezing when the toxic paint carried towards them although no-one owned up to spraying the Clerk of Works car!

Serious preparations for some kind of aerodrome defence resulted in hundreds of earth-filled sandbags being placed round doors, windows and hastily-dug slit trenches. Dozens of gas detector posts were stuck in the ground, an event which brought a shudder to those old enough to remember the previous war.

In the third week of December, a new sound broke the stillness when the Hawker Hurricanes of No. 3 Squadron led by Squadron Leader Gifford entered the circuit to make their landings and, because of the camouflaged landing area, they were not too sure where the boundary began.

The second heavy snowfall of winter engulfed the area in the last two weeks of January 1940 during which three Blenheims of No. 500 Squadron forced-landed in a snowstorm. Under a dark heavy sky airmen toiled to free the aerodrome of the white, virgin blanket. Sorely disillusioned 'erks' found the task intolerable and made igloos and snowmen, the former as refuge and the latter bore a remarkable likeness to the Station Warrant Officer!

No. 16 Squadron based at Old Sarum, another Army Co-operation unit and the last of its kind this side of the Channel, moved to Hawkinge on February 16 with eighteen

Lysanders. They began to work furiously in field support duties until their embarkation to France in April.

By now the Recruit Training Pool had closed and the station now came under Fighter Command. Later that month a convoy of Queen Mary trailers arrived originating from RAF Henlow with thirteen aircraft and equipment belonging to No. 1 Pilotless Aircraft Unit. It was an impressive array of bits and pieces that was unloaded into a hangar where airmen poked and prodded, lifted sheeting and discussed its usefulness. Mechanics and riggers were, however, disillusioned when they learned that these prize possessions, now totalling twenty-six Tiger Moths and some Queen Bees, were to remain dismantled.

That month also saw the arrival of Flying Officer Scott-Farnie to set up a listening post at the aerodrome using short-wave receivers. Long before hostilities began Great Britain, like many other countries, had operated long-range monitoring of foreign broadcasts which became the forerunner of radio intelligence. It was not then highly technical nor highly organised but, even before the fall of France, listening to German transmissions proved invaluable. Naturally translators were needed and eventually German-speaking WAAFs maintained a twenty-four hour watch. These girls, specially selected and promoted to the rank of sergeant, moved from the original cramped conditions to Maypole Cottage, an old secluded building near the village, and once established the wireless unit became instrumental in discovering frequencies used by Luftwaffe units and German 'E' Boats.

On March 1, Squadron Leader Eayrs arrived to form No. 416 (AC) Flight and some quite obsolete aircraft were flown in from St. Athan a couple of weeks later. Everything about this unit seemed a bit vague. Airmen borrowed tools and equipment and by April 1 it was disbanded only to be reformed nineteen days later!

During March, No. 16 Squadron maintained their working-up routine and it was whilst an affiliation exercise was taking place that Sergeant Lomay's Hurricane (No. 3 Squadron) spun into the ground near the aerodrome.

Local contractors had already started building the dispersal pens, three of which were located behind the White Horse Inn backing on to Killing Wood, the other three being on the opposite side of the aerodrome on Gibraltar Lane.

Although Hawkinge had been found an unsuitable field from which to use Blenheims the previous year, it was now a matter of urgency to use the aerodrome to provide a jump-off for low-level attacks on German troops surrounding the BEF in France and both Nos. 25 and 604 'County of Middlesex' Squadrons participated in these sorties, refuelling and rearming at the aerodrome.

As the French and British Armies were being pushed back towards the Channel coast, a mammoth evacuation programme was prepared code named 'DYNAMO', under the command of Vice-Admiral Ramsey at Dover. Hawkinge became an important part of this complex organisation when an HQ was set up there named 'Back Component', under the direction of Air Vice-Marshal C. H. B. Blount. His task was not to be envied. Through the various intelligence channels, he was expected to collate evidence to assist with evacuating thousands of troops along an area of coast which hourly diminished in size as defensive positions were overrun. Information was extremely scarce, mainly due to the lack of adequate wireless equipment, and therefore he relied to a great extent on reports given by returning aircrews, especially the Army Co-operation units. Additionally, further information was gleaned from the intercepted messages received by the experimental wireless section.

Maypole Cottage was the location of the 'Y' Service at Hawkinge. The 'Y' Service, which grew during the war into a vast world-wide network of listening posts intercepting the enemy's wireless traffic, provided the raw-material for the Ultra codebreakers.

Above and below: The Haskard Target (building 110) built in 1934, was used for the instruction of No. 2 (AC) Squadron. A large hessian 'map' was supported some three feet from the floor and, while the crew members played on the top, erks crawled underneath setting off puffs of smoke to simulate shell bursts. In May 1940, the building was used as the nerve centre for the Dunkirk evacuation. Now sadly vandalised and having caught fire once, it stands forgotten on the eastern end of the camp site. Roy Humphreys firmly believes it should be preserved in view of its unique history.

The aerodrome soon became overcrowded with aircraft. Lysanders, Hurricanes, Spitfires and Blenheims flew in from the fighting areas showing signs of battle damage. The majority were refuelled quickly and dispersed to other aerodromes but others, looking much the worse for wear and obviously too dangerous to fly, were wheeled into the hangars. One Lysander, attacked by a large force of Bf 109s over Boulogne, was in a sorry mess. Pilot Officer Scotter successfully brought his machine back to Hawkinge only to discover to his amazement that the cockpit was practically severed from the remainder of the fuselage. Fuel tank, undercarriage and wings were all hanging by the merest thread of metal.

No. 2 Squadron, like others, suffered severe casualties both in aircraft and crews. Before Dunkirk they had operated single machines at ten minute intervals, deep into France without fighter cover of any sort. On May 26, in answer to urgent calls for assistance, eight Lysanders of the squadron took off from Hawkinge to drop supplies to the troops defending Calais. As the metal containers filled with water, food and ammunition were being dropped from as low as fifty feet, the aircraft were subjected to murderous ground fire. Two machines were brought down in as many minutes and the remainder were damaged. The shortage of Lysanders became acute, so much so that a later dropping sortie over the same area included of all things, obsolete Hector biplanes. Of the 170 or so Lysanders that went to France, eighty-eight are known to have been lost through enemy action, while others were destroyed by our own forces owing to lack of fuel or unfinished repairs. The price in manpower too was high for about 120 aircrew were lost.

The gradual build up of enemy activity after the Dunkirk evacuation brought many strangers to the aerodrome. Pilots flew in with petrol gauges reading empty, hydraulics shot away, ammunition expended, engines smoking, tail sections crumpled and trailing fabric like bunting. Some of the hasty landings would have made the hair of any instructor stand on end. Aircraft clipped the perimeter trees and hedges, ploughed through fences and dug deep grooves in the turf. Machines stood up on their propellors, some cartwheeled, others skidded across the field on their canopies. Even a pirouette was not uncommon.

As a front line satellite aerodrome, used primarily for rearming and refuelling fighter aircraft, the personnel of No. 11 Servicing Flight set up a remarkable record of thoroughness, efficiency and determination, administering to the needs of countless fighters which dropped in without warning or ceremony before, during and after combat. Such exploits of combat would never have been achieved without the conscientious efforts of the ground crews whose cheerfulness and devotion to duty dispelled the fears of many a young fighter pilot. Vomit and blood were washed from cockpit floors, damaged aircraft were repaired and patched with speed and efficiency, and injured pilots were removed carefully from their damaged machines.

Following the advice of many Army officers, aerodrome defences had, by now, taken on some semblance of order. Trenches and dugouts were established but there was still no provision for the use of heavy calibre anti-aircraft guns. All anti-aircraft units were at that time under the direction of Fighter Command and Air Vice-Marshal Dowding was forced to move the majority of the available heavy guns to protect industrial towns and cities. The aerodrome was therefore in a very vulnerable position regarding its defence. By the end of May, four 40mm Bofors units had been sited within the perimeter on more or less static sites. There were of course the official complement of eight

One of the aerodrome defences. Hamilton Forts were sunken concrete cylinders out on the aerodrome which could be raised pneumatically in the event of an attack by paratroopers to provide a protected, light machine gun fire position. Roy Humphreys has been instrumental in persuading the farmer to keep this one in situ.

The other three have been removed — this one lies beside the western boundary fence.

.303in Lewis machine guns (which had always been allocated to aerodrome defence since the First World War) and, in addition there were four 20mm Hispano cannons and one 20mm Oerlikon that had somehow been salvaged from a sunken ship off Dover. Other Bofors units were sited outside the perimeter. These were completely mobile with crews living in almost bivouac conditions having just a canvas sheet, drawn between tractor and the ground, for protection. One or two lorries carried machine guns in the roof of the cab and one in particular, being armoured, was called the Armadillo.

Towards the end of June, the experimental Parachute and Cable (PAC) device was installed. This bizarre weapon was invented to supplement the deficiencies of aerodrome defence and the rockets, based on the Schurmully marine device, were fired from a tube-like contraption resembling a length of guttering about four feet long attached to a swivel base plate. They were set off in batches of eight by a unit containing a four-volt battery. Coiled in a box near the base plate was a long length of piano-type wire attached to each rocket. Theoretically, the rocket projectile would reach a height of about 600 feet trailing the wire behind it when a sudden jerk released a small parachute which suspended the wire in the path of enemy aircraft.

Hawkinge never had a conventional control tower; this long, low building (No. 30) served as a combined Flying Control and Operations Block (Imperial War Museum).

This well-meaning device was unsuccessful when operated at Hawkinge, although a successful claim was made for it a year later during a 'tip and run' raid. The first trials of the PAC equipment (whether fired by accident or design has never been established) resulted in a hilarious shambles. The 3-inch projectiles flew up into the sky in all directions each crossing the path of another allowing the wires to become hopelessly entangled. The combined weight of the enmeshed wire proved too much for the little parachutes which sank to earth before the rockets had given of their best to litter the aerodrome fizzing and burning like giant squibs at a Guy Fawkes gala night.

Wooden poles were stuck into the largest fields surrounding Hawkinge to combat expected glider landings, road blocks were set up either side of the village and important installations were mined with eight-foot lengths of drainpipe which, wired together in batches of six, were to be fired from a central point.

On July 2 the German air force supreme command issued orders in respect of the air onslaught against Britain and from that day onward small bomber groups escorted by fighters roamed the Channel areas. During the battles which followed, Hawkinge received hundreds of fighters for refuelling and rearming and, in addition, particular squadrons used it as a daytime base.

The watch office still stands — the photo *centre* was taken in 1973. In 1979, an anti-vandal measure has been to brick up the windows.

REINDENE WOOD

ALKHAM VALLEY

HAWKINGE VILLAGE

'B' FLIGHT DISPERSAL

KILLING WOO

TERLINGHAM
MANOR FARM

'A' FLIGHT DISPERSAL

ARGROVE WOOD

Squadrons using Hawkinge on a day-to-day basis included No. 501 'County of Gloucester' and Nos. 32, 72, 64 and 610 'County of Chester'. No. 79 Squadron flew down in the first week of July under the command of Squadron Leader J. H. Hayworth. Flying Hurricanes, they were engaged every day in pitched battles against odds of over four to one.

It was as the result of one of these early bomber group interceptions on July 4 that Pilot Officer K. R. Gillman, flying a Hurricane of No. 32 Squadron, forced-landed at Hawkinge at about 7.00 p.m. His tail section was extensively damaged and in fact very little rudder control was available but, fortunately, Gillman was unhurt. The attack by a force of Dornier 17s was concentrated on a convoy just east of Dover; No. 79 Squadron had scrambled eight available Hurricanes at about 2.00 p.m. and within minutes had lost the first one when Sergeant H. Cartwright was seen to crash into the sea off St. Margaret's Bay.

In the early hours of July 5, a Heinkel 111 of 8 Staffel, KG1, ploughed into the sea off Lydden Spout near Dover. The crew of five swam ashore and were captured by an anti-aircraft gun crew who conveyed them to Hawkinge. Locked in the guard room beside the main gate, they soon became VIPs as many airmen thought up excuses to take a look at the enemy from close quarters. That evening saw a Spitfire crash-land on the aerodrome after Sub-Lieutenant F. D. Paul of the Fleet Air Arm attached to No. 64 Squadron had tangled with a Bf 109 over the Channel. He brought the damaged aircraft back and managed to get the wheels down but made a very shaky cross-wind landing.

On Sunday, July 7, a large convoy was under attack off Dover at 2.30 p.m. with over forty Dornier 17Zs of KG2 milling around the sky. No. 79 Squadron was scrambled from Hawkinge and soon lost their CO, Squadron Leader J. D. C. Joslin, whose Hurricane crashed near Chilverton Elms. On the following day yet another convoy was under attack in the Dover Straits and No. 79 Squadron, which had already suffered heavy losses during the past two months, lost another two aircraft this day. Nine Hurricanes were scrambled from Hawkinge and were promptly bounced by a superior number of Bf 109s. Pilot Officer J. E. R. Wood was the first to go down in flames and his body was later picked up by a naval launch. Flying Officer E. W. Mitchell was killed when his Hurricane crashed at Temple Ewell, Dover where the wreckage burned for over an hour. Flying Officer R. F. Smythe of No. 32 Squadron managed to bring his crippled Hurricane back to Hawkinge with the engine on fire having been hit by cannon shells over Dungeness.

By this time, No. 79 Squadron was in need of a rest and was subsequently sent out of the fighting area to Turnhouse, Scotland on July 10. They had only just left the aerodrome when Sergeant R. Carnall, flying a Hurricane of No. 111 Squadron, dropped on to the turf in a near dive putting the spinner into the ground.

On July 12, Winston Churchill, now Prime Minister, arrived at the aerodrome in his personal Flamingo transport aircraft to chat informally with pilots. They gave a good account of their experiences. The Prime Minister stayed overnight and, before turning in, had a deep and serious talk with Air Vice-Marshal Keith Park who had, incidently, escorted the Flamingo to Hawkinge.

The following day, Sergeant A. E. Binham of No. 64 Squadron wrestled with the controls of his Spitfire after being hit a number of times by Dover-based anti-aircraft batteries. He landed the machine wheels up on the field beside Barnhurst Lane and, understandably having just been brought down by his own side, stood swearing at the damage.

Of all the tragedies associated with the aerodrome, that which involved No. 141 Squadron was the most poignant. No. 141 arrived at Hawkinge in the early hours of Friday, July 19 with their Boulton Paul Defiants. They had been the first to be so equipped but later, because of unsuitability for daylight fighting operations, the aircraft were quickly relegated to the night-fighter role. A week before their arrival (when they were at West Malling), the squadron had received the new constant-speed propellor, the three-bladed prop which increased performance (speed-wise) of the aircraft, but the deficiencies in firepower and manoeuverability were not considered at this stage. However, the Defiant was at that time a comparatively new fighter for which the RAF held such high hopes. It was a slim Merlin-powered monoplane with a crew of two — pilot and gunner — but, unlike the Hurricane and Spitfire, carried no forward firing armament in its wings. It was armed instead with a four-gun, power-operated turret situated about midway along the fuselage just aft of the cockpit.

Only two squadrons, Nos. 141 and 264, had originally been equipped with the Defiant. The latter squadron had scored a measure of success over the Dunkirk beaches during the evacuation by shooting down thirty-seven enemy aircraft on two successive sorties. This score has since been disputed but, nevertheless, however misguided the reports may have been, this first action by No. 264 Squadron spoke well of the new fighter.

No. 141 Squadron (unlike its twin No. 264) did not shoot in anger until July 19. Resplendent in their new camouflage paint, coded TW-, the aircraft were a magnificent sight. The commanding officer, Squadron Leader W. Richardson, was fascinated by the

gleaming motifs painted on the sides of the fuselages under the cockpits — *Cock o' the North, Cock-a-Hoop, Cocksure, Cocked for Firing*, to name but a few.

Lunch on this particular Friday was suddenly interrupted by the wail of the Folkestone siren at 12.10 p.m. Eight minutes later the Luftwaffe were dropping bombs in and out of Dover harbour and were being heavily engaged by local AA batteries. No. 141 Squadron were immediately scrambled to patrol at approximately 5,000 feet above the Channel south of Dungeness point. Only nine of the original twelve Defiants got airborne at 12.30 p.m. for two developed engine trouble within seconds of starting up and one machine packed up during its take-off run. The remaining nine were soon climbing out to the west in sections of three, line astern and in typical RAF formation — a formation which incidentally was later dropped and replaced by the 'loose finger four' configuration, for which the Luftwaffe fighter units were noted.

Continuing their course beyond Dungeness, they were soon vectored to a point some ten miles north of Cap Gris Nez where it was hoped to intercept the German bombers returning from their missions over Dover. It was Flight Lieutenant Loudon who first gave warning of approaching enemy fighters. About twenty or so Bf 109s of II/JG2 (the famous Richthofen Geschwader) were diving at them from out of the sun. The perfectly-formated Defiants altered course slightly to bring their guns to bear on the targets but the young German pilots were not willing to patronise this unfavourable position. The most vulnerable part of the Defiant was the underside and the leader of the 109 pack dived below the formation then screamed upward until the Messerschmitts were hanging on their propellors whilst each pilot selected a target and fired in short bursts.

Almost immediately two Defiants broke away belching flame and smoke as they plummeted to the sea below. Pilot Officer J. R. Kemp, his gunner Sergeant R. Crombie, Pilot Officer A. Howley and Sergeant A. G. Curley, were unable to get out of the 'flamers'. The remaining seven jockeyed for position in a desperate attempt to give their gunners a chance to get in a burst. Flashing aircraft were now tumbling over onto their backs below the Defiants. Sergeant Powell was the first to send a Messerschmitt down in flames from the now seething mass of spiralling machines which shed ammunition cases and other debris as they banked, spun, screamed and roared their way around the sky.

All the Defiants had been hit in the first attack. Pilot Officer I. N. McDougall wrestled with the controls of his machine after it had spun over on to its back and dived for the sea with traces of white glycol from a punctured tank splattering against the windshield. He ordered his gunner, Sergeant J. F. Wise, to bale out — an almost impossible task in a Defiant for the turret was one of the most inescapable contraptions ever devised. Sergeant Wise, however, managed the impossible and cleared the spinning machine. McDougall was about to follow when the engine suddenly picked up and coughed into life. Battling with a machine that was reluctant to fly, he brought it back to Hawkinge where he made a perfect landing although Sergeant Wise was lost. Flight Lieutenant M. J. Loudon watched two more Defiants burst into flames and spin for the sea when he was brought up with a jolt and suddenly found himself the target for half a dozen 109s coming in from both sides. Caught between this murderous cross-fire, he put the nose of the plane down in an attempt to increase speed and at the same time instructed his gunner, Pilot Officer E. Farnes, to bale out which he did. With engine compartment ablaze, Loudon nursed the stricken machine back towards the coast and managed to put it down in a belly landing just east of the aerodrome. Pilot Officer Farnes was later picked up by the Ramsgate lifeboat exhausted, but otherwise alright.

Cock o' the North, ablaze from stem to stern, skimmed the waves in a desperate attempt to reach home. Unable to regain height, the Rhodesian-born pilot, Flight Lieutenant I. D. G. Donald, struggled to maintain control as the blazing aircraft streaked across Dover. Over the Elms Vale area the Defiant followed the valley until its engine ceased. Flying no further, it dived into the side of a hill just four miles from base and exploded on impact, killing the pilot and gunner, Pilot Officer A. C. Hamilton. (A plaque now hangs in the University of Rhodesia in its honour.)

Of the nine aircraft of No. 141 Squadron scrambled, only four got back, and one of these crashed. The squadron's first action of the war had ended in terrible tragedy with six Defiants lost, four pilots and six gunners killed. The squadron (or, to be more precise, what was left of it) moved to Biggin Hill soon afterwards where survivors were released from further action and were rested.

This disastrous event, culminating in the near destruction of a complete fighter squadron, caused a reappraisal of obvious deficiences and limitations of the Defiant.

A Defiant of No. 141 Squadron comes in to land at Hawkinge after a dusk patrol (Imperial War Museum).

There was no let up in the attacks during July. On the 25th, No. 111 Squadron, at Hawkinge for the day, scrambled to the Dover area at 2.30 p.m. to assist No. 64 Squadron in engaging Ju 88s over a convoy where they were, in turn, joined by No. 32 Squadron. Pilot Officer Daw, although injured, refused to leave his battered Hurricane and, with the fabric torn to shreds and with an evil-sounding engine, eventually forced-landed near Dover.

At the end of the month, the Fox Film Unit arrived to make various instructional films which coincided with the erection of more dispersal huts.

The month of August saw the first enemy air attack on the aerodrome in its entire history. On Monday, August 12 the Luftwaffe prepared for its biggest effort so far in the softening up process in preparation for Hitler's 'Adler Tag' offensive due to begin the following day.

At Hawkinge the station personnel were gloomy. Roused by the Tannoy at the unearthly hour of 5.00 a.m., they reluctantly crawled from their bunks and, as the mists rose from the turf, 'erks' flitted between buildings as the station gradually came to life. The 'Baby Buffs' (Buffs Regiment) blew into their hands as they waited for the tea urn to arrive. Duty at Hawkinge was, as one put it thirty years later, 'very boring'. Having recently joined the army these young soldiers had fired a few practice rounds into the butts at Lydden Spout before being split into three groups for aerodrome defence in the south-

east. The only highlight of their short career so far was shouting: 'Who goes there?' to young airmen returning from clandestine courtships, invading the perimeter fences late at night. As the soldiers, like all army personnel, were known to the RAF as 'brown jobs', the young Buffs always took great delight in marching these captured swains to the guardroom at rifle point.

During the past week, Hawkinge had seen very little action although patrols had been flown from the sector stations and Nos. 32, 501 and 610 Squadrons had arrived on odd days. A few aircraft had been left behind for repairs and one or two Hurricanes of No. 32 Squadron and a Spitfire of No. 610 were lodged in a hangar as temporarily unserviceable. The dispersal areas at Killing Wood and Gibraltar Lane were empty, the huts had been swept clean ready for the next unit and the 'trolley accs' stood in their sandbagged emplacements.

At about 7.40 a.m., the Observer Corps at Dover Castle reported seeing large formations of enemy aircraft heading in towards them. The sky was suddenly filled at about 10,000 feet with aircraft stretching from Deal to Dungeness. No. 610 Squadron was scrambled at once from Biggin Hill, No. 32 was put on stand-by and, within seconds of the enemy being sighted by No. 610, the pilots of 32

were sitting in their cockpits eager to get airborne. No. 610 were soon heavily engaged in individual dogfights over the whole of the Romney Marsh areas as the German fighter-bombers made their attack on the radar station at Rye.

At noon, No. 32 Squadron was ordered to Hawkinge to relieve No. 501 as enemy activity increased. They arrived from Biggin Hill in pairs, their Hurricanes clipping the treetops most of the way. The last to land was their CO, Squadron Leader M. Crossley, DFC, who had joined No. 32 Squadron before the war flying Gauntlets and was popularly known as 'The Red Knight'. He already had seven confirmed victories and by the end of the Battle of Britain was to score twenty-two, gaining the DSO.

The pilots lay around in groups talking and smoking while their Hurricanes were being refuelled. They watched the vapour trails strung across the sky like shredded cotton wool as No. 610 Squadron patrolled overhead. By this time, five of the radar stations had been put out of action, two convoys in the Thames Estuary had been dive-bombed and Portsmouth had been heavily attacked by over one hundred and fifty raiders. It was 2.30 p.m. when suddenly the pilots were galvanised into action and, with the jangling bell still ringing in their ears, ran for their aircraft,

Thanks to the Fox photographic unit's visit to Hawkinge, we have these excellent shots of No. 32 Squadron during the battle. *Above:* **This one shows aircraft and personnel of 'A' Flight at their dispersal beside Gibraltar Road.** *Bottom:* **The dispersal in September 1979 with its carpet of parched and blackened stubble.**

donning their cumbersome parachute packs as they climbed into their cockpits. No. 610 Squadron was already in sight of the aerodrome and came in to land as the Hurricanes of No. 32 climbed to 8,000 feet to patrol between Hawkinge and Dover as cover for their relieving unit now being refuelled. By keeping at least one squadron in the air on patrol, Air Vice-Marshal Park was able to intercept any likely raiders. With the radar stations extensively damaged and some non-operational, the Observer Corps were now the only means of reporting enemy formations.

After a quiet and uneventful patrol, No. 32 returned to the aerodrome to refuel having been airborne for only one hour. Refuelling at Hawkinge was by no means a leisurely business and within fifteen minutes all serviceable machines were ready if needed. The petrol bowsers with their earthpins trailing along behind were trundling back to the fuel dump when the scramble signal was given. Within seconds the Hurricanes started up and moved out to their take-off positions. Their leader raised his hand and motioned fore and aft to indicate he was ready to start rolling, the section leaders acknowledged with the thumbs up sign and the machines moved forward as one.

One aircraft remained sitting on the grass near Killing Wood, looking forlorn and helpless with its engine cover removed. With an arm reaching into the complicated machinery, an airman balanced on the wing root while another stood close by taking the full measure of wrath from the irate pilot.

Thirty minutes elapsed — the pilot had long since walked back to the dispersal and the two airmen, now engrossed in technicalities, completely failed to hear the drone of unfamiliar aero engines.

At about 4.45 p.m., fifteen Ju 88s of II/KG76 had been observed forming up over the French coast near Abbeville having taken off from Evreux some twenty miles north-west of Paris. No. 32 Squadron were patrolling the Margate area when the 88s were coming in over the Channel towards Dungeness. Three miles from Dymchurch the German formation split into two separate groups, both maintaining a height of 5,000 feet. While the first group continued inland heading for Lympne, the second group turned parallel with the coast until it reached a position opposite Sandgate and then altered course to Hawkinge.

The aerodrome lay undefended by a fighter squadron and the only means of defence at the time were the three 30cwt Bedford trucks mounting a Lewis machine gun each, and a three-ton truck sporting an Hispano cannon. At the first snarl of the twin Jumos under boost from the leading machine, the two mechanics ran from the Hurricane to the nearest slit trench. No warning had sounded and the station personnel were taken by complete surprise.

The first three enemy machines in line abreast made a mess of their bombing run for a mixture of HEs and incendiaries ploughed into the ground from a point in the centre of the field to the tarmac in front of the hangars. As they screamed overhead, a solitary Hispano from somewhere near the fuel dump opened up spraying the sky like a garden hose. The next three raiders were more accurate, their bombs falling among buildings. The large workshop opposite the old Officers'

GZ-I, P3522 about to scramble (Fox).

Mess went up with a terrific bang and disappeared in a sheet of flame and smoke. Engine parts, tools and sundry bent and twisted items hurled through the air with terrible force. No. 3 hangar received direct hits through the roof causing two of the massive iron doors to buckle and collapse, trapping an airman and two civilians.

The main equipment stores also received a direct hit; the building seemed to erupt from inside showering the area with burning clothes and boxes. Two houses, formerly used by married personnel but now used to billet airmen, were blown to pieces, killing and wounding the inhabitants. Ammunition stored in the corner of the bombed hangar began to explode sending bullets and tracers in all directions. Each bomb explosion produced a sound wave that reverberated against the sides of the hangar. The successive detonations gave off a cacophony of blast, echo, blast effect. The ground shook and trembled underfoot, paving slabs cracked, telephone wires snapped as the poles were uprooted and trees shed their leaves. Leaving chaos in their wake, the last of the bombers

disappeared into the haze, its engines pouring out blue vapour.

It was all over in minutes. Billowing clouds of smoke hung in the sky like a huge black shroud and white-hot metal and stones sizzled on the ground everywhere. There was silence for a time — even the birds had stopped singing. Then, as if by a prearranged signal, blue-overalled airmen appeared from the slit trenches everywhere. Some stood and stared at the shambles around them while others, bewildered and stunned by the crash of bombs, shook their heads vigorously.

Airmen picked their way through the maze of bomb craters edged with chalk and smouldering like small volcanoes. The station ambulance — a 30cwt Bedford — its roof covered with earth, made its way over roads littered with debris to the collapsed buildings. Close to the watch office a small 15cwt van burned fiercely and a tree lay torn from the ground, its roots staring up at the blackened sky.

The Buffs detachment were already helping to free the trapped civilians from the collapsed door section and through the gaping, twisted

opening, an aeroplane wing could be seen burning. The red, white and blue roundel hung in blistered shreds. Trestles and steps were smashed to matchwood, an anvil torn from its bench had been hurled with sickening force at a starter battery in which it had become embedded. The fire truck and crash tender arrived and soon water cascaded over the burning scene; foam engulfed the little van, its tyres now a black mass of smouldering rubber, its shattered windscreen littering the ground.

Miraculously, the watch office remained unscathed and, although the telephone system was inoperable, the R/T network was still working. No. 32 Squadron, now low on fuel and completely out of ammunition, broke off their engagement and made for home; some inland made for Biggin Hill but five came back to Hawkinge. They appeared over the smoking aerodrome in line astern and looking down at the devastation below started to use the R/T. Squadron Leader Crossley realised that none of his brood could make Biggin Hill

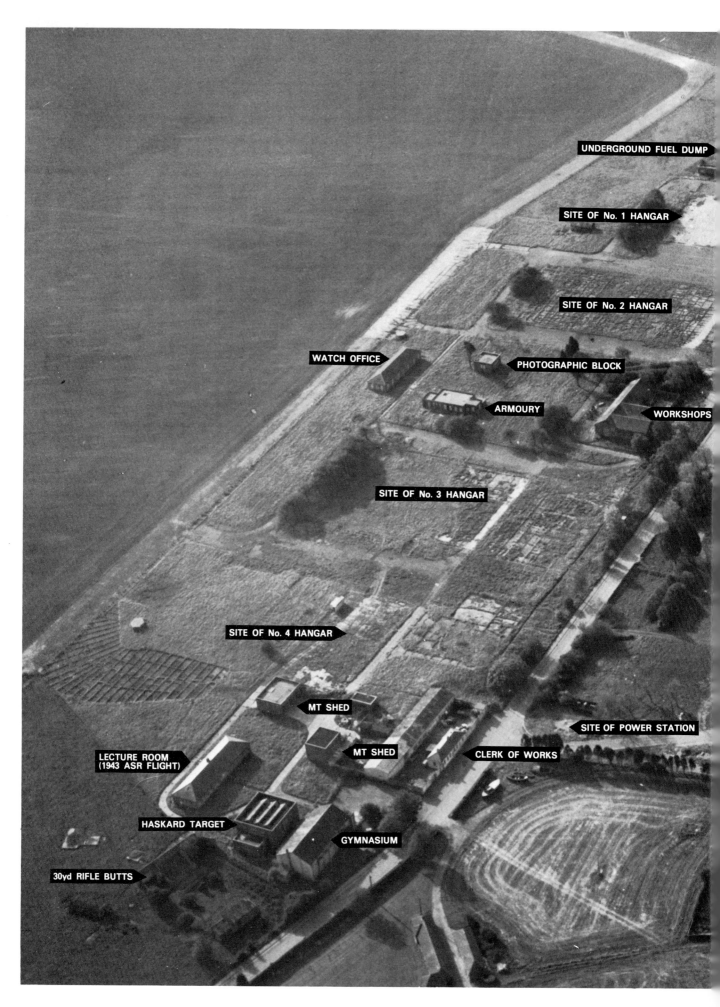

UNDERGROUND FUEL DUMP

SITE OF No. 1 HANGAR

SITE OF No. 2 HANGAR

WATCH OFFICE

PHOTOGRAPHIC BLOCK

ARMOURY

WORKSHOPS

SITE OF No. 3 HANGAR

SITE OF No. 4 HANGAR

MT SHED

SITE OF POWER STATION

MT SHED

LECTURE ROOM
(1943 ASR FLIGHT)

CLERK OF WORKS

HASKARD TARGET

GYMNASIUM

30yd RIFLE BUTTS

OFFICERS' QUARTERS

OFFICERS' MESS

BIJOU COTTAGE

MORTUARY

GUARD ROOM

SITE OF OLD
OFFICERS' MESS

NAAFI

MARRIED QUARTERS

SEWAGE BUILDING

'So we must laugh and drink from the deep blue cup of the sky' — John Masefield. Pilots of No. 32 Squadron take a brief respite from action at their Hawkinge dispersal in July 1940. From L-R are Pilot Officer R. F. Smythe, Pilot Officer K. R. Gillman, Pilot Officer J. E. Procter, Flight Lieutenant P. M. Brothers, Pilot Officer D. H. Grice, Pilot Officer P. M. Gardner and Pilot Officer A. F. Eckford. All survived the battle and the war except for Keith Gillman who went missing in action on August 25, 1940 (Fox Photos).

The spot where the weary pilots rested during that distant summer has changed little as our picture, taken on September 27, 1979, shows.

and, as Manston and Lympne had been knocked out for the time being, it was imperative to 'pancake' at Hawkinge. Calling the local controller he asked for permission to land and received a rather apologetic reply with instructions to avoid the craters at all costs. With undercarriages down, the Hurricanes prepared to land, anxiously watched by those below for no one at that time knew whether unexploded bombs were on the field. Not wishing to tempt fate, the five pilots put their machines down gently and everyone gave a sigh of relief. Normally ground crews would be out servicing the aircraft almost immediately but all were otherwise engaged dealing with the chaos.

The pilots had no sooner stepped down from their machines and begun to take off their parachutes when a small formation of twin-engined aircraft appeared from the direction of Paddlesworth. As the first bullets were fired from the nose guns of the raiders, ground personnel dashed for cover. Bombs exploded simultaneously with the sound of the Tannoy blaring out a warning to take cover. No. 5 hangar erupted, showering the village with bricks and mortar. This second attack by the same unit was, like the first, over in a few minutes for the Ju 88s screamed out to sea unhindered. No one stirred from the shelters for some considerable time and when eventually they did emerge, they found that although incendiaries were burning and spluttering everywhere, not one of the Hurricanes had been damaged. Most of No. 5 hangar was, however, a heap of rubble.

The task of filling craters began the following day. Parties of airmen had been working throughout the night to shift the tons of rubble that had blocked the roads. Windows were boarded up and scarred and cracked walls were shored temporarily. Aerodrome Road was like a canal in parts as the water used to fight the fires ran down to find its level.

A large party of troops arrived from

Shorncliffe Camp to assist with the clearing up and were under command of a young subaltern. Obtaining a Lewis machine gun from the armoury, he vowed 'to get a jerry if the opportunity presented itself'. In fact, he very nearly succeeded in getting a Hurricane of No. 56 Squadron which, heavily damaged and flown by Flying Officer Brooker, crashed on to the field at 4.30 p.m. On the next day, Pilot Officers Smythe and Barton of No. 32 Squadron had both brought their damaged machines back to Hawkinge and were following around the circuit ready to land

when the young 2nd Lieutenant raised the Lewis and would have fired but for the timely shout of: 'They're ours!' Both Hurricanes, unable to lower their undercarriages and at near stalling speed, dropped on to the grass in a cloud of dust.

Thursday, August 15 broke fine and warm with just a slight haze over the Channel. It enabled the Luftwaffe to exert its biggest attack of the 'Adler Tag' offensive using every fighter, bomber and dive-bomber they could lay hands on.

At Hawkinge it had been a quiet morning

No. 32 Squadron start their engines on the 'A' Flight dispersal. The aircraft in the centre GZ-C, N2459 flown by Pilot Officer D. H. Grice, was shot down in flames on August 15 south of Harwich. 'Duggie' Grice was rescued and taken to hospital badly burned (Fox Photos).

with just the usual reconnaissance flights to Dover and the arrival from Shorncliffe of army trucks loaded with eager youngsters who were to put the finishing touches to the battered turf. No. 501 Squadron was at standby, their Hurricanes already refuelled.

On the other side of the Channel at Bonningues, near Calais, the Luftwaffe chief of staff of the II Fliegerkorps, Oberst Paul Deichman, prepared to send off his first sorties of over one hundred aircraft. At 11.00 a.m. the armada, consisting of sixty Ju 87s heavily escorted by Bf 109s, left the coast of France and were spotted by radar. The Stukas of II/StG1 under the command of Hauptmann Keil were to attack Lympne with their 500 and 250kg bombs. Meanwhile over two dozen Stukas of IV(St)/LG1 commanded by Hauptmann von Brauchitsch, the son of the German general, headed for Hawkinge similarly loaded. Above them, weaving and wheeling in loose formation, were the 109 fighters of JG26 led by Major Adolf Galland.

No. 501 Squadron were suddenly scrambled to patrol the coast. Just to the north of the aerodrome, an old horse-drawn binder clattered around a cornfield, its mechanism spewing forth corn stooks. By this time the Stuka Gruppen had come within range of the Dover guns. Led by Hauptmann Keil, the Stukas headed for Lympne in a westerly direction while the second group continued inland out of range of the guns.

Led by von Brauchitsch the second formation turned for Hawkinge. The farmers had stopped to repair their ailing binder and were so engrossed that they failed to hear or see the approaching German dive-bombers until they were over Swingfield. Then suddenly the crash of Bofors guns defending the airfield burst upon their eardrums with frightening alarm as the gull-winged raiders began their descent. The screaming, snarling engines merged with the thunder of exploding bombs, most of which were released too soon due to the formidable barrage. Some of the 250kg bombs went astray and uprooted a tree or two in Reinden Wood, others straddled the cemetery and open fields to the north of the sewage works. Vital electric cables were also severed which put the Dover radar system out of action.

'E' block, used by the sergeant pilots, disappeared in a huge cloud of smoke and flame covering the nearby slit trenches with earth and rubble. The guns failed to find a target but Nos. 501 and 54 Squadrons had already attacked the fleeing raiders from Lympne and were now heading for Hawkinge. The two squadrons had been powerless to stop the raids taking place but their timely intervention prevented Hawkinge taking a severe beating. One of the first to go down in flames was a Stuka flown by Leutnant von Rosen and

he and his gunner were killed. Sergeant N. A. Lawrence of No. 54 Squadron bagged two Stukas and then was himself shot down, 'ditching' in the sea off Folkestone. Another was shot down by Sergeant Farnes of No. 501 Squadron and the next went down under the guns of Sergeant D. A. S. McKay, bringing his total of confirmed victories to seven. He was attacked later whilst landing at Hawkinge to rearm and refuel when a Bf 109 followed him down but he fortunately evaded the fusillade of bullets.

On the afternoon of August 15, the radar plots were so numerous that the whole picture of operations became confused. Eleven RAF fighter squadrons, something like 130 Hurricanes and Spitfires, were scrambled to intercept enemy formations. No. 32 Squadron had been despatched to Hawkinge immediately after the morning raid and by 2.30 p.m. the pilots were sitting in their cockpits on standby wondering if they would be attacked on the ground before they could get up.

Galland's fighters escorted the German bombers over many points along the coast and the sky became filled with aircraft of every description. Heinkel IIIs and Dornier 17s, Junkers 88s and Messerschmitt Bf 110s ranged over a wide area and at varying heights.

Within twenty minutes No. 32 Squadron was hurtling over the perimeter hedges to intercept Bf 109s over Harwich. Hawkinge was again without a fighter squadron for protection when aircraft of KG1 and KG2 dropped their bombs on the already crater-scarred field. Open ground and trees received stray bombs but no casualties or real damage were suffered by the station buildings. The aerodrome defences opened up and the majority of personnel who were not engaged with vital work, on hearing the warning whistle, retired quickly to shelters and trenches.

By now the aerodrome surface was scarred with dozens of brown and white circles. Local unemployed together with a Home Defence detachment began work with picks and shovels and even a steam roller complete with machine gun ventured out on to the field to flatten the mounds while visiting pilots snatched a meal and a nap. Food and sleep became luxuries.

Three days later, on August 18, No. 615 Squadron came down to operate Channel patrols. This was the same day that the Rt. Hon. Anthony Eden chose to visit the 'drome, and at 12.40 p.m. on this brilliant Sunday, the Squadron was scrambled. Twelve Hurricanes took off in three sections of four in perfect

Twenty-eight years later, fictional-coded Spitfires of Harry Saltzman's air force (then reputed to be the 35th largest in the world!) take off over the old dispersal with the pillbox in Gibraltar Lane suitably dressed for the film 'Battle of Britain.'

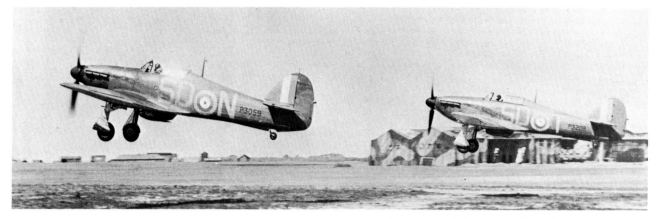

copy-book formation, heading towards Dover in a slow but steady climb. Even before they reached the sea they received a course alteration. Now, with the sun behind them, the climbing aircraft flew north towards the Thames Estuary. Hawkinge lay far to the south when, at slightly less than 20,000 feet, the first attack was made by Bf 109s. One of the first aircraft hit was a reserve machine which had the distinction of being one of the very first batch of fifty Hurricanes built. Pilot Officer Looker, overcoming a constant stream of difficulties, eventually managed to crash land at Croydon.

While Looker was battling with his damaged machine, Hawkinge received its third attack. The dew-soaked grass at Hawkinge covered by ground mist played havoc with the guns, and the crews constantly wiped dry the sights and breech mechanisms as the Red Alert had been in operation since early morning. By midday the sun had disappeared behind cloud and at 1.15 p.m. the telephone rang in the control room. The Observer Corps at Dover had seen a small enemy formation heading towards the aerodrome. The Tannoy suddenly blared out a warning to all personnel and whistles blew from the furthermost corners of the station. Personnel were instructed if not engaged on vital work to take shelter. White-aproned cooks disappeared into dugouts carrying the inevitable tea canister. The post corporal dived from his bicycle into a convenient hedge. But a petrol bowser crew stood their ground knowing that if a squadron came in they would be needed.

The sector controller sent No. 615 back towards Hawkinge to intercept the raiders. Nos. 32 and 610 Squadrons were at stand-by on the ground at Biggin Hill while No. 501 were patrolling the coast near Margate. At 1.20 p.m., six Dornier 17Zs came over the village at about 100 feet escorted by half-a-dozen Bf 109s. Bullets and cannon shells ripped into the sodden turf from the village

Erroneously captioned in past publications as 'Hurricanes of 501 Squadron taking off from Rochford and/or Gravesend,' this photograph was, in fact, taken at Hawkinge in August 1940. The damage visible to No. 5 hangar dates the photo some time after August 12 but before August 18 when both these aircraft were shot down (together with two others) by Oberleutnant Schoepfel of JG26. The photo, taken from 'B' Flight dispersal, could possibly show No. 501 Squadron taking off for this fatal combat when Pilot Officer K. N. T. Lee baled out wounded from SD-N, P3059 and Pilot Officer J. W. Bland was killed in SD-T, P3208 (Imperial War Museum).

Pilots of No. 501 Squadron at 'B' Flight dispersal at Hawkinge. L-R: standing, Flying Officer S. Witorzenc, Flight Lieutenant G. E. B. Stoney (killed on August 18) and Sergeant F. Kozlowski; sitting, Flying Officer R. L. Dafforn, Sergeant P. C. P. Farnes, Pilot Officer K. N. T. Lee, Flight Lieutenant J. A. A. Gibson and Sergeant H. C. Adams (killed as a Pilot Officer on September 6). The aircraft in the background coded KW is a No. 615 Squadron machine. Although the picture was released on August 16, it would seem to have been taken prior to August 12 as No. 5 hangar, which can be seen intact in the background, was partially wrecked on that date (Central Press).

Although No. 5 hangar no longer stands, the scene of the scramble is easily pin-pointed by the surviving buildings on the skyline. Behind the long, low lecture room (building 101) stands the Intelligence Office (building 110) and the gymnasium (No. 108). (Hawkinge has seen three changes of building numbering — we have used the WWII numbers throughout.)

112

'The fighting man shall from the sun
 Take warmth, and life from the glowing earth,'
Captain The Hon. Julian Grenfell. Died of wounds May 26, 1915.

Officer and NCO pilots of No. 610 'County of Chester' Squadron lounge in the sun at 'A' Flight dispersal to await the next scramble from Hawkinge in July 1940 (Fox Photos).

perimeter to Elvington Lane. The bowser crew threw themselves to the ground half expecting to be engulfed in flames. The Dorniers roared over the aerodrome leaving the fighters to tackle the gun emplacements. The crash of the Bofors was deafening as salvo after salvo concentrated on the fleeing bombers but without much success as they were flying fast and too close to the ground for AA fire to be effective. Gunners ducked quickly as cannon shells ripped into the sandbagged gunpits.

Meanwhile No. 501 Squadron met a horde of Messerschmitts near Canterbury at about 1.30 p.m. and lost four Hurricanes in as many minutes to the guns of a single Messerschmitt piloted by Oberleutnant G. Schoepfel. Sergeant McKay jumped by the 109 near Canterbury parachuted out from his burning Hurricane near Blean Wood. Pilot Officer J.

W. Bland was killed instantly but Pilot Officers F. Kozlowski and K. N. T. Lee managed to bale out. Meanwhile, another Hurricane had been shot down near the sector station at Biggin Hill. Later that afternoon, the sixth screamed into the ground near Chilham at about 5.40 p.m. and, although the pilot Flight Lieutenant G. Stoney baled out, he died later of his injuries.

In the period immediately following this last attack on the aerodrome, enemy activity in the vicinity was slight and this brief respite enabled repair crews to erect temporary sheeting to the roof of No. 2 hangar which had

been blown off by a stick of bombs, pieces of metal landing near the village. This period was not without incident however as Nos. 32, 501 and 610 Squadrons arrived on alternate days for the usual coastal patrols.

On the 22nd, a Spitfire of No. 610 Squadron, flown by Sergeant D. F. Corfe became the victim of a Messerschmitt attack when his unit was bounced by top cover fighters protecting Erprobungsgruppe 210's Bf 110s busily engaged over convoy 'Totem' in the Dover Straits. Sergeant Corfe managed to find Hawkinge with his burning Spitfire and just cleared the wreckage before the machine

This is another well-known photograph that is often wrongly identified as to its location. Our comparison pin-points the spot. The scene is little changed except for the missing bulk of No. 1 hangar. Beyond the stubble lies the derelict aviation fuel dump with the same houses on the far side of Aerodrome Road.

exploded. On the following day, whilst Corfe's battered Spitfire's wreckage was still being cleared from the field, a Hurricane of No. 32 Squadron with Pilot Officer Pfeiffer at the controls attempted a landing on only one wheel as the other had been shot away. On touching the ground the remaining leg collapsed and the aircraft did a neat pirouette. Pfeiffer walked away shaken but unhurt.

On August 24 it was the turn of No. 32 Squadron to patrol from Hawkinge. Scrambled to intercept a heavy raid over Dover, the squadron found themselves ranging over the whole of south-eastern England at heights between 2,000 and 20,000 feet. At about 3.15 p.m., Pilot Officer Pniak was clobbered by a Bf 109 and, having received a slight leg injury, was forced to bale out. A calm, confident and extremely determined young man, he was soon flying another Hurricane from Hawkinge within the hour. At approximately 4.15 p.m. his new steed received cannon shells in the engine which stopped everything. He brought the ailing machine back but only managed to drop it into a field north of Lyminge.

This top scoring squadron was rested the following day. So far they had earned one DSO and five DFCs, losing five pilots killed and one taken prisoner-of-war. Even on their last day they lost two pilots attacking Dorniers over Dover. They were replaced on August 27 by No. 79 Squadron who, after refuelling at Biggin Hill, were sent to Hawkinge. They were sipping mugs of tea from Annie's tea-van on the 28th when they were scrambled. Squadron Leader Heyworth led the Spitfires towards Deal and they wasted little time in shooting down an He 59 seaplane.

No. 610 Squadron shared facilities on the 26th and during a dogfight over Folkestone at lunchtime lost a Spitfire. Sergeant P. Else baled out severely wounded. Minutes previously, Pilot Officer K. Webster had brought his damaged Spitfire over the eastern perimeter. The undercarriage had collapsed and the nose dug into the soft earth covering a bomb crater. It somersaulted and burst into flames, killing the pilot.

For three months Arthur Edney had watched the air battles increase in intensity and, outside the comparative safety of his cottage near the aerodrome, dodged falling ammunition cases and other debris which always rained from the heavens. It was on Wednesday, August 28 whilst haymaking that he experienced his narrowest escape.

The drone of high flying aircraft and the chatter of machine guns did nothing to disturb the colourful cock pheasants strutting about the hedgerows. They somehow seemed immune from man's hysterical desire to kill one another. Arthur and his two sisters stopped toiling, not because the haycart had reached its capacity but because they heard a sound so harsh and unnatural from above. Gyrating windmill fashion a smoking, metallic blur fell from the sky and, with a sickening crunch, the blackened aircraft hit the ground. Arthur ran to the crater's edge where a blue vapour hovered like incense. He looked down at the remains of one of Hitler's Messerschmitts which had bored down through fifteen feet of flintstone and clay. A strange smell of petrol, engine coolant, burnt harness and cordite invaded his nostrils. He stood back and, with indescribable feelings, saw the pilot, Oberleutnant Erich Kircheis, descend towards the village of Denton under a silk canopy.

The following day Sergeant Ginger Lacey of No. 501 Squadron, one of the top scoring pilots of Fighter Command, positioned his Hurricane behind a Bf 109 of 3/JG3 right over the aerodrome. Bofors gunners stood almost spellbound whilst watching the dogfight. They cheered when they saw Oberleutnant Floerke bale out. While Floerke floated earthwards, Flight Lieutenant A. A. Gibson and Sergeant W. J. Green also abandoned their Hurricanes.

Tea and wads from Annie — photo taken later in 1942 (Hartwell).

On Sunday September 1, the radar station at Dover was put out of action after one of several heavy raids made on aerodromes and towns along the coast. The third and fourth attacks made on this day were carried out

A 20mm Oerlikon cannon MG-FFM recovered from the Messerschmitt flown by Oberleutnant Kircheis, Nr. 5395 which was shot down on August 28 and now on display at the Brenzett Aeronautical Museum in Kent.

simultaneously on Lympne and Hawkinge in the late afternoon. It had been a glorious day of sunshine and blue skies but now, as the sun was beginning to change from bright yellow to orange, five Messerschmitts screamed over the aerodrome. Shouts of, 'Engage Target!' could be heard before the Bofors opened up producing a polka-dot pattern above the village rooftops. They flew on through this barrage as if it had not been there and over the aerodrome. The gunners, still firing, traversed with them until one raider received a direct hit which blew a sizeable piece from its port wing tip. Over Elham the raiders turned back to the aerodrome with the sun behind them sending the gunners into a quandary. They made small targets as they dived singly. Eight 125kg bombs were dropped, smashing into the shell of No. 3 hangar, blowing a small building to pieces and uprooting some trees in Killing Wood.

The following day yet another squadron moved to Hawkinge for a stint at front line patrols. This was No. 72 Squadron which, commanded by Squadron Leader A. R. Collins, arrived from Croydon and they were soon joined by Wing Commander R. B. Lees, the squadron's former CO, flying his own Spitfire. It was not long before they were at stand-by and later scrambled to intercept raiders over Dover. Squadron Leader Collins, his Spitfire in poor shape, limped back to the aerodrome to crash in a cloud of dust in the centre of the field. The crash tender bumped over the tufts and mounds to find the pilot trapped in the mangled wreckage. He was extricated with great difficulty and within minutes of being rescued was calling for another aeroplane. Sergeant Norfolk returned at roughly the same time but could only manage to put his aircraft into a nearby field. He walked away from the wreck just before it blew up.

Flight Lieutenant E. Graham took over command of the squadron for the next sortie but was shot down near Lympne. Squadron Leader Collins, who had been found a recently serviced Spitfire, was shot up again but managed to return to base. Wing Commander Lees was also wounded but reached Hawkinge. As a result of activities that day this squadron claimed eighteen enemy aircraft out of thiry-five known to have been shot down but lost three of their own aircraft.

The squadron arrived again on the 4th from Croydon to intercept returning enemy bombers. They were tired and in need of rest for they had been continuously engaged in running dogfights. At lunchtime a large formation of German bombers was sighted in the Dover area and No. 72 Squadron scrambled to assist fourteen other squadrons in the ensuing battle.

The following day they were down to nine Spitfires which included the reserve. It was the same story in nearly every fighter unit. The Royal Air Force was down to its last few fighters. The situation was now desperate and Air Vice-Marshal Park said as much in his written report to the AOC-in-C of Fighter Command, Air Chief-Marshal Sir Hugh Dowding.

At Hawkinge the station sick quarters were moved to the comparative safety of Meriden House, some two-and-a-half miles away.

Two days later, on Friday, September 6, Kesselring sent off an enormous formation of Heinkels, Dorniers and Junkers escorted by Bf 109s. At 5.30 p.m., Feldwebel Werner Gottschalk took off in his Bf 109 fighter with others of II/LG2 and set course for the Thames Estuary. Somewhere above Chatham, where the London gun-belt began, his aircraft spun over on to its back. One must assume from this that a shell had burst very close. He turned back towards the coast and was losing height rapidly when he was attacked by British fighters near Canterbury. He survived that ordeal and, within sight of the coastline, his engine gave up. Realising he was not high enough to glide to safety over the Channel, he turned along the ridge of the North Downs. Meanwhile, the watch office personnel at Hawkinge noticed a strange aircraft heading towards the aerodrome with flaps and wheels locked down for a landing.

A battalion of Buffs had been on Red Alert for over a week, half expecting an invasion of the station. The light AA regiment battery, manning the 40mm guns, were now very trigger happy. But Werner Gottschalk, avoiding at all costs the indignity of baling out over the sea, brought his little fighter in to make a perfect landing with a dead engine. It trundled along the grass towards an empty hangar which had been made useless by bombing as if it had every right to be there. Then someone, somewhere, saw and recognised the black Luftwaffe markings on the fuselage. Gottschalk jumped down from the cockpit as just about every machine gun on the aerodrome opened fire. He ran into the hangar for cover and was quickly captured and taken to the guard room.

The following day yet another attack, more conventional, was mounted against Hawkinge. The Observer Corps at Folkestone had spotted the small formation of Bf 109s and 110s clipping the waves but they were unable to predict the target. At the precise moment when the telephone rang in the watch office the first section of Messerschmitts arrived at Hawkinge from the direction of Sandgate and opened fire on gun emplacements at Gibraltar Lane sending bullets and cannon shells into the sandbags. The second wave, this time the twin-engined Bf 110s, followed in a shallow dive from about 1,000 feet releasing their bombs on to the aerodrome. An office building disappeared in a cloud of smoke and debris while trees and a wall collapsed nearby. The next wave, made up of fighters, strafed the gunsites at Argrove and Terlingham. As they sped over the village they were followed by three Bf 110s making their bombing run from the direction of the Danes. The first machine bagged the hostel building which collapsed in a heap of rubble. The second, upset by the terrific barrage from the now excited gunners, appeared to slide into his attack sideways. The raider righted itself over the cemetery gates and the pilot, fast running out of target, released his bombs in the direction of the village. The machine practically stood on its tail as the bombs exploded against two houses at the corner of Aerodrome Road. The third machine veered off releasing its bombs in a field at Mill Lane. There was a dugout in the corner of this field which had been built by soldiers in the First

This is believed to be a photograph of Feldwebel Werner Gottschalk's Bf 109E-7/B which landed at Hawkinge to a special reception committee on September 6 (Flight).

World War. Well preserved over the years, the large oak beams in the roof were stoutly supported by pine logs. Neither had moved or rotted and the whole structure would have withstood considerable battering but one bomb found its mark and a direct hit on the shelter took six lives.

In all, eighteen bombs had been dropped and one soldier had been killed on the aerodrome itself and twelve personnel wounded. The Officers' Mess and No. 1 hangar received hits and the Station HQ was destroyed. The grass landing area itself began to look in a sorry state due to the combination of recently filled in craters, a hot dry summer and constant use by hundreds of fighters. In certain areas it was more like a dust bowl where large patches of brown dirt mixed with chalk made life difficult. Propellers threw up great clouds of the stuff and it covered everything and everybody. Dirt mingled with sweat; it clung to the skin giving a clownish appearance to the hardworking ground crews who sweated, swore, joked and worked long hours round the clock to maintain serviceable aircraft.

September 15, now the official anniversary of the Battle of Britain, was a day to compare with the 7th, with large formations of enemy aircraft crossing the coastline at several points throughout the day and night. The station personnel were apprehensive as they watched the hundreds of tell-tale vapour trails increase minute by minute. They waited for the 'softening up' attack but fortunately this did not materialise. Operation 'Seeloewe', Hitler's invasion plan for England, was put back yet again. The RAF had proved invincible. The German bomber force was now down to twenty machines per squadron instead of the usual thirty.

It was at this time that Air Vice-Marshal Park became aware of certain defects in the defence system. The radar stations, even when operating at their optimum, were usually unable to pinpoint with complete accuracy the height and formation strengths of the enemy forces and, more often than not, this information was left to the imagination of the operators. The build up of enemy forces over the coastal aerodromes of France could only be hinted at and their composition was largely unknown until spotted by either the Observer Corps posts or our defending fighter squadrons.

It was through this lack of precise in-

This house stands on the site of the shelter in Mill Lane, Hawkinge which received a direct hit on September 7 killing six civilians.

Above: **The original Officers' Mess (building 28 see pages 94-95) hit on September 7 and finished off on October 27 (Air Commodore W. K. Beiseigel).** Below: **The sweeping drive still remains with evidence of the attack** (photo right) **still visible in the front wall.**

formation afforded by the radar units and the inability of the Observer Corps to collate information in bad weather conditions that the first 'spotter' techniques were introduced from Hawkinge. A lone Spitfire borrowed from No. 92 Squadron then at Manston arrived at Hawkinge on September 15, 1940. Piloted by Flight Lieutenant A. R. Wright, it flew two missions that day. The job of the spotter pilot, if scrambled early enough, was to climb above enemy formations and collect information about them before they reached their proposed targets. The information required was: type of aircraft, numbers, whether with fighter escort, direction of the raiders, and whether formations were split up into different groups. The early morning sortie on the 15th was a failure as Wright had been scrambled too late and the afternoon mission nearly cost him his life. Although guns were carried, instructions were not to engage the enemy in combat but he inadvertently met two Bf 109s over Dungeness which were climbing to intercept. Wright dived straight at them, split them up and followed one down nearly to the sea. He was unable to see whether the 109 pulled out or not but as the flying characteristics of the 109 were opposite to the Spitfire in a dive, it seemed unlikely that the Messerschmitt pilot would have regained control.

The same day the station workshops evacuated the aerodrome and Hockley Soul in Alkham valley was taken over as a rest camp and was known as Hawkinge 'D'.

In October, three months after the start of the Battle of Britain, Goering decided that his bomber losses were not conducive to the air superiority for which he had hoped. He had

lost about 1,650 aircraft and, in an attempt to stem these losses, introduced the fighter-bomber techniques which wrought such havoc on the south-east coastal towns. The success of his Erprobungsgruppe 210 was (according to Goering) unquestionable although the Bf 110 was outclassed by RAF fighters. Nevertheless, he ordered that all Jagdgeschwadern were to provide one Staffel each for these new fighter-bomber operations and subsequently the Bf 109s were fitted with bomb racks under the fuselage.

On Saturday October 5, the Polish squadron No. 303 were up and waiting for the two formations of Bf 110s of Gruppe 210 en route for West Malling aerodrome north of Maidstone. Bomb-carrying Bf 109s were also in the area and, after releasing their 250kg bombs these reverted to the fighter role. The Poles accounted for four Bf 110s and lost only one Hurricane and pilot. Flight Lieutenant W. Januszewicz had tangled with a 109E-4B and brought his damaged machine over the airfield. Unfortunately it somersaulted in the middle of the 'drome and the pilot was killed.

Hawkinge came under attack for the sixth time on October 9. It was a dull grey day with intermittent rain squalls and high winds. The gunners had donned their groundsheets and covered the shell racks. Field canisters rattled and shook in the three-ton-truck which made its way to the Argrove gunsite carrying the mid-day meal and, as the tailboard clattered open, the Folkestone siren started to wail. Mess tins forgotten, the crews raced for their guns as orders were shouted. In seconds, the barrels were traversing in the direction of the sea. Even so, the gunners were completely taken by surprise when the six

Messerschmitt Bf 109E-4B fighter-bombers, their wing cannons blazing, flew in over the Downs at nought feet.

The many-coloured unit insignia, together with yellow tail fins and engine covers, stood out against the grey blotch camouflage and even greyer backcloth of rain-sodden cloud. With the familiar shouts of 'ON! . . . ON! . . . ON! . . . ' the Bofors at the Terlingham emplacements opened fire with barrels elevated at near zero. Shells burst through the trees over the Danes as huge clods of earth were flung into the air from exploding bombs. Four exploded harmlessly within fifty yards of the remains of No. 3 hangar, the fifth demolished a wooden tower used by No. 2 Squadron in the late thirties while the sixth buried the gun simulator building in a pile of rubble but, as neither were any longer in use, their loss did not affect the running of the aerodrome.

The fleeing raiders were intercepted by Spitfires of No. 222 Squadron. Flying Officer E. H. Thomas shot one down near Postling. The German fighter belly-landed in a field and Thomas watched the pilot, Feldwebel Fritz Schweser, set fire to it before surrendering to local farmhands.

On Friday, October 11, towns in the south-east were raided by bomb-carrying Bf 109s. Folkestone and Canterbury were two of the worst hit. Whilst intercepting one of these raids, Pilot Officer Allen of No. 66 Squadron was shot down. Allen, however, managed to get his Spitfire back to the aerodrome although he was severely concussed in the landing.

Having suffered heavy losses in the past two months during daylight raids, the Luftwaffe

now switched its bombers to night operations leaving only fighter-bombers to fly on low-level strafing and bombing sorties. Numerous raids were made on Hawkinge throughout October on these low-level missions, some carried out by single aircraft. At lunchtime on the 14th, for example, a Messerschmitt Bf 110 dropped two 250kg bombs right in the middle of the squash court. The NAAFI nearby lost all its windows but there were no serious casualties among airmen relaxing inside. Half-an-hour later a single Bf 109 streaked in to plant another bomb among the station buildings. It produced a spectacular fountain from a fractured water main, cut telephone wires and killed one soldier.

The following day, a Hurricane of No. 257 Squadron, trailing torn fabric from tail and wings, approached the aerodrome from over the village rooftops. The pilot held off at near stalling speed allowing the wing area to gain lift from the strong wind prevalent. But the nose dropped. The propellor dug into the ground and the undercarriage collapsed sending the aircraft over on to its back. Pilot Officer North slid back the hood, undid his harness and fell out uninjured.

German fighter-bombers were back again on October 27 free flying over Kent. London and the south-east had been under Red Alert from the early morning of the previous day. The siren at Folkestone had given warning at 7.45 a.m. on this bright Sunday morning, keeping the gunners on their toes. Binoculars scanned the horizon as fighter after fighter dropped in from all directions. Some had lost contact with their units while others had

exhausted their ammunition and petrol in chasing elusive enemy formations. Many had wireless troubles caused by dampness which always seemed to effect the sensitive electrical apparatus when the aircraft were flying in excess of 20,000 feet.

By 11.00 a.m. a fairly large formation of German fighter-bombers crossed the coast at Deal heading for Margate and Ramsgate. The watch office personnel were apprehensive as reports came in from the blitzed towns. Taking advantage of the mass of white cumulus cloud which had now materialised, eight Bf 109 fighter-bombers headed towards the aerodrome. The first unit to spot the raiders after the initial warning given by the Observer Corps, was the Royal Marine 3.7in gun battery at Swingfield. They sent up a terrific salvo, joined by other batteries at Lydden Spout and Capel le Ferne. The enemy aircraft changed course and sheered off inland. But for the black smudges dotting the clouds, the sound of brass shell cases banging against each other as they were thrown into a pile, everything again became normal. The gunners watched and waited in silence.

The now familiar sound of Merlin engines broke the silence as Spitfires of No. 74 Squadron scrambled from Biggin Hill, spreading out as they vectored to Dungeness. Led by the indomitable 'Sailor' Malan, they failed to intercept and lost the scent. With No. 74 Squadron out of the way the raiders came

back over the aerodrome at no more than 800 feet. It was a shrewd move. The four fighter-bombers, in line abreast, were over the station before the gunners realised what was happening. They watched four bombs fall before they could fire a round. The camp post office erupted in a cloud of black smoke sending tiles, bricks and timber flying in all directions. The original Officers' Mess built in the twenties received a direct hit blowing out the west wing and the remaining roof. Two bombs exploded in the coal yard blasting Welsh coal into the cemetery.

Shouts of 'Engage Target! . . . Engage Target! . . . ' could be heard as the Bofors frantically spewed out shells which curved towards the fleeing raiders. Machine gun bullets ripped into trees and buildings as the next four aircraft made their bombing run. Through black, billowing smoke they appeared at an even lower height than the previous wave, and amply demonstrated the risk they took. Bombs fused to explode on impact created havoc, the blast of high explosive blending with exploding 40mm shells. As if drawn by a powerful magnet one fighter-bomber with bits and pieces falling off it eventually crashed into the sea off Folkestone.

Below left: The Hawkinge air-raid warning siren now on display at the Brenzett Aeronautical Museum. *Below:* The control box in the guardhouse photographed in 1973.

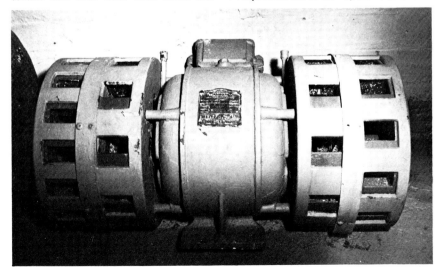

According to British official sources, the Battle of Britain was reckoned to be over by the end of October. The German view, however, extends the battle to May 1941. Whichever is acceptable, as far as Hawkinge is concerned, November marked the beginning of the RAF's ability to wage its own retaliatory air battles with the posting in of the newly-formed No. 421 Flight. Hurricanes and Spitfires had been used by the unit from Gravesend and West Malling until it re-equipped with Spitfires at Biggin Hill. Nine aircraft were allocated and on the morning of November 15 they flew to Hawkinge. This short trip was not without incident either, for Sergeant Don McKay, an experienced fighter pilot of so many air battles, spotted a lone Dornier near Folkestone. Already credited with seven confirmed and four probables, he promptly disposed of the German bomber into the Channel.

The unit soon got into its stride and was soon involved in shipping spotter techniques as well, bringing to the aerodrome a sense of pride and purpose totally divorced from any previous role.

For some time, German long range guns at Cap Gris Nez had been hurling shells in the general direction of Dover and Folkestone aided by a single spotter aircraft flying over the Channel. Soon after No. 421 Flight arrived, staff on duty at the Observer Post on the Dover Castle ramparts reported sighting this spotter. A shell had already struck a water tower at the aerodrome demolishing the sergeants' mess billiard room wall. Others had exploded from time to time in the vicinity of the village. On November 23, Pilot Officer Lawrence immediately scrambled to make an interception and returned some thirty minutes later to report he had shot down a Bf 110 before the crew knew of his existence.

Another pilot from Hawkinge set a possible speed record for combat when he shot down a Heinkel He 60 reconnaissance seaplane on November 26. The presence of the seaplane and its fighter escort approaching Dungeness was given by the 'Y' Service unit at Capel Le Ferne by direct telephone link, instead of going through the sector control at Biggin Hill. Flight Lieutenant O'Meara scrambled in the nearest aircraft available to him at the time, which happened to be an ancient blue-painted Spitfire originally used for the early high spotter patrols and still retained at the station. Of doubtful vintage and fitted with special bulges in the perspex canopy to give better pilot visibility, the aircraft was kept in a specially reserved dispersal away from other squadron machines.

O'Meara arrived in the area plotted by 'Y' and found the Heinkel without much difficulty. He attacked the seaplane from the beam without really thinking of the possibilities of a fighter escort and watched the aircraft dive into the sea. He arrived back at Hawkinge just fourteen minutes from take off and was greeted with the news that sector had just sent through a request to intercept!

A most unusual and unprecedented incident occurred at Hawkinge on the afternoon of November 29, 1940. A recently-serviced Spitfire stood at 'A' Flight dispersal. In the cockpit was a young eighteen-year-old rigger with the nickname of 'Texas'. His one ambition was to become a fighter pilot but the CO kept turning down his requests. No one noticed anything amiss when 'Texas' fired the cartridge starter. It was quite normal for riggers to move aircraft from one position to another about the aerodrome as this saved bothering pilots. The Merlin engine spluttered into life and the rigger allowed the engine to warm up.

Minutes later the aircraft moved leisurely and somewhat haphazardly down the slope then, with a roar, gathered speed as the throttle was opened. A further burst of power shot the aircraft bouncing across the grass. The speed built up considerably.

The gunners, ever watchful, paid little heed; to them, it was just another Spitfire being moved. Watch office personnel were baffled and asked each other for confirmation. Unauthorised movements fouled-up aerodrome discipline. Then the inevitable happened. The Spitfire was not trimmed for take-off, and neither was the propellor in fine pitch, and it came to a rather sticky end in an agonising screech of tortured metal when the starboard wing was torn off.

With only a cut hand to show for his misdeed, 'Texas' climbed down from the wreckage. He stood back inconspicuously with the gathering crowd, regaining what composure he could under the circumstances. Amidst babbling voices all asking for the pilot he turned to slink away into obscurity, but this was not to be. A Flight Lieutenant, red-faced and near to apoplexy, screamed at the disillusioned rigger, who wished the ground would open up and swallow his six-foot frame.

'Texas' was taken under escort to the gate guardroom after receiving a dressing down by his CO. With the lashing tongue still ringing in his ears he felt deflated and dejected. Naturally the Air Ministry took a serious view of the whole escapade and at his court-martial he received a six-month sentence. 'Texas' was

further to astound the CO by escaping from the guardroom the day prior to his removal to the dreaded 'glasshouse'! The national press made light of the whole affair by referring to the popular song of the time, *If I Only Had Wings.*

The remarkable proficiency attained by the gunners in aircraft identification suddenly took a turn for the worse when, at about 11.00 a.m. on a dull November morning, they blotted their copybook. A thin, twin-tailed, twin-engined aircraft arrived unannounced over the aerodrome at about 200 feet and proceeded to make the usual left-hand circuit approach for landing. The gunners, however, were too quick off the mark for although the Red Alert had not been given they opened up with everything they had. The visitor veered away, dived to hedge-top height and, with its undercarriage retracting, flew inland at high speed. Several hits had been observed on the aircraft before it dived away and, as a green Very light shot into the air, the gunners were busy congratulating themselves. Unfortunately, their rejoicing was short-lived. Hurried telephone calls were made to the gun emplacements where an embarrassed young lieutenant explained the striking similarity between a Hampden and a Dornier 17Z!

Flight Lieutenant R. A. B. Learoyd had taken part in a raid on the night of August 12/13, 1940 along with four other Hampdens of Nos. 49 and 83 Squadrons which were to attack an aqueduct forming part of the Dortmund-Ems canal. The first two aircraft were shot down before they were able to release their bomb load and the second two, badly shot up by the accurate flak defences and crippled, veered away from the target. The fifth aircraft, piloted by Learoyd, flew to within 150 feet of the target in the face of intense flak and blinding searchlights to release his bombs at the base of the aqueduct. His aeroplane, struck many times by flak, climbed into the clouds and made good its escape although heavily damaged. Avoiding pursuing night-fighters, he struggled with the controls of the Hampden and brought it back, thus saving his crew and earning himself the highest award for gallantry — the Victoria Cross.

Learoyd was on a few days' holiday with fellow officers in Blackpool from his squadron which was then based at Scampton in Lincolnshire. It had been arranged that, on the day in question, a pilot would 'ferry' a Hampden to Blackpool where his friends were due to spend a few more days. Learoyd would then fly the aircraft to Hawkinge en route to the presentation of the Honorary Freedom of his then home town, the Cinque Port of New Romney. Learoyd flew over New Romney where the normal procedure on these occasions was to fly around his house a couple of times to signal his arrival before proceeding to a pre-arranged landing at either Lympne or Hawkinge. On this occasion, the flight to Hawkinge had been cleared and he flew down with the original pilot sitting on the mainspar behind the pilot's seat and the regular crew in their correct positions.

After passing over Ashford he lost height and arrived over his house at about a hundred feet or so, did three circuits and flew straight from there to Hawkinge at little more than 500 feet. He recalled some thirty years afterwards that it 'was a damned silly thing to do' but, being stationed in Lincolnshire, had not realised how trigger-happy they were in the south. He was informed later however that his clearance had not been received ahead of his arrival. All the time he was flying round the house and all the way to Hawkinge he had been subjected to small-arms fire but knew nothing of this at the time.

Reaching Hawkinge he lowered the undercarriage and prepared to land. However,

Hawkinge from the south-east in October 1979. Killing Wood is in the foreground.

whilst in circuit he happened to look up and outwards and saw a number of small black puffs. By the time he realised what they signified the gunners found their range and the aircraft was hit a number of times. The poor pilot sitting behind Learoyd received a lump of metal in a leg and the instrument panel more or less disintegrated. Retracting the undercarriage, Learoyd quickly dived to hedge-top height and flew inland. After a short while, two fighters approached and after firing the colour of the day escorted the Hampden to West Malling. From there, Learoyd scrounged a car and returned to New Romney for the ceremony and, somewhat impressed by the accuracy of the defences, recounted his experiences. It is interesting to record that although the Hampden was hit no less than thirty-two times, mostly by machine gun fire, an inquiry was later held at Dover Castle to ascertain why it had taken so long to hit a sitting and unsuspecting target!

On December 5, Bf 109s again bombed the station although causing little damage and no casualties.

Although No. 421 Flight was primarily

119

engaged in reporting on the movements of enemy aircraft and shipping, it soon became apparent that these lads were gleefully performing duties beyond those asked of them. They were eager to cross swords with the enemy on every occasion even to the extent of getting into the air on any pretext whatsoever in the hope of running into the Luftwaffe. On December 7, Sergeant J. Gillies flying the blue-painted Spitfire (P7498), chased and harassed a Do 17Z right across the Channel shooting bits from it at every opportunity. When about five miles from the French coast he broke for home leaving the smoking German machine weaving and twisting above the waves. He ran out of fuel on the return journey but pressed on in a glide that enabled him to put down in a field just one mile from the aerodrome.

An even more impressive glide return to Hawkinge was performed in February 1941 by Flight Lieutenant Billy Drake, an event which made headlines in the national press and was mentioned in BBC news bulletins the next day. On February 2, Flight Lieutenant Drake was on a reconnaissance flight at about 30,000 feet over northern France when his engine suddenly stopped. At that time he was some seventy miles from Hawkinge but decided to glide back. In an area infested with German fighters it was a chance that paid off. Drake, an experienced pilot, had the watch office personnel biting their finger nails with apprehension as he glided over the Channel to make a perfect landing. Other pilots had attempted this feat with varying degrees of success and some had lost their lives as a result.

On January 11, 1941, No. 421 Flight heard they were to expand to squadron strength. As a small unit they had been in action almost continuously since their inception three months before. They had carried out no less than 199 patrols from Hawkinge alone, destroying ten enemy aircraft, damaging nine more and claiming four probables. This was no mean feat for a handful of pilots.

Thus, a new fighter squadron was born at Hawkinge — No. 91 (F) Nigerian — which became legendary as the 'Jim Crow' squadron. Based on the successful operations of the former flight, No. 91 Squadron continued in style and became one of the most professional reconnaissance/fighter units in Fighter Command. The Archbishop of Canterbury conducted the service of dedication when the Squadron officially came into being on February 16.

Three more raids were made on Hawkinge during February, no damage or casualties being caused in the attacks on the 4th and 16th but Sergeant McKay's Spitfire (P7735) was set alight by the only bomb dropped on the 8th. It was lunchtime when a lone red-nosed BF 109E of II/LG2, piloted by Werner Schlather, made its run in from the Alkham valley. Five thousand feet below, airmen were

Three E-type blast pens protected aircraft at both 'A' and 'B' Flight dispersals. *Above:* 'B' Flight on the edge of Killing Wood in 1942 and *below* in October 1979.

marching back to the aerodrome from St. Michael's church where the Archbishop of Canterbury had preached the sermon. The column of airmen scattered to all points of the compass as Schlather strafed them and, before the defences were aware of his presence, he managed to get in a burst or two at Spitfires in 'B' flight dispersal. The Messerschmitt climbed up into a loop immediately over the centre of the aerodrome, made a neat Immelmann turn and flipped over into a dive to shoot up 'A' Flight. His third attempt was his last, however, for he made the fatal mistake of banking round

tightly over the village for the next run. The port wing tip crumpled under the blast from a Bofors shell; the undercarriage dropped down indicating that the hydraulics had gone and in seconds the climbing fighter stalled. It lost height rapidly and screamed into a field near Arpinge Farm.

Today in the cemetery adjacent to the aerodrome, standing among others, is a tombstone simply inscribed 'Werner Schlather'. His body, together with the remains of his red-painted fighter, were found by Hawkinge personnel twelve feet below ground.

Above: Then and now. New Zealander Flight Lieutenant G. C. Pannell in the cockpit of 'Onitsha Province' DL-K of No. 91

Squadron in one of the 'A' Flight pens on the western side of Gibraltar Road (Imperial War Museum).

The following month there were three casualties when a Bf 109 dropped a bomb at 5.00 p.m. on March 10, quite close to 'B' Flight dispersal. A sharp bank to port and the raider was down out of sight, side-slipping round Sugarloaf Hill and out over Folkestone before the gunners knew what had happened.

Another Bf 109, perhaps the same one, was back again the next day to plant a bomb on the Aerodrome Road.

Two days later it was a perfect moonlight night and, at 2.30 a.m., high explosive bombs straddled nearby fields although none fell closer than one mile from the aerodrome.

Hit and run raids on Hawkinge continued throughout the spring of 1941, two Bf 109s dropping four bombs on April 10; five 109s returning three days later (one of which was damaged by AA fire), and machine gun strafing attacks on May 8 and 11.

On Friday, May 16, the aerodrome was attacked no less than four times on the one day. The first of these was made at about 1.00 p.m. when most airmen were finishing their mid-day meal. Wing Commander Fry, the station CO, was on the steps of the Officers' Mess filling his pipe when, without warning of any kind, not even a whistle blast, two yellow-nosed Bf 109s slipped in under the radar screens and began to strafe the gun emplacements near Gibraltar Lane. They were not alone as another two followed strafing the aircraft standing at dispersal pens at Killing Wood. As usual with this type of raid the defences were caught napping and the raiders were hurtling out to sea before a shell was fired. Assessing the damage afterwards revealed that only one Spitfire had been damaged and this was repairable.

Most probably pleased with this attack, the Luftwaffe came back at 2.30 p.m. with four Messerschmitts, each making a different approach. No. 91 Squadron was smugly pleased that it was being singled out in this

Above: **One lucky lady surrounded by the pilots and administrative staff of No. 91 'Nigeria' Squadron in front of the new Officers' Mess in 1942 (Kent Messenger).** *Below:* **Built in 1937, after standing derelict for nearly ten years, the building has now been renovated to be used as the Hawkinge Youth Adventure Centre.**

way. Its reputation at stake, the Royal Observer Corps actually spotted the aircraft this time along the coast near Deal and continued to plot them on course as they swung inland over the southern collieries. No one could be sure of their target for these hit-and-run raiders bombed and machine-gunned towns and villages at random but this time the station was alerted.

In line abreast the raiders skimmed the treetops at Reinden Wood and opened fire as

they approached the village. Cannon shells and machine gun bullets ripped across the grass, but the squadron had already taken off and were now out over the Channel waiting to pounce. The Bofors put up a fierce barrage, their barrels nearly parallel with the ground. One Messerschmitt suddenly turned over on its back and dived down beyond the Downs although no one saw a tell-tale pall of smoke which would have indicated a crash. The PAC rockets, set off too late to be effective, swished

121

Above: Pilots of No. 91 'Nigeria' Squadron at their dispersal behind Hawkinge village in September 1942. Squadron Leader J. E. F. 'Moses' Demozay stands in front of the Spitfire VB while Flight Lieutenant 'Chris' Le Roux sits astride the cowling of DL-H. From the left are 'Shag' O'Shaugnessy, Flying Officer Bishop, the squadron IO, 'Scotty' Downer, 'Johnny' Downs, 'Geoff' Pannell, unknown, 'Ronny' Ingram, Roger 'Sammy' Hall, unknown. Note the sticky tape across the window panes of the cottage on the right as a preventive measure against splintering by blast (Kent Messenger). *Below:* The pilots, aircraft and sticky tape have long since disappeared but the cottages remain. A rusting and corroded Nissen crew room still stands nearby.

into an empty sky. Out over the Channel the squadron's Spitfires disposed of two raiders as they turned for the French coast and only one enemy fighter managed to reach its base. Although one airman was killed and five others injured by flying debris, little damage was inflicted on the aerodrome.

The third attack was made in the evening at about 7.00 p.m. and consisted of a much larger force of fighter-bombers which attacked in waves of three. A similar raid was being made on Lympne at the same time, both carried out using the new Messerschmitt Bf 109Fs for the first time. Fortunately this third attack had also been spotted enabling No. 91 Squadron to be vectored to patrol the coast between Deal and Dungeness. What might have been a severe raid was thwarted by the sheer weight of anti-aircraft shells which plastered the evening sky in one huge barrier of defence. Bombs were dropped rather haphazardly across the aerodrome and sections of the perimeter fencing collapsed. A wooden dispersal hut disappeared in a cloud of earth and smoke and one eyewitness recalls

it 'falling to the ground, disintegrating plank by plank as if in a slow-motion film'.

Soon afterwards the squadron landed at Hawkinge having picked their way cautiously between the bomb craters although the dusk patrol was advised to land at West Malling. Helped by low cloud, the raiders had made good their escape by hugging the sea but, even so, two were brought down.

Three hours later Canterbury received a heavy raid and it was from this direction that two aircraft arrived over Hawkinge at 10.30 p.m. streaking in at low level to release their HEs before speeding out over Folkestone. Buildings were damaged by blast, two air raid shelters (which fortunately were empty) were blown up and the temporary roof to No. 2 hangar, which had been extensively damaged the year before, caved in. A couple of Spitfires of questionable vintage together with the CO's 'taxi' were also damaged.

So ended a rather hectic day in the life of the aerodrome. Airmen worked non-stop throughout the night filling in the craters and clearing up the bomb damage. Damaged

aircraft were patched up, the torn dispersal bays were re-sandbagged as were the gun emplacements and, by the 18th, the station was back to normal.

Another aspect of the air war at Hawkinge was the work of its air-sea rescue unit. The most pressing problem during the Battle of Britain had been to rescue fighter pilots brought down in the Channel and North Sea and it was for this reason that Fighter Command borrowed a small number of Lysander aircraft from the army co-operation squadrons. With rubber dinghies attached to the wheel spats, this slow but highly manoeuvrable aircraft was a most welcome sight to a 'ditched' airman. Usually the Lysander was accompanied by one or two fighter aircraft to ward off any likely enemy attack for, although it carried twin Browning machine guns, it was a sitting duck for any prowling enemy fighter. The first Lysanders to operate from Hawkinge in the air sea rescue role were obtained from 'B' Flight of No. 4 Army Co-operation Squadron which arrived at nearby Manston in December 1940. Daily,

a single machine was despatched to Hawkinge on stand by, returning to its home base at night.

However nearly a year was to elapse before the single Lysander was finally replaced by a complete operational rescue unit when, in June 1941, 'A' Flight of No. 277 (ASR) Squadron was formed. A month later the flight received two Walrus amphibians, the single-engined, three-seater pusher type biplane designed in the early thirties for fleet spotter work.

The two amphibians initially allotted to the Hawkinge ASR flight provided a new experience for flying personnel. Landings at sea became a new feature and it was not long before 'A' Flight were engaged in some very hair-raising incidents.

Pressure on existing air-sea rescue squadrons at that time in the English Channel caused the Air Ministry to review the Boulton Paul Defiant in the hope that it would be better suited than the Lysander. Defiants were being released in ever increasing numbers from the night-fighter squadrons which were being equipped with Beaufighters and, by February of that year, trials began to test the Defiant's ASR suitability. At least in terms of speed, the Defiant had the edge on the Lysander although the Ministry failed to realise other more important disadvantages. Nevertheless, in May 1942, No. 277 (ASR) Squadron received its complement of six Defiants to supplement the four Lysanders already on strength.

Modifications to the Defiant's wings were made at squadron level to accommodate the 'M' type dinghy. It turned out to be the first disadvantage because only one such dinghy could be carried under each wing compared to the four carried by the 'Lizzie'. However, the increased numerical strength of the squadron was a valuable asset when the unit operated from Shoreham during the Dieppe raid in August of that year but within six months of its introduction, it was plainly evident that the Defiant was not at all suitable. For one thing, they were taking up valuable time in engine overhauls and hangar space was at a premium since only No. 1 hangar survived the bombing raids of 1940. Pilots were disillusioned with their performance and the rather high stalling speed and wide turning circle — both important factors in ASR work — were an insufferable imposition. Once again the Defiant, whose role in service with various RAF commands had proved considerably less than spectacular, gradually disappeared from air-sea rescue squadrons leaving the Lysander supreme until the arrival of the ASR Spitfire.

In June 1942 Hawkinge became host to additional fighter squadrons and these were the first aircraft to use the aerodrome for sweeps and 'Rhubarbs' over France which allowed selective targets further afield to be attacked by using wing drop-tanks. Three corrugated blister hangars had been hastily erected to accommodate them and only afforded the most simple type of protection for engine servicing and the like. No. 65 Squadron was the first to arrive, commanded by Squadron Leader Bartley, who had fought with No. 92 Squadron during the Battle of Britain as a Pilot Officer. The next to arrive was No. 41 Squadron under the command of Squadron Leader Fee. Both units flew Spitfire Vbs, and the latter took up coastal patrols and fighter sweeps in pairs, similar to the 'Jim Crows' ranging along the French, Belgian and Dutch coasts with some night sorties thrown in for good measure. However, by July both squadrons were moved north pending their posting overseas.

After a delay of over a month, Operation Jubilee (the Dieppe raid) was finally carried out on August 19, 1942. Like other aerodromes in the south-east, Hawkinge became a kind of stronghold. Movements in and around the aerodrome were curtailed to a minimum with everyone entering the station

With the formation of No. 277 Air-Sea Rescue Squadron in June 1941, a different sort of scramble became commonplace at Hawkinge. They took over building 101 (the lecture block) as their HQ seen here next to the stop-butt for the 30-yard rifle range (Imperial War Museum).

Checking the dingy fitted to a Lysander of No. 227 (ASR) Squadron outside the old sports pavilion (building 113) used for ASR stores (Kent Messenger).

SITE Nº I (AIRFIELD)

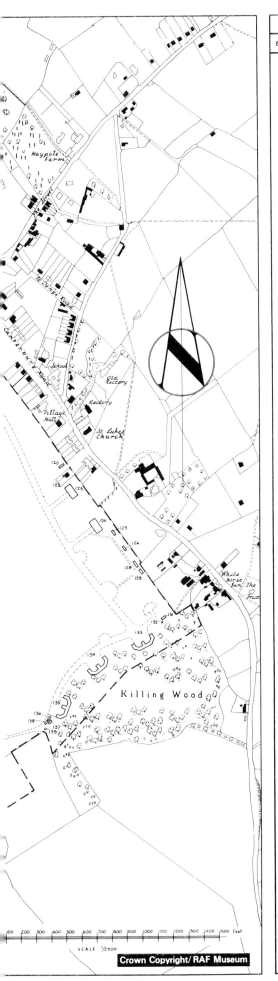

Crown Copyright/ RAF Museum

SCALE 1/2500

BLDG Nº	DESCRIPTION SITE Nº 1 (AIRFIELD).	CONSTR'N
1	TRANSFORMER	
2	MARRIED OFFICERS QRS. GP IV	P.B.
3	LATRINE BLOCK (Part of GP IV Qr.)	P.B.
4	GARAGE	P.B.
5&6	MARRIED OFFICERS QRS GP V	P.B.
7	Do. Do. Do	P.B.
8	Do. Do. Do	P.B.
9	OFFICERS MESS & QRS	P.B.
10	Do. QRS	†
11	BLISTER HANGAR	C.I.
12	PETROL INSTALLATION (Aviation)	
13		
14	PETROL INSTALLATION (Aviation)	
15		
16	PETROL INSTALLATION (M.T.)	
17		
18	GAS DEFENCE HUT	†&C.I.
19	FIRE TENDER & N.F.E.	†.B.
20	WATCH HUT. (Temporary)	†
21	BULK OIL INSTALLATION	
22	FLIGHT SHED Nº1	†.B.
23	STORE	P.B.
24	INFLAMMABLE STORE	C.I.
25	LUBRICANT STORE	†.B
26	BIJOU COTTAGE (St.Engrs QRS)	P.B
27	BOWSER SHED Nº3	†.B
28	FLIGHT SHED Nº 2 (War Damaged)	
29	COMPASS PLATFORM	P.C
30	OPERATIONS BLOCK	P.B.
31	LINK TRAINER	P.B.
32	OIL STORE	†
33	ARMOURY	P.B
34	WORKSHOPS (Ex Main Stores)	P.B
35	PARACHUTE STORE	P.B
36	LATRINES	†.B
37	BOOSTER PUMP HOUSE	†.B.
38	WATER TANK	Cast Iron
39	RESERVOIR	P.C
40	FIRE PARTY BLOCK	P.B
41	SERGEANTS MESS	†.B.&T.
42	BARRACK BLOCK (Single Storey)	P.B
43	AMBULANCE GARAGE	P.B.
44	SICK QUARTERS	P.B.
45	LATRINES	
46	E.W.S. Nº 2	P.C.
47	RATION STORE	P.B.
48	MORTUARY	P.B
49	GAS DEFENCE HUT.	†
50	BARRACK BLOCK (War Damaged)	†.B
51	Do. Do.	†.B
52	INCINERATOR	C.I.
53	ABLUTIONS (SUMMER CAMP)	C.I.
54	PIGGERIES	Brick
55	LATRINES (SUMMER CAMP)	C.I.
56	W/T MAST	St.
57	BARRACK BLOCK	
58	E.W.S. Nº1	P.C
59	TENNIS COURT (O.R's)	Tarmac
60	INSTITUTE	P.B.
61	GROCERY STORE	P.B.
62	BARRACK BLOCK.	P.B.
63	DINING ROOM	P.B.&T
64	BYE PRODUCTS	P.B
65	FLAGSTAFF	Timber
66	BARRACK BLOCK	P.B
67	STATION H.Q. (War Damaged) (Ex. officers QRS)	
68		
69	GUARD HOUSE	P.B.
70	MARRIED W.O.s QRS. (2 Nº)	P.B
71	Do. Do. Do. (1 Nº)	P.B
72	Do. O.R's Do. (4 Nº)	P.B.
	A.M.W.D COMPOUND (73-77)	
73	STORE	N.
74	Do.	N.
75	Do.	N.
76	Do.	N.
77	Do. (War Damaged)	†.
78	M.G. POST	†.B.
79	W/T MAST.	St.
80	MARRIED O.R's QRS (2 Nº)	P.B.
81	Do. Do Do (4 Nº)	P.B
82	Do. Do. Do (4 Nº)	P.B
83	Do. Do. Do. (2 Nº)	P.B.
84	STAND-BY SET	
85	FUEL STORE	P.B.
86	DIESEL OIL TANK	
87	POWER HOUSE	†.B.
88	ENCROACHMENT. TEL.KIOSK&LET.BOX.	
89	BLISTER HANGAR	C.I
90	FLIGHT SHED (War Damaged.)	
91	BULK PARAFFIN TANK	
92	DUTY CREW ROOM (Temporary)	†.
93	CRASH PARTY HUT. Do.	†.
94	TEST BUTT	†.
95	LATRINES (O.R's)	C.I.
96	E.W.S. Nº3 [War Damaged]	P.C.
97	BLACKSMITH & WELDERS SHOP.	P.B
98	FUEL STORE	†.
99	SLEEVE STREAMER MAST	
100	M.T. TANKERS SHED	P.B
101	A.S.R HQ (Ex Photographic Block)	P.B.
102	MINIATURE ARTILLARY RANGE	P.B
103	A.M.W.D. YARD & SHEDS	†.
104	R.M. SWITCH UNIT	
105	A.M.W.D. OFFICE	

BLDG Nº	DESCRIPTION	CONSTR'N
106	CONTRACTORS YARD & STORE	P.B.
107	A.M.W.D. AGRICULTURE MACHY SHED	†
108	GYMNASIUM	†.B.
109	ENCROACHMENT. DRESSING RM.	†
110	INTELLIGENCE OFFICE (Ex Haskard Target)	†.B.
111	M.G. RANGE	P.B.&P.C
112	BOMB DROPPING TEACHER	†.
113	A.S.R. STORES ETC. (Ex Sports Pavilion)	†.
114	HUT	N
115	PYROTECHNIC STORE	P.B.
116	EXPLOSIVES STORE	P.B.
117	BARRIER GUARD HUT	†&C.I.
118&119	BLISTER HANGARS	C.I.
120	'B' FLIGHT OFFICE	N
121		
122	GAS DEFENCE HUT	
123&124	BLISTER HANGARS	C.I.
125	'B' FLIGHT CREW ROOM	N
126	'B' Do. ARMOURY	N
127		
128	'B' FLIGHT SLEEPING SHELTER	P.B.
129	'B' Do. OFFICE	T.B.
130		
131	'B' FLIGHT PILOTS ROOM	N
132	TRANSFORMER	
133-135	AIRCRAFT SHELTER PENS	B.&Earth
136	HUT.	†
137	HUT (GUN SITE)	N
138	HUT	†
139	ABLUTIONS	N
140		
141		
142		
143		
144		
145	HUT.	N
146	HUT	N
147	HUT	N
148		
149		
150		
151	COMPASS PLATFORM	
152	TRANSFORMER.	
153	PREDICTOR TRANS.	†.
154	HUT	†.
155	HUT	†.
156	HUT (GUN SITE)	N
157	LATRINES	N
158	Do.	N
159	AMMUNITION STORE (RAF REG)	†.B.
160	'A' FLIGHT ARMOURY	N.
161	- " - WIRELESS SECTION	†.B.
162		†.B.
163		P.B
164	- " - DISPERSAL HUT	†.B.
165	GAS DEFENCE HUT	C.I.
166	AIRCRAFT SHELTER PEN	B.&Earth
167	HUT	N.
168	AIRCRAFT SHELTER PEN.	B.&Earth
169	HUT	N.
170	HUT	N.
171	HUT	N.
172	BATTLE H.Q. L.A.A	†.B
173	AIRCRAFT SHELTER PEN	B.&Earth
174	SPEECH BROADCASTING	P.B
175		
176	OLD BATTLE H.Q.	P.B.
177	FLYING CONTROL	†.
178	FLARE PATH HUT	†.
179	OLD BATTLE H.Q.	P.C
180		
181		
182		
183		
184		
185		
	W.T. ETC. (186-193)	
186	W.T. & R.T. BLOCK	P.B
187		
188		
189	H.F-D.F (Bullet & Blast Proof Hut)	†.
190	LATRINE	C.I.
191		
192	D.F. TOWER (War Damaged)	
193	D.F. TOWER Do. Do.	
194		
195		
	SEWAGE DISPOSAL WORKS	
196	STORE	†.B.
197	SEDIMENTATION TANKS (2 Nº)	P.C.
198	PERCOLATING FILTER	P.C.
199	Do. Do.	P.C.
200	HUMUS CHAMBER	P.C.
201		
	REQUISITIONED PROPERTIES	
202(a)	'BOX COTTAGE (War Damaged)	Brick
202(b)	SHED (Demolished)	Do.
203(a)	'WOODLAND DANE	Do.
203(c)	SHED.	Do.
203(c)	Do.	Do.
203(d)	Do.	Do.
204(a)	'ROSEMARIE'	Timber
204(b)	SHED	Do.
205	'VIEW DE FRANCE'	Do.

Right: **Our aerial shot shows the northern extension to the aerodrome, squeezed in between the cemetery and the village in 1943, to try to cater for the increasing number of larger aircraft seeking to land in difficulties.** *Above:* **However this B-17F Fortress from the 365th Bomb Squadron, 305th Bombardment Group chose to land in the opposite direction on September 15, 1943 and so ended up on the edge of Terlingham Manor Farm (Crown Copyright).**

B-17 HERE

scrutinised and special passes issued to all personnel.

The night before the raid took place two Spitfire squadrons flew in and were quickly dispersed. No. 416 Squadron was the first to touch down commanded by Squadron Leader Chadburn, His unit had only been operational since February of that year. The other squadron was No. 616 'South Yorkshire', the last auxiliary squadron to be formed in 1938.

Very few German aircraft were seen in the initial stages of the landing as Spitfires and Typhoons swarmed over the whole area in an umbrella of protection but, as the day's operations wore to a close, packs of FW 190s appeared. Dozens of fighters returned to the coastal aerodromes for re-arming and refuelling during the day, some of which were members of the American 'Eagle' squadrons based at Biggin Hill. In the late evening, a damaged Spitfire of No. 616 Squadron crash-landed in a field just east of the aerodrome.

On November 6, Squadron Leader Palmer, VC, a hero of the First World War, arrived to take charge of the RAF Regiment who had now taken over the defences of Hawkinge. His appointment coincided with a batch of new aircraft silhouette posters which were pasted in the huts. However, they did not help when, four days later, a Liberator belonging to the 93rd USAAF Bomb Group crashed at the aerodrome. There were very few B-24s in the United Kingdom at that time and this particular machine had been detached to fly anti-submarine patrols.

On February 2, 1943 an exercise was held in a lighter vein by the station CO. Twenty-seven 'would-be' escapers made up from pilots and airmen of both No. 91 and No. 277 Squadrons, together with other officers, were dropped from a lorry in the Elham area and were told to make their own way back to the 'drome undetected. The RAF Regiment put out about 100 men, fully armed to search for them. Only seven escapers actually got through. Squadron Leader Harries purloined an army uniform from a house in Elham, and managed to get through the cordon without being challenged. Pilot Officer Hartwell (No. 277 Squadron) and Warrant Officer Waddington (No. 277) temporarily borrowed a local farmer's milk float and, with the assistance of Land Army girls, they dressed in dungarees. They both arrived back at camp, calmly guiding their horse and cart through the barriers to deliver eggs to the Officers' Mess!

In April 1943, No. 91 Squadron moved to Northolt to re-equip with the latest Griffin-engined Spitfire Mk. XII. Their place at Hawkinge was taken by No. 41 Squadron which had received its Mk XIIs in February. This squadron flew on shipping strikes and scrambled to intercept tip-and-run raiders.

Take-offs from Hawkinge were now more hair-raising for the XII was not without its drawbacks. A pronounced swing to the right was caused by the four blades as opposed to the left swing inherent in the three-bladed types. Full left rudder was applied as a matter of course which resulted in some crazy flying and Spitfires were observed leaving the ground in a most ungainly manner. Even landings caused quite a stir among the 'tarmac critics' when XIIs were seen approaching the field sideways but the idiosyncrasies of the mark were soon mastered.

Hawkinge had always been known as a difficult aerodrome on which to land with anything more than two engines and, with a four-engined bomber descending it was like trying to land on a pocket handkerchief. Additional N-S length had been provided by taking over a meadow on the northern side of Aerodrome Road. Ground personnel alerted when a stricken bomber was making for the aerodrome rushed out to remove fences across the road thus increasing the landing length into the meadow.

This had already been done on July 9, when a seriously-damaged Lancaster of No. 460 Squadron with two engines knocked out after a raid on Cologne managed, after repeated attempts, to finally settle on the grass. Brakes squealed in protest but in vain. The smoking Lancaster continued on its original course towards the village failing to negotiate a turn to port which would have taken it into the meadow. Instead it tore into a hastily-evacuated Nissen hut which split apart like a ruptured melon. From the resultant mass of twisted metal there emerged only one crew member who could walk. All the remainder had suffered serious injury, one of whom was only extricated some four hours later.

Another four-engined bomber, this time a B-17 Fortress, also crash-landed at Hawkinge two months later. It swerved off the grass to finally stop outside the aerodrome near Terlingham Manor Farm. Then, in November, a Boston of No. 88 Squadron, piloted by Pilot Officer Gibson who had been badly wounded during a bombing operation on the Pas de Calais, managed to put down at Hawkinge in an almost perfect, three-pointer.

WAR GRAVES PLOT

RUNWAY EXTENSION
ACROSS ROAD

Crashed at Hawkinge. *Above:* **A Spitfire IIA burned beyond recognition in the centre of the aerodrome (Imperial War Museum).**

No. 91 Squadron finally left Hawkinge for good in the third week of June 1943. Later destined to join No. 85 Group of the 2nd Tactical Air Force they had, during their stay, been a most popular unit and had grown from the early reconnaissance unit days, proving without doubt to be one of the finest fighter squadrons. Their high morale, keenness of spirit and dedicated flying won them a fantastic record at this front line station. They had notched up seventy-seven enemy aircraft destroyed, twenty-seven probables and seventy-eight damaged, and in doing so gained a DSO, eleven DFCs, four Bars to the award and five DFMs. Truly a magnificent effort by some of the finest pilots in the Royal Air Force.

Hawkinge was not to remain long without a resident fighter squadron and on June 21 No. 501 'County of Gloucester' Squadron arrived flying Spitfire Vbs under the command of Squadron Leader B. Barthold. This particularly well-known fighter unit had often scrambled from the aerodrome back in the summer months of 1940 and, by the close of that series of famous engagements, had claimed 149 enemy aircraft destroyed. They were now to fly recce patrols, occasional 'Rhubarb' and bomber escort sorties and the inevitable escort duties for the resident rescue

unit. No. 501 Squadron received a full complement of the latest MK IX Spitfires before the end of the year. A common sight at the aerodrome during their stay were Spitfires returning from sorties festooned with an assortment of continental shrubbery protruding from radiators and telegraph wire trailing from tail wheels. Local observer corps posts were ringing the station in increasing numbers explaining that a Spitfire of the squadron had just passed overhead trailing wire from the elevators. Damaged fins and elevators were a constant worry to the engineering officer, not to mention the damage caused by these dangling cheese cutters which sliced neatly through trees and tiles with ease.

Visiting squadrons during this period were from all nationalities: the Belgians with No. 350; the Dutch with their No. 322 Squadron and the Czech No. 313 Squadron.

The RAF Regiment manning the defences around the periphery were so keen to have a go irrespective of what nationality the aircraft was that, subsequently, they had to be rationed with ammunition. They felt that their own contribution to the war effort since the virtual disappearance of the Luftwaffe in the area, was sadly lacking in intensity. They seldom had anything to fire at now except the

occasional stray American fighter which always seemed to approach the aerodrome from under the cliffs and continued at near nought feet along the North Downs. Quite naturally, the gunners wished to illustrate their preparedness, and blasted away. It was good practice anyway.

The new year had barely begun when Hawkinge came under German attack for the first time in several months. On January 21, 1944 aircraft attacked the aerodrome at 9.00 p.m., setting a hut alight, damaging others, and causing injuries to personnel. Night fighters shot down three German aircraft in the vicinity. (Earlier that day, a Liberator had belly-landed on the grass returning damaged from a bombing raid.)

The following month, Prince Bernhardt of the Netherlands visited No. 322 Squadron to present medals to his officers and airmen.

February also saw the arrival of a flight of No. 137 Squadron (part of the 2nd TAF) flying Typhoons. The remainder of the squadron was based at Lympne and although bomber escort missions were flown during that month, bombing sorties carrying 500-pounders did not begin until March. Ample targets in France were provided for the Typhoons, softening up the German defences prior to the Normandy invasion. In April, No.

F ort.   H gc

Eye witness sketches of crashes in 1944. Lieutenant B. C. Sherren was stationed at Hawkinge and drew these at the time. *Above:* 'Fort Sack' on May 1, 1944.

137 re-equipped with rocket-firing Typhoons and, although the squadron had moved to nearby Manston, aircraft occasionally operated from Hawkinge to sweep the Channel, blasting 'E' boats, coastal trawlers and flak ships.

In April, No. 501 Squadron left Hawkinge for Friston and, as preliminary D-Day attacks were stepped up, the station received many VIPs who arrived for talks at Dover Castle, a frequent visitor being General Bernard Montgomery.

The build-up to D-Day resulted in many crashes by returning crippled aircraft as is illustrated by station records of the period:

1.4.44. At 14.00hrs 3 Liberators landed after attacking Stuttgart.

2.4.44. No. 501 Squadron Spitfire (AA743) crashed on take-off.

20.4.44. An American Liberator crashed just west of airfield. There were 4 survivors.

21.4.44. A Boston and 3 Marauders landed — one Marauder belly-flopped; there were no casualties.

27.4.44. A Liberator landed at dusk on 3 engines. Crew OK.

30.4.44. C.O concerned regarding airmen walking across airfield when so many lame aircraft were trying to make their landings.

1.5.44. B-17 Fortress crashed on drome; crew OK.

However, the official records, with their laconic entries, disguise the true dramas as is illustrated in the landing of the Fortress on May 1.

On this day the American 92nd Bomb Group raided the towns of Le Gistmont and Rheims, and a B-17F christened *Fort Sack* assigned to the 325th Bomb Squadron had two of its four engines knocked out. It was the ASR Spitfire V which found the crippled Fortress trailing smoke about half-way over the Channel. The Spitfire guided the bomber back to the coast at the time when personnel were thinking of their NAAFI break. A dozen or so airmen, bunched together and fooling about, were cycling on the perimeter track when, from out of nowhere, or so it seemed, there appeared *Fort Sack* bearing down on them at great speed. The B-17, its silver surface reflecting the sun's rays, just managed to clear the western end of the field before flopping onto the grass, bouncing with such force that one of its undercarriage legs collapsed. The machine had by this time covered over half the available landing distance and was perilously near the village when a wingtip dug into the ground, slewing the aircraft round into the aerodrome extension. The perplexed airmen leaped as one from their cycles, turned them round and fled the way they had come, pedalling furiously. The Fortress came to rest in a huge cloud of dust near the cemetery gates with one wing shielding an absolutely terrified gun crew.

An even more-spectacular landing concerning a B-17 occurred early in 1945, perhaps the most dramatic landing of all. This happened on the afternoon of January 5, when a very lame B-17 suddenly loomed up over the trees at Killing Wood with every intention of landing. The undercarriage was locked down but the port inner engine was missing.

Wing Commander Mike Crossley was Station Commander at the time and saw it all. 'Now as you know', Mike remembered, 'Hawkinge aerodrome was hardly suitable for gigantic four-engined bombers even when they are in the capable hands of the pilot, let alone the navigator as this one turned out to be, the pilot and co-pilot both having been killed during the raid. It was soon evident that the man in charge could not or did not know how to get his remaining throttles right back as the poor old B-17 came sailing across the grass at about ten feet and at about 30 mph above stalling speed. When he saw he couldn't make it he slammed open the throttles and, with a ghastly sort of yawing swoop, just missed the Flying Control Office with his wing tips and then disappeared below the immediate horizon of trees.

'The tarmac was by this time dotted with running figures and, as the B-17 disappeared, everybody stopped and just listened for the crash. Nothing happened except that the roar of the three engines kept on and on with every ear following the general line of sound.

'Suddenly the darned thing appeared again at the same spot of entry as last time and still going too fast and too high. The Flying Control Office, rather unsportingly, fired a red Very light at him, but the unfortunate chap was in no mood to watch a firework display. He came in just the same. Well more or less the same thing happened, but this time a little higher and we were able to watch his unhappy progress round the circuit. There was no question in our minds as to whether he was going to crash or not; it was simply a matter of where he would crash.

'He slammed the nose down and came skidding in across the field with his tail very high looking for all the world as if searching for something. Well the field soon ran out and he charged through a fence hit a bank and came to rest straddled across the road. The tail section broke away and deposited the tail

Avenga   H'ge.

Above: **Avenger June 9, 1944.** *Below:* **Liberator March 1, 1944.**

Lib. H'ge.

gunner on the further side of the road where I found him forlornly sitting when I arrived on the scene only moments later. The last I saw of Master Sergeant Katz — I shall never forget his name — he was strolling off down the road, pursued by the MO in the ambulance, repeating over and over again — ''show me the bastard who will make me fly again . . . show me the b . . . ' The heroic navigator survived, as did Katz, but the rest of the crew were gonners, whether from the sortie or the crash I cannot remember.'

The remarkable job of patching up crashed aircraft was the responsibility of Flight Lieutenant E. Johns, a station engineer of considerable talents who later received the MBE for his magnificent services at Hawkinge. Johns had dealt with practically every type of aeroplane known to the RAF from Moth trainers to heavy bombers. The Hawkinge mechanics and fitters serviced damaged aircraft with dedicated intensity. Very few machines were scrapped without a detailed inspection and were repaired wherever it was possible, in hangars, on the peri-track or under trees near the White Horse dispersal. Inclement weather was no deterrent as portable lights were set up under canvas awnings.

On May 23, 1944, Hawkinge was host to a most unusual type of aircraft, namely the American Grumman Avenger (TBF-1C). Twenty-four of these aircraft arrived from the Royal Naval Air Station at Eglington flown by pilots of Nos. 854 and 855 Squadrons of the Fleet Air Arm who occupied themselves during daylight hours by weapon training before becoming operational on May 31.

By the first week in June, all aircraft had received black and white invasion stripes beneath the wings and around the fuselage. Even the amphibians of No. 277 (ASR) Squadron got their paint job. On the morning of June 5 all station personnel were confined to camp and, just before dawn on the 6th, hundreds of fighters broke the morning stillness and took off in the twilight to take up their positions for the biggest invasion in the history of warfare. The aerodrome once again played host to squadrons designated the task of creating a false warning in the Pas de Calais area. Each day Hawkinge received flights or squadrons from the 2nd Tactical Air Force and an additional watch tower had been constructed to cope with the increased traffic.

Above: Fifteen years after its closure, except for the missing station sign board, the camp remained remarkably undamaged with much of the equipment and fittings still intact. *Below:* However, by 1979, deterioration of the fabric was very evident. The gate post has been hit by a construction lorry as have two of the guard room verandah supports. The fire party block on the left has also been demolished.

The only loss to the resident Fleet Air Arm squadrons took place during the first phase of operations on June 7 when JZ452 failed to return from patrol.

From June 11 to 19, anti-submarine patrols were flown by both squadrons to the west of the 'Neptune/Overlord' convoy routes between the Isle of Wight and Cherbourg. These were in addition to the ASPs flown between the North Foreland and Beachy Head. An attack was delivered on a submerging U-boat on June 12 but as there were no signs of wreckage or oil on the sea it was not claimed.

Then, from the beginning of July, the two squadrons commenced night 'Rover' patrols against shipping off the French, Belgian and Dutch coasts.

Exactly seven days after the Normandy landings, the Germans launched their first revenge weapon, the V1 pilotless robot bomb. The V1 was considerably smaller than a conventional fighter aircraft and was thus harder to hit especially as it flew at around 400 mph. When British fighters followed one it was necessary to approach with extreme caution to within 200 yards or less. At this range a kill had a devastating effect as the explosion of the one-ton warhead often engulfed the attacking machine causing it to crash.

A plan of defence was imperative when it was discovered that the total number of V1s flying over the coast was increasing daily. Anti-aircraft guns of various calibres and aircraft of Fighter Command combined to cover both the North Downs and the Channel. Barrage balloons were the last means of defence and were strung up in a belt round the south-east of London.

The name 'Diver' was subsequently used officially by the RAF to describe fighter patrols to combat the V1 and these became commonplace over south-east England.

The first unit to arrive at Hawkinge for Diver patrols was No. 402 Squadron, a Canadian unit named 'Winnipeg Bears'. They arrived on August 9 with their new Spitfire Mk XIVs under the command of Squadron Leader W. G. Dodd. The long-nosed 'fourteens' were often seen flying through the anti-aircraft barrage following a V1 and, on August 16, the squadron shot down three 'Divers'. One of these failed to explode and went into a shallow glide before crashing into a field near Pledge Farm, tearing through a hedge, missing a tractor by a few feet and spilling the green contents of its warhead across the field.

Hawkinge had already experienced the new weapon when a V1 crashed near No. 6 Bofors site on July 29. Five days later another exploded just behind the flying control office, seriously damaging the Capel 'Y' Service telephone room and slightly injuring two operators. Another blew up over the sick quarters on August 24 causing some damage.

Sharing Hawkinge at the same time during August and September were the Belgians of No. 350 Squadron who arrived for their second stay now under the command of Squadron Leader M. G. L. Donnet. They were engaged in the ever increasing Diver patrols, flying their new Mk XIVs and scored their first kill on August 15.

Above: **The hallowed ground beloved of station Warrant Officers and drill instructors (Shoesmith & Etheridge).** *Below:* **Although the barrack blocks still stand, they are now being converted into private living accommodation.**

No. 402 Squadron left Hawkinge at the end of September as did the Belgian unit which moved to Lympne to make room for No. 132 Squadron of No. 83 Group, 2nd TAF.

Another Canadian unit arrived on September 30 — No. 441 'Silver Fox' Squadron (RCAF) which began bomber escort duties. September had seen two more heavy bomber crashes at Hawkinge when a Lancaster with two engines out overshot the aerodrome on the 11th with another from No. 582 Squadron crash-landing on the 24th. The former aircraft hit a brick air-raid shelter, killing one crew member and injuring three others.

By the end of the year these squadrons had been relieved by No. 611 'West Lancashire' and No. 451 — an Australian unit which had recently arrived in the UK from the Continent.

Winter had taken hold of grass-surfaced Hawkinge with a vengeance, making the movement of aircraft extremely difficult; rutted tracks and hard tufts of grass caused slight accidents to machines controlled by unwary pilots and in January 1945 operations were almost at a standstill. Certain areas of the aerodrome had also become dumping grounds and boxes of ammunition lay beneath the trees whilst spare wheels wings and tail units littered the floor of what was once No. 2

hangar. Engine crates were stacked outside the workshop where personnel of No. 86 MU had left them after hectic engine changes.

The Officers' Mess, ante-room and hall were beginning to look like a scrapdealer's yard for over mantlepieces, on corner tables and even hanging from ceilings, were the twisted and bent but highly-prized relics of an airman's war. Black swastikas and crosses, coloured emblems and shields all denoted the fast disappearance of the Luftwaffe's crack fighter units. It was a far cry from the summer days of 1940.

The new year saw the gradual run down of the station as the ground war moved further east beyond the range of UK-based Spitfires. The Australian squadron moved out in early February and No. 277 (ASR) Squadron was officially disbanded on the 15th of that month.

Although No. 611 Squadron were promised re-equipping with the North American Mustang only one sortie was flown with the new aircraft before the squadron transferred to Hunsdon.

After the rush and tumble of so many visiting squadrons, the sudden inactivity was somehow fraught with a kind of uncertainty and a substantial part of the normal working day was spent on a frenzied clean-up campaign. Surrender of the German armed forces on May 8 gave strength and purpose to airmen on their off-duty hours. The stillness of many a night was broken periodically by returning revellers from their binges in Folkestone and the collapse of the Third Reich produced a variable concoction of schoolboy antics from all quarters. A Hillman van was seen hurtling round the perimeter track with at least thirty people on board until the petrol gave out and WAAFs on the station began to check their kit when various articles of female underwear were seen flying from the most exposed places. The VE-Day celebrations went on for some time and no one seemed to mind what happened for the next day or so.

Later, activity of a different sort induced a greater sense of responsibility among airmen when returning POWs were brought to the aerodrome from the continent. The Dutch Royal Family also arrived and were escorted back to Holland from the station. King Peter of Yugoslavia also returned to his country from Hawkinge.

Inevitably, with the collapse of Japan on August 14, more celebrations broke out but the station personnel at last realised that peace was finally at hand and that demobilisation was just around the corner.

Pilots were scarce now and so were aircraft. A few Martinets remained and, in contrast, several Vengeances had been flown in and parked rather haphazardly near the one and only remaining hangar. These latter aircraft, formerly in Naval service, were to be converted and modified for drogue towing, necessitating alterations to the fuel tanks and the attachment of a wind-driven winch to the starboard side of the rear cockpit. Six airmen were employed on this particular task, posted in from their parent unit based at Hornchurch.

Modified aircraft were taxied back and forth from their original parking area and the workshop by the fitters and mechanics who, it seemed, were exempt from the mandatory discipline from any form of NCO. As it was, nobody thought of asking them what they were supposed to be doing. Enjoying complete freedom from petty rules and instructions they found unforeseen pleasure in guiding these fat-bellied brutes round the tarmac perimeter on any pretext.

Eventually, modifications were completed and the airmen were out of a job. They returned to their unit only to be told that they had been permanently posted to Hawkinge. They returned but communications had fouled up somewhere for it was discovered that no one knew their correct destination. In all, seven trips, back and forth to Hawkinge,

The station church dedicated to St. Hugh of Lincoln (Shoesmith & Etheridge).

The church was demolished in the late 1960s at the same time as No. 1 hangar. The foundation and altar steps are now all that remain.

were carried out in as many weeks. Their final reception at the aerodrome was one of complete disbelief for this little band of nomads realised with a deal of apprehension that they were all alone. The aerodrome was completely deserted — both personnel and aircraft had disappeared.

Thereafter the Air Ministry decided to make Hawkinge the new location for No. 3 Armament Practice School (APS) until a more permanent site could be found. Wing Commander H. C. Kennard, who had served with No. 66 Squadron during the summer of 1940, was the now Station Commander and received the first squadrons, Nos. 1 and 122, both flying Mk IX Spitfires, which arrived for their peace-time training programme during September. The Ministry did not, however,

Beautiful lines . . . shapely . . . quick to react . . . lovely in a tight corner . . . ! Hawkinge's guardian angels.

waste any time in relocating the APS and on November 7 this moved to the north of England leaving Hawkinge non-operational and reduced to care and maintenance.

The words 'care and maintenance' were like a sentence of death. No more would squadrons arrive to be cared for, their aircraft fussed over, young pilots revered and respected. No more would the mess corridors echo with the boisterous shouts of youthful fighter pilots. Gone were the days of scrambles, nervous tension and soiled cockpits. Gone also the cheerful competition of 'kills', the hollow sadness over lost friends and the binges at the local.

For the next eleven months, the station was manned only by civilians but, in July 1947, the arrival of the WAAF Technical Training Unit under the command of Group Officer N. Dinnie brought life back to the old 'drome. Courses were run in drill and administration for other ranks and refresher courses for WAAF officers. Those who passed out successfully from Hawkinge found themselves posted to Recruit Training Centres in various parts of the British Isles. One of the most notable NCOs who served there at that time was Sergeant Whitton-Brown, daughter-in-law of the great aviator. Parades were a major feature of the type of training which the WAAFs were subjected to throughout their stay and, not the least, was a visit from HRH The Duchess of Gloucester who presented a silver cup to a long-serving member.

After the war, the immortal Spitfire appeared on static display at many RAF stations. These aircraft were, in the main, no longer serviceable and were given a place of honour at or near the main gate or entrance. RAF Hawkinge was no exception and a fine specimen, a Mark IX which had served with No. 433 (RCAF) in 1944, stood on the site of the old Sergeants' Mess which had been bombed in 1940.

In December 1955, the Home Gliding Centre was set up at the aerodrome to train ATC cadets who arrived for one week courses

under the expert guidance of RAF pilots and experienced civilians. The thrills of gliding were, to say the least, quite tame compared with powered flight. Accidents happened of course and the most notable to occur was a glider controlled by a young seventeen-year-old which managed to land on the roof of the village hairdresser's shop!

Gliders were stored in canvas hangars on the eastern boundary and, while they were not original Bessoneau-type structures, they did follow the same flimsy principle. A particularly devastating storm occurred in January 1958 which blew down these fine tapestries causing infinite damage to the aerofoils within. A dozen or so airmen were posted to the aerodrome the following month to carry out repairs to the collapsed glider hangars and they, in turn, brought unforseen problems with them.

Restoration began almost immediately by stripping the framework of canvas and replacing broken wooden spars, no mean task in the middle of winter on a particularly draughty aerodrome. Dressed in an assortment of bits of uniform and civilian attire, the 'erks' wore anything which came to hand and looked like mountain bandits from Outer Mongolia, and were in direct contrast to the smartly dressed drill instructors and other RAF personnel. Apart from making themselves very unpopular with the instructors by whistling after the girls marching to and from classrooms, the so called 'bandits' used the NAAFI building which had not been in use for a long time. Nightly sing-song and beer sessions round a soaking piano provided trainees and some staff with a congenial, if somewhat bawdy, insight into service life.

It was dusk on Friday, December 8, that Royal Air Force Station Hawkinge disappeared from public view with dignity and ceremony and entered into a world of obscurity. A cold wind blew across the aerodrome as RAF and WRAF personnel, marched and paraded with the Central Bands of the Royal Air Force. Prayers and blessings

The only female form we found on the camp site in September 1979 was this faded pin-up left by a long-forgotten airman on his locker.

took place in front of No. 1 hangar, the only survivor to have withstood the ravages of war. The Last Post was played as the RAF Ensign was slowly lowered for the last time. Finally, in the presence of that most senior and distinguished of a long line of station commanders, Marshal of the Royal Air Force, Sir William Dickson, the march past took place.

Speeches over, eminent guests were whisked away into the darkness. It had been a nostalgic moment for most and all had been proud to be present on this sad occasion to pay tribute to this once famous station.

Seven years went by until one quiet Sunday afternoon in mid-June 1968 when film director Harry Saltzman arrived with his entourage to transform the old aerodrome back to its former wartime colour and sounds to produce

Right: **When MK356 was taken to RAF Locking on the closure of Hawkinge, there was a storm of protest from Folkestone Council which wanted to retain it for display on the Leas (E. Kettle).** *Below:* **Today it is part of the RAF collection at St. Athan in South Wales although, Folkestone would dearly like it returned.**

The Spitfire IX gate guardian MK356 was re-coded M5690 indicating that it was a non-flying instructional airframe. (The correct description should have been 5690M.)

scenes for his epic film *Battle of Britain*. Wooden dispersal huts and large mock hangars were erected on the exact locations of the originals. Bomb craters appeared in the field to simulate the attacks of 1940. Static machines, Spitfires of various marks, some no longer airworthy, stood almost proudly on the grass as if given a new lease of life. For two weeks film sequences were shot in a mixture of bright sunlight and occasional rain showers.

It is difficult to describe the emotions of those present as many had first-hand experience of the battles fought over south-east England. Many memories were revived as thoughts travelled back to the events of thirty years before. However, in no time at all, it was

all over and the aerodrome returned to its former placid existence. Cattle once again grazed over the green expanse which had, for over fifty years, been a legend in the defence of England.

By 1964 the Ministry of Defence could find no further use for the small, grass-surfaced aerodrome, and fifty acres of land and buildings were offered for auction on July 9. Three years later a final package of seventy-seven acres went under the auctioneers hammer at the Royal Star Hotel, Maidstone. The aerodrome had finally gone.

Today, however, much remains to be seen of Hawkinge for the nostalgic visitor or ex-serviceman. Several of the buildings on the

aerodrome itself still stand, some occupied for industrial or agricultural purposes, the remainder fortunately having largely escaped the attentions of vandals. Across the road the old guardhouse overlooks the accommodation area currently being converted by the local council for the construction of a housing estate. Nearby the second Officers' Mess stands intact, ready for its new role as a young persons' hostel.

Overlooking the English Channel, by and large Hawkinge still remains to be viewed as a typical Battle of Britain aerodrome and, although the sounds of battle are gone, it stands as a ghostly memorial to its former glories.

After so many years of study devoted to the history of Hawkinge, Roy Humphreys was upset that nothing existed to record its former glories. It was entirely due to his personal efforts that this memorial now stands on a small plot in front of the gymnasium beside Aerodrome Road. So that part of the station life could be permanently preserved, Roy chipped out the compass-swinging circle *(above right)* from the concrete floor of No. 3 hangar *(above left)* and had it incorporated in the memorial which was dedicated on April 29, 1978. He now regularly maintains the small plot and has installed seats for visitors who wish to sit and contemplate the exciting events that have taken place at Hawkinge over more than sixty-five years of aviation.

Gravesend

BY RAY MUNDAY

Gravesend (Chalk) Airport lay two miles south of the River Thames at 5125N and 0024E. Opened in June 1932, it became a thriving pre-war aerodrome. The picture *above* looking south-east shows the flying control building, clubhouse and hangars (Flight). *Below:* Forty-four years later, urban sprawl has completely engulfed the aerodrome, only a small loop of perimeter track remaining on the eastern side of Thong Lane.

Gravesend Airport was established in June 1932 at Thong Lane, Chalk, on high ground overlooking the River Thames. Two small hangars and a combined control tower and clubhouse, together with the usual ancillary buildings, were built on the eastern edge of the 148-acre grass site. Captain Edgar Percival often used the fields when he flew in to visit his brother who was a doctor practising in Gravesend and it is reputed to have been his idea for the airport to be sited there. A flying school, air-taxi service and workshops were established and, at a later date, a large barn hangar, 130 feet x 100 feet, was erected.

The airport was named London East — Gravesend and the aim was to encourage airlines to use the airport as an alternative landing place to Croydon. Croydon was, at that time, the main airport for London but it often became shrouded by fog caused by coal fires and it was forced to close for many hours at a time. Airliners of KLM, Swissair, Sabena and Deutsche Lufthansa did in fact use the airport on diversion but not on the scale that had been hoped for by the operating company.

In 1933, Edgar Percival established his works in the small hangars and it was from Gravesend that he turned out the Gulls and Mew Gulls which were arguably the most successful sports and racing aircraft of their day. Many races were won, and records broken, by aircraft built by Percival. Jean Batten, Beryl Markham, Amy Mollison, Alex Henshaw and Percival himself, all set records in Percival aircraft, several of the attempts starting and finishing at Gravesend.

When Percival transferred his works to Luton, he was replaced at Gravesend in March 1937 by Essex Aero Limited whose Managing Director was R. J. Cross, held by some to be the finest aero engineer when it came to modifying and preparing aircraft for racing and record attempts. The famous De Havilland Comet G-ACSS was flown by Alec Clouston and Victor Ricketts in March 1938, when they set new records for the England to New Zealand and return flight, whilst Mew Gull G-AXEF was in the hands of Alex Henshaw in February 1939 when new records were set for the England to Capetown round

Above: **De Havilland DH83 Fox Moth G-ACGN of Gravesend Aviation Ltd., on the apron outside the 'Law' hangar in 1934. A four-passenger charter aircraft of the company, it could be hired for about one shilling and sixpence (7½ pence) per mile (via P. Connolly).**
Below: **Looking across the back gardens of the Riverview Park estate to where the hangars once stood.**

trip. Both these aircraft were prepared for the attempts by Essex Aero, and both survive to this day.

With the expansion of the RAF in the late 1930s, No. 20 Elementary and Reserve Flying Training School was set up in late 1937 at Gravesend and pilots were trained for both the RAF and the Fleet Air Arm. Gradually the emphasis shifted from civil aircraft to service types and in September 1939 the aerodrome was requisitioned by the government and it became a satellite of Biggin Hill in No. 11 Group of Fighter Command.

Pilots were accommodated in the control tower as well as at Cobham Hall, the nearby home of the Darnley family. The Laughing Waters roadhouse on the A2 road was also used to accommodate ground crews as well as local commandeered houses. Aircraft were dispersed around the aerodrome, together with hastily erected Nissen huts and machine gun emplacements.

No. 20 ERFTS moved out shortly after war was declared and No. 32 Squadron moved in in January 1940. No. 32 Squadron spent three

months at Gravesend with Hurricanes and were followed by No. 610 'County of Chester' Squadron who flew their Spitfires during the Dunkirk evacuation. Many scraps with numerically superior fighter forces occurred and the Squadron lost two commanding officers during this spell, Squadron Leaders Franks and Smith, both being killed in action. Replacing No. 610 Squadron when they moved away to Biggin Hill in July was No. 604 'County of Middlesex' Squadron equipped with Blenheim 1Fs. This fighter version of the twin-engined Blenheim had been converted at the Southern Railway works at Ashford by installing a four-gun pack slung under the fuselage. Numerous night patrols were carried out together with searchlight co-operation patrols but, in spite of several emergency night take-offs, no contact was made with the enemy. No. 72 Squadron also spent some weeks at Gravesend at this time whilst detached from Biggin Hill.

With the Battle of Britain now entering its early stages, No. 501 'County of Gloucester' Squadron moved into Gravesend on July 27,

1940. This was an Auxiliary Air Force Unit flying Hurricanes and, at this stage of the war, many of the pilots were the original Auxiliary members. Amongst illustrious names, two Sergeant Pilots are well remembered: J. H. 'Ginger' Lacey and D. A. S. McKay, both surviving the battle and the war.

On July 29, a large formation of Ju 87s and escorting Bf 109s was engaged and the Squadron claimed six of the enemy shot down and six damaged. No. 501 Squadron used Hawkinge aerodrome as their forward base, to which the aircraft departed soon after first light each day. Constant patrols took place, often engaging enemy aircraft which were attacking shipping convoys in the Channel or in harbour. Sometimes a return would be made to Gravesend during the day, but often this would not be until the evening. On August 1 for example, No. 501 was at readiness at Hawkinge by 4.42 a.m.

On August 4, the Squadron carried out air-to-air firing practice at Holbeach range, Sutton Bridge, which, in the situation that they faced, must have seemed superfluous. Gradually the pace of the battle stepped up and, because of the constant strain on the pilots' nerves, accidents occurred. Pilot Officer Parkin undershot when landing at Gravesend and Sergeants Howarth and Wilkinson collided on the ground in bad weather. None of the pilots was injured, but much needed aircraft were written off.

On August 8 the battle started in earnest and, on each succeeding day, No. 501 Squadron continued to carry out interception patrols, sometimes finding the enemy aircraft and engaging them in combat but at other times encountering only empty skies. On three days, the 9th, 10th and 11th, the sky had

Above: **The 'Faithful Annies' of No. 20 Elementary Reserve Flying Training School aligned before Gravesend's control tower in 1939. The fluttering White Ensign distinguishes the naval section of No. 20 ERFTS. Avro Anson N5291, after long service with various training units, was struck off charge on February 7, 1945 (S. Parsonson).** *Below:* **Does some latter-day Sappho wax lyrical in the groves of surburbia and do modern Leanders find their Hellespont in Gravesend Reach? The same view in October 1979 across Sapho (sic) Park from Leander Drive.**

plenty of cloud cover but on the 12th the day was fine and clear and a force of thirty-plus Ju 87s was encountered at 3,000-4,000 feet between Deal and Ramsgate. Several aircraft were claimed as destroyed but Flying Officer K. Lukaszewicz was lost in this action. Later in the day (and on the following day) the Squadron operated from Gravesend as bombing had temporarily closed Hawkinge for flying, but, by 4.00 a.m. on the 15th, the twelve Hurricanes were back at Hawkinge engaging successive waves of attackers. On the 18th two pilots were killed, Pilot Officer J.

W. Bland and Flight Lieutenant G. E. B. Stoney, and four other pilots had to bale out of their doomed Hurricanes after hectic dog-fights had broken out over southern Kent. When the remnants of the squadron returned to base, they were ordered to defend Biggin Hill which was under attack. Overcast conditions, together with rain and high winds, combined to enable the Squadron to get some rest during the next two days.

On August 24 the day was fine and clear and a large formation of enemy aircraft was engaged before landing at Hawkinge. At

Four-hundred-year-old Cobham Hall has seen many historic events — from providing a honeymoon suite for King Charles I to providing quarters for RAF aircrew from Gravesend in WWII.

The modern motel 'The Inn on the Lake' on the M2 stands on the site of the former Laughing Waters hotel burnt down in the 1960s and used during the battle for ground crew accommodation.

12.45 p.m. another large force was intercepted after it had carried out a devastating attack on Manston aerodrome. On this day Pilot Officer P. Zenker was shot down by Bf 109s and killed. Throughout the remainder of August and into September the same pattern of operations was carried out. Some days were hectic, particularly the 30th when enemy bombing smashed Biggin Hill, the sector station, causing telephone communication to be put out of action. On September 2, bombs fell on Gravesend aerodrome injuring two soldiers, and Flying Officer A. T. Rose-Price was killed on the day that he joined No. 501 Squadron, when his Hurricane, L1578, was shot down near Ashford. The action continued every day with the resources of No. 11 Group being stretched to the limit.

In the afternoon of September 4, fifteen He 111s approached Gravesend aerodrome but turned away before the Hurricanes could take off. On this day further bombs were dropped in the vicinity of the aerodrome. Early in the morning of the 6th, the squadron engaged a force of approximately 100 enemy aircraft over Ashford and lost three pilots in the subsequent dog-fights: Pilot Officer H. C. Adams in V6612; Sergeant O. V. Houghton in V6646 and Sergeant G. W. Pearson in P3516. The following day the squadron intercepted the largest formations of the Luftwaffe that they had met to date comprising four waves of bombers escorted by Messerschmitt Bf 109s and 110s.

At midday on September 10, orders were received for No. 501 Squadron to move to Kenley.

On September 11, No. 66 Squadron moved into Gravesend with their Spitfires — they had been one of the first squadrons to be equipped with the new fighter back in 1938. They had some experienced fighter pilots, amongst whom Flight Lieutenant Bob Oxspring and Pilot Officer 'Dizzy' Allen survived the war and have described some of their experiences in recently published books. The squadron continued the action with daily interception patrols either from Gravesend or Hawkinge

Above: **A Debden-based Bristol Blenheim IF of No. 29 Squadron at Gravesend in 1939, possibly during the August air exercises of that year (S. Parsonson).** *Bottom:* **'And innocence is closing up his eyes' — Michael Drayton 1563-1631. A dimunitive resident of Whinfell Way, Gravesend, all unaware of what has gone before, dribbles his rubber ball over the spot that the machine of war once straddled.** *Below:* **The partially-reconstructed hangar from Gravesend was re-erected at Northfleet Industrial Estate after the closure of the aerodrome in 1956 (Ray Munday).**

and, on September 15, No. 66 Squadron was in the thick of the fighting.

After this date the weather deteriorated but regular interceptions and dog-fights caused the loss of five pilots whilst the squadron was at Gravesend — Flight Lieutenant K. McL. Gillies in X4320 on October 4; Pilot Officer G. H. Corbett in R6779 and Sergeant R. A. Ward in N3043 on the 8th; Pilot Officer H. W. Reilley in R6800 on the 17th and Pilot Officer J. R. Mather in P7539 on the 27th.

As the attacks on England decreased by day

with the Luftwaffe switching to night bombing, No. 66 Squadron was posted on October 30 to West Malling.

On October 7, 1940, No. 421 Flight was formed at Gravesend on the personal instigation of the Prime Minister whilst No. 66 Squadron was still stationed there. This flight was used to patrol the sky high over the Channel to report on the build up of the Luftwaffe air fleets for their attacks on England. The flight was formed with a nucleus of personnel from No. 66 Squadron

Gravesend in November 1940 courtesy of Luftflotte Kdo. 2 (via Christopher Elliott).

and used the same code on their aircraft — LZ — but with a hyphen placed between the L and the Z. When originally formed, No. 421 Flight was equipped with Hurricanes until the Commanding Officer, Flight Lieutenant Patrick Green, personally requested the Air Officer Commanding, to allow them to fly Spitfires. Whilst at Gravesend, Sergeant C. A. H. Ayling was shot down and killed on October 11.

Although we are told that the Ultra code secrets contributed little to the defence of Britain at this period of the war, it is interesting to conjecture if Mr. Churchill and Air Marshal Sir Hugh Dowding used the special flight to confirm facts that they already knew from the code deciphers, thus being able to use the available defending force to the best advantage. No. 421 Flight moved to West Malling on October 30.

On November 3, No. 141 Squadron with Defiant night fighters moved to Gravesend from Gatwick and were joined shortly afterwards by No. 85 Squadron flying Hurricanes. The latter was commanded by Squadron Leader Peter Townsend. These two squadrons operated in the night fighter role until 1941 when various squadrons, mainly flying Spitfires, spent time at Gravesend.

On October 20, 1940, Spitfire II 'AMANGABAD', P7445 of No. 421 Flight returned to Gravesend badly chewed for this memorable landing. The pilot, Sergeant A. W. P.

RAF photo taken June 29, 1950 showing the 1942-43 extensions (Crown Copyright).

Spears was unhurt despite the extensive damage (Donald Elliott). The cottages of Sara Park, basking in the October sun, look across the spot where the aircraft came to grief.

The aerodrome landing area was still grass with the N-S and E-W strips 933 yards in length and the NE-SW direction fifty yards longer. The main SE-NW dimension was 1,333 yards. During 1942 and 1943 extensions were constructed lengthening the N-S to 1,700 yards and the E-W to 1,800 yards. Fuel storage at this time amounted to 32,000 gallons of aviation and 1,500 of MT spirit and 400 gallons of oil. Close on 650,000 rounds of small-arms ammunition were available.

The extensions enabled the aerodrome to accommodate three squadrons and three USAAF fighter units were attached to the station for a short time. Occasionally, bomber aircraft returning from raids on the Continent would land at Gravesend owing to shortage of fuel or injuries to the crew. On one such occasion, nineteen American Marauders arrived unexpectedly; nevertheless the station fed the 105 US airmen, refuelled and made emergency repairs to the aircraft and despatched them to their home base within three hours.

In the early part of 1944, during the 'little blitz' when the enemy attempted to re-open the night assault on London, several bombs fell on or near the aerodrome but it did not suffer serious damage. Airmen from

Gravesend sometimes gave assistance to the local authorities when incendiary bombs fell in the district.

In April 1944 it was decided to base No. 140 Wing at Gravesend with the Mosquito bombers of Nos. 21, 464 (Australian) and No. 487 (New Zealand) Squadrons. These aircraft were used to soften up targets in France prior to the D-Day invasion. However, these operations were brought to a premature close when the V1 flying bombs commenced operations against southern England. The intensity of these pilotless aircraft, flying at high speed in the vicinity of Gravesend aerodrome, and the necessity to ring the area with captive barrage balloons, forced the wing to move to Thorney Island. After this sudden, enforced closure, Gravesend became the control centre for guidance of aircraft through the balloon defences and, with the cessation of hostilities in Europe, Gravesend was put on a care and maintenance basis with the large hangar being used for the demobilisation of naval personnel from Chatham.

After the war, the buildings were used for a time for storage of surplus service equipment. Essex Aero then took over the large hangar and attempted a limited amount of aircraft work but they were heavily committed in other areas and, apart from some ATC gliding, the aerodrome was only used for industry. Essex Aero had attempted to revitalise the aerodrome but Gravesend Borough Council refused to allow the wartime additions to be consolidated into the post-war aerodrome. This effectively extinguished the airfield as such and Essex Aero went into liquidation in April 1956. The Air Ministry finally relinquished control in June and, since that time, the large private housing estate of Riverview Park has been built on the area of the pre-war aerodrome and two schools and a sports centre with playing fields occupy most of the wartime extensions.

Today, all that is left in situ of Gravesend aerodrome are several lengths of perimeter track. The large barn hangar was dismantled and re-erected on the Northfleet Industrial Estate, albeit without the workshops and offices down each side. The fourteen pilots who died during the Battle of Britain whilst flying from Gravesend are commemorated on a plaque in the Thong Lane Sports Centre.

Above: **Hurricane Mk Is of No. 79 Squadron parked at Gravesend during the last year of peace. The houses of Thong village lie behind AL-M with Randall and Shorne Woods in the distance (S. Parsonson).** *Bottom:* **Looking down Sirdar Strand forty years later, beyond the spot where the fighters once stood to the same woods in the background.**

The plaque to the fourteen pilots that died flying from Gravesend (Ray Munday).

Manston

BY THE LATE

FLYING OFFICER WILLIAM FRASER

Flying began at Manston in 1916 when the Admiralty sought to replace their inadequate landing facilities at Detling (near Maidstone) and Westgate on the nearby cliff top. The first wooden huts were erected on the recently-acquired land beside the A253 to Ramsgate in February, the first aircraft moving in during May. By the end of the year two separate units had been established at Manston: the operational War Flight and a training school for flying the Handley-Page bomber.

The strategic position of Manston for the defence of the capital was demonstrated the following year when German Gothas began to bomb London. Enemy formations were intercepted on July 7 and August 22, one Gotha on the latter raid being brought down close to Manston at Vincent's Farm.

Meanwhile, the Admiralty were firmly committed to the permanent establishment of the aerodrome and work began on additional

Top: Looking the length of the workshop of No. 1 Section of the School of Technical Training 1936/37, a veritable treasure cave of vintage aircraft. Among the more readily identifiable are, from left to right, a Westland Wapiti, a Vickers Vildebeest, a De Havilland Gipsy Moth and the tail of a Saro Cloud flying boat. *Above:* October 1979 and Manston aerodrome is now under German occupation! At least the site of the old workshop is, being utilized for the storage of Volkswagen cars.

The present-day RAF Officers' Mess was once Pouce's Farmhouse, requisitioned during WWI as quarters for the Station CO.

Today the Manston CO lives in Holmecroft, another cottage taken over during the First War expansion of the aerodrome.

Avro Ansons and North American Harvard trainers in front of the old watch office at Manston aerodrome on October 2, 1939. The early-pattern roundels and camouflage are of interest as are the gas detector paint diamonds forward of the fins. Civilians seem to be in firm control of aircraft marshalling — either this or the Homburg-hatted gentleman in the right foreground is executing a nifty Highland fling! (Popperfoto).

Forty years later in October 1979, the new control tower dominates the skyline and all traces of the former signals square and watch office have gone.

facilities. These included permanent hangars to replace the canvas structures, underground hangars, a huge workshop and accommodation for over 3,600 officers and men. At the same time many underground shelters lined with railway sleepers were excavated in the chalk.

On the amalgamation of the Royal Naval Air Service with the Royal Flying Corps into the new Royal Air Force on April 1, 1918, it was provisionally decided that three bomber training squadrons should be stationed at No. 203 Training Depot Station, Manston. The War Flight was also increased to three flights from No. 219 Squadron which still had its headquarters at Westgate.

With the Armistice in November 1918, Manston was partly used as a demobilisation centre although its role in training men for the new RAF continued. In 1920 the first elements arrived for the establishment of the School of Technical Training (Men) and, later that year, the RAF Permanent Building Committee held a conference on site to tie up the loose ends following the wartime acquisition of the area. Pouce's farmhouse, requisitioned from a German alien Fraulein Luhn, was retained, in spite of the post-war objections of the former owner, to become the Commanding Officer's residence. Holmcroft (formerly known as Rose Cottage) and two cottages adjoining the headquarters offices were also retained.

The following year the OC, Wing Commander Primrose, unveiled the War Memorial which still stands in Manston village.

In 1924 work began on the married quarters in Manston Court Road and, at the same time, the wartime underground hangars were demolished, the work being inspected by the Chief of the Air Staff, Air Marshal Sir Hugh Trenchard. The after effects of the underground tunnelling had an unfortunate consequence shortly thereafter when a hole some twenty to thirty feet across and ten feet deep appeared in the centre of the parade ground. Further subsidence occurred in February 1929.

A succession of squadrons were posted to Manston during the inter-war years and by the beginning of 1936 the station was once again in course of expansion. Extra huts were erected to accommodate the new arrivals but these were not sufficient to house a further increase in personnel which took place in June 1938 and a tented camp had to be erected on the outskirts to provide for 700 men.

Intensive bombing, the construction of the huge emergency runway and dispersals and post-war changes have now completely altered the face of the aerodrome compared with what it was like during the Battle of Britain. This is Manston as it was photographed at 10.35 a.m. on January 11, 1939 from 11,000ft.

GAS HUT

NORTHERN GRASS

PARADE GROUND

PUBLIC ROAD

OLD WATCH OFFICE

SITE OF PRESENT-DAY
CONTROL TOWER

A253

Led by a Warrant Officer, airmen emerge from the gas hut at Manston in 1938 after one of the most unpopular parades, the testing of gas masks. The corporal is slightly out of fashion wearing the 'dog collar' tunic (Charles E. Brown).

'Seagull to Manston Tower. On the northern grass now'. The noxious vapours apparently agreed with the hawthorn bush which now approximates the site of the hut. The hangar was destroyed in the bombing.

During the worsening international crisis in September that year the aerodrome was camouflaged, bomb and ammunition dumps set up and the station prepared against ground attack by the digging of trenches and erection of machine gun posts. On the declaration of war, the School for Technical Training was dispersed to other sites and No. 3 Squadron arrived to occupy the aerodrome with Nos. 235 and 253 Fighter Squadrons being formed on the station. Over the next few months, all three squadrons were transferred, their places being taken up by No. 79 and No. 600 'City of London' Squadron.

In March 1940 Polish personnel, over-flowing from Eastchurch on the Isle of Sheppey, began to arrive. That same month a Blenheim from No. 600 Squadron crashed on the aerodrome and burst into flames. For a vain rescue attempt to free one of the passengers in which he was badly burned, the pilot, Flying Officer Anthony Tollemache, was awarded the Empire Gallantry Medal, being one of the first recipients of the George Cross instituted by King George VI which replaced the EGM.

Squadrons from Manston were now constantly over France keeping the Luftwaffe from the Dunkirk beaches. No. 264 Squadron was operating from Manston in Defiants which had all their firepower emanating from the rear cockpits. It took the Germans a short time to catch on to this and, attacking from the rear, many of them were cut to pieces over Dunkirk. The station was visited at the end of

The base of the hangar now forms a convenient car park for the control tower.

May by Marshal of the Royal Air Force Lord Trenchard, Captain Harold Balfour, MP, the Under Secretary of State for Air, and General Ironside, the GOC Home Forces. Meanwhile the Poles, after assembling at Manston, were sent off to Blackpool. Wing Commander R. B. Jordan took over for a short period in June and recalls, 'I was only there for Dunkirk and was responsible for re-fuelling, re-arming and feeding the squadrons which flew in from various fighter stations in No. 11 Group. They operated from Manston during the day or night and returned to their own base when

they had finished their patrols. They were hectic days!'

The beginning of the month had seen the first German bombs on Manston. High explosive and incendiaries were dropped near the explosive store but no damage was done, and some of them failed to explode. Following this incident, No. 1 'M' Balloon Unit was sent to assist in the defence of the station. Before July was over, the Duke of Kent, the Secretary of State for Air and the Inspector General of the RAF had all visited Manston, looking at the preparations being made for the blow

Left: Station parade at Manston in 1938 (Charles E. Brown).
Right: No hobnails ring to bellowed commands at Manston's old parade ground today — the whole square has now been completely grassed and many of the huts demolished.

which must inevitably fall, knowing that across the channel the Luftwaffe was preparing for Eagle Day.

At Manston activity increased as the squadrons from other No. 11 Group stations came and went from their dispersals at this forward aerodrome. August came but the weather was bad and 'Adlertag' was postponed. On the 11th the preliminaries were under way with attacks on shipping and raids on Dover and Portland. Next day, the enemy was over Kent in force, bombing the radar stations and the aerodromes of Manston, Lympne, and Hawkinge. At 12.50 p.m. Manston was attacked and bombed at low altitude by fifteen Bf 110s and some Heinkels. As the bombs fell, No. 65 Squadron were taking off in their Spitfires and somehow most of them managed to get off the ground. The raid lasted for five minutes and in that time two hangars were damaged, workshops were destroyed and one civilian clerk was killed. When the chalk dust had settled, the aerodrome was seen to be pitted with about a hundred bomb-craters and was unserviceable until the next day, although Nos. 65 and 54 Squadrons managed to land their Spitfires.

The next attack was made by nine Bf 110s at 12.10 p.m. on the 15th. Two of the enemy aircraft were destroyed, one by a Royal Artillery Bofors and one by a RAF Hispano machine gun fitted to a ground mounting and fired by No. 600 Squadron air gunners from the ground. Four hangars were damaged and one large crater was made in the centre of the aerodrome.

The next day the station was attacked again, this time by eight Bf 109s. One Blenheim and one Spitfire were destroyed by machine gun fire and two other Blenheims damaged but there were no casualties. On the 18th, at 3.30 p.m., twelve Heinkel 111s raked Manston with cannon and machine gun fire in a surprise attack. There had been no warning and crews servicing Spitfires were caught out in the open — one airman was killed, fifteen were injured and two Spitfires were destroyed. More attacks were made on the 20th and 22nd and hangars in the East Camp were damaged but there were no casualties.

On August 24, No. 264 Defiant Squadron was ordered from Hornchurch to Manston to provide defensive cover for the battered aerodrome. At 12.50 p.m. one section of the squadron was in the air, whilst the remainder was refuelling, when twenty bombers complete with a heavy fighter escort came hurtling down on to the station. Ground defences opened up and No. 600 Squadron's personnel fired any weapon they could find while the Defiants were trying desperately to get off the ground. This was the worst attack yet and seven men were killed, the landing ground being covered with craters. Unexploded bombs were everywhere, buildings and aircraft were burning fiercely, communications had been cut and the station was completely isolated. The local Fire Brigades and RAF personnel fought to control the blaze and rescue weapons and stores.

This raid is incorrectly dated in the station record of operations as occurring on the 25th. Also no mention is made of the alleged mutiny of ground personnel who, according to other sources, took cover in the underground shelters and refused to come out. The record book briefly states that: 'Later it was decided to evacuate permanently all administrative personnel and those not required in connection with Station defence and servicing of aircraft. Accommodation for evacuated personnel was found in Westgate.' From August 28 to September 5 the Operations Record Book is blank although there is no evidence that pages have been removed from the original now in the Public Record Office at Kew — Ed.

On August 28, the station was inspected by the Prime Minister, Winston Churchill. He saw an aerodrome that was barely serviceable, craters everywhere and flagged unexploded bombs. The next day he wrote to the Secretary of State and Chief of Air Staff saying that he was perturbed at the time being taken to repair damaged aerodromes, suggesting that mobile repair companies should be formed and properly equipped for the task.

August 1940 — Manston under attack! The craters from four sticks of bombs can be seen straddling the aerodrome (US National Archives).

A classic battle scene at a forward aerodrome. The refuelling trailer has just completed its task, the parachutes lie ready on the tailplanes, the trolley accs are connected and the erks stand by their kites. Spitfires of No. 65 Squadron at readiness, August 1940.

After the chalk dust had settled, Manston began sorting itself out and tried to return to normal. Command of the station had passed in September to Squadron Leader G. A. L. Manton, one of whose first jobs was to do some explaining to Wing Commander Reginald Presland who arrived on leave from overseas and called at the station to look at his private aeroplane which he had left there. The aeroplane had been blitzed during the previous month and Squadron Leader Manton tried to soften the blow by saying that the High Commissioner for Egypt had also lost his private aeroplane in the same attack and that, in any case, a battalion of cockney soldiers had stolen the instruments from the aircraft! Wing Commander Presland understandably did not find much consolation in this argument.

Lysander aircraft were attached to Manston from No. 4 Army Co-operation Squadron, their task being to assist in aircrew rescue operations, working with the high speed launches in Ramsgate harbour and other rescue craft and lifeboats in the district. Minor air attacks took place in September, October, November and December but little damage was done.

On October 17, Oberleutnant Walter Rupp flying a Bf 109E-4/B of 3/JG53 kindly made the RAF a present of his Messerschmitt (c/n 1106) when he force-landed at Manston after being damaged over Gravesend. Five weeks later on November 27, a second German aviator, Leutnant Wolfgang Teumer from 6/JG52, made a wheels-up landing at Manston under similar circumstances in his Bf 109E-3/B (c/n 4101).

The new year saw the German raiders back again. In January, two Bf 109s bombed the aerodrome, little damage was done and the intruders were driven off. Later that month the dispersal HQ at Westgate was bombed by a Ju 88; two brick lodges were demolished but no one was hurt. In February, the aerodrome was bombed and machine-gunned by thirty Messerschmitts; one airman was killed on his way to a shelter trench, one Spitfire was damaged and there was further damage to the aerodrome surface and buildings. Two minor raids took place in March but none of these incidents affected the serviceability of the station.

By now Manston was playing a double role as far as fighter operations were concerned. Its position as a forward striking base was unequalled and not only were day and night fighter squadrons based there to help carry the air war to Germany's doorstep, but it was used by many other squadrons based further inland, to land, refuel and be briefed by the Manston Intelligence Staff on their way to the continent.

Part of Manston's role was to act as a base for anti-shipping strikes and to attempt to deny the English Channel to the German Navy and, during the first nine months of 1941, squadrons based at the aerodrome had sunk 44,600 tons of enemy shipping.

On October 5, 1941, Wing Commander R. P. Gleave arrived to take over command of the station. The Air Officer Commanding No. 11 Group, Air Vice-Marshal Leigh-Mallory, had told him to go there and turn Manston into an operational station with all that that implied. On arrival, the new Station Commander could see what the AOC meant. The state of the aerodrome was deplorable. Nothing had been done about dismantling the framework of the bombed and burnt-out hangars which had concrete floors and which were badly needed as hardstandings for dispersals. This was one of the first jobs to be undertaken and the wrecked buildings, when they were dismantled, provided many hundreds of tons of desperately needed steel. The airmen's accommodation had also been badly damaged, but Mr. Lee, the Works Department Superintendent, knocked down the worst buildings, salvaged what material he could and used it to repair other huts. A vast water tower sat beside and dwarfed the Air Traffic Control Building. It was a flying hazard and had been redundant for a long time as the camp had a full-sized water main running through it. Wing Commander Gleave fought to have it removed but was repeatedly baulked by the Air Ministry. Eventually he threatened to get the Army to blow it up and obtained the desired permission to dismantle it. It is one of Manston's legends that, when the demolition gang arrived, they found painters about to repaint it!

The grass-surfaced aerodrome had three landing lanes: the E-W on a bearing of 278°T was 200 x 1,600 yards; the NE-SW on 233°T measuring 200 x 1,900 yards and the NW-SE direction of 159°T 200 x 1,100 yards. The E-W and NE-SW directions had been lengthened by projecting spurs beyond the main landing area. Petrol storage of 44,000 gallons of aviation fuel and 3,600 gallons of MT was provided for refuelling by trailer. Munition storage existed for forty tons of bombs and five million rounds of small arms ammunition.

The danger of invasion was still considered a strong possibility and the capture of Manston was believed to be one of the German's pre-requisites to the establishment of the Luftwaffe in Britain. The Army provided a battalion of soldiers for the defence of the aerodrome and all station personnel were

Not an anti-invasion measure but physical training at Manston in 1938. With a channel breeze whipping their shorts about their legs, a group of long-suffering airmen form a captive audience to the prowess of a 'javelin pilot' (Charles E. Brown).

Thirty-nine years on and No. 3 hangar, the most westerly, is the only one in North Camp to have survived Manston's stormy past. It now houses 'E' Flight of No. 22 Squadron, one of whose Wessex helicopters stands on the apron.

armed to man the defence localities and buildings. Guns from wrecked aircraft were mounted on home-made stands and a 30mm cannon 'appeared' from nowhere, accompanied by thirty rounds — it had, it is believed, once been used in trials on a special mounting in a flying boat but had somehow made its own way to Manston. The aerodrome itself was mined with Cortex — threaded through conduits running across the landing surface. It was inspected by the Army at intervals and one can imagine the consternation caused one day when it was discovered the field mice had eaten through the Cortex and jeopardised the defence plan! The GOC 12th Corps — Lieutenant-General Montgomery — visited Manston at the end of March 1942 and his visit was shortly followed by warning of a possible paratroop raid. In the event, this did not materialise.

The position of Manston on the projecting spur of northern Kent made it extremely attractive to the crews of crippled aircraft returning from continental missions endeavouring to set down on the first piece of available dry land. The Station Commander had been watching the increasing numbers of emergency landings and had begun to worry about the aerodrome itself. For aircraft flying by night which had not been shot up, it was bad enough, but the 'lame ducks' of Bomber

Command were now trying to make Manston in every imaginable kind of trouble. The aerodrome was comparatively limited for landings of larger aircraft, some without flaps or brakes and many aircraft overshot and added to the damage already sustained. Wing Command Gleave had already pleaded for the construction of a really large runway and 'lead-in' lights but, so far, he had not been successful.

On the night of August 28/29, 1942, his worst fears were to be realised. Landing activity started at 8.15 p.m. when the Northolt Polish Spitfire Wing, comprising Nos. 302, 306, 308 and 317 Squadrons, started landing in the gathering darkness. There were forty-five aircraft in all. At one minute to midnight, a Wellington of No. 305 (Polish) Squadron crash-landed on the beginning of the flare-path. This aircraft had been attacked by three night fighters in succession on its way to Saarbrucken and had caught fire. The rear-gunner had been killed during one of the attacks and the navigator, wireless operator and front gunner had baled out over enemy territory. However, the bombs had been jettisoned and the captain and second pilot had succeeded in getting it back to Manston. Before 1.00 a.m. another three Wellingtons and three Stirlings had landed and, at 4.00 a.m., a Stirling of No. 218 Squadron landed

from Munich. He had been told to avoid the obstruction caused by the first Wellington and consequently landed too far to the right, sweeping through a line of the Polish Wing's Spitfires. The Stirling destroyed one Spitfire which burst into flames and swept on into a dispersal bay already occupied by an Albacore where it came to rest in a tangle of metal. Shortly after this incident, a Stirling of No. 7 Squadron landed short of fuel with his engines cutting. The fire raging below and the obstruction on the flare-path made landing a very tricky business and he also landed too far to the right. Fortunately he careered through a gap in the line of Spitifres with the Medical Officers, the Fire Party and others scattering out of his way. The aircraft hit a long wooden hut and cannoned into a Bellman hangar, damaging both buildings considerably. Fortunately the two men who normally slept in the hut were out working. Another Wellington followed and the last bomber to come in was another Stirling of No. 218 Squadron which was so short of petrol that it was unable to taxi in completely after landing, all engines cutting for lack of fuel. That morning Wing Commander Gleave inspected the north-west perimeter which was in a sorry state, littered with wreckage. The damage to aircraft and buildings on the ground was terrible — the Albacore was crushed beneath the Stirling and a Spitfire had been flattened by a Stirling's wheel. He had the scene of carnage photographed in every detail and sent the result to the Air Officer Commanding. (*Unfortunately there now seems no trace of these photographs — Ed.*) Air Vice-Marshal Leigh-Mallory sent them immediately to the Air Ministry, an act which had the desired effect of obtaining approval, in principle, for the construction of the new runway although there was to be no sign of it for some time yet.

When Wing Commander D. F. B. Sheen took over as Station Commander in November, he noted on his arrival that there were some seventeen wrecks around the station perimeter, visible evidence of Manston's work in bringing in damaged bombers. By this time there was scarcely a night when the station was not asked for help, and, in the tower, the emergency frequency (Darky) was manned by WAAF operators who quickly gained the reputation for being very efficient and calm, even in the worst emergencies. Within ten days of his arrival, the new Station Commander had seen a Wellington crash in flames on the aerodrome, killing four of the crew.

Towards the end of the year, an Air Commodore from the Airfield Board of the Air Ministry came to the station to examine

The hangar visible behind the airmen was another casualty of the bombing. The base now forms a convenient site for the aircraft dump. Shallow depressions in the former sports field are all that remain of the defensive slit trenches.

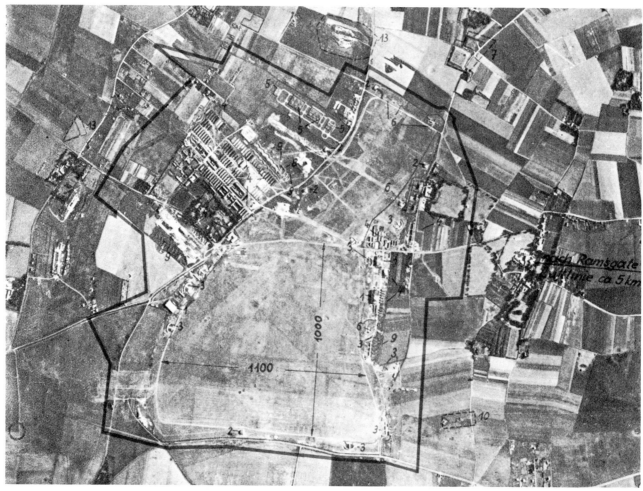

Above: **This extract from an October 1942 Luftwaffe target map shows that all except two hangars have been dismantled.**

Below: **Charles E. Brown's oblique taken on October 31, 1945 looking east along the huge crash runway built 1943-44.**

the possibility of the construction of a 3,000-yard runway. Wing Commander Sheen had been pressing without much success for at least a £5,000 improvement to a taxi-track and expressed his amazement at the calm assumption of the Air Commodore that the runway could go there — it only meant shifting some houses and diverting the main road at a cost of about £1,000,000! He remembers the answer he was given: 'He told me it was no good going for chicken-feed — one had to go for the big stuff and he would get his million pounds.'

The year finally ended with the Navy having the last word. Lieutenant Garthwait, who was the new CO of No. 841 Squadron, landed in an Albacore and a burst tyre caused his undercarriage to collapse, the shock of landing detaching one of his flares which set fire to the aircraft. Luckily, Lieutenant Garthwait and Sub-Lieutenant Waiting were able to get out and run to a safe distance before the petrol tank exploded; this in turn set off the four 100 pound bombs, followed quickly by the four 250 pounders. The aerodrome had to be declared unserviceable for a period although a flarepath was quickly put down for emergency landings.

During April 1943, Manston was used as a base for the 'bouncing bomb' experiments which were taking place at a nearby beach at Reculver. Wing Commander Guy Gibson flew from the aerodrome on several occasions, the famous ace even adding to the mounting accident tally by crashing in a nearby field while flying a Magister!

The following month Manston received its third German visitor, royally welcomed by the station pilots. In the early hours of May 20, Unteroffizier Heinz Ehrhardt of 1/SKG10 approached Manston (where the runway lights had been switched on for a returning Typhoon) after having crossed the Thames Estuary from Clacton, believing that he had crossed the Channel. As soon as he had landed at what he thought was St. Omer in France, he was pounced on by a group of No. 609 Squadron pilots who were pleased to inform him he was, in fact, in England and his FW 190A-4/U8 aircraft (c/n 5843) was snatched with delight. When the interrogation team arrived they were considerably put out to discover that the German had been entertained throughout the night with cocoa and cigarettes.

Exactly four weeks later, Unteroffizier Werner Ohne, also of 1/SKG10, became Manston's fourth passive 'victory'. Taking off on June 20 at 2.00 a.m., in an FW 190A-5/U8 (c/n 2596), he became disorientated and, with an unserviceable radio, he identified the visual beacon of Manston as that of his own base and came in to make a perfect landing.

The contract for the construction of the 'crash' runway was awarded to John Laing and Son Ltd. and work officially began on June 15, 1943. The specification called for a 3,000 yard runway 250 yards wide (five times

as wide as a normal runway) together with an aircraft dispersal loop over 2,000 yards long leading off the western end and twelve crash bays off the southern edge of the new runway, the whole lot linked by a motor vehicle road. The work was to include the installation of lighting and drainage and the re-grading of 392 acres of adjacent land.

There was some delay in the commencement of the work as the Air Ministry had not fully requisitioned the site for the extension and the level details for the runway were only released in stages between July 11 and August 18. A chalk quarry, which was to provide nearly a quarter of a million cubic yards of fill, was not requisitioned until July 22.

Altogether over 370,000 cubic yards of soil had to be excavated on site for the new constructions, the labour force involved rising to a peak of 694 men on October 19. A total of 149 lorries were used on the job together with other heavy plant. More than 379,000 square yards of concrete had to be laid seven inches thick with an additional tarmac preparation by Messrs. Chittenden and Simmonds of 462,500 square yards. The outfall for the 19,000 yards of drains had to be taken under the Ramsgate-Canterbury railway, through the then existing minefields to discharge down the chalk cliffs into the sea.

All the time the work was proceeding, the aerodrome had to be kept fully operational and a temporary landing lane was marked out on the eastern side of the 'drome. Some of the excavated earth was used to create mounds for

the Bofors guns to provide a better field of fire. At the same time, the NE-SW landing lane was graded to take out the bumps and hollows.

The 174 acres of paved area were completed in forty-three weeks and, at 2.45 p.m. on April 5, 1944, the new runway was brought into operation. During its first three weeks it fully justified the time and money on its construction with fifty-six emergency landings being recorded. On April 22 the station record comments:

'More crashes and forced landings today. Manston is rapidly becoming a Pranger's Paradise! Hectic day with the damaged aircraft coming to rest in the most unaccountable and awkward positions about the airfield. But for the prompt action of the crash parties and servicing wing, we could have been mistaken for a large dispersed salvage dump! Five Fortresses, two Thunderbolts, two Albacores, one Spitfire, two Marauders.' This same period saw many urgent calls for the duty Medical Officer as 33 American and 11 British casualties were lifted out of battle-damaged aircraft.

'The 'aircraft doctors' were also busy, and the servicing wing, assisted by No. 86 MU detachment and an American contingent, which had arrived under Captain John Patrick English, repaired thirteen British and thirty American aircraft by the end of the month. Fuel bowsers were always active from crack of dawn and 1,613 aircraft were refuelled during this period; 179 of these had, in fact, made emergency landings short of fuel.'

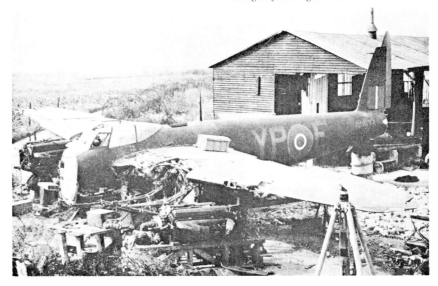

On the night of August 24, 1942, Mosquito DD673 piloted by Squadron Leader N. J. Starr overshot its landing run and collided with a steam roller. We were fortunate to be able to trace the driver and hence pinpoint the location — now used as the 'dispersal' for the 'foamer'. Despite its ungainly appearance, the Emergency Foam Landing Equipment has provided safe landings for a number of aircraft in difficulties.

Manston's prime position for mounting sweeps over the continent, shipping attacks and for providing a forward base for bomber escorts led to further increases in its operational strength. However, mounting successes by Manston squadrons were matched by mounting crashes and the station was even 'attacked' by friendly aircraft when a Liberator dropped eight bombs on June 13 while attempting a crash landing.

By June 1944 the tally of emergency landings had increased to 779 and it was appreciated that because of the increase in crippled aircraft using the aerodrome, many with wounded aboard, medical facilities must

likewise be increased. It was felt it would be better to try to treat wounded airmen on the spot rather than patch them up and let them suffer the ordeal of a journey to an inland hospital. The planned expansion led to the casualty centre being converted to a sixty-bed hospital with provision for thirty-five more casualties at Westgate. The medical staff was built up with postings from the American forces, the Princess Mary's RAF Nursing Service and the Royal Navy. Some equipment had to be improvised such as the use of tin shears to cut through metal-impregnated, electrically-heated flying clothing and zip fasteners. The work of Manston's hospital

Manston in 1958. Today the loop dispersal in the foreground has been dismantled.

staff under Squadron Leader Dr. Ian MacGregor was responsible for saving the lives of countless airmen.

In July, a welcome interlude was provided by two more Germans presenting the station personnel with their aircraft. Both incidents occurred on the night of July 20/21 and, although the two Bf 109G-6s (c/n 163240 and 412951) were from different Staffels (3/JG301 and 1/JG1) they both flashed their downward recognition lights while circuiting the aerodrome and were naturally encouraged to land by the air traffic controller. This increased Manston's 'bag' of German aircraft to six.

During August, the US Eighth Air Force posted Detachment A of the 16th Mobile Reclamation and Repair Squadron to Manston, a 250-strong unit, to co-ordinate and assist in the work concerning American aircraft and personnel.

The following month the facilities at Manston were strained to breaking point with the arrival of thousands of airborne troops with their gliders and tugs en route for Operation Market Garden.

Manston was one of the three emergency airfields in Britain with 3,000 yard runways equipped to handle returning aircraft in difficulty. (The others were at Carnaby in Yorkshire and Woodbridge in Suffolk.) One of the landing aids provided was the Fog Investigation and Dispersal Operation equipment — FIDO for short. This consisted of petrol burners installed at close intervals along the runway which were lit to disperse fog sufficiently to enable an aircraft to land safely. During a period of bad weather at Manston in September 1944 alone, FIDO assisted in the safe return of nineteen aircraft.

For a time after the end of the war, Manston's future looked uncertain but, in December 1945, the location of the aerodrome made it suitable for an equally important role in peace-time. Transport Command set up No. 91 Staging Post there on April 1, 1946. The airfield was listed as an RAF and Civil Customs Aerodrome and this designation was confirmed on July 15 when it was transferred from Fighter to Transport Command. Skyways Ltd. had already begun to operate York aircraft between Manston and the Middle East and Switzerland.

Manston's crash record was increased on June 1, 1948 when an Air Ministry Film Unit deliberately crashed a Mosquito at the end of the E-W runway. During the following two months there were fourteen other 'incidents' — not that the airfield should be considered as dangerous for its long, wide runway had a special attraction to aircraft in difficulties. This spate of accidents culminated in the Battle of Britain Day 'At Home' on September 18 when a Mosquito stalled into the crowd after performing a slow roll, killing both the crew and several spectators.

On July 14, 1950 Manston reverted to the control of Fighter Command so that the airfield could more easily be put at the disposal of the US Strategic Air Command which was then seeking additional bases in the UK. SAC used Manston as a base for its rotational wings, the first to arrive being the 20th Fighter Bomber Wing equipped with F-84E Thunderstreaks which stayed until December 1950. The 20th was followed by the 31st Fighter Escort Wing who, in turn, were replaced by the 12th Fighter Escort Wing in July 1951. By November that year, bases in the Midlands had been prepared for the SAC and the 12th moved inland in November. For a time during the Korean war, Manston was the home of the 123rd Fighter Bomber Wing, then undergoing training. During this time the Americans lost several F-84s on the aerodrome, one fatal accident occurring at an air display, the aircraft exploding over the airfield and crashing on the runway.

When the 123rd left in July 1952 the airfield was assigned to the Third Air Force, USAFE and it was during this period that its most notorious peacetime incident occurred in August 1955. An American negro, Napoleon Green, who was awaiting trial for an assortment of charges, escaped from custody, broke into the armoury and helped himself to arms and ammunition. Tired of waiting in ambush for Captain Mercer Ader, the US military police chief, Green loosed off some shots at some policemen in their billet, sprayed officers and cars and indiscriminately wounded servicemen and civilians, men and women. An RAF corporal on a bicycle was shot in the back and killed. After commandeering a car, Green drove to Broadstairs and he was finally cornered and shot dead on the beach at Joss Bay.

In April 1956 Manston saw an increase in RAF personnel when it was re-opened as a Master Diversion Airfield. Two months later the station was able to acquire a Spitfire LF Mk16 TB752 as a gate guardian to the great interest of the American servicemen based there. It was also the centre of attraction for a planeload of Russians who were diverted to Manston when Heathrow was fogbound. While the Americans hastened to hide away their most interesting aircraft, the Russians sat tight in their TU104, not wanting to disembark until permission had been received from their embassy. When they finally emerged after a five-hour wait, the Spitfire proved of more interest than the US aircraft! A humorous sequel occurred when the Russians asked for the TU104 to be refuelled — they rejected tanker after tanker after one of their technicians had personally sampled each one!

Between January 1, 1957 and June 30, 1958, Manston was under sole USAF control. When the 406th Fighter Interceptor Wing was inactivated, the airfield was closed as an operational base and put on a 'care and maintenance' basis.

For the next eight months there was a hiatus while its future was decided. Then, in March 1959, it was announced that the aerodrome would once again become part of No. 11 Group Fighter Command, linked with West Malling. Silver City Airways, forced to look for new premises with the closure of Blackbushe Airport, also obtained permission to operate from Manston, being based on the eastern 'civilian' side of the aerodrome. As soon as the airfield had been reopened, the emergency landings began again, the first being four Belgian military aircraft followed by a Royal Navy Vampire and a USAF C-47. Meanwhile the civilian side of Manston 'Airport' continued to expand, both Skyways and British European Airways using the facilities.

In 1961 the Search and Rescue Helicopter Flight was established, soon becoming an integral part of post-war Manston. Another change was the station's transfer to No. 3 Group Bomber Command which occurred on October 1, 1962; gliding training for Air Training Corps was begun the following year introducing four Chipmunk aircraft to give the cadets flying experience.

Early in 1963, Manston's role as a crash 'drome caused it to be selected for installation of the Pyrene Prototype Runway Foamer — a device which lays a foam carpet enabling an aircraft to land wheels up with a greatly-reduced fire risk. The equipment was not used for real until March the following year when an RAF Valiant performed a successful landing. Three more military 'foam' landings occurred in 1966 before a British Eagle Britannia full of passengers successfully indicated the benefit of the system to civilian aircraft when it slithered to a halt on April 20, 1967. The emergency operation was carried out so swiftly that the Board of Trade reported that the passengers were in more danger of being run down by the fire engines!

A nostalgic look at the past was given in 1968 when two Heinkel 111s and fifteen Messerschmitts flew in over the cliffs and landed en route from Spain ready for Air Registration Board inspection before their participation in the film *Battle of Britain*. Tremendous advance publicity had led to hundreds of sightseers flocking to see the 'raiders'.

Today Manston remains an Emergency Landing Airfield. The Search and Rescue Flight, which had performed such a sterling service during its eight years existence, was posted in March 1969 but not before it had its final fling by rounding up twenty-seven Pakistanis illegally attempting to enter the country by boat on the Romney Marshes!

Rochford

BY BILL GENT

In 1914, Rochford was established as a military aerodrome for Home Defence Squadrons to operate against German Zeppelin and Gotha attacks on London. Sited on farmland half-a-mile south of Rochford village and two miles north of Southend Central, it was bounded on the north by Rochford golf course and to the east by the Liverpool Street Railway Line and the B1013. Here squadrons were grouped and taught formation flying tactics and methods of night fighting before going on to France. Various aircraft (BE2cs, SE5As, Sopwith Camels, etc.) were ferried from the factories through Rochford to France.

On August 2, 1917, No. 61 Squadron was formed at Rochford and on the 12th they intercepted ten Gothas which managed to bomb Rochford before being chased back across the Channel.

During a daylight raid on Southend on December 6, 1917, one of the raiding Gothas was hit by anti-aircraft guns and crash-landed on Rochford golf course although, unfortunately, this aircraft caught fire before any useful information could be gained. Local gossip has it that a British officer, seeing the German signal pistol, reached for it and it went off accidentally, firing a flare directly into the aircraft.

After the First World War the land was derequisitioned and it reverted to farmland until 1933 when Southend Corporation purchased it for airport development. The municipal aerodrome was formally opened on September 18, 1935. A thriving flying club and a unit of the RAF Volunteer Reserve used the aerodrome, with Auxiliary Squadrons and the Civil Air Guard coming in for summer camps until the RAF selected Rochford as a satellite to the fighter base at Hornchurch.

Sunning themselves on the south-eastern corner of Rochford aerodrome in July 1940, four pilots of No. 54 Squadron relax between convoy protection patrols. In the background one of the squadron's Spitfires stands at readiness while the London (Fenchurch Street) to Southend train puffs past. From left to right are Flying Officer J. L. Allen, DFC, Pilot Officers E. J. Coleman, G. D. Gribble and A. R. McL. Campbell, a Canadian. Of the four, only Campbell survived the war. Johnny Allen was killed in action on July 24 and possibly this was the last picture taken of him. Pilot Officer Gribble was killed on June 4, 1941 and Coleman later in the war (Crown Copyright).

On October 16, 1979, Winston G. Ramsey, editor of *After the Battle,* ruminates on the fate of the young pilots who once occupied the same spot. The former secluded corner of the aerodrome is now a car park, only a small fragment of the original hedge remaining.

In November 1939, No. 54 Squadron flew into Rochford and, throughout the Battle of Britain, this squadron, together with No. 74, alternated between there and Hornchurch.

Patrolling over the Thames Estuary in January 1940, No. 54 Squadron damaged an He 111 chalking up the first interception to Rochford.

At the end of May, the Rochford squadrons fought above the Dunkirk beaches where

many local boats were helping with the evacuation of the British Expeditionary Force.

The following month, flying a sortie from Rochford on 18th, Flight Lieutenant 'Sailor' Malan of No. 74 Squadron became the first single-seater pilot of World War II to destroy an enemy aircraft by night. Nine days later he made another record when he scored two kills in one night.

June 18, 1940 is remembered locally as the

day when the first bombs of the war fell in the area when a large formation of German aircraft tried to put Canewdon radar station (two miles to the north of Rochford) out of action.

Whilst protecting shipping and convoys, Rochford pilots reported that He 59 float-planes with Red Cross markings were being used in the Channel for acts other than air-sea rescue. Shortly after receiving orders that, if detected in warlike operations, these float planes should be intercepted, Rochford pilots forced one down on the Goodwin Sands on July 9.

On August 26, thirty Do 17s with an escort of Bf 109s and 110s were spotted by radar forming up and crossing the Channel. Six Spitfires from No. 65 Squadron at Horn-church, led by Flight Lieutenant Saunders, were scrambled to intercept. The 130-odd German raiders were spotted at 20,000ft, some ten thousand feet below, by the six British fighters and they dived to break up the formation. While the Bf 110s formed their defensive circles, Flight Lieutenant Saunders went after the bombers flying in the direction of Southend. Seeing a Dornier he opened fire at 400 yards and, as he closed to 250 yards, both engines began to smoke. The German then went in a diving turn towards the aerodrome and Saunders stopped firing when he realised it was going to attempt a belly landing which it successfully accomplished. (This Dornier later proved useful to Air Ministry technical experts.) During the dog-fight, Rochford police station and several cottages had been sprayed with bullets and two people watching the battle in their gardens had been wounded.

Two days later on the 28th, between 200 and 300 bombs were dropped in the Rochford area at noon leaving thirty craters on the aerodrome, buildings and haystacks ablaze and the railway line blocked. All services and telephones were temporarily put out of action.

Early in the morning of September 2 No. 249

Above: On August 26, 1940, Dornier Do 17Z, U5 + LK of 2/KG2 sprawls like a dead bat in the centre of Rochford aerodrome. *Bottom:* On October 16, 1979, a Handley Page Dart-Herald, G-BCWE of British Island Airways, rolls past the spot where the Dornier ended its flying days thirty-nine years before.

Squadron was scrambled from North Weald. Over Rochester they engaged a German formation and three of their aircraft were shot down but not before they had severely damaged a Dornier 17 over Chatham. Unable to return to France Oberleutnant Rohr made for Rochford aerodrome where he made a successful crash-landing, sliding to a halt a few yards away from the Area Senior Medical Officer. It was later reported that when the unarmed MO pulled the wounded pilot from the aircraft he found the rear machine gun pointed at him with the gunner behind it. Cautiously approaching, he found the gunner was dead but with his finger still on the trigger!

With the German concentration of barges and landing craft in Belgian canals and off the French coast for Operation Sealion, the Roch-ford squadrons raided these areas on day and night sorties and it was during this period that

Jeffrey Quill, the Spitfire test pilot, flew from Rochford to further assess the machine's capabilities under combat conditions.

After September 1940, the Luftwaffe day attacks lessened and night raids against the docks took precedence. This change of strategy brought re-organization in the defences and Rochford was made independent of Hornchurch and re-named RAF Southend and on January 9, 1941 the station was made a forward base for offensive fighter operations.

Two days previously, the aerodrome had been hit by a lone raider which dropped eight bombs, scoring three hits on the aerodrome, Then, on May 11, 1941, the station was dive-bombed and strafed by sixteen Bf 109s. The Operation Room and ambulance garage were demolished, one airman being killed and several wounded but the ground defences shot down one raider which crashed beside No. 1 hangar.

SCHEDULE OF BUILDINGS.

Bldg. No	BUILDING.
1	STORES WORKSHOPS.
2	OIL STORE.
3	GUARD ROOM.
4	LINK TRAINER & ELECTRICAL W/SHOP
5	PARACHUTE STORE.
6	HANGAR. 175' × 94' (BELLMAN.)
7	Do: Do: Do:
8	C.I. HUT. OFFICES.
9	PETROL STORE.
10	AMBULANCE SHELTER.
11	FIRE CREW.
12	STORES.
13	ABLUTIONS HUT.
14	BARRACK HUT.
15	WATER TANK Nº1. 20,000. GALLS (FIRE)
16	Do: Nº2. Do: Do:
17	Do: Nº3. Do: Do:
17A & B	Do: Nº4 & 5. Do: Do:
18	WATCH OFFICE.
19	CINE CAMERA. GUN WORKSHOP.
20	DINING ROOM. COOK HOUSE & N.A.A.F.I.
21	C.O.s BATTLE H.Q. & STATION CONTROL ROOM.
22	BARRACK HUT. (NISSEN)
23	ABLUTIONS.
24	BARRACK HUT. (NISSEN)
24A	LATRINE.
25	AIRCRAFT PENS. (BLENHEIM) A to F.
26	SLEEPING SHELTER.
27	Do: Do:
28	CAMOUFLAGE STORE.
29	DESTRUCTOR.
29A	COAL COMPOUND.
30	GROUNDSMENS' HUT.
31	M.G. POST.
31A	Do: Do:
31B	Do: Do:
31C	Do: Do:
32A	A.A. GUN POSITION.
33	S.A.A. STORE. (TEMPORARY.)
34	PETROL STORE.
35	M.I. ROOM.
36	COAL STORE FOR H.Q. OFFICES.
37	COUNTY OF LONDON SUPPLY. KIOSK.
38	ELECTRIC FEEDER PILLAR.
39	A.B.C. PLINTHS.
40	FILM PROJECTION ROOM.
41	FILM ASSESSING ROOM. STORE & OFFICE
42	Do: HUT.
43	Do: LATRINE.
44	P.A.C.
45	Do:
46	GAS CHAMBER.
47	PICKET. HAMILTON. FORT.
47A	Do: Do:
47B	Do: Do:
48	FLIGHT OFFICES & REST ROOM.
49	BLISTER HANGAR. E.O.
50	Do: Do: Do:
51	FLIGHT OFFICES & REST ROOM.
52	FIRE POOL HUTS A. 30' × 12' B. 15' × 12'
53	CREW ROOM.
54	BELT FILLING ROOM.
55	DECONTAMINATION CENTRE.
56	FLIGHT OFFICE.
57	TECHNICAL LATRINE.
58	W.D. OFFICE & STORE.
59	BLISTER HANGAR. E.O.
60	Do: Do: Do:
61	GAS DEFENCE CENTRE.
62	AVIATION PETROL INSTN. 12,000 GALS: (U.G)
64	PICKET POST.
65	SPEECH BROADCASTING INSTALLATION
66	FLIGHT OFFICES.
67 - 69	S.A.A. STORES.
70	CANNON TEST BUTT.
71-72	LATRINE & DRYING ROOM.
73	FUSING SHED.
74	DETONATOR STORE.
75-76	BOMB STORES. 2 Nº: 28' × 21'.
77	S.A.A. STORES.
78	A. W/T & ELEC. WKSHP. B. WKSHP. C. DROGUE STORE. D. ARMOURY.
79	GAS EQUIPMENT STORE. 14' × 10'
80	PYROTECHNIC STORE.
81	OFFICERS QTRS. AT EASTWOODBURY.
82	N.A.A.F.I. STAFF QUARTERS.

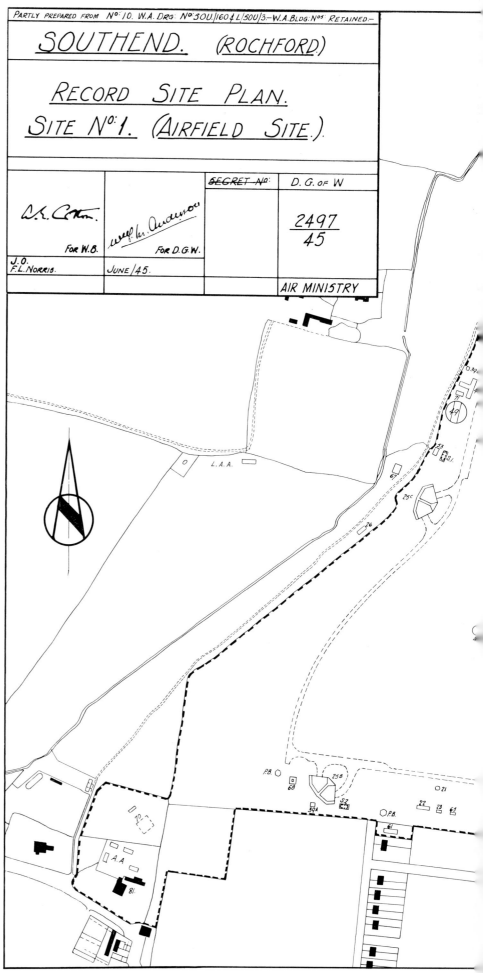

SOUTHEND. (ROCHFORD)

RECORD SITE PLAN.
SITE Nº 1. (AIRFIELD SITE.)

PARTLY PREPARED FROM Nº 10. W.A. DRG: Nº 30U./160 & L/50U/3.—W.A. BLDG: Nºs RETAINED:—

SECRET Nº | D.G. OF W
2497 / 45

FOR W.B. | FOR D.G.W.
J.O. F.L. NORRIS. | JUNE / 45.

AIR MINISTRY

In February 1942, No. 313 (Czech) Squadron arrived at Southend followed later by No. 411 (Canadian) Squadron, No. 121 (Eagle) Squadron, No. 350 (Belgian) Squadron and No. 453 (Australian) Squadron. The Whirlwind, the first British single-seat, twin-engined fighter and low-level fighter-bomber, also came to Southend for a few sorties against enemy ground targets.

At mid-day on October 26, 1942 a large bombing raid damaged 100 houses in Rochford and a Bf 109, crippled by the guns of No. 2830 RAF Regiment, crashed into No. 350 Squadron's dispersal, killing a Belgian warrant officer and injuring two other airmen.

With the Normandy invasion in 1944, Squadrons from Southend crossed to the bridgehead airstrips and their places were temporarily taken by other units equipping and training before going on to Europe.

The position of the airfield on the northern edge of the Estuary made RAF Southend a well-placed refuge for RAF and USAAF bombers and fighters returning to England, although on September 1, 1944 RAF Southend returned to satellite status and was thereafter reduced to a 'care and maintenance' base only.

In 1946 the aerodrome was again derequisitioned and it opened to commercial traffic early in 1947. A municipal air centre and flying school was formed on March 27 and one of the subsequent part-time instructors was Mr Richard Kilnor who had flown Spitfires with No. 65 Squadron during the Battle of Britain from this same airfield. (The flying school closed in January 1964.)

Customs facilities were inaugurated in 1948 and, in the same year, Southend was used as a maintenance base for civil aircraft operating on the Berlin Airlift.

In 1951 the terminal building was constructed and the apron areas, taxiways and concrete runways were laid and extended. Car ferry services to Europe were inaugurated by Silver City from Southend in 1954 using Bristol Freighters on the 'Channel Air Bridge'.

In the mid-fifties, Aviation Traders (Engineering) Ltd. designed and built the ATL 90 Accountant at Southend airport — a turbo-prop airliner which was one of the many contenders designed at this time as a replacement for the DC3 although only one prototype was built. The ATL 98 Carvair, conceived by Sir Freddie Laker in the early sixties as a freighting conversion of the DC4, was designed and twenty-two were built at Southend.

Southend has had a good post-war accident-free record, one of the few incidents occuring to a Channel Airways Viscount G-APPU on May 4, 1968. Returning from Rotterdam, the aircraft made a normal touchdown about 3,200ft from the upwind end of the main runway, the surface of which was wet. However at the end of its run it failed to stop and it overshot the end of the runway by about 100ft with the starboard wing obstructing the railway track. There were no injuries.

Over the years, Southend Airport has been the home of numerous airlines but today only British Island Airways and British Midlands remain. Helicopter Hire also operate from the airfield, supplying helicopters for filming, police work and crop-spraying. There are two flying clubs, several firms maintaining light aircraft and two crop-spraying companies using fixed-wing aircraft.

The most significant development, as far as aviation enthusiasts are concerned, was the opening of the Historic Aircraft Museum on May 27, 1972. Located on the southern boundary alongside Aviation Way, the museum had its beginnings in the old British Historic Aircraft Museum which was to be located at Biggin Hill. Early on, a switch was made to Southend, one of the two aircraft then on the strength of the museum, a Sea Fury, being moved by road from Biggin Hill in the middle of the night towed by a Land-Rover.

Subsequent exhibits arrived by both road and air and the collection was building up nicely when the organiser went bankrupt. The property developers who took over the project, erecting a purpose-designed aircraft museum building with an airport hotel and discotheque, also went bankrupt and the museum was placed in the hands of the Official Receiver. In the interim, Queens Moat Houses Ltd. took over the running of the complex but the lack of permanent maintenance staff together with the frequent moving of aircraft to stage exhibitions in the display hall has led to many aircraft deposited on loan being removed by their owners. Nevertheless the museum has attracted many thousands of

visitors to Rochford during its precarious period of existence.

More recently, the publication of new regulations by the Civil Aviation Authority concerning overshoots on one engine brought the whole future of the aerodrome into question. The work to be carried out at Southend to comply with the new ruling necessitated the demolition of several houses

and farm buildings near the airport. As only two commercial airlines then operated from the aerodrome (both of which could easily be moved to Stansted), it was initially doubtful if the local authority would provide the necessary finance to purchase the properties and re-house the occupants. However it is now understood that Southend Corporation have decided to carry out the necessary work.

Rochford, now renamed Southend Municipal Airport, taken on October 19, 1979 looking north-east. Post-war alterations can clearly be compared with the plan of the aerodrome as it was at the end of the war reproduced on the preceding pages. We made a detailed search for the sunken Hamilton Forts but these have all been removed.

SECTOR E
North Weald

BY WILF NICOLL

On Saturday, September 11, 1915, soon after the fall of darkness, a solitary Zeppelin purred its way high above the deserted beaches of Norfolk, entering far into the county before turning on to a southerly heading for its intended target — London. However, when rolling fog banks appeared below accurate navigation became impossible and, after a meandering flight over most of Suffolk and Essex, the bewildered navigator calculated that their goal had been reached and all their bombs were unloaded. Returning safely to base they jubilantly reported a successful attack on the British capital. In actual fact, the startled recipients of eight high explosive and fifty-two incendiary bombs were the blissfully sleeping inhabitants of the village of North Weald Bassett. The 'Weald' had received its baptism of fire, fortunately without casualties or damage.

In order to combat the growing Zeppelin menace, a small number of landing grounds were established on the eastern approaches to London. It seemed natural that North Weald should be chosen as the site of one of these, if only to extract retribution for one lost night's sleep and so, on land requisitioned from the Pullers of Great Weald Hall, the War Office laid out an aerodrome on the north side of the Epping-Ongar road, to the west of the village. It became operational in August 1916 and was the base for a flight of BE2cs of No. 39 (Home Defence) Squadron.

With the increasing regularity of German airship raids, North Weald's participation in the defence of the capital was not long delayed. At 11.00 p.m. on September 2, 1916, a single BE2c rose from the aerodrome with Second Lieutenant C. S. Ross at the controls. After a two-hour uneventful patrol between North Weald and Hainault he crashed on return to base. At 1.00 a.m. a second patrol took off with Second Lieutenant J. I. Mackay patrolling between North Weald and Joyce Green. An hour later, at 10,000 feet over Joyce Green, he spotted the searchlight-illuminated shape of an airship somewhere over north London. Opening the throttle to its limit he sent his BE2c juddering in pursuit and arrived within a mile of his proposed target when the monster was lit from within by an orange

glow. Suddenly it burst into flames, falling 11,500 feet to crumple into a glowing mass near the village of Cuffley. A young pilot named William Leefe-Robinson had beaten him to fame.

Then, on Sunday, October 1, at 10.00 p.m., Second Lieutenant W. J. Tempest lifted his BE2c from between the tar pot flares of North Weald aerodrome to climb into the darkness to patrol between Hainault and Joyce Green. One-and-three-quarter hours later at an altitude of 14,500 feet, his attention was drawn to sudden searchlight activity over north London. One by one the blue-white beams sloped across the sky like fluorescent tubes to lock into a pyramid. At a distance of fifteen miles, Tempest could just make out a flickering silvery spot of light at the apex, like a moth in a torch beam. Vibrating across the intervening space at his maximum speed of 82 mph, he flew through the edge of an 'ack ack' barrage emerging unscathed and succeeded in overhauling the object trapped in the beams. The gargantuan dimensions of the German naval airship L31 filled the sky before him as he dived at the huge bulk firing all the way. Allowing the momentum of his dive to carry him along the underside, he fired further bursts as he passed along its length. As the mixture of incendiary and explosive bullets

entered the Zeppelin's belly, he noticed an intense red glow shining through the fabric. Tempest barely had time to pull his aircraft out of the way before the airship, now a tumbling holocaust, roared past him to crash at Potters Bar. Its commander, 32-year-old, Mannheim-born, Kapitanleutnant Heinrich Mathy, the Zeppelin 'ace', jumped to his death rather than burn with his ship. Tempest was awarded an immediate DSO.

As the British defences took the measure of the Zeppelins, so the raids dwindled but, in May 1917, a new menace appeared in the shape of the Gotha. In September the two detached flights of No. 39 Squadron which had operated from Sutton's Farm and Hainault Farm moved into North Weald from whence the squadron operated as a complete unit throughout the year of the Gotha attacks on London. In October 1918, No. 39 transferred to the Western Front, the aerodrome remaining unoccupied until Nos. 75 and 44 Squadrons moved in briefly before disbanding on June 13 and December 31, 1919.

The general revulsion towards militarism which swept the country after the Armistice did much to reduce the strength of the armed forces. With the subsequent paring of defence expenditure RAF squadrons were disbanded and aerodromes neglected and it was not until

1923 that the service began its slow climb back to strength.

Reconstruction for North Weald began in 1926/27, the station being formed with effect from September 27, 1927. Wing Commander A. G. R. Garrod was posted to command with Flight Lieutenant W. M. Yool as adjutant. Two weeks later, on Tuesday, October 11, Squadron Leader C. H. Elliott-Smith led the Armstrong Whitworth Siskin 111As of No. 56 Squadron from Biggin Hill to North Weald to become the first of the station's resident units.

January 6, 1928 brought a change in command with the appointment of Wing Commander William Sholto Douglas. On March 17, 1928, No. 56 Squadron, led by its new CO, Squadron Leader A. Lees, took part in an air demonstration for the King of Afghanistan at Hendon.

The second of North Weald's squadrons, No. 29, arrived on April 1, Squadron Leader M. L. Taylor leading the unit's Siskin 111As from Duxford. During 1932 both squadrons re-equipped with Bristol Bulldogs and in 1933 a scene reminiscent of 'The Desert Song' was enacted in front of the hangars when both units and their aircraft were inspected by the Emir of Katsina and his royal entourage, all clad in colourful burnouses.

In March 1935, No. 29 Squadron traded

Photograph taken in July 1941 looking north-west at North Weald with its landing surface broken up with painted lines representing fields. A meandering stream 'flows' along the N-S runway to a pond at the intersection before continuing along the E-W runway — all of which must have made landings rather disconcerting! No. 2 hangar, which stood in the centre, was demolished in the bombing of the station during the Battle of Britain

their Bulldogs for Hawker Demon two-seat day fighters and in August 1936 departed for duty at Amriya, Egypt during the Abyssinian crisis, returning to North Weald three months later.

After No. 29's departure, a new unit was 'born' at North Weald as part of the RAF's expansion programme when No. 151 Squadron, under the command of Squadron Leader W. V. Hyde, was formed from 'B' Flight of No. 56 on August 4, 1936, both units flying the Gloster Gauntlet. In July 1937, the more powerful Gladiators replaced the Gauntlets and, less than a year later, No. 56 received the first of its Hurricanes, the third squadron to be selected to fly the type. (No. 151 was not similarly equipped until November 1938.)

A stylized version of the No. 56 Squadron crest still visible in July 1979 above the main entrance to one of the barrack blocks.

On September 30, 1937, two of No. 29 Squadron's Demons collided over the aerodrome and crashed in the fields adjacent to Weald Hall Lane killing the occupants. In November the squadron moved to Debden.

When Prime Minister Neville Chamberlain stepped from the Lockheed Electra at Heston airport in September 1938, waving his pledge from Hitler and declaring that it heralded 'peace in our time', Fighter Command utilized the next few months of grace to bring itself to full combat readiness. For the North Weald units under their new commanding officers, Squadron Leader E. V. Knowles of No. 56 and Squadron Leader E. M. 'Teddy' Donaldson of No. 151, it became a point of honour that each should match the other in efficiency. Attack exercises, practice 'scrambles', battle climbs, air drills and formations and lots of firing practice — the latter being something that Teddy Donaldson,

With No. 3 hangar in the background, pilots of No. 56 Squadron prepare for the night-flying exercises on August 9, 1937. Described at the time as the largest air defence exercise ever carried out at night, it involved about 400 aircraft (Radio Times).

In front of the site of the bombed No. 2 hangar, Wilf Nicoll and Gordon Ramsey study the Ordnance Survey map of the area in preparation for the night-frying exercise on July 24, 1979 code-named 'Sustenance — Fish and Chips'.

162

one of the best shots in the service, insisted upon. Every flying day was now filled to capacity. Nevertheless in the evenings, when there was no night flying practice, there were places to relax and enjoy the fullness of life in that last dwindling period of peace. 'The Talbot' and the 'Queen's Head' in North Weald or 'The Cock' at Epping were favourites and London was only twenty miles away.

In May 1939, No. 17 Squadron arrived from Kenley, switching their Gauntlets for No. 56's Hurricanes and staying briefly before taking up their war station at Debden in September. Friday, September 1 brought the German invasion of Poland and at North Weald the Hurricanes were dispersed around the perimeter of the aerodrome with tents erected close by as temporary crew rooms. 'Tannoy' loudspeakers, connected with the operations room, were strung around the field at the makeshift dispersals. Saturday, September 2, brought the first day of mobilization and on Sunday at 11.15 a.m. the balloon went up. A signal received that day from No. 11 Group headquarters at Uxbridge read: 'War has broken out with Germany only'. Some pilots were disappointed; they could have taken on the world.

Into North Weald came the Blenheim Is of No. 604 'County of Middlesex' Squadron, one of which was flown by John Cunningham with his gunner Jimmy Rawnsley, later to achieve fame as the top scoring night-fighter team. Relegated at first to east coast shipping patrols, the squadron began night-fighter training in October.

Occupying 400 acres between Weald Hall Lane, Church Lane and the Epping-Ongar road, North Weald, now 'E' Sector Station within No. 11 Group, had continually been improved and additional fields had been taken over on the northern boundary which gave originally four grass-surfaced runways. The longest from NE-SW covered 1,233 yards, the second from E-W 1,033 yards and the remaining two of 993 and 883 yards ran from SE-NW and N-S respectively. Two permanent runways, 50ft wide, ran N-S (933 yards) and E-W (923 yards). A fifty-four foot wide asphalt perimeter track extended half-way around the aerodrome on the western side. Aircraft were accommodated in two C-type hangars, four blister hangars and four 'extra over blister' hangars. Fuel supplies totalled 96,000 gallons of aviation spirit, 4,000 gallons of MT fuel and 2,000 gallons of oil. Refuelling was carried out by means of bowsers and trailer tankers. Type 2 flying control was provided and night landing facilities consisted of Glim lamps and goose neck flares. Two satellite landing grounds were provided at Hunsdon and Stapleford Tawney. The contemporary Air Ministry notes mention fog prevalence as considerable.

The station air raid alarm was sounded on both September 4 and 5, the all clear coming after fifteen to thirty minutes. At 6.25 a.m. on Wednesday, September 6, the North Weald controller scrambled six Hurricanes of No. 56 Squadron to investigate a report of a 'bogey' (an unidentified aircraft) over West Mersea. Minutes later two more flights of Hurricanes were despatched and the air raid sirens were sounded in the east coast and Estuary towns. The Chatham anti-aircraft batteries joined in and Spitfires from No. 74 Squadron were scrambled from Hornchurch. In cloudy conditions, the fighters attacked each other in the Southend area and two Hurricanes were shot down by the Spitfires. Pilot Officer Hulton-Harrop died in the wreck of L1985 but Pilot Officer 'Tommy' Rose managed to bale out of L1980 only slightly injured. It was only on the return to North Weald that it was realised that the Luftwaffe was not involved and the RAF had shot down its own aircraft. Throughout Fighter Command the incident became known as the 'Battle of Barking Creek' and, on the following day, Group

Above: Hedgehog! Hurricane N2522 US-P of No. 56 Squadron comes to grief in a hedge bordering the Epping-Ongar road after overshooting the N-S runway. *Below:* Roadhog! Passing the scene of the Hurricane's mishap thirty-nine years later, a driver under instruction on an LTE double-decker bus makes one of his early sorties from the aerodrome.

Captain M. B. Frew took over command of the station with the unenviable task of collating the facts leading to the tragic events of the previous day.

In October, No. 56 Squadron moved to the forward aerodrome at Martlesham Heath leaving a detachment at the 'Weald'. At intervals during the autumn months, the Hurricanes of No. 151 were scrambled to intercept German mine layers over the Thames estuary but without engaging.

The savage winter of 1939-40 cut flying programmes severely but, in mid-January 1940, the pilots of No. 604 Squadron hauled their Blenheims into the freezing air and left for Northolt while a similarly equipped unit, No. 25 Squadron, arrived in their place. One of the brightest events in a dark month was the arrival of the new station commander, Wing Commander Francis Victor Beamish. One of the RAF's most forceful and energetic personalities, he led by example and was to prove a tower of strength during the Weald's ordeal in the forthcoming battle.

On January 23, 1940, a decision was taken by the War Cabinet for the sale of twelve Hurricanes to Finland to aid that country's fight against the Russian aggressor. On February 2, after No. 56 Squadron returned from Martlesham, a number of ground crews from Nos. 56 and 151 were ordered to station headquarters where they were asked if any

would volunteer for a special assignment. Of the sixteen men who volunteered, half were from No. 56 and half from No. 151. They were then told their destination and duties — the servicing of the twelve aircraft sold to Finland. By the 19th of the month they were on their way. For those left at North Weald there was also a taste of the Arctic and the station's three snow ploughs and two sweeps were kept operating to capacity during February when hundreds of tons of snow had to be removed from the runways.

March and April followed the pattern of the early months of the war and it seemed as though the 'Phoney War' was here to stay. On May 10, 1940 it all changed with the inexorable drive of the Wehrmacht towards the sea. As the battle raged throughout the Low Countries, Luxembourg and into France, the squadrons of the Advanced Air Striking Force and the Air Component were seriously depleted in their fight against a numerically superior enemy. To counter the losses sustained by the Hurricane squadrons, the War Cabinet, without the approval of the C-in-C of Fighter Command, Sir Hugh Dowding, ordered the transfer of fresh units from the UK to aerodromes in France as reinforcements.

On May 15, Squadron Leader Donaldson led No. 151 Squadron on patrol from a French aerodrome to destroy six Ju 87 'Stuka' dive

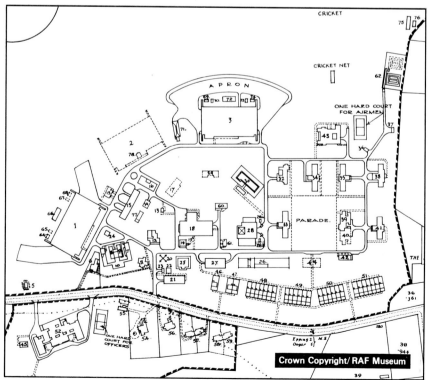

Crown Copyright/ RAF Museum

bombers over Valenciennes, damaging another five. Late in the afternoon of May 16, one flight of No. 56 Squadron led by Flight Lieutenant Ian Soden flew to the aerodrome at Norrent Fontes in France, operating from Vitry-en-Artois. By the 18th the flight had been destroyed and, of the six pilots, Soden was dead as was 'Tommy' Rose who had survived the 'Barking Creek' fiasco.

The following day, while again operating from Vitry, Pilot Officer Bryan John Wicks of No. 56 Squadron was shot down and posted missing. After nearly two weeks he arrived back at North Weald via Belgium and France, leaving Dunkirk under technical arrest as a fifth columnist.

May 28, found 'Teddy' Donaldson with No. 151 over the Dunkirk area. Donaldson was attacking an He 111 when he ran out of ammunition. In sheer frustration he carried out a mock head-on attack whereupon the German pilot jettisoned his bombs and promptly baled out — without his parachute!

In July, the Luftwaffe commenced attacks in strength on the coastal convoys and both squadrons were heavily engaged in protection patrols. On July 9, six Hurricanes from No. 151 engaged a force of 100 enemy aircraft over an east coast convoy. Flight Lieutenant Ironside, the flight commander, nearly blinded by his own blood from severe facial injuries sustained when a cannon shell exploded on the canopy, returned to North Weald and pulled off a miraculously safe landing.

On the opening day of the battle, July 10,

'B' Flight of No. 56 Squadron left early in the morning for the forward aerodrome at Manston and later they were in action over convoy 'Bread' off the North Foreland.

There followed an almost daily procession of savage battles over the crawling lines of little ships running the gauntlet along the south and east coasts. From the melee of whirling aircraft over the south-bound convoy 'Booty' on July 12, a Hurricane bearing the DZ code of No. 151 was seen gliding with a dead engine towards the sea off Orfordness. Flying Officer James Allen, a young New Zealander, was missing from the Mess that evening. The following day No. 56 Squadron despatched eleven aircraft to patrol between Dover and Calais. At about 3.45 p.m. they ran into a dive-bombing attack on a Channel convoy. Sergeants James Roy Cowsill and Joseph Whitfield were hit by the Bf 109 escorts and sent spinning into the cold waters of the Channel.

Twenty-five-year-old Pilot Officer Jack Royston Hamar had been with No. 151 Squadron since early 1940. A veteran of the Dunkirk and convoy battles, he had destroyed six enemy aircraft and probably others. For his proficiency and heroism he was awarded the Distinguished Flying Cross on July 23, 1940. The following day, taking off from North Weald, his Hurricane inexplicably dived into the ground from 500 feet. They took his body back to his home town of Knighton in Radnorshire.

During an early morning attack on Dover harbour on Monday, July 29, Hurricane P3879 was shot down by Bf 109s, carrying Flight Sergeant Cecil John Cooney of No. 56 Squadron to his death. Later in the day twelve Hurricanes of No. 151 Squadron tackled forty Bf 110s of Erpro 210 and ZG26 over a Channel convoy without loss.

On Sunday, August 11, No. 56 Squadron lost a young pilot through the kind of tragic error that occurs all too frequently in war. At 1.00 p.m. his Hurricane, N2667, was attacked by a Spitfire of No. 74 Squadron and shot down into the Thames Estuary. Sergeant Ronnie Baker was picked up dead by a rescue launch.

The days passed in a welter of activity with the loss of familiar faces becoming a common feature of daily life. On August 12, Geoff Page of No. 56 fell to the cross-fire of a group of Dornier gunners; his header tank exploded

Above: Traffic halts on the Epping road while a Hurricane I bearing the pre-war code (GG) of No. 151 Squadron drops down over the boundary hedge — No. 1 hangar in the background. *Below:* Twenty-nine years after the beginning of the Second World War, the hangars were again the backdrop for another war: this time during the re-enactment of one of the bombing raids on the station for the film 'Battle of Britain'.

North Weald
Flugplatz

Lange(ostw.Greenw): 0 ° 9' 0", Breite:51°43 0"
Mißweisung~10°40'(Mitte 1938)

1)	2 Flugzeughallen etwa	7 000 qm
2)	12 Werkstätten u. Nebengebäude etwa	4 500 qm
3)	56 Unterkunftsgebäude etwa	11 000 qm
4)	4 große Unterkunftsgeb. im Bau	
5)	Baustelle	
6)	7 umwallte Gebäude(Muni Häuser oder Befehlsstelle	etwa 1 500 qm
7)	13 Luftschutzunterstände etwa	
	bebaute Fläche etwa	24 000 qm

Erweiterung des Platzes möglich

A good illustration of the depth of German pre-war intelligence concerning the Royal Air Force's front line bases. *Top left:* This Luftwaffe reconnaissance photograph forms the basis for a target map dated May 24, 1939. *Left:* Although we could not trace a British site plan for the same year, this Air Ministry sheet of the camp site dated 1928 approximates the same layout. The footnotes given to each by the opposing air forces are reproduced here in facsimile form. The majority of the German interpretation is very loose although the pre-war Operations Room (RAF building 30) has been correctly described as a 'Befehlsstelle'.

· REFERENCE ·

1.	AEROPLANE SHED		41.	CIVILIAN QTRS [BARRACK BLOCK 'A' TYPE]
2.	" " [SITE ONLY]		42.	SHOPS & STORES [ADJUTANTS]
3.	" "		43.	INSTITUTE.
4.	COMPASS PLATFORM		44.	CHURCH & CINEMA [SITE ONLY]
5.	BOMB STORE [EXISTING]		45.	SQUASH RACQUETS COURT.
6.	WOs QUARTER.		46.	ONE W.Os QUARTER [WO TYPE]
7.	WORKSHOP. [CARPENTERS]		47.	TWO " QUARTERS [D°]
8.	W/T LECTURE ROOM & LIBRARY		48.	SEVEN 'b' TYPE MARRIED AIRMENS QTRS
9.	GENERAL LECTURE ROOM.		49.	SIX " " " " "
10.	MACHINE SHOP [CARPENTERS]		50.	SIX " " " " "
11.	OFFICES [STATION]		51.	SEVEN " " " " "
12.	GUARD HOUSE.		52.	OFFICERS MESS & QUARTERS.
13.	LATRINES [TECHNICAL]		53.	W/T STATION.
13A	ENGINE TEST HOUSE.		54.	ONE GP III MARRIED OFFICER'S QTR [WO TYPE]
14.	BLACKSMITHS' SHOP		55.	GARAGE FOR GROUP III QUARTER.
15.	ENGINE WORKSHOPS.		56.	ONE GP IV MARRIED OFFICERS QTR [WO TYPE]
16.	ARMOURY, ARMᵗ INSTRᴺ, WORKSHOP & PHOTO		57.	TWO GP V " " QTRS
17.	ARMOURY [SITE ONLY]		58.	ONE GP V " " QTR [SITE ONLY]
18.	MAIN STORES.		59.	ONE GP V " " " ["]
19.	FIRE PARTY & TENDER HOUSE.		60.	LUBRICANT & LIQUID CONTAINERS STORE.
20.	FLAGSTAFF.		61.	INFLAMMABLE STORE.
21.	POWER HOUSE.		62.	No 1 SECTION BULK PETROL STORAGE [AVIATION]
22.	COOLING POND.		63.	No 2 " " " " [SITE ONLY]
23.	OIL TANKS.		64.	PUMP HOUSE [SITE ONLY]
24.	WATER TOWER.		65.	PETROL EXPENSE STORAGE TANK [SITE]
25.	RESERVOIR.		66.	PILOTS' ROOM & LOCKER ROOM
26.	W & B & CONTRACTORS YARDS.		67.	PETROL EXPENSE STORAGE TANK [SITE]
27.	FUEL STORE.		68.	PUMP HOUSE. [SITE ONLY]
28.	M.T. YARD.		69.	PUMP HOUSE.
28A	D° PETROL INSTALLATION.		70.	PETROL EXPENSE STORAGE TANK.
28B	D° " "		71.	GUN TESTING BUTT.
29.	OFFICES [SITE ONLY]		72.	PILOTS' ROOM & LOCKER ROOM.
30.	OPERATIONS BLOCK.		73.	PETROL EXPENSE STORAGE TANK.
31.	MACHINE GUN RANGE.		74.	PUMP HOUSE.
32.	SERGEANTS' MESS.		75.	PAVILION [PROPOSED]
33.	BARRACK BLOCK 'C' TYPE.		76.	D° LATRINE [PROPOSED]
34.	" " " "		77.	PARACHUTE STORE.
35.	" " " "		78.	DUTY PILOTS BLOCK.
36.	MORTUARY		33A	ACCOM. FOR 11 AIRMEN PILOTS. [DUTY PILOTS ROOM]
37.	INCINERATOR			
38.	SICK QUARTERS			
39.	DINING ROOM & COOKHOUSE			
40.	" " " [EXTENSION NECESSARY IF SQUADRONS BECOME MOBILE]			

Above: **Hurricanes of No. 151 Squadron soar from the grass in June 1940 while two more from No. 56 taxy towards the top of the runway. The GPO wireless masts formed both a landmark and a potential hazard (Imperial War Museum).** *Right:* **Today poplars dominate the North Weald skyline. A glider from the Essex Gliding Club settles on the same runway.**

and the Hurricane fell like a blazing brand. Fighting his way out of the consuming flames at 15,000 feet, he fell through 10,000 feet of space before his charred hands could manipulate the rip cord. He did not return to operational flying until 1943.

At 4.20 p.m. on Eagle Day, August 13, Sergeant Hillwood charged a Bf 110 head-on over Sheerness and was shot down for his temerity. The 56 Squadron pilot baled out, landed in the sea and swam two miles to a Sheppey beach.

August 18, 1940 brought a change in command for No. 151 Squadron when Squadron Leader J. A. G. Gordon, who had succeeded 'Teddy' Donaldson, was admitted to Rochford Hospital suffering severe burns. Two days later his successor Squadron Leader Eric Bruce King arrived on the station.

On Saturday, August 24, the Luftwaffe attacks on aerodromes began and these were to continue daily until the first week of September. The day began with clear skies

but the promise of fine, sunny weather did nothing to allay the fears of the Sector Controllers in the south. At 3.40 p.m., eight Hurricanes of No. 151 Squadron were scrambled to intercept a raid approaching from the east. Climbing hard, the pilots were confronted with the awesome sight of a mass of Do 17s, He 111s, Bf 110s and Bf 109s stacked in layers from 15,000 feet upwards. As the squadron went in to attack the Heinkels of KG53, they were joined by nine more Hurricanes of 'Treble One' squadron which selected the Dorniers for their special opening gambit — the head-on attack in line abreast. The bulk of the enemy bombers

jettisoned their bomb loads and turned for the coast but the remainder pressed on to North Weald where they dropped nearly 200 bombs. Both the officers' and airmen's married quarters were severely damaged and the power house also suffered badly. A large number of missiles fell along the Epping-Ongar road damaging the water and gas mains. Several delayed-action bombs were included in the downpour and some of these exploded the following day, the others being successfully dealt with by the Station Demolition Squad. Nine members of the Essex Regiment, who were in a shelter which received a direct hit, were killed and ten other personnel injured.

In the bombing attack of August 24, 1940, nine members of the 7th Battalion, The Essex Regiment, stationed at North Weald for aerodrome defence, were killed. We felt it was important to establish exactly where they lost their lives. By an incredible coincidence, one of the readers of *After the Battle* **magazine, Mr.**

John Smith of Hertford, was not only a seventeen-year-old private *(photo below)* **in 'G' Company but was in the very shelter when it received a direct hit. On Saturday, January 26, 1980, we took him back to the aerodrome to indicate exactly what happened.**

Company HQ was in this house within the perimeter, now derelict.

The Essex Regiment were billeted in the nearby MT hangar. Bunks were set in rows inside and parades were held on the concrete forecourt.

Intimation of the raid had come the previous afternoon when a lone Dornier flew a complete circuit of the aerodrome. No shots were fired in defence until it was leaving. An airman remarked to the soldiers, all teenagers, that: 'We will cop it now as that was a recce plane'. *Above:* John Smith indicates the direction from where the bombers came.

'All Army and Air Force personnel man your aerodrome action stations!' When the Tannoy order was broadcast at about 4.30 p.m., the soldiers ran out of the hangar towards their shelter (exactly like that in the photo *below*). A stick of bombs began falling parallel to the main road hitting the ground all around the soldiers, the thundering explosions rocking the ground. Private Smith was last in through the entrance . . . just as he sat down a

bomb hit the far end of the shelter blowing his best friend Private Miles into the tree and burying all the others. Altogether nine men died and John Smith spent the next five months in hospital — his ankle was almost severed and he suffered a severe head wound. Today there is no sign of the shelter but the force of the explosion is graphically illustrated by the two barrack block wings destroyed.

Eight of his mates now lie in St. Andrew's Churchyard, North Weald.

The fire-ravaged skeleton of a No. 25 Squadron Blenheim lies in the gutted cavern of No. 2 hangar after the September 3 raid.

Today only the guide rails to the massive doors remain to indicate its position.

The defending pilots claimed three He 111s destroyed with two Bf 109s as probables. No. 151 lost one Hurricane in a crash landing, the pilot being admitted to Ramsgate Hospital. Four other Hurricanes were damaged. One, V7380 flown by Squadron Leader King, had the propellor shot away in combat with a Bf 110, but was skilfully glided back and brought safely down. Six days later, in Hurricane V7369, he led No. 151 on patrol over the Thames Estuary when the squadron engaged an enemy force of 130 aircraft. Eric King was shot down by the escorting Bf 109s, his remains were found in his burnt-out Hurricane at Temple Street, Strood. In the same battle, twenty-eight-year-old Polish pilot, Sergeant Feliks Gmur fell to the Messerschmitts' guns, his Hurricane R4213 pile-driving into a field at Jacks Hatch, Epping Green.

During the early morning of Saturday, August 31, the Chain Home Radar at Canewdon in Essex gave warning of the approach of a massive force of aircraft estimated at 200 plus. Nearing the coast, the great column split into a number of separate raids, one of which headed in the direction of North Weald. A dozen Hurricanes of No. 56, scrambled earlier, met the raiders in the vicinity of Colchester, but before they could mount an attack they were 'bounced' by the escorting Bf 109s and 110s, losing four of their number without scoring. The Dorniers penetrated to the 'Weald. One of the four lost was Flight Lieutenant Percy 'Mouse' Weaver and neither he nor his aircraft have ever been found. Only hours after his death in action, the award of his DFC was announced. The squadron itself had almost ceased to exist, having lost eleven aircraft in five days of savage battles.

On Sunday, September 1, No. 249 Squadron led by Squadron Leader John Grandy arrived from Boscombe Down to relieve the hard pressed No. 56. Without a commander and reduced to seven Hurricanes, they left for Boscombe to reform and rest. On the same day No. 151 left for Digby in Lincolnshire, it too being without a commanding officer and reduced to ten serviceable aircraft and twelve pilots. From Digby came No. 46 Squadron to take up residence eventually at the satellite of Stapleford. Another 'posting in' was No. 25 Squadron with their new commanding officer Squadron Leader Mitchell, leaving one flight on detachment at Martlesham.

No. 249 had barely settled in at North Weald when they were committed to action. The following day one of their Hurricanes was

The steel doors at the northen end of the adjacent No. 1 hangar still retain the scars of bomb splinters.

lost and two damaged in crash landings, the pilots escaping unhurt.

At 9.40 a.m. on Tuesday, September 3, a force of thirty Do 17s escorted by fifty Bf 110s crossed high over the south-east corner of Kent. Turning inland, they followed the course of the Thames glittering in the early morning sun 20,000 feet below. Between Canvey Island and Tilbury the ponderous mass swung north over Essex.

At North Weald, No. 249 had just landed and were refuelling when the station warning sounded. Those Hurricanes that had completed the operation, roared across the field in a race to get airborne before the bombs started falling. Others, their tanks only partially replenished, hurried after them and by the time the raiding force appeared at 15,000 feet from the north-east, all the station's serviceable aircraft were in the air. Three Blenheims of No. 25 Squadron also managed to clear the station and climb towards the west.

At a serious height disadvantage, No. 249 climbed as steeply and as rapidly as they could to deflect the Dorniers from their bombing run, but the bombs were already falling. Both No. 151 and No. 25 Squadrons' hangars were hit and gutted by fire. The MT yard was badly

damaged and several lorries set alight. Living quarters were again damaged and the old Operations Room hit and partly destroyed. The new Operations Block took a direct hit on the roof and survived. The Tannoy and station warning systems were put out of action and the main stores were severely damaged. In fact there were few buildings that did not carry scars from this raid. Over 200 bombs, some delayed-action, landed squarely on the aerodrome. Most fell in the south and south western corner of the landing ground and although heavily cratered, it was not rendered unserviceable for daytime use. One airman and one civilian died, seven were seriously injured and thirty slightly hurt.

Wing Commander Francis Victor Beamish, who had flown regularly with his units since his appointment as Station Commander, received official recognition of his leadership and drive at an investiture at Buckingham Palace on September 4, 1940 when he received his DSO from the hands of HM King George VI.

On September 5, as a contingency measure against further bombing attacks, station headquarters was moved to Blake Hall, the Operations Room to a building at Marden Ash, sick quarters to Bury Lodge, Bury Lane,

The standard pre-war Operations Block (building 30) now often used by ATC Cadets on weekend camps.

The Operations Block (building 94), used during the Battle of Britain until September 5, still bears the evidence of the direct hit.

and the MT Pool to Potter Street. No. 151 Squadron HQ transferred to Digby, and No. 56 Squadron HQ to Boscombe Down.

With the enemy's tactical change on September 7, when London became the primary target and continued as such over the next few weeks, the southern aerodromes were relieved of the Luftwaffe's attentions. Losses had been severe among the squadrons defending their own and other bases and, in the seven days of unrelenting struggle, No. 249 Squadron was reduced to seven serviceable aircraft.

On September 17, at 2.30 a.m. a solitary bomber dropped two random 100kg bombs. One exploded close to the side of the western perimeter track, the other in a nearby field. Throughout the remainder of the month, Wing Commander Beamish flew operationally at every opportunity. On September 19 he returned to North Weald in a No. 249 Squadron Hurricane which looked like the proverbial colander. With the hydraulic system shot away and no brakes he set the bullet-torn machine down like a crate of eggs and walked away unhurt.

Pilots now flew with a reckless disregard for their own lives, manifesting all the symptoms of sheer fatigue. On September 27, a South African, Pilot Officer Percy Burton of No. 249, rammed a Bf 110, killing himself and the enemy in the massive disintegration of both aircraft.

Also during the month No. 25 Squadron scored their first double victory when Pilot Officer Herrick shot down a Do 17 and an He 111 on the same night. A few nights later he destroyed another He 111. These were to be the last claims made while flying Blenheims for soon afterwards the squadron was re-equipped with Beaufighters.

On October 2, the station received a visit from Sir Hugh Dowding and on the following day by Captain Balfour, the Under Secretary of State. On the 8th, No. 25 Squadron departed to Debden and No. 257 Squadron, led by Squadron Leader 'Bob' Tuck, arrived from Martlesham.

On Saturday, October 19, a member of the American press visited the station in the person of Mr. C. Olsson, a journalist on the staff of *Life* magazine. Unfortunately, as far as his copy was concerned, he had chosen one of the quietest days during the whole of the battle. However, as if on cue, a Hurricane of No. 249 Squadron, V6635, arrived over the base in obvious trouble. Pilot Officer A. R. F. Thompson brought it in for a forced landing without injury to himself and Mr. Olsson departed satisfied.

Sunday, October 27, brought a rash of German attacks on aerodromes in the south and east. Heavy cloud formations assisted the raiders in their tasks but failed to save the Dornier that carried out a single-handed raid on North Weald. Dropping through the cloud

Above: The Operations Room — still used for 'operations' of sorts but hardly in keeping with its historic past. *Below:* The first location for the dispersed Sector E operations was behind what was called the Drill Hall at Cooper's Hill, Marden Ash near Ongar, about four miles from the aerodrome. This is now the Haunt Social Centre but the actual building which housed the Operations Room itself was pulled down in the 1960s. Operations remained here for 2½ years until more suitable accommodation had been prepared at Blake Hall (near Bobbingworth) which was already the location of North Weald Station HQ.

On the outbreak of war, Blake Hall, owned by the Capel-Cure family for 200 years, was being used by the family's London firm of insurance brokers as a dispersed location for its records and office staff who were accommodated in the estate riding school buildings. Early in 1940. the Hall was taken over by the Royal Army Medical Corps and all the furniture was moved and locked away in the library (on the left in the photo *above*) for safe keeping. After the bombing of North Weald, the Air Ministry took over the Hall on September 5 for the station headquarters without advising Major George Capel-Cure who was then living with his family in Shropshire. The first he knew of the take-over was when an urgent telegram arrived from the local vicar to ask someone to come quickly to rescue the contents of the Hall which had been unceremoniously dumped in the garden. With the absence of his son in the Army, his daughter-in-law, Mrs. Nigel Capel-Cure, reached the Hall after passing the checkpoints in what was now a defence area with difficulty. With the help of two airmen she was able to rescue most of the family's belongings, storing them wherever she could in the neighbourhood.

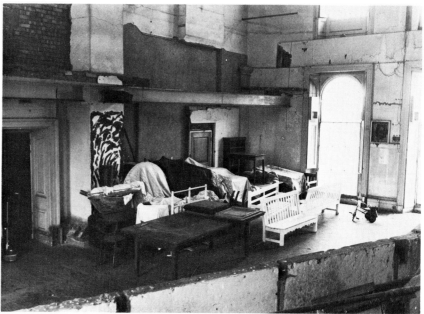

Thereafter the RAF had to be left to their own devices. To enable the Operations Room, currently in makeshift accommodation at Marden Ash, to be incorporated with the Station HQ, the south-west wing was completely gutted, the library and drawing room ceilings removed and five bedrooms and two bathrooms ripped out above. A huge red-brick extension was added and numerous Nissen huts constructed in the grounds. This then became the operations centre for Sector E for the remainder of the war.

On the death of his father in 1943, title to the Hall had passed to Major Nigel Capel-Cure *(far left)* but it was not until 1948, after a prolonged battle with the Air Ministry, that re-possession of the family home was possible. The state of the Hall was appalling and two years' restoration work was necessary before the building was made habitable. Major Capel-Cure had the red-brick extension demolished, the air-raid shelters and Nissen huts dismantled and the grounds reinstated but the compensation was insufficient to rebuild the interior of the Operations Room. In 1950, when the family moved back, this wing was virtually sealed off and left. To the editor, finding the room in 1980 was a unique and exciting experience although the Major finds it difficult to match our enthusiasm for the desecration of his family home! Although the floor and the joists to the upper balcony were removed when the extension was demolished and the dangerous overhanging plate glass taken out, the lower tiers still remain. (Access to the upper balcony was from the extension built on the south-west wing.) Parts of the 'Tote' boards *(above right)* can still be seen and some contemporary maps *(right)* have survived. The ventilation plant was removed *(above)* but much of the trunking has been left. The editor hopes he has persuaded Major Capel-Cure to look on the room with a new historical eye, for in years to come it will be an integral part of the long history of Blake Hall.

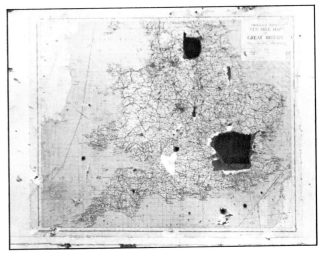

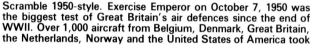

Scramble 1950-style. Exercise Emperor on October 7, 1950 was the biggest test of Great Britain's air defences since the end of WWII. Over 1,000 aircraft from Belgium, Denmark, Great Britain, the Netherlands, Norway and the United States of America took part. *Left:* **Pilots of No. 72 Squadron scramble for their de Havilland Vampire F3 jet fighters at North Weald (Central Press).** *Right:* **Twenty-nine years later, the weed-choked and rubble strewn blast pens are now repositories for steel pipes.**

base, the German salvoed his bombs then hurriedly popped back into cover. Only one bomb fell on the camp, doing no damage, the remainder all dropping close to the GPO Wireless Station at Weald Gullet. No. 249 Squadron had taken off just prior to the attack and it was Pilot Officer Millington who spotted the Do 17 emerging from cloud cover and gave chase. Catching up with it over the Thames Estuary he delivered a long burst which sent it tumbling down into the cloud once more. He followed but on emerging under the cloud layer could find no trace of it.

On Tuesday, October 29, No. 249 Squadron had just become airborne and No. 257 were commencing their take-off run when, at 4.40 p.m., a formation of Bf 109s of 3/Erpro 210 flashed over the camp, scattering 100kg bombs and machine gunning as they went. Bullets struck the buildings like hammer blows and traversed the field with geysering spouts of earth and divots.

Roaring and bouncing across the grass, the Hurricanes, unable to deviate, were at their most vulnerable. The first 'vic' of three, led by Bob Tuck, had just become airborne and were about forty feet up over the end of the runway when a 100kg bomb exploded below and to the right. Hurricane V6852, piloted by Sergeant A. G. Girdwood, took the full blast under the starboard wing which threw it towards Tuck's aircraft. The stricken Hurricane half-rolled and passed inverted over the other aircraft before nose-diving into the ground and bursting into flames. 'Jock' Girdwood, a much respected NCO pilot, was burned to death.

About forty-five 100kg bombs were dropped, twenty-seven landing on the camp mostly on the landing area, and two on open ground near the Officers' Mess. The guard room, just rebuilt after damage in a previous raid, was virtually demolished, a Bellman hangar also suffered further damage which rendered it useless and a 30cwt lorry and mechanical crane stored inside were destroyed. Several dispersal huts were also destroyed or damaged and a Miles Magister — the station hack — came to a sticky end. Nineteen fatal casualties occurred with another forty-two injured. Despite the cratering of the aerodrome surface, it still remained serviceable for daytime use. Only one of the raiders was shot down — the leader of the brilliantly-executed attack — Staffelkapitan Otto Hintze who baled out and was captured.

On the penultimate day of the battle, No. 249 Squadron intercepted and turned a force of Bf 109s heading for North Weald, destroying one and damaging another before the enemy fled towards the mouth of the Thames.

On November 7, No. 257 Squadron returned to Martlesham while No. 46 moved to North Weald from Stapleford. On Armistice Day, Monday November 11, No. 46 Squadron was scrambled to meet a force of hostiles approaching Harwich. Off the Orfordness coast they found No. 257's Hurricanes lining up for an attack on ten Fiat BR20 bombers and twenty-two Fiat CR42 biplane fighters of the Regia Aeronautica. After the initial attack by No. 257, the enemy formation was split and stood little chance against the speed and fire power of the Hurricanes. That their losses were so small speaks highly of the skill and heroism of the Italian pilots and crews. No. 46 pulled down their share and returned to base without loss.

The remainder of the month was given over to coastal patrols but, in December, No. 249 commenced flying 'Rhubarbs' over France while No. 46 returned north to Digby. No. 56 Squadron returned to its home base with a new CO, Squadron Leader H. M. Pinfold, remaining until June 1941 when it left for Martlesham.

In May 1941 No. 249 Squadron had left for duty in Malta and No. 242 Squadron flew in from Stapleford to replace them, staying only until July. They were to return to North Weald in August 1942 having been reformed in April after decimation in Java.

In June 1941 came the first of the American 'Eagle' Squadrons, No. 71. Equipped with Spitfire VAs, they flew their first operations over France in September, losing three pilots. In August No. 222 'Natal' Squadron took up residence and were actively engaged on fighter sweeps over the continent until their departure in August 1942.

December 1941 brought the second of the 'Eagle' squadrons, No. 121, to North Weald while in the same month No. 71 moved out. Equipped with Spitfire VBs, No. 121 operated with No. 222 Squadron on 'Circus' and 'Rhubarb' operations, both units being committed to action against the German capital ships during the 'Channel Dash' in February 1942.

In June No. 121 moved to Rochford and the first of the 'Wealds' Norwegian units, No. 331 Squadron, arrived to take its place. When No.

222 Squadron departed in August, No. 332 Norwegian Squadron came as a replacement unit and, together, the Norwegians flew 'Rhubarbs', 'Ramrods', 'Rodeos' and 'Roadsteads'. Both squadrons left the station briefly in August to take part in the ill-fated Dieppe raid 'Operation Jubilee' — No. 331 flying from Manston on that occasion and No. 32 from Redhill.

From 1942 to 1944 a steady stream of British, Commonwealth and Allied fighter squadrons left their mark at North Weald but after D-Day activity was gradually scaled down until the station found itself in a quiet backwater. Operational flying ceased completely in early 1945.

On June 23-24, 1945 a rally of Observer Corps members took place on the aerodrome and on July 1 the station was transferred to No. 46 Group, Transport Command. In July, No. 304 'Mazonia' Polish Squadron arrived with Wellington Mk C15s and Warwick Mk C3s to be joined by No. 301 Polish Squadron in August on transport operations. Due to the unsuitability of the North Weald runways for heavily laden aircraft, both units moved to Chedburgh in September.

From October 1945 to September 1948 the station was used as No. 9 Personnel Despatch Centre and various selection boards were also established there.

In 1949, North Weald returned to Fighter Command and in March No. 601 'County of London' Squadron, Royal Auxiliary Air Force moved in closely followed by No. 604 'County of Middlesex' Squadron. Both were equipped with Spitfire LF 16es. In June the formation of the Royal Auxiliary Air Force Traffic Control took place and in 1950 North Weald's first jets arrived, both squadrons converting to De Havilland Vampire F3s. In March 1950 they were joined by No. 72 Squadron also flying the Vampire. Conversion to Meteors came for all three units in 1952.

During April 1953, No. 72 Squadron left the 'Weald' which in October became once more a Sector Operations Centre and the Headquarters of the Metropolitan Sector.

In December 1953, No. 111 Squadron was reformed at North Weald and equipped with Hawker Hunters. With these aircraft they became, under the brilliant direction of their commanding officer, Squadron Leader Roger Topp, the premier formation aerobatic team in world aviation. As the 'Black Arrows', with their twenty-two all-black Hunters, they set new standards in aerobatic techniques and

thrilled thousands during their displays at Farnborough and elsewhere.

From 1953 to 1959 the aerodrome became a base for various Reserve Flights. In 1957 the auxiliary squadrons were disbanded and on April 2 of that year Fighter Command Modification Centre was formed.

In August 1958, 'Treble One' left North Weald and three months later on November 15 the station was relegated to care and maintenance status. On September 1, 1964, it was further reduced to an inactive (guarded) state, but received a new lease of life when it was transferred to the Army Department on January 4, 1966.

During the 1960s the aerodrome became an active gliding centre. On September 7, 1969 a K13 glider BGA 1510 was being launched by car tow on the pilot's first solo when the cable snapped at about 600 feet. The glider turned to starboard, the turn steepening and developing into a spin from which no recovery was made, the pilot being seriously injured in the crash. Then, on July 4, 1976, a Piper PA-28R-200-2 registration G-BBOP was preparing to land at North Weald. During a descending turn on to the final approach, the aircraft collided with an eighty-two feet high radio mast and crashed to the ground killing both occupants.

Between 1977 and 1979 the future of the old aerodrome was in the balance. Various plans were discussed and rejected but in August 1979 the Epping Forest District Council decided to take advantage of the MOD's bargain offer and purchased the station complex for the princely sum of £660,000.

Today North Weald echoes to the roar of double-decker red buses and articulated lorries as budding London Transport drivers rumble up and down the huge runways making occasional stops to pick up phantom passengers. The other group of drivers, intent on obtaining their Heavy Goods Vehicle licence, steer their ungainly charges around the perimeter tracks. One wonders if they are ever tempted to line up on the runway threshold, open the throttle wide and go

The wartime expansion of North Weald. The aerodrome photographed two years after the end of the war showing the runway extensions to the north and west, completion of the perimeter track and additional dispersals (Crown Copyright). In 1951, a further 2,000ft spur was added to the northern end of the 4,350ft N-S runway to enable the airfield to cater for jet aircraft and two T2 hangars Nos. 4 and 5, removed from Willingale, re-erected on the western side. The M11 motorway now just touches the south-western dispersal but has left the flying area untouched. Although the Ministry of Defence still own most of the buildings, Epping Forest District Council hope to develop the aerodrome into a leisure centre. *Overleaf:* **North Weald in October 1979.**

hammering down the massive expanse of asphalt hoping by some miracle to emulate the past users and rise unfettered to the skies.

By the old main gate of North Weald stands a stone monolith which was erected to commemorate the Norwegians who flew and died while serving on the station. Unveiled on June 19, 1952, by the Crown Princess of Norway, Princess Astrid, it could equally be a tribute to the pilots of all nationalities who died 'in ops' from the 'Weald'. For after all, they were all brothers in arms.

NORTHERN 'JET' EXTENSION

POST-WAR CONTROL TOWER

FIRST OPS BLOCK

SECOND OPS BLOCK

SITE OF SHELTER

MT HANGAR

TO ONGAR

Martlesham Heath

BY WILF NICOLL

Martlesham Heath, situated seven miles east-north-east of Ipswich on the eastern side of the A12 Woodbridge road, was a natural site for an aerodrome consisting as it does of some 2,631 acres of fairly level sandy soil overlying gravel which provided a reasonable degree of drainage.

Towards the end of 1916, a centre was formed at Martlesham Heath by Bertram Hopkinson for the official testing of prototype aircraft but it was not until January of the following year that the Royal Flying Corps moved its Testing Squadron under the command of Henry Tizard from Upavon to take up residence. The station was then officially opened on the 16th of the month.

In October, 1917, the title Aeroplane Experimental Station was bestowed upon Martlesham with Lieutenant Colonel H. L. Cooper posted to command. Its pilots were required to fly every type and class of aircraft from fighters to bombers and the accurate assessment of captured enemy types was part and parcel of their hazardous duties.

Throughout 1918, extensive testing and re-design work took place on the Vickers F.B.27 later to be named the Vimy and, although too late to see service in the Great War, it achieved immortality as the aircraft that carried Alcock and Brown on their record breaking flight between Newfoundland and Ireland in June 1919. Not without its early troubles, tests were delayed on the F.B.27s due to trouble with the airscrews and on September 11, 1918, the third prototype, B9954, stalled on take-off with a full load of bombs which exploded in the subsequent crash, killing the pilot.

In 1919 it was decided by the newly-formed Air Ministry that the aerodrome site should be leased on a more secure basis and towards this end negotiations were set in motion, finally reaching fruition on November 14, 1921 when a five year lease was taken out with the owner, the Right Honourable Ernest George Pretyman M.P. In 1923 this was extended to one of nine hundred and ninety nine years.

On October 6, 1922 there occurred a mysterious incident when a large wooden hangar containing the entire collection of captured enemy aircraft caught fire in the early hours and was totally destroyed.

During 1924 a brilliant young Flying Officer pilot was posted to Martlesham where he did valuable work on the various flight testing programmes. After five years he resigned his commission and joined the staff of the Vickers-Armstrong Aircraft Company where as Joseph 'Mutt' Summers he brought all his skill and expertise to test flying the prototype of Reginald J. Mitchell's brain-child, the Spitfire. Later he was also to fly the prototype Wellington and was involved deeply in the early tests of Barnes Wallis's 'bouncing' bombs.

Situated as it was on open heathland, Martlesham presented a picture of great natural beauty during late summer and autumn. The gorse, which grew in great profusion, dotted the heath like solar flares with wine-coloured rivers of heather in between. They also presented a potential hazard as was evidenced in August 1930 when a bush fire of frightening dimensions swept towards the airfield, lasting for three weeks before succumbing to the Herculean efforts of the station and local fire brigades.

Station headquarters September 1979.

On July 6, 1936 the new king Edward VIII arrived at Martlesham with his brother the Duke of York (later King George VI) as part of his inspection tour of the Royal Air Force. Among the many new types he inspected were the Spitfire, Hurricane, Battle, Blenheim, Wellington, Hampden and Lysander — names which in a few short years would be as well-known to the public as they were to the members of the service. During the test flying of the Spitfire the qualities of this supreme aircraft were not apparently appreciated by everyone. One day at Martlesham a Group Captain was watching it perform and was heard to say to a colleague in scathing tones 'There's a racehorse for you'. Then turning to the Hurricane parked nearby, he added 'That's more like an aeroplane'. Rumour has it that his opinion changed rapidly during the summer of 1940.

Despite the hazardous nature of the flying that was carried out at Martlesham, the

The King reviews his air force. As part of his inspection tour of the RAF on July 9, 1936, King Edward VIII visited Martlesham where he saw the latest types of aircraft. Accompanied by the Chief of the Air Staff, Sir Edward L. Ellington and the station CO, Group Captain Maund, he prepares to enter the Bristol 130 prototype bomber transport K3583, christened Bombay in April 1937. Behind is the Armstrong Whitworth AW23 prototype bomber transport K3585 later developed as the Whitley bomber (Popperfoto).

number of serious accidents was small indeed. It was inevitable however that from time to time a bad one would occur involving serious injury to those involved and sometimes even death. One such tragic event happened on May 28, 1937 when a Hawker Demon two seater fighter of No. 64 Squadron was carrying out spin and recovery exercises over the aerodrome. The pilot failed to recover from his last spin and the aircraft crashed on to the middle of the aerodrome killing both occupants.

In the wake of the Munich crisis in the autumn of 1938, plans were put into operation to place Martlesham in a state of readiness for the outbreak of war that now seemed inevitable. Primitive attempts at camouflage were carried out on buildings and the aerodrome surface, security was reviewed and tightened and aircraft dispersed around the vast aerodrome perimeter. In June, 1939 the station was visited by Sir Hugh Dowding, the AOC of Fighter Command, when the plans for Martlesham's assimilation into the nation's air defence system were no doubt discussed at length in Station Headquarters.

On September 1, the day that Hitler's invasion of Poland began, the Aircraft and Armament Experimental Establishment moved west to Boscombe Down, Wiltshire. With the outbreak of war, Martlesham's days of experimental testing were over and the station was relegated to the status of a forward aerodrome in the North Weald 'E' Sector of No. 11 Group, Fighter Command.

During the early days of the 'phoney war', squadrons arrived and departed on a rotational basis, none of them staying for any length of time. Work on surface improvement went on apace to furnish better take-off and landing facilities for aircraft operating under combat conditions. Anything considered to be a potential hazard to flying was forcefully and sometimes brutishly dealt with, even to the extent of levelling the burial mounds of the ancient dead, the round barrows which had stood sacrosanct for centuries on the north-west of the aerodrome.

In the spring of 1940 Parachute and Cable Rocket apparatus was planted across the face of the aerodrome although this was never used operationally in its defence.

Throughout that first wartime spring the Hurricanes from North Weald and Debden alternated in their tenancy of the 'Heath' from

where they flew incessant coastal patrols. But as Europe suddenly erupted with the invasion of the Low Countries and France, patrols were extended to cover the beaches of Belgium and Northern France giving the pilots their first chance to tangle with the Luftwaffe's experienced fighter elite.

The Battle of Britain was heralded in at Martlesham in rousing style. At 5.15 a.m. on Wednesday July 10, 1940, a number of unidentified enemy aircraft appeared from the clouds and scattered eighteen 50kg bombs along the edge of the aerodrome without causing either casualties or damage. At 1.20 a.m. the following morning and again at 4.59 a.m. 'Red Alert' warnings were received at the station but no attack was made on the aerodrome.

On Friday, July 12, the Hurricanes of 'A' Section, No. 17 Squadron, led by Flying Officer Count M. E. Czernin, arrived from Debden at 10.00 a.m. and in a number of skirmishes with the enemy in the vicinity of the convoy 'Booty' off Orfordness claimed one Do 17 and two He 111s destroyed. At 7.48 p.m. the same evening, the Defiants of 'A' Flight, No. 264 Squadron landed from Duxford.

Shortly after 3.00 a.m. on Sunday, July 14, an Armstrong Whitworth Whitley V of No. 77 Squadron, serial N1365 based at Driffield, staggered from the east towards the aerodrome with its starboard propeller feathered. As it crossed the aerodrome at a low altitude three crew members, Sergeants Silverwood, Barrie and Amos abandoned the stricken aircraft and parachuted to safety. The captain, Flying Officer Piddington, and his second pilot Sergeant Fenning then brought the bomber in for a forced landing. The starboard engine had seized up after being struck by flak over Holland and the return journey over the North Sea had been accomplished on one engine.

On Tuesday, July 23, a De Havilland Flamingo touched down at 11.23 a.m. bringing Neville Chamberlain, Brigadier General Gourlay and General Hylor on an inspection of the station as part of their tour of the east coast defences. Later in the day further visits were made by General Taylor, the Inspector General of Fortifications, and Air Commodore Saunders.

By July 25, the station had become almost exclusively an advanced operational base with

numerous squadrons arriving and departing each day. It was on this date that the signal 'Air Raid Message Purple' was introduced into the station warning system. On receipt of the signal all vehicle headlights had to be extinguished.

During the early hours of the following day, two Vickers Wellingtons and one Whitley were forced by severe weather conditions to refuel at Martlesham before proceeding on to their respective bases. After their departure there was some consternation amongst the service police and station defence personnel with the discovery of a small bomb container laden with incendiaries which had apparently been jettisoned by one of the bombers on its approach.

Bad weather again prevailed on Saturday, July 27, with the most violent thunderstorms breaking over the southern half of the country. At 12.30 p.m. the heavens opened up over Martlesham with a rainstorm of tropical intensity which lasted for an hour-and-a-half, flooding all the low-lying buildings and producing a sizeable lake on the landing ground. The following day was spent improving the serviceability of the storm drains.

By Monday, July 29, the surface of the aerodrome had dried out sufficiently to enable both Nos. 17 and 85 Squadrons to carry out operations. During the course of the day both units claimed one enemy bomber each in separate actions. After a running battle between No. 151 Squadron's Hurricanes and the Bf 110s of Erprobungsgruppe 210 and Zerstorergeschwader 26 over the Thames estuary, Flying Officer C. D. Whittingham was forced to make an emergency landing in Hurricane P3119 at Martlesham. The pilot was unhurt and his aircraft only slightly damaged.

On the 30th No. 85 Squadron scored again when it intercepted one of two Bf 110s of Gruppe 210 shadowing an east coast convoy. The German pilot in an effort to shake off his pursuers took his aircraft down to wave-top height. With inexperienced pilots on his tail this tactic might have worked but the two Hurricanes now pursuing him were flown by Flight Lieutenant H. R. 'Hammy' Hamilton and Sergeant Geoffrey 'Sammy' Allard, two of the finest fighter pilots in the RAF. After a chase of thirty-five miles, at times only six feet above the waves, the Bf 110 was sent crashing into the sea, taking with it Leutnant Herold and his gunner.

For some time staff accommodation had posed a problem for Station HQ and on the last day of July a request was transmitted to Air Ministry to sanction the requisitioning of Kesgrave Hall, three-and-a-half miles east of Ipswich, and a number of private houses in Deben Avenue.

A draft of 150 airmen arrived from Blackpool Ground Crew Reception Centre on Thursday, August 1, presumably for ground defence duties. However, as neither of the stations at Bawdsey or Orfordness had a complement of defence personnel, the draft was split equally between these two establishments.

Throughout the previous two days a series of mysterious explosions filled the security personnel with a great deal of unease. A search of the surrounding areas produced nothing in the way of evidence as to the cause or location of these until the Royal Navy hesitantly disclosed that they were having trouble with their river mines!

On August 9th Major General Majendie came to discuss details of the aerodrome defences and at 5.00 p.m., The Right Honourable Anthony Eden arrived en route to Heston. During the course of the day a further forty-eight recruits arrived for General Duties. August 10 saw all WAAF personnel evacuated from the Officers' Married Quarters where they had been temporarily billeted and transferred to Kesgrave Hall, now requisitioned for this purpose.

Where the feet of the mighty trod, the ubiquitous car has now taken over, the site being used as a car park for the Martlesham Squash Club — the new building on the left. The hangar in the background was used by No. 15 Squadron which had the responsibility for testing new developments in armaments and bombing technology. 'B' Flight housed its bomber aircraft in this hangar which replaced a previous wooden hangar built by German prisoners from the First War which burned down on October 6, 1922.

177

On August 11, the day that Air Vice-Marshall Keith Park visited the station, No. 85 Squadron was despatched to intercept a large enemy force attacking a north-bound convoy. As Yellow section approached a formation of twenty Bf 110s, by some freak of reception a voice was heard over their R/T singing *September in the Rain,* a popular song of the period in guttural broken English. Seconds after the squadron went into the attack, the singing stopped.

Since the opening of the battle, night flying patrols had been stepped up in an endeavour to combat the solitary nocturnal raiders despatched by the Luftwaffe to seek targets of opportunity. No. 25 Squadron, flying from Martlesham, took an active part in these patrols flying their twin-engined Blenheims whenever the weather permitted. On August 8, 1940 they received formal notice that they were to be immediately re-equipped with the new, more powerfully-engined and armed Bristol Beaufighter but for one reason or another the Blenheims lingered on for some time after. At midnight on August 12, Pilot Officer Corry was landing from an otherwise uneventful patrol when he overshot the landing ground, ran into the boundary barbed wire and overturned, fortunately without injury to himself or his crew.

Adler Tag, August 13, brought No. 17 Squadron to the station at 2.30 p.m. on a semi-permanent posting, while No. 85 Squadron left for Debden minus two Hurricanes which collided head-on while taxiing for take off.

Just before 3.00 p.m. on Thursday, August 15, No. 17 Squadron were ordered off by the controller to patrol the Harwich area as warning had been received of an indeterminate number of hostiles approaching from the south-east. One section of Hurricanes had just managed to clear the

Post-Battle of Britain Luftwaffe reconnaissance photo (dated August 26, 1942) showing the runway extensions to the south-west and south-east. Today a re-alignment of the A1093 cuts across the aerodrome in front of the former eastern technical area to give access to the new Martlesham Heath Village being constructed in the centre of the drome. Extract from Ordnance Survey Sheet 169 (Crown Copyright).

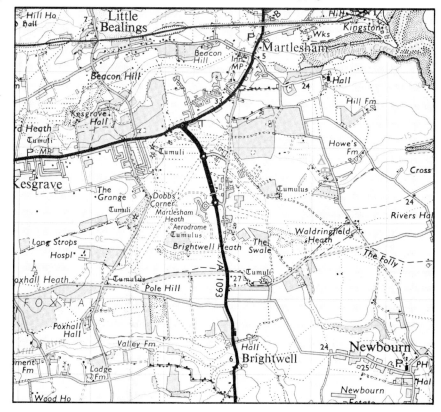

178

aerodrome when sixteen Bf 110s and nine Bf 109s of Gruppe 210 swept across, fast and low, scattering the startled station staff with cannon and machine gun fire, to lay their bombs accurately over the camp and landing ground. Thirty seconds later the station warning sounded. Four-and-a-half minutes later the enemy had gone. Emerging from the slit trenches in which they had rapidly taken shelter, airmen were met with the awesome sight of the aftermath of a precision hit-and-run raid and it was obvious to all that the station had been badly clobbered. A mounting column of smoke and dust hovered above Martlesham. Two hangars were rendered completely unserviceable, No. 25 Squadron's night-flying equipment store had been blown to smithereens, two 500kg bombs had fallen on the main camp road wrecking the guard room, coppersmith's shop, joiner's shop and severing the water main. The blast from two more broke every window and piece of glass in the Officers' Mess and raised the roof — something the pilots had been doing for years but not so literally. Two large craters had been left in the aerodrome itself although these had been filled in and levelled by 7.00 p.m. By far the greatest amount of damage had been caused when a visiting Fairey Battle, which had been set ablaze in the strafing and laden with 1,000lbs. of bombs, blew up with such force that it wrecked the watch office. Of the seven casualties inflicted among station personnel, only two were serious. Hauptmann Walter Rubensdorffer, after the successful execution of a brilliant raid, led his team of specialists safely back to Denain. (A few hours later he was to make a simple navigational error and attack the wrong target. It was to cost him his life.)

The following day was fully taken up with station repairs and clearance but on the 17th a red warning at noon gave a clear indication that a lesson had been well and truly learned as airmen and airwomen set records in the dash to the shelters that remained unbroken for years. However, the hazards of wartime service life had not escaped the Officers' Mess cat; when the secretary opened the safe at noon on August 18 she was found reposing on the usual contents with a family of five newborn kittens!

On August 26 Sergeant Sellars of No. 111 Squadron force landed his Hurricane near the Mess due to severe battle damage received in the defence of the unit's base at Debden. The following day the station had an unusual visitor in the shape of a 'Bison'. This consisted of a motor car chassis surmounted by a concrete box of gigantic dimensions liberally punctured with gun slits and topped by a structure which can only be described as a Heath Robinson aviary. Strict instructions confined it to a maximum speed of four miles per hour and that only on smooth ground otherwise the tyres would catch alight by induced friction when they rubbed against the wings. Two days later, the strange, unloved contraption groaned out of the station at a snail's pace en route for Ipswich Airport for which it had been originally intended.

Another departure was scheduled for the 31st when No. 25 Squadron (minus one flight) returned to North Weald and tragedy; seventy-two hours later three of their Blenheims were mistakenly attacked by Hurricanes of No. 46 Squadron.

During the first week of September, the leaderless No. 257 Squadron arrived to take up station at Martlesham. Demoralised and apathetic after the hefty losses they had taken during the past few weeks, they now indifferently awaited the arrival of their new commanding officer. Squadron Leader Roland Stanford Tuck, DFC had already carved his name in the annals of RAF history as one of its finest and most successful fighter pilots and over the next few weeks he moulded the group of disgruntled pilots into a skilled fighting unit. On the first day of the month,

'Dropping down the corridors of air with wheels outstretched to bond again with earth'. The Hurricanes of No. 257 Squadron return to Martlesham on Armistice Day, 1940 after their combat with the Regia Aeronautica (Imperial War Museum).

the squadron tangled with a large enemy force over Essex losing two Hurricanes and one pilot. Two more, badly mauled, flown by Pilot Officer Grundy and Sergeant Nutter returned to Martlesham for emergency landings.

During the night of September 4, the night-fighter Blenheims of No. 25 Squadron claimed two He 111s destroyed over the sea; consequently the welcome one of the pilots received on his return to Martlesham was ungracious to say the least. Pilot Officer Rofe's aircraft was caught by searchlights over the aerodrome and heavily engaged by the anti-aircraft guns which twice threw the Blenheim into a spin before it managed to evade the attentions of the 'friendly' gunners and make a safe landing. What Pilot Officer Rofe threw at the gunners is not recorded.

In the late afternoon of Saturday, September 7, the greatest daylight raid mounted by the Germans to date was inexorably pressing on towards London. In the company of the other squadrons committed to that battle, No. 257 threw itself furiously against the northern flank of the bomber stream.

From the savage skirmishing, two of its pilots and their Hurricanes disappeared from the sight of men. That is until September, 1979, exactly thirty-nine years later, when the Wealden Aviation Archaeology Group excavated the site of an aircraft crash at Elmley, Spitend Point on the Isle of Sheppey and brought into the light of day the mortal remains of Flight Lieutenant H. R. A. Beresford. Of his colleague, Flying Officer L. R. G. Mitchell, no trace has ever been found.

While London was still burning from the massive pounding it had received during the night of the 7th, Signal A 443 — Alert No. 1 — was received at Martlesham at 5.20 a.m. the following morning. This message, implying that invasion was imminent, had been despatched to all fighter stations from Fighter Command Headquarters, Bentley Priory at 9.50 p.m. on September 7. As no priority was marked on the Martlesham signal it was not decoded until 10.30 a.m. by which time the Germans could have been knocking on the gates of Ipswich had the invasion taken place!

September 15, that hot, still Sunday, found

No roar of Merlins split the air over Martlesham's western boundary on September 15, 1979. The fragmented runway surface is moss and weed covered and new undergrowth burgeons everywhere.

Martlesham's fighters returning to the aerodrome battle-torn and exhausted at the close of the long day. During the course of three patrols, a total of seven hours or more in the air, they claimed five destroyed for two Hurricanes damaged.

By mid-September the aerial armadas had disappeared from the daytime skies, their place being taken by small packs of bomb-carrying Bf 109s and 110s and, as the nature of the battle changed, so too did the role of Martlesham's squadrons. Situated as it was well to the north-east of the capital and close to the North Sea, its units found themselves once more relegated to standing coastal and convoy patrols.

October came, affording them a measure of relief with the diminishing tempo of battle. Within the first two weeks of the month No. 257 Squadron moved to the sector station at North Weald while No. 17 Squadron arrived from Debden to take up residence.

On Tuesday, October 22 the Army headed for Martlesham on a simulated rescue operation to save the station from capture by imaginary invaders. To this end a survey team armed with maps, charts, tape measures and three tanks set out to find the quickest route to the aerodrome. After the destruction of a sign post, a pheasant covert and yards of Dannert wire they were forced to retreat ignominiously when they reached a small bridge over a lane which could accommodate neither the width nor the weight of the tanks. A long and serious conference was held on the spot at the conclusion of which it was decided that the tanks could never thunder to Martlesham's rescue by that particular route. (They returned victorious on the 24th having found an alternative one!)

Saturday, October 26 and the dining halls and messes were filling with airmen speculating on the tea-time menu when the aerodrome defences sprang into action. As beads of tracer latticed the early evening sky, all thoughts of bodily sustenance were forgotten. If any paused to look skyward in their dash for the shelters they might have espied the centre of so much attention — a solitary He 111 throbbing across the 'drome at 6,000 feet. No hits were registered and the visitor departed. On Sunday, conversation still tended to centre on the Heinkel's visit and what it portended. The answer came at 4.42 p.m., four minutes after the station warning sounded, when twenty bomb-carrying Bf 109s erupted out of cloud at 7,000 feet over the aerodrome. The station's Bofors and Hispanos burst into life but the Jabos with cannon and machine guns blazing pressed home their attack and planted their bombs across the face of Martlesham, disappearing almost as suddenly as they had arrived leaving only a pall of dust and smoke to mark their passage. Station workshops had again been hit but damage was slight and the only crater in the aerodrome surface was immediately filled and levelled by a party of Royal Engineers. A visiting Lysander was slightly damaged by the blast from a 500kg bomb which burst nearby and the station lighting was out of action for about two hours. One of the most remarkable escapes occurred when the battery-charging room took a direct hit, destroying the building. The duty man emerged from the wreckage, his clothing in shreds but with only superficial injuries.

On November 7 the men and machines of No. 257 Squadron returned to Martlesham, taking over No. 25 Squadron's hangar. Armistice Day, November 11, dawned clear and cold. Squadron Leader Tuck, having spent a restless night with a painful ear condition, called on the Station Medical Officer and was advised not to fly that day. Consequently he was off the station when nine Hurricanes of No. 257 were scrambled just before 2.00 p.m. to intercept an enemy force heading for Harwich. Climbing hard out to sea, they spotted their targets, ten twin-

Above: Hurricanes of No. 242 Squadron return to Martlesham on March 27, 1941 from one of the many interminable coastal patrols flown by them during their tenancy of the Suffolk base (Fox Photos). Below: On September 15, 1979 only cottony cumulus drifted above the former aerodrome. The house on the edge of the plantation has gone, only the base and overgrown garden remaining.

engined aircraft escorted by twenty-two *biplane* fighters. Passing the formation, No. 257 turned and approached it from the rear noticing for the first time another group of Hurricanes closing in on its left flank. These were the aircraft of No. 46 Squadron scrambled from North Weald. Puzzled as to their identity Flight Lieutenant Peter 'Cowboy' Blatchford led the Squadron in line abreast towards the strange craft, identifying them as Italian as the Hurricanes closed in. In the melee off Orfordness, during which they lost three Fiat BR 20 bombers and three Fiat CR 42 fighters, the Italian airmen fought back courageously against their attackers before being deflected from their mission. All the RAF fighters returned safely to their bases.

Unless the weather was particularly atrocious, coastal and convoy patrols still had to be flown and valuable lives were still lost although not always to the human enemy. On December 17, 1940, No. 257 Squadron moved north to the Norfolk aerodrome of Coltishall while No. 242 Squadron, led by their indestructible commander, Douglas Bader, flew in to Martlesham with their new Mk. IIA Hurricanes. Here, as at Coltishall, they continued the old pattern of patrolling the convoy lanes.

Meanwhile preparations had been under way for Fighter Command to take the offensive in the form of sweeps over enemy-occupied countries by fighter wings of two or more squadron strength. The first of these code-named 'Circus' operations took place on January 10, 1941 when No. 242 from Martlesham rendezvoused with the two North Weald squadrons to escort six Blenheims of No. 114 Squadron in an attack on targets in the Foret de Guines area. Henceforth the monotony of standing patrols was alleviated by increasing numbers of 'Circus' operations interspersed with the odd 'Rhubarb' where two aircraft took off, usually in the most dismal weather conditions and utilizing low cloud cover, attacked targets of opportunity a few miles inland of the enemy's coastline. But none of this was accomplished without cost and, in just over a month, No. 242 lost six experienced pilots.

On March 18, 1941 Douglas Bader, now promoted to Wing Commander, left the Squadron to command the new Tangmere Wing at its Sussex base. Squadron Leader Treacy was posted to command No. 242 which left Martlesham in April 1941.

From 1941 to November 1943 a steady stream of British, Commonwealth and Allied squadrons arrived for varying periods of

Above: **Where deadly fighters once roared full tilt towards the skies, imbibers sit and sip at ease. 'The Douglas Bader' public house, Martlesham's latest reminder of its past, stands on a small section of the old main runway.** *Right:* **Sir Douglas Bader after pulling the first pint at the opening ceremony on Friday, September 14, 1979 (Tolly Cobbold).**

residence and the nearby town of Ipswich, where most of Martlesham's transitory residents disported themselves when off duty, became as cosmopolitan as London, Paris, Sydney or New York.

One October day in 1943, the air over the station was split by the unmistakable sound of Pratt and Whitney Double Wasps as the P-47 Thunderbolts of the 356th Fighter Group, United States Eighth Air Force, made a roaring low-level pass across the aerodrome before landing to take over their new residence. They were to remain at Martlesham for the remainder of the war in Europe, converting to P-51 Mustangs during their stay and finally departing in October/November 1945. In the latter month the aerodrome was transferred from Eighth Fighter Command, USAAF to Fighter Command, Royal Air Force and later still in the year on December 12, it was taken on the strength of Coastal Command.

Post-war Martlesham became once more an RAF base and a new sound filled the skies over East Anglia. The jet age had well and truly arrived and once more it seemed as though the station would play an active role in the defence system of the United Kingdom. Fighter squadrons, some of which had added battle honours to their standards at Martlesham during the war, now returned jet-winged. But despite the lengthening of the main runway it rapidly became evident that the aerodrome was no longer suitable as a base for high-speed operational jet aircraft. Furthermore air traffic movements from the nearby RAF and USAF bases at Woodbridge and Bentwaters encroached upon the Martlesham circuit.

In the late 1940s, the station became once more the testing place for service equipment when the Bomb Ballistics and Blind Landing Unit was established, becoming in 1950 the Armament and Instrument Experimental Unit. The wheel had come full circle and once more the name 'Martlesham', as in the twenties and thirties, came to stand for an accuracy and thoroughness that was second to none in the examination of aircraft and their equipment. In January 1951, No. 140 Flight Royal Air Force Police were briefly based there before disbanding on January 1, 1953.

Four-and-a-half years later on June 30, 1957 the A and IEU suffered the same fate. The following year the station was the base for a short period of No. 22 (Search and Rescue) Squadron operating Westland Whirlwind helicopters, the unit providing a valuable rescue service along the East Anglian Coast.

In 1959 the song of the Merlin brought music to the ears of many of Martlesham's ghosts. Memories of the past were re-awakened with the return to the aerodrome of the unmistakable shapes of the Spitfire and Hurricane. However, the Royal Air Force's Battle of Britain Flight stayed only long enough to participate in the Battle of Britain fly-past over Central London before departing for Coltishall.

On the last day of 1962 the station was transferred to the London District under 'care and maintenance'. The last test programme was carried out at Martlesham the following year when rough ground taxi-ing trials were carried out on two aircraft, the Avro 748, later to become the Andover transport in RAF service, and the Rolls-Royce Dart-powered Handley Page Herald. On March 24, the care and maintenance unit was disbanded and the following day the station was further reduced to inactive (guarded) status. On April 9 Martlesham was officially closed on the disposal of Air Ministry assets.

In the next few years with the re-development of the aerodrome site, numerous small industries sprang into existence, finding ideal, ready-made accommodation among the old service buildings. Overshadowing all is the massive complex of the Post Office Research Centre. On the opposite side to the former technical area stands the modern headquarters of the Suffolk County Constabulary. The aerodrome itself now lies mainly beneath an expanding modern village community: a collection of multi-coloured, box-shaped dwellings without character, tradition or an identity of their own. Fragmentary sections of the once great runways are still extant and, in the approximate centre of the main one, Tolly Cobbold, the Suffolk brewers, opened a public house on September 14, 1979 to serve the citizens of the new community. Mindful of Martlesham's illustrious past, the brewery directors had chosen the date of the unveiling well for the hostelry itself is named after one of the old RAF station's better known inhabitants, 'The Douglas Bader'.

Tucked away on the western side of the heath is the Watch Office looking weather-beaten and much ill-used but still bravely defying the passage of time with its green ramparts of gorse gathered protectively about it. On the locked and padlocked door is a rough hand-painted notice which reads 'J.A.I. Produts' (sic). How are the mighty fallen!

Overleaf: **October 19, 1979. Martlesham Heath Village sprawls across the aerodrome.**

Stapleford Tawney

BY PETER NORRIS

Lying on the A113 road between Chigwell and Ongar to the north-east of London, the aerodrome was originally opened on June 23, 1934 as an operating base for Hillman's Airways, formed three years previously by Edward Hillman, an Essex businessman, as a charter company. After two years of general charter and taxi work, Hillman had commenced a scheduled service to Paris on April 1, 1933 from Maylands Aerodrome near Harold Wood at Romford in Essex using six new de Havilland DH 84 Dragons with the return fare of £5.10.0, undercutting all rivals. The service was a big success and the airline, together with the expansion of work on the charter side, soon outgrew the small field at Maylands. Hillman therefore obtained 180 acres of land near the village of Stapleford Tawney on a 25-year lease and laid out an aerodrome 1,300 yards by 900 yards. Three hangars were built with a concrete apron in front plus a small passenger and administration building, the aerodrome being known as the Essex Aerodrome.

Within a few weeks of moving in, a Stapleford-Liverpool-Isle of Man-Belfast service was inaugurated followed in December by an extension to Glasgow plus a GPO mail contract over the route. On December 12 Hillman's Airways became a limited company but, tragically, Edward Hillman died suddenly eighteen days later at the age of forty-five.

Despite the premature death of its founder, the company continued to expand and, by the summer of 1935, was operating the following services: Paris four daily; Liverpool-Glasgow-Belfast two daily; Ostend, Brussels, Antwerp three daily; and Ramsgate-Ostend one daily.

Extra equipment in the shape of eight DH 89 Dragon Rapides had been acquired to cope with the additional services but the expansion programme had put a severe financial strain on the company. In October it was announced that the company expected to lose £28,000 at the end of the financial year and was accepting a take-over bid from Whitehall Securities Corporation Ltd.

Whitehall already owned two airlines, United Airways and Spartan Air Lines both based at Heston and, after formally acquiring

Hillmans on December 11th, the three companies were merged to form British Airways Ltd. which commenced operations on January 1, 1936 with Heston as its main London terminus.

Operations were still carried out from Stapleford for a time including the inauguration of a service to Malmo, Sweden on February 17 with DH 86s, but within a few months all services were transferred to Heston and Stapleford was left empty with the exception of a few private owners for the next two years.

In 1938, with the RAF expansion programme in full swing, the aerodrome was re-opened for use by No. 21 Elementary and Reserve Flying Training School operated under contract from the Air Ministry by Reid and Sigrist Ltd. for the training of RAFVR pilots. Tiger Moths were used for basic training with Hawker Harts, Hinds and Audaxes for the more advanced work. In his book *Wing Leader*, 'Johnnie' Johnson writes of his training at the aerodrome recalling that the relative serenity of the area was often shattered by formations of Hurricanes flying over from North Weald.

Shortly after the outbreak of war, the aerodrome was requisitioned and No. 21 E & RFTS moved out. Additional land was acquired and a two-and-a-quarter-mile concrete perimeter track 18ft wide constructed together with six double dispersal pens and various buildings for accommodation. The grass surface landing area measured 1,000 yards N-S; 800 yards E-W; 1,150 yards SE-NW with the main NE-SW direction 1,220 yards. The aerodrome surface was painted with tar lines giving a field pattern from the air and on completion, the aerodrome was handed over to No. 11 Group as a satellite for North Weald capable of handling one fighter squadron.

The first recorded use of the aerodrome by North Weald squadrons was in late March 1940 when Hurricanes of Nos. 56 and 151 Squadrons were flown over after the last operation of the day for an overnight stop in case of enemy night attacks on the parent

Top: **The Essex Aerodrome in March 1935 which was expanded in 1939 into a satellite for North Weald, four miles to the north (Flight). Forty years later *(right)*, the aerodrome still retains its wartime perimeter track although the landing area is restricted to two strips NE-SW and E-W.**

station. Shortly after dawn the aircraft returned to North Weald to prepare for the day's operations.

This shuttle procedure continued for the next few weeks but the first squadron to be permanently based at Stapleford was No. 151 Squadron which moved in from Martlesham Heath on August 29, mounting several patrols the same day. On the first sortie, the squadron encountered fifty Bf 109s although without scoring. On a later patrol, Pilot Officer A. G. Wainwright flying a Hurricane was shot down by a Bf 109 but baled out and was admitted to Epping Hospital with fractured ribs. The following day the squadron once again mounted a number of patrols and, on the second of these, a large formation of seventy-plus bombers with a hundred-plus fighter escort was intercepted resulting in a Do 215, Ju 88 and He 111 being claimed although the squadron lost two pilots — Squadron Leader E. B. King and Sergeant F. Gmur.

The action on the 31st started early with a Luftwaffe raid on North Weald during which No. 151 Squadron shot down a confirmed Bf 109 from the fighter escort. On the second patrol a Do 17 was confirmed shot down near Hornchurch and the third patrol resulted in a Do 215 being brought down over the Thames Estuary. The squadron lost two aircraft but both pilots, although injured, managed to parachute to safety.

After a somewhat short stay, the squadron was ordered to move on September 1 and, after mounting two patrols in the morning, it departed for Digby and No. 12 Group for a rest having been in constant action since early May, including detachment to France before the Armistice.

Taking over their aircraft were the pilots of No. 46 Squadron. This unit had seen action in Norway earlier in the year and, during the evacuation, had flown its Hurricanes onto the aircraft carrier HMS *Glorious*. Unfortunately the ship was sunk on the way home and the squadron lost all its aircraft and many of its personnel. After regrouping at Digby, the squadron was once again ready for action and mounted its first patrol from Stapleford shortly after arrival with a flight of twelve Hurricanes over Rochford at 4.35 p.m.

The squadron's Operational Record Book (Form 540) gives an interesting description of their new base:

'The aerodrome was found to have a pronounced slope down towards the hangars, there were several ridges running across the 'drome and the surface was extremely rough. The aircraft were dispersed around the wood which ran along one edge of the landing field, crews and equipment were housed in hurricane and bell tents and a marquee. There were two corrugated iron huts and several trenches for protection from blast. A

small stream running through the wood was used by the airmen for washing purposes'.

On September 2 the squadron mounted a number of patrols, the first of which was something of a farce as the squadron received orders to patrol 'Watchford'. After some head scratching and map searching, the squadron set off and patrolled Watford north-west of London without result. On returning to base, the squadron learned that it should have patrolled Rochford, some fifty miles in the opposite direction! On the last patrol of the day, the squadron had a Bf 109 kill confirmed but also lost Pilot Officer J. C. D. L. Bailey who was shot down in Hurricane P3067 near Eastchurch.

From now on the squadron was in daily contact with the Luftwaffe and on September 3 the squadron intercepted thirty Ju 88s escorted by fifty Bf 109s and Bf 110s attacking North Weald. In the ensuing battle four Hurricanes were shot down and Sergeant G. H. Edworthy reported as missing. Later three Hurricanes bounced what they thought were three Ju 88s flying in formation; tragically they proved to be three Blenheims from No. 25 Squadron returning to North Weald. Two were shot down and one pilot, Pilot Officer D. W. Hogg, killed. By the end of September, five other pilots had been lost: Flying Officer R. P. Plummer, shot down on September 4 and who died in hospital ten days

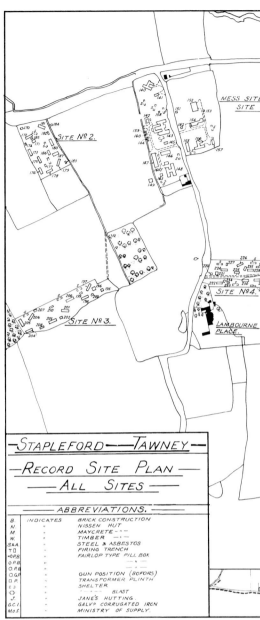

—STAPLEFORD——TAWNEY—

—RECORD SITE PLAN—

—— ALL SITES ——

——— ABBREVIATIONS. ———

B.	INDICATES	BRICK CONSTRUCTION
N.	"	NISSEN HUT
M.	"	MAYCRETE "
W.	"	TIMBER —"
S.&A	"	STEEL & ASBESTOS
T.O	"	FIRING TRENCH
F.O.P.B	"	FAIRLOP TYPE PILL BOX
O.P.B	"	" "
O.P.B	"	
O.G.P	"	GUN POSITION (BOFORS)
O.P.	"	TRANSFORMER PLINTH
C.J.	"	SHELTER
O.	"	" — " BLAST
J.	"	JANE'S HUTTING
G.C.I.	"	GALVᴼ CORRUGATED IRON
M.o.S.	"	MINISTRY OF SUPPLY.

BLDNs	BUILDING	CONSᵀ
	TECHNICAL SITE	
1	HANGAR & ARMOURY OFFICE (PART).	S & A
2	SEWAGE PUMP HOUSE.	B
3		
4	TRANSFORMER PLINTH	
5		
6		
7	M.T BULK PETROL. (2/1000 GAL. U.G.)	
8	SUB STATION ON PLINTH.	
9		
10		
11		
12	FIRE HOSE STORE.	
13	N.A.A.F.I. FOR 511	N
14	TECHNICAL LATRINES	B
15	OFFICERS MESS FOR 33	N
16	SQUADRON OFFICES (B TYPE HUT)	N
17	RESERVE WATER TANK. (14,500 GAL.)	
18	FIRE PUMP HOUSE. 15' x 7'	B
19	CREW ROOM 20' x 20'	N
20	PARAFFIN TANK. (500 GAL.)	S & A
21		
22	OIL STORE.	B
23	BULK PETROL INSTALLATION (2/2600 GAL. U.G.)	
24	WORKS SERVICES HUT & YARD	N
25	STORE	N
26	CONTRACTORS HUT & YARD	
27	W.D AGRIC. IMPLEMENTS SHELTER	G.C.I
28	FUEL YARD	
29	AVIATION PETROL INSTALLⁿ. (2/1000 GAL) (NOT USED)	
30	OVER BLISTER HANGAR.	
31	Do Do Do.	
32	STANDING (SITE OF O.B.H)	
33	Do (Do Do)	
37	S.A.A STORE	B
38	BATTLE H.Q	B
39	BULK AVIATION PETROL & PUMP HOUSE (12,000 GAL U.G.)	
40		
41	ARMY DEFENCE ACC. (GUN CREW).	J.
42	Do Do Do	N.
43	Do Do Do LATRINE	B
44	SLEEVE STREAMER MAST	
45	S.A.A. STORE.	B
47	ARMY DEFENCE ACC. AND ABLUTS.	N.
48	Do Do	N.
49	Do Do	N.
50	Do Do LATRINES	G.C.I
51	Do ACC	N
52	SLEEPING SHELTER	C.
53	STORE 30' x 20' (B TYPE)	N
54	FLIGHT OFFICES	
55	LATRINES & DRYING ROOM	
56/1	HARDSTANDING 60' x 62'	
56/2	Do	
56/3	Do	
56/4	Do	
56/5	Do	
56/6	Do	

An example of the dispersed sites which accompanied wartime aerodromes and which were just as essential to the running of the station. At Stapleford Tawney only the outlines of a few concrete bases remain to be seen today.

later; Sub-Lieutenant J. C. Carpenter, who had been seconded from the Fleet Air Arm, on the 8th; Sergeant W. A. Peacock on the 11th; Sergeant G. W. Jeffreys on the 18th when his parachute failed to open and Pilot Officer J. D. Crossman, an Australian, on the last day of the month.

October began quietly for No. 46 Squadron until the 15th when a patrol over Sevenoaks and Gravesend was bounced by a flight of Bf 109s. Two Hurricanes were shot down and Pilot Officer P. S. Gunning killed; in return one Bf 109 was claimed as destroyed.

Bad weather restricted operations during the next ten days, the first casualty occuring on the 22nd when Sergeant J. P. Morrison was shot down over Dungeness. Three days later Pilot Officer W. B. Pattullo damaged a Bf 109 in a combat during the morning but then crashed into a house in Romford later in the day. Although he was taken to hospital alive, he died the following day.

Then on the 29th came both victory and tragedy. The day dawned fair but later clouded over in the east. During an engagement in the afternoon south of the Thames, Flight Lieutenant Rabagliati accounted for a Bf 109 and Pilot Officer Reid damaged another. Then the Hurricane flown by Sergeant H. E. Black (who had only joined the squadron the previous week) was hit and set on fire. Although he managed to bale out

with an injured leg, he died of his wounds in Ashford Hospital ten days later.

A patrol in the Dover-Deal area on November 1 sighted several aircraft at 20,000 feet and, on interception, the pilots identified them as Italian Savoia Marchetti three-engined bombers and one was chased out to sea with its port engine damaged but it managed to escape. As there are no reports of Savoia Marchettis being used by the Italians from Belgium, it is almost certain that these were Cant Z1007s which were operating from there at this time.

Operations continued with a Do 215 damaged on November 5 and a Bf 110 damaged on the 7th although flights from the aerodrome were being hampered by the rainy weather which made the grass surface boggy. On the 8th the aerodrome was declared unserviceable and the squadron moved to North Weald from which, three days later, it was involved in the famous battle with Italian CR 42s and BR 20s near Orford Ness.

Another unit based at Stapleford at that time was No. 419 Flight although its role and equipment are unknown and it moved to Stradishall on October 9. Unlike North Weald, its parent station five miles to the north, Stapleford escaped lightly from the attentions of the Luftwaffe, only one raid being reported on the night of October 7 when a number of incendiaries plus two bombs fell

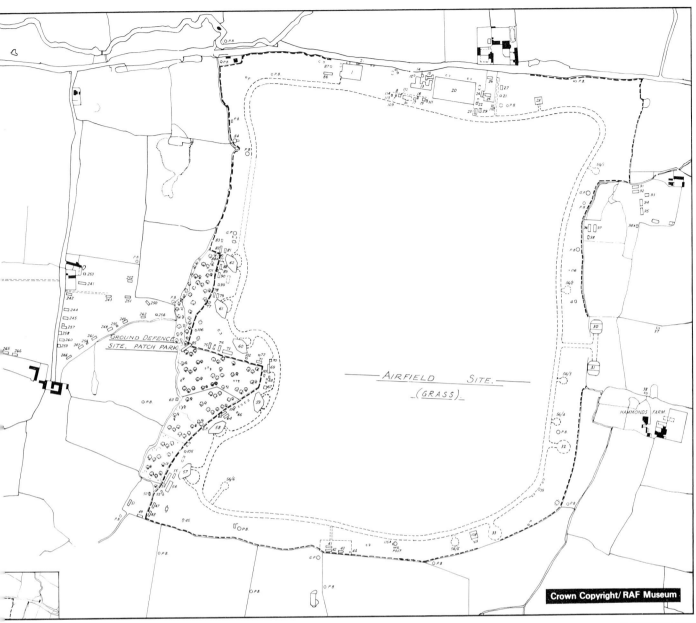

GROUND DEFENCE SITE. PATCH PARK

AIRFIELD SITE.
(GRASS).

HAMMONDS FARM.

Crown Copyright/ RAF Museum

BLD.N°	BUILDING	CON.°⁷
57	AIRCRAFT PEN (S.E.)	
58	Do Do Do	
59	Do Do Do	
60	Do Do Do	
61	Do Do Do	
62	Do Do Do	
63	S.A.A. STORE	N
64	GAS CLOTHING STORE.	N
65	LUBRICANT & INFLAMMABLE STORE.	N
66	FIRE HOSE STORE	B
67	RESERVE WATER TANK.	
68	STORE	B
69	SPEECH BROADCASTING BLDG.	B
70	N.F.E. STORE & WORKSHOPS.	B
71	WATCH OFFICE	N
72	FIRE HOSE STORE	B
73	FLIGHT OFFICES	B
74	LATRINES & DRYING ROOM	B
75	SLEEPING SHELTER	B
77	S.A.A. STORE	B
78	DECONTAM CENTRE (TEMPORARY).	N
79	Do Do Do	N
81	ARMY DEFENCE ACC. GUN CREW 54'×15'.	N.
82	Do Do Do Do	J.
83	Do Do Do LATRINE	B
84	SEWAGE DISPOSAL WORKS	B
85	BARRACK HUT. 90 × 20'. (B TYPE)	M
86	ARMY DEFENCE ACC. GUN CREW 66 × 18	B
87	Do Do Do LATRINES.	B
88	COOKHOUSE & 10'×10' STORE. (ARMY DEFENCE)	½ N.
88A		G.C.I.
89	BARRACK HUTS (Do Do)	N.
90	Do Do Do (Do Do)	N
91	ARMY DEFENCE ACC.	N
92	Do Do Do	½ N.
93	Do Do Do	N.
94	Do Do Do GAS CLOTHING	N.
95	Do Do Do	N.
96	Do Do Do GUN CREW	N.
97	Do Do Do	N.
98	Do Do Do LATRINES	B
98A		
99	Do Do 11' 6"×12' GAS CLOTHING STORE.	B
101	ABLUTS & LATRINES.	B
102	AIRMEN'S	W.
103	TEMPORARY STORE	
104	AIRMEN'S LATRINES.	G.C.I.
105	Do Do	Do
106	Do Do	Do
108	CANNON TEST BUTT	B
109	OIL STORE, 15'×4'6"	B
110	DOPE STORE	B
111	FIRE HOSE REEL SHELTER 12'×6'	B
112	RESERVE WATER TANK. 14,500 GAL	B
113	FIRE HOSE REEL SHELTER, 15'×4'6'	B
114	AVIATION PETROL INSTALL™ (2/1000 GAL U.G.)	B
115A	QUADRANT SHELTER 4'×4'	B
116	SL STREAMER MAST (POLE)	W

BLD.N°	BUILDING	CON.°⁰
	W.A.A.F. ACCOMMODATION.	
	(LAMBOURNE PLACE).	
	QUARTERS FOR 2 OFFICERS, 4 SGTS. & 40 A.C.W.	
	ALL RANKS MESS WITH R.A.F. INSTITUTE WITH R.A.F.	
	MESS SITE (N° 1)	
140	SICK QUARTERS, (10 BEDS)	B
141	BATH BLOCK	B
142	STAND BY SET HOUSE	B
143	DINING ROOM, (FOR 511)	B
144	AIRMENS LATRINES (15 W.C's, 8 U.)	B
145	RATION STORE.	B
146	GROCERY & LOCAL PRODUCE STORE.	B
147	AIRMENS ABLUTIONS.	B
148	INSTITUTE (FOR 510)	B
149	WATER STORAGE TANK, 30,000 GAL H.L.	B
151	PICKET POST	B
152	FUEL COMPOUND	
153	GAS CLOTHING STORE	B
154	DECONTAMINATION CENTRE, TYPE KM	B
155	MEDICAL INSPECTION (USED AS A/M QRS).	B
156	SERGEANTS MESS (FOR 50)	B
157	Do BATH BLOCK (3 W.C's, 2 U. 6 SHOWERS. 12 BASINS)	B
158	FIRE HOSE SHELTER	B
159	TRANSFORMER PLINTH	N
160	W.D. OFFICE	B
161	FIRE TRAILER SHELTER	B
162	Do	
163	RESERVE WATER TANK	
	SITE N° 2	
170	PICKET POST	B
171	RESERVE WATER TANK.	
172	OFFICERS' QUARTERS.	M
173	Do	M
174	Do LATRINE (3 W.C's, 1 U.)	M
175	SERGEANTS' QUARTERS.	M
176	Do	B
177	Do LATRINES (2 W.C's, 1 U.), & DRYING RM.	M
178	AIRMEN'S BARRACK HUT.	M
179	Do Do Do	M
180	Do Do Do	M
181	Do Do Do	B
182	Do LATRINES (2 W.C's, 1 U.), & DRYING RM.	B
183	Do Do Do Do	M
184	SEWAGE PUMP HOUSE	M
185	OFFICERS ABLUTIONS	B
186	SERGEANTS & AIRMEN'S ABLUTIONS.	B
187	AIRMEN'S BARRACK HUT.	M

BLD.N°	BUILDING	CON.°⁰
	SITE N° 3.	
195	PICKET POST	B
196	RESERVE WATER TANK.	
197	OFFICERS' QUARTERS	M.
198	SERGEANTS' QUARTERS.	M
199	Do LATRINES, (2 W.C's, 1 U.)	N
200	OFFICERS QUARTERS	M
201	Do	M
202	Do LATRINES (3 W.C's, 1 U.), & DRYING RM	M
203	AIRMEN'S BARRACK HUT	M
204	Do Do Do	M.
205	Do Do Do	M.
206	Do Do Do	M.
207	Do LATRINES (2 W.C's, 1 U.), & DRYING RM	B
208	Do Do Do Do	B
209	OFFICERS' ABLUTIONS	B
210	SERGEANTS' & AIRMEN'S ABLUTIONS.	B
	SITE N° 4. (GROUND DEFENCE SITE) PATCH PARK.	
220	PICKET POST	B
221	RESERVE WATER TANK.	
222	OFFICERS' QUARTERS	M
223	Do LATRINES (2 W.C's, 1 U.)	M
224	SERGEANTS' QUARTERS.	M
225	Do Do	M
226	Do Do	M
227	Do LATRINES (2 W.C's, 1 U.), & DRYING RM	M
228	AIRMEN'S BARRACK HUT	M
229	Do Do Do	B
230	Do Do Do	B
231	Do Do Do	B
232	Do LATRINES (2 W.C's, 1 U.), & DRYING RM	B
233	Do Do Do Do	B
234	OFFICERS' ABLUTIONS	B
235	SERGEANTS' & AIRMEN'S ABLUTIONS.	B
	SITE N° 5.	
241 & 242	BARRACK HUTS 36'×16'	M o S
243	Do HUT.	M
244 249	Do HUTS.	M o S
250 252	Do Do	N.
253 256	AIRMENS LATRINES (8 BUCKETS & 4 U.B)	G.C.I.
257	Do ABLUTIONS	W
258	HARDSTANDINGS	
259		
260	COOKHOUSE	W.
261	ORDERLY ROOM	M o S
262	SERGEANTS BARRACK HUT.	M o S
263 265	BARRACK HUTS	M o S
266	Do HUT 36'×16'	M o S
267	LATRINE.	G.C.I.

The aerodrome photographed on February 3, 1943. Hedges have been painted on the surface to break up the outline and the hangars camouflaged.

on the aerodrome causing many craters but no damage.

The aerodrome remained without aircraft until the following spring, probably due to the state of the landing ground, when No. 242 Squadron arrived from Martlesham Heath on April 9 equipped with Hurricanes. The squadron got off to a bad start when, on the first day's operations (20th), three aircraft collided in cloud over the channel, all three pilots being killed including the CO, Squadron Leader Treacy, who had taken over from Squadron Leader Douglas Bader shortly before moving in.

Squadron Leader Whitney-Straight took over command three days later but this was to prove an unlucky month for the squadron with two more pilots being killed for only one Ju 88 destroyed. May brought an improvement in fortunes with two He 111s confirmed on the 11th and the squadron carried out a number of offensive sweeps over France and Belgium until moving to North Weald on the 22nd.

Next to arrive was No. 3 Squadron which flew in from Martlesham Heath on June 23. Also equipped with Hurricanes, like its predecessor it undertook various sweeps and convoy patrols although these came to an end at the end of the month, and detachments were sent to Hunsdon on a nightly basis for night-flying practice with Turnbinlite-equipped Bostons and Havocs of No. 1451 Flight. This routine continued for the whole of

July and part of August, the squadron also undertaking various night patrols and intruder work from Manston and Shoreham until the squadron moved to Hunsdon on August 10.

Meanwhile, an unusual unit had moved in during June, this being No. 2 Camouflage Unit equipped with a mixture of Oxfords, Dominies and Tiger Moths. This unit was responsible to various government departments for carrying out the aerial examination of camouflaged factories, fuel dumps and other installations.

Apart from this unit, the aerodrome remained empty until December when No. 277 Squadron was formed on the 22nd from the air-sea rescue flights at Martlesham Heath, Hawkinge, Friston and Tangmere, equipped with Lysanders and Walruses. The squadron was responsible for ASR work in the sea areas adjacent to No. 11 Group. A new flight was set up at Shoreham while the two at Friston and Tangmere were withdrawn. Stapleford became the squadron HQ and was responsible for major maintenance and pilot conversion, no operational flying being carried out from the aerodrome. The headquarters was located in Dudbrook Hall five miles from the aerodrome, this also being the home of the station HQ.

Early in 1942, a number of new buildings were erected including billets close to the main hangar, messes and other buildings and eight blister hangars. Petrol storage was provided for 8,480 gallons of aviation spirit and 1,000 gallons of MT fuel.

In April the squadron started receiving Defiants and, by mid-May, had twelve on charge. Tragically, one of these crashed on approach to Croydon on April 25 killing both the pilot and his passenger, a civilian Rolls-Royce representative. Other types used by the squadron as hacks were Tiger Moths and a Koolhoven FK 43 which had escaped from Holland in May 1940 and which still retained its Dutch Army serial 965. The squadron remained at Stapleford until December 7 when it moved to Gravesend.

In March 1943, the aerodrome was transferred to No. 34 Wing, Army Co-operation Command, and became a satellite of Sawbridgeworth. On the 14th, No. 656 Squadron arrived from Westley, Bury St. Edmunds; this was an air observation post unit equipped with Auster Is and IIIs plus a few Tiger Moths. After a few months of working-up exercises, the squadron was mobilised and left for India via Liverpool Docks on August 12.

Meanwhile No. 34 Wing had been disbanded in June and the aerodrome was

now put under the control of No. 12 Group. These moves were part of the build up to the formation of the 2nd Tactical Air Force which formed on November 15, Stapleford still remaining a satellite of Sawbridgeworth.

The winter months saw the arrival of a large number of ground personnel attached to the 2nd TAF including Signals, RAF Regiment and two Repair and Salvage units, Nos. 420 and 421. The majority of these units left for the south coast advanced landing grounds in the spring of 1944 in preparation for D-Day.

June 15 saw the arrival of what must be the aerodrome's largest-ever aircraft visitor when a Colonel Seamour made a short visit from and returned to nearby Chipping Ongar in a Marauder. By this time, No. 142 Flight, London Gliding Command was based on the aerodrome equipped with Cadet gliders, the unit giving instruction to cadets during the weekends and evenings.

No. 2 Camouflage Unit moved out in September, this proving to be Stapleford's last wartime powered aircraft unit.

With the V-weapon barrage now in full swing, various rockets landed in the vicinity of the aerodrome and on November 20 a V2 exploded in the centre of the aerodrome making a crater 60 feet in diameter. This was followed on February 23, 1945 by another rocket which landed on the main camp buildings during working hours at 3.30 p.m. causing widespread damage and killing seventeen personnel with a further fifty injured.

In April the last few ground units were posted away and on May 11 the aerodrome was reduced to a care and maintenance status under North Weald. The Army are known to have used the aerodrome as a drop zone for paratroops from Halifaxes operating from

The underground battle headquarters situated adjacent to Hammond's Farm *(photo below)* **has been preserved by the farmer, Mr. Mugleston. The vertical entry shaft** *(left)* **and the overgrown emergency exit** *(right).*

Wethersfield and Earls Colne in 1945 and 1946. American forces cleared all the southern pillboxes and defence works leaving the rubble piled on the perimeter track but after this the aerodrome became disused and finally reverted to agriculture.

In 1953, 'Buster' and Roger Frogley, founders of the Herts and Essex Aero Club, decided to sell their aerodrome at Broxbourne in Hertfordshire so that the valuable gravel on which it lay could be extracted. The club's new home was to be Stapleford and the hangars were renovated and flying began again using Tiger Moths and Austers.

In 1955 Edgar Percival, the famous pre-war light aircraft designer, formed a new company under his name and set up a production line at Stapleford for his EP 9 crop-spraying aircraft, the first flight taking place on December 21, 1955. Nearly forty aircraft were built until the company was sold and the production line moved to Blackpool in 1958.

Today, although Herts and Essex still own the airfield, pilot training is carried out under the auspices of the Stapleford Flying Club. Thurston Aviation also operated a large fleet of air taxis, mainly Aztecs and Navajos, until they moved to Stansted at the end of 1978.

When asked by the editor to caption this picture, Wilf Nicoll remarked: 'Please sir! Don't know what this is. Looks as though a constipated seagull has flown over'. (It's actually a sealed up Hamilton Fort, Wilf!)

Stapleford Tawney's gate guardian. Other aerodromes have aircraft displayed by their main entrance, some of which may have had no connection with the station. Stapleford has the former NAAFI hut which dispensed refreshment and entertainment to the off-duty airmen and, at times, did much to lighten the gloom of a wartime existence. Now occupied by the Thorn Electrical Group.

SECTOR F
Debden

BY KEITH BRAYBROOKE

Three miles south-east of Saffron Walden, on the southern side of the A130 road, lies the former RAF station of Debden, its lifetime spanning the years 1937-1975. It was one of the many aerodromes constructed during the extensive expansion period of the Royal Air Force during the mid-thirties and, significantly, the only one specifically intended for fighters, though its history, briefly outlined here, became varied and distinguished.

The aerodrome was originally grass-surfaced, the buildings forming the functional complex on the eastern side comprising three C-type hangars to accommodate three squadrons with adjacent technical and administrative buildings and barracks — all brick-built in the stylish design common to the expansion period aerodromes.

The landing area provided for four landing and take-off directions. The NE-SW was 1,150 yards; the E-W 1,200 yards and the SE-NW 1,250 yards whilst the main 1,600 yard dimension lay on the N-S axis. Petrol storage totalled 72,000 gallons of aviation fuel and 5,000 of motor spirit. A million rounds of small arms ammunition was in store immediately available for use.

The station opened on April 22, 1937 receiving Nos. 87, 80 and 73 Squadrons, all Gladiator equipped. The transition from biplane to monoplane took place the following year, Hurricanes re-equipping Nos. 85 and 87 Squadrons in 1938 and No. 29 Squadron receiving Blenheim 1Fs in 1939. This was the status at Debden when hostilities commenced.

War was barely a week old when Nos. 85 and 87 Squadrons were ordered to France, Nos. 17 and 504 Squadrons taking their place at Debden. Apart from a short spell within No. 12 Group, Debden was an 'F' Sector Station of No. 11 Group Fighter Command

'The harvest truly is plenteous, but the labourers are few' — Matthew IX. v. 37.
Above: **On a clover-studded dispersal in 1940 close to Rectory Farm, pilots of No. 17 Squadron sit in the August sunshine between sorties. On the cowling from left to right: Flying Officer D. H. W. Hanson, Flight Lieutenant W. J. Harper, Flying Officer G. R. Bennette. On the wing from the left: Pilot Officer L. W. Stevens, Pilot Officer C. E. Pitman and Sergeant G. Griffiths, DFM. On September 3, David Hanson was shot down after destroying a Do 17. He attempted a landing but was eventually forced to bale out at 100 feet and was killed.** *Below:* **Debden disembowelled. The ravaged earth of the aerodrome is dumped unceremoniously by juggernaut tippers over the former dispersal.**

and as such played a key role in the Battle of Britain. A large area of East Anglia came under the aegis of the Debden Operations Room but the quiet period during the early months of the war provided the opportunity for completion of buildings, two intersecting runways of 1,300 x 50 yards running E-W and N-S and additional 35ft taxiways enabling aircraft to be dispersed in surrounding countryside. The E-W runway was later extended to 1,600 yards.

Ground defence was provided initially by units of the Territorial Army later supplemented by the 41st AA Brigade. Debden's squadrons were frequently detached to forward aerodromes for varying periods, firstly to Wattisham then, from mid-December, regularly to Martlesham Heath. A 'Q' site was established at Great Yeldham and in June an aerodrome at nearby Castle Camps was made operational as Debden's first satellite.

The return of the weakened fighter squadrons from France meant a period of hurried re-strengthening and, at Debden, No. 85 Squadron, under their new CO, Squadron Leader Peter Townsend, together with some of the 'old hands' including Sammy Allard and Dickie Lee, re-mustered and was the first to use Castle Camps. Much of the duty hitherto undertaken by Debden squadrons was of routine patrol and convoy protection with No. 29 Squadron undertaking considerable night flying. It was one of their aircraft which caused the first bombs to fall on Debden on June 25 when the attacker used the returning Blenheim's flarepath as its marker. Shortly after, No. 29 Squadron moved to Digby, Debden becoming all Hurricane-equipped ready to fight the imminent battle during which time it was under command of Wing Commander J. L. F. Fuller-Good.

On July 10, the official beginning of the battle, Debden suffered slight bomb damage from a Do 17 which approached the aerodrome at 5.15 a.m. and circled at 9,000ft about 500 yards from the boundary. When it was engaged by AA fire, it dropped twenty-two small HE bombs, five of which landed near the married quarters breaking some windows.

Both No. 17 and No. 85 Squadrons were frequently scrambled during the next few weeks to intercept raids over a wide area of East Anglia, the Thames Estuary and Kent.

For the last two weeks of August, both squadrons moved south, being replaced by No. 111 and No. 601 Squadrons which arrived to join newly arrived No. 257 Squadron. During this period the Luftwaffe concentrated its attacks on key fighter stations and, on August 26, Debden received its first heavy raid in mid-afternoon resulting in considerable damage and casualties.

Raid No. 20 on August 26 moved in to Braintree from the south-east and was then plotted turning east. The plot was then lost by the Observer Corps for the next warning of the imminent raid on Debden was the dropping of bombs onto the aerodrome. More than a hundred HE and incendiary rained down, scoring direct hits on the Sergeants' Mess, NAAFI, the airmen's block, the WAAF quarters, the MT yard, equipment section, parade ground as well as the landing area itself. One trench received a direct hit and four RAF personnel and one civilian were killed. Electric and water mains were damaged and several unexploded bombs remained buried in parts of the camp.

The following day Marshal of the Royal Air Force Lord Trenchard visited Debden to inspect the damage. Earlier that morning the alarm had been raised when a Lysander circled the aerodrome acting in a suspicious manner. Not wishing to take any chances, a Hurricane from No. 601 Squadron was ordered up to investigate and, if not satisfied, to force down the aircraft. This was done and when the pilot climbed down from the cockpit he hotly declared he was on affiliation work with ground troops at Thaxted!

On August 31, Debden received its second heavy raid. The Operations Record Book described the attack in detail:

'Two formations of enemy aircraft approached the aerodrome from the south at about 0830 hours. The first formation passed slightly to the west at about 0833 hours at 15,000 feet and left the Sector. Bombs were heard in the distance dropping to the north.

'The second formation came up on the same course. They were thirty Dornier 17s in layers of three Vics in line astern, (three aircraft per Vic), the layers being stepped up in echelon to 16,000 feet with twenty Me 110 escorting to port and the same number to starboard 500 feet above.

'Before reaching Debden, they changed course to the east and then to north-west and approached Debden out of the sun. Bombing commenced at 0838 hours from 15,000 feet. Just before the bombs dropped, a puff of smoke, possibly a smoke bomb, appeared under the formation. This was not AA fire as fire from ground defences was not opened because of the height of the raiders.

'The bombs fell in sticks beginning south of the aerodrome and straddling the station in a general direction of north-west. The enemy aircraft then circled the aerodrome anti-clockwise singly in line astern and were attacked and broken up by fighter aircraft . . .

'Nine Hurricanes of No. 111 Squadron at Castle Camps, the satellite aerodrome, took off at 0810 hours to patrol Debden at 15,000 feet and engaged the raiders, a combat taking place to the north of the aerodrome and later in the Clacton area. Two enemy aircraft were destroyed, three probably destroyed and three others damaged.

'Hurricanes of No. 601 Squadron took off from Debden at 0827 hours and patrolled base at 15,000 feet and attacked the formation when proceeding north-north-west over Debden with the result that two enemy machines were destroyed and one probably destroyed, one other being damaged.

'No. 257 Squadron forward at Martlesham were airborne at 0830 hours and ordered to patrol Debden at 15,000 feet. They had almost reached Debden when they sighted two formations of enemy bombers at 16,000 feet flying east and several smaller formations of Me 110s at the same height behind the bombers. These they attacked destroying five and damaging another three.

'In all, about 100 HE and incendiary bombs were dropped, some of the incendiaries falling on the north side of the landing ground. The Sick Quarters and a Barrack Block received direct hits and were badly damaged. The Sergeants' Mess, NAAFI and the Cookhouse, three wooden huts, a hangar and a lock-up garage were also damaged by hits.

Pilots and a Gladiator of No. 87 Squadron at Debden in 1938 with No. 3 hangar in the background. On the left in the group of pilots by the wing tip is Pilot Officer R. L. 'Laurie' Lorimer who, with Flying Officer G. H. J. Feeny and Sergeant Dewdney, flew tied-together aerobatics in their Gladiators at the Villacoublay Air Display the same year. Lorimer was killed in action in France serving with No. 1 Squadron in May 1940, Feeny posted missing in action the following month, and Dewdney killed in an accident.

On November 15, 1979, reconstruction work was in full swing transforming Debden into Carver Barracks to be used as a base for an armoured reconnaissance regiment. Only No. 3 of the three hangars remains standing. This was the hangar through which Flying Officer R. H. A. 'Dickie' Lee flew a Hawker Fury for a sequence in the George Formby comedy film 'It's in the Air'. Lee went missing after combat on August 18, 1940.

BOUNDARY OF 1939 AERODROME

OPERATIONS BLOCK

Our photograph taken in July 1977 shows RAF Debden largely intact with official vandalism limited to the demolition of the watch office, building 34.

The location plan on the opposite page shows extent of the aerodrome in May 1939 and the site plan gives the use for each building in the camp.

· P E R M A N E N T ·	I N D E X	· H=H U T T I N G ·			
NO.	**BUILDING.**	**NO.**	**BUILDING**	**NO.**	**BUILDING.**
1	GAS CHAMBER.	44	PETROL, M/T, BULK INSTⁿ. 5.000.GALˢ.	7	SHELTER, FIRE TENDER, & N.F.E.
2	INCINERATOR (SITE FOR)	45	WORKS SERVICES BUILDINGS.	8	STORE, LUBRICANT & INFLAMMABLE.
3	STORE, PRACTICE BOMBS.	46	STORE, RATION.	9	PETROL COMPOUND.
4	" , S.A. AMMUNITION & DETONATOR (Gp.XII).	47	MESS, SERGEANTS for 105 & QUARTERS 14 Nᵒ.	10	WORKSHOPS. MAIN.
5	" , PYROTECHNIC & GROUP IX & XI.	48	QUARTERS, SINGLE SERGEANTS. 18 Nᵒ.	11	STORES, MAIN.
6	TEST BUTT, M/G.	49	DINING Rⁿ. & INSTITUTE for 400.	12	ARMOURY.
7	TEST HOUSE, ENGINE. (SITE FOR)	50	BARRACK BLOCK, A TYPE,3 N.C.Oˢ & 84 MEN.	13	OFFICES. M.T.
8	RANGE, M/G, 25 YARDS, 4 POINT.	51	" " , R " ,3 " 84 "	14	SHED. M.T. (BESSONNEAU)
9	PETROL, AVIATION, BULK INSTⁿ. 1/72,000.GALˢ.	52	" " , R " ,3 " 84 "	15	STORE, PARACHUTE.
10	GARAGES, SINGLE OFFICERS. 10 BAYS.	53	" " , Q " ,3 " 68 "	16	W/T. TRANSMITTING HUT.
11	COURT, SQUASH RACQUETS	54	BARRACK BLOCK. (SITE FOR.)	17	BARRACK HUTS. (A ᵀᴼ L) (12. N.C.Oˢ & 300. O/Rˢ)
12	QUARTERS, SINGLE OFFICERS. 30 Nᵒ.	55	" (" ").	18	" " (1. " & 27 ")
13	MESS, OFFICERS for 45.	56	COURTS, TENNIS, AIRMENS.	19	ABLUTION & LATRINES.(AIRMEN)
14	COURTS, TENNIS, OFFICERS. (SITE FOR)	57	GAS DECONTAMINATION.	20	" " "
15	QUARTER, MARRIED OFFICER, GROUP V.	58	FLAGSTAFF.	21	BATH HOUSE. (N.C.Oˢ & AIRMEN)
16	" , " " , " V.	59	SICK QUARTERS.	22	QUARTERS, SINGLE SERGEANTS.(15)
17	" , " " , " IX.	60	MORTUARY & AMBULANCE GARAGE.	23	STORE, RATION. A&B
18	" , " " , " V.	61	OPERATIONS BLOCK.	24	MESS, SERGEANTS.(80)
19	" , " " , " V.	62	OFFICES, STATION HEADQUARTERS.	25	DINING ROOM.
20	" , " " , " V.	63	GUARD HOUSE & FIRE PARTY & TENDER.	26	STORE, GROCERY.
21	" , " " , " II.	64	STAND-BY SET HOUSE.	27	INSTITUTE.
22	HOCKEY GROUND	65	CHURCH & CINEMA. (SITE FOR).	28	FUEL COMPOUND.
23	COURTS, TENNIS, SERGEANTS. (SITE FOR.)	66	SHOP & STORE, GROCERY.	29	EDUCATION HUT.
24	HEATING (CENTRAL) STATION.	67	QUARTERS, MARRIED AIRMEN. 44 Nᵒ.	30	GARAGE, AMBULANCE & MORTUARY.
25	SHED, PETROL TANKERS, 4.BAYS.	68	" " W/Oˢ. 2 Nᵒ.	31	SICK QUARTERS.
26	STORE, PARACHUTE.	69	PAVILION, SPORTS. (SITE FOR)	32	OFFICES, STATION. PHOTO.& W/T RECᵈ.
27	STORE, LUBRICANT & INFLAMMABLE STORE.	70	FOOTBALL GROUND, RUGBY.	33	GARAGE, FIRE TENDER.
28	OIL, BULK INSTⁿ. (SITE FOR)	71	CRICKET "	34	GUARD HOUSE & FIRE PARTY.
29	STORE, FUEL.	72	FOOTBALL " , ASSOCⁿ.	35	MESS. OFFICERS.
30	STORES, MAIN.	73	CRICKET NET SITES. (SITE FOR)	36	QUARTERS, SINGLE OFFICERS. (18)A & B
31	LATRINES, TECHNICAL.	74	NEON BEACON PIT. (" ")	37	BATH HOUSE, OFFICERS.
32	SHED, PETROL TANKERS, 4.BAYS.	75	MACHINE GUN PIT.	38	STORE, PYROTECHNICS.
33	SHELTER, FIRE TENDER & N.F.E. STORE.	75A	" " "	39	GAS CHAMBER & PRACTICE BOMB STORE
34	OFFICE, WATCH. (WITH TOWER).	75B	" " "	40	ELECTRICITY SUB STATION.
35	SHED, AIRCRAFT. C TYPE. 225'×150'.			41	OFFICE & STORE, MESS SECRETARY.
36	" , " " "			42	" " .MESSING OFFICER.
37	" , " " "			43	WORKSHOP & STORE, WORKS SERVICES.
38	COMPASS PLATFORM	1.		44	LATRINES, TECHNICAL.
39	SHED, PETROL TANKER, 4 BAYS.	2	RANGE. M.G.	45	OFFICES, WORKS SERVICES.
40	LATRINES, TECHNICAL.	3	TEST BENCH, ENGINES. (PLATFORM)	46	LATRINE & STORE. " "
41	WORKSHOPS, MAIN.	4	TEST BUTT, M.G.	47	INCINERATOR
42	ARMOURY.	5	LATRINES, TECHNICAL. (A, B & C)	48	COMPASS PLATFORM
43	SHEDS, M/T, 9 LARGE BAYS.	6	OFFICE, WATCH.	49	SEWAGE DISPOSAL WORKS.
43A	SHED, M/T, DETACHED BAY.			50	" " " TOOL HOUSE.

192

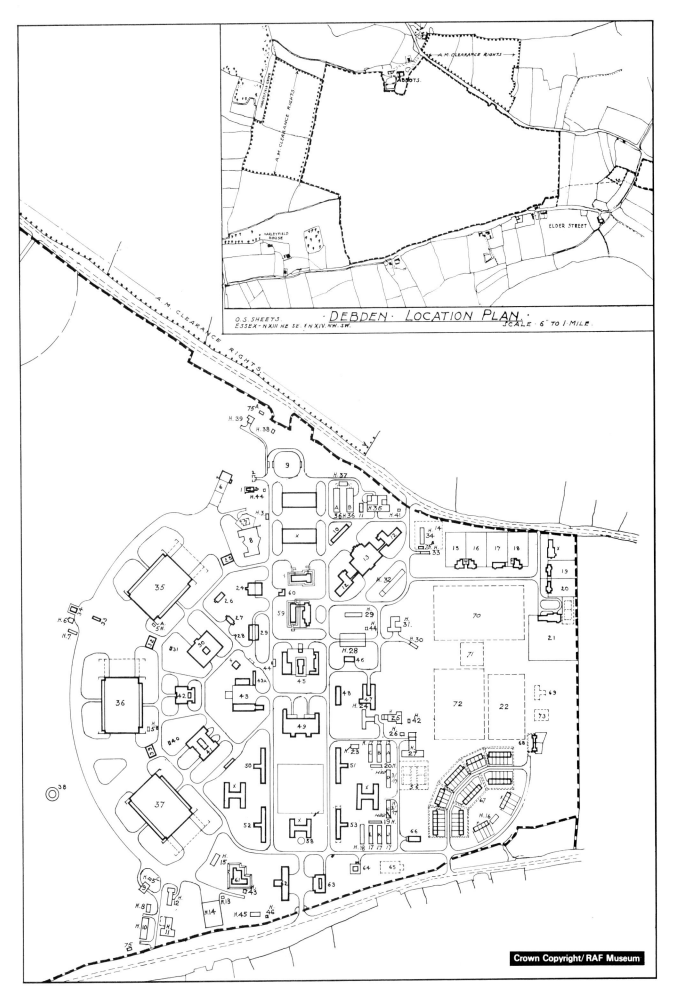

DEBDEN · LOCATION PLAN ·

O.S. SHEETS.
ESSEX · N.XIII NE SE: & N.XIV. NW. SW.
SCALE · 6" TO 1 MILE ·

193

'The operational side of the Station functioned throughout and there was no failure of lighting or communications in the Operations Room.

'One civilian and one airman were killed and twelve RAF personnel were injured.'

After this raid it was considered prudent to move the Operations Room away from the aerodrome and a temporary hut was established in a disused chalk pit near Saffron Walden beside the A130 until the Saffron Walden Grammar School was requisitioned for its use. A trophy which resulted from the raid of August 26 was a map removed from

Right: **The Operations Block for Sector F on the south-western corner of the camp (see plan).** *Below:* **As the Debden Operations Room is the only one of the new style No. 11 Group Sector blocks to have remained in Ministry hands since the Battle of Britain, the interior has remained largely intact.**

the leading Dornier after it was shot down near Debden. This map, which clearly showed the attacker's course, was proudly framed and displayed in the Officers' Mess until the end of the war.

Early September saw squadron changes with the return of No. 17 and the arrival of No. 73 Squadron to the Debden sector. Daylight combats remained fierce but when the Luftwaffe changed to heavier bombing after dark, No. 73 Squadron was designated a night-fighter unit and was joined by No. 25 Squadron who were working-up on the new Beaufighter. Defiants of No. 264 Squadron and the rejuvenated No. 85 Squadron were also involved in night defence duties at Debden until the end of 1940.

Right: **The quarry beside the A130 just to the south of Saffron Walden, the location of the temporary dispersed ops room, now occupied by the buildings of the Scott and Bowe Company. No trace of the original operations set-up remains.**

The gymnasium at the Dame Bradbury Private School (formerly Saffron Walden Grammar School) to which Sector Operations moved after their temporary stay in the chalk pit. Carefree children now play where the destinies of men were once charted.

During the period of August to November 1940, contemporary claims made by Debden's fighters were 110 aircraft destroyed, thirty-three probables and sixty damaged for a loss of thirty-three aircraft destroyed and eleven pilots killed.

Their Majesties King George VI and Queen Elizabeth visited Debden on January 28, 1941. More startling, on February 14, a Heinkel 111 landed but took off again before action could be taken. Havocs of No. 85 Squadron were busy in night defence from Debden but moved soon after the establishment of a Hurricane Operational Training Unit, No. 52 OTU, which stayed until August. Additional hangars (one Bellman and eleven blister type) were added to the south and west plus further

provision of hardstandings and revetments around the perimeter. Bostons of No. 418 Squadron (RCAF), formed at Debden in 1941, commenced their operations on March 26, 1942 but it was the Spitfire which was the predominant aircraft in 1942 with the formation of the Debden Wing. A second satellite aerodrome opened at Great Sampford in April with No. 65 Squadron as its first tenants. They, in company with Nos. 111, 350 and No. 71 'Eagle' Squadrons were constantly active, but it was when the latter was joined by the other two 'Eagle' squadrons (Nos. 121 and 133) that led to the transfer of all three to the USAAF on September 29, 1942 to become the 4th Fighter Group.

During their tenure they became one of the

most famed units of the US Eighth Air Force and the Group emerged to become the highest scoring unit within the European Theatre with over 1,000 victories, firstly with the Spitfires then P-47 Thunderbolts and finally the P-51 Mustang. Before their departure in 1945, the American pilots had held exercises with Meteors of No. 616 Squadron, the jets heralding a new era in aviation.

After the war Debden returned to the RAF and functioned within Technical Training Command, firstly as the Empire Radio School, then Signals Division, changing to Debden Division of the RAF Technical College in 1951. Aircraft of many varied types

Carver Barracks, October 19, 1979.

On September 29, 1942, the official transfer of the Eagle Squadrons from the Royal Air Force to the United States Army Air Corps took place at Debden. Here the Stars and Stripes takes its place alongside the RAF Ensign before the latter is lowered at the termination of the ceremony. The photograph was taken from the NAAFI (building 49) and the Press Censorship Bureau have indicated that the guardroom (No. 63) and the station headquarters (No. 62) and two barrack blocks must be deleted.

Before the parade, AOC-in-C Fighter Command, Air Chief Marshal Sir Sholto Douglas makes his last inspection of Eagle Squadron personnel followed by their new commander General Carl Spaatz Commander of the Eighth Army Air Force (USAF).

The Guidon Party having fallen in, soldiers of the 13th/18th Hussars await inspection by the Adjutant Captain N. S. Southward who returns a snappy salute to a Squadron Officer. This was a rehearsal for the Armistice Day service in Saffron Walden.

Friday, November 9, 1979, 9.30 a.m. and the 13th/18th Hussars, (Queen Mary's Own) fall in for a pre-Armistice Day Adjutant's inspection parade. Nicknamed 'the Lilywhites' from the buff-coloured facings originally adopted by the 13th Hussars and now worn by the band, amalgamation with the 18th Hussars came in 1922 at Aldershot when Queen Mary consented to become the first Colonel-in-Chief of the new Regiment. The unit had returned from its third posting to Northern Ireland in May.

were flown during this period until 1960 when flying ceased and the station became the base for the RAF Police Depot and functioned as such for the next fifteen years. HRH Princess Margaret conducted a Royal Review at the station on June 5, 1973 but Debden's days were numbered and the closing ceremonial culminating with a fitting fly-past by a Spitfire and Hurricane took place on April 25, 1975.

On September 30, 1975, the site was transferred to the Army department of the Ministry of Defence and demolition of many of the buildings, including two of the hangars, commenced in 1978 preparatory to its re-opening as Carver Barracks. Named after Field-Marshal Lord Carver, the first unit to occupy the new barracks, which are being specially converted for an armoured reconnaissance regiment, is the 13th/18th Royal Hussars, Queen Mary's Own.

The Regiment's first big local parade was held in Saffron Walden on Armistice Day 1979 and we were fortunate to be able to photograph the dress rehearsal on the parade ground on November 9 making a fitting comparison to that held on the same spot by members of the Royal Air Force and USAAF in 1942.

The end of an identity. Only one concrete letter of the station identification code 'DB' remained in November 1979.

'And the walls came tumbling down'. What the German bombing failed to do has now been accomplished. The last wall of the two hangars about to go.

SECTOR G
Duxford/Fowlmere

BY ALISTER RABY

For the Battle of Britain period the histories of Duxford and Fowlmere have to be considered together as the latter had no separate identity, operating throughout as a satellite of the main station. Both aerodromes dated back to the latter years of the First World War although Fowlmere was slightly older, being in use early in 1917 as a landing ground for No. 75 (Home Defence) Squadron. Then, in mid-1917, both Duxford and Fowlmere were selected as sites for fully-fledged aerodromes which were needed for the rapidly expanding training programme for the Royal Flying Corps. Contracts were let to P. & W. Anderson Ltd. of Aberdeen and work started in October, both aerodromes being built to

On May 4, 1939, during a press day at Duxford, a simulated air raid alarm sent the heavily encumbered pilots of No. 19 Squadron lumbering for their Spitfire Is much to the amusement of the more comfortably attired erk. Time and experience would soon reduce the amount of equipment with which they loaded themselves in these early practice scrambles (Central Press).

almost identical patterns as the photographs show, each having six hangars (170ft by 100ft), an aircraft repair shed and a hutted camp for living and administration purposes. They opened before completion in March 1918 as mobilisation stations for six new RFC DH9 day-bomber squadrons. When construction was finished at the end of August, the two aerodromes assumed their planned role as Nos. 31 and 35 Training Depot Stations under the control of No. 26 Wing in Cambridge. However, within three months the war was over and, from the beginning of 1919, both Duxford and Fowlmere were more concerned with demobilisation and the

disbandment of squadrons returning from the Continent.

At the end of March 1920 Fowlmere was put on care and maintenance for disposal and in October 1922, just five years after building work had started, the demolition firm of Bennett and Blowers moved in and within a few years there was no trace left of the former aerodrome or its buildings. Duxford was more fortunate in being selected as one of the RAF's first post-war training stations, opening as No. 2 Flying Training School in May 1920.

Many famous pilots on short service commissions gained their wings at Duxford,

On October 13, 1979, two members of the Imperial War Museum's airfield staff, in the time-honoured posture of stipendiary guardians, stroll past the enigmatical smile on the face of the ex-No. 57 Squadron Handley Page Victor tanker on static display.

including the record-breakers Jim Mollison and Charles Black. However, the training role was short-lived for, in 1923, the government adopted the recommendations of the Steel-Bartholomew Committee for the defence of south-east England against air attack. This involved the establishment of an Air Fighting Zone extending from Duxford in the north to Devizes in the south. Three new fighter squadrons, Nos. 19, 29 and 111, were formed from flights and personnel of the FTS which moved to Digby in May 1924. Duxford

Ever since a long-forgotten clerk captioned the photograph above as Duxford, everyone has published it as such. However, our author Alister Raby did not accept this and has now correctly identified it as depicting its identical sister aerodrome at Fowlmere. Compare with the picture *below* **of Duxford (Imperial War Museum and P. H. T. Green).**

then commenced its thirty-eight years as a fighter station initially in No. 6 Group.

The next year the RAF was reorganised on an area basis, Duxford becoming part of Fighting Area. A station flight was formed, responsible for training members of the newly established Cambridge University Air

Squadron and many ex-CUAS pilots eventually fought in the Battle of Britain. Other functions of the station flight were daily, high-altitude meteorological sorties and flight research for the University Aeronautics Department. Flight Lieutenant Frank Whittle assisted in this latter work while studying for

Within five years of it opening, the massive Belfast hangars at Fowlmere were completely demolished together with all other buildings. During WWII, the technical area was located on the opposite side around Manor Farm (Cambridgeshire Collection).

an engineering degree in the mid-thirties as well as working on his first jet engine.

In 1928, Nos. 29 and 111 Squadrons left but No. 19 stayed on as the resident squadron — going from Grebes to Siskins and then to Bulldogs until becoming the first unit to be equipped with the Gloster Gauntlet in 1935. With this new type, the squadron was chosen to carry out formation drill over Duxford on the occasion of King George V's Jubilee Review of the Royal Air Force on July 6, 1935.

On the formation of Fighter Command in July 1936, Fighting Area became No. 11 Group and in the same month a new expansion squadron, No. 66, was formed from No. 19 Squadron's 'C' Flight. Continued expansion resulted in the formation in 1937 of a more northerly No. 12 Group, controlled from Watnall, of which Duxford became the southern outpost. Meanwhile more land had been acquired and permanent station buildings and married quarters constructed to the north of the A505.

Thursday, August 4, 1938 is possibly the most significant date in Duxford's history for on that day Jeffrey Quill delivered Spitfire I K9789 to No. 19 Squadron, commanded by Squadron Leader H. I. Cozens. Before joining Supermarine's, Quill, like several other well-known test pilots, had served with Duxford's Station Flight. By the end of 1938 both No.19 and No. 66 were fully re-equipped and Duxford was the RAF's first Spitfire station. Both squadrons were used for the trials of improvements and new equipment, such as variable pitch propellers and VHF radio and, by September 1939, Duxford was ready with its Spitfires for any challenge that might come.

On the outbreak of war both Nos. 11 and 12 Groups were under the control of Duxford 'old boys'. Air Vice-Marshal Keith Park had commanded No. 111 Squadron there in 1927/28 and the AOC of No. 12 Group, Air Vice-Marshal Trafford Leigh Mallory brought his Bristol Fighter squadron (No. 8) to Duxford for disbandment in 1919.

From the first day of the war, Duxford's relatively inland position resulted in the introduction of a pattern of operations from forward aerodromes, these being established initially from Watton and Horsham St. Faith. Nos. 19 and 66 Squadrons took turns to operate mainly coastal patrols in which they were soon joined by a newly-formed Duxford squadron, No. 222, flying Blenheim Is. Life was fairly uneventful until the New Year when a section of No. 66 flying from Horsham shot down an He 111 attacking a trawler off Cromer. Squadron Leader Cozens left No. 19 Squadron on promotion to a staff appointment.

Early in February 1940, Flying Officer Douglas Bader was posted to No. 19 Squadron. Just seven years before he had been

'and from the tents,
The armourers, accomplishing the knights,
With busy hammers closing rivets up,
Give dreadful note of preparation.'

Henry V, William Shakespeare

Perhaps the best known picture of the Battle of Britain — Fowlmere, September 1940.

The men and machines have gone — only the earth abides. The re-arming scene in September 1979 with the partially demolished Manor Farm in the background.

Above: Flight Lieutenant Brian Lane seems to be photographed against his wishes at Manor Farm. *Right:* Thirty-nine years later on the same spot, Martin Sheldrick pin-points the photographic locations for Wilf Nicoll.

Lunch in the 'Officers' Mess' at Fowlmere, September 1940. The picture gives a clear indication of the very basic facilities existing on satellite aerodromes (Imperial War Museum).

September 1979 and gone is the snow-white linen and the genteel patter of mess silver on crockery. Now a trailer with a tank of liquid manure occupies the site of the old nissen hut.

Squadron Leader Brian Lane, third from left, relaxes with some of his lads in the adjoining crew room after acquiring his 'scraper ring' on the death of former CO Philip Pinkham on September 5. The furnishings are spartan but comfortable with the usual Lloyd-

Loom chairs in evidence (Imperial War Museum). Only the concrete bases of the Nissen huts remain. Broken and rusting farm implements replace the furniture and the conversation of the long-lost men is superceded by the twittering of sparrows.

Pilot Officer Wallace Cunningham, Sub-Lieutenant A. G. Blake nicknamed 'The Admiral', a Fleet Air Arm pilot killed during the battle on October 29 at Chelmsford, and Flying Officer F. N. Brinsden clutching an overfed spaniel enjoy a respite in the September sun outside the Fowlmere crew rooms. The Fowlmere photos are some of the best taken during the battle (Imperial War Museum). Occupying exactly the same position as the 1940 pilots, Wilf Nicoll, our ex-wireless operator/air gunner steeped in the history of the Royal Air Force, tries to enjoy a respite in a most uncomfortable service camp chair.

Above: **Briefing 1940. Utilizing an old kitchen table from one of the farm cottages, Brian Lane briefs his No. 19 Squadron pilots (Imperial War Museum).**
Right: **Martin Sheldrick is that rare breed of farmer who is sensitive to the history that was made on the land that he inherited. At Manor Farm, Fowlmere, in September 1979, he briefs Wilf Nicoll on exactly the same spot. We are indebted to Martin for the generous loan of photographs collected from former pilots who have re-visited the drome.**

discharged from the RAF from Duxford as permanently unfit after a flying accident in which he lost his legs. He was soon joining in routine patrols but there was still little action. In March No. 222 began to exchange its Blenheims for Spitfires and Bader joined them as a flight commander but in May they left, replaced by No. 264 Squadron flying the new two-seat Defiant turreted fighter. Within days

The controller's caravan. The signals' tent is on the left.

Although the crew rooms have gone the spot is unmistakable.

Above: With radiator flaps wide open, three Spitfires of No. 92 Squadron taxi over Fowlmere's sunburned grass to the downwind end of the runway (Imperial War Museum). *Bottom:* The neatly harrowed fields of the old aerodrome in 1979. In the background, the wooded slopes of Heydon and Chrishall Granges.

the Germans were sweeping through the Low Countries and into France and No. 19 Squadron opened its score on May 11 with a Ju 88, the Defiants claiming a Ju 88 and an He 111 off the Dutch coast the following day. On May 26 No. 19 Squadron claimed thirteen aircraft over Dunkirk for the loss of four of their own including their new CO, Squadron Leader Geoffrey Stephenson (he eventually turned up in Colditz where he was joined in 1944 by his old friend Douglas Bader).

At the end of May No. 66 Squadron ended its four-year association with Duxford moving to the new aerodrome at Coltishall and the following month No. 19 Squadron moved to the nearby WW1 aerodrome site at Fowlmere which had been reopened as a satellite aerodrome (G1) with minimum facilities. The station commander at Duxford at this time was Wing Commander A. B. Woodhall, a Great War veteran, who also acted as 'G' Sector Controller.

In July 1940 a special flight was formed at Duxford. Operated by No. 5 Radio Maintenance Unit (Later No. 74 Signals Wing), its function was to check and maintain the chain of RDF (radar) stations between the Thames and the Wash. The equipment for this vital, if unspectacular, work was made up of impressed civilian Cierva Autogiros and DH Hornet Moths.

Compare the plan of the aerodrome in 1944 (PSP runways were laid by American engineers to overcome the drainage problem) with the aerial oblique on pages 206-7. Taken in October 1979 just after ploughing, the outline of the perimeter track is clearly visible.

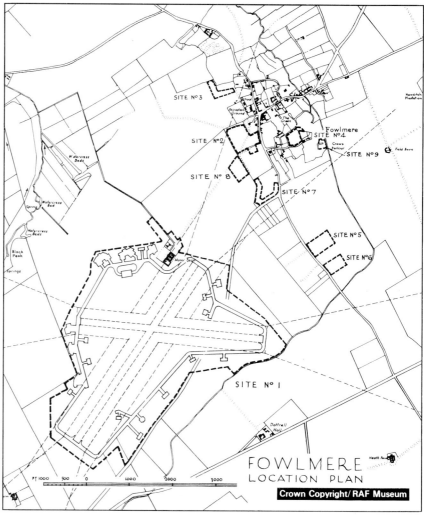

FOWLMERE
LOCATION PLAN

Crown Copyright/RAF Museum

No. 19 Squadron's move to Fowlmere coincided with a decision to re-equip them with the first cannon-armed Spitfires, continuing their role as the trials squadron for that aeroplane. Ironically, operational difficulties with the cannons limited their participation in the early stages of the Battle of Britain which was just beginning. Their new CO, Squadron Leader P. C. Pinkham, complained that stoppages were making the squadron practically non-operational.

Duxford's first Hurricanes arrived in July with the formation of a squadron made up of Czech pilots who had escaped from France — No. 310. These replaced the Defiants of No. 264 Squadron as their success had been limited once the Germans had learnt to distinguish them from Hurricanes.

It was not until well into the third phase of the battle — when the Luftwaffe sought to attack the sector aerodromes and destroy RAF ground installations — that Duxford came into its own. As No. 12 Group to the north of the main fighting was comparatively rested

Above left: **After the battle, the primitive facilities at Fowlmere were expanded with the addition of a single T2 hangar and standard RAF watch office. Today only the former remains** *(photo above)* **having been reclad in coated aluminium in 1975** *(photo below).*

Below: **Martin Sheldrick's contribution to history. Concerned that a beautiful RAF wall mural in one of the buildings was deteriorating, he brought up a mobile generator for lighting and engaged a photographer to record it in colour.**

A Charles E. Brown study of fitters of No. 19 Squadron (the first to be equipped with the Spitfire) with their aircraft lined up across the all-grass aerodrome at Duxford.

In 1968 the same high ground was the background for other photographs during the re-enactment of the Battle of Britain for the film of the same name. An early scene is the Luftwaffe strafing attack on a French aerodrome in May 1940 led very convincingly for the cameras by Commandante Pedro Santa Cruz of the Spanish Air Force.

and out of things, at the end of August Air Vice-Marshal Leigh Mallory decided to bring down the Hurricanes of No. 242 Squadron, now commanded by Squadron Leader Douglas Bader, from Coltishall to Duxford to join Nos. 19 and 310 Squadrons on daily standby. Flying as a squadron under Wing Commander Woodhall's guidance, Bader's men claimed twelve enemy aircraft for the loss of none of their own in the defence of North Weald on August 30. Leigh Mallory was impressed and authorised Bader to lead the other two Duxford squadrons as a wing and several days were spent practising three-squadron formation take-offs. No. 19 Squadron also gave up its cannon Spitfires, reverting to eight machine guns. On the morning of September 5 Squadron Leader P. C. Pinkham was shot down and killed by a Bf 109 and Squadron Leader B. J. Lane became No. 19's fourth commanding officer in nine months.

The Duxford Wing achieved no real success until September 9 by which time the Luftwaffe had turned its attention to London when the Duxford squadrons claimed twenty destroyed for the loss of four Hurricanes and two pilots (a Canadian Pilot Officer K. M. Sclanders of No. 242 and Flying Officer J. E. Boulton of No. 310). On the strength of this victory two more squadrons were added to the Wing, No. 302 (Polish) with Hurricanes and No. 611, an auxiliary squadron, with Spitfires. Each day some sixty Hurricanes and Spitfires were dispersed around Duxford and the satellite of Fowlmere and, by Sunday, September 15, Bader's 'big wing', now more formally known as No. 12 Group Wing, was ready for action. On this historic day the five-squadron wing took to the air three times against all out Luftwaffe attacks on London. By the evening their immediate after-the-battle claim was at least 42½ victories for the loss of four aeroplanes and one Polish pilot, Flight Lieutenant T. P. Chlopik, from No. 302 Squadron.

Thereafter the Wing continued to operate from Duxford with varying success. At No. 11 Group, Park was sceptical of their tactics as he considered such a large formation un-wieldy, climbing at the rate of the slowest aeroplane and often late to engage. Leigh Mallory at Watnall, however, was convinced of the overwhelming effectiveness of the large formation when properly positioned. While this is not the place to study the controversy in detail, it is enough to record that the Duxford Wing become a household word.

Duxford and Fowlmere, unlike the front line stations to the south, had escaped lightly. Some 100 bombs, jettisoned rather than aimed around Fowlmere on the morning of Saturday, August 31 had caused no damage to the station. A delayed-action bomb dropped on Duxford the same night was towed away and exploded safely.

By the end of the battle the Wing's claim was 152 enemy aircraft destroyed for the loss of thirty pilots and rather more aeroplanes. Post-war checking of records would reduce this figure but, more important, the battle had been won and, on October 26, Sir Archibald Sinclair, the Secretary of State for Air, flew in to congratulate the Wing on its performance. A few weeks later President Benes of Czechoslovakia arrived to present decorations to Wing Commander Woodhall and a number of British and Czech pilots.

There was now a radical change of role for Duxford. Nos. 19 and 310 Squadrons remained, although largely relegated to inhospitable Fowlmere, now retitled WA.1 from where they carried out coastal patrols as well as sweeps and escort duties over occupied Europe.

Then, in December 1940, the Air Fighting Development Unit moved up from Northolt bringing a variety of types for handling and tactical trials. Their equipment included several captured enemy aeroplanes which were later transferred to a separate Enemy Aircraft Flight. A special Aircraft Gun Mounting Establishment was formed to deal with the sort of installation snags which had bedevilled No. 19 Squadron's abortive attempt to introduce the cannon-armed Spitfire into service. Stirlings, Halifaxes and later Lancasters also arrived at Duxford to develop evasive tactics with the AFDU.

Group Captain Vasse, the CO of the AFDU, took over from Woodhall as station commander and, in June 1941, No. 19 Squadron ended its eighteen-year association with Duxford and moved south along with its Czech companions. Duxford was to continue its role of introducing new types into service. The first to arrive was the American Airacobra which No. 601 Squadron tried unsuccessfully to lick into shape. It was soon joined by No. 56 Squadron with its Typhoons which, despite teething troubles with the Sabre engine, was turned into a very useful strike fighter. Early in 1942, the Allison-engined North American Mustang arrived for trials — the verdict being that with a Rolls-Royce Merlin it would be a war-winning aeroplane — and so it proved.

In July 1942 the dummy superstructure of a destroyer was set up on Fowlmere. This represented Louis Mountbatten's *Kelly* and was filmed under attack by a Ju 88 of Duxford's Enemy Aircraft Flight for the film *In Which We Serve*.

By early 1943, American Air Force P-38 Lightnings and P-47 Thunderbolts were being tried out by the AFDU and, at the beginning of April, Duxford was handed over to the USAAF as a fighter base. It became Station 357 and the home of the 78th Fighter Group, operating at first with Thunderbolts and later with the Duxford-inspired Merlin-Mustang. Soon afterwards Fowlmere became an aerodrome in its own right as Station 378 with the Mustangs of the 339th Fighter Group. Both groups were part of the 66th Fighter Wing with headquarters at Sawston Hall.

At the time of the transfer to the Eighth Air Force, the grass landing area at Duxford measured 1,600 yards by 2,000 yards. This allowed a 1,500 yard take-off run on the NE-SW and SE-NW diagonals; a thousand yards from N-S and 1,400 yards from E-W although this approach was restricted by 40ft-high trees at one end. During the rainy, wet conditions that existed in the latter months of 1944 (which caused the Americans to nickname Duxford 'Duckpond') the heavier US fighters had difficulty operating from the grass and engineers had to lay down a 6,000ft pierced steel planking runway on a NE-SW axis across the grass by extending the aerodrome at the eastern end. An additional forty-seven steel mat hardstandings were added to the existing twenty-six tarmac dispersals.

The similar conditions which existed at Fowlmere ('Hen Puddle' to the Americans) necessitated two PSP runways being laid, one of 1,600 yards running NE-SW and the other of 1,400 yards on an E-W axis, the 339th moving to Bassingbourn while the work was being carried out. A T2 hangar was added to the small RAF technical site which had grown up around the farm buildings on the northern perimeter.

By the end of the war the 78th Fighter Group claimed nearly 1,400 enemy aeroplanes destroyed in the air and on the ground for the loss in action of 264 of their own.

When the Air Ministry's plans for the post-war future of the two aerodromes were made known, they were virtually a carbon copy of the decision taken following the First World War.

As far as Fowlmere was concerned, after the 339th Fighter Group left in October 1945, the station was disbanded. By 1947 agricultural ploughing of the land re-commenced following the lifting of the tracked runways and the perimeter track and other buildings were cleared during the course of several

years. The single T2 hangar was retained by the Ministry of Works until 1957 when the land was sold back to the former owners, the major part to F. F. Sheldrick & Sons Ltd of Manor Farm and the remainder to Mr. F. Pepper of Black Peak Farm. In 1975 the preservation of the T2 hangar was assured when the Sheldrick family had it reclad in coated aluminium.

Duxford, on the other hand, was to be retained by the RAF as a peacetime station. On December 1, 1945, the aerodrome was officially handed back by the Americans and No. 165 Squadron moved in, equipped initially with Spitfires. However the coming of the jet era necessitated operation from permanent runways and the aerodrome was closed for flying between October 1949 and July 1951 for the construction of a 6,000ft by 150ft concrete runway and twenty-eight of the dispersals were protected with parallel concrete blast walls.

Duxford's last operational phase began in August 1951 with the Meteors of Nos. 64 and 65 Squadrons, later replaced by Javelins and Hunters. However, the threat from the south-east, which had originally called Duxford into being as a fighter station in 1923, was now replaced by one from more northerly latitudes. In a defence situation, where every half-minute might count, Duxford was no

longer in the right place and the decision was taken that it should close. On August 1, 1961, it was erased from Fighter Command's Order of Battle and the last of Duxford's fighters flew away.

For several years the future of the aerodrome was uncertain and it was still on 'care and maintenance' when Harry Saltzman began looking for locations to film his epic *Battle of Britain*. Its largely unchanged character made it an ideal 'set' and the hangars were re-camouflaged and flight lines of Hurricanes and Spitfires faced similar lines of Messerschmitts and a pair of Heinkels of the Spanish Air Force (albeit with Merlin engines). During the summer days of 1968 these aeroplanes took off to re-enact the battle of 1940, leaving familiar vapour trails across the sky. On June 21 and 22 fiction overtook reality when one of the hangars was blown up (after considerable difficulty) during a German 'attack', resulting in far more damage than ever occurred during the war years.

This bizarre episode renewed interest in Duxford and this subsequently led to the Imperial War Museum, together with the enthusiastic assistance of the members of the Duxford Aviation Society, establishing what is now probably Europe's most important historic aviation centre in association with the

In April 1939, Duxford was still a simple, square-shaped grass aerodrome. Only in 1944 was the first runway added (constructed of pierced steel planking) being replaced in 1949-51 by a single 6,000ft concrete runway on a NE-SW axis suitable for jet fighters.

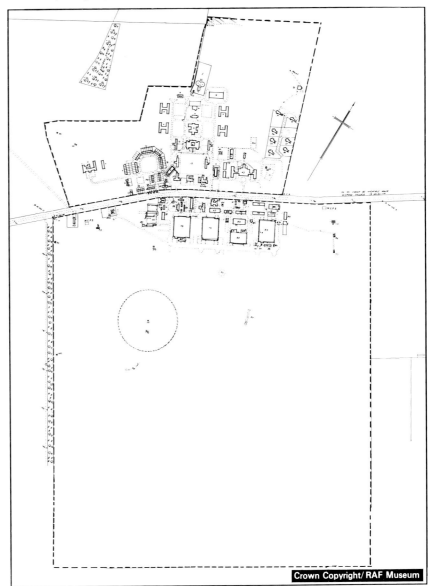

Above: **Not the beginning of the British space programme but the Duxford fire fighting force in September 1940. The airman in the white asbestos 'space' suit was required to walk into the heart of any conflagration for the purposes of rescue or recovery of bodies. His rate of pay for this was about two shillings (10p) per day (Imperial War Museum).**
Below: **The same corner in October 1979, with the IWM's midget submarines in the background.**

Cambridgeshire County Council. However, the plans for the total preservation of the aerodrome came too late as the Department of the Environment had already scheduled the construction of the London-Cambridge M11 motorway to cross the eastern end of the runway. The public enquiry held in March 1976 saw Sir Douglas Bader fight his last battle for the aerodrome but all was to no avail: the Ministry neatly sidestepped all arguments by pointing out that the wartime aerodrome would be left intact and only the post-war runway extension would be lost. By August 1977 contractors plant had moved in and is still in evidence in our aerial photograph taken in October 1979.

Following the restoration of the WWI hangars, which house examples of many of the types of aeroplane which have been based at Duxford, work began on repainting all the buildings in a wartime camouflage scheme in keeping with its former history.

Today the aerodrome is a thriving attraction for hundreds of thousands of visitors

The Officers' Mess. It was extended post-war but now stands boarded up to the north of the A505.

Recent alterations to Duxford include the removal of several dispersals and part of the perimeter track (foreground) and the bisection of the eastern end by the M11 London-Cambridge motorway.

a year. Altogether over sixty different types of aircraft are to be seen ranging from the Tiger Moth to Concorde. Many of them, owned by Duxford Aviation Society members and loaned to the Imperial War Museum, fly regularly. Of special period interest are the Skyfame Cierva Autogiro G-ACUU, which as HM580 flew with Duxford's radar calibration flight in the 1940s, and Tony Haigh Thomas's Hornet Moth G-ADLY (then W9388) which did similar work from a Scottish base. One of Duxford's proudest exhibits is the Shuttleworth Spitfire, AR501, an ex-310 Czech Squadron aeroplane, restored in its original markings. Frequently airborne from Duxford, it provides a unique living link with the Battle of Britain of forty years ago.

The hangar goes up . . . or rather down. Unauthorised alterations by Spitfire Productions Ltd., for 'Battle of Britain'.

SECTOR W
Exeter

BY MICHAEL PAYNE

When Exeter Airport was formally opened by Sir Kingsley Wood on July 30, 1938, the grass landing area was only a fraction of the size of the present airfield. It had already been in use for about a year and boasted a terminal building, one hangar and a refuelling point. Jersey Airways and Railway Air Services were the principal operators but there was plenty of activity when the Civil Air Guard scheme was inaugurated. A number of blue and silver D.H. Hornet Moths were operated as trainers until the outbreak of war. During this period a second, larger hangar was constructed to the west of the terminal buildings and this was occupied by a detachment from the RAE Farnborough with an assortment of Fairey Battles, a Wellesley, a Virginia, a Harrow and one of the Fairey P.4/34 prototypes. This aircraft was used in the experiments in which aircraft were flown into balloon cables. Empire Air Day 1938 saw a huge crowd along the eastern side of the aerodrome and a variety of service aircraft arrived to take part in the flying display.

In September 1939, the two Handley Page 42s of Imperial Airways were flown in together with the short Scylla and Syrinx, and these, as well as all the buildings, were camouflaged. Occasional visitors also at this time were the

Top: **Fitters and armourers of No. 601 'County of London' Squadron swarm over one of the unit's Hurricanes on the eastern fringe of the perimeter at Exeter sometime after the squadron's withdrawal from Tangmere in September 1940 (Imperial War Museum).** *Below:* **Today the eastern extension to the E-W runway runs across the middle distance.**

three Junkers Ju 52/3M aircraft of British Airways, though these were based at Whitchurch. At about this time, one of the Shorts was dismantled and its fuselage was used as a temporary office.

RAF Station Exeter was officially inaugurated in the presence of Nos. 213 and 87 Squadrons on July 6, 1940.

Soon after this, work began on extending the aerodrome both to the east and to the north-west. On the eastern side a farmhouse and a lane disappeared and a large tract of farmland and orchard was levelled and added to the aerodrome. This area was in use during the Battle of Britain as a dispersal area for the Hurricanes of Nos. 213 and 601 Squadrons, the ground crews working round the perimeter under canvas and the pilots billeted in the city. Towards the village of Honiton Clyst in the north-west, a small hill had to be removed and this work continued well into 1941 before it was possible to lay the whole length of the main E-W runway. The aerodrome was most conspicuous from the air with its great gash of red-brown soil where the earth-moving contractors were hard at work.

The dimensions of the grass surface landing area were as follows: N-S, 850 yards; NE-SW, 1,050 yards; E-W, 1,500 yards and SE-NW, 1,100 yards. The runways constructed were the E-W on 074°T, 2,000 x 50 yards; the SE-NW on 120°T, 1,450 x 50 yards and the N-S, 1,000 x 50 yards. The perimeter track was 50 feet wide. There were two hangars at this time, storage facilities for 72,000 gallons of aviation fuel and 5,000 gallons of MT spirit. Refuelling was by means of tankers. Munitions consisted of a thirty-ton bomb store and over five million rounds of ammunition.

At the outbreak of the Battle of Britain, No. 700 General Construction Company, Royal Engineers, was stationed on the aerodrome under canvas ready to repair any damage caused by enemy action. A detachment of the Devonshire Regiment (one NCO and twenty men) was also on hand for guard duties.

During the battle, Exeter operated the Hurricanes of Nos. 87, 213 and 601 Squadrons. The aerodrome itself was attacked by one twin-engined aircraft on August 21 which dropped four bombs on Army tents on the perimeter, killing two servicemen. A further two casualties died after admission to hospital and another twenty-one men, including one civilian, were injured.

It was on September 12 that the Station Commander, Wing Commander Dewar, DSO, DFC, took off from Exeter to fly to

The Operations Room for W Sector at Poltimore, three miles north of the aerodrome, is the only one, out of the ten sectors covered in this book, which is still used operationally. Now improved to withstand nuclear attack, it was taken over in 1947 by No. 21 Group, Royal Observer Corps. The unit changed its designation rather appropriately to No. 10 Group in 1953.

Tangmere but he failed to arrive and was reported missing. Temporary command was assumed by Squadron Leader R. S. Mills of No. 87 Squadron.

At the beginning of 1941, a new shape appeared in the skies around Exeter when the then secret Westland Whirlwind twin-engined fighters of No. 263 Squadron flew in from Scotland. However, operations proved difficult in the muddy conditions of that winter and they remained only until February, leaving the station to the Hurricanes of No. 504 and the Spitfires of No. 66 Squadron. These were joined in April by the Defiants of No. 307 (Polish) Squadron which provided the night-fighter defence for Exeter and Plymouth. No. 307 Squadron were to remain at Exeter until mid-April 1943, flying successively the Beaufighter Mk II, Mk I, Mk VI, and, in 1943, the Mosquito Mk II.

During the first half of 1941 five German attacks were carried out against Exeter, the one on April 5 destroying one hangar and damaging sixteen aircraft. The following year

another raid hit the aerodrome on February 12 although one of the attacking Do 217s was shot down by AA fire two miles east of the aerodrome beside the A30.

From 1941, a succession of Spitfire squadrons operated from Exeter with Mk IIs and Mk Vbs, — Nos. 317, 308, 421, 19, 310, 131, and (in the first part of 1943) a detachment from No. 124 Squadron flying the Spitfire HF Mk VI. From September 1943 until April 1944, No. 616 Squadron flew a mixture of Mk VI and Mk VII Spitfires, all having the extended wing-tips and a non-matt finish. In January 1944, No. 610 Squadron arrived flying Spitfire Mk Vbs with the customary clipped wing tips. These aircraft were gradually replaced by the new Griffon-powered Mk XIV. They stayed until April when they flew out to Culmhead (formerly named Church Stanton).

The Polish night-fighter squadron moved to Fairwood Common in April 1943, to be replaced by No. 125 Squadron (Beaufighters), and later by No. 406 Squadron. For a brief

Overleaf: **The drome looking south-west in June 1941.**

213

period in late 1942, a number of Havoc Turbinlite aircraft of No. 536 Squadron were based at Exeter with their companion night fighter Hurricanes of No. 247 Squadron. But they recorded no successes and their vacated dispersal area was occupied first by the Typhoons of No. 257 Squadron and then by those of No. 266 Squadron. During this period of the war, it was a frequent sight to see the aerodrome crowded with light bombers of No. 2 Group with a massive escort of visiting Spitfires, with Bostons, Mosquitos and, once or twice, the Venturas of No. 464 Squadron setting out to raid targets in Normandy or Brittany. USAAF P-38 Lightnings and P-47 Thunderbolts of the Ninth Air Force also used Exeter as a forward base on many occasions until, in April 1944, the aerodrome became Station 463 of the USAAF, being occupied entirely by the Dakotas, Hadrians and Horsas of the 440th Troop Carrier Group, USAAF, in preparation for the D-Day landings in June.

Various 'lodger' units also used Exeter. A detachment of the Gunnery Research Unit (GRU) flew a Wellington Mk Ic, a Wapiti, a Battle (T) and several Lysander and Defiant target tugs (all coded HP). From 1943, Nos. 695 and 691 Squadrons provided searchlight and AA co-operation flights with Oxfords, Martinets and disarmed Hurricanes, though they moved temporarily to Winkleigh (in mid-Devon) during the American 'occupation' in 1944. Black-painted Swordfishes of the Royal Navy hunted for E-boats in the Channel, also based on Exeter, during the nights of early 1943 but their stay was only short.

As the war moved eastwards across the Continent, Exeter became a backwater and, in January 1945, the Station was transferred to Flying Training Command and No. 3 Glider Training School moved in with Hotspur gliders and Master tugs. Soon after VE-Day, No. 329 Squadron's Spitfires arrived for a short stay but the last truly operational RAF units to use Exeter were the Mosquitos of No. 151 Squadron and the new Meteors of No. 222 Squadron.

When the station was disbanded as an RAF base in July 1946, it reverted to the status of a civil airport and was officially transferred to the Ministry of Civil Aviation in January 1947. No. 10 Reserve Flying School was formed in 1949, flying Tiger Moths (later Chipmunks), and by this time Chrislea Aircraft Ltd. were producing the 'Ace' at the northern side of the airfield. From 1951, Exeter was the home of No. 3 CAACU, a target facilities unit manned by civilian personnel and flying Spitfire Mk 16s, Mosquitos, Vampires and Meteors at different periods.

The airfield now has three runways, the main E-W having a length of 6,120ft, with unobstructed approaches in all directions. There is now a new and more extensive hardstanding area in front of the Terminal Building but at the same time there are many of the original wartime installations still in existence and still in use. Dispersal bays, hardstanding pads around the perimeter track, hutments and the old station workshops and motor transport bays, remain today though many of these buildings now serve different purposes. For example, the hutted camp to the south is now part of a flourishing industrial estate. Sector W operations were located in the grounds of Poltimore House, some three miles north of the aerodrome. There in 'Camp B' (the aerodrome was Camp A), a semi-underground Operations Room was constructed. Although this was closed down at the end of the war it was re-activated in 1947 as the No. 21 Group HQ. Royal Observer Corps. In 1953 the unit was redesignated No. 10 Group, a fitting change of title and one in keeping with the former use of the Operations Room by Fighter Command.

Our comparison photograph taken on November 1, 1979.

SECTOR Y
Middle Wallop

BY NORMAN PARKER

Middle Wallop, five miles west of Andover, was planned as a bomber station but started life as the home of No. 15 Flying Training School. The aerodrome began with a grass landing area measuring 1,000 yards SE-NW; 1,250 yards E-W; 1,200 yards N-S and 1,400 yards NE-SW — the latter two directions being extended subsequently to 1,600 and 19,000 yards respectively. A 50ft concrete perimeter track ran around the aerodrome and five C-type hangars were constructed on the northern side. Provision was later made for the storage of five million rounds of small arms ammunition and 144,000 gallons of fuel.

When the station became operational on June 12, 1940, it was still under active construction with open trenches in abundance. Only one hangar had been completed together with three barrack blocks, stores, headquarters and the essential guardroom. In order to provide temporary accommodation,

officers were put up at Andover whilst airmen had to be satisfied with tents. Three mobile kitchens provided the only cooking facilities. Group Captain P. E. Maitland was the first Station CO.

In May, ground defences were increased and a searchlight erected between Nos. 3 and 5 hangars. The air-raid siren was installed on the 26th and all personnel were issued with small arms, rifles or revolvers, in case of attack by parachutists. The camouflaging of the buildings had begun before the end of the month using a scheme of black and dark green and Royal Engineers arrived for defence duties and began erecting barbed-wire entanglements.

Meanwhile, as a signal had been received from Training Command HQ to the effect that the station might be needed for operational fighters at short notice, the parachute section was ejected from the Operations Room. By the end of the month total station personnel numbered 1,067.

A few days later an incident occurred which provided a good test for the new defences. At five minutes past midnight on June 7, the Duty Pilot reported that flares were dropping over the aerodrome. One minute later a report came in of twelve parachutists dropping to the north-west of the station. Within eight

minutes, all posts had been manned and warnings telephoned to the Local Defence Volunteers.

During the next hour, two phone calls were received from members of the public reporting sightings of parachutists. At 12.51 a.m., the mobile defence column was despatched to Knock Wood. No sooner had Brigadier Lewis and his men set out than a message was received from nearby RAF Boscombe Down that an experiment was underway involving aircraft towing flares! Too late to recall the column, the scare escalated and, at 1.21 a.m., the Andover police phoned through a warning of enemy landings and a 'Red Alert' air-raid warning had been received. Half-an-hour later Group Captain Maitland arrived and, after assessing what had taken place, managed to calm the situation and by 3.10 a.m. the station was finally stood down.

Middle Wallop fell within No. 10 Group Fighter Command with its headquarters at Rudloe Manor near Box. Wallop became an operational sector station with 'Y' Sector Operations Room in what is today the station church. Aircraft operated from the forward

Left and above: The birth pangs of a Royal Air Force station. The view from the Operations Block looking south past airmen's 'H' blocks to the five C-type hangars (Public Record Office).

Left and above: Tents and huts provide temporary living accommodation prior to the completion of the OR's married quarters. Today the Rations Store and NAAFI are on the left.

Left and above: With the corner of No. 2 hangar on the left, this was the WWII station armoury under construction which now houses the Army Air Corps photo section (Public Record Office).

Left and above: An Airspeed Oxford of No. 15 FTS is parked outside No. 2 hangar (centre) surrounded by a welter of building materials. Today construction work is taking place on a new flight simulator building (Public Records Office).

Nos. 4 and 5 hangars near completion in May 1940 with the fire and crash tender bays beginning to take shape. The unfinished bulk of No. 3 hangar fills the background. Temporary personnel accommodation in the foreground (Public Record Office).

base of Warmwell and from Boscombe Down and Chilbolton in August and September respectively.

Several night-fighting experimental units were established in the summer of 1940, the most successful of which was No. 604 Squadron, which, under the command of a youthful Squadron Leader John Cunningham, went on to become a top scoring night-fighter unit.

The first fighter unit to be located at the aerodrome was an Auxiliary Squadron, No. 601, which flew its Hurricanes to Middle Wallop before No. 15 Flying Training School left for Brize Norton.

At 9.00 a.m. on June 12, 1940, the Operations Record Book was opened and history began. Wing Commander D. N. Roberts, was both the Station Commander and Sector Controller.

A number of squadrons were briefly based at Middle Wallop during this period; No. 236 with Blenheim 1s; No. 1 RCAF with Hurricanes and No. 50, also with Hurricanes, but all had moved before the Battle of Britain began. The squadrons chiefly involved were Nos. 234 and 238 with Hurricanes and the Yorkshire Auxiliary Squadron No. 609 with Spitfires. No. 152 also flew Spitfires at Warmwell, the other aerodrome in the Wallop

sector at that time. All Wallop squadrons used Warmwell as an advance base, flying down early in the morning and returning at dusk as operational areas demanded attention.

Daily patrols were maintained during the lull before the storm but not until August 8 did the battle really begin in earnest. A large convoy codenamed 'Peewit' was attacked by heavy German forces off the Isle of Wight during the defence of which No. 609 Squadron claimed three Bf 110s and two Ju 87s whilst No. 238 Squadron claimed two Bf 110s and a Bf 109 and four unconfirmed kills with a loss of two of their own pilots. For the next three weeks fighting was continuous as attack after attack was made against south coast targets, Middle Wallop aerodrome itself being bombed with varying degrees of success on the 13th, 14th, 15th and 21st.

On August 13, a vast force of enemy bombers supported by Bf 109 fighters launched Adlertag. Junkers Ju 87 dive-bombers turned over Lyme Regis for their

attack on Middle Wallop but their fighter escort, short on fuel, had turned for home and No. 609 Squadron shot down six out of the nine aircraft in one unit. Ju 88s flying high above the Solent, also headed for Wallop but missed their target, bombing Andover instead. Only one Ju 88 found the aerodrome, dropping five bombs which landed in the village of Nether Wallop just behind No. 238 Squadron's dispersal points. By evening, the two squadron's claimed eighteen destroyed and three probables all without loss to themselves.

The following day another heavy attack developed with a large number of He 111s heading for Middle Wallop. Many bombs were dropped but only one aircraft, a Ju 88, bombed with any success. Diving out of the cloud, the crew dropped four bombs, one of which hit No. 609 Squadron's hangar. That one bomb blew the windows out, stripped the roof and blew the heavy iron door off its track as it was being closed. Three Blenheims and

A peaceful Sunday in October 1979 and the helicopters of the Army Air Corps are safely hangared for the weekend.

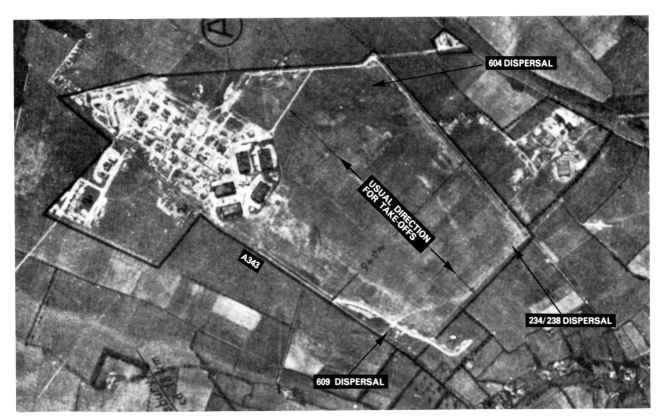

Above: This October 1940 Luftwaffe photo of Middle Wallop indicates the extent of the aerodrome during the Battle of Britain (via Christopher Elliott).

Below: This British low-level oblique of the camp site, unfortunately undated but circa 1946-47, clearly shows the destruction of hangar No. 5 (Crown Copyright).

several Spitfires were written off. Three airmen were killed and one wounded and also three civilian workers employed by contractors lost their lives with two others wounded. However, retribution in the shape of a Spitfire flown by Sergeant Feary of No. 609 Squadron was only seconds away. As the Ju 88 pulled out of its dive, he opened fire and the aircraft crashed five miles away near Grately Station. The tally at the end of the day was four Ju 88s and one He 111 destroyed without loss.

Yet another attack took place on the 15th but a miscalculation by the leader caused the twelve 1,000kg bombs to fall wide and, although two hangars were hit, one aircraft destroyed and five others damaged, there were no casualties. Again the Middle Wallop sector

Right: **No. 609 Squadron line up at Middle Wallop, August 1940. L-R: Pilot Officer John Curchin, Flight Lieutenant J. H. G. 'Butch' MacArthur, Pilot Officer David Crook, Pilot Officer John Appleby, Pilot Officer 'Shorty' Keough (an American), Pilot Officer Geoffrey Gaunt, Squadron Leader H. S. George Darley and Pilot Officer Noel Agazarian (Crown Copyright).**
Below: **The dispersal today — the 'drome was extended later in the war removing the hedges which existed in 1940.**

Time for a quick cuppa between sorties. Pilots and 'battle bowlered' ground crews of No. 609 Squadron at their dispersal in August 1940. The pilot on the right is Sergeant A. N. Feary who was shot down by Bf 109s over Yeovil on October 7, 1940 and killed after baling out too low (Crown Copyright).

pilots were very successful, claiming thirteen aircraft destroyed plus six probables although one pilot, Pilot Officer C. H. Hight, a New Zealander from No. 234 Squadron, was killed and two others were missing.

Although the station rejoiced in a brief respite on the 16th, attacks were still heavy but were confined to the coastline where the limited range of the Bf 109 could be used to advantage. Casualties mounted on both sides but generally in favour of the RAF. This day too was a special day for Fighter Command; No. 249 Squadron from Boscombe Down in the Wallop Sector were on patrol between Lyndhurst and Romsey when Red Section, under the command of Flight Lieutenant John Nicolson, broke off to attack three Ju 88s — an action which led to the only award of the Victoria Cross to a pilot of Fighter Command during the Second World War.

During the battle, the No. 609 Squadron dispersal was in the south-western corner of the aerodrome, virtually beside the main Andover-Salisbury road (now the A343). There was no proper perimeter track at that time, only the rough track visible on the German reconnaissance photo. Near the corner, the CO, Squadron Leader G. N. Darley, and his wife were able to rent a house just the other side of the hedge. 'This had a

The shambles that was No. 5 hangar after the bombing raid of August 14, 1940. Just inside can be seen the wing of a mangled Spitfire while the massive steel door has been blown from its track. Three airmen were crushed to death when it was blasted onto them as they struggled to close it to save the aircraft inside. All photos taken by an unknown airman. *Below:* The orderly appearance of No. 5 hangar in October 1979 belies the destruction inflicted upon it thirty-nine years before.

Right: **As Middle Wallop had been conceived as a bomber station, there was no provision for a proper Sector Operations Room. The first improvised location was in a wooden hut, completely bare of any blast protection, behind the Station HQ. Meanwhile a standard ops block was hurriedly being built on the corner of the camp site to which Wing Commander David Roberts and his staff transferred in mid-August.**

field telephone to the dispersal', recalls George Darley, 'so that if we were called to readiness from fifteen minutes standby, I was always the first there — much to the disgust of the pilots who had to come from the Officers' Mess. The house came complete with excellent air-raid shelter — useful during raids. My wife knew my aircraft so never waved to me whilst coming in to land but waved to everybody else! I don't suppose many wives were so closely involved with a squadron during the Battle of Britain.'

Middle Wallop, meanwhile, began to patch up the damage and dealt with a number of unexploded bombs on the 17th. Thereafter only very occasionally did an enemy aircraft penetrate the fighter screen to try and bomb the station and, on each of the five visits between the main attacks in August up to the end of November, the bombs dropped did little or no damage although, at one stage, one 500kg unexploded bomb closed the main Andover Road for two days.

As the emphasis of attack moved across the country, so the Wallop Sector Controller, Wing Commander Roberts, deployed his forces to meet each threat as it developed. The battle raged up and down the south coast, Vickers Armstrong's Supermarine factories at Woolston and Itchen both being destroyed but, despite the loss, their products continued to destroy the attackers with only a temporary reduction in supply.

Below: **This is the interior of the wooden hut, still with its raised balcony, cleverly converted into the station church.**

SECOND OPERATIONS BLOCK

AIRMEN'S DINING HALL AND NAAFI

SICK QUARTERS

A343

224

STATION HQ

FIRST OPERATIONS BLOCK

SERGEANTS' MESS

MT YARD

GUARD ROOM

Following the Fighter Command policy of dispersing Operations Rooms away from aerodromes, Wallop House was taken over in Nether Wallop village — now a nursing home.

A fourth move was made in June 1943 to a purpose-built Operations Block on the northern side of Over Wallop village. The building still stands although derelict.

Above: **A near miss on one of the airmen's barrack blocks during the raid on August 14. (The filled-in crater is visible on the aerial photograph on the previous page, taken on February 15, 1941. It** is the centre block on the far side of the parade ground.) *Below:* Traces of wartime camouflage still remain but the pock-marked brickwork has been neatly repaired.

By the end of the battle, the Wallop Sector had expanded to include a squadron of Hurricanes at Boscombe Down, another at Chilbolton as well as the resident squadron at Warmwell, No. 152. However, with the onset of the long winter nights, the secondary role of night-fighting assumed the greater importance. No. 604 received the first of the new Beaufighters, the Long Air Mine (aircraft trailing bombs on the end of 2,000ft of piano wire) continued development at Middle Wallop by No. 420 Flight which had arrived in September and the Helmore Turbinlite Havocs appeared on the scene. Of these, the airborne radar had the only real success for the Long Air Mine frightened the populace and the airborne searchlight robbed its pilot of effective night vision.

The following year saw the air war beginning to move across the Channel and taking the offensive to the Continent. As the number of squadrons at Wallop increased so did the station and its facilities. The aerodrome almost doubled in area as did the dispersal areas.

During the preparations for the invasion of Europe, Middle Wallop was transferred to the USAF in December 1943 as a base for tactical reconnaissance units until they moved to advanced landing grounds in France in July 1944. During September, No. 3501 Central Servicing Unit was established to undertake second and third line servicing for the 2nd Tactical Air Force in France and many hundreds of Spitfires, Typhoons, Hurricanes, Tempests, Mustangs and Mosquitoes flew back for base inspections during this period. When this unit moved to Odiham in February 1945, Middle Wallop became HMS *Flycatcher*, a Royal Navy Unit to form up a series of mobile naval air operations bases (MONABS) for service in the Far East. However, the end of hostilities led to the abandonment of further operational activities.

The station was returned to Fighter Command on April 10, 1946. The gaunt framework of the wrecked hangar still remained and it stayed that way even when flying re-started with No. 227 Operational Conversion Unit. This subsequently became the Air Observation Post School, then the Light Aircraft School and, finally, the Army Air Corps. On October 1, 1958, the station was formally passed to Army control and it was only in the sixties that the hangar was rebuilt, the blast walls around the dispersals removed and new accommodation constructed for married personnel.

Today the aerodrome remains the largest and only active military grass airfield and is the centre of training for the Army Air Corps and also the location of the Museum of Army Flying.

Pilot Officer David Crook, author of one of the most acclaimed books on the Battle of Britain, 'Spitfire Pilot' published in June 1942, takes off from Middle Wallop in September 1940 (Crown Copyright).

Above: Pilot Officers D. M. Crook and G. N. Gaunt of No. 609 Squadron at Middle Wallop in September 1940. Geoff Gaunt, trapped in a burning Spitfire, died on September 15 when he was shot down near Kenley by enemy fighters. His identity was not established until four days later. David Crook was killed in 1944. *Below:* Our author, Norman Parker, describes the fate of the two pilots to Sergeant Docherty of the Army Air Corps at Middle Wallop in October 1979. Danebury and Chattis Hill in the background.

228

Warmwell

BY IVAN MASON

Opened in May 1937 as part of the Armament Group RAF, the station was first known as RAF Woodsford and was the home of No. 6 Armament Training Camp. The aerodrome was situated to the south of the Wareham to Dorchester railway and stretched nearly a mile westwards from Woodsford crossing. The grass field had a twelve foot tarmac perimeter track enclosing a useful length of some 1,900 yards from NE-SW and SE-NW; 1,750 yards from E-W and 800 yards from N-S. The watch office lay halfway along the northern boundary and later looked out on a row of dispersal pads on the western half of the field. One convex-roofed hangar was sited in the south-east corner adjacent to the camp site and was later replaced by two T2s.

Armament training was to operate in

With the canvas gun-port patches blown and powder-fouling streaking the wing undersurfaces, Spitfire PR-L is speedily re-armed at Warmwell during the late afternoon of July 9, 1940 after No. 609 Squadron's engagement with a force of Ju 87s and Bf 109s over Weymouth Bay (Crown Copyright). *Bottom:* The overgrown dispersal in February 1980 beside Dick o' the Banks road.

conjunction with two bombing and gunnery ranges on the nearby Chesil Beach. The 1,200 yard western range ran from Langton Ferry to Herbury and the central one stretched 1,400 yards from the old church at Fleet to Hythe. Both local fishermen and naturalists raised objections, the former to the loss of fishing grounds and the latter to possible disturbance to the swannery at Abbotsbury but, in spite of the opposition, the ranges were completed. On September 23, 1937 the *Dorset Chronicle* noted that 'bombers from Woodsford are coming over daily and there is considerable activity in the air'. However, as late as November, *The Times* recorded hopefully that the air-to-ground gunnery range was not yet functioning.

In July 1937 a Station Flight was formed with Avro Tutors and Westland Wallaces and the first squadrons arrived to use the aerodrome. These were Nos. 206 and 220, both with Avro Ansons, taking part in the annual Coastal Defence Exercise. They were the precursors of more than twenty regular and auxiliary squadrons which used the station for air firing and summer camps over the next two years. Other regular visitors were the advanced training squadrons of the Flying Training Schools.

On April 1, 1938, the Armament Training Camp was retitled No. 6 Armament Training School and from July 1 the station was known as Warmwell. On September 4, 1939, No. 6 ATS again changed its name, this time to No. 10 Air Observer School. For another two months the unit continued to operate its varied fleet of Battles, Hinds, Overstrands, Sidestrands, Henleys, Seals and Wallaces, which numbered more than sixty aircraft.

A further change took place on November 6 when the Central Gunnery School was created from a nucleus of No. 10 AOS and equipped with Battles, Whitleys, Wellingtons, Masters, Defiants and Hampdens. The remaining part of the unit then became No. 10 Bombing and Gunnery School. The station settled down to its busy but orderly programme of training until the events of May and June 1940 showed an air onslaught on Britain to be imminent. During that month plans for the extension of air defence west of Southampton were put into operation. Warmwell was transferred to No. 10 Group, Fighter Command, as a forward aerodrome in Middle Wallop Sector 'Y' and No. 10 Bombing and Gunnery School moved out to Dumfries on July 13. The Spitfires of No. 609 Squadron moved from Northolt to Middle Wallop on July 4 and operated from Warmwell on a daytime basis. No. 152 Squadron, also with Spitfires, arrived from Acklington to take up residence on July 12 for the defence of Portland naval base. Thus the meagre forces of Fighter Command in the area were disposed and the battle began.

At first, the Warmwell Spitfires had little success and by the end of July the pilots of No. 609 Squadron admitted to being despondent. They had been in action since Dunkirk and had paid a high price for their victories. Never lacking in courage, their small flights or sections took on huge formations of the enemy. On July 9 for example, Green section set off to patrol Weymouth at 6.30 p.m. After an uneventful forty-five minute patrol, some Ju 87s were sighted. The three Spitfires attacked but were set upon by escorting Bf 110s. Using cloud cover, Pilot Officer D. M. Crook stalked a Ju 87 and sent it flaming into the sea. Meanwhile Flying Officer Drummond-Hay fell prey to the Bf 110s and he too dived into the sea.

Two days later, five aircraft of 'B' Flight intercepted a morning attack on a convoy south of Weymouth. Against what the surviving pilots described as 'ridiculous odds' they attacked, shooting down two Ju 87s. The enemy escort fighters accounted for two Spitfires. Flight Lieutenant P. H. Barran and Pilot Officer T. M. Mitchell did not return.

Another convoy patrol on July 27 led to a

During the Battle of Britain, Warmwell had only very primitive facilities. This tent was the crew room for No. 609 Squadron, pitched on the northern boundary beside the road from Higher Woodsford to West Stafford. Anyone taken short had to use the field in the background! Standing L-R: Pilot Officer A. C. 'Red' Tobin (American), Pilot Officer P. Ostaszewski (Polish), Flying Officer H. M. Goodwin, Flying Officer Paul Edge, Pilot Officer Michael Appleby, Flight Lieutenant Frank Howell, Squadron Leader H. S. George Darley, Flight Lieutenant J. H. G. 'Butch' MacArthur, Sergeant A. N. Feary, Pilot Officer F. Nowierski (Polish), Pilot Officer C. N. 'Teeny' Overton and, crouching in front, Pilot Officers M. E. 'Mike' Staples, David Crook and R. G. 'Mick' Miller.

confused action in which Pilot Officer J. R. Buchanan was killed and, having lost four pilots in three weeks' operations from Warmwell, the squadron had reason to feel depressed.

The 609 pilots had much to complain about apart from the fighting itself. They considered Warmwell a poor station. Their dispersal was located on the northern side of the aerodrome and it consisted of a canvas tent which often blew down. Meal hours were fixed and the door of the mess hall was locked afterwards so that pilots on operations during meal times went without food. One senior officer even told the pilots: 'I used to run a fighter squadron and we always had meals on time!'

No. 152 Squadron had seen no action before its arrival in mid-July and claimed no victories during its first month in action though taking part in several combats. Then came August 11 and their first loss. During a mid-Channel combat, Pilot Officer J. S. B. Jones baled out but was killed and his body recovered by the Germans to be buried at Le Havre. The following day an even worse fate befell the squadron with the deaths of Pilot Officer D. C. Shepley and an Australian,

Flight Lieutenant L. C. Withall. Neither pilot was ever found.

August 13 gave the squadrons the chance to get their own back as Pilot Officer Crook of No. 609 Squadron describes in this extract from his book *Spitfire Pilot*:

'At about 4 p.m. we were ordered to patrol Weymouth at 15,000 feet. We took off, thirteen machines in all, with the C.O. leading, and climbed up over Weymouth. After a few minutes I began to hear a German voice talking on the R.T., faintly at first and then growing in volume. By a curious chance this German raid had a wave-length almost identical with our own and the voice we heard was that of the German Commander talking to his formation as they approached us across the Channel. About a quarter of an hour later we saw a large German formation approaching below us. There were a number of Junkers 87 dive-bombers escorted by Me 109s above, and also some Me 110s about two miles behind, some sixty machines in all.

'A Hurricane squadron attacked the Me 110s as soon as they crossed the coast and they never got through to where we were.

'Meanwhile the bombers with their fighter

From a reliable source, information has been received of an impending attack on WARMWELL aerodrome this morning.   Aircraft to be ready to leave at 0700 hours.

This message must be treated as OFFICER ONLY and should not be transmitted by telephone.   Air Ministry and Admiralty are in possession of this information.

M.I.14.
1040 hrs.
20.8.40.   Lieut.Colonel. G.S.

Distribution :

D.D.M.I.(I) (for D.M.I)
G.H.Q. Home Forces.
G.H.Q.(Adv.)(I),Home Forces.
M.O.3.

MOST SECRET. (20)   B 39   OFFICER ONLY.

Information has been received from a reliable source that attacks will be made on the following aerodromes this morning as follows as from 1000 hours :
WARMWELL as from 1000 hours ;
KEMBLE , ABINGDON, BRIZE NORTON, ABBOTS INCH, as from 0600 hours;

This message must be treated as OFFICER ONLY and should not be transmitted by telephone.   Air Ministry and Admiralty are in possession of this information.

M.I.14.
0600 hohrs.
          Lieut. for
          Lieut. Colonel, G.S.

(20)

OFFICER ONLY.   38   MOST SECRET.

From a reliable source, information has been received of an impending attack on WARMWELL aerodrome this morning. Aircraft to be ready to leave at 0700 hours, As on 22.8.40.

This message must be treated as OFFICER ONLY and should not be transmitted by telephone.   Air Ministry and Admiralty are in possession of this information.

M.I.14.
0152 hours.
23.8.40.   for Lieut.-Colonel, G.S.

Distribution :-

D.D.M.I.(I) (for D.M.I.).
G.H.Q., Home Forces.
G.H.Q. (Adv.) (I), Home Forces.
M.O.3.

OFFICER ONLY.   B 37   MOST SECRET.

1.   Reliable source states that air attacks are to be expected during the course of today, 22nd. August, on WARMWELL and BRIZENORTON aerodromes and also possibly on RISSINGTON aerodrome.

- - - - - -

and the one below
This message/must be treated as OFFICER ONLY and should not be transmitted by telephone. The Air Ministry and Admiralty are in possession of this information.

- - - - -

2.   An equally reliable source reports that photographic reconnaissances of various targets including possibly LANDS END and NEWQUAY ST. EVAL aerodromes will be made during 22 August.

M.I.14.
0215 hrs.
22.8.40.   for Lieut.Colonel. G.S.

Distribution : D.D.M.I.(I) for D.M.I.
G.H.Q. Home Forces.
G.H.Q. (Adv) (I), Home Forces.
M.O.3.
File.

OFFICER ONLY.   B 40   MOST SECRET.

It is reliably reported that air attacks are to be expected during the course of today, 25th. August, 1940, on WARMWELL, LITTLE RISSINGTON and ABINGDON aerodromes and reconnaissances of aerodromes by a single aircraft in the area SOUTHAMPTON - ALDERSHOT - BRIGHTON.

. . . . .

This message should be treated as OFFICER ONLY and should not be transmitted by telephone. The Air Ministry and Admiralty are in possession of this information.

M.I.14.
0740 hrs.
25.8.40.   for Lieut. Colonel. G.S.

Distribution :   D.D.M.I.(I) for D.M.I.
G.H.Q. Home Forces.
G.H.Q.(Adv) (I), Home Forces.
M.O.3.
File.

This is the first time to our knowledge that British Ultra intelligence has been reproduced in facsimile form. These briefs were based on decoded Luftwaffe signals which had been transcribed via the Enigma code machine. Compare these bulletins with the Warmwell Operations Record Book for the same period. Ultra gave Sir Hugh Dowding a unique insight into German intentions during the battle (Public Record Office).

---

escort still circling above them, passed beneath us. We were up at almost 20,000 feet in the sun and I don't think they ever saw us till the very last moment. The CO gave a terrific ''Tally ho'' and led us round in a big semi-circle so that we were now behind them, and we prepared to attack.

'Mac, Novi (one of the Poles), and I were flying slightly behind and above the rest of the squadron, guarding their tails, and at this moment I saw about five Me 109s pass just underneath us.

'I immediately broke away from the for-mation, dived on to the last Me 109, and gave him a terrific burst of fire at very close range. He burst into flames and spun down for many thousands of feet into the clouds below, leaving behind him a long trail of black smoke.

'I followed him down for some way and could not pull out of my dive in time to avoid going below the clouds myself. I found that I was about five miles north of Weymouth, and then I saw a great column of smoke rising from the ground a short distance away. I knew perfectly well what it was and went over to have a look. My Me 109 lay in a field, a tangled heap of wreckage burning fiercely, but with the black crosses on the wings still visible. I found out later that the pilot was still in the machine. He had made no attempt to get out while the aircraft was diving and he had obviously been killed by my first burst of fire. He crashed just outside a small village. and I could see everybody streaming out of their houses and rushing to the spot.'

(Peter Cornwell makes an interesting comment on the confusion of the official records concerning this claim. Confirmation

	13·35	"Yellow"	Nothing of interest to report.
	23·30	"Purple"	
Warmwell	20/8/40 22·30	"Yellow"	Our aircraft flew over domestic
			side of Camp at approx 3500 ft.
Warmwell	21/8/40 07·00	"Red"	"Red" sounded
	08·00	"White"	

R.A.F. Form 540

See instructions for use of this form in K.R. and A.C.I., para 2196, a 3 War Manual, Pt. II., chapter XX., and notes in R.A.F. Pocket Book.

. . . 400,000 12/37—McC & Co—51-5658

OPERATIONS RECORD BOOK

of (Unit or Formation) R.A.F. Warmwell

Page No. 2

No. of pages used for day

Place	Date	Time	Summary of Events	References to Appendices
Warmwell	21/8/40	09·50	"Yellow" Not broadcast.	
		10·40	"White" do	
		14·38	"Yellow" do	Isolated aircraft none
		14·51	"White" do	of which came into the
		17·12	"Yellow" do	immediate vicinity of
		18·09	"White" do.	the aerodrome.
Warmwell	22/8/40	10·15	"Yellow" Broadcast on Station.	
		11·32	"White"	
		12·37	"Yellow" Not broadcast.	
		12·58	"White" do	
		15·32	"Yellow" do	
		16·23	"White" do	
		17·22	"Yellow" do	
		17·53	"White" do	
		18·25	"Yellow" do	
		18·50	"White" do	
		22·30	"Purple" do	
Warmwell	25/8/40	10·05	"Yellow" Broadcast on Station.	
		10·40	"White" do	
		11·50	"Yellow" do	
		12·15	"White" do.	
		17·00	"Red". Syren sounded and at 17·25 hours	
			an enemy attack commenced. Approx	
			20 bombs were dropped (varying sizes),	

Page No.

Place	Date	Time	Summary of Events	References to Appendices
Warmwell	25/8/40	17·25	Sick Quarters were burnt out, two	
			hangars damaged, numbers of windows	
			broken in different parts of the Camp.	
			Huts also were damaged.	
			9 unexploded bombs located in the	
			Camp. 1 exploded at 0200 hrs 26th; one	
			at 0430 hrs; one at 10·30 hrs 27th; one at 14·00	
			hrs; one at 23·35 hrs and one at 0645 hrs (28th).	
Warmwell	26/8	1110	"Yellow" – Not broadcast. As a result of the	
		13·59	"Yellow" do attack, communication	

of the combat was given by Flying Officer Nowierski (Novi) but stating that the aircraft Crook brought down fell into Poole Harbour. Pilot Officer Crook's logbook, preserved in the Public Record Office, AIR4/21 5854, simply states that He rocked violently and then turned over and dived away and burst into flames and crashed near Hardy's Monument behind Weymouth.' According to official records, no Bf 109s are reported to have crashed on land in that area on that day.)

'I climbed up through the clouds again to rejoin the fight,' continues Crook, 'but there was nothing to be seen, and so I returned to the aerodrome, where all the ground crews were in a great state of excitement, as they could hear a terrific fight going on above the clouds but saw nothing except several German machines falling in flames.

'All the machines were now coming in to land and everybody's eyes were fixed on the wings.

'Yes — they were all covered with black streaks from the smoke of the guns — everybody had fired.

'There was the usual anxious counting —

only ten back — where are the others — they should be back by now — I hope to God everybody's OK — good enough, here they come! Thank God, everybody's OK!

'We all stood round in small groups talking excitedly, and exchanging experiences. It is very amusing to observe the exhilaration and excitement which everybody betrays after a successful action like this!

'It soon became obvious that this had been our best effort yet.

'Thirteen enemy machines had been destroyed in about four minutes' glorious fighting. Six more were probably destroyed or damaged, while our only damage sustained was one bullet through somebody's wing. I think this was the record bag for one squadron in one fight during the whole of the Battle of Britain.'

On 16th, No. 152 Squadron scored their first confirmed victory on a patrol over the Isle of Wight when Pilot Officer Beaumont attacked three Bf 109s and shot down two of them. A further ten aircraft were claimed on the 18th and another on the 21st. Then on August 25 Warmwell received its first direct attack.

Alarms had sounded throughout the day and both squadrons had engaged the enemy during the afternoon. In a combat off Portland No. 152 Squadron claimed three destroyed and one probable but lost Pilot Officers R. M. Hogg and T. S. Wildblood. Meanwhile the Spitfires of No. 609 Squadron patrolled the Swanage area and intercepted a large enemy formation. In the ensuing scattered fighting they shot down six or seven of the enemy for no loss to themselves.

The raid on Warmwell began just before 5.30 p.m. Some twenty bombs destroyed the station sick quarters, damaged hangars and other buildings and left a few craters on the aerodrome. Some delayed-action bombs exploded during the following two days but the raid caused no casualties.

After the hectic events of the 25th, the rest of August seemed quiet by comparison. The enemy was still active and No. 152 Squadron destroyed a Heinkel off Portland on 27th. Neither squadron suffered losses and no more bombs fell in the immediate area.

During much of September No. 609 Squadron were often called to the defence of London but did not operate from Warmwell. No. 152 Squadron continued to patrol Portland and shot down a Ju 88 on 17th and the destruction of another Ju 88 on the 19th was the result of a ground-controlled interception. As the aircraft approached from the sea, two Spitfires of Green section were directed to it and it was promptly shot down by Sergeant Holland; a reminder that most of the success of the Warmwell fighters, as with all the others, was due to early detection of the enemy by radar. There was always good liaison with the nearby installation at Worth Matravers.

Wide ranging battles took place on 25th and on the 26th when nine Spitfires attacked some thirty Ju 88s over the Isle of Wight and shot down three although Sergeant J. McBean Christie of 152 was lost. Another battle took place on September 27 and on the last day of the month four enemy aircraft were destroyed. In the afternoon of October 7 both squadrons intercepted a raid by Ju 88s heading for Yeovil. In spite of their efforts the town was bombed but at least four of the enemy were destroyed. No. 152 Squadron lost Pilot Officer H. J. Akroyd and No. 609 Sergeant A. N. Feary.

The rest of the month was relatively quiet as was most of November though actions on 28th caused the loss of two pilots from each of the squadrons. No. 609 Squadron moved into Warmwell on the 29th and the year came to a close with no other major activity having taken place.

On February 24, 1941, No. 609 Squadron left Warmwell for Biggin Hill and No. 234 Squadron arrived from St. Eval to replace them.

A surprise raid by three He 111s on April 1 caused ten deaths and resulted in the station being evacuated at night except for essential defences. No. 152 Squadron left on April 9 to be replaced briefly by No. 118. In June the Central Gunnery School moved out but the Chesil ranges continued in use following the opening by No. 10 Group of a fighter squadron practice camp at Warmwell in November and a steady stream of fighter squadrons passed through making use of the local facilities.

Looking north at Warmwell's desecrated features in October 1979. In 1973, the whole of the area on which the aerodrome was situated was given over to gravel extraction.

On November 11 a Hurricane of No. 32 squadron crashed into the ammunition dump, killing the pilot, Sergeant Howlett, and two soldiers. Also in November No. 402 (RCAF) Squadron arrived for a four month stay during which it pioneered the operation of the Hurribomber in raids over France.

To assist in the gunnery practice, No. 1487 Target Towing Flight was formed on November 20 equipped with twelve Lysanders, remaining at Warmwell until September 1943.

The Canadians left on March 4, 1942 to be replaced by No. 175 Squadron which formed the following day with Hurricane IIBs and stayed until October 10. Meanwhile No. 266 Squadron (Typhoon 1Bs) and No. 263 (Whirlwinds) arrived in September. No. 266 was replaced by another Typhoon squadron, No. 257, in January 1943, Warmwell being used as a base for fighter sweeps over France. The Whirlwinds departed in December of that year and on January 17, 1944 No. 257 Squadron left.

Warmwell was transferred to the Middle Wallop sector of No. 11 Group on March 15, 1944 to become the home of the Lightnings of 474th Fighter-Bomber Group, US Ninth Air Force, the Americans referring to Warmwell as Station 454. (They were not the first American unit to use Warmwell as a detachment of the 30th Fighter Squadron of the Eighth Air Force flying Spitfires used the station in July 1942.)

When the group left in August 1944, No. 17 Armament Practice Camp formed and was joined later by No. 14 APC. These were visited by squadrons of the 2nd Tactical Air Force from their continental bases for range practice.

Aircraft of the air-sea rescue squadrons were based on the station from 1941 onwards: No. 276 (1941-44), No. 275 (April-August 1944) and No. 277 (from August 1944).

From November 1944 to May 1945 the station was transferred back to Colerne Sector in No. 10 Group. In June the station was switched again to No. 11 Group, hosting armament practice camps for the squadrons of 2nd TAF. However, when these camps finished in October, the work of RAF Warmwell was ended. Reduced to care and

maintenance status, the buildings were called into temporary use in the early post-war years as a buffer depot for the storage of food.

In 1973 Warmwell was taken over for gravel extraction, and ECC Quarries and Amey Roadstone have done such an extensive job that virtually the whole area of the aerodrome has disappeared off the face of the map. Only the odd huts on the north side and the T2 hangars remain, most of the intervening land having been completely removed. Dorset County Council is currently using part of the workings as a refuse tip. The camp area, which in April 1945 accommodated nearly eight hundred personnel, is mostly a new housing estate with an adjacent caravan site. The watch office is the only remnant of the station to be given a new long lease of life as it has been bought by an enterprising builder and converted into a private house.

Believe it or not this is the Warmwell watch office. In 1952 it was purchased from the Air Ministry for use as a private dwelling with the proviso that the original structure would remain intact in case it was needed for a future emergency. Now clad with brickwork and tiles, renamed Egdon House.

SECTOR Z
Northolt

BY PETER NORRIS

Lying fourteen miles to the west of London on the A40 Western Avenue, Northolt can claim to be the oldest operational RAF station with flying units, having had RAF units in constant residence since 1915.

The aerodrome was officially opened in March, 1915 when No. 4 Reserve Aeroplane Squadron arrived from Farnborough, the site having been selected a few months earlier by Major W. S. Brancker (later Sir Sefton Brancker), Deputy Director of Military Aeronautics at the War Office, during an aerial search for sites suitable for aerodromes for the rapidly expanding Royal Flying Corps.

An interesting story surrounds the requisitioning of the land as it is said the official sent to carry out the task held his map upside down and requisitioned land to the south of the Great Central Railway (completed only shortly before in 1907) instead of

the north where, in 1912, a proposed Harrow Aerodrome was to be sited.

A total of 283 acres were acquired and work began in January 1915 with the clearing of hedges and trees. From the Greenford-Ruislip road known as West End Lane which forms the eastern boundary, a road was built into the aerodrome near the northern boundary. To the left of this road quarters for officers and men were built consisting of long wooden barrack huts, a regimental institute and an officers mess. Next came a line of six flight sheds, each 200ft x 60ft, then a twin hangar of the same size with a connecting corridor and, finally, at the western end, a Napier-type hangar 170ft x 70ft all of wooden construction. Behind the flight sheds, on the opposite side of the road, ran a line of eight workshops. The guard room stood near the gate to West End Lane.

The aerodrome itself consisted of three strips laid out from north to south stretching from the hangars across a brook which was bridged with iron plates and up the hill on the eastern side of the line of the present Western Avenue (not built until 1936). The aerodrome was named Northolt after the nearby Northolt Junction railway station (since renamed South Ruislip). Shortly thereafter additional land

Above: **The air exercises of August 1939 get under way and the pilots of No. 111 Squadron hurry as best they can for their Hurricanes while fitters stand by the handles of the inertial starters. There would appear to be a shortage of trolley accumulators (Fox Photos).** *Below:* **With the familiar outlines of the Officers' Mess behind, a No. 32 Squadron Westland Whirlwind sits on the helicopter pad in front of the squadron offices during a particularly wet October day in 1979.**

was requisitioned to enable the landing area to be extended to the west.

The aerodrome was designated one of the seven Home Defence night landing grounds, having primitive lighting for night operations. The first recorded flight took place on the night of June 4/5, 1915 during a Zeppelin raid.

The first known casualty came on January 31, 1916 when Major Penn-Gaskell hit a tree on the west side of the aerodrome. He had taken off that night to check on the weather prior to letting any of his pilots take off to intercept Zeppelins attacking the Midlands and he died four days later from his injuries. Another night take-off exactly two months later

resulted in a similar fatal accident when Lieutenant John Bailey of No. 11 Reserve Aeroplane Squadron was killed. The two incidents were seized upon by an outspoken Member of Parliament, Mr. Noel Pemberton-Billing, as a result of which public indignation caused the Government to set up a committee to study the organisation of the British flying services.

During the first winter of operations, the lack of drainage caused serious waterlogging of the landing surface. An improvised solution was to cover an area of eight square acres in the middle of the aerodrome with clinker. Tracks from the hangars were also surfaced with ash, a temporary expedient which lasted until 1925 when the aerodrome was properly drained. The clinker patch was a characteristic feature of Northolt and, although now

crossed by the N-S runway, remains of the cinder tracks leading from the hangars can still be seen from the air today.

By this time, the Fairey Aviation Company, which had opened a factory in Hayes, was using the aerodrome for flight testing, fuselages being towed from Hayes and assembled on the aerodrome. The company was also involved in a remarkable aircraft known as the Kennedy Giant, designed by J. C. H. McKenzie-Kennedy who had worked with Igor Sikorsky in Russia. On his return to England, and with the half-hearted backing of the Air Ministry, he contracted with Fairey Aviation and the Gramophone Company Ltd. (also in Hayes) to build his design for a giant four-engined bomber. The aircraft was taken by road to Northolt in sections but, with a wing span of 140ft, it was too large for any

hangar and was built in the open early in 1917. After many problems and design changes (there was a snag with the centre of gravity and the wings had to be moved back after assembly had been completed), the first flight was undertaken by Lieutenant F. T. Courteney, then an instructor with No. 35 TS. Using the natural slope of the aerodrome towards the south, he only managed a short hop of about 100ft, the aircraft proving badly underpowered. No further attempts were made to fly the machine and it was eventually dumped in the north-western corner where it slowly rotted away.

With the entry of the United States into the war, Northolt received many Americans for flying training and also taught flying skills to forty Russian Tzarist cadets in 1917.

In early 1918, the RFC/RAF training

programme underwent a review as a result of which Northolt's three training squadrons were amalgamated into a single unit — No.30 Training Depot Station — which was to be responsible for training single-seat fighter pilots only. To deal with the increasing number of pupils, a building programme was put in hand for a new officers' mess and an NCOs' mess and quarters. A WRAF hostel was planned (although never built) on the opposite side of West End Lane.

The one and only contact with the enemy by aircraft flying from Northolt in the First War took place on June 13, 1917 when a Bristol Fighter from No. 35 Training Squadron intercepted Gothas over Ilford, Essex. During the encounter the observer, Captain C. H. C. Keevil, was killed.

However, although Northolt had little First War operational history, its role as a training aerodrome was full of incidents. One evening some officers were quietly drinking their gins at the top of the gentle slope outside the Mess

(a wooden building on the same site as the present RAF Officers' Mess) when a Short-horn, which was plodding slowly round the circuit on a pupil's first solo flight, gave an amusing demonstration of the amount of redundant structure in an aeroplane of those days. On his first landing attempt, the pilot lost one of his wheels. Undeterred, he pushed on round the circuit with pieces hanging down. At his second attempt some of the undercarriage struts fell off and so it went on, during repeated circuits and attempts to land, until the aeroplane quietly disintegrated during its final brush with the ground.

Then there was the Shorthorn flown by 'Dud' Mudge on his first solo which crashed into a hangar while landing at Northolt. The nose of the nacelle, with the pilot sitting in it, went through the wall of the hangar while the pusher engine continued to roar at full throttle outside as if it was trying to push the building over. The pilot sat inside the hangar unable to quieten the motor outside because the throttle

Northolt, circa 1929 with Siskins, Gipsy Moths, Fairey IIIFs and an Avro 504N of No. 24 Communications Squadron.

control had broken in the crash. On at least one other occasion a Shorthorn landed right on top of a hangar, as also did a Martinsyde.

With the end of the war, the air force training programme had shrunk rapidly and, by May 1919, Northolt's career as a fighter training aerodrome ceased altogether. Nevertheless, its proximity to the RAF Depot (later HQ) at Uxbridge meant a new role as a communications landing ground and the South-Eastern Communications Flight arrived at Northolt. In 1920 a Coastal Area Flight arrived and in 1923 these two flights were merged to become the Inland Area Communications Flight. Meanwhile, the aerodrome had been thrown open for civil use and the Central Aircraft Company moved in to operate a flying school and a charter organisation as well as the manufacturing of aircraft.

The station history of the period records another unusual, yet lucky, flying accident when Lieutenant C. L. Startup and Air Mechanic Carpenter were flying at 1,000 feet over Harrow. The petrol tank of their Avro 504 burst and the aircraft caught fire and blazed to such an extent that the cockpit became untenable. Both airmen climbed out onto the wings and from this position the pilot succeeded in retaining sufficient control to make a hurried landing. Both occupants were injured but survived.

An interesting description of the aerodrome was recorded by the chief test pilot of the Fairey Company, Captain Norman Macmillan, when he took up his appointment in January 1924:

'A large white-painted wooden gate was the aerodrome entrance. Inside and near the gate were the guardroom, the low wooden buildings of the Station Headquarters and the old Officers' Mess. A tarmac roadway ran due west from the gate, its surface potholed for lack of upkeep. On the right of this roadway were the assorted domesticities of an air station. There were no women in uniform. (The First World War WRAF had been disbanded and the WAAF had not been formed.)

'The backs of low wooden sheds bordered the left side of the roadway and at the far end rose two unequal, larger hangars. The Fairey Aviation Company rented one from the Air Ministry and prototype and production Fairey landplanes were assembled there for flight. Wings were transported in the Company's lorries which towed the fuselages on their own wheels from the factory at Hayes about five miles away.

'At some periods one or more Bessoneau hangars (temporary structures developed in the 1914-18 war for field use with wood-truss frames and canvas covering), stood beyond the Fairey Hangar to house additional aircraft.

'In front of the row of low wooden sheds a continuous stretch of tarmac hard-standing bordered the aerodrome. This tarmac continued to form an apron to the two individual hangars, the entrances of which faced east and west.

'The roadway and hangars were sited on a slight hump of ground which ran like a faint ridge along the whole length of what was then the aerodrome.

'From the hangars the grass surface sloped gently down to a 'bottom' and then the ground began to rise gently towards the south. On this slope farmers still worked and grazed animals and a wire 'animal' fence marked the southern and western borders of the landing ground. When the wind blew from the south there was little room to land even the relatively slow aircraft of those days after crossing over the hangars. A narrow un-built-on gap between the Fairey hangar and the western boundary of the aerodrome made it possible to approach below hangar level and often pilots took advantage of this fairway.'

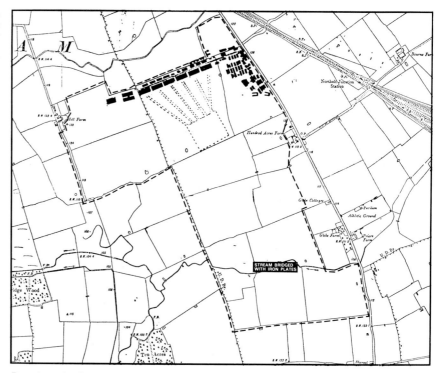

Based on the Ordnance Survey plan of the period, this was the extent of the aerodrome in 1918 showing the clinker paths and the clinker patch in the centre.

During 1925, proper drainage was installed and the clinker patch grassed over. The size of the aerodrome (which had contracted in 1919 when requisitioned land was released) was enlarged with an extension to the west. Work also began on permanent buildings to replace those built during the First World War, barrack blocks, a dining room and airmen's mess being among the first. An Operations Block and Station HQ were added in the late twenties.

In 1930 three of the flight sheds were demolished and work commenced on an A-type hangar. That year Fairey Aviation moved out to the Great West aerodrome (later reconstructed, enlarged and expanded into Heathrow airport). The Auxiliary Air Force, the 'Territorial Army' of the air providing a reserve for the regular RAF, formed its first two squadrons, Nos. 600 (City of London) and 601 (County of London) at Northolt in 1925. The main inter-war squadron based at Northolt was No. 41 whose twelve-year tenure ended when they were posted to Aden during

the Italian-Abyssinian War in 1935. During 1927 to 1933 No. 24 Communication Squadron was also based there bringing many high ranking officials and military personnel as well as royalty to the station. The late Duke of Windsor (then Prince of Wales) and the late Prince George (then Duke of Kent) both learned to fly under the instruction of Squadron Leader D. S. Don, CO of No. 24 Squadron.

On June 12, 1934, No. 111(F) Squadron arrived, the unit making history in January 1938 when they became the first squadron in the RAF to receive the new Hawker Hurricane monoplane fighter.

On May 1, 1936 the station was transferred to No. 11 Group Fighter Command. In 1939, Northolt became one of the first RAF aerodromes to have runways and two, each of 800 yards heading NE-SW and N-S, were laid down with a connecting perimeter track. Five H-type barrack blocks were also completed in the north-eastern corner.

On the outbreak of war, Northolt resident

Below left: Five months after the delivery of their first Hurricane, No. 111 Squadron demonstrated their new fighters before the Parliamentary Air Committee and other Members of Parliament when they visited Northolt on April 27, 1938. The Air Minister, The Right Honourable Sir Kingsley Wood, MP, leans over the cockpit while a squadron pilot patiently explains that the front is the end with the propeller (Fox Photos). *Below right:* A gleaming Hawker Siddeley HS125 of No. 32 Squadron stands on the rain-swept apron before No. 6 hangar which now houses the squadron's aircraft and offices.

squadrons were Nos. 111 and 601 but these were replaced by a successsion of units which came and went in the months before the Battle of Britain began. An important step took place on January 14, 1940 with the arrival of Group Captain S. F. Vincent who was to command the station throughout the battle.

Earlier that month work had begun to camouflage the aerodrome with the intention of allowing the station buildings to blend into the landscape — to the horror of Group Captain Vincent who had other ideas:

'I was just in time to prevent the camouflage "experts" hiding the hangars with their wavy stripes of green and black and brown', wrote the Group Captain later, 'and so achieving just what one wanted to avoid — that is, a large black space in the midst of the surburban areas of Ruislip, Northolt, Harrow and Uxbridge. I said: "No, make it show up as much as possible but paint houses on the hangars and if possible on the runways, tarmac, etc. Keep the barrack blocks, messes

Group Captain Vincent's handywork photographed by the Luftwaffe on August 31, 1940. Note how closely the 'fields' represent the original ones on the survey on the opposite page. Western Avenue, built in 1936, cuts across the bottom of the photo.

and stores as buildings. Let them all be seen like the surroundings''. With great difficulty I won my battle and my drawings were copied and each hangar became two rows of small houses with a 'garden' blank down the middle with wonderful results — our pilots from other aerodromes frequently failing to find us for instance! Anyway I am quite certain I foxed the Germans.'

The perimeter track and runways had large black blobs representing trees and bushes and, for final effect, a meandering stream was painted down each runway with a pond where they intersected. The open grass areas were

marked with tar lines to represent hedges, these faithfully following the pre-1915 field pattern. A new section of perimeter track, which looped away from the west end of the aerodrome, was built providing access to a number of new dispersals and a total of thirteen twin dispersal pens were built on various parts of the aerodrome together with huts for maintenance and aircrews. Bofors guns were placed in position, trenches dug and a detachment of the 2nd Battalion, The London Scottish Regiment, posted in for aerodrome defence duties, spent most of March and April wiring up the perimeter.

Below left: **Another episode in the MPs' visit to Northolt. Grouped before the open doors of No. 5 hangar, the visitors watch a formation take-off by Hurricanes of No. 111 Squadron (Flight).** *Below left:* **The doors of No. 5 hangar were firmly closed on October 25, 1979, not so much for security but to keep out the driving rain.**

On May 18 the Spitfires of No. 609 (West Riding) Squadron flew into Northolt. For ten days the squadron saw no action although the time was put to good use with practice flying and the fitting of armour plate behind the pilot's seat. Then, on May 30, the squadron mounted its first operation — a patrol over Dunkirk to cover the evacuation now in progress. No contact was made with the Luftwaffe but on the way home part of the squadron became lost resulting in a number of forced landings and the death of Flight Lieutenant Desmond Ayres who crashed, out of fuel, near Harwich. The following days saw the squadron on frequent patrols over the French coast. By June 2, when the squadron flew its final patrol over Dunkirk, five pilots had been killed for the squadron tally of three He 111s, two Bf 109s, one Do 17 and one Bf 110 claimed as destroyed. Winston Churchill made two visits to France (on June 11 and 13) to try to persuade the French to keep fighting. On both occasions the squadron was chosen to act as escort for Churchill's Flamingo from Hendon, making a rendezvous over the south coast before flying to France. Both trips passed off without incident.

A few days later, the remains of No. 1 Squadron began to arrive having been evacuated from the Continent. Its surviving Hurricanes arrived on June 20 and the squadron immediately began to set about working up into an operational unit.

On July 4, No. 609 moved west to Middle Wallop being replaced by No. 257 which flew in from nearby Hendon. The new squadron went quickly into action and a dawn patrol on the 9th found a Do 17 over Kent at 22,000ft and claimed it as damaged. Another dawn patrol on the 19th intercepted a Do 17 near Brighton and chalked it up as destroyed but unfortunately Hurricanes of No. 145 Squadron were also on the scene and they too entered a claim. As a result the victory was split between the two squadrons.

On the same day No. 1 Squadron, which up to this date had had a number of uneventful patrols, intercepted an He 111 over the South Downs and, in the running battle that

'The beating of the guns grows louder.
Not long boys, now' — The Assault, Robert Nichols.
Above: **The pilots of No. 111 Squadron relax in front of No. 5 hangar at Northolt before the start of the last big peacetime air exercise on August 8, 1939. Note the mast for flying 'weather' flags (Radio Times).** *Below:* **Yesterday's saplings have grown to maturity to screen No. 5 hangar which, in October 1979, housed No. 207 Squadron.**

followed, the squadron lost one Hurricane, the pilot escaping unhurt. The Heinkel escaped only to be shot down off Brighton minutes later by No. 145 squadron. The squadron's first confirmed victory since returning to England came a few days later while on detachment at Tangmere on the 25th with a Bf 109 destroyed. For a short period the squadron swapped places with No. 43 Squadron which was being rested at Northolt after losing a number of pilots during weeks of intensive action. This swap lasted until August 1 when both squadrons returned to their original bases.

August 2 was a red letter day for Northolt — the occasion being the formation of No. 303 (Kosciuszko) Squadron, the RAF's second

Polish fighter squadron but the first to go into action. This was the start of an association between the Northolt and Polish squadrons that was to last for almost four years; a connection still maintained today with the Polish War Memorial situated just outside the south-eastern boundary of the aerodrome. The majority of the Polish pilots had seen action in both Poland and France before coming to England and were eager to get back into the air for another crack at the Luftwaffe. However, because the majority of the pilots could not speak English, it was decided to put them all on a crash course so at least they would be able to understand the basic commands given by the sector controllers. At the same time they were also to be given instruction in flying Hurricanes. Although a Polish Squadron Leader and Flight Leaders were appointed, these positions were duplicated by RAF personnel, the officers being respectively: Squadron Leader R. G. Kellett, Flight Lieutenant Athol Forbes and Flight Lieutenant Johnny Kent.

By the middle of August, No. 257 had lost eight Hurricanes with four pilots killed and on the 15th it was moved to Debden. Its place at Northolt was taken two days later by No. 1 (RCAF) Squadron — the aerodrome now being host to three squadrons, each of a different nationality. The Royal Air Force No. 1 Squadron had returned to Northolt on August 1, the duplication of unit number with the Canadians no doubt causing some confusion.

No. 1 (RCAF) Squadron had arrived in England late in June bringing with them a number of Canadian-built Hurricanes. Having worked up at Middle Wallop and Croydon, the squadron arrived at Northolt fully operational, the Squadron CO, Squadron Leader E. A. McNabb, already having one Do 17 to his credit while flying from Croydon on a familiarisation flight. On August 26, while on its second patrol from Northolt, the squadron intercepted a formation of Do 17s and claimed three destroyed and three damaged. Three Hurricanes were shot down, one pilot, Flying Officer R. L. Edwards, being killed. On the last day of the month the squadron was surprised by Bf 109s near Dover and three Hurricanes were shot down although the pilots managed to escape. Later in the day however the tables were turned and two Bf 109s were downed.

Meanwhile the Poles had spent August furiously training. At first the pilots, being unused to retractable undercarriages, had written off two or three Hurricanes in belly landings when they forgot to lower the gear and, as a quick remedy, an airman with a Very pistol was stationed at the end of the runway ready to remind any forgetful pilots with a red flare. Interception was practised with Blenheims and, on the 30th, while on practice north of London, a large formation of Do 17s was spotted. This proved too much for one of the Polish pilots, Flying Officer Paszkiewicz, who attacked the formation and shot one of the bombers down in flames. As a result of this successful encounter, No. 303 Squadron was declared operational the following day and in their first scramble intercepted six Bf 109s claiming four destroyed and two damaged.

No. 1 Squadron (RAF) was also in the thick of it losing a number of aircraft and three pilots (Pilot Officer D. O. M. Browne, Pilot Officer J. A. J. Davey and Sergeant M. M. Shanahan) during August. Claims entered

Two NAAFI girls and a Fairey Battle warm up to their tasks at Northolt during the 1938 air exercises. Before an admiring and appreciative group of erks, the ladies of the urn dispense char and charm. Theirs was a job essential to service morale but which received scant recognition among the higher echelons (Flight).

'If only the NAAFI would arrive'. All stoicism has been drained as Flight Lieutenant Ann McKillop, Wilf Nicoll and Peter Norris look longingly through the falling rain towards the latent comforts of the Officers' Mess, Northolt on October 25, 1979.

A Naafi beauty with a hairstyle like an Old Bailey judge gives out a welcome cup of 'char' and her best 'come hither' glance to an unusually shy airman.

The tea is absent but the glance is there. RAF Northolt's stunning PRO brightens an otherwise dull, wet day as she smiles for the photographer. Peter Norris and Wilf Nicoll put on brave faces.

No. 5

No. 6

OPERATIONS BLOCK BUILDING 27

during this period included four He 111s, one Ju 88 and one Bf 110 all destroyed on the 16th. A Bf 109, a Do 17 and a Bf 110 on the 18th; two Do 17s on the 28th and two He 111s on the 30th. Although Northolt was, as yet, untouched by bombing (perhaps due to the CO's camouflage scheme) Group Captain Vincent formed a Station Defence Flight consisting of a couple of Gladiators and Hurricanes which were allocated to the Station Flight for use by the AOC and other HQ Fighter Command personnel at nearby Bentley Priory. Using pilots from the Station Flight, the flight was to be used to defend the station in case of enemy attack while the home based squadrons were in the air. Vincent flew on a couple of sorties in August but made no contact with the enemy.

Being close to central London, Northolt attracted numerous visitors. Winston Churchill dropped in on a number of occasions while passing the aerodrome en route for Chequers to make unofficial visits to the station's squadrons. On July 17 he visited the aerodrome officially accompanied by his wife together with Lord Beaverbrook, Minister of Aircraft Production, and the Right Honorable Sir Archibald Sinclair, Secretary of State for

In May 1940, Sector Z Operations Room was sited in a W/T hut building 40 (now demolished). Just before the Battle of Britain began, it moved to building 27, the standard style, pre-war ops block, now used by the Education Section minus the earth embankment *photo below* **(Photo above copyright British Airways).**

Air, to see a display of RAF aircraft including a number of prototypes. The Prime Minister paid a further visit on August 26 to view a captured Do 17 and Bf 109. The Duke of Kent also toured the station on August 28.

September saw all three squadrons hard at work. No. 1, after its run of casualties in mid-August, had not suffered any further losses and was sent to Wittering on the 9th for a rest. Shortly before leaving, the squadron had become the first unit to use the Fairey Aerodrome at Heathrow which had been brought into use for night dispersals.

Their place was taken by No. 229 Squadron from Wittering equipped with Hurricanes. The squadron went straight into action and on the 11th they lost three Hurricanes although all the pilots survived. The Canadians also lost two aircraft this day, both pilots baling out, and the Poles three aircraft with two pilots killed (Flying Officer A. Cebrzynski and Sergeant S. Wajtowicz). All these losses occurred within the space of twenty minutes during dog fights with Bf 109s. On September 15 all three squadrons were in action and lost a total of eight aircraft with three pilots killed. The Canadians lost Flying Officer R. Smithers, the Poles Sergeant M. Brzezowski

This is the actual Operations Room in building 27, now used as a classroom.

On May 16, 1940, plans had been set in motion for the dispersal of Sector operations by the requisitioning from London Transport of a shop in Victoria Road next to Ruislip Manor underground station. It was empty at the time but now houses an estate agent. Operations moved there in August being visited by the King on September 26 by which time the Oxfam shop had also been taken over. Facilities were primitive for although toilets had been added for the WAAFs, airmen had to use the station WC! The operations table itself almost filled the shop. Also it was only possible to receive communications from the pilots necessitating a telephone relay back to the aerodrome for messages to be transmitted to the aircraft. The delays this caused together with the cramped conditions led to the return of operations to building 27 until more adequate premises could be found. This came with the take over of Eastcote Place, a mansion set in its own grounds in Eastcote Road. In 1968 it was converted into flats and town houses were built in the grounds.

and No. 229 a Belgian, Pilot Officer G. L. J. Doutrepont. The Station Defence Flight was also airborne, Group Captain Vincent in a Hurricane attacking single-handed a formation of eighteen Do 17s head on, possibly shooting down five of them.

Also at Northolt on that day was 'B' Flight of No. 264 Squadron with Defiants having arrived on the 12th for night operations. Although the squadron was scrambled twice during the afternoon on base patrols, it saw no action. A few days later the flight moved to the satellite aerodrome at Luton to continue its night operations

No. 1 (RCAF), being the first Canadian squadron in England, received a string of visitors including the Canadian ambassador, a party from Canadian Press and, on September 25, the famous Canadian First World War Ace, Air Marshal 'Billy' Bishop, VC. For Bishop this was a sentimental journey for it was at Northolt in 1916 that he learnt to fly before going on to fame with seventy-two confirmed victories.

At 8.55 p.m. that evening the station was bombed for the first time, a lone aircraft dropping a stick across the north-east corner, three bombs landing on or near the barrack blocks, one on the Parachute and Cable (PAC) defence and two on the adjacent railway line. No casualties were caused and damage was slight.

The following day brought another important visitor, H M King George VI. Arriving at 2.30 p.m., he toured the station visiting all the squadrons at their dispersals. Just as he had completed his tour, Nos. 229 and 303 were scrambled. Group Captain Vincent invited the King to listen to their progress from the 'Z' Sector Operations Room which was now housed in two commandeered shops in Ruislip. The aircraft were sent to intercept a raid approaching Portsmouth and the King listened to the R/T as the Hurricanes closed in. However the raid which consisted of He 111s and Bf 110s was not bound for Portsmouth but for the Supermarine works at Woolston. The King remained until the combat was finished and then returned to the aerodrome to watch the aircraft land and meet the pilots. Group Captain Vincent later put his thoughts onto paper:

'The visit of the King was a most inspiring day. Everything went off as if faked for the occasion! The squadrons took off to intercept a raid on Southampton while he was there. He watched the interception from the Sector

The aftermath of the raid on October 6 — Sergeant Antoni Siudak's Hurricane P3120 and a huge, water-filled crater. Without the photographs to prove it, it would be difficult to imagine the havoc once wrought between Nos. 5 and 6 hangars (Polish Institute).

244

Operations Room and heard the Leader's 'Tally Ho' and subsequent orders, etc.

'We then returned to the aerodrome and saw the first Hurricane land. On going up to it we found its starboard wing thoroughly riddled by enemy fire and found that the pilot had shot down a Me 109 and so it went on, until we found that pilots from Northolt had destroyed sixteen enemy aircraft for no loss to us, with the exception of one who landed at Thorney Island but with the pilot OK *(but see crash list for September 26 — Ed.)*. Everything else during the King's visit was of the same order and he overstayed his programme time by about two hours.'

The Northolt Squadrons claimed 148 aircraft destroyed in September with twenty-five probables and fifty-two damaged. Two of those destroyed were credited to Group Captain Vincent while flying the Station Flight Hurricane N3250 on the 30th when he came upon three Bf 109s. Attacking from behind, one of the pilots shot down the leading aircraft and Vincent quickly shot down another thus becoming, as far as is known, the only RAF pilot to have credited victories in both world wars.

At 12.10 p.m. on October 6, a lone Ju 88 appeared out of the clouds to the north of the aerodrome and roared in at 200 feet towards the southern perimeter machine gunning the outer buildings. As the aircraft passed over the C-hangar, it dropped two bombs which landed instead between the hangars. The blast killed an airman acting as lookout on the hangar roof (AC2 H. E. Stennett buried at Northwood Cemetery) and also Sergeant A. Suidak taxi-ing a Polish Hurricane. The blast also damaged a Station Flight Hurricane L1684 parked nearby. Turning away, the Ju 88 then machine gunned its way towards No. 229's dispersal point. Two of the British squadron's aircraft were up on a base patrol and intercepted the attacker over the aerodrome. Although scoring several hits, the aircraft seemingly escaped to safety into cloud only to crash a little later at Leatherhead, Surrey.

On October 9, the Canadian squadron was sent north for a rest, swopping places at Prestwick with another Hurricane squadron No. 615. No. 303 Squadron also went north a few days later changing places with another Polish unit No. 302 at Leconfield. A few days before the move, 303 lost Sergeant Josef Frantisek, a Czech, who had been with the Polish Air Force since 1939. He had escaped to France, then England where he joined Kosciuszko Squadron, going on to become the top scoring pilot of the Battle of Britain with seventeen confirmed victories. His death was a mystery for, as the squadron approached Staines while returning from a patrol, Frantisek broke away from the formation and dived away to the east. His aircraft crashed at Ewell and no clue could be found to the cause of the crash. The total Polish claim for their six weeks in battle was 126 destroyed for eight pilots killed, a record unmatched by any other squadron.

With poor weather and the switch to night bombing, the new squadrons found combats less frequent and the bad weather also brought its own problems as No. 302 Squadron were to discover to their cost. On October 18 a flight of Hurricanes became lost over Surrey and in the resulting disaster, one aircraft crashed near Detling, another at Thames Ditton while two others, short of fuel, attempted to land at Kempton Park racecourse. Tragically both failed in the attempt and altogether four pilots were killed.

As the month closed, the Battle of Britain officially came to an end. Northolt's score for October stood at 22½ destroyed, three probables and fifteen damaged. The station had remained fully operational throughout the battle.

As the new year opened Fighter Command went on to the attack with sweeps over oc-

HM King George VI signs the No. 303 Squadron History Book as a memento of his visit. Looking on in the centre is Group Captain Stanley Vincent. The book is now preserved at the Polish Institute. The King signed on the page opposite a drawing introducing the British phase of the squadron's history executed by Flight Lieutenant Johnny Kent.

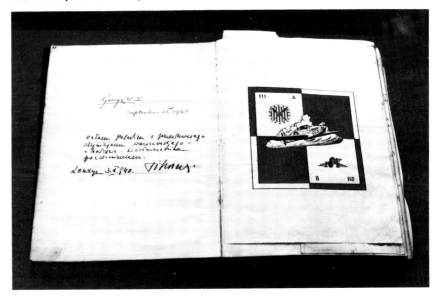

cupied France. All the old squadrons were posted away in early January and it was the newly-returned Hurricanes of Nos. 1 and 303 Squadrons along with 601 that opened Northolt's offensive operations.

As 1941 progressed, further Polish units (now in the process of re-equipping with Spitfires) arrived at Northolt and, by May, all the squadrons based there were Polish and, with the odd exception, were to remain so until April 1944. As well as the previously mentioned units, the other Polish squadrons were Nos. 306, 308, 315, 316 and 317.

When the satellite at Heston gained station status in April 1942, Northolt was reduced to two squadrons with two Polish squadrons at Heston, all four operating as a wing. The Dieppe raid in August 1942 saw the wing flying a total of eight sorties in support of the landings, the Northolt squadrons claiming 16½ aircraft destroyed for no losses. The following August, the Northolt Spitfires became the first to fly as a wing over Germany.

In November 1943 the squadrons were absorbed into the 2nd Tactical Air Force. Northolt was designated No. 131 airfield and,

together with Heston (No. 133 airfield), formed the 18th Fighter Wing, No. 84 Group, 2nd TAF. Both aerodromes were brought up to three-squadron strength and remained so until early April 1944 when all the squadrons moved to advanced landing grounds near the south coast in preparation for D-Day thus bringing to a close Northolt's days as a fighter aerodrome.

However, mention must be made of the Special Service Flight formed at Northolt in September 1942. This was equipped with a special conversion of the Spitfire IX for high-altitude work to counter Ju 86 bombers which roamed England at will at altitudes of over 40,000ft. On September 10, 1942, a Spitfire flown by Pilot Officer Prince Emmanuel Galitzine (born in Russia, but brought to England at the age of one in 1919) intercepted a Ju 86P at 42,000ft north of Southampton, damaging the port wing — possibly the highest combat to take place during the Second World War.

On March 25, 1943, RAF Transport Command was created out of the old Ferry Command which since July 18, 1941 had been engaged mainly in flying aircraft across the

245

Above: **Two Hurricanes of No. 615 'County of Surrey' Squadron about to settle on the grass in the south-east corner of the drome in October 1940. The tarmac beneath them is the perimeter track (Crown Copyright).** *Opposite:* **Today the NW-SE runway built in 1945 can be seen in the background.**

Atlantic to this country. Air Chief Marshal Sir Frederick Bowhill, who had commanded Ferry Command in Montreal, was made AOC-in-C of the new command. He established his headquarters at Stanmore, and Northolt became the Command's main London terminal. As a transport aerodrome, Northolt's first requirement was for a longer main runway. Work had already commenced on extending the main NE-SW runway and in April 1944, the short N-S runway, which had been little used for some time, was closed so that it could be used as additional parking space.

Prior to these works, little new construction had been carried out since 1940 although a B1-type hangar was later erected to the west of the main group and in 1943 fourteen blister hangars were put up on various sites around the aerodrome.

Northolt remained a fighter station until April 1944. By then transport traffic had increased to such an extent that the aerodrome could no longer be used as a Sector Station. As far as fighter operations were concerned, it became instead a forward aerodrome in the Tangmere Sector. In addition, Northolt was now in extensive use by photographic reconnaisance squadrons. In April 1944, these included No. 16 PRS (Spitfires), No. 140 PRS (Mosquitos) and a night photographic reconnaisance squadron, No. 69, equipped with Wellington Xs.

At this time, a flight of Transport Command equipped with Avro Yorks were also based at Northolt and in May — when HM the King inspected the station — the Station Flight was raised to the status of a squadron and became known as the ADGB Communications Squadron. Early in June a special Douglas C-54B, Skymaster (DC-4) was delivered to Northolt for the use of the Prime Minister. During this same month the flow of passengers through the station began to swell with the addition of casualties and prisoners-of-war arriving from Normandy.

The closing months of the war saw a steady growth in the importance of Northolt as a transport aerodrome. By November 1944 — when high-intensity night lighting was installed — there were 7,506 movements during the month. Northolt was now London's acknowledged main airport. It was to continue in this role until the new aerodrome,

construction of which started at Heathrow in 1945, could be developed to replace it.

Notable transport flights made from Northolt during 1944 included the first non-stop capital to capital flight between London and Washington on July 20/21 by the famous Liberator (AL578) *Marco Polo.* The flying time was 19 hours 46 minutes. The return flight was made non-stop from New York to Northolt in just under 18 hours. A non-stop flight from Northolt to Cairo was made by a York aircraft on November 16, 1944, the flying time being 10 hours 25 minutes.

The USAAF was a large-scale user of Northolt during 1944 but in December all American units left the station. All this time Northolt had been operating with the single, NE-SW runway but it had long been clear that a second runway was essential. In addition, a new apron and more perimeter tracks were an obvious necessity. In December 1944, a new NW-SE runway was surveyed. Initially laid in pierced steel planking (PSP), construction started early in 1945. During this period the NE-SW runway was resurfaced and work started on an aircraft parking apron to face the new passenger and freight buildings which were also under construction on the south side of the aerodrome adjacent to the A40 Western Avenue.

In February 1945, five Dakotas of No. 271 Squadron were based at Northolt to operate a scheduled passenger service to Brussels. These operations, in conjuction with similar services from Croydon, heralded the revival — initially under the aegis of No. 110 Wing of No. 46 Group — of scheduled British air services to the Continent.

On December 20, 1945, the Government stated in a White Paper that Northolt and Croydon would be used as London's airports for European and domestic services in the immediate post-war period. Then, on January 24, 1946, the Parliamentary Secretary to the Ministry of Civil Aviation (which had been formed on May 1, 1945) stated in the House of

With Western Avenue in the foreground and West End Road on the right, this was Northolt in May 1942 showing the work under way extending the NE-SW runway. The WWI clinker paths are visible as is the clever camouflaging of the hangars as a row of houses.

Commons that, as European services were taken over from the RAF by civil air transport, these services would be operated from Northolt. Foreign airlines would also be permitted to use the aerodrome.

From February 1, 1946, regular services were operated by Dakotas of the European Division of BOAC (which became British European Airways on August 1) from Northolt to Paris, Brussels and Amsterdam. On February 4, 1946, Northolt became officially a civil airport on loan from the Air Ministry to the Ministry of Civil Aviation. The first foreign civil aircraft to use it is believed to have been a Sabena DC-3 from Brussels which was diverted from Croydon because the grass landing area there was waterlogged.

By now the NW-SE runway, relaid in concrete, was ready for use together with a new control tower on the north-western corner. All BEA maintenance was carried out in the old RAF hangars on the northern side until 1952 when their new engineering base at Heathrow gradually took over the work. As more and more facilities came into use at Heathrow, BEA gradually transferred their flight operations. Their final BEA flight, a Dakota to Jersey, left in October 1954 and the aerodrome then reverted to RAF control. Since 1946 almost five million passengers had passed through Northolt on 300,000 flights.

Throughout this period, the RAF continued to use the aerodrome and operated scheduled Dakota services to Berlin, Warsaw and Vienna. An RAF handling party was based at Northolt throughout the period and its strength built up once the RAF regained control. By May 1, 1955, the RAF had

Above: **With its brand new NW-SE runway, this was London's new airport just three weeks before opening.** *Below:* **Twenty years later, this photo indicates the expansion of the terminal buildings on the south side (Crown Copyright).**

transferred the VIP reception area from No. 5 hangar on the north side to a modified section of the civilian passenger terminal on the opposite side of the aerodrome. A programme to repair and renovate the buildings was put in hand and this work, together with resurfacing of the runways and taxiways was completed by mid-1957. The last remaining WW1 hangars — the twin and Napier types — were demolished about this time, the last of the old First World War flight sheds already having disappeared sometime during the war.

Flying incidents at Northolt have been very rare in the post-civilian era and, when one considers the proximity of London Heathrow and the density of traffic in the local area, Northolt's safety record over the last thirty years is indeed remarkable.

On June 1, 1960 an Anson aircraft of Bomber Command Communication Squadron suffered an engine failure soon after take off from the northern end of the NE-SW runway. The aircraft failed to maintain height and pancaked onto the Express Dairy premises in South Ruislip. The aircraft came to rest poised in a precarious position on the roof of the building thirty feet above the ground. Fortunately there was no fire and no serious injuries resulted from the mishap. Then October 25 saw the unheralded arrival of a Pan American Boeing 707 bound for London Heathrow. The pilot inadvertently set up a visual approach pattern on the Harrow gasholder and the NE-SW runway (on a bearing of 26/08) at Northolt, mistaking these two very similar landmarks for the Southall gasholder and runway 23 Left at Heathrow. No casualties resulted from this error as the Northolt air traffic pattern was not in use by other aircraft at the time and the Captain successfully brought the Boeing to a halt at the end of the 5,500ft runway, albeit with little or no rubber left on the tyres. The aircraft was subsequently stripped of its seating and successfully flown out. Then, on April 28, 1964, a Lufthansa Boeing 707 made a similar approach to the NE-SW runway but, fortunately, the pilot became aware of his mistake, due largely to the alertness of the ATC Duty watch. A red Very seemed to convince the 707 captain that he was in error and a low overshoot of the runway resulted. As a result of these two incidents, it was decided that the bigraph for Northolt should be

changed from NH to NO since it was considered that the large white letters NH painted on the Harrow gasholder were too easily confused with the LH painted on the Southall gasholder. However, the boot was on the other foot on May 3, 1964 when a Spanish DC4 made an approach to Hendon in mistake for Northolt. The captain of this aircraft subsequently explained that the error was caused by one of his passengers, who had once previously landed at Northolt, advising him that Hendon was Northolt!

Early in 1969, the southern taxiway was resurfaced and the building of a new Education Centre begun. During the night of Easter Monday, an electrical power surge caused a 'one-armed-bandit' in the Sergeants' Mess to explode and the fire quickly spread through the spirits in the bar. By morning the rest of the Mess, which was largely of wooden construction, was almost completely gutted. Plans for the Education Centre were hurriedly changed and the new building instead became the Sergeants' Mess.

In April 1969 Northolt was in the headlines again. Squadron Leader Lecky Thompson took off in a Harrier jump jet from Northolt on a practice run to New York as part of the Daily Mail Transatlantic Air Race. Six hours and thirty seven minutes later he landed at Floyd Bennet Naval Air Station, the first vertical take off jet to fly the Atlantic. (His time makes an interesting comparison with the eighteen-hour flight of the *Marco Polo* Liberator from New York to Northolt in 1944.)

A hair-raising incident occurred on January 9, 1970. An Indian Air Force Constellation making an approach to the northern end of the NE-SW runway was cleared by Northolt GCA to 1,350 feet but descended instead to 500 feet while still five miles away. The normal

For nine years Northolt was London's main airport. View looking east (British Airways).

overshoot procedure of a climb straight ahead or a turn to the north would have taken the aircraft periously close to the suburb of Harrow on the Hill which was already above the aircraft's flight path. The controller therefore had little option but to instruct the Constellation to turn south and climb across the approach path into Heathrow. Unfortunately an Olympic Airways Boeing 727 was, at that time, on just such an approach. The two aircraft passed so close to each other that the 727 crew reported being able to hear the noise of the Constellation's engines. The Constellation eventually managed to land at Northolt after its fourth attempt.

On April 18, 1973 a student pilot from Denham on his second solo flight in a Beagle Pup suddenly had his cabin door come open in flight. The inexperienced student panicked and made for the first piece of concrete he could see which was the south side apron at Northolt. In making his approach he just cleared the newly-built ATC Tower and, during his landing run on the pan, passed under the wing of a parked C-130 Hercules. Needless to say, he failed the course!

In April 1979 plans were announced for a new passenger and operations building to be constructed on the southern side to replace the wartime building which is still in use.

Today Northolt, as London's military aerodrome, is occupied by No. 207 Squadron equipped with Devons with the task of flying Strike Command staff within the UK. No. 32 Squadron, operating HS 125s, Whirlwinds, Andovers and a Gazelle, likewise is responsible for transporting Government ministers, senior civil servants and high ranking military personnel.

The Casualties

Introduction by the Editor

HM King George VI with the Dean of Westminster during the ceremony dedicating the Battle of Britain Chapel in Westminster Abbey on July 10, 1947 (Radio Times).

In 1942 it was decided by the Air Ministry to extract from the records a list of all those pilots who had lost their lives as a result of the fighting during the Battle of Britain — August 8 to October 31, 1940 — as a pre-requisite to the creation of a national memorial. These dates were later amended to include the period July 10 - August 7. The list included a total of 449 aircrew lost and a minute was attached to the list to advise that if the discrepancy was spotted with the 375 casualties given in the Air Ministry Battle of Britain booklet published in 1941, a suitable explanation could be provided. Many of the missing were still officially listed as 'Death since presumed' but, at that stage of the war, the possibility that a serviceman was a prisoner-of-war could not be ruled out. The list of names when finalised on November 26, 1942 was not to be published as foreign Allied personnel were listed and all such casualties were always withheld from the press for the sake of the next of kin still living in the occupied countries.

On July 10, 1947 — the seventh anniversary of the first day of the battle — His Majesty King George VI unveiled the Battle of Britain Memorial in Westminster Abbey. It had been decided to dedicate the easternmost of the five small chapels forming the chevet of Henry VII's Chapel to the memory of the men of the Royal Air Force killed in the Battle of Britain. The Chapel had originally been built between 1503 and 1519 as the burial place for King Henry VII and his uncle King Henry VI, although it was never used as such. Instead Oliver Cromwell, General Ireton, Admiral Blake and others including John Churchill, the first Duke of Marlborough, were placed in the vault only to be removed in the seventeenth and eighteenth centuries.

In September 1940 a fragment from a German bomb pierced the east wall of the Chapel and the hole was retained covered with glass.

The centrepiece of the Chapel was the Memorial Window extending across the entire east wall. Designed and painted by Hugh Easton, the lower panes contained the badges of sixty-three of the squadrons that took part

The King removes the RAF Ensign from the Roll of Honour (Radio Times).

in the battle. (In 1960 the number of units serving under Fighter Command during the battle was officially amended to seventy-one.)

The Roll of Honour on parchment bound in blue leather originally rested on a wrought-iron lectern north of the Chapel. The book was designed and executed by William F. Matthews, illustrated by Miss Daisy Alcock and presented by Bruce S. Ingram. Inscribed at the beginning of the Roll was the wording: 'Detailed in this record are those members of the flying forces of the Allied Nations who lost their lives as a result of fighting in the Battle of Britain. July 10-October 31, 1940'.

When the total number of aircrew who were to be included in the Roll was announced in March 1947 as 1,495, it immediately raised questions from the public over the discrepancy with the previously published total of 375. Mr. E. H. Keeling, the Honorary Secretary of the Battle of Britain Memorial, gave the official answer in a letter to *Flight* magazine published on April 17:

'Your correspondent Mr. F. J. Seward asks how the inclusion of 1,500 names in the Roll of Honour to be placed in the Abbey when the King unveils the Memorial Chapel on July 10 can be reconciled with the figure of 375 published in 1941.

The Roll of Honour includes:-
    448 in Fighter Command
    718 in Bomber Command
    280 in Coastal Command
    14 in other RAF Commands
    34 in The Fleet Air Arm.

Those killed in other than Fighter Command are included in the Roll because their attacks on enemy shipping, invasion barges and bases of various kinds, were an essential contribution to the winning of the Battle which is deemed to have begun on July 10 and ended on October 31, 1940'. *(Note that the figures given in Mr. Keeling's reply only total 1,494).*

The book now records 1,503 personnel. Covering such a broad spectrum, including even Flying Training Command and Maintenance Command, and not based on the battle as fought by Fighter Command, the rules for inclusion seem extremely vague.

Nothing was done officially to define the qualifications for the classification of a Battle of Britain airman until November 9, 1960 when the Air Ministry published AMO N850. (The delay in publishing the information was explained by the need to examine captured German documents concerning the Battle of Britain.) The AMO stated for the first time the precise squadrons which were deemed to have fought in the battle under the control of Fighter Command and it also stated the exact requirements for the award of the Battle of Britain rosette to the 1939-45 Star: 'Any pilot or aircrew must have flown at least one operational sortie with any of the seventy-one accredited squadrons or flights between 0001 hours on July 10 and 2359 hours on October 31, 1940. (As a result, six additional squadron badges were added to the Westminster Abbey window in 1961 but the two Fleet Air Arm units were still omitted.)

There was still no mention by name of those who had fought in the battle and it was left to an RAF serving officer, Flight Lieutenant John H. Holloway, who decided to undertake, as a personal challenge, the compilation of a complete list of 'The Few'. This task took him fourteen years of his spare time and must surely be one of the most praiseworthy pieces of research ever undertaken.

'In 1955 I was stationed at Royal Air Force, Kenley during the making of the film *Reach for the Sky*', explains Flight Lieutenant Holloway who retired from the RAF in 1958. 'As a Flight Lieutenant, I was able to move freely between messes and was, therefore, in a very good position to collect many autographs of Battle of Britain pilots and crew in my personal copy of the book *Reach for the Sky*. Having been closely associated with some of

Detail from one of the four panels included in the Memorial Window depicting Visions symbolising the Redemption — a Squadron Leader kneels before the Christ Child who raises His hand in blessing. The Virgin Mary stands, by tradition, on the crescent moon. Three other panels show a Sergeant Pilot, Pilot Officer and Flying Officer (Radio Times).

"The Few" in my squadron (No. 615) as a wireless mechanic and having been called upon to assist in the re-arming, re-fueling as well as the servicing of the wireless equipment in their aircraft during the height of the air battles over London, Kenley and Biggin Hill, I knew first hand of the tremendous spirit and courage of these pilots. It became an obsession with me to collect their autographs and this I continued to do during the following months, travelling around the country, seeking them out which was not too easy with the limited information I had of "The Few". In consequence, I was more likely to collect, at that time, signatures of the better known at the expense of the lesser known but, even so,

no less heroic in this vital battle which meant so much to the world as a whole.

'After quite a few months, I was successful in collecting a hundred or so signatures, including that of Sir Winston Churchill at the foot of his famous quotation to "The Few", an impossible task of course through his secretaries but not so difficult through Lady Churchill, for such a worthy cause.

'It soon became apparent and indeed it was pointed out to me by a senior RAF staff officer that such a collection, if extended to include the signatures of all "The Few" and collated together in a more appropriate book, could become a museum piece. Although this meant my hopes of it becoming my personal property

THE SEVENTY-ONE ACCREDITED SQUADRONS AND OTHER UNITS WHICH
SERVED UNDER FIGHTER COMMAND IN THE BATTLE OF BRITAIN

Fighter Command

Squadrons	Name	Code	Radio call sign	Aircraft	No. of Casualties
No. 1	'Cawnpore'	JX	ACORN	Hurricane	7
No. 3		QO		Hurricane	1
No. 17		YB	EDEY	Hurricane	5
No. 19		QV	LUTON	Spitfire	6
No. 23		YP		Blenheim	8
No. 25		ZK		Blenheim/Beaufighter	5
No. 29		RO		Blenheim	8
No. 32		GZ	JACKO	Hurricane	2
No. 41		EB	MITOR	Spitfire	11
No. 43	'China-British' (1941)	FT		Hurricane	14
No. 46	'Uganda'	PO	ANGEL	Hurricane	14
No. 54		KL	RABBIT	Spitfire	6
No. 56	'Punjab'	US	BAFFIN	Hurricane	8
No. 64		SH	FREEMA	Spitfire	7
No. 65	'East India'	YT		Spitfire	8
No. 66		LZ	FIBUS	Spitfire	8
No. 72	'Basutoland'	RN	TENNIS	Spitfire	9
No. 73		TP		Hurricane	4
No. 74		ZP	DYSOE	Spitfire	12
No. 79	'Madras Presidency'	NV	PANSY	Hurricane	4
No. 85		VY	HYDRO	Hurricane	7
No. 87	'United Provinces'	LK	SUNCUP	Hurricane	7
No. 92	'East India'	QJ	GANNIC	Spitfire	14
No. 111		JU	WAGON	Hurricane	11
No. 141		TW		Defiant	10
No. 145		SO	PATIN	Hurricane	13
No. 151		DZ		Hurricane	11
No. 152	'Hyderabad'	SN	MAIDA	Spitfire	14
No. 213	'Ceylon'	AK		Huricane	15
No. 219	'Mysore'	FK		Blenheim/Beaufighter	6
No. 222	'Natal'	ZD	KOTEL	Spitfire	9
No. 229		KE	KETA	Hurricane	5
No. 232		EF		Hurricane	—
No. 234	'Madras Presidency'	AZ	CRESSY	Spitfire	5
No. 238		VK		Hurricane	17
No. 242	'Canadian'	LE	LORAG	Hurricane	5
No. 245	'Northern Rhodesia'	DX		Hurricane	2
No. 247	'China-British'	HP		Gladiator	—
No. 249	'Gold Coast'	GN	GANER	Hurricane	8
No. 253	'Hyderabad'	SW	VICEROY	Hurricane	11
No. 257	'Burma'	DT	ALERT	Hurricane	11
No. 263	'Fellowship of the Bellows'	HE		Hurricane/Whirlwind	1
No. 264	'Madras Presidency'	PS		Defiant	18
No. 266	'Rhodesia'	UO		Spitfire	7

Flights

No. 421		L-Z		Hurricane/Spitfire	1
No. 422				Hurricane	—
Fighter Interception Unit		ZQ		Hurricane/Blenheim/Beaufighter	—

Auxiliary Squadrons

No. 501	'County of Gloucester'	SD	MANDREL	Hurricane	19
No. 504	'City of Nottingham'	TM		Hurricane	6
No. 600	'City of London'	BQ		Blenheim/Beaufighter	9
No. 601	'County of London'	UF	WEAPON	Hurricane	14
No. 602	'City of Glasgow'	LO	VILLA	Spitfire	5
No. 603	'City of Edinburgh'	XT	VIKEN	Spitfire	13
No. 604	'County of Middlesex'	NG		Blenheim/Beaufighter	1
No. 605	'County of Warwick'	UP	TURKEY	Hurricane	8
No. 607	'County of Durham'	AF		Hurricane	9
No. 609	'West Riding'	PR	SORBO	Spitfire	7
No. 610	'County of Chester'	DW	DOGROSE	Spitfire	11
No. 611	'West Lancashire'	FY	CHARLIE	Spitfire	2
No. 615	'County of Surrey'	KW		Hurricane	6
No. 616	'South Yorkshire'	YQ		Spitfire	6

Commonwealth and Allied Squadrons

No. 1 Canadian		YO	CARIBOU	Hurricane	3
No. 302 (Polish)	'City of Poznan'	WX	CALEB	Hurricane	7
No. 303 (Polish)	'Warsaw—Kosciuszko'	RF	APANY	Hurricane	9
No. 310 (Czech)	'Czecho-Slovak'	NN	CALLA	Hurricane	4
No. 312 (Czech	'Czecho-Slovak'	DU	SILVO	Hurricane	1

Coastal Command

No. 235		QY		Blenheim	14
No. 236		FA		Blenheim	10
No. 248		WR		Blenheim	16

Fleet Air Arm

No. 804		K6		Sea Gladiator/Martlet	—
No. 808				Fulmer (flown solo)	—

Note: Aircraft were switched between units during the battle and sometimes squadron code letters were not changed immediately.

would not be possible I accepted this and, at the beginning of my self-imposed task, I decided that the most appropriate book, in which to collect these signatures would be Dennis Richard's publication *The Royal Air Force 1939-45 Volume 1, The Fight at Odds* covering the Battle of Britain.

'How could I hope to obtain the signatures of all "The Few" when no complete and accurate list had ever been compiled? The compilation of such a list of those qualified to this title became to me Phase One in my long and arduous research ahead. I first contacted Battle of Britain pilot, Group Captain Tom Gleave, CBE, historian in the Cabinet Office Historical Section in London who introduced me to Mr. Nermey, head of the Air Historical Branch, explaining my project and asking for his assistance. This he readily gave although some doubt was expressed by his staff as to whether or not I would succeed where others had failed in the past.

'The Air Historical Branch staff were most co-operative and allowed me access to all the official records in use during the period covering the Battle of Britain i.e. 0001 hours July 10, 1940 to 2359 hours October 31, 1940. Most of my spare time for the next four years was spent going through the records and extracting the names of the qualifiers. Certain conditions had to be met for pilots and crew to qualify for this the most highly-prized of all the awards — the gold rosette worn on the ribbon of the 1939-45 star signifying that the wearer was a Battle of Britain airman and consequently one of those immortalised by Sir Winston Churchill in his famous quotation to "The Few".

'These conditions meant a careful examination of the flight records of sixty-seven different squadrons plus some subsidiary units from July 10 to October 31, 1940. Eventually, a provisional list with some 3,500 names was produced but, since in the flight records no initials were given (simply rank and name), duplication was bound to exist in my provisional list for several reasons. In many instances, pilots and crews were transferred between Battle of Britain squadrons and, in some cases, even flew with three different squadrons during the period under review. Also, promotion in the officer ranks was fairly rapid and many sergeants were commissioned during this period. Furthermore, there were in the list such common names as Smith (32), Brown (18), Johnson (14), Baker (10), Scott (11) and Jones (10).

'Obviously my next step would have to be to identify each entry with initials and, after many more months of further research with the valuable assistance of the Airmen and Officers Records establishment, initials and the squadrons associated with each airman were produced. By this means, duplication was, in most cases, eliminated leaving 2,946 qualifiers.

'In 1961, the first ever completed list of "The Few" giving their rank (1940), initials, name, nationality and squadrons served with during the Battle of Britain was made available to the public as an appendix to that classic publication on the Battle of Britain *The Narrow Margin* and the public, who had previously known only of the symbolic "Few", now knew who they were by name. It was now also possible to summarize for the first time the nationalities of those who played their part in the Battle of Britain alongside the Royal Navy and Royal Air Force: Americans, Australians, Belgians, Canadians, Czechoslovakians, Free French, Irish, Jamaicans, New Zealanders, Palestinian, Poles, South Africans and Southern Rhodesians.

'As a result of my research, the members of the Battle of Britain Fighter Association showed their gratitude to me with the presentation of a silver-mounted Spitfire. Needless to say it is my most treasured possession.

The 25th Battle of Britain anniversary banquet held in the Guildhall gave John Holloway an opportunity to collect a considerable number of names. The Spitfire on display is K9942 frequently flown by Flight Lieutenant James Nicolson, the Battle of Britain VC and the only airman in Fighter Command to receive the supreme award.

'Phase Two of my project constituted the collection of the signatures of those of "The Few" still living but, before I could do this, I had first to obtain their latest known addresses and to trace their whereabouts.

'After the passing of yet another year, and once again with most valuable assistance of Air Ministry staff, most of the addresses were found and I was to discover that "The Few" were resident in countries all over the world. I also knew that of the 2,946 qualifiers, only about 1,600 were alive and that of those that had died some 500 had been killed in the Battle of Britain itself.

'My next job was to write to those living explaining my project and inviting them to partake in it. Meanwhile, I was also kept busy collecting for the second time those signatures recorded in the book *Reach for The Sky*. Fortunately, all co-operated by signing again including Sir Winston Churchill. Once I had obtained Sir Winston's signature, for obvious reasons, it would have been too unwise and too costly to circulate the book so I introduced a system whereby loose sheets were circulated on which the signatures could be recorded, each sheet providing space for sixty to seventy signatures. These loose sheets would then be inserted into the final product.

'Fortunately for me I was able to find volunteers in Canada, Australia, New Zealand and America who undertook to circulate a loose sheet in their own countries and this they did without thought of reimbursement, thereby saving me a lot of time and expense in postage. Owing to the great distances to be covered and remote addresses, this took about two years to complete and to the following I owe a great deal for their services;

Canada	Wing Commander J. P. Falkowski DFC, VM
New Zealand	Flight Lieutenant M. R. Andrews
Australia	Mr. Scieluna
America	Mr. J. E. Lauder

I am especialy indebted to Wing Commander J. P. Falkowski who extended his efforts beyond Canada by going to Poland to collect several signatures from Polish pilots resident there.

'The United Kingdom and the remaining countries I tackled myself travelling all over the country collecting signatures. How enjoyable it was, meeting these fighter boys, reminiscing over a beer and how interested they were in my project going through the records to see how their squadron friends had fared after twenty years.

'To collect 'Bee' Beamont's signature I went to Preston in Lancashire and whilst I waited for him in his office he was 'upstairs' breaking the sound barrier in a prototype fighter aircraft. On another occasion I went to an address in Hertfordshire to collect the signature of a pre-war weekend flier with an auxiliary squadron who blossomed forth into a famous Battle of Britain pilot, now an estate agent. I arrived early one morning at a most inopportune time when he had been up all night with a housing estate problem but, in spite of this and weary though he was, he still had time to give me his signature and have a chat about the project over a cup of tea. How interested he was and for a brief nostalgic moment his troubles seemed to leave him.

'Unfortunately, to travel perhaps 200 miles or so to meet them personally, however enjoyable this was, did not produce signatures quickly enough and so, in the main, the method of postal circulation of the loose sheets was used and eighteen of these were kept in circulation. Even so, each sheet took about a week in transit for the reward of only one signature. I attended all the Battle of Britain re-unions and any other functions where I was likely to pick up a signature. The 25th Battle of Britain anniversary banquet held at the Guildhall in London brought together many of "The Few" and I was able to collect a few more signatures and also meet two of my helpers, both Battle of Britain aircrew, Wing Commander Falkowski from Canada and Flight Lieutenant Andrews from New Zealand, to discuss their progress in obtaining signatures and to laden them with further work when they returned home. On yet another occasion, I took a trip to France to pick up a rather elusive signature and, on many other occasions, the services of a BOAC air hostess, Miss Barbara Mullett, my next door neighbour, were offered to convey letters to overseas countries resolving the problems of stamped addressed envelopes for replies.

'There were setbacks such as the lost sheet and one that accidently slipped from the envelope into a puddle of water and was ruined. Unfortunately, both sheets contained about sixty signatures which had to be recollected but, in all fairness to the unhappy signator who dropped the sheet in the water, he sent me a cheque to cover all expenses in the replacement and he can be happy to know that no signature was lost through the incident. I recall in 1962 one signature being obtained from a pilot who was desperately ill in the RAF Hospital at Uxbridge. His friend insisted that he take the book to his bedside and I was told how glad and proud he was to sign. He died within the next few days but his signature is there on the page opposite that of Sir Winston's.

'By 1966 I had collected over 800 live signatures including that of the popular "Sailor" Malan who signed for me when he was in England for medical treatment. Tragically, he died soon after returning to South Africa but his signature as one of "The Few" has gone down to posterity in my collection.

'At this time I was reminded by those of "The Few" who were alive that my collection would be incomplete without the signatures of those who had died and so Phase Three then began. This meant, firstly, finding the addresses of about 1,400 next of kin and then writing to all the mums, dads and wives wherever they were in the world, inviting them to send me a signature of their lost ones. One would have thought it would be difficult to find a signature after all those years, twenty-six to be exact, but they found them from all kinds of sources — private letters, school books, driving licences, marriage licences, diaries, flying log books, passports and many other sources; even from a Blood Donor's certificate, a Prayer Book, a masonic certificate and a menu from a Stalag prisoner-of-war camp. How proud they were to be able to add the signature to be placed with those of the living in the collection and how grateful were they not to have been forgotten. To read these letters, many full of sadness, gave me an insight to their feelings on the Battle of Britain. I felt quite guilty in opening up old wounds. From one mother I received a diary written by her about her son who was killed in the Battle of Britain when he was only twenty years of age and to me it is the most beautifully composed document I have ever been privileged to read. When such a diary can end with these words: "He was the loveliest and most precious gift that God could bestow on any mortal here on earth and I, his mother, shall mourn him all the rest of my days", little imagination is required to visualize the heartfelt entries that preceded these words.

'Where relatives were unable to find a signature or letters sent by me to the next of kin were returned marked "Gone away", "Deceased" or "Unknown", the Air Ministry came to my aid and were able to help in many cases by providing a copy of the missing signatures for this rather special, unique and "one off" project. When presented to the Imperial War Museum in October 1969, the total number of signatures stood at 2,200. In addition, the signatures were added of the designers of the Spitfire and Hurricane, R. J. Mitchell and Sir Sidney Camm.

'The signatures are housed in a handsome leather-bound, double-fronted cover on the left flap of which are engraved the words "The Battle of Britain" and on the right the simple yet so symbolic words: "The Few". Laid down the centre of the two books and secured into the cover binding is the Battle of Britain tie worn exclusively by "The Few". This beautifully designed tie, the most coveted in the world, was presented by its designer Mr. T. Herbert-Jones ARPS, FRSA, of Gieves Limited of Bond Street, London and he modified it a little so that it would symbolise a book-marker. Mr. Jones, an ardent admirer of "The Few", is the sole distributor of this tie and all applications for it are handled by him personally. If the applicants name does not appear in my compiled list of "The Few", a copy of which Mr. Jones holds, there is no hope of a tie being issued at any price.

'The medal ribbon displayed immediately above the tie is the 1939-45 Star. To distinguish all aircrew personnel who took part operationally in the Battle of Britain, a gilt rose emblem was awarded for wearing on the full size ribbon. On the miniature medal ribbon, worn on evening dress, a small bar is worn bearing the words "Battle of Britain". With certain awards, a silver rosette indicates a further similar award but the introduction of a gold rose is unique in the long history of all British military decorations and medals.

'A handsome oak showstand has been made to support the books, the RAF crest and wording being hand-carved by a leading London craftsman.

'Pilots and aircrew of fourteen nations flew in the Battle of Britain and these included seven Americans, six of whom were killed later in the war *(Research for this book indicates that other Americans enlisted in the RAF, some as Canadians — Ed.)* Now that I

The fruits of fourteen years of dedicated labour. John Holloway presents 'The Few' to the Imperial War Museum, London on October 21, 1969 (Keystone).

Display of 'The Few' at the Imperial War Museum beside the dress jacket worn by Air Chief-Marshal Lord Dowding.

had the original signatures of these seven pilots and their complete service records; a reproduction of Sir Winston Churchill's famous quotation to ''The Few'' signed by Sir Winston; solid silver models of the Spitfire and Hurricane aircraft and all the relevant statistics, I decided to produce a Battle of Britain Tableau to commemorate these seven pilots and present the exhibit to the Smithsonian Institution in Washington. This exhibit was presented, on my behalf, to the Director of the Institution Mr. Michael Collins (Apollo 11 space astronaut) by the British Ambassador to the United States, Sir Peter Ramsbotham on September 15, 1976 in my presence.

'I also decided to make up small personal souvenir albums and some 500 were produced and distributed to next of kin and others who had helped'.

'If my work has brought some satisfaction to ''The Few'' and their relatives then I feel that all the expenses incurred and the effort involved over the fourteen years it took me to compile the book will have been well worthwhile. After all, it was little enough to do for those who did so much.'

Following Flight Lieutenant Holloway's mammoth self-imposed task, it was left to others to dot the 'i's and cross the 't's. Using this list as a basis, Squadron Leader F. E. Dymond produced a listing entitled 'They Fell in the Battle' for inclusion in the new Battle of Britain Museum at Hendon. The basic intention of this Roll is to list all those killed on operational flying duties from the accredited squadrons during the accepted period and, with the approval of the Battle of Britain Fighter Association, to exclude pilots killed accidentally. As a result, following his first draft produced in 1978, Squadron Leader Dymond has since deleted Pilot Officer C. H. Bacon, Flight Lieutenant J. A. Davies, Pilot Officer D. Hastings, Sergeant D. R. Stoodley and Pilot Officer I. W. Sutherland from the Museum list giving a current total of 498 pilots and aircrew.

In the production of the list of casualties for inclusion in this book, our editorial policy has not been to set ourselves up as judge or jury to decide who was to be included and who omitted. Instead we have chosen to give a complete record of every pilot or aircrew member that lost his life or died as a result of wounds received in one of the accredited units during the period of the battle. The foundation of this record lies in Peter Cornwell's listing of aircraft losses and only after the

most painstaking cross-checking and meticulous research has a completely accurate compilation been possible. By marrying up every name against a recorded aircraft loss and vice-versa, any possible discrepancies have been eliminated. Even so, the ability to examine every query in detail has only been possible with the generous help of the staff of the Ministry of Defence AR9 department (which deals with RAF casualties) and the Commonwealth War Graves Commission at Maidenhead, Berkshire who have supported our work enthusiastically. Additionally the gravestones of every casualty buried in the United Kingdom have been checked and photographed. As a result, our work has uncovered a serious error in the records which has lain unnoticed for forty years.

On June 27, 1940 (thirteen days before the beginning of the battle) the Air Ministry published AMO 416 which amended the conditions of service for wireless operators and air gunners. Paragraph 2 stated:

'*Promotion to sergeant.* — (i) With effect from 27th May, 1940, airmen mustered as

wireless operator (air gunner) or air gunner who do not already hold the rank of sergeant will be promoted to the rank of temporary sergeant and will take precedence among themselves according to the date of their promotion or classification in their present mustering.'

As the effective date for this promotion (which was to be carried out by individual commanding officers) was May 27, therefore one should not find any wireless operators/air gunners serving in the Battle of Britain below the rank of sergeant. We found eight, all of whom were killed during the battle.

A further Air Ministry Order, No. 803 dated October 31, 1940 confirmed a similar arrangement for air observers with effect from September 14, 1940.

In 1942, when the first Roll of Honour was in preparation, the error was spotted and a minute, dated November 26, appended to the list stated that: 'In this section are 8 airmen whose ranks are shown as below Sergeant. It will be remembered that it was decided in 1940 that no airman below that rank should take part in air operations against the enemy. All 'live' airmen were immediately promoted as well as all casualties, the effective date in the latter case being prior to the date of the casualty. C.7.Cas at the Record Office have been advised and are now taking the action which should have been taken by the units long ago. The procedure will take some time as non-effective files will have to be withdrawn. We should ensure that if this scroll is to be prepared the correct rank should be shown, after confirming that action is complete and the next of kin informed.' The airmen concerned were LAC A. L. Austin, AC2 C. F. Cooper, AC2 A. Jackson, AC2 N. Jacobson, AC2 J. P. McCaul, AC2 R. I. Payne, AC1 J. B. Warren and LAC J. P. Wyatt. (The inconsistencies of this first listing can be illustrated with the Blenheim of No. 600 Squadron which crashed on October 3 where, of the three crewmen killed, only the name of Pilot Officer C. A. Hobson is included.)

In spite of the fact that the error had been spotted, nothing was done and the whole matter was forgotten . . . forgotten that is until we came on the scene thirty-seven years later and set about visiting the graves of all those that had died and began cross-checking the various lists of names. (John Holloway includes these airmen with the rank of sergeant on his Roll but it was a presumption

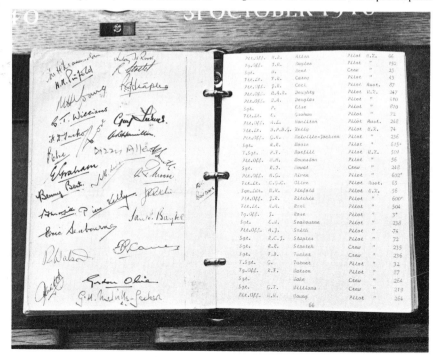

on his part to do so as the records state otherwise.)

However when we put forward our evidence for the eight names to be amended, the official reply was that, 'We have re-checked our casualty records . . . and can confirm that the ranks of the airmen listed in your letter are correct.' This, in effect, was a neat and excellent example of the bureaucratic 'side-step'. Naturally the records would indicate that they were because they had never been corrected in the first place!

Another contentious area is the correct rank held by many officers during the period under review. Due to the deaths in action of squadron or flight commanders, promotions in the field were inevitable as leadership gaps had to be filled as rapidly as possible. This has led to considerable confusion as to the actual rank held by a casualty at the time of his death.

The normal 'Substantive' peacetime rank was complicated by a wartime structure which made provision for 'War Substantive', 'Temporary' and 'Acting' ranks (both paid and unpaid). Basically, during the Battle of Britain, Full Substantive rank only applied to officers holding regular commissions; War Substantive was awarded to officers receiving time promotions and also to officers holding Temporary or Acting rank for certain periods; Temporary rank was for promotions by the Air Ministry to fulfil vacancies in the war establishment and Acting rank was bestowed by Commands and Groups to officers performing, temporarily, duties of certain higher ranks. Officers could hold Acting ranks of two or, exceptionally, three grades higher than their substantive rank for a considerable period before promulgation to a War Substantive rank. At least twenty-two Battle of Britain airmen held Acting ranks at the time of their deaths and we have been unable to establish just why some were confirmed in their Acting rank when they died whereas others were reduced one grade to their supposedly substantive rank. For example, both Richard Lee and Robert Jeff held the rank of Acting Flight Lieutenant yet, whereas Bob Jeff is confirmed a full Flight Lieutenant, 'Dickie' Lee is now only accorded the rank of Flying Officer. The policy of the Commonwealth War Graves Commission is to ignore the word 'Acting' and, to avoid confusion, we have followed their lead in our list.

Readers will also note that a discrepancy exists with eleven Polish officers concerning

The Tableau presented to the Smithsonian Institution on September 15, 1976.

their ranks. This also goes back to 1940 when the Polish pilots were incorporated into the Royal Air Force, either in RAF units or one of the Polish squadrons. The Air Ministry could not agree with the Polish authorities on the equivalent ranks between the Royal Air Force and Polish Air Force and this resulted in many Polish personnel being given a rank one grade lower with their pay correspondingly reduced. This remained a sore point with the Polish airmen throughout the war and much correspondence on the subject is on file at the Polish Institute in London. When the Polish authorities came to construct their memorial at Northolt, they decided to give their officers what they considered was the equivalent of their appropriate Polish rank. This has therefore resulted in these eleven airmen being listed in the records and on the memorial as holding a different rank.

Other errors, omissions or irreconcilable details are indicated in the text or captions. Two graves were found unmarked by any stone (Pilot Officer J. D. Lenahan and Pilot Officer R. A. Marchand) and that of Pilot

Officer M. Ravenhill was found to be a marked family grave but uninscribed with his name or date of death. Comments have been made where necessary regarding those private headstones which are illegible or otherwise in a bad state of repair. We have also retained the original county names throughout as we feel this is more in keeping with the period under review.

The following chapter contains a total of 537 men who were killed in the battle or who died later of wounds received. Six were only boys of eighteen years of age — George Brash, Maxwell Digby-Worsley, Norman Jacobson, Laurie Rasmussen, Ronald Tucker and Daniel Wright. The youngest was Aircraftman 2nd Class Jacobson (rightfully a sergeant) who has no known grave.

RAF Casualty List Day by Day

JULY		AUG.		SEP.		OCT.	
		1	5	1	6	1	6
		2	1	2	4	2	—
		3	—	3	6	3	3
		4	1	4	12	4	1
		5	1	5	8	5	2
		6	1	6	7	6	2
		7	—	7	16	7	9
		8	20	8	2	8	8
		9	1	9	6	9	5
10	2	10	—	10	—	10	6
11	3	11	25	11	18	11	4
12	4	12	11	12	1	12	5
13	5	13	14	13	3	13	3
14	1	14	4	14	4	14	1
15	—	15	11	15	16	15	6
16	1	16	11	16	—	16	2
17	1	17	—	17	3	17	5
18	8	18	10	18	3	18	5
19	11	19	4	19	—	19	2
20	7	20	1	20	5	20	5
21	2	21	—	21	1	21	2
22	1	22	2	22	—	22	4
23	—	23	—	23	2	23	1
24	3	24	10	24	2	24	3
25	7	25	13	25	5	25	6
26	1	26	7	26	3	26	4
27	2	27	4	27	20	27	6
28	1	28	10	28	10	28	—
29	3	29	1	29	2	29	5
30	—	30	9	30	8	30	9
31	5	31	9			31	—
	68		**176**		**173**		**120**

FLIGHT LIEUTENANT P. H. BARRAN

Flight Lieutenant Philip Henry Barran was born April 20, 1909 at Chapel Allerton, Leeds. He served in the Royal Air Force before the war and prior to the Battle of Britain was stationed at Northolt with No. 609 'West Riding' Squadron. In the first few days of July 1940, the squadron moved west to Middle Wallop and on the 11th of the month was sent to the newly completed forward aerodrome at Warmwell. On that day, the readiness flight of six Spitfires was scrambled to the aid of a convoy off Portland. The flight split into two, one half tackling the dive-bombers, the other fending off the escorting Messerschmitt Bf 109s. In the battle against odds of six to one, Philip Barran's Spitfire was severely damaged forcing him out of the fight to return to base. Five miles from shore, his Spitfire burst into flames and he had to bale out, parachuting into the sea. Although a rescue boat picked him up, he succumbed to wounds, severe burns and shock before reaching land.

ADAMS, P/O H. C. British. No. 501 Squadron 6:9:40 22yrs. Tandridge (St. Peter) Churchyard, Surrey. North of church.

AEBERHARDT, P/O R. A. C. British. No. 19 Squadron 31:8:40 19yrs. Whittlesford (SS Mary & Andrew) Churchyard, Cambridgeshire A.7.

AKROYD, P/O H. J. British. No. 152 Squadron. Seriously injured 7:10:40. Died 8:10:40 27yrs. Warmwell (Holy Trinity) Churchyard, Dorset. South part.

ALLEN, F/O J. H. L. New Zealander. No. 151 Squadron 12:7:40 25yrs. Runnymede Memorial Panel 5.

ALLEN, F/O J. L., DFC, British. No. 54 Squadron 24:7:40 24yrs. Margate Cemetery, Kent. Section 50 Grave 15936.

ALLGOOD, Sgt. H. H. British. Nos. 85-253 Squadrons 10:10:40 25yrs. Cambridge (St. Mark) Burial Ground, Grantchester, Cambridgeshire. Grave 139.

ALLTON, Sgt. L. C. British. No. 92 Squadron 19:10:40 20yrs. Nuneaton (Oaston Road) Cemetery, Warwickshire. Section D Grave 88.

AMBROSE, P/O R. British. No. 151 Squadron 4:9:40 21yrs. Epping Cemetery, Essex. Section Z Grave 3.

'Their name liveth for evermore'. The Stone of Remembrance in every large Commonwealth War Graves Commission cemetery was designed by Sir Edwin Lutyens in 1918 to give an impression of majesty and tranquility. The words from Ecclesiasticus were chosen by Rudyard Kipling. This is the Bergen op Zoom War Cemetery in the Netherlands where Sergeant George Collett lies buried — killed on August 22, 1940.

ANDREAE, F/O C. J. D. British. No. 64 Squadron 15:8:40 23yrs. Runnymede Memorial Panel 5.

ANDREW, Sgt. S. British. No. 46 Squadron 11:9:40 21yrs. North Ferriby (All Saints) Churchyard, Yorkshire. Grave 141.

ANDRUSZKOW, Sgt. T. Polish No. 303 Squadron 27:9:40 19yrs. Northwood Cemetery, Ruislip-Northwood, Middlesex. Section H Grave 208. Also commemorated on the Polish Memorial, Northolt.

ARTHUR, P/O C. J. British. No. 248 Squadron 27:8:40 22yrs. Runnymede Memorial Panel 7

ASH, F/Lt. R. C. V. British. No. 264 Squadron 28:8:40 31yrs. St. Andrews Western Cemetery, Fife. Section D Grave 6D.

ASHTON, P/O D. G. British. No. 266 Squadron 12:8:40 20yrs. Runnymede Memorial Panel 7.

ATKINS, Sgt. F. P. J. British. No. 141 Squadron 19:7:40 26yrs. Boulogne Eastern Cemetery, France. Plot 13 Row A Grave 18.

ATKINSON, P/O A. A. British. No. 23 Squadron 30:10:40 32yrs. Clymping (St. Mary) Churchyard, Sussex.

ATKINSON, P/O H. D., DFC, British. No. 213 Squadron 25:8:40 22yrs. Market Weighton Cemetery, Yorkshire. Row 1R Grave 7.

ATKINSON, P/O R. British. No. 213 Squadron 17:10:40 19yrs. Gillingham (Woodlands) Cemetery, Kent. Section F Grave 578

AUSTIN, LAC, A. L. British. No. 604 Squadron. Seriously injured 25:8:40. Died 26:8:40 25yrs. Northwood Cemetery, Ruislip-Northwood, Middlesex. Section H Grave 180.

AYERS, Sgt. D. H. British. No. 74 Squadron 23:9:40 26yrs. Ipswich Cemetery Section X.H. Grave 407.

One of the earliest principles of the work of the Commission was that there was to be no distinction between officers and men in the form or nature of the memorials or headstones as each were owed an equal debt of gratitude. Commission headstones differ only in respect of nationalities. *Below left:* The standard headstone for servicemen from the United Kingdom and Commonwealth. *Centre:* The distinctive design selected for Polish dead and *right* that for Czechoslovakians approved in 1949.

As the standard headstone only was permitted as a gravemarker overseas, the Commission pressed for a similar system to be adopted for those who died within the United Kingdom. Some 1,300 service plots were established in civil cemeteries and churchyards throughout the country and while many Battle of Britain casualties will be found buried in these plots, either in the one nearest to their crash site or that closest to their station, it was confirmed in March 1941 that the next of kin could elect to make their own arrangements. Thus it is that the graves of many aircrew killed in the battle will be found marked with private memorials, most in this category being located in their home towns. Typical of these service plots is that at Maidstone Cemetery which contains 134 graves of which sixteen are of officers, NCOs and men killed in a bombing raid on Detling aerodrome on August 13, 1940. Within the ranks lies Pilot Officer John Bailey who was shot down on September 2.

AYLING, Sgt. C. A. H. British. No. 66 Squadron/421 Flight 11:10:40 28yrs. Pembroke (Monkton, St. Nicholas) Cemetery. Grave 107.

BACON, F/O C. H. British. No. 610 Squadron 30:9:40 21yrs. Windermere (St. Mary's) Cemetery, Westmorland. Section B.1 Grave 52.

BADGER, S/Ldr. J. V. C., DFC, British. No. 43 Squadron. Seriously wounded 30:8:40. Died 30:6:41 29yrs. Halton (St. Michael and All Angels) Churchyard, Buckinghamshire. Plot 3 Row B Grave 111.

BAILEY, P/O J. C. L. D. British. No. 46 Squadron 2:9:40 20yrs. Maidstone Cemetery, Kent. Plot CCI Grave 90.

BAKER, Sgt. B. British. No. 264 Squadron 26:8:40 27yrs. Runnymede Memorial Panel 11.

BAKER, Sgt. E. D. British. No. 145 Squadron 8:8:40 28yrs. Runnymede Memorial Panel 11.

BAKER, Sgt. R. D. British. No. 56 Squadron 11:8:40 23yrs. Letchworth Cemetery Hertfordshire. Section A Division G Grave 193.

BANN, Sgt. S. E. British. No. 238 Squadron 28:9:40 26yrs. Macclesfield Cemetery, Cheshire. Plot A Grave 938.

BARKER, Sgt. J. K. British. No. 152 Squadron 4:9:40 23yrs. Etaples Military Cemetery, France. Plot 69 Row A Grave 5.

BARON, P/O R. V. British. No. 219 Squadron 12:10:40 40yrs. Sittingbourne & Milton (Sittingbourne) Cemetery (old ground). Section W Grave 48.

BARRAN, F/Lt. P. H. British. No. 609 Squadron 11:7:40 31yrs. Leeds (Lawns Wood) Cemetery. Section B Unconsecrated Grave 392.

BARRY, F/O N. J. M. South African Nos. 3-501 Squadrons 7:10:40 22yrs. Finghall (St. Andrew) Churchyard Yorkshire. North of church.

BAXTER, Sgt. S. British. No. 222 Squadron 14:9:40 24yrs. Newcastle-upon-Tyne (West Road) Crematorium. Panel 1.

The private memorials form a contrast to these orderly burial grounds — Sergeant Ronald Baker who rests at Letchworth Cemetery is believed to have been shot down by his own side on August 11.

Pilot Officer Noel Benson lies with his mother and father at Great Ouseburn in Yorkshire, the eldest of two sons who both lost their lives in the Second World War. (His brother Brian, a Captain in the RASC, was killed in Germany in April 1945.) Nicknamed 'Broody', Noel was a contemporary of Richard Hillary and Peter Pease in No. 603 'City of Edinburgh' Squadron and had a fortunate escape on July 23 when he managed to return his combat-damaged aircraft over seventy-five miles out in the North Sea. He was shot down in flames over Kent on August 28.

BAYLEY, Sgt. E. A. British. Nos. 32-249 Squadrons 10:10:40 29yrs. Bromley (St. Lukes) Cemetery, Kent. Grave 198.

BEAUMONT, P/O W., DFC, British. No. 152 Squadron 23:9:40 26yrs. Runnymede Memorial Panel 7.

BEEDHAM, P/O J. J. I. British. No. 245 Squadron 7:10:40 20yrs. Glenavy Roman Catholic Churchyard, County Antrim, Northern Ireland. Plot 4 West Side Grave 20.

BELEY, P/O R. W. G. Canadian No. 151 Squadron 12:8:40 20yrs. Margate Cemetery, Kent. Section 50 Grave 15938.

BELL, F/O J. S. British. No. 616 Squadron 30:8:40 23yrs. Lincoln (Eastgate or St. Peter's) Cemetery. Section A Grave 483.

BENNETT, P/O C. C. Australian. No. 248 Squadron 1:10:40 23yrs. Runnymede Memorial Panel 7.

BENSON, P/O N. J. V. British. No. 603 Squadron 28:8:40 21yrs. Great Ouseburn (St. Mary) Churchyard Extension, Yorkshire. Section L Grave 3.

BENZIE, P/O J. Canadian. No. 242 Squadron 7:9:40 25yrs. Runnymede Memorial Panel 7.

BERESFORD, F/Lt. H. R. A. British. No. 257 Squadron 7:9:40 24yrs. Originally remembered on Runnymede Memorial Panel 4, now buried in Brookwood Military Cemetery. Plot 24 Row D Grave 14.

BERRY, Sgt. A. British. No. 264 Squadron 24:8:40 23yrs. Runnymede Memorial Panel 12.

BERRY, F/Sgt. F. G., DFM, British. No. 1 Squadron 1:9:40 26yrs. Harrow (Pinner) New Cemetery, Middlesex. Section G5 Grave 92.

BICKERDIKE, P/O J. L. New Zealander No. 85 Squadron 22:7:40 21yrs. Wimbish (All Saints) Churchyard, Essex.

BIRCH, Sgt. R. R. G. British. No. 19 Squadron 13:7:40 23yrs. Whittlesford (SS Mary & Andrew) Churchyard, Cambridgeshire. Row B Grave 6.

BLACK, Sgt. H. E. British. Nos. 257-32-46 Squadrons. Seriously wounded 29:10:40. Died 9:11:40 26yrs. Ibstock (St. Denys) Churchyard, Leicestershire. Grave 1242.

BLAKE (F.A.A.), Sub/Lt A. G. British. No. 19 Squadron 29:10:40 23yrs. Langley (St. Mary) Churchyard, Slough, Buckinghamshire. Row 13 Grave 3.

BLAND, P/O J. W. British. No. 501 Squadron 18:8:40 30yrs. Gravesend Cemetery, Kent. Plot B.12 Grave 1241.

Miss Pamela Beresford in the 14th century village church at Hoby, Leicestershire where her father was Rector for twenty-six years. On the wall is the family memorial stone commemorating her brother's death. On Saturday, September 29, 1979, the remains of Flight Lieutenant Hugh Beresford were uncovered during the excavation of a crash site on the Isle of Sheppey for a BBC TV documentary (Daily Express).

On August 15, No. 1 Squadron (RAF) scrambled from Northolt. A section of three aircraft were surprised by an enemy formation described later by the one surviving pilot as consisting of over fifty Bf 109s. Pilot Officer Dennis Browne *(left)* and Sergeant Martin

Shanahan *(right)* were both shot down and, as their bodies were never found, were commemorated on the Runnymede Memorial. Unfortunately it seems that an administrative mix-up incorrectly recorded their dates of death as August 16.

BOLTON, Sgt. H. A. British. No. 79 Squadron 31:8:40 21yrs. Hartlepool (Stranton) Cemetery. Plot 10 Division A Church of England Grave 258.

BONSEIGNEUR, P/O C. R. Canadian No. 257 Squadron 3:9:40 22yrs. Saffron Walden Cemetery, Essex. War graves plot Compartment 40 Grave 2.

BOOTH, Sgt. G. B. British. No. 85 Squadron. Seriously injured 1:9:40. Died 7:2:41 20yrs. Crystal Palace District Cemetery. Section H3 Grave 18056.

BOROWSKI, F/O J. Polish. No. 302 Squadron 18:10:40 28yrs. Northwood Cemetery, Ruislip-Northwood, Middlesex. Section H Grave 269.

BOULTON F/O J. E. British. Nos. 603-310 Squadrons 9:9:40 20yrs. Bandon Hill Cemetery, Beddington, Surrey. Section R Grave 28.

BOWEN, F/Lt. C. E. British. No. 607 Squadron 1:10:40 24yrs. Runnymede Memorial Panel 4.

BOWEN, P/O N. G. British. No. 266 Squadron 16:8:40 20yrs. Wallingford Cemetery, Berkshire. Section R Grave 60.

BOYLE, F/O J. G. Canadian. No. 41 Squadron. 28:9:40 26yrs. Lynsted (SS Peter & Paul) New Churchyard, Kent. North side Row F Grave 1.

BRANCH, F/O G. R., EGM (George Cross), British. No. 145 Squadron 11:8:40 26yrs. Quiberville Churchyard, France. Grave 6. East of church.

BRASH, Sgt. G. B. British. No. 248 Squadron 1:10:40 18yrs. Runnymede Memorial Panel 12.

BRIMBLE, Sgt. J. J. British. No. 73 Squadron 14:9:40 23yrs. Runnymede Memorial Panel 12.

BRITTON, P/O H. W. A. British. No. 17 Squadron 6:8:40 19yrs. Wimbish (All Saints) Churchyard, Essex.

BROADHURST, P/O J. W. British. No. 222 Squadron 7:10:40 23yrs. Hornchurch Cemetery, Essex. Section A Grave 1339.

BROWNE, P/O D. O. M. British. No. 1 Squadron 16:8:40 22yrs. Runnymede Memorial Panel 7.
Both Pilot Officer Browne and fellow pilot Sergeant Shanahan appear in the Official Casualty Returns as 'missing' on August 16, 1940 and their dates of death are recorded as such. However the Form 540, No. 1 Squadron Operations Record Book gives the date of his last operation as August 15 as does a squadron history published in 1971.

BRUCE, F/Lt. D. C. British. No. 111 Squadron 4:9:40 22yrs. Runnymede Memorial Panel 4.

BRUMBY, Sgt. N. British. Nos. 615-607 Squadrons 1:10:40 20yrs. Hull Northern Cemetery, Yorkshire. Compartment 218 Grave 46.

BRYSON, P/O J. S. Canadian. No. 92 Squadron 24:9:40 27yrs. North Weald Bassett (St. Andrew) Churchyard, Essex. Row 1 Grave 4.

BRZEZOWSKI, Sgt. M. Polish. No. 303 Squadron 15:9:40 20yrs. Polish Memorial, Northolt.

BUCHANAN, P/O J. R. British. No. 609 Squadron 27:7:40 25yrs. Runnymede Memorial Panel 7.

BUCHIN, P/O M. S. H. C. Belgian. No. 213 Squadron 15:8:40 34yrs. Runnymede Memorial Panel 7. Also has a memorial grave in the Pelouse d'Honneur Cemetery of Brussels at Evere.

BUCK, Sgt J. A. British. No. 43 Squadron 19:7:40 24yrs. Stretford Cemetery, Lancashire. Section P.1. Joint Grave 362.

BUCKLAND, P/O F. W. British. No. 74 Squadron 8:10:40 20yrs. Brighton (Woodvale) Borough Crematorium. Panel 1.

BULMER (F.A.A.), Sub/Lt. G. G. R. British. No. 32 Squadron 20:7:40 20yrs. Lee-on-Solent Fleet Air Arm Memorial. Bay 1 Panel 3.

BURGOYNE, P/O E. British. No. 19 Squadron 27:9:40 25yrs. Burghfield (St Mary) Churchyard, Berkshire. North of Church.

BURTON F/O P. R-F. South African. No. 249 Squadron 27:9:40 23yrs. Tangmere (St. Andrew) Churchyard, Sussex. Row 1 Grave 480.

BURY-BURZYMSKI, P/O J., VM, Polish. No. 303 Squadron 24:10:40 25yrs. Leconfield Churchyard, Yorkshire.

BUTTERFIELD, Sgt. S. L., DFM, British. No. 213 Squadron 11:8:40 27yrs. Boulogne Eastern Cemetery, France. Plot 11 Row A Grave 16.

CALE, P/O F. W. Australian. No. 266 Squadron 15:8:40 25yrs. Westminster City Cemetery, Ealing. Plot 16 Grave 13060.

CAMBRIDGE, F/Lt W. P. British. No. 253 Squadron 6:9:40 28yrs. Reading (Henley Road) Cemetery, Eye and Dunsden, Berkshire. Block 3 Grave 4726.

CAMPBELL, P/O K. C. British. No 43 Squadron 29:7:40 28yrs. Lympne (St. Stephen) Churchyard, Kent. Grave 12D.

CAMPBELL, P/O N. N. Canadian. No. 242 Squadron 17:10:40 27yrs. Scottow Cemetery, Norfolk. Grave 244.

CARDELL, P/O P. M. British. No. 603 Squadron 27:9:40 23yrs. Great Paxton (Holy Trinity) Churchyard, Huntingdonshire.

CARDNELL, P/O C. F. British. No. 23 Squadron 8:8:40 22yrs. Highgate Cemetery, St. Pancras. Square 23, Grave 32149.

CARPENTER (F.A.A.), Sub/Lt. J. C. British. Nos. 229-46 Squadrons. 9:9:40 21yrs. Lee-on-Solent Fleet Air Arm Memorial. Bay 1 Panel 3.
This officer is officially listed as 'missing' on September 9, 1940. However, No. 46 Squadron records show that they took off from Stapleford at 11.30 a.m. on September 8, 1940 and engaged an enemy formation at 12.15 p.m. over the Isle of Sheppey. Sub-Lieutenant Carpenter appears to have gone down at about 12.30 p.m. and his naval record shows that he was reported 'missing' in a signal from No. 46 Squadron timed 8.20 p.m. on September 8, 1940. A further signal from Rear Admiral Naval Air Stations timed 7.14 p.m. on September 9 notified that the officer had been 'killed in crash'. Unfortunately neither of these signals can now be traced in Admiralty records and we can only assume that as the officer's death was notified on September 9, 1940, this date has been recorded for naval administrative purposes.

CARTER, F/O P. E. G. British. Nos. 73-302 Squadrons. 18:10:40 21yrs. Croydon (Queen's Road) Cemetery. Section A.A.2. Grave 34255.

CASE, P/O H. R. British. No. 72 Squadron 12:10:40 24yrs. Withycombe (St. Nicholas) Churchyard, Somerset.

CAWSE, P/O F. N. British. No. 238 Squadron 11:8:40 25yrs. Cayeux-sur-Mer Communal Cemetery, France. Plot 1 Grave 8.

CEBRZYNSKI, F/O A. Polish. No. 303 Squadron. Seriously injured 11:9:40. Died 19:9:40 28yrs. Northwood Cemetery, Ruislip-Northwood, Middlesex. Section H Grave 187. Also commemorated on the Polish Memorial, Northolt.

CHALDER, P/O H. H. British. Nos. 266-41 Squadrons. Seriously wounded 28:9:40. Died 10:11:40 25yrs. Newcastle-upon-Tyne (St. Nicholas) Cemetery. Section W Grave 300.

Missing Fleet Air Arm personnel are commemorated on their special memorial at Lee-on-Solent. Some fifty-six Fleet Air Arm aircrew were seconded to RAF Fighter Command to help fight the battle of whom nine were killed. Six have no known graves and their names are inscribed on the memorial.

Sub-Lieutenant Jack Carpenter has no known grave and, although some Hurricane fragments have been recovered on Bearstead Golf Course at Maidstone, they cannot be positively identified as coming from P3201. In spite of our evidence regarding the error in his date of death, the Naval Branch of the Ministry of Defence have refused to amend their records or authorise the correction of those held by the CWGC.

Missing over the Channel on August 12 while serving with No. 257 Squadron — Pilot Officer John Chomley from Southern Rhodesia.

The Royal Air Force pays tribute to its dead. This is Scottow Cemetery, Norfolk where Canadian Pilot Officer Norman Campbell is buried, far from his home in St. Thomas, Ontario. A young Senior Aircraftwoman lays flowers on November 7, 1978 as Jaguar aircraft from nearby Coltishall thunder overhead (Eastern Daily Press).

CHALONER LINDSEY, P/O P. British. No. 601 Squadron 26:7:40 20yrs. Wimereux Communal Cemetery, France. Plot 7 Row B Grave 4.

CHALUPA, Sgt. J. Czechoslovakian. No. 310 Squadron 16:10:40 21yrs. Brookwood Military Cemetery. Plot 28 Row D Grave 10.

CHLOPIK, F/Lt. T. P. Polish. No. 302 Squadron 15:9:40 32yrs. Southend-on-Sea (Sutton Road) Cemetery, Essex. Plot R Grave 12265. Also commemorated on the Polish Memorial, Northolt.

CHOMLEY, P/O J. A. G. British. No. 257 Squadron 12:8:40 20yrs. Runnymede Memorial Panel 7.

CHRISTIE, Sgt. J. McB. British. No. 152 Squadron 26:9:40 22yrs. Renfrew (Arkleston) Cemetery. Section L Row T Grave 51.

CLARKE, P/O A. W. British. No. 504 Squadron 11:9:40 20yrs. Runnymede Memorial Panel 7.

CLARKE, Sgt. G. S. British. No. 248 Squadron 1:10:40 19yrs. Runnymede Memorial Panel 12.

CLENSHAW, Sgt. I. C. C. British. No. 253 Squadron 10:7:40 22yrs. Kelvedon (St. Mary) Churchyard Extension, Essex. Grave 413.

CLIFTON, P/O J. K. G. British. No. 253 Squadron 1:9:40 21yrs. Staplegrove (St. John) Churchyard, Somerset. Row Q Grave 9.

COBDEN, P/O D. G. New Zealander. No. 74 Squadron 11:8:40 26yrs. Ostende New Communal Cemetery, Belgium. Plot 9 Row 3 Grave 24.

COLLARD, F/O P. DFC. British. No. 615 Squadron 14:8:40 24yrs. Oye-Plage Communal Cemetery, France. Row 1, Grave 10.

COLLETT, Sgt. G. R. British. No. 54 Squadron 22:8:40 24yrs. Bergen op Zoom War Cemetery, Netherlands. Plot 14 Row A Grave 4.

COMELY, P/O P. W. British. No. 87 Squadron 15:8:40 19yrs. Runnymede Memorial Panel 7.

CONNORS, F/Lt. S. D. P. DFC and Bar. British. No. 111 Squadron 18:8:40 28yrs. North Berwick Cemetery. Section B Grave 123.

COONEY, F/Sgt. C. J. British. No. 56 Squadron 29:7:40 26yrs. Runnymede Memorial Panel 10.

COOPER, AC2 C. F. British. No. 600 Squadron 3:10:40 20yrs. Heath Town (Holy Trinity) Churchyard, Wolverhampton (old graveyard) Row 38 Grave 63

'At the going down of the sun and in the morning we will remember them.' So reads the inscription on the grave of the first airman killed in the Battle of Britain, now sadly overgrown in St. Mary's Churchyard, Kelvedon in Essex. Sergeant Ian Clenshaw died on a dawn patrol from Kirton-in-Lindsey aerodrome (Sector M in No. 12 Group) on July 10.

POST OFFICE TELEGRAM

Charges to pay

s. ____ d. ____

RECEIVED

_____ m

From _____

No. ____ 12

OFFICE STAMP

Prefix. Time handed in. Office of Origin and Service Instructions. Words. _____ m

2

To

402 BB 1.11 RUISLIP TELEX OHMS 24

IMPORTANT = MR COOPER 53 ROWLANDS AVENUE HEATH TOWN

WOLVERHAMPTON =

REGRET YOU INFORM YOU YOUR SON 1003497 COOPER KILLED

3 RD OCTOBER LETTER FOLLOWS = RECORDS TELEX RUISLIP +

+ 53 1003497 3 RD

For free repetition of doubtful words telephone " TELEGRAMS ENQUIRY " or call, with this form **B or C**
at office of delivery.   Other enquiries should be accompanied by this form and, if possible, the envelope.

Charges to pay

s. ____ d. ____

RECEIVED AM 8 59 53 2 1003497 SIX HUND +

From BM

OFFICE TELEGRAM

No. ____

OFFICE STAMP

21

Prefix. Time handed in. Office of Origin and Service Instructions. Words. _____ m

15

To

115 BB 8.5 REDHILL T OHMS 81

PRIORITY MRS E COOPER 53 ROWLANDS AVE HEATHTOWN

WOLVERHAMPTON

= REFERENCE AC 2 COOPER CHARLES FREDERICK 1003497
GOVERNMENT WILL SEND DECEASED HOME IF YOU WISH AND CANNOT
AFFORD EXPENSE NO OTHER TRAVELLING EXPENSES WILL BE
ALLOWED STOP OTHERWISE FUNERAL WILL BE HERE AND DATE
ADVISED LATER STOP IF YOU WISH TO ATTEND AND CANNOT AFFORD
EXPENSES A RETURN RAILWAY WARRANT FOR TWO PERSONS
(ONE RELATIVE) WILL BE ISSUED ON PRODUCTION OF THIS
TELEGRAM AT NEAREST POLICE STATION STOP =
COMMANDING OFFICER 600 TH SQUADRON +

POST OFFICE TELEGRAM

Charges to pay
——— s. ——— d.
RECEIVED
——————— m
From
AM 8 26

Prefix. Time handed in. Office of Origin and Service Instructions. Words _____ m
47
47 6.33 UPLANDS TS OHMS 25
To _____

No. _____
OFFICE STAMP

BM COOPER 53 ROWLANDS AVE HEATHTOWN WOLVERHAMPTON =

BODY OF LAC COOPER LEAVING PADDINGTON 4.5 PM
TRAIN MONDAY 7.10.40 TIME ARRIVAL WOLVERHAMPTON
NOT KNOWN = O/C RAF KENLEY ++ 53 4.5 PM 7.10.40 ++

For free repetition of doubtful words telephone "TELEGRAMS ENQUIRY" or call, with this form
at office of delivery. Other enquiries should be accompanied by this form and, if possible, the envelope. B or C

How insensitive these telegrams read forty years later announcing the death of their eldest son Charles to Mr. and Mrs. Cooper in October 1940. He was the wireless operator in a Blenheim which crashed in a rainstorm on a routine patrol flying from Redhill. Charles Cooper is one of the eight airmen who are still listed in Ministry of Defence records with aircraftman ranks due to their units not carrying out Air Ministry Order A416 of June 27, 1940 which stated the minimum rank for a wireless operator/air gunner was to be Sergeant. As the order was backdated to May 27 — before the battle began — there is no doubt that their ranks are incorrect but the CWGC, although wishing to help, cannot act without MoD authorisation. The latter is not forthcoming.

COOPER-KEY, P/O A. M. British. No. 46 Squadron 24:7:40 21yrs. Scopwick Church Burial Ground, Lincolnshire. Row 2 Grave 32.

COPCUTT, Sgt. R. British. No. 248 Squadron 20:10:40 20yrs. Runnymede Memorial Panel 13.

COPEMAN, P/O J. H. H. British. No. 111 Squadron 11:8:40 27yrs. Middlekerke Communal Cemetery, Belgium. Row A Grave 26.

CORBETT, P/O G. H. Canadian. No. 66 Squadron 8:10:40 21yrs. Upchurch (St. Mary) Churchyard Extension, Kent. South-west corner.

CORCORAN, Sgt. H. British. No. 236 Squadron 20:7:40 27yrs. Runnymede Memorial Panel 13.

COVERLEY, F/O W. H. British. No. 602 Squadron 7:9:40 23yrs. Scarborough (Dean Road) Cemetery, Yorkshire. Section C, Grave 7A.

COWSILL, Sgt. J. R. British. No. 56 Squadron 13:7:40 20yrs. Runnymede Memorial Panel 13.

COX, P/O K. H. British. No. 610 Squadron 28:8:40 24yrs. Birmingham Municipal Crematorium. Column 1. (Ashes since scattered at old Castle Bromwich aerodrome.)

COX, F/O P. A. N. British. No. 501 Squadron 27:7:40 25yrs. Runnymede Memorial Panel 5.

COX, Sgt. R. C. R. British. No. 248 Squadron 27:8:40 30yrs. Kviberg Cemetery, Gothenburg, Sweden. Plot 3 Row B Grave 6.

CROFTS, F/O P. G. British. No. 605 Squadron 28:9:40 22yrs. Tilford (All Saints) Churchyard, Surrey. South-east corner.

CROMBIE, Sgt. R. British. No. 141 Squadron 19:7:40 29yrs. Runnymede Memorial Panel 13.

CROSSMAN, P/O J. D. Australian. No. 46 Squadron 30:9:40 22yrs. Chalfont St. Giles Churchyard, Buckinghamshire. Grave 13.

CRUTTENDEN, P/O J. British. No. 43 Squadron 8:8:40 20yrs. Runnymede Memorial Panel 7.

CULVERWELL, Sgt. J. H. British. No. 87 Squadron 25:7:40 25yrs. Cardiff (Cathays) Cemetery. Section E. J. Grave 114.

CUNNINGHAM, F/Lt. J. L. G. British. No. 603 Squadron 28:8:40 23yrs. Runnymede Memorial Panel 4.

CURLEY, Sgt. A. G. British. No. 141 Squadron 19:7:40 33yrs. Runnymede Memorial Panel 13.

CUTTS, F/O J. W. British. No. 222 Squadron 4:9:40 20yrs. Runnymede Memorial Panel 5.

D'ARCY-IRVINE, F/O B. W. J. British. No. 257 Squadron 8:8:40 22yrs. Runnymede Memorial Panel 5.

DAVEY, P/O J. A. J. British. No. 1 Squadron 11:8:40 20yrs. Sandown Cemetery, Isle of Wight. Section A Grave 14.

DAVIES, P/O A. E. British. No. 222 Squadron 30:10:40 23yrs. Tanworth (or Tanworth-in-Arden) St. Mary Magdalene Churchyard Extension, Warwickshire. South of chancel. Grave 1601.

DAVIES, Sgt. J. W. British. No. 600 Squadron 7:9:40 22yrs. Roundhaye (St. John) Churchyard, Leeds. Section C Joint Grave 180.

DAVIES-COOKE, F/O P. J. British. Nos. 72-610 Squadrons. 27:9:40 23yrs. Rhydymwyn (St. John) Churchyard, Cilcain, Flintshire.

DAVIS, F/Lt. C. R. DFC Born American, possibly naturalised British at age 21. No. 601 Squadron 6:9:40 29yrs. Storrington (St. Mary) Churchyard, Sussex.

DE MANCHA, P/O R. A. British. No. 43 Squadron 21:7:40 23yrs. Runnymede Memorial Panel 8.

DEMETRIADI, F/O R. S. British. No. 601 Squadron 11:8:40 21yrs. Cayeux-sur-Mer Communal Cemetery, France. Plot 1 Grave 7.

DEWAR, W/C J. S., DSO, DFC, British. Nos. 87-213 Squadrons. 12:9:40 33yrs. North Baddesley (St. John the Baptist) Churchyard, Hampshire. North-west part.

DEWEY, P/O R. B. British. Nos. 611-603 Squadrons. 27:10:40 19yrs. Hornchurch Cemetery, Essex. Section A Grave 1341.

DICKIE, P/O W. G. British. No. 601 Squadron 11:8:40 24yrs. Runnymede Memorial Panel 8.

DICKINSON, Sgt. J. H. British. No. 253 Squadron 30:8:40 21yrs. Egton (St. Mary) Churchyard Egton-with-Newland, Lancashire. Grave N1.

DIFFORD, F/O I. B. South African. No. 607 Squadron 7:10:40 30yrs. Tangmere (St. Andrew) Churchyard, Sussex. Row 3 Grave 483.

DIGBY-WORSLEY, Sgt. M. P. British. No. 248 Squadron 19:8:40 18yrs. Runnymede Memorial Panel 13.

DIXON, Sgt. F. J. P. British. No. 501 Squadron 11:7:40 21yrs. Abbeville Communal Cemetery Extension, France. Plot 8 Row C Grave 14.

DONALD F/Lt. I. D. G., DFC, British. No. 141 Squadron 19:7:40 22 yrs. Tilford (All Saints) Churchyard, Surrey. South-west corner.

DOULTON, F/O M. D. British. No. 601 Squadron 31:8:40 31yrs. Runnymede Memorial Panel 5.

Wing Commander John Scatliff Dewar, DSO, DFC, was born at Mussoori, Lahore Province, India in 1907 and, contrary to some previously published articles, was not related to the family of whisky distillers. He was educated at Kings College, Canterbury and entered the service through the Royal Air Force college at Cranwell. He was a brilliant student and pilot with 'exceptional' ratings and he eventually became a test pilot at Martlesham Heath. In September 1939, Squadron Leader Dewar took No. 87 Squadron to France and, in recognition of his leadership and success in extricating the squadron in May 1940 (in spite of a broken shoulder), was one of the first four officers to receive the double award of the DSO and DFC. What happened on his last flight from Exeter to Tangmere on September 12 has never been exactly determined as his body was found washed up on a Sussex beach. As Commanding Officer of Exeter, he was the highest ranking officer to be killed in the Battle of Britain.

DOUTREPONT, P/O G. L. J. Belgian. No. 229 Squadron 15:9:40 27yrs. Exhumed and repatriated to Pelouse d'Honneur Cemetery of Brussels at Evere on 20:10:1949. Tomb II-12.

DOWNER, P/O A. R. British. No. 263 Squadron. Seriously injured 20:7:40. Died 21:7:40 22yrs. Great Northern London-Cemetery. Section AC Grave 950.

DRAKE, P/O G. J. South African. No. 607 Squadron 9:9:40 20yrs. Originally remembered on Runnymede Memorial Panel 8, now buried in Brookwood Military Cemetery. Plot22 Row E Grave 2.

DREW, S/Ldr. P. E. British. No. 236 Squadron 1:8:40 30yrs. Biville Churchyard, France. (North-west part, near west wall.)

DRUMMOND, F/O J. F. DFC. British. No. 92 Squadron 10:10:40 21yrs. Thornton Garden of Rest, Lancashire (North of Liverpool on B5422) Section A Grave 3.

DUSZYNSKI, Sgt. S. Polish. No. 238 Squadron 11:9:40 24yrs. Polish Memorial, Northolt.

DYKE, Sgt. L. A. British. No. 64 Squadron 27:9:40 22yrs. Runnymede Memorial Panel 13.

DYMOND, Sgt. W. L. DFM. British. No. 111 Squadron 2:9:40 23yrs. Runnymede Memorial Panel 13.

EDRIDGE, P/O H. P. M. British. No. 222 Squadron 30:10:40 21yrs. Roman Catholic Cemetery, Perrymead, Widcombe, Bath, Somerset (off Prior Park Road). Grave 107.

EDWARDS, P/O H. D. Canadian. No. 92 Squadron 11:9:40 24yrs. Folkestone New Cemetery, Kent. Plot O Grave 31.

The three Belgian pilots who were buried in England were exhumed after the war to be reburied as national heroes in the Belgian Pelouse d'Honneur Cemetery in Brussels. Pilot Officer Georges Doutrepont was originally buried in the military plot in Northwood Cemetery at Ruislip-Northwood *above left* **but now lies in Tomb 12** *above* **at Evere.**

EDWARDS, F/O R. L. Canadian. Nos. 401-1 (RCAF) Squadrons 26:8:40 (no date of birth given in records). Brookwood Military Cemetery. Plot 3 Row C Grave 1A.

EDWORTHY, Sgt. G. H. British. No. 46 Squadron 3:9:40 25yrs. Runnymede Memorial Panel 13.

Of the nine Czechoslovakians killed during the battle, only two are buried in the Czech national plot (No. 28) at Brookwood — Sergeant Jan Chalupa and Pilot Officer Emil Fechtner. Two Czechs were never found (Sergeant Vladimir Horsky and Pilot Officer Jaroslav Sterbacek) and the others lie buried in cemeteries all over England.

EGAN, Sgt. E. J. British. No. 501 Squadron 17:9:40 19yrs. Originally remembered on Runnymede Memorial Panel 14, now buried at Brookwood Military Cemetery. Plot 24 Row D Grave 16.

ELCOME, Sgt. D. W. British. No. 602 Squadron 26:10:40 21yrs. Runnymede Memorial Panel 14.

ELEY, Sgt. F. W. British. No. 74 Squadron 31:7:40 21yrs. Wrenbury (St. Margaret) Churchyard, Wrenbury Cum Frith, Cheshire. Centre Part Row 4 Grave 11.

ELLIS, Sgt. J. H. M. British. No. 85 Squadron 1:9:40 21yrs. Runnymede Memorial Panel 14.

ELSDON, Sgt. H. D. B. British. No. 236 Squadron 18:7:40 28yrs. Runnymede Memorial Panel 14.

ENGLISH, P/O C. E. British. No. 605 Squadron 7:10:40 28yrs. Newcastle-upon-Tyne (SS Andrews and Jesmond) Cemetery, Northumberland. Section B Consecrated Joint Grave 213.

EYLES, Sgt. P. R. British. No. 92 Squadron 20:9:40 24yrs. Runnymede Memorial Panel 14.

FARROW, Sgt. J. R. British. No. 229 Squadron 8:10:40 24yrs. Northwood Cemetery, Ruislip-Northwood, Middlesex. Section H Grave 230.

FEARY, Sgt. A. N. British. No. 609 Squadron 7:10:40 28yrs. Warmwell (Holy Trinity) Churchyard, Dorset. South part.

The story of Sergeant Eddie Egan (above) is a tribute to the perseverence of amateur aviation archaeologists. His body was never found in 1940 and he was listed as a missing airman on the Runnymede Memorial. Thirty-six years later his crash site was located at Bethersden and the aircraft excavated together with his remains. Although a Croydon inquest identified these as being of Sergeant Egan, the Ministry of Defence refused to

FECHTNER P/O E., DFC, Czechoslovakian. No. 310 Squadron 29:10:40 24yrs. Brookwood Military Cemetery. Plot 28 Row E Grave 1.

FENEMORE, Sgt. S. A. British. No. 501 Squadron 15:10:40 20yrs. Liverpool (Allerton) Cemetery, Lancashire. Section 2D, Church of England Grave 218.

FERRISS, F/Lt. H. M., DFC, British. No. 111 Squadron 16:8:40 22yrs. Chislehurst (St. Mary) Roman Catholic Churchyard, Chislehurst-Sidcup, Kent.

FINNIE, P/O A. British. No. 54 Squadron 25:7:40 24yrs. Margate Cemetery, Kent. Section 50 Grave 15937.

FISHER, F/O B. M. British. No. 111 Squadron 15:8:40 23yrs. Eton (St. John) Church Cemetery, Buckinghamshire. Grave 41.

FISKE, III P/O W. M. L. American. No. 601 Squadron. Seriously burned 16:8:40. Died 17:8:40 29yrs. Boxgrove (SS Mary & Blaise) Churchyard, Sussex. Section F Grave 2.

FLEMING, P/O R. D. S., British. No. 249 Squadron 7:9:40 20yrs. Golders Green Crematorium, Hendon. Panel 2.

FLETCHER, Sgt. J. G. B. British. No. 604 Squadron 25:8:40 20yrs. Forest Row Cemetery, Sussex. Grave 1289.

FLOOD, F/Lt. F. W. Australian. No. 235 Squadron 11:9:40 25yrs. Runnymede Memorial Panel 4.

accept the findings and he was buried at Brookwood as an unknown airman (above). Not to be thwarted by officialdom, four wreck groups combined on a re-dig of the site to find the aircraft identification plate. This small two-inch piece of brass was found and the Ministry relented and instructed the Commonwealth War Graves Commission to replace the headstone.

FORRESTER, P/O G. M. British. No. 605 Squadron 9:9:40 26yrs. Odiham Cemetery, Hampshire. North side. Grave 425.

FRANCIS, P/O C. D. British. No. 253 Squadron 30:8:40 19yrs. Runnymede Memorial Panel 8.

FRANTISEK, Sgt. J., DFM, Czechoslovakian. No. 303 Squadron 8:10:40 27yrs. Northwood Cemetery Ruislip-Northwood, Middlesex. Section H Grave 246.

FRASER, Sgt. R. H. B. British. No. 257 Squadron 22:10:40 20yrs. Glasgow (Craigton) Cemetery. Section FF. Grave 2213.

FRITH, Sgt. E. T. G. British. No. 92 Squadron. Seriously injured 9:10:40. Died 17:10:40 26yrs. Oxford (Botley) Cemetery, North Hinksey, Berkshire. Plot J/I Grave 3.

GAMBLEN, F/O D. R. British. No. 41 Squadron 29:7:40 25yrs. Runnymede Memorial Panel 5.

GANE, P/O S. R. British. No. 248 Squadron 20:10:40 20yrs. Trondheim (Stavne) Cemetery, Norway. AIV British. A.1.

GARDINER, Sgt. E. C. British. No. 219 Squadron 30:10:40 27yrs. Pontefract Cemetery, Yorkshire. Section U Grave 125.

GARFIELD, Sgt. W. J. British. No. 248 Squadron 13:9:40 25yrs. Bergen (Mollendal) Church Cemetery, Norway. Row B Grave 5.

GARVEY, Sgt. L. A. British. No. 41 Squadron 30:10:40 26yrs. Birmingham (Witton) Cemetery, Warwickshire. Section 56 Grave 10373.

GAUNT, P/O G. N. British. No. 609 Squadron 15:9:40 24yrs. Salendine Nook Baptist Chapel Yard, Huddersfield, Yorkshire. Section D Grave 337.

GILLAN, F/O J. British. No. 601 Squadron 11:8:40 26yrs. Runnymede Memorial Panel 5.

GILLIES, F/Lt. K. McL. British. No. 66 Squadron 4:10:40 27yrs. Thornton Garden of Rest, Lancashire. (North of Liverpool on B5422 road to Lunt.) Section A Grave 50.

GILLMAN, P/O K. R. British. No. 32 Squadron 25:8:40 19yrs. Runnymede Memorial Panel 8.

GIRDWOOD, Sgt. A. G. British. No. 257 Squadron 29:10:40 22yrs. Paisley (Hawkhead) Cemetery, Renfrew. Section A, Grave 2026.

GLEDHILL, Sgt. G. British. No. 238 Squadron 11:8:40 19yrs. Criquebeuf-en-Caux Churchyard, France. South-east corner.

GLOWACKI, P/O W. J. Polish. No. 605 Squadron 24:9:40 26yrs. Guines Communal Cemetery, France. Military Plot Grave 1. Also commemorated on the Polish Memorial, Northolt.

GLYDE, F/O R. L., DFC, Australian. No. 87 Squadron 13:8:40 26yrs. Runnymede Memorial Panel 5.

GMUR, Sgt. F. Polish. No. 151 Squadron 30:8:40 25yrs. Epping Cemetery, Essex. Section Z Grave 2. Also commemorated on the Polish Memorial, Northolt.

GOLDSMITH, F/O C. W. South African. No. 603 Squadron, Seriously injured 27:10:40. Died 28:10:40 23yrs. Hornchurch Cemetery, Essex. Section A Grave 1340.

GOODALL, P/O H. I. British. No. 264 Squadron 8:10:40 25yrs. Poole (Parkstone) Cemetery, Dorset. Section V Grave 87.

GOODWIN, Sgt. C. British. No. 219 Squadron 30:9:40 21yrs. Hull Northern Cemetery. Compartment 214 Grave 32.

GOODWIN, F/O H. McD. British. No. 609 Squadron 14:8:40 25yrs. Chaddesley Corbett (St. Cassian) Churchyard, Worcestershire. North-west corner.

GORDON P/O W. H. G. British. No. 234 Squadron 6:9:40 20yrs. Mortlach Parish Churchyard, Banff. Grave 1032.

GORE, F/Lt. W. E., DFC, British. No. 607 Squadron 28:9:40 25yrs. Runnymede Memorial Panel 4.

GOTH, P/O V. Czechoslovakian. No. 501 Squadron 25:10:40 25yrs. Sittingbourne & Milton (Sittingbourne) Cemetery, Kent. Old ground. Section W Grave 141.

GOULDSTONE, Sgt. R. J. British. No. 29 Squadron 25:8:40 19yrs. Ryarsh (St. Martin) Churchyard, Kent.

GOUT, P/O G. K. British. No. 234 Squadron 25:7:40 24yrs. St. Eval Churchyard, Cornwall. Row 1 Grave 13.

GRAY, Sgt. M. British. No. 72 Squadron 5:9:40 20yrs. Fulford Cemetery, North Yorkshire. Plot 13 Row W Grave 7.

GREEN, P/O A. W. V. British. No. 235 Squadron 11:9:40 21yrs. Runnymede Memorial Panel 8.

GREEN, P/O M. D. British. No. 248 Squadron 20:10:40 20yrs. Runnymede Memorial Panel 8.

GREENSHIELDS (F.A.A.), Sub/Lt. H. L. British. No. 266 Squadron 16:8:40 22yrs. Calais Southern Cemetery, France. Plot P Grave 18.

GREENWOOD, Sgt. E. G. British. No. 245 Squadron 21:10:40 22yrs. Runnymede Memorial Panel 14.

GREGORY, P/O F. S. British. No. 65 Squadron 13:8:40 21yrs. Enfield Crematorium, Middlesex. Panel 1.

GRICE, F/O D. N. British. No. 600 Squadron 8:8:40 28yrs. Charing (Kent County) Crematorium.

Sergeant Pilot Tim Frith (left) was the youngest son of Mr. and Mrs. Arthur Frith of Cowley, Oxford. He went to school at Bedford House and Southfields and later joined the staff of Morris Motors Limited. He was a keen sportsman and member of the YMCA. Flying from Biggin Hill, he was shot down in flames near Ashford on October 9 and died eight days later from his burns.

Oxford Cemetery at Botley lies two miles to the west of the city. The majority of the war graves are concentrated in the Commission plot as this was selected as a Royal Air Force Regional Cemetery and the total number of Second World War burials is 580. Tim Frith is one of the twelve servicemen not buried in this plot and having private headstones.

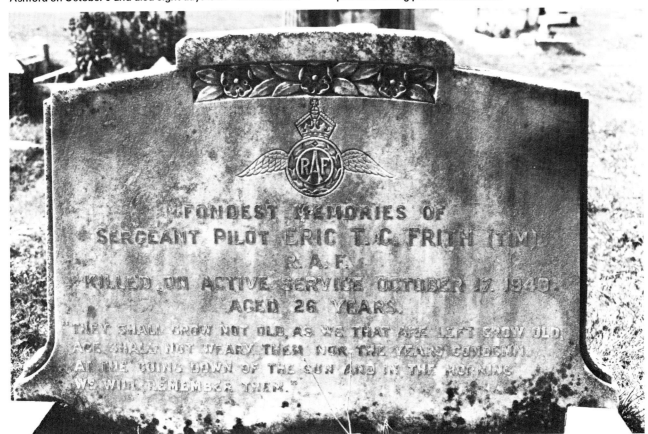

Flying Officer Franciszek Gruszka was flying with No. 65 Squadron when he crashed into a marsh near Canterbury on August 18. The pilot was not recovered and in 1948 his name was included on the Polish Memorial at Northolt (which is intended to commemorate all Polish aircrew who died operationally whether they have graves or not). On March 28, 1971, parts of a Spitfire including the engine were excavated at Westbere, positively identified as R6713, the aircraft Gruszka was flying. Police were present as it was anticipated that the pilot's remains would be recovered. Athough it was stated at the time that no evidence of the pilot was found, in 1976 a team from RAF Bicester was detailed to re-excavate the site. On this occasion human remains were uncovered which were later buried at Northwood Cemetery with full military honours.

GRUSZKA, F/O F. Polish. No. 65 Squadron 18:8:40 30yrs. Originally remembered on the Polish Memorial Northolt, now buried at Northwood Cemetery, Ruislip-Northwood, Middlesex. Section H Grave 202.

GUNN, P/O H. R. British. No. 74 Squadron 31:7:40 27yrs. Ostende New Communal Cemetery, Belgium. Plot 9 Row 3 Grave 20.

GUNNING, P/O P. S. British. No. 46 Squadron 15:10:40 29yrs. North Weald Bassett (St. Andrew) Churchyard, Essex. Row 2 Grave 9.

GUNTER, P/O E. M. British. No. 501 Squadron 27:9:40 20yrs. Aldeby (St. Mary) Churchyard, Norfolk.

GURTEEN, P/O J. V. British. No. 504 Squadron 15:9:40 24yrs. Hendon Crematorium. Panel 5.

GUY, Sgt. L. N. British. No. 601 Squadron 18:8:40 25yrs. Runnymede Memorial Panel 14.

HAIGH, Sgt. C. British. No. 604 Squadron 25:8:40 23yrs. Swinton (St. Margaret) Churchyard, Yorkshire. Section E Row D Grave 42.

HALL, F/Lt. N. M., AFC, British. No. 257 Squadron 8:8:40 24yrs. Criel Communal Cemetery, France. Grave 10.

HALTON, Sgt. D. W. British. No. 615 Squadron 15:8:40 21yrs. Runnymede Memorial Panel 14.

HAMAR, P/O J. R., DFC British. No. 151 Squadron 24:7:40 25yrs. Knighton Cemetery, Radnorshire. Row K Grave 9.

HAMILTON, P/O A. C. British. No. 141 Squadron 19:7:40 28yrs. Folkestone New Cemetery, Kent. Plot O Grave 12.

HAMILTON, F/Lt. H. R. Canadian. No. 85 Squadron 29:8:40 23yrs. Folkestone New Cemetery, Kent. Plot O Grave 26.

HANSON, F/O D. H. W. British. No. 17 Squadron 3:9:40 22yrs. Mappleton (All Saints) Churchyard, Yorkshire.

HANZLICEK, Sgt. O. Czechoslovakian. No. 312 Squadron 10:10:40 29yrs. Liverpool (West Derby) Cemetery. Section 11 Roman Catholic Collective Grave 392.

HARDACRE, F/O J. R. British. No. 504 Squadron 30:9:40 24yrs. Fawley (All Saints) Churchyard, Hampshire. Old portion. Row 2 Grave 8.

HARGREAVES, P/O F. N. British. No. 92 Squadron 11:9:40 21yrs. Runnymede Memorial Panel 8.

Franciszek Gruszka was given a British Commonwealth-style headstone as he was serving with an RAF squadron (No. 65) when he was killed. He was buried in Georges Doutrepont's old grave, No. 202, at Northwood Cemetery, Middlesex.

HARRISON, P/O D. S. British. No. 238 Squadron 28:9:40 29yrs. Tangmere (St. Andrew) Churchyard, Sussex. Row 1 Grave 482.

HARRISON, P/O J. H. British. No. 145 Squadron 12:8:40 22yrs. Runnymede Memorial Panel 8.

HARROLD, P/O F. C. British. No. 501 Squadron 28:9:40 23yrs. Cherry Hinton (St. Andrew) Churchyard, Cambridge.

HASTINGS, P/O D. British. No. 74 Squadron 8:10:40 25yrs. Tynemouth (Preston) Cemetery, Northumberland. Section C Unconsecrated Grave 12984.

HAWKINGS, Sgt. R. P. British. No. 601 Squadron 18:8:40 25yrs. Filton (St. Peter) Churchyard, Gloucester. North-east of church. Row 17 Grave 3

HAWLEY, Sgt. F. B. British. No. 266 Squadron 15:8:40 23yrs. Runnymede Memorial Panel 15.

HAWORTH, F/O J. F. J. British. No. 43 Squadron 20:7:40 23yrs. Runnymede Memorial Panel 5.

HEAD, Sgt. F. A. P. British. No. 236 Squadron 1:8:40 25yrs. Runnymede Memorial Panel 15.

HELCKE, Sgt. D. A. British. No. 504 Squadron 17:9:40 24yrs. Herne Bay Cemetery, Kent. Section DDR Grave 16.

HEWITT, P/O D. A. Canadian. No. 501 Squadron 12:7:40 20yrs. Runnymede Memorial Panel 8.

HEYWOOD, P/O N. B. British. No. 257 Squadron 22:10:40 22yrs. Stretford Cemetery, Manchester. Section N.1 Grave 210.

HIGGINS, Sgt. W. B. British. No. 253 Squadron 14:9:40 26yrs. Whitwell (St. Lawrence) Churchyard, Derbyshire.

HIGGS, F/O T. P. K. British. No. 111 Squadron 10:7:40 23yrs. Noordwijk General Cemetery, Netherlands. Plot 1 Joint Grave 8.

HIGHT, P/O C. H. New Zealander. No. 234 Squadron 15:8:40 22yrs. Bournemouth East Cemetery (in Gloucester Road), Boscombe, Hampshire. Row S.1 Grave 144.

HILL, P/O H. P. New Zealander. No. 92 Squadron 20:9:40 20yrs. Folkestone New Cemetery, Kent. Plot O Grave 30.

HILLCOAT, F/Lt. H. B. L. British. No. 1 Squadron 3:9:40 25yrs. Runnymede Memorial Panel 4.

HLAVAC, Sgt. J. Czechoslovakian. No. 56 Squadron 10:10:40 26yrs. Warmwell (Holy Trinity) Churchyard, Dorset. South part.

HOBSON, P/O C. A. British. No. 600 Squadron 3:10:40 21yrs. Banstead (All Saints) Churchyard, Surrey. West of church.

HOGG, P/O D. W. British. No. 25 Squadron 3:9:40 23yrs. Glasgow (Eastwood) Cemetery. Section H (New Part) Grave 278.

HOGG, P/O R. M. British. No. 152 Squadron 25:8:40 21yrs. Runnymede Memorial Panel 8.

HOLDER, Sgt. R. British. No. 151 Squadron 26:10:40 23yrs. Bidford-on-Avon Burial Ground, Warwickshire. Grave 217.

HOLLAND, P/O D. F. British. No. 72 Squadron 20:9:40 23yrs. St. Andrews Churchyard, Chaddleworth, Berkshire. North part.

HOLLAND, Sgt. K. C. Australian. No. 152 Squadron 25:9:40 20yrs. Weymouth Crematorium, Weymouth and Melcombe Regis, Dorset.

HOMER, F/O M. G., DFC, British. No. 242 Squadron 27:9:40 21yrs. Swanage (Godlingston) Cemetery, Dorset. Plot A Consecrated Grave 792.

HOOD, S/Ldr. H. R. L., DFC, British. No. 41 Squadron 5:9:40 32yrs. Runnymede Memorial Panel 4.

HOPE, F/O R. British. No. 605 Squadron 14:10:40 27yrs. Woking (St. John's) Crematorium, Surrey. Panel 2.

HORSKY, Sgt. V. Czechoslovakian. No. 238 Squadron 26:9:40 26yrs. Runnymede Memorial Panel 15.

HOUGHTON Sgt. O. V. British. No. 501 Squadron 6:9:40 19yrs. Allesley (All Saints) Churchyard Extension, Coventry. Centre B 29.

HOVE, van den d'ERTSENRYCK, P/O A. E. A. Belgian. Nos. 501-43 Squadrons 15:9:40. 32yrs. Exhumed and repatriated to Pelouse d'Honneur Cemetery of Brussels at Evere on 20:10:49.

A tragic photo. Before this picture left the camera, two of these men were dead. Pilots of No. 43 Squadron relax in the sun outside the Officers' Mess at Tangmere on Saturday, September 7, 1940. L-R, standing: Pilot Officer H. C. Upton, Pilot Officer A. E. A. van den Hove d'Ertsenryck and Pilot Officer D. Gorrie. L-R, seated: Pilot Officer F. R. Carey, Flight Lieutenant J. I. Kilmartin, Squadron Leader C. G. Lott, Flight Lieutenant R. C. Reynell and Squadron Leader C. B. Hull. Dick Reynell and Caesar Hull were killed in combat about three hours later and Albert van den Hove d'Ertsenryck died in action on September 15. George Lott had only just been discharged from hospital after being blinded in the right eye during combat on July 9, 1940 (J. Beedle).

The day after Pilot Officer Albert Emmanuel Alix van den Hove d'Ertsenryck was posted to No. 501 Squadron at Kenley, his Hurricane P2760 was severely damaged in a combat over Ashford. Although he attempted to bring the aircraft down, it exploded 200ft over East Stour Farm at Chilham. His remains were taken to St. Stephen's Churchyard at Lympne near Hythe, Kent. Although he was exhumed and reburied in Brussels in 1949 (photo left), his original grave is still retained in the form of the small memorial above.

HOWES, P/O P. British. No. 603 Squadron 18:9:40 21yrs. Woking (St. John's) Crematorium, Surrey. Panel 3.

HOWLEY, P/O R. A. Canadian. No. 141 Squadron 19:7:40 20yrs. Runnymede Memorial Panel 27.

HUGHES, Sgt. D. E. New Zealander. No. 600 Squadron 3:10:40 28yrs. Whyteleafe (St. Luke) Churchyard, Caterham and Warlingham, Surrey. Row E Grave 32.

HUGHES, F/Lt. D. P., DFC, British. No. 238 Squadron 11:9:40 22yrs. Runnymede Memorial Panel 4

HUGHES, F/Lt. P. C., DFC, Australian. No. 234 Squadron 7:9:40 23yrs. Sutton (or Sutton-in-Holderness) St. James Churchyard, Hull. Row G Grave 4.

HULL, S/Ldr. C. B., DFC, South African. No. 43 Squadron 7:9:40 27yrs. Tangmere (St. Andrew) Churchyard, Sussex. Row 1 Grave 477.

HUNTER, S/Ldr. P. A., DSO, British. No. 264 Squadron 24:8:40 27yrs. Runnymede Memorial Panel 4.

HURST, P/O P. R. S. British. No. 600 Squadron 23:10:40 20yrs. Catterick Cemetery, Yorkshire. Church of England Section Row M Grave 14.

HUTLEY, P/O R. R. British. No. 213 Squadron 29:10:40 22yrs. Tangmere (St. Andrew) Churchyard, Sussex. Row 2, Grave 484.

IRELAND, Sgt. S. British. No. 610 Squadron 12:7:40 22yrs. Knockbreda Church of Ireland Churchyard, Newtownbreda, Northern Ireland. Section E Grave 78.

IRVING, F/Lt. M. M. British. No. 607 Squadron 28:9:40 29yrs. Runnymede Memorial Panel 4.

ISAAC, Sgt. L. R. British. No. 64 Squadron 5:8:40 24yrs. Runnymede Memorial Panel 15.

JACKSON, AC2 A. British. No. 29 Squadron 13:10:40 29yrs. Mexborough Cemetery, Yorkshire. Section D Unconsecrated Grave 642.

JACOBSON, AC2 N. British. No. 29 Squadron 25:8:40 18yrs. Runnymede Memorial Panel 27.

JANUSZEWICZ, F/O W. Polish. No. 303 Squadron 5:10:40 29yrs. Northwood Cemetery, Ruislip-Northwood, Middlesex. Section H Grave 231. Also commemorated on the Polish Memorial, Northolt, but as a Flight Lieutenant.

JASTRZEBSKI, F/Lt. F. Polish. No. 302 Squadron 25:10:40 34yrs. Kiel War Cemetery, Germany. Plot 4 Row H Grave 6. Also commemorated on the Polish Memorial, Northolt.

JAY, P/O D. T., DFC, British. No. 87 Squadron 24:10:40 19yrs. Exeter Higher Cemetery, Heavitree, Exeter, Devon. Section ZK Grave 33.

JEBB, F/O M. British. No. 504 Squadron. Seriously injured 15:9:40. Died 19:9:40 22yrs. Hendon Crematorium. Panel 5.

JEFF, F/Lt. R. V., DFC and Bar, CdeG, British. No. 87 Squadron 11:8:40 27yrs. Runnymede Memorial Panel 4.

JEFFREY, F/O A. J. O., DFC, British. No. 64 Squadron 25:7:40 22yrs. Flushing (Vlissingen) Northern Cemetery, Netherlands. Row A Joint Grave 5.

JEFFERYS, Sgt. G. W. British. No. 46 Squadron 18:9:40 20yrs. Winterbourne Earls (St. Michael) Churchyard, Winterbourne, Wiltshire.

JENKINS, P/O D. N. O. British, No. 253 Squadron 30:8:40 21yrs. Bagendon (St. Margaret) Churchyard, Gloucestershire. South-east corner.

JOHNSON, P/O C. E. British. No. 264 Squadron 28:8:40 35yrs. Folkestone New Cemetery, Kent. Plot O Grave 27.

JOHNSON, Sgt. J. I. British. No. 222 Squadron 30:8:40 26yrs. Towcester Cemetery, Northamptonshire. Row G Grave 2.

JOHNSTON, P/O J. T. Canadian. No. 151 Squadron 15:8:40 26yrs. Folkestone New Cemetery, Kent. Plot O. Grave 16.

JONES, P/O J. S. B. British. No. 152 Squadron 11:8:40 21yrs. Ste. Marie Cemetery, Le Havre, France. Division 64 Plot 6 Row B Grave 7.

JONES, P/O J. T. British. No. 264 Squadron 24:8:40 21yrs. Runnymede Memorial Panel 8.

JOTTARD, P/O A. R. I. G. Belgian. No. 145 Squadron 27:10:40 28yrs. Runnymede Memorial Panel 8. Also has a memorial grave in the Pelouse d'Honneur Cemetery of Brussels at Evere.

JOWITT, Sgt. L. British. No. 85 Squadron 12:7:40 28yrs. Runnymede Memorial Panel 16.

KARASEK, Sgt. L. R. British. No. 23 Squadron 25:9:40 23yrs. Over Wallop (St. Peter) Churchyard, Hampshire. Row A Grave 2.

KAY, Sgt. A. British. No. 248 Squadron 13:9:40 24yrs. Runnymede Memorial Panel 16.

KAY-SHUTTLEWORTH, F/O Lord R. U. P. British. No. 145 Squadron 8:8:40 27yrs. Runnymede Memorial Panel 4.

KEAST, Sgt. F. J. British. No. 600 Squadron 8:8:40 31yrs. Whitstable Cemetery, Kent. Section 4A Grave 16.

KEEL, Sgt. G. E. British. No. 235 Squadron 9:10:40 20yrs. Portsmouth Eastney (or Highland Road) Cemetery, Hampshire. Section M (south wall) Row 2 Grave 4.

Altogether, the CWGC is responsible for the maintenance of 23,589 burial places in 140 countries throughout the world. This is Flushing (Vlissingen) Northern Cemetery in the Netherlands where Flying Officer Alistair Jeffrey lies buried.

Squadron Leader Caesar Barraud Hull, DFC, was born at Shanganie, Southern Rhodesia in 1914 and educated at St. John's College, Johannesburg, South Africa. He commenced his flying career as an aircrew cadet in the South African Air Force Reserve. He was appointed to a short service commission in the Royal Air Force and, on August 8, 1936, joined No. 43 Squadron at Tangmere as a Pilot Officer. In May 1940 he was posted as a flight commander to No. 263 Squadron which was despatched to Norway to provide air cover for the evacuation of British troops. His exploits against the overwhelming Luftwaffe forces are legendary. Badly wounded, he was flown home and after recovery rejoined the Squadron at Drem on July 3. On September 1, he returned to Tangmere to command his old unit and, six days later, was shot down into the grounds of Purley High School and killed.

A form of unofficial testimonial issued to next of kin, this one from Squadron Leader G. D. Garvin to one of the Defiant gunners, Pilot Officer Charles Johnson, who perished in the last daytime sortie by this type of aircraft before it was withdrawn as unsuitable for combat.

KEMP, P/O J. R. New Zealander. No. 141 Squadron 19:7:40 25yrs. Runnymede Memorial Panel 8.

KENNARD-DAVIS, P/O P. F. British. No. 64 Squadron. Seriously injured 8:8:40. Died 10:8:40 19yrs. Brookwood Cemetery, Surrey. St. Cyprian's Avenue Grave 202344. (Not Military Cemetery.)

KENNEDY, F/Lt. J. C. Australian. No. 238 Squadron 13:7:40 23yrs. Warmwell (Holy Trinity) Churchyard, Dorset. South part.

KENNER, P/O P. L. British. No. 264 Squadron 28:8:40 21yrs. Brentwood (London Road) Cemetery, Essex. Plot L Grave 106.

KESTIN (F.A.A.), Sub/Lt. I. H. British. No. 145 Squadron 1:8:40 23yrs. Lee-on-Solent, Fleet Air Arm Memorial. Bay 1, Panel 6.

KEYMER, Sgt. M. British. No. 65 Squadron 22:8:40 24yrs. Bazinghen Churchyard, France. Western corner.

KIDSON, P/O R. New Zealander. No. 141 Squadron 19:7:40 26yrs. Runnymede Memorial Panel 9.

KING, S/Ldr. E. B. British. No. 151 Squadron 30:8:40 29yrs. Highgate Cemetery, St. Pancras. Square 74 Grave 40453.

KING, P/O F. H., DFM, British. No. 264 Squadron 24:8:40 24yrs. Runnymede Memorial Panel 9.

KING, P/O M. A. British. No. 249 Squadron 16:8:40 19yrs. Fawley (All Saints) Churchyard, Hampshire. Old portion Row 2 Grave 7.

KING, F/O P. J. C. British. No. 66 Squadron 5:9:40 19yrs. Farnborough (St. Botolph) Churchyard, Warwickshire. South-east corner.

KIRK, Sgt. T. B. British. No. 74 Squadron. Seriously wounded 20:10:40. Died 22:7:41 22yrs. East Harlsey (St. Oswald) Churchyard, Yorkshire. New part Row 2 Grave 29.

KIRKPATRICK, P/O J. C. Belgian. No. 235 Squadron 9:10:40 25yrs. Runnymede Memorial Panel 9. Also has a memorial grave in the Pelouse d'Honneur Cemetery of Brussels at Evere.

KIRTON, Sgt. D. I. British. No. 65 Squadron 8:8:40 21yrs. Dover (St. James's) Cemetery, Kent. Section KV Grave 22.

KREPSKI, P/O W. Polish. No. 54 Squadron 7:9:40 23yrs. Polish Memorial, Northolt, but as a Flying Officer.

KWIECINSKI, Sgt. J. Polish. No. 145 Squadron 12:8:40 23yrs. Polish Memorial, Northolt.

LAMBERT, F/O H. M. S. British. No. 25 Squadron 15:9:40 22yrs. Reading (Henley Road) Crematorium, Eye and Dunsden, Berkshire. Panel 1.

LANGLEY, P/O G. A. British. No. 41 Squadron 15:9:40 24yrs. Abington (SS. Peter and Paul) Churchyard, Northamptonshire. Grave 1300.

LANSDELL, Sgt. J. British. No. 607 Squadron 17:9:40 23yrs. Hempnall (St. Margaret) Churchyard, Norfolk (old part behind church).

LARICHELIERE. P/O J. E. P. Canadian. No. 213 Squadron 16:8:40 27yrs. Runnymede Memorial Panel 9.

Another aspect of the work of the CWGC is the provision for engraved memorials to those who were cremated. The stone illustrated, which includes the name of Flying Officer Hugh Lambert who died while based at North Weald, is at Reading Crematorium which stands in the grounds of the cemetery in Henley Road, Eye and Dunsden, Berkshire.

THE BATTLE OF BRITAIN AUGUST 28th 1940

In the short time P/O C. . Johnson had been with the squadron, he had been very successful. He was recalled from leave, to take part in the activities at Hornchurch as he knew his job thoroughly and was reliable. The squadron can ill-afford his loss.

ours Sincerely,

Squadron Leader, Commanding, No. 264 Squadron, R. .F.,

LECKY, P/O J. G. British. No. 41 Squadron 11:10:40 19yrs. Tilford (All Saints) Church-yard, Surrey. South-west of church.

LEE, F/O R. H. A., DSO, DFC, British. No. 85 Squadron 18:8:40 23yrs. Runnymede Memorial Panel 6.

LENAHAN, P/O J. D. British. No. 607 Squadron 9:9:40 20yrs. Cranbrook Cemetery, Kent. Section O Grave 58.

LITCHFIELD, P/O P. British. No. 610 Squadron 18:7:40 25yrs. Runnymede Memorial Panel 9.

LITTLE, Sgt. R. British. No. 238 Squadron 28:9:40 22yrs. Runnymede Memorial Panel 16.

LLOYD, Sgt. P. D. British. No. 41 Squadron 15:10:40 23yrs. High Beech (Holy Innocents) Churchyard, Essex.

LOCKTON, Sgt. E. E. British. No. 236 Squadron 20:7:40 22yrs. Runnymede Memorial Panel 16.

LOVELL-GREGG, S/Ldr. T. G. New Zealander. No. 87 Squadron 15:8:40 27yrs. Warmwell (Holy Trinity) Churchyard, Dorset.

LOVETT, F/Lt. R. E., DFC, British. No. 73 Squadron 7:9:40 26yrs. Hendon Cemetery. Section J9 Grave 39576.

One of the two graves of Battle of Britain aircrew in this list that we found unmarked belongs to Pilot Officer John Lenahan at Cranbrook Cemetery, Kent. However, when we checked with the CWGC, they informed us that the stone had temporarily been removed to add an additional inscription to his mother.

One of the most tragic losses during the battle was that of Sergeant Lloyd. Philip David Lloyd was born in Loughton on the fringe of Epping Forest. He attended the Boys' High School and then commenced employment in the office of the Chigwell Urban District Council (as had a future RAF fighter 'ace' then Pilot Officer but now Air Vice-Marshal Johnny Johnson). About the time of the Munich crisis he joined the RAF Volunteer Reserve learning to fly at nearby Stapleford Tawney aerodrome. On Saturday, August 24, 1940, Sergeant Pilot Philip Lloyd married the girl he had known since his schooldays in the Church of the Holy Innocents, deep in the forest at High Beach. They were parted after two weeks when he took up his posting as a replacement pilot with No. 41 Squadron then resting at Catterick. Tuesday, September 3 saw the return of No. 41 to Hornchurch and the mounting fury of the battle. Over the next few weeks, the squadron took hefty losses, but Sergeant Lloyd seemed to bear a charmed life. Then, in the early morning of Tuesday, October 15, the 23-year-old pilot set off on a routine coastal patrol from which he never returned. On October 27, his body was discovered on the beach at Herne Bay and, a few days later, Philip Lloyd returned for ever to the little church where he had been married just two months before.

LUKASZEWICZ, F/O K. Polish. No. 501 Squadron 12:8:40 27yrs. Polish Memorial, Northolt.

McAVITY, F/O G. F. British. No. 3 Squadron 19:10:40 29yrs. Olrig New Cemetery, Caithness. Section A Grave 109.

McCAUL AC2 J. P. British. No. 219 Squadron 30:9:40 28yrs. Leigh Cemetery, Lancashire. Section 25 Grave J8.

MacCAW, F/O D. C. British. No.· 238 Squadron 8:8:40 24yrs. Senneville-sur-Fecamp Churchyard, France. Grave 5.

MACDONALD, P/O D. K. British. No. 603 Squadron 28:8:40 22yrs. Runnymede Memorial Panel 9.

MACDONALD, F/Lt. H. K. British. No. 603 Squadron 28:9:40 28yrs. Edinburgh (Warriston) Crematorium Panel 3.

McDONOUGH, P/O B. M. Australian. No. 236 Squadron 1:8:40 23yrs. Runnymede Memorial Panel 9.

McGIBBON, P/O J. British. No. 615 Squadron 29:9:40 25yrs. Faslane Cemetery, Rhu, Dumbartonshire. Section R Grave 55.

MACHIN, Sgt. W. H. British. No. 264 Squadron 24:8:40 20yrs. Birmingham (Handsworth) Cemetery. Section 22 Church of England Class B Grave 12885.

MACINSKI, P/O J. Polish No. 111 Squadron 4:9:40 24yrs. Polish Memorial, Northolt, but as Flying Officer.

McINTOSH, Sgt. P. R. C. British. No. 605 Squadron 12:10:40 20yrs. Shirley (St. John) Churchyard, Croydon, Surrey. Section N Grave 276.

McKENZIE, P/O J. W. British. No. 111 Squadron 11:8:40 20yrs. Runnymede Memorial Panel 9.

MACKINNON, Sgt. D. D. British. No. 236 Squadron 13:7:40 21yrs. Villerville Communal Cemetery, France. Grave 1.

McNAY, Sgt. A. L. British. No. 73 Squadron 5:9:40 22yrs. Runnymede Memorial Panel 17.

MAFFETT, P/O G. H. British. No. 257 Squadron 31:8:40 24yrs. Windsor Road Cemetery, Bray, Berkshire. Section O Grave 42.

MAIN, Sgt. A. D. W. British. No. 249 Squadron 16:7:40 22yrs. Dundee Crematorium, Angus.

MALES, P/O E. E. British. No. 72 Squadron 27:9:40 20yrs. Great Northern London Cemetery. Section K Grave 1383.

MANGER, P/O K., DFC, British. No. 17 Squadron 11:8:40 23yrs. Runnymede Memorial Panel 9.

Royal Air Force
Martlesham Heath,
Woodbridge,
Suffolk.
22-8-40

My Dear Mum & Dad,

Just a line to let you know that I am at the above address: we came here four days ago for four or five days but it looks as if we will stay here for another ten days or so. We start at 0430 hrs and go on until 2130 hrs with about 35 minutes off for each meal. Last Tuesday I had a cup of cocoa at 0400 and breakfast at 1115, a plate of soup at 1400 hrs and dinner at 2000 hrs. Actually it was a very bad day and now things are much better although we still get up before 0400 hrs.

You remember the other day when the Hun sent over about 60 aircraft heading towards London via the Thames estuary: well it was 247(F) squadron who headed them off. When they were turning round in formation other fighters joined us and we had quite a good scrap while it lasted. I got in about three attacks — the first at the leading bombers: we were also in formation. The next was alone and I was lucky enough to have a crack at the leader of a sub-formation of five Heinkel 111s. I think it was probably rather unpleasant for them as I found them above me and I fired from a position where they could not fire at me. I think the leader was damaged. The third and last attack was on the middle of the main formation and I picked out a Dornier 215. I attacked him from above and dived down on him. The intelligence people have given me the aircraft as shot down as there was quite a glow in the fuselage as I dived away. I suggested that the glow may have been the sun but they think he was destroyed. The amazing part of the whole show was that my aircraft was not even scratched let alone hit — the Hurricane certainly is a grand aircraft.

I think you had better write to Debden as I do not know when I shall leave here.

I am off on a convoy patrol in a few minutes so I must finish to catch the post.

Love to you both.

Nine days after Pilot Officer Gerard Maffett wrote this last letter to his parents, twelve Hurricanes from his squadron encountered an enemy force over Clacton which outnumbered them four to one. Two Hurricanes were lost, one flown by Gerard crashing onto the foreshore at Walton-on-the-Naze. Today he is unique among all the casualties of the battle as his grave is still marked with the original 1940 Imperial War Graves Commission cross at the special wish of his mother who died in 1975 aged 100.

VOLUNTEER FOR FLYING DUTIES

You can be accepted

NOW

For the **R.A.F.** as a

PILOT (AGE 18 TO 30)

AIR OBSERVER (AGE 18 TO 32)

WIRELESS OPERATOR/ AIR GUNNER (AGE 18 TO 32)

APPLY

R.A.F. SECTION
COMBINED
RECRUITING CENTRE

'He was the loveliest and most precious gift that God could bestow on any mortal here on earth, and I, his mother, shall mourn him all the rest of my days'. So wrote Mrs. Constance Marchand at the end of her diary which she later had privately printed.

The grave of Pilot Officer Roy Marchand in Bromley Hill Cemetery at Lewisham was marked with the most impressive of all the private headstones on this list of Battle of Britain aircrew. Roy was also the young pilot depicted on the well-known RAF wartime recruiting posters *opposite* (Tony Graves).

After Mrs. Marchand died on March 22, 1971 in Switzerland, her husband gave permission for the London Air Museum to remove the complete headstone and curb for display in their museum.

When the latter folded, the headstone was transported to a farm in Kent where the editor photographed it in December 1979 *left* and also the grave as it is today *right*.

Flight Lieutenant Ian James Muirhead, DFC, was born in West Ham, his family later moving to Carlisle. He joined the Royal Air Force before the war and on the outbreak of hostilities was serving as a Flight Sergeant pilot with No. 151 Squadron at North Weald. Early in 1940 he received his commission and in March was posted as a Pilot Officer to No. 605 Squadron. He took part in the air fighting over France and on one occasion was shot down behind the German lines. Successfully evading capture, he returned to the UK and his squadron. The next few months were spent at the Scottish aerodrome at Drem and it was not until September 8 that No. 605 came south to join the battle, flying from Croydon. On October 7, 1940 he was shot down over south London by Bf 109s but baled out unhurt. Eight days later, he met his death near Gillingham when his Hurricane crashed to earth at Spekes Bottom after combat with enemy fighters over Maidstone. *Above:* As he was and *right* as depicted by artist Cuthbert Orde.

P/O. I.J. MUIRHEAD. D.F.C.   605 Squadron

MANTON, Sgt. E. British. No. 610 Squadron 28:8:40 25yrs. Hawkhurst Cemetery, Kent. Plot A Grave J62 (New cemetery beside A229 south of village).

Official Casualty Records state that this officer was killed in action on August 28, 1940 contrary to the details shown in the Form 540. No. 610 Squadron Operations Record Book which indicates that he was shot down on August 29. The Burial Register of Hawkhurst Cemetery also shows the date of death of 'Sergeant (Pilot) Edward Manton 81001 RSF (Aux) 610 Squadron August 28, 1940.

MARCHAND, P/O R. A. British. No. 73 Squadron 15:9:40 22yrs. Bromley Hill Cemetery, Lewisham. Block I Grave 230.

MAREK, Sgt. F. Czechoslovakian. No. 19 Squadron 14:9:40 27yrs. Eastbrookend Cemetery, Barking, Essex. Square C2 Grave 691.

MARSH, Sgt. H. J. British. No. 238 Squadron 13:8:40 27yrs. Runnymede Memorial Panel 17.

MATHER, P/O J. R. British. No. 66 Squadron 27:10:40 25yrs. Ifield (St. Margaret) Churchyard, Crawley, Sussex.

MATTHEWS, F/O H. K. F. British. No. 603 Squadron 7:10:40 28yrs. Crystal Palace District Cemetery. Section P9 Grave 14775.

MAXWELL, Sgt. W. British. No. 264 Squadron 26:8:40 23yrs. Runnymede Memorial Panel 17.

MAY, Sgt. L. D. British. No. 601 Squadron 25:10:40 21yrs. Runnymede Memorial Panel 17.

MEAKER, P/O J. R. B., DFC, British. No. 249 Squadron 27:9:40 21yrs. West Dean Cemetery, Sussex. Grave 243.

MEESON, Sgt. C. V. British. No. 56 Squadron 20:9:40 21yrs. Loughton Burial Ground, Loughton, Essex. Section E Grave 749.

MESNER, Sgt. B. W. British. No. 248 Squadron 13:9:40 29yrs. Runnymede Memorial Panel 17.

MILEY, F/O M. J. British. No. 25 Squadron 15:9:40 22yrs. North Weald Bassett (St. Andrew) Churchyard, Essex. Row 1 Grave 2.

MILLER, P/O R. F. G. Australian. No. 609 Squadron 27:9:40 20yrs. Radford Semele (St. Nicholas) Churchyard, Warwickshire. South-east of churchyard.

MILLINGTON, P/O W. H., DFC., Australian. No. 249 Squadron 30:10:40 23yrs. Runnymede Memorial Panel 9.

MILLS-SMITH, Sgt. F. British. No. 601 Squadron 25:10:40 22yrs. Runnymede Memorial Panel 17.

MITCHELL, P/O G. T. M. British. No. 609 Squadron 11:7:40 29yrs. Willian (All Saints) Churchyard, Letchworth, Hertfordshire. East of church.

MITCHELL, F/O L. R. G. British. No. 257 Squadron 7:9:40 24yrs. Runnymede Memorial Panel 6.

MOBERLY, F/O G. E. British. No. 616 Squadron 26:8:40 25yrs. Caterham and Warlingham (Caterham) Burial Ground, Surrey. Section A Grave 179.

MONTGOMERY, P/O C. R. British. No. 615 Squadron 14:8:40 26yrs. Oye-Plage Communal Cemetery, France. Row 1 Grave 19.

MONTGOMERY, Sgt. H. F. British. No. 43 Squadron 14:8:40 26yrs. Senneville-sur-Fecamp Churchyard, France. Grave 6.

MOODY, P/O H. W. British. No. 602 Squadron 7:9:40 30yrs. Runnymede Memorial Panel 9.

MORRISON, Sgt. J. P. British. No. 46 Squadron 22:10:40 25yrs. Newcastle-upon-Tyne (St. Andrews and Jesmond) Cemetery. Section O Unconsecrated Grave 277.

MOSS, (F.A.A.) Sub/Lt. W. J. M. British. No. 213 Squadron 27:8:40 23yrs. Lee-on-Solent Fleet Air Arm Memorial. Bay 1 Panel 3.

MUDIE, P/O M. R. British. No. 615 Squadron. Badly wounded 14:7:40. Died 15:7:40 24yrs. Esher Cemetery, East Molesey, Surrey. Class A Grave 1596.

MUIRHEAD, F/Lt. I. J., DFC, British. No. 605 Squadron 15:10:40 27yrs. Holme Cultram (St. Mary) Churchyard, Holme Abbey, Cumberland.

NEVILLE, Sgt. W. J. British. No. 610 Squadron 11:8:40 26yrs. Runnymede Memorial Panel 17.

NOBLE, Sgt. D. British. No. 43 Squadron 30:8:40 20yrs. East Retford Cemetery, Nottinghamshire. Section AK Grave 232.

NOKES-COOPER, F/O B. British. No. 236 Squadron 1:8:40 32yrs. Bayeux War Cemetery, France. Plot 29 Row K Grave 7.

NORRIS, Sgt. P. P. British. No. 213 Squadron 13:8:40 22yrs. Etaples Military Cemetery, France. Plot 46 Row B Grave 22.

O'BRIEN, S/Ldr. J. S., DFC, British. No. 234 Squadron 7:9:40 28yrs. Orpington (St. Mary Cray) Cemetery. Plot E Division 3 Grave 131.

OELOFSE, P/O J. R. S. South African. No. 43 Squadron 8:8:40 23yrs. Tangmere (St. Andrew) Churchyard, Sussex. Row 2 Grave 479.

As the Allied armies moved across the Continent in 1944-45, the Army Graves Registration Service were responsible for laying out all cemeteries. Graves were usually marked with white wooden or pressed steel crosses (the same as those now used in the Pelouse d'Honneur — see the three Belgian graves illustrated in this chapter). *Above:* This was the graveyard at Terschelling in Holland in 1945 where Sergeant Kenneth Parker was laid to rest. *Below:* These military cemeteries were progressively handed over to the Commonwealth War Graves Commission for permanent headstones and the Cross of Sacrifice (designed by Reginald Blomfield) to be added. Unlike the other combatants, as a general rule, British graves were never moved or concentrated into larger cemeteries.

OLDFIELD, Sgt. T. G. British. No. 92 Squadron 27:9:40 21yrs. Chertsey (St. Stephens) Church Burial Ground, Surrey. Plot F Grave 314.

O'MALLEY, F/O D. K. C. British. No. 264 Squadron 4:9:40 29yrs. Kirton-in-Lindsey Burial Ground, Lincolnshire. Block A Grave 181.

O'NEILL F/O D. H. British. No. 41 Squadron 11:10:40 25yrs. Streatham Park Cemetery, Mitcham. Square 7A Grave 12104.

ORGIAS, P/O E. New Zealander. No. 23 Squadron 25:9:40 25yrs. Over Wallop (St. Peter) Churchyard, Hampshire. Row A Grave 1.

OSTOWICZ, F/O A. Polish. No. 145 Squadron 11:8:40 29yrs. Polish Memorial, Northolt.

PANKRATZ, F/Lt. W. Polish. No. 145 Squadron 12:8:40 36yrs. Polish Memorial, Northolt.

PARKER, Sgt. K. B. British. No. 92 Squadron 15:10:40 25yrs. Terschelling (Westerschelling) General Cemetery, Netherlands. Grave 25.

PARKINSON, Sgt. C. British. No. 238 Squadron. Seriously injured 20:7:40. Died 21:7:40 25yrs. Stoke (St. Michael) Churchyard, Coventry. Block D Row 4 Grave 14.

PARNALL, F/Lt. D. G. British. No. 249 Squadron 18:9:40 25yrs. St. Gennys (St. Genesius) Churchyard, Cornwall.

PARNALL, P/O S. B. British. No. 607 Squadron 9:9:40 30yrs. Golders Green Crematorium, Hendon. Panel 3.

PASZKIEWICZ, F/O L. W., DFC, Polish. No. 303 Squadron 27:9:40 32yrs. Northwood, Ruislip-Northwood Cemetery, Middlesex. Section H Grave 224. Also commemorated on the Polish Memorial, Northolt, but as a Flight Lieutenant..

PATERSON, F/Lt. J. A., MBE, New Zealander. No. 92 Squadron 27:9:40 20yrs. Orpington (St. Mary Cray) Cemetery. Plot E Division 3 Grave 129.

PATTERSON, (F.A.A.) Midshipman P. J. British. No. 242 Squadron 20:8:40 19yrs. Fleet Air Arm Memorial, Lee-on-Solent. Bay 1 Panel 3.

PATTERSON, P/O R. L. British. No. 235 Squadron 18:7:40 26yrs. Runnymede Memorial Panel 9.

PATTINSON, F/O A. J. S. British. No. 92 Squadron 12:10:40 21yrs. Poole (Parkstone) Cemetery, Dorset. Section E Grave 46.

PATTISON, Sgt. K. C. British. No. 611 Squadron. Seriously injured 11:10:40. Died 13:10:40 27yrs. Nottingham Southern Cemetery, West Bridgeford. Section O16 Grave 26.

PATTULLO, P/O W. B. British. No. 46 Squadron. Seriously injured 25:10:40. Died 26:10:40 21yrs. North Weald Basset (St. Andrew) Churchyard, Essex. Row 2 Grave 8.

PAUL, (F.A.A.) Sub/Lt. F. D. British. No. 64 Squadron. Captured 25:7:40. Died 30:7:40 24yrs. Hardinghen Churchyard, France. Military Plot Grave 1.

One of the first families to lose two brothers in the Royal Air Force during the Second World War was that of Mr. and Mrs. J. B. Parnall of Walthamstow, then in Essex but now a borough of London. James (left) was killed in the Battle of France on May 14, 1940 and Stuart in the Battle of Britain on September 9, 1940. Their parents had this composite photograph made up from two separate pictures taken in December and January 1940 and this has been kindly supplied by their sister Estelle.

It is only since the beginning of the 20th century that the ancient custom of cremation instead of burial has been followed to any extent in the United Kingdom. The Cremation Society of England felt there was a need for a crematorium to serve the needs of the Metropolis and the London Cremation Company was formed in 1902. This is now called Golders Green Crematorium and Pilot Officer Stuart Boyd Parnall's name is included on the third of the three bronze panels of the CWGC Memorial which was designed by the Commission's Chief Architect and Artistic Adviser, Sir Edward Maufe, RA.

Ludwik Witold Paszkiewicz was a religious, serious-minded, 32-year-old serving officer in the Polish Air Force, flying obsolete fighters in the defence of his country during the German invasion in September 1939. With the fall of Poland, he made his way to France where he enlisted in the French Air Force and flew as a fighter pilot until that country's capitulation. He was then one of over four thousand Polish airmen who were evacuated by sea to the United Kingdom where he joined the Royal Air Force, being

posted to No. 303 Squadron on its formation on August 21, 1940. Nine days later while, on a training flight, he claimed the unit's first victory by shooting down a Do 17. Just four weeks later, Flying Officer Paszkiewicz was shot down at Borough Green in Kent and killed. During his brief operational career with the RAF he had accounted for six enemy aircraft (Polish Institute).

285

On September 6, 1940, a Hurricane crashed on Cowleas Farm at Hothfield. It would seem that although the pilot was identified at the time, this record became lost between examination at the mortuary and the funeral. Four days after the crash, an unknown British airman was buried at St. Stephen's Churchyard at Lympne eleven miles away. When the CWGC came to mark the grave permanently after the war, rather unusually for an unidentified serviceman, the date of death was included on the headstone. Sergeant Geoffrey Pearson of No. 501 Squadron was the only pilot missing on that date and we believe this is his grave.

PAYNE, AC2 R. I. British. No. 23 Squadron 25:9:40 31yrs. Treeton (St. Helen) Churchyard Extension, Yorkshire. Section NG Grave 36.

PEACOCK, Sgt. W. A. British. No. 46 Squadron 11:9:40 20yrs. Runnymede Memorial Panel 18.

PEARSON, Sgt. G. W. British. No. 501 Squadron 6:9:40 21yrs. Runnymede Memorial Panel 18.
Believed to be the dead airman recovered from his wrecked Hurricane at Cowleas Farm, Hothfield on this date and buried as an 'unknown airman' at St. Stephen's Churchyard, Lympne on 10:9:40.

PEARSON, Sgt. I. British. No. 65 Squadron 16:10:40 20yrs. Strathmiglo Parish Churchyard, Fife. Section K Grave 29.

PEASE, F/O A. P. British. No. 603 Squadron 15:9:40 22yrs. Middleton Tyas (St. Michael and All Angels) Churchyard, Yorkshire.

PEEL, F/O C. D. British. No. 603 Squadron 17:7:40 21yrs. Runnymede Memorial Panel 6.

PERRY, Sgt. H. T. British. No. 23 Squadron 30:10:40 23yrs. Saffron Walden Cemetery, Essex. Compartment 51 Grave 6.

PETERS, F/O G. C. B. British. No. 79 Squadron 29:9:40 27yrs. Rathnew Cemetery, County Wicklow, Eire. Grave 2252.

PETERSON, F/O O. J. Canadian No. 1 (RCAF)-401 Squadrons 27:9:40 24yrs. Brookwood Military Cemetery, Woking. Plot 3 Row K Grave 1A.

PHILIPPART, P/O J. A. L. Belgian. No. 213 Squadron 25:8:40 31yrs. Exhumed and repatriated to Pelouse d'Honneur, Cemetery of Brussels at Evere on 20:10:1949. Tomb II-11.

PHILLIPS, F/Sgt. N. T. British. No. 65 Squadron 8:8:40 31yrs. Chatham Cemetery, Kent. Section T Grave 54.

PIATKOWSKI, P/O S. Polish. No. 79 Squadron 25:10:40 28yrs. Pembrey (St. Illtyd) Churchyard, Carmarthenshire. Row 1 Collective Grave 11. Also commemorated on the Polish Memorial, Northolt, but as a Flying Officer.

PIDD, Sgt. L. British. No. 238 Squadron 15:9:40 22yrs. Woodmansey (St. Peter) Churchyard, Yorkshire.

When we visited Saffron Walden cemetery, we were surprised to find that Sergeant Tom Perry was only accorded the rank of Aircraftman 1st Class. When we pointed out the discrepancy to the CWGC, they were only too pleased to admit that an error had been made and to immediately order a replacement headstone. This error is not to be confused with the more serious one we discovered of the eight airmen who should have been promoted to the rank of Sergeant in 1940 but whom we found still listed as LACs, AC1s or AC2s.

The production of the book you are holding was the reason for the 'promotion' of Sergeant Perry from Aircraftman 1st Class.

PIGG, F/O O. St. John, British. No. 72 Squadron 2:9:40 22yrs. Durham (St. Oswald's) Burial Ground. Row 1 Grave 90.

Official Casualty Records state that this officer was killed in action on September 2, 1940. However two independent contemporary sources state otherwise:
Ashford ARP Centre
September 1, 1940 message timed at 14.38 hours.
'RAF 'plane down (at) Elvey Farm, Pluckley at 11.15 hours. 'Plane burnt out, pilot's fate unknown.'
Local Casualty Clearance Officer's Records
'Ashes of Flying Officer O. St. John Pigg No. 39678 collected from Elvey Farm, Pluckley nr Ashford. Notified 28/9/40. Collected 2/10/40 — Pluckley. Coffined body despatched to Durham.'

PINKHAM, S/Ldr. P. C., AFC, British. No. 19 Squadron 5:9:40 25yrs. Kingsbury (St. Andrew) Churchyard, Wembley. Section H Extension Grave 4.

PLUMMER, F/O R. P. British. No. 46 Squadron. Seriously burned 4:9:40. Died 14:9:40 28yrs. Haywards Heath (Western Road) Cemetery. Plot AC Grave 164.

PONTING, P/O W. A. British. No. 264 Squadron 24:8:40 30yrs. Runnymede Memorial Panel 9.

POSENER, P/O F. H. South African. No. 152 Squadron 20:7:40 23yrs. Runnymede Memorial Panel 9.

PYMAN, P/O L. L. British. No. 65 Squadron 16:8:40 23yrs. Calais Southern Cemetery, France. Plot Q Grave 18.

RAMSAY, P/O J. B. British. No. 151 Squadron 18:8:40 21yrs. Runnymede Memorial Panel 9.

Exeter Higher Cemetery at Heavitree is the last resting place for two Battle of Britain Hurricane pilots — Pilot Officer Dudley Jay, DFC, Mentioned in Despatches and Flying Officer Julian Topolnicki. Until 1949 it contained a third — Pilot Officer Jacques Phillipart — until he was exhumed for burial in Belgium.

287

RAMSHAW, Sgt. J. W. British. No. 222 Squadron 4:9:40 24yrs. Beverley (Queensgate) Cemetery, Yorkshire. Block 35 Grave 15.

RASMUSSEN, Sgt. L. A. W. New Zealander. No. 264 Squadron 4:9:40 18yrs. Kirton-in-Lindsey Burial Ground, Lincolnshire. Block A Grave 182.

RAVENHILL, F/O M. British. No. 229 Squadron 30:9:40 27yrs. Sheffield (City Road) Cemetery, Yorkshire (Beside A616 to Eckington). Section K Grave 5903.

REDDINGTON, Sgt. L. A. E. British. No. 152 Squadron 30:9:40 26yrs. Runnymede Memorial Panel 18.

REECE, Sgt. L. H. M. British. No. 235 Squadron 18:7:40 26yrs. Runnymede Memorial Panel 18.

REILLEY, P/O H. W. American but joined RAF as a Canadian. No. 66 Squadron 17:10:40 22yrs. Gravesend Cemetery, Kent. Plot B14 Grave 1271.

REYNELL, F/Lt. R. C. Australian. No. 43 Squadron 7:9:40 28yrs. Brookwood Cemetery, Surrey. St. Bartholomew's Avenue Grave 202417. (Not Military Cemetery.)

RHODES, P/O R. A. British. No. 29 Squadron 25:8:40 19yrs. Runnymede Memorial Panel 9.

RHODES-MOORHOUSE, F/Lt. W. H., DFC, British. No. 601 Squadron 6:9:40 26yrs. Parnham Private Cemetery, Beaminster, Dorset.

RICALTON, F/O A. L. British. No. 74 Squadron 17:10:40 26yrs. Sittingbourne and Milton (Sittingbourne) Cemetery, Kent. Old ground. Section W Grave 142.

RICHARDSON, Sgt. C. J. British. No. 29 Squadron 31:7:40 29yrs. Runnymede Memorial Panel 18.

RIDLEY, Sgt. M. British. No. 616 Squadron 26:8:40 24yrs. Folkestone New Cemetery, Kent. Plot O Grave 23.

RIGBY, P/O R. H. British. No. 236 Squadron 18:7:40 24yrs. Ste. Marie Cemetery, Le Havre, France. Division 67 Row D Grave 10.

RIMMER, F/Lt. R. F. British. No. 229 Squadron 27:9:40 21yrs. Hoylake (Grange) Cemetery, Cheshire. Section D Grave 79.

RINGWOOD, Sgt. E. A. British. No. 248 Squadron 27:8:40 20yrs. Runnymede Memorial Panel 18.

RITCHIE, Sgt. R. D. British. No. 605 Squadron 9:8:40 24yrs. Leslie Cemetery, Fife. West wall border Grave 103.

ROSE-PRICE, F/O A. T. British. No. 501 Squadron 2:9:40 21yrs. Runnymede Memorial Panel 6.

ROUND, Sgt. J. H. British. No. 248 Squadron 19:8:40 27yrs. Runnymede Memorial Panel 19.

ROZWADOWSKI, P/O M. Polish. No. 151 Squadron 15:8:40 25yrs. Polish Memorial, Northolt, but as a Flying Officer.

RUSHMER, F/Lt. F. W. British. No. 603 Squadron 5:9:40 30yrs. Runnymede Memorial Panel 4.

ST. JOHN, F/O P. C. B. British. No. 74 Squadron 22:10:40 23yrs. Amersham Consecrated Cemetery, Buckinghamshire (behind St. Mary's churchyard). Grave 2661.

SAMOLINSKI, P/O W. M. C. Polish. No. 253 Squadron 26:9:40 23yrs. Polish Memorial, Northolt, but as a Flying Officer.

SANDERS, F/O D. J. British. No. 54 Squadron 7:9:40 21yrs. Catterick Cemetery, Yorkshire. Church of England Section Row M Grave 13.

SAUNDERS, Sgt. A. F. C. British. No. 600 Squadron 7:9:40 19yrs. Wandsworth Cemetery, London. Block 32 Grave 40.

SAWYER, S/Ldr. H. C. British. No. 65 Squadron 2:8:40 25yrs. City of London Crematorium, Manor Park, East Ham, London. Panel 16.

The ashes of Flight Lieutenant Willie Rhodes-Moorhouse lie beneath this simple stone.

William Henry Rhodes-Moorhouse was born in 1914 at Brompton Square, London, moving later to the family home at Parnham House, Beaminster. As he grew up he moulded his life on the image of the gallant father he never came to know. Second Lieutenant William Barnard Rhodes-Moorhouse won the first Victoria Cross to be awarded for gallantry in the air. On April 26, 1915, he single-handedly carried out a successful bombing raid on the railway at Courtrai, Belgium. Severely wounded by ground fire, he nevertheless returned his flimsy aircraft safely to base and delivered his report before collapsing from the effects of his wounds, dying in hospital the following day. At his request, his body was brought home to Parnham for burial. Young Willie, educated at Eton, acquired his pilot's licence when he was seventeen, maintaining his private aircraft at Heston. A sportsman of great ability, his mercurial nature found an affinity in the fast downhill dash on the ski slopes of Europe. A skier of Olympic excellence, he participated in the Winter Games of 1937/38. At St. Moritz, a group of young men came together who would later face sterner tests of their courage and skill. For Willie Rhodes-Moorhouse, Max Aitken, Roger Bushell and American William Fiske greater trials were still to come. All, with the exception of Billy Fiske, were at that time members of No. 601 'County of London' Auxiliary Air Force Squadron, unofficially known as the 'Millionaire's Squadron'. Willie had joined the unit in between

travelling extensively around the world and getting married. He had over 1,000 flying hours to his credit before entry but was still required to undergo basic flying training to RAF standards. On the outbreak of war, No. 601 was flying Blenheim 1F fighters at Biggin Hill and, on November 29, 1939, six of its aircraft (with six more from No. 25 Squadron) carried out the first long-range fighter strike of the war when they attacked the German mine-laying seaplane base at Borkum. Early in 1940, Hurricanes replaced the Blenheims and the squadron moved to Tangmere in time for the Dunkirk withdrawal and the Battle of Britain. On July 15, 1940 a reunion took place in the Officers' Mess with the arrival of Pilot Officer Billy Fiske, now posted to No. 601. In the mounting fury of the battle, Willy Rhodes-Moorhouse was to gain the award of the DFC but lose much more. Dick Demetriadi, his brother-in-law, died in combat on August 11 and his friend Billy Fiske succumbed to burns and wounds less than a week later. Roger Bushell, as commander of No. 92 Squadron, had been in German captivity since Dunkirk but was later murdered by the Gestapo in 1944. High over Tunbridge Wells on a September morning, Willie Rhodes-Moorhouse fought his last battle against overwhelming odds. They laid his ashes in his father's grave on the hill overlooking Parnham House. Of the young winter sportsmen from that distant Olympic meeting, only one survived — Max Aitken.

SCHWIND, F/Lt. L. H. British. No. 213 Squadron 27:9:40 27yrs. Crowborough Burial Ground, Sussex. Grave 1723.

SCLANDERS, P/O K. M. Canadian. No. 242 Squadron 9:9:40 24yrs. Whyteleafe (St. Luke) Churchyard, Surrey. Row G Grave 34.

SCOTT, Sgt. E. British. No. 222 Squadron 27:9:40 35yrs. Runnymede Memorial Panel 19.

SCOTT, Sgt. J. A. British. No. 74 Squadron 27:10:40 22yrs. Wembley (Alperton) Burial Ground, Plot DD Grave 93.

SCOTT, F/O W. J. M. British. No. 41 Squadron 8:9:40 25yrs. Dundee Western Cemetery, Angus. Compartment 19 Grave 25C.

SEARS, P/O L. A. British. No. 145 Squadron 8:8:40 19yrs. Runnymede Memorial Panel 10.

SHANAHAN, Sgt. M. M. British. No. 1 Squadron 16:8:40 25yrs. Runnymede Memorial Panel 19.
Both Sergeant Shanahan and Pilot Officer Browne appear in the Official Casualty Returns as 'missing' on August 16, 1940 and their dates of death are recorded as such. The Form 540, No. 1 Squadron Operations Record Book, gives the date of his last operation as August 15, as does a squadron history published in 1971.

SHARP, Sgt. B. R. British. No. 235 Squadron 11:9:40 27yrs. Runnymede Memorial Panel 19.

SHAW, F/O I. G. British. No. 264 Squadron 24.8.40 21yrs. Runnymede Memorial Panel 6.

SHAW, P/O R. H. British. No. 1 Squadron 3:9:40 24yrs. Runnymede Memorial Panel 10.

SHEPHERD, Sgt. F. E. R. British. No. 611 Squadron 11:9:40 22yrs. Whyteleafe (St. Luke) Churchyard, Surrey. Row G Grave 33.

SHEPLEY, P/O D. C. British. No. 152 Squadron 12:8:40 22yrs. Runnymede Memorial Panel 10.

SHEPPERD, Sgt. E. E. British. No. 152 Squadron 18:10:40 23yrs. Ryde (Binstead) Cemetery, Isle of Wight. Section D Grave 8.

SHEPPERD, Sgt. G. E. British. No. 219 Squadron 30:9:40 23yrs. Catterick Cemetery, Yorkshire. Church of England Section Row M Grave 8.

SHORROCKS, P/O N. B. British. No. 235 Squadron 11:9:40 29yrs. Runnymede Memorial Panel 10.

SIBLEY, Sgt. F. A. British. No. 238 Squadron 1:10:40 26yrs. Runnymede Memorial Panel 19.

SILVER, Sgt. W. G. British. No. 152 Squadron 25:9:40 27yrs. Portsmouth Milton Cemetery (in Milton Road), Hampshire. Plot U Row 23A Grave 13.

SIM, Sgt. R. B. British. No. 111 Squadron 11:8:40 23yrs. Runnymede Memorial Panel 19.

SIMPSON, F/O G. M. New Zealander. No. 229 Squadron 26:10:40 21yrs. Runnymede Memorial Panel 6.

SIUDAK, Sgt. A. Polish. No. 303 Squadron 6:10:40 31yrs. Northwood Cemetery, Ruislip-Northwood, Middlesex. Section H Grave 225. Also commemorated on the Polish Memorial, Northolt.

SLATTER P/O D. M. British. No. 141 Squadron 19:7:40 26yrs. Runnymede Memorial Panel 10.

SLY, Sgt. O. K. British. No. 29 Squadron 13:10:40 20yrs. Runnymede Memorial Panel 19.

SMITH, Sgt. A. D. British. No. 66 Squadron. Seriously injured 4:9:40. Died 6:9:40 22yrs. Whyteleafe (St. Luke) Churchyard, Surrey. Row D Grave 33.

SMITH, S/Ldr. A. T. British. No. 610 Squadron 25:7:40 34yrs. Delamere (St. Peter) Churchyard, Cheshire. South part.

On August 12, 1940, Pilot Officer Douglas Shepley failed to return from a sortie south of the Isle of Wight. Having already lost a son and daughter in the war his mother, together with his wife of just six weeks, decided to collect enough money to replace the Spitfire in which he had been lost. In less than fifteen weeks, they raised the necessary £5,700 to purchase a new aeroplane *(below)* These cuttings tell of their exploit. The 'Shepley Spitfire', W3649, was first issued to No. 602 'City of Glasgow' Squadron on August 16, 1941. Thereafter it served with No. 303 Polish Squadron before being switched to No. 485 New Zealand Squadron on November 24, 1941. It was lost on March 28, 1942 whilst being flown by one of the Royal Air Force's most illustrious pilots, Group Captain Francis Beamish, DSO and Bar, DFC, AFC. His body was never found and he is commemorated on Panel 64 of the Runnymede Memorial.

MOTHER AND WIFE TO BUY A SPITFIRE

THE mother and wife of a Sheffield pilot reported missing after his Spitfire was shot down over the Channel have started a fund to buy a new Spitfire.

He is Pilot-Officer Douglas Clayton Shepley, youngest son of Mr. and Mrs. Jack Shepley, of Woodthorpe Hall, Homesfield. His brother and sister both lost their lives on war service.

"We both have the greatest urge to buy a Spitfire to replace the one in which my son was brought down," said Mrs. Shepley.

"Even those who do not know us will perhaps have heard of our great losses and sympathise with our desire to do something to help this most wonderful R.A.F."

Mr. and Mrs. Shepley's only daughter, Miss Jeanne Shepley, was killed in the sinking of ss. Yorkshire while returning to join her unit of the F.A.N.Y.S., and another son, Flight-Lieut. George Rex Shepley, D.F.C., was shot down near Dunkirk when single-handed he attacked powerful squadrons of enemy 'planes.

Anxious to co-operate with Spitfire funds, Oscar Deutsch is offering free use of his 200 Odeon cinemas to local mayors for concerts.

At a special meeting held at the Bolsover Colliery pithead baths yesterday it was decided by the workmen to allocate a penny in every 10s. earned towards the cost of buying Spitfire 'planes.

The Mayor has headed the Buxton list with £50, and the local M.P., Captain Hugh Molson, has given £25. It is hoped to reach £6,000 in a few weeks.

HER SON'S SPITFIRE IS REPLACED

IN less than 15 weeks £5,700 has been raised by the Shepley Spitfire Fund. Yesterday a cheque was sent to Lord Beaverbrook, Minister of Aircraft Production, with the request that it should be used to buy a plane to be called "The Shepley Spitfire."

Pilot Officer Douglas C. Shepley, youngest son of Mr. and Mrs. Jack Shepley, of Woodthorpe Hall, Holmesfield, Sheffield, was reported missing on August 22nd after his Spitfire had been brought down in the English Channel.

On the following day his mother and her daughter-in-law—a bride of only six weeks—started a fund to replace the fighter in which this 21-year-old pilot is presumed to have lost his life.

CHILDREN HELPED

Response to the appeal came from many quarters. Money was collected in large and small sums, mostly small, and among the thousands who subscribed were many children who raised money by holding jumble sales of toys, making lavender bags for sale, and giving concerts.

Older sympathisers organised dances, whist drives, American teas, concerts, and jumble sales, and made house-to-house, theatre, shop, publichouse, and club collections.

GENEROUS ENCOURAGEMENT

Thanking, through the "Telegraph and Independent," all who have helped so generously, Mrs. Jack Shepley and Mrs. Douglas Shepley state that, although at first they did not intend to publish any names of contributors, they feel they have to thank the Press, and Messrs. T. B. and W. Cockayne, Ltd., for the publicity and encouragement given.

They also mention the Sheffield A.R.P. organisation which has come in at the end with a magnificent donation, the result of collections at all Wardens' Posts.

Thirty-nine years later, another tribute was paid to the young Sheffield pilot with the naming of a new pub in Mickley Lane, Totley. Mr. Seymour Shepley, Douglas's brother, was given the honour of pulling the first pint in his memory.

Spitfire to be Named "Shepley"

LORD BEAVERBROOK, Minister of Aircraft Production, in acknowledging the receipt of £5,700 from the "Shepley Spitfire Fund" has assured Mrs. J. T. Shepley, of Woodthorpe Hall, Holmesfield, near Sheffield, that a plane shall be named "The Shepley Spitfire.

Lord Beaverbrook has sent Mrs. Shepley a letter which the family wish to share with all who have contributed to the fund.

Mr. J. T. Shepley told "The Star" that he and his wife were deeply touched by the remarks of Lord Beaverbrook and feel that it conveys a message which will hearten everyone who reads it. Lord Beaverbrook wrote:—

"Dear Mrs. Shepley,—I have been deeply moved by the gift which you and your daughter-in-law have sent me.

"Will ou allow me, in sending you my heartfelt sympathy in the tragic losses you have sustained, to tell you how proud, I am convinced, your sons and daughter would be to know of the tribute you have paid to their memory.

"Through suffering and self-sacrifice the people of our country will march forward to victory. Those whom we have lost already have most splendidly pointed the way.

"Now, by your contribution for the purchase of a Spitfire, which shall assuredly be named as you desire, you have registered your determination that their sacrifice shall not be in vain.

"You, and all those generous-hearted people who have contributed to the sum you send me, have given proof of the unconquerable spirit of our race. You have given also a guarantee of a future which will be the justification of all the trials and sorrows we must endure to-day.

"I send you this expression of my profound gratitude.

"Yours sincerely,

"(signed) BEAVERBROOK."

SMITH, P/O D. N. E. British. No. 74 Squadron 11:8:40 24yrs. Ostende New Communal Cemetery, Belgium. Plot 9 Row 3 Grave 22.

SMITH, F/O D. S. British. No. 616 Squadron. Seriously wounded 27:9:40. Died 28:9:40 26yrs. Highley (St. Mary) Churchyard, Shropshire. South-east part.

SMITH, (F.A.A.) A/Sub/Lt. F. A. British. No. 145 Squadron 8:8:40 (no date of birth in records). Lee-on-Solent Fleet Air Arm Memorial. Bay 1 Panel 3.

At St. Luke's Churchyard at Whyteleafe, a special plot was set aside which became known as 'Airmen's Corner'. During the 1939-45 war it was exclusively reserved for airmen who died while based at Kenley and Croydon. Altogether there are forty WWII graves of which six concern the Battle of Britain — Sergeant David Hughes, Pilot Officer Kirkpatrick Sclanders, Sergeant Fred Shepherd, Sergeant Arthur Smith, Flying Officer Alec Trueman and Sergeant Peter Walley. We visited Whyteleafe just after the annual Battle of Britain service held on September 16, 1979.

292

SMITH, Sgt. K. B. British. No. 257 Squadron 8:8:40 21yrs. Runnymede Memorial Panel 19.

SMITHER, F/O R. Canadian. Nos. 1 (RCAF)-401 Squadrons 15:9:40 27yrs. Brookwood Military Cemetery. Plot 3 Row H Grave 1.

SMITHERS, P/O J. L. British. No. 601 Squadron 11:8:40 24yrs. Ste. Marie Cemetery, Le Havre, France. Division 67 Row R Grave 5.

SOLOMON, P/O N. D. British. No. 17 Squadron 18:8:40 26yrs. Pihen-les-Guines Communal Cemetery, France. Row A Grave 4.

SPRAGUE, Sgt. M. H. British. No. 602 Squadron 11:9:40 21yrs. Tangmere (St. Andrew) Churchyard, Sussex. Row 2 Grave 481.

STANLEY, Sgt. D. O. New Zealander. No. 151 Squadron. Seriously injured 26:10:40. Died 27:10:40 24yrs. Scopwick Church Burial Ground, Lincolnshire. Row 2 Grave 33.

STARR, S/Ldr. H. M. British. No. 253 Squadron 31:8:40 25yrs. Swindon (Radnor Street) Cemetery, Wiltshire. Block E Grave 8235.

STEBOROWSKI, F/O M. J. Polish. No. 238 Squadron 11:8:40 31yrs. Polish Memorial, Northolt, but as a Flight Lieutenant.

STEPHENS, Sgt. C. British. No. 23 Squadron 8:8:40 24yrs. Coychurch (St. Crallo) Churchyard, Coychurch Lower, Glamorganshire.

STERBACEK, P/O J. Czechoslovakian. No. 310 Squadron 31:8:40 26yrs. Runnymede Memorial Panel 10.

STEVENS, Sgt. R. E. British. No. 29 Squadron 13:10:40 20yrs. Runnymede Memorial Panel 19.

STOCKS, Sgt. N. J. British. No. 248 Squadron 20:10:40 18yrs. Runnymede Memorial Panel 19.

STONEY, F/Lt. G. E. B. British. No. 501 Squadron 18:8:40 29yrs. Sefton (St. Helen's) Churchyard, Lancashire.

STOODLEY, Sgt. D. R. British. No. 43 Squadron 24:10:40 21yrs. Salisbury (London Road) Cemetery, Wiltshire. Section M Grave 382.

STUCKEY, Sgt. S. G. British. No. 213 Squadron 12:8:40 26yrs. Runnymede Memorial Panel 20.

STUDD, P/O J. A. P. British. No. 66 Squadron 19:8:40 22yrs. Touchen End (Holy Trinity) Churchyard, Bray, Berkshire. Row 8 Grave 15.

SUTTON, P/O N. British. No. 72 Squadron 5:10:40 26yrs. St. Helens Cemetery, Lancashire. Section 58 Grave 281.

SYDNEY, F/Sgt. C. British. No. 92 Squadron 27:9:40 25yrs. Orpington (St. Mary Cray) Cemetery, Kent. Plot E Division 3 Grave 130.

SYLVESTER, P/O E. J. H., DFC. British. No. 501 Squadron 20:7:40 26yrs. Runnymede Memorial Panel 10.

TANNER, F/Sgt. J. H. British. No. 610 Squadron 11:8:40 25yrs. Calais Southern Cemetery, France. Plot P Grave 17.

THOMAS, F/O C. R. D. British. No. 236 Squadron 18:7:40 22yrs. Quiberville Churchyard, France. Grave 2.

THOMAS, P/O R. C. British. No. 235 Squadron 9:10:40 29yrs. Cardiff (Cathays) Cemetery. Section P Grave 1094.

THOMPSON, Sgt. J. B. British. No. 25 Squadron 31:7:40 24yrs. Magheragall Church of Ireland Churchyard, County Antrim, Northern Ireland. Grave 194.

TOOGOOD, Sgt. L. V. British. No. 43 Squadron 27:10:40 20yrs. Portsmouth (Kingston) Cemetery (in St. Mary's Road), Hampshire. Plot 98 (Billing) Row I Grave 13.

TOPOLNICKI, F/O J. Polish. No. 601 Squadron 21:9:40 30yrs. Exeter Higher Cemetery, Heavitree, Devon. Section ZK Grave 32. Also commemorated on the Polish Memorial, Northolt.

Another 'aerodrome churchyard' is that established during the Second World War at Holy Trinity, Warmwell, Dorset. Included in the twenty-three burials are Pilot Officer Harold Akroyd, Sergeant Alan Feary, Sergeant Jaroslav Hlavac — a Czech, Flight Lieutenant John Kennedy, Squadron Leader Terence Lovell-Gregg and Sergeant Sid Wakeling — all killed in the Battle of Britain.

TRUEMAN, F/O A. A. G. Canadian. No. 253 Squadron 4:9:40 26yrs. Whyteleafe (St. Luke) Churchyard, Surrey. Row E Grave 37.

TUCKER, Sgt. R. Y. British. No. 235 Squadron 18:7:40 18yrs. Runnymede Memorial Panel 20.

TURNER F/Lt. D. E. British. No. 238 Squadron 8:8:40 30yrs. Runnymede Memorial Panel 5.

TURNER, Sgt. R. C. British. No. 264 Squadron 28:8:40 25yrs. Reading (Henley Road) Cemetery, Eye and Dunsden, Berkshire. Block 4 Grave 7614.

TWEED, Sgt. T. R. British. No. 56 Squadron 15:9:40 26yrs. SS Mary and Melores Cemetery, Amesbury, Wiltshire. Row 2 Grave 79.

VINYARD, Sgt. F. F. British. No. 64 Squadron 6:10:40 24yrs. Runnymede Memorial Panel 20.

WADHAM, Sgt. J. V. British. No. 145 Squadron 12:10:40 21yrs. Carisbrooke Cemetery, Newport, Isle of Wight. Section A Grave 14.

WAITE, Sgt. E. British. No. 29 Squadron 31:7:40 24yrs. Runnymede Memorial Panel 20.

WAKEHAM, P/O E. C. J. DFC. British. No. 145 Squadron 8:8:40 19yrs. Runnymede Memorial Panel 10.

WAKELING, Sgt. S. R. E. British. No. 87 Squadron 25:8:40 21yrs. Warmwell (Holy Trinity) Churchyard, Dorset. South part.

WALCH, F/Lt. S. C. Australian. No. 238 Squadron 11:8:40 23yrs. Runnymede Memorial Panel 5.

WALLEY, Sgt. P. K. British. No. 615 Squadron 18:8:40 20yrs. Whyteleafe (St. Luke) Churchyard, Surrey. Row F Grave 32A.

WALSH, Sgt. J. P. British. No. 616 Squadron 4:8:40 20yrs. Harrow Cemetery, Middlesex. Section 13 Grave 1909.

WANT, Sgt. W. H. British. No. 248 Squadron 19:8:40 28yrs. Runnymede Memorial Panel 20.

WAPNIAREK, P/O S. Polish. No. 302 Squadron 18:10:40 24yrs. Northwood Cemetery Ruislip-Northwood, Middlesex, Section H Grave 268. Also commemorated on the Polish Memorial, Northolt, but as a Flying Officer..

WARD, Sgt. R. A. British. No. 66 Squadron 8:10:40 23yrs. Croydon (Mitcham Road) Cemetery, Surrey. Plot DD Grave 28475.

WARNER, F/Lt. W. H. C. British. No. 610 Squadron 16:8:40 21yrs. Runnymede Memorial. Panel 5.

WARREN, AC1 J. B. W. British. No. 600 Squadron 8:8:40 19yrs. Calais Southern Cemetery, France. Plot O Grave 32.

WARREN, Sgt. S. British. No. 1 Squadron 9:10:40 22yrs. Runnymede Memorial. Panel 20.

WATERSTON, F/O R. McG. British. No. 603 Squadron 31:8:40 23yrs. Edinburgh (Warriston) Crematorium. Panel 4.

WATSON-PARKER, Sgt. P. I. British. No. 610 Squadron 13:7:40 22yrs. Cudham (SS Peter and Paul) Churchyard, Orpington, Kent. Section N Grave 24.

WATTS, Sgt. R. D. H. British. No. 235 Squadron 11:9:40 35yrs. Runnymede Memorial Panel 20.

WAY, F/Lt. B. H. British. No. 54 Squadron 25:7:40 22yrs. Oostduinkerke Communal Cemetery, Belgium. Row C Grave 53.

WEAVER, F/Lt. P. S., DFC, British. No. 56 Squadron 31:8:40 25yrs. Runnymede Memorial Panel 5.

WEBSTER, P/O F. K. British. No. 610 Squadron 26:8:40 26yrs. Sandown Cemetery, Isle of Wight. Section E Grave 40.

WEBSTER, F/Lt. J. T., DFC, British. No. 41 Squadron 5:9:40 24yrs. Darlington Crematorium, County Durham. Panel 4.

WENDEL, F/O K. V. New Zealander. No. 504 Squadron 7:9:40 24yrs. Faversham Borough Cemetery, Kent. Section E Grave 20.

WESTMORELAND, Sgt. T. E. British. No. 616 Squadron 25:8:40 27yrs. Runnymede Memorial, Panel 20.

WHALL, Sgt. B. E. P., DFM, British. No. 602 Squadron 7:10:40 22yrs. Amersham Consecrated Cemetery, Buckinghamshire (behind St. Mary's church). Grave 2585.

WHITBREAD, P/O H. L. British. No. 222 Squadron 20:9:40 26yrs. Ludlow New Cemetery, Shropshire. Section A Row 2 Grave 29A.

Lawrence Whitbread was born in 1914 in Ludlow and attended the local Grammar School. He was a keen sportsman and entered the RAF on a short service commission at the RAF college at Cranwell. Posted to No. 222 Squadron as a Pilot Officer in October 1939, he served with that unit for the remainder of his operational career. It was while the squadron was based at Hornchurch in September that he was attacked by four enemy fighters, crash-landing in the garden of Pond Cottage near Rochester. Although he was thrown clear, he had been caught in a burst of machine gun fire down his left-hand side. Examination of his diary revealed he had been flying with a frost-bitten hand brought on from sleeping in his Spitfire — something which he should have reported to the MO. Our artist George Campbell visited the well-kept grave in Ludlow unknowingly on the anniversary of his death. At the graveside he met Laurie's sister who had come to pay her respects and who was only too pleased to describe something of his life and death to an interested stranger. George Campbell was so moved by their meeting that he decided to paint Laurie's portrait *(opposite)* from photographs as a gift to her. Lawrence Whitbread is highly regarded by the people of Ludlow — a road being named after him and the church of St. Lawrence being floodlit on September 20 each year in his memory.

WHITFIELD, Sgt. J. J. British. No. 56 Squadron 13:7:40 25yrs. Runnymede Memorial Panel 21.

WHITLEY, P/O D. British. No. 264 Squadron 28:8:40 21yrs. Bedford Cemetery. Section E Grave 849.

WICKINGS-SMITH, P/O P. C. British. No. 235 Squadron 11:9:40 22yrs. Runnymede Memorial Panel 10.

WIGHT, F/Lt. R. D. G., DFC, British. No. 213 Squadron 11:8:40 24yrs. Cayeux-sur-Mer Communal Cemetery, France. Plot 1 Grave 9.

WILCOX, F/O E. J. British. No. 72 Squadron 31:8:40 23yrs. Staplehurst (All Saints) Churchyard, Kent.

WILDBLOOD, P/O T. S. British. No. 152 Squadron 25:8:40 20yrs. Runnymede Memorial Panel 10.

WILKES, Sgt. G. N. British. No. 213 Squadron 12:8:40 21yrs. Runnymede Memorial Panel 21.

WILKINSON, S/Ldr. R. L. British. No. 266 Squadron 16:8:40 30yrs. Margate Cemetery, Kent. Section 50 Grave 15939.

WILLIAMS, S/Ldr. C. W. British. No. 17 Squadron 25:8:40 30yrs. Runnymede Memorial Panel 4.

WILLIAMS, P/O D. G. British. No. 92 Squadron 10:10:40 20yrs. Salisbury (London Road) Cemetery, Wiltshire. Section M Grave 378.

WILLIAMS, F/Sgt. E. E. British. No. 46 Squadron 15:10:40 28yrs. Runnymede Memorial Panel 11.

WILLIAMS, P/O W. S. New Zealander. No. 266 Squadron 21:10:40 20yrs. Stradishall (St. Margaret) Churchyard, Suffolk.

WILSON, P/O R. R. Canadian. No. 111 Squadron 11:8:40 20yrs. Runnymede Memorial Panel 10.

WINTER, P/O D. C. British. No. 72 Squadron 5:9:40 26yrs. South Shields (Harton) Cemetery, County Durham. Section O Grave 11795.

WISE, Sgt. J. F. British. No. 141 Squadron 19:8:40 20yrs. Runnymede Memorial Panel 21.

WITHALL, F/Lt. L. C. Australian. No. 152 Squadron 12:8:40 29yrs. Runnymede Memorial Panel 5.

WOJCICKI, Sgt. A. Polish. No. 213 Squadron 11:9:40 26yrs. Polish Memorial, Northolt.

WOJTOWICZ, Sgt. S. Polish. No. 303 Squadron 11:9:40 24yrs. Northwood Cemetery, Ruislip-Northwood, Middlesex. Section H Grave 209. Also commemorated on the Polish Memorial, Northolt.

WOODGER, P/O D. N. British. No. 235 Squadron 24:8:40 20yrs. Runnymede Memorial Panel 10.

WOODS-SCAWEN, P/O C. A., DFC, British. No. 43 Squadron 2:9:40 22yrs. Folkestone New Cemetery, Kent. Plot O Grave 25.

WOODS-SCAWEN, F/O P. P., DFC, British. No. 85 Squadron 1:9:40 24yrs. Caterham and Warlingham (Caterham) Burial Ground, Surrey (rear of St. Mary's church). Section A Grave 180.

WOODWARD, F/O H. J., DFC, British. No. 23 Squadron 30:10:40 24yrs. Heckmondwike Cemetery, Yorkshire. General Section L Grave 51.

WORSDELL, P/O K. W. British. No. 219 Squadron 30:10:40 20yrs. Nutfield Cemetery, Surrey. Plot B (Consecrated) Grave 474.

WRIGHT, Sgt. D. L. British. No. 235 Squadron 24:8:40 18yrs. Chasetown (St. Ann) Churchyard, Burtonwood, Staffordshire. New Section Row L Grave 1593.

WRIGHT, Sgt. J. British. No. 79 Squadron. Seriously injured 4:9:40. Died 5:9:40 24yrs. New Kilpatrick (or Hillfoot) Cemetery, Dunbartonshire. Section D Grave 741.

'Thy will be done. R.I.P.' The simplest of epitaphs but the most tragic. Bereavement could not be worse than it was for Mr. Philip Woods-Scawen and his wife Kathleen of Farnborough, Hampshire. They lost both their sons in the Battle of Britain, the second the day after the first. *Below:* Mr. Woods-Scawen displays the twin Distinguished Flying Crosses posthumously awarded to his sons by the King.

Patrick Philip Woods-Scawen was the elder of two brothers born at Karachi, India. Both were educated at Salesian College at Farnborough and joined the Royal Air Force before the war. In 1939, Patrick was serving with No. 85 Squadron in France throughout the 'Phoney War' period and after, remaining with the squadron until his death in action on September 1, 1940. He was the first of the brothers to be killed and the last to be found, his body lying undiscovered until September 6. Charles Anthony Woods-Scawen, like his elder brother, entered the RAF before the war. Early in 1940 he was posted to No. 43 Squadron where he was known as 'Wombat'. He flew with the squadron over France and on June 7 was forced to bale out of his Hurricane, landing behind the German lines. Successfully evading capture, he eventually found his way back to Tangmere and further action. In all, he had to take to his parachute seven times. On the last occasion he baled out too low and was killed on impact with the ground. His death occurred on September 2, 1940 within twenty-four hours of that of his brother.

WYATT, LAC. J. P. British. No. 25 Squadron 15:9:40 32yrs. Melplash (Christ Church) Churchyard, Netherbury, Dorset. West part.

YOUNG, P/O J. H. R. British. No. 74 Squadron 28:7:40 22yrs. Pihen-les-Guines War Cemetery, France. Plot 1 Row E Grave 2.

YOUNG, Sgt. R. B. M. New Zealander. No. 264 Squadron 8:10:40 22yrs. Northwood Cemetery, Ruislip-Northwood, Middlesex. Section H Grave 253.

ZALUSKI, Sgt. J. S. Polish. No. 302 Squadron 17:10:40 24yrs. Northwood Cemetery, Ruislip-Northwood, Middlesex. Section H Grave 252. Also commemorated on the Polish Memorial, Northolt.

ZENKER, P/O P. Polish. No. 501 Squadron 24:8:40 26yrs. Polish Memorial, Northolt, but as a Flying Officer.

ZUKOWSKI, P/O A. Polish. No. 302 Squadron 18:10:40 29yrs. Northwood Cemetery, Ruislip-Northwood, Middlesex. Section H Grave 297. Also commemorated on the Polish Memorial, Northolt, but as a Flying Officer.

TWO OF " THE FEW "

F./O. P. P. WOODS-SCAWEN, D.F.C., R.A.F.

P./O. C. A. WOODS-SCAWEN, D.F.C., R.A.F.

R.A.F.

DEDICATED TO P. P. AND C. A. WOODS-SCAWEN

O, what do we owe them who fought out
the foemen,
And smiling-faced hurled themselves into
the blue ;
Who recked not of numbers but while in
our slumbers
In the grey of the dawn gave their young
lives for you ?

Say that their glory shall live in our story,
Nor shamed by the deeds of our worthies
of yore ;
Now all the world rings, the Lion has wings,
And none are more brave than the heroes
who soar.

" Per terram per mare," and now in the
air.
Britannia, their deeds will yet make us free ;
And hard in the wake of Nelson and Drake
Are our sons of the air as well as the sea.

Then let us remember, and while there's
an ember
Of love for those young hearts at rest in the
grave,
To show by each deed the land that they
freed
Is worthy of all that those dear lads gave.

R. J. C.

The Runnymede Memorial

After the 1939-1945 War, the Air Council Committee on War Memorials presented to the Air Council their recommendations for the commemoration of those members of the Air Forces of the British Commonwealth and Empire who, while serving in or in association with the Royal Air Force, lost their lives and have no known grave. These recommendations, approved by the Air Council in February 1948, were referred to the Imperial War Graves Commission, in order that the Commission might plan and build memorials in accordance with them. The Commission also had to consider proposals from some of the Commonwealth Governments for the commemoration of other units of their respective Air Forces.

It was decided that in the United Kingdom there should be one such memorial to airmen who lost their lives while serving from bases in the United Kingdom, Iceland, the Faroe Islands, Northern Ireland and the Azores, and from bases on the Continent of Europe in France, Holland, Belgium, Germany, Denmark, Norway, Finland, Luxembourg, Czechoslovakia and Russia. They served in Bomber, Fighter, Coastal, Transport, Flying Training and Maintenance Commands, and came from all parts of the British Commonwealth and Empire.

When it came to choosing a site for the memorial, Sir Arthur Longmore, the RAF representative on the Commission, wanted to preserve a close association with aircraft and favoured a position near the new London Airport at Heathrow. (It will be remembered that fighters on night dispersal from Northolt frequently used Heathrow, or the Great West Aerodrome as it was then called, during the battle.) Lieutenant-Colonel Reginald Murphy, the Commission's chief officer for the United Kingdom took a number of long exploratory walks along the Thames near Windsor and eventually came upon a site on Cooper's Hill, part of a wooded ridge that swept down to the river at historic Runnymede. It was an excellent spot and from the hilltop, broad views could be obtained of Windsor and Heathrow. By the autumn of 1949 six acres of land had been generously donated by Sir Eugen and Lady Effie Millington-Drake and work had begun on the construction by Messrs. Holloway & Sons.

October 17, 1953 and HM Queen Elizabeth II unveils the memorial on Cooper's Hill at Runnymede to all the airmen (including Czechs and Belgians but not Poles) who went missing serving with the Royal Air Force in northern Europe during the Second World War. Of the 537 airmen who were killed in the Battle of Britain, 175 have no known grave (Central Press).

The Queen places a wreath of pink carnations, orchids and Lilies-of-the-Valley in front of the central arch (Keystone).

On October 17, 1953, the new Runnymede Memorial was inaugurated by HM Queen Elizabeth II. Designed by Sir Edward Maufe and constructed in Portland stone with Westmorland green slate roofs, it consists of a cloister planned to record the names of 20,547 missing airmen. On the far side of the cloister there is a tower reminiscent of an aerodrome watch office, containing a vaulted room or shrine as a place for contemplation. At the southern side of the site are entrance gates to a central avenue which leads to a three-arched portico giving access to the cloisters. The cloisters on the edge of the wooded hill overlooking the Thames have curved wings terminating in two look-outs, one facing towards Windsor and the other towards the London Airport. The tower has a central arched opening above which are three sculptured figures representing Justice, Victory and Courage, and the turret is surmounted by a crown. On the river side of the shrine is a balcony giving a fine view of the Thames Valley and, on a clear day, of seven counties. Two spiral staircases lead to a gallery from which a further staircase gives access to the roof.

The names of the missing are inscribed on the stone reveals of the narrow windows in the cloister and the look-outs. The light coming through the window slits will illuminate the reveals, giving them something of the appearance of partially-opened stone books, on which the names can easily be read.

In the centre of the cloister rests the Stone of Remembrance. Above the three-arched entrance to the cloister is a great stone eagle with the Royal Air Force motto 'Per Ardua ad Astra'. On each side is the inscription: 'In this cloister are recorded the names of twenty thousand airmen who have no known grave. They died for freedom in raid and sortie over the British Isles and the lands and seas of Northern and Western Europe.' In the beautifully engraved glass of the great window of the shrine (by John Hutton) two angels hold a scroll on which appear verses from Psalm 139.

The number of names engraved on the memorial in 1953 was 20,466, but since that date the burial places of twelve airmen have been discovered, three of them Battle of Britain pilots formerly listed as missing. When it is necessary to replace the panels, these names will be removed (Keystone).

The Polish Air Force Memorial, Western Avenue, Northolt

Three years after the close of the Second World War, a monument was erected beside the Western Avenue on the north-eastern edge of Northolt aerodrome — a monument devoted to the memory of Polish pilots who had lost their lives. Many of them had taken off on their last flight from this aerodrome.

The monument was erected out of funds contributed by the members of the Polish Armed Forces and by the British public. The ceremony of its unveiling on November 2, 1948, might be looked upon as a winding up of the history of the Polish Air Force in Great Britain.

The monument has its own history. The idea originated as early as 1943 among the airmen stationed at Northolt and at first was to have taken the shape of a tablet to the memory of Polish airmen killed in the Battle of Britain. The war, however, continued, affording little opportunity for the realisation of the idea — while the number of airmen killed increased. Thus, in the summer of 1945, a committee was formed to honour the fallen airmen in some suitable way. The committee was composed of Air Vice-Marshal M. Izycki, KCB, as chairman, Squadron Leader S. Laszkiewicz as treasurer, Flight Lieutenant Osiatynski as secretary, and Group Captains J. Bajan, CBE, and A. Gabszewicz, DSO and Bar, DFC. The committee invited Air Chief-Marshal Sir Roderic Hill to become Honorary Chairman of the Committee and co-opted the then OC of Northolt station, Group Captain R. G. A. Ford.

It was fortunate that a well-known Polish sculptor, M. Lubelski, the creator of a number of monuments in Poland, and recently liberated by the Allied Armies from a forced labour camp in Germany, happened to be in London at the time. The committee entrusted him with the planning of the monument.

The artist used stone slabs — two forming the base and the third, placed vertically, a column on which perches an eagle, about to take off for flight. The design was very simple and unostentatious. An appeal was set in motion, the cost of the monument being estimated at £3,000. At the request of the committee, Marshal of the Royal Air Force Viscount Portal of Hungerford appealed to the British people in the following letter:

' . . . The part played during the Battle of Britain and during later operations over the Continent by the Polish

Top: Construction work nearing completion on the memorial built by William Wood and Sons Limited and Bath and Portland Stone Limited. The site was given for a peppercorn rent for 999 years by the Middlesex County Council. *Above:* The memorial is unveiled on November 2, 1948 by Marshal of the Royal Air Force Lord Tedder, Chief of Air Staff (Radio Times).

fighter pilots who served with the RAF has as yet no visible memorial in this country.

'At the present time when the Polish Air Force which served with the RAF is about to be disbanded I hope and believe that many British people would like to show their gratitude to those Polish pilots who were amongst the "Few" in the Battle of Britain and have never been among the last among the many who won the Battle of Europe . . . '

This appeal was supported by the 'Father of the RAF', Marshal of the Royal Air Force Viscount Trenchard, who wrote:

'I am sure England will never forget that Poland was most brutally attacked on September 1, 1939 but, in spite of the overwhelming disaster which took place to that nation, as many of those young Polish fighters as could escaped from their country and came to England to take part in the first great fight in defending these islands. They lived with us and died with us in all the battles in the war, and Northolt was their main station.

'Their action must be remembered, and nothing should be allowed in any way to interfere with our honouring to the best of our means those Polish members of the Royal Air Force who, when stationed in these islands, laid down their lives both for their own country and for ours.'

These letters, published in *The Daily Telegraph* on June 24 and July 2, 1946, opened the fortnight's campaign launched by Lord Camrose for collecting funds for the monument. Contributions began to flow in, accompanied by many letters:

'I take a more than great interest in this Fund,' wrote Air Vice-Marshal S. F. Vincent, of South-East Asia Command and formerly Senior Air Staff Officer of Fighter Command, 'because I was the station commander at Northolt during 1940 and the Battle of Britain when the first and greatest Polish Squadron, No. 303, started their operations from this country.'

The conclusion of the unveiling ceremony — The Last Post. Services are held annually by the Polish Air Force Association.

'In air fighting the selfish pilot may build up a considerable score for himself at the expense of his fellows in the formation because, unless the leaders are well supported by those behind them, they fall an easy prey to the enemy fighters,' wrote Wing Commander R. G. Kellett, DSO, DFC, first OC No. 303 Polish Fighter Squadron. 'In this connection it is greatly to the credit of the Polish airmen that the three English pilots who commanded the squadron and flights survived the Battle of Britain.'

By the end of 1946 the Committee had at its disposal a total of £8,172 7s. 1d. Events, however, occurred which altered the original modest intentions of the Committee. Firstly, Northolt aerodrome was taken over by civil aviation and, due to the resulting reorganisation, the site originally selected for the monument lost much of its significance. In addition, it was suggested that the monument should honour the memory of all Polish airmen killed in Great Britain. The Committee accepted this suggestion and decided to adapt the monument accordingly. As there was difficulty in finding a suitable alternative location in London, the original idea was resumed that the monument should be erected at Northolt — on the site it now occupies.

M. Lubelski did not alter his original conception of the monument but he added to it an effective and striking stone setting. The site for the monument was granted to the Committee by the Middlesex County Council but the formalities were not completed until the end of 1947. Meanwhile the Committee had settled all details of the inscriptions to be placed on the monument.

It was decided that it should be engraved with the names of 1,241 members of the crews who were killed in operational flights out of the total list of 2,408 — the other losses were caused by flying accidents and it was unfortunately impossible, owing to lack of space, to include their names on the monument.

Group Captain Gabszewicz suggested the inscription in Polish and English on the face of the monument: 'To the memory of the fallen Polish airmen', and The Reverend Gogolinski, Chief Chaplain to the Polish Air Force, suggested the inscription on the back of the monument (II Tim. iv. 7) 'I have fought a good fight. I have finished my course. I have kept the faith.'

The elevation of the monument was carried out by Bath and Portland Stone Limited and the bronze eagle, sculptured by M. Lubelski, was cast by Morris Singer Company Limited who also made the letters of the inscriptions.

When at last, in December 1947, the final permits were granted, and thanks to the kindness of the Ruislip-Northwood Urban District Council the care of the monument was ensured, fresh difficulties nearly forced the Committee to alter their plans: the cost of labour had risen and caused an increase in the cost of erection by approximately £2,000, a sum which exceeded the money available to the Committee. It was therefore necessary to agree to substitute York stone for the originally planned Portland stone for the base of the monument which brought down the cost to within the means of the Committee. Work on the foundations and the stone work was entrusted to William Wood and Sons Limited. The execution of the lists of the fallen was entrusted to Mr. Ralph, a well-known stone mason.

The memorial is selective in that only the names of 1,241 Polish airmen (out of the total of 2,408 killed) are inscribed on the surrounding wall. Thus, of the thirty-one Poles who lost their lives in the Battle of Britain, Flying Officer Jan Borowski, who crashed at Kempton Park on October 18, and Pilot Officer Jan Bury-Burzymski, VM, who died during dogfight practice on October 24, are omitted. Airmen are arranged in rank order — the reason for the discrepancies with their Royal Air Force ranks has been discussed in the introduction to the Casualties.

Work began in May 1948. The foundation stone was blessed by Reverend Gogolinski in the presence of the Inspector of the Polish Air Force and the members of the Committee. On November 2, 1948, on All Souls' Day, the unveiling ceremony took place. It was attended by the President of the Polish Republic, M. August Zaleski, representatives of the British Government, numerous dignitaries of the British and American Armed Forces and some 3,000 guests. After a few words spoken by Air Commodore S. Karpinski, introducing Marshal of the Royal Air Force Viscount Portal, Lord Tedder unveiled the monument and Reverend Gogolinski paid tribute in prayer to those killed. M. August Zaleski deposited a wreath while the Polish and British national anthems were played. Lord Tedder deposited wreaths on behalf of the RAF and the British people — and the British national anthem concluded the ceremony. The trumpeters sounded the Last Post and slowly, after laying flowers, the public began to withdraw.

The Battle of Britain VC

BY ANDY SAUNDERS

Forty years separates these photographs taken in the little Yorkshire village of Kirkby Wharfe. *Left:* James Nicolson with his wife Muriel shortly after his release from hospital with their new baby James born in September 1940. *Right:* Andy Saunders, our author for this chapter, interviews Mrs. Nicolson on the same spot in 1980.

It is a sad fact that only one pilot of RAF Fighter Command received the nation's highest award for valour during the Battle of Britain (and, indeed, throughout the entire war) despite numerous acts of undoubted courage and heroism on the part of other pilots. The story of Flight Lieutenant James Brindley Nicolson will be well known but it is considered important to dispel some of the previously published myths surrounding this particular award and the stories which have grown up in the Southampton area where Nicolson was shot down on August 16, 1940.

On that day, Flight Lieutenant Nicolson was leading Red Section of No. 249 Squadron from Boscombe Down in a squadron formation patrolling between Poole and Romsey at 15,000ft. They took off around 1.05 p.m. Nicolson's section consisted of Pilot Officer Martyn King (Red 2) and Squadron Leader Eric King (Red 3) who was flying as a supernumerary acquiring combat experience prior to assuming command of No. 151 Squadron at Rochford.

Whilst flying towards Romsey, action was sighted over Gosport and Nicolson led his section off to investigate. Nicolson states in his combat report that twelve Spitfires engaged the enemy (wrongly identified in some official reports as Ju 88s) so he turned his section back to re-join the squadron. Slowly climbing to 17,000ft and with the sun behind them, Red Section were caught in the fatal fighter trap and 'bounced' in an attack out of the sun.

All three aircraft were hit simultaneously; Pilot Officer King's and Nicolson's aircraft being critically damaged whilst Squadron Leader King's aeroplane was hit and damaged causing him to return to base. What happened in the unfortunate Martyn King's final moments will never be known, only that he managed to vacate his doomed Hurricane and parachute gently down to about

1,500ft. At this juncture, his canopy collapsed and he fell into the garden of No. 3 Clifton Road, Shirley, Southampton crashing through a tall tree and leaving part of his parachute on the chimney stack. He died in the arms of Fred Poole who, living nearby, had seen him descending and had rushed to where he lay on the lawn. He was buried in Fawley Cemetery on August 21. The Operational Record Book for No. 249 Squadron states that Martyn King's parachute failed because it had been hit by a cannon shell. The tattered remnants of his parachute were a grim memorial that remained hanging on the chimney for some three months after his death.

During an engagement with the enemy near Southampton on August 16, 1940, Flight Lieutenant Nicolson's aircraft was hit by four cannon shells, two of which wounded him whilst another set fire to the gravity tank. When about to abandon his aircraft owing to flames in the cockpit, he sighted an enemy fighter. This he attacked and shot down although as a result of staying in his burning aircraft, he sustained serious burns to his hands, face, neck and legs.

Flight Lieutenant Nicolson has always displayed great enthusiasm for air fighting and this incident shows that he possesses courage and determination of a high order by continuing to engage the enemy after he had been wounded and his aircraft set on fire. He displayed exceptional gallantry and disregard for the safety of his own life.

London Gazette
November 15, 1940.

Left: This is believed to be the wreckage of Flight Lieutenant Nicolson's Hurricane scattered across the playing field at Rownhams School. Above: April 1980. The crash site is near the fence line bordering the gardens of Rownhams Way (Paul Strudwick).

The crash site of the second Hurricane was in this field between the Southampton-Salisbury railway line and the A3057 (Paul Strudwick).

Above: The garden of No. 30 Clifton Road where Pilot Officer King died. The house is now divided into student's flats and the nine-foot chimney stack (on the right side of the house) was demolished two years ago as it was considered unsafe. During the war a small chapel stood on the site of the garage, the house being occupied by a clergyman at the time. Right: Martyn King's grave in Fawley Cemetery.

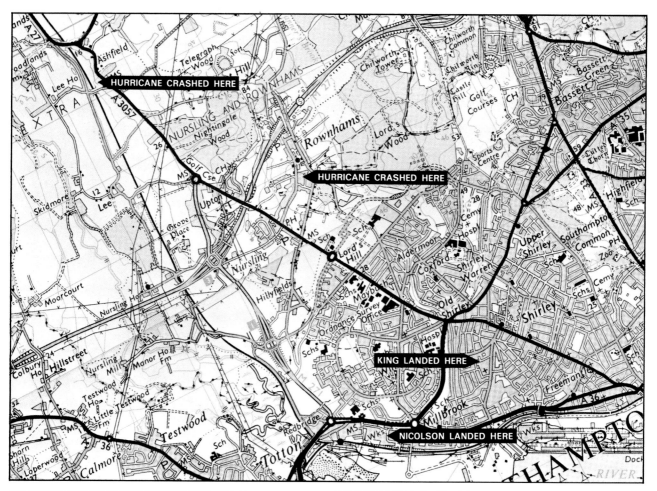

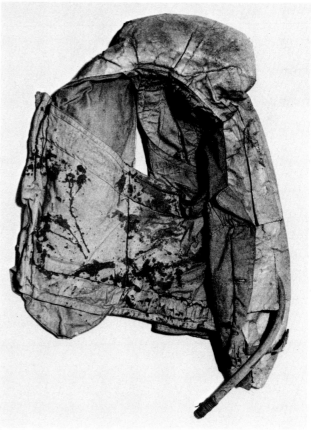

This is the first time to our knowledge that photographs of Flight Lieutenant Nicolson's burned and tattered uniform and his Mae-West with its pellet holes and bloodstains have ever been published. Stored for forty years, we are indebted to Mrs. Nicolson for her permission to include them. It is solely due to the enterprise of Andy Saunders that both items will be displayed in the forthcoming Tangmere Memorial Museum to be opened at Westhampnett aerodrome in 1981.

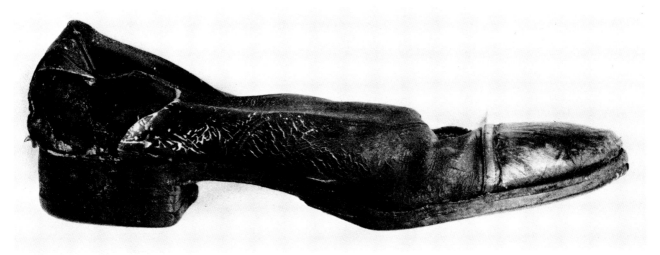

His left shoe damaged by the cannon shell.

Meanwhile Nicolson, his cockpit a mass of flame, prepared to bale out but was overtaken by a Bf 110, possibly his attacker. He made an attack on this aircraft which twisted and turned in its efforts to elude him. His left hand was holding the throttle open in the midst of the flames and molten metal was dripping on his feet from the dashboard. He had already received shrapnel wounds to his left foot from a cannon shell. He later explained to his young wife Muriel that he lost sight of the German aircraft and then prepared to bale out.

His parachute opened and, as he floated down in a cloudless sky, he saw the skin on his hands 'hanging down like a little boy's trousers'. A German aircraft circled around him and he told his wife that he 'played dead on his parachute'. Then he saw he was heading in the direction of the high-tension cables which run north to south through the western suburbs of Southampton. Approaching the ground, he judged that he would miss the wires and land near a boy riding a bicycle along a road. He could see the lad was approaching a left-hand turning and he was just about to surprise him with a cry from the sky of: 'Turn left!', when a Home Guard sergeant opened up on Nicolson with a shotgun, the pellets hitting him on his right side.

The cyclist, who turned out to be a butcher's delivery boy, ran over to him as he landed and, looking down at the severely burned and bleeding airman, shouted at the sergeant: 'Did you do this?' When the NCO replied that he had, the lad hit out, a fight started and it was only the arrival of a policeman and an ambulance that saved the sergeant from being lynched. Although the vehicle was intended for Nicolson, it was used instead to evacuate the severely-beaten sergeant!

A nurse, who had arrived on the scene, was horrified to see how badly the pilot was injured: his trousers were burned to shreds, he had third degree burns from the waist downwards and was bleeding where the pellets had struck him. She gave him a shot of morphia but not before he had dictated a telegram for his pregnant wife in Yorkshire advising her that he was safe. (Muriel relates how she was in the company of her sister for lunch that day and she suddenly had a premonition that something was wrong and that 'Nick' was in trouble.)

Nicolson was taken to the Royal Southampton Hospital in an old Albion lorry from where he was later

'Nick' chats to the matron of the Royal Air Force convalescent home situated in the Palace Hotel, Torquay (Fox Photos).

Lucky man! Escorted by his mother, sister Bobby, wife Muriel and younger sister 'Cupie', 'Nick' poses for photographs after the award of the Victoria Cross on November 25, 1940. Afterwards the family went for a celebration dinner at the Grosvenor Hotel.

moved to the RAF hospital at Halton and then to the RAF convalescent hospital at Torquay. It was there on November 15 that he learned he had been awarded the supreme British decoration for gallantry. On Sunday, November 24, he was summoned to attend the King at Buckingham Palace at 12.30 p.m. the following day for a private investiture. He was told that he could bring two other persons with him and naturally 'Nick' wanted to share the occasion with Muriel and also his mother. His two sisters, who had met him on the spur of the moment when he arrived in London, accompanied him to the Palace. When the King was told that they were waiting for Nicolson in an ante-room, he insisted they be present while the Victoria Cross was pinned on their brother's tunic.

Being the only Battle of Britain pilot to receive the award, 'Nick' felt that he should not have been especially singled out. He told Muriel that others had deserved the VC more than he did and he felt particularly conscious of the fact that he had survived whilst many others had not. At first he refused to put the mauve ribbon on his uniform until he was reprimanded for being improperly dressed. Later, Mrs. Nicolson had an opportunity to ask Sir Hugh Dowding why only one VC had been awarded to a Battle of Britain pilot. His answer was that the act for the award had to be witnessed and that this was always difficult where single-seater aircraft were concerned. (Twenty-one VCs were awarded to the Royal Air Force in the Second World War but only one of these was to a Fighter Command pilot.)

It is worth observing that the visit of some top brass to the squadron soon after the event undoubtedly had some bearing on the promulgation of Nicolson's award. On that very afternoon the AOC, Sir Christopher Quintin Brand, visited the squadron followed on the 19th by the Inspector General of the RAF and HRH The Duke of Kent on August 28.

As to the locations of the crashes of the two Hurricanes, the hectic actions of the period and the passage of forty years has made it difficult for researchers and historians to establish with one hundred per cent accuracy the respective sites. What is known is that one Hurricane fell in an open field at Lee to the south of Romsey, mid-way between the A3057 and the Southampton/Salisbury railway line, and another fell on what is now the playing field at Rownhams School. Both crashes were on August 16, 1940 and are certainly the Hurricanes of King and Nicolson. The wrecked machine at Lee was visited, amongst others, by Mr. F. Hunt of Millbrook — then a young boy. On asking one of the guards its nationality, he was told, 'German sonny', despite some evidence of RAF markings. Mr. Bert Angel also went to the scene and recalls seeing the eight .303 Browning machine guns strewn around the field. The Rownhams crash was visited by Mr. Phillips of Rownhams Farm who vividly remembered seeing 'bits and pieces of wreckage strewn all over the place'. The Press clearly stated in 1945 that James Nicolson's aircraft crashed at Rownhams and the majority of opinion now conforms to that view.

However an unresolved argument still exists over the identity of the German aircraft attacked by Nicolson. Local legend claims that one of the several crashed enemy machines in the immediate vicinity was the 'plane attacked by Nicolson'. The Messerschmitt Bf 110 at North Baddesley has since been excavated by enthusiasts and claimed by them to be Nicolson's 'victim' but this is certainly not the case as it crashed on August 13. A check with the aircraft losses in this book for August 16 would seem to indicate that there are no Bf 110 land crashes which can be attributed to Flight Lieutenant Nicolson on that day. Nicolson himself believed the aircraft crashed in the sea.

'Nick' landed in a field belonging to a Mr. Strange at Burrowdale Road, Millbrook and one of the first on the

Above: **Flight Lieutenant Nicolson's combat report was dictated while in hospital and signed by the CO of No. 249, Squadron Leader John Grandy.** *Below:* **His entry in his personal flying log book confirms he was flying GN-A at the time. Note the discrepancy between the times given in the two documents.**

Squadron Leader Nicolson (pictured taking the salute outside Leeds Town Hall at Warships Week in 1942) returned to flying in April 1941 with familiarisation flights in a Miles Master. After being checked out at No. 54 OTU, he served at Finningly, Hunsdon and Hibaldstow before being posted as Station Commander to Alipore, Calcutta in 1942. The last entry in his log book is for a Tiger Moth flight on November 2, 1944 at Chittagong. 'Nick' had already been asked to stand as a candidate for the Member of Parliament for York in the elections to be held at the end of the war when he went missing over the Bay of Bengal in May 1945.

In April 1980 we were privileged to be able to photograph the award cast in bronze from the cascables of two of the Chinese guns captured in the Crimea from the Russians now at the Royal Artillery Depot at Woolwich. Examining the obverse, the date reads '10 NOV 1940'. Normally, when the Cross is given for a specific action, then it is that date which is inscribed. When awarded for sustained effort the date shown is the publication date of the citation in the London Gazette. James Nicolson's VC conforms to neither custom and Military Secretary 3 branch of the Ministry of Defence, depository of the complete records on the Victoria Cross, can give no explanation for the mis-dating.

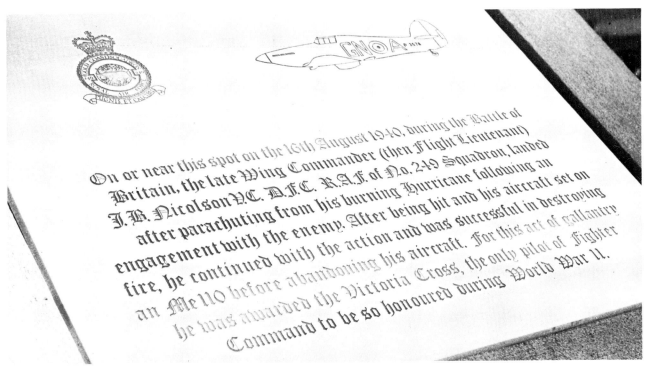

On or near this spot on the 16th August 1940, during the Battle of Britain, the late Wing Commander (then Flight Lieutenant) J.B. Nicolson V.C. D.F.C. R.A.F. of No. 249 Squadron, landed after parachuting from his burning Hurricane following an engagement with the enemy. After being hit and his aircraft set on fire, he continued with the action and was successful in destroying an Me 110 before abandoning his aircraft. For this act of gallantry he was awarded the Victoria Cross, the only pilot of Fighter Command to be so honoured during World War II.

scene was Mrs. Phyllis Lewis along with Police Constable Eric Coleman. Mrs. Lewis clearly recalls Nicolson's smouldering tunic and his dictation of a telegram to PC Coleman for his wife saying that he was safe. (The telegram was sent from nearby Redbridge Post Office.) Today this area is an industrial estate the actual site of his landing being occupied by Mullard's factory. In 1970, Mullards erected a memorial on or near the spot where he landed and this was unveiled by Muriel Nicolson on Sunday, August 16, 1970 — the 30th anniversary of the event. At the ceremony was Eric Coleman, the policeman to whom Nicolson had dictated his telegram. In 1970 he was a Chief Superintendent in the Southampton Police and he still had the original

dictated note which he presented to Mrs. Nicolson. Also present at the ceremony were two other men who went to Nicolson's aid, Mr. F. Lisle and Mr. E. A. Dukes.

Tragically, Nicolson (by then a 29-year-old Wing Commander with the VC and DFC) did not survive the war. On May 2, 1945 at 2.50 a.m., he died when the No. 355 Squadron Liberator in which he was flying as a passenger in a raid on Rangoon crashed in the Bay of Bengal at 2052N, 8933E after an engine caught fire. He has no known grave and is commemorated on Column 445 of the Singapore Memorial. Apart from this and the memorial at the Mullard factory, he is also remembered on one of the RAF's fleet of VC10 aircraft (XV107) which is named after him.

Exactly thirty years after 'Nick' landed at Millbrook, his widow unveiled this memorial stone in the grounds of the Mullard Southampton factory on the Millbrook Industrial Estate.

The Aircraft Losses

PETER D. CORNWELL

Introduction

The air battles fought over southern England during the summer of 1940 are well documented and to the casual observer another book on the subject may appear excessive, possibly even superfluous. This is not so, for this volume is unique. Unlike previously published accounts, this work finally attempts to establish with certainty the actual losses suffered by the Luftwaffe and RAF Fighter Command during the period July 10 - October 31, 1940 — a truly accurate assessment of which must surely form the basis of any informed comment on the subject. Yet, unaccountably, no two books on the Battle of Britain seem to conform on this vital aspect of our recent past as any serious student of aviation history will readily attest. This is a disturbing situation when previous accounts and even official statistics fail to agree on details still within the living memory of the actual participants.

Emerging forty years after the events they describe, these pages define losses in both men and machines with hitherto unpublished accuracy and detail, part of the results of research which has absorbed my interest over the past twenty years. Presented in diary form, the period included in this account follows that established by the 'official' British history. This is an arbitrary choice, particularly from the German viewpoint, but adopted here merely for ease of comparison with existing records. Similarly, the curious expedient of comparing only those losses suffered by RAF Fighter Command to those of the entire Luftwaffe is also perpetuated.

Despite the plethora of material already published, the Battle of Britain still remains an emotive subject and one that I therefore have attempted to approach dispassionately as an academic. The observant reader will note that I have largely ignored the contentious area of claims and victories. This was quite deliberate and I make no apology for so doing. Identifying the victors and the vanquished was not the aim of this work and to offer such opinions, however seemingly well founded, would be at best speculative and at worst irresponsible on such a broad scale. It would be particularly so if one were forced to base such judgements on existing accounts, many of which are shown to be unreliable.

I have concentrated in this volume on determining the actual losses suffered by both sides, basing my findings on surviving contemporary documents, my initial approach being made to official RAF sources and to the Air Historical Branch in particular. I owe sincere thanks to Mr. L. A. Jackets of that department for his generous assistance in allowing me privileged access to documents and files relevant to the period and to Mr. E. H. Turner, Mr. S. H. Bostock and Mr. G. Gateley for guiding me so diligently through the wealth of research material then in their custody and for suggesting alternative sources. Also I am most appreciative of the ready willingness of Mr. D. Bateman to answer many last minute queries. Much of this material has since passed into the Public Records Office at Kew where students may now consult such documents as the Squadron Operations Record Books (Forms 540) with comparative ease.

These fascinating volumes contain details of flights made by each pilot together with a daily summary of the squadron's activities, individual combat reports (Forms 'F') being filed separately as an appendix. They were usually compiled by the Duty Officer and these records sometimes reveal the pressures of a front-line unit beyond their bald statement of actual events. Often based upon cryptic notes hastily scribbled between combat sorties flown from forward aerodromes, they inevitably contain errors and ambiguous entries. Yet, often unverified, these documents form the basis of previously published accounts as well as official records and statistics relating to the Battle of Britain. A good illustration is provided by the entry on Saturday, September 14 for the loss of an aircraft and crew from the Shoreham-based Fighter Interception Unit. The Form 540 in the ORB fails to give the serial of the aircraft concerned but the official Air Ministry file on the incident states that the aircraft was a Blenheim L5721 — an irreconcilable statement as the serial L5721 was issued to a Fairey Battle with No. 9 Bombing and Gunnery School on June 14. Francis K. Mason tried to solve this mystery in *Battle over Britain*, McWhirter Twins Limited, 1969, pp 568-569, where he stated that the aircraft was Beaufighter R2059 and that its last operation took place on the night of September 12/13. However, Beaufighter R2059 was damaged in an accident on September 9, was repaired by No. 4 Maintenance Unit at Bristol and was still 'on charge' in 1945. The actual aircraft was, in fact, Blenheim *Z5721* which took off from *Tangmere* and was lost on *September 14*, the crew being made prisoners-of-war. Contemporary accounts on how the aircraft came to be lost also conflict, the pilot stating that they were hit by flak over Calais whilst one of the crewmen said that they ran out of petrol!

Accepting, therefore, the limitations of wartime records and ignoring earlier publications, I have, wherever possible, chosen to seek corroboration from other contemporary sources during preparation of this work. Some were available to me amongst those records already referred to but much had to be compiled from basic sources. By the simple yet arduous process of tracing the history of every Hurricane and Spitfire airframe available to RAF Fighter Command between July and December 1940, I was able to correct many previous errors and plug gaps in existing records. More important, this analysis revealed far more losses to RAF aircraft than have hitherto been recorded. Many such incidents are included here for the very first time.

Casualties to pilots and aircrew, another sorely vexed question, suffered similar scrutiny during preparation of this volume. I was particularly pleased to be involved in the research on the list of casualties presented elsewhere in this book which should be accepted as the only credible one yet published.

Few German documentary sources survived the end of the war, so I was especially fortunate in obtaining access to an original copy of the Luftwaffe Quartermaster General's returns for 1940. These established a basis for the German losses detailed in this account. Though they are highly subjective, like most contemporary documents, they are subject to interpretation for errors abound. Again, wherever possible, I have sought corroboration from other sources. For help in seeking out valuable extra information relating to Luftwaffe losses of the period, I am indebted to the staffs of the Bundesarchiv Zentralnachweisstelle, Koblenz; the Deutsche Dienststelle (WASt) in Berlin and the Volksbund Deutsche Kriegsgraberfursorge e.V. Kassel. Mr. L. Stevens also proved an abundant source of information on German aircrew buried in the UK and I am grateful for his early assistance.

Whenever an aircraft came to grief in wartime, the civil authorities were often involved and most of them kept log books which offered a significant source of fascinating information and verification of details already gleaned. Archives outside the official libraries were scoured for such records and my thanks are also due to those Chief Constables and County Archivists who allowed me access to police records and ARP reports relating to aircraft casualties in their localities. Incorporating such details makes this work the most specific account yet published as to where aircraft actually fell in 1940. Parish burial registers and the files of local Casualty Clearance Officers provided additional notes on aircrew losses whilst the wartime records of the Royal National Lifeboat Institution proved an excellent source of information on incidents occurring off shore. These were kindly made available to me through Christopher Elliott to whom I owe sincere thanks.

Jim Beedle volunteered admirable assistance in vetting my details on No. 43 Squadron's losses whilst Alan Brown and Terry Parsons also gave invaluable advice on the manuscript. Many kind friends and patient correspondents sustained my interest over the years and often provoked lines of inquiry which I may well have otherwise overlooked. A special mention therefore to Dennis Knight, Michael Payne and my good friend Bruce Robertson who generously provided me with a great deal of unique material from his own collection. To these and others too numerous to mention who offered advice, guidance and encouragement during the years of research, my humble thanks. Not least of all to Ann, Simon and Alex who accepted my prolonged absences from the family over a particularly difficult period which coincided with final manuscript preparation — my special thanks.

Finally, my appreciation to the editorial team for their skill and patience during production of this book and to the editor Winston Ramsey in particular. From the outset his obviously keen interest in this project plus his total commitment to 'getting it right' proved a valuable stimulus.

However carefully researched and meticulously compiled these records may be, I accept that they must inevitably remain incomplete and will almost certainly be shown to contain errors. Nevertheless, I offer them as the first honest attempt to establish a correct basis for the actual losses suffered by both sides during the Battle of Britain.

Aviation Archaeology and the Battle of Britain

The rise of interest in aviation archaeology over recent years, where enthusiasts have grouped themselves together to excavate wartime aircraft wrecks, has provided some interesting footnotes to many of the entries included in this narrative.

Schoolboy witnesses to wartime crashes often coveted souvenirs of such events and the immediate post-war years saw a developing interest in and the collection of such memorabilia. Early enthusiasts such as Ken Anscombe, Christopher Elliott, Peter Foote and Dennis Knight were among the first to establish important personal collections and eventually to contemplate the then rather eccentric notion of excavating the remains of aircraft which had crashed during the war.

Their activities captured the imagination of like-minded enthusiasts who initiated similar ventures and thus the first generation of aviation archaeologists was born. The late 1950s and early 1960s witnessed the early excavations by groups which later evolved into such organisations as the Ashford and Tenterden Recovery Group, the Halstead War Museum, the Kent Battle of Britain Museum and London Air Museum. Inevitably others disbanded as interest waned, their finds, undocumented and unresearched, being scattered and lost to us forever.

These early recovery operations were generally somewhat haphazard affairs and evoked a curiously ambivalent attitude on the part of the Ministry of Defence which eventually became directly involved following some disturbing early discoveries. A growing public interest in the history of aviation and the Second World War in particular, provided aviation archaeologists with much publicity, often adverse, in the news media, and created some concern among modern historians.

The events of our recent past form part of our national heritage and the unbridled activities of amateur enthusiasts in the sphere of aircraft recovery is to be condemned. It is true to say that the vast majority of excavations already undertaken have proved of no real historical value. Despite the best of declared intentions by the groups concerned, the motives of many remain questionable and acquisition is often more important than inquisition. All too infrequently, a recovery is effected whereby valuable historical matter is revealed or corroboration of ambiguous contemporary evidence is obtained but this is often accidental and even then it is the subject of little real research or careful documentation.

As the aviation archaeology movement gathered momentum in the late 1960s, competition between groups became fierce and the frenzied level of their activities finally provoked a note of guidance to recovery groups which was issued by the Ministry of Defence in March 1975. This document sought to exert a degree of indirect control on groups by the exercise of self-discipline and relied upon their willingness to adopt certain standards. As a guide line it was well conceived and it had much to commend it but, regrettably, it carried no great legislative weight and, as a result, was of little real value in protecting crashed military aircraft of historical interest.

In November 1979, in response to a great deal of media attention to the recovery of crashed aircraft where bombs and human remains had been uncovered, the Air Force Board Secretariat withdrew permission for all outstanding digs. The revised notes of guidance issued in February 1980 attempted to lay down new rules which, if observed, would avoid many of the problems raised on earlier recoveries and they also clearly re-affirmed that all crashed UK military aircraft remained Crown property until ownership rights have been relinquished. However this new document, without the backing of the law, still falls short of what is required to protect a dwindling resource of national importance and it is to be hoped that the authorities will tighten their control on groups in general. Aviation archaeologists sincere in their interests and intentions should welcome such control which would be in the best interests of their own movement at large.

To this end, the British Aviation Archaeological Council, as a liaison between such groups and the Ministry of Defence, could provide a useful vehicle whereby direct control might be exercised. Sadly, an initiative in this area seems lacking and excavations continue apace, history being the poorer as a result.

It is my sincere belief that some of the groups currently involved in aviation archaeology are at least conscious of their huge responsibility as custodians of a rich historical heritage. It is my fear that they are unaware of means to protect such a heritage and ill-equipped to do so. I applaud their diligence, their enthusiasm and their enterprise but I suspect that any true benefit from their individual efforts is, at present, minimal. Hopefully this book will, in some part, help provide lasting documentation on some of their discoveries to date. It is a singular mark of their obviously serious intentions that many groups involved in aviation archaeology were pleased to co-operate in the preparation of this work and I offer them all my thanks as follows.

Mike Llewellyn, a prime-mover among aviation archaeologists, was generous with his time and hospitality

in providing vital backgrounds to the hundreds of crash sites he has investigated over the years, many of which are included in this narrative. It was Mike who, in 1972, afforded me the opportunity of associating myself with what I considered to be a truly worthwhile enterprise — creation of the Kent Battle of Britai*. Museum at Chilham Castle. At that time there was no officially sponsored museum where the public could remind itself of the events of 1940 and inspect tangible relics of those days. Indeed the 'official' museums possess very little directly attributable to the Battle of Britain. As a sincere and humble tribute to all airmen who flew, fought and died in the skies over southern England, the Kent Battle of Britain Museum remains unique. To its curator, Mike Llewellyn, for the privilege of allowing me a small personal contribution to history and for five years well spent in the good company of his dedicated volunteers, I shall remain indebted.

I am also indebted to Jim Howard and Simon Parry of the Air Historical Group for their valuable contribution to this work and to Keith Hiscock, Peter Rushen and Mike Skeels of the Essex Aviation Group, whose professional presentation of items gleaned from their files was much appreciated.

Lashenden Air Warfare Museum provided useful material resulting from their 'digs' as did Peter Dimond and Chris Goss of the Southern Area Wartime Aircraft Preservation Society who added considerably to my knowledge of wartime events in Hampshire.

Steven Vizard, whose private collection of 1940 memorabilia rivals many museum collections, also made a significant contribution.

Particular thanks for information to Brenzett Aeronautical Museum and its chairman, Dave Buchanan, whose quiet courtesy veils an impressive ability to organize the most ambitious recovery projects.

I would also like to express my grateful appreciation to Andy Saunders for his enthusiastic involvement with this venture. He not only volunteered a wealth of information relating to Sussex crashes but also profuse notes on excavations organised together with colleagues Brian Connolly, Steve Hall and Pat Burgess of the Wealden Aviation Archaeological Group.

Finally, a special word of thanks to my good friend Tony Graves whose persuasive talents often convinced even me that a bleak dawn spent in some rural backwater awaiting the arrival of a JCB is a worthwhile experience and who usually proved correct. For his time in compiling notes on the countless sites he has investigated together with John Tickner over recent years and for details of the many aircraft they so diligently unearthed for the London Air Museum, many thanks.

The following organizations also rendered valuable assistance: Derbyshire Historical Aviation Society, Devon Aircraft Research and Recovery Team, Dumfries and Galloway Aviation Group, Essex Historical Aircraft Society, Fenland Aircraft Preservation Society, Gwalia Aviation Research Group, Historic Aircraft Archaeologist Group, Humberside Aircraft Preservation Society, Kettering Aircraft Research Group, Lincolnshire Aircraft Recovery Group, Norfolk & Suffolk Aviation Museum, North East Aircraft Museum, Scotland West Aircraft Investigation Group, Solway Aviation Archaeology Group, South West Aircraft Recovery Group and the Warplane Wreck Investigation Group.

Peter D. Cornwell

Girton, Cambridgeshire
March, 1980.

The Royal Air Force

Wednesday, July 10

In 1951, Noordwijk General Cemetery in the Netherlands still contained temporary wartime grave markers. The grave of Pilot Officer Tom Higgs, who collided with a Dornier on the afternoon of the first day of the battle, is the fifth from the left.

56 SQUADRON, NORTH WEALD

Hurricane P3554. Hit in engine during combat with Bf 110s over convoy off Dungeness 2.00 p.m. Crash-landed Manston with engine seized. Flight Lieutenant E. J. Gracie unhurt. Aircraft a write-off.

66 SQUADRON, COLTISHALL

Spitfire N3042. Hit by return fire from Do 17 engaged off Winterton 8.30 a.m. Returned to base. Pilot Officer C. A. Cooke unhurt. Aircraft repairable.

74 SQUADRON, HORNCHURCH

Spitfire P9446. Forced-landed following combat with Bf 109s over the Channel off Dover 11.05 a.m. Sergeant E. A. Mould unhurt. Aircraft damaged but repairable.

Spitfire K9863. Damaged in combat with Do 17s and Bf 109s over Dover 11.05 a.m. Forced-landed Manston. Pilot Officer J. C. Freeborn unhurt. Aircraft damaged but repairable.

Spitfire P9398. Hit in radiator during combat with Do 17s and Bf 109s over Dover 2.00 p.m. Crash-landed at Lympne. Pilot Officer D. G. Cobden unhurt. Aircraft repairable.

111 SQUADRON, CROYDON

Hurricane P3671. Attacked by Oblt. Oesau of III/JG51 during combat over the Channel off Folkestone 1.00 p.m. Collided with Do 17 of 3/KG2 and lost a wing at 6,000ft. Flying Officer T. P. K. Higgs baled out but killed. Aircraft lost.

Hurricane P3459. Damaged in combat with Bf 109s off Folkestone 1.15 p.m. Returned to base. Flying Officer H. M. Ferris unhurt. Aircraft damaged but repairable.

Hurricane P3663. Damaged in port wing during action off Folkestone. Crashed on landing at Hawkinge 2.00 p.m. Sergeant R. Carnall unhurt. Aircraft damaged but repairable.

Hurricane P3676. Damaged in attack by Spitfire over Hawkinge 7.00 p.m. Pilot Officer B. M. Fisher unhurt. Aircraft damaged but repairable.

253 SQUADRON, KIRTON-IN-LINDSEY

Hurricane P3359. Lost control flying in bad visibility on dawn patrol. Crashed near Humber coast. Sergeant I. C. C. Clenshaw killed. Aircraft a write-off.

610 SQUADRON, BIGGIN HILL

Spitfire L1000. Hit in port mainplane by Bf 109 during combat over Dover 11.15 a.m. Crashed on landing at Hawkinge. Squadron Leader A. T. Smith unhurt. Aircraft DW-D damaged but repairable.

611 SQUADRON, TERNHILL

Spitfire N3051. Starboard flap badly damaged in landing on waterlogged runway. Flying Officer D. H. Watkins unhurt. Aircraft repairable.

Thursday, July 11

66 SQUADRON, COLTISHALL

Spitfire N3182. Hit by return fire from Do 17 engaged ten miles south-east of Yarmouth 6.20 a.m. Returned to base. Squadron Leader R. H. A. Leigh unhurt. Aircraft repairable.

85 SQUADRON, MARTLESHAM HEATH

Hurricane P2716. Shot down in sea off Harwich during attack on Do 17 of II/KG2 6.15 a.m. Squadron Leader P. W. Townsend baled out and rescued by *Cap Finisterre*. Aircraft VY-F lost.

87 SQUADRON, EXETER

Hurricane P3387. Returned to base damaged in combat with Bf 110s of III/ZG76 south of Portland 12.01 p.m. Flying Officer R. L. Glyde unhurt. Aircraft repairable.

145 SQUADRON, TANGMERE

Hurricane P3400. Shot down during combat over the Channel and ditched off Selsey Bill 6.25 p.m. Squadron Leader J. R. A. Peel rescued semi-conscious by Selsey lifeboat. Aircraft lost.

Hurricane P2951. Glycol system damaged in combat over the Channel 6.30 p.m. Landed at base engine seized. Flying Officer G. R. Branch unhurt. Aircraft repairable.

236 SQUADRON, THORNEY ISLAND

Blenheim L6816. Hit in engine and mainplane by return fire from He 111 engaged over Start Point 12.30 p.m. Landed St. Eval. Pilot Officer B. M. McDonough, Sergeant F. A. P. Head believed unhurt. Aircraft damaged but repairable.

242 SQUADRON, COLTISHALL

Hurricane P3088. Crashed following routine patrol 6.10 a.m. cause not stated. Pilot Officer R. D. Grassick unhurt. Aircraft damaged but repairable.

501 SQUADRON, MIDDLE WALLOP

Hurricane N2485. Shot down by Oblt. Franziket of III/JG27 in combat over convoy ten miles south-east of Portland Bill 8.00 a.m. Sergeant F. J. P. Dixon baled out but drowned despite search by Weymouth lifeboat. Aircraft lost.

601 SQUADRON, TANGMERE

Hurricane P3681. Set alight by bullet in gravity tank during attack on He 111s over the Channel off Selsey Bill. Crashed at Cranmore, Isle of Wight 6.20 p.m. Sergeant A. W. Woolley baled out badly burned and wounded. Aircraft a write-off.

609 SQUADRON, WARMWELL

Spitfire L1095. Shot down by Oblt. Dobislav of III/JG27 during combat over convoy off Portland 8.05 a.m. Pilot Officer G. T. M. Mitchell missing (washed ashore near Newport, Isle of Wight). Aircraft lost.

Spitfire L1069. Severely damaged in combat with Bf 109s of III/JG27 over convoy off Portland 8.10 a.m. Abandoned five miles off Portland Bill whilst trying to reach coast. Flight Lieutenant P. H. Barran baled out wounded and badly burned. Rescued from sea but died before reaching land. Aircraft lost.

611 SQUADRON, TERNHILL

Spitfire N3052. Starboard wheel damaged hitting a chock on take-off. Returned to base 11.00 a.m. Flying Officer D. H. Watkins unhurt. Aircraft repairable.

Right: **Sergeant Fred Dixon's body was washed up in France and was buried in Abbeville Communal Cemetery.**

The Barran family grave in Leeds (Lawns Wood) Cemetery. Thirty-one-year-old Philip, or 'Pip' as he was nicknamed, of No. 609 Squadron was buried here in July 1940, his mother in 1953 and father in 1956.

Friday, July 12

29 SQUADRON, DIGBY

Blenheim L6646. Undercarriage hydraulics failure. Forced-landed at base 2.50 a.m. Pilot Officer J. R. D. Braham and Sergeant W. J. Gregory unhurt. Aircraft damaged but repairable.

79 SQUADRON, TURNHOUSE

Hurricane N2609. Collided with Miles Master at Sealand during transit flight. Pilot unhurt. Aircraft damaged but repairable.

85 SQUADRON, MARTLESHAM HEATH

Hurricane P2557. Crashed into the sea off Felixstowe during attack on He 111 of II/KG53 8.50 a.m. Sergeant L. Jowitt missing. Aircraft lost.

Right: **'Mitch' Mitchell was washed up on the Isle of Wight near Newport. On July 25 he was buried at Letchworth in a grave now neglected and overgrown.**

145 SQUADRON, TANGMERE

Hurricane N2703. Overturned during forced-landing north-west of Ringwood during routine patrol 12.30 p.m. Sub-Lieutenant F. A. Smith slightly hurt. Aircraft a write-off.

151 SQUADRON, NORTH WEALD

Hurricane P3304. Returned to base badly damaged by return fire from Do 17 of II/KG2 engaged over convoy off Orfordness 9.45 a.m. Wing Commander F. V. Beamish unhurt. Aircraft damaged but repairable.

Hurricane P3152. Rudder controls shot away in action against Do 17s of II/KG2 over convoy off Orfordness, 9.45 a.m. Dead-stick landing at Martlesham Heath. Squadron Leader E. M. Donaldson unhurt. Aircraft damaged but repairable.

Hurricane P3275. Hit in engine by return fire from Do 17 of II/KG2 engaged over convoy off Orfordness 9.45 a.m. Ditched in sea. Flying Officer J. H. L. Allen missing. Aircraft lost.

234 SQUADRON, ST. EVAL

Spitfire N3231. Returned with broken rudder cable after engaging Ju 88 which bombed base 4.38 p.m. Pilot Officer W. H. G. Gordon unhurt. Aircraft damaged but repairable.

257 SQUADRON, NORTHOLT

Hurricane L2101. Landing accident at base. Pilot Officer G. H. Maffett unhurt. Aircraft damaged but repairable.

Hurricane P3707. Landing accident at base. Pilot Officer The Hon. D. A. Coke believed unhurt. Aircraft damaged but repairable.

501 SQUADRON, MIDDLE WALLOP

Hurricane P3084. Shot down into the Channel off Portland during attack on a Do 17 3.45 p.m. Pilot Officer D. A. Hewitt missing despite search by Weymouth lifeboat. Aircraft lost.

610 SQUADRON, BIGGIN HILL

Spitfire P9502. Lost control in dive through cloud during dogfight practice. Crashed at Titsey Park. Sergeant S. Ireland killed. Aircraft DW-Q a write-off.

Site excavated by the London Air Museum which recovered a complete Rolls-Royce Merlin engine, propeller boss with two blades still attached, .303in Browning machine-gun with 'P9502' stencilled on the ammunition feed mechanism, blind-flying panel and one complete undercarriage leg.

Saturday, July 13

19 SQUADRON, DUXFORD

Spitfire R6688. Stalled attempting steep turn during dogfight practice. Crashed and burned out 7.00 p.m. Sergeant R. R. G. Birch killed. Aircraft a write-off.

25 SQUADRON, MARTLESHAM HEATH

Blenheim   . Lost starboard propeller and reduction gear during convoy patrol. Forced-landed. Flying Officer A. Lyall unhurt. Aircraft believed repairable.

Right: **Sergeant Ireland's remains were taken back to his native home of Newtownbreda just outside Belfast, Northern Ireland.**

Excavation of Sergeant Sydney Ireland's Spitfire in Titsey Park — the first Battle of Britain crash site excavated by the London Air Museum (Patrick Smith Associates). *Below:* The evidence of identity on the ammunition feed chute.

The churchyard of SS Mary and Andrew at Whittlesford is the burial ground for RAF Duxford. There are thirty graves from the 1939-45 war including one Czech and one of the Polish Air Force. Two Battle of Britain pilots lie buried here — Sergeant Raymond Birch, killed on July 13, and Pilot Officer Raymond Aeberhardt who died on the last day of August.

43 SQUADRON, TANGMERE

Hurricane P3466. Hit in petrol tank by return fire from He 111 engaged off south coast 11.30 a.m. Returned to base. Pilot Officer D. G. Gorrie unhurt. Aircraft repairable.

Hurricane P3531. Hit in port mainplane and aileron by return fire from He 111 engaged off Sussex coast 11.30 a.m. Returned to base. Pilot Officer R. A. De Mancha unhurt. Aircraft repairable.

56 SQUADRON, NORTH WEALD

Hurricane N2402. Damaged in attack by Oblt. Foezoe of 4/JG51 whilst engaging Ju 87s of II/StG1 over the Channel off Calais 4.45 p.m. Flight Lieutenant J. H. Coghlan slightly injured. Aircraft repairable.

Hurricane P2922. Shot down by Oblt. Foezoe of 4/JG51 in combat over the Channel off Calais 4.45 p.m. Sergeant J. J. Whitfield missing. Aircraft lost.

Hurricane N2432. Shot down in combat over the Channel off Calais 4.45 p.m. by Fw. John of 4/JG51. Sergeant J. R. Cowsill missing. Aircraft lost.

Hurricane P2985. Damaged forced-landing near Detling 5.00 p.m. following combat over the Channel. Sergeant R. D. Baker unhurt. Aircraft damaged but repairable.

64 SQUADRON, KENLEY

Spitfire K9795. Hit by AA fire during combat with Bf 109s over Dover 5.45 p.m. Belly-landed Hawkinge. Sergeant A. E. Binham unhurt. Aircraft damaged but repairable.

238 SQUADRON, MIDDLE WALLOP

Hurricane P2950. Believed wounded by return fire during destruction of Do 17 of 2(F)/123 over Chesil Beach. Stalled and crashed at Southdown, Littlemore trying to avoid HT cables during landing 3.20 p.m. Flight Lieutenant J. C. Kennedy killed. Aircraft a write-off.

263 SQUADRON, GRANGEMOUTH

Hurricane P2991. Night-flying accident during unauthorised patrol. Crashed at Carstairs Junction Public School, Lanark attempting to land in built-up area 2.15 a.m. Flight Lieutenant W. O. L. Smith unhurt. Aircraft a write-off.

603 SQUADRON, MONTROSE

Spitfire L1024. Engine seized during routine flight. Forced-landed at base. Pilot Officer D. K. MacDonald unhurt. Aircraft repairable.

610 SQUADRON, BIGGIN HILL

Spitfire R6807. Crashed at Skid House, Tatsfield during routine patrol 11.36 a.m. Cause not stated. Sergeant P. I. Watson-Parker killed. Aircraft a write-off.

Flight Lieutenant John Kennedy of Sydney, New South Wales lies over 10,000 miles from home in Warmwell Churchyard and Sergeant Patrick Watson-Parker is buried in SS Peter and Paul Churchyard at Cudham in Kent.

Sunday, July 14

111 SQUADRON, CROYDON

Hurricane P2958. Crashed on take-off from Hawkinge forward base Pilot Officer A. G. A. Fisher unhurt. Aircraft damaged but repairable.

615 SQUADRON, KENLEY

Hurricane L1584. Shot down by Bf 109s of II/JG51 in combat over convoy off Dover 3.30 p.m. Crashed in sea. Pilot Officer M. R. Mudie baled out badly wounded and rescued by Navy. Admitted to Dover Hospital but died 15.7.40. Aircraft lost.

Monday, July 15

17 SQUADRON, DEBDEN

Hurricane P3482. Flying accident. Crashed during routine patrol. Pilot Officer D. L. Dawbarn unhurt. Aircraft a write-off.

92 SQUADRON, PEMBREY

Spitfire P9434. Forced-landed near Liskeard 8.30 p.m. due to storm and loss of bearings during return flight from AFDU Northolt. Flight Lieutenant R. R. S. Tuck unhurt. Aircraft damaged but repairable.

145 SQUADRON, TANGMERE

Hurricane P3517. Forced-landed at Wickham in bad visibility 10.00 p.m. Flying Officer P. W. Dunning-White unhurt. Aircraft believed undamaged.

Robin Hood of the Devon Aircraft Research and Recovery Team with the Merlin retrieved from the mouth of the River Dart, 145ft below the surface. The aircraft was hit by return fire from a Dornier 17 over Old Mill Creek. Sub-Lieutenant Bramah was able to climb with smoke coming from the engine before baling out, being rescued by the destroyer Scimitar. It is hoped to display the engine, together with the complete story and eye witness reports of the incident, in Dartmouth Museum (Herald Express).

213 SQUADRON, EXETER

Hurricane N2541. Shot down near Dartmouth following attack on Do 17 over Portland 1.20 p.m. Crashed in sea. Sub-Lieutenant H. G. K. Bramah baled out injured. Aircraft lost.

Rolls-Royce Merlin engine recovered by Totnes Sub-Aqua Club, July 1979 and donated to the Devon Aircraft Research and Recovery Team believed to be from the submerged wreckage of this aircraft.

249 SQUADRON, CHURCH FENTON

Hurricane L1715. Crashed on landing at Acklington. Sergeant H. J. Davidson unhurt. Aircraft damaged but repairable.

266 SQUADRON, WITTERING

Spitfire N3245. Damaged in heavy landing following night-flying practice. Flight Lieutenant S. H. Bazley unhurt. Aircraft repairable.

609 SQUADRON, WARMWELL

Spitfire P9467. Crashed on landing from routine patrol. Pilot Officer J. Curchin unhurt. Aircraft damaged but repairable.

611 SQUADRON, TERNHILL

Spitfire N3060. Propeller damaged when collided with trolley-accumulator whilst taxiing into dispersal. Sergeant E. N. Kelsey unhurt. Aircraft undamaged.

Tuesday, July 16

73 SQUADRON, CHURCH FENTON

Hurricane P3647. Cross-country flight to Prestwick to arrange billets. Caught in deteriorating weather and attempted forced-landing with undercarriage not locked down. Crashed at Workington 1.00 p.m. Pilot Officer J. D. Smith unhurt. Aircraft damaged but repairable.

249 SQUADRON, CHURCH FENTON

Hurricane P3057. Hit an obstacle during night take-off 00.15 a.m. Pilot Officer J. R. B. Meaker unhurt. Aircraft repairable.

Hurricane P2995. Engine failed on take-off. Crashed and burned out in Copmanthorpe Wood 00.50 a.m. Sergeant A. D. W. Main killed. Aircraft a write-off.

603 SQUADRON, TURNHOUSE

Spitfire   . Hit in starboard mainplane by return fire from He 111 of 9/KG26 shot down twenty-five miles north-east of Frazerburgh 4.10 p.m. Returned to base. Pilot Officer J. S. Morton unhurt. Aircraft repairable.

Wednesday, July 17

32 SQUADRON, BIGGIN HILL

Hurricane N2588. Forced-landed near Dungeness due to loss of oil pressure 4.25 p.m. Flying Officer J. B. W. Humpherson unhurt. Aircraft damaged but repairable.

64 SQUADRON, KENLEY

Spitfire P9507. Crashed Hempstead Lane, Hailsham 2.00 p.m. with serious damage caused by surprise solo attack over the Channel by Lt. Wick of I/JG2. Flying Officer D. M. Taylor wounded admitted to Eastbourne Hospital. Aircraft damaged but repairable.

92 SQUADRON, PEMBREY

Spitfire P9368. Hit by return fire from Ju 88 engaged over Bristol 7.15 p.m. Returned to base. Pilot Officer C. H. Saunders unhurt. Aircraft repairable.

145 SQUADRON, TANGMERE

Hurricane P3163. Returned to base damaged by return fire from Ju 88 engaged near St. Catherine's Point 3.30 p.m. Squadron Leader J. R. A. Peel unhurt. Aircraft repairable.

603 SQUADRON, TURNHOUSE

Spitfire K9916. Missing from operational sortie circumstances unknown. Flying Officer C. D. Peel missing. Aircraft lost.

Thursday, July 18

145 SQUADRON, TANGMERE

Hurricane P3381. Hit by return fire during attack on He 111 twenty miles south of Bognor 1.05 p.m. Returned to base. Flight Lieutenant A. D. McN. Boyd unhurt. Aircraft repairable.

152 SQUADRON, WARMWELL

Spitfire P9440. Hit in mainplane by Bf 109 during attack on Do 17s off the Isle of Wight 10.30 a.m. Pilot Officer C. Warren unhurt. Aircraft damaged but repairable.

Spitfire   . Damaged by Bf 109s during engagement over the Isle of Wight 10.30 a.m. Returned to base. Pilot Officer I. N. Bayles unhurt. Aircraft repairable.

235 SQUADRON, BIRCHAM NEWTON

Blenheim N2541. Failed to return from operational sortie 10.00 a.m. Pilot Officer R. L. Patterson. Sergeant R. Y. Tucker and Sergeant L. H. M. Reece missing. Aircraft lost.

236 SQUADRON, THORNEY ISLAND

Blenheim L6779. Believed shot down by Major Schellmann of JG2 during photo-recce mission over Le Havre 12.15 p.m. Deteriorating weather and intense AA fire over Cap de la Hague. Pilot Officer C. R. D. Thomas killed and Sergeant H. D. B. Elsdon missing. Aircraft lost.

Blenheim L6639. Believed that claimed by Oberfw. Schnell of II/JG2 12.15 p.m. Lost during photo-recce mission over Le Havre with bad weather and intense AA fire over Cap de la Hague. Pilot Officer R. H. Rigby and Sergeant D. D. Mackinnon killed. Aircraft lost.

266 SQUADRON, WITTERING

Spitfire N3170. Collided with stationary tractor whilst taxi-ing at base. Pilot Officer D. G. Ashton unhurt. Aircraft damaged but repairable.

Spitfire N3244. Forced-landed at Heckington due to engine trouble. Pilot Officer R. J. B. Roach unhurt. Aircraft damaged but repairable.

603 SQUADRON, TURNHOUSE

Spitfire R6755. Hit in glycol system by return fire from He 111 engaged over Aberdeen 4.40 p.m. Forced-landed near Old Meldrum. Pilot Officer G. K. Gilroy unhurt. Aircraft damaged but repairable.

603 SQUADRON, MONTROSE

Spitfire L1049. Collided with Miles Master at base. Pilot unhurt. Aircraft damaged but repairable.

609 SQUADRON, WARMWELL

Spitfire R6636. Glycol system damaged by return fire from Ju 88 engaged off Swanage 3.15 p.m. Forced-landed on Studland Beach and covered by sea at high tide. Flying Officer A. R. Edge unhurt taken off by RN launch. Aircraft damaged but repairable.

Spitfire R6634. Shot down by return fire from Ju 88 engaged five miles off Swanage 3.15 p.m. Flight Lieutenant F. J. Howell baled out and rescued by RN Auxiliary vessel. Aircraft lost.

610 SQUADRON, BIGGIN HILL

Spitfire P9452. Shot down by Hptmn. Tietzen of II/JG51 in combat over the Channel north of Calais 10.00 a.m. Pilot Officer P. Litchfield missing. Aircraft DW-T lost.

Friday, July 19

1 SQUADRON, NORTHOLT

Hurricane P3471. Hit in glycol tank by return fire from He 111 of III/KG55 pursued whilst out of ammunition. Forced-landed in flames outside Brighton 6.15 p.m. Pilot Officer D. O. M. Browne unhurt. Aircraft a write-off.

32 SQUADRON, BIGGIN HILL

Hurricane P3144. Believed that shot down by Uffz. Mayer of III/JG51 in combat over Dover. Crashed at Hougham 4.25 p.m. Flight Sergeant G. Turner baled out badly burned and admitted to Dover Hospital. Aircraft a write-off.

43 SQUADRON, TANGMERE

Hurricane P3140. Shot down off Selsey Bill during combat with Bf 109s of III/JG27. Believed that claimed by Oblt. Adolph. Crashed in Channel off Felpham 5.15 p.m. Flight Lieutenant J. W. C. Simpson baled out with bullet in ankle and suffered broken collar-bone in heavy landing at West Worthing. Admitted to Worthing Hospital. Aircraft lost.

Hurricane P3531. Shot down off Selsey in combat with Bf 109s of III/JG27. Probably that claimed by Fw. Lehmann. Crashed in sea 5.15 p.m. Sergeant J. A. Buck baled out wounded but drowned. Aircraft lost.

Hurricane P3468. Damaged in attack by Fw. Blazytko of III/JG27 during action over the Channel off Selsey 5.15 p.m. Returned to base. Sergeant J. L. Crisp believed unhurt. Aircraft repairable.

Our artist George Campbell seeks out the grave of Pilot Officer Ronald Rigby in St. Marie Cemetery at Le Havre, France. His crewman, Sergeant Donald Mackinnon, lies at Villerville Communal Cemetery across on the south side of the Seine Estuary.

64 SQUADRON, KENLEY

Spitfire P9369. Hit in cockpit and starboard aileron during combat over Dover 4.00 p.m. Possibly that attacked by Oblt. Lignitz of III/JG51. Returned to base. Pilot Officer J. J. O'Meara unhurt. Aircraft repairable.

Spitfire K9991. Believed that attacked by Lt. Kolbow. Collided with Bf 109 of III/JG51 during combat over Dover 4.00 p.m. Returned to base with wing-tip damaged. Flying Officer H. J. Woodward unhurt. Aircraft repairable.

141 SQUADRON, WEST MALLING

Defiant L7001. Badly damaged in attack by Bf 109s of III/JG51 over the Channel 12.45 p.m. Crashed near Hawkinge due to engine failure. Flight Lieutenant M. J. Loudon wounded in arm admitted to Canterbury Hospital. Pilot Officer E. Farnes baled out uninjured and rescued from sea. Aircraft a write-off.

In abandoning this aircraft, Pilot Officer Farnes became only the second airman ever to have saved his life by using the X-type static-line parachute manufactured by the GQ Parachute Company. As such, he was awarded a commemorative gold lapel badge inscribed P/O E. Farnes. July 19, 1940'. Forty years later this very badge was discovered by a man digging in his garden at Headington, Oxford.

Defiant L7009. Shot down by Bf 109s of III/JG51 and crashed at Elmsvale Road, Dover 12.45 p.m. Flight Lieutenant I. D. G. Donald and Pilot Officer A. C. Hamilton both killed. Aircraft a write-off.

Defiant L6974. Shot down into the Channel off Dover during combat with Bf 109s of III/JG51 12.45 p.m. Pilot Officer J. R. Kemp and Sergeant R. Crombie missing. Aircraft lost.

Sergeant James Buck (left) was a Volunteer Reservist called to No. 43 Squadron just prior to the outbreak of war. On July 19, flying from Tangmere with 'A' Flight, his Hurricane was shot down when they were bounced by a numerically superior force of enemy fighters. Jimmy Buck, wounded, baled out and landed in the sea. Lack of air-sea rescue facilities delayed the search for him and next day his body was recovered from the Channel. Also in this picture taken at Wick in April 1940 are (L-R) Pilot Officer C. A. Woods-Scawen (killed on September 2), Flight Lieutenant C. B. Hull (killed September 7) Pilot Officer W. C. Wilkinson (killed on June 7 prior to the battle) and Sergeant G. W. Garton who survived the war a Wing Commander (Imperial War Museum).

Sergeant Buck of Chorltonville, Manchester was buried in Stretford Cemetery.

Flight Lieutenant Ian David Graham Donald, DFC, from Epsom and Pilot Officer Arthur Charles Hamilton *(photo left)* from Harrow were two victims in the 'slaughter of the innocents' which took place off Dover on Friday, July 19, 1940. A pilot/air gunner team in a Defiant of No. 141 Squadron, their debut in action proved to be their last. Their unit, although the first to fly the Defiant, had never seen action with the aircraft and by July 19 the Luftwaffe were wise to the limitations of the machine and chopped them down piecemeal. Pilot Officer Hamilton is buried in the cemetery beside Hawkinge aerodrome and Flight Lieutenant Donald, whose grave was terribly overgrown when we discovered it, beside All Saints church at Tilford, Surrey *(below)*.

Defiant L6995. Shot down into the Channel off Dover during combat with Bf 109s of III/JG51 12.45 p.m. Pilot Officer R. A. Howley and Sergeant A. G. Curley missing. Aircraft lost.

Defiant L7015. Shot down into the Channel off Dover during combat with Bf 109s of III/JG51 12.45 p.m. Pilot Officer R. Kidson and Sergeant F. P. J. Atkins killed Aircraft lost.

Defiant L7016. Shot down into the Channel off Dover during combat with Bf 109s of III/JG51 12.45 p.m. Pilot Officer J. R. Gardner baled out wounded, rescued from sea and admitted to Canterbury Hospital. Pilot Officer D. M. Slatter missing. Aircraft lost.

Defiant L6983. Hit in engine during combat with Bf 109s of III/JG51 over the Channel off Dover 12.45 p.m. Returned to base. Pilot Officer I. N. McDougall unhurt. Sergeant J. F. Wise baled out and missing. Aircraft repairable.

145 SQUADRON, TANGMERE

Hurricane P2770. Hit in glycol and hydraulic system by return fire from He 111 of III/KG55 engaged over Sussex coast 6.20 p.m. Forced-landed Shoreham aerodrome. Pilot Officer M. A. Newling slightly concussed admitted to Shoreham Hospital. Aircraft damaged but repairable.

238 SQUADRON, MIDDLE WALLOP

Hurricane P2946. Crash-landed cause not stated. Sergeant H. J. Marsh believed unhurt. Aircraft damaged but repairable.

603 SQUADRON, TURNHOUSE

Spitfire K9995. Damaged in combat with enemy aircraft. Returned to base. Sergeant J. R. Caister unhurt. Aircraft damaged but repairable.

616 SQUADRON, LECONFIELD

Spitfire   . Collided with obstruction at base during night-flying practise 00.50 a.m. Squadron Leader M. Robinson unhurt. Aircraft repairable.

Sergeant Cecil Parkinson of No. 238 Squadron from Counden, Coventry now lies in St. Michael's Churchyard, Stoke.

Saturday, July 20

32 SQUADRON, BIGGIN HILL

Hurricane P3679. Attacked by Hptmn. Tietzen of II/JG51 in action over Dover 6.00 p.m. Returned to base. Sergeant W. B. Higgins slightly injured. Aircraft damaged but repairable.

Hurricane N2670. Shot down by Oblt. Priller of II/JG51 in combat off Dover 6.00 p.m. Sub-Lieutenant G. G. R. Bulmer missing. Aircraft lost.

Hurricane N2532. Engine and gravity tank badly damaged in attack by Oberfw. Illner of II/JG51 during combat off Dover. Forced-landed near Hawkinge and burned out 6.20 p.m. Squadron Leader J. Worrall unhurt. Aircraft GZ-H a write-off.

43 SQUADRON, TANGMERE

Hurricane P3964. Shot down into the Channel during investigation of a He 115 south of the Needles 6.00 p.m. Flying Officer J. F. J. Haworth baled out but missing. Aircraft lost.

Hurricane P3784. Forced-landed beside River Arun at Amberley with engine seized 7.40 a.m. Sergeant H. J. L. Hallowes unhurt. Aircraft damaged but repairable.

152 SQUADRON, WARMWELL

Spitfire K9880. Shot down by Oblt. Homuth of 3/JG27 in combat over the Channel off Swanage 4.35 p.m. Pilot Officer F. H. Posener missing. Aircraft lost.

236 SQUADRON, THORNEY ISLAND

Blenheim L1300. Shot down during escort mission by Hptmn. Neumann of JG27. Crashed in the Channel off Cherbourg 6.20 p.m. Sergeant E. E. Lockton, Sergeant H. Corcoran missing. Aircraft ND-A lost.

238 SQUADRON, MIDDLE WALLOP

Hurricane P3766. Shot down in flames by Oblt. Homuth of 3/JG27 in combat over the Channel fifteen miles south of Swanage 1.15 p.m. Sergeant C. Parkinson baled out and picked up by HMS *Acheron* but died from his injuries the following day.

249 SQUADRON, CHURCH FENTON

Hurricane P3154. Forced-landed at Wellburn Hall, Yorks. following engine failure due to misunderstanding of petrol system. Flying Officer J. R. C. Young unhurt. Aircraft GN-H damaged but repairable.

263 SQUADRON, GRANGEMOUTH

Hurricane P2917. Crashed attempting forced-landing. Cause not stated. Pilot Officer A. R. Downer fatally injured, died next day in Edinburgh Infirmary. Aircraft a write-off.

501 SQUADRON, MIDDLE WALLOP

Hurricane P3082. Shot down by Lt. Zirkenbach of I/JG27 in combat over the Channel off Cherbourg 4.30 p.m. Pilot Officer E. J. H. Sylvester missing. Aircraft lost.

603 SQUADRON, TURNHOUSE

Spitfire R6752. Crash-landed on the aerodrome following delivery flight. Pilot Officer R. G. Manlove (ferry pilot) unhurt. Aircraft repairable.

610 SQUADRON, BIGGIN HILL

Spitfire N3201. Tail shot away by Oberfw. Schmid of I/JG51 in combat over Hawkinge 6.30 p.m. Pilot Officer G. Keighley baled out slightly wounded landing at Lydden. Aircraft DW-S a write-off.

Sunday, July 21

43 SQUADRON, TANGMERE

Hurricane P3973. Collided with Bf 109 flown by Lt. Kroker of 7/JG27 in combat ten miles south of the Needles at 3.15 p.m. Pilot Officer R. A. De Mancha missing. Aircraft lost.

Hurricane P3971. Starboard aileron jammed by 20mm cannon shell during combat with Hptmn. Gerlitz of III/JG27 ten miles south of the Needles 3.15 p.m. Returned to base. Squadron Leader J. V. C. Badger unhurt. Aircraft repairable.

54 SQUADRON, ROCHFORD

Spitfire N3184. Engine failure during convoy patrol fifteen miles east of Clacton. Crashed in sea 9.20 a.m. Pilot Officer J. L. Kemp baled out and rescued by Royal Navy destroyer. Aircraft lost.

73 SQUADRON, PRESTWICK

Hurricane P3470. Undercarriage collapsed in heavy landing after a night-flying exercise. Sergeant A. E. Scott unhurt. Aircraft damaged but repairable.

Hurricane P3034. Stalled from 5ft causing undercarriage to collapse after night-flying practice 2.45 a.m. Sergeant J. J. Griffin unhurt. Aircraft damaged but repairable.

Hurricane P3470. Nosed-over and undercarriage collapsed in landing at base on water-logged runway 6.30 p.m. Sergeant R. V. Ellis believed unhurt. Aircraft damaged but repairable.

238 SQUADRON, MIDDLE WALLOP

Hurricane P3767. Port mainplane damaged by return fire from Do 17 of 4(F)/14 brought down at Blandford 3.00 p.m. Returned to base. Flying Officer C. T. Davis unhurt. Aircraft repairable.

501 SQUADRON, MIDDLE WALLOP

Hurricane L2038. Forced-landed at Ford 10.30 a.m. during routine patrol. Cause not stated. Flight Sergeant P. F. Morfill believed unhurt. Aircraft repairable.

Pilot Officer Alan Downer crashed on July 20 and died the following day.

Monday, July 22

In the late afternoon of Monday, July 22, Pilot Officer John Bickerdyke crashed en route to Castle Camps satellite aerodrome *(above)*. His grave in All Saints' Churchyard, Wimbish, 11,500 miles from his home in Nelson, New Zealand, is sadly neglected.

85 SQUADRON, MARTLESHAM HEATH

Hurricane P3895. Crashed prior to landing at Castle Camps satellite aerodrome 5.35 p.m. Pilot Officer J. L. Bickerdike killed. Aircraft a write-off.

92 SQUADRON, PEMBREY

Spitfire R6597. Night landing accident. Overshot flare-path and crashed at base 2.20 a.m. Sergeant R. H. Fokes unhurt. Aircraft damaged but repairable.

235 SQUADRON, BIRCHAM NEWTON

Blenheim P4835. Forced-landed at Horsham St. Faith due to engine failure approx. 11.00 a.m. Pilot Officer D. N. Woodger, Sergeant W. H. J. Westcott and Sergeant P. R. Prosser unhurt. Aircraft believed undamaged.

601 SQUADRON, TANGMERE

Hurricane L1772. Forced-landed at Rose Green, Pagham due to engine failure 5.38 p.m. Pilot Officer J. K. U. B. McGrath unhurt. Aircraft a write-off.

611 SQUADRON, DIGBY

Spitfire K9950. Landed at base with undercarriage retracted. Reason not stated. Sergeant A. D. Burt unhurt. Aircraft damaged but repairable.

611 SQUADRON, TERNHILL

Spitfire N3062. Forced-landed on beach at Colwyn Bay due to failure of coolant system. Pilot Officer D. A. Adams unhurt. Aircraft damaged but repairable, moved onto promenade to avoid incoming tide.

Above: Pilot Officer Ricardo De Mancha (who had an Italian father and English mother) failed to return from a combat on Sunday afternoon, July 21 (Jim Beedle).

Hornchurch, Thursday, June 27, 1940. Pilot Officer John Laurence Allen receives his DFC from King George VI. Twenty-seven days later he was killed after his Spitfire was disabled by a Bf 109 near Margate. He was seen making for Foreness in a con-trolled descent with a dead engine which restarted after a few minutes. He then made for Manston when the engine died again and, in attempting to turn towards Foreness a second time, he stalled, spun in and crashed. He now lies buried at Margate.

Tuesday, July 23

3 SQUADRON, WICK

Hurricane P2862. Collided on take-off with 269 Squadron Hudson and crashed on aerodrome 12.35 p.m. Pilot Officer D. L. Bisgood seriously injured. Aircraft a write-off.

232 SQUADRON, SUMBURGH

Hurricane P2861. Ditched in sea off Shetlands following engine failure. Sergeant A. F. Butterick rescued unhurt. Aircraft lost.

247 SQUADRON, ROBOROUGH

Gladiator   . Damaged at Usworth during transit flight to base. Flying Officer T. W. Gillen unhurt. Aircraft damaged.

Gladiator   . Damaged at Turnhouse during transit flight to base. Pilot Officer Doughty unhurt. Aircraft damaged.

257 SQUADRON, NORTHOLT

Hurricane P3641. Crashed on landing at Hendon cause not stated. Pilot Officer J. A. G. Chomley unhurt. Aircraft damaged but repairable.

603 SQUADRON, MONTROSE

Spitfire N3026. Landed at base undercarriage up. Reason not stated. Squadron Leader G. L. Denholm unhurt. Aircraft damaged but repairable.

Spitfire N3229. Hit by return fire from Do 17 engaged seventy-five miles east of Aberdeen 3.30 p.m. Returned to base. Flight Lieutenant F. W. Rushmer unhurt. Aircraft damaged but repairable.

Spitfire   . Hit by return fire from Do 17 engaged seventy-five miles east of Aberdeen 3.30 p.m. Pilot Officer N. J. V. Benson unhurt. Aircraft repairable.

Wednesday, July 24

46 SQUADRON, DIGBY

Hurricane P2685. Crash-landed near base. Cause unknown. Flying Officer A. M. Cooper-Key killed. Aircraft a write-off.

54 SQUADRON, ROCHFORD

Spitfire P9389. Forced-landed at Great Bainden Farm, Mayfield and later returned to base damaged following attack on Do 17s bombing Channel convoy off Dover 8.45 a.m. Pilot Officer A. Finnie unhurt. Aircraft repairable.

Spitfire P9549. Returned to base damaged following attack on Do 17s bombing Channel convoy 8.50 a.m. Pilot unhurt. Aircraft damaged but repairable.

Spitfire R6812. Engine damaged in combat with Bf 109s of Stab III/JG26 over Margate. Stalled attempting to reach Manston. Crashed and burned out near the Old Charles Inn, Margate 12.30 p.m. Flying Officer J. L. Allen killed. Aircraft a write-off.

Spitfire R6710. Damaged in attack by Bf 109 of Stab III/JG26 over Margate 12.45 p.m. Returned to base cockpit shattered. Pilot Officer H. K. F. Matthews unhurt. Aircraft damaged but repairable.

Spitfire N3192. Ran out of fuel pursuing an enemy aircraft. Forced-landed at Sizewell near Orfordness 12.50 p.m. Sergeant G. R. Collett slightly injured. Aircraft written-off.

64 SQUADRON, KENLEY

Spitfire L1035. Hit in bottom tank during attack on Do 17 over the Goodwin Sands 9.00 a.m. Returned to base. Sub-Lieutenant F. D. Paul unhurt. Aircraft repairable.

66 SQUADRON, COLTISHALL

Spitfire N3041. Crashed in sea during routine operational patrol. Cause unknown 7.20 p.m. Sergeant A. D. Smith believed unhurt. Aircraft lost.

74 SQUADRON, HORNCHURCH

Spitfire L1001. Landed at base undercarriage retracted during practice landings 11.15 a.m. Flying Officer W. H. Nelson unhurt. Aircraft repairable.

145 SQUADRON, TANGMERE

Hurricane P3516. Crashed on take-off from Westhampnett satellite 5.00 p.m. Pilot Officer J. E. Storrar believed unhurt. Aircraft damaged but repairable.

151 SQUADRON, NORTH WEALD

Hurricane P3316. Crashed on aerodrome from 500ft shortly after take-off 2.10 p.m. Cause unknown. Pilot Officer J. R. Hamar killed. Aircraft a write-off.

Thursday, July 25

32 SQUADRON, BIGGIN HILL

Hurricane P3677. Forced-landed near Dover after combat with Bf 109s 12.50 p.m. Pilot Officer V. G. Daw slightly injured admitted to hospital. Aircraft damaged but repairable.

43 SQUADRON, NORTHOLT

Hurricane N2665. Failed to close throttle on landing after night-flight 10.15 p.m. Overshot runway and crashed into boundary hedge. Pilot Officer R. Lane unhurt. Aircraft damaged but repairable.

54 SQUADRON, ROCHFORD

Spitfire R6707. Shot down following destruction of Bf 109 over convoy between Dover and Deal. Crashed in Channel 3.00 p.m. Flight Lieutenant B. H. Way killed. Aircraft lost.

Spitfire P9387. Crash-landed near Dover following combat with Bf 109s 3.00 p.m. Pilot Officer D. R. Turley-George unhurt. Aircraft a write-off.

Flight Lieutenant Basil Hugh Way (front row, second from right), born in Newark, Nottinghamshire, entered Cranwell Royal Air Force College in 1937 where he won the Groves Memorial Prize for the best all-round pilot performance. He was posted to No. 54 Squadron at Hornchurch in January, 1940 and a few months later was appointed 'B' Flight Commander. On July 25, he led nine Spitfires against a massive force of sixty Ju 87s which were attacking a Channel convoy when they were overwhelmed by a tidal wave of escorting fighters. 'Wonky' Way was shot down into the sea between Dover and Deal and lost without trace — that is, until the vagaries of the tides and currents washed the 22-year-old pilot's remains ashore on a Belgian beach to be buried in Oost-Dunkerke Cemetery.

Welsh-born Pilot Officer Jack Hamar, DFC, from Knighton, Radnorshire was a veteran of the Dunkirk and early coastal battles along the shores of southern Britain. Tall and exceptionally strong, he was popular with all members of No. 151 Squadron and his death on July 24, 1940, when his Hurricane inexplicably crashed after take-off, left a gap in the unit's ranks not easily filled. His award of the DFC had been made only the previous day.

Spitfire R6816. Shot down during combat with Bf 109s over Channel convoy off Dover 6.10 p.m. Crashed at Kingsdown. Pilot Officer A. Finnie killed. Aircraft a write-off.

56 SQUADRON, NORTH WEALD

Hurricane P3479. Returned to base with damage sustained in combat with Ju 87s and Bf 109s over destroyers off Dover 6.00 p.m. Squadron Leader G. A. L. Manton slightly injured. Aircraft damaged but repairable.

64 SQUADRON, KENLEY

Spitfire P9421. Failed to return following combat with enemy aircraft off Dover 2.55 p.m. Crashed in sea. Flying Officer A. J. O. Jeffrey killed. Aircraft lost.

Spitfire L1055. Air-system damaged by Ju 87 over Channel off Dover 3.10 p.m. Forced-landed at Hawkinge. Squadron Leader A. R. D. MacDonnell unhurt. Aircraft damaged but repairable.

Spitfire N3231. Crashed on landing at base due to damage sustained in combat over Dover 4.00 p.m. Flying Officer H. J. Woodward unhurt. Aircraft damaged but repairable.

Spitfire R6700. Forced-landed Lympne with main supercharger bearing failure after combat off Folkestone 5.00 p.m. Flight Lieutenant L. F. Henstock unhurt. Aircraft SH-K repairable.

Spitfire L1035. Crashed in Channel during combat off south coast 5.45 p.m. Sub-Lieutenant F. D. Paul captured severely wounded (died 30.7.40). Aircraft lost.

87 SQUADRON, EXETER

Hurricane P3596. Night-flying accident. Crashed and burned out at Hullavington during early morning. Sergeant J. H. Culverwell killed. Aircraft a write-off.

152 SQUADRON, WARMWELL

Spitfire K9901. Glycol tank hit by return fire from Ju 87. Aircraft ditched 10.50 a.m. five miles south of Portland. Flying Officer E. C. Deansley wounded, rescued by SS *Empire Henchman* and landed at Lyme Regis where admitted to hospital. Aircraft lost.

Spitfire P9327. Damaged in attack by Hptmn. Schlichting of III/JG27 over Channel off Portland 11.30 a.m. Returned to base. Squadron Leader P. K. Devitt unhurt. Aircraft damaged but repairable.

Tuesday 1.15p.m.
21.5.40

Dear Mother & Father,

At last we are able to get time off for a letter or two.

How are all of you at home? I trust very well. Have been moving from place to place, so have never heard from anyone at home in Birmingham.

Have been having a real rough time, lost nearly all my clothes and had been sleeping in any old place, plus getting into some real hot places.

Have been posted down to Tangmere to help form a new squadron. My old squadron pulled in every pilot in the last raid, even including the C/O and we came back almost halved in number, so we just can't carry on the squadron.

We have bagged about forty German planes in the last four days but their numbers are terrific. Have been going in for about six of us to forty and fifty of theirs, the air was thick. I think we lost the Flight Commander yesterday, what a nice chap, they said he was engaged by about ten fighters and went down fighting madly.

Our squadron have been flying every day and we are very tired plus, on top of that, we have had orders to stop the advance at all costs. Believe me, to see the German dive-bombers in their hundreds cutting at our poor troops makes you only too glad to help — its terrible.

Please do not send parcels or letters because of my constant change of address.

Been flying Hurricanes and Spitfires, 'what about that Father?'

Cheerio for now,

With God's good grace I might be seeing you all one of these days.

Your son,
Eric.

By kind permission of Mr. Maurice E. Bann, brother of the late Sergeant Eric Bann of No. 238 Squadron killed on September 28, we are able to reproduce a series of letters Eric wrote to his parents in Macclesfield. They span virtually the entire Battle of Britain period and this first one was written when the squadron was covering the Dunkirk evacuation.

222 SQUADRON, KIRTON-IN-LINDSEY

Spitfire P9443. Damaged by return fire from He 111 engaged off Mablethorpe 7.00 a.m. Returned to base. Pilot Officer T. A. Vigors unhurt. Aircraft damaged but repairable.

Spitfire P9325. Forced-landed four miles north-west of base out of fuel after combat with He 111 off Mablethorpe 7.00 a.m. Flying Officer J. W. Cutts unhurt. Aircraft repairable.

234 SQUADRON, ST. EVAL

Spitfire P9493. Crashed near Porthtowan during routine night patrol 11.45 p.m. Cause unknown. Pilot Officer G. K. Gout killed. Aircraft a write-off.

610 SQUADRON, BIGGIN HILL

Spitfire R6693. Stalled attempting to land at Hawkinge after combat with Bf 109s over the Channel. Crashed and burned out in disused engine testing shed 3.40 p.m. Squadron Leader A. T. Smith killed. Aircraft DW-A a write-off.

Spitfire R6595. Damaged in combat with Bf 109s over Channel convoy 3.20 p.m. Returned to base. Pilot Officer F. T. Gardiner wounded in arm. Aircraft DW-O repairable.

Pilot Officer Geoffrey Gout attended the New Beacon School in Sevenoaks, Kent. He was a keen motorist and raced at Brooklands. Now his remains lie beneath this slab in the churchyard at St. Eval.

Friday, July 26

Squadron Leader Andrew Smith of No. 610 Squadron was killed at Hawkinge on July 25. He was married and came from Manley. This is his simple grave at St. Peter's Churchyard, Delamere, Cheshire.

92 SQUADRON, PEMBREY

Spitfire N3167. Crashed on landing at base on burst tyre after routine night patrol 1.30 a.m. Sergeant S. M. Barraclough unhurt. Aircraft damaged but repairable.

238 SQUADRON, MIDDLE WALLOP

Hurricane P3702. Damaged in head-on attack on Bf 109s of I/JG27 over the Channel off Swanage 12.00 p.m. Sergeant R. Little unhurt. Aircraft damaged but repairable.

266 SQUADRON, WITTERING

Spitfire N3118. Damaged landing at base in heavy rain. Squadron Leader D. G. H. Spencer unhurt. Aircraft repairable.

601 SQUADRON, TANGMERE

Hurricane P3886. Returned to base with engine trouble 9.40 a.m. Flying Officer H. J. Riddle unhurt. Aircraft undamaged.

Hurricane P2753. Shot down in Channel two miles off St. Catherine's Point by Oblt. Dobislav of III/JG27 10.00 a.m. Pilot Officer P. Chaloner Lindsey missing. Aircraft UF-T lost.

603 SQUADRON, TURNHOUSE

Spitfire N3288. Nosed over on landing in mud at Dyce. Pilot Officer G. K. Gilroy unhurt. Aircraft repairable.

616 SQUADRON, LECONFIELD

Spitfire P9383. Undercarriage wrecked in heavy landing at base following dawn practice flight. Pilot Officer W. L. B. Walker unhurt. Aircraft damaged but repairable.

Pilot Officer James Buchanan of Iden, Sussex, 25-year-old Volunteer Reserve pilot with No. 609 'West Riding' Squadron missing after combat south of Weymouth on July 27.

Saturday, July 27

232 SQUADRON, SUMBURGH

Hurricane P3411. Parked aircraft. Hit by Blenheim on take-off. Aircraft damaged.

236 SQUADRON, THORNEY ISLAND

Blenheim L1119. Forced-landed in orchard near Detling out of petrol 12.06 p.m. Sergeant N. P. C. Barron and Sergeant J. Lowe unhurt. Aircraft ND-C damaged but repairable.

501 SQUADRON, GRAVESEND

Hurricane P3808. Shot down by Fw. Fernsebner of III/JG52 in combat over Dover harbour 5.45 p.m. Flying Officer P. A. N. Cox missing. Aircraft lost.

609 SQUADRON, WARMWELL

Spitfire N3023. Shot down by Oblt. Framm of I/JG27 in combat over convoy off Weymouth 10.20 a.m. Pilot Officer J. R. Buchanan missing. Aircraft lost.

Sunday, July 28

19 SQUADRON, DUXFORD

Spitfire R6627. Crashed on landing at base following attack on Ju 88 6.00 p.m. Sergeant H. A. C. Roden unhurt. Aircraft damaged but repairable.

41 SQUADRON, MANSTON

Spitfire P9429. Attacked by Major Moelders of JG51 in combat off Dover 2.35 p.m. Crashed on landing at base. Flying Officer A. D. J. Lovell wounded in thigh admitted to Margate Hospital. Aircraft damaged but repairable.

74 SQUADRON, HORNCHURCH

Spitfire P9336. Shot down by Bf 109s of 9/JG26 in combat off Dover. Crashed onto roof of Buckland Mill, north of Dover 2.20 p.m. Sergeant E. A. Mould baled out wounded to Dover Military Hospital. Aircraft a write-off.

Pihen-les-Guines War Cemetery is the last resting place for two Battle of Britain pilots, Pilot Officer James Young killed on July 28 and Pilot Officer Neville Solomon.

Spitfire P9547. Crashed in Channel near Goodwin Sands 2.20 p.m. Believed shot down by Oblt. Muencheberg III/JG26. Pilot Officer J. H. R. Young killed. Aircraft lost.

Spitfire R6706. Damaged in action with Bf 109s over Dover. Possibly that attacked by Obfw. Schmid of I/JG51 2.35 p.m. Returned to base. Pilot Officer J. C. Freeborn unhurt. Aircraft damaged but repairable.

Spitfire R6779. Attacked by Oberleutnant Leppla of I/JG51 whilst pursuing Major Moelders of JG51 over Channel. 2.40 p.m. Landed Manston with engine seized. Pilot Officer P. C. F. Stevenson unhurt. Aircraft damaged but repairable.

87 SQUADRON, EXETER

Hurricane P2855. Crashed into parked aircraft during early morning take-off in poor visibility. Pilot Officer C. W. W. Darwin admitted to hospital with head injuries. Aircraft a write-off.

Hurricane P3225. Aircraft involved in collision above. Damaged but repairable.

92 SQUADRON, PEMBREY

Spitfire N3287. Abandoned over Exeter due to deteriorating weather conditions and R/T failure during night patrol over Swansea Bay. Crashed near Chudleigh 3.50 a.m. Pilot Officer T. S. Wade baled out unhurt. Aircraft a write-off.

245 SQUADRON, ALDERGROVE

Hurricane N2593. Stalled and crashed at base due to mishandling. Cause not stated. Sergeant P. Killick seriously injured. Aircraft a write-off.

257 SQUADRON, NORTHOLT

Hurricane P3622. Seriously damaged in combat with Bf 109s of JG26 over Channel off Dover 2.00 p.m. Landed Hawkinge. Sergeant R. V. Forward believed unhurt. Aircraft a write-off.

611 SQUADRON, DIGBY

Spitfire K9970. Landed at base undercarriage retracted following re-call from air-firing practice flight. Pilot error. Pilot Officer J. W. Lund unhurt. Aircraft damaged but repairable.

Monday, July 29

41 SQUADRON, MANSTON

Spitfire N3038. Missing following combat with Ju 87s and Bf 109s over Dover 7.45 a.m. Flying Officer D. R. Gamblen missing. Aircraft lost.

Spitfire N3100. Undercarriage collapsed in landing at base following combat off Dover 7.50 a.m. Flying Officer W. J. M. Scott believed unhurt. Aircraft a write-off.

Spitfire N3264. Flaps damaged in combat off Dover. Crashed on landing at base 8.00 a.m. Pilot Officer G. H. Bennions believed unhurt. Aircraft a write-off.

Spitfire N3113. Crashed on landing at base damaged in action off Dover 8.00 a.m. Flight Lieutenant J. T. Webster believed unhurt. Aircraft damaged but repairable.

Spitfire N3112. Crashed on landing at base damaged in action off Dover 8.05 a.m. Pilot Officer J. N. Mackenzie believed unhurt. Aircraft damaged but repairable.

43 SQUADRON, NORTHOLT

Hurricane L1955. Crashed and burned out at Brabourne Lees due to engine failure. 8.15 a.m. Pilot Officer K. C. Campbell killed. Aircraft a write-off.
Rolls-Royce Merlin engine recovered from Brabourne Leas by Brenzett Aeronautical Museum believed to be from this machine. Engine currently being rebuilt.

56 SQUADRON, NORTH WEALD

Hurricane P3612. Attacked by Bf 109 in action over Dover Harbour 7.45 a.m. Returned to base. Pilot Officer M. H. Mounsdon unhurt. Aircraft repairable.

Hurricane P3879. Shot down by Bf 109. Crashed and exploded in Channel off Dover 7.45 a.m. Flight Sergeant C. J. Cooney killed. Aircraft lost.

64 SQUADRON, KENLEY

Spitfire R6643. Damaged by Ju 87 in combat over Channel. Escorted back to coast by Gibson of 501 Squadron and forced-landed near St. Margaret's Bay 7.30 a.m. Sergeant A. E. Binham unhurt. Aircraft damaged but repairable.

Inquisitive or helping? Brenzett Aeronautical Group members get lots of interested black and white spectators at a dig at Brabourne Lees. *Centre:* Although positive identification of the airframe was not forthcoming, this is the engine plate from the Merlin believed to be from L1955 of No. 43 Squadron. *Bottom:* The engine was recovered virtually undamaged and Bob Cole is currently stripping and rebuilding the complete unit and believes the engine can still be made to run after thirty-odd years underground.

66 SQUADRON, COLTISHALL

Spitfire N3042. Crashed in sea off Orfordness after attack on He 111 approx. 2.50 p.m. Pilot Officer L. W. Collingridge injured rescued and admitted to Ipswich Hospital. Aircraft lost.

85 SQUADRON, MARTLESHAM HEATH

Hurricane P3150. Airscrew and port mainplane hit by return fire from Do 17 of III/KG76 forty miles east of Felixstowe 3.05 p.m. Returned to base. Flying Officer P. P. Woods-Scawen unhurt. Aircraft repairable.

151 SQUADRON, NORTH WEALD

Hurricane P3119. Attacked by Bf 110s of III/ZG26 during convoy patrol. 4.00 p.m. Forced-landed Martlesham Heath. Flying Officer C. D. Whittingham unhurt. Aircraft repairable.

Hurricane P3306. Attacked by Bf 110s of III/ZG26 during convoy patrol. 4.00 p.m. Forced-landed Rochford. Flying Officer R. M. Milne unhurt. Aircraft damaged but repairable.

302 SQUADRON, LECONFIELD

Hurricane P3217. Landed at base cross-wind on first familiarisation flight. Pilot Officer K. Lukaszewicz unhurt. Aircraft damaged but repairable.

501 SQUADRON, GRAVESEND

Hurricane   . Hit in port mainplane during combat with Ju 87s over Dover 7.45 a.m. Returned to base. Pilot Officer J. W. Bland unhurt. Aircraft repairable.

610 SQUADRON, BIGGIN HILL

Spitfire P9503. Damaged by return fire from Do 17 of Stab KG2 engaged over Channel off Dungeness 1.15 p.m. Landed at base on punctured tyre. Pilot Officer S. C. Norris unhurt. Aircraft DW-D damaged but repairable.

Tuesday, July 30

219 SQUADRON, CATTERICK

Blenheim L1109. Undercarriage damaged on take-off. Forced-landed at base 1.20 p.m. Sergeant T. Birkett and Sergeant E. R. Lacey unhurt. Aircraft damaged but repairable.

236 SQUADRON, THORNEY ISLAND

Blenheim   . Crashed at Carew Cheriton during return flight from Bircham Newton in bad weather 7.00 p.m. Flight Lieutenant R. M. Power and crew injured. Aircraft a write-off.

603 SQUADRON, MONTROSE

Spitfire   . Hit by return fire from He 111 of 8/KG26 shot down south-east of Montrose 12.05 p.m. Returned to base. Flight Lieutenant F. W. Rushmer unhurt. Aircraft repairable.

Spitfire   . Hit by return fire from He 111 of 8/KG26 shot down south-east of Montrose 12.05 p.m. Returned to base. Pilot Officer A. P. Pease unhurt. Aircraft repairable.

Wednesday, July 31

Sergeant Fred Eley's grave (in the foreground) at Wrenbury, Cheshire. The almost-illegible inscription on the granite headstone states that he was 'Killed in action over Folkestone Harbour July 31, 1940'. His memory is perpetuated in St. Margaret's with a stained glass window and his photo in an 'In Memoriam' book in the church.

25 SQUADRON, MARTLESHAM HEATH

Blenheim L1408 involved in collision over the Bristol Channel with L6722 during test of AI radar system Sergeant J. B. Thompson killed, AC2 E. J. Toy and Mr. D. M. Gordon missing. Aircraft lost.

As AC2 Toy was serving with No. 32 MU and Mr. D. M. Gordon was a civilian technical assistant their names are not included in our list of casualties.

29 SQUADRON, DIGBY

Blenheim L6722. Collision with L1408 above. Sergeant E. Waite, Sergeant C. J. Richardson and LAC T. Ward missing. Aircraft lost.

LAC Ward was serving with No. 32 MU and therefore his name does not appear on our list of casualties from the accredited squadrons.

Blenheim L8509. Landed at Wellingore undercarriage up due to pilot error. Crew unhurt. Aircraft damaged but repairable.

74 SQUADRON, HORNCHURCH

Spitfire P9398. Shot down in flames off Folkestone Pier 4.00 p.m. Sergeant F. W. Eley killed. Believed that claimed by Hptmn. Tietzen of 4/JG51. Aircraft lost.

Spitfire P9379. Shot down into Channel off Folkestone 4.00 p.m. Pilot Officer H. R. Gunn killed. Believed that claimed by Oblt. Foezoe of 4/JG51. Aircraft lost.

Spitfire R6983. Returned to base badly damaged in attack by Lt. Hohagen of 4/JG51 over the Channel off Dover 4.00 p.m. Flight Lieutenant D. P. D. G. Kelly unhurt. Aircraft damaged but repairable.

234 SQUADRON, ST. EVAL

Spitfire P9365. Crashed on landing after routine night patrol 1.28 a.m. Sergeant W. W. Thompson unhurt. Aircraft a write-off.

263 SQUADRON, GRANGEMOUTH

Hurricane P2990. Undershot flare-path during night landing at base and wrecked. Pilot believed unhurt. Aircraft a write-off.

501 SQUADRON, GRAVESEND

Hurricane P3646. Crashed and burned out at Lydden following combat with Ju 87s and Bf 109s over Dover 7.00 p.m. Pilot Officer R. S. Don baled out injured admitted to Canterbury Hospital. Aircraft a write-off.

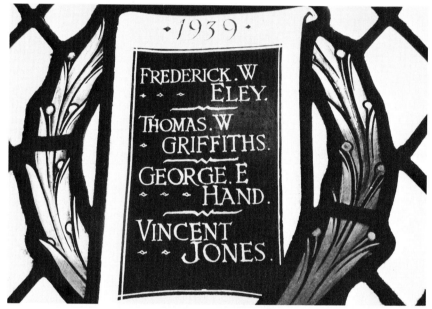

Hurricane P3349. Undershot runway and crashed on landing following combat over Dover 9.50 p.m. Pilot Officer E. G. Parkin injured admitted to Gravesend Hospital. Aircraft damaged but repairable.

Only four airmen who died in the Battle of Britain are buried in Ireland. One lies in Eire and the others in Northern Ireland. Sergeant Joe Thompson was the only one recovered after the Blenheim collision on July 31.

Thursday, August 1

145 SQUADRON, WESTHAMPNETT

Hurricane P3155. Shot down by return fire during attack on Hs 126 and crashed in Channel ten miles south of Hastings at 3.00 p.m. Sub-Lieutenant I. H. Kestin killed. Aircraft lost.

236 SQUADRON, THORNEY ISLAND

Blenheim N3601 shot down during bomber escort mission 5.15 p.m. Believed victim of ground defences in attack on Querqueville aerodrome or possibly brought down by Oblt. Adolph of III/JG27. Squadron Leader P. E. Drew, Flying Officer B. Nokes-Cooper both killed. Aircraft ND-K lost.

Blenheim N2774 shot down during bomber escort mission 5.15 p.m. Either victim of ground defences at Querqueville aerodrome or possibly that shot down by Oblt. Duellberg of III/JG27. Pilot Officer B. M. McDonough, Sergeant F. A. P. Head both missing. Aircraft ND-N lost.

Blenheim N3603 returned to base with severe damage to tail caused by AA fire during ground attack on Querqueville aerodrome 5.20 p.m. Possibly also attacked by Oberfw. Richter of III/JG27. Sergeant Smith, Sergeant A. H. Piper both unhurt. Aircraft ND-M damaged but repairable.

504 SQUADRON, CASTLETOWN

Hurricane L1957 undercarriage damaged in bad approach following night-flying practice. Further damaged in crash-landing at Wick. Pilot Officer H. N. Hunt unhurt. Aircraft damaged but repairable.

602 SQUADRON, DREM

Spitfire P9461 tore off a wing on landing in heavy ground mist 1.30 a.m. Flight Lieutenant J. D. Urie unhurt. Aircraft a write-off.

Spitfire K9892. Overshot flarepath on landing at base in severe ground mist 1.30 a.m. Visibility restricted to fifty yards. Pilot Officer H. W. Moody unhurt. Aircraft LO-N damaged but repairable.

616 SQUADRON, LECONFIELD

Spitfire K9829 returned to base damaged in radio and engine bearer by return fire from Ju 88 engaged at 1.05 p.m. Sergeant M. Ridley unhurt. Aircraft damaged but repairable.

Friday, August 2

65 SQUADRON, HORNCHURCH

Spitfire R6799 crashed on take-off from base on night patrol 11.35 p.m. and burned out. Squadron Leader H. C. Sawyer killed. Aircraft a write-off.

The Cross of Sacrifice at Bayeux War Cemetery. In the background the spires of the Cathedral of Our Lady dating back to the 11th century. Here lies Flying Officer Benjamin Nokes-Cooper killed on August 1. The captain of Blenheim N3601, Squadron Leader Peter Drew, lies in Biville Churchyard near the west coast of the Cherbourg peninsula.

Spitfire N3128. Crashed on take-off and completely wrecked. Exact details not recorded. Pilot believed unhurt. Aircraft a write-off.

219 SQUADRON, CATTERICK

Blenheim L8692. Overshot runway at Leeming during practice landing without flaps 3.15 p.m. Undercarriage deliberately raised to avoid running onto the Great North Road. Pilot Officer W. G. M. Lambie and Sergeant R. Bell both unhurt. Aircraft FK-M damaged but repairable.

504 SQUADRON, CASTLETOWN

Hurricane L1945 nosed over on landing due to bad approach 5.45 p.m. Sergeant D. A. Helcke unhurt. Aircraft damaged but repairable.

603 SQUADRON, TURNHOUSE

Spitfire R6717 crashed at Inkhorn, Aberdeenshire exact circumstances unknown. Sergeant I. K. Arber believed unhurt. Aircraft a write-off.

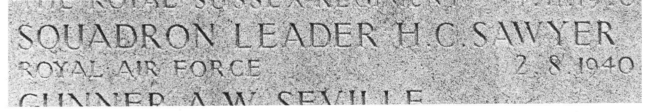

One of the seventy servicemen cremated at the City of London Crematorium was Squadron Leader Henry Sawyer of St. John's Wood.

Saturday, August 3

248 SQUADRON, SUMBURGH

Blenheim   . Forced-landed in cornfield at Tranent 2.16 p.m. cause not stated. Sergeant J. H. Round, Sergeant W. H. Want and Sergeant G. Yates unhurt. Aircraft WR-S damaged but repairable.

65 SQUADRON, HORNCHURCH

Spitfire P9516. Forced-landed at Kenley during routine flight. Pilot unhurt. Aircraft damaged but repairable.

Sunday, August 4

236 SQUADRON, THORNEY ISLAND

Blenheim L8684 landed at Ford with severe damage to oil system following attack by fighters off Le Havre 4.45 p.m. Pilot Officer C. B. G. Peachment, Sergeant J. Lowe both unhurt. Aircraft ND-D damaged but repairable.

616 SQUADRON, LECONFIELD

Spitfire N3271. Spun into the ground from 5,000ft during dog fight practice. Exact cause unknown. Sergeant J. P. Walsh killed. Aircraft a write-off.

Monday, August 5

41 SQUADRON, HORNCHURCH

Spitfire N3234. Wrecked in crash landing near Sandwich shortly after take-off from Manston. Pilot believed unhurt. Aircraft a write-off.

John Walsh was born in Harrow in 1920 but from childhood was known to his family and friends as 'Pat'. He was educated at Harrow County School where he became a prefect. Completing his schooling, he then entered the Civil Service and in February 1939 took the first step towards his ambition to become a pilot by joining the RAFVR. He qualified as a sergeant pilot and was posted to No. 616 'South Yorkshire' Squadron at Leconfield as a replacement pilot. Having acquired a small car, he took the opportunity to visit his family whenever possible, one such visit taking place on July 28, 1940. The following Sunday — August 4 — Pat Walsh was detailed for dogfight practice during which his Spitfire spun into the ground from 5,000 feet.

64 SQUADRON, KENLEY

Spitfire L1029. Failed to return from squadron sortie following surprise attack by enemy fighters over the Channel 8.50 a.m. Sergeant L. R. Isaac missing. Aircraft lost.

Spitfire K9991. Landed at Hawkinge with serious damage to fuselage and internal control cables caused by 20mm cannon shell following combat with Bf 109s off the French coast 9.00 a.m. Pilot Officer A. G. Donahue unhurt. Aircraft damaged but repairable.

65 SQUADRON, HORNCHURCH

Spitfire P9436. Hit in petrol tank during combat with Bf 109s of JG54 over the Channel east of Dover 9.00 a.m. Attacked by Oblt. Seiler. Forced-landed Manston following mid-air fire. Sergeant Walker suffered slight shoulder injury. Aircraft damaged but repairable.

219 SQUADRON, CATTERICK

Blenheim L1168. Undercarriage retracted too soon after take-off and jammed. Aircraft forced to land wheels up. Sergeant A. J. Hodgkinson unhurt. Aircraft repairable.

Blenheim   . Belly-landing at base due to faulty undercarriage caused in take-off accident. Pilot Officer T. Birkett unhurt. Aircraft damaged but repairable.

On August 5, 1940, 24-year-old Sergeant Lewis Isaac was one of six pilots of No. 64 Squadron despatched from Kenley on dawn patrol over the Kent coast. They had barely arrived on their patrol line when, out of the early morning haze, the Bf 109s of 1/JG54 fell upon them, sending Sergeant Isaac's Spitfire hurtling into the Channel. The young Welsh pilot's body was never recovered.

Although his father was a major in the Royal Corps of Signals, 'Billie' Britton chose to join the Royal Air Force being posted to No. 17 Squadron. Following the unexplained crash on August 6, the 19-year-old Scottish lad was buried in a secluded corner of All Saints Churchyard at Wimbish. The churchyard is rather difficult to find, being situated up a small farm track.

Tuesday, August 6

17 SQUADRON, DEBDEN

Hurricane N2456. Crashed and burned out in Debden Park shortly after take-off on routine air test 10.15 a.m. Cause unknown. Pilot Officer H. W. A. Britton killed. Aircraft a write-off.

32 SQUADRON, BIGGIN HILL

Hurricane V7205. Wrecked in forced-landing at base reason not stated. Pilot believed unhurt. Aircraft a write-off.

72 SQUADRON, ACKLINGTON

Spitfire L1078. Crashed on landing following uneventful patrol 12.40 p.m. Sergeant R. C. J. Staples unhurt. Aircraft a write-off.

219 SQUADRON, CATTERICK

Blenheim . Collided with HT cables and crashed into a river during searchlight co-operation flight. Pilot Officer J. C. Carriere, Sergeant C. Beveridge both superficially injured. Aircraft a write-off.

232 SQUADRON, SUMBURGH

Hurricane R4090. Replacement aircraft crashed on delivery to unit. Pilot unhurt. Aircraft a write off.

234 SQUADRON, ST. EVAL

Spitfire P9366. Crashed on landing from routine night patrol 11.05 p.m. Flying Officer P. W. Horton unhurt. Aircraft a write-off.

616 SQUADRON, LECONFIELD

Spitfire R6702. Returned to base with damage caused by debris and return fire from Ju 88 attacked twenty miles north-east of Flamborough 5.00 p.m. Squadron Leader M. Robinson unhurt. Aircraft damaged but repairable.

Spitfire . Returned to base with slight damage received in attack on Ju 88 in company with Squadron Leader Robinson 5.00 p.m. Sergeant M. Ridley unhurt. Aircraft repairable.

Spitfire . Returned to base with slight damage received in attack on Ju 88 above. 5.00 p.m. Flight Lieutenant R. O. Hellyer unhurt. Aircraft repairable.

Wednesday, August 7

65 SQUADRON, HORNCHURCH

Spitfire R6617. Crashed and burned out on take-off 1.05 p.m. Flight Lieutenant C. G. C. Olive unhurt. Aircraft a write-off.

248 SQUADRON, SUMBURGH

Blenheim L9456. Ditched off St. Abbs Head due to petrol shortage. Towed into land by trawler. Pilot Officer R. H. Haviland, Pilot Officer M. L. Wells, Sergeant A. Kay picked up from their dinghy by a trawler and landed at South Shields. Aircraft WR-R salvaged and repairable.

253 SQUADRON, TURNHOUSE

Hurricane P3457. Crashed during night flight cause not stated. 9.00 p.m. Pilot Officer D. N. O. Jenkins unhurt. Aircraft a write-off.

263 SQUADRON, GRANGEMOUTH

Whirlwind P6966. Crashed at Lanton Farm, Stenhousemuir near Stirling during training flight. Pilot Officer I. M. McDermott baled out slightly injured. Aircraft a write-off.
The first production aircraft. Major investigation and recovery masterminded by Steve Vizard. Combined efforts enabled the excavation of the remains of both Rolls-Royce Peregrine engines and all major components and equipment.

501 SQUADRON, GRAVESEND

Hurricane P3041. Collided with Sergeant Wilkinson during landing approach at base in poor visibility 8.40 a.m. Sergeant E. F. Howarth unhurt. Aircraft damaged but repairable.

Hurricane P3083. Collided with Sergeant Howarth in landing at base in poor visibility 8.40 a.m. Sergeant W. A. Wilkinson unhurt. Aircraft SD-E damaged but repairable.

616 SQUADRON, LECONFIELD

Spitfire R6696. Crashed and exploded three miles from base during night-flying practice 2.45 a.m. cause unknown. Flying Officer D. S. Smith believed baled out unhurt. Aircraft a write-off.

Spitfire K9817. Undershot runway and hit perimeter fence landing after night-flying practice. Sergeant T. E. Westmoreland unhurt. Aircraft damaged but repairable.

Thursday, August 8

23 SQUADRON, COLLY WESTON

Blenheim L1448. Crashed near Peterborough on night patrol 11.48 p.m. Cause unknown but presumed to have been temporary loss of control. Pilot Officer C. F. Cardnell, Sergeant C. Stephens both killed. Aircraft YP-K a write-off.

43 SQUADRON, TANGMERE

Hurricane P3267. Engine seized following destruction of Ju 87 in combat over the Channel 4.40 p.m. Forced-landed at Ford Farm, Whitwell, Isle of Wight. Pilot Officer H. C. Upton unhurt. Aircraft damaged but repairable.

Hurricane P3466. Slightly damaged during combat with enemy aircraft ten miles south of the Isle of Wight 4.40 p.m. Returned to base. Sergeant C. A. L. Hurry unhurt. Aircraft repairable.

Hurricane P3781. Shot down in combat with enemy aircraft ten miles south of the Isle of Wight 4.45 p.m. Crashed in sea. Pilot Officer J. Cruttenden missing. Aircraft lost.

EXCAVATION OF THE SOLE WESTLAND WHIRLWIND TO CRASH IN THE BATTLE.

Westland Whirlwind, serial number P6966, was delivered to No. 25 Squadron in June 1940 and was then transferred to No. 263 Squadron during the following month. P6966 was the first production aircraft, one of the eight of the type to fly during the battle, and after its loss it featured in the Whirlwind handling manual (which was not printed at the time of the crash).

The accident occurred on August 7, 1940. Whilst P6966, piloted by Pilot Officer I. M. McDermott, was taking off, the aircraft suffered a burst tyre. However, McDermott managed to prevent the wing touching the ground and was able to get the aircraft airborne. Once in the air, the watch office informed McDermott that his undercarriage was visibly damaged and they advised him to climb to a safe height and then bale out, rather than attempt a landing with the damaged landing gear. McDermott accordingly baled out, parting company with P6966 just north of Stirling, the aircraft crashing into a large field at Lanton Farm, Stenhousemuir, then owned by a Mr. Adam. During his descent by parachute, McDermott was circled by a Spitfire and, on landing, he sprained his ankle and was captured by the local Home Guard who mistook him for a German. The RAF then spent two to three days trying to recover P6966, but without much success.

There the matter rested, until Steve Vizard, aided by Alan Brown, searched for a suitable Whirlwind for excavation. The first site that was investigated in June 1979 was a 1941 Whirlwind crash but the only item of interest recovered was a rusted prop boss. Undaunted, they made a visit to the Air Historical Branch and searching the 'P' aircraft cards, discovered the location of the crash site of

P6966 — the first production aircraft delivered in June 1940 — the remains of which were excavated in October 1979.

P6966 at Lanton Farm. After considerable effort and many phone calls the present landowner, Mr. Watson (who had taken over the farm from Mr. Adam) was traced. Permission to dig was then obtained from the Ministry of Defence and Mr. Watson and the local hire of a Hymac digger was also arranged.

On October 12, 1979, Steve Vizard, Terry Parsons, Tony Graves, Andy Saunders, Bill Hamblin, John Ellis and Peter Foote motored to Scotland in a Range Rover and a lorry for bringing back any parts recovered. Although the party arrived late in the evening an immediate search of the field was made by torchlight for a stake that the farmer had promised he would place on the impact point. When found it turned out to be a peg six inches high!

The next morning everyone assembled at the site and at 8.00 a.m. digging commenced. At a depth of eight feet, some engine parts, wing panels and cowling were discovered and soon after, one of the two Rolls Royce 885-horse power Peregrine engines was found together with prop blades. The digger then moved over to the approximate position of the other engine and soon afterwards, fuel tanks, an oil cooler and a fire extinguisher were uncovered and a complete undercarriage leg and tyre. The other Peregrine engine was found soon afterwards in superb condition. The final excavation was thirty feet square by twenty-five feet deep. Apart from the fact that the digger continually broke down the dig was highly successful and the party retired to the hotel weary but triumphant.

GORDON RAMSEY

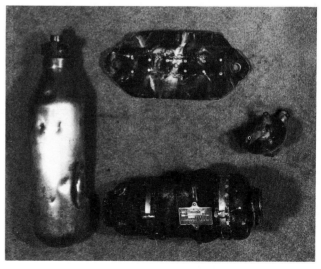

Sergeants' Mess RAF Station, Tangmere, Sussex.

Well Mother and Father I'm back with the B.E.F, London, Saturday night — one of the lucky ones. What a scene on Euston Station — never seen anything like it — crowds gave us boys a wonderful welcome. I managed to get May to come down, my word what a grand re-union and weekend — we both enjoyed ourselves. I only wish we could have come up to Macclesfield to pay you a visit. I have actually been back three days but was given an instructional course before being released.

Never in my life have I witnessed such wonderful spirit shown by the British boys. Thank God, although I could not be as brave myself, that I am British. Regular orders were coming through for all, 'Fight on until you drop, then get up and fight.' That order has been carried out to a man. All the boys were arriving in London Saturday night still wet, after swimming to the rescue boats. Mothers, fathers, wives, sweethearts were all waiting there. Some poor devils just stood looking dazed when they realized that their man had payed the price, their faces almost haunted.

Well Father, tell boys at 'Fairies' to not grumble about all the extra work, we need all your help. All the boys are now anxiously waiting to get fresh planes and get over there to try and save those wonderful boys who remained solid whilst the rest were got aboard for old England. We have been flying this afternoon, not much wasted time, but to see those remaining boys' faces, full of hope for our return, even sleep and food does not interest us.

Thank you very much for the parcel and letter, nice to have clean clothes though May has now come to my help, Money. clothes, food, she was grand, but I had lost all, not a thing. I even had to borrow a cigarette from a stranger. All the boys were the same, but old England was very kind for cigarettes were dished out at Euston.

No, the daily paper photograph is not me, rather swanking, but I am not a coming pilot but am almost a veteran having taken part through squadron operations throughout the whole of the heavy actions.

Cheerio for now, all my kind regards to all in Macclesfield.

To you at home may I wish you all good health and luck. When I come back home again for a rest I might be more lucky and visit home.

God Bless.

Your loving son
Eric

The graves of the crew of the No. 23 Squadron Blenheim which crashed on August 8 near Peterborough. *Left:* Pilot Officer Charles Cardnell in the terribly overgrown Highgate Cemetery in North London. Cemetery officials had to work for fifteen minutes to clear, first a path to the grave and then the undergrowth which completely covered it. *Above:* His gunner, Sergeant Cyril Stephens, lies in St. Crallo's Church, Coychurch.

PILOT OFFICER
J.R.S. OELOFSE
(OF SOUTH AFRICA)
PILOT
ROYAL AIR FORCE
8TH AUGUST 1940   AGE 23

Hurricane P3468. Shot down in combat with enemy aircraft ten miles south of the Isle of Wight 4.45 p.m. and crashed in sea. Pilot Officer J. R. S. Oelofse killed. Aircraft lost.

Hurricane P3202. Returned to base port wing severely damaged by cannon-fire from Bf 110 during combat off the Isle of Wight 4.40 p.m. Flight Lieutenant F. R. Carey slightly wounded in arm. Aircraft repairable.

Hurricane P3214. Damaged in combat with Bf 110s of V/LG1 ten miles south of the Isle of Wight 4.45 p.m. Returned to base. Pilot Officer C. A. Woods-Scawen slightly wounded with shell splinters in legs. Aircraft damaged but repairable.

64 SQUADRON, KENLEY

Spitfire P9369. Believed victim of surprise attack by Hptmn. Trautloft of III/JG51. Forced-landed at Great Couldham, Capel-le-Ferne 11.10 a.m. Sergeant J. W. C. Squier injured admitted to hospital. Aircraft a write-off.

Spitfire L1039. Caught fire during combat with Bf 109s of JG51 north of Dover 12.05 p.m. Crashed and burned out near West Langdon. Pilot Officer P. F. Kennard-Davis baled out seriously wounded but died two days later in Royal Victoria Hospital, Dover. Aircraft a write-off.

65 SQUADRON, HORNCHURCH

Spitfire K9911. Shot down in flames during combat with Bf 109s over Manston 11.40 a.m. Believed that claimed by Oblt. Fronhoefer of 9/JG26. Crashed and burned out. Sergeant D. I. Kirton killed. Aircraft a write-off.

Spitfire K9905. Shot down during action with Bf 109s of III/JG26 over Manston 11.45 a.m. Crashed and burned out. Probably that claimed by Oblt. Muencheberg. Flight Sergeant N. T. Phillips killed. Aircraft a write-off.

Spitfire L1094. Attacked by Oberfw. Grzymalla of III/JG26 during combat over Manston 11.55 a.m. Returned to base. Pilot believed unhurt. Aircraft damaged but repairable.

Flight Sergeant Norman Taylor Phillips of No. 65 Squadron shot down over Manston on August 8 now at rest in the family grave at Chatham Cemetery, Kent.

Pilot Officer Peter Kennard-Davis, who died on August 10 from wounds received in an air battle on the 8th, lies with his grandparents in a neat family grave beside St. Cyprian's Avenue in the London Necropolis Cemetery at Brookwood.

SERGEANT PILOT DAVID KIRTON

KILLED AUGUST 8, 1940

David Ian Kirton from Dover joined the RAF before the war and from May 1939 underwent flying training at No. 22 Elementary Reserve Flying Training School at Cambridge. On qualifying as a sergeant pilot, in July 1940 he was posted to No. 65 Squadron at Hornchurch. He survived the early skirmishings for almost a month before falling in flames over Manston on August 8. He was 21 years old at the time of his death and now lies buried in St. James's Cemetery, Dover.

145 SQUADRON, WESTHAMPNETT

Hurricane P2955. Failed to return from combat with enemy aircraft over the Channel south of the Isle of Wight 9.05 a.m. Believed that shot down by Uffz. Sippel of I/JG27. Pilot Officer L. A. Sears missing. Aircraft lost.

Hurricane P3381. Believed that shot down by Fw. Mueller of I/JG27 in combat over the Channel south of the Isle of Wight 9.15 a.m. Crashed in sea. Sergeant E. D. Baker missing. Aircraft lost.

Hurricane P2957. Missing following action against Ju 87s and Bf 110s over convoy south of Isle of Wight 4.40 p.m. Pilot Officer E. C. J. Wakeham missing. Aircraft lost.

Hurricane P3163. Failed to return from combat with Ju 87s and Bf 110s over convoy south of Isle of Wight 4.40 p.m. Flying Officer Lord R. U. P. Kay-Shuttleworth missing. Aircraft lost.

Hurricane P3545. Missing following combat south of the Isle of Wight 4.45 p.m. Crashed in sea. Sub-Lieutenant F. A. Smith missing. Aircraft lost.

The Shuttleworth family can trace their lineage back to the year 1330 when Henry de Shuttleworth married Agnes, daughter of William de Hacking. Their first born, a son, became Ughtred de Shuttleworth of Gawthorpe. One ancestor named Richard fought as a colonel in Cromwell's New Army, five of his sons also serving the Parliamentary cause. A later Richard was knighted by Charles II for services to the Royalists. Born on October 30, 1913, Richard Ughtred Paul Kay-Shuttleworth, was the first son of Captain, The Honourable Laurence Kay-Shuttleworth and his wife Selina but when he was barely 3½ years old his father was killed in action in France. He was educated at Eton and Balliol College, Oxford and joined the RAFVR before the war. With the death of his grandfather, the 1st Baron Shuttleworth of Gawthorpe in 1939, he succeeded to the baronetcy. Just before the Battle of Britain commenced Lord Shuttleworth was posted to No. 145 Squadron. When based at Westhampnett the squadron flew virtually every day in defence of one or other of the Channel convoys. On Thursday, August 8, Flying Officer Lord Kay-Shuttleworth died an heroic death in the company of heroes fighting the Battle of Convoy CW9 — codenamed 'Peewit'.

Flying Officer Dennis Neve Grice, DFC, from Ealing (above left), Sergeant Francis John Keast from Whitstable and AC1 John Benjamin William Warren from Chelmsford (above right) were all members of the same Blenheim crew from No. 600 'City of London' Squadron. On Thursday, August 8, 1940 they were flying in the vicinity of their base at Manston when they were attacked by enemy fighters and shot down, their aircraft falling towards the town of Ramsgate. Instead of abandoning the stricken Blenheim, Dennis Grice stayed at the controls and lifted the aircraft clear of the town, only to crash almost immediately afterwards into the sea.

152 SQUADRON, WARMWELL

Spitfire R6811. Shot down in combat with Bf 109s of II/JG53 off Swanage. Crashed and burned out at Marsh Farm, Bestwall at 4.15 p.m. Sergeant D. N. Robinson unhurt. Aircraft a write-off.

Spitfire   . Damaged in combat with Bf 109s of II/JG53 off Swanage. Forced-landed at Spyway, Langton Matravers 4.20 p.m. Pilot Officer W. Beaumont unhurt. Aircraft damaged but repairable.

234 SQUADRON, ST. EVAL

Spitfire N3278. Forced-landed at Pensilva and wrecked having run out of petrol during routine patrol 10.15 a.m. Sergeant J. Szalgowski unhurt. Aircraft a write-off.

238 SQUADRON, MIDDLE WALLOP

Hurricane P3823. Shot down in combat with elements of III/JG27 and V/LG1 over convoy 'Peewit' south of the Isle of Wight 12.45 p.m. Flight Lieutenant D. E. Turner missing. Aircraft lost.

Hurricane P3617. Shot down in combat with enemy aircraft over convoy 'Peewit' south of the Isle of Wight 12.50 p.m. Crashed in sea. Flying Officer D. C. MacCaw killed. Aircraft lost.

Hurricane P2947. Ditched in the Channel 1.40 p.m. after attack on He 59 during search mission for earlier squadron losses. Squadron Leader H. A. Fenton rescued from sea by HMS *Bassett* and admitted to Haslar Hospital, Gosport with slight injuries. Aircraft lost.

257 SQUADRON, NORTHOLT

Hurricane P2981. Shot down in combat with Bf 109s of III/JG27 off St. Catherine's Point 12.00 p.m. Flight Lieutenant N. M. Hall killed. Aircraft lost.

Hurricane R4094. Failed to return following action off St. Catherine's Point 12.00 p.m. Sergeant K. B. Smith missing. Aircraft lost.

Hurricane P3058. Missing following combat with Bf 109s of III/JG27 off St. Catherine's Point 12.05 p.m. Flying Officer B. W. J. D'Arcy-Irvine missing. Aircraft lost.

303 SQUADRON, NORTHOLT

Hurricane R4100. Crashed on landing after routine training flight. Sergeant M. Belc unhurt. Aircraft damaged but repairable.

Hurricane V7245. Landed undercarriage up following training flight. Sergeant J. Frantisek unhurt. Aircraft damaged but repairable.

600 SQUADRON, MANSTON

Blenheim L8665. Shot down by Oblt. Sprick of III/JG26. Crashed in flames into the sea off Ramsgate 11.55 a.m. Flying Officer D. N. Grice, Sergeant F. J. Keast, AC1 J. B. W. Warren all killed. Aircraft ZO-A lost.
Fragments from this aircraft collected at the time and donated to the Kent Battle of Britain Museum.

609 SQUADRON, WARMWELL

Spitfire P9322. Damaged in attack by Bf 110 of V/LG1 over the Isle of Wight 12.00 p.m. Returned to base. Pilot Officer M. J. Appleby unhurt. Aircraft repairable.

610 SQUADRON, HAWKINGE

Spitfire R6765. Severely damaged in combat with Bf 109s of JG51 over base 11.30 a.m. Pilot unhurt. Aircraft DW-T damaged but repairable.

Spitfire L1045. Forced-landed near Wittersham following combat with Bf 109s of JG51 over base 11.20 a.m. Pilot believed unhurt. Aircraft damaged but repairable.

Friday, August 9

The bodies of Dennis Grice and Frank Keast were recovered from the sea. Grice was cremated at Charing, Kent and his name is commemorated on the Memorial Panel *(above left)*. Frank Keast is buried in the family grave at Whitstable *(above right)* but John Warren was washed up in France and is now buried at Calais.

64 SQUADRON, KENLEY

Spitfire R6995. Damaged by 20mm cannon shell during combat with enemy fighters. Returned safely to base 4.40 p.m. Sergeant J. Mann unhurt. Aircraft damaged but repairable.

Spitfire R6639. Severely damaged in combat over Hawkinge 5.37 p.m. Forced-landed Hawkinge. Pilot unhurt. Aircraft damaged but repairable.

Spitfire R6992. Forced-landed at Hawkinge with damage sustained in combat 5.40 p.m. Pilot unhurt. Aircraft damaged but repairable.

266 SQUADRON, WITTERING

Spitfire L1059. Hit an obstacle landing at Hatfield in bad visibility 7.00 a.m. Sergeant A. W. Eade unhurt. Aircraft damaged but repairable.

303 SQUADRON, NORTHOLT

Hurricane P3645. Wrecked in taxi-ing accident at base. Flying Officer L. W. Paszkiewicz unhurt. Aircraft a write-off.

600 SQUADRON, MANSTON

Blenheim L8679. Engine failure during night operations. Came under fire from own AA defences. Abandoned aircraft crashed near Westgate 11.00 p.m. Flying Officer S. P. le Rougetel, baled out unhurt and rescued from the sea by Margate lifeboat. Sergeant Smith baled out and swam ashore at Westgate. Aircraft ZO-O a write-off.

605 SQUADRON, DREM

Hurricane L2103. Developed glycol leak during section patrol off the east coast and crashed into the sea one mile off Dunbar, East Lothian 4.45 p.m. Sergeant R. D. Ritchie presumed overcome by fumes and neck broken in crash. Picked up by the *Eunmara*. Aircraft lost.

Saturday, August 10

23 SQUADRON, COLLY WESTON

Blenheim   . Engine failure during night patrol. Forced-landed at Coltishall 1.00 a.m. Flight Lieutenant R. M. B. D. Duke-Woolley, Flying Officer D. A. P. McCullen both unhurt. Aircraft YP-P repairable.

Blenheim   . Forced-landed at Sutton Bridge following engine failure during routine night patrol 1.50 a.m. Pilot Officer A. J. Willans, Sergeant Johnson both unhurt. Aircraft YP-Z repairable.

234 SQUADRON, ST. EVAL

Spitfire P9468. Landed undercarriage up from routine patrol. Reason not stated. Sergeant A. S. Harker unhurt. Aircraft damaged but repairable.

Robert Douglas Ritchie was a 24-year-old Scot born in the old Kingdom of Fife. He joined the Royal Air Force Volunteer Reserve before the war and in September 1939 was absorbed into the Royal Air Force. When the Battle of Britain began, he was serving as a sergeant pilot with No. 605 'County of Warwick' Squadron then based at Drem, East Lothian on the southern shore of the Firth of Forth. Often patrolling within sight of his home near Loch Leven, he died on August 9. His body was recovered from the sea and taken back to Leslie Cemetery for burial.

Sunday, August 11

1 SQUADRON, NORTHOLT

Hurricane   . Forced-landed at Tangmere with damaged aileron controls following attack by friendly fighter over the Sussex coast 11.10 a.m. Pilot Officer R. H. Shaw unhurt. Aircraft repairable.

Hurricane P3172. Damaged in combat with Bf 110s and crashed and burned out on Sandown golf course in attempted forced-landing 11.20 a.m. Pilot Officer J. A. J. Davey killed. Aircraft a write-off.

17 SQUADRON, DEBDEN

Hurricane P3539. Returned to base damaged in combat with Bf 110s off the east coast 11.50 a.m. Flying Officer D. H. W. Hanson unhurt. Aircraft damaged but repairable.

Hurricane P3760. Missing following combat with Bf 110s off the east coast 11.50 a.m. Pilot Officer K. Manger missing. Aircraft lost.

Hurricane P3892. Damaged in combat with Bf 110s off Orfordness 11.50 a.m. Returned to base. Pilot Officer L. W. Stevens unhurt. Aircraft repairable.

56 SQUADRON, NORTH WEALD

Hurricane N2667. Reputedly shot down by solitary Spitfire during convoy patrol 1.00 p.m. Crashed in sea. Sergeant R. D. Baker baled out but dead when picked up. Aircraft lost.

64 SQUADRON, KENLEY

Spitfire P9450. Damaged in combat with Bf 109s off Dover and unable to lower undercarriage on return to base 10.45 a.m. Sergeant J. Whelan unhurt. Aircraft repairable.

Spitfire N3293. Returned to base with damage caused by cannon-fire from enemy fighter engaged off Dover 12.00 p.m. Pilot Officer C. J. D. Andreae unhurt. Aircraft repairable.

John Davey from Leamington, Warwickshire won a cadetship to the Royal Air Force College at Cranwell from RAF Halton. When he was shot down on the Isle of Wight he was buried near where he fell in the local cemetery at Sandown.

Pilot Officer Kenneth Manger, DFC, came from St. John's Wood, London. He failed to return from combat over the North Sea and is now remembered at Runnymede.

74 SQUADRON, HORNCHURCH

Spitfire P9393. Shot down in the Channel one mile off Dover following solo attack on twelve Bf 109s 8.10 a.m. Pilot Officer P. C. F. Stevenson baled out and rescued from the sea by MTB after drifting eleven miles out. Aircraft lost.

Spitfire R6757. Failed to return from combat with Bf 110s thirty miles east of Harwich 12.15 p.m. Crashed in sea. Pilot Officer D. G. Cobden killed. Aircraft lost.

Spitfire R6962. Failed to return from combat with Bf 110s thirty miles east of Harwich 12.15 p.m. Crashed in sea. Pilot Officer D. N. E. Smith killed. Aircraft lost.

85 SQUADRON, MARTLESHAM HEATH

Hurricane   . Returned to base with mainplane damaged by return fire from Bf 110 engaged over convoy off east coast 12.00 p.m. Sergeant H. H. Allgood unhurt. Aircraft VY-A repairable.

87 SQUADRON, EXETER

Hurricane P3598. Damaged in action with Bf 109s off Portland Bill 10.45 a.m. Forced-landed near Warmwell. Pilot Officer A. C. R. McLure wounded in leg. Aircraft damaged but repairable.

Hurricane V7231. Last seen diving to attack enemy aircraft off Portland Bill 10.45 a.m. Flight Lieutenant R. V. Jeff missing. Aircraft lost.

Hurricane V7233. Shot down in combat with enemy fighters off Portland Bill 10.50 a.m. Pilot Officer J. R. Cock baled out slightly injured and swam ashore. Aircraft lost.

111 SQUADRON, CROYDON

Hurricane P3105. Shot down into the Channel during combat off Margate 2.20 p.m. Pilot Officer J. H. H. Copeman killed. Aircraft lost.

Hurricane P3922. Believed shot down by Bf 109 during combat off Margate 2.20 p.m. crashed in the sea. Pilot Officer J. W. McKenzie missing. Aircraft lost.

Hurricane P3595. Failed to return from combat with Bf 109s escorting Do 17s over Margate 2.25 p.m. Presumed crashed in sea. Pilot Officer R. R. Wilson missing. Aircraft lost.

Hurricane P3548. Crash-landed near Martlesham Heath having run out of fuel following combat with enemy aircraft over Thanet 2.50 p.m. Sergeant H. S. Newton unhurt. Aircraft a write-off.

Above: This was Ostende New Communal Cemetery in Belgium shortly after the end of the war. Among the graves marked with temporary crosses is that of Pilot Officer Donald Cobden (right), No. 74 Squadron of Christchurch, New Zealand, shot down over the North Sea on August 11. Bottom: This is Ostende Cemetery today — the graves of the First World War are in the foreground with those of the Second, now with permanent headstones, in the background. (Two other fellow squadron members lie with him in Row 3 — Pilot Officer Denis Smith killed the same day and Pilot Officer Harold Gunn killed on July 31.)

Malayan-born, Flight Lieutenant Robert Voase Jeff was with No. 87 Squadron at Debden in 1937 where he was known as 'Social-type Jeff' because he wore the smartest uniform on the station. He served with the squadron in France from 1939 where he shot down the first He 111 to crash on French soil and was awarded the Croix de Guerre avec Palme by General Vuillemin (above). On the squadron's return to the United Kingdom he fought throughout the early part of the battle, acquiring a DFC and Bar, until August 11 when he was last seen diving on an enemy aircraft off Portland Bill (Imperial War Museum).

The remains of Sergeant Sam Butterfield, DFM, now lie in Boulogne Eastern Cemetery.

Robert Black Sim was born in Kilmarnock, North Ayrshire in 1917. He joined the Royal Air Force before the outbreak of war and early in July 1940 was posted as a replacement sergeant pilot to No. 111 Squadron at Croydon. Just over one month later, on Sunday, August 11 when the squadron was heavily engaged against overwhelming odds over the Thames Estuary, Sergeant Bob Sim became separated from his unit in the build up of cloud and was pounced on by enemy fighters. Shot down into the sea, no trace of him or his aircraft were ever found.

Hurricane P3942. Failed to return from combat with Bf 109s escorting Do 17s engaged off Margate 2.20 p.m. Presumed crashed in Channel. Sergeant R. B. Sim missing. Aircraft lost.

145 SQUADRON, WESTHAMPNETT

Hurricane P2951. Missing following combat with enemy fighters south of Swanage 10.30 a.m. Crashed in sea. Flying Officer G. R. Branch killed. Aircraft lost.

Hurricane P3164. Forced-landed on the Isle of Wight with damage sustained in combat with enemy fighters south of Swanage 10.30 a.m. Squadron Leader J. R. A. Peel slightly injured. Aircraft damaged but repairable.

Hurricane V7294. Shot down during combat with enemy fighters south of Swanage 10.35 a.m. Reputedly crashed on the Isle of Wight. Flying Officer A. Ostowicz missing. Aircraft a write-off.

Hurricane P2918. Damaged in combat with enemy fighters south of Swanage 10.35 a.m. and forced-landed near Christchurch. Pilot Officer A. N. C. Weir unhurt. Aircraft damaged but repairable.

152 SQUADRON, WARMWELL

Spitfire R6614. Crashed in mid-Channel during combat with Bf 109s 11.00 a.m. Pilot Officer J. S. B. Jones baled out but killed. Aircraft lost.

213 SQUADRON, EXETER

Hurricane N2708. Hydraulics damaged by return fire from Ju 88 engaged over Portland. Crashed on landing 10.25 a.m. Pilot Officer A. I. Osmand unhurt. Aircraft AK-C damaged but repairable.

Hurricane N2661. Returned to base with damage to oil tank, wings and engine following destruction of Ju 88 off Portland 10.30 a.m. Pilot Officer J. A. L. Phillipart unhurt. Aircraft AK-H damaged but repairable.

Hurricane N2650. Failed to return following combat over Portland 11.00 a.m. Flight Lieutenant R. D. G. Wight killed. Aircraft AK-O lost.

Pilot Officer John Jones of No. 152 Squadron (via Andy Saunders).

Hurricane P3789. Failed to return following combat over Portland 11.00 a.m. Sergeant S. L. Butterfield killed. Aircraft AK-P lost.

Hurricane P3585. Engine set alight following destruction of Bf 110 over Portland 11.00 a.m. Forced-landed on Lulworth range. Sergeant E. G. Snowden unhurt. Aircraft AK-M damaged but repairable.

Flight Lieutenant Stuart Crosby Walch was born and raised in Tasmania. He joined the Royal Air Force before the war and was posted to No. 238 Squadron on its formation in May 1940 at Middle Wallop flying Hurricanes. He was actively engaged in the no-quarter battles over the convoys in July, accounting for three enemy fighters in fifteen days. For his qualities of leadership and aggression in the air, he was appointed a flight commander and, on Sunday, August 11, led the squadron into battle over Portland harbour. Four aircraft failed to return one of which, flown by Stuart Walch, was last seen tumbling into Lyme Bay.

238 SQUADRON, MIDDLE WALLOP

Hurricane P2978. Shot down into the Channel during combat two miles east of Weymouth 10.40 a.m. Sergeant G. Gledhill killed. Aircraft lost.

Hurricane P2827. Starboard wing damaged in action off Portland 10.45 a.m. Returned to base. Sergeant H. J. Marsh unhurt. Aircraft damaged but repairable.

Hurricane P3124. Returned to base starboard wing and glycol system damaged in combat two miles east of Weymouth 10.45 a.m. Sergeant L. Pidd slightly injured. Aircraft damaged but repairable.

Hurricane R4097. Shot down into the Channel during combat two miles east of Weymouth 10.45 a.m. Flight Lieutenant S. C. Walch missing. Aircraft lost.

Hurricane P3819. Shot down into the sea off Portland 10.48 a.m. Flying Officer M. J. Steborowski missing. Aircraft lost.

Hurricane P3222. Shot down by Bf 109 in combat off Weymouth 10.50 a.m. Crashed into the sea. Pilot Officer F. N. Cawse killed. Aircraft lost.

601 SQUADRON, TANGMERE

Hurricane P3885. Shot down during combat off Portland 10.45 a.m. crashed into the sea. Pilot Officer J. L. Smithers killed. Aircraft lost.

Hurricane R4092. Shot down into the Channel during combat off Portland 10.50 a.m. Flying Officer R. S. Demetriadi killed. Aircraft lost.

Hurricane P3783. Failed to return from combat off Portland 10.50 a.m. Flying Officer J. Gillan missing. Aircraft lost.

Hurricane L2057. Failed to return following combat over the Channel off Portland 10.55 a.m. Pilot Officer W. G. Dickie missing. Aircraft lost.

'These fragmentary notes are written after a visit paid to the squadron this afternoon to find out what I could about Richard who failed to return after the great battle of Portland last Sunday, August 11. Our boats, which were out from the start of the battle, did not find him (probably he came down too far out over the sea) and, contrary to what one heard, no E-boats were in the vicinity. Nor were other sea craft seen on the sea by the other machines. The squadron consisting of twelve machines was, upon this occasion, led by his brother-in-law Flight Lieutenant William Rhodes-Moorhouse, DFC, who himself got into and out of trouble and lost contact with the others. There were seven or eight British squadrons out (about ninety machines in all) engaging an enemy of 250 to 300 machines. The fight started at over 20,000 feet up and developed into a dogfight. At about 10,000 feet — twenty miles south of Swanage — another machine of the same squadron, quite by chance, saw Richard flash past him in pursuit of an enemy machine. Petrol was at that time coming out of his tank on the port side. Apparently he had not much chance of getting back and chose to continue the pursuit to make the attack on the enemy machine.

'When the boats returned and Richard had not been picked up, Squadron Leader Ward and three other machines went out at 7.00 p.m. to search the sea. They covered an area of thirty miles flying at only fifty feet above the sea but could find no trace of Richard. He must have gone down without being able to bale out which suggests that he had been shot. All hope of his being alive has now been abandoned. Whether before making the supreme sacrifice he brought down any enemy machines that day and if so how many will never be known but, on the occasion before that last one, he destroyed a Messerschmitt 110.'

Stephen Demetriadi (his father), August 13, 1940.

Sunday, August 11, 1940 — the worst day for RAF casualties throughout the entire battle. Twenty-five airmen lost their lives, more than double the number on the 'Day of the Innocents' July 19 (11 dead) or the so-called 'hardest day' of August 18 (10 dead)

or 'Battle of Britain' day — September 15 (16 dead). These are the two pilots killed from No. 610. *Left:* Flight Sergeant John Tanner and *right* Sergeant Bill Neville. Flight Sergeant Tanner is now buried at Calais but Sergeant Neville was never found.

609 SQUADRON, WARMWELL

Spitfire R6769 returned to base leaking glycol and with severe damage to starboard aileron and rudder following combat over the Channel off Swanage 10.35 a.m. Pilot Officer J. C. Dundas unhurt. Aircraft PR-D damaged but repairable.

610 SQUADRON, BIGGIN HILL

Spitfire R6918. Failed to return from patrol over the Channel off Calais 11.30 a.m. Flight Sergeant J. H. Tanner killed. Aircraft DW-D lost.

Spitfire R6630. Missing following patrol over the Channel off Calais 11.30 a.m. Sergeant W. J. Neville missing. Aircraft DW-X lost.

615 SQUADRON, KENLEY

Hurricane N2328. Overturned on landing at Hawkinge 8.45 p.m. Pilot Officer J. A. P. McClintock unhurt. Aircraft damaged but repairable.

616 SQUADRON, LECONFIELD

Spitfire R6698. Collided with stationary aircraft on take-off losing port oleo leg. Crashed on landing 6.28 p.m. Pilot Officer L. H. Casson unhurt. Aircraft damaged but repairable.

Pilot Officer William Dickie 24-year-old from Dundee. Missing August 11, now remembered on Panel 8 of the Runnymede Memorial.

Monday, August 12

32 SQUADRON, BIGGIN HILL

Hurricane N2596. Shot down during combat over Dover 5.00 p.m. Crashed near Hawkinge. Pilot Officer A. R. H. Barton unhurt. Aircraft a write-off.

43 SQUADRON, TANGMERE

Hurricane R4108. Forced-landed Tangmere following action over the Channel 11.15 a.m. Sergeant A. L. M. Deller unhurt. Aircraft damaged but repairable.

Hurricane R4110. Returned to base with damage to engine and oil tank caused by return fire from He 111s engaged over the Channel 12.45 p.m. Pilot Officer C. A. Woods-Scawen unhurt. Aircraft repairable.

54 SQUADRON, HORNCHURCH

Spitfire R6815. Forced-landed at Lympne damaged in action against Bf 109s off Dover 8.30 a.m. Pilot Officer J. L. Kemp injured. Aircraft damaged but repairable.

Spitfire R6914. Damaged in combat with Bf 109s and crash-landed at Denton 8.40 a.m. Pilot Officer D. R. Turley-George admitted to Kent and Canterbury Hospital with shrapnel wounds to head. Aircraft damaged but repairable.

Spitfire N3160. Damaged by Bf 109 during front gun exercise on ditched enemy pilot in mid-Channel. Forced-landed near Dartford 8.45 a.m. Pilot Officer E. F. Edsall unhurt. Aircraft damaged but repairable.

56 SQUADRON, NORTH WEALD

Hurricane   . Hit in glycol tank by return fire from Do 17 of KG2 attacked ten miles north of Manston where forced-landed 5.30 p.m. Pilot Officer F. B. Sutton unhurt. Aircraft repairable.

Hurricane P2970. Shot down during attack on Do 17s of KG2 ten miles north of Margate 5.50 p.m. Crashed in flames two miles off Epple Bay. Pilot Officer A. G. Page baled out badly burned and rescued by tender transferring to Margate lifeboat. Aircraft US-X lost.

64 SQUADRON, KENLEY

Spitfire X4060. Damaged in attack by Bf 109 during interception of Do 17s off Dover 5.35 p.m. Landed at Hawkinge. Flight Lieutenant L. F. Henstock unhurt. Aircraft SH-N damaged but repairable.

Spitfire X4018. Shot down by Bf 109s during engagement over the south coast. Crashed and burned out at Sellinge 5.40 p.m. Pilot Officer A. G. Donahue baled out burned. Aircraft a write-off.

65 SQUADRON, HORNCHURCH

Spitfire R6712. Slightly damaged in bombing attack on aerodrome 12.45 p.m. Engine stopped by blast on point of take-off. Pilot Officer K. G. Hart unhurt. Aircraft repairable.

145 SQUADRON, WESTHAMPNETT

Hurricane R4180. Missing following combat with Ju 88s and Bf 110s south of the Isle of Wight 12.30 p.m. Pilot Officer J. H. Harrison missing. Aircraft lost.

Hurricane P3391. Failed to return from combat with enemy aircraft south of the Isle of Wight 12.30 p.m. Sergeant J. Kwiecinski missing. Aircraft lost.

Hurricane P3736. Set alight in mistaken attack by suspected Spitfire over the Isle of Wight 12.30 p.m. Crashed and burned out at base. Flight Lieutenant A. H. McN. Boyd unhurt. Aircraft damaged but repairable.

Hurricane R4176. Missing following combat with enemy aircraft south of the Isle of Wight 12.30 p.m. Flight Lieutenant W. Pankratz missing. Aircraft lost.

151 SQUADRON, NORTH WEALD

Hurricane P3302. Shot down by Bf 109s off Ramsgate 11.00 a.m. crashed in sea. Flying Officer A. B. Tucker rescued by launch and admitted to Ramsgate Hospital with back wounds. Aircraft lost.

Hurricane P3304. Shot down in action with Bf 109s off Ramsgate 11.00 a.m. crashed in sea. Pilot Officer R. W. G. Beley rescued from sea but died of wounds at Manston. Aircraft lost.

Hurricane P3780. Badly damaged in combat over Ramsgate 11.00 a.m. landed Rochford. Pilot Officer K. B. L. Debenham unhurt. Aircraft damaged but repairable.

Robert Beley's headstone at Margate.

Middle Wallop
Friday.

Dear Mother and Father,

At last I have found time to write and thank you all for the nice letters and grand parcels. I am very sorry for not having written sooner but things have been impossible just lately.

First let me wish you, Mother, many happy returns of the day, trusting that you are well and cheery of spirit. I only wish that I could have managed to make a trip home upon your birthday. It would have been very nice.

Have been having lots of fun just lately. Have been missing for three days. Poor old May's heart was in her mouth but I got 24 hours leave upon arriving back at the base just to go and prove to the dear girl that I was really O.K.

The C/O and two of us were out on early morning patrol when along came a shower of bombers to attack our convoy. In we went, roaring all over the sky with odds of seven to one, but this time I could not dodge quick enough and I was knocked for six right into the English Channel. Gosh it was so cold so early in the morning. Well I broke all swimming records and was eventually picked up by a boat and landed at Portsmouth. There they detained me just to make sure that I was all right. However, apart from a few gallons of sea water in my stomach, I was otherwise O.K. and I have been doing plenty of flying since. I was also very pleased to find that the other two were O.K. and had managed to shoot down one bomber and drive the rest home, before they even touched the convoy.

How's every one at home? Please convey my kind regards to all, also, in case I don't get chance to write, please thank Miss Warhurst, and Auntie Hilda for their nice parcels. I will write to them as soon as I get a few moments to spare.

Cheerio for now, all my kind regards to Father and Maurice, trusting both are keeping well.

Your loving son,
Eric.

May's birthday 7th August
Have 24 hours leave 5-6th August from Monday until noon Tuesday. Do you think any of you could get down to Birmingham? Should very much like to see you.

Sidney George Stuckey joined the Royal Air Force some years before the war and was serving as a sergeant pilot with No. 73 Squadron on the outbreak of hostilities. He is pictured here (centre) with other pilots of the squadron in France. He fought with No. 73 throughout the campaign in France until June 18 when it returned to Britain to Church Fenton to recover its strength in pilots and aircraft. After a spell of leave he was posted to No. 213 Squadron at Exeter and it was from a sortie from that aerodrome on Monday, August 12 that he failed to return (Imperial War Museum).

152 SQUADRON, WARMWELL

Spitfire P9456. Failed to return from combat with enemy aircraft south of the Isle of Wight 12.20 p.m. Flight Lieutenant L. C. Withall missing. Aircraft lost.

Spitfire   . Missing following attack on Ju 88s south of the Isle of Wight 12.20 p.m. Pilot Officer D. C. Shepley missing. Aircraft lost.

213 SQUADRON, EXETER

Hurricane   . Returned to base damaged in port elevator and starboard fuel tank following destruction of Bf 110 off the Isle of Wight 12.30 p.m. Sergeant G. D. Bushell unhurt. Aircraft AK-D repairable.

Hurricane P2854. Missing following combat with enemy aircraft off Bognor 12.44 p.m. Sergeant G. N. Wilkes missing. Aircraft AK-M lost.

Hurricane P2802. Failed to return from action over the Channel off Bognor 12.45 p.m. Sergeant S. G. Stuckey missing. Aircraft AK-R lost.

257 SQUADRON, NORTHOLT

Hurricane P3662. Missing following combat with enemy aircraft off Portsmouth 1.00 p.m. Pilot Officer J. A. G. Cholmley missing. Aircraft lost.

Hurricane P3776. Severely damaged in combat over Portsmouth 1.00 p.m. Crash-landed. Flying Officer the Hon. D. A. Coke slightly wounded and admitted to Royal Naval Hospital at Haslar. Aircraft damaged but repairable.

263 SQUADRON, GRANGEMOUTH

Whirlwind P6970. Tailwheel collapsed on landing at base. Squadron Leader H. Eelies unhurt. Aircraft repairable.

266 SQUADRON, TANGMERE

Spitfire N3175. Hit in oil system by return fire from Ju 88 over the Isle of Wight. Forced-landed and burned out on Bembridge aerodrome 12.20 p.m. Pilot Officer W. S. Williams unhurt. Aircraft a write-off.

Spitfire P9333. Believed shot down in flames during combat with enemy aircraft off Portsmouth 12.35 p.m. Pilot Officer D. G. Ashton missing. Aircraft lost.

303 SQUADRON, NORTHOLT

Hurricane P3890. Landed undercarriage up after training flight. Sergeant Gallus unhurt. Aircraft damaged but repairable.

501 SQUADRON, GRAVESEND

Hurricane P3397. Forced-landed outside Dover following combat with Bf 109s off Westgate 11.30 a.m. Squadron Leader A. L. Holland unhurt. Aircraft damaged but repairable.

Hurricane P3803. Missing following combat with enemy fighters west of Ramsgate 12.55 p.m. Flying Officer K. Lukaszewicz missing. Aircraft lost.

Hurricane N2329. Undercarriage collapsed on landing at Hawkinge due to damaged runway 4.50 p.m. Sergeant J. H. Lacey unhurt. Aircraft repairable.

Hurricane P2986. Tipped up on landing at Hawkinge due to damage to runway 5.05 p.m. Flight Lieutenant J. A. Gibson unhurt. Aircraft damaged but repairable.

504 SQUADRON, CASTLETOWN

Hurricane L1999. Forced-landed at Evanton due to oil pressure failure during air-firing practice 5.30 p.m. Flying Officer M. Jebb unhurt. Aircraft repairable.

600 SQUADRON, MANSTON

Blenheim   . Damaged in bombing attack on Manston. No personnel casualties. Aircraft damaged but repairable. One other Blenheim also suffered slight damage.

Pilot Officer Dennis Garth Ashton, a 20-year-old pilot from Keyworth, Nottinghamshire, flew Spitfires with No. 266 Squadron. At the beginning of August 1940 they left the quiet backwater of Wittering and flew south to Tangmere where on the twelfth of the month he was in action during a savage fight over Portsmouth. His aircraft was reported as seen going down in flames. No trace of either it or its young pilot were ever found.

609 SQUADRON, WARMWELL

Spitfire K9841. Returned to base with starboard aileron and mainplane damaged following combat with enemy fighters off Swanage 12.30 p.m. Pilot Officer N. leC. Agazarian unhurt. Aircraft damaged but repairable.

Spitfire K9997. Damaged in combat with Bf 110s off the Isle of Wight 12.40 p.m. Returned to base. Pilot Officer H. McD. Goodwin unhurt. Aircraft damaged but repairable.

Spitfire R6692. Returned to base wings badly strained following high speed vertical attack on Ju 88 over mid-Channel 12.50 p.m. Flying Officer J. C. Newberry unhurt. Aircraft repairable.

610 SQUADRON, BIGGIN HILL

Spitfire L1044. Shot down in flames during combat over New Romney 8.00 a.m. Crashed in sea. Pilot Officer E. B. B. Smith baled out. Rescued from the sea and admitted to Dover Hospital with burns. Aircraft DW-H lost.

Spitfire R6806. Damaged in port wing, aileron and fuel tank in attack by Bf 109 over New Romney 8.00 a.m. Further damaged in heavy landing at base. Flying Officer F. T. Gardiner slightly wounded in leg. Aircraft DW-N repairable.

Spitfire R6621. Damaged in combat with enemy fighters off Dover 8.00 a.m. Pilot unhurt. Aircraft damaged but repairable.

Spitfire P9495. Severely damaged in action with Bf 109s over Romney 8.05 a.m. Pilot believed unhurt. Aircraft DW-K a write-off.

Tuesday, August 13

43 SQUADRON, TANGMERE

Hurricane P3972. Abandoned over Cocking Down damaged by cross-fire from He 111s engaged over Petworth 6.49 a.m. Flight Lieutenant T. P. Dalton-Morgan baled out slightly wounded. Aircraft a write-off.

Hurricane R4102. Crash-landed and burst into flames on Northend Farm, Milland near Midhurst 7.27 a.m. hit by return fire from He 111s intercepted over Petworth. Flying Officer C. A. Woods-Scawen unhurt. Aircraft a write-off.
Site identified by the Southern Area Wartime Aircraft Preservation Society but little aircraft wreckage remains.

Hurricane V7221. Emergency landing at base following combat sortie 7.00 a.m. Hit in glycol system and radiator. Sergeant D. Noble unhurt. Aircraft repairable.

56 SQUADRON, NORTH WEALD

Hurricane P3479. Abandoned over Sheppey when radiator exploded following attack by Bf 110 4.15 p.m. Pilot Officer C. C. O. Joubert baled out slightly injured landing at Copton Farm, Faversham. Aircraft a write-off.

Hurricane N2429. Shot down in combat with Bf 110s over Sheppey 4.15 p.m. Believed crashed near Seasalter. Flying Officer P. F. M. Davies baled out severely burnt. Aircraft US-T a write-off.

Hurricane R4093. Shot down in head-on attack by Bf 110 off Sheerness 4.20 p.m. Crashed in sea. Sergeant P. Hillwood baled out unhurt and swam two miles to land at Sheppey. Aircraft US-P lost.

Universally accepted by aviation archaeology wreck groups as the hallmark of a successful dig, this particular example of an RAF fighter aircraft control column recovered by Steve Vizard of the private Tonbridge Aircraft Museum from Coldblow Lane, Detling in 1976 defies accurate identification. Location alone is insufficient to establish provenance.

Hurricane P3587. Wrecked in forced-landing at Hawkinge after combat over the Thames Estuary 4.30 p.m. Flying Officer R. E. P. Brooker unhurt. Aircraft a write-off.

64 SQUADRON, KENLEY

Spitfire K9805. Forced-landed at base following action with enemy aircraft over Chichester 7.40 a.m. Pilot Officer P. J. Simpson unhurt. Aircraft damaged but repairable.

65 SQUADRON, HORNCHURCH

Spitfire R6766. Crashed at Eastry during night-flying practice 7.15 p.m. Cause unknown. Pilot Officer F. S. Gregory baled out too low and killed. Aircraft a write-off.

74 SQUADRON, HORNCHURCH

Spitfire K9871. Forced-landed West Malling unable to lower undercarriage following destruction of Do 17 off Whitstable 7.00 a.m. Pilot Officer H. Szczesny unhurt. Aircraft damaged but repairable.

Spitfire R6759. Damaged in combat with enemy aircraft over north Kent coast 7.00 a.m. Pilot unhurt. Aircraft damaged but repairable.

Spitfire N3091. Shot down by return fire from Do 17 over the Thames Estuary 7.05 a.m. Abandoned following explosion in cockpit. Flight Lieutenant S. Brezezina baled out unhurt. Aircraft lost.

85 SQUADRON, MARTLESHAM HEATH

Hurricane L1889. Severely damaged in taxiing collision prior to take-off for Debden 2.00 p.m. Pilot unhurt. Aircraft damaged but repairable.

Hurricane P3409. Taxi-ing accident at base 2.00 p.m. Collided head-on with L1889 prior to take-off. Pilot unhurt. Aircraft damaged but repairable.

87 SQUADRON, EXETER

Hurricane P3387. Hit by return fire from Ju 88 engaged south of Selsey Bill 8.00 a.m. crashed in sea. Flying Officer R. L. Glyde missing. Aircraft lost.

111 SQUADRON, CROYDON

Hurricane P3880. Returned to base severely damaged in attack on Do 17s over north Kent 7.30 a.m. Sergeant W. L. Dymond unhurt. Aircraft damaged but repairable.

Hurricane P3888. Damaged in engagement over north Kent 7.30 a.m. Returned safely to base. Sergeant J. T. Craig unhurt. Aircraft repairable.

Hurricane P3530. Crashed on landing at base following combat with Do 17s over north Kent 7.40 a.m. Pilot Officer A. G. McKintyre unhurt. Aircraft damaged but repairable.

Sussex-born Sergeant Philip Purchall Norris, twenty-two years old, was a pilot with No. 213 Squadron at Exeter. On the day of the 'Adlerangriff' the squadron was scrambled to assist two other squadrons in protecting the Portland naval base. After the battle it was found that Philip Norris was missing and later his body was washed ashore in France. He is now buried at Etaples, the town near Le Touquet known to the WWI British soldier as 'Eat Apples'.

152 SQUADRON, WARMWELL

Spitfire R6608. Damaged by Bf 109 during attack on Bf 110 off Portland 4.00 p.m. Returned to base. Pilot Officer R. F. Inness slightly wounded in elbow. Aircraft a write-off.

213 SQUADRON, EXETER

Hurricane P3348. Failed to return from action over Portland 4.50 p.m. Sergeant P. P. Norris killed. Aircraft AK-B lost.

238 SQUADRON, MIDDLE WALLOP

Hurricane P2989. Forced-landed at Eartham near Tangmere with damaged oil tank following attack by Bf 109 south of the Isle of Wight 7.27 a.m. Sergeant L. G. Batt unhurt. Aircraft damaged but repairable.

Hurricane P3764. Shot down by Bf 109 and crashed in the Channel off the Isle of Wight 7.30 a.m. Sergeant E. W. Seabourne rescued from sea with burns. Aircraft lost.

Hurricane P3177. Believed shot down by Bf 109s during combat over Portland 4.30 p.m. Sergeant H. J. Marsh missing. Aircraft lost.

Hurricane P3805. Shot down in combat over Portland 4.30 p.m. Crashed Bredy Farm, Burton Bradstock. Sergeant R. Little unhurt. Aircraft a write-off.

257 SQUADRON, NORTHOLT

Hurricane P3601. Hit in glycol, petrol tanks and oil cooler by return fire from Ju 88 engaged over Selsey 3.30 p.m. Returned to base. Pilot Officer C. F. A. Capon unhurt. Aircraft damaged but repairable.

Hurricane P3623. Returned to base damaged in attack on Ju 88s over Tangmere 7.30 a.m. Sergeant D. J. Hulbert unhurt. Aircraft damaged but repairable.

266 SQUADRON, EASTCHURCH

Spitfire N3178. Damaged in bombing attack on base 7.10 a.m. No personnel casualties. Aircraft damaged but repairable.

601 SQUADRON, TANGMERE

Hurricane P3383. Returned to base damaged in combat with Bf 110s over Portland 12.15 p.m. Pilot Officer W. M. L. Fiske unhurt. Aircraft damaged but repairable.

Hurricane P3884. Damaged in combat over Portland 12.15 p.m. Returned to base. Pilot Officer M. D. Doulton unhurt. Aircraft damaged but repairable.

Hurricane P2690. Shot down by enemy fighters over Portland and crashed in the Channel off Whitnose, Weymouth Bay 12.15 p.m. Pilot Officer H. C. Mayers baled out and picked up by MTB. Treated for slight shrapnel wounds at Portland Hospital. Aircraft lost.

Hurricane P2920. Severely damaged by return fire from Ju 88 engaged over Sussex coast 7.00 a.m. Returned to base. Flying Officer W. C. Clyde slightly wounded in legs. Aircraft damaged but repairable.

609 SQUADRON, WARMWELL

Spitfire R6690. Dead-stick landing at base due to damaged glycol system following combat over the Channel 4.25 p.m. Pilot Officer J. C. Dundas unhurt. Aircraft repairable.

Sergeant Pilot 'Tony' Marsh, No. 238 Squadron, missing over Portland, August 13.

Flying Officer Henry MacDonald Goodwin *(left)* joined No. 605 'County of Warwickshire' Squadron, Auxiliary Air Force together with his brother Barrie in late 1938. Shortly after the outbreak of war 'Mac', as he was known to his service colleagues, transferred to No. 609 'West Riding' Squadron with which unit he served until his death in action on August 14, 1940 at the age of twenty-five. When last seen alive, he was in pursuit of an enemy aircraft far out over the Channel, his body being washed ashore on the south coast some days later. His 23-year-old brother Barrie perished in a flying accident in Scotland on June 24, 1940. Today they lie side by side at St. Cassian's Churchyard at Chaddesley Corbett. Their cousin, Ronald Goodwin, became CO of No. 605, their original squadron, in 1948-49 just before the Royal Auxiliary Air Force was disbanded.

Wednesday, August 14

23 SQUADRON, COLLY WESTON

Blenheim   . Starboard engine seized during night patrol 3.50 a.m. Emergency landing at base. Pilot Officer Pattinson, Sergeant MacAdam both unhurt. Aircraft YP-Q repairable.

32 SQUADRON, BIGGIN HILL

Hurricane P3171. Severely damaged by Bf 109s in combat over Dover 1.15 p.m. Landed Hawkinge. Pilot Officer Smythe unhurt. Aircraft a write-off.

Hurricane P3146. Forced-landed Hawkinge following attack by Bf 109s over Dover 1.30 p.m. Pilot Officer A. R. H. Barton unhurt. Aircraft damaged but repairable.

Hurricane V7223. Forced-landed near Dover following combat with Bf 109s 1.30 p.m. Pilot Officer B. Wlasnowalski unhurt. Aircraft damaged but repairable.

43 SQUADRON, TANGMERE

Hurricane L1739. Failed to return following interception of He 111 forty miles south of Beachy Head 7.15 p.m. Crashed in sea. Sergeant H. F. Montgomery killed. Aircraft lost.

65 SQUADRON, HORNCHURCH

Spitfire R6602. Severely damaged by Bf 109s in combat over the Channel 12.45 p.m. Forced-landed Manston. Pilot Officer L. L. Pyman unhurt. Aircraft damaged but repairable.

Spitfire R6884. Damaged in combat over Manston 12.45 p.m. Returned to base R/T damaged. Sergeant M. Keymer unhurt. Aircraft repairable.

92 SQUADRON, PEMBREY

Spitfire N3285. Hit by return fire from Ju 88 engaged north-west of Cardiff 5.45 p.m. Forced-landed on mountainside near Aberdare. Sergeant R. E. Havercroft unhurt. Aircraft damaged but repairable.
Site identified and investigated by the Gwalia Aviation Research Group but no wreckage discovered.

151 SQUADRON, NORTH WEALD

Hurricane P3310. Shot down into the sea off Christchurch in attack on Do 17s 7.00 a.m. Sergeant G. Atkinson baled out and rescued from sea. Admitted to hospital suffering from shock. Aircraft lost.

213 SQUADRON, EXETER

Hurricane R4099. Returned to base damaged by return fire from He 111 intercepted over Lyme Bay 7.50 a.m. Pilot Officer H. D. Atkinson slightly wounded by shell splinters in the arm. Aircraft damaged but repairable.

Oye Plage Communal Cemetery — the last resting place for two Hurricane pilots from Kenley shot down on August 14 — Peter Collard *(right)* and Cecil Montgomery *(opposite)*.

600 SQUADRON, MANSTON

Blenheim L1521. Aircraft burned out following bombing attack on base. No personnel losses. Aircraft a write-off.

Blenheim   . Aircraft burned out following bombing attack on base. Write-off.

Blenheim   . Aircraft burned out following bombing attack on base. Write-off.

609 SQUADRON, WARMWELL

Spitfire N3024. Missing following sporadic independent actions over the south coast 5.30 p.m. Flying Officer H. McD. Goodwin killed. Aircraft lost.

Spitfire R6961. Returned to base with slight damage to spinner and mainspar following destruction of Ju 88 five miles south-west of base 5.40 p.m. Pilot Officer J. C. Dundas unhurt. Aircraft repairable.

610 SQUADRON, BIGGIN HILL

Spitfire K9947. Forced-landed at Wye following destruction of Bf 109 in combat off Folkestone 12.30 p.m. Sergeant B. E. D. Gardner admitted to Ashford Hospital with bullet wounds in arm. Aircraft DW-M repairable.

Spitfire L1009. Severely damaged in combat over Folkestone 12.30 p.m. Pilot believed unhurt. Aircraft DW-B damaged but repairable.

615 SQUADRON, KENLEY

Hurricane P3380. Damaged by Bf 110 in combat over Dover 12.45 p.m. Returned to base. Flying Officer J. R. H. Gayner unhurt. Aircraft repairable.

Hurricane P3109. Failed to return from combat off Dover 12.45 p.m. Crashed in sea. Flying Officer P. Collard killed. Aircraft lost.

Hurricane P3160. Missing following combat over the Channel off Dover 12.50 p.m. Crashed in sea. Pilot Officer C. R. Montgomery killed. Aircraft lost.

Hurricane L1983. Undercarriage collapsed on landing at Hawkinge following combat off Dover 1.00 p.m. Pilot Officer E. B. Rogers unhurt. Aircraft damaged but repairable.

Thursday, August 15

1 SQUADRON, NORTHOLT

Hurricane P3047. Crashed in sea south of Harwich following combat with Bf 109 3.00 p.m. Flight Lieutenant M. H. Brown baled out slightly injured in face and hands. Rescued by a trawler. Aircraft lost.

Hurricane R4075. Failed to return from combat with enemy fighters off Harwich 3.00 p.m. Pilot Officer D. O. M. Browne missing. Aircraft lost.

Hurricane P3043. Missing following combat with enemy fighters off Harwich 3.00 p.m. Sergeant M. M. Shanahan missing. Aircraft lost.

Both the above pilots, Pilot Officer Browne and Sergeant Shanahan, appear in the Official Casualty Returns as 'missing' on August 16, 1940 and their dates of death are recorded as such. The Form 540, No. 1 Squadron Operations Record Book states otherwise as does a squadron history published 1971.

PILOT OFFICER CECIL MONTGOMERY, No. 615 SQUADRON.

Hurricane P3678. Slightly damaged by Bf 109 in combat over the sea off Harwich 3.00 p.m. Returned to base. Pilot Officer J. F. D. Elkington unhurt. Aircraft repairable.

17 SQUADRON, DEBDEN

Hurricane P3891. Shot down by Bf 109s and crash-landed outside Felixstowe on dead engine 3.45 p.m. Flying Officer W. J. Harper wounded in face and leg. Admitted to Felixstowe Hospital. Aircraft damaged but repairable.

32 SQUADRON, BIGGIN HILL

Hurricane N2459. Shot down in flames by Bf 109s. Crashed in sea at Pye Sands, Pennyhole Bay south of Harwich 3.25 p.m. Pilot Officer D. H. Grice baled out burned, rescued by MTB and admitted RN Hospital, Shotley. Aircraft GZ-C lost.

Hurricane N2671. Force-landed with glycol leak following action with Bf 109s off Harwich 3.35 p.m. Pilot Officer B. Wlasnowalski unhurt. Aircraft damaged but repairable.

Hurricane P3522. Damaged in attack on Do 215s off Selsey Bill 6.00 p.m. Landed at Tangmere. Sergeant B. Henson unhurt. Aircraft damaged but repairable.

43 SQUADRON, TANGMERE

Hurricane P3971. Hit in glycol system by return fire from Ju 88 of 4/LG1 engaged over Emsworth. Returned to base with engine and cockpit hood damaged 5.30 p.m. Squadron Leader J. V. C. Badger unhurt. Aircraft damaged but repairable.

Hurricane R4107. Returned to base with two bullets in main spar following combat sortie 5.45 p.m. Pilot Officer C. A. Woods-Scawen unhurt. Aircraft FT-B repairable.

54 SQUADRON, HORNCHURCH

Spitfire N3097. Shot down by Bf 109 following destruction of Ju 87s. Crashed in sea off Dover 11.45 a.m. Sergeant N. A. Lawrence rescued by Royal Navy admitted to Dover hospital with shock. Aircraft lost.

Spitfire R7015. Crashed at Hythe during combat with Bf 109s over Dover 11.45 a.m. Sergeant W. Klozinsky admitted to Ashford hospital with injuries. Aircraft a write-off.

Spitfire R6981. Chased back across Channel from Calais Marck by Bf 109s and severely damaged. Believed crashed and burned out at Pope Street, Godmersham near Ashford 7.00 p.m. Flight Lieutenant A. C. Deere baled out at 1,500ft and sprained a wrist. Delivered to East Grinstead Hospital. Aircraft a write-off.
Panel from this aircraft donated to the Brenzett Aeronautical Museum.

Spitfire R7019. Forced-landed near Maidstone damaged after combat with Bf 109s 7.05 p.m. Pilot Officer H. K. F. Matthews unhurt. Aircraft damaged but repairable.

64 SQUADRON, KENLEY

Spitfire N3230. Forced-landed Hawkinge with glycol system damaged following action with Bf 109s over Dungeness 3.20 p.m. Pilot Officer E. G. Gilbert unhurt. Aircraft damaged but repairable.

Spitfire R6990. Failed to return from combat with Bf 109s over the Channel 3.20 p.m. Flying Officer C. J. D. Andreae missing. Aircraft lost.

Spitfire K9964. Forced-landed at Calais Marck following action with Bf 109s over the Channel off Dungeness 3.25 p.m. Pilot Officer R. Roberts captured. Aircraft SH-W lost.

79 SQUADRON ACKLINGTON

Hurricane   . Returned to base damaged in combat with enemy aircraft off the coast 1.00 p.m. Pilot unhurt. Aircraft damaged but repairable.

At 5.45 p.m. on August 15, a Hurricane broke away from a dogfight over Greenwoods Farm, Sidlesham trailing smoke and flames. The aircraft headed west but then turned sharply to port and the pilot was seen to bale out. Unfortunately his parachute, when it opened, was seen to be on fire and he fell faster and faster until he landed in a pond near the Selsey gasholder. Later, when the body was recovered from deep in the mud, it was found that his harness had burnt through and he had fallen free of his parachute. The pilotless Hurricane dived, swooped and turned erratically before it crashed into a barn *(above).* The engine buried itself deep in the concrete floor, the rest of the wreckage smashing through the rear wall. The crash set fire to an adjacent building and the scorch marks are still visible today. Basil Fisher *(below left)* was an Etonian and it was in St. John's Cemetery at Eton that his remains were laid to rest (S. Hall/A. Saunders).

Holy Trinity Churchyard, Warmwell.

87 SQUADRON, EXETER

Hurricane P3215. Shot down in combat with enemy fighters over Portland 6.00 p.m. Crashed into a wood at Abbotsbury attempting to reach Warmwell aerodrome. Squadron Leader T. G. Lovell-Gregg killed. Aircraft a write-off.

Hurricane P3465. Forced-landed at Symondsbury near Bridport following combat over Portland 6.00 p.m. Sergeant J. Cowley slightly injured admitted to Bridport hospital. Aircraft a write-off.

Hurricane P2872. Shot down by Bf 110 and crashed into the sea off Portland 6.05 p.m. Pilot Officer P. W. Comeley missing. Aircraft lost.

Memorial Grave, Brussels, Belgium.

Hurricane R2687. Damaged by Bf 109 in combat over Portland 6.10 p.m. Forced-landed on Field Barn Farm, Radipole. Pilot Officer D. T. Jay unhurt. Aircraft damaged but repairable.

111 SQUADRON, CROYDON

Hurricane R4195. Landed at West Malling damaged by return fire from Do 17s over Thames Estuary 3.00 p.m. Sergeant W. L. Dymond unhurt. Aircraft damaged but repairable.

Hurricane P3961. Damaged in glycol system in attack on Do 17s over the Thames Estuary 3.00 p.m. Landed at Hawkinge on dead engine. Flying Officer H. M. Ferris unhurt. Aircraft damaged but repairable.

Hurricane P3595. Severely damaged in combat with Ju 88s and Bf 110s over Thorney Island 6.00 p.m. Landed at Hawkinge. Pilot Officer A. G. McIntyre slightly wounded. Aircraft a write-off.

Hurricane P3944. Shot down in flames during action against Ju 88s and Bf 110s over Selsey. Crashed at Greenwoods Farm, Sidlesham 5.51 p.m. Flying Officer B. M. Fisher baled out but killed. Aircraft a write-off.

Site investigated by both the Southern Area Wartime Aircraft Preservation Society and the Wealden Aviation Archaeological Group. Surface fragments discovered scattered about the farm yard.

151 SQUADRON, NORTH WEALD

Hurricane V7409. Radio aerial shot away during combat with Bf 109s west of Dover 3.30 p.m. Returned to base. Pilot Officer K. B. L. Debenham unhurt. Aircraft damaged but repairable.

Hurricane L1975. Forced-landed at Eastwell Park near Ashford with engine damaged in combat with Bf 109s over Dover 7.12 p.m. Pilot Officer J. L. W. Ellacombe unhurt. Aircraft damaged but repairable.

Hurricane P3941. Shot down by Bf 109s and crashed into the Channel off Dymchurch 7.15 p.m. Pilot Officer J. T. Johnston picked up dead. Aircraft lost.

Hurricane P3065. Shot down in combat with Bf 109s over Dover 7.15 p.m. Crashed at Shorncliffe. Sub-Lieutenant H. W. Begg wounded. Aircraft DZ-G a write-off.

Hurricane P3940. Damaged in combat west of Dover 7.15 p.m. Returned to base. Squadron Leader J. A. G. Gordon wounded. Aircraft repairable.

Hurricane V7410. Failed to return from combat with Bf 109s over the Channel off Dover 7.20 p.m. Pilot Officer M. Rozwadowski missing. Aircraft lost.

152 SQUADRON, WARMWELL

Spitfire K9954. Severely damaged by Bf 109 in combat off Portland but reached base 5.30 p.m. Flight Lieutenant B. P. A. Boitel-Gill unhurt. Aircraft a write-off.

Spitfire R6910. Returned to base damaged and rudder jammed following combat off Portland 5.30 p.m. Pilot Officer H. J. Ackroyd unhurt. Aircraft damaged but repairable.

Spitfire R6968. Severely damaged in combat with enemy aircraft off Portland 5.30 p.m. Returned to base. Pilot unhurt. Aircraft damaged but repairable.

Folkestone New Cemetery, Kent.

213 SQUADRON, EXETER

Hurricane V7227. Missing following action off Portland 5.45 p.m. Pilot Officer M. S. H. C. Buchin missing. Aircraft AK-C lost.

Hurricane W6669. Hit in wing by 20mm cannon shell during combat with Bf 110s off Portland 5.45 p.m. Returned to base. Sergeant R. D. Dunscombe unhurt. Aircraft AK-Q damaged but repairable.

219 SQUADRON, CATTERICK

Blenheim L8698. Hit by return fire from enemy aircraft engaged off Scarborough 2.00 p.m. Crash-landed at Driffield. Sergeant O. A. Dupee wounded in right arm. Sergeant T. H. Bannister unhurt. Aircraft damaged but repairable.

Bournemouth East Cemetery, Hampshire.

Hurricane P3582 was shot down during the attack on Hawkinge on August 15 (Flight).

234 SQUADRON, MIDDLE WALLOP

Spitfire R6988. Shot down by enemy fighters and crashed in Bournemouth 6.15 p.m. Pilot Officer C. H. Hight killed. Aircraft a write-off.

Spitfire N3277. Damaged in combat with enemy fighters off Swanage 6.15 p.m. Forced to land near Cherbourg. Pilot Officer R. Hardy captured. Aircraft AZ-H lost.

Spitfire R6985. Failed to return following combat with enemy fighters off Swanage 6.20 p.m. Believed crashed in Channel. Pilot Officer V. Parker captured. Aircraft lost.

Spitfire P9363. Believed severely damaged during combat with enemy fighters over the Channel and crashed near Twyford 6.25 p.m. Pilot baled out unhurt. Aircraft a write-off.

257 SQUADRON, NORTHOLT

Hurricane L1703. Abandoned following mid-air fire during routine patrol 12.05 p.m. and believed collided with balloon cable and crashed at Larbourne Farm, West Drayton. Pilot Officer C. G. Frizell baled out unhurt. Aircraft a write-off.
Crash site now believed to be a gravel pit and investigated by the Air Historical Group but nothing found.

266 SQUADRON, HORNCHURCH

Spitfire N3189. Missing following destruction of He 115 off Dunkirk 5.15 p.m. Believed crashed in Channel. Sergeant F. B. Hawley missing. Aircraft lost.

Spitfire N3181. Returned to base severely damaged by 20mm cannon fire during attack on Ju 88 off Dover 6.50 p.m. Flight Lieutenant D. L. Armitage unhurt. Aircraft damaged but repairable.

Spitfire N3168. Crashed in flames on the bank of River Medway at Teston following combat over Kent 6.50 p.m. Pilot Officer F. W. Cale baled out into River Medway and killed. Aircraft a write-off.

501 SQUADRON, GRAVESEND

Hurricane P3582. Shot down during combat with Ju 87s attacking Hawkinge 11.30 a.m. Possibly that crashed at Alkham. Flight Lieutenant J. A. A. Gibson baled out unhurt. Aircraft a write-off.

Hurricane P3040. Shot down during engagement with Ju 87s over Hawkinge 11.30 a.m. Flight Lieutenant A. R Putt baled out unhurt. Aircraft a write-off.

Hurricane V7230. Returned to base damaged following attack on Ju 87s over Hawkinge 11.30 a.m. Flying Officer S. Witorzenc believed unhurt. Aircraft damaged but repairable.

601 SQUADRON, TANGMERE

Hurricane V7253. Crashed near Selsey during combat with enemy fighters 5.45 p.m. Pilot Officer J. K. McGrath unhurt. Aircraft damaged but repairable.

Hurricane P3232. Shot down in combat over Winchester 5.50 p.m. Abandoned at height over Durley. Flying Officer G. N. S. Cleaver baled out with severe facial injuries landing near Lower Upham and admitted to hospital. Aircraft a write-off.

604 SQUADRON, MIDDLE WALLOP

Blenheims L6723, L8676. Destroyed in bombing attack on base by Ju 88s 5.00 p.m. No personnel losses.

Blenheim L6610. Crash-landed at base damaged following attack by Spitfire flown by Pilot Officer D. M. Crook of 609 Squadron 6.00 p.m. Pilot unhurt, Air Gunner slightly wounded. Aircraft a write-off.

605 SQUADRON, DREM

Hurricane P3827. Forced-landed one mile from Usworth following combat off the east coast 2.10 p.m. Flying Officer C. W. Passy unhurt. Aircraft a write-off.

Hurricane P3308. Hit by return fire from He 111s off Newcastle 2.20 p.m. Returned to base slightly damaged. Flight Lieutenant A. A. McKellar unhurt. Aircraft repairable.

Hurricane P2717. Forced-landed near Hart Railway station following combat off Newcastle 2.20 p.m. Pilot Officer K. S. Law badly injured admitted to West Hartlepool Hospital. Aircraft damaged but repairable.

615 SQUADRON, KENLEY

Hurricane P3162. Damaged by Bf 109s in combat off Folkestone 12.00 p.m. Landed Hawkinge. Pilot Officer D. Evans unhurt. Aircraft repairable.

Hurricane L1829. Damaged in combat with Bf 109s over Folkestone. 12.05 p.m. Returned to base badly damaged in rear fuselage. Pilot Officer A. J. J. Truran slightly injured. Aircraft KW-W damaged but repairable.

Hurricane P2801. Shot down in combat with Bf 109s. Crashed and burned out at Seal 12.05 p.m. Sergeant D. W. Halton missing. Aircraft a write-off.

616 SQUADRON, LECONFIELD

Spitfire K9807. Undercarriage wrecked in heavy landing after routine practice flight 5.35 p.m. Pilot Officer W. L. B. Walker unhurt. Aircraft damaged but repairable.

'Per Ardua ad Astra' is the inscription on the headstone for Pilot Officer Francis Cale's grave at Westminster City Cemetery at Ealing, Middlesex.

Friday, August 16

1 SQUADRON, NORTHOLT

Hurricane P3173. Shot down over Thorney Island. Crashed and burned out at Manor Farm, Chidham 1.05 p.m. Pilot Officer J. F. D. Elkington baled out injured and admitted to hospital. Aircraft a write-off.
Major recovery by the Wealden Aviation Archaeological Group 1975. Complete Rolls-Royce Merlin engine, armour plate and cockpit components including the control column unearthed.

Hurricane P2751. Set alight by return fire from He 111 over Surrey 5.30 p.m. Returned to base. Squadron Leader D. A. Pemberton unhurt. Aircraft repairable.

Hurricane P3653. Hit in glycol tank during attack on He 111s 5.30 p.m. Crash-landed near Farnham. Pilot Officer P. V. Boot unhurt. Aircraft damaged but repairable.

Hurricane P2686. Damaged in explosion of He 111 shot down near Petworth 5.25 p.m. Returned to base. Pilot Officer G. E. Goodman unhurt. Aircraft repairable.

Hurricane   . Returned to base with two longerons severed in attack by Bf 110 over the South Downs 5.35 p.m. Pilot Officer N. P. W. Hancock unhurt. Aircraft repairable.

19 SQUADRON, DUXFORD

Spitfire R6904. Returned to base damaged during combat with Bf 110s off Harwich 5.30 p.m. Sergeant H. A. C. Roden unhurt. Aircraft repairable.

43 SQUADRON, TANGMERE

Hurricanes P3971, R4108, R4110, V7364. Destroyed in bombing attack on base 1.00 p.m. No personnel losses. Aircraft a write-off.

Hurricane N2621. Shot down by Bf 109 following destruction of Ju 87 off Sussex coast 1.15 p.m. Crashed near Parkhurst, Isle of Wight. Pilot Officer C. A. Woods-Scawen slightly injured. Aircraft a write-off

Hurricane L1742. Tail damaged by cannon fire during attack on Ju 87s off Selsey 1.15 p.m. Returned to base. Pilot Officer D. G. Gorrie unhurt. Aircraft repairable.

Hurricane P3216. Crash-landed on Selsey beach with damage to oil system following attack on Ju 87 off Sussex coast 1.20 p.m. Flying Officer H. C. Upton unhurt. Aircraft damaged but repairable.

Hurricane L1736. Developed glycol leak and caught alight on routine patrol 6.00 p.m. Sergeant J. L. Crisp baled out but broke a thigh in heavy landing. Aircraft FT-H a write-off.

56 SQUADRON, NORTH WEALD

Hurricane V7368. Set alight in surprise attack by enemy aircraft during section patrol 12.02 p.m. Pilot Officer L. W. Graham baled out slightly injured. Aircraft a write-off.

Hurricane P3547. Hit by return fire from Do 17 and forced-landed at over 100 mph south of Whitstable 5.15 p.m. Burned out. Flight Sergeant F. W. Higginson slightly injured. Aircraft US-A a write-off.

The control column, completely intact, recovered from the excavation of the crash site of Hurricane P3173 of No. 1 Squadron by the Wealden Aviation Archaeological Group.

64 SQUADRON, KENLEY

Spitfire L1038. Damaged by Bf 109 in combat over the Dover straits 1.05 p.m. Forced-landed Hawkinge. Sergeant J. Mann slightly wounded. Aircraft damaged but repairable.

Spitfire P9554. Shot down by Bf 109 during return to base from Hawkinge. Crashed at Blackboy, Uckfield 5.10 p.m. Squadron Leader A. R. D. MacDonnell baled out unhurt landing Possingworth Park. Aircraft a write-off.
Excavated by Halstead War Museum

Spitfire L1068. Severely damaged by cannon fire during combat with He 111s 5.30 p.m. Returned to base. Pilot Officer P. J. Simpson unhurt. Aircraft damaged but repairable.

65 SQUADRON, HORNCHURCH

Spitfire K9915. Failed to return following combat over the Channel off Deal 5.30 p.m. Crashed in sea. Pilot Officer L. L. Pyman killed. Aircraft lost.

Spitfire R6618. Burned out at Manston following strafing attack by Bf 109s. No personnel losses. Aircraft a write-off.

111 SQUADRON, CROYDON

Hurricane R4193. Collided with Do 17 of 7/KG76 during head-on attack over Marden 12.45 p.m. Crashed on Brandenbury Farm, Collier Street. Flight Lieutenant H. M. Ferriss killed. Aircraft a write-off.

Hurricane P3029. Shot down during combat with enemy aircraft over Kent 12.30 p.m. Crashed at Palmers Green Farm, Brenchley, near Paddock Wood. Sergeant R. Carnall slight burns. Aircraft a write-off.

Hurricane V7222. Returned to base with damage sustained in combat over Kent 12.30 p.m. Flight Lieutenant S D. P. Connors unhurt. Aircraft repairable.

Hurricane N2482. Damaged by attacks from six Bf 109s engaged over the Channel 12.20 p.m. Returned to base. Sergeant T. Y. Wallace unhurt. Aircraft repairable.

The grave of Flight Lieutenant Henry Ferriss, DFC, at St. Mary's RC Churchyard in Chislehurst, Kent.

213 SQUADRON, EXETER

Hurricane   . Failed to return from combat off Portland 1.00 p.m. Pilot Officer J. E. P. Laricheliere missing. Aircraft AK-R lost.

234 SQUADRON, MIDDLE WALLOP

Spitfire R6967. Engine set alight by Bf 109 in attack over Gosport 5.32 p.m. Crashed between Southwick and Widley. Flying Officer K. S. Dewhurst baled out unhurt landing near Widley. Aircraft a write-off.
Site investigated by the Wealden Aviation Archaeological Group in November 1975. Many small fragments recovered.

Spitfire X4016. Shot down into the sea off Portsmouth during combat with Bf 109s 5.35 p.m. Flying Officer F. H. P. Connor baled out unhurt rescued by Royal Navy launch. Aircraft lost.

Spitfire N3242. Damaged in combat with Bf 109s over Portsmouth 5.45 p.m. Pilot unhurt. Aircraft damaged but repairable.

Spitfire R6896. Returned to base with damage sustained in combat with Bf 109s over Portsmouth 6.00 p.m. Flight Lieutenant P. C. Hughes unhurt. Aircraft damaged but repairable.

249 SQUADRON, BOSCOMBE DOWN

Hurricane P3576. Shot down in flames during engagement with Bf 110s over Southampton 1.52 p.m. Believed crashed at Rownhams School. Flight Lieutenant J. B. Nicolson baled out badly burned and fired at by LDV whilst in parachute. Admitted to Royal Southampton Hospital. Aircraft GN-A a write-off.

Hurricane P3616. Shot down by enemy fighters over Southampton 1.55 p.m. Believed crashed at Toothill, near Lee. Pilot Officer M. A. King baled out but killed when parachute collapsed during descent. Aircraft a write-off.
Largely a surface crash and cleared by the authorities at the time. Many small fragments remain scattered over an acre field. Site investigated by numerous groups and individuals.

Hurricane P3870. Returned to base with slight damage caused by enemy fighter attack over Southampton 1.52 p.m. Squadron Leader E. B. King unhurt. Aircraft repairable.

266 SQUADRON, HORNCHURCH

Spitfire R6768. Shot down in combat with Bf 109s. Crashed and burned out at Eastry 12.35 p.m. Squadron Leader R. L. Wilkinson killed. Aircraft a write-off.
Site investigated by Steve Vizard March 1980 and small pieces recovered.

Spitfire N3240. Failed to return from combat with Bf 109s over Canterbury 12.40 p.m. Believed crashed near Stoneheap Farm. Little Mongeham. Sub-Lieutenant H. L. Greenshields missing. Aircraft a write-off.

Spitfire X4030. Severely damaged in combat with Bf 109s over Canterbury 12.40 p.m. Sergeant A. W. Eade unhurt. Aircraft damaged but repairable.

Spitfire N3095. Shot down in flames at Adisham during combat with Bf 109s 12.45 p.m. Pilot Office N. G. Bowen killed. Aircraft a write-off.

Spitfire P9312. Set alight in combat with Bf 109s and abandoned over Canterbury 12.45 p.m. Believed that which crashed near Wickhambreux. Flight Lieutenant S. H. Bazley baled out with burns and minor injuries. Aircraft a write-off.

Spitfire K9864. Severely damaged in combat with Bf 109s over Canterbury and forced-landed near Oare, Faversham 12.55 p.m. Pilot Officer J. F. Soden slightly wounded in legs. Aircraft a write-off.

600 SQUADRON MANSTON

Blenheim . Destroyed in strafing attack on base by Bf 109s. No personnel losses. Another Blenheim also damaged but repairable.

Sub-Lieutenant Henry La Fone Greenshields, 22-year-old Fleet Air Arm pilot serving with No. 266, now buried at Calais Southern Cemetery *(opposite).* In 1976 his sister received this letter — a sad obituary to a brave pilot.

601 SQUADRON, TANGMERE

Hurricane P3358. Damaged by return fire from Ju 87 over Bognor and forced-landed in flames back at base 1.00 p.m. Pilot Officer W. M. L. Fiske badly burned admitted to hospital but died of shock and injuries the next day. Aircraft a write-off.

602 SQUADRON, WESTHAMPNETT

Spitfire K9881. Landed at base damaged following action against Ju 87s attacking Tangmere 2.00 p.m. Pilot Officer T. G. F. Ritchie unhurt. Aircraft damaged but repairable.

Spitfire P9463. Crash-landed in flames on return to base after combat with Ju 87s attacking Tangmere 2.00 p.m. Pilot Officer H. W. Moody unhurt. Aircraft damaged but repairable.

610 SQUADRON, BIGGIN HILL

Spitfire R6802. Failed to return from combat with Bf 109s off Dungeness 5.15 p.m. Flight Lieutenant W. H. C. Warner missing. Aircraft DW-Z lost.

Spitfire . Attacked by Bf 109 over Dungeness 5.20 p.m. Returned to base R/T damaged. Pilot Officer D. McT. Gray unhurt. Aircraft DW-D repairable.

615 SQUADRON, KENLEY

Hurricane P2963. Severely damaged by Bf 110 during attack on He 111 over Newhaven 5.30 p.m. Returned to base. Pilot Officer P. H. Hugo wounded in both legs. Aircraft a write-off.

April 28, 1976

Dear Mr. & Mrs. Greenshields,

You will not know who I am but I have wanted to write this letter since the end of the war and could not for reasons as will be seen below.

I am French born and lived in Calais from the time I was born to the end of 1946. On August 16, 1940 I witnessed the fight of a British plane with German ones and saw it pass over my house and eventually fall onto the bank of the canal a few hundred yards behind my house. We all ran to this point to see if we could help in any way but alas there was nothing we could do. To this day I have never forgotten this and I have wanted to write to the parents of this brave young man whose courage in trying to avoid falling on an inhabited area saved so many lives. The Germans, when they removed his body from the plane, presented a guard of honour but we too stood there and prayed very hard for him and thanked him from the very bottom of our hearts for his sacrifice and courage.

His death also had a tragic link with my own life as my father was killed by a German vehicle on August 15, 1940, and it was not until about one hour after your son's death that my mother and I were told of his death as the Germans had removed all his belongings before taking him to the hospital mortuary and only gave the belongings back to the French Police that evening, after a torturing twenty-four hours wondering about his fate.

To this date I have always associated your son and my father in my prayers on the anniversary of my father's death and each time I visit my father's grave I visit your son's, as I did weekly all throughout the time I was in Calais until 1946.

Your son was buried under the name of Henri Lafon (a Canadian's name so it seemed) because his identity disc has been badly damaged and all they could read was the Christian name, which must have been Henry, and the second name but the surname has disappeared. I have just read these details in the book written by a friend of mine in Calais, called 'Calais the Forbidden Zone June 1940-August 1941'. Until then I was not sure which grave was your son's as two airmen had died on that day and been buried side by side under whatever names had been deciphered from the identity discs and papers available at the time, and when they were formally identified and the proper name engraved on the headstones I was never sure which was your son's grave and used to pray on both. In case I would ever find out I had taken the address of both from the cemetery registry and this is how I have now traced you and hope this letter will find you.

I want to say a very big thank you for your son's courage and ultimate sacrifice and how brave he was in the face of the enemy and how very proud you should be to have had such a son. Our deepest thanks will go for ever to all those brave young men who gave their whole so that we could be free from the horrors of the Nazi occupation and once again be able to live without constant fear and oppression. I sincerely hope this letter from the past has not revived your sorrow too much but will give you a small measure of comfort in knowing how your son really died and so bravely.

Yours most sincerely,

Mrs. R. J. Park

William Meade Lindsley Fiske, wealthy stockbroker, film producer and international sportsman from Chicago, was a close friend of the pilots of the 'Millionaire's Squadron, No. 601 'County of London' and, although the American authorities severely frowned on foreign enlistment, his influential friends enabled him to join the Royal Air Force in September 1939. The publicity that this event attracted (especially as his wife in the photo *above* was the ex-Countess of Warwick, a noted society figure at the time) made his death on August 17 all the more significant and, on July 4, 1941, American Independence Day, the Secretary of State for Air, Sir Archibald Sinclair, unveiled a Memorial Plaque *(above right)* in the crypt of St. Paul's Cathedral. Over the ensuing years Fiske has been portrayed as the only American to die in the Battle of Britain. Our research for this book leads us to believe that several other Americans enlisted under the guise of Canadians to avoid the displeasure of the US State Department. The fact that Ministry of Defence records list them as Canadians is not proof of their nationality. Friends of Pilot Officer Hugh Reilley, killed on October 17, were told to keep quiet about him being an American as he had wangled a Canadian passport. 'Billy' Fiske buried at Boxgrove churchyard *(below)* should therefore only be described as 'an American killed in the battle'.

SQUADRON LEADER R. L. H. WILKINSON

Squadron Leader Rodney Levett Wilkinson assumed command of No. 266 Squadron at Wittering on July 6, 1940. On August 1 he led his unit to Tangmere where it was involved in the bitter fighting over the south coast and the Channel. A further move was made to Hornchurch on August 13 and it was while leading the squadron from there that he was shot down in combat three days later and killed. He is now buried in the war graves section at Margate Cemetery.

Saturday, August 17

43 SQUADRON, TANGMERE

Hurricane L1836. Believed to be the aircraft which returned to base severely over-stressed due to vertical dive at speed in pursuit of Do 215 over Winchester 5.30 p.m. Sergeant H. J. C. Hallowes unhurt. Aircraft damaged but repairable.

235 SQUADRON, THORNEY ISLAND

Blenheim N3540. Overshot runway and crashed on landing following routine night patrol 9.35 p.m. Sergeant S. J. Hobbs, Sergeant H. W. Ricketts, Sergeant T. A. Maslen all unhurt. Aircraft a write-off.

302 SQUADRON, LECONFIELD

Hurricane P3927. Caught fire on training flight and crashed attempting emergency landing at Wheel. Pilot Officer Glowczynski admitted to Beverley Hospital seriously burned. Aircraft a write-off.

Sunday, August 18

1 SQUADRON, NORTHOLT

Hurricane P3757. Damaged in combat over Dungeness 2.00 p.m. Returned to base. Pilot Officer G. E. Goodman unhurt. Aircraft damaged but repairable.

17 SQUADRON, DEBDEN

Hurricane V7407. Returned to base with damage sustained in attack from Bf 109 off Dover 1.00 p.m. Squadron Leader C. W. Williams unhurt. Aircraft repairable.

Hurricane   . Returned to base severely damaged by Bf 109s in combat over Dover 1.00 p.m. Sergeant D. J. North-Bomford unhurt. Aircraft damaged but repairable.

Hurricane L1921. Missing following engagement with Bf 109s off Dover 1.05 p.m. Crashed in sea. Pilot Officer N. D. Solomon killed. Aircraft lost.

Hurricane P3209. Forced-landed Manston following combat off Dover and destroyed in strafing attack by Bf 109s 2.15 p.m. Sergeant G. Griffiths unhurt. Aircraft damaged but repairable.

32 SQUADRON, BIGGIN HILL

Hurricane P3147. Set alight during action over Biggin Hill 1.45 p.m. Abandoned over Brenchley. Pilot Officer J. F. Pain baled out slightly wounded landed at Horsmonden and admitted to hospital. Aircraft a write-off.

Hurricane V7363. A 20mm cannon shell exploded in cockpit during combat over Biggin Hill 1.45 p.m. Crashed at Skeynes Park Farm, Edenbridge. Flight Lieutenant H. a'B. Russell baled out seriously wounded applied tourniquet during parachute descent and admitted to Edenbridge Hospital. Aircraft a write-off.
   Major recovery undertaken by the London Air Museum. Shattered remains of Rolls-Royce Merlin engine excavated plus propeller boss, blind-flying panel and waistcoat discovered in compressed remnants of cockpit map storage box. Cockpit clock presented to the pilot in 1979.

Waistcoat belonging to Flight Lieutenant Russell recovered from the crumpled map compartment by the London Air Museum.

Pilot Officer Neville Solomon, killed August 18, now buried at Pihen-les-Guines, France.

Hurricane V6536. Hit by return fire in gravity tank during combat over Biggin Hill. 1.45 p.m. Forced-landed at Otford. Sergeant B. Henson slightly wounded in face. Aircraft damaged but repairable.

Hurricane N2461. Shot down in combat with Bf 109s 5.30 p.m. Crashed at Wigmore. Squadron Leader M. N. Crossley baled out unhurt landing at Gillingham. Aircraft GZ-F a write-off.

Hurricane V6535. Shot down in combat with Bf 109s 5.35 p.m. Believed crashed Ruckinge. Pilot Officer R. C. C. de Grunne baled out badly burned admitted to hospital. Aircraft a write-off.
Site excavated by the Brenzett Aeronautical Museum in 1973. Some fragments of airframe and minor components recovered. Canvas from rear fuselage with painted serial 'V6535' displayed in the Kent Battle of Britain Museum

Hurricane R4106. Crashed at Rose Garden Cottage, Chartham Hatch following combat with Bf 109s over Canterbury 5.29 p.m. Sergeant L. H. B. Pearce baled out slightly wounded. Aircraft a write-off.
Site excavated by London Air Museum in February 1979. Complete Rolls-Royce Merlin engine recovered together with instrument panel, control column, full armour plate, tail wheel and both undercarriage legs. Control locking tools found and aircraft serial number stencilled on plywood fuselage covering confirmed identity beyond dispute.

Hurricane R4081. Forced-landed at Biggin Hill 1.45 p.m. following combat with enemy fighters. Pilot Officer A. F. Eckford unhurt. Aircraft damaged but repairable.

43 SQUADRON, TANGMERE

Hurricane R4109. Damaged by Bf 109s of II/JG27 during attack on Ju 87s attacking base. Crash-landed at Holme Street Farm, Pulborough 2.26 p.m. Flight Lieutenant F. R. Carey wounded in right knee admitted to Royal West Sussex Hospital, Brighton. Aircraft damaged but repairable.

65 SQUADRON, HORNCHURCH

Spitfire R6713. Crashed Westbere, near Canterbury during flight patrol from Rochford 1.30 p.m. Flying Officer F. Gruszka killed. Aircraft a write-off.
Site identified by the Kent Battle of Britain Museum in 1971 an exploratory dig revealed rudder fabric, radio aerial mast, first-aid kit, rudder-bar pedals and pilot's parachute. Identity confirmed 'R6713' being stencilled on one of the .303in Browning machine-gun ammunition feed chutes. Later complete excavation undertaken at the request of the Ministry of Defence 1976 when complete instrument panel and windscreen were recovered together with remains of pilot who was buried with full military honours following an inquest to establish identity. Some items also held by Brenzett Aeronautical Museum.

85 SQUADRON, DEBDEN

Hurricane P2923. Last seen in pursuit of enemy formation thirty miles off the east coast 5.50 p.m. Flying Officer R. H. A. Lee missing. Aircraft VY-R lost.

Hurricane P3649. Damaged in collision with He 111 in combat over the Thames Estuary 5.40 p.m. Returned to base minus starboard wing tip. Pilot Officer J. E. Marshall unhurt. Aircraft damaged but repairable.

Hurricane V7249. Damaged by return fire from Ju 88 engaged over the Thames Estuary 5.45 p.m. Crashed in sea. Pilot Officer J. A. Hemmingway baled out and rescued by lightship twelve miles east of Clacton. Aircraft lost.

92 SQUADRON, PEMBREY

Spitfire N3040. Abandoned over Horsmonden damaged by return fire from Ju 88 2.15 p.m. Crashed by Tucks Cottages, near Park Farm. Flight Lieutenant R. R. S. Tuck baled out and slightly injured in heavy landing. Aircraft a write-off.
Surface fragments displayed at the Kent Battle of Britain Museum. Pieces also form part of the Vizard collection.

Display board of some of the smaller items recovered at Chartham Hatch by the London Air Museum. The museum closed in 1977 and all their exhibits are currently in store.

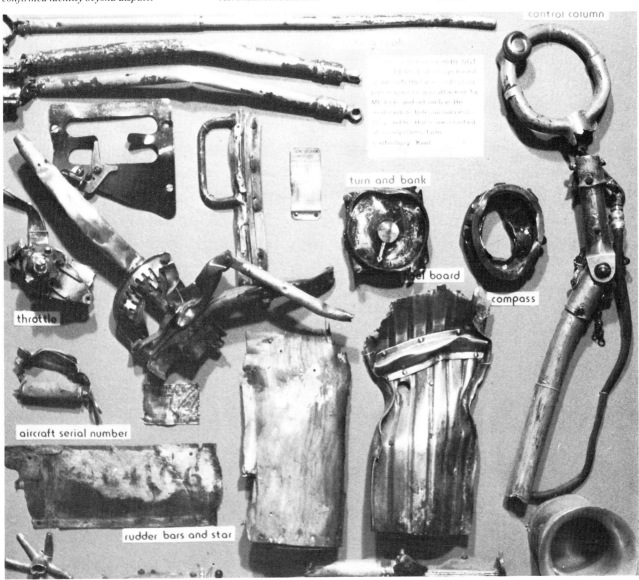

The excavation of Franciszek Gruszka's Spitfire. The Kent Battle of Britain Museum displayed these items *(above and below)* including sections of the pilot's parachute harness, following their dig in 1971. As the pilot had never been found in 1940, the Ministry of Defence re-dug the site in 1975 and recovered human remains.

Above: Dipstick cover at Chilham Castle and *below* flight computer at Brenzett Aeronautical Museum.

111 SQUADRON, CROYDON

Hurricane P3399. Forced-landed on Woodcote Bank golf course with damage sustained in attack on Do 17s attacking Kenley 1.15 p.m. Pilot Officer P. J. Simpson unhurt. Aircraft damaged but repairable.

Hurricane R4187. Shot down by AA fire whilst attacking Do 17s bombing Kenley. Believed crashed at The Oaks, Wallington 1.18 p.m. Flight Lieutenant S. D. P. Connors killed. Aircraft a write-off.

Hurricane N2340. Shot down in combat with enemy aircraft over Kenley. Crashed at Oxted 1.20 p.m. Sergeant A. H. Deacon baled out unhurt. Aircraft a write-off.

Dickie Lee was the living example of the public image of the fighter pilot. Tall, good looking, extrovert with a preference for loud blondes and nearly always at loggerheads with authority over his penchant for low flying. His inherent flying skill can still be seen in an old comedy film of the late thirties when he flew a Hawker Fury through a hangar at Debden. With no less a personage as Lord Trenchard as his godfather, it was ordained that he should make his career in the Royal Air Force. To this end, he entered Cranwell College in 1937 and was posted to No. 85 Squadron at Debden the following year. Service in France followed the outbreak of war where the squadron sustained heavy losses. He returned to the UK in May 1940 and for a short period served with No. 56 Squadron at North Weald before rejoining No. 85. On Sunday, August 18, thirteen Hurricanes of No. 85 engaged an enemy force estimated at 200 aircraft, fifteen miles east of Foulness Island. Flying Officer Richard Hugh Anthony Lee, DSO, DFC, in single-handedly chasing three Bf 110s out to sea, flew to an unknown grave (Imperial War Museum).

Hurricane P3943. Set alight by return fire from Do 17 of 9/KG76 during low-level attack on Kenley 1.15 p.m. Abandoned over Botley Hill Farm, Tatsfield. Sergeant H. S. Newton baled out unhurt. Aircraft a write-off.
Excavations by Halstead War Museum revealed propeller boss and remains of shattered airframe. Some fragments also held by Kent Battle of Britain Museum.

151 SQUADRON, NORTH WEALD

Hurricane P3871. Mainplane and oil tank damaged by cross-fire during attack on Ju 88 east of Chelmsford 5.30 p.m. Forced-landed Martlesham. Wing Commander F. V. Beamish unhurt. Aircraft damaged but repairable.

Hurricane P3940. Shot down in combat with Bf 110s over Rochford crashed and burned out at Tabriums Farm, Battlesbridge 5.30 p.m. Squadron Leader J. A. G. Gordon baled out badly burned admitted to Rochford Hospital. Aircraft a write-off.

Hurricane R4181. Failed to return from combat with enemy aircraft over Chelmsford 5.30 p.m. Pilot Officer J. B. Ramsay missing. Aircraft lost.

152 SQUADRON, WARMWELL

Spitfire   . Returned to base with damage following action with Ju 87s and Bf 109s south-east of Isle of Wight. 3.00 p.m. Pilot Officer W. Beaumont unhurt. Aircraft repairable.

Spitfire   . Damaged in combat with enemy aircraft off the Isle of Wight 3.05 p.m. Pilot unhurt. Aircraft repairable.

257 SQUADRON, DEBDEN

Hurricane P3708. Shot down by Bf 110 in combat over Thames Estuary and crashed at Nazewick Farm, Foulness 6.00 p.m. Sergeant A. G. Girdwood baled out wounded in foot admitted to Foulness Hospital. Aircraft a write-off.

266 SQUADRON, HORNCHURCH

Spitfires X4061, X4066. Landed Manston to refuel and caught in strafing attack by Bf 109s 2.30 p.m. Aircraft burned out and write-offs.

Spitfires K9850, L1088, N3127, R6762, R6920, X4063. Severely damaged in strafing attack by Bf 109s 2.30 p.m. Aircraft damaged but repairable.

Squadron Leader John Gillan, CO of No. 111 Squadron, briefs his pilots at Northolt. Flight Lieutenant Stanley Connors, DFC and Bar, shot down by friendy anti-aircraft fire on August 18 over Kenley, is arrowed. His body was taken back to his native town of North Berwick in East Lothian where he is now remembered by a simple wooden cross on the wall of the cemetery.

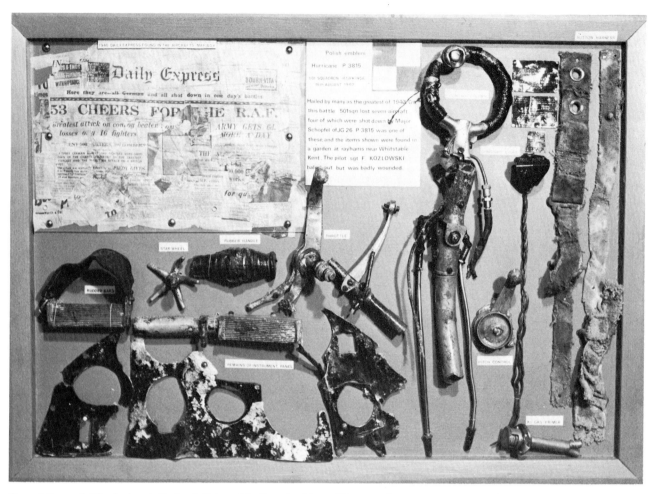

The victims of Oberleutnant Gerhard Schoepfel. Based with Jagdgeschwader 26 at Caffiers, seven miles south of Calais, Schoepfel was leading the unit on August 18 due to the temporary absence of its commander Adolf Galland. Flying ahead of the bombers on their mission to attack Fighter Command's aerodromes, their first contact with British fighters came near Canterbury. 'Suddenly I noticed a Staffel of Hurricanes underneath me', wrote Schoepfel later. 'They were using the English tactics of the period, flying in close formation of threes, climbing in a wide spiral'. Virtually sitting ducks, four of the Hurricanes were dispatched in as many minutes earning Schoepfel the award of the Ritterkreuz on September 11. *Above:* Display of remains of Pilot Officer Kozlowski's aircraft excavated by the London Air Museum. A newspaper dated August 9 was found in the remains of the cockpit. *Below:* Items from Pilot Officer Bland's machine collected by Steve Vizard. *Below right:* Mr. Jack Matthews of the Lashenden Air Warfare Museum, displays the pilot's head armour from Sergeant McKay's Hurricane.

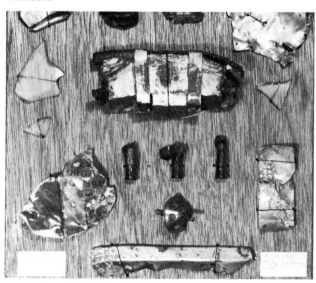

501 SQUADRON, GRAVESEND

Hurricane P3059. 'Bounced' by Bf 109s of JG26 over Canterbury 1.30 p.m. Shot down by Oblt. G. Schoepfel. Pilot Officer K. N. T. Lee admitted to hospital with leg wounds. Aircraft SD-N a write-off.

Hurricane P3815. Shot down by Oblt. G. Schoepfel of JG26 over Canterbury 1.30 p.m. Crashed and burned out on Rayhams Farm near Whitstable. Pilot Officer F. Kozlowski seriously injured admitted to hospital. Aircraft a write-off.

Major back-garden excavation organised by London Air Museum 1979. Complete Rolls-Royce Merlin engine with propeller boss recovered with instrument panel, control column, maps and legible copy of Daily Express dated August 9, 1940.

Hurricane N2617. Shot down by Oblt. Schoepfel of JG26 in surprise attack over Canterbury 1.32 p.m. Sergeant D. N. E. McKay baled out over Dargate slightly burned. Aircraft a write-off.

Reputed to be the aircraft excavated at Lenham, Kent by Lashenden Air Warfare Museum. Recovery revealed armour plate, gun-sight, radio aerial mast and rudder stern post. Tail wheel and one main wheel in Kent Battle of Britain Museum collection.

Hurricane P3208. Crashed at Calcott Hill, Sturry following attack by Oblt. G. Schoepfel of JG26 1.35 p.m. Pilot Officer J. W. Bland killed. Aircraft SD-T a write-off.

Site investigated by the Historic Aircraft Archaeologists Group. Surface fragments and a lead mass balance weight also collected by Steve Vizard.

Hurricane R4219. Shot down in action with enemy aircraft over Biggin Hill area 12.05 p.m. Crashed Cronks Farm, East Seal. Flying Officer R. L. Dafforn baled out unhurt. Aircraft a write-off.

Pieces in the Vizard collection.

Hurricane P2549. Shot down in combat with Bf 110s over Thames Estuary 5.46 p.m. Crashed near Stile Farm, Chilham. Flight Lieutenant G. E. B. Stoney killed. Aircraft a write-off.

Flight Lieutenant George Stoney laid to rest at St. Helen's Churchyard, Sefton.

504 SQUADRON, CASTLETOWN

Hurricane P2993. Became lost above thick cloud during weather test flight. Crash-landed at St. Fergus, Aberdeen 10.30 p.m. Sergeant H. D. B. Jones unhurt. Aircraft damaged but repairable.

601 SQUADRON, TANGMERE

Hurricane R4191. Failed to return from combat with Bf 109s of II/JG27 off Sussex coast 2.15 p.m. Sergeant L. N. Guy missing. Aircraft lost.

Hurricane L1990. Shot down in combat with Bf 109s of II/JG27 over Sussex coast. Crashed off Summer Lane, Nyetimber, Pagham 2.50 p.m. Reputedly shot down by Uffz. Born. Sergeant R. P. Hawkings killed. Aircraft a write-off.

Hurricane V7305. Hit in oil system by Bf 109 flown by Lt. Wiesinger of 4/JG27 during attack on Ju 87s over Selsey. Engine seized over aerodrome boundary causing aircraft to crash on landing 3.00 p.m. Flight Sergeant A. H. D. Pond unhurt. Aircraft damaged but repairable.

602 SQUADRON, WESTHAMPNETT

Spitfire L1005. Severely damaged in combat with Ju 87s and Bf 109s over Ford 2.30 p.m. Landed Tangmere. Flying Officer C. J. Mount unhurt. Aircraft damaged but repairable.

Spitfire X4110. Severely damaged in combat with Bf 109s over Ford 2.35 p.m. Landed at base minus flaps, on burst tyre. Flight Lieutenant J. D. Urie wounded in legs. Aircraft damaged but repairable.

Spitfire X4161. Forced-landed at Ford on burst tyre causing aircraft to nose over following combat with Bf 109s 2.40 p.m. Pilot Officer H. W. Moody unhurt. Aircraft damaged but repairable.

Spitfire K9969. Hit in port wing and petrol tank by Bf 109 and further damaged in collision with Poling RDF mast. Flew through HT cables prior to crash-landing at Norway Farm, Rustington 2.41 p.m. Flying Officer P. J. Ferguson wounded and suffering shock. Aircraft damaged but repairable.

Spitfire L1019. Hit by return fire from Ju 87 attacked over Ford. Ditched at Elmer Sands, Middleton 2.55 p.m. Sergeant B. E. P. Whall unhurt. Aircraft LO-G a write-off.

'In love and in gratitude to our dear son who was killed in the Battle of Britain — Mother'. The family grave of Sergeant Redvers Hawkins in St. Peter's Churchyard, Filton, Gloucestershire.

610 SQUADRON, BIGGIN HILL

Spitfire R6694. Hit by Bf 109 during return to base and further damaged hitting a bomb crater on landing 1.50 p.m. Pilot Officer C. O. J. Pegge unhurt. Aircraft DW-F damaged but repairable.

Spitfire R6993. Returned to base damaged by cross-fire from He 111s engaged over Dungeness 2.00 p.m. Flight Lieutenant J. Ellis unhurt. Aircraft DW-W repairable.

615 SQUADRON, KENLEY

Hurricanes P3158, P3487, R4186. Destroyed in low-level bombing attack on Kenley by 9/KG76 1.00 p.m. No personnel losses. Aircraft write-offs.

Hurricane P2966. Shot down in combat with Bf 109s and crashed into Robsacks Wood at Sevenoaks Weald 1.15 p.m. Flight Lieutenant L. M. Gaunce baled out with slight burns admitted to Holmesdale Hospital. Aircraft a write-off.
Rolls-Royce Merlin engine and other major components excavated from a depth of 20ft by Halstead War Museum in 1969. Some fragments also in the Kent Battle of Britain Museum and the Vizard collection.

Hurricane R4221. Crash-landed at Orpington following combat with Bf 109s 1.15 p.m. Pilot Officer P. H. Hugo wounded, admitted to Orpington Hospital. Aircraft KW-J a write-off.

Hurricane L2075. Forced-landed at Kenley damaged in combat with enemy fighters 1.20 p.m. Pilot unhurt. Aircraft damaged but repairable.

Hurricane P2768. Shot down in flames and crashed on Morden Park golf course 1.30 p.m. Sergeant P. K. Walley killed. Aircraft a write-off.

Hurricane L1592. Severely damaged by Bf 109s over Sevenoaks and fired on by station defences whilst forced-landing at Croydon 2.00 p.m. Pilot Officer D. J. Looker admitted to Croydon Hospital with severe shock and concussion. Aircraft KW-Z struck off charge.
This aircraft survived the war and completely refurbished can now be seen at the Science Museum in London.

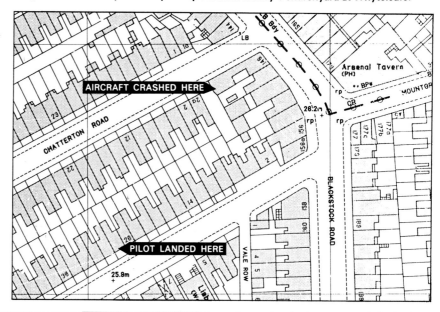

Sergeant Peter Walley buried by his squadron in Kenley's churchyard at Whyteleafe.

Although pilots were often saved to fight again by taking to their parachutes, there was always a risk to life when their aircraft crashed to the ground especially if this was in a built-up area. Pilot Officer Birch abandoned his aircraft over north London late on August 19 — the map indicates where it fell near the Arsenal football stadium (Ordnance Survey). *Left:* The Hurricane crashed behind Messrs. G. & L. Mull's bakers shop (on the corner) after first hitting the roof. The repair work is still visible. *Right:* Locals thought the pilot on the roof of No. 28 Gillespie Road was a German although he kept calling out that he was English!

Monday, August 19

1 SQUADRON, NORTHOLT

Hurricane P3684. Blundered into London balloon barrage during night patrol and crashed and burned out in Chatterton Road, Finsbury Park 11.30 p.m. Pilot Officer C. N. Birch baled out unhurt landing on roof of 28 Gillespie Road. Aircraft a write-off.

66 SQUADRON, COLTISHALL

Spitfire N3182. Crashed in sea three miles south of Orfordness, victim of return fire from He 111 engaged 5.20 p.m. Pilot Officer J. A. P. Studd baled out and rescued by Aldeburgh lifeboat but failed to regain conciousness. Aircraft lost.

92 SQUADRON, PEMBREY

Spitfire L1080. Damaged in bombing attack on Bibury satellite aerodrome by Ju 88 3.00 p.m. Aircraft damaged but repairable. Three more Spitfires slightly damaged.

Spitfire R6703. Hit by return fire in attack on Ju 88 over the Solent. Forced-landed and exploded at Norton, Selsey 3.20 p.m. Pilot Officer T. S. Wade unhurt. Aircraft a write-off.

248 SQUADRON, SUMBURGH

Blenheim   . Missing following reconnaissance of south Norwegian coast 11.30 a.m. Sergeant J. H. Round, Sergeant W. H. Want, Sergeant M. P. Digby-Worsley all missing. Aircraft WR-S lost.

602 SQUADRON, WESTHAMPNETT

Spitfire P9423. Crashed and burned out on Colworth Farm, Toad Hall, North Berstead 2.50 p.m. having been set alight by return fire from Ju 88 engaged off Bognor. Pilot Officer H. W. Moody baled out landing outside Arundel with burns to hands. Aircraft a write-off.
Site excavated by the Wealden Aviation Archaeological Group in 1979. Little recovered apart from remains of shattered Rolls-Royce Merlin engine and reduction gear.

Tuesday, August 20

65 SQUADRON, HORNCHURCH

Spitfire R6818. Engine damaged in attack by Bf 109 during combat over the Thames Estuary. Forced-landed Havengore Island, Foulness 3.30 p.m. Pilot Officer K. G. Hart unhurt. Aircraft a write-off.

236 SQUADRON, ST. EVAL

Blenheim Z5729. Damaged by AA fire over Pembroke Dock 3.51 p.m. Returned to base. Pilot Officer G. L. Campbell, Sergeant S. Archer both unhurt. Aircraft ND-H repairable.

242 SQUADRON, COLTISHALL

Hurricane P2967. Dived vertically into sea and exploded five miles north-east of Winterton 1.45 p.m. Cause unknown. Midshipman P. J. Patterson killed. Aircraft lost.

600 SQUADRON, MANSTON

Blenheim   . Damaged in enemy raid on base 3.00 p.m. No personnel losses. Aircraft damaged but repairable.

Although his home was in Paignton, Devon, Pilot Officer John Studd was laid to rest in Touchen End in Berkshire. Unusually, his grave has two headstones.

Wednesday, August 21

56 SQUADRON, NORTH WEALD

Hurricane P3153. Shot down by return fire from Do 17 of 8/KG2 intercepted over East Anglia. Forced-landed and burned out 6.15 p.m. Flying Officer R. E. P. Brooker unhurt. Aircraft a write-off.

152 SQUADRON, WARMWELL

Spitfire   . Slightly damaged by return fire from Do 17 engaged west of the Needles 4.50 p.m. Returned to base. Pilot Officer R. M. Hogg unhurt. Aircraft repairable.

236 SQUADRON, ST. EVAL

Blenheim   . Parked aircraft destroyed in bombing raid by Ju 88s 1.50 p.m. No crew losses. Three aircraft write-offs.

238 SQUADRON, MIDDLE WALLOP

Hurricane   . Damaged in combat with Ju 88s over St. Eval 5.25 p.m. Details not clear. Pilot believed unhurt. Aircraft damaged but repairable.

302 SQUADRON, LECONFIELD

Hurricane P3934. Forced-landed near base with engine trouble following engagement with Ju 88s off Bridlington 4.30 p.m. Pilot Officer S. J. Chalupa unhurt. Aircraft damaged but repairable.

604 SQUADRON, MIDDLE WALLOP

Blenheim   . Damaged in bombing attack on base. No personnel casualties. Aircraft damaged but repairable.

611 SQUADRON, DIGBY

Spitfire II P7290. Damaged by return fire from Do 17 off Skegness 12.45 p.m. Returned to base damage to spinner, mainplane and starboard tailplane. Flying Officer D. H. Watkins unhurt. Aircraft damaged but repairable.

Spitfire II P7304. Returned to base damaged in starboard tailplane, aileron and engine cowling following attack on Do 17 off Skegness 12.40 p.m. Pilot Officer M. P. Brown unhurt. Aircraft damaged but repairable.

Spitfire II P7303. Nosed over on landing on burst tyre following combat with Do 17 off Skegness 1.05 p.m. Also hit by return fire. Pilot Officer J. W. Lund unhurt. Aircraft repairable.

Spitfire II P7292. Hit by return fire from Do 17 engaged off Skegness. Returned to base damaged in glycol and hydraulic systems 1.20 p.m. Squadron Leader J. E. McComb unhurt. Aircraft damaged but repairable.

Spitfire II P7305. Hit a chock left on the runway and nosed over on landing 2.05 p.m. Sergeant A. S. Darling unhurt. Aircraft damaged but repairable.

Thursday, August 22

29 SQUADRON, DIGBY

Blenheim   . Struck by lightning during RDF trial flight 4.40 p.m. Returned to base. Sergeant A. J. A. Roberts, Pilot Officer P. A. Tomlinson both unhurt. Aircraft damaged but repairable.

32 SQUADRON, BIGGIN HILL

Hurricane P3205. Crashed on landing at Hawkinge 10.40 a.m. Pilot Officer J. Pfeiffer unhurt. Aircraft damaged but repairable.

54 SQUADRON, HORNCHURCH

Spitfire R6708. Shot down in combat with enemy fighters 1.15 p.m. Crashed into the Channel off Deal. Sergeant G. R. Collett killed. Aircraft lost.

65 SQUADRON, HORNCHURCH

Spitfire L1094. Landed Manston severely damaged in combat with Bf 109s over the Channel 7.30 p.m. Possibly that attacked by Fw. Philipp of II/JG26. Sergeant H. C. Orchard unhurt. Aircraft damaged but repairable.

Spitfire   . Landed at Manston with damage sustained in combat with Bf 109s off Dover 7.30 p.m. Pilot unhurt. Aircraft repairable.

Spitfire K9909. Shot down in combat with Bf 109s over the sea off Dover 7.35 p.m. Believed that claimed by Lt. Krug of II/JG26. Sergeant M. Keymer killed. Aircraft lost.

151 SQUADRON, NORTH WEALD

Hurricane   . Damaged in attack by Bf 109 during convoy patrol. Returned to base. Flight Lieutenant R. L. Smith unhurt. Aircraft repairable.

152 SQUADRON, WARMWELL

Spitfire R6829. Hit by return fire from Ju 88 and forced-landed near Beaford 3.40 p.m. Pilot Officer W. Beaumont unhurt. Aircraft damaged but repairable.

610 SQUADRON, BIGGIN HILL

Spitfire R6695. Shot down in flames during combat with Bf 109s over Folkestone 2.15 p.m. Crashed and burned out at Hawkinge. Sergeant D. F. Corfe unhurt. Aircraft DW-P a write-off.

615 SQUADRON, KENLEY

Hurricane P3901. Damaged in attack by a friendly Hurricane 1.15 p.m. Forced-landed outside Deal. Pilot Officer D. H. Hone unhurt. Aircraft damaged but repairable.

616 SQUADRON, KENLEY

Spitfire R6926. Attacked by Bf 109s over Dover and set alight. Crashed in flames at Runninghill, Elham 7.32 p.m. Flying Officer H. S. L. Dundas baled out and admitted to Kent and Canterbury Hospital with arm and leg wounds. Aircraft a write-off.

Spitfire   . Returned to base with damaged mainplane caused by 20mm cannon shell in surprise attack by Bf 109s over Dover 7.40 p.m. Pilot Officer L. H. Casson unhurt. Aircraft repairable.

Friday, August 23

1 SQUADRON, NORTHOLT

Hurricane P2980. Ran out of fuel during night patrol. Crashed at Hunts Farm, Withyham 4.09 a.m. Sergeant H. J. Merchant unhurt apart from superficial cuts. Aircraft a write-off.

32 SQUADRON, BIGGIN HILL

Hurricane P2795. Crashed landing on one wheel at Hawkinge 7.15 a.m. due to combat damage. Pilot Officer J. Pfeiffer unhurt. Aircraft damaged but repairable.

Hurricane P3900. Forced-landed at Hawkinge, exact circumstances unknown. Pilot unhurt. Aircraft damaged but repairable.

65 SQUADRON, HORNCHURCH

Spitfire R6620. Reputedly damaged in combat 1.45 p.m. Details not stated. Pilot unhurt. Aircraft damaged but repairable.

232 SQUADRON, SUMBURGH

Hurricane P3104. Damaged by return fire from He 111 engaged eight miles west of Fair Isle 9.00 a.m. Returned to base. Flight Lieutenant M. M. Stephens unhurt. Aircraft damaged but repairable.

602 SQUADRON, WESTHAMPNETT

Spitfire X4160. Returned to base with slight damage caused by collision with unidentified RAF fighter 7.00 p.m. Pilot Officer T. G. F. Ritchie unhurt. Aircraft repairable.

Saturday, August 24

32 SQUADRON, BIGGIN HILL

Hurricane   . Shot down in combat with Bf 109s and believed crashed in Dover Harbour 3.15 p.m. Pilot Officer K. Pniak baled out slightly injured. Aircraft lost.

Hurricane V6568. Crashed at Lyminge following combat with Bf 109s over Folkestone 4.15 p.m. Pilot Officer R. F. Smythe wounded admitted to Royal Masonic Hospital, Hammersmith. Aircraft a write-off.

Hurricane V6572. Shot down in combat with Bf 109s over Folkestone 4.20 p.m. Crashed at Rhodes Minnis near Lyminge. Pilot Officer K. Pniak baled out and injured ankle and knee in heavy landing. Admitted to hospital. Aircraft a write-off.

Excavated in October 1979 by the Brenzett Aeronautical Museum, which recovered a propeller boss and reduction gear and other minor components.

Sergeants' Mess RAF Station, St. Eval, Cornwall.
Dear Mother and Father,
    How's my good people at Macclesfield? I trust you are keeping well and in good spirit.
    Well here I am an old crock so soon. I am afraid that our duty at the front line has told its tale upon our systems. Our engagements have been really hectic and, unfortunate for us, we've always been there first, waiting for enforcement, with the final result we are all down with nerve trouble and have been sent to this rest camp.
    We received a telegram from Air Ministry congratulating us upon our very good work and wishing us good rest but the cost has been heavy. Just Gordon Batt and I remain among the sergeants and many of our officers have gone. Just a very sad memory remains and worse for me, poor Tony Marsh, my section leader and I were the last two in action and I think I must have done too much flying for I fainted and I, poor Tony's guard, left him to the mercy of all. Oh dear, I did feel bad, when I learned he never came back.
    This place brings back pleasant memories, for it was round here that my dear May and I spent our lovely holiday last year, Newquay, Carbis Bay, surf-riding and all that. We are getting out one day in three and I hope to visit some of these places. We are of course still flying for it keeps us fresh and helps nerves and have consequently flown over many places in Cornwall and Devon. Our new sector covers all Cornwall and most Devon but its quiet and the 'Hun' does not come over in large numbers. Gosh, at our last place, I began to dream of those hundreds we were always meeting.
    What do you think of our efforts? Never did I think for one minute that we could hold back so large a number — planes just tumbled out of the sky. God but these grand lads are just giving their very all and some are very tired boys.
    You will have to forgive me for not having written before this but we have never left duty, our food and sleep have been obtained there.
    How's Father getting along these days? I trust he's keeping well and getting just a little time off to enjoy this nice weather. We shall, I understand, be here for three weeks until we have become re-fitted and new pilots plus our troubles put right. I hope and wish that I could get May down for a short time. I don't think we shall get any time off or leave for we have proved good metal for the RAF and they require us back again.
    Oh well, cheerio for now, all my kind regards.
                    Your loving son
                    Eric

One of the earliest aircraft archaeology groups was the one at Ashford and Tenterden now amalgamated into the Brenzett Aeronautical Museum. Many years of experience have proved the absolute necessity of adequate research before a dig commences. This site, determined from 1945 aerial photographs and local eye witness reports, is that of the second crash of Pilot Officer Pniak on August 24. Once the approximate crash site, on high ground mid-way between Rhodes Minnis and Lyminge, had been determined, a six-inch scrape is made to remove surface rubbish and give a clean reading on metal detectors. The ground is then carefully cut away around the site with a mechanical digger until wreckage is reached when hand spades are used. This particular dig in the hard Kent chalk revealed the prop boss (seen *below* being cleaned by Dave Buchanan and John Elgar-Whinney) and many small parts taken away for further examination including the throttle control *(below right)*.

Hurricane V6567. Crashed at Tedders Lees, near Elham 4.30 p.m. following combat with Bf 109s. Pilot Officer E. G. A. Seghers baled out unhurt, landing in the sea. Aircraft a write-off.

Hurricane P3481. Crashed near Lyminge during combat with Bf 109s over Folkestone 4.30 p.m. Squadron Leader M. N. Crossley unhurt. Aircraft a write-off.

54 SQUADRON, HORNCHURCH

Spitfire X4019. Badly damaged by enemy fighters in combat over Manston 10.40 a.m. Returned to base. Pilot Officer A. R. McL. Campbell wounded. Aircraft damaged but repairable.

Spitfire P9389. Crashed at School Lane, Kingsdown 3.43 p.m. following combat with enemy fighters. Pilot Officer C. Stewart baled out landing in Thames Estuary. Picked up by Royal Navy admitted to Canterbury Hospital. Aircraft a write-off.

65 SQUADRON, HORNCHURCH

Spitfire R6884. Shot down in combat off Margate 3.35 p.m. Exact details not recorded. Aircraft lost.

66 SQUADRON, COLTISHALL

Spitfire X4052. Forced-landed at base after routine patrol 5.10 p.m. Cause unknown. Pilot Officer R. W. Oxspring unhurt. Aircraft repairable.

85 SQUADRON, CROYDON

Hurricane L1933. Believed victim of Dover AA defences. Forced-landed Hawkinge and over-ran runway due to flap damage 8.30 a.m. Pilot Officer J. Lockhart slightly wounded. Aircraft damaged but repairable.

151 SQUADRON, NORTH WEALD

Hurricane V7306. Returned to base damaged following combat with Bf 109s over Ramsgate 11.30 a.m. Flight Lieutenant R. L. Smith unhurt. Aircraft repairable.

Hurricane R4183. Shot down in combat with Bf 109s over Ramsgate, crashed and burned out 11.30 a.m. Pilot Officer K. B. L. Debenham seriously wounded admitted to Ramsgate hospital. Aircraft a write-off.

Hurricane P3273. Shot down by Bf 109s over Ramsgate. Crashed Plumford Farm, Ospringe 11.55 a.m. Sergeant G. T. Clarke wounded admitted to hospital. Aircraft damaged but repairable.

Hurricane P3739. Returned to base damaged in combat with Bf 110s 3.55 p.m. Pilot Officer I. S. Smith unhurt. Aircraft repairable.

Hurricane V7380. Airscrew shot off by Bf 110 in combat over base 4.00 p.m. Landed safely. Squadron Leader E. B. King unhurt. Aircraft damaged but repairable.

234 SQUADRON, MIDDLE WALLOP

Spitfire N3239. Shot down by Hptmn. Mayer and Lt. Zeis of 1/JG43 in combat 4.40 p.m. Crashed on the Isle of Wight. Pilot Officer J. Zurakowski unhurt. Aircraft a write-off.

235 SQUADRON, THORNEY ISLAND

Blenheim Z5736. Attacked by 1 (RCAF) Squadron Hurricanes over Thorney Island and badly damaged. Crashed on landing 4.40 p.m. Sergeant K. E. Naish, Sergeant W. G. Owen both unhurt. Aircraft damaged but repairable.

Sergeant Daniel Leslie Wright, an 18-year-old wireless operator/air gunner from Lichfield, Staffordshire was a victim of war's tragic irony. On August 24, after the heavy raid on Portsmouth by the Ju 88s of LG1, three Blenheims of No. 235 Squadron were mistakenly attacked over their Thorney Island base by the Hurricanes of No. 1 RCAF Squadron. The crews of two aircraft escaped unhurt but the third crashed into Bracklesham Bay carrying its crew to their deaths. Only the body of Danny Wright *above* was recovered; no trace was found of the pilot, Pilot Officer David Woodger. Danny's simple epitaph reads: 'Thy will be done'.

Blenheim T1804. Shot down by 1 (RCAF) Squadron Hurricanes and crashed into Bracklesham Bay 4.45 p.m. Pilot Officer D. N. Woodger missing, Sergeant D. L. Wright killed. Aircraft lost.

Blenheim N3531. Damaged in attack by 1 (RCAF) Squadron Hurricanes over base 4.45 p.m. Landed safely. Flight Lieutenant F. W. Flood and crew unhurt. Aircraft repairable.

263 SQUADRON, GRANGEMOUTH

Hurricane L1803. Caught fire during routine night training flight. Crashed and burned out. Pilot Officer D. Stein baled out over Grangemouth Docks arrested on landing but released later. Aircraft a write-off.

264 SQUADRON, HORNCHURCH

Defiant L7013. Attacked by Bf 109s over Thanet and badly damaged. Forced-landed Manston 8.20 a.m. when Very cartridges exploded in cockpit. Flying Officer E. W. Campbell-Colquhoun, Pilot Officer G. Robinson both unhurt. Aircraft PS-U damaged but repairable.

Defiant L7021. Severely damaged in tail by return fire from Ju 88 attacked over Manston 12.40 p.m. Returned to base. Pilot Officer D. Whitley, Sergeant R. C. Turner both unhurt. Aircraft damaged but repairable.

Defiant N1535. Last seen in pursuit of Ju 88s following attack on Manston 12.40 p.m. Squadron Leader P. A. Hunter, Pilot Officer F. H. King missing. Aircraft PS-A lost.

Defiant L6966. Lost following combat with Ju 88s and Bf 109s over the Channel off Thanet 12.40 p.m. Believed shot down by Major Luetzow of JG3. Pilot Officer J. T. Jones, Pilot Officer W. A. Ponting missing. Aircraft lost.

Defiant L7027. Failed to return from combat with Bf 109s off Manston 12.45 p.m. Possibly shot down by Major Luetzow of JG3. Flying Officer I. G. Shaw, Sergeant A. Berry missing. Aircraft lost.

Defiant . Damaged in collision with another aircraft during scramble from base 3.40 p.m. Flying Officer D. H. C. O'Malley, Pilot Officer A. O'Connell both unhurt. Aircraft damaged but repairable.

Defiant L6965. Shot down during combat with Bf 109s of JG51 over base 4.00 p.m. Pilot Officer R. S. Gaskell slightly injured, Sergeant W. H. Machin died of wounds. Aircraft a write-off.

501 SQUADRON, GRAVESEND

Hurricane P3141. Missing following engagement with Do 17s and Bf 109s four miles north-west of Dover 10.15 a.m. Pilot Officer P. Zenker missing. Aircraft lost.

Hurricane L1659. Crashed at Hawkinge following action against Ju 88s and Bf 109s attacking Manston 1.00 p.m. Sergeant W. J. Green unhurt. Aircraft damaged but repairable.

Hurricane L1865. Shot down in combat with Bf 109s 4.35 p.m. Crashed Pells Farm, West Kingsdown. Pilot K. R. Aldridge baled out over Ryarsh and admitted to hospital with broken arm. Aircraft a write-off.
Site investigated by the London Air Museum and few surviving fragments recovered.

604 SQUADRON, MIDDLE WALLOP

Blenheim L6681. Crashed near Odiham during night patrol 11.40 p.m., cause not stated. Flying Officer H. Speke, Sergeant S. H. J. Shirley both unhurt. Aircraft damaged but repairable.

609 SQUADRON, WARMWELL

Spitfire L1082. Severely damaged in attack by Bf 110s over Ryde 4.50 p.m. Returned to base. Pilot Officer A. Mamedoff unhurt. Aircraft damaged but repairable.

Spitfire X4104. Returned to base damaged following attack by Bf 110s over Ryde 4.50 p.m. Flight Lieutenant F. J. Howell unhurt. Aircraft damaged but repairable.

Above: **Squadron Leader P. A. Hunter discusses tactics with the pilots of No. 264 Squadron at Hornchurch in August 1940. Philip Hunter teamed up with his gunner LAC F. H. King** *(above right)* **in May 1940. As pioneers of a new conception in fighter tactics evolved for the Boulton Paul Defiant, they achieved a remarkable measure of success in the early days. During six days in May they accounted for nine enemy aircraft, which brought the rewards of the DSO to Philip Hunter and the DFM and rapid promotion to Fred King. But the German pilots now had the measure of the Defiant and, during three separate actions in four days, the squadron lost eleven Defiants with five pilots and nine gunners dead. Leaning on the tailplane is Sergeant E. R. Thorn who, with his gunner Sergeant F. J. Barker, were to survive the battle to become the top scoring Defiant team (Imperial War Museum).**

The aircraft in which Philip Hunter and Fred King lost their lives on August 24 somewhere over the Channel.

610 SQUADRON, BIGGIN HILL

Spitfire R6686. Crashed in flames at Hammill near Eastry 8.50 a.m. following attack by Hptmn. Foezoe of 4/JG51 during combat off Ramsgate. Sergeant S. J. Arnfield baled out but broke ankle on landing admitted to Victoria Hospital, Deal. Aircraft DW-S a write-off.

Spitfire R6641. Returned to base damaged after combat with Bf 109s off Dover 11.45 a.m. Pilot Officer E. S. Aldous unhurt. Aircraft DW-X damaged but repairable.

Spitfire X4102. Shot down by Bf 109 in combat over Dover and crash-landed near Shepherdswell 12.00 p.m. Pilot Officer D. McI. Gray wounded, admitted to Waldershare Hospital. Aircraft DW-K a write-off.

Spitfire   . Shot down in combat with Bf 109s over the Thames Estuary. Crash-landed at Fyfield 4.30 p.m. Pilot Officer C. Merrick slightly wounded admitted to Ongar Hospital. Aircraft DW-D a write-off.

615 SQUADRON, KENLEY

Hurricane V7318. Engine damaged in combat with enemy aircraft over the Thames Estuary. Forced-landed at Longfield, Gravesend 4.10 p.m. Pilot Officer D. H. Hone unhurt. Aircraft damaged but repairable.

Two other Defiant gunners missing on August 24. *Left:* Pilot Officer Bill Ponting from Whetstone, Middlesex and *right* Sergeant Alan Berry of Longsight, Manchester. Both are commemorated on the Runnymede Memorial.

SERGEANT BILL MACHIN, No. 264 SQUADRON. DIED OF WOUNDS, AUGUST 24, 1940.

To

SERGEANT W. H. MACHIN

Defiant Squadron R.A.F.

Killed in Action

24th August, 1940

" See, Icarus, the wax melts fast
It falls, as I fall too,
And now my soul takes wings at last
That I may fly to you."

Sergeant William Howard Machin, 20 years old, was the son of Edmund and Ivy Machin of Handsworth, Birmingham. Shot down over Hornchurch, he died of his wounds. After his death his family produced this card 'In Memoriam'.

THE summer loved he when the sky
   Was rich with golden blue,
When all the fields and mountains high
   The sweet contentment knew
Of Life, of Youth, of carefree Love,
   Of sunbeams-dancing near,
When fleecy clouds do float above
   To shed a happy tear.

The summer knew his restless mind
   That used to roam afar,
And rest awhile a dream to find
   On some celestial star;
Or maybe in the water's depth,
   Through which he used to glide,
And wake the ripples as they slept
   To kiss his very side.

Too soon that summer when the world
   In chaos rose again,
And armed friend 'gainst brethren hurled
   The hellish tide to stem,
Of Doubt and Lies, of Sin and Greed
   That swept the modern shore
And clamoured blood its belly feed,
   And bones, and human gore.

Then this last summer, sadder now,
   Did see him ere he died,
His right to live to prove, then bow
   His head to Fate beside.
There's many thus who pledge their hearts
   To answer Freedom's call,
But few are they whom Freedom asks
   To glorify their all.

And so when summer comes again
   To warm our peaceful land,
The hills and fields and marshy fen,
   The willows as they stand
Beside the stream and share our tears
   For him who died to give
Fresh life to summer through the years;
   He gladly died—we live.

T. LEWIS GREEN, September, 1940

Sunday, August 25

17 SQUADRON, DEBDEN

Hurricane R4199. Port mainplane shot off in head-on attack on Bf 110. Crashed in the sea off Portland 5.45 p.m. Squadron Leader C. W. Williams missing. Aircraft lost.

Hurricane V7407. Shot down in combat with Bf 110s and Bf 109s and crashed in the sea off Portland 5.48 p.m. Flight Lieutenant A. W. A. Bayne baled out and rescued unhurt. Aircraft lost.

29 SQUADRON, DIGBY

Blenheim L1330. Believed shot down in combat over Wainfleet and crashed in sea 10.00 p.m. Pilot Officer R. A. Rhodes and AC2 N. Jacobson missing, Sergeant R. J. Gouldstone killed. Aircraft lost.

32 SQUADRON, BIGGIN HILL

Hurricane V6547. Shot down by Bf 109 in combat over the Channel 7.00 p.m. Pilot Officer J. Rose baled out and rescued from sea. Aircraft lost.

Hurricane N2433. Failed to return from combat over the Channel off Dover 7.00 p.m. Pilot Officer K. R. Gillman missing. Aircraft lost.

54 SQUADRON, HORNCHURCH

Spitfire R6969. Believed forced-landed at Brook End, Birchington damaged by Bf 109s over Dover 7.20 p.m. Pilot Officer M. Shand wounded. Aircraft damaged but repairable.

73 SQUADRON, CHURCH FENTON

Hurricane P3758. Shot down by British AA defences during night patrol and crashed west of Beverley 1.30 a.m. Sergeant V. A. B. Leng baled out unhurt. Aircraft a write-off.

Hurricane   .   Collided with petrol bowser whilst taxi-ing at base. Pilot Officer A. McFadden unhurt. Aircraft repairable.

Squadron Leader Cedric Watcyn Williams, Commanding Officer of No. 17 Squadron missing on August 25, chats to Pilot Officer H. A. C. Bird-Wilson at Debden.

We chose to use the portrait — so well known during the war years — of Pilot Officer Keith Gillman on our cover as the epitome of 'The Few'. It was taken at Hawkinge in July 1940, just a month before he went missing over the Channel. After the war, Mr. and Mrs. Gillman presented the Gillman Trophy to the Life Guard Association to be competed for annually in their swimming competitions. During 1979 it rested in the bar of the Dover Sports Centre having been won by the Dover branch. 'Colt' Gillman is now remembered on Panel 8 of the Runnymede Memorial.

Sergeant Ronald Gouldstone was the air gunner in a night fighter Blenheim of No. 29 Squadron shot down on the night of August 25. The deaths of all three crewmen were officially recorded as August 25 although Ronald's grave at St. Martin's Churchyard at Ryarsh, Kent is inscribed August 26. It was in this aircraft that the youngest airman to be killed during the Battle of Britain lost his life — AC2 Norman Jacobson of Grimsby, Lincolnshire.

Pilot Officer Richard Hogg of No. 152 'Hyderabad' Squadron at Debden shortly after the re-forming of the squadron on October 1, 1939. A native of the Channel Islands, 21-year-old Dick Hogg failed to return to Warmwell on August 25, 1940.

Warmwell is the last resting place for another pilot killed on August 25 — Sergeant Sidney Wakeling. Aged 21.

85 SQUADRON, CROYDON

Hurricane P3402. Forced-landed Gravesend cause not stated. Pilot unhurt. Aircraft damaged but repairable.

87 SQUADRON, EXETER

Hurricane V7250. Shot down in flames in combat over Portland. Believed crashed at New Barn outside Dorchester 6.05 p.m. Sergeant S. R. E. Wakeling killed. Aircraft a write-off.

92 SQUADRON, PEMBREY

Spitfire N3268. Severely damaged in attack on Do 215 off St. Gowans Head. Glided fifteen miles to land on dead engine and forced-landed 6.20 p.m. Flight Lieutenant R. R. S. Tuck slightly injured in leg. Aircraft a write-off.
    Site identified by the Gwalia Aviation Research Group.

152 SQUADRON, WARMWELL

Spitfire R6810. Shot down by enemy fighters in combat over the Channel 5.30 p.m. Pilot Officer R. M. Hogg missing. Aircraft lost.

Spitfire R6994. Failed to return from combat over the Channel 5.30 p.m. Pilot Officer T. S. Wildblood missing. Aircraft lost.

Timothy Seddon Wildblood was born in Egypt on March 3, 1920. He went to school at Colmes Rectory at Allton (1926-28), The Towers, Crowthorne (1928-33) and Wellington College from 1933 to 1937. On completion of his education, he won a King's Cadetship to the RAF College, Cranwell in January 1938 and he entered B Squadron on January 13. Commissioned on October 1, 1939, he was posted to No. 152 Squadron at Acklington. Although he failed to return on August 25, the Air Ministry did not release the fact until the publication of Casualty List No. 45 on September 10. He was Mentioned in Dispatches on March 17, 1941 and his death was confirmed the following month.

213 SQUADRON, EXETER

Hurricane N2646. Badly damaged in combat with Bf 109 and forced-landed at Burton Bradstock 5.45 p.m. Sergeant E. G. Snowden unhurt. Aircraft damaged but repairable.

Hurricane P3200. Failed to return from combat over Warmwell 6.00 p.m. Pilot Officer H. D. Atkinson killed. Aircraft lost.

Hurricane V7226. Shot down in combat over Warmwell and crashed in sea 6.05 p.m. Pilot Officer J. A. L. Phillipart baled out but killed. Aircraft AK-I lost.

First buried in Exeter Higher Cemetery, Jacques Phillipart now lies in Brussels.

602 SQUADRON, WESTHAMPNETT

Spitfire N3226. Shot down in combat with enemy fighters and crashed in sea off Portland 5.45 p.m. Sergeant M. H. Sprague baled out unhurt and rescued from sea. Aircraft lost.

Spitfire P9381. Shot down in combat with enemy fighters over Dorchester. Crashed and burned out on Galton Heath 5.47 p.m. Flying Officer W. H. Coverley baled out unhurt. Aircraft a write-off.

604 SQUADRON, MIDDLE WALLOP

Blenheim L6782. Crashed near Witheridge, Exeter exact circumstances unknown during operational sortie at night. Sergeant J. G. B. Fletcher and Sergeant C. Haigh both killed. LAC A. L. Austin died following day. Aircraft a write-off.

609 SQUADRON, WARMWELL

Spitfire R6986. Returned to base badly damaged by 20mm cannon fire from Bf 110 engaged over Swanage 5.30 p.m. Over-ran runway on landing due to flap damage. Flying Officer P. Ostaszewski slightly wounded in the arm. Aircraft damaged but repairable.

Spitfire R6961. Overshot Bf 110 during combat over Swanage and damaged by return fire. Returned to base 5.35 p.m. Pilot Officer D. M. Crook unhurt. Aircraft damaged but repairable.

610 SQUADRON, BIGGIN HILL

Spitfire K9931. Shot down in combat with Bf 109s over Dover 7.20 p.m. Crashed and burned out on Stoneheap Farm near Northbourne. Pilot Officer F. T. Gardiner slightly wounded admitted to Waldershare Hospital. Aircraft DW-P a write-off.

616 SQUADRON, KENLEY

Spitfire R6966. Failed to return from combat with Bf 109s over Canterbury 7.00 p.m. Sergeant T. E. Westmoreland missing. Aircraft lost.

Spitfire K9819. Failed to return from combat with Bf 109s over Canterbury area 7.00 p.m. Sergeant P. T. Wareing reported as POW. Aircraft lost.

Pilot Officer Harold Atkinson's grave at Market Weighton, Yorkshire.

Of the three airmen killed in the No. 604 Squadron Blenheim on the night of August 25, Sergeant John Fletcher lies at Forest Row, Sussex *(left)* Sergeant Cyril Haigh at Swinton, Yorkshire *(right)* and LAC Albert Austin at Northwood military plot.

Monday, August 26

1 (RCAF) SQUADRON, NORTHOLT

Hurricane P3069. Damaged by return fire from Do 215 over North Weald 3.30 p.m. Squadron Leader E. A. McNab unhurt. Aircraft damaged but repairable.

Hurricane P3874. Shot down in attack on Do 215 over North Weald 3.30 p.m. Crashed at The Hydes, Little Bardfield. Flying Officer R. L. Edwards killed. Aircraft a write-off.

Hurricane P3872. Severely damaged in attack on Do 215 over North Weald 3.35 p.m. Flying Officer Desloges unhurt. Aircraft damaged but repairable.

Hurricane P3869. Forced-landed at Biddenden exact circumstances unknown. Pilot unhurt. Aircraft repairable.

43 SQUADRON, TANGMERE

Hurricane P3903. Damaged in attack by Bf 109 during combat off Portsmouth 4.40 p.m. Returned to base. Pilot Officer A. E. A. van den Hove d'Ertsenryck unhurt. Aircraft repairable.

Hurricane P3220. Reputedly crashed at Wittering following combat with He 111s over Portsmouth 4.45 p.m. Pilot Officer R. Lane wounded and badly burned admitted to Royal West Sussex Hospital, Brighton. Aircraft a write-off.

Hurricane P3202. Crashed at Ratham Mill, Bosham following combat over Portsmouth 4.45 p.m. Pilot Officer C. K. Gray baled out wounded in right arm. Aircraft a write-off.

Tail wheel and remains of tyre recovered from this location by the Wealden Aviation Archaeological Group.

Flying Officer Robert Edwards of the Royal Canadian Air Force was shot down near Thaxted, Essex and now lies in the Canadian section at Brookwood Military Cemetery.

> *Sergeants' Mess.*
> *RAF Station,*
> *St. Eval,*
> *Cornwall.*
> *August 1940.*
>
> *Dear Mother and Father,*
> *Thank you very much for your letters. I am very sorry for not having written sooner, but dear old 'Gerry' has followed us down here, and we have been quite busy knocking 'em' down. All the people round here are very happy and at rest for they have got to know that we are down here and our reputation has followed us for all they say is here come those fighter boys of the crack squadron. Talk about free beer when we go into any of these Cornish taverns. My word, we feel very proud of these kind people's thoughts towards us.*
> *Have received many letters and parcels and letters from all of you and I am trying very hard to reply and offer my many thanks to all. Maurice, Messrs. Slaters, The Vicar, Mayor's Comfort Fund, all are very kind.*
> *I am trying very hard to get Maurice posted down to my squadron. It would be fine for I could keep a brother's eye upon him, plus help in any way, and we could go out together. I am very sure that Maurice would enjoy helping in our squadron in its good work, plus seeing and helping his brother with the good work, so here's hoping.*
> *This good Cornish air has healed our war sores and very soon all of us hope to be again back in action, driving back the invader. I understand that many in our squadron are soon to be recognised for their good work done.*
> *A further pleasant surprise, May is coming down for a few days this coming weekend and, to top the bill, my Flight Commander has given me a few days leave to enjoy myself along with my wife, so here's to a very pleasant weekend.*
> *I read in the local Macclesfield paper that soon the seventeenth Spitfire will soon be given to the nation. 'Bravo Macc!' All the boys of the RAF are amazed at this grand town. How I wish that I could be the lucky local boy to fly the plane.*
> *Well cheerio to all,*
> *Your loving son*
> *Eric.*

Hurricane R4231. Severely damaged in combat over Portsmouth 4.45 p.m. Returned safely to base. Pilot Officer C. A. Woods-Scawen unhurt. Aircraft damaged but repairable.

Hurricane V7259. Shot down in head-on attack on He 111s over Portsmouth and abandoned over Birdham 4.50 p.m. Pilot Officer H. L. North baled out wounded in head and shoulder. Admitted to Royal West Sussex Hospital, Brighton. Aircraft a write-off.

Hurricane V7308. Belly-landed at base badly damaged in combat over Portsmouth 4.55 p.m. Pilot Officer G. C. Brunner wounded and admitted to Royal West Sussex Hospital, Brighton. Aircraft damaged but repairable.

56 SQUADRON, NORTH WEALD

Hurricane V7340. Shot down by Bf 109 in combat over Canterbury 12.30 p.m. Crashed in River Stour near Grove Ferry, Upstreet. Pilot Officer B. J. Wicks baled out unhurt. Aircraft a write-off.

Hurricane P3473. Wrecked forced-landing at Courtsend, Foulness following combat with Bf 109s 12.30 p.m. Sergeant G. Smythe unhurt. Aircraft a write-off.

85 SQUADRON, CROYDON

Hurricane V7381. Returned to base with damage received in attack on Do 17s over the Thames Estuary 3.30 p.m. Sergeant J. H. M. Ellis unhurt. Aircraft damaged but repairable.

Hurricane P3966. Shot down by Bf 109 in combat over Eastchurch and crashed on Pitsea Marshes 4.00 p.m. Pilot Officer J. A. Hemmingway baled out unhurt. Aircraft a write-off.

111 SQUADRON, DEBDEN

Hurricane V7222. Severely damaged in head-on attack by Bf 110 over Marks Tey 3.20 p.m. Returned to base. Flight Lieutenant D. C. Bruce unhurt. Aircraft damaged but repairable.

Hurricane R4096. Crashed near Martlesham Heath following combat with enemy aircraft over Essex 3.35 p.m. Sergeant R. F. Sellars slightly injured admitted to hospital suffering shock. Aircraft damaged but repairable.

234 SQUADRON, MIDDLE WALLOP

Spitfire X4023. Landed back at base with undercarriage up after combat with Bf 109s over Portsmouth 5.20 p.m. Pilot Officer P. W. Horton unhurt. Aircraft damaged but repairable.

Spitfire P9494. Forced-landed near East Grinstead 5.30 p.m. following combat with Bf 109s. Sergeant M. C. B. Boddington unhurt. Aircraft damaged but repairable.

249 SQUADRON, BOSCOMBE DOWN

Hurricane P2910. Forced-landed Tangmere with frozen radiator 5.15 p.m. Squadron Leader J. Grandy unhurt. Aircraft repairable.

Hurricane P3660. Forced-landed Tangmere with broken tail wheel 5.15 p.m. following uneventful patrol. Pilot Officer P. R. F. Burton unhurt. Aircraft repairable.

257 SQUADRON, DEBDEN

Hurricane V6563. Burned out following bombing attack 3.30 p.m. No personnel losses. Aircraft a write-off.

On leave from air gunnery school, Sergeant Walter Maxwell, a 23-year-old air gunner from Meols, Cheshire, was later posted to No. 264 Squadron on August 4, 1940. His short operational life lasted three weeks and one day.

264 SQUADRON, HORNCHURCH

Defiant L7005. Crash-landed at Marshside, Chislet during action with Bf 109s over Thanet 12.10 p.m. Sergeant E. R. Thorn, Sergeant F. J. Barker both slightly injured. Aircraft a write-off.

Defiant L7024. Returned to base damaged in combat with Bf 109s over Thanet 12.15 p.m. Pilot Officer H. I. Goodall, Sergeant R. B. M. Young both unhurt. Aircraft damaged but repairable.

Defiant L6985. Shot down by Bf 109s following destruction of Do 17 over Thanet and crashed two miles off Herne Bay 12.26 p.m. Flight Lieutenant A. J. Banham baled out and rescued from sea, landing at Herne Bay. Sergeant B. Baker missing. Aircraft lost.

Defiant L7025. Shot down by Bf 109s and crashed in sea two miles off Herne Bay 12.26 p.m. Flying Officer I. R. Stephenson baled out injured and rescued from sea. Landed at Herne Bay, admitted to Canterbury Hospital. Sergeant W. Maxwell missing. Aircraft lost.

310 SQUADRON, DUXFORD

Hurricane R4184. Returned to base with slight damage to glycol system following attack on Do 17s over Clacton 3.15 p.m. Flying Officer G. L. Sinclair unhurt. Aircraft repairable.

Hurricane P3157. Severely damaged by Bf 109 in combat over the Thames Estuary. Forced-landed near Upminster 3.15 p.m. Sergeant E. M. C. Prchal slightly wounded. Aircraft damaged but repairable.

Hurricane P3960. Shot down in attack on Do 17s over Clacton. Crashed and burned out at Rumbolds Farm, Goldsands, Southminster 3.40 p.m. Pilot Officer V. Bergman baled out slightly wounded. Aircraft a write-off.

Hurricane P3887. Shot down by return fire from Do 17s in attack over Wickham Bishops. Crashed at Maldon 3.55 p.m. Squadron Leader G. D. M. Blackwood baled out unhurt. Aircraft a write-off.

601 SQUADRON, DEBDEN

Hurricane V7238. Crashed and burned out believed rear of Captain's Wood, Great Totham 4.00 p.m. during routine patrol. Sergeant A. W. Woolley unhurt. Aircraft a write-off.

602 SQUADRON, WESTHAMPNETT

Spitfire X4188. Shot down in flames by Hptmn. Mayer of I/JG53 in action over Selsey Bill 4.43 p.m. Crashed in sea. Sergeant C. F. Babbage baled out, rescued from sea and admitted to Bognor Hospital. Aircraft lost.

Spitfire X4187. Shot down by Lt. Zeis of I/JG53 in combat over Selsey Bill. Landed wheels up at Tangmere 4.35 p.m. Flying Officer C. H. Maclean seriously wounded admitted to hospital. Aircraft damaged but repairable.

Spitfire K9995. Believed damaged by return fire from He 59 attacked over the Channel 7.20 p.m. Pilot unhurt. Aircraft damaged but repairable.

610 SQUADRON, BIGGIN HILL

Spitfire R6595. Severely damaged by Bf 109 in combat over Folkestone and crashed in flames attempting to land at Hawkinge. 12.40 p.m. Pilot Officer F. K. Webster killed. Aircraft DW-O a write-off.
Site excavated by Brenzett Aeronautical Museum and complete remains recovered.

Spitfire P9496. Shot down in combat with Bf 109s over Folkestone 12.40 p.m. Crashed and burned out at Paddlesworth. Pilot believed unhurt. Aircraft a write-off.

Spitfire R6970. Shot down by Bf 109s in action over Folkestone and crashed and burned out at Castle Hill, Hawkinge 12.42 p.m. Sergeant P. Else baled out seriously wounded. Admitted to Kent and Canterbury Hospital. Aircraft DW-M a write-off.

615 SQUADRON, KENLEY

Hurricane R4121. Shot down into the sea off Sheerness by Bf 109s 3.10 p.m. Pilot Officer J. A. P. McClintock baled out unhurt. Aircraft lost.

Hurricane R4111. Shot down by Bf 109 and crashed in flames west of Herne Bay pier 3.15 p.m. Flight Lieutenant L. M. Gaunce baled out, rescued from sea and admitted to Herne Bay Hospital with shock. Aircraft lost.

Hurricane V6564. Crash-landed Rochford damaged in combat with Bf 109s over Thames Estuary 3.40 p.m. Pilot Officer D. H. Hone wounded and admitted to Southend Hospital. Aircraft a write-off.

Hurricane P2878. Damaged in combat over Portsmouth. Crashed and burned out at Warrendown, Forest Side 4.50 p.m. Flying Officer J. R. H. Gayner baled out and admitted to Idsworth House Hospital with minor injuries. Aircraft a write-off.
First excavated by the Southern Area Wartime Aircraft Preservation Society in September 1971 but badly-burned Rolls-Royce engine left in situ. Later re-excavated by the Wealden Aviation Archaeological Group and engine and other smashed components recovered.

616 SQUADRON, KENLEY

Spitfire R6701. Shot down in combat off Dover 12.00 p.m. Pilot Officer W. L. B. Walker baled out wounded in foot and rescued by Royal Navy. Admitted to Halton Hospital. Aircraft lost.

Spitfire R6632. Forced-landed Bekesbourne following attack by Bf 109 over Dungeness 12.00 p.m. Flying Officer J. S. Bell unhurt. Aircraft a write-off.

Spitfire N3275. Hit in glycol system by Bf 109 over Dungeness and crash-landed on perimeter of Eastchurch aerodrome where burned out 12.05 p.m. Flying Officer E. F. St. Aubin admitted to Minster County Hospital with burns. Aircraft a write-off.

Spitfire R6758. Believed shot down by Hptmn. Foezoe of 4/JG51 over Dover 12.15 p.m. Sergeant M. Ridley killed. Aircraft a write-off.

Spitfire R7018. Shot down into the Channel off Dover by Hptmn. Foezoe of 4/JG51 at 12.15 p.m. Flying Officer G. E. Moberley killed. Aircraft lost.

Spitfire K9827. Shot down in surprise attack by Bf 109. Forced-landed and burned out at Crundale House Farm, Wye 1.15 p.m. Sergeant P. Copeland admitted to Ashford Hospital. Aircraft a write-off.

Spitfire R6633. Shot down by Bf 109s and forced-landed at Adisham 1.20 p.m. Pilot Officer R. Marples wounded in leg by cannon splinters admitted to Kent and Canterbury Hospital. Aircraft a write-off.

Tuesday, August 27

1 SQUADRON, NORTHOLT

Hurricane P3897. Held by searchlights and lost control 1.00 a.m. Abandoned aircraft crashed and burned out at Lacey Green, Buckinghamshire. Pilot Officer C. A. G. Chetham baled out unhurt landed at Amersham. Aircraft a write-off.

72 SQUADRON, ACKLINGTON

Spitfire K9922. Aircraft severely damaged in landing accident. Pilot unhurt. Aircraft a write-off.

92 SQUADRON, PEMBREY

Spitfire P9548. Damaged in forced-landing near Bristol having lost bearings during night flight from Bibury 10.45 p.m. Pilot Officer F. N. Hargreaves unhurt. Aircraft a write-off.

145 SQUADRON, DREM

Hurricane P3898. Damaged in forced-landing during aerobatic practice 11.30 a.m. Sergeant J. V. Wadham unhurt. Aircraft damaged but repairable.

Since 1918 the Webster family have run the Stag Inn at Lake on the Isle of Wight. Frank Kinnersley Webster was born in Burma but grew up on the island. He joined the Volunteer Reserve before war began and served with No. 610 Squadron. The picture *(above)* was taken of Frank (right) with fellow sergeants at Hove. He was killed trying to land his damaged Hurricane at Hawkinge and was taken back to the Isle of Wight to be buried with his father.

Pilot Officer Charles Arthur, Sergeant Eric Ringwood and Sergeant Ralph Cox made up the crew of a No. 248 Squadron Blenheim despatched from Sumburgh, Shetlands on an armed reconnaissance of the south Norwegian coast. The aircraft failed to return and Pilot Officer Arthur and Sergeant Ringwood were never seen again. The body of Sergeant Cox *(below left)* was discovered on the Swedish coast near Gothenburg and now lies in Kviberg Cemetery *above.*

152 SQUADRON, WARMWELL

Spitfire R6831. Hit by return fire from Ju 88 and crashed in sea eight miles off Portland 12.30 p.m. Pilot Officer W. Beaumont baled out unhurt. Aircraft lost.

213 SQUADRON, EXETER

Hurricane N2336. Lost control and struck sea during routine patrol 12.58 p.m. Cause unknown. Sub-Lieutenant W. J. M. Moss killed. Aircraft AK-G lost.

247 SQUADRON, ROBOROUGH

Gladiator N5701. Flew through trees at Werrington, Devon on dummy landing approach following night patrol over Plymouth from St. Eval. Sergeant R. T. Thomas unhurt. Aircraft a write-off.

248 SQUADRON, SUMBURGH

Blenheim   Failed to return from reconnaissance sortie to south Norwegian coast 12.00 p.m. Crashed in sea. Pilot Officer C. J. Arthur, Sergeant E. A. Ringwood both missing, Sergeant R. C. R. Cox killed. Aircraft WR-U lost.

501 SQUADRON, GRAVESEND

Hurricane R4222. Hit in glycol tank by return fire from Do 215 over the Channel 11.30 a.m. Returned to base. Squadron Leader H. A. V. Hogan unhurt. Aircraft damaged but repairable.

Wednesday, August 28

54 SQUADRON, HORNCHURCH

Spitfire R6832. Shot down by another Spitfire during attack on Bf 109 and crashed near Frid Wood, Stockbury 1.00 p.m. Flight Lieutenant A. C. Deere baled out unhurt over Detling. Aircraft a write-off.
  Excavations by the Kent Battle of Britain Museum in October 1973 revealed remains of Rolls-Royce Merlin engine, tail wheel strut, windscreen frame and gun firing-button.

Spitfire X4053. Shot down in combat with Bf 109s over Ramsgate 5.15 p.m. Believed crashed into Westbere Lake near Canterbury. Squadron Leader D. O. Finlay baled out wounded. Aircraft a write-off.

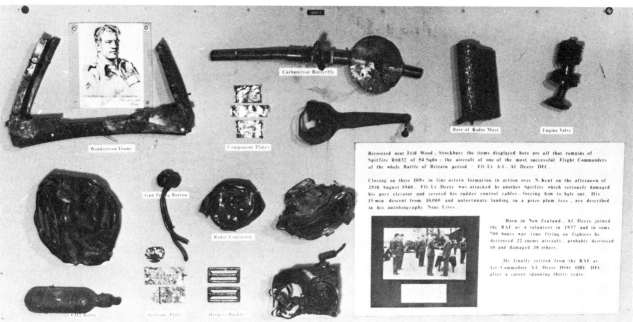

Relics from Al Deere's Spitfire R6832, shot down by another unidentified Spitfire, on display at the Kent Battle of Britain Museum.

ON FEB 3 1940, FLTLT (LATER GPCP) PETER TOWNSEND
OF NO43 SQN SHOT DOWN A HEINKEL INTO THE SNOW
NEAR SNEATON CASTLE YORKS., THE FIRST GERMAN
A/C TO BE DESTROYED OVER ENGLAND SINCE WW1

K K

56 SQUADRON, NORTH WEALD

Hurricane R4117. Crashed and exploded near Share and Coulter, West End, Herne Bay following combat with Bf 109s over the Thames Estuary 1.10 p.m. Pilot Officer W. H. Constable-Maxwell baled out slightly injured. Aircraft a write-off.

Hurricane V7382. Forced-landed Scocles Farm, Eastchurch. Damaged by return fire from Do 17 engaged over the Thames Estuary 1.30 p.m. Flying Officer P. S. Weaver unhurt. Aircraft damaged but repairable.

Hurricane R4198. Shot down believed by Spitfire in combat over the Thames Estuary 5.00 p.m. Pilot Officer F. B. Sutton baled out badly burned and admitted to Canterbury Hospital. Aircraft a write-off.

Hurricane N2523. Shot down by Bf 109 following destruction of another over Hawkinge 5.10 p.m. Petrol tank exploded and aircraft crashed in flames into a wood at Ladwood Farm, Acrise. Sergeant G. Smythe baled out unhurt. Aircraft a write-off.
Few surviving fragments excavated by Brenzett Aeronautical Museum in 1977. Items in the Vizard collection believed to be from this same aircraft.

79 SQUADRON, BIGGIN HILL

Hurricane P3938. Forced-landed Appledore Station near Tenterden with glycol system damaged in combat over Hythe 9.10 a.m. Flight Lieutenant G. D. L. Haysom unhurt. Aircraft damaged but repairable.

85 SQUADRON, CROYDON

Hurricane P3467. Damaged by Bf 109 during attack on another 4.20 p.m. Returned to base. Sergeant F. R. Walker-Smith unhurt. Aircraft damaged but repairable.

151 SQUADRON, NORTH WEALD

Hurricane L2005. Set alight during combat over the Thames Estuary and crashed into a bungalow at Millthorpe, Godmersham 4.30 p.m. Pilot Officer J. W. E. Alexander baled out badly burned. Admitted to hospital. Aircraft a write-off.

Hurricane P3320. Crash-landed at Eastchurch following combat over the Thames Estuary 4.35 p.m. Sergeant L. Davies wounded. Aircraft damaged but repairable.

219 SQUADRON, CATTERICK

Blenheim L1524. Undershot runway on landing in sudden rain storm 1.45 a.m. Sergeant H. F Grubb, Sergeant S. Austin both unhurt. Aircraft repairable.

264 SQUADRON, HORNCHURCH

Defiant N1576. Returned to base severely damaged in attack on He 111 over Dover 9.00 a.m. Pilot Officer W. F. Carnaby, Pilot Officer C. C. Ellery both unhurt. Aircraft damaged but repairable.

Defiant L6957. Petrol tank holed during attack on He 111 over Folkestone 9.00 a.m. Returned to base. Sergeant A. J. Lauder, Sergeant V. R. Chapman both unhurt. Aircraft damaged but repairable.

Defiant L7021. Crashed in flames on Luddenham Marsh, Faversham 9.20 a.m. during combat with Bf 109s. Squadron Leader G. D. Garvin baled out with minor injuries. Flight Lieutenant R. C. V. Ash baled out but killed. Aircraft a write-off.

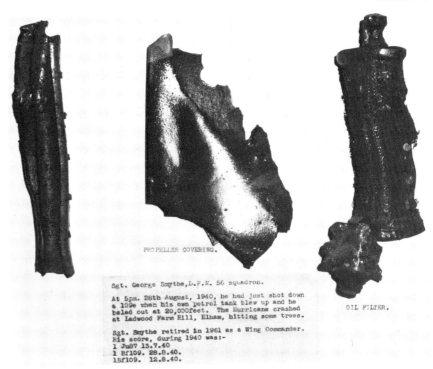

PROPELLER COVERING.

OIL FILTER.

Sgt. George Smythe, D.F.M. 56 squadron.

At 5pm. 28th August, 1940, he had just shot down a 109e when his own petrol tank blew up and he baled out at 20,000feet. The Hurricane crashed at Ladwood Farm Hill, Elham, hitting some trees.

Sgt. Smythe retired in 1961 as a Wing Commander. His score, during 1940 was:-
1 Ju87 13.7.40
1 Bf109. 28.8.40.
1Bf109. 12.8.40.

Display of wreckage from Sergeant George Smythe's Hurricane N2523 at Brenzett.

IN PROUD
AND LOVING MEMORY
OF
ROBERT CLIFFORD VACY ASH
FLIGHT LIEUTENANT R.A.F.
DIED IN ACTION AUGUST 28TH 1940
AGED 31.

TO HIM THAT OVERCOMETH IS GIVEN TO EAT OF THE TREE OF LIFE THAT GROWETH IN THE MIDST OF THE PARADISE OF GOD.
TO HIM SHALL BE GIVEN THE MORNING STAR.

One of the twenty-one war graves in St. Andrews Western Cemetery, Fife.

In the early morning of Wednesday, August 28, 1940, twelve Defiants of No. 264 took off from Hornchurch on what was destined to be the last daytime sortie carried out by that type of aircraft. The men in them must have rated their chances of survival pretty low as, during the previous four days, the squadron had lost seven aircraft in combat and nine crew members.

Defiant N1574. Shot down by Bf 109 in combat over Thanet 8.55 a.m. Crashed in Kingswood, Challock Forest. Pilot Officer D. Whitley, Sergeant R. C. Turner both killed. Aircraft a write-off.

Major recovery by the Kent Battle of Britain Museum at Cutlers Farm, Molash revealed shattered Rolls-Royce Merlin engine and Defiant' aircraft identity plate together with assorted wreckage. Site later visited by London Air Museum and further surface fragments recovered. Engine plate recovered by Steve Vizard 1980.

Defiant L7026. Shot down in combat with Bf 109s of JG26 over Thanet 8.55 a.m. Crashed in flames on Sillibourne Farm, Hinxhill. Pilot Officer P. L. Kenner, Pilot Officer C. E. Johnson both killed. Aircraft a write-off.

Major recovery by the Kent Battle of Britain Museum. Complete Rolls-Royce Merlin engine discovered at a depth of fourteen feet with propeller boss, one blade still attached. Control column, escape axe from rear turret, parachute buckles and charred parachute silk also unearthed plus quantities of oil and petrol which rendered operations quite hazardous.

Once again the Defiant proved to be a vulnerable death trap and Pilot Officer Peter Kenner *left* and his gunner Pilot Officer Charles

Johnson *right* perished in L7026 — the second aircraft in the line up at the top of the page.

Sergeant Robert Turner, DFM, *(left)* crewed up with Pilot Officer David Whitley when he was posted to No. 264 Squadron as a turret gunner early in 1940. Considering the losses sustained by the two Defiant squadrons, Nos. 141 and 264, Sergeant Turner and his pilot lasted a shade longer than most. Both however were killed in the last daylight action fought by Defiants during the Battle of Britain. Robert Turner, Christ's Hospital scholar, was buried at Eye and Dunsden *(above)* and David Whitley at Bedford *(below left).*

The crash sites of both Defiants lost on August 28 have been excavated by the Kent Battle of Britain Museum. *Below:* The engine from L7026 recovered from Sillibourne Farm and *above* a display board of items from N1574 at Cutlers Farm, Molash.

Defiant N1569. Severely damaged in combat with Bf 109s of JG26 and forced-landed at Court Lodge Farm, Petham 9.05 a.m. Pilot Officer J. R. A. Bailey, Sergeant O. A. Hardy both unhurt. Aircraft damaged but repairable.

603 SQUADRON, HORNCHURCH

Spitfire R6751. Failed to return from combat with Bf 109s over Dover 4.45 p.m. Flight Lieutenant J. L. G. Cunningham missing. Aircraft XT-U lost.

Spitfire L1046. Failed to return from combat with Bf 109s over Dover 4.45 p.m. Pilot Officer D. K. MacDonald missing. Aircraft lost.

Spitfire R6989. Seriously damaged in combat with Bf 109s off Dover 4.50 p.m. Returned to base. Flying Officer I. S. Ritchie wounded admitted to Oldchurch Hospital, Romford. Aircraft XT-X damaged but repairable.

Spitfire N3105. Crashed in flames on Great Hay Farm, Leigh Green, Appledore Road, Tenterden during combat with Bf 109s 8.30 p.m. Pilot Officer N. J. V. Benson killed. Aircraft XT-P a write-off.

610 SQUADRON, BIGGIN HILL

Spitfire P9511. Shot down in combat with Bf 109s over Dover and crashed into a house at Stelling Minnis 5.00 p.m. Pilot Officer K. H. Cox killed. Aircraft a write-off.

615 SQUADRON, KENLEY

Hurricane R4116. Hit in the engine by return fire from Do 17 over Sandwich. Forced-landed at Snoadstreet Farm, Throwley 9.15 a.m. Pilot Officer S. J. Madle injured admitted to Hothfield Hospital. Aircraft a write-off.
Surface fragments collected by Brenzett Aeronautical Museum.

Thursday, August 29

85 SQUADRON, CROYDON

Hurricane P2879. Severely damaged in combat with Bf 109s off Eastbourne 3.45 p.m. Sergeant G. B. Booth unhurt. Aircraft damaged but repairable.

Hurricane L1915. Set alight by Bf 109s in combat over the Channel. Glided back to land and crashed at Brigden Hill Farm, Ashburnham 4.00 p.m. Sergeant J. H. M. Ellis baled out unhurt. Aircraft VY-B a write-off.

Hurricane V7350. Shot down by Bf 109s in combat off Sussex coast. Crashed on Underwood Farm, near River Dudwell, Etchingham 4.28 p.m. Sergeant F. R. Walker-Smith baled out wounded in foot, landed at Hawkhurst. Aircraft a write-off.
Major recovery by the Etchingham Aviation Society and now exhibited at Robertsbridge Aviation Society Museum.

Hurricane V6623. Attacked by Bf 109s over Winchelsea. Crashed near Camber Castle ruins, Rye foreshore 6.15 p.m. Flight Lieutenant H. R. Hamilton killed. Aircraft VY-L a write-off.

151 SQUADRON, STAPLEFORD

Hurricane P3382. Crashed near Basildon during routine night patrol 7.40 p.m. Pilot Officer A. G. Wainwright baled out and admitted to Epping Hospital with broken ribs. Aircraft a write-off.

Contemporary souvenir from Pilot Officer Madle's Hurricane R4116 now displayed at Brenzett Aeronautical Museum.

219 SQUADRON, CATTERICK

Blenheim   . Forced-landed at Sywell during return flight from St. Athan. Sergeant T. Birkett unhurt. Aircraft repairable.

501 SQUADRON, GRAVESEND

Hurricane R4223. Crashed near Hawkinge during combat with Bf 109s 7.20 p.m. Sergeant W. J. Green baled out and rescued from sea off Folkestone. Aircraft a write-off.

Hurricane P3102. Shot down by Bf 109s in combat over Hawkinge. Crashed at Ladwood Farm, Acrise 7.30 p.m. Flight Lieutenant J. A. A. Gibson baled out slightly injured landing at Mill Hill Farm, Ottinge. Aircraft a write-off.

603 SQUADRON, HORNCHURCH

Spitfire N3267. Cockpit damaged in combat with Bf 109s over Deal 4.00 p.m. Returned to base. Flying Officer C. J. Boulter slightly wounded. Aircraft XT-S damaged but repairable.

Spitfire P9459. Forced-landed at Bossingham following combat with enemy fighters over Deal 4.10 p.m. Flight Lieutenant F. W. Rushmer slightly wounded. Aircraft XT-N damaged but repairable.

Spitfire R6753. Shot down by Bf 109s and crashed near New Romney 6.42 p.m. Pilot Officer D. J. C. Pinckney baled out slightly burned and admitted to hospital. Aircraft XT-G a write-off.
Wreckage recovered by the Brenzett Aeronautical Museum during summer 1976. Many interesting relics unearthed including the aircraft 'Form 700' from the cockpit and currently being prepared for eventual display.

Spitfire L1021. Separated from squadron and shot down by Bf 109 whilst acting as 'weaver' to 85 Squadron Hurricanes. Crash-landed near Lympne 7.00 p.m. Pilot Officer R. H. Hillary unhurt. Aircraft XT-M a write-off.

Folkestone New Cemetery is also the last resting place of Canadian Harry Hamilton *(left)*, a Flight Lieutenant with No. 85 Squadron from King's County, New Brunswick.

610 SQUADRON, BIGGIN HILL

Spitfire X4011. Damaged in combat with Do 215s and Bf 110s over Mayfield. Crashed at Gatwick 4.00 p.m. Pilot Officer A. C. Baker unhurt. Aircraft DW-O a write-off.

Spitfire R6629. Shot down in combat over Mayfield area 4.00 p.m. Crashed at Great Wigsell Estate, Hurst Green. Sergeant E. Manton killed. Aircraft DW-E a write-off.

Official Casualty Records state that this officer was killed in action on August 28, 1940 contrary to the details shown in the Form 540, No. 610 Squadron Operations Record Book. The burial register of Hawkhurst Cemetery also shows the date of death of 'Sergeant (Pilot) Edward Manton 810081 RAF (Aux) 610 Squadron 28 August 1940.'

Major recovery by the Robertsbridge Museum which excavated complete surviving remains and all major components. Some fragments in the Kent Battle of Britain Museum.

'The strife is o'er, The battle done, Now is the victor's triumph won' — the inscription on the headstone belonging to Sergeant Edward Manton. All the evidence points to an incorrect date of death in the records and on the stone.

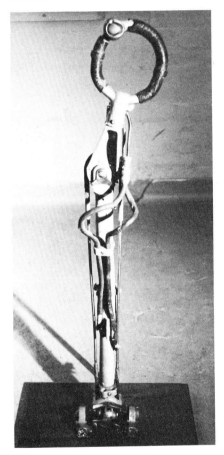

Virtually mint control column, one of the best recovered from a crash site from Spitfire R6753 now on display at Brenzett.

Friday, August 30

32 SQUADRON, BIGGIN HILL

Hurricane N2540. Destroyed in enemy attack on base. No personnel losses. Aircraft a write-off.

43 SQUADRON, TANGMERE

Hurricane P3179. Shot down by Bf 109 during combat over the Sussex coast. Crashed near junction of Portland and Woodhouse Road, Hove 11.50 a.m. Sergeant D. Noble killed. Aircraft a write-off.

On August 30, No. 43 Squadron lost two pilots. Dennis Noble, a 20-year-old from East Retford, Nottinghamshire, had arrived on August 3 direct from No. 6 Operational Training Unit at Sutton Bridge. He lasted just twenty-seven days — his remains were taken back to his home town for burial *(below)* in the town cemetery.

Another loss to the squadron was its Commanding Officer, John 'Tubby' Badger, DFC, who survived as its leader for fifty-one days. After he was shot down, he fought his injuries for nine months before death came on June 30, 1941. He was laid to rest at St. Michael and All Angels, Halton *(below)*.

On the morning of August 30, Pilot Officer E. J. Morris collided with a Heinkel over the borders of Sussex and Surrey. His Hurricane crashed on Lodge Farm, South Holmwood *(above)* the He 111 less than a mile to the south. The comparison photograph *(below)* of the site today during the WAAG investigation, courtesy Stuart Hall and Andy Saunders.

Hurricane V6548. Shot down in combat with Bf 109s and crashed south of Woodchurch 5.35 p.m. Squadron Leader J. V. C. Badger grievously wounded admitted to Ashford Hospital. (Died 30.6.41) Aircraft a write-off.

56 SQUADRON, NORTH WEALD

Hurricane N2668. Crash-landed and burned out following action with Bf 110s over Essex 4.45 p.m. Flying Officer R. E. P. Brooker unhurt. Aircraft a write-off.

Hurricane R2689. Crashed and burned out near Halstead following destruction of He 111 in combat over Essex 4.45 p.m. Possibly that down at Palmers Farm, Coggeshall. Flight Lieutenant E. J. Gracie believed unhurt. Broken neck discovered next day. Aircraft a write-off.

66 SQUADRON, COLTISHALL

Spitfire R6715. Shot down into the sea twenty miles east of Aldeburgh during attack on Do 17 5.00 p.m. Pilot Officer J. H. T. Pickering unhurt, rescued by lightship. Aircraft lost.

74 SQUADRON, KIRTON-IN-LINDSEY

Spitfire X4022. Crashed and burned out following collision with X4027 during routine patrol 11.00 a.m. Sergeant W. M. Skinner baled out unhurt. Aircraft a write-off.

Spitfire X4027. Forced-landed following mid-air collision with X4022 during patrol 11.00 a.m. Pilot Officer E. W. G. Churches unhurt. Aircraft damaged but repairable.

79 SQUADRON, BIGGIN HILL

Hurricane P3203. Collided with He 111 of 10/KG1 during combat over Reigate 11.10 a.m. Crashed on Lodge Farm, South Holmwood, Brockham. Pilot Officer E. J. Morris baled out unhurt, landing near Dorking. Aircraft a write-off.

Few surviving fragments excavated by the Wealden Aviation Archaeological Group in September 1979.

Hurricane   . Returned to base damaged following combat over Surrey with Bf 109s 12.10 p.m. Pilot Officer W. H. Millington unhurt. Aircraft damaged but repairable.

Hurricane   . Damaged in rudder during combat with Bf 109 over base 6.20 p.m. Pilot Officer P. F. Mayhew unhurt. Aircraft repairable.

85 SQUADRON, CROYDON

Hurricane V6624. Shot down in attack on He 111s of IV/KG1 and crashed at Langley Farm, Smarden 11.40 a.m. Pilot Officer J. E. Marshall baled out unhurt. Aircraft VY-D a write-off.

Believed to be the aircraft recovered from neighbouring Tanden Farm by the Kent Battle of Britain Museum. Excavations revealed complete Rolls-Royce Merlin engine, both undercarriage legs and tail wheel, plus cockpit instruments, control column and rudder bar pedals. Subsequently, re-excavated by Steve Vizard in 1979 who unearthed the remains of a smashed Rolls-Royce Merlin engine, propeller hub, 'ROTOL' badge and some cockpit components but nothing to determine exact identity.

92 SQUADRON, PEMBREY

Spitfire N3249. Crashed on landing due to ground mist after night flight from Bibury 1.00 a.m. Sergeant R. E. Havercroft unhurt. Aircraft QJ-P damaged but repairable.

Sergeant Feliks Gmur, shot down at Epping Green, lies in Epping Cemetery.

111 SQUADRON, DEBDEN

Hurricane R4112. Returned to base with damage to port wing following combat with Bf 110s over Manston. Flying Officer B. H. Bowring unhurt. Aircraft repairable.

151 SQUADRON, STAPLEFORD

Hurricane V7369. Crashed and burned out in Temple Street, Strood, 11.51 a.m. during routine squadron patrol. Cause unknown. Squadron Leader E. B. King killed. Aircraft a write-off.

Control column and many manufacturers plates recovered from under the road at this location by the Lashenden Air Warfare Museum. Items also in the Vizard collection.

Hurricane R4213. Shot down in combat with enemy aircraft over the Thames Estuary 4.00 p.m. Crashed Jacks Hatch, Epping Green. Sergeant F. Gmur killed. Aircraft a write-off.

Hurricane P3119. Damaged in combat over the Thames Estuary 4.00 p.m. Forced-landed. Pilot Officer J. L. W. Ellacombe unhurt. Aircraft damaged but repairable.

222 SQUADRON, HORNCHURCH

Spitfire R6719. Damaged in combat with Bf 109s and forced-landed at Daniyns Hall Farm, Warwick Lane, Rainham 12.10 p.m. Sergeant I. Hutchinson unhurt. Aircraft damaged but repairable.

Squadron Leader Eric King served with Nos. 253 and 249 Squadrons before being posted to No. 151 Squadron (then at North Weald), on August 21. His first command lasted only nine days . . . ending in a burnt-out aircraft in Strood on the River Medway. Thirty years later, the crash site was investigated by the Lashenden Air Warfare Museum — Trevor Matthews displays the burned joystick they recovered *(below left)*. The gun button was locked on 'fire'. After considerable effort and two visits, we tracked down Eric King's overgrown grave in Highgate Cemetery *(below)*.

Spitfire P9325. Forced-landed at Eastchurch 4.00 p.m. with severe damage following combat over Canterbury. Sergeant S. Baxter unhurt. Aircraft a write-off.

Spitfire R6720. Damaged in combat with enemy aircraft over Canterbury and crash-landed on Bekesbourne aerodrome 4.19 p.m. Pilot Officer W. R. Assheton unhurt. Aircraft damaged but repairable.

Spitfire P9375. Crashed in flames near Cherry Orchard Lane, Rochford 4.30 p.m. following combat with enemy fighters. Pilot Officer J. M. V. Carpenter baled out unhurt. Aircraft a write-off.

Spitfire P9364. Returned to base with damaged mainspar after attack on He 111 over Billericay 5.15 p.m. Flying Officer J. W. Cutts unhurt. Aircraft repairable.

Spitfire K9826. Shot down by Bf 109s. Crashed and burned out at Marley near Barham 6.00 p.m. Pilot Officer H. P. M. Edridge baled out with burns to face, landing at Broome Park. Aircraft ZD-X a write-off.

Spitfire R6628. Shot down by Bf 109s. Crashed and burned out at Longhampark Lodge, Bishopsbourne 6.02 p.m. Sergeant J. I. Johnson killed. Aircraft a write-off.

Spitfire P9443. Crash-landed near Sittingbourne following combat with Bf 109s, 6.10 p.m. Flight Lieutenant G. C. Matheson seriously injured. Aircraft a write-off.

Spitfire P9323. Shot down in combat with Bf 109s and crashed on South Lees Farm, Minster, Sheppey 6.29 p.m. Sergeant A. W. P. Spears baled out unhurt. Aircraft ZD-F a write-off.

253 SQUADRON, KENLEY

Hurricane P3802. Forced-landed near Maidstone following combat with Bf 109s 11.15 a.m. Flight Lieutenant G. A. Brown wounded in shoulder admitted to Preston Hall Hospital. Aircraft a write-off.
Control column in Steve Vizard collection taken from a wrecked Hurricane at the time of its crash at Mereworth Woods near West Malling said to be from this machine.

Hurricane L1965. Shot down in combat with Bf 109s 11.15 a.m. Believed crashed near Monks Hill, Biddenden. Pilot Officer C. D. Francis missing. Aircraft a write-off.

Hurricane P3921. Shot down in combat with enemy fighters over Redhill 11.20 a.m. Crashed at Woldingham. Pilot Officer D. N. O. Jenkins baled out but killed by enemy fighters. Aircraft a write-off.

Hurricane P2960. Hit in engine by 20mm cannon shell during combat over Redhill 11.30 a.m. Returned to base. Squadron Leader H. M. Starr unhurt. Aircraft damaged but repairable.

Hurricane P3717. Returned to base damaged in attack from Bf 110 in action over Redhill 11.35 a.m. Pilot Officer W. M. C. Samolinski unhurt. Aircraft damaged but repairable.

Hurricane P3213. Shot down by Fw. Koch of II/JG26 in combat over Dungeness 5.15 p.m. Believed crashed at Cuckolds Corner, Plurenden Manor near Woodchurch. Sergeant J. H. Dickinson baled out but killed. Aircraft a write-off.

Hurricane P3412. Returned to base severely damaged by 20mm cannon during combat with Bf 109s over Dungeness 5.20 p.m. Flying Officer J. H. Wedgewood unhurt. Aircraft damaged but repairable.

This neat and tidy grave at Towcester Cemetery, Northamptonshire belongs to Sergeant Joseph Inkerman Johnson, 'Natal' Squadron pilot killed on August 30.

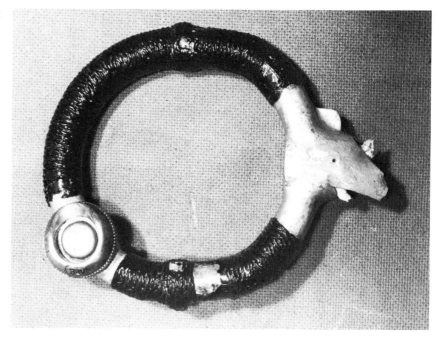

This joystick, now owned by Steve Vizard, was picked up in Mereworth Woods in 1940 and is believed to have come from Hurricane P3802.

The Commonwealth War Graves Commission headstone in the foreground in the picturesque churchyard of St. Margaret's at Bagendon, Gloucestershire marks the last resting place of Pilot Officer David Jenkins of No. 253 Squadron.

The headstone in St. Mary's Churchyard at Egton-with-Newland which marks the grave of father and son — Norman Dickinson who died in 1933 and Sergeant John Dickinson killed on August 30, 1940.

501 SQUADRON, GRAVESEND

Hurricane P8816. Forced-landed with radiator damaged by return fire from He 111s intercepted over the Thames Estuary 5.15 p.m. Sergeant J. H. Lacey unhurt. Aircraft damaged but repairable.

603 SQUADRON, HORNCHURCH

Spitfire R6754. Returned to base damaged in tail following combat with Bf 110s over Deal 11.10 a.m. Sergeant A. R. Sarre unhurt. Aircraft XT-F damaged but repairable.

Spitfire L1067. Shot down in combat with Bf 110s over Deal 11.15 a.m. Crashed at Hope Farm, Snargate. Squadron Leader G. L. Denholm baled out unhurt. Aircraft XT-D a write-off.
Major recovery by the Brenzett Aeronautical Museum on September 22, 1973. Instrument panel, most major controls and components together with many manufacturers plates recovered plus portion of engine cowling bearing traces of 'BLUE PETER'.

John Swift Bell now lies with his mother and father in Lincoln.

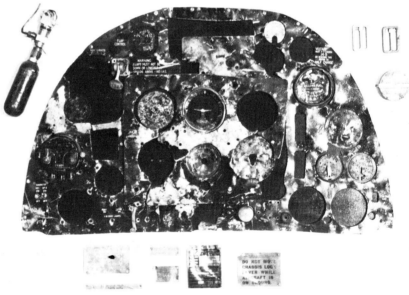

Spitfire L1067 was excavated by the Brenzett team. *Above:* Dave Buchanan, chairman of the group, shows George Denholm the cowling from his aircraft which still bears the legend 'Blue Peter' (Brenzett). *Below:* Instrument panel and artifacts on display. (This aircraft must not be confused with the officially-named 'Blue Peter' Spitfire AD540 sponsored by the Newmarket and Racing Industry Spitfire Fund.)

Spitfire X4163. Returned to base with punctured oil tank following attack by Bf 109s over Canterbury 4.40 p.m. Flying Officer R. McG. Waterston unhurt. Aircraft XT-O repairable.

Spitfire R7021. Tail shot off in combat with Bf 109s, 4.55 p.m. Crashed at Addington Park, near West Malling. Sergeant A. R. Sarre baled out unhurt. Aircraft XT-X a write-off.

616 SQUADRON, KENLEY

Spitfire X4248. Shot down in head-on attack on Bf 109s over West Malling. Crashed and burned out near Percival Farm, Wrotham 12.02 p.m. Flying Officer J. S. Bell killed. Aircraft a write-off.

Spitfire L1012. Misjudged landing approach at base following action over West Malling 12.10 p.m. and overshot runway. Sergeant J. Hopewell unhurt. Aircraft damaged but repairable.

Pilot Officer Raymond Andre Charles Aeberhardt from Walton-on-Thames joined the Royal Air Force before the war and was a 19-year-old pilot flying Spitfires with No. 19 Squadron at Fowlmere, Cambridgeshire when the Battle of Britain began. On August 31, 1940, the squadron intercepted an enemy force attacking Debden aerodrome and, in the ensuing fight, Ray

Aeberhardt's Spitfire received damage to its hydraulic system. He left the fight and nursed his aircraft back to Fowlmere where he was forced to attempt a landing without flaps. His Spitfire somersaulted on to its back and caught fire, the young pilot dying in the holocaust. Today this striking memorial marks his grave in the churchyard at Whittlesford.

Saturday, August 31

1 SQUADRON, NORTHOLT

Hurricane V7375. Set alight by Bf 110 in combat over Chelmsford. Crashed and burned out on Ovington Hall Farm, Halstead 8.45 a.m. Sergeant H. J. Merchant baled out and admitted to Halstead Hospital with burns. Aircraft a write-off.

1 (RCAF) SQUADRON, NORTHOLT

Hurricane P2971. Abandoned over Cranbrook during combat with Bf 109s 9.15 a.m. Crashed at Staplehurst. Flying Officer Hyde baled out with burns. Aircraft a write-off.

Hurricane P3858. Shot down by Bf 109s in combat over Cranbrook 9.15 a.m. Crashed and burned out at Upper Street, Broomfield. Flying Officer Sprenger baled out unhurt landing at Little Bay Court, Ulcombe. Aircraft a write-off.

Hurricane N2530. Shot down in combat with Bf 109s over Cranbrook 9.20 a.m. Flight Lieutenant V. B. Corbett baled out with burns landing near Wittersham level crossing. Aircraft a write-off.

Hurricane P3869. Crashed and burned out at Gravesend during attack on Do 215s at 5.00 p.m. Flying Officer Desloges baled out severely burned. Aircraft a write-off.

17 SQUADRON, DEBDEN

Hurricane R4091. Forced-landed at Yalding 6.25 p.m. Damaged in combat with Bf 109s over Maidstone. Sergeant G. A. Steward unhurt. Aircraft damaged but repairable.

19 SQUADRON, DUXFORD

Spitfire X4231. Shot down during attack on Do 17s ten miles east of base 8.30 a.m. Crashed in flames near Little Shelford. Flying Officer T. J. B. Coward baled out severely wounded in leg landing on Royston — Newmarket Road. Admitted to Addenbrooke's Hospital, Cambridge. Aircraft a write-off.

Spitfire R6958. Shot down in combat over the Thames Estuary 8.45 a.m. Flying Officer F. N. Brinsden baled out unhurt. Aircraft a write-off.

Spitfire R6912. Flaps damaged in combat causing aircraft to overturn on landing 8.50 a.m. Burned out. Pilot Officer R. A. C. Aeberhardt killed. Aircraft a write-off.

54 SQUADRON, HORNCHURCH

Spitfire X4235. Caught on take-off in bombing attack 1.15 p.m. Crashed in River Ingrebourne outside aerodrome perimeter. Sergeant J. Davis unhurt. Aircraft damaged but repairable.

Spitfire R6895. Caught on take-off in bombing and crashed inverted onto runway from 100ft 1.15 p.m. Flight Lieutenant A. C. Deere slightly injured. Aircraft a write-off.

Spitfire X4236. Caught in bombing attack during take-off 1.15 p.m. Lost one wing and crashed on runway. Pilot Officer E. F. Edsall unhurt. Aircraft KL-L a write-off.

Spitfire X4054. Shot down possibly by friendly Hurricane following destruction of Bf 109. Crashed and burned out near Great Hollanden Farm, Hildenborough 7.28 p.m. Sergeant D. G. Gibbins baled out unhurt landing at Tinley Lodge, Shipbourne. Aircraft a write-off.

56 SQUADRON, NORTH WEALD

Hurricane R4197. Shot down in combat with enemy fighters over Colchester 8.38 a.m. Pilot Officer M. H. Mounsdon injured. Aircraft a write-off.
Pristine landing lamp taken from the aircraft in 1940 donated to the Kent Battle of Britain Museum.

Hurricane V6628. Abandoned during combat with enemy fighters over Colchester 8.40 a.m. Sergeant C. Whitehead baled out unhurt. Aircraft a write-off.

Hurricane V7378. Shot down by enemy fighters over Colchester 8.45 a.m. Crashed into River Blackwater at West Point, Osea Island. Flight Lieutenant P. S. Weaver missing. Aircraft lost.

Hurricane V7341. Shot down by Bf 110 during attack on Do 17s over Colchester. Crashed near White Hart Lane, Springfield 9.05 a.m. Flying Officer I. B. Westmacott baled out injured landing at Little Baddow. Admitted to Chelmsford Hospital. Aircraft a write-off.

72 SQUADRON, BIGGIN HILL

Spitfire P9438. Crashed near New Romney during combat over Dungeness 6.35 p.m. Flight Lieutenant F. M. Smith baled out wounded and badly burned. Aircraft a write-off.

Spitfire P9457. Shot down in combat over Dungeness. Crashed in Hungerford Field, Chickenden Farm, Staplehurst 7.10 p.m. Flying Officer E. J. Wilcox killed. Aircraft a write-off.

79 SQUADRON, BIGGIN HILL

Hurricane N2345. Crashed at The Grange, Water Lane, Limpsfield following combat over base 9.30 a.m. Pilot Officer G. H. Nelson-Edwards slightly injured. Aircraft a write-off.

Hurricane V7200. Shot down in combat over Kenley 4.00 p.m. Crashed attempting a forced-landing at Haliloo Farm, Warlingham. Sergeant H. A. Bolton killed. Aircraft a write-off.
Location visited by the Air Historical Group with no result.

Hurricane P3050. Set alight in combat with Bf 109s over Romney 6.00 p.m. Crash-landed on Conghurst Farm, Hawkhurst. Pilot Officer W. H. Millington wounded in left thigh and badly burned. Admitted to Croydon Hospital. Aircraft a write-off.

Hurricane P3877. Damaged by Bf 109 during attack on Do 17s over base and crashed on landing 6.50 p.m. Pilot Officer E. J. Morris wounded. Aircraft damaged but repairable.

Edgar Wilcox from Mitcham, Surrey buried in All Saints Churchyard, Staplehurst, Kent. The town was in the heart of the battle and several aircraft came down in the surrounding area. One unusual grave belongs to an unknown airman killed in 'September 1940' although investigations as to his identity remain uncorroborated at time of publication.

Flight Lieutenant Percy Stevenson Weaver, DFC, a native of Bath, Somerset, joined the Royal Air Force before the war and in September 1939 was a Flying Officer with No. 56 Squadron at North Weald where he was known to his fellow pilots as 'Mouse'. He participated in the air battles over the convoys in the early build up to the battle and, in mid-August, his natural talent for leadership earned him the command of a flight. On August 28, he forced-landed his severely battle-damaged Hurricane on farmland near Eastchurch and walked away unhurt, but only three days later, in a bitter dogfight over east Essex, he was overwhelmed by enemy fighters and sent spinning into the muddy depths of the River Blackwater. A popular and much respected pilot, he was sadly missed in the squadron. His award of the DFC was gazetted only hours after his death and the following day the remnants of No. 56 were withdrawn from the battle area.

Sergeant Pilot Henry Bolton came from West Hartlepool. After his death on August 31, he was taken back to County Durham and now lies buried in the family grave.

85 SQUADRON, CROYDON

Hurricane P3166. Shot down by Bf 110 during attack on Bf 109s over Tunbridge Wells. Crashed at Bedgebury Park near Badgers Oak, Goudhurst 1.00 p.m. Squadron Leader P. W. Townsend baled out wounded in foot landing Cranbrook Road, Hawkhurst. Admitted to Hawkhurst Cottage Hospital. Aircraft VY-Q a write-off.
Crash site investigated by Halstead War Museum which discovered some remaining fragments and remains of Rolls-Royce engine. Pieces also held by the Kent Battle of Britain Museum and London Air Museum.

Hurricane V6581. Attacked by Bf 110 during combat over Tunbridge Wells. Crashed between Northiam and Newenden 1.30 p.m. Pilot Officer P. A. Worrall baled out slightly wounded in thigh and admitted to Croydon Hospital. Aircraft a write-off.
Major recovery undertaken by Robertsbridge Museum which excavated complete surviving remains of the aircraft.

Hurricane N2544. Shot down in action over the Thames Estuary. Crash-landed in flames at Fanton Chase, Shotgate 6.30 p.m. Pilot Officer W. T. Hodgson unhurt. Aircraft VY-G damaged but repairable.

Hurricane   Damaged in combat over the Thames Estuary 6.00 p.m. Returned to base. Pilot Officer J. E. Marshall unhurt. Aircraft VY-D repairable.

Hurricane L2071. Returned to base with fabric stripped from wings following vertical dive in pursuit of Bf 110 west of Sittingbourne 6.05 p.m. Sergeant G. B. Booth unhurt. Aircraft repairable.

111 SQUADRON, DEBDEN

Hurricane P2888. Shot down in combat with Bf 110s over Felixstowe 9.20 a.m. Crashed and burned out. Sergeant J. T. Craig baled out injured admitted to Epping Hospital. Aircraft a write-off.

Sergeants' Mess,
RAF Station
Middle Wallop,
Tuesday.

My Dear Mother and Father,
Thank you both for the nice letters and also the postal order. I was very pleased to hear from Father, chatty news about things and people I know so well always provides interest.
I've been having plenty of fun just lately, plenty of anxious moments waiting for the word go and then plenty of action when up there. I had a peculiar coincidence this weekend for whilst out on patrol early Sunday morning, my section bumped right into Ju 88s. We just marked a man each. I myself chased my man from Portsmouth to Bristol. All the way up he kept me at bay by means of his cannon firing in the rear. However, we had a chase through the clouds over Bristol and then he foxed me by cutting his engines and I went sailing right under him. A very anxious moment followed whilst I got off his tail. Eventually he turned tail for the coast and I was after him with everything that I had got, the engine flat out with my emergency pulled flat-out. I thought my ears were going to burst for we were diving from 25,000. Well I didn't see him come down though all his guns were out of action. When I arrived back at our base, the other two were still going at it. Eventually, Gordon Batt came down at Rissington and I asked the C/O if I could go up in Batt's car to see if he was OK. I found him fine though his machine was being repaired. Before leaving Wallop I was told that we were free for 24 hours and so we continued on to Birmingham for Sunday evening. They were very surprised to see me and very pleased.
Mother, we three sergeants have formed a section 'Yellow' and I want to know if you could get us three silk yellow scarves or squares and, bye the bye, I would very much like to pay my debts so please make out your bill and send same along.
Have you found any cheap scooter bikes Father? We are hoping to run them for next to nothing, petrol and oil free, and plenty of mechanics to carry out repairs.
Ah well, cheerio for now,
All my kind regards to the good people in Macclesfield.
Your loving son,
Eric.

151 SQUADRON, STAPLEFORD

Hurricane P3301. Shot down by Bf 109s in combat over the Thames Estuary. Forced-landed Foulness 10.25 a.m. Pilot Officer F. Czajkowski wounded in right shoulder admitted to Shoeburyness hospital. Aircraft a write-off.

Hurricane P3312. Hit by broadside from Ju 88 and abandoned as gravity fuel tank exploded 1.30 p.m. Pilot Officer J. L. W. Ellacombe baled out with burns and admitted to St. Lukes Hospital, Bradford. Aircraft damaged but repairable.

222 SQUADRON, HORNCHURCH

Spitfire P9337. Shot down in flames by Bf 109 over Ashford 6.12 p.m. Believed crashed near Huntbourne, St. Michaels, Tenterden. Pilot Officer C. G. A. Davies burned. Aircraft a write-off.

Spitfire N3233. Landed at Eastchurch damaged by 20mm cannon-fire from Bf 109 6.15 p.m. Flight Lieutenant A. I. Robinson slightly wounded. Aircraft damaged but repairable.

249 SQUADRON, BOSCOMBE DOWN

Hurricane L2067. Forced-landed near Whitchurch 2.00 p.m. due to engine failure during routine patrol. Pilot Officer R. E. N. E. Wynn unhurt. Aircraft damaged but repairable.

253 SQUADRON, KENLEY

Hurricane L1830. Shot down by enemy fighters on squadron interception patrol. Believed crashed near Grove Ferry 8.25 a.m. Squadron Leader H. M. Starr fell dead at Hammill Brickworks near Eastry. Aircraft a write-off.

Hurricane P3115. Shot down in flames during attack on Ju 88s and crashed near Hazel Wood, Mace Farm, Cudham 1.02 p.m. Squadron Leader T. P. Gleave baled out grievously burned and admitted to Orpington hospital. Aircraft a write-off.
Surface wreckage recovered by members of Flairavia Flying Club, Biggin Hill and Rolls-Royce Merlin engine donated to the Imperial War Museum currently on loan to the Essex Aviation Group. Site visited by many groups and individuals over the years and pieces now in Halstead War Museum, Kent Battle of Britain Museum and London Air Museum.

Radnor Street Cemetery at Swindon — last resting place for No. 253 Squadron Commanding Officer, Harold Starr, shot down on the morning of August 31.

Hurricane P3713. Severely damaged in attack on Ju 88s over base 1.45 p.m. Pilot unhurt. Aircraft damaged but repairable.

Hurricane P3714. Returned to base severely damaged following attack on Ju 88s over base 1.50 p.m. Pilot unhurt. Aircraft damaged but repairable.

257 SQUADRON, DEBDEN

Hurricane R3175. Shot down in combat with Bf 110s over Clacton. Crashed at Walton-on-the-Naze 8.56 a.m. Pilot Officer G. H. Maffett killed. Aircraft DT-S a write-off.
Complete cockpit section of airframe including instrument panel and windscreen recovered 1972/3 by team led by Lieutenant G. H. Rayner, RN. Now displayed in Battle of Britain Museum at Hendon.

Hurricane P4903. Hit in petrol tank during combat with Bf 110s over Clacton. Crashed in Colne Creek, near Aldborough Point 9.00 a.m. Pilot Officer J. A. McD. Henderson baled out injured and burned. Rescued from sea and admitted to Brightlingsea Naval Hospital. Aircraft lost.
Large portion of airframe together with wing spar and undercarriage leg recovered by the Essex Aviation Group during July 1979.

The engine from Tom Gleave's Hurricane P3115 *above* as found in Hazel Wood, Cudham by the Flairavia Flying Club and *below* currently on display in the Essex Aviation Group collection at Duxford (Essex Aviation Group).

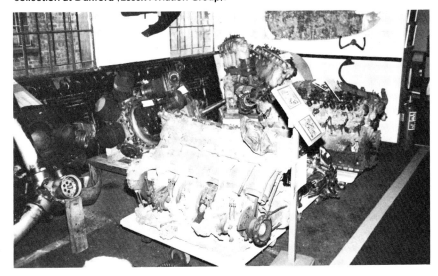

RECOVERY OF THE LARGEST BRITISH BATTLE OF BRITAIN RELIC.

Hawker Hurricane Mk I P3175 is the largest relic of a British fighter, shot down in the Battle of Britain, which has been recovered and put on display. Its completeness is due to the preserving qualities of the crash site environment and its careful excavation by hand; each fragment uncovered being kept for examination and possible reassembly into a component that could be added to the main part of the recovered aircraft.

The aeroplane was originally built by the Gloster Aircraft Company and delivered to No. 10 Maintenance Unit in June 1940. It was officially taken on charge on June 29 and issued to No. 257 Squadron on August 9. Inspection of the Operation Record Book first mentions P3175 as being flown by Pilot Officer G. H. Maffett on August 18, coded DT-S, and it remained his aircraft until the final crash on August 31, 1940.

On that day, nine Hurricanes took off from Martlesham Heath at 8.25 a.m. led by Flight Lieutenant H. R. A. Beresford and were ordered to patrol Debden at 15,000ft. The squadron climbed towards Debden. At 14,000ft they encountered two large formations of Ju 88s with various formations of Bf 110s at 16,000ft. Being unable to catch up with the Ju 88s, the squadron turned their attention to the Bf 110s.

At least six Bf 110s were claimed as destroyed by the squadron but two Hurricanes were also lost including P3175 which crashed on the Essex foreshore near Stone Point at Walton-on-the-Naze at 8.50 a.m. This area was occupied by the army during the war and was cordoned off from the general public. As far as is known, no concerted effort was made to recover the remains and so one can only assume that the wreckage lying above ground level was gradually taken away by personnel from the army camp so that, by the time the land was reopened to the public, little remained to mark the crash site. The soft mud of the salt marshes no doubt helped to cover the remains as well.

Geoff Rayner (now a Lieutenant in the Royal Navy) first remembers seeing the site about 1961 and by that time only a few locals, mostly school children, knew of the crashed aircraft in the marshes. The type was unknown. By the latter half of the 1960s, all that remained visible above the marsh surface was a three foot section of aluminium spar. Geoff's rather crude attempt at digging at this

Above: **All that could originally be seen in 1970 of P3175 which crashed at Walton-on-the-Naze on August 31 killing the pilot Gerard Maffett.**

Above: **Part of the wing uncovered at the initial investigation in August 1972.**

Using hand shovels, the major excavation begins. Cut-outs between spars for the undercarriage show clearly at this stage.

More work exposes the main spar and engine bearers. The Hurricane was lying inverted at 30 degrees.

time revealed part of a fuel tank but the going in the salt marsh was extremely difficult. By August 1971, coastal erosion had exposed another section of the wreckage a few feet away from the spar and, as it was now more accessible and more people were using the beach, souvenir hunting speeded up. Soon the spar was down to six inches high.

With the exposure of the other section and a bit of detective work, Geoff Rayner was able to work out that it was probably a Hurricane and was able to estimate its orientation under the mud. In late 1972, a couple of exploratory digs at selected places enabled him to locate the wing leading edge and part of the fuselage framework near the engine at a depth of four feet. It was definitely a Hurricane. The mud had proved to be an excellent preservative and damage was mainly due to impact and fire. Corrosion was minimal. Geoff estimated that the aircraft lay inverted at a shallow angle of about 30 degrees and consisted of the complete fuselage as far back as the rear of the cockpit, a third of the port wing and a stub of the starboard wing. The undercarriage was also intact.

It was obviously going to be quite a task to recover the remains intact and so the assistance of the local Air Training Corps was sought. In April 1973 it was all hands to the shovels and a hole up to twenty feet across revealed the airframe lying as expected. The top of the engine was located at a depth of five feet with its base nearer eight feet deep. The mud from the hole was used to make a parapet around it and keep out the high tide. As the site was flooded by spring tides but not at neaps, it was planned that the recovery would take place at a weekend coinciding with a neap tide. Work on enlarging the hole was undertaken during the week before and the parapet was increased just in case the tides were higher than predicted. All went smoothly until the actual lift of the remains from the hole. The airframe would only move so far as it was still attached to the engine which was found to be stuck fast. A second attempt was

made the following weekend, this time using heavier equipment, and was successful. Once the airframe had been lifted from the hole, fire damage was seen to be more severe than was at first apparent from the relatively intact undersurface revealed during the early stages of digging. The engine was recovered a few weeks later, intact except for a broken carburettor, complete with the stubs of the three wooden propeller blades.

The long process of cleaning off the mud — a very sticky and stubborn substance — then began. Identification was proved from the maker's name plate and various panel markings including pencil inscriptions on two of the expended cartridge case chutes. Pencil writing can also still be seen on some of the woodwork

Soon after the recovery, the RAF Museum at Hendon was contacted but they felt that they would be unable to do anything constructive with the remains for some considerable time. Meanwhile the cleaning continued. Regular contact was kept with the museum over the years and, when finally plans were announced for the formation of a Battle of Britain Museum, a natural home had been found. The remains were moved to Hendon in June 1977 for a concerted effort to finish the cleaning and reassemble the pieces for the museum opening in November 1978.

Today, displayed in its crashed state against a natural foreshore background, the remains of the aeroplane in which Pilot Officer Gerard Maffett died are the first exhibit to be seen by visitors as they enter the museum.

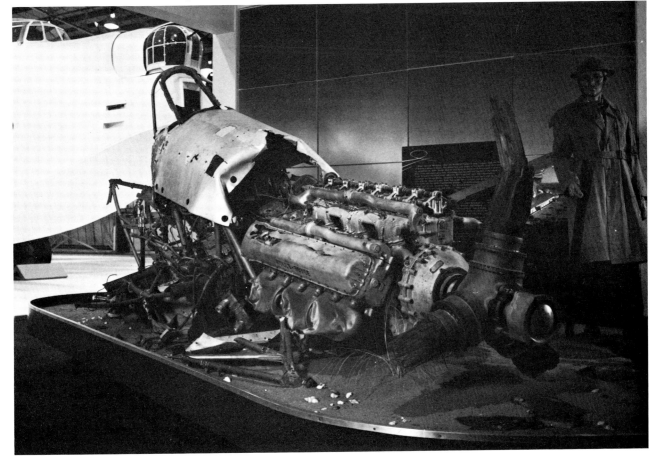

310 SQUADRON, DUXFORD

Hurricane P3159. Shot down by Bf 109s in attack on Do 215s over the Thames Estuary 1.30 p.m. Crashed and burned out south of Wennington church near Romford. Pilot Officer J. Sterbacek missing. Aircraft a write-off.
Undercarriage and six Browning machine-guns recovered by the Essex Historical Aircraft Society during excavations on August 13, 1978.

Hurricane P8814. Shot down by Bf 109s escorting Do 215s engaged over the Thames Estuary 1.30 p.m. Pilot Officer M. Kredba baled out unhurt. Aircraft a write-off.

Hurricane P3889. Damaged in wings and port undercarriage during combat over the Thames Estuary 1.35 p.m. Pilot Officer E. Fechtner unhurt. Aircraft damaged but repairable.

Hurricane V6621. Returned to base damaged in combat over the Thames Estuary 1.40 p.m. Pilot Officer J. M. Maly unhurt. Aircraft damaged but repairable.

501 SQUADRON, GRAVESEND

Hurricane V6540. Shot down in combat with Bf 109s over Gravesend. Crashed and burned out 1.15 p.m. Sergeant A. Glowacki baled out slightly injured. Aircraft a write-off.

Pilot Officer Jaroslav Sterbacek from Blansko, Czechoslovakia lost his life fighting with the Royal Air Force on the last day of August 1940. In the same month, but thirty-eight years later, the Essex Historical Aircraft Society recovered six of the eight .303in Browning machine guns from the crash site near Romford (Essex Historical Aircraft Society).

601 SQUADRON, DEBDEN

Hurricane P3263. Badly damaged in combat with Bf 109s engaged in attack on base 9.15 a.m. Crash-landed. Pilot Officer T. Grier unhurt. Aircraft damaged but repairable.

Hurricane P3735. Hit in gravity petrol tank following destruction of Bf 109 in combat over Gravesend 1.30 p.m. Crashed and burned out. Sergeant R. N. Taylor baled out unhurt. Aircraft a write-off.

Hurricane R4215. Shot down in combat with Bf 109s over the Thames Estuary 1.35 p.m. Believed crashed in sea. Flying Officer M. D. Doulton missing. Aircraft lost.

Hurricane N2602. Crashed and burned out following combat with Bf 109s off Gravesend 1.35 p.m. Sergeant A. W. Woolley baled out burned and admitted to hospital. Aircraft a write-off.

Hurricane V7260. Crashed and burned out following combat with Bf 109s over the Thames Estuary 1.40 p.m. Pilot Officer H. T. Gilbert baled out unhurt. Aircraft a write-off.

602 SQUADRON, WESTHAMPNETT

Spitfire L1040. Hit in glycol tank during action against Ju 88s and Bf 109s over Dungeness 6.30 p.m. Landed at Ford. Sergeant D. W. Elcome unhurt. Aircraft repairable.

603 SQUADRON, HORNCHURCH

Spitfire X4273. Believed victim of mid-air collision with Lt. Binder of I/JG3 during combat over London 6.30 p.m. Broke up over Woolwich and crashed near Repository Road. Flying Officer R. M. Waterston killed. Aircraft XT-K a write-off.
Complete leading edge of port wing recovered from Woolwich Arsenal dump by the Kent Battle of Britain Museum thought to be from this aircraft.

No. 14 Hereford Road, Wanstead, Essex — then and now. The engine of Spitfire X4271 fell in the front garden of No. 12. The only casualty was a dog although the road was cordoned off for two weeks while the wreckage was cleared.

Spitfire R6835. Hit in compressed air system by 20mm cannon shell during combat with Bf 109s over Southend 6.30 p.m. Returned to base. Flying Officer B. J. G. Carbury slightly wounded. Aircraft XT-W. damaged but repairable.

Spitfire X4271. Set alight during combat over the Thames 6.20 p.m. Crashed into No. 14 Hereford Road, Wanstead. Pilot Officer G. K. Gilroy baled out and attacked by crowds on landing. Admitted to King George Hospital, Ilford. Aircraft XT-N a write-off.

Sunday, September 1

1 SQUADRON, NORTHOLT

Hurricane P3276. Crashed following combat with Bf 109s east of Tonbridge 11.30 a.m. Flight Sergeant F. G. Berry killed. Aircraft damaged but repairable.

1 (RCAF) SQUADRON, NORTHOLT

Hurricane P3963. Shot down in action against Do 215s and Bf 110s 2.25 p.m. Crashed and burned out at Shipbourne. Flying Officer B. V. Kerwin baled out with burns. Aircraft a write-off.

Hurricane P3068. Returned to base with severe damage to tail unit following attack on Do 215s and Bf 110s over Maidstone area 2.30 p.m. Pilot Officer E. W. B. Beardmore unhurt. Aircraft damaged but repairable.

Hurricane R4171. Shot down in action against Do 215s escorted by Bf 110s 2.30 p.m. Crashed near West Malling. Flying Officer A. Yuile baled out unhurt. Aircraft a write-off.

54 SQUADRON, HORNCHURCH

Spitfire   Damaged in combat with He 111s and Bf 110s over Maidstone 11.00 a.m. Returned safely to base. Pilot Officer C. F. Gray unhurt. Aircraft repairable.

72 SQUADRON, CROYDON

Spitfire L1092. Forced-landed at West Malling on dead engine due to severe damage to cooling system caused by Bf 109 in combat over Beachy Head 11.30 a.m. Pilot Officer B. Douthwaite unhurt. Aircraft damaged but repairable.

Spitfire P9448. Reported shot down in combat with Bf 109s over Beachy Head 11.30 a.m. Flying Officer R. A. Thompson wounded. Aircraft a write-off.

Flight Sergeant Frederick George Berry, DFM, joined the Royal Air Force as an apprentice at the age of fifteen. After three years of training as a tradesman, he volunteered and was selected for pilot training. He joined No. 43 Squadron as a sergeant pilot in 1936 at the age of twenty-two and was later posted to No. 1 Squadron in 1938 with which unit he served with distinction throughout the campaign in France and the Battle of Britain until his death in action near Tonbridge on September 1, 1940 (Imperial War Museum). He was buried at Harrow New Cemetery, Middlesex.

Spitfire P9458. Shot down in combat with Bf 109s crashed and burned out on Elvey Farm, Pluckley 11.15 a.m. Flying Officer O. St. J. Pigg killed. Aircraft a write-off.

Official Casualty Records state that this officer was killed in action on September 2, 1940. However, our evidence for this entry on September 1 is based on two independent contemporary accounts as follows:
Ashford ARP Centre
September 1, 1940, message timed at 14.38 hours.
'RAF 'plane down (at) Elvey Farm, Pluckley at 11.15 hours. 'Plane burnt out, pilot's fate unknown.'
Local Casualty Clearance Officer's Records
'Ashes of Flying Officer O. St. John Pigg No. 39678 collected from Elvey Farm, Pluckley nr Ashford. Notified 28/9/40. Collected 2/10/40 — Pluckley. Coffined body despatched to Durham.'

Excavated by the Kent Battle of Britain Museum which recovered a shattered Rolls-Royce Merlin engine, pilot's seat and head armour and remains of parachute. Site later investigated by the London Air Museum and few remaining surface fragments collected.

Spitfire L1056. Severely damaged in combat with Bf 109 over Beachy Head. Landed undercarriage up at West Malling 11.40 a.m. Sergeant M. H. Pocock wounded in left leg and wrist admitted to hospital. Aircraft damaged but repairable.

Spitfire K9938. Returned to base tail unit severely damaged in combat with Bf 109s off Dungeness 1.50 p.m. Sergeant N. R. Norfolk unhurt. Aircraft repairable.

Flying Officer Oswald St. John Pigg.

Head armour and pieces of engine recovered from the orchard where Oswald Pigg crashed by the Kent Battle of Britain Museum. The 22-year-old Flying Officer, the son of a Northumberland vicar, is buried at Durham.

Spitfire X4034. Attacked by Bf 109 over Lympne 1.50 p.m. Returned to base with damage to oil system. Flight Lieutenant E. Graham unhurt. Aircraft repairable.

Spitfire X4109. Believed shot down in surprise attack by enemy fighters over Maidstone and crashed near Ham Street. Flying Officer D. F. B. Sheen baled out unhurt. Aircraft a write-off.

79 SQUADRON, BIGGIN HILL

Hurricane   Crashed on landing following combat with Bf 109 over base 2.45 p.m. Flight Lieutenant G. D. L. Haysom believed unhurt.

Hurricane   Severely damaged in combat with Bf 109s over base 2.45 p.m. Pilot Officer L. T. Bryant-Fenn wounded admitted to hospital.

Hurricane L2062. Crashed in Court Road Orchard near 'Highways' Chelsfield following combat with Bf 109s over base 2.45 p.m. Pilot Officer B. R. Noble wounded and admitted to hospital. Aircraft a write-off.
   According to the report from the salvage unit that visited this site on September 23, the pilot's body still remained in the wreckage. However there is no mention of his identity and only Sergeant J. H. M. Ellis of No. 85 Squadron remains unaccounted for on this date and he is known to have been flying P2673. Post-war, the site was excavated by the Halstead War Museum which is said to have discovered traces of human remains.

Glendon Bulmar Booth from Sydenham joined the RAFVR before the war and, on qualifying as an NCO fighter pilot, was posted to No. 85 Squadron on July 15, 1940, flying Hurricanes from Debden and Martlesham. August 19 brought a squadron move further south to Croydon. On September 1, Pat Woods-Scawen led his last patrol during which the squadron was cut to ribbons. Sergeant Glen Booth, the tall, quiet youth, jumped too late from his blazing Hurricane. Fire had spread to his parachute pack and canopy and, as the silk shrivelled and charred, he crashed to earth breaking his back and limbs. Admitted to Purley Hospital, he lingered in agony for five months. He was just twenty years old. His mother and father are now buried with him at Crystal Palace.

85 SQUADRON, CROYDON

Hurricane P5171. Returned to base damaged following combat with Bf 109s over Dover 11.45 a.m. Sergeant G. Goodman unhurt. Aircraft damaged but repairable.

Hurricane N2477. Forced-landed at Lympne due to loss of oil pressure and caught in bombing attack 1.45 p.m. Sergeant G. Allard unhurt. Aircraft VY-L damaged but repairable.

Hurricane V7343. Crashed at Oxted following combat with Bf 109s over Tunbridge Wells 2.15 p.m. Flying Officer A. V. Gowers baled out badly burned and wounded admitted to Caterham Hospital. Aircraft a write-off.

Hurricane L2071. Shot down by Bf 109s in combat over Tunbridge Wells area 2.15 p.m. crashed at Sanderstead. Sergeant G. B. Booth baled out with burns and parachute alight, further injured in heavy landing and admitted to Purley Hospital (died 7.2.41). Aircraft VY-O a write-off.

Hurricane P3150. Shot down in combat with Bf 109s during combat over Kenley area 2.15 p.m. Flying Officer P. P. Woods-Scawen baled out but killed due to paracahute failure. Body found 6.9.40 in the grounds of The Ivies, Kenley Lane. Aircraft a write-off.

Hurricane P2673. Failed to return following combat with Bf 109s over Kenley area 2.15 p.m. Sergeant J. H. M. Ellis missing. Aircraft VY-E lost.

Hurricane P3151. Landed at base undercarriage jammed up following combat with Bf 109s over Kenley 2.15 p.m. Pilot Officer A. G. Lewis unhurt. Aircraft VY-Y damaged but repairable.

253 SQUADRON, KENLEY

Hurricane P5185. Shot down in combat with Do 215s and Bf 110s over Dungeness 2.00 p.m. Believed crashed at Clapper Lane, Staplehurst. Pilot Officer J. K. G. Clifton killed. Aircraft a write-off.

Site excavated by Steve Vizard 1977 but nothing found to establish identity beyond dispute.

603 SQUADRON, HORNCHURCH

Spitfire L1020. Forced-landed during routine operational sortie 4.45 p.m. Cause not stated. Pilot Officer P. M. Cardell unhurt. Aircraft XT-L a write-off.

616 SQUADRON, KENLEY

Spitfire R6778. Hit in port wing and oil tank by cannon fire during attack on Do 215 over base 2.20 p.m. Pilot Officer L. H. Casson unhurt. Aircraft a write-off.

Monday, September 2

43 SQUADRON, TANGMERE

Hurricane P3903. Crash-landed at Bell Corner near Old Romney following combat with Bf 109s over east Kent 1.30 p.m. Pilot Officer D. A. R. G. LeR. Du Vivier admitted to casualty clearing station Benenden with leg wounds. Aircraft a write-off.

Despite ambiguous contemporary evidence, believed to be the Hurricane excavated by Brenzett Aeronautical Museum at this site on September 20, 1975. A complete recovery involving all major components but failing to discover any irrefutable evidence as to identity.

Granite memorial cross to John Clifton on his grave in St. John's Churchyard, Staplegrove, Somerset.

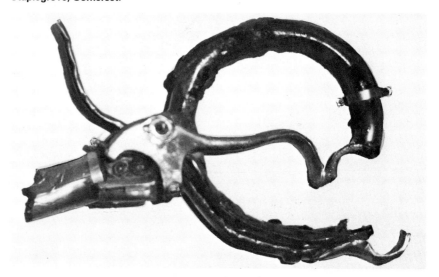

This control column, displayed by Brenzett Aeronautical Museum, was recovered in 1975 at Bell Corner, Romsey, although Peter Cornwell has still to be convinced that this is from Hurricane P3903 (Brenzett label the exhibit incorrectly as N7885).

Hurricane P3786. Shot down in combat with Bf 109s over east Kent 1.30 p.m. Crashed at Warehorne near Ashford. Flying Officer M. K. Carswell baled out injured admitted to Ashford Hospital. Aircraft a write-off.

Hurricane V7420. Set alight in combat with Bf 109s over east Kent and attempted to crash-land at Fryland near Ivychurch 1.30 p.m. Pilot Officer C. A. Woods-Scawen baled out too low and killed. Aircraft a write-off.

Complete surviving remains of aircraft recovered by the Brenzett Aeronautical Museum in 1977.

46 SQUADRON, STAPLEFORD

Hurricane P3067. Shot down in combat over the Thames Estuary 5.30 p.m. Pilot Officer J. C. L. D. Bailey killed. Aircraft a write-off.

Hurricane P3597. Forced-landed at Borden near Sittingbourne 5.36 p.m. following combat over Thames Estuary. Flight Lieutenant A. C. Rabagliati unhurt. Aircraft damaged but repairable.

72 SQUADRON, CROYDON

Spitfire   Returned to base damaged following attack on Do 17s and fighter escort over Herne Bay 12.45 p.m. Pilot Officer B. Douthwaite unhurt. Aircraft repairable.

Spitfire X4105. Damaged in combat with Bf 110s over Herne Bay 12.45 p.m. Returned safely to base. Squadron Leader A. R. Collins slightly wounded. Aircraft damaged but repairable.

Spitfire K9938. Crashed and burned out on Garrington Farm near Bekesbourne emergency landing ground 1.00 p.m. following combat over Herne Bay. Sergeant N. R. Norfolk unhurt. Aircraft a write-off.

Spitfire X4241. Believed shot down in combat with enemy aircraft over Lympne 4.10 p.m. Flight Lieutenant E. Graham unhurt. Aircraft DW-S a write-off.

Spitfire K9840. Severely damaged during combat south of Dungeness 4.15 p.m. and crashed on return to Hawkinge. Wing Commander R. B. Lees wounded. Aircraft damaged but repairable.

Spitfire R6806. Severely damaged in combat over the Thames Estuary 5.30 p.m. but returned to base. Squadron Leader A. R. Collins wounded. Aircraft DW-N a write-off.

Having crashed less than a mile north-east of their museum building, it was only natural that the Brenzett Aeronautical Group would investigate the site of Hurricane V7420 flown by Pilot Officer Charles 'Tony' Woods-Scawen — the second of the two brothers to die in September 1940. Following the successful recovery of much of his aircraft, John Elgar-Whinney, a member of the group, constructed these very unusual and highly-prized trophies from pieces from the engine for presentation to outstanding ROC posts and crews by No. 1 Group, Royal Observer Corps.

111 SQUADRON, DEBDEN

Hurricane P3875. Shot down in combat with Bf 109s over the Thames Estuary 12.50 p.m. Sergeant W. L. Dymond missing. Aircraft a write-off.

Hurricane R7400. Landed at Castle Camps satellite aerodrome with damage to cockpit sliding hood after combat with Bf 109s over the Thames Estuary 12.50 p.m. Pilot Officer P. J. Simpson unhurt. Aircraft repairable.

Hurricane   . Landed at Rochford slightly damaged by Bf 109 over the Thames Estuary 1.00 p.m. Pilot Officer J. R. Ritchie unhurt. Aircraft repairable.

Hurricane R4228. Forced-landed at Detling following attack on He 111s over Thames Estuary and caught in bombing attack at 1.00 p.m. Flight Lieutenant H. S. Giddings unhurt. Aircraft damaged but repairable.

222 SQUADRON, HORNCHURCH

Spitfire X4280. Forced-landed back at base following head-on attack by Bf 110 5.45 p.m. Flight Lieutenant A. I. Robinson wounded in leg. Aircraft damaged but repairable.

Spitfire K9799. Returned to base damaged following combat 5.45 p.m. Pilot unhurt. Aircraft damaged but repairable.

Spitfire   . Damaged in combat with enemy aircraft over base 5.45 p.m. Pilot unhurt. Aircraft repairable.

236 SQUADRON, ST. EVAL

Blenheim T1947. Damaged in night-flying accident. Landed across flare path 11.15 p.m. Pilot Officer Salter unhurt. Aircraft damaged but repairable.

TO THE EVERLASTING MEMORY OF
DAVID HARRY W. HANSON
FIGHTER PILOT
KILLED IN THE BATTLE OF
BRITAIN 3 SEPTEMBER 1940
AGED 22

249 SQUADRON, NORTH WEALD

Hurricane V7352. Crash-landed near Chartham following combat with enemy fighters over Rochester 8.00 a.m. Pilot Officer R. E. N. E. Wynn wounded. Aircraft damaged but repairable.

Hurricane P2988. Shot down in flames by Bf 110 of 5/ZG26 in combat over Rochester 8.00 a.m. Crashed on Eccles Recreation Ground near Rainham. Pilot Officer H. J. S. Beazley unhurt baled out over Gillingham landing in Boxleywood. Aircraft a write-off.

Hurricane P3384. Hit by return fire from Bf 110 of II/ZG26 engaged over Rochester 8.00 a.m. Crash-landed at Meopham. Pilot Officer P. R. F. Burton unhurt. Aircraft damaged but repairable.

253 SQUADRON, KENLEY

Hurricane P2946. Shot down in combat with Bf 109s over Thanet 8.15 a.m. Believed that which crashed at Longport, Crundale. Sergeant J. Metham slightly injured. Aircraft a write-off.

Hurricane V6640. Crashed near Rye following action over the Sussex coast 1.00 p.m. Flying Officer D. B. Bell-Salter baled out wounded and injured in heavy landing due to damaged parachute. Admitted to Rye Hospital. Aircraft a write-off.

303 SQUADRON, NORTHOLT

Hurricane R4178. Damaged in combat with Bf 109s over the Channel and forced-landed near Elvington near Dover 6.05 p.m. Pilot Officer M. Feric unhurt. Aircraft damaged but repairable.

501 SQUADRON, GRAVESEND

Hurricane   . Damaged in combat with enemy aircraft over base 8.05 a.m. Sergeant W. B. Henn injured. Aircraft damaged but repairable.

Hurricane V7230. Forced landed at Horton Priory, Sellindge after combat with enemy aircraft over north Kent 8.25 a.m. Pilot Officer S. Skalski injured. Aircraft repairable.

Hurricane L1578. Failed to return from combat over Dungeness 4.30 p.m. Flying Officer A. T. Rose-Price missing. Aircraft lost.

Hurricane V7234. Shot down during combat south of Ashford 4.30 p.m. Sergeant H. C. Adams believed unhurt. Aircraft damaged but repairable.

603 SQUADRON, HORNCHURCH

Spitfire X4250. Returned to base cockpit hood shattered in combat over Hawkinge 8.15 a.m. Sergeant J. Stokoe unhurt. Aircraft XT-X repairable.

Spitfire R6752. Landed undercarriage up due to damage sustained in combat with Bf 109s over the Thames Estuary 1.35 p.m. Pilot Officer J. G. E. Haig unhurt. Aircraft XT-E. damaged but repairable.

Spitfire N3056. Shot down in combat with enemy fighters over Maidstone 5.25 p.m. Sergeant J. Stokoe baled out wounded admitted to Leeds Castle Hospital. Aircraft XT-B a write-off.

All Saints Church Mappleton, Yorkshire. Just beside the church door lies the grave of Flying Officer David Hanson of nearby Rolston. A plaque inside the church commemorates his memory

616 SQUADRON, KENLEY

Spitfire X4181. Engine set alight in attack by Bf 110 over the Maidstone area and crashed on Brook Farm, Capel, near Tonbridge 4.35 p.m. Flight Lieutenant D. E. Gillam baled out unhurt. Aircraft a write-off.
Site excavated by Steve Vizard 1976.

Douglas Hogg was the only one to die in the tragic encounter on September 3 when three No. 25 Squadron Blenheims were set upon by Hurricanes mistaking them for Ju 88s attacking North Weald.

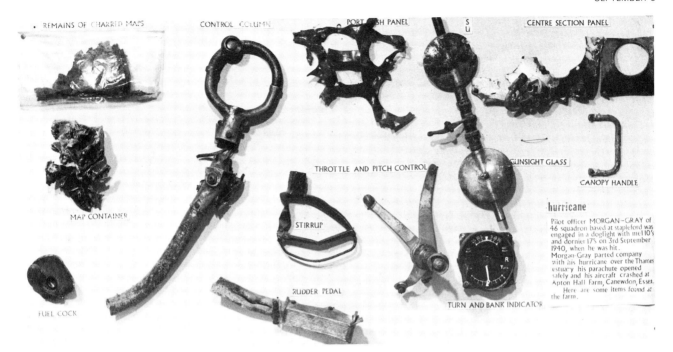

REMAINS OF CHARRED MAPS · CONTROL COLUMN · PORT DASH PANEL · CENTRE SECTION PANEL

MAP CONTAINER

THROTTLE AND PITCH CONTROL

STIRRUP

FUEL COCK

RUDDER PEDAL

GUNSIGHT GLASS

CANOPY HANDLE

TURN AND BANK INDICATOR

hurricane

Pilot officer MORGAN-GRAY of 46 squadron based at stapleford was engaged in a dogfight with me110's and dornier 17's on 3rd September 1940, when he was hit. Morgan-Gray parted company with his hurricane over the Thames estuary his parachute opened safely and his aircraft crashed at Apton Hall Farm, Canewdon, Essex. Here are some items found at the farm.

Tuesday, September 3

Above: **In 1973 the London Air Museum carried out a complete excavation of the crash site of Hurricane P3063, abandoned by Pilot Officer Morgan-Gray over Rochford.** *Below:* **The control column and head armour (Tony Graves).**

1 SQUADRON, NORTHOLT

Hurricane P3782. Crashed at Parkhouse Farm, Chart Sutton 11.30 a.m. Exact circumstances not stated. Pilot Officer R. H. Shaw missing. Aircraft a write-off.

Hurricane P3044. Failed to return from squadron patrol 11.30 a.m. cause unknown. Flight Lieutenant H. B. L. Hillcoat missing. Aircraft lost.

17 SQUADRON, DEBDEN

Hurricane R4224. Forced-landed near North Weald following attack by Bf 110 10.20 a.m. Squadron Leader A. G. Miller unhurt. Aircraft damaged but repairable.

Hurricane P3892. Landed at Castle Camps satellite aerodrome radiator damaged in combat with enemy aircraft 10.30 a.m. Pilot Officer D. H. Wissler unhurt. Aircraft repairable.

Hurricane P3673. Shot down in flames by enemy fighters. Crashed and burned out near Handleys Dairy Farm, Ingrave, Essex 10.30 a.m. Sergeant D. Fopp baled out burned landing at Presseys Farm, Hutton and admitted to hospital. Aircraft VY-D a write-off.
Paddock excavated by the London Air Museum and many minor components recovered.

Hurricane P3539. Shot down following destruction of Do 17 and crashed on Brickhouse Farm, Foulness 10.55 a.m. Flying Officer D. H. W. Hanson baled out at 100ft and killed. Aircraft damaged but repairable.

25 SQUADRON, NORTH WEALD

Blenheim L1512. Shot down over base in attack by RAF Hurricane and crashed near Greensted Green 11.15 a.m. Pilot Officer D. W. Hogg killed, Sergeant E. Powell baled out unhurt. Aircraft a write-off.

Blenheim L8650. Forced-landed at Hatfield Heath following attack by RAF Hurricane over North Weald 11.15 a.m. Pilot Officer E. Cassidy unhurt. Aircraft damaged but repairable.

Blenheim L1409. Returned to base damaged in attack by RAF Hurricane. Squadron Leader W. W. Loxton unhurt. Aircraft damaged but repairable.

46 SQUADRON, STAPLEFORD

Hurricane P3114. Hit by Bf 109 during attack on Ju 88 over Rochford 10.35 a.m. Returned to base heavily damaged. Pilot Officer P. W. Le Fevre unhurt. Aircraft damaged but repairable.

Hurricane P3063. Set alight during attack on Do 215 over Rochford and crashed at Apton Hall Farm, Canewdon 10.30 a.m. Pilot Officer H. Morgan-Gray baled out wounded. Aircraft a write-off.
Major recovery by the London Air Museum in 1973. Complete Rolls-Royce Merlin Engine excavated together with the propeller boss, reduction gear, instrument panel and control column, head armour, gun-sight, pilot's maps, tail wheel and undercarriage legs.

Hurricane P3064. Failed to return from combat over the Essex coast. Believed that crashed in Redwood Creek, River Crouch 10.35 a.m. Sergeant G. H. Edworthy missing. Aircraft lost.
Machine-gun access panel and other small pieces recovered with great difficulty from deep mud by the London Air Museum in 1974.

Hurricane . Landed at Debden with damage sustained in combat over the Essex coast 10.35 a.m. Flight Sergeant E. E. Williams slightly wounded. Aircraft damaged but repairable.

Hurricane P3024. Shot down in combat over Canewdon and crashed into the sea-wall at Beckney Farm, south Fambridge 10.45 a.m. Sergeant E. Bloor baled out with slight burns on face landing at Scaldhurst Farm, Canewdon. Aircraft a write-off.
Pieces recovered from alongside the sea-wall by the London Air Museum in 1973.

THE UNKNOWN BATTLE OF BRITAIN PILOT'S MEMORIAL GARDEN AT CHART SUTTON NEAR MAIDSTONE, KENT

Parkhouse Farm lies some six miles south-east of Maidstone on a southward facing slope overlooking the Weald of Kent. It was here that on September 3, 1940 a Hurricane crashed at the edge of an apple orchard near a small stream. Fragmentary remains of the pilot were removed for burial and, according to the notes of the village policeman, they were interred at Sittingbourne. As the engine and cockpit had plunged deep into the Wealden clay beyond recovery, the surface was tidied and the site left. Local people remember that one of the machine guns lay against a tree nearby for several days afterwards and that creaking noises were heard from the hot buried wreckage underground. Several local people remember the plane coming over and crashing but, as another Spitfire also crashed nearby, it is now difficult to separate their recollections of the two crashes. The crash was so severe that no identification of the pilot or the aircraft serial was possible.

Reference to published records of losses on that day makes it possible to hazard a guess as to the pilot's identity but this is not sufficient proof to convince the Ministry of Defence. Additionally the authorities have made it clear that as remains were removed for burial the site must not be called a grave.

An old couple living in a farm cottage nearby (now derelict) marked the site with a rough wooden cross and planted flowers including rose bushes. They informally tended this garden until their death — probably during the late 1950s. The site was then neglected and became overgrown until 1970 when Headcorn Royal Air Forces Association branch was formed. Our founder members heard the story and approached the farmer who gave them permission to clear the undergrowth and restore the garden.

The work was done and, on the Sunday preceding Battle of Britain Sunday in September 1970, a Memorial Service was held in Chart Sutton church followed by a Service of Dedication at the garden. Wing Commander Scholes, the Commanding Officer of RAF Biggin Hill, attended with members of his

REPORT TO SQUADRON LEADER GOODMAN
R.A.F. DEPOT. 29-9-40.

HURRICANE P 3782.   Parkhouse Farm, Chart, Sutton.

I located site of crash as above, inspected crater made by aircraft with P.C. Whyman No: **265**, Kent County Constabulary, stationed at Sutton Vallence. He informed me that this aircraft was removed by an R.A.F. Squad with a long, low, loader on Saturday the 26th September. This P.C. found billeting accommodation for the Squad. The site has been completely cleared.

Signed ___*A V Nicholls*___

Although the Ministry of Defence cannot positively identify the aircraft at Chart Sutton, either by serial number or occupant, the above contemporary report would seem to give the pilot as Robert Shaw of No. 1 Squadron.

The war graves plot at Sittingbourne and Milton Cemetery. Documentary evidence indicates that one of the graves of the two unknown airmen (second from left at the back or extreme left in front) contains the fragmentary remains of Pilot Officer Shaw.

unit, the Mayor of Maidstone and RAFA members and friends. Canon Alec Goodrich, a former RAF chaplain, officiated. That first Sunday it poured with rain but the service has been held in perfect weather on the same Sunday ever since. Over the years, support and attendances have steadily grown and, in most years, we have had a fly-past by a Hurricane or a Spitfire from the Battle of Britain Memorial Flight. In 1977 we had one of each aircraft and they stayed overhead for almost ten minutes.

In 1977 we had filled the local church to capacity so we were delighted when the headmaster of Sutton Valence School, a large public school in the next village, offered us their chapel for the next Memorial Service. In September 1978 the Service moved there, the

Central Band of the RAF attended and we held a parade on the square nearby. Groups taking part included RAF Biggin Hill, No. 1 Group, Royal Observer Corps, Maidstone, Ashford ATC, the RAFA and Royal British Legion. We were honoured to receive Dame Anna Neagle, DBE, as our most distinguished guest. The congregation approached 400 and a fleet of coaches moved everyone to Chart Sutton for the wreath laying ceremony and fly-past then back to the school for tea in the dining hall.

In 1979 the event ran on similar lines. Air Chief-Marshal Sir David Evans, AOC-in-C Strike Command, flew to Headcorn to attend, and The Queen's Colour Squadron, RAF, provided a full ceremonial Guard of Honour and the lining parties at the chapel and at the garden. The Service for the 40th Anniversary of the Battle of Britain will be held on September 7, 1980.

ANDREW CLARKE
Chairman RAFA Headcorn Branch.

Trumpeters of the Central Band of the RAF sound 'The Last Post' at the service held at Parkhouse Farm on Sunday, September 9, 1979 (Geoffrey Cardew).

222 SQUADRON, HORNCHURCH

Spitfire L1010. Abandoned over Burnham having developed a glycol leak during routine patrol 7.30 a.m. Crashed at Lower Raypits, Canewdon. Sergeant R. B. Johnson baled out slightly injured. Aircraft a write-off.

Major recovery by the London Air Museum in 1973. Complete Rolls-Royce Merlin engine excavated together with propeller boss all three blades still attached, instrument panel, control column, rudder bar pedals, maps, first-aid kit, radio mast and tail wheel. Rudder bar pedal subsequently presented to the pilot.

Right: The complete prop assembly (metal on L-series Spitfires) from Sergeant Reg Johnson's aircraft being raised at Canewdon under the instruction of Tony Graves. *Below:* Tony indicates the position of the crash site on one of the maps recovered from the wreckage. *Bottom left:* The seat was virtually intact complete with cushion and Sutton harness. *Bottom right:* The propeller and other parts when displayed at the London Air Museum now closed (Tony Graves).

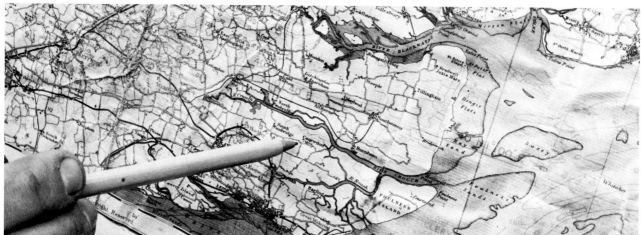

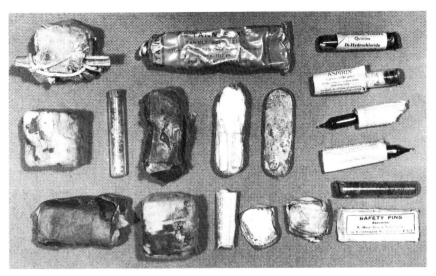

249 SQUADRON, NORTH WEALD

Hurricane V6635. Damaged by AA fire during routine patrol over Dover and crashed on landing at base 3.55 p.m. Sergeant P. A. Rowell slightly concussed. Aircraft repairable.

253 SQUADRON, KENLEY

Hurricane P3610. Crashed into a wood at Nonnington during squadron sortie 7.00 a.m. Exact cause not stated. Pilot Officer L. C. Murch unhurt. Aircraft a write-off.

257 SQUADRON, DEBDEN

Hurricane P3518. Shot down in combat with enemy fighters over Ingatestone 10.45 a.m. Crashed at Lodge Farm, Galleywood, Essex. Pilot Officer C. A. Bon Seigneur baled out but fell dead at the Grove, Ingatestone. Aircraft a write-off.
Crash-site excavated by the Essex Historical Aircraft Society in 1974. Rolls-Royce Merlin engine recovered together with propeller, cockpit instruments and remains of airframe.

Hurricane L1585. Shot down by enemy fighters and crashed and burned out 10.45 a.m. Reputedly fell near 'Brook and Parsonage'. Pilot Officer D. W. Hunt baled out severely burned admitted to Billericay Hospital. Aircraft a write-off.

Above: Sergeant Johnson's first-aid kit recovered in mint condition.

Above: **The Essex Historical Aircraft Society excavating the crash site of Hurricane P3518 flown by Pilot Officer Camille Robespierre Bon Seigneur (Essex Historical Aircraft Society). He baled out but his parachute failed to open and he was buried in the front row of the war graves plot at Saffron Walden** *(below).*

Hurricane P3704. Damaged by enemy fighters in combat over the Chelmsford area 10.45 a.m. Pilot Officer K. C. Gundry unhurt. Aircraft damaged but repairable.

Hurricane P3705. Slightly damaged in engagement over Chelmsford 10.45 a.m. Sergeant R. C. Nutter slightly wounded. Aircraft repairable.

303 SQUADRON, NORTHOLT

Hurricane R2688. Engine damaged by Bf 109 during attack on another Bf 109 over the Channel. Landed at Woodchurch near Tenterden 11.20 a.m. Sergeant S. Wojtowicz slightly injured. Aircraft damaged but repairable.

Hurricane V7246. Slightly damaged by Bf 109 over Dungeness 11.20 a.m. Returned safely to base. Flying Officer Z. Henneberg unhurt. Aircraft repairable.

310 SQUADRON, DUXFORD

Hurricane P8811. Shot down during attack on Bf 110s west of Chelmsford 10.00 a.m. Reputed to have crashed on Rookes Farm. Sergeant J. Kopriva baled out unhurt. Aircraft a write-off.

603 SQUADRON, HORNCHURCH

Spitfire X4277. Shot down in flames into the Channel by Hptmn. Bode of II/JG26 during combat off Margate 10.04 a.m. Pilot Officer R. H. Hillary baled out grievously burnt rescued by Margate life-boat and admitted to hospital. Aircraft XT-M lost.

Spitfire X4185. Abandoned over Creeksea Church, Burnham due to damage suffered in attack by Hptmn. Bode of II/JG26 in combat over the Channel off Margate 10.08 a.m. Flying Officer D. Stewart-Clarke baled out wounded admitted to Chelmsford Hospital. Aircraft XT-Z a write-off.

616 SQUADRON, KENLEY

Spitfire R6963. Forced-landed at base circumstances not known. Pilot unhurt. Aircraft damaged but repairable.

Wednesday, September 4

25 SQUADRON, NORTH WEALD

Blenheim Hit by AA during attack on enemy aircraft on night interception patrol 3.00 a.m. Tail unit badly damaged. Pilot Officer B. J. Rofe, Sergeant J. B. McCormack both unhurt. Aircraft ZK-J.

43 SQUADRON, TANGMERE

Hurricane L1836. Damaged in combat with Bf 110s off Sussex coast 1.30 p.m. Forced-landed at Ford following mid-air fire caused by damaged glycol tank. Pilot Officer Van den Hove d'Ertsenryck unhurt. Aircraft damaged but repairable.

46 SQUADRON, STAPLEFORD

Hurricane P3052. Shot down in combat with enemy fighters 1.15 p.m. crashed and burned out on the railway line at Rectory Road, Hawkwell. Flying Officer R. P. Plummer baled out landing at Stambridge with extensive burns to both legs. Admitted to Rochford Hospital (died 14.9.40). Aircraft a write-off.

Hurricane P3066. Shot down by Bf 109s in action over Rochford 1.15 p.m. Pilot Officer C. F. Ambrose baled out unhurt. Aircraft a write-off.

Richard Plummer, buried at Haywards Heath, was seriously burned in his crash on September 4 and died in hospital ten days later.

Hurricane P3031. Overturned landing on one wheel at base following combat over Rochford 1.25 p.m. Flying Officer F. Austin unhurt. Aircraft damaged but repairable.

Hurricane V7201. Forced-landed at Chigborough Farm, Goldhanger Road, Heybridge with undercarriage damaged by Bf 109 in combat over Rochford 1.40 p.m. Pilot Officer R. H. Barber admitted to Epping Hospital with fractured jaw and neck. Aircraft repairable.

66 SQUADRON, KENLEY

Spitfire P9316. Shot down in combat over the Thames Estuary 9.50 a.m. crashed near Howe Green Farm, Purleigh. Pilot Officer A. N. R. L. Appleford baled out slightly wounded. Aircraft a write-off.

Spitfire N3048. Shot down in combat over Ashford and crashed near Mersham 10.00 a.m. Sergeant A. D. Smith baled out seriously wounded admitted to No. 7 Casualty Clearing Station at Benenden (died 6.9.40). Aircraft a write-off.
Locality investigated by the Historic Aircraft Archaeologist Group 1978 and some surface fragments found. Exact crash site remains undiscovered.

Spitfire N3044. Forced-landed at Great Cowbridge Farm, near Billericay following combat over the Thames Estuary 10.07 a.m. Flight Lieutenant F. P. R. Dunworth slightly wounded. Aircraft damaged but repairable.

Spitfire N3032. Badly damaged by Bf 109s during combat over Dover 1.30 p.m. Returned to base. Pilot Officer P. J. C. King unhurt. Aircraft damaged but repairable.

Spitfire X4052. Damaged in combat with Bf 109s over Thanet and forced-landed outside Canterbury 1.35 p.m. Flight Lieutenant G. P. Christie slightly wounded. Aircraft damaged but repairable.

Spitfire R6689. Shot down in action with Bf 109s over Ashford 1.40 p.m. Believed crashed on crossroads at Chequertree Farm. Pilot Officer C. A. Cooke baled out slightly wounded, landed at Ham Street. Aircraft a write-off.
Site investigated by Steve Vizard

72 SQUADRON, CROYDON

Spitfire R6971. Set alight during combat with Bf 110s and crashed on Culvers Farm, Hartfield 1.05 p.m. Pilot Officer E. E. Males baled out unhurt landing at Holtye. Aircraft a write-off.
Many small components and fragments excavated by the Wealden Aviation Archaeological Group in August 1979.

Spitfire P9460. Believed shot down in combat with Bf 110s over the Tenterden area 1.15 p.m. Pilot Officer R. D. Elliott unhurt. Aircraft a write-off.

Spitfire N3229. Severely damaged in head-on attack by Bf 110 over Tenterden 1.20 p.m. Returned to base. Pilot Officer D. F. Holland unhurt. Aircraft damaged but repairable.

73 SQUADRON, CHURCH FENTON

Hurricane P3456. Forced-landed near Cambridge during routine flight from Duxford 8.00 p.m. cause not stated. Sergeant P. O'Byrne unhurt. Aircraft damaged but repairable.

Badge from the extreme tip of the prop boss, a much sought after relic, recovered by the Wealden Group from Spitfire R6971 at Hartfield.

79 SQUADRON, BIGGIN HILL

Hurricane P3676. Severely damaged by Bf 110s in action over base 1.40 p.m. Crashed at Surbiton. Sergeant J. Wright wounded admitted to hospital (died 5.9.40). Aircraft a write-off.

111 SQUADRON, CROYDON

Hurricane Z2315. Forced-landed at Catts Green Farm, Ewhurst with damage to oil system following combat with Bf 109s over the Channel 9.00 a.m. Flight Lieutenant H. S. Giddings unhurt. Aircraft JU-E damaged but repairable.

Hurricane R4172. Shot down in combat with Bf 109s 9.15 a.m. Believed crashed in the Channel five miles east of Folkestone. Flight Lieutenant D. C. Bruce missing. Aircraft lost.

Hurricane Z2309. Presumed crashed in the Channel five miles east of Folkestone during combat with Bf 109s 9.15 a.m. Pilot Officer J. Macinski baled out but missing. Aircraft lost.
  Reputed to be the aircraft recovered from Dene Farm, West Stourmouth by the Brenzett Aeronautical Museum in 1976.

Hurricane Z2308. Returned to base damaged in combat with Bf 109s off Folkestone 9.20 a.m. Flying Officer B. H. Bowring unhurt. Aircraft damaged but repairable.

151 SQUADRON, DIGBY

Hurricane V7406. Flying accident at base, cause not stated. Crashed and burned out. Pilot Officer R. Ambrose killed. Aircraft a write-off.

152 SQUADRON, WARMWELL

Spitfire R6909. Believed shot down by return fire from Do 17 engaged twenty-five miles off Bognor. Crashed in the sea. Sergeant J. K. Barker baled out but killed. Aircraft lost.

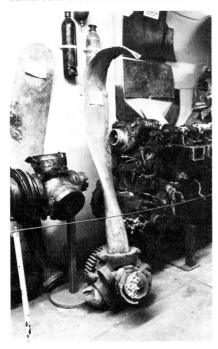

Propeller recovered by the Ashford and Tenterden Group from another aircraft (Spitfire X4278 No. 222 Squadron, Flying Officer Cutts) which crashed at the beginning of September at Chart Sutton with a missing pilot. The recovery of this aircraft on Amberfield Farm adds weight to the argument that Pilot Officer Shaw's aircraft crashed on Parkhouse Farm.

Sergeant John Barker of No. 152 Squadron is buried at Etaples.

Sergeant John Wright buried in Dumbartonshire.

John William Ramshaw was born in Beverley, Yorkshire and attended Spencer Council School and Beverley Grammar School. In 1934 he commenced employment as a clerk in Hull with the Halifax Building Society. Imbued with a love of flying, he took private lessons before joining the RAFVR and, with the outbreak of war, was absorbed into the ranks of the RAF. As a sergeant pilot he was subsequently posted to No. 222 Squadron at Kirton-in-Lindsey. On August 29, 1940 the squadron moved south to Hornchurch and flew into action the following day. On September 4, he was shot down near Yalding in Kent. Rescuers plucked him from the wreckage of his Spitfire but he died before reaching hospital. John Ramshaw had lasted just five days in the front line. On Thursday, September 12, a large number of the inhabitants of Beverley attended his funeral in Queensgate Cemetery to pay their respects. The coffin, draped with the Union Jack, was carried by six sergeants of the Royal Air Force followed by a contingent of airmen. One of those present was Irene Williams, his young fiancee.

222 SQUADRON, HORNCHURCH

Spitfire P9378. Believed victim of AA during attack on Bf 109s. Crashed at Boughton Monchelsea 1.20 p.m. Pilot Officer J. M. V. Carpenter blown out of the cockpit landed safely with slight wounds. Aircraft a write-off.

Spitfire X4278. Shot down by Bf 109s in combat over Maidstone 1.30 p.m. Crashed and burned out on Amberfield Farm, Chart Sutton. Flying Officer J. W. Cutts missing. Aircraft ZD-D a write-off.
   Major recovery by the Ashford and Tenterden Recovery Group 1972. Complete remains, propeller boss and blades displayed at Brenzett Aeronautical Museum. Personal effects in Vizard collection.

Spitfire K9962. Crashed at Collier Street near Yalding during combat with Bf 109s 1.35 p.m. Sergeant J. W. Ramshaw severely injured, dead on arrival at West Kent Hospital. Aircraft a write-off.

234 SQUADRON, MIDDLE WALLOP

Spitfire X4182. Engine damaged in combat with Bf 110s over the Sussex coast 1.50 p.m. Returned to base. Sergeant Z. Olenski unhurt. Aircraft repairable.

253 SQUADRON, KENLEY

Hurricane V6638. Shot down in combat over base. Crashed in Nork Way, Banstead 10.00 a.m. Flying Officer A. A. G. Trueman killed. Aircraft a write-off.

264 SQUADRON, KIRTON-IN-LINDSEY

Defiant N1628. Crashed on take-off. Flying Officer D. K. C. O'Malley, Sergeant L. A. W. Rasmussen both killed. Aircraft a write-off.

601 SQUADRON, TANGMERE

Hurricane R4214. Forced-landed near Goring with damage sustained in combat with Bf 110s over Worthing 1.45 p.m. Flying Officer J. S. Jankiewicz wounded. Aircraft damaged but repairable.

602 SQUADRON, WESTHAMPNETT

Spitfire   . Damaged in combat over Beachy Head 1.10 p.m. Returned safely to base. Pilot unhurt. Aircraft repairable.

Spitfire K9955. Returned to base severely damaged following combat over Beachy Head 1.10 p.m. Pilot unhurt. Aircraft damaged but repairable.

603 SQUADRON, HORNCHURCH

Spitfire X4263. Forced-landed at Elstead near Ashford due to engine failure. Sergeant A. R. Sarre unhurt. Aircraft damaged but repairable.

The crew of the Defiant N1628 of No. 264 Squadron which crashed taking off at Kirton-in-Lindsey aerodrome are buried in the same 'station' cemetery. *Left:* Flying Officer Derek O'Malley of Henley-on-Thames and *right* Sergeant Laurie Rasmussen from Auckland, New Zealand.

Squadron Leader Philip Pinkham, AFC, lies in St. Andrew's Churchyard, Kingsbury in north London.

Thursday, September 5

17 SQUADRON, DEBDEN

Hurricane P2994. Returned to base aileron and rudder badly damaged in combat over Gravesend 3.20 p.m. Sergeant L. H. Bartlett unhurt. Aircraft repairable.

19 SQUADRON, DUXFORD

Spitfire N3286. Returned to base severely damaged following combat with Bf 109s over Hornchurch 10.10 a.m. Pilot Officer W. J. Lawson unhurt. Aircraft damaged but repairable.

Spitfire P9422. Shot down by Bf 109 in combat over the Thames Estuary 10.15 a.m. Believed crashed in Whitehorse Wood, Birling, Kent. Squadron Leader P. C. Pinkham killed. Aircraft a write-off.

Spitfire P9391. Damaged by Bf 109s in action over Hornchurch 10.15 a.m. Returned safely to base. Pilot Officer E. Burgoyne unhurt. Aircraft repairable.

41 SQUADRON, MANSTON

Spitfire N3098. Damaged in combat over the Thames Estuary 10.20 a.m. Forced-landed at Stanford-le-Hope. Sergeant R. A. Carr-Lewty unhurt. Aircraft damaged but repairable.

Spitfire R6635. Collided with P9428 during combat with Do 17s and escort of Bf 109s over the Thames Estuary 3.25 p.m. Crashed and burned out on Bonvills Farm, North Benfleet. Flight Lieutenant J. T. Webster killed. Aircraft a write-off.

Spitfire X4021. Severely damaged in attack on Do 17s over Maidstone 3.30 p.m. Pilot Officer R. W. Wallens badly wounded in leg admitted to hospital. Aircraft a write-off.

Spitfire P9428. Believed to have collided head-on with another Spitfire during attack on Do 17s over the Thames Estuary 3.30 p.m. Squadron Leader H. R. L. Hood missing. Aircraft lost.

Spitfire N3162. Returned to base damaged by Bf 109 during destruction of He 111 over the Thames Estuary 3.30 p.m. Pilot Officer E. S. Lock slightly wounded in left leg. Aircraft damaged but repairable.

Spitfire R6885. Shot down in combat over the Thames Estuary 3.35 p.m. Believed crashed in sea. Flying Officer A. D. J. Lovell baled out unhurt. Aircraft a write-off.

64 SQUADRON, LECONFIELD

Spitfire P9563. Crashed near Hartington during routine section patrol 8.20 a.m. Cause not stated. Sergeant D. E. Lloyd unhurt. Aircraft damaged but repairable.

66 SQUADRON, KENLEY

Spitfire N3043. Damaged in combat with Bf 109 and forced-landed at base minus an aileron 4.00 p.m. Pilot Officer H. R. Allen unhurt. Aircraft LZ-X damaged but repairable.

Spitfire N3060. Shot down in combat with Bf 109s over Medway 4.00 p.m. Flying Officer P. J. C. King baled out but killed due to parachute failure. Aircraft a write-off.

Spitfire K9944. Shot down in combat with Bf 109s 4.05 p.m. Flight Lieutenant G. P. Christie wounded admitted to RN Hospital, Gillingham. Aircraft a write-off.

Flying Officer Peter King is buried in the overgrown churchyard at Farnborough, Warwickshire.

Spitfire N3029. Forced-landed with damage sustained in combat with Bf 109s over north Kent 4.05 p.m. Pilot Officer R. J. Mathers unhurt. Aircraft damaged but repairable.

72 SQUADRON, CROYDON

Spitfire X4013. Shot down by Bf 109 and crashed into Covert Wood, Elham 2.25 p.m. Pilot Officer D. C. Winter killed attempting to abandon aircraft too low. Aircraft lost.

Spitfire N3093. Crashed into Elham Park Wood during combat with Bf 109s 2.25 p.m. Sergeant M. Gray killed. Aircraft lost.

Spitfire X4034. Shot down in flames by Bf 109 during combat over Hawkinge. Crashed at Wildage Farm, Bladbean 2.25 p.m. Flying Officer D. F. B. Sheen baled out wounded. Aircraft a write-off.

Cockpit instruments in Steve Vizard collection.

'To the Glorious Memory of our dearly loved son Sergeant Pilot Malcolm Gray, 72 Fighter Squadron (Spitfire) RAF, killed in action in Defence of Britain, September 5, 1940 aged 20 years Faithful unto Death'.

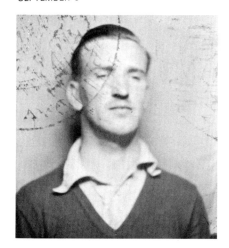

Above: **White House Farm, North Fambridge, Essex, September 5, 1940, 3.30 p.m. The smouldering crater marks the impact point of the Hurricane flown by Sergeant Alex McNay** *(above left). Below:* **Thirty-nine years later the scene is unchanged except for the members of the London Air Museum opening up the crater (Tony Graves).** *Left:* **A map was found inscribed 'McNay' and pieces of the pilot's harness** *(below).* **Although Alex McNay, born in Glasgow, is listed as missing, Tony Graves states that 'no tangible remains of the pilot were discovered'.**

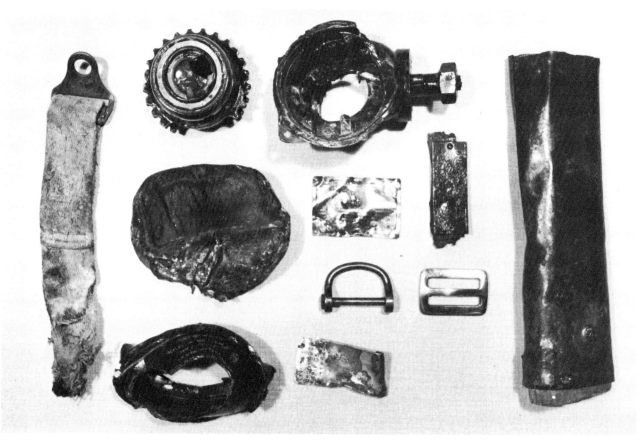

73 SQUADRON, DEBDEN

Hurricane P3110. Shot down in surprise attack during interception of Ju 88. Crashed near Steels Farm, West Hanningfield 3.25 p.m. Pilot Officer R. D. Rutter baled out and admitted to Billericay Hospital with bullet in ankle. Aircraft TP-G a write-off.

Excavations by the Essex Historical Aircraft Society revealed Rolls-Royce Merlin engine and fragments of airframe identified as being from the area of cockpit.

Hurricane P3224. Crashed and burned out at White House Farm, North Fambridge following combat over Burnham 3.30 p.m. Sergeant A. L. McNay missing. Aircraft TP-L a write-off.

Site identified and excavated by London Air Museum in September 1979. Shattered remnants of burned-out Rolls-Royce Merlin engine recovered together with head armour and tail wheel. Traces of burned parachute silk found and compressed maps in remains of map storage box discovered bearing legend 'McNAY'. Remains of airframe collected by the Essex Historical Aircraft Society.

Hurricane P3204. Believed that crashed south-east of Nevendon Hall following combat over Burnham 3.30 p.m. Flight Lieutenant R. E. Lovett baled out unhurt. Aircraft TP-H a write-off.

Hurricane P2975. Armour plate pierced during action over Burnham 3.30 p.m. Returned safely to base. Sergeant G. W. Garton unhurt. Aircraft damaged but repairable.

Hurricane P2984. Returned to base badly damaged following combat over Burnham 3.30 p.m. Sergeant A. E. Marshall unhurt. Aircraft TP-A damaged but repairable.

Hurricane P2815. Forced-landed at Wallasea Yacht Club 3.45 p.m. with damage sustained in combat over Burnham. Squadron Leader M. W. S. Robinson unhurt. Aircraft TP-B damaged but repairable.

79 SQUADRON, BIGGIN HILL

Hurricane P5207. Damaged in attack on Do 17s over base 10.40 a.m. Returned to base. Flight Lieutenant G. D. L. Haysom unhurt. Aircraft damaged but repairable.

The Essex Historical Aircraft Society excavated No. 73 Squadron Hurricane P3110 flown by Pilot Officer Rutter.

111 SQUADRON, CROYDON

Hurricane   . Damaged in combat with Bf 109s 10.00 a.m. Flight Lieutenant H. S. Giddings unhurt. Aircraft repairable.

Hurricane 314. Hit in port wing by cannon fire during combat with Bf 109s over the Kent coast 10.10 a.m. Flying Officer B. H. Bowring unhurt. Aircraft repairable.

Hurricane 312. Forced-landed near Lullingstone Castle following combat with Bf 109s over north Kent 10.10 a.m. Sergeant F. H. Silk slightly wounded. Aircraft repairable.

222 SQUADRON, HORNCHURCH

Spitfire X4057. Hit by AA during attack on Bf 109 over Dover. Crashed and burned out near Pineham 3.00 p.m. Sergeant D. J. Chipping baled out wounded. Aircraft a write-off.

249 SQUADRON, NORTH WEALD

Hurricane V6625. Shot down by Bf 109 during combat over the Thames Estuary 3.30 p.m. Flight Lieutenant R. A. Barton unhurt. Aircraft a write-off.

253 SQUADRON, KENLEY

Hurricane P5181. Forced-landed at Charing cause not stated. Pilot unhurt believed to have been Pilot Officer W. M. C. Samolinski. Aircraft a write-off.

303 SQUADRON, NORTHOLT

Hurricane R4175. Returned to base damaged following action against Bf 109s over Rochford 3.15 p.m. Sergeant J. Frantisek unhurt. Aircraft repairable.

Hurricane P2985. Shot down by Bf 109 in combat over Gillingham 3.45 p.m. Aircraft crashed at Bonvills Farm, North Benfleet. Pilot Officer W. Lapkowski baled out with broken leg and burns and landed at Rectory Road, Hawkwell. Admitted to Rochford Hospital. Aircraft a write-off.

Major recovery by the Essex Aviation Group on September 9, 1978. Excavations to a depth of twenty feet revealed a complete compressed fuselage and the Rolls-Royce Merlin engine.

Tail wheel and carbon dioxide bottle with clearly readable inscription recovered by the Essex Aviation Group from the crash site of Hurricane P2985 of the Polish No. 303 Squadron abandoned by Pilot Officer Lapkowski just north of Southend.

501 SQUADRON, GRAVESEND

Hurricane V6644. Shot down by Bf 109s in combat over Canterbury 10.00 a.m. Pilot Officer S. Skalski injured admitted to Herne Bay Hospital. Aircraft a write-off.

603 SQUADRON, HORNCHURCH

Spitfire X4261. Failed to return following combat with Do 17s and Bf 109s escort over Biggin Hill 10.00 a.m. Possibly that which crashed on Buckmans Green Farm, Smarden. Flight Lieutenant F. W. Rushmer missing. Aircraft lost.

Wreckage of a Spitfire recovered from this site by the London Air Museum in 1970. Date of incident documented by legend '5th September 40' etched in a wooden beam of a nearby barn. Excavations revealed shattered Rolls-Royce Merlin engine, two propeller blades, one still attached to the propeller boss, remains of instrument panel and one undercarriage leg. Also discovered were a silver half-hunter pocket watch, box of 'Swan Vestas' matches and partial remnants of scorched parachute silk but nothing tangible to establish beyond question the identity of the aircraft.

Spitfire X4264. Believed shot down at Marden by Bf 109s during action over the Biggin Hill area 10.00 a.m. Pilot Officer W. P. H. Rafter wounded admitted to West Kent Hospital, Maidstone. Aircraft a write-off.

Intact propeller boss with two blades still attached recovered by Lashenden Air Warfare Museum.

Friday, September 6

1 SQUADRON, NORTHOLT

Hurricane P2686. Shot down south of Penshurst by return fire from Bf 110s 9.30 a.m. Pilot Officer G. E. Goodman baled out with sprained shoulder. Aircraft a write-off.

Possibly the site investigated by Steve Vizard at Brownings Farm, Chiddingstone Causeway. Luxor goggle frames amongst the various items recovered.

43 SQUADRON, TANGMERE

Hurricane V7257. Returned to base damaged by Bf 109s during attack on Ju 88s over the Channel off Dungeness 9.30 a.m. Flight Lieutenant R. C. Reynell unhurt. Aircraft repairable.

Hurricane V6542. Crashed at base following combat with Bf 109s off Dungeness 9.50 a.m. Flight Lieutenant T. F. Dalton-Morgan wounded in knee. Aircraft damaged but repairable.

64 SQUADRON, LECONFIELD

Spitfire K9903. Crashed during routine patrol flight 8.30 p.m. cause not stated. Sergeant H. W. Charnock believed unhurt. Aircraft a write-off.

72 SQUADRON, CROYDON

Spitfire N3070. Shot down in head-on attack on Bf 109 over Maidstone crashed and burned out at Wanshurst Green 1.15 p.m. Pilot Officer R. D. Elliott baled out unhurt. Aircraft a write-off.

Spitfire   . Returned to base damaged in combat with Bf 109s over Maidstone 1.15 p.m. Pilot unhurt. Aircraft repairable.

Right: **The Merlin from Pilot Officer Rafter's Spitfire on display at the Lashenden Air Warfare Museum.**

Flight Lieutenant Frederick Rushmer was posted missing in action when he failed to return to Hornchurch on September 5 and no trace of either him or his aircraft was ever found. In 1970, the London Air Museum excavated a Spitfire crash site at Smarden and personal effects were recovered *(right)* **together with much of the aircraft (Tony Graves).**

Above: **Steve Vizard believes these Luxor goggle frames recovered from Penshurst once belonged to Pilot Officer Goodman although Peter Cornwell is reluctant to positively identify them as such without better evidence.**

253 SQUADRON, KENLEY

Hurricane P3032. Crashed at Kingsnorth during routine squadron patrol 9.15 a.m. Cause unknown. Acting Squadron Leader W. P. Cambridge baled out but killed. Aircraft a write-off.

73 SQUADRON, DEBDEN

Hurricane P2875. Shot down in combat with enemy fighters over the Thames Estuary 9.20 a.m. Pilot Officer H. W. Eliot baled out wounded and admitted to Twickenhurst Hospital with burns. Aircraft a write-off.

111 SQUADRON, CROYDON

Hurricane P3425. Slightly damaged in attack on Ju 88s over Kenley 9.00 a.m. Flying Officer B. H. Bowring unhurt. Aircraft repairable.

Hurricane L1892. Crash-landed following combat with Ju 88s over Kenley 9.10 a.m. Sergeant L. J. Tweed injured. Aircraft damaged but repairable.

Hurricane V7386. Attacked by Bf 109s over the Thames Estuary 6.10 p.m. Forced-landed near Dartford. Flying Officer B. H. Bowring slightly wounded. Aircraft damaged but repairable.

Pilot's silk scarf, photographs and German 7.92mm bullet removed from his arm on this day presented to the Kent Battle of Britain Museum.

234 SQUADRON, MIDDLE WALLOP

Spitfire X4036. Shot down in combat with Bf 109s and crashed on Howbourne Farm. Hadlow Down 9.10 a.m. Pilot Officer W. H. G. Gordon killed. Aircraft AZ-G a write-off.

Crash-site investigated by the Wealden Aviation Archaeological Group 1974 but no wreckage found.

Spitfire X4183. Shot down in flames by Bf 109s and exploded over Quickbourne Lane, Northiam 9.20 a.m. Sergeant W. H. Hornby baled out with facial injuries. Aircraft a write-off.

Spitfire N3279. Damaged by Bf 109 over Beachy Head and crashed on landing back at base 10.15 a.m. Pilot Officer J. Zurakowski unhurt. Aircraft damaged but repairable.

Spitfire N3061. Hit by return fire from Ju 88 engaged off Portland 1.45 p.m. Crashed in the sea. Pilot Officer P. W. Horton baled out slightly injured picked up by RN launch and landed at Weymouth. Aircraft lost.

249 SQUADRON, NORTH WEALD

Hurricane R4229. Shot down in combat with Bf 109s over Maidstone 8.45 a.m. Squadron Leader J. Grandy baled out slightly wounded and admitted to Maidstone Hospital. Aircraft a write-off.

Pilot Officer William Gordon *(left)* **was born in Aberdeen, his family later moving to Banffshire. On September 6, 1940 his squadron was heavily engaged by Bf 109s over the Sussex coastline, losing three Spitfires. Bill Gordon was the only fatality and his body was taken back to Mortlach Churchyard** *above* **(A. Saunders).**

Flight Lieutenant William Percival Cambridge *(top right)* **from Caversham, Berkshire was born in 1912 in India where his father held a government engineering post. Educated at Bromsgrove Public School, Worcestershire, he later took up a career in the Indian sugar industry. An intense interest in aviation led him to join the Royal Air Force in 1936. He was an all-round sportsman and was a popular and enthusiastic member of the Berkshire Wanderers Rugby Football Club. On the outbreak of war, two important events took place in his life: the first was that he got married and the second was his posting to No. 253 Squadron on its formation in October 1939. With the advent of the Battle of Britain, No. 253 flying Hurricanes was stationed at Turnhouse near Edinburgh moving south to Kirton-in-Lindsey for a short spell in July before returning to Scotland. Bill Cambridge was now senior flight commander and one of the squadron's four trained night-flying pilots. No. 253 was posted to Kenley on August 29. Over the next two days they were well and truly blooded, losing both their CO, Squadron Leader Starr, and their super-numary, Squadron Leader Tom Gleave, on August 31. Bill Cambridge was appointed acting CO and thereafter led the squadron into battle daily until September 6. He was killed after only nine days in action. After his funeral service on September 12 at St. Peter's Caversham, he was laid to rest at Henley Road Cemetery at Eye and Dunsden, Berkshire. On his death his acting rank was ignored and he is officially listed as a Flight Lieutenant.**

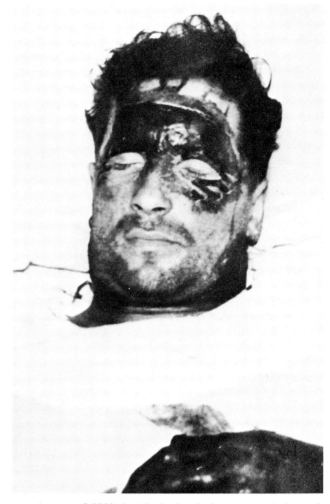

Surrounded by highly inflammable aviation spirit, fighter pilots suffered horrific burns if trapped in their confined cockpits. A graphic example occurred on September 6 when the Hurricane of Squadron Leader Krasnodebski (above) of No. 303 Squadron was set alight in a combat over Dartford, Kent. He took to his parachute at 8,000ft but had already been severely burned. Archibald McIndoe had set up a burns treatment unit at East Grinstead and his plastic surgery on his 'guinea pigs' became internationally renowned, enabling many airmen to return to a normal life (Polish Institute).

303 SQUADRON, NORTHOLT

Hurricane V7290. Shot down by return fire from He 111 9.15 a.m. crashed at Fletchers Farm, Pembury. Sergeant S. Karubin slightly injured admitted to Farnborough Hospital. Aircraft a write-off.

Major recovery by Halstead War Museum which holds complete remains including the Rolls-Royce Merlin engine.

Hurricane V7284. Severely damaged by return fire from Do 215. Forced-landed at Biggin Hill minus starboard aileron 9.20 a.m. Squadron Leader R. G. Kellett slightly wounded in leg. Aircraft damaged but repairable.

Hurricane R4179. Shot down in combat with Bf 109s over west Kent 9.20 a.m. Crash-landed and wrecked hitting an embankment. Flight Lieutenant A. S. Forbes slightly injured. Aircraft damaged but repairable.

Hurricane P3974. Shot down in combat with Bf 109s. Crashed near HT cables between Hextable and Wilmington 9.20 a.m. Squadron Leader Z. Krasnodebski baled out badly burned admitted to Farnborough Hospital. Aircraft a write-off.

Site investigated by the London Air Museum. Many small fragments litter the area.

Hurricane R4175. Returned to base damaged following combat with Bf 109s over west Kent 9.25 a.m. Sergeant J. Frantisek unhurt. Aircraft repairable.

Hurricane R2685. Forced-landed at base following engine fire at 11,000ft during routine patrol 1.55 p.m. Flight Lieutenant J. A. Kent unhurt. Aircraft repairable.

Hurricane P3089. Shot down by Bf 109 during solo attack on Bf 110 whilst flying on patrol with No. 1 Squadron. Crash-landed near Lenham 6.20 p.m. Flying Officer W. Januszewicz unhurt. Aircraft repairable.

501 SQUADRON, GRAVESEND

Hurricane V6612. Shot down in combat over Ashford 9.00 a.m. Crashed at Clavertye, near Elham. Pilot Officer H. C. Adams killed. Aircraft a write-off.

Hurricane V6646. Shot down in combat over Ashford 9.00 a.m. Crashed into Long Beech Wood, Charing. Sergeant O. V. Houghton killed. Aircraft a write-off.

Hurricane P3516. Failed to return following combat over the Ashford area 9.00 a.m. Believed crashed near Kempton Manor, Hothfield. Sergeant G. W. Pearson missing. Aircraft lost.

There is a strong possibility that Sergeant Pearson's body was recovered but was buried as an 'Unknown Airman' at St. Stephen's Churchyard, Lympne on September 10, 1940.

Nineteen-year-old Sergeant Oliver Houghton (No. 501 Squadron) from Coventry now buried in All Saints Churchyard at Allesley.

Hugh Charles Adams from Oxted, Surrey joined the RAFVR about 1938 and, on the outbreak of war, was called into the Royal Air Force where he was passed through the various stages of pilot training emerging as a sergeant pilot in July 1940. On the 17th of the month he was posted to No. 501 'County of Gloucester' Squadron at Middle Wallop as a replacement and flew with them for the remainder of his short life. On September 2 he was shot down in combat for the first time but escaped unhurt bringing his damaged machine back to Gravesend. He then received his commission as Pilot Officer but, on September 6, was shot down again and killed in action. His grave can be found in the rather neglected churchyard of St. Peter's Tandridge.

Possibly the best Merlin engine ever recovered is that from Willie Rhodes-Moorhouse's Hurricane displayed at Chilham Castle.

Carl Davis was born of American parents in South Africa and held a US passport. When he was thirteen he came to Britain to attend Sherbourne School going on to Trinity College, Cambridge before spending a couple of years at McGill University, Montreal. (He was the brother-in-law of Flight Lieutenant Sir Archibald Hope who also fought in the Battle of Britain.) Carl Davis certainly was not a South African as stated in several other publications as prior to January 1, 1949, all citizens of the Dominions held British citizenship. Although extensive enquiries have been made, it has not proved possible to obtain confirmation from the American authorities whether or not he renounced his American citizenship when he was 21 (in 1932) as did his sister. Flight Lieutenant Davis, DFC, was shot down and killed on September 6 and was buried in St. Mary's Churchyard, Storrington, Sussex.

601 SQUADRON, TANGMERE

Hurricane V6647. Shot down by Bf 109 during action over Mayfield 9.30 a.m. Crashed at Kippings Cross near Pembury. Pilot Officer H. T. Gilbert baled out wounded. Aircraft a write-off.

Hurricane P3382. Shot down by Bf 109s in combat over Mayfield 9.30 a.m. Abandoned over Sutton Valence. Flying Officer J. Topolnicki baled out wounded admitted to Leeds Castle Hospital. Aircraft a write-off.

Hurricane P3363. Shot down in combat with Bf 109s 9.30 a.m. Crashed inverted and burned out in back garden of cottage at Matfield, Brenchley, near Tunbridge Wells. Flight Lieutenant C. R. Davis killed. Aircraft UF-W a write-off.
Surviving wreckage displayed at the Kent Battle of Britain Museum includes the voltage regulator cover and parachute shroud lines.

Hurricane P8818. Shot down by Bf 109s in combat over Tunbridge Wells 9.30 a.m. Crashed near High Brooms Viaduct, Southborough. Flight Lieutenant W. H Rhodes-Moorhouse killed. Aircraft a write-off.
Major recovery by the Kent Battle of Britain Museum 1976. Beautiful intact Rolls-Royce Merlin engine with propeller boss and supercharger excavated together with radiator, tail wheel, cockpit components, remains of Sutton harness and pilot's wrist-watch.

602 SQUADRON, WESTHAMPNETT

Spitfire R6834. Returned to base damaged following combat with Bf 109s over Hailsham 1.02 p.m. Pilot Officer T. G. F. Ritchie slightly wounded in legs admitted to Chichester Hospital. Aircraft damaged but repairable.

Spitfire N3227. Shot down in combat with Bf 109s over Hailsham. Crashed and burned out at Pelsham Farm, Peasmarsh 1.30 p.m. Sergeant G. A. Whipps baled out unhurt. Aircraft a write-off.
Some small fragments excavated by the Wealden Aviation Archaeological Group in 1975.

Spitfire R6601. Returned to base damaged in combat with Bf 109s over Hailsham 1.20 p.m. Pilot Officer H. W. Moody unhurt. Aircraft damaged but repairable.

Spitfire R6600. Damaged in combat with Bf 109s over Hailsham 1.20 p.m. Returned safely to base. Flying Officer P. J. Ferguson unhurt. Aircraft damaged but repairable.

603 SQUADRON, HORNCHURCH

Spitfire X4260. Brought down by Hptmn. von Bonin of I/JG54 in sporadic engagement over the Channel off Manston 1.30 p.m. Landed in France. Sergeant J. R. Caister captured. Aircraft XT-D lost.

Saturday, September 7

41 SQUADRON, HORNCHURCH

Spitfire N3266. Forced-landed between Confield Tye and Tinsleys Farm at West Hanningfield following action over southern Essex 5.45 p.m. Sergeant R. C. Ford unhurt. Aircraft damaged but repairable.

Spitfire P9430. Crashed and partly burned out at Leonard Drive, Drakes Farm, Rayleigh 6.08 p.m. after combat over base. Sergeant J. McAdam unhurt. Aircraft a write-off.
Site investigated by the Essex Aviation Group but no traces of wreckage now remain.

Spitfire X4318. Undercarriage wrecked in forced-landing in Kemsleys Field, Star Lane, Brickfields, Great Wakering 6.20 p.m. following combat with enemy aircraft over base. Pilot Officer O. B. Morrogh-Ryan unhurt. Aircraft damaged but repairable.

43 SQUADRON, TANGMERE

Hurricane V7309. Crashed and burned out at Babylon Farm, Sutton Valence following combat over the Ashford area. Sergeant A. L. M. Deller baled out unhurt. Aircraft a write-off.

Hurricane V6641. Shot down by Bf 109 in combat over south London 4.45 p.m. Crashed in Purley High School grounds. Squadron Leader C. B. Hull killed. Aircraft a write-off.
Crash-site investigated by London Air Museum and some small fragments including exploded .303 ammunition discovered on surface.

Hurricane V7257. Crashed at Crown Point, Blackheath during combat with Bf 109s over south London 4.45 p.m. Flight Lieutenant R. C. Reynell baled out wounded and fell dead near 'Greyladies'. Aircraft a write-off.
Crash-site investigated by the London Air Museum in January 1977. Few scattered surface fragments collected.

Flight Lieutenant Richard Carew Reynell, Australian by birth, was a serving officer in the Royal Air Force before the war and a pilot with one of the premier fighter squadrons of the RAF — No. 43. As a member of their Fury aerobatic team, his flying thrilled thousands during the peacetime displays both at home and abroad. His flying skills eventually led him to Hawker Aircraft Limited as a test pilot but on August 26, 1940 he returned to No. 43 at Tangmere as a flight commander where he renewed his long friendship with Caesar Hull — a friendship that was to end tragically in the deaths of both men on September 7 over London. Richard Reynell was buried in an obscure corner of Brookwood Cemetery which lies on the opposite side of the Woking-Pirbright road to the Military Cemetery. It took us a considerable time to locate the grave which lies in thick undergrowth about eighty yards due south of the south-eastern end of St. Bartholomew's Avenue. Here our author Peter Cornwell checks the details.

Tony Graves looks down at the spot on Blackheath where Dick Reynell's Hurricane crashed. The engine had broken free and landed on the convent in the background. Reynell came down about 100 yards behind the cameraman (Mercury Photos).

The operational life of Flying Officer Donald Sanders lasted a mere four days. On Monday, September 2, 1940, No. 54 Squadron was withdrawn from Hornchurch to the Yorkshire base of Catterick for rest and re-mustering. The following day the 21-year-old pilot was posted in as a replacement, fresh from his Operational Training Unit. On September 7, while undergoing further training, his Spitfire crashed from a low altitude, killing him instantly. He was buried in Catterick Cemetery where there are, altogether, forty-two burials from the 1939-45 war. Here also lies Pilot Officer Peter Hurst killed on October 23 and Sergeant George Shepperd who died on September 30.

54 SQUADRON, CATTERICK

Spitfire P9560. Crashed from low altitude during training flight 12.05 p.m. Exact cause unknown. Flying Officer D. J. Sanders killed. Aircraft a write-off.

Spitfire R6901. Failed to return from operational sortie over the Flamborough area 2.30 p.m. Believed lost bearings due to R/T failure and crashed in sea. Pilot Officer W. Krepski missing. Aircraft lost.

66 SQUADRON, KENLEY

Spitfire X4321. Forced-landed at Hawkinge following combat 12.30 p.m. Pilot Officer C. A. W. Bodie unhurt. Aircraft LZ-F damaged but repairable.

Spitfire N3225. Damaged in combat with enemy aircraft and forced-landed 12.35 p.m. Pilot Officer I. J. A. Cruickshanks believed unhurt. Aircraft damaged but repairable.

Many of the aircraft shot down during the battle and listed in these pages lived to fight another day. A typical example is X4321 from No. 66 Squadron *(below)* which crash-landed near Barnhurst Lane, Hawkinge on September 7 and was back in service by December 19, 1940.

HURRICANE 111 SQDN.

SGT. T. J. WALLACE D.F.M.

Above: The extensive collection of serial number and instruction plates from Hurricane P3025 flown by Sergeant Wallace of No. 111 Squadron on September 7 at Brenzett.

Flight Lieutenant Reginald Eric Lovett, DFC, a regular officer with No. 73 Squadron, went with the unit to France at the outbreak of war where, due to a series of misfortunes, he acquired the nickname 'Unlucky' Lovett. On May 10, 1940, he came very close to death when he was shot down and trapped in his blazing Hurricane. He managed to crash-land but had to be rescued from the cockpit by which time his hands were virtually useless. Rushed to hospital, he miraculously survived and was flown back to the UK where, after weeks of further treatment, he returned to his squadron, then resting at Church Fenton. On Thursday, September 5, No. 73 Squadron was posted south to Debden to reinforce the hard pressed No. 11 Group squadrons. Within four hours of their arrival, they were thrown into action over the mouth of the Thames losing four Hurricanes with one pilot killed. Ray Lovett baled out and survived. Two days later, during the German onslaught on London, 'Unlucky' Lovett was shot down for the last time. They buried him in Hendon Cemetery — close by his parents home at Golders Green (Imperial War Museum).

72 SQUADRON, CROYDON

Spitfire R7022. Forced-landed at Eynsford following action against He 111s and Bf 109s over the Thames Estuary 6.15 p.m. Sergeant J. White slightly injured in leg and forehead. Aircraft damaged but repairable.

Spitfire X4254. Badly damaged by Bf 109 in combat over the Thames Estuary 6.20 p.m. Crash-landed at Biggin Hill. Flying Officer T. A. F. Elsdon severely injured in knee and shoulder. Aircraft damaged but repairable.

73 SQUADRON, DEBDEN

Hurricane P3234. Shot down in combat with enemy aircraft and crashed on Fritze Farm, Stock near Billericay 5.00 p.m. Flight Lieutenant R. E. Lovett killed. Aircraft TP-E a write-off.

Hurricane P3863. Severely damaged by Bf 110 and forced-landed near Dammerwick Farm, Burnham Marshes following engine failure 5.20 p.m. Sergeant A. E. Marshall slightly injured. Aircraft TP-C damaged but repairable.

Orpington Cemetery in Star Lane at St. Mary Cray was the one used by Biggin Hill. In the front row *above* lies Squadron Leader Joseph O'Brien, DFC, of No. 234 Squadron, killed on September 7, Flight Sergeant Charles Sydney and Flight Lieutenant James Paterson, both of No. 92 Squadron and both shot down on September 27. Here also are fifteen of the thirty-nine personnel killed in the bombing of Biggin on August 30 including one of the WAAFS, ACW1 Edna Button, a Deaconess of the Methodist Church of New Zealand, who came from Tasmania.

Flight Lieutenant Paterson Clarence Hughes, DFC, hailed from Haberfield, New South Wales. In 1935, at the age of seventeen, he joined the Royal Australian Air Force as a cadet at Point Cook and, two years later, applied for and received a commission in the Royal Air Force. He served with Nos. 64 and 247 Squadrons until November 1939 when he was transferred to No. 234 Squadron at Leconfield, East Yorkshire. In Hull he met and courted Kathleen Brodrick and, just before the unit moved to its new base at St. Eval, Cornwall, they were married. On September 7, 1940, one month after his wedding, Pat Hughes was killed when the Dornier he was attacking blew up with such force that it wrecked his Spitfire. In twenty-four days of intensive combat he had accounted for fifteen enemy aircraft and shared in the destruction of others. He was awarded the DFC posthumously. The photo *above* was taken on a picnic with his fiancee outside Leconfield on Sunday, June 9, 1940.

Pat Hughes was very fond of his dog 'Flying Officer Butch' and he took him everywhere with him including flying. His aircraft crash site was first excavated by the Halstead War Museum but, regretably, the curator Ken Anscombe, has refused to assist us with information or photographs of any of their digs. Pieces from this Spitfire are held in other collections and Steve Vizard kindly allowed us to photograph relics *below* in his private Tonbridge Aviation Museum.

On September 13, after a service in St. James', Sutton-in-Holderness, Hull, he was laid to rest in the churchyard. The inscription on his headstone is common to so many of those airmen killed in the battle: 'Never in the field of human conflict was so much owed, by so many to so few'.

79 SQUADRON, BIGGIN HILL

Hurricane   . Landed at West Malling with damage sustained in combat over base 5.45 p.m. Pilot Officer D. W. A. Stones slightly wounded.

111 SQUADRON, CROYDON

Hurricane P3025. Severely damaged by Bf 109 over the Channel 6.30 p.m. Glided back to English coast and abandoned south of Ashford. Crashed on Gammons Farm, Newchurch. Sergeant T. J. Wallace baled out slightly wounded. Aircraft a write-off.

Site excavated on August 24, 1974 by the Brenzett Aeronautical Museum. Rolls-Royce Merlin engine, cockpit instruments and controls and many interesting components recovered.

222 SQUADRON, HORNCHURCH

Spitfire X4089. Glycol system damaged in combat over Rochester 5.45 p.m. Returned safely to base. Flying Officer B. Van Mentz unhurt. Aircraft repairable.

Spitfire N3169. Forced-landed in Sutton Valence following action south of Maidstone 6.25 p.m. Sergeant J. H. H. Burgess unhurt. Aircraft damaged but repairable.

234 SQUADRON, MIDDLE WALLOP

Spitfire P9466. Shot down in combat with enemy aircraft over St. Mary Cray 6.25 p.m. Crashed near Biggin Hill. Squadron Leader J. S. O'Brien killed. Aircraft a write-off.

Spitfire X4009. Crashed at Darks Farm, Bessels Green during combat with enemy aircraft 6.30 p.m. Flight Lieutenant P. C. Hughes killed. Aircraft a write-off.

Site excavated by Halstead War Museum in 1969. Many pieces including the tail wheel and instrument panel recovered from below fifteen feet of clay. Base of propeller, mass balance weight and gun firing button in Kent Battle of Britain Museum. Maps and undercarriage warning horn in the Vizard collection.

Pilot Officer John Benzie, a Canadian with No. 242 Squadron, went missing on the afternoon of September 7. After a five-week search, the London Air Museum traced the suspected crash site. These were some of the items found. Remains of the pilot were handed to the local police but their whereabouts are now unknown.

242 SQUADRON, COLTISHALL

Hurricane P3061. Returned to base severely damaged by Bf 109 in combat over the Thames Estuary 5.00 p.m. Squadron Leader D. R. S. Bader unhurt. Aircraft damaged but repairable.

Hurricane P3207. Slightly damaged in combat with Bf 109s over the Thames Estuary 5.00 p.m. Returned safely to base. Sub-Lieutenant R. J. Cork slightly injured. Aircraft repairable.

Hurricane P2962. Failed to return from combat over the Thames Estuary 5.00 p.m. Pilot Officer J. Benzie missing. Aircraft lost.

Aircraft excavated near the railway line at Blackacre, Theydon Bois by the London Air Museum believed to be this machine. Pilot's remains recovered and subject to inconclusive inquest held at Epping. Complete Rolls-Royce engine with propeller boss, reduction gear, cockpit instruments and controls including the control column, armour plate, Sutton harness and parachute excavated together with tail wheel and both undercarriage legs. Subsequent local display of relics raised £200 for the Royal Air Force Benevolent Fund.

Hurricane P3715. Undercarriage wrecked in forced-landing on old aerodrome at Stow-St.Maries due to damaged radiator following combat over Thames Estuary 5.25 p.m. Pilot Officer D. W. Crowley-Milling unhurt. Aircraft LE-M damaged but repairable.

249 SQUADRON, NORTH WEALD

Hurricane R4114. Shot down in combat with Bf 109s over Maidstone 5.00 p.m. Crashed at Hollingbourne. Pilot Officer R. D. S. Fleming killed. Aircraft a write-off.

Hurricane V6574. Crashed at Eastchurch following combat with Bf 109s over Maidstone area 5.00 p.m. Sergeant R. Smithson wounded. Aircraft repairable.

Hurricane R4230. Abandoned over Maidstone following combat with Bf 109s and believed crashed at Eastling 5.05 p.m. Sergeant F. W. G. Killingback baled out wounded. Aircraft a write-off.

Hurricane V6610. Hit in engine by return fire from He 111 engaged over Maidstone. Crash-landed at Potter Street, Harlow 5.05 p.m. Pilot Officer R. G. A. Barclay unhurt. Aircraft damaged but repairable.

Hurricane P3594. Caught fire during attack on He 111 pursued over the Channel 5.20 p.m. Flying Officer P. H. V. Wells baled out wounded and admitted to Canterbury Hospital. Aircraft a write-off.

Hurricane N2440. Believed hit by AA fire during attack on Do 17s 6.00 p.m. Sergeant J. M. B. Beard baled out unhurt. Aircraft a write-off.

257 SQUADRON, DEBDEN

Hurricane P3049. Shot down in combat over the Thames Estuary 5.30 p.m. Crashed at Elmley, Spitend Point, Sheppey. Flight Lieutenant H. R. A. Beresford missing. Aircraft DT-D a write-off.

Site identified by the Kent Battle of Britain Museum in 1971 and partial excavation revealed 'P3049' serial painted on some of the fragments recovered. Complete excavation by the Wealden Aviation Archaeological Group for BBC TV in September 1979 unearthed remaining wreckage including the tail wheel, control column, aircraft identity plate, parachute pack and pilot's remains. Following statutory inquest, Flight Lieutenant Beresford buried at Brookwood Military Cemetery on November 16, 1979 with full military honours.

In 1979 the BBC decided that aircraft archaeology would be the subject of one of their 'Inside story' series of television documentaries. They therefore contacted the British Aviation Archaeological Council, who referred them to the Wealden Aviation Archaeological Group, to request their co-operation. With the title in mind of 'Missing — no known grave', the site chosen for excavation was at Elmley on the Isle of Sheppey in Kent. This crash site had already been investigated by the Kent Battle of Britain Museum in 1971 and abandoned due to the difficulty of digging in the marshy ground but not before the identity of the aircraft had been established as P3049. The pilot of this Hurricane on its last sortie was Flight Lieutenant Hugh Beresford (portrait *above* displayed by his sister) who was listed as missing and commemorated on the Runnymede Memorial. This site therefore offered the BBC all the ingredients they wanted with the possibility of a military funeral to round off their programme nicely (Associated Newspapers).

Hurricane V7254. Shot down during action over the Thames Estuary 5.30 p.m. Believed crashed in sea. Flying Officer L. R. G. Mitchell missing. Aircraft lost.

Hurricane P3709. Returned to base with damage sustained in combat over the Thames Estuary 5.30 p.m. Sergeant P. T. Robinson unhurt. Aircraft damaged but repairable.

Hurricane V7317. Severely damaged in combat over the Thames Estuary and forced-landed near Sittingbourne 5.35 p.m. Sergeant D. J. Hulbert unhurt. Aircraft damaged but repairable.

303 SQUADRON, NORTHOLT

Hurricane V6605. Returned to base with slight damage following action against Bf 109s off the Essex coast 5.00 p.m. Flying Officer Z. Henneberg unhurt. Aircraft repairable.

Hurricane R4217. Damaged by return fire from Do 17 engaged over the Thames Estuary 5.00 p.m. Returned to base. Flight Lieutenant A. S. Forbes slightly wounded. Aircraft damaged but repairable.

Hurricane P3890. Shot down by Bf 109 during attack on Do 17s over the Thames Estuary 5.00 p.m. crashed near Canterbury Gate, Selsted. Pilot Officer J. Daszewski baled out severely wounded in thigh and admitted to Waldershire Hospital. Aircraft a write-off.

Hugh Beresford's parachute *above,* when opened out, was completely undamaged *right* (S. Hall/ A. Saunders).

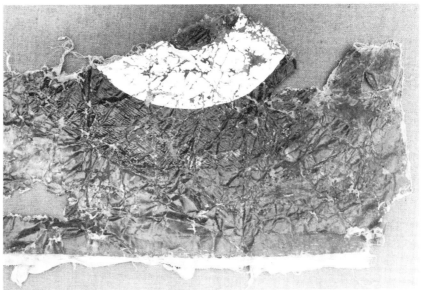

Left: Control column recovered during the dig for the cameras on September 29, 1979 and *above* part of the roundel still visible on the fuselage fabric. The news media soon got on to the story and features appeared in the popular press during the following week although the involvement of the BBC was not mentioned. Naturally it made the story all the more newsworthy to say the aircraft had lain undiscovered for thirty-nine years until it was 'accidently' found. *Below:* Part of a wing spar from the earlier dig on the site in Steve Vizard's collection.

Grave No. 14 in Row D of Plot 24 at Brookwood was chosen as the last resting place for Hugh Beresford's remains. *Right:* The grave is dressed with artificial grass on the morning of the burial.

The funeral, coming within the production period of this book, provided us with the ideal opportunity to portray all the elements of a full British military funeral. Led by Squadron Leader, The Reverend Roger Huddleston and flanked by six officers from RAF Odiham and six airmen from The Queen's Colour Squadron, the cortege leaves the Canadian Records and Reception Building.

With self-loading rifles in the position 'Reverse Arms', Flying Officer K. P. Ottaway leads the escort party.

Led by Bandmaster Warrant Officer Tilley, the band of the Royal Air Force College, Cranwell in winter full dress uniform.

After turning right down Lincoln Avenue and left into Long Lane, the procession halts at the Royal Air Force Shelter.

The Queen's Colour Squadron bearer party comprising Leading Aircraftmen Kevin Andrews, Adrian Blaker, Glynn Ford, Martin Heath, Denis Lalor and Stephen Strain carried the coffin to the graveside.

Caps are removed by the 'hat-man', LAC Bayford. The Odiham bearer party: Flight Lieutenants Wayne Gregory, Mark Hewitt, Mike Hodgson, Paul Longden, Phil Pynegar and Graham Thomas, then took over the task of lowering the coffin.

The committal. The rifle and sword position by the escort party from The Queen's Colour Squadron is 'Rest on your arms reverse'.

Apart from the BBC documentary team, ITN covered the funeral as a news item but, oddly, BBC TV news did not.

The Volley. With the advent of the self-loading rifle, one blank now has to be fired by a third of the firing party at a time to give the three volleys. The only alternative would be either to add the unsightly, yellow blank-firing attachment to the muzzles, to enable the SLR to re-load a second and third cartridge or to use live rounds.

Last respects. Each member of the bearer parties salutes the grave before marching off. The three WRAF personnel about to lay the wreaths are Corporal Tanya Crispin, and Senior Aircraftwomen Jane Kirby and Carol Storey.

Hugh Beresford's headstone of Botticino limestone from a quarry in the Italian alps is engraved by the CWGC in Arras, France.

March 1980. The headstone, set in a headstone beam for absolute regularity, is erected at Brookwood.

The back garden of No. 40 Roding Road, Loughton, Essex where the Hurricane of Flying Officer Pisarek of No. 303 Squadron crashed. Three people in an air-raid shelter in the garden were killed. Tony Graves displays Pisarek's shoe left behind in the cockpit and found in May 1976. The engine, which embedded itself beneath the shelter foundations, could not be extracted.

Hurricane R4173. Shot down by Bf 109 and crashed in back garden of No. 40 Roding Road, Loughton 5.05 p.m. Flying Officer M. Pisarek baled out unhurt. Aircraft a write-off.

Small suburban back garden excavated by the London Air Museum which recovered remains of Rolls-Royce Merlin engine, complete instrument panel, control column, maps, head armour, both undercarriage legs and tyres, and serial number 'R4173' stencilled on remains of fuselage. Also discovered was the pilot's shoe left in the cockpit, confirming contemporary accounts (Excavation covered in detail in After the Battle magazine No. 13).

310 SQUADRON, DUXFORD

Hurricane V7437. Crashed near Capel Fleet, Harty Marshes, Sheppey 6.10 p.m. following combat over the Thames Estuary. Sergeant J. Koukal baled out grievously burned and admitted to hospital. Aircraft a write-off.

Major recovery by Kent Battle of Britain Museum 1972. Intact Rolls-Royce Merlin engine and radiator excavated with head-armour, cockpit components including the control column, complete radio and section of plywood tail wheel housing bearing stencilled serial 'V7437'. Czech pilot's badge, given by Sergeant Koukal to a local resident who gave him first-aid, subsequently also donated to the museum.

Hurricane V6643. Damaged by Bf 110 in combat over Southend. Forced-landed on Whitmans Farm, Purleigh 6.20 p.m. damaging undercarriage. Pilot Officer V. Goth unhurt. Aircraft NN-Y damaged but repairable.

504 SQUADRON, HENDON

Hurricane L1615. Shot down in combat over the Thames Estuary 5.00 p.m. Crashed Sandbanks Farm near Graveney, Faversham. Flying Officer K. V. Wendel badly burned died of injuries. Aircraft a write-off.

Site investigated by the Kent Battle of Britain Museum and few remaining surface fragments recovered.

Hurricane P3021. Forced-landed at Eastchurch with 20mm cannon shell through cockpit hood and petrol tank following combat over the Thames Estuary 5.10 p.m. Sergeant B. M. Bush unhurt. Aircraft repairable.

Above: With pots and cylinders flapping, this is the 'engine' recovered from Capel Fleet. Sergeant Koukal abandoned the aircraft on the evening of September 7 baling out at 22,000ft and delayed opening his parachute for 11,000ft to try to extinguish his burning clothes. On landing, his uniform re-ignited causing him seventy per cent burns. He spent two years in hospital under Archibald McIndoe undergoing twenty-two operations. After the crash site had been excavated in 1972, Koukal came from Czechoslovakia to visit the Kent Battle of Britain Museum and met Mrs. Carrie Wright whose husband had torn the burning clothes from his body in 1940. By way of showing his appreciation, Koukal presented Mrs. Wright with his Czech pilot's badge now in the care of the museum.

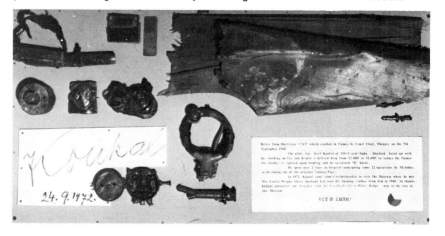

Flying Officer Kenneth Wendel was a pioneer member and pupil of the Auckland Flying Corps in New Zealand. He now lies in the war graves plot at Faversham Borough Cemetery, Kent.

Sergeant Bert Saunders was buried in Wandsworth Cemetery after he was killed in the Blenheim crash at Rainham. The neat grave is a stark contrast to that of his fellow crewman (bottom).

600 SQUADRON, HORNCHURCH

Blenheim L6684. Port engine failed on landing approach. Crashed on back from 200ft at East Close, Rainham and partially burned out, 3.50 p.m. Sergeant A. F. C. Saunders and Sergeant J. W. Davies killed. Aircraft a write-off.

602 SQUADRON, WESTHAMPNETT

Spitfire N3228. Radiator damaged by return fire from Do 17 engaged over south London 5.30 p.m. Returned to base. Pilot Officer O. V. Hanbury unhurt. Aircraft repairable.

Spitfire N3198. Shot down during combat with enemy aircraft over the Biggin Hill area 5.30 p.m. Crashed in flames at Fosters Farm, Hayesden Lane near Tonbridge. Flying Officer W. H. Coverley baled out badly burned died of injuries. Aircraft a write-off.

Site excavated by Steve Vizard.

Spitfire X4256. Failed to return from combat over the Biggin Hill area 5.30 p.m. Pilot Officer H. W. Moody missing. Aircraft lost.

Spitfire K9839. Crash-landed west of Wrotham glycol tank damaged by return fire from Do 17 engaged over Biggin Hill 5.30 p.m. Pilot Officer E. W. Aries unhurt. Aircraft LO-Q damaged but repairable.

603 SQUADRON, HORNCHURCH

Spitfire L1057. Belly-landed back at base due to damage received in combat over London 5.20 p.m. Pilot Officer A. P. Pease unhurt. Aircraft repairable.

Spitfire X4250. Forced-landed at base with cannon shell in mainplane following combat over south London 5.30 p.m. Squadron Leader G. L. Denholm unhurt. Aircraft XT-X repairable.

Spitfire P9467. Shot down in combat over the Thames 5.30 p.m. Sergeant A. R. Sarre baled out slightly wounded. Aircraft a write-off.

Spitfire N3196. Forced-landed at Sutton Valence following combat with enemy fighters over south London 5.30 p.m. Pilot Officer B. G. Stapleton unhurt. Aircraft damaged but repairable.

609 SQUADRON, WARMWELL

Spitfire N3280. Returned to base tail damaged following combat over south London 5.45 p.m. Pilot Officer A. K. Ogilvie unhurt. Aircraft repairable.

Spitfire N3113. Engine damaged by enemy fighters in combat over south London 5.50 p.m. Returned safely to base. Flying Officer J. D. Bisdee unhurt. Aircraft repairable.

Spitfire R6915. Hit in oil sump by return fire from He 111 and forced-landed at White Waltham 6.00 p.m. Pilot Officer N. leC. Agazarian unhurt. Aircraft repairable.

Flying Officer Bill Coverley was mortally wounded in combat on September 7 while serving with No. 602 Squadron. His was a family of military tradition as the headstone at Scarborough shows.

The grave of Sergeant John Davies at St. John's Churchyard, Roundhay near Leeds was one of the most overgrown and consequently one of the most difficult we had to locate. We found his brother killed in 1941 had been buried with him.

Sunday, September 8

41 SQUADRON, HORNCHURCH

Spitfire R6756. Crashed in flames during squadron patrol off Dover area. Presumed victim of Bf 109 attack 12.15 p.m. Flying Officer W. J. M. Scott killed. Aircraft a write-off.

43 SQUADRON, TANGMERE

Hurricane L1727. Crashed at Gedney Dye, Lincolnshire due to engine seizure during ferry flight to Usworth. Pilot Officer C. K. Gray unhurt. Aircraft damaged but repairable.

46 SQUADRON, STAPLEFORD

Hurricane P3525. Returned to base damaged by Bf 109 in action over Sheppey 12.25 p.m. Sergeant S. Andrew unhurt. Aircraft repairable.

Hurricane P3201. Missing following attack on enemy aircraft over Sheppey 12.30 p.m. Believed crashed on Bearsted Golf Course, Maidstone. Sub-Lieutenant J. C. Carpenter missing. Aircraft lost.

This officer is officially listed 'missing' on September 9, 1940. However, No. 46 Squadron records show that they took off from Stapleford at 11.30 a.m. on September 8, 1940, and engaged an enemy formation at 12.15 p.m. over the Isle of Sheppey. Sub-Lieutenant Carpenter, appears to have gone down at about 12.30 p.m. and his naval record shows that he was reported 'missing' in a signal from No. 46 Squadron timed 8.20 p.m. on September 8, 1940. A further signal from Rear Admiral Naval Air Stations timed 7.14 p.m. on September 9 notified that the officer had been 'killed in crash'. Unfortunately neither of these signals can now be traced in Admiralty records and we can only assume that as the officer's death was notified on September 9, 1940, this date has been recorded for naval administrative purposes.

Excavated by Ron Gammage a local enthusiast. Surface fragments also collected by Steve Vizard but do not establish identity of crash beyond question.

Hurricane V6631. Crashed at Hollingbourne following combat over Sheppey 12.30 p.m. Flight Lieutenant N. W. Burnett wounded admitted to hospital. Aircraft a write-off.
Excavated by the Kent Battle of Britain Museum which recovered the supercharger, blind-flying panel and control column. Site later investigated by Steve Vizard and many surface fragments found including the GLOSTER' maker's plate confirming V6631.'

Hurricane P3053. Shot down by Bf 109 during attack on two more. Crash-landed on Meopham Green 12.35 p.m. Pilot Officer P. R. McGregor unhurt. Aircraft damaged but repairable.

600 SQUADRON, REDHILL

Blenheim L1111. Lost following R/T failure during night patrol 9.30 p.m. Abandoned at 6,000ft over Basingstoke, petrol exhausted. Crashed near Odiham. Pilot Officer H. B. L. Hough, Sergeant E. C. Barnard, Sergeant Smith all baled out unhurt. Aircraft ZO-N a write-off.

605 SQUADRON, CROYDON

Hurricane L2061. Shot down by Bf 109 in combat over Tunbridge Wells at 12.30 p.m. Crashed and burned out at Trottiscliffe. Pilot Officer J. Fleming baled out and admitted to hospital with burns and shock. Aircraft a write-off.
Excavated by Ron Gammage. Remains now in the Vizard collection.

The immaculate headstone on the Scott family grave at Dundee.

By diligent search, Steve Vizard has often found items missed by the major wreck groups. This the tiny brass identification plate found at Hollingbourne confirming the identity of the Gloster-made Hurricane V6631.

Small fragments of aircraft are of equal interest to Steve Vizard. This is his display from Pilot Officer Fleming's Hurricane L2061 from No. 605 Squadron.

Monday, September 9

1 (RCAF) SQUADRON, NORTHOLT

Hurricane P3081. Shot down south of base during combat with enemy fighters. Flying Officer Millar baled out wounded and burned. Aircraft a write-off.

19 SQUADRON, DUXFORD

Spitfire P9431. Returned to base with bullets through windscreen and gravity tank following combat over North Weald 5.55 p.m. Sub-Lieutenant A. G. Blake unhurt. Aircraft repairable.

Spitfire P9546. Returned to base with bullet through port mainspar following combat with Bf 109s over London 6.00 p.m. Pilot Officer W. Cunningham unhurt. Aircraft repairable.

66 SQUADRON, KENLEY

Spitfire N3049. Shot down in combat with Bf 109s over East Grinstead 5.55 p.m. Believed crashed at Cowden. Pilot Officer G. H. Corbett baled out slightly injured. Aircraft a write-off.

85 SQUADRON, CHURCH FENTON

Hurricane P2827. Crashed practising dusk landing at base. Sergeant H. H. Allgood believed unhurt. Aircraft damaged but repairable.

92 SQUADRON, BIGGIN HILL

Spitfire L1077. Crash-landed at Midley near Rye following combat with enemy aircraft over base 5.30 p.m. Pilot Officer C. H. Saunders admitted to RAMC Brookland with shrapnel in leg. Aircraft a write-off.
Various surface wreckage donated to Kent Battle of Britain Museum said to have originated from this crash.

Spitfire P9372. Shot down in combat with enemy aircraft over base 5.30 p.m. Pilot Officer W. C. Watling baled out badly burned on face and hands. Aircraft a write-off.

Spitfire R6596. Returned to base severely damaged following combat over base 5.50 p.m. Pilot Officer B. Wright unhurt. Aircraft damaged but repairable.

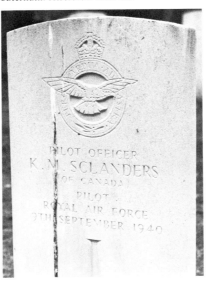
The smashed gun-sight once used by Flight Sergeant Wunsche, recovered by the Wealden group from Newtimber.

222 SQUADRON, HORNCHURCH

Spitfire X4058. Crash-landed at Southfleet with three 20mm cannon shells in the engine following combat with Bf 109s 5.45 p.m. Pilot Officer T. A. Vigors unhurt. Aircraft damaged but repairable.

Spitfire P9469. Returned to base minus large section of tailplane shot off by Bf 109 in action over Wrotham 5.50 p.m. Pilot Officer J. W. Broadhurst unhurt. Aircraft repairable.

242 SQUADRON, COLTISHALL

Hurricane P3087. Shot down in combat with Do 17s and Bf 110s over Thames Haven 5.45 p.m. Crashed at Marden Park Farm, Caterham. Pilot Officer K. M. Sclanders killed. Aircraft a write-off.

Hurricane P2831. Hit by return fire from Do 17 over the Thames Estuary 5.45 p.m. Crashed at Kenley. Sergeant R. E. V. H. Lonsdale baled out unhurt landing at Caterham. Aircraft a write-off.

249 SQUADRON, NORTH WEALD

Hurricane P3667. Forced-landed at Cooling during routine squadron patrol 5.20 p.m. cause not stated. Sergeant H. J. Davidson unhurt. Aircraft repairable.

253 SQUADRON, KENLEY

Hurricane V6639. Returned to base cockpit side panel broken open 5.50 p.m. Flying Officer R. F. Watts unhurt. Aircraft damaged but repairable.

Hurricane   . Forced-landed at Cobham Park Farm following combat with Ju 88s 6.15 p.m. Pilot unhurt. Aircraft repairable.

303 SQUADRON, NORTHOLT

Hurricane P3700. Shot down by Bf 109s in combat over Beachy Head. Crashed and burned out at Saddlescombe Farm, Poynings, Newtimber 5.55 p.m. Flight Sergeant K. Wunsche baled out with slight burns landing near Devils Dyke and admitted to Hove Hospital. Aircraft a write-off.
Major recovery undertaken by the Wealden Aviation Archaeological Group September 1979. Remains of shattered Rolls-Royce Merlin engine, propeller hub, head armour and cockpit components including the gun-sight all unearthed.

Hurricane P3975. Shot down in action with Bf 109s over Beachy Head forced-landed near Cambridgeshire Farm, Falmer 6.00 p.m. Sergeant J. Frantisek unhurt. Aircraft RF-U damaged but repairable.

310 SQUADRON, DUXFORD

Hurricane P3888. Lost control following collision with Flight Lieutenant Sinclair during attack on enemy aircraft over Croydon 5.35 p.m. Hit a Do 215 amidships and crashed in Ninehams Road, Kenley. Flying Officer J. E. Boulton killed. Aircraft a write-off.

Hurricane R4084. Crashed at Purley Way, Wallington following collision with Flying Officer Boulton 5.35 p.m. Flight Lieutenant G. L. Sinclair baled out and sprained ankle landing in a wood at Caterham. Aircraft a write-off.

Hurricane P3142. Crash-landed at Oxted out of fuel following combat with Bf 109s 5.45 p.m. Pilot Officer Rypl unhurt. Aircraft damaged but repairable.

Only two British pilots were killed on September 9 and these are their headstones: Kirkpatrick Sclanders at Whyteleafe and John Boulton at Bandon Hill, both in Surrey.

Pilot Officer George Forrester's grave at Odiham. Born in Newcastle in 1914, he came from Dorset where he lived with his wife Frances at Upper Bassett.

602 SQUADRON, WESTHAMPNETT

Spitfire K9910. Crash-landed in a wood at Crocker Hill, Boxgrove following combat with Bf 109s over Mayfield. Flying Officer P. C. Webb slightly injured with broken wrist. Aircraft a write-off.

Spitfire N3282. Landed near Arundel after combat with Bf 109s over Mayfield 6.00 p.m. Sergeant B. E. P. Whall injured neck. Aircraft repairable.

605 SQUADRON, CROYDON

Hurricane P2765. Hit by cross-fire during attack on He 111s of KG53 over Farnborough 5.30 p.m. Cockpit side shot away and abandoned over Bordon near Petersfield. Crashed at the Straits, Kingsley. Pilot Officer J. Humphreys baled out wounded in the hand. Aircraft a write-off.

Major recovery from a back garden by the Southern Area Wartime Aircraft Preservation Society during April 1979. Intact Rolls-Royce Merlin engine with propeller still attached excavated with cockpit instruments, remains of Sutton harness and large quantity of airframe on part of which was stencilled 'P2765' confirming the aircraft identity.

Hurricane L2059. Shot down by crossfire from He 111s over Farnborough and collided with He 111 of Stab III/KG53. Fell minus starboard wing north of Alton 5.30 p.m. Pilot Officer G. M. Forrester fell dead at Southfield Farm. Aircraft a write-off.

Site investigated by the Wealden Aviation Archaeological Group and also by the Southern Area Wartime Aircraft Preservation Society which collected a few surface fragments.

607 SQUADRON, TANGMERE

Hurricane P3574. Shot down in combat with Do 17s and Bf 109 escort over Mayfield 5.30 p.m. Crashed Lime Trees Farm, Goudhurst. Pilot Officer S. B. Parnall killed. Aircraft a write-off.

Fragments in the Vizard collection.

Hurricane P3117. Crashed Mount Ephraim, Cranbrook following combat against Do 17s and Bf 109s over Mayfield 5.35 p.m. Pilot Officer J. D. Lenahan killed. Aircraft a write-off.

Crash site investigated by John Ellis in March 1980. Crater in Union Orchard still visible but only small parts recovered.

Only four of 'The Few' have been honoured with post-war military funerals — Hugh Beresford, George Drake, Eddie Egan and Franciszek Gruszka. The first was Pilot Officer George James Drake from South Africa (top right with his mother just before leaving for the UK) who went missing on September 9. The Ashford and Tenterden group first started looking for the site of the crash in September 1971 and many weeks were spent searching woodland and making local enquiries in the Mayfield area where his last combat was known to have taken place. Eventually the crash site was pin-pointed at Goudhurst, some ten miles away to the north-east, in March 1972. Excavation of the spot took place on May 21/22 when the remains of the pilot were recovered. An inquest followed in November and, two weeks later, George Drake was laid to rest at Brookwood Military Cemetery. Above: George's brothers Eric (left) and Arthur (right) flew from South Africa for the funeral. Here Dave Buchanan shows them the control column and engine from the wreck, both now on display at the Brenzett Aeronautical Museum.

Hurricane P2728. Shot down at Bockingfold Farm, Goudhurst during combat with enemy aircraft over the Mayfield area 5.30 p.m. Pilot Officer G. J. Drake killed. Aircraft a write-off.

No attempt at recovery made until crash-site excavated by Ashford and Tenterden Recovery Group on May 21, 1972. Intact Rolls-Royce Merlin engine and complete air-frame unearthed together with remains of pilot. Following an inquest on November 7, Pilot Officer Drake was buried with full military honours at Brookwood Military Cemetery on November 22, 1972.

Hurricane P2912. Forced-landed near Knock-holt engine seized following combat with Bf 109s over Mayfield 5.30 p.m. Sergeant P. A. Burnell-Phillips slightly wounded in ankle. Aircraft repairable.

Hurricane P2680. Crashed at Stilstead Farm, East Peckham during combat with Do 17s and Bf 109 escort 5.30 p.m. Sergeant R. A. Spyer slightly wounded. Aircraft a write-off.

Major recovery undertaken by the Kent Battle of Britain Museum which unearthed an intact Rolls-Royce Merlin engine and super-charger, armour plate, control column, gun-sight, rudder bar pedals, complete wing armament of four .303in Browning machine-guns and portion of airframe bearing sten-cilled serial 'P2680'. Maps, aircraft 'Form 700' and gloves bearing name 'Spyer' later discovered by Steve Vizard.

Hurricane   . Believed crashed and burned out at Squires Field, Pevensey following combat with enemy aircraft over Mayfield 5.35 p.m. Pilot baled out. Aircraft a write-off.

611 SQUADRON, DIGBY

Spitfire II P7320. Forced-landed near Henlow out of fuel during routine patrol flight from Fowlmere 6.35 p.m. Sergeant F. E. R. Sheppherd unhurt. Aircraft damaged but repairable.

FIGHTER INTERCEPTION UNIT, SHOREHAM

Beaufighter R2059. Forced-landed at Tang-mere when cockpit roof flew off during night patrol and collided with unlighted truck. Pilot Officer G. Ashfield unhurt. Aircraft damaged but repairable.

Above: The site of the crash at Bockingfold Farm (Brenzett). *Below:* Evidence of identity of the airframe is usually mandatory if the Ministry of Defence are to accept the responsibility of naming the pilot. The group found the serial number still clearly sten-cilled on this piece of plywood.

Below: Followed by Arthur and Eric Drake, the bearer party from RAF Odiham carry the remains of their brother to his grave (Central Press).

Tuesday, September 10

25 SQUADRON, NORTH WEALD

Blenheim L1440. Wrecked in belly-landing following loss of an airscrew during routine patrol. Sergeant K. B. Hollowell unhurt. Aircraft damaged but repairable.

72 SQUADRON, CROYDON

Spitfire K9841. Hit by return fire in attack on Do 215 and further damaged when undercarriage collapsed in forced-landing at Little Hutchings Farm, Etchingham 5.30 p.m. Pilot Officer E. E. Males unhurt. Aircraft QJ-R a write-off.

312 SQUADRON, DUXFORD

Hurricane L1644. Crashed and burned out south of Cambridge. Cause not stated. Sergeant J. Keprt baled out unhurt. Aircraft a write-off.

602 SQUADRON, WESTHAMPNETT

Spitfire L1040. Crashed Felpham Golf Course during night-flying practice 8.45 p.m. Sergeant D. W. Elcombe unhurt. Aircraft a write-off.

Spitfire L1002. Damaged forced-landing at Tangmere following night-flying training 9.15 p.m. Pilot Officer O. V. Hanbury unhurt. Aircraft damaged but repairable.

Spitfire X4270. Slightly damaged landing at Tangmere after night-flying 9.15 p.m. Pilot Officer C. J. Mount unhurt. Aircraft repairable.

Wednesday, September 11

1 (RCAF) SQUADRON, NORTHOLT

Hurricane P3534. Shot down during attack on He 111s over Tunbridge Wells 4.12 p.m. Crashed at Lakestreet Manor, Mayfield. Flying Officer T. B. Little baled out wounded in leg and landed at Rotherfield. Admitted to Kent and Sussex Hospital, Tunbridge Wells with burns to face and side. Aircraft a write-off.
Site excavated by the Wealden Aviation Archaeological Group in February 1980 down to a depth of four feet. Only small parts recovered.

Hurricane V6670. Crashed and burned out near Romney following engagement with He 111s over Tunbridge Wells 4.20 p.m. Flying Officer P. W. Lochnan unhurt. Aircraft a write-off.

17 SQUADRON, DEBDEN

Hurricane P3892. Returned to base with damage received in combat with enemy fighters over the Thames Estuary 4.20 p.m. Sergeant L. H. Bartlett unhurt. Aircraft damaged but repairable.

19 SQUADRON, DUXFORD

Spitfire N3046. Severely damaged in combat with Bf 109s over London 4.05 p.m. Returned to base. Flying Officer F. Dolezal slightly wounded in leg. Aircraft damaged but repairable.

Spitfire P9546. Forced-landed following engagement with Bf 109s over London 4.15 p.m. Flight Sergeant G. C. Unwin unhurt. Aircraft damaged but repairable.

Crankshaft and pistons from No. 46 Squadron Hurricane V6549 at Brenzett. Belgian pilot, Sergeant R. de Cannart d'Hamale, was killed in a later crash in November — outside our strict period of the Battle of Britain which ended on October 31.

Spitfire X4059. Crashed on landing at base on punctured tyres after combat over London 4.20 p.m. Flying Officer L. A. Haines unhurt. Aircraft damaged but repairable.

41 SQUADRON, HORNCHURCH

Spitfire N3059. Oil cooler severely damaged in surprise attack by Bf 109 during 'spotter' patrol of Dungeness 4.30 p.m. Returned safely to base. Sergeant I. E. Howitt unhurt. Aircraft damaged but repairable.

Spitfire X4325. Shot down during attack on Ju 88 and abandoned over Sevenoaks 4.35 p.m. Pilot Officer G. A. Langley baled out unhurt. Aircraft a write-off.

Spitfire X4343. Returned to base damaged following combat with Bf 110s over Maidstone 4.40 p.m. Pilot Officer G. H. Bennions slightly wounded in left heel. Aircraft damaged but repairable.

46 SQUADRON, STAPLEFORD

Hurricane P3525. Crashed and burned out during uneventful patrol 11.00 a.m. cause unknown. Sergeant S. Andrew killed. Aircraft a write-off.

Hurricane V6549. Shot down during combat over north Kent 3.30 p.m. Crashed at School Fields, Sandhurst. Sergeant R. E. de C. d'Hamale baled out believed landing unhurt at Hurst Green. Aircraft a write-off.
Remains of shattered Rolls-Royce Merlin engine recovered by the Brenzett Aeronautical Museum.

Hurricane V7232. Failed to return from combat over the Thames Estuary 3.30 p.m. Presumed crashed into sea. Sergeant W. A. Peacock missing. Aircraft lost.

Hurricane P3094. Crash-landed and burned out in West Lordine Wood, Staplecross 3.40 p.m. following combat over the Thames Estuary. Pilot Officer P. R. McGregor injured admitted to hospital. Aircraft a write-off.
Excavated by the Wealden Aviation Archaeological Group in 1973. Remains of shattered Rolls-Royce Merlin engine, propeller hub and minor components recovered.

Sergeant Stanley Andrew from Swanland, Yorkshire enlisted in the Volunteer Reserve in 1937. Already a regular with six months service by September 1939, he fought in 1940 at Narvik. He now lies beside All Saints Church, North Ferriby.

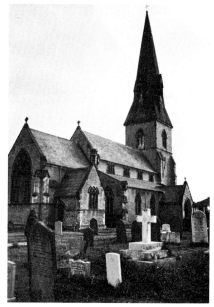

66 SQUADRON, GRAVESEND

Spitfire X4339. Forced-landed damaged following combat 6.55 p.m. Pilot Officer I. J. A. Cruickshanks unhurt. Aircraft damaged but repairable.

72 SQUADRON, CROYDON

Spitfire R6710. Returned to base damaged following interception of enemy formation over Gravesend 4.00 p.m. Pilot Officer B. Douthwaite slightly wounded. Aircraft a write-off.

73 SQUADRON, DEBDEN

Hurricane P2796. Shot down in combat with Bf 110s over Sheppey 4.10 p.m. crashed Warren Farm, Boxley near Detling. Sergeant H. G. Webster baled out unhurt. Aircraft a write-off.

Hurricane P3868. Believed damaged in combat with Bf 110s over the Sheppey area 4.10 p.m. Returned safely to base. Sergeant R. V. Ellis unhurt. Aircraft repairable.

92 SQUADRON, BIGGIN HILL

Spitfire K9793. Failed to return following combat with enemy aircraft over Dungeness 4.15 p.m. Presumed crashed into sea. Pilot Officer F. N. Hargreaves missing. Aircraft lost.

Spitfire R6613. Crashed following combat with Bf 109s over Folkestone 6.50 p.m. Flight Lieutenant J. A. Paterson believed unhurt. Aircraft a write-off.

Spitfire P9464. Shot down in combat with Bf 109s and crashed into a wood at Evegate Manor Farm, Smeeth 7.00 p.m. Pilot Officer H. D. Edwards killed (wreck discovered 7.10.40). Aircraft a write-off.
Site excavated by the Kent Battle of Britain Museum October 1974 and Rolls-Royce Merlin engine recovered with tail wheel, both undercarriage legs, control column, rudder bar pedals, parachute release buckle and assorted aircraft wreckage.

213 SQUADRON, TANGMERE

Hurricane V6667. Shot down into the Channel one mile off Selsey Bill 4.00 p.m. during combat with Bf 110s. Sergeant A. Wojcicki missing. Aircraft AK-P lost.

Hurricane P3780. Hit in glycol and gravity petrol tank by unseen aircraft during combat over Selsey Bill 4.00 p.m. Crashed in sea. Flight Lieutenant J. E. J. Sing baled out unhurt. Aircraft AK-A lost.

219 SQUADRON, CATTERICK

Blenheim L1272. Tail wheel damaged in heavy landing at Bassingbourn. Squadron Leader J. A. Leathart unhurt. Aircraft repairable.

222 SQUADRON, HORNCHURCH

Spitfire R6638. Forced-landed on Parsonage Farm, Fletching 4.40 p.m. damaged in combat over Maidstone. Pilot Officer W. R. Assheton unhurt. Aircraft damaged but repairable.

Spitfire P9364. Cockpit hood shattered by Bf 109 during attack on He 111 over Tunbridge Wells 5.00 p.m. Returned safely to base. Sergeant E. Scott unhurt. Aircraft repairable.

'In loving memory of Harry of Winnipeg, Manitoba, Canada. Nobly he lived, gloriously he died. We will remember him.' Pilot Officer Edwards at Folkestone New Cemetery.

229 SQUADRON, WITTERING

Hurricane P3038. Shot down in combat over Biggin Hill 4.00 p.m. Pilot Officer M. Ravenhill baled out and admitted to Shorncliffe Hospital suffering from shock. Aircraft a write-off.

Hurricane P3463. Windscreen damaged by Bf 109 during attack on He 111 over the Biggin Hill area 4.00 p.m. Flight Lieutenant R. F. Rimmer slight facial cuts. Aircraft damaged but repairable.
Bullet-holed rear-view mirror from this aircraft donated to the Wealden Aviation Archaeological Group by the family of the late Flight Lieutenant Rimmer.

Hurricane N2466. Set alight during engagement with He 111s over Maidstone 4.10 p.m. Abandoned aircraft exploded over Linton and Boughton areas. Pilot Officer K. M. Carver baled out burned and admitted to hospital. Aircraft a write-off. A/C PARTS DUG UP IN MAR 81.

235 SQUADRON, THORNEY ISLAND

Blenheim . Shot down by Bf 109 during escort mission for FAA Albacores attacking Calais. Crashed into sea 5.30 p.m. Pilot Officer P. C. Wickings-Smith, Pilot Officer A. W. V. Green and Sergeant R. D. H. Watts missing. Aircraft QY-E lost.

Blenheim . Failed to return from escort mission for FAA Albacores attacking Calais 5.30 p.m. Presumed shot down into sea by Bf 109s. Flight Lieutenant F. W. Flood, Pilot Officer N. B. Shorrocks and Sergeant B. R. Sharp missing. Aircraft QY-G lost.

238 SQUADRON, MIDDLE WALLOP

Hurricane P3096. Shot down in combat involving Ju 88s south of Tunbridge Wells 4.10 p.m. Believed that which crashed near Withyham Post Office. Pilot Officer W. Tower-Perkins baled out wounded and admitted to Tunbridge Wells Hospital with burns. Aircraft a write-off.
Site investigated by Steve Vizard but only small fragments recovered.

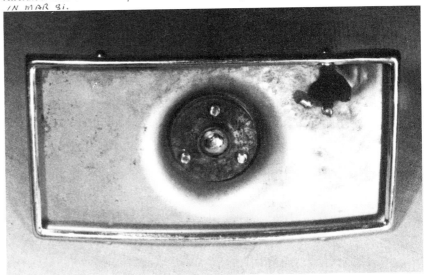

This bullet-holed rear view mirror from Hurricane P3463 was given to the Wealden group by the Rimmer family. Flight Lieutenant Rimmer had kept it as a souvenir until his death on September 27.

303 SQUADRON, NORTHOLT

Hurricane V7242. Shot down by Bf 109s in combat south of London 4.25 p.m. crashed and burned out in chalk pit at Westerham. Sergeant S. Wojtowicz killed. Aircraft a write-off.

Hurricane V7465. Forced-landed at Heston damaged in combat over south London 4.30 p.m. Flight Lieutenant A. S. Forbes wounded. Aircraft repairable.

Hurricane V6665. Shot down in combat south of London 4.30 p.m. crashed at Pembury. Flying Officer A. Cebrzynski severely injured died 19.9.40. Aircraft a write-off.

501 SQUADRON, KENLEY

Hurricane P5200. Shot down in action with Bf 109s over Maidstone 3.45 p.m. Sergeant T. G. Pickering unhurt. Aircraft a write-off.

504 SQUADRON, HENDON

Hurricane P3429. Undercarriage collapsed on take-off 3.10 p.m. Pilot Officer M. Rook unhurt. Aircraft damaged but repairable.

Hurricane N2471. Oil pressure failure shortly after take-off 3.15 p.m. Returned safely to base. Pilot Officer J. V. Gurteen unhurt. Aircraft damaged but repairable.

The posthumous award — the bitter-sweet honour presented to so many wives of fighting men. A photo released in June 1941, Mrs. Joan Hughes holds the Distinguished Flying Cross she had just received from the King on behalf of her late husband, Flight Lieutenant David Price Hughes of No. 238 Squadron, missing on September 11 (Keystone).

On the afternoon of September 11, two Blenheims from No. 235 Squadron at Thorney Island (a Coastal Command unit fighting under the auspices of Fighter Command) were shot down on an escort mission to Calais. No trace of the aircraft or the six crewmen was ever found. Sergeant Reginald Watts from Far Colton, Northamptonshire (above) was the wireless op/air gunner on QY-E.

Hurricane V7240. Failed to return following interception of Ju 88 formation south of Tunbridge Wells 4.15 p.m. Flight Lieutenant D. P. Hughes missing. Aircraft lost.

Hurricane R2682. Failed to return from combat with Ju 88s pursued over Romney Marsh 4.15 p.m. Aircraft crashed at Little Scotney Farm, Lydd. Sergeant S. Duszynski missing. Aircraft a write-off.
Remains of aircraft recovered by the Ashford and Tenterden Recovery Group in 1973.

249 SQUADRON, NORTH WEALD

Hurricane V6682. Shot down in combat with He 111s over the Thames Estuary and north Kent 4.20 p.m. Crashed near Benenden. Sergeant W. L. Davis baled out wounded. Aircraft a write-off.

253 SQUADRON, KENLEY

Hurricane P2883. Returned to base damaged following combat over the Sussex coast 3.45 p.m. Pilot unhurt. Aircraft damaged but repairable.

266 SQUADRON, WITTERING

Spitfire II P7313. Hit by return fire from He 111 and abandoned over Billericay 4.20 p.m. Pilot Officer R. J. B. Roach baled out unhurt. Aircraft a write-off.

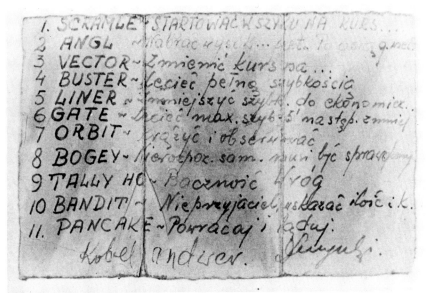

1. SCRAMBLE ~ STARTOWAĆ W SZYKU NA KURS...
2. ANGL ~
3. VECTOR ~ Zmienić kurs na...
4. BUSTER ~ Lecieć pełną szybkością
5. LINER ~ Zmniejszyć szyb. do ekonom....
6. GATE ~ Lecieć max. szyb. 5' następ. zmniej
7. ORBIT ~ Krążyć i obserwować
8. BOGEY ~ Nierozp. sam. musi być sprawdz....
9. TALLY HO ~ Baczność wróg
10. BANDIT ~ Nieprzyjaciel, wskazać ilość i k.
11. PANCAKE ~ Powracaj i ląduj.

When a pilot from a particular aircraft is missing, there is a strong probability that he was still in the aircraft when it crashed. Pilots who baled out, even if killed for some reason, were spotted and recovered. When the Ashford and Tenterden Group dug up the Hurricane at Little Scotney Farm near Lydd on January 13, 1973, they positively identified it as R2682. This aircraft had been lost whilst being flown by a Polish pilot Sergeant Stanislaw Duszynski *(above)* and, whilst his parachute *(bottom right)*, his shoe, pieces of uniform and personal notes *(top right)* were found, it seems strange that no human remains were recovered. The results of the dig were fully reported to the Ministry of Defence AR9 branch that deals with RAF casualties with the suggestion that a further attempt could be made to recover remains but that digging would be difficult in the 'running sand'. (Much of Romney Marsh is waterlogged as it lies below sea level.) No official decision was made to attempt another excavation.

HURRICANE Mk. II. R2682
Pilot:- SGT. S. DUSZYNSKI
(POLAND)

Another Polish pilot killed on September 11 was Sergeant Antoni Wojtowicz of No. 303 buried at Northwood.

Spitfire X4269. Returned to base starboard wing damaged following combat with Bf 110s over Selsey Bill 4.20 p.m. Sergeant C. F. Babbage unhurt. Aircraft damaged but repairable.

605 SQUADRON, CROYDON

Hurricane P3828. Landed at Redhill due to engine trouble developed during combat over the Croydon area 4.15 p.m. Flying Officer R. Hope unhurt. Aircraft repairable.

611 SQUADRON, DIGBY

Spitfire II P7298. Set alight during combat over Croydon 4.00 p.m. Reputedly hit by AA fire from Brooklands. Abandoned aircraft crashed behind 'Walton and Hersham Motors', Weybridge. Sergeant F. E. R. Shepherd baled out but parachute destroyed by abandoned aircraft. Aircraft a write-off.
Crash site subject to extensive post-war redevelopment and investigated by the Air Historical Group without success.

Spitfire II P7321. Severely damaged by return fire from He 111 engaged over Croydon 4.15 p.m. Crashed on dead engine near Kenley. Sergeant S. A. Levenson unhurt. Aircraft damaged but repairable.

Visitors to war cemeteries should always be careful not to be mislead by facts which are not immediately apparent from headstone inscriptions. For example, Flying Officer Arsen Cebrzynski was described on the first wartime list of Battle of Britain casualties as 'Killed 11-9-40'. In actual fact he was wounded on that date and died eight days later.

Hurricane P3770. Shot down in combat over Kent coast 4.00 p.m. Crashed and burned out south of Rookelands, near Newchurch, Romney Marsh. Pilot Officer A. W. Clarke missing. Aircraft a write-off.
Site excavated by the Kent Battle of Britain Museum and remains of shattered Rolls-Royce engine unearthed together with many fragments including the map storage box containing complete set of maps, pilot's silk inner gloves and pocket handkerchief marked 'CLARKE' in indelible pencil. Site also investigated by the Historical Aircraft Archaeology Group which collected many surface fragments. London Air Museum recovered complete wing-tip with navigation lamp from nearby ditch.

602 SQUADRON, WESTHAMPNETT

Spitfire L1027. Severely damaged in combat with enemy fighters over Selsey Bill 4.15 p.m. Pilot Officer S. N. Rose slightly wounded. Aircraft damaged but repairable.

Spitfire N3282. Shot down in combat with Bf 110s south of Selsey Bill 4.20 p.m. crashed into the Channel. Sergeant M. H. Sprague killed (washed ashore at Brighton 10.10.40). Aircraft lost.

This map was recovered by the Kent Battle of Britain Museum from a Hurricane crash site near Newchurch, Kent. Although personal effects established the identity of the missing pilot, no human remains were reported as being found.

Sergeant Mervyn Sprague, a 21-year-old from Richmond, Surrey, was a pilot with No. 602 Squadron and is now buried at Tangmere.

No. 611 Squadron Sergeant Pilot Frederick Shepherd, married from Prestatyn, Flintshire, buried at Whyteleafe.

On September 12, Wing Commander John Dewar, DSO, DFC, Commanding Officer of RAF Exeter, set off to fly to Tangmere. He never arrived and his body was washed up on September 30. This is his grave in the churchyard of St. John the Baptist, North Baddesley, Hampshire. Tuesday the 12th was the lull before the storm — rain and cloud hampered enemy operations on that day and Johnny Dewar was the only casualty — and the highest ranking during the entire battle.

Thursday, September 12

213 SQUADRON, TANGMERE

Hurricane V7306. Failed to arrive at Tangmere on routine flight from Exeter. Exact circumstances not recorded. Wing Commander J. S. Dewar killed. (Body washed ashore at Kingston Gorse, Sussex on 30.9.40.) Aircraft a write-off.

Friday, September 13

238 SQUADRON, MIDDLE WALLOP

Hurricane P3830. Forced-landed Perrylands Wood, Hellingly 4.55 p.m. having run out of fuel. Pilot Officer J. R. Urwin-Mann unhurt. Aircraft repairable.

248 SQUADRON, SUMBURGH

Blenheim . Failed to return from reconnaissance of Feje-Stadlandet sector of Norwegian coast 7.00 a.m. Sergeant W. J. Garfield killed, Sergeant B. W. Mesner, Sergeant A. Kay both missing. Aircraft WR-V lost.

501 SQUADRON, KENLEY

Hurricane P2793. Radiator shot off during destruction of He 111 over Maidstone 1.45 p.m. Believed crashed at Abbey Farm Leeds. Sergeant J. H. Lacey baled out with slight burns. Aircraft a write-off.
Site excavated 1977 by Steve Vizard.

FIGHTER INTERCEPTION UNIT, SHOREHAM

Blenheim Z5721. Failed to return from night operational patrol and crashed in Channel off Calais. Exact circumstances not clear. Flight Lieutenant R. G. Ker-Ramsay, Warrant Officers G. Dixon and E. L. Byrne baled out and made PoW. Aircraft lost.

Sergeant Bertram Mesner was one of seven boys living with their sister in Halley Road, Forest Gate, then in Essex. During a short leave in the summer of 1940 he returned to Forest Gate where he married a local girl on July 13. Two months later he and his crew failed to return from an armed reconnaissance off the Norwegian coast.

Saturday, September 14

19 SQUADRON, DUXFORD

Spitfire R6625. Crashed near Horndon-on-the-Hill, Orsett during routine patrol 4.20 p.m. Cause unknown but presumed victim of oxygen failure. Sergeant F. Marek killed (on attachment from 310 squadron). Aircraft a write-off.
Major recovery operation by the Essex Historical Aircraft Society unearthed Rolls-Royce Merlin engine, propeller, undercarriage components, cockpit controls and instruments and remains of rear airframe totally compressed by force of impact with the ground. (Excavation described in detail in After the Battle magazine No. 10.)

41 SQUADRON, HORNCHURCH

Spitfire R6605. Shot down by Bf 109s during squadron patrol. Exact circumstances unclear. Squadron Leader R. C. F. Lister baled out wounded. Aircraft a write-off.

43 SQUADRON, USWORTH

Hurricane P2682. Caught in leader's slipstream and made heavy landing on one wheel at base. Pilot Officer C. K. Gray unable to correct fully due to arm injuries sustained 26.8.1940. Aircraft damaged but repairable.

66 SQUADRON, GRAVESEND

Spitfire X4327. Shot down in combat with Bf 109s over Maidstone 7.00 p.m. Pilot Officer R. H. Robbins seriously injured admitted to Leeds Castle Hospital. Aircraft a write-off.

Spitfire N3029. Forced-landed a mile southeast of base due to engine failure 7.20 p.m. Sergeant P. H. Willcocks unhurt. Aircraft a write-off.

A particularly wet and muddy dig was carried out at Horndon-on-the-Hill by the Essex Historical Aircraft Society in 1975. The group continued in pouring rain as the event was somewhat special — it was the exact day almost to the hour that the Spitfire of Sergeant

Frantisek Marek had crashed thirty-five years previously. The Czech pilot was buried in Eastbrookend Cemetery albeit with an incorrect date of death (September 16). *After the Battle* magazine were able to get this changed after publication of the story.

72 SQUADRON, BIGGIN HILL

Spitfire K9960. Abandoned following combat over Ashford. Crashed and burned out at Orlestone 6.30 p.m. Sergeant H. J. Bell-Walker baled out unhurt. Aircraft a write-off.

73 SQUADRON, DEBDEN

Hurricane L1981. Returned to base damaged following attack by Spitfire during combat over Tilbury 4.00 p.m. Pilot unhurt. Aircraft TP-B damaged but repairable.

Hurricane V7209. Forced-landed at West Malling with radiator damage following attack by Spitfire during combat over Tilbury 4.00 p.m. Flight Lieutenant M. L. ff. Beytagh unhurt. Aircraft repairable.

Hurricane L2039. Shot down during combat over Tonbridge area 4.00 p.m. crashed at Newenden. Squadron Leader M. W. S. Robinson baled out wounded and admitted to Kent and Sussex hospital. Aircraft TP-F a write-off.

Hurricane P2542. Shot down in combat over the Tonbridge area 4.00 p.m. Suspected location currently under investigation. Sergeant J. J. Brimble missing. Aircraft TP-D lost.

Hurricane P3209. Landed at Gravesend with damage sustained in combat over the Thames Estuary 4.05 p.m. Sergeant V. A. B. Leng unhurt. Aircraft repairable.

Hurricane   . Shot down over Maidstone during combat with enemy aircraft 4.05 p.m. Crashed at Clapper Lane, Staplehurst. Sergeant J. J. Griffin baled out and admitted to West Kent Hospital with dislocated shoulder and leg injuries. Aircraft TP-L a write-off.
Surface wreckage recovered by Steve Vizard for his private collection

Hurricane V7446. Damaged by Bf 109 in combat over the Thames Estuary and forced-landed near Dover 4.10 p.m. Sergeant A. E. Marshall unhurt. Aircraft TP-E damaged but repairable.

74 SQUADRON, COLTISHALL

Spitfire II P7352. Returned to base damaged in port wing, air intake and spinner by return fire from Bf 110 10.00 a.m. Flying Officer J. C. Mungo-Park unhurt. Aircraft repairable.

92 SQUADRON, BIGGIN HILL

Spitfire R6624. Shot down by Bf 109s and crashed at Sole Street House, near Faversham 7.00 p.m. Sergeant H. W. McGowan baled out wounded and admitted to Faversham Hospital. Aircraft a write-off.

Spitfire X4051. Returned to base with damage caused by Bf 109s in combat over Canterbury 7.10 p.m. Sergeant J. Mann injured admitted to Orpington Hospital. Aircraft repairable.

222 SQUADRON, HORNCHURCH

Spitfire X4265. Forced-landed at Detling damaged in combat with Bf 109s 4.00 p.m. Sergeant I. Hutchinson unhurt. Aircraft repairable.

Spitfire X4275. Severely damaged in combat with Bf 109s and crashed attempting to land near Rochford 4.15 p.m. Sergeant S. Baxter killed. Aircraft a write-off.

Spitfire X4249. Abandoned over Aveley due to damage sustained in action with Bf 109s 4.20 p.m. Crashed south of Cockhide Farm. Sergeant R. B. Johnson baled out unhurt. Aircraft a write-off.
Small fragments and minor components from cockpit area together with remains of shattered Rolls-Royce Merlin engine recovered by the Essex Historical Aircraft Society in August 1974.

An unusual relic was found at Staplehurst where Sergeant Griffin of No. 73 Squadron landed by parachute after being shot down over Maidstone. In 1976, Steve Vizard found this small identity tag left by the pilot over thirty-five years before.

229 SQUADRON, NORTHOLT

Hurricane N2592. Forced-landed at Heston damaged by unseen enemy aircraft during operational sortie 4.15 p.m. Pilot Officer J. W. Hyde unhurt. Aircraft damaged but repairable.

253 SQUADRON, KENLEY

Hurricane P5184. Crashed in flames on Swanton Farm, Bredgar following combat with Bf 109s 6.00 p.m. Sergeant W. B. Higgins killed. Aircraft a write-off.

St. Lawrence Churchyard, Whitwell, Derbyshire.

Hurricane P3804. Shot down in combat with Bf 109s and crashed at Stone near Faversham 6.10 p.m. Sergeant J. A. Anderson baled out and admitted to Faversham Hospital with severe burns. Aircraft a write-off.

501 SQUADRON, KENLEY

Hurricane N2329. Forced-landed at base exact circumstances unknown. Pilot unhurt. Aircraft damaged but repairable.

Leading Aircraftman John Pile Wyatt from Melplash, Dorset, a 32-year-old observer, joined No. 25 Squadron at North Weald, Essex in late July 1940. On September 15 he was killed in a flying accident involving two Blenheims, the full circumstances of which were never clear although the squadron was at this time developing its night fighter role with the aid of primitive AI equipment. This is his grave at Christ Church, Melplash.

Sunday, September 15

1 (RCAF) SQUADRON, NORTHOLT

Hurricane P3080. Attacked by Bf 109s and shot down over Tunbridge Wells 12.10 p.m. Flying Officer A. D. Nesbitt baled out wounded admitted to hospital. Aircraft a write-off.

Hurricane P3876. Shot down by Bf 109s in combat over Tunbridge Wells 12.10 p.m. Flying Officer R. Smither killed. Aircraft a write-off.

Hurricane L1973. Returned to base severely damaged following combat with Bf 109s and He 111s south of London 2.45 p.m. Flying Officer A. Yuile wounded. Aircraft damaged but repairable.

19 SQUADRON, DUXFORD

Spitfire R6991. Forced-landed due to damage sustained in combat 3.00 p.m. Sub-Lieutenant A. G. Blake unhurt. Aircraft damaged but repairable.

Spitfire X4070. Failed to return following combat with enemy fighters 3.05 p.m. and posted missing. Believed ditched just off French coast with severe damage. Sergeant J. A. Potter wounded POW (capture confirmed 4.10.40). Aircraft lost.

Spitfire P9431. Crash-landed with glycol tank damage following action with Bf 109s 3.10 p.m. Sergeant H. A. C. Roden slightly injured. Aircraft a write-off.

25 SQUADRON, NORTH WEALD

Blenheim   . Flying accident exact details not stated but possible collision involving two aircraft. Flying Officer M. J. Miley, Flying Officer H. M. S. Lambert and LAC J. P. Wyatt killed. Pilot Officer B. G. Hooper believed unhurt. Aircraft a write-off.

September 15 — Battle of Britain Day — is still regarded by many as the climax to the battle although contemporary British claims have been disproved by post-war research. Ross Smither, killed just after noon, lies at Brookwood.

41 SQUADRON, HORNCHURCH

Spitfire P9324. Shot down in combat with Bf 109s 12.30 p.m. Believed that which crashed and burned out at Wick House, Bulphan near Thurrock. Pilot Officer G. A. Langley killed. Aircraft a write-off.

46 SQUADRON, NORTH WEALD

Hurricane N2599. Returned to base with slight damage to starboard mainplane following combat over London 12.30 p.m. Sergeant C. A. L. Hurry unhurt. Aircraft repairable.

56 SQUADRON, BOSCOMBE DOWN

Hurricane P3660. Crashed one mile north-west of High Post aerodrome near base circumstances unknown. Sergeant T. R. Tweed killed. Aircraft a write-off.

73 SQUADRON, DEBDEN

Hurricane P3865. Shot down by Bf 109s in combat over Maidstone and crashed at Nouds Farm, Teynham 12.20 p.m. Pilot Officer R. A. Marchand killed. Aircraft TP-K a write-off.

Major recovery by the London Air Museum. Remains of shattered Rolls-Royce Merlin engine excavated together with propeller boss, cockpit components and control column, intact gun-sight and remains of Sutton harness and pilot's parachute. Some fragments also displayed by the Kent Battle of Britain Museum.

92 SQUADRON, BIGGIN HILL

Spitfire R6767. Returned to base with 20mm cannon damage to wing following combat with Bf 109s over Canterbury 12.15 p.m. Flight Sergeant C. Sydney unhurt. Aircraft repairable.

Spitfire P9513. Hit by return fire from Do 17s over Ashford 3.00 p.m. Returned to base severely damaged. Pilot Officer A. C. Bartley unhurt. Aircraft damaged but repairable.

Spitfire R6606. Shot down in combat west of Ashford 2.50 p.m. Pilot Officer R. H. Holland baled out and slightly injured on landing. Admitted to hospital at East Grinstead. Aircraft a write-off.

Gerald Archibald Langley, born at Stony Stratford, was educated at Wolverton Grammar School. In 1936, the family moved to Northampton where he entered the employment of the Prudential Assurance Company. In March 1939, he joined the Royal Air Force Volunteer Reserve and received his commission in May 1940. Flying Spitfires with No. 41 Squadron at Hornchurch, Pilot Officer Gerry Langley was the unit's only casualty on Sunday, September 15, when his aircraft was shot down by enemy fighters at Bulphan, Essex. Gerry was buried in the grave in the foreground at St. Peter and Paul's Churchyard at Abington.

Sergeants' Mess, RAF Middle Wallop, Hants.

Dear Mother and Father,   *11/9/40*

    Letting you know that I have arrived safely.

    Old 238 have been right in the thick of it, London every day. Good job I was far away for my leave, all the others recalled.

    Domagala in hospital (Polish Sergeant M. Domagala), *also Tower-Perkins* (Pilot Officer W. Tower-Perkins) *May's pal. My Flight Commander Mr. Hughes* (Flight Lieutenant D. P. Hughes) *and one of the other Polish boys killed. Things have been rather warm.*

    Away for flying now, was flying us soon as I landed.

    Cheerio and thank you both.

        Love Eric.

Sergeant Thomas Tweed, 26-year-old No. 56 Squadron pilot, lies in St. Mary and Melorus Church Cemetery at Amesbury, Wiltshire. He was married and came from Worksop.

Above: The London Air Museum located the crash site of Pilot Officer Roy Marchand's Hurricane between Sittingbourne and Faversham in Kent at Nouds Farm, Teynham. The excavation successfully recovered all the major components — small pieces are displayed *below.* The group came in for bitter criticism when they later removed Roy Marchand's headstone from his grave, albeit with the permission of his father.

229 SQUADRON, WITTERING

Hurricane N2537. Shot down by enemy fighters in combat over Sevenoaks area. Crashed on Staplehurst Railway Station 11.50 a.m. Pilot Officer G. L. J. Doutrepont killed. Aircraft a write-off.
Small fragments collected from the crash-site by the Kent Battle of Britain Museum and also by the London Air Museum.

Hurricane V6616. Shot down in attack on Do 215s and Bf 110s over Sevenoaks 12.00 p.m. Pilot Officer R. R. Smith baled out with leg wounds. Aircraft a write-off.

238 SQUADRON, MIDDLE WALLOP

Hurricane L2089. Shot up in combat with He 111s and Bf 110s over Kenley 3.00 p.m. Returned to base tail damaged. Pilot Officer V. C. Simmonds unhurt. Aircraft damaged but repairable.

Hurricane P2836. Crashed into an oak tree at Kent College, Pembury during combat with He 111s and Bf 110s engaged over Kenley 3.00 p.m. Sergeant L. Pidd baled out but landed dead. Aircraft a write-off.
Crash site excavated by Brenzett Aeronautical Museum on March 1, 1975.

Hurricane P3920. Severely damaged during attack on He 111s 3.05 p.m. Forced-landed at West Malling. Flight Lieutenant M. V. Blake unhurt. Aircraft damaged but repairable.

Hurricane P3462. Returned to base damaged in combat over Kenley 3.10 p.m. Flying Officer C. T. Davis unhurt. Aircraft repairable.

Hurricane P3833. Damaged in combat with He 111s and Bf 110s over Kenley and forced-landed out of fuel at Gulledge Farm, Imberhorne near East Grinstead 4.35 p.m. Pilot Officer A. R. Covington unhurt. Aircraft damaged but repairable.

242 SQUADRON, COLTISHALL

Hurricane V6576. Forced-landed following combat over London 12.45 p.m. Flight Lieutenant G. E. Ball unhurt. Aircraft repairable.

Hurricane P2884. Shot down by Bf 109s over Rye following destruction of Do 17 over the Channel. Crashed at Church Field, Udimore 2.40 p.m. Flight Lieutenant G. S. ff. Powell-Sheddon baled out and admitted to Rye Hospital with dislocated left shoulder. Aircraft a write-off.
Excavated by the Ashford and Tenterden Recovery Group October 28, 1972. Items displayed by Brenzett Aeronatical Museum.

249 SQUADRON, NORTH WEALD

Hurricane P3660. Severely damaged by Bf 109 following attack on He 111 south-east of London 2.35 p.m. Crash-landed at West Malling. Pilot Officer K. T. Lofts unhurt. Aircraft a write-off.

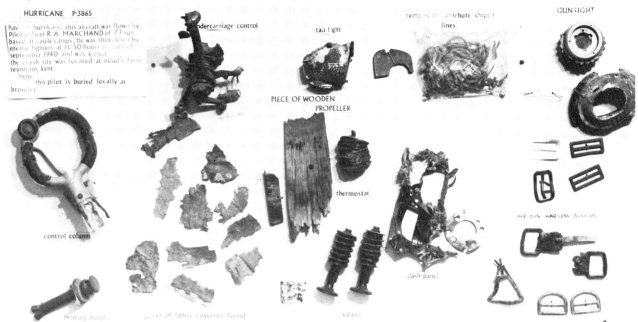

HURRICANE P-3865

undercarriage control
tail light
remains of parachute shroud lines
GUNSIGHT
PIECE OF WOODEN PROPELLER
thermostat
control column
VARIOUS HARNESS BUCKLES
dash panel
Priming Pump
pieces of fabric covering found
valves

Georges Doutrepont arrived in England in the company of eight of his countrymen on July 7, 1940 ready to join the Royal Air Force. Altogether twenty-nine Belgian pilots escaped from the continent to continue the fight. Pilot Officer Doutrepont was shot down late on the morning of the 15th crashing into Staplehurst railway station in Kent.

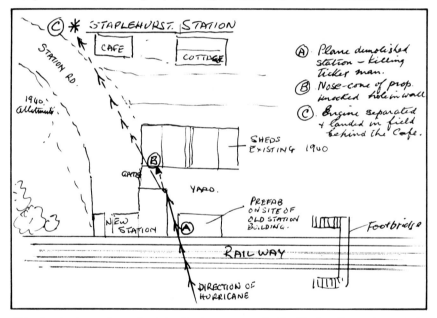

This sketch shows the path of the Hurricane as recalled by Mr. Ron Roots *(below)*, the present-day booking clerk, who indicates the impact point of the spinner.

Above: **An early Battle of Britain excavation attempted way back in the 1960s, Alan Brown is now in the forefront of wreck research and recovery.** *Below:* **Exhibit from the crash at the Kent Battle of Britain Museum.**

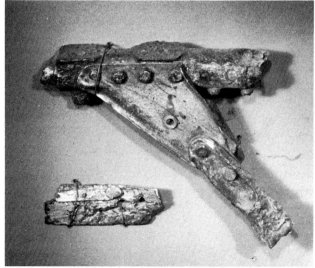

HURRICANE L1998 238 SQDN.

SGT. L. PIDD

Hawker Hurricane, L1998, 238 Squadron, Middle Wallop.
Crashed into woodland at the rear of the Kent College
at Pembury, on Sunday 15-9-1940 at 15.00 hours after
being shot down by a Messerschmitt 110, near Tonbridge,
Kent, the pilot Sgt. L. Pidd, baled out but was killed
when his parachute failed to open.
The Group wish to express their thanks to the Bursar
of the College for permission to recover this aircraft
on 1-3-1975.

Sergeant Leslie Pidd of No. 238 Squadron, 22-year-old son of George and Hilda Pidd of Dunswell, Yorkshire, was shot down on the afternoon of September 15. Although he baled out he was dead when he reached the ground. Sergeant Eric Bann from the same squadron saw him die and in his letter to his parents, written on the following day *(below)* described how Sergeant Pidd was machine gunned on his parachute. An interesting contrast to this contentious issue was given by Air Chief-Marshal Sir Hugh Dowding in his post-battle report (written in 1941 but not published until 1946): ' This is perhaps a convenient opportunity to say a word about the ethics of shooting at aircraft crews who have baled out in parachutes. Germans descending over England are prospective prisoners-of-war and, as such, should be immune. On the other hand, British pilots descending over England are still potential combatants. Much indignation was caused by the fact that German pilots sometimes fired on our descending airmen (although, in my opinion, they were perfectly entitled to do so), but I am glad to say that in many cases they refrained.' The exhibit *(above left)* is at Brenzett and Leslie Pidd's overgrown grave is in St. Peter's Churchyard, Woodmansey.

Above: **The Ashford and Tenterden group excavated Flight Lieutenant Powell-Sheddon's No. 242 Squadron Hurricane at Udimore in 1972. Incredibly these oak leaves *(below)* were found impressed on the front of the engine having been carried into the ground thirty years before.**

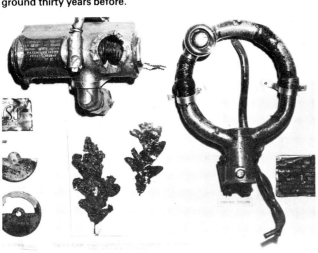

Sergeants Mess,
RAF,
(Name deleted)
Hants.
Monday.
16/9/40

My Dear Mother and Father,
What about the RAF yesterday? My gosh, for every bomb dropped upon the King and Queen old 238 gave them hell. We got 12 'Huns' in one scrap. We just went in as one man and held our fire until very close range then blew them right out of their cockpits. We're all just mad for revenge. Never again shall any one of us give any mercy for our poor Flight Commander and yesterday the Yorkshire boy Sgt. Pidd fell victims to these swines, machine gunning whilst coming down by parachute. Now, after seeing poor Pidd go, shall I ever forgive the 'Hun'.
I am afraid that the weather will curb our activity for it is raining hard. Still it will give rest to the overworked though, mind you, we're for them now and will be quite content to fly any time.
Have felt much brighter after my visit home. Thank you all for the sincere kind actions shown to me, I really enjoyed myself and of course so did May.
Cheerio for now, all my kind regards to the people of Macclesfield.
Your loving son,
Eric.
PS. Domagala quite well, will have to undergo an operation before fit for flying again. He's raising the place down — wants to be back among the Germans.

Sergeant Michael Brzezowski, a 20-year-old from No. 303 Squadron, failed to return on the afternoon of September 15.

253 SQUADRON, KENLEY

Hurricane V6698. Damaged during attack on Do 215 formation over the Channel 3.30 p.m. Forced-landed at Hawkinge. Pilot Officer A. R. H. Barton unhurt. Aircraft damaged but repairable.

257 SQUADRON, DEBDEN

Hurricane P3642. Forced-landed at Croydon with damage sustained in combat over the Thames Estuary 12.30 p.m. Returned to base later. Pilot Officer C. F. A. Capon unhurt. Aircraft damaged but repairable.

Hurricane V7254. Slightly damaged in combat over the Thames Estuary 12.35 p.m. Landed at Biggin Hill returning to base later. Flight Lieutenant P. M. Brothers unhurt. Aircraft repairable.

302 SQUADRON, DUXFORD

Hurricane P2954. Shot down in surprise attack by enemy aircraft over North Weald and crashed at Marks Farm, Woodham Road, Battlesbridge 2.45 p.m. Flight Lieutenant T. P. Chlopik fell dead at Rawreth believed injured baling out. Aircraft WX-E a write-off.

Hurricane   . Returned to base damaged in surprise attack by enemy aircraft over North Weald 3.05 p.m. Sergeant J. Kowalski unhurt. Aircraft repairable.

303 SQUADRON, NORTHOLT

Hurricane P2903. Returned to base with damage sustained in combat with Bf 109s over the Kent coast 12.45 p.m. Pilot Officer W. Lokuciewski wounded in leg. Aircraft damaged but repairable.

Hurricane P3939. Shot down in combat with Bf 109s over Dartford 3.00 p.m. Sergeant T. Andruszkow baled out unhurt. Aircraft RF-M a write-off.

Reputed to be the aircraft excavated by the London Air Museum at Lower Stoke. Major recovery revealed a complete Rolls-Royce Merlin engine, propeller boss, reduction gear, head armour, remains of instrument panel, control column, pilot's maps, tail wheel and remnants of roundel from fuselage.

Hurricane V7465. Slightly damaged in combat with Bf 109s over north Kent 3.00 p.m. Returned safely to base. Squadron Leader R. G. Kellett unhurt. Aircraft repairable.

Hurricane L2099. Returned to base with damage received in combat with Bf 109s over Gravesend 3.05 p.m. Flying Officer W. Zak unhurt. Aircraft repairable.

Hurricane V6673. Damaged in combat with Bf 109s over the Thames 3.00 p.m. Returned to base. Sergeant S. Wojciechowski unhurt. Aircraft repairable.

Hurricane R2685. Returned to base with slight damage following combat with Bf 109s over north Kent coast 3.00 p.m. Pilot Officer M. Feric unhurt. Aircraft repairable.

Hurricane V6684. Slightly damaged during engagement over Gravesend 3.05 p.m. Returned safely to base. Flying Officer W. Urbanowicz unhurt. Aircraft repairable.

Hurricane 3577. Failed to return from combat with Bf 109s over the Thames off Gravesend 3.05 p.m. Presumed crashed in the Estuary. Sergeant M. Brzezowski missing. Aircraft lost.

310 SQUADRON, DUXFORD

Hurricane R4085. Shot down in combat with enemy fighters over the Thames Estuary. Crashed and burned out half mile south of Billericay church 2.42 p.m. Squadron Leader A. Hess baled out unhurt. Aircraft a write-off.

One of the most well-known crashes of the entire battle was the Dornier which crashed into the forecourt of Victoria Station. Sergeant Holmes helped in its destruction but was shot down himself over Chelsea. This is a fragment from his parachute now displayed at Chilham Castle..

Hurricane R4087. Shot down by enemy fighters in combat over the Thames. Believed crashed and burned out half mile north-west of B1011 and A13 junction outside Pitsea 2.30 p.m. Sergeant J. Hubacek baled out slightly injured in right foot admitted to Chatham Hospital. Aircraft a write-off.

Aircraft remains excavated from under a road at Stoke, Isle of Grain by the London Air Museum thought to be this aircraft. Few fragments found do not confirm identity. Pieces also in the Vizard collection.

501 SQUADRON, KENLEY

Hurricane V7433. Forced-landed with radiator damaged in combat with Bf 109s over Ashford 12.35 p.m. Squadron Leader H. A. V. Hogan unhurt. Aircraft damaged but repairable.

Hurricane P2760. Severely damaged by Bf 109s during attack on Do 17s over Ashford. Exploded over East Stour Farm, Chilham wreckage falling into River Stour 12.45 p.m. Pilot Officer A. E. A. van den Hove d'Ertsenryck killed. Aircraft a write-off.

Locality investigated by the Kent Battle of Britain Museum which recovered two wing spar attachments.

All that could be found from Pilot Officer Albert Emmanuel Alix van den Hove d'Ertsenryck's Hurricane which exploded in the air near Chilham.

504 SQUADRON, HENDON

Hurricane P2725. Shot down in attack on Do 17s over London 12.15 p.m. Abandoned over Chelsea, crashed and burned out. Sergeant R. T. Holmes baled out unhurt landing in Ebury Bridge Road. Aircraft a write-off.

Portion of parachute silk, a contemporary souvenir, donated to the Kent Battle of Britain Museum.

John Vinter Gurteen was born in 1916 and came from Suffolk. He won a scholarship to the United States under the English Speaking Union and was a Volunteer Reserve pilot with No. 504 Squadron when he was shot down over south London just after mid-day on the 15th. His remains were cremated at Hendon and now his name is inscribed on the Portland stone panel of the screen wall beside the Cross of Sacrifice.

Hurricane L1913. Believed returned to base with damage to oil cooler following combat over London 12.25 p.m. Flight Lieutenant M. E. A. Royce unhurt. Aircraft damaged but repairable.

Hurricane N2481. Shot down in combat over southern outskirts of London. Dived full throttle onto a house at Hartley near Longfield 12.58 p.m. Pilot Officer J. V. Gurteen killed. Aircraft a write-off.

Hurricane N2705. Crashed near Dartford following combat over south-east London 2.45 p.m. Flying Officer M. Jebb admitted to Dartford hospital with burns (died of injuries 19.9.40). Aircraft a write-off.

602 SQUADRON, WESTHAMPNETT

Spitfire X4412. Forced-landed at Shoreham with engine disabled by return fire from Do 17 engaged over Beachy Head 3.20 p.m. Sergeant C. F. Babbage unhurt. Aircraft damaged but repairable.

603 SQUADRON, HORNCHURCH

Spitfire X4324. Shot down in combat with enemy aircraft and crashed in Kingswood near Chartway Street, Kent 3.05 p.m. Flying Officer A. P. Pease killed. Aircraft a write-off.

Surface fragments recovered during investigation of crash site by Kent Battle of Britain Museum and also London Air Museum and Steve Vizard.

Spitfire R7019. Hit by return fire from Do 17 and crashed on Warren Farm, Fairlight near Hastings 3.10 p.m. Squadron Leader G. L. Denholm baled out unhurt landing near Guestling Lodge. Aircraft a write-off.

605 SQUADRON, CROYDON

Hurricane L2122. Shot down during engagement with Do 17s and Bf 109s over Croydon 11.40 a.m. Crashed at Drux Farm, Plaxtol. Pilot Officer R. E. Jones baled out slightly injured. Aircraft a write-off.

Major recovery by Malling Aircraft Archaeologists. Items now in Lashenden Air Warfare Museum and Vizard collection.

Hurricane L2012. Hit by return fire during attack on Do 17 at 11.40 a.m. Lost control and collided amidships with enemy aircraft over Marden losing port wing. Crashed at 'The Leas', Yalding. Pilot Officer T. P. M. Cooper-Slipper baled out slightly hurt. Aircraft a write-off.

Fragments in Vizard collection. Rolls-Royce Merlin engine, propeller boss and blades, and quantities of smashed airframe in Lashenden Air Warfare Museum also attributed by them to this aircraft.

607 SQUADRON, TANGMERE

Hurricane V6688. Set alight in head-on attack on two Do 17s over Appledore 2.55 p.m. Collided with both and abandoned over Cranbrook. Pilot Officer P. J. T. Stephenson baled out and slightly wounded. Aircraft a write-off.

Flying Officer Arthur Peter Pease, son of Sir Richard and Lady Pease of Richmond, was killed in action at 3.05 p.m on September 15. If you would learn about Peter Pease it is recommended that you read Richard Hillary's classic account of the air war, 'The Last Enemy'. In it he tells beautifully the whole tragic story of the gifted young men who flew and fought and died with debonair gallantry in that now distant summer of 1940. Peter Pease was taken home to the family grave in the little Yorkshire churchyard of St. Michael and All Angels at Middleton Tyas.

609 SQUADRON, WARMWELL

Spitfire K9997. One wheel damaged in collision with crash tender on landing approach at Middle Wallop. Crashed on landing 12.30 p.m. Pilot Officer E. Q. Tobin unhurt. Aircraft damaged but repairable.

Spitfire R6690. Believed shot down by Bf 110 during attack on enemy bombers over London. Crashed and burned out near Kenley 12.30 p.m. Pilot Officer G. N. Gaunt killed (identified 19.9.40). Aircraft a write-off.

Crash site at Sutton visited by Steve Vizard and relics found believed to be from this machine.

Spitfire R6922. Hit by return fire during attack on Do 17 over Rye 3.10 p.m. Returned to base severely damaged. Flying Officer J. C. Dundas unhurt. Aircraft damaged but repairable.

611 SQUADRON, DIGBY

Spitfire II P7303. Severely damaged by return fire from He 111 in combat south of London 2.50 p.m. Returned to base. Flying Officer T. D. Williams unhurt. Aircraft damaged but repairable.

Monday, September 16

92 SQUADRON, BIGGIN HILL

Spitfire R6616. Undercarriage collapsed due to side-slip on landing 11.00 a.m. Pilot Officer H. P. Hill unhurt. Aircraft repairable.

257 SQUADRON, DEBDEN

Hurricane P3642. Forced-landed during training flight to Hendon. Cause not stated. Sergeant D. J. Hulbert unhurt. Aircraft damaged but repairable.

605 SQUADRON, CROYDON

Hurricane N2589. Severely damaged in attack by Bf 109 flown by Major Moelders of JG51 over north Kent 7.50 a.m. Landed at Detling. Pilot Officer E. J. Watson wounded. Aircraft damaged but repairable.

At 11.40 a.m. on the morning of September 15, Pilot Officer Cooper-Slipper of No. 605 collided with a Dornier over Marden. He managed to bale out and landed only slightly hurt, his Hurricane crashing at Yalding. The Lashenden Air Warfare Museum display these items said to be from his aircraft and have investigated the Dornier crash site with positive results.

Geoffrey Norman Gaunt (his picture appears on page 227 in the chapter on Middle Wallop) was a cousin of the film star James Mason. He was missing during a mid-day battle on the 15th but it was not until four days later that the RAF station at Kenley informed No. 609 Squadron that a Spitfire wreck had been located. The machine had fallen from 20,000ft and had completely disintegrated on hitting the ground. Geoff Gaunt was only identified by the name in his collar band. On September 26 he was buried in the Salendine Nook Baptist Chapelyard in Huddersfield. David Crook describes in 'Spitfire Pilot' how he arrived at the chapel too late for the ceremony: 'Unfortunately the Magister had something wrong . . . I was rather late in starting. I landed at Yeadon and raced over to Huddersfield by car and arrived at the church about fifteen minutes after the service had finished. Everybody had gone. The grave was still open and I walked over to it and stood there for a moment looking at the inscription on the coffin of this very gallant and delightful friend.'

616 SQUADRON, KIRTON-IN-LINDSEY

Spitfire L1036. Ditched in North Sea twenty miles north of Cromer 10.30 a.m. having run out of fuel following pursuit of Ju 88. Sergeant T. C. Iveson unhurt brought ashore at Yarmouth by MTB. Aircraft lost.

Tony Graves (being photographed with a propeller blade from Flying Officer Briese's Hurricane V6669 recovered in 1940 and given to the London Air Museum) has, together with John Tickner, been involved with aviation archaeology for more than a decade. Their major personal triumph was the Eddie Egan recovery.

Tuesday, September 17

1 (RCAF) SQUADRON, NORTHOLT

Hurricane V6669. Crash-landed at High Halstow 3.30 p.m. with damaged oil system following combat with Bf 109s. Flying Officer Briese unhurt. Aircraft damaged but repairable.

Crash site investigated by London Air Museum and many small fragments and minor components recovered. One propeller blade donated by a local resident.

In September 1976 a Hurricane was discovered by the London Air Museum in a wood at Bethersden, Kent which contained the remains of its pilot. Careful research suggested he was Sergeant Edward Egan who had been presumed killed in action on September 17, 1940, had no known grave and was therefore commemorated on the Runnymede Memorial. Although the museum's evidence satisfied the Coroner that the remains were those of Sergeant Egan, the Ministry of Defence insisted on further information which would prove this beyond any doubt and therefore the Commonwealth War Graves Commission were obliged to carry out the burial as that of an unknown airman although Egan's relatives were present. A consortium of wreck societies therefore elected to re-dig the crash site and Steve Hall of the Wealden group found the tiny manufacturer's plate *(below)* confirming the aircraft identity. With this positive proof, the Ministry of Defence relented and a new headstone was placed on the grave at Brookwood Military Cemetery bearing Edward Egan's full details and a personal inscription chosen by his sister: 'In Treasured Memory of a Much Loved one of The Few'. The plate on the coffin obviously still remains as it was (Daily Mail).

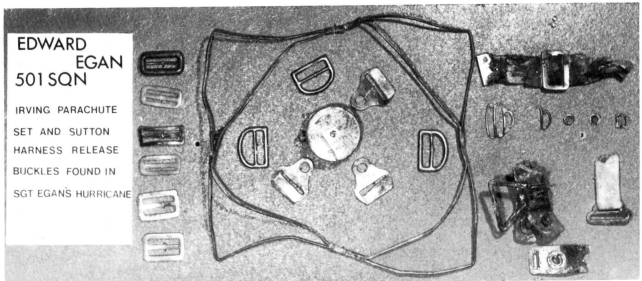

EDWARD EGAN 501 SQN — IRVING PARACHUTE SET AND SUTTON HARNESS RELEASE BUCKLES FOUND IN SGT EGAN'S HURRICANE

Right: **Obituary notice for Sergeant Denis Helcke of No. 504 Squadron. The phrase 'Killed in action' appears on many graves of 'The Few' although whether an accident can be classed as 'in action' is debatable. The RAF Battle of Britain Museum state that they do not include accidental deaths on their roll of operational casualties although, in this case, Denis Helcke's name is included.**

41 SQUADRON, HORNCHURCH

Spitfire X4178. Returned to base with damage caused by Bf 109 in combat off Manston 3.35 p.m. Flying Officer J. G. Boyle unhurt. Aircraft repairable.

Spitfire R6887. Severely damaged in combat with Bf 109s over Dover 3.40 p.m. Pilot Officer J. N. Mackenzie unhurt. Aircraft a write-off.

Spitfire N3266. Badly damaged by Bf 109 in action off Dover 3.45 p.m. Pilot Officer H. H. Chalder unhurt. Aircraft damaged but repairable.

Spitfire X4409. Forced-landed at Stelling Minnis following combat with Bf 109s over Manston 3.45 p.m. Pilot Officer H. C. Baker unhurt. Aircraft repairable.

73 SQUADRON, DEBDEN

Hurricane   . Attacked by suspected friendly Hurricane during patrol over Hornchurch 4.10 p.m. Forced-landed on Wick Farm, Burnham with damaged petrol tank. Sergeant A. E. Marshall unhurt. Aircraft TP-A repairable.

151 SQUADRON, DIGBY

Hurricane R4185. Flew into the ground during pursuit of He 111 through low cloud 5.30 p.m. Sergeant J. Winstanley injured admitted to hospital. Aircraft a write-off.

152 SQUADRON, WARMWELL

Spitfire   . Landed at Colerne with engine seized having been hit in oil cooler by return fire from Ju 88 2.00 p.m. Pilot Officer E. S. Marrs unhurt. Aircraft repairable.

501 SQUADRON, KENLEY

Hurricane V7357. Shot down during solo attack on Bf 109 formation over Ashford 3.40 p.m. Believed crashed Winstead Court. Sergeant J. H. Lacey baled out unhurt. Aircraft a write-off.

Hurricane P3820. Shot down in flames by Bf 109 in surprise attack over Ashford 3.40 p.m. crashed Daniels Wood, Tuesnoad Farm, Bethersden. Sergeant E. J. Egan killed. Aircraft a write-off.

Site located and excavated by the London Air Museum on September 11, 1976. Remains of shattered and badly burned Rolls-Royce Merlin engine recovered together with propeller boss, reduction gear, remnants of instrument panel, cockpit controls including the control column, tail wheel and both undercarriage legs. Also recovered were the pilot's remains and parachute pack riddled with 7.9mm bullets. Inquest at Croydon February 25, 1977 identified pilot as Sergeant Egan who was buried with full military honours at Brookwood Military Cemetery as an unknown airman'. Crash-site re-excavated in November 1978 by London Air Museum assisted by members of Brenzett Aeronautical Museum, Kent Battle of Britain Museum and the Wealden Aviation Archeological Group and the aircraft identity plate eventually found confirming identity beyond dispute. MoD authorised headstone to be changed to one including name. Bulkhead armour and base of control column in Kent Battle of Britain Museum.

504 SQUADRON, HENDON

Hurricane V7529. Lost control following dummy attack by RAF fighters over Faversham 4.00 p.m. ARP reported crashed Shepherds Hill, Selling. Sergeant D. A. Helcke baled out but hit aircraft and fell dead near Selling. Aircraft a write-off.

607 SQUADRON, TANGMERE

Hurricane P3929. Shot down by Hptmn. Neumann of I/JG27 and forced-landed on Tuesnoad Farm, Bethersden 3.35 p.m. Pilot Officer G. H. E. Welford slightly wounded. Aircraft damaged but repairable.

Site investigated by the London Air Museum and many fragments collected from a nearby hedgerow. Some pieces also in Kent Battle of Britain Museum collection.

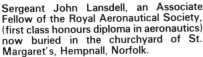

Sergeant John Lansdell, an Associate Fellow of the Royal Aeronautical Society, (first class honours diploma in aeronautics) now buried in the churchyard of St. Margaret's, Hempnall, Norfolk.

George William Jeffreys, born in Hemel Hempstead, came from Winterbourne in Wiltshire. He joined the Volunteer Reserve before the war and was serving with No. 46 Squadron at Stapleford Tawney when he was killed in one of the many instances during the battle of a malfunctioning parachute. His grave lies in St. Michael's Churchyard at Winterbourne Earls.

Hurricane P3933. Shot down by Hptmn. Neumann of I/JG27 and crashed at the 'Bell' at Beltring 3.40 p.m. Sergeant J. Lansdell killed. Aircraft a write-off.

Fragments recovered from hop-garden by London Air Museum in 1976.

611 SQUADRON, DIGBY

Spitfire II P7305. Overturned on landing at Fowlmere following collision with stationary Spitfire in bad visibility 5.00 p.m. Pilot Officer J. W. Lund unhurt. Aircraft damaged but repairable.

Wednesday, September 18

1 (RCAF) SQUADRON, NORTHOLT

Hurricane P3859. Shot down in combat over the Thames Estuary 10.30 a.m. Pilot Officer E. W. B. Beardmore baled out slightly wounded. Aircraft a write-off.

19 SQUADRON, DUXFORD

Spitfire N3265. Forced-landed following engine seizure during routine patrol 10.50 a.m. Pilot Officer F. Hradil unhurt. Aircraft damaged but repairable.

Spitfire X4170. Forced-landed at Eastchurch with glycol tank damaged following combat over the Thames Estuary 1.30 p.m. Pilot Officer W. J. Lawson unhurt. Aircraft repairable.

25 SQUADRON, NORTH WEALD

Blenheim   . Returned to base damaged by return fire from enemy aircraft intercepted during night patrol 10.50 p.m. Pilot Officer B. J. Rofe, Sergeant J. B. McCormack both unhurt. Aircraft ZK-H damaged but repairable.

41 SQUADRON, HORNCHURCH

Spitfire X4317. Returned to base slightly damaged in combat with Bf 109s west of Gravesend 1.00 p.m. Pilot Officer G. H. Bennions unhurt. Aircraft repairable.

46 SQUADRON, STAPLEFORD

Hurricane V7442. Shot down in action over Chatham 12.30 p.m. Sergeant G. W. Jefferys baled out but killed due to parachute failure. Aircraft a write-off.

Hurricane V6554. Shot down in combat over Chatham believed that which crashed at Chestnut Avenue, Walderslade 12.36 p.m. Pilot Officer P. W. le Fevre baled out with minor injuries. Aircraft a write-off.

Items from an aircraft recovered at nearby Bredhurst by Steve Vizard said to be from this aircraft.

London Air Museum display of relics from No. 66 Squadron Spitfire R6603.

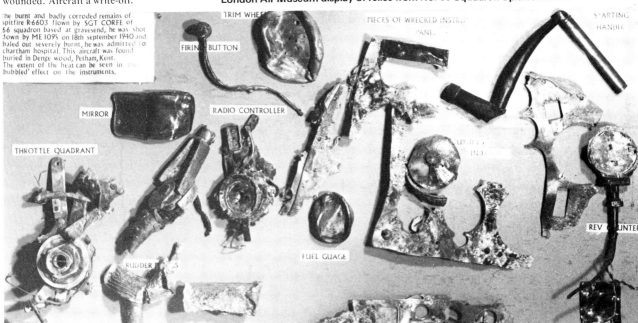

the burnt and badly corroded remains of spitfire R6603 flown by SGT CORFE of 66 squadron based at gravesend, he was shot down by ME 109's on 18th september 1940 and baled out severely burnt, he was admitted to chartham hospital. This aircraft was found buried in Denge wood, Petham, Kent. The extent of the heat can be seen in the bubbled effect on the instruments.

Hurricane P3816. Shot down in combat and believed crashed in Chatham 12.56 p.m. Sergeant C. A. L. Hurry baled out wounded and burned admitted to Chatham Hospital. Aircraft a write-off.

Brown painted fuselage panel embossed 'P3816' taken from the crash-site in 1940 and subsequently donated to the Kent Battle of Britain Museum.

66 SQUADRON, GRAVESEND

Spitfire R6603. Shot down in action over Canterbury area 10.30 a.m. Believed crashed in Denge Wood, Petham. Sergeant D. F. Corfe injured admitted to Chartham Hospital. Aircraft a write-off.

Major recovery undertaken by the London Air Museum complete Rolls-Royce Merlin engine excavated from chalk together with two propeller blades, propeller boss and spinner bearing traces of red paint, cockpit components and controls, rear-view mirror, tail wheel and both undercarriage legs.

Spitfire R6925. Shot down in combat over the Thames Estuary 5.00 p.m. Pilot Officer R. J. Mathers baled out uninjured. Aircraft a write-off.

72 SQUADRON, BIGGIN HILL

Spitfire R6704. Shot down in surprise attack by Bf 109 during squadron patrol over Gravesend 10.30 a.m. Sergeant H. J. Bell-Walker seriously wounded. Aircraft damaged but repairable.

Spitfire P9368. Seriously damaged in combat with Bf 109s and forced-landed at Martin Mill, Dover 10.30 a.m. Pilot Officer J. P. Lloyd seriously wounded. Aircraft damaged but repairable.

Spitfire X4337. 'Bounced', by Bf 109s over north Kent and forced-landed at Hawkinge 10.30 a.m. Pilot unhurt. Aircraft damaged but repairable.

73 SQUADRON, DEBDEN

Hurricane . Smashed propeller and damaged port wing in heavy landing following first flight with unit 10.25 a.m. Pilot Officer K. M. Millist unhurt. Aircraft TP-C repairable.

92 SQUADRON, BIGGIN HILL

Spitfire N3193. Crashed and burned out at Hollingbourne 9.55 a.m. following combat with Bf 109s. Pilot Officer R. Mottram slightly burned and admitted to Orpington Hospital on return to unit. Aircraft a write-off.

Above: **The Essex Historical Aircraft Society uncovering the wreckage of Flight Lieutenant Parnall's No. 249 Squadron Hurricane at Margaretting.** *Below:* **Denis Geach Parnall, twenty-five years old, was taken back to his native Cornwall for burial in the local churchyard of St. Gennys. His grave is the one with the Celtic cross.**

Spitfire N3283. Severely damaged in combat with Bf 109s and crashed at Appledore due to engine failure during forced-landing 10.00 a.m. Pilot Officer A. C. Bartley unhurt. Aircraft damaged but repairable.

Spitfire K9991. Crash-landed at Debden following combat with He 111s off the Essex coast 5.40 p.m. Flight Lieutenant J. A. Paterson unhurt. Aircraft damaged but repairable.

222 SQUADRON, HORNCHURCH

Spitfire R6772. Crashed and burned out at Clock House Farm, Challock after combat with Bf 109s over Canterbury 1.53 p.m. Sergeant I. Hutchinson baled out slightly wounded landing at Molash. Aircraft a write-off.

249 SQUADRON, NORTH WEALD

Hurricane V6694. Shot down during patrol over Gravesend 1.25 p.m. crashed and burned out by the A12 road near Furness Farm, Furze Hill, Margaretting, Essex. Flight Lieutenant D. G. Parnall killed. Aircraft a write-off.

Major recovery undertaken by the Essex Historical Aircraft Society. Rolls-Royce Merlin engine. unearthed together with propeller, undercarriage legs, cockpit controls and instruments and many shattered airframe components.

302 SQUADRON, DUXFORD

Hurricane P3086. Believed hit by debris from Ju 88 engaged over the Chelmsford area 5.40 p.m. Crash-landed at Sandon Lodge Farm, Danbury. Sergeant E. Patarak unhurt. Aircraft damaged but repairable.

303 SQUADRON, NORTHOLT

Hurricane . Damaged by RAF fighters in combat over mid-Kent 1.15 p.m. Returned safely to base. Pilot unhurt. Aircraft repairable.

501 SQUADRON, KENLEY

Hurricane V6600. Shot down by Bf 109s in combat over Tonbridge and crashed near Clapper Lane, Staplehurst 9.33 a.m. Sergeant C. J. Saward baled out unhurt. Aircraft a write-off.

Hurricane V6620. Crashed near Charing following combat against He 111s with Bf 109 escort over West Malling 12.30 p.m. Squadron Leader H. A. V. Hogan baled out unhurt. Aircraft a write-off.

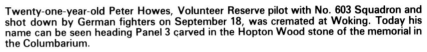

E RECORDED THE NAMES OF ONE H
IETEEN MEMBERS OF HIS MAJESTY'S
DIED IN THE SERVICE OF THEIR COU

SSMAN, RN.	PILOT OFFICER (PILOT) P. HOWES		MAJOR J. C. S. M
31.10.1941	ROYAL AIR FORCE	18.9.1940	GENERAL LIST
)FC.	LT-COL. H. C. E. HULL, DSO.		SQUADRON LEA
26.3.1941	THE QUEEN'S ROYAL REGIMENT	18.11.1939	ROYAL AIR FORCE
ER	MAJOR F. T. B. JOHNSON		CHIEF OFFICER
9.8.1944	THE LOYAL REGIMENT	3.8.1942	

603 SQUADRON, HORNCHURCH

Spitfire X4323. Shot down by Bf 109s and crashed at Kennington near Ashford 9.50 a.m. Pilot Officer P. Howes killed. Aircraft a write-off.

Spitfire K9803. Fuselage badly damaged by 20mm cannon-fire in combat over Maidstone 10.00 a.m. Returned to base. Sergeant G. T. Bailey unhurt. Aircraft damaged but repairable.

Twenty-one-year-old Peter Howes, Volunteer Reserve pilot with No. 603 Squadron and shot down by German fighters on September 18, was cremated at Woking. Today his name can be seen heading Panel 3 carved in the Hopton Wood stone of the memorial in the Columbarium.

Thursday, September 19

257 SQUADRON, DEBDEN

Hurricane V6558. Forced-landed at Bawdsey during uneventful convoy patrol 1.20 p.m. Cause not stated. Flight Lieutenant P. M. Brothers unhurt. Aircraft damaged but repairable.

Friday, September 20

41 SQUADRON, HORNCHURCH

Spitfire X4101. Damaged in combat and forced-landed at Lympne 5.00 p.m. Pilot Officer G. H. Bennions unhurt. Aircraft damaged but repairable.

56 SQUADRON, BOSCOMBE DOWN

Hurricane L1595. Flying accident during formation practice 11.30 a.m. Crashed west of Bulford Camp near Amesbury. Sergeant C. V. Meeson killed. Aircraft US-S a write-off.

72 SQUADRON, BIGGIN HILL

Spitfire X4410. Shot down in combat with enemy fighters in combat over Canterbury 10.20 a.m. Believe crashed at Stiff Street near Sittingbourne. Pilot Officer D. F. Holland baled out severely wounded and died shortly after admission to hospital. Aircraft a write-off.

Fuselage panel bearing traces of camouflage paint and pilot's 'wings' insignia recovered by local civil authorities in 1940 and subsequently donated to the Kent Battle of Britain Museum. Some surface fragments collected by Steve Vizard.

92 SQUADRON, BIGGIN HILL

Spitfire X4417. Shot down by Major Moelders of JG51 in combat over Dungeness. Crashed and burned out at West Hougham 11.34 a.m. Pilot Officer H. P. Hill killed. Aircraft a write-off.

Spitfire N3248. Shot down into the Channel off Dungeness by Major Moelders of JG51 at 11.34 a.m. Sergeant P. R. Eyles missing. Aircraft lost.

Denis Holland was educated at Newbury, Berkshire and began a career as a civil pilot when he was fifteen. He had obtained both his 'A' and 'B' certificates by the time he was seventeen and he became the youngest Air Guard instructor in Great Britain the following year. When war broke out he had served for five years in the Volunteer Reserve and had a total of 3,000 hours logged. Daring and born to flying, he was nicknamed 'Dutch' when he joined the RAF. By Friday, September 20, he had seven confirmed victories. He baled out that morning after being in combat over Canterbury but landed badly wounded. His last words to the doctor after admission to hospital were: 'I am all right, old pal, Dutchy can take it'. After he died, they took him back to Berkshire where he was laid in the family plot at St. Andrew's Chaddlesworth.

SERGEANT CHARLES MEESON, DIED SEPTEMBER 20, 1940

Pilot Officer 'Laurie' Whitbread, although mortally wounded, managed to land his Spitfire almost intact, sliding across

Hermitage Road at Higham to end up in this small stagnant pond. He was thrown clear but had been killed.

222 SQUADRON, HORNCHURCH

Spitfire N3203. Crashed at Pond Cottage, Hermitage Farm, Higham, Rochester 11.15 a.m. following surprise attack by Bf 109s. Pilot Officer H. L. Whitbread killed. Aircraft a write-off.

Spitfire R6840. Badly damaged in surprise attack by Bf 109s over Thames Estuary 11.35 p.m. Crashed through perimeter fence on landing. Pilot Officer E. F Edsall unhurt. Aircraft damaged but repairable.

Spitfire K9993. Shot down in surprise attack by Bf 109s over the Thames Estuary 11.35 a.m. Crashed and burned out at West Hanningfield. Pilot Officer W. R. Assheton baled out with slight burns landing at Latchingdon and admitted to St. Peter's Hospital, Maldon. Aircraft a write-off.

Pilot Officer Howard Hill, son of Jack and Dorothy Hill of Spring Creek, Marlborough, New Zealand. He was twenty years old when shot down by the German ace Major Moelders and now lies in the military plot in Folkestone New Cemetery beside Hawkinge aerodrome.

253 SQUADRON, KENLEY

Hurricane R2686. Crashed and burned out following attack by Bf 109 11.30 a.m. Pilot Officer A. R. H. Barton slightly wounded admitted to Ashford Hospital. Aircraft a write-off.

Hurricane V6736. Crashed following attack by Bf 109s over Maidstone area 11.30 a.m. Sergeant R. A. Innes believed unhurt. Aircraft a write-off.

Hurricane P5179. Damaged in attack by Bf 109s during patrol over Maidstone 11.30 a.m. Pilot unhurt. Aircraft damaged but repairable.

Sergeant Charles Victor Meeson lived with his parents in a large rambling house in Loughton, Essex called 'Brooklyn' (now the site of the county library). An early entrant into the Royal Air Force on the outbreak of war, Charles Meeson qualified as an NCO pilot and, in late August 1940, was posted as a replacement to No. 56 Squadron at North Weald a few days before the withdrawal of the unit to Boscombe Down for rest and refit. On the 20th of the month he suffered an accident while engaged on formation practice, his Hurricane crashing and carrying him to his death. Although the old house in Loughton has gone, Charles Meeson lies re-united with his parents in the town's burial ground.

605 SQUADRON, CROYDON

Hurricane V6722. Badly damaged by 20mm cannon in attack by Bf 109 11.30 a.m. Returned safely to base. Pilot Officer W. J. Glowacki unhurt. Aircraft damaged but repairable.

463

Flying Officer Julian Topolnicki, a Polish pilot with No. 601, buried in the Commonwealth War Graves Commission section at Exeter Higher Cemetery.

Saturday, September 21

29 SQUADRON, DIGBY

Blenheim L1507. Damaged hitting a floodlight on landing at Ternhill following evening patrol 9.05 p.m. Sergeant V. H. Skillen, Aircraftman D. W. Isherwood both unhurt. Aircraft repairable.

92 SQUADRON, BIGGIN HILL

Spitfire N3032. Believed forced-landed near Hildenborough 6.45 p.m. following combat over Sevenoaks. Pilot unhurt. Aircraft damaged but repairable.

601 SQUADRON, EXETER

Hurricane L1894. Crashed and burned out on take-off on training flight 11.30 a.m. Flying Officer J. Topolnicki killed. Aircraft a write-off.

Sunday, September 22

19 SQUADRON, DUXFORD

Spitfire X4351. Destroyed in bombing attack on base 3.30 p.m. No casualties. Aircraft a write-off.

85 SQUADRON, CHURCH FENTON

Hurricane V6668. Damaged in forced-landing near Clitheroe low on fuel in bad visibility. Flight Lieutenant G. Allard unhurt. Aircraft damaged but repairable.

Hurricane V7349. Forced-landed near Burnley out of fuel in bad visibility. Pilot Officer J. E. Marshall unhurt. Aircraft damaged but repairable.

Hurricane V7440. Damaged in forced-landing outside Burnley low on fuel in deteriorating weather conditions. Pilot Officer J. A. Hemmingway unhurt. Aircraft damaged but repairable.

501 SQUADRON, KENLEY

Hurricane V7498. Forced-landed during weather test flight 7.50 a.m. Pilot Officer P. R. Hairs unhurt. Aircraft repairable.

Monday, September 23

65 SQUADRON, TURNHOUSE

Spitfire K9904. Crashed on landing from routine practice flight 4.05 p.m. Sergeant Hine unhurt. Aircraft damaged but repairable.

72 SQUADRON, BIGGIN HILL

Spitfire X4063. Believed crash-landed and burned out near Sittingbourne following combat with Bf 109s over Gravesend 10.30 a.m. Pilot Officer B. W. Brown unhurt. Aircraft a write-off.

73 SQUADRON, CHURCH FENTON

Hurricane P8812. Shot down by Bf 109s over Sheppey and crashed at Ludgate, Lynstead near Rodmersham 10.55 a.m. Sergeant V. A. B. Leng baled out and injured in heavy landing. Admitted to Chatham Hospital. Aircraft a write-off.
Excavated by the London Air Museum which recovered an intact Rolls-Royce Merlin engine, propeller boss, cockpit components including head armour and one complete undercarriage leg.

Hurricane V7445. Shot down by Bf 109s over Sheppey and crashed in the Swale, Elmley. 11.00 a.m. Sergeant F. S. Perkins baled out unhurt. Aircraft TP-A a write-off.

Hurricane P3226. Crashed near Lightship 93 following attack by Bf 109s 11.03 a.m. Pilot Officer D. S. Kinder rescued from Thames Estuary and admitted to RN Hospital, Chatham with severe burns. Aircraft lost.

Hurricane L2036. Crashed in Thames Estuary near Lightship 93 following attack by Bf 109s 11.05 a.m. Pilot Officer Hobart rescued from sea and admitted to RN Hospital, Chatham with severe burns. Aircraft lost.

74 SQUADRON, COLTISHALL

Spitfire II P7362. Abandoned aircraft during routine patrol 1½ miles south-east of Southwold 11.30 a.m. Cause unknown. Sergeant D. H. Ayers baled out but lost. (Body recovered 4.10.40.) Aircraft lost.

92 SQUADRON, BIGGIN HILL

Spitfire P9371. Crashed attempting forced-landing near West Malling following combat with Bf 109s over Gravesend 10.00 a.m. Pilot Officer A. J. S. Pattinson severely wounded in thigh admitted to Preston Hall Hospital, Maidstone. Aircraft a write-off.

152 SQUADRON, WARMWELL

Spitfire R7016. Failed to return from operational sortie and believed crashed in Channel. Cause unknown. Pilot Officer W. Beaumont missing. Aircraft lost.

229 SQUADRON, NORTHOLT

Hurricane P2879. Shot down whilst acting as 'weaver' on squadron patrol. Abandoned aircraft crashed on St. Mary's Marshes, Hoo 10.50 a.m. Pilot Officer P. O. D. Allcock baled out wounded landing at Westcliff and admitted to Southend Hospital. Aircraft a write-off.

Middle Wallop,
Sunday.

Dear Mother, Father and 'Sandy',
Thanks very much for the letter, very sorry for not having written sooner but have been going great guns.

Have been having a real hectic week, the invasion having started in real earnest. Have been right in the thick of it, our squadron managed to bag 21 planes on Thursday. Never in all my life have I had such a flying day and never before have I seen so many planes. However, yours truly managed again to come out O.K. Thank God. However we lost our Flight Commander and Section Leader, poor fellows, then followed our Commanding Officer. Today I have just come back from a further great fight. I think our report in the news tomorrow will even better Thursday's record but were again first there and consequently suffered our losses. Only one pilot returned from 'B' Flight so we now have only pilots without C/O or Flight Commander. I think they will have to make me a Squadron Leader. I am pleased to say that my 'bag' keeps going up.

Have made great friends with a young Polish Air Force pilot, two having joined our squadron. His tale of how the Germans machine gunned all his people and his life hunted by 'Gestapo' police before he eventually managed to escape to England, well it just made my blood boil. He does not want to live, only seek revenge upon the 'Germans' who have killed and taken all that matters in life. Poland he states is just Hell, its people and food ravaged by blood-thirsty men of the 'Gestapo'.

My leave has gone for six, even my 24 hours today has gone. Still never mind, may God keep me alive and I'll be with you all one of these fine days, so don't worry or be disappointed with this cruel news.
All my kind regards to you all,
Eric

David Ayers from Herne Bay, Kent was a student at Kent College, Canterbury from 1926 to 1931. He was a pre-war member of the RAF Volunteer Reserve. When his body was recovered from the North Sea on October 4, he was laid to rest in the beautifully maintained cemetery at Ipswich not far from his last patrol.

John Bryson, Pilot Officer with No. 92 Squadron, came from Montreal, Canada. He crashed near North Weald and was buried at St. Andrews.

234 SQUADRON, ST. EVAL

Spitfire R6896. Failed to return from routine section patrol 11.00 a.m. Believed crashed in Channel off French coast. Pilot Officer T. M. Kane captured. Aircraft lost.

257 SQUADRON, DEBDEN

Hurricane P2960. Shot down by Bf 109 during patrol over the Thames Estuary 9.52 a.m. Crashed at Grove, Eastchurch. Sergeant D. J. Aslin baled out and admitted to Minster Hospital with burns. Aircraft a write-off.

Tuesday, September 24

17 SQUADRON, DEBDEN

Hurricane P3878. Crashed into the sea off Chatham following attack by Bf 109 9.05 a.m. Pilot Officer H. A. C. Bird-Wilson baled out burned and rescued from sea. Admitted to RN Hospital, Chatham. Aircraft YB-W lost.

Hurricane P3168. Crashed on landing at base due to damage suffered in attack by Bf 109 over the Thames Estuary 9.15 a.m. Pilot Officer D. H. Wissler wounded in left arm and admitted to Saffron Walden Hospital. Aircraft damaged but repairable.

41 SQUADRON, HORNCHURCH

Spitfire N3118. Shot down during squadron patrol off Dover and crashed in the Channel 1.45 p.m. Sergeant J. McAdam baled out rescued from the sea and admitted to Dover Hospital. Aircraft lost.

Spitfire R6604. Crashed outside Dover following combat with Bf 109s over the Channel 1.50 p.m. Sergeant E. V. Darling unhurt. Aircraft damaged but repairable.

72 SQUADRON, BIGGIN HILL

Spitfire   . Severely damaged in combat with enemy aircraft over Swanley 8.20 a.m. Believed returned safely to base. Flight Sergeant Steere unhurt. Aircraft damaged but repairable.

92 SQUADRON, BIGGIN HILL

Spitfire X4037. Shot down by Bf 109s 9.00 a.m. Crashed and burned out near North Weald. Pilot Officer J. S. Bryson killed. Aircraft a write-off.

Spitfire X4356. Crash-landed on Higham Marshes damaged in starboard mainplane and glycol system by Bf 109 in action over Maidstone 9.03 a.m. Sergeant W. T. Ellis unhurt. Aircraft damaged but repairable.

Spitfire X4427. Returned to base with severe damage to mainplane sustained in combat with Bf 109s over Maidstone 9.15 a.m. Squadron Leader R. C. F. Lister wounded in wrist and legs admitted to Farnborough Hospital. Aircraft damaged but repairable.

151 SQUADRON, DIGBY

Hurricane P3306. Tail knocked off in collision with V7432 during formation practice 10.20 a.m. Sergeant J. McPhee baled out unhurt. Aircraft a write-off.

Hurricane V7432. Collided with P3306 during formation practice 10.20 a.m. Forced-landed in a paddock at Waddington. Pilot Officer J. K. Haviland unhurt. Aircraft damaged but repairable.

Pilot Officer D. H. Wissler with Hurricane YB-W, P3878, which crashed into the sea off Chatham on the morning of September 24 after being abandoned by Pilot Officer Bird-Wilson. Pilot Officer Wissler survived the battle to meet death in action on November 11, (Armistice Day) 1940.

601 SQUADRON, EXETER

Hurricane R4120. Overshot runway and overturned on landing after training flight 12.05 p.m. Pilot Officer D. B. Ogilvie slightly injured admitted to hospital. Aircraft damaged but repairable.

605 SQUADRON, CROYDON

Hurricane P3832. Shot down by Bf 109s in combat over the French coast 4.30 p.m. Pilot Officer W. J. Glowacki killed. Aircraft lost.

615 SQUADRON, PRESTWICK

Hurricane V7239. Wrecked in forced-landing having run out of fuel. Sergeant Finch slightly injured. Aircraft a write-off.

616 SQUADRON, KIRTON-IN-LINDSEY

Spitfire N3058. Forced-landed out of fuel having lost bearings during return flight from Duxford 7.00 p.m. Pilot Officer J. H. Rowden unhurt. Aircraft damaged but repairable.

Wednesday, September 25

1 (RCAF) SQUADRON, NORTHOLT

Hurricane V6749. Forced-landed near Cookham during routine patrol 12.10 p.m. Cause not stated. Flying Officer R. W. Norris unhurt. Aircraft damaged but repairable.

23 SQUADRON, MIDDLE WALLOP

Blenheim L8369. Stalled and crashed manoeuvring to land with flaps and undercarriage lowered. Fell at Broughton near Stourbridge 9.30 p.m. Pilot Officer E. Orgias, Sergeant L. R. Karasek and AC2 R. I. Payne all killed. Aircraft YP-B a write-off.

43 SQUADRON, USWORTH

Hurricane P5191. Landed wheels up at Hetton-le-Hole following engine failure due to mishandling of fuel cock. Pilot Officer Langdon unhurt. Aircraft damaged but repairable.

85 SQUADRON, CHURCH FENTON

Hurricane L1854. Crashed attempting forced-landing near base. Exact details not recorded. Pilot believed unhurt. Aircraft a write-off.

As a Kings Scout Master, Rotherham-born Reginald Irving Payne was an active campaigner for youth organisations and activities. When war was declared in September 1939, he was in a reserved occupation and could, had he wished, sat out the war in comparative safety and comfort. But such was not Reg Payne's way. Instead he volunteered for air crew duties in the Royal Air Force and after completing training as a wireless operator/air gunner he was posted to No. 23 Squadron on September 23, 1940. Two nights later the Blenheim in which he was flying stalled and crashed while attempting to land at Middle Wallop, killing the entire crew. *Above:* Reg Payne's grave at St. Helen's, Treeton was one of the most overgrown we photographed — especially compared with those of his two fellow crewmen. He is also one of those airmen never promoted in 1940 and still incorrectly attributed with the rank of AC2 instead of sergeant. This error in the records has been fully discussed in the chapter on the Casualties.

Left: **Eric Orgias, the pilot, from Napier, Hawke's Bay, New Zealand, held a diploma in sheep farming at the Massey Agricultural College, Palmerston North.** *Right:* **Laurence Karasek, the observer.**

152 SQUADRON, WARMWELL

Spitfire P9463. Believed shot down by enemy aircraft in action over Portsmouth. Exact fate uncertain. Sergeant W. G. Silver killed. Aircraft a write-off.

Spitfire   . Damaged in action over Yeovil 11.45 a.m. Returned to base. Pilot Officer G. J. Cox unhurt. Aircraft repairable.

Spitfire   . Returned to base with slight damage following combat south of Bristol 11.45 a.m. Pilot Officer E. S. Marrs unhurt. Aircraft repairable.

Spitfire X4177. Hit in petrol tank by return fire from He 111 engaged west of Bristol 11.55 a.m. Forced-landed at Skew Bridge, Newton St. Loe three miles west of Bath. Squadron Leader P. K. Devitt unhurt. Aircraft damaged but repairable.

Spitfire N3173. Crashed near Church Farm, Woolverton following attack on He 111s west of Bristol 12.00 p.m. Sergeant K. C. Holland killed. Aircraft a write-off.

Sergeant Bill Silver with his wife Evelyn and one year old daughter Joyce. Sergeant Silver was killed over Portsmouth while flying with No. 152 Squadron and was buried in Milton Road Cemetery in Portsmouth. In later years, his widow remarried and made a new life for herself in Victoria, Australia, but Joyce died tragically after the birth of her first baby when only twenty-six.

234 SQUADRON, ST. EVAL

Spitfire X4182. Crashed near St. Mawgan on return from routine sortie 6.45 p.m. Cause not stated. Pilot Officer MacKay baled out and seriously injured. Aircraft a write-off.

238 SQUADRON, MIDDLE WALLOP

Hurricane P3222. Forced-landed outside Padstock following engagement with enemy aircraft 12.05 p.m. Later returned to base. Sergeant D. S. Harrison unhurt. Aircraft repairable.

Hurricane N2597. Forced-landed on Charmy Down following action against He 111s and Bf 110s south of Yeovil 3.40 p.m. Sergeant F. A. Sibley unhurt. Aircraft a write-off.

609 SQUADRON, WARMWELL

Spitfire L1008. Belly-landed at Glastonbury with engine trouble following destruction of Bf 110 near Portishead Point 12.00 p.m. Sergeant J. Hughes-Rees unhurt. Aircraft damaged but repairable.

Spitfire N3280. Hit by Bf 109 during combat south of Bristol 12.00 p.m. Landed back at base on burst tyre. Pilot Officer A. K. Ogilvie unhurt. Aircraft damaged but repairable.

Thursday, September 26

152 SQUADRON, WARMWELL

Spitfire K9982. Crashed into the Channel twelve miles south of the Needles following combat with Bf 109s 4.40 p.m. Flying Officer E. C. Deanesley baled out wounded and rescued by RN launch landing at Swanage. Aircraft lost.

Spitfire K9882. Shot down by Bf 109s in combat over the Channel off Swanage 4.50 p.m. Crashed into the sea. Sergeant J. M. Christie picked up dead. Aircraft lost.

229 SQUADRON, NORTHOLT

Hurricane V6745. Forced-landed at Hambledon after combat with Bf 110s over Southampton 4.30 p.m. Sergeant S. W. Merryweather wounded and slightly burned. Aircraft RE-Y a write-off.

238 SQUADRON, MIDDLE WALLOP

Hurricane P2983. Forced-landed at Lee-on-Solent following combat with Bf 110s over the Isle of Wight 4.30 p.m. Squadron Leader H. A. Fenton unhurt. Aircraft repairable.

Hurricane P3464. Returned to base damaged in combat with Bf 110 over the Isle of Wight 4.30 p.m. Sergeant J. V. Kucera believed unhurt. Aircraft damaged but repairable.

Hurricane P3098. Shot down in combat with Bf 110s over the Solent 4.30 p.m. Presumed crashed in the sea. Sergeant V. Horsky missing. Aircraft lost.

Hurricane P3830. Shot down by Bf 110 in combat over the Isle of Wight west of Newport 4.35 p.m. Pilot Officer R. A. Kings baled out unhurt. Aircraft a write-off.

Hurricane L1998. Returned to base severely damaged in combat with Bf 110s over the Isle of Wight 4.35 p.m. Sergeant J. Jeka unhurt. Aircraft damaged but repairable.

Arkleston Cemetery in Renfrew contains burials from both world wars — thirteen from 1914-18 and forty-four from 1939-45. One of the latter is John McBean Christie from No. 152 Squadron.

Sergeants' Mess, RAF Middle Wallop, Hants.
26/9/40 Thursday

My Dear Mother and Father,

How's things Macclesfield way? Still enjoying the grand peaceful comfort. My word the boys could not understand how I managed to find anywhere free from bombs. Things are really warm, never a night without a visit from 'Jerry' and all day long we are knocking him away from London. Still such is the day's work.

I wonder if you could forward to me my alarm clock in case. I am having great trouble in getting up these days for we are going to bed and getting up at very odd times, just according to our 'friends' ebb and flow.

You will perhaps be very pleased to learn that Domagala is getting along quite nicely, very anxious to be back with us again. His friend Jeka has been doing some very good work. My work has been relieved by the help of this very formidable pilot. Our squadron may well be called the International Squadron for we have in our midst English, Scotch, Irish, New Zealanders, Australians, Polish, Czechs and Canadians. Not so bad but they are all a grand lot and good to know.

Have had a letter from May, she's very busy once again but feeling much better after the rest.

Met one of the boys from Rissington yesterday. He tells me that my old pal Sgt. Friendship has now the DFM and Bar and has also been made a Pilot Officer. Good boy, we had some grand times together.

My report and recommendation for commission has now gone through. My word, my C/O did give me a nice report and he added that I was strongly recommended for a Pilot Officer, so now I await the Air Ministry. I suppose they wonder what I am doing, first refused then accepted. Anyway, may it make or break me, I have now decided to hold the first commission in our family.

Ah well, cheerio for now, all my kind regards,
Your loving son,
Eric.

253 SQUADRON, KENLEY

Hurricane P2958. Shot down in action over the Channel 11.00 a.m. Crashed in the sea. Flight Lieutenant G. R. Edge baled out and rescued by motor-boat. Admitted to hospital in Ashford. Aircraft lost.

Hurricane V7470. Failed to return from combat over the Channel 11.00 a.m. Believed crashed in the sea. Pilot Officer W. M. C. Samolinski missing. Aircraft lost.

303 SQUADRON, NORTHOLT

Hurricane V6673. Forced-landed at Biggin Hill damaged in action over Southampton 4.30 p.m. Sergeant M. Belc unhurt. Aircraft damaged but repairable.

Hurricane V7465. Returned to base minus port wing tip following combat over Southampton 4.30 p.m. Flight Lieutenant A. S. Forbes unhurt. Aircraft damaged but repairable.

Hurricane P3544. Damaged in combat over Southampton. Forced-landed between Charity and Wyton Farms near Fareham 5.45 p.m. Flying Officer W. Januszewicz unhurt. Aircraft RF-H damaged but repairable.

602 SQUADRON, WESTHAMPNETT

Spitfire X4411. Returned to base with radiator damage following attack on He 111 over the Solent 4.40 p.m. Pilot Officer A. L. Edy unhurt. Aircraft repairable.

607 SQUADRON, TANGMERE

Hurricane P5205. Shot down in engagement with enemy aircraft over the Isle of Wight 4.20 p.m. Flight Lieutenant C. E. Bowen baled out unhurt over Kaylthorpe. Aircraft a write-off.

609 SQUADRON, WARMWELL

Spitfire N3288. Mainspar severely damaged by return fire from He 111 engaged over Christchurch 4.35 p.m. Returned to base. Pilot Officer A. K. Ogilvie unhurt. Aircraft damaged but repairable.

Spitfire R6979. Returned to base starboard wing and aileron damaged by 20mm cannon-fire during combat over Christchurch 4.40 p.m. Squadron Leader H. S. Darley unhurt. Aircraft repairable.

Friday, September 27

1 (RCAF) SQUADRON, NORTHOLT

Hurricane P3647. Shot down at Hever during combat with Ju 88s and Bf 110s over north Kent 9.15 a.m. Flying Officer O. J. Peterson killed. Aircraft a write-off.

Hurricane P3899. Forced-landed at Gatwick with damage sustained in action against Ju 88 and Bf 110 over north Kent 9.20 a.m. Flying Officer P.W. Lochnan unhurt. Aircraft damaged but repairable.

Hurricane P3672. Damaged in action over north Kent 9.25 a.m. Forced-landed at Kenley. Flying Officer Sprenger unhurt. Aircraft damaged but repairable.

17 SQUADRON, DEBDEN

Hurricane V6553. Attacked by Bf 109s over the Thames Estuary 9.30 a.m. Returned to base aileron and rudder damaged. Sergeant L. H. Bartlett unhurt. Aircraft repairable.

Pilot Officer Eric Burgoyne photographed by a member of No. 19 Squadron, Pilot Officer Peter Howard-Williams, at Fowlmere. After he was killed on September 27, he was taken back to his village church of St. Mary's Burghfield in Berkshire for burial.

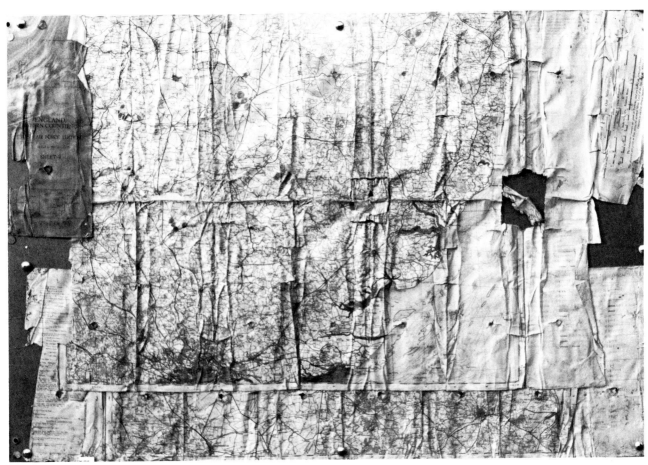

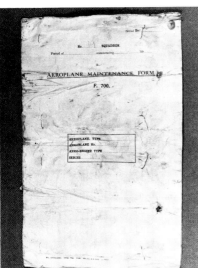

This bullet-holed quarter-inch map, the Royal Air Force edition of Sheet 9 (Eastern Counties), was recovered from the wreckage of the Spitfire flown by Sergeant Cox of No. 19 Squadron. The London Air Museum also recovered the Form 700 *left*, also pierced by a bullet, confirming the identity of the aircraft as X4237. *Below:* This was the complete display of relics from this aircraft that could be seen in the museum (which was situated at 139 North Cray Road, Bexley, Kent) before it closed (Kentish Times).

19 SQUADRON, DUXFORD

Spitfire X4352. Shot down in combat with Bf 109s over Canterbury and crashed at Coldred 12.30 p.m. Pilot Officer E. Burgoyne killed. Aircraft a write-off.

Spitfire X4237. Shot down by Bf 109s during action over the Canterbury area 12.20 p.m. Crashed at Wye Court Farm, Wye. Sergeant D. G. S. R. Cox wounded. Aircraft a write-off.

Site excavated by London Air Museum in February 1974. Items recovered include shattered Rolls-Royce Merlin engine, three badly twisted propeller blades, complete blind-flying panel, aircraft clock stopped at precise time of impact, remains of pilot's leather flying helmet and canvas oxygen mask, maps and aircraft 'Form 700' bearing the aircraft serial number.

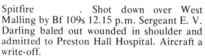

Relics from the No. 41 Squadron Spitfire abandoned by Sergeant Usmar over Mereworth. This crash site has been investigated by at least two groups. *Above:* Piece from the tailplane in the Lashenden Air Warfare Museum and *right* the spinner badge owned by Steve Vizard.

41 SQUADRON, HORNCHURCH

Spitfire   . Shot down by Bf 109s during squadron patrol over West Malling and crashed at Swanton Lane, Mereworth 12.15 p.m. Sergeant F. Usmar baled out and admitted to Preston Hall Hospital with leg wounds. Aircraft EB-S a write-off.

Site investigated by the Lashenden Air Warfare Museum and few surviving fragments recovered including part of tailplane. Pieces also held by Steve Vizard.

Ernest Males from Southgate, London was twenty years old when he was killed on the morning of September 27 whilst serving with No. 72 Squadron.

Spitfire   . Shot down over West Malling by Bf 109s 12.15 p.m. Sergeant E. V. Darling baled out wounded in shoulder and admitted to Preston Hall Hospital. Aircraft a write-off.

Spitfire R6755. 'Bounced' by Bf 109s during squadron patrol 3.45 p.m. Crashed and burned out at East Malling. Flight Lieutenant E. N. Ryder baled out unhurt. Aircraft a write-off.

46 SQUADRON, STAPLEFORD

Hurricane P3756. Forced-landed at Rochester with engine damaged in combat with enemy aircraft over north Kent 1.20 p.m. Pilot Officer K. Mrazek unhurt. Aircraft damaged but repairable.

64 SQUADRON, LECONFIELD

Spitfire X4032. Failed to return from routine section patrol 10.30 a.m. circumstances unknown. Sergeant L. A. Dyke missing. Aircraft lost.

66 SQUADRON, GRAVESEND

Spitfire P9519. Hit by AA fire during attack on Ju 88 and crash-landed near Orpington 3.45 p.m. Pilot Officer G. A. Corbett unhurt. Aircraft damaged but repairable.

72 SQUADRON, BIGGIN HILL

Spitfire X4340. Shot down in combat with Bf 109s over Sevenoaks 9.40 a.m. Crashed Shadwell Dock, Stepney. Pilot Officer E. E. Males killed. Aircraft a write-off.

Spitfire N3068. Shot down by Bf 109 during combat over Sevenoaks 9.40 a.m. Crashed at West Wickham. Flying Officer P. J. Davies-Cook killed. Aircraft a write-off.

Spitfire   . Forced-landed with damage to header tank following combat with Bf 109s over Sevenoaks 9.45 a.m. Sergeant J. White unhurt. Aircraft damaged but repairable.

73 SQUADRON, DEBDEN

Hurricane N2337. Damaged in combat with Bf 110s over Kenley 9.40 a.m. Forced-landed at Kenley. Sergeant A. E. Marshall unhurt. Aircraft TP-A damaged but repairable.

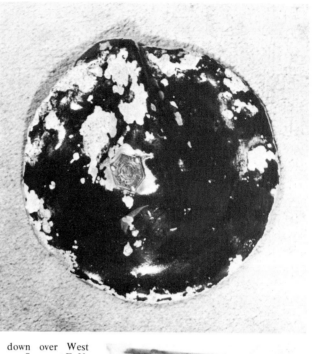

Flight Sergeant Charles Sydney joined the RAF as an apprentice when he was fifteen. He later volunteered for flying duties and was posted to No. 19 Squadron at Fowlmere on August 18, 1940. He was transferred to No. 266 for about two weeks and moved again to No. 92 at Biggin Hill on September 10. Seventeen days later he was dead, shot down early on the morning of September 27. He is now buried in the Biggin Hill 'station' churchyard at St. Mary Cray, Orpington.

Hurricane P3785. Returned to base with bullet through centre section following combat with Bf 110s over Kenley 9.40 a.m. Sergeant R. Plenderleith unhurt. Aircraft damaged but repairable.

Hurricane P3209. Forced-landed near Staffhurst Wood, Limpsfield with engine damaged in combat with Bf 110s over Kenley 9.45 a.m. Sergeant P. O'Byrne unhurt. Aircraft damaged but repairable.

92 SQUADRON, BIGGIN HILL

Spitfire X4422. Shot down in combat with enemy aircraft over Sevenoaks. Crashed and burned out at Sparepenny Lane, Farningham 9.20 a.m. Flight Lieutenant J. A. Paterson killed. Aircraft a write-off.
Site excavated by unknown amateur enthusiasts. Relics also in the Vizard collection.

Spitfire X4480. Damaged by Bf 109 in combat over Sevenoaks 9.30 a.m. Returned to base minus large section of tailplane. Pilot Officer J. Mansel-Lewis unhurt. Aircraft repairable.

Spitfire P9544. Hit by return fire from Do 17 engaged over Brighton 9.40 a.m. Forced-landed and overturned on Macehill, Lewes Race Course. Pilot Officer T. S. Wade unhurt. Aircraft damaged but repairable.

Spitfire R6767. Reputedly crashed at Kingston-on-Thames following combat with enemy aircraft 9.40 a.m. Flight Sergeant C. Sydney killed. Aircraft a write-off.
Said to be under the 'Birds-Eye' works in Station Avenue, Walton. Local research by the Air Historical Group failed to locate any tangible relics.

Spitfire R6622. Shot down by Bf 109s (?) and crashed at Hesketh Park, Dartford 3.18 p.m. Sergeant T. G. Oldfield killed. Aircraft a write-off.

Spitfire R6760. Crashed on landing at base following combat with Ju 88 over Kent/Sussex borders 3.30 p.m. Sergeant H. Bowen-Morris unhurt. Aircraft damaged but repairable.

152 SQUADRON, WARMWELL

Spitfire   . Damaged by return fire from Ju 88 engaged south of Bristol 9.30 a.m. Returned safely to base. Pilot Officer E. S. Marrs unhurt. Aircraft repairable.

Spitfire   . Slightly damaged when starboard gun panel broke loose during combat south of Bristol 11.45 a.m. Returned to base. Flying Officer R. F. Inness unhurt. Aircraft repairable.

Spitfire   . Port mainplane damaged by Bf 109 in combat south of Bristol 11.50 a.m. Landed at base on burst tyre. Pilot Officer I. N. Bayles unhurt. Aircraft damaged but repairable.

213 SQUADRON, EXETER

Hurricane P3979. Crash-landed with damage caused by Bf 110 in combat over Whitchurch 9.15 a.m. Flying Officer J. M. Strickland unhurt. Aircraft AK-V damaged but repairable.

Hurricane N2401. Shot down in combat with enemy fighters over Gatwick 9.25 a.m. Crashed onto Wilderness Golf Course, Seal, near Sevenoaks. Flight Lieutenant L. H. Schwind killed. Aircraft AK-Q a write-off.
Major recovery undertaken by Halstead War Museum in 1970 after an eight year search for the exact site. Shattered remains of Rolls-Royce Merlin engine unearthed together with rocker gear, propeller boss and hydraulic pump. Fragments also held by the Kent Battle of Britain Museum.

Flying Officer Paul Davies-Cooke was killed while flying with No. 72 Squadron at Biggin Hill. He was taken back to Rhydymwyn Churchyard at Cilcain, Flintshire where he was laid to rest in the family plot beside St. John's Church. Although with the changes to county boundaries, one should now refer to Flintshire as Clwyd, the editor made the decision to retain the original county names in this book as being more in keeping with the period.

222 SQUADRON, HORNCHURCH

Spitfire R6720. 'Bounced' by Bf 109s during patrol over Maidstone and crashed near Wennington, Rainham, Essex 12.00 p.m. Sergeant R. H. Gretton seriously wounded in back admitted to Oldchurch Hospital. Aircraft damaged but repairable.

Spitfire P9364. Failed to return from operational sortie 4.00 p.m. Exact circumstances unknown but believed crashed at Greenway Court, Hollingbourne. Sergeant E. Scott missing. Aircraft lost.

229 SQUADRON, NORTHOLT

Hurricane V6782. Shot down in combat with Bf 109s. Exploded over Franchise Manor Farm, Burwash 3.30 p.m. Flight Lieutenant R. F. Rimmer killed. Aircraft RE-T a write-off.

Site investigated by Steve Vizard and some surface fragments collected.

Hurricane N2436. Returned to base with damage sustained during attack on Ju 88 over south-east London 3.45 p.m. Pilot Officer R. E. Bary unhurt. Aircraft RE-A damaged but repairable.

Hurricane P3603. Hit by cross-fire from Ju 88s and forced-landed at Lingfield 3.45 p.m. Flight Lieutenant W. A. Smith unhurt. Aircraft RE-X a write-off.

242 SQUADRON, COLTISHALL

Hurricane V6576. Forced-landed near Sandwich with engine on fire after combat with Bf 109s off Dover 12.30 p.m. Flight Lieutenant G. E. Ball unhurt. Aircraft repairable.

Below: **Flying Officer Lionel Schwind is buried in Crowborough Burial Ground, Sussex. His brother Sergeant Gordon Schwind (killed on May 26, 1940) lies buried in Belgium. Lionel's grave is marked with the imposing Celtic cross in the foreground.**

Above: **St. Stephen's Church Burial Ground at Chertsey, Surrey — final resting place for Sergeant Trevor Oldfield, Royal Auxiliary Air Force, killed with No. 92 Squadron.**

Flight Lieutenant Reginald Frank Rimmer flew as a Pilot Officer with No. 66 Squadron at Duxford before the war but was later posted to No. 229 Squadron at Wittering and flew with that unit from the beginning of the Battle of Britain. During late August, the squadron was based at Bircham Newton but returned south, closer to the capital, in early September. On the 27th of the month, 21-year-old Reg Rimmer was shot down by enemy fighters over Kent, his Hurricane exploding in mid-air before he could bale out. He was buried at the Grange Cemetery at Hoylake, Cheshire *(right)* near his home at Meols. After the war, his family erected this memorial plaque *(below left)* at Franchise Manor Farm, Burwash in Kent beside the crash site. With its deterioration over the years, the Wealden Aviation Archaeology Group together with the Heathfield Royal Air Force Association dedicated a new memorial *(below right)* on June 18, 1977. In the interim, Steve Vizard had investigated the site and recovered these pieces *(bottom)* from a depth of four feet (A. Saunders).

473

Hurricane P2967. Shot down in combat with Bf 109s and crashed in flames at Bluetown, Mintching Wood, Milstead near Sittingbourne 12.25 p.m. Flying Officer M. G. Homer killed. Aircraft a write-off.

Site identified by the Kent Battle of Britain Museum and some fragments collected from nearby hedgerow. Pristine lawn of an immaculate modern bungalow subsequently excavated by the Wealden Aviation Archaeological Group in 1979 with assistance from London Air Museum. Shattered Rolls-Royce Merlin engine, propeller hub, rudder bar pedals and other cockpit components recovered together with oxygen and compressed-air bottles.

249 SQUADRON, NORTH WEALD

Hurricane V6729. Landed at Gatwick with damage from Bf 110s engaged over Redhill 9.35 a.m. Flight Lieutenant R. A. Barton unhurt. Aircraft damaged but repairable.

Hurricane V6559. Damaged in combat with Bf 110s over Redhill 9.40 a.m. Pilot Officer H. J. S. Beazley slightly wounded in foot. Aircraft repairable.

Hurricane V6683. Collided with Bf 110 during combat over Redhill area. Crashed at Wellers Field, Station Road, Hailsham 9.50 a.m. Flying Officer P. R-F. Burton killed. Aircraft a write-off.

Area of crash-site investigated by the Wealden Aviation Archaeological Group in 1972. Fragments still to be seen scattered about on the surface.

Hurricane P3834. Shot down by return fire from Ju 88 and crashed at Brake Field, Giffords Farm, Dallington 3.20 p.m. Pilot Officer J. R. B. Meaker baled out but hit tailplane and fell dead at Warren Field, Brightling Park. Aircraft a write-off.

Hurricane V6622. Shot down during attack on Ju 88s south of London 3.50 p.m. Forced-landed at West Malling. Pilot Officer R. G. A. Barclay unhurt. Aircraft damaged but repairable.

253 SQUADRON, KENLEY

Hurricane V6691. Damaged in combat with enemy fighters north of Hastings 9.30 a.m. Returned safely to base. Pilot unhurt. Aircraft damaged but repairable.

Flying Officer Michael Giles Homer, a 21-year-old pilot from Swanage, Dorset, wearing the ribbon of the Distinguished Flying Cross awarded to him for bombing operations early in the war. In September 1940, he transferred to fighters and No. 1 Squadron at Northolt (A. Saunders). On September 21 he was posted to No. 242 Squadron at Coltishall but in less than seven days he was dead, shot down near Sittingbourne. His parents had his remains sent back to Dorset where they now lie in the town cemetery.

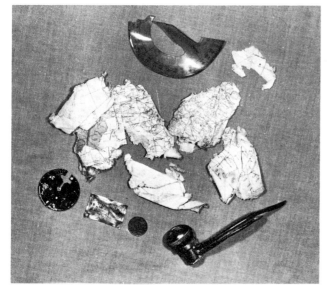

Fragments of maps, a buckled protractor, a halfpenny, an instrument face, plate and the gun firing button from Flying Officer Homer's Hurricane recovered by the Wealden group in 1979.

Percival Ross-Frames Burton was born in South Africa and died in a collision with a German fighter over Hailsham. Although flying from North Weald, he was taken to the station churchyard at Tangmere for burial.

James Reginald Bryan Meaker hailed from Kinsale, County Cork, Eire, and could have chosen to spend the war in comfortable neutrality. Instead he joined the Royal Air Force before the war and was eventually posted to No. 46 'Uganda' Squadron. From April 24 to 27, 1940, he served with No. 263 Squadron in Norway flying Gladiators from frozen lakes against the superior might of the Luftwaffe until the unit was forced to withdraw through lack of aircraft. Returning to the UK on May 2, he was posted to No. 249 'Gold Coast' Squadron when it was reformed with Hurricanes later in the month. In August, the squadron came south to join in the battle and on September 27, Pilot Officer Jimmy Meaker, DFC, in abandoning his stricken Hurricane, hit the tailplane and fell thousands of feet to earth, his parachute unopened. Buried in West Dean Cemetery, Sussex, his mother and father now lie in their grave nearby.

Hurricane   . Returned to base with superficial damage caused by enemy fighters engaged north of Hastings 9.35 a.m. Pilot unhurt. Aircraft repairable.

303 SQUADRON, NORTHOLT

Hurricane   . Returned to base damaged following combat with He 111 and Bf 109 over Horsham 9.20 a.m. Pilot Officer M. Feric unhurt. Aircraft repairable.

Hurricane V7289. Shot down in combat over Horsham area 9.35 a.m. Crashed Blundel Lane, Stoke D'Abernon. Flying Officer W. Zak baled out and admitted to Leatherhead Hospital with burns. Aircraft a write-off.
Large sections of airframe recovered by the Air Historical Group in October 1977.

Hurricane   . Damaged in combat over Horsham 9.30 a.m. Returned to base radiator damaged. Flying Officer Z. Henneberg unhurt. Aircraft repairable.

Hurricane L1696. Crashed at Crowhurst Farm, Borough Green during combat with enemy aircraft 9.35 a.m. Flying Officer L. W. Paskiewicz killed. Aircraft RF-M a write-off.
Major recovery by Malling Aircraft Archaeologists. Rolls-Royce Merlin engine excavated together with propeller boss with one blade still attached, main undercarriage components and pilot's parachute. Propeller presented to the Sikorski Museum. Rudder bar pedals and compass donated to Tony Graves for London Air Museum. Pieces also in Steve Vizard collection. Bulk of remains now in Lashenden Air Warfare Museum.

Hurricane V7246. Shot down in flames in combat over the Horsham area. Crashed at Holywych Farm, Cowden 9.35 a.m. Sergeant T. Andruskow killed. Aircraft a write-off.
Fragments in the Vizard collection.

Hurricane V6684. Returned to base bullets through airscrew and cockpit canopy following destruction of Ju 88 off Sussex Coast 3.15 p.m. Flight Lieutenant J. A. Kent unhurt. Aircraft RF-J repairable.

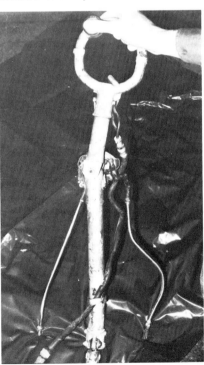

In October 1977, the crash site of Hurricane V7289 from No. 303 Squadron was excavated by the Air Historical Group. Amongst the many items of interest recovered were the complete control column and the tail wheel (Air Historical Group).

Paskiewicz corner in the Lashenden Air Warfare Museum at Headcorn aerodrome, near Ashford, Kent. *Below left:* The museum presented one of the prop blades to the Sikorski Museum at 20, Princes Gate, London — displayed for our photo by the assistant archivist Captain Waclaw Milewski. *Below right:* The top of the control column now owned by Steve Vizard. Flying Officer (or Flight Lieutenant) Ludwik Paskiewicz is now buried at Northwood.

Above: **The impact point of the No. 501 'County of Gloucester' Squadron Hurricane, abandoned by Pilot Officer Gunter, in the hop garden near Sittingbourne before excavation by the London** Air Museum (Tony Graves). *Right:* **A rare find as aluminium disintegrates with prolonged burial.** *Below:* **Part of the smashed dashboard.**

310 SQUADRON, DUXFORD

Hurricane V6608. Shot down by Bf 109 in engagement over Thanet 12.20 p.m. Believed crashed on Woodsdale Farm, Godmersham. Flying Officer G. L. Sinclair baled out unhurt landing at Chilham. Aircraft a write-off.

Location investigated by the Kent Battle of Britain Museum but very little discovered. Precise crash-site probably not located.

501 SQUADRON, KENLEY

Hurricane V6672. Shot down in combat with Bf 110 over Godstone 9.15 a.m. Sergeant V. H. Ekins baled out and admitted to Sevenoaks Hospital. Aircraft a write-off.

Hurricane V6645. Shot down in action against Do 17s with Bf 109 escort and crashed near Teynham Court, Sittingbourne 12.25 p.m. Pilot Officer E. M. Gunter baled out but killed due to parachute failure. Aircraft a write-off.

Site excavated by the London Air Museum September 1976 and an intact Rolls-Royce Merlin engine recovered together with propeller boss, cockpit instruments and controls. One undercarriage leg unearthed complete with tyre and magnesium-alloy hub still intact.

504 SQUADRON, FILTON

Hurricane P3415. Landed at Gammons Farm, Kilmington, Axminster with damage suffered in combat over Bristol 12.05 p.m. Possibly that claimed by Oberleutnant Roedel of 4/JG27. Sergeant C. Haw unhurt. Aircraft damaged but repairable.

602 SQUADRON, WESTHAMPNETT

Spitfire X4414. 'Bounced' by Bf 109 and hit in glycol tank. Forced-landed at Bivelham Forge Farm, Mayfield 9.20 a.m. Pilot Officer D. H. Gage unhurt. Aircraft damaged but repairable.

Spitfire X4160. Damaged by Bf 109s following attack on Ju 88 off Dungeness 9.25 a.m. Returned safely to base. Sergeant C. F. Babbage unhurt. Aircraft repairable.

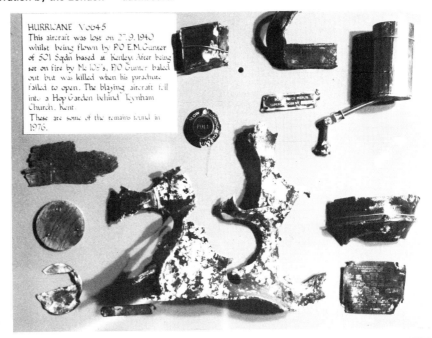

HURRICANE V6645
This aircraft was lost on 27.9.1940 whilst being flown by P/O E.M. Gunter of 501 Sqdn based at Kenley. After being set on fire by Me 109's, P/O Gunter baled out but was killed when his parachute failed to open. The blazing aircraft fell into a Hop Garden behind Teynham Church, Kent.
These are some of the remains found in 1976.

Edward Gunter's grave in a quiet corner of St. Mary's Churchyard, Aldeby, Norfolk.

603 SQUADRON HORNCHURCH

Spitfire N3244. Pilot believed wounded in combat with Bf 109s over the Channel. Attempted to regain English coast but forced to abandon aircraft quarter-of-a-mile off Folkestone 12.45 p.m. Pilot Officer P. M. Cardell baled out but parachute failed to open. Picked up dead by shore boat. Aircraft lost.

Philip Melville Cardell from Huntingdonshire served very briefly with the ill-fated No. 263 Squadron after its return from Norway. On July 3, 1940, he was posted to No. 603 'City of Edinburgh' Squadron and was based at Montrose with 'B' Flight. 'Bewildered, excited and a little lost,' according to Richard Hillary, he was known to his fellow pilots as 'Pip'. August 10, found the squadron flying south to Hornchurch and immediate action. One by one he saw his friends go down, 'Broody' Benson was first, followed by Colin Pinkney, Dick Hillary and Peter Pease. On the first day of September he forced-landed a veritable wreck of an aircraft at Hornchurch after a sortie, walking away unhurt. On September 27, 'Pip' Cardell's Spitfire was badly hit in a fight over the Channel. His efforts to bring his failing aircraft back to land were unsuccessful and he was forced to bale out. His parachute failed him and he fell into the sea within sight of Folkestone beach. A fellow pilot endeavoured to attract the attention of people near the shoreline to Pilot Officer Cardell's plight without success. In a desperate effort to save his friend, Pilot Officer Dexter crash-landed his Spitfire on the beach and commandeered a rowing boat only to recover the dead body of 'Pip' Cardell. His family took his body back to Great Paxton for burial in the churchyard beside his home. They also decided to give him something different from a sad gravestone. The year before he died, Philip had beautified the farmhouse garden and constructed a pond with a sundial. The family therefore moved this to mark his grave — the most unusual yet fitting memorial. (Unfortunately the date on the marker is completely incorrect stating that Philip was killed on '1 Sept, 1940'.)

Spitfire X4250. Forced-landed on Folkestone beach 12.50 p.m. during attempt to rescue Pilot Officer Cardell. Pilot Officer P. G. Dexter unhurt commandeered the boat which recovered Pilot Officer Cardell's body. Aircraft damaged but repairable.

609 SQUADRON, WARMWELL

Spitfire X4107. Collided head-on with Bf 110 of 9/ZG26 and exploded over Chesilbourne near Kingcombe 11.45 a.m. Main wreckage fell east of Doles Ash. Pilot Officer R. F. G. Miller killed. Aircraft a write-off.

Spitfire X4234. Damaged by machine-gun fire during combat over Poole Harbour 12.15 p.m. Returned to base. Pilot Officer M. E. Staples unhurt. Aircraft damaged but repairable.

616 SQUADRON, DUXFORD

Spitfire R6702. Believed crashed at Workhouse Cottage, Throwley near Faversham 12.20 p.m. having been shot down by Bf 109s whilst acting as 'weaver'. Flying Officer D. S. Smith seriously wounded admitted to Faversham Cottage Hospital (died following day). Aircraft a write-off.

The Miller's of Radford Semele, Warwickshire were another family that lost two brothers in the Royal Air Force in 1940. John, aged twenty-three, a Wellington pilot with No. 149 Squadron, was lost on August 12 and Rogers with No. 609 Squadron collided with a Bf 110 on September 27. Both lie side by side in St. Nicolas Churchyard.

Donald Sydney Smith came from the village of Highley, seven miles from Bridgnorth, Shropshire. He was educated at Bridgnorth Grammar School and later at Winchester College where he joined the Royal Air Force Volunteer Reserve. After graduation, he was appointed geography master at Droxford Senior School and later at Highley School where his father was headmaster. Eventually he gave up teaching to make his career in the Royal Air Force and was gazetted as Pilot Officer in May 1938. A period of attachment to the Fleet Air Arm convinced him that his preference lay with fighters and he applied for a transfer to

Fighter Command. A posting to No. 616 'South Yorkshire' Squadron flying Spitfires at Leconfield was the answer to the young pilot's prayer. In May 1940 the squadron commenced night-flying practice and, on the night of August 7, Pilot Officer Smith had a lucky escape when he was forced to abandon his Spitfire which crashed and exploded near the base. Then, on Friday, September 27, while flying from Duxford, Pilot Officer Don Smith was shot down and grievously wounded whilst acting as 'weaver' for the formation. He died the following day and was taken back to St. Mary's Churchyard near his home.

Macclesfield Courier

AND HERALD

CHESHIRE ADVERTISER, CONGLETON COURIER, AND STOCKPORT EXPRESS

Registered for Transmission in the United Kingdom. | THURSDAY, OCTOBER 3rd, 1940 | 130th Year of Publication.

Prisoner of War

REPORTED MISSING many weeks ago. Private Arthur Tucker, 21-years-old son of Mr. and Mrs. Tucker. of 3 Hullev Place, Hurdsfield

prisone
quite a
fined.
It wa
notifica
news th
comes a:
anxious
before tl
Lincolns
sportsma

Whit

The

AN APP
H. E
whitewash
order to a:
As anyor
very effecti
difficulties i
ing in the
ever-present
The sudden
the footpath
unwarily, se.
The Mayor
stones would
the Infir ar
good many b
winter. It w
which would
might save a

NO E

RETIRING T

HAD PEACE
at present,
clesfield, in com
other municipali
throes of electic
November 1st.
But the war h
for the time bein
are looked upon
Consequently, for
field will have no
every probability
whose terms of offi
1st will remain in
Several of them
what they intend to
they give is that th
Those whose ter... o. once end next month are:

Air Raid Victims

Husband Killed—Wife Injured

...tion that we have continued superior to all that ambition or that despotism

Nazi Warplane Exhibit

MACCLESFIELD'S ...pular and ener-
r. W. Garfield
g to arrange for
an aeroplane in
vith the Mayor's

the Town Clerk
on Friday that
obably arrange
raft Production
damaged Ger-
Macclesfield for
ith the Mayor's

will be on exhi
econd week in

ritten to Mr.
assuring him
taken of the

Plundered Alderley

e Police are
obbery which
eptember 21,
ewellery was

n the resi-
away, and
found the
away.
t week at
ks Heath.
forced off.
ag.

'ize

LOSS

Herbert
Vithing-
aternity
d most

ed else-
of age,

lember
senior,
days
t was
year

1931,
ain's

club
re is
eing

... for annual competition to commemorate his association with the club.
The Club representatives at the funeral on Tuesday were: Mr. H. Kearsley (secre-

---

Sergt.-Pilot S. E. Bann

DEATH IN ACTION AGAINST ENEMY

HERO of all the air-minded boys in the town, Sergeant-Pilot S. E. Bann, of 121 Bond Street, fighter pilot who had expressed a wish to fly Macclesfield's Spitfire, was killed in air combat last week-end.

To Sergeant-Pilot Bann, our local 'Cobber Kain,' danger had become the breath of life in recent times. His letters home conveyed the impression that he was literally straining at the leash to ' get at ' the enemy, and the fact that he was recently shot down into the English Channel did little to damp his ardour.

He first came into the news when it was learned that he was one of the pilots engaged in an aerial dog-fight, a description of which was excitedly broadcast by the B.B.C. as it was actually taking place. This certainly was something to write home about, and he told his parents:—

" Yesterday six of us ran into 25 enemy fighters. My first thought was: ' Here goes—I'll fight,' but four of them to one of us made things too bad. I ducked and fought just like a madman. I looked up once, and the air was full of machines and lead, all milling round for that final burst."

Something of the wonderful spirit of our fighter pilots was shown in another letter in which Sergeant-Pilot Bann described another air combat as " lots of fun." On the occasion to which he so euphemistically referred, he was shot down into the English Channel because, as he said, he did not dodge quickly enough.

High praise of his colleagues has been a feature of all communications to his parents. " Those grand lads are giving their very all; our Flight Commander is absolutely fearless," he has told them.

Can one wonder at the successes gained by the R.A.F. over the disillusioned Luftwaffe when we have men of the calibre of Sergeant-Pilot Bann manning our deadly little fighters ?

It is with intense regret that we learn of his death, and we sympathise greatly with his family; but they can find comfort in the knowledge that their son died defending his home and the women and children of his land from the threat from the air.

He was deeply touched by a story told him by a young Polish pilot with whom he had become friendly. The plight of ravaged Poland under the domination of the conqueror made his blood boil. The Polish pilot concerned lived only for revenge.

So Sergeant-Pilot Bann will not realise his cherished ambition and sit at the controls of the town's Spitfire. Nevertheless, he has set a glorious example of courage, gameness and determination. It is believed he had " bagged " quite a number of enemy 'planes.

Twenty-six years of age, Sergeant-Pilot Bann was married only early this year, and he had gone to reside in Birmingham. He was a native of Macclesfield, and received his education at Athey Street School and Manchester College of Technology, being at the latter place a student of aeronautical engineering. Later he went to Sheffield Training College. Three years ago he joined the Volunteer Reserve Section of the R.A.F. His bride at his wedding in March was Miss Agnes May Butler, of Birmingham.

Five weeks ago his cousin, Sergeant-Observer Jack Bann, of Ivy Road, was reported missing, and no further news has been received concerning him. Sergeant-Pilot Bann's brother, Maurice, is also in the R.A.F.

The funeral is to take place at the Borough Cemetery some time this week-end.

R.D.C. AIRCRAFT FUND

MACCLESFIELD Rural District Council at a meeting of their General Purposes Committee last Tuesday, decided to support the Cheshire Aircraft Victory Fund.

Each member of the Council has pledged his support to the district effort and, in addition, all clerks of parish councils and parish meetings are to be circularised asking them to take steps to ensure the success of the scheme in their respective parishes.

THE SPITFIRE FUND

Saturday, September 28

29 SQUADRON, DIGBY

Blenheim L1371. Hit in starboard wing by British AA fire during evening patrol 7.10 p.m. Returned to base. Pilot Officer J. Buchanan, Sergeant G. A. Waller both unhurt. Aircraft damaged but repairable.

41 SQUADRON, HORNCHURCH

Spitfire X4409. Shot down during combat over Charing. Possibly that which exploded over East Stour Farm, Chilham 10.30 a.m. Pilot Officer H. H. Chalder baled out seriously wounded landing at Garlinge Green. Admitted to Chartham Hospital (died 10.11.40). Aircraft a write-off.

Sergeant Eric Bann, whose letters we have been following throughout the battle, with his wife May on their wedding day.

Spitfire X4426. Shot down in combat over Charing. Crashed and burned out on Erriotts Farm, Dadmans, Lynstead 10.37 a.m. Flying Officer J. G. Boyle killed. Aircraft a write-off.
Relics in the Vizard collection.

Spitfire X4345. Crash-landed at Pluckley following combat over Charing 10.40 a.m. Pilot Officer E. S. Aldous slightly injured. Aircraft a write-off.

Spitfire R6619. Returned to base fuselage badly damaged by 20mm cannon shells in combat with Bf 109s over Hornchurch 1.45 p.m. Pilot Officer G. H. Bennions unhurt. Aircraft damaged but repairable.

66 SQUADRON, GRAVESEND

Spitfire X4322. Shot down in combat over Mayfield and crashed at Batts Wood, Bivelham Forge Farm. Pilot Officer A. B. Watkinson baled out wounded in shoulder and leg. Aircraft a write-off.

Spitfire N3170. Forced-landed following combat over Mayfield. Sergeant B. Wright unhurt. Aircraft damaged but repairable.

213 SQUADRON, EXETER

Hurricane . Severely damaged by intense return fire from Bf 110 off Selsey Bill 3.00 p.m. Forced-landed back at base. Flying Officer R. W. Kellow unhurt. Aircraft AK-H damaged but repairable.

Two pilots were lost on the 28th by No. 41 Squadron at Hornchurch. *Above:* Harry Chalder was mortally wounded at 10.30 a.m. although he fought for life for another twelve days. He is buried at Newcastle-upon-Tyne. *Below:* Three minutes later, John Boyle, the son of a Canadian doctor from Ottawa, was shot down in the same combat. He is buried at SS Peter and Paul Churchyard at Lynsted, Kent.

I beg to acknowledge receipt of your letter of the 26th November, 1940 and, although you have given me something to think about, I will try to give you the facts as near as possible as I know them. On the fatal day your son was engaged with other splendid fellows of the RAF in aerial combat with the enemy over this district and his machine later crashed.

I cannot give you any detail as to what caused his machine to crash but can only assume that it was hit by enemy fire. While the fight was still in progress, the machine your son was piloting was seen flying at great speed towards Portsmouth, probably hoping to regain its base as I believe that it was on fire although not to any great extent.

When at a good height over Brading Marshes your son was seen to bale out quite safely but watchers who saw him come down say that his parachute did not open and this was found to be correct when Police and Military recovered his body shortly after. As regards the machine, this continued for a considerable distance out of control, pilotless, before finally crashing on the north side of Bembridge Downs about a mile away.

The machine was in little pieces strewn over about 200 yards of ground and I can only assume that the petrol tank exploded otherwise this would not have happened in the way it did.

As far as I could see, your son was not wounded by the enemy as no gunshot wounds could be found on him at all but it was perfectly obvious that he died from a fractured skull as when he was examined by a doctor his skull was found to be badly fractured over the left eye caused through striking the ground.

There was no chance of life when found I am sorry to say, had there been I would have worked hours as also would my men to have brought him round but, under the circumstances, I could see that it was perfectly hopeless from the first.

One blessing is that your son did not suffer for death according to the doctor was instantaneous.

I agree with you that at that time these gallant men must have been very much overworked but they have performed a most marvellous feat against overwhelming odds and have earned the gratitude of all the civilised world and such is the spirit of the British RAF that their names will live for ever as the saviours of our country of which we are all so proud.

Extract from a letter to Mrs. C. Bann from Inspector W. Butcher, Isle of Wight Constabulary, on the death of her son on September 28, 1940.

Hurricane   . Hit by return fire from Bf 110 engaged over the Isle of Wight 3.10 p.m. Crashed in the sea off Culver Cliffs, Bembridge. Pilot Officer J. M. Talman baled out unhurt rescued by Bembridge life-boat and landed at Ryde. Aircraft AK-A lost.

238 SQUADRON, MIDDLE-WALLOP

Hurricane N2400. Shot down into the sea during combat with Bf 109s over the Isle of Wight 2.45 p.m. Sergeant R. Little missing. Aircraft lost.

Hurricane V6776. Severely damaged by Bf 109s over Fareham 2.59 p.m. Sergeant S. E. Bann baled out over Brading Marshes but killed when parachute failed. Aircraft a write-off.

Hurricane V6778. Landed at Andover out of fuel following combat over the Isle of Wight 2.45 p.m. Crashed attempting take-off with empty fuel tanks 3.15 p.m. Pilot Officer V. C. Simmonds unhurt. Aircraft damaged but repairable.

Hurricane P3836. Shot down in combat with Bf 109s over the Solent 2.50 p.m. Crashed in the sea. Pilot Officer D. S. Harrison killed (washed ashore at Brighton 9.10.40). Aircraft lost.

249 SQUADRON, NORTH WEALD

Hurricane V6617. Shot down during combat over Faversham and crashed at Blackett's Farm, Tonge 2.20 p.m. Pilot Officer A. G. Lewis baled out badly burned and admitted to Faversham Cottage Hospital. Aircraft GN-R a write-off.
Site excavated by Kent Battle of Britain Museum and remains of burned out Rolls-Royce Merlin engine, control column and various fragments recovered.

One private headstone in the war graves section in St. Andrew's Churchyard belongs to Pilot Officer David Harrison from Burnham.

Pilot Officer Frederick Cecil Harrold *(above left)* flew Hurricanes with No. 501 'County of Gloucester' Squadron throughout the month of July 1940 but, on August 26, was posted to No. 151 Squadron at North Weald. On September 1, he accompanied the squadron to Digby but then returned to No. 501 at Kenley on September 26. Two days later he was in action with the squadron over southern Kent. Watchers at Ulcombe saw a Hurricane come screaming down towards their village to bury itself in Strawberry Plantations *(above)*. Frederick Harrold was buried at Cherry Hinton near his home in Cambridge. Three decades later, when the London Air Museum excavated the crash site, one of the items found was the Form 700 (Tony Graves).

501 SQUADRON, KENLEY

Hurricane V7497. Attacked by Bf 109s over Deal and shot down 10.10 a.m. Crashed and burned out at Chartway Street, East Sutton. Pilot Officer E. B. Rogers baled out unhurt. Aircraft a write-off.

Hurricane P3417. Shot down by Bf 109s and crashed in Strawberry Plantations, College House, Ulcombe 10.10 a.m. Wreck burned out. Pilot Officer F. C. Harrold killed. Aircraft SD-W a write-off.
Major recovery by the London Air Museum in August 1975 revealed shattered Rolls-Royce Merlin engine, propeller boss and reduction gear. Remains of instrument panel, cockpit controls, full armour plate, maps and aircraft 'Form 700' together with pilot's gauntlets also unearthed. Cockpit instruments and parachute release buckle found on site shortly afterwards by Steve Vizard.

Hurricane P3605. Crashed on landing following combat with Bf 109s over Deal 10.35 a.m. Flying Officer D. A. E. Jones unhurt. Aircraft damaged but repairable.

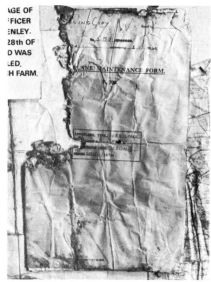

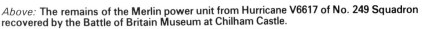

Above: **The remains of the Merlin power unit from Hurricane V6617 of No. 249 Squadron recovered by the Battle of Britain Museum at Chilham Castle.**

603 SQUADRON, HORNCHURCH

Spitfire L1076 'Bounced' by Bf 109s over Gillingham 10.20 a.m. Shot down on to Brompton Barracks. Flight Lieutenant H. K. McDonald killed. Aircraft a write-off.

605 SQUADRON, CROYDON

Hurricane V6699. Shot down by Bf 109s over Ticehurst and exploded in a paddock at Earle Down, Red Pale, Dallington 1.55 p.m. Flying Officer P. G. Crofts baled out but fell dead at South View Farm, Warbleton. Aircraft a write-off.

Hurricane P3828. Attacked by Bf 109s and shot down over Ticehurst. Crashed Bewl Bridge, Lamberhurst 2.20 p.m. Flying Officer R. Hope baled out unhurt landing at Ticehurst. Aircraft a write-off.

Rolls-Royce Merlin engine, propeller boss, cockpit instruments and controls including the control column, complete head armour and both undercarriage legs recovered from swampy area over a period of six months by the London Air Museum in 1964. Site also excavated by Wealden Aviation Archaeological Group on March 18, 1972 and both main wheel tyres and remains of radio recovered together with assorted wreckage.

Flying Officer Hope's Hurricane P3828 crashed at Bewlbridge Farm. The site was first excavated by Tony Graves of the London Air Museum (who recovered the items *below*) and then by the Wealden group which recovered the wreckage *above*. The construction of the Bewl Bridge Reservoir has now flooded the crash site (S. Hall/A. Saunders).

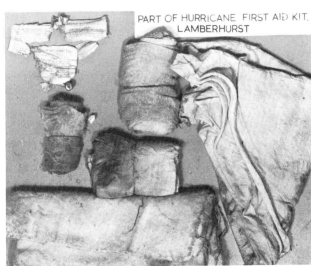

PART OF HURRICANE FIRST AID KIT. LAMBERHURST

607 SQUADRON, TANGMERE

Hurricane P3108. Shot down in action with Bf 109s east of Selsey 3.00 p.m. Believed crashed in sea. Flight Lieutenant W. E. Gore missing. Aircraft lost.

Hurricane R4189. Crashed in the Channel east of Selsey during combat with Bf 109s 3.00 p.m. Flight Lieutenant M. M. Irving missing. Aircraft lost.

611 SQUADRON, DIGBY

Spitfire II P7369. Crashed on landing at Ternhill 3.30 p.m. circumstances not stated. Pilot Officer J. R. G. Sutton suffered slight facial injuries. Aircraft a write-off.

Sunday, September 29

66 SQUADRON, GRAVESEND

Spitfire N3035. Forced-landed following combat with enemy fighters 5.20 p.m. Sergeant P. H. Willcocks wounded. Aircraft damaged but repairable.

79 SQUADRON, PEMBREY

Hurricane P3203. Hit by return fire from He 111 engaged off coast 6.30 p.m. Crashed in the Irish sea. Pilot Officer G. H. Nelson-Edwards baled out unhurt rescued by SS *Dartford* and landed at Milford Haven. Aircraft lost.

Hurricane P5177. Failed to return from interception of He 111s over the Irish sea 6.30 p.m. Crashed in sea. Flying Officer G. C. B. Peters killed. Aircraft lost.

Hurricane P5178. Forced-landed in the Irish Republic following interception of He 111s over the Irish sea 6.35 p.m. Pilot Officer P. F. Mayhew unhurt. Aircraft impounded.

Flying Officer Peter Guerin Crofts, No. 605 Squadron, shot down on September 29 at Dallington in East Sussex. Peter managed to bale out but somehow fell free of his parachute and hit the ground at South View Farm. His family buried him at All Saints Tilford and erected the memorial *above* on the spot where he fell (S. Hall/A. Saunders).

145 SQUADRON, DREM

Hurricane V7422. Damaged in taxi-ing accident at base. Sergeant J. McConnell unhurt. Aircraft damaged but repairable.

253 SQUADRON, KENLEY

Hurricane P2677. Shot down by Bf 109 and crashed in flames at New Road, Denton near Newhaven 4.25 p.m. Sergeant A. Edgeley baled out landing at South Heighton with shoulder wound. Admitted to Horton Hospital. Aircraft a write-off.

Hurricane V6621. Set alight in attack by another Hurricane during combat with Bf 109s over Weybridge. Crashed and burned out on Longridge Farm, Chailey 4.35 p.m. Pilot Officer R. C. Graves baled out and admitted to Brockley Park Hospital, Haywards Heath with burns. Aircraft a write-off.
  Excavated by the Wealden Aviation Archaeological Group in October 1979. Propeller hub and many other relics unearthed.

Hurricane P3609. Rudder controls shot away and petrol tank hit in attack by Hurricane during combat with Bf 109s over Weybridge 4.30 p.m. Flight Lieutenant R. M. B. D. Duke-Woolley unhurt. Aircraft damaged but repairable.

504 SQUADRON, FILTON

Hurricane L1913. Reputedly hit by AA fire during night sortie over the Midlands. Abandoned over Nuneaton, Warwickshire. Pilot baled out believed unhurt. Aircraft a write-off.

601 SQUADRON, EXETER

Hurricane   . Damaged in landing accident. Exact details not recorded. Sergeant F. H. R. Hulbert unhurt. Aircraft repairable.

615 SQUADRON, PRESTWICK

Hurricane V7312. Dived into ground from 7,000ft during routine practice flight. Cause unknown. Pilot Officer J. McGibbon killed. Aircraft a write-off.

Flight Lieutenant Maurice Irving (third from right) from Newcastle-upon-Tyne, killed on September 28, was one of the few remaining original auxiliary members of No. 607 'County of Durham' Squadron.

Flight Lieutenant William Ernest Gore, DFC, from Stockton-on-Tees, was an electrical engineer before the war and a weekend member of No. 607 'County of Durham' Squadron, Auxiliary Air Force. After the outbreak of war he served in France, flying Gloster Gladiator biplanes during the squadron's attachment to the Air Component of the British Expeditionary Force. Decimated in the Flanders campaign, the squadron returned to Usworth in June 1940 to refit, but moved south to Tangmere during the Battle of Britain. On September 28 this well-liked and respected flight commander was shot down into the Channel east of Selsey. His body was never found.

Steve Hall from the Wealden Aviation Archaeological Group investigates the site of the crash of Pilot Officer Grave's Hurricane of No. 253 Squadron on Longridge Farm at Chailey. Only small items were recovered (S. Hall/ A. Saunders).

Far from his home in New South Wales, Australian Pilot Officer John Crossman lies in Chalfont St. Giles, Buckinghamshire.

Monday, September 30

1 (RCAF) SQUADRON, NORTHOLT

Hurricane V7288. Port elevator severely damaged by Bf 109 causing aircraft to nose-over on landing 5.00 p.m. Flying Officer D. P. Brown unhurt. Aircraft damaged but repairable.

41 SQUADRON, HORNCHURCH

Spitfire P9394. Attacked by Bf 109s off Dungeness and engine set alight. Forced-landed at Hawkinge 2.20 p.m. Sergeant R. A Beardsley unhurt. Aircraft damaged but repairable.

Spitfire X4344. Crash-landed at base starboard wing damaged by 20mm cannon fire following combat with Bf 109s over Dungeness 2.25 p.m. Flying Officer A. D. J. Lovell unhurt. Aircraft damaged but repairable.

46 SQUADRON, STAPLEFORD

Hurricane   . Shot down by enemy fighters and crashed in flames at Tablehurst Farm, Forest Row 1.30 p.m. Pilot Officer J. D. Crossman killed. Aircraft a write-off.

Crash-site located by the Wealden Aviation Archaeological Group and investigated in September 1979 but no relics recovered.

56 SQUADRON, BOSCOMBE DOWN

Hurricane P2866. Crashed following combat with Bf 109s and Bf 110s over Bournemouth 11.30 a.m. Flying Officer K. T. Marston believed unhurt. Aircraft a write-off.

Hurricane P3655. Crashed following engagement with Bf 109s and Bf 110s over Bournemouth 11.30 a.m. Sergeant Ray wounded suffered a broken arm. Aircraft US-R a write-off.

Hurricane P3870. Forced-landed at Warmwell with damage from return fire by Do 215 engaged over Portland 5.00 p.m. Pilot Officer B. J. Wicks unhurt. Aircraft repairable.

Hurricane L1764. Crash-landed on Chesil Bank opposite Abbotsbury Swannery 5.00 p.m. following attack on Do 215s and Bf 110s over Portland. Pilot Officer M. H. Constable-Maxwell unhurt. Aircraft US-M a write-off.

Hurricane P3088. Crashed following combat with Do 215s and Bf 110 escort over Portland 5.00 p.m. Flight Lieutenant R. S. J. Edwards believed baled out unhurt. Aircraft US-N a write-off.

Hurricane N2434. Shot down in combat with Do 215s and Bf 110s over the Portland area 5.00 p.m. Crashed at Okeford Fitzpaine. Sergeant P. H. Fox believed baled out wounded in leg. Aircraft a write-off.

Hurricane P2910. Damaged by return fire from Do 215 intercepted over Portland 5.05 p.m. Forced-landed at Warmwell. Flight Lieutenant H. M. Pinfold unhurt. Aircraft repairable.

During the war there was a Royal Air Force station beside Gare Loch at Rhu in Dunbartonshire, Scotland, and, three miles away along the A814, lies the little village of Shandon. It was here that James McGibbon grew up to join the RAF and serve with No. 615 'County of Surrey' Squadron based, at the end of September 1940, at Prestwick. Pilot Officer McGibbon met his death during a routine patrol and was buried in the family grave at Rhu.

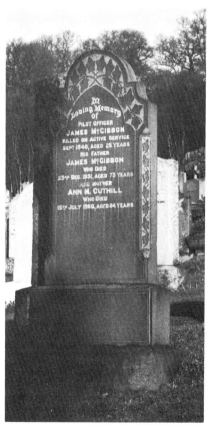

SERGEANT LESLIE REDDINGTON. KILLED SEPTEMBER 30, 1940

As a youth, Leslie Arthur Edwin Reddington followed the occupational pattern of most Coventry lads — he became apprenticed to one of the great engineering factories in the city. In the case of Les Reddington it was the foundry of the Daimler Engineering Works. A brilliant young man, he taught mathematics and engineering drawing at Coventry Technical College in the evenings and was always ready to share his knowledge with youngsters struggling to learn their trade. Later he married and settled down to raising a family, his wife presenting him with a baby girl in 1936. Two years later, after the Munich crisis, he joined the Royal Air Force Volunteer Reserve and had amassed a number of flying hours by the time war broke out. In September 1939 he was called into the Royal Air Force and after training was posted to No. 152 Squadron at Middle Wallop in August 1940. His second daughter was born in February 1941 and named Lesley after her father. Sergeant Reddington never saw her. On Monday, September 30 he was shot down over Portland and no trace of him nor his aircraft was ever found.

On the last night of September, Blenheim L1261 from No. 219 Squadron crashed one mile south-west of Accrington shortly after taking off, killing all the crew. The pilot, Sergeant Charles Goodwin aged twenty-one *left* was buried at his home town of Kingston-upon-Hull.

64 SQUADRON, LECONFIELD

Spitfire P9564. Crashed four miles north of base during routine sortie 10.30 a.m. Cause not stated. Sergeant A. F. Laws believed unhurt. Aircraft a write-off.

87 SQUADRON, EXETER

Hurricane   . Returned to base slightly damaged following combat over Portland 5.00 p.m. Sergeant H. Walton slightly wounded. Aircraft repairable.

92 SQUADRON, BIGGIN HILL

Spitfire X4069. Damaged by Lt. Wiesinger of 4/JG27 in combat over Brighton 5.00 p.m. Forced-landed at Shoreham. Pilot Officer B. Wright slightly wounded by cannon shell splinters in thigh admitted to Southlands Hospital, Shoreham. Aircraft a write-off.

151 SQUADRON, DIGBY

Hurricane P2826. Hit by return fire from Ju 88 intercepted off the Humber 7.20 a.m. Returned to base. Flying Officer K. H. Blair unhurt. Aircraft damaged but repairable.

Hurricane P5182. Returned to base severely damaged by return fire from Ju 88 engaged over the North Sea 7.30 a.m. Sergeant D. B. F. Nicholls unhurt. Aircraft a write-off.

152 SQUADRON, WARMWELL

Spitfire   . Caught in cross-fire during attack on enemy bombers over Portland 4.45 p.m. Landed on one wheel back at base with damage to cockpit hood and petrol tank. Pilot Officer E. S. Marrs unhurt. Aircraft repairable.

Spitfire L1072. Believed crashed into sea during combat over Portland 4.45 p.m. Sergeant L. A. E. Reddington missing. Aircraft lost.

219 SQUADRON, CATTERICK

Blenheim L1261. Disintegrated and crashed during routine night patrol 9.40 p.m. Exact cause uncertain. Sergeant C. Goodwin, Sergeant G. E. Shepperd and AC2 J. P. McCaul all killed. Aircraft a write-off.

John McCaul of the RAF Volunteer Reserve, also killed in the Blenheim, is one of the forgotten ones. According to Ministry of Defence records his rank was AC2 — hence his headstone *(above)* at Leigh Cemetery in Lancashire. There is no doubt that he should have been promoted to sergeant following the Air Ministry orders in 1940 promoting all aircrew to that rank.

The air gunner on L1261 was Sergeant George Shepperd *(left)* from Sidcup, Kent who was buried in the station churchyard near the squadron's base at Catterick.

222 SQUADRON, HORNCHURCH

Spitfire P9492. Forced-landed at Denham damaged following action over south-west London 1.45 p.m. Sergeant I. Hutchinson wounded. Aircraft a write-off.

Spitfire . Shot down by Bf 109 and crash-landed near Sittingbourne Paper Mills 5.45 p.m. Aircraft later exploded. Flight Lieutenant G. C. Matheson unhurt. Aircraft a write-off.

229 SQUADRON, NORTHOLT

Hurricane N2647. Returned to base with damage sustained in combat with Bf 109s 10.35 a.m. Sergeant R. J. O'Manney slightly wounded. Aircraft damaged but repairable.

Hurricane P3422. Severely damaged by Bf 109s in combat over north Kent 10.40 a.m. but returned safely to base. Pilot Officer R. A. L. Du Viver unhurt. Aircraft damaged but repairable.

Venner switch, owned by Steve Vizard, from N2652 dug by the Halstead group.

The Ravenhill family grave at Sheffield City Road Cemetery No. 5903 in Section K. Flying Officer Malcolm Ravenhill was buried here in October 1940 having been killed while serving with No. 229 Squadron at Northolt on September 30 although there is no mention of his name on the headstone. His is one of the two unmarked graves of aircrew killed in the battle.

Hurricane P2815. Shot down by Bf 109s 10.40 a.m. Crashed and burned out at Church Road, Ightham. Flying Officer M. Ravenhill killed. Aircraft a write-off.

Shattered remains of airframe and some minor components recovered by the Halstead War Museum in March 1970.

Hurricane N2652. Shot down by Bf 109s in combat over Edenbridge 10.40 a.m. Crashed at Ightham Place. Pilot Officer N. K. Stansfeld baled out slightly wounded. Aircraft a write-off.

Site excavated by the Halstead War Museum in March 1970 and complete remains recovered. To illustrate the problems of identification in aircraft archaeology, the serial number of this aircraft '2652' was discovered on pieces of airframe recovered by Kent Battle of Britain Museum during an exploratory dig at Elmley, Isle of Sheppey (see entry for P3049 on September 7, 1940). Both aircraft were subsequently found to have been under repair at 4 MU Rolls-Royce during the first week of July 1940 and indicates the extent of 'cannibalisation' of aircraft prevalent at that time.

Hurricane P3227. Damaged in combat with Bf 109s over north Kent and crash-landed west of Ash 10.50 a.m. Pilot Officer F. A. Robshaw slightly wounded. Aircraft RE-R damaged but repairable.

Hurricane R4112. Hit by return fire during solo attack on Do 215 formation. Forced-landed on beach at Lydd 2.00 p.m. Pilot Officer V. M. M. Ortman unhurt. Aircraft damaged but repairable.

Hurricane V7411. Forced-landed during squadron patrol 4.45 p.m. Believed damaged in combat over Kent. Sergeant C. G. Hodson slightly injured. Aircraft damaged but repairable.

Hurricane P3037. Abandoned during squadron patrol over Kent 4.45 p.m. Believed shot down in combat. Pilot Officer L. B. R. Way baled out unhurt. Aircraft a write-off.

238 SQUADRON, MIDDLE WALLOP

Hurricane L1702. Collided with Pilot Officer Simmonds' aircraft during routine patrol. Crashed near Shaftesbury 2.00 p.m. Pilot Officer R. A. Kings baled out but injured in heavy landing due to damaged parachute. Admitted to hospital. Aircraft a write-off.

Hurricane N2474. Crashed near Shaftesbury following collision with Pilot Officer King's aircraft 2.00 p.m. Pilot Officer V. C. Simmonds baled out unhurt. Aircraft a write-off.

302 SQUADRON, LECONFIELD

Hurricane P3925. Taxied into stationary aircraft at base. Sergeant J. Zaluski unhurt. Aircraft repairable.

Hurricane P3924. Slightly damaged in taxi-ing collision mentioned above. No casualties. Aircraft repairable.

Charles Harvey Bacon, a Demi of Magdalene College, Oxford, joined the RAFVR at the age of nineteen and was serving with No. 610 'County of Chester' Squadron when he crashed to his death on Alnmouth beach. His simple grave lies in St. Mary's Church, Windermere.

303 SQUADRON, NORTHOLT

Hurricane P3663. Crash-landed on beach near Lydd severely damaged in combat with Bf 109s over mid-Channel 2.00 p.m. Pilot Officer J. Radomski unhurt. Aircraft damaged but repairable.

Hurricane   . Shot down during combat with Bf 109s 5.00 p.m. Sergeant M. Belc baled out unhurt. Aircraft a write-off.

501 SQUADRON, KENLEY

Hurricane L1657. Forced-landed at Pembury following combat with Bf 109s over Maidstone 9.00 a.m. Flying Officer N. J. M. Barry unhurt. Aircraft damaged but repairable.

504 SQUADRON, FILTON

Hurricane P2987. Forced-landed following combat with enemy aircraft over Yeovil 5.00 p.m. Pilot Officer E. M. Frisby unhurt. Aircraft damaged but repairable.

Hurricane P3021. Crash-landed near Yeovil following action over south-west coast 5.00 p.m. Sergeant B. M. Bush unhurt. Aircraft damaged but repairable.

Hurricane P3774. Forced-landed following combat over Yeovil area 5.00 p.m. Sergeant W. H. Banks unhurt. Aircraft TM-V repairable.

Hurricane P3414. Shot down in combat over the south-west coast 5.00 p.m. Crashed in sea. Flying Officer J. R. Hardacre killed (washed ashore at Yarmouth 10.10.40). Aircraft TM-K lost.

Hurricane V6731. Returned to base damaged following attack on He 111 over Yeovil 5.10 p.m. Flight Lieutenant M. E. A. Royce unhurt. Aircraft damaged but repairable.

602 SQUADRON, WESTHAMPNETT

Spitfire P9510. Damaged by return fire from Ju 88 engaged over Selsey Bill 4.15 p.m. Returned to base. Pilot Officer J. S. Hart unhurt. Aircraft damaged but repairable.

609 SQUADRON, WARMWELL

Spitfire R6915. Hit in glycol tank during attack on He 111 north of base 5.30 p.m. Returned safely to base. Pilot Officer N. le C. Agazarian unhurt. Aircraft repairable.

610 SQUADRON, ACKLINGTON

Spitfire   . Crashed on Alnmouth beach due to flying accident. Flying Officer C. H. Bacon killed. Aircraft a write-off.

Flying Officer John Hardacre was serving with No. 504 'City of Nottingham' Squadron when he was shot down into the Channel on September 30. The Solent tides washed his body ashore on the Isle of Wight ten days later and the squadron took him to All Saints Churchyard at Fawley *(below)* where they laid him next to his fellow-servicemen in the small war graves plot.

Tuesday, October 1

3 SQUADRON, TURNHOUSE

Hurricane P326l. Forced-landed near Chryston, Lanarkshire due to lack of fuel. Pilot error. Pilot Officer J. Lonsdale unhurt. Aircraft a write-off.

41 SQUADRON, HORNCHURCH

Spitfire X4559. Shot down during combat with Bf 109s over Henfield 2.55 p.m. Crashed on Heatenthorn Farm, near Alborne. Pilot Officer G. H. Bennions baled out grievously wounded landing at Dunstalls Farm. Admitted to Horsham Hospital. Aircraft EB-J a write-off.

Site excavated by the Wealden Aviation Archaeological Group in November 1974 with Mr. Bennions in attendance. Remains of Rolls-Royce engine, propellor hub and blade recovered. Landowner of crash site has since named one of his racehorses 'Bennions Spitfire'.

238 SQUADRON, CHILBOLTON

Hurricane P3599. Missing following combat with enemy fighters over Poole Harbour 11.10 a.m. Sergeant F. A. Sibley missing. Aircraft lost.

Hurricane R4099. Shot down by Bf 109 during action over Poole 11.10 a.m. Pilot Officer A. R. Covington unhurt. Aircraft a write-off.

248 SQUADRON, SUMBURGH

Blenheim   . Failed to return from reconnaissance mission to the Norwegian coast. Pilot Officer C. C. Bennett, Sergeant G. S. Clarke, Sergeant G. B. Brash missing. Aircraft lost.

302 SQUADRON, LECONFIELD

Hurricane   . Forced-landed at Bramcote port gun cowling torn loose during routine patrol. Pilot Officer W. E. Karwowski unhurt. Aircraft repairable.

George Bennions, left, with ex-Sergeant J. A. Potter of No. 19 Squadron (shot down and made POW on September 15). On October 1 George was serving with No. 41 Squadron at Hornchurch when he abandoned his Spitfire over West Sussex. In 1974 the Wealden group excavated the crash site in his presence (Peter Foote).

607 SQUADRON, TANGMERE

Hurricane P2900. Shot down during combat with Bf 110s over the Isle of Wight 10.50 a.m. Flight Lieutenant C. E. Bowen missing. Aircraft lost.

Hurricane V6686. Shot down during combat with Bf 110s over the Isle of Wight 10.50 a.m. Sergeant N. Brumby killed. Aircraft lost.

611 SQUADRON, DIGBY

Spitfire II P7376. Undercarriage failure. Forced-landed at base. Sergeant R. A. Angus unhurt. Aircraft damaged but repairable.

Wednesday, October 2

17 SQUADRON, DEBDEN

Hurricane V7659. Forced-landed near Pulham out of fuel following destruction of Do 17 of Stab KG2 10.10 a.m. Flying Officer H. P. Blatchford unhurt. Aircraft undamaged.

Hurricane P3788. Forced-landed near Pulham out of fuel following destruction of Do 17 of Stab KG2 10.15 a.m. Pilot Officer F. Fajtl unhurt. Aircraft damaged but repairable.

The pilot of the No. 248 Squadron Blenheim lost on the first day of October, Pilot Officer Clarence Bennett from Adelaide, Australia. All the crew failed to return from a flight to Norway.

Norman Brumby came from Kingston-upon-Hull and attended Boulevard Secondary School. He joined the Volunteer Reserve in 1938 and saw service in France before being killed with No. 607.

Hurricane P3536. Forced-landed out of fuel following destruction of Do 17 of Stab KG2 10.20 a.m. Pilot Officer J. K. Ross unhurt. Aircraft undamaged.

41 SQUADRON, HORNCHURCH

Spitfire X4545. Collided with stationary aircraft on take-off 1.30 p.m. Sergeant J. K. Norwell slightly injured. Aircraft a write-off.

Spitfire   . Damaged in collision with X4545 above 1.30 p.m. Aircraft repairable.

235 SQUADRON, THORNEY ISLAND

Blenheim N3531. Collided with tractor on take-off 5.45 p.m. Flight Lieutenant P. A. M. Stickney, Pilot Officer D. C. Howe, Sergeant O. J. Dee unhurt. Aircraft QY-F damaged but repairable.

603 SQUADRON, HORNCHURCH

Spitfire P9553. Shot down following destruction of Bf 109 in action over Croydon 10.30 a.m. Crashed and burned out. Pilot Officer P. G. Dexter baled out wounded in leg. Aircraft a write-off.

Thursday, October 3

236 SQUADRON, ST. EVAL

Blenheim Z5743. Undercarriage collapsed whilst taxying at base. Pilot Officer A. F. Y. Lees believed unhurt. Aircraft damaged but repairable.

248 SQUADRON, SUMBURGH

Blenheim   . Damaged by return fire from Do 215 engaged 8.45 a.m. Returned to base. Pilot Officer A. L. Fowler wounded in face and eyes by perspex splinters. Aircraft WR-U damaged but repairable.

600 SQUADRON, REDHILL

Blenheim   . Suffered engine failure during routine patrol in heavy rain. Crashed into trees on high ground at Broadstone Warren, Forest Row 3.55 a.m. Pilot Officer C. A. Hobson, Sergeant D. E. Hughes, AC2 C. F. Cooper killed. Aircraft BQ-M a write-off.

The Gillies family grave in the Thornton Garden of Rest. Here lies the 27-year-old commander of 'A' Flight of No. 66 Squadron, Liverpool-born Flight Lieutenant Kenneth Gillies, killed on October 4.

Pilot Officer Colin Hobson's grave at All Saints Banstead in Surrey. Of the three crew members killed in the Blenheim from No. 600 Squadron, 'Tony's' was the only name put forward on the 1942 provisional Roll of Honour. The air gunner, Sergeant David Hughes from Taranaki, New Zealand, is buried in Whyteleafe and AC2 Charles Cooper, the wireless operator, at Heath Town, Wolverhampton. Charles Cooper is one of those aircraftmen who should have been promoted to sergeant.

Friday, October 4

66 SQUADRON, GRAVESEND

Spitfire X4320. Missing following interception of He 111 off east coast 4.00 p.m. Crashed into sea. Flight Lieutenant K. McL. Gillies killed (washed ashore at Covehithe 21.10.40) Aircraft lost.

266 SQUADRON, WITTERING

Spitfire II P7296. Forced to land at Little Bytham, Lincolnshire in adverse weather. Sergeant S. A. Goodwin unhurt. Aircraft damaged but repairable.

501 SQUADRON, KENLEY

Hurricane V6733. Forced-landed at Great Bentley Farm, Cuckfield due to deteriorating weather during routine patrol 5.05 p.m. Flying Officer D. A. E. Jones unhurt. Aircraft damaged but repairable.

Hurricane V7498. Forced-landed at Ockley Manor Farm, Keymer due to adverse weather during routine patrol 5.20 p.m. Sergeant J. H. Lacey unhurt. Aircraft SD-E damaged but repairable.
Control column donated to the Wealden Aviation Archaeological Group said to have originated with this particular aircraft.

605 SQUADRON, CROYDON

Hurricane V6784. Forced-landed at Pitchfont Farm, Limpsfield due to low cloud at base 4.55 p.m. Pilot Officer C. E. English unhurt. Aircraft UP-E damaged but repairable.

This control column donated to Wealden Aviation Archaeological Group is believed to be from Hurricane V7498 of Sergeant James Lacey, better known as 'Ginger', who was the top-scoring fighter pilot during the Battle of Britain with a total of eighteen credited victories.

Saturday, October 5

1 (RCAF) SQUADRON, NORTHOLT

Hurricane P3873. Shot down during combat with enemy fighters over Canterbury. Crashed at Deering Farm, Smarden. Flying Officer H. de M. Molson baled out wounded and admitted to Chartham Hospital. Aircraft a write-off.

Major recovery by the London Air Museum which unearthed the shattered remains of a Rolls-Royce Merlin engine, propeller boss, centre-section panel and a few cockpit instruments. Fragments also in Kent Battle of Brtitain Museum coillection.

41 SQUADRON, HORNCHURCH

Spitfire N3225. Returned to base damaged in wing during combat with Bf 109s over Thames Estuary 12.15 p.m. Flying Officer A. D. J. Lovell unhurt. Aircraft repairable.

66 SQUADRON, GRAVESEND

Spitfire N3285. Returned to base with damage sustained in combat with Bf 109s over Tenterden 11.45 a.m. Pilot Officer C. A. W. Bodie unhurt. Aircraft repairable.

Spitfire X4543. Returned to base damaged in combat with Bf 109s over Tenterden 11.50 a.m. Sergeant B. Wright unhurt. Aircraft repairable.

Spitfire X4473. Shot down during combat with Bf 109s over Tenterden 11.50 a.m. Believed forced-landed at Detling. Pilot Officer J. B. Kendal slightly injured and admitted to Preston Hall Hospital, Maidstone. Aircraft damaged but repairable.

72 SQUADRON, BIGGIN HILL

Spitfire X4544. Mid-air collision shortly after take-off 9.45 a.m. Returned to base. Sergeant R. C. J. Staples unhurt. Aircraft repairable.

Spitfire K9989. Mid-air collision shortly after take-off. Crashed and burned out 9.50 a.m. Pilot Officer N. Sutton killed. Aircraft a write-off.

Spitfire K9935. Damaged by Bf 109 in action over the Channel 10.20 a.m. Returned to base. Flight Sergeant J. Steere unhurt. Aircraft repairable.

238 SQUADRON, CHILBOLTON

Hurricane P3611. Shot down by Bf 109s in combat over Shaftesbury. Crashed and burned out near Mere 2.20 p.m. Squadron Leader J. R. MacLauchlan baled out and admitted to Shaftesbury Hospital with burns. Aircraft a write-off.

Site excavated by Torbay Aircraft Museum and many shattered and burnt-out components recovered.

302 SQUADRON, LECONFIELD

Magister   . Damaged forced-landing out of fuel. Flight Lieutenant Laguna, Flight Lieutenant J. A. Thomson unhurt. Aircraft damaged but repairable.

Pilot Officer Norman Sutton was tragically killed in a mid-air collision with a fellow pilot on October 5, 1940. His Spitfire plunged to earth carrying him to his death shortly after taking off, the other pilot succeeding in parachuting to safety.

Relics from P3873 recovered by the London Air Museum included the Ki-gas primer.

303 SQUADRON, NORTHOLT

Hurricane P3892. Crashed in flames at Stowting following action with Bf 109s 12.00 p.m. Flying Officer W. Januszewicz killed. Aircraft a write-off.

307 SQUADRON, KIRTON IN LINDSEY

Defiant L7035. Undercarriage retracted in error whilst taxi-ing at base 4.00 p.m. Sergeant B. Malinowski, LAC Ostrowski unhurt. Aircraft damaged but repairable.

603 SQUADRON, HORNCHURCH

Spitfire K9807. Shot down during combat with Bf 109s over Dover 11.55 a.m. Crashed near Chilham. Pilot Officer J. S. Morton baled out burned. Aircraft a write-off.

607 SQUADRON, TANGMERE

Hurricane P3668. Damaged in combat with Bf 109s over Swanage 2.00 p.m. Forced-landed. Pilot believed unhurt. Aircraft damaged but repairable.

Hurricane P3756. Damaged in combat with Bf 109s over Swanage 2.00 p.m. Forced-landed. Pilot believed unhurt. Aircraft damaged but repairable.

Hurricane V6742. Damaged in combat with Bf 109s over Swanage 2.00 p.m. Forced-landed. Pilot believed unhurt. Aircraft damaged but repairable.

Hurricane P3554. Crashed at Woodhorn Farm, Aldingbourne after combat with Bf 109s over Swanage 2.00 p.m. Pilot baled out unhurt. Aircraft a write-off.
Fully excavated by the Wealden Aviation Archaeological Group in September 1979. Intact Rolls-Royce Merlin engine recovered together with complete instrument panel and control column. Aircraft identity plate also discovered confirming identity.

Control column, foot stirrup and rudder pedals from Hurricane P3554 which crashed at Woodhorn Farm, Aldingbourne after being shot down by Bf 109s. These parts and many others, including the instrument panel, the intact Rolls-Royce Merlin engine and the aircraft identity plate were excavated by the Wealden Group in September 1979.

609 SQUADRON, WARMWELL

Spitfire N3223. Abandoned over Salisbury Plain 6.15 p.m. due to undercarriage failure following routine patrol. Crashed near Chisenbury. Flying Officer T. Nowierski baled out unhurt. Aircraft a write-off.

616 SQUADRON, KIRTON IN LINDSEY

Spitfire L1001. Nosed over on landing due to undercarriage fault. Sergeant K. A. Wilkinson unhurt. Aircraft damaged but repairable.

Sunday, October 6

1 (RCAF) SQUADRON, NORTHOLT

Hurricane L1684. Severely damaged in bombing attack by lone raider 1.15 p.m. Aircraft damaged but repairable.

64 SQUADRON, LECONFIELD

Spitfire R6683. Crashed into sea during routine section patrol 2.20 p.m. Cause unknown. Sergeant F. F. Vinyard missing. Aircraft lost.

72 SQUADRON, BIGGIN HILL

Spitfire K9940. Severely damaged in bombing attack on base. No personnel casualties. Aircraft damaged but repairable.

229 SQUADRON, NORTHOLT

Hurricane P3716. Crash-landed near Leatherhead out of fuel and with radio unserviceable following routine squadron patrol 2.05 p.m. Flight Lieutenant W. A. Smith unhurt. Aircraft damaged but repairable.

303 SQUADRON, NORTHOLT

Hurricane P3120. Destroyed in bombing attack on base by lone raider 1.15 p.m. Sergeant A. Suidak killed. Aircraft a write-off.

Hurricane P3217. Believed severely damaged in bombing attack by lone raider 1.15 p.m. Aircraft damaged but repairable.

Monday, October 7

1 (RCAF) SQUADRON, NORTHOLT

Hurricane P2993. Badly damaged in combat with Bf 109. Landed at Biggin Hill. Flying Officer A. D. Nesbitt believed unhurt. Aircraft damaged but repairable.

41 SQUADRON, HORNCHURCH

Spitfire N3267. Shot down by return fire from Do 17 engaged over Folkestone 10.45 a.m. Pilot Officer D. A. Adams baled out landing at Douglas Farm, Postling. Aircraft a write-off.
Relics held by Malcolm Petitt, an amateur enthusiast.

Spitfire X4178. Returned to base damaged by return fire from Do 17 engaged over Folkestone 10.45 a.m. Pilot Officer J. N. Mackenzie unhurt. Aircraft repairable.

56 SQUADRON, BOSCOMBE DOWN

Hurricane P3514. Shot down during combat with enemy aircraft south of Yeovil 4.00 p.m. Believed crashed at Alton Pancras. Sergeant D. H. Nichols baled out and injured in heavy landing. Aircraft a write-off.

66 SQUADRON, GRAVESEND

Spitfire X4326. Damaged in combat. Precise details not stated. Pilot Officer H. M. T. Heron unhurt. Aircraft LZ-N damaged but repairable.

152 SQUADRON, WARMWELL

Spitfire R6608. Forced-landed at Sutton Scotney out of fuel after combat over Lyme Regis 4.40 p.m. Pilot Officer R. M. D. Hall unhurt. Aircraft repairable.

The grave of Pilot Officer Joseph Beedham of No. 245 Squadron who was killed on October 7 whilst landing Hurricane N2707 at Turnhouse. The aircraft suffered engine failure, killing Joe Beedham and wrecking the aircraft.

Three of Hornchurch's Battle of Britain dead are interred in the military plot of Hornchurch Cemetery. All died in combat in the space of twenty days in October 1940, the youngest, Pilot Officer Bob Dewey of Portsmouth, was only nineteen. Pilot Officer Johnny Broadhurst from Crayford was aged twenty-three when he died as was South African Flying Officer Claude Goldsmith.

Spitfire N3039. Shot down during combat with enemy fighters over Lyme Regis 4.40 p.m. Crashed and burned out at Nutmead, Shillingstone. Pilot Officer H. J. Akroyd severely burned (died 8.10.40). Aircraft a write-off.

222 SQUADRON, HORNCHURCH

Spitfire P9469. Shot down during attack on enemy bombers 4.50 p.m. Crashed and burned out at Baileys Reed Farm, Hurst Green, Salehurst. Pilot Officer J. W. Broadhurst baled out but killed landed Longhurst. Aircraft a write-off.
Major recovery by Robertsbridge Aviation Museum.

238 SQUADRON, CHILBOLTON

Hurricane V6777. Shot down by Bf 109s in action over Blandford 4.20 p.m. Crashed at Shatcombe Farm, Wynford Eagle. Pilot Officer A. R. Covington baled out slightly injured and admitted to Blandford Hospital. Aircraft a write-off.

245 SQUADRON, TURNHOUSE

Hurricane N2707. Engine failure during landing. Pilot Officer J. J. I. Beedham killed. Aircraft a write-off.

257 SQUADRON, DEBDEN

Hurricane P3620. Forced-landed Eglantine Road, Horton Kirby 11.30 a.m. Pilot unhurt. Aircraft damaged but repairable.

264 SQUADRON, LUTON

Defiant N1578. Crashed on take-off cause not stated. Pilot Officer G. H. Hackwood, Flying Officer A. O'Connell both injured and admitted to hospital. Aircraft a write-off.

303 SQUADRON, NORTHOLT

Hurricane P3089. Crashed and caught fire on take-off from decoy aerodrome at Borstal, Chatham 2.20 p.m. where landed following combat with Bf 109s. Pilot Officer B. Mierzwa unhurt. Aircraft damaged but repairable.

501 SQUADRON, KENLEY

Hurricane V6800. Shot down by Bf 109 in combat over Wrotham. Crashed Lane End, Darenth 10.40 a.m. Flying Officer N. J. M. Barry fell dead at Wilmington. Aircraft a write-off.

Hurricane V6799. Forced-landed outside Folkestone starboard wing badly damaged in destruction of Bf 109 by collision over the Channel 2.05 p.m. Pilot Officer K. W. Mackenzie slight facial injuries. Aircraft SD-X damaged but repairable.

601 SQUADRON, EXETER

Hurricane R4218. Hit in glycol tank during combat with Bf 110s over Portland. Forced-landed south of Axminster 4.05 p.m. Pilot Officer H. C. Mayers slightly injured. Aircraft a write-off.

602 SQUADRON, WESTHAMPNETT

Spitfire X4160. Damaged by Ju 88 off Beachy Head. Spun-in near Court Farm, Lullington whilst attempting forced-landing 5.50 p.m. Sergeant B. E. P. Whall severely injured died on admission to Princess Alice Hospital, Eastbourne. Aircraft a write-off.

603 SQUADRON, HORNCHURCH

Spitfire N3109. Shot down in combat with Bf 109s of II/JG26. Crashed Hurst Farm, Godmersham Park 10.45 a.m. Flying Officer H. K. F. Matthews killed. Aircraft a write-off.

Site excavated by the Kent Battle of Britain Museum February 1976 and propeller hub with two blades still attached recovered together with control column, rudder bar pedals and various cockpit instruments and components. Parachute buckles and clips also discovered plus microphone housing from oxygen mask and personal effects including key, loose change and nail file.

Nathaniel John Merriman Barry, born in South Africa, was educated at Pembroke College, Cambridge, where he studied mechanical engineering. In 1938 his introduction to flying came with his joining the Cambridge University Gliding Club and, the following year on the outbreak of war, he joined the RAF. On receiving his wings and commission as Pilot Officer, 'Nate' Barry was appointed Aide-de-Camp to Air Vice-Marshal de Crespigny. Unhappy in his air staff appointment, he constantly agitated for an operational posting to a fighter squadron. At the end of September 1940 his wish was granted with a posting to No. 3 Squadron flying Hurricanes. Shortly afterwards, he transferred to No. 501 Squadron with which unit he met his death in action over Wrotham, Kent on October 7 at the age of twenty-two. He lies interred at Finghall Cemetery, 6,000 miles from his native land, in a little country churchyard nestling in a valley of the Yorkshire Wolds.

605 SQUADRON, CROYDON

Hurricane V7305. Shot down during combat with Bf 109s over south London 11.45 a.m. Crashed and burned out at Bexley. Pilot Officer I. J. Muirhead believed baled out unhurt. Aircraft a write-off.

Hurricane P3677. Shot down by Bf 109s over Westerham 2.00 p.m. Crashed and burned out Park Farm, Brasted. Pilot Officer C. E. English killed. Aircraft a write-off.

607 SQUADRON, TANGMERE

Hurricane L1728. Mid-air collision during squadron patrol. Crashed at Eartham Farm, Slindon 4.00 p.m. Flying Officer I. B. Difford killed. Aircraft a write-off.

Hurricane P3860. Collided with Flying Officer Difford during squadron patrol. Crashed near Slindon 4.00 p.m. Pilot Officer A. M. W. Scott baled out unhurt. Aircraft a write-off.

Sergeant Basil Ewart Patrick Whall, DFM, joined the Royal Air Force Volunteer Reserve in 1936 and at the outbreak of war was posted as a sergeant pilot to No. 605 'County of Warwick' Squadron. In April 1940, he transferred to No. 263 Squadron and fought with them throughout the Norwegian campaign flying Gladiators against insuperable odds, both human and elemental. Eventually, without aircraft or bases, the squadron made a forced withdrawal back to the UK in June. On July 5 he was posted to No. 602 'City of Glasgow' Squadron at Drem converting to Spitfires. August 14 saw the squadron's move to the south to take up residence at Westhampnett from where Sergeant Whall was to fight the remainder of his short war and earn himself a DFM. Four days after his arrival he was forced to ditch his aircraft but escaped unscathed. He was rather more unlucky on Monday, September 9 when he crash-landed after combat, injuring his neck but saving his Spitfire. Then, almost a month to the day, his luck ran out. On October 7 he was returning from action off Brighton when his aircraft inexplicably flew into the ground, injuring him so severely that he died (A. Saunders). Basil Whall was buried at Amersham where, later in October, he was joined by his step-brother Peter St. John, killed on the 22nd.

609 SQUADRON, WARMWELL

Spitfire N3238. Shot down in surprise attack by Bf 109s over Yeovil. Crashed at Watercombe Farm, south of Warmwell 4.30 p.m. Pilot unable to regain control. Sergeant A. N. Feary baled out too low and killed. Aircraft a write-off.

Wing spar section collected from local resident by the Wealden Aviation Archaeological Group in August 1979.

Spitfire X4472. Forced-landed at Meriden Wood Down, Winterbourne Houghton with engine damaged in attack by Bf 109s 4.30 p.m. Flight Lieutenant F. J. Howell unhurt. Aircraft damaged but repairable.

Spitfire N3231. Shot down in flames in surprise attack by enemy fighters over Yeovil 4.30 p.m. Crashed at Vale Farm, Sutton Waldron. Pilot Officer M. E. Staples baled out wounded and admitted to Blandford Hospital. Aircraft a write-off.

Spitfire R6915. Hit by cannon-fire during attack on Bf 110 over Dorchester 4.35 p.m. Returned to base. Flying Officer J. C. Dundas slightly wounded in legs by shell splinters. Aircraft damaged but repairable.
This aircraft survived the war and, completely refurbished, can now be seen at the Imperial War Museum in London.

Sergeant Alan Norman Feary aged twenty-eight years from Derby was one of the stalwarts of No. 609 'West Riding' Squadron. On October 7, patrolling the Weymouth area with 'B' Flight, his aircraft was seen spinning earthwards after an engagement with enemy fighters. He recovered but almost immediately spun again, recovering before entering a third spin. He then abandoned his stricken machine but had left it too late . . . his parachute failed to open properly and he was killed when he struck the earth near Watercombe Farm. He lies buried in Holy Trinity Churchyard, Warmwell, among the aerodrome's other dead warriors.

Flying Officer Henry Key Fielding Matthews, a 28-year-old pilot, served with No. 603 'City of Edinburgh' Squadron. He died when his Spitfire was shot down at Godmersham Park on October 7, 1940. We found his grave at Crystal Palace badly neglected.

Charles English, born 1912 in Newcastle-upon-Tyne, served as a Pilot Officer with No. 605 'County of Warwick' Squadron at Drem, Midlothian which flew south to Croydon on September 8, 1940. On October 4 the Geordie pilot survived a crash-landing in foul weather near Westerham, Kent but three days later, in a vicious dogfight over the same area, was shot down and killed. Buried with him in the same Newcastle grave is his brother who was killed as a sergeant pilot in 1941.

'At the going down of the sun and in the morning, we will remember . . . ' The memorable words dedicated to fighting men are inscribed on the headstone of Flying Officer Ivor Difford in Tangmere Churchyard.

October fatalities from No. 66 Squadron at Gravesend. Pilot Officer George Corbett (left) shot down and killed on the morning of September 8 and now buried in a well-kept grave at St. Mary's, Upchurch *(right)* and Flight Lieutenant Ken Gillies who went missing over the North Sea on October 4 and whose body was washed ashore on the 21st (Kent Battle of Britain Museum).

Tuesday, October 8

1 SQUADRON, WITTERING

Hurricane P3169. Landed at Spalding having lost bearings following air-firing practice 1.25 p.m. Sergeant N. Cameron unhurt. Aircraft undamaged.

66 SQUADRON, GRAVESEND

Spitfire R6779. Shot down in combat with Bf 109s 9.30 a.m. Crashed and burned out on Bayford Marshes, Upchurch. Pilot Officer G. H. Corbett killed. Aircraft a write-off.

Spitfire N3043. Shot down in combat with Bf 109s over north Kent 11.55 a.m. Crashed near Rochester. Sergeant R. A. Ward killed. Aircraft LZ-K a write-off.

72 SQUADRON, BIGGIN HILL

Spitfire K9847. Forced-landed at Halstead due to engine failure 10.00 a.m. Sergeant N. V. Glew unhurt. Aircraft damaged but repairable.

Spitfire   . Damaged in combat with Bf 109s 10.40 a.m. Returned to base. Pilot unhurt. Aircraft repairable.

Spitfire   . Damaged in combat with Bf 109s 10.40 a.m. Returned to base. Pilot unhurt. Aircraft repairable.

74 SQUADRON, COLTISHALL

Spitfire II P7329. Mid-air collision during practice attacks over base 3.40 p.m. Crashed near Gillingham. Pilot Officer D. Hastings killed. Aircraft a write-off.

Spitfire II P7373. Collided with Pilot Officer Hastings during practice attacks. Crashed at Gillingham near base 3.40 p.m. Pilot Officer F. W. Buckland killed. Aircraft a write-off.

229 SQUADRON, NORTHOLT

Hurricane V6820. Lost formation in cloud and fell out of control over Bovingdon 12.05 p.m. Disintegrated at 200ft. Sergeant J. R. Farrow killed. Aircraft a write-off.

Rufus Arthur Ward, aged twenty-three years from Croydon, was an RAF reservist before the war. He flew as a sergeant pilot with No. 66 Squadron and on October 8, 1940, he became the unit's third combat fatality in four days when his Spitfire was shot down by Bf 109s near Rochester.

Sergeant John Farrow of Eastleigh died flying with No. 229 Squadron at Northolt.

Pilot Officer Douglas Hastings, married living in North Shields, collided with a fellow officer from No. 74 Squadron, Pilot Officer Frank Buckland, during dogfight practice and both crashed to earth near Beccles. Douglas Hastings was buried in the family plot at Tynemouth *(left)* and Frank Buckland was cremated at Brighton where his name is now inscribed on the memorial panel.

Josef Frantisek pictured *above* on joining the Polish Air Force and *below* by Cuthbert Orde just twenty days before his death

264 SQUADRON, LUTON

Defiant N1627. Crashed at Marlow cause unknown. Pilot Officer H. I. Goodall, Sergeant R. B. M. Young killed. Aircraft a write-off.

303 SQUADRON, NORTHOLT

Hurricane R4175. Crashed at Cuddington Way, Ewell, Surrey during routine patrol 9.40 a.m. Cause unknown. Sergeant J. Frantisek killed. Aircraft a write-off.

604 SQUADRON, MIDDLE WALLOP

Blenheim L1281. Overshot flare path landing from night patrol. Crashed and wrecked. Pilot Officer D. Bayliss and crew unhurt. Aircraft a write-off.

611 SQUADRON, TERNHILL

Spitfire II P7291. Crashed landing at base. Reason not stated. Pilot Officer J. D. Humphreys (of 29 Squadron) unhurt. Aircraft damaged but repairable.

Buried with many of his comrades at Northwood, Group Captain Vincent, the Northolt CO, sent this letter of condolence to the squadron.

Royal Air Force Station,
Northolt, Ruislip,
Middlesex.

9th October 1940.

Dear *Kellett*

I feel I must put on paper my sympathy with you and No. 303 Squadron at the loss of Sergeant FRANCZISEK, also to record my admiration of his magnificent work with the Squadron. I trust the Squadron will not take his loss badly, but always look upon it with the wonderful example he has set for the start of the Squadron. His name should stay for ever in the Squadron History as a really fine fighter.

I am proud to have known him myself, and to have had him at Northolt.

Yours

Squadron Leader R.G. Kellett, D.F.C.,
No. 303 (Polish) Squadron,
Northolt.

Wednesday, October 9

1 SQUADRON, WITTERING

Hurricane V7376. Failed to return from section cloud formation flight over the Wash 11.15 a.m. Sergeant S. Warren missing. Aircraft lost.

41 SQUADRON, HORNCHURCH

Spitfire X4558. Forced-landed with damage sustained in combat with Bf 109s over base 4.15 p.m. Squadron Leader D. O. Finlay unhurt. Aircraft damaged but repairable.

92 SQUADRON, BIGGIN HILL

Spitfire . Shot down believed by Bf 109s and crashed at Smeeth, Ashford 12.50 p.m. Sergeant E. T. G. Frith baled out badly burned admitted to Willesborough Hospital (died 17.10.40). Aircraft a write-off.

234 SQUADRON, ST. EVAL

Spitfire R6621. Crashed on landing at base 7.30 p.m. following destruction of Do 17 off Newquay. Sergeant C. H. Bell unhurt. Aircraft damaged but repairable.

235 SQUADRON, THORNEY ISLAND

Blenheim N3530. Missing following combat with enemy aircraft over the Channel 5.30 p.m. Pilot Officer J. C. Kirkpatrick missing, Pilot Officer R. C. Thomas, Sergeant G. E. Keel killed. Aircraft QY-S lost.

Thursday, October 10

56 SQUADRON, BOSCOMBE DOWN

Hurricane P3421. Shot down in combat with Bf 109s over Wareham 12.20 p.m. Crashed at Manor Farm, Worgret. Sergeant J. Hlavac killed. Aircraft a write-off.

92 SQUADRON, BIGGIN HILL

Spitfire X4038. Mid-air collision during attack on Do 17 over Tangmere 8.15 a.m. Crashed east of Brighton pieces falling at Fallowfield Crescent, Hove. Pilot Officer D. G. Williams killed. Aircraft a write-off.

Sergeant George Keel *(left)*, a 20-year-old air gunner, joined No. 235 Squadron, Coastal Command at Thorney Island on August 13, 1940. On October 9 the Blenheim in which he was flying was shot down into the Channel killing all the crew members. George Keel was buried at Portsmouth.

Spitfire R6616. Collided with Pilot Officer Williams during attack on Do 17 over Tangmere 8.15 a.m. Crashed and burned out in Jubilee Field, Portslade. Flying Officer J. F. Drummond wounded in leg and arm, baled out too low and killed. Aircraft a write-off.

Spitfire X4552. Hit in glycol tank by return fire from Do 17 engaged over Tangmere. Crash-landed near Poynings station 8.35 a.m. Sergeant W. T. Ellis unhurt. Aircraft QJ-C a write-off.

238 SQUADRON, CHILBOLTON

Hurricane P3984. Shot down during attack on enemy fighters over Warmwell 1.00 p.m. Crashed near Corfe Castle viaduct. Pilot Officer R. F. T. Doe baled out wounded landing at Brownsea Island admitted to Poole Hospital. Aircraft a write-off.

The observer, Pilot Officer Richard Thomas, lies in Cardiff in the cemetery known locally as Cathays. The Belgian pilot, James Kirkpatrick, was never found but he has a memorial grave in Brussels.

Victims of the collision during the early morning combat on October 10. No. 92 Squadron lost two pilots in the incident: Pilot Officer Desmond Williams, now buried in Salisbury, and Flying Officer John Drummond in the Garden of Rest at Thornton.

Sergeant Edward Alan Bayley, pictured with his baby daughter Angela, was born in Eastbourne, Sussex. He learned to fly privately at Wilmington in 1933 and was an experienced Volunteer Reserve pilot with No. 32 Squadron at Biggin Hill by September 1939. He remained with the squadron but was posted to No. 249 Squadron at North Weald in September 1940. On Thursday, October 10, during a routine patrol over the Thames Estuary, his Hurricane dropped from formation and, in a steepening dive, fell away towards the earth. Sergeant Bayley made no attempt to abandon his aircraft and it carried him to his death deep in Cooling Marsh. He was buried in the cemetery at St. Luke's, Bromley.

Of the nine Czechoslovakian pilots who lost their lives during the Battle of Britain, two died on October 10. Sergeant Jaroslav Hlavac whilst serving with No. 56 Squadron, now buried at Holy

Trinity, Warmwell, and Sergeant Otta Hanzlicek with the Speke-based Squadron, No. 312. He lies in a joint grave, No. 392 in West Derby Cemetery, Liverpool, with another Czech killed in 1941.

249 SQUADRON, NORTH WEALD

Hurricane V7537. Crashed at Shades House, Cooling Marsh during routine patrol 3.47 p.m. Believed due to oxygen failure. Sergeant E. A. Bayley killed. Aircraft a write-off.

Surface relics in the London Air Museum.

253 SQUADRON, KENLEY

Hurricane L1928. Crashed into houses at Albion Place, Maidstone 3.55 p.m. Cause unknown. Sergeant H. H. Allgood killed. Aircraft a write-off.

Cellar excavated by Kent Battle of Britain Museum during redevelopment of site and later investigated by Steve Vizard.

312 SQUADRON, SPEKE

Hurricane L1547. Caught fire during routine patrol, cause unknown. Crashed into mud of River Mersey. Sergeant O. Hanzlicek baled out into river at Oglett and killed. Aircraft a write-off.

Site investigated by the Warplane Wreck Investigation Group without result. The first Mk I production aircraft.

421 FLIGHT, GRAVESEND

Spitfire II   . Damaged by cannon-fire during combat with Bf 109s. Forced-landed at base. Sergeant M. A. Lee unhurt. Aircraft repairable.

Above: **Albion Place, Maidstone, on the afternoon of Thursday, October 10, 1940 (South Eastern Newspapers Ltd). Demolished houses burn where the No. 253 Squadron Hurricane crashed piloted by Sergeant Harold Allgood** *(left)* **(Kent Battle of Britain Museum). Today the site has been redeveloped for offices** *(below).* **Sergeant Allgood's drogue parachute was collected by one of the soldiers who cleared the site in 1940 and was given to a woman driver from the West Kent Regiment. Now in Steve Vizard's collection.**

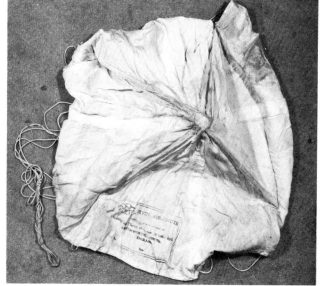

Harold Allgood's remains were sent for interment near his home at Cambridge. St. Mark's Burial Ground is extremely difficult to find and it took us three visits before we traced his overgrown grave. His brother Edwin, lost over the North Sea in May 1942, is also remembered on the headstone.

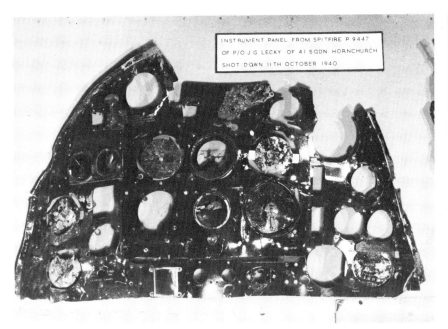

INSTRUMENT PANEL FROM SPITFIRE P 9447
OF P/O J G LECKY OF 41 SQDN HORNCHURCH
SHOT DOWN 11TH OCTOBER 1940

Friday, October 11

41 SQUADRON, HORNCHURCH

Spitfire X4042. Mid-air collision during battle climb to engage Bf 109s. Crashed near Crooked Billet, Ash 4.24 p.m. Flying Officer D. H. O'Neill baled out but parachute failed. Aircraft a write-off.

Spitfire X4554. Collided with Flying Officer O'Neill during battle climb to engage Bf 109s. Crashed and burned out at South Ash Manor, West Kingsdown 4.24 p.m. Sergeant L. R. Carter baled out unhurt. Aircraft a write-off.

Spitfire P9447. Shot down in combat with Bf 109s 4.30 p.m. Crashed at Preston Hall, Maidstone. Pilot Officer J. G. Lecky baled out but killed. Aircraft a write-off.

Major excavation by the Kent Battle of Britain Museum at Great Bells Farm, Eastchurch, Isle of Sheppey revealed complete Rolls-Royce Merlin engine, propeller blade with 20mm cannon shell lodged in it, tail wheel, number plate, radio aerial mast, cockpit instrument panel, control column, rudder bar pedals and other interesting relics. Remains of pilot's leather helmet inscribed 'LECKY' together with 'Luxor' goggle frames and canvas oxygen mask also recovered but the circumstances of this loss still in doubt.

56 SQUADRON, BOSCOMBE DOWN

Hurricane P3866. Forced-landed Warmwell due to engine failure 2.15 p.m. Pilot Officer C. C. O. Joubert unhurt. Aircraft US-V damaged but repairable.

66 SQUADRON, GRAVESEND

Spitfire N3121. Crashed near Newhook on approach to Eastchurch aerodrome in bad visibility 10.00 a.m. Sergeant P. H. Willcocks unhurt. Aircraft damaged but repairable.

Spitfire X4562. Shot down believed by Major Moelders of JG51 in combat over Canterbury 11.15 a.m. Crashed and burned out in Covert Wood, Elham. Pilot Officer J. H. T. Pickering injured admitted to Kent and Canterbury Hospital. Aircraft a write-off.

Instrument panel and propellor blade struck by a German cannon shell recovered from Great Bells Farm, Eastchurch and displayed at Chilham Castle. Although a pilot's helmet named 'Lecky' was uncovered at the site, items of clothing could have been loaned by other pilots during the battle as were maps. Therefore the airframe serial number is usually essential to prove positive identification.

Tilford Churchyard in Surrey was the scene of the burial of John Gage Lecky in the presence of a great company of mourners in October 1940. John Lecky was born in Yokohama, Japan where his father was a language officer with the British Embassy. He was sent to Highfield Preparatory School, Liphook at the age of seven and later attended Wrekin College, Shropshire and the RAF College, Cranwell. He was commissioned on March 9, 1940 and first served with an army co-operation unit. However his dream was to be a fighter pilot and he achieved a posting to No. 41 Squadron where he scored his first confirmed victory on his second sortie. On his next flight the following day he was shot down and killed. Of the many floral tributes to the 19-year-old pilot, the most moving was one from his puppy — 'With love from Chips to his Master'.

Spitfire X4255. Crash-landed at Hawkinge 11.40 a.m. after oil tank exploded over the Channel during pursuit of Bf 109s. Attacked by Major Moelders of JG51. Pilot Officer H. R. Allen severely concussed. Aircraft damaged but repairable.

72 SQUADRON, BIGGIN HILL

Spitfire K9870. Shot down in flames by Bf 109 during combat over convoy off Deal 7.59 a.m. Crashed Milton Regis, Sittingbourne. Pilot Officer H. D. Pool baled out wounded. Aircraft a write-off.

Spitfire R6777. Taxi-ing accident prior to take-off 10.30 a.m. Sergeant N. V. Glew unhurt. Aircraft repairable.

73 SQUADRON, DEBDEN

Hurricane V6676. Shot down whilst acting as 'weaver' to rest of squadron and crashed at Dillywood, Frindsbury 11.08 a.m. Sergeant R. Plenderleith baled out with slight burns and admitted to Chatham Hospital. Aircraft a write-off.

Site investigated by Steve Vizard and Alan Brown in February 1980 and small pieces recovered.

Throughout Pembrokeshire there are 361 burials from the 1939-45 war in sixty-five different cemeteries and churchyards. Sergeant Charles Ayling's brilliant white Portland stone grave marker is a focal point in Monkton St. Nicholas Cemetery near Pembroke.

249 SQUADRON, NORTH WEALD

Hurricane V6728. Crashed on landing due to pilot error 3.25 p.m. Pilot Officer J. J. Solak unhurt. Aircraft GN-Z repairable.

253 SQUADRON, KENLEY

Hurricane V6570. Shot down during combat over Tunbridge Wells 12.00 p.m. Pilot Officer L. C. Murch baled out injured and admitted to hospital with broken arm. Aircraft a write-off.

Hurricane L1666. Crashed during interception patrol 4.30 p.m. cause not stated. Sergeant R. A. Innes believed unhurt. Aircraft repairable.

312 SQUADRON, SPEKE

Hurricane L1807. Reputedly damaged in combat over Chester 6.15 p.m. Pilot Officer J. A. Jaske unhurt. Aircraft repairable.

421 FLIGHT, GRAVESEND

Spitfire II P7303. Crashed near Newchurch during combat with enemy aircraft over Hawkinge 4.00 p.m. Sergeant C. A. H. Ayling killed. Aircraft a write-off.

Few surviving fragments excavated from chalk by the Brenzett Aeronautical Museum in 1978.

611 SQUADRON, TERNHILL

Spitfire II P7356. Returned to base with damage caused by return fire from Do 17 engaged off Holyhead 6.30 p.m. Flying Officer T. D. Williams unhurt. Aircraft damaged but repairable.

Spitfire II P7323. Became lost on return from sortie. Crashed at Crooksey Green, near Kidderminster 7.45 p.m. Sergeant K. C. Pattison critically injured admitted to Barnsley Hall Hospital, Bromsgrove (died 13.10.40). Aircraft a write-off.

Saturday, October 12

3 SQUADRON, MONTROSE

Hurricane R4077. Taxi-ing accident at base. Sergeant J. Biel unhurt. Aircraft repairable.

29 SQUADRON, DIGBY

Blenheim L1472. Engine failure shortly after take-off from Wellingore. Forced-landed 3.50 p.m. Pilot Officer J. Buchanan unhurt. Aircraft damaged but repairable.

41 SQUADRON, HORNCHURCH

Spitfire   . Engine cut on take-off. Crashed at Globe Road, Hornchurch 4.40 p.m. Sergeant J. McAdam unhurt. Aircraft a write-off.

72 SQUADRON, BIGGIN HILL

Spitfire P9338. Lost formation and crashed at Capel-le-Ferne near Folkestone 9.20 a.m. Cause unknown. Pilot Officer H. R. Case killed. Aircraft a write-off.

Sergeant Ken Pattison, RAFVR, of No. 611 Squadron was buried in Nottingham Southern Cemetery at West Bridgford.

PILOT OFFICER HERBERT ROBERT CASE, No. 72 SQUADRON, KILLED OCTOBER 12, 1940

Pilot Officer Herbert Case was a 24-year-old Royal Air Force Volunteer Reserve pilot with No. 72 'Basutoland' Squadron based at Biggin Hill. His home was in Withycombe in Somerset and after he was killed on October 12 near Folkestone, his parents requested that he be buried in their local churchyard of St. Nicholas.

Aberconway Pattinson, born in Chelsea but with his home in Bournemouth, was killed on October 12 when his Spitfire X4591 was shot down north-west of Folkestone. He is now buried in Parkstone Cemetery at Poole.

92 SQUADRON, BIGGIN HILL

Spitfire X4591. Shot down by Bf 109 in combat over Hawkinge 4.40 p.m. Crashed and burned out in Bartholomews Wood, Postling Wents. Pilot Officer A. J. S. Pattinson killed. Aircraft a write-off.
Site excavated by local amateur enthusiasts and results unknown. Also investigated by the Historic Aircraft Achaeological Group.

145 SQUADRON, TANGMERE

Hurricane P3896. Attacked by Bf 109s over Hastings. Crashed in Blackbrooke Wood, Guestling 10.22 a.m. Sergeant Thorpe injured baled out landed at Coghurst and admitted to Buchanan Hospital, Hastings. Aircraft a write-off.
Area of crash investigated by the Wealden Aviation Archaeological Group in 1975. Many small parts collected fron undergrowth.

Hurricane V7251. Returned to base severely damaged following combat with Bf 109s over the Channel off Dungeness 10.30 a.m. Pilot Officer P. W. Rabone unhurt. Aircraft a write-off.

Hurricane V7426. Shot down by Bf 109s over Hastings 10.40 a.m. Crashed Coursehorn Farm, Chittenden, near Cranbrook. Sergeant J. V. Wadham killed. Aircraft a write-off.

219 SQUADRON, REDHILL

Blenheim L1113. Experienced unexpected engine vibration during routine night patrol. Engines throttled back as precaution causing high speed stall. Crashed at Court Lodge Farm, Ewhurst 9.40 p.m. Pilot Officer R. V. Baron baled out but parachute failed. Sergeant G. M. Mead baled out unhurt. Aircraft a write-off.

249 SQUADRON, NORTH WEALD

Hurricane V7313. Shot down in combat with Bf 109s over Eastchurch 9.50 a.m. Adjutant G. Perrin baled out slightly wounded admitted to hospital. Aircraft a write-off.

John Wadham was educated at Ryde School on the Isle of Wight and then went to the Grammar School at Newport. He had begun an apprenticeship with the furnishing firm of Shepperd and Hedgers in Southampton but also joined the RAF Volunteer Reserve prior to the outbreak of war. Pilot Officer Wadham was killed while serving with No. 145 Squadron and was taken back to Newport for burial.

257 SQUADRON, NORTH WEALD

Hurricane P3704. Crashed Saffrey Farm, Owens Court, Selling after combat with Bf 109s over Deal 9.50 a.m. Pilot Officer J. Redman unhurt. Aircraft damaged but repairable.

Hurricane R4195. Forced-landed at Detling with damage sustained in combat with Bf 109s over Deal 9.50 a.m. Pilot Officer K. C. Gundry slightly wounded by shell splinters. Aircraft repairable.

Hurricane V7298. Shot down in combat with Bf 109s over Dungeness. Crashed High House Farm, Stone 5.00 p.m. Pilot Officer C. F. A. Capon baled out slightly wounded. Aircraft a write-off.

Major recovery by the Wealden Aviation Archaeological Group in April 1978. Rolls-Royce Merlin engine, cockpit instruments and components including the control column and rudder bar pedal assembly all salvaged.

421 FLIGHT, GRAVESEND

Spitfire II P7441. 'Bounced' by Bf 109s at over 20,000ft during spotting flight. Crashed Coldbridge, Boughton Malherbe. Flight Lieutenant C. P. Green baled out over Pembles Cross Farm, Egerton wounded in neck and arm. Admitted to hospital. Aircraft a write-off.

Site excavated by local enthusiast Ron Gammage. Items in the Vizard collection.

602 SQUADRON, WESTHAMPNETT

Spitfire X4541. Damaged by return fire from Ju 88 engaged over the Channel, overturned forced-landing at Iford Farm, Iford near Lewes 3.40 p.m. Sergeant C. F. Babbage unhurt. Aircraft LO-M damaged but repairable.

Spitfire P9446. Returned to base main spar damaged by return fire from Ju 88 engaged over the Channel off Beachy Head 3.40 p.m. Pilot Officer J. S. Hart unhurt. Aircraft damaged but repairable.

605 SQUADRON, CROYDON

Hurricane P3022. Shot down in action against Bf 109s over the Channel off Dungeness 12.30 p.m. Sergeant P. R. C. McIntosh killed. Aircraft lost.

615 SQUADRON, NORTHOLT

Hurricane L2101. Forced-landed at Chiddingfold due to engine trouble. Pilot Officer N. D. Edmond unhurt. Aircraft damaged but repairable.

Date: October 12, 1940. Time: 1540 hours. Location: Iford Farm, Iford, Sussex. Spitfire X4541 comes to grief in an emergency landing but the Pilot Cyril Babbage of No. 602 Squadron was unhurt (Fox).

The neglected grave of Sergeant Peter McIntosh of No. 605 Squadron in St. John's Churchyard, Croydon.

507

Sunday, October 13

17 SQUADRON, DEBDEN

Hurricane P3536. Shot down by AA during squadron patrol over Chatham crashed Rochester 1.50 p.m. Pilot Officer J. K. Ross baled out wounded admitted to Gravesend hospital. Aircraft a write-off.

29 SQUADRON, TERNHILL

Blenheim L6637. Shot down in error by 312 Squadron Hurricanes. Crashed in flames off the Point of Aire near the Morecambe Light 6.00 p.m. Sergeant R. E. Stevens, Sergeant O. K. Sly missing. AC2 A. Jackson killed. Aircraft lost.

Blenheim L7135. Damaged in attack by 312 Squadron Hurricanes off east coast 6.00 p.m. Returned to base. Pilot Officer J. D. Humphreys, Sergeant E. H. Bee, A/C J. F. Fizell unhurt. Aircraft repairable.

46 SQUADRON, STAPLEFORD

Hurricane   . Forced-landed at Biggin Hill following attack by Bf 109s over Dungeness. Sergeant Pearce wounded. Aircraft repairable

66 SQUADRON, GRAVESEND

Spitfire N3285. Damaged in combat with Bf 109s over Maidstone 4.20 p.m. Returned to base. Pilot Officer C. A. W. Bodie unhurt. Aircraft damaged but repairable.

Spitfire X4479. Forced-landed near Halling Ferry 4.00 p.m. following combat with Bf 109s over Maidstone. Squadron Leader R. H. A. Leigh unhurt. Aircraft damaged but repairable.

Spitfire X4543. Crash-landed at Hornchurch following combat with Bf 109s over Maidstone 4.10 p.m. Sergeant H. Cook unhurt. Aircraft a write-off.

FIGHTER INTERCEPTION UNIT, SHOREHAM

Blenheim L6805. Operating as target aircraft for AI-equipped Boston and suffered engine failure due to mishandling of fuel cocks. Crashed through landing obstructions near Lancing College 2.00 p.m. Flying Officer C. A. G. Clark and one NCO unhurt. A/C Mitchell suffered broken collar-bone. Aircraft a write-off.

Monday, October 14

73 SQUADRON, DEBDEN

Hurricane   . Forced-landed near Haverhill during routine patrol 6.45 p.m. Cause not stated. Pilot Officer A. McFadden unhurt. Aircraft TP-G undamaged.

Hurricane   . Forced-landed at Bartlow 6.50 p.m. during routine squadron patrol. Cause not stated. Squadron Leader A. D. Murray unhurt. Aircraft TP-L undamaged.

152 SQUADRON, WARMWELL

Spitfire R6763. Landed without benefit of undercarriage following dog-fight practice 3.15 p.m. Sergeant J. S. Anderson unhurt. Aircraft damaged but repairable.

Another of our aircraftmen-cum-sergeants, AC2 Arthur Jackson of No. 29 Squadron, lies beneath the Commonwealth War Graves Commission headstone in the middle distance in this picture of Mexborough Cemetery, Yorkshire. Not only has he the wrong rank but, to add insult to injury, the 29-year-old pilot was killed by his own side.

Flying Officer Ralph Hope of No. 605 'County of Warwick' Squadron (second cousin to Neville Chamberlain), an auxiliary pilot who joined the squadron before the war and flew with it until his tragic death at the age of twenty-seven on October 14. On this day of low cloud and drizzle, he chased a Heinkel 111 into the Inner Artillery Zone where his Hurricane struck a barrage balloon cable. A squadron veteran of Dunkirk, the convoy and September battles over London, it was ironic that Ralph Hope should succumb to our own defences (A. Saunders). His remains were cremated at Woking.

No. 46 Squadron lost Peter Stackhouse Gunning on October 15 and buried him in St. Andrew's Churchyard, North Weald.

213 SQUADRON, TANGMERE

Hurricane V6541. Damaged landing on waterlogged runway at Merston. Pilot unhurt. Aircraft damaged but repairable.

601 SQUADRON, EXETER

Hurricane P5208. Overshot runway landing after formation practice 6.40 p.m. Sergeant E. Weightman unhurt. Aircraft undamaged.

Hurricane P3393. Overshot runway landing after formation practice 6.45 p.m. Sergeant R. A. Millburn unhurt. Aircraft damaged but repairable.

605 SQUADRON, CROYDON

Hurricane P3107. Inadvertently flew into the Inner Artillery Zone during routine patrol and believed collided with balloon cable but possible victim of AA defences. Crashed South Norwood 12.50 p.m. Flying Officer R. Hope killed. Aircraft a write-off.

616 SQUADRON, KIRTON-IN-LINDSEY

Spitfire X4330. Unable to lower undercarriage following routine sortie. Crash-landed at base 4.07 p.m. Sergeant R. V. Hogg unhurt. Aircraft YQ-G damaged but repairable.

Tuesday, October 15

29 SQUADRON, TERNHILL

Blenheim K7135. Destroyed by a single bomb dropped during enemy raid on aerodrome. Aircraft a write-off.

Blenheim L6741. Damaged during enemy bombing raid on aerodrome. Aircraft repairable.

41 SQUADRON, HORNCHURCH

Spitfire X4178. Shot down in surprise attack by Hptmn. Foezoe of 4/JG51. Crashed in Channel 9.00 a.m. Sergeant P. D. Lloyd killed (washed ashore near Kings Hall, Herne Bay 27.10.40). Aircraft lost.

46 SQUADRON, STAPLEFORD

Hurricane N2480. Shot down in combat with Bf 109s over the Thames Estuary. Crashed and burned out in chalk pit at Little Thurrock 1.05 p.m. Pilot Officer P. S. Gunning killed. Aircraft a write-off.

Hurricane V6550. Shot down in combat with Bf 109s over the Thames Estuary. Crashed in Gravesend 2.30 p.m. Flight Sergeant E. E. Williams missing. Aircraft a write-off.

Hurricane V6789. Abandoned over the Thames Estuary during combat with Bf 109s. Crashed at Gravesend 2.40 p.m. Sergeant A. T. Gooderham baled out slightly burnt. Aircraft a write-off.

Sergeant Philip Lloyd of No. 41 Squadron was shot down over the sea on October 15. His body was not recovered until twelve days later and was buried in a secluded corner of the Church of the Holy Innocents, deep in Epping Forest at High Beech, Essex.

92 SQUADRON, BIGGIN HILL

Spitfire R6642. Shot down in combat with Bf 109s over the Thames Estuary 10.00 a.m. Reputedly crashed in sea off Hoo Marina. Sergeant K. B. Parker killed. Aircraft lost.

Surviving remains recovered under extremely hazardous conditions from tidal estuary by the London Air Museum using 45-gallon oil drums as flotation bags. Rolls-Royce Merlin engine, propeller boss all three blades still attached, both undercarriage legs, tail wheel, cockpit instruments and controls, intact armoured cockpit windscreen and gunsight recovered but nothing to identify the aircraft beyond dispute. Main wheel tyre held by Kent Battle of Britain Museum.

ROLLS-ROYCE MERLIN mk II ENGINE AND THREE BLADED DE-HAVILLAND PROP. these remains were found on the mudflats at hoo marina, kent, they come from a spitfire of 92 sqn which was shot down on 15th oct 1940, the pilot sgt parker baled out but has never been found.

GUNSIGHT AND 303 SHELLS:

A most unusual find by the London Air Museum reputedly from Sergeant Parker's Spitfire R6642 was the pilot's armoured glass windscreen, completely unbroken and in mint condition. Note the inscription is incorrect — Kenneth Parker is buried in Holland.

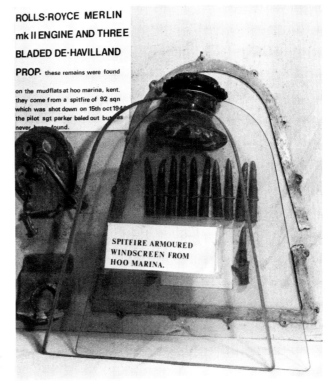

ROLLS-ROYCE MERLIN mk II ENGINE AND THREE BLADED DE-HAVILLAND PROP. these remains were found on the mudflats at hoo marina, kent, they come from a spitfire of 92 sqn which was shot down on 15th oct 1940, the pilot sgt parker baled out but was never found.

SPITFIRE ARMOURED WINDSCREEN FROM HOO MARINA.

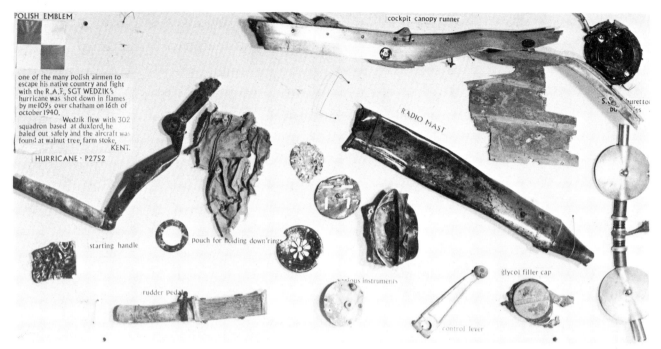

POLISH EMBLEM

one of the many Polish airmen to escape his native country and fight with the R.A.F., SGT WEDZIK's hurricane was shot down in flames by me109s over chatham on 16th of october 1940.
Wedzik flew with 302 squadron based at duxford, he baled out safely and the aircraft was found at walnut tree, farm stoke, KENT.

HURRICANE · P2752

cockpit canopy runner

RADIO MAST

S.U. carburettor bodies

starting handle

pouch for holding down rings

rudder pedal

various instruments

glycol filler cap

control lever

Spitfire R6838. Shot down in combat with Bf 109s. Crashed Wybornes Farm, High Halstow 11.47 a.m. Flight Lieutenant C. B. F. Kingcome baled out wounded admitted to RN Hospital, Chatham. Aircraft a write-off.

Orchard location investigated by London Air Museum. Many scattered fragments remain.

Spitfire . Shot down during action with Bf 109s. Crashed on mudflats off Allhallows 11.50 a.m. Pilot Officer J. W. Lund rescued from sea by HMS *Nysan.* Aircraft a write-off.

145 SQUADRON, TANGMERE

Hurricane V7337. Attacked by Bf 109s over Christchurch Bay 1.00 p.m. Abandoned over New Milton. Pilot Officer J. Machacek baled out wounded in leg and admitted to Lymington hospital. Aircraft a write-off.

213 SQUADRON, TANGMERE

Hurricane V6544. Crash-landed following combat with Bf 109 over the Swanage area 12.45 p.m. Flight Lieutenant J. M. Strickland unhurt. Aircraft AK-V damaged but repairable.

222 SQUADRON, HORNCHURCH

Spitfire L1089. Forced-landed near Hawkinge having run low on fuel and being damaged in combat with Bf 109s 2.30 p.m. Sergeant J. T. Dunmore unhurt. Aircraft damaged but repairable.

Spitfire K9795. Forced-landed at Tillingham Hall, near Horndon 4.20 p.m. due to engine failure. Undercarriage damaged. Pilot Officer H. P. M. Edridge unhurt. Aircraft damaged but repairable.

229 SQUADRON, NORTHOLT

Hurricane P3124. Shot down in flames during combat with Bf 109s 10.00 a.m. Crashed on to buildings at South Street Farm, Stockbury. Squadron Leader A. J. Banham baled out burned. Aircraft a write-off.
Site excavated 1978 by the Historic Aircraft Archaeological Group said to be this aircraft. Few fragments recovered from depth of only four feet included valves from the shattered Rolls-Royce Merlin engine and various maker's plates but none confirming identity beyond dispute. Relics also in Vizard collection.

Relics recovered from Sergeant Wedzik's Hurricane P2752 displayed by the London Air Museum. (Note the date on the Letraset caption is incorrect.)

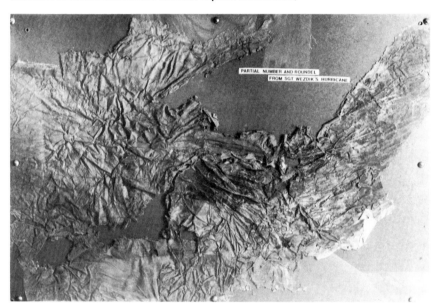

PARTIAL NUMBER AND ROUNDEL FROM SGT WEDZIK'S HURRICANE

Hurricane P3456. Tail surfaces badly damaged in combat with Bf 109s 10.05 a.m. Returned to base. Flight Lieutenant W. A. Smith unhurt. Aircraft damaged but repairable.

253 SQUADRON, KENLEY

Hurricane V6756. Crashed at Dunton Green being severely damaged in combat 8.30 a.m. Sergeant E. H. C. Kee unhurt. Aircraft damaged but repairable.

257 SQUADRON, NORTH WEALD

Hurricane V7351. Forced-landed at Hawkinge following engagement with Bf 109s over the Thames Estuary 12.30 p.m. Pilot Officer G. North unhurt. Aircraft damaged but repairable.

302 SQUADRON, NORTHOLT

Hurricane P3812. Forced-landed at Slough damaged in combat over the Thames Estuary. Squadron Leader W. A. J. Satchell unhurt. Aircraft damaged but repairable.

Hurricane R2684. Forced-landed at Wrotham due to engine failure. Pilot Officer J. L. Malinski unhurt. Aircraft damaged but repairable.

Hurricane P2752. Shot down in flames during combat with Bf 109s over Chatham 11.30 a.m. Crashed Walnut Tree Farm, Stoke. Sergeant M. Wedzik baled out admitted to Chatham Hospital. Aircraft WX-R a write-off.

Excavated by the London Air Museum 1969. Shattered Rolls-Royce Merlin engine recovered plus control column, first-aid kit and partial instrument panel, undercarriage legs and tyres.

312 SQUADRON, SPEKE

Hurricane V6846. Crashed near Dalton-in-Furness having lost bearings and low on fuel during routine patrol. Major J. K. Ambrus believed unhurt. Aircraft damaged but repairable.

Hurricane V6811. Abandoned over Dalton-in-Furness having lost his bearings and low on fuel. Pilot Officer T. Vybiral believed unhurt. Aircraft a write-off.

Hurricane V6542. Forced-landed near Carnforth lost and low on fuel during routine patrol. Flight Lieutenant H. A. G. Comerford unhurt. Aircraft a write-off.

421 FLIGHT, GRAVESEND

Spitfire II P7444. Damaged in combat with Bf 109s. Wrecked in attempted forced-landing at Blackham Farm, Broadoak 11.00 a.m. Sergeant M. A. Lee wounded admitted to hospital. Aircraft damaged but repairable.

Spitfire X4612. Forced-landed following engine seizure due to big-end failure. Pilot Officer K. A. Lawrence unhurt. Aircraft damaged but repairable.

501 SQUADRON, KENLEY

Hurricane V6722. Crashed at Postern Gate Farm, Godstone following action with Bf 109s over Redhill 8.15 a.m. Sergeant S. A. Fenemore killed. Aircraft a write-off.
 Remains excavated by London Air Museum include the smashed Rolls-Royce Merlin engine, propeller boss, yellow tip of a propeller blade, partial instrument panel and implements left by wartime recovery crew.

Hurricane P5194. Damaged in action with Bf 109s over Sheppey 1.10 p.m. Forced-landed at Rochford. Sergeant R. W. E. Jarrett wounded. Aircraft damaged but repairable.

Hurricane V6787. Landed at Rochester with glycol leak developed during combat with Bf 109s over Sheppey 1.10 p.m. Flying Officer R. C. Dafforn unhurt. Aircraft damaged but repairable.

601 SQUADRON, EXETER

Hurricane V6666. Crashed on landing undercarriage not locked. 6.40 p.m. Pilot Officer J. W. Seddon unhurt. Aircraft damaged but repairable.

605 SQUADRON, CROYDON

Hurricane N2546. Shot down in combat with Bf 109s over Maidstone. Crashed at Spekes Bottom, Darland near Gillingham 11.45 a.m. Flight Lieutenant I. J. Muirhead killed. Aircraft a write-off.

609 SQUADRON, WARMWELL

Spitfire P9503. Attacked by Bf 109s over Southampton 12.40 p.m. Returned to base damaged in wing. Flying Officer J. C. Dundas unhurt. Aircraft repairable.

Stanley Fenemore, the son of William and Gertrude Fenemore of Whitewell, County Antrim, Northern Ireland, was a Volunteer Reserve pilot with No. 501 Squadron. His Hurricane V6722 was shot down near Godstone and he was buried in Liverpool, now re-united with his family. Tony Graves, seen *below* with his daughter on the memorial seat beside the field in which Sergeant Fenemore crashed, excavated the site in 1976. These are some of the relics recovered.

Spitfire X4539. Hit in cockpit during surprise attack by Bf 109s over Southampton 12.40 p.m. Returned to base. Pilot Officer N. le C. Agazarian unhurt. Aircraft repairable.

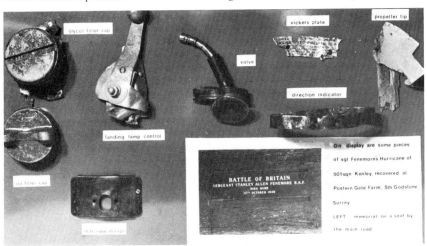

Wednesday, October 16

AIRCRAFT						A.M. Form 78.

Contract No. *962371/38*

Type *HURRICANE I*   R.A.F. No. *P. 3318*   Contractor *BROOKLANDS*

Type of Engine *MERLIN. III*   Engine Nos. *148170*

	(1)	(2)	(3)	(4)	(5)	(6)	(7)	(8)	(9)
Taken on Charge of	27 MU	3 Sqdn	1 store	20 MU	1 Sqdn	3 MU	15 MU	11 Gp	607 Sqd
Date taken on Charge	20/3/40	10.4.40	6.7.40	23.8.40	1.9.40	3/11/40	-41.40	2 Mar.	16.5.41
Authority	1632 A	1623	CAT B	.233	1623 A	1623 A	1627	1623 A	1623

	(10)	(11)	(12)	(13)	(14)	(15)	(16)	(17)	(18)
Taken on Charge of	14 Sqdn	331 SQ	55 OTU	47	55 OTU				
Date taken on Charge	6.6.41	7.8.41	26.8.41						
Authority	1623D	1623D	1623						

Date	Unit to whom allotted	Authority	Date	Unit to whom allotted	Authority
30.1.40	27. M. U.	2624			
2..?	27 M.U.	1???			
14.12.40	18 M.U.	13720			

(487) Gp.697 Wt.13105 6/39 C&SLtd

Aircraft cards were made out for every single aircraft which saw service in the RAF to record each movement of the aircraft, whether for repair or squadron service. The cards are now preserved at the Air Historical Branch in London and, although they provide an invaluable reference source, they have been known to be incorrect. This is the card for Hurricane P3318 which forced-landed on October 16 and which was finally lost in a flying accident on November 11, 1941 (Air Historical Branch).

Authority	Reason for Allotment	Special Fitments, etc.	Write off or Strike off Details		
			Date	Extent of Damage	Source of Informat'n
2624	RESERVE AIRCRAFT		30.1.1940	F.B.O. (3)	
			18.9.?		
			11.11.41	F.A	

Date *16.11.41.*
Authority *438/3/P3318/22*
Unit *55 OTU*
Total Flying Hours
Remarks :-

1 SQUADRON, WITTERING

Hurricane P3318. Forced-landed during local flying practice 2.15 p.m. Sergeant J. Prihoda unhurt. Aircraft believed undamaged.

29 SQUADRON, TERNHILL

Blenheim K7135. Damaged in bombing raid by Ju 88 on base 7.21 a.m. Aircraft damaged but repairable.

Blenheim L6741. Damaged in bombing raid on base by Ju 88 7.21 a.m. Aircraft damaged but repairable.

65 SQUADRON, TURNHOUSE

Spitfire R6714. Crashed following flying accident over Gateside 4.00 p.m. Sergeant I. Pearson killed. Aircraft a write-off.

Ian Forbes Pearson was born at Gateside in the County of Fife to John and Agnes Pearson of Bannaty Mill Farm. Serving as an RAFVR sergeant pilot with No. 65 Squadron, his family saw him crash within a mile of the farm. They buried him at Strathmiglo Parish Churchyard just two miles from his home.

249 SQUADRON, NORTH WEALD

Hurricane V6878. Hit by return fire from Do 215 engaged over Kent and forced-landed at Rolvenden near Tenterden 1.10 p.m. Pilot Officer K. T. Lofts unhurt. Aircraft a write-off.

264 SQUADRON, LUTON

Defiant N1621. Damaged on return to base following destruction of He 111 of 2/KGr.126 over Brentwood 1.30 a.m. Pilot Officer F. D. Hughes, Sergeant F. Gash unhurt. Aircraft damaged but repairable.

302 SQUADRON, NORTHOLT

Hurricane P3935. Hit balloon cable in bad visibility losing fourteen inches from starboard wing. Landed at Heston. Sergeant Kosarz unhurt. Aircraft damaged but repairable.

310 SQUADRON, DUXFORD

Hurricane P3143. Crashed near Ely during routine training flight. Cause unknown. Sergeant S. J. Chalupa killed. Aircraft NN-D a write-off.

Personnel of No. 310 Czechoslovakian Squadron at Duxford. This Hurricane, P3143, carried Sergeant Jan Chalupa to his death near Ely, Cambridgeshire on October 16.

504 SQUADRON, FILTON

Hurricane R4178. Forced-landed near Whitchurch and ran into a pond 3.15 p.m. Pilot Officer R. E. Tongue unhurt. Aircraft damaged but repairable.

601 SQUADRON, EXETER

Hurricane V6649. Crashed in avoiding Flying Officer Riddle (V7236) who was landing in the wrong direction following a weather test 11.45 a.m. Flight Lieutenant Sir Archibald Hope Bt. unhurt. Aircraft damaged but repairable.

Thursday, October 17

46 SQUADRON, STAPLEFORD

Hurricane P3539. Propeller and under-carriage damaged in belly-landing at Parkers Farm, Woodend, Abbess Roding due to lack of fuel and poor visibility 12.00 p.m. Sergeant R. de C. d'Hamale unhurt. Aircraft PO-Y damaged but repairable.

66 SQUADRON, GRAVESEND

Spitfire R6800. Shot down by Major Moelders of JG51 in combat over Westerham 3.25 p.m. Crashed and burned out at Crockham Hill, Sevenoaks. Pilot Officer H. W. Reilley killed. Aircraft LZ-N a write-off.

74 SQUADRON, BIGGIN HILL

Spitfire II P7360. Shot down in combat with Bf 109s over Maidstone 3.40 p.m. Crashed near Hollingbourne. Flying Officer A. L. Ricalton killed. Aircraft a write-off.

The grave of Hugh Reilley at Gravesend, unsung American hero shot down by the German ace Major Moelders. It has always been assumed that William Fiske was the only American killed in the Battle of Britain but Hugh Reilley, anxious to fight with the Royal Air Force, crossed the border into Canada and obtained a Canadian passport. Only a few close friends knew his real nationality and his secret died with him on October 17.

Pilot Officer Ronald Atkinson *(left)* from Gillingham, Kent joined the Royal Air Force Volunteer Reserve before the war and, when the Battle of Britain started, was serving as a Blenheim pilot with No. 600 'City of London' Squadron at Manston. In August 1940 he was posted to No. 111 Squadron with a change of aircraft to Hurricanes, transferring on September 19 to No. 213 Squadron at Exeter. On October 17, at the age of nineteen, while flying from Tangmere, he was shot down and killed after combat with enemy fighters. He was buried at Gillingham. *Above:* The London Air Museum uncovered the wreckage of P3174 in 1975. The caption card on the board below is incorrect — Pilot Officer H. D. Atkinson was killed on August 25.

213 SQUADRON, TANGMERE

Hurricane P3174. Shot down in combat with Bf 109s 4.30 p.m. Crashed at Weeks Farm, Egerton, near Pluckley. Pilot Officer R. Atkinson killed. Aircraft AK-G a write-off.

Site excavated by the London Air Museum in 1975. Top of pilot's seat unearthed together with windscreen frame and many small components. Parachute harness buckles, quick release buckle and loose change also discovered.

Hurricane V6866. Shot down in combat with Bf 109s over Tenterden 4.30 p.m. Forced-landed. Sergeant G. Stevens unhurt. Aircraft AK-D damaged but repairable.

242 SQUADRON, COLTISHALL

Hurricane V6575. Presumed damaged by return fire from Do 17 engaged off Yarmouth 9.00 a.m. Crashed in sea. Pilot Officer N. N. Campbell killed. Aircraft a write-off.

Hurricane P3207. Damaged by return fire from Do 17 engaged off Yarmouth 9.00 a.m. Returned to base. Pilot Officer M. K. Brown unhurt. Aircraft repairable.

253 SQUADRON, KENLEY

Hurricane P3537. Crashed at Gains Hill, Yalding due to engine failure. Pilot Officer T. Nowak unhurt. Aircraft a write-off.
Site investigated by Steve Vizard

Hurricanes N2455, N2588, P2865, V6757. Severely damaged in bombing attack on base at 8.00 p.m. Aircraft damaged but repairable.

266 SQUADRON, WITTERING

Spitfire X4164. Damaged in landing accident. Sergeant C. E. Ody unhurt. Aircraft repairable.

302 SQUADRON, NORTHOLT

Hurricane V6753. Lost bearings on routine patrol and damaged in forced-landing near Slough. Flight Lieutenant H. Czerny unhurt. Aircraft damaged but repairable.

Hurricane V7417. Overturned attempting forced-landing at Colliers End 10.05 a.m. Sergeant J. S. Zaluski killed. Aircraft WX-T damaged but repairable.

Hurricane V6735. Forced-landed near Sittingbourne 5.30 p.m. Cause not stated. Pilot Officer S. Kleczkowski unhurt. Aircraft WX-M repairable.

421 FLIGHT, GRAVESEND

Hurricane II . Forced-landed at Detling on seized engine 9.30 a.m. following violent evasive action to avoid Bf 109s. Sergeant A. W. P. Spears unhurt. Aircraft LZ-V repairable.

Hurricane II . Crashed on landing following combat with Bf 109s 2.20 p.m. Flight Sergeant J. Gillies injured. Aircraft LZ-O repairable.

501 SQUADRON, KENLEY

Hurricane V6703. Severely damaged in bombing attack on base at 8.00 p.m. Aircraft damaged but repairable.

615 SQUADRON, NORTHOLT

Hurricane P2754. Collided with Sergeant Hammerton on take-off 9.15 a.m. Flying Officer A. P. Gray unhurt. Aircraft repairable.

Hurricane P3111. Collided with Flying Officer Gray on take-off 9.15 a.m. Sergeant J. Hammerton unhurt. Aircraft repairable.

Friday, October 18

145 SQUADRON, TANGMERE

Hurricane V6856. Overshot runway on landing and collided with stationary aircraft 10.35 a.m. Pilot Officer M. A. Newling unhurt. Aircraft a write-off.

Hurricane V6876. Hit by another aircraft whilst parked 10.35 a.m. Aircraft damaged but repairable.

152 SQUADRON, WARMWELL

Spitfire R6607. Crashed at Tadnoll Mill near Dorchester during afternoon. Exact circumstances not recorded. Sergeant E. E. Shepperd killed. Aircraft a write-off.

234 SQUADRON, ST. EVAL

Spitfire R6983. Crashed on landing from routine dawn patrol 8.25 a.m. Flying Officer J. S. Young unhurt. Aircraft repairable.

249 SQUADRON, NORTH WEALD

Hurricane P3463. Ran out of petrol in landing circuit. Forced-landed on Padfields Farm, Church Road, Thornwood Common 4.30 p.m. damaging undercarriage. Adjutant H. Bouquillard unhurt. Aircraft repairable.

Hurricane P5206. Damaged in forced-landing near base. Cause not stated. Possibly that down at Maylands, Romford 7.00 p.m. Pilot believed unhurt. Aircraft damaged but repairable.

Flying Officer Peter Edward Carter was one of the four pilots from No. 302 Polish Squadron at Northolt who became disorientated in foul weather conditions on the afternoon of October 18. Three were Polish nationals whilst the fourth, Peter Carter, came from Croydon. He is buried there today in Queen's Road Cemetery.

Edmund Eric Shepperd was born in Binstead, Isle of Wight in 1917 and was barely two years old when his father died on April 8, 1919 of wounds received in the Great War. Educated at schools in Binstead and Ryde, he excelled both academically and athletically becoming a keen tennis player. Some years before the war, he joined the Royal Air Force as a regular, serving on a number of overseas stations. In July 1940 he was a sergeant pilot with No. 152 Squadron at Warmwell and he fought with the unit throughout the battle, accounting for four enemy aircraft. On Friday, October 18, his Spitfire inexplicably ploughed into the ground near Dorchester. He now lies buried beside the father he scarcely came to know.

Aleksiej Zukowski crashed after running out of fuel and died a Pilot Officer. His Polish comrades buried him at Northwood but credited him with the rank of Flying Officer after the war.

302 SQUADRON, NORTHOLT

Hurricane P3872. Crashed attempting forced landing on Nutwood Farm, Thames Ditton on return from patrol in bad weather conditions 4.05 p.m. Pilot Officer S. Wapniarek killed. Aircraft WX-R a write-off.

Site excavated by the Air Historical Group which recovered some engine and cockpit components, instruments, control column, propeller boss and tail wheel tyre.

Hurricane V6571. Ran out of fuel having lost bearings in deteriorating weather conditions after routine patrol. Crashed Harp Farm, Boxley, near Detling 4.05 p.m. Pilot Officer A. Zukowski killed. Aircraft WX-Q a write-off.

Hurricane P3931. Crashed at Kempton Park Race Course returning from routine patrol in deteriorating weather conditions 4.10 p.m. Flying Officer P. E. G. Carter baled out at 50ft and killed. Aircraft WX-V a write-off.

Hurricane P3930. Crashed and burned out on Kempton Park Race Course returning from patrol in deteriorating weather conditions at 4.10 p.m. Flying Officer J. Borowski killed. Aircraft WX-X a write-off.

Hurricane   . Forced-landed having lost bearings in poor visibility 4.25 p.m. Pilot Officer B. Bernas unhurt. Aircraft WX-Y repairable.

616 SQUADRON, KIRTON-IN-LINDSEY

Spitfire N3066. Aircraft severely damaged in forced-landing at Broughton having run out of fuel due to inexperience. Sergeant R. Ivey unhurt. Aircraft damaged but repairable.

Saturday, October 19

3 SQUADRON, CASTLETOWN

Hurricane P3260. Crashed attempting slow roll during AA co-operation exercise. Flying Officer G. F. McAvity died of injuries. Aircraft a write-off.

92 SQUADRON, BIGGIN HILL

Spitfire R6922. Crashed on Tuesnoad Farm, Smarden. Circumstances unknown. Sergeant L. C. Allton killed. Aircraft a write-off.

Crash site excavated by the London Air Museum and complete Rolls-Royce Merlin engine recovered together with propeller boss, all three blades still attached, cockpit instruments and controls, remains of pilot's parachute, cigarette case, and 'Luxor' goggle frames. Wartime recovery operations were abandoned when a hurricane lamp was knocked over accidentally igniting trapped fuel. The burned-out remains of the lamp were also recovered together with the rest of this aircraft.

249 SQUADRON, NORTH WEALD

Hurricane V6635. Forced-landing following routine patrol over Harwich 6.00 p.m. Cause not stated. Pilot Officer A. R. F. Thompson unhurt. Aircraft repairable.

421 FLIGHT, GRAVESEND

Hurricane II Z2352. Forced-landed at Clement Street, Old Swanley 2.51 p.m. Cause not stated. Flying Officer Parrott slightly injured. Aircraft LZ-U damaged but repairable.

615 SQUADRON, NORTHOLT

Hurricane 311. Belly-landed at base due to undercarriage failure 4.50 p.m. Adjutant R. Mouchotte unhurt. Aircraft from Canadian production batch (previously L1760) damaged but repairable.

The most northerly grave of a Battle of Britain airman buried in the United Kingdom belongs to Flying Officer George McAvity, a Canadian pilot from Hampton, New Brunswick, who lies in Olrig Cemetery in Caithness.

Leslie Allton, born in 1920 in Nuneaton, attended King Edward VI Grammar School from 1931 to 1937 during which time he was School Captain, Captain of Football, Hockey and Cricket (above).

Before the war he was a keen weekend flier with the RAFVR and during the Battle of Britain served with No. 266 Squadron, transferring to No. 92 Squadron at Biggin Hill at the end of September.

He was killed on October 19 when he crashed at Tuesnoad Farm, Smarden and was buried in his home town.

Thirty-odd years later, the London Air Museum uncovered the burnt and blackened wreckage. Some of the items which came to light were the pilot's goggles and his cigarette case. Another incredible find was this hurricane lamp which it is believed was lost by local souvenir hunters in 1940 when it ignited the petrol vapour in the crater (Tony Graves).

Sunday, October 20

46 SQUADRON, STAPLEFORD

Hurricane V6790. Forced-landed near Buntingford cause unknown. Pilot believed unhurt. Aircraft damaged but repairable.

66 SQUADRON, GRAVESEND

Spitfire X4599. Damaged in combat 11.40 a.m. Returned to base. Sergeant H. Cook unhurt. Aircraft *PLYMOUTH AND SOUTHSEA I* damaged but repairable.

74 SQUADRON, BIGGIN HILL

Spitfire II P7370. Shot down at Coxheath in combat with enemy fighters over Maidstone 2.55 p.m. Sergeant T. B. Kirk baled out severely wounded and admitted to Preston Hall Hospital Maidstone. Died of wounds 22.7.41. Aircraft a write-off.
    Site excavated 1976 by Steve Vizard who recovered Rolls-Royce Merlin engine, propeller boss and cockpit components.

Spitfire II P7426. Shot down in action with Bf 109s over south London and crashed at Cowden 3.00 p.m. Sergeant C. G. Hilken baled out wounded and admitted to Orpington Hospital. Aircraft a write-off.

Spitfire II P7355. Severely damaged in oil cooler during combat with Bf 109s over south London 3.05 p.m. Crash-landed with engine seized. Pilot Officer B. V. Draper unhurt. Aircraft a write-off.

92 SQUADRON, BIGGIN HILL

Spitfire N3113. Damaged by return fire from Bf 110 of 7(F)/LG2 shot down at Horsmonden 12.50 p.m. Forced-landed at Waterfield near Tonbridge. Flying Officer J. W. Villa unhurt. Aircraft damaged but repairable.

Spitfire X4412. Returned to base damaged by return fire from Bf 110 of 7(F)/LG2 shot down at Horsmonden 12.50 p.m. Pilot unhurt. Aircraft damaged but repairable.

248 SQUADRON, SUMBURGH

Blenheim P6952. Shot down in attack on enemy aircraft off coast of Norway 9.30 a.m. Flight Lieutenant G. M. Baird captured. Sergeant R. Copcutt missing. Warrant Officer D. L. Burton captured wounded and admitted to hospital in Stavanger. Warrant Officer S. V. Wood captured wounded and admitted to hospital in Oslo. Aircraft WR-X lost.

On October 20, No. 248 Squadron at Sumburgh in the Shetlands despatched two Blenheims to the Norwegian coast on a reconnaissance mission. Both failed to return. Captain of L9453 was Pilot Officer Sidney Gane now buried in Trondheim, Norway.

One of the most beautiful headstones, simple yet explicit, is that which marks the grave of Sergeant Thomas Kirk. Harlsey Castle has a direct, private entrance to St. Oswald's Churchyard where the Kirk family plot is situated.

Blenheim L9453. Failed to return from reconnaissance sortie over the Norwegian coast. Pilot Officer S. R. Gane killed. Pilot Officer M. D. Green, Sergeant N. J. Stocks missing. Aircraft WR-Z lost.

421 FLIGHT, GRAVESEND

Spitfire II P7445. Extensively damaged in rudder, elevator and radiator by enemy cannon fire. Returned to base. Sergeant A. W. P. Spears unhurt. Aircraft *AMANGABAD* damaged but repairable.

605 SQUADRON, CROYDON

Hurricane V6844. Propeller shot off during combat with Bf 109s over New Romney 10.00 a.m. Returned to base. Pilot Officer P. D. Thompson unhurt. Aircraft repairable.

Hurricane V6755. Controls badly damaged in combat with Bf 109s over New Romney 10.00 a.m. Returned to base. Pilot Officer J. H. Rothwell unhurt. Aircraft damaged but repairable.

Monday, October 21

245 SQUADRON, TURNHOUSE

Hurricane P3657. Dived into Loch Neagh and exploded. Cause unknown. Sergeant E. G. Greenwood killed. Aircraft a write-off.

266 SQUADRON, WITTERING

Spitfire X4265. Landed Stradishall to refuel and crashed on take-off 12.50 p.m. Reason unknown. Pilot Officer W. S. Williams killed. Aircraft a write-off.

615 SQUADRON, NORTHOLT

Hurricane V7601. Damaged in landing at Heathrow. Pilot Officer L. N. Landels unhurt. Aircraft damaged but repairable.

Stradishall Churchyard in Norfolk beside St. Margaret's church was used for burials by the nearby RAF station. Pilot Officer Wycliff Williams from New Zealand crashed taking off from the aerodrome on October 21.

Tuesday, October 22

46 SQUADRON, STAPLEFORD

Hurricane R4074. Shot down in combat with enemy fighters over Dungeness. Crashed near Newchurch church 4.50 p.m. Sergeant J. P. Morrison killed. Aircraft a write-off.

Surface fragments believed to be from this aircraft recovered by the Kent Battle of Britain Museum.

74 SQUADRON, BIGGIN HILL

·Spitfire II P7431. Shot down in combat with Bf 109s. Crashed at South Nutfield, Surrey 3.30 p.m. Flying Officer P. C. B. St. John killed. Aircraft a write-off.

Site investigated by the London Air Museum and some surface fragments collected. Subsequently complete remains of aircraft excavated by Halstead War Museum.

Spitfire II P7364. Crashed at Hadlow Place, near Tonbridge 3.30 p.m. following combat with Bf 109s. Pilot Officer R. L. Spurdle baled out unhurt. Aircraft a write-off.

249 SQUADRON, NORTH WEALD

Hurricane V6566. Forced-landed at Fitzwalters Meadows, Hall Lane, Shenfield due to engine failure 3.09 p.m. Pilot Officer A. R. F. Thompson unhurt. Aircraft damaged but repairable.

257 SQUADRON, NORTH WEALD

Hurricane R4195. Came under AA fire during combat with Bf 109s over Folkestone. Crashed three-quarters-of-a-mile south of Lydd church 4.46 p.m. Pilot Officer N. B. Heywood killed. Aircraft a write-off.

Hurricane V6851. Shot down in combat with Bf 109s over Folkestone. Crashed and burned out at Moat Farm, Shadoxhurst 4.50 p.m. Sergeant R. H. B. Fraser killed. Aircraft a write-off.

Crash site excavated by the Brenzett Aeronautical Museum.

Hurricane P2835. Attacked by Bf 109s over Folkestone and severely damaged. Landed at Gatwick 5.10 p.m. Sergeant R. C. Nutter unhurt. Aircraft damaged but repairable.

The Morrison family grave in St. Andrew's and Jesmond Cemetery — one of the five burial grounds owned by the Newcastle-upon-Tyne Corporation. Here lie mother, father and son — Sergeant Joseph Morrison — a Volunteer Reserve pilot shot down while flying with No. 46 Squadron from Stapleford on October 22.

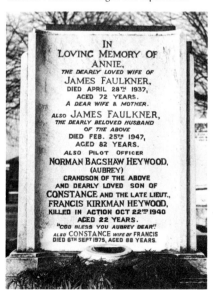

Pilot Officer Norman Heywood, shot down by friendly defences, was buried in Stretford Cemetery in Lime Road.

Flying Officer Peter St. John, step-brother to Sergeant Basil Whall killed on October 7, was himself shot down and killed on the 22nd. His grave can be found at Amersham behind St. Mary's Churchyard.

605 SQUADRON, CROYDON

Hurricane V6783. Shot down by Bf 109s over base 2.30 p.m. Crash-landed near Dorking. Pilot Officer J. A. Milne slightly wounded in action but fractured hip in landing. Aircraft a write-off.

Wednesday, October 23

600 SQUADRON, CATTERICK

Blenheim L1272. Crashed into hillside at Kirkby Malzeard, Yorks. during practice flight through cloud 10.55 a.m. Pilot Officer P. R. S. Hurst killed. Aircraft BQ-X a write-off.

616 SQUADRON, KIRTON-IN-LINDSEY

Spitfire   . Undercarriage leg torn off and mainplanes damaged in heavy landing having misjudged approach to base. Sergeant Wilson unhurt. Aircraft damaged but repairable.

Thursday, October 24

43 SQUADRON, USWORTH

Hurricane V7303. Dusk-flying accident at base 7.25 p.m. Made six attempts to land cross-wind and finally stalled at 250ft. Sergeant D. R. Stoodley killed. Aircraft a write-off.

87 SQUADRON, EXETER

Hurricane P3404. Collided with Pilot Officer Cock during routine patrol. Crashed and burned out. Pilot Officer D. T. Jay baled out but believed to have hit the tailplane as he did not pull his ripcord and killed. Aircraft a write-off.

Hurricane   . Tail surfaces severely damaged when hit by P3404 during routine patrol. Forced-landed at base. Pilot Officer J. R. Cock unhurt. Aircraft repairable.

Above: Brenzett group members investigating the crash site of Sergeant Robert Fraser's Hurricane at Shadoxhurst on June 30, 1973. A Glasgow-born Volunteer Reserve pilot with No. 257 Squadron at North Weald, he now lies in a weed-covered grave in Craigton Cemetery. *Below:* Parts recovered are now displayed in the group's museum in Kent. (Note the correct spelling of the pilot's name is Fraser.)

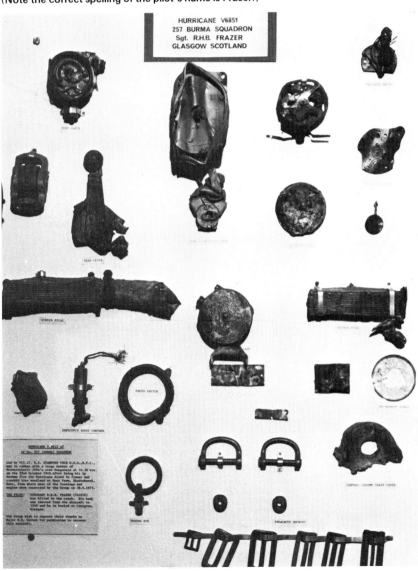

Pilot Officer Dudley Trevor Jay was serving in No. 87 Squadron at Debden just prior to the outbreak of war, moving to their new base at Seclin in France when the unit was attached to the Air Component. On its return to the United Kingdom, the squadron retired to Church Fenton to rebuild their strength before moving to Exeter. Trevor Jay survived the shambles of the French campaign, the battles for the Channel convoys and the mounting savagery over the south coast towns and ports. Then, one week before the end of the battle, Flying Officer John Cock was leading a formation of four Hurricanes on a routine patrol when without warning his engine cut. Nos. 2 and 3 pulled away to the sides but Trevor Jay, flying in the box position, could not avoid a collision. The propellor of Jay's aircraft hit the tail of Cock's, smashing the blades although Cock recovered and made it back to Exeter. Jay started a controlled glide but at 1,800 feet abandoned the Hurricane. The two remaining pilots who had escorted him down watched, horror struck, as he fell tumbling towards the earth, his parachute unopened. The 19-year-old veteran, who won himself a DFC, was found dead and his squadron laid him to rest in the war graves section of Exeter Higher Cemetery (N. Franks).

Our artist, George Campbell, seeks out the grave of Sergeant Donald Stoodley in London Road Cemetery, Salisbury. His overgrown plot was found in Section M with most of the other war graves although it was marked with a private curbstone. Donald came from Southampton but died at Usworth serving with No. 43 Squadron.

111 SQUADRON, MONTROSE

Hurricane P3046. Take-off accident exact details unknown. Sergeant M. J. Mansfield unhurt. Aircraft damaged but repairable.

141 SQUADRON, COTTESMORE

Defiant L6994. Landed without undercarriage locked down following hydraulic pump failure. Crashed on landing at base. Pilot Officer E. F. Edwards unhurt. Aircraft damaged but repairable.

151 SQUADRON, DIGBY

Hurricane V6537. Crashed during training flight 6.30 p.m. Details not stated. Flying Officer C. D. Whittingham unhurt. Aircraft damaged but repairable.

303 SQUADRON, LECONFIELD

Hurricane V6807. Crashed during dog-fight practice 5.20 p.m. Pilot Officer J. Bury-Burzymski killed. Aircraft a write-off.

Friday, October 25

41 SQUADRON, HORNCHURCH

Spitfire II P7371. Forced-landed at Hawkinge with 20mm cannon shell through starboard camshaft casing after combat with Bf 109s off Dungeness 4.00 p.m. Sergeant R. A. Beardsley unhurt. Aircraft repairable.

Spitfire II P7442. Forced-landed west of Tandridge Lodge, Tandridge out of fuel following combat with Bf 109s 4.30 p.m. Pilot Officer J. N. Mackenzie unhurt. Aircraft believed undamaged.

46 SQUADRON, STAPLEFORD

Hurricane V6804. Crashed into house in Woodstock Avenue, Romford 12.07 p.m. following routine patrol. Cause unknown. Pilot Officer W. B. Patullo recovered from wreck and admitted to Oldchurch Hospital but died next day. Aircraft a write-off.

The station churchyard at Leconfield. The small war graves plot beside St. Catherine's contains the graves of nineteen airmen, seven of whom are Polish. Many died in local incidents as did Pilot Officer Jan Bury-Burzymski of No. 303 Squadron who crashed during dogfight practice in Hurricane V6807 on October 24.

Likewise another churchyard serving an RAF aerodrome is the one at St. Illtyd's Pembrey. Of the thirty-four service burials, twenty-nine are from the Second World War including seven belonging to the Polish Air Force. Pilot Officer Stanislaw Piatkowski was killed while serving with No. 79 Squadron.

66 SQUADRON, GRAVESEND

Spitfire X4170. Shot down in combat with Bf 109s over Tunbridge Wells. Crashed in orchard near Capel 9.00 a.m. Pilot Officer R. W. Oxspring baled out slightly injured. Aircraft a write-off.
Site excavated by Malcolm Petitt.

79 SQUADRON, PEMBREY

Hurricane N2708. Crashed near Carew Cheriton after routine patrol. Cause unknown. Pilot Officer S. Piatowski killed. Aircraft a write-off.
Crash site identified and at time of press under consideration for excavation by the Gwalia Aviation Research Group.

92 SQUADRON, BIGGIN HILL

Spitfire X4480. Forced-landed at Penshurst aerodrome following combat with Bf 109s 1.30 p.m. Pilot Officer J. Mansell-Lewis unhurt. Aircraft undamaged.

111 SQUADRON, MONTROSE

Hurricane V6539. Night landing accident at base 8.00 p.m. Sub-Lieutenant T. V. Worrall unhurt. Aircraft damaged but repairable.

145 SQUADRON, TANGMERE

Hurricane   . Forced-landed and exploded at High Beeches, Haywards Heath Golf Course 12.19 p.m. due to engine failure during squadron patrol. Pilot Officer B. M. de Hemptinne unhurt. Aircraft a write-off.

Hurricane P3926. Forced-landed at Barn Farm field, Brightling 12.30 p.m. with damage sustained in combat with Bf 109s over Tenterden. Pilot Officer R. D. Yule wounded in leg admitted to Pembury hospital. Aircraft SO-Y a write-off.

151 SQUADRON, DIGBY

Hurricane L2047. Night landing accident at base 9.45 p.m. Cause not stated. Sergeant Grant unhurt. Aircraft damaged but repairable.

238 SQUADRON, CHILBOLTON

Hurricane P3349. Hit a boundary hedge and telephone lines in dangerous low flying near base 6.00 p.m. Pilot Officer J. S. Wigglesworth unhurt. Aircraft repairable.

249 SQUADRON, NORTH WEALD

Hurricane P3615. Shot down in combat with Bf 109s over north Kent 12.00 p.m. Believed crashed on Rankins Farm, Linton. Sergeant J. M. B. Beard baled out wounded and admitted to Pembury hospital. Aircraft a write-off.
Aircraft wreckage recovered from this site by Steve Vizard but nothing found to establish identity beyond dispute.

Hurricane V7409. Forced-landed at Rochester following combat with Bf 109s over north Kent 12.00 p.m. Adjutant H. Bouquillard wounded and admitted to RN Hospital at Chatham. Aircraft damaged but repairable.

Hurricane V6692. Lost bearings during routine patrol and landed near Colchester 10.00 a.m. Sergeant M. K. Macejowski unhurt. Aircraft believed undamaged.

257 SQUADRON, NORTH WEALD

Hurricane V6741. Ran off landing-strip at Penshurst due to brake failure following combat with Bf 109 over the Channel 2.10 p.m. Sergeant H. F. W. Shead unhurt. Aircraft repairable.

Plate from the oxygen regulator found by Steve Vizard at Rankin's Farm at Linton, believed to be from Hurricane P3615 abandoned by Sergeant Beard.

On the afternoon of October 25, two Hurricanes from No. 501 Squadron collided during combat over Tenterden, Kent. Pilot Officer McKenzie managed to bale out and Steve Vizard picked up a myriad of small parts left behind on the surface after the crash site was excavated by Ron Gammage. Pilot Officer Vilem Goth was less fortunate and is buried at Sittingbourne.

302 SQUADRON, NORTHOLT

Hurricane V7593. Failed to return from patrol over the Channel. Last seen gliding toward the enemy coast 10.50 a.m. Flight Lieutenant F. Jastrzebski killed. Aircraft WX-V lost.

306 SQUADRON, CHURCH FENTON

Hurricane L1717. Crashed on landing wheels up after first solo flight on type. Sergeant Waskiewicz unhurt. Aircraft repairable.

308 SQUADRON, BAGINGTON

Hurricane V6914. Forced-landed on golf links cause not stated. Pilot Officer F. Szyszka unhurt. Aircraft damaged but repairable.

501 SQUADRON, KENLEY

Hurricane P5193. Believed shot down in combat with Bf 109s over Cranbrook 3.15 p.m. Sergeant S. A. H. Whitehouse unhurt. Aircraft repairable.

Hurricane N2438. Reputedly shot down during combat with Bf 109s over Cranbrook 3.15 p.m. Pilot Officer V. R. Snell believed unhurt. Aircraft a write-off.

Hurricane P2903. Collided with Pilot Officer McKenzie during combat with Bf 109s over Tenterden. Crashed in orchard at Manor Farm, Staplehurst 3.25 p.m. Pilot Officer V. Goth killed. Aircraft a write-off.
Surface fragments in the Steve Vizard private collection.

Hurricane V6806. Crashed into Brewers Wood, Tolehurst Farm 3.25 p.m. after mid-air collision with Pilot Officer Goth during combat over Tenterden. Pilot Officer K. W. McKenzie baled out unhurt. Aircraft a write-off.
Major recovery by local enthusiast Ron Gammage. Fragments also in the Kent Battle of Britain Museum and the Vizard Collection.

601 SQUADRON, EXETER

Hurricane V6917. Collided with Sergeant Mills-Smith during section training flight 3.00 p.m. Crashed in sea off Exmouth. Sergeant L. D. May missing. Aircraft lost.

Hurricane P3709. Crashed into sea off Exmouth after mid-air collision with Sergeant May during section training flight 3.00 p.m. Sergeant F. Mills-Smith missing. Aircraft lost.

603 SQUADRON, HORNCHURCH

Spitfire P7350. Believed shot down in combat with Bf 109s over Hastings 10.10 a.m. Pilot Officer B. Martel unhurt. Aircraft damaged but repairable.

Spitfire P7325. Crashed Stonelink Farm, Brede following combat with Bf 109s over Sussex coast 10.15 a.m. Pilot Officer J. Soden baled out and injured right leg in landing at 'Perryfields' admitted to East Sussex Hospital, Hastings. Aircraft a write-off.

Spitfire P7309. Shot down in combat with Bf 109s over Hastings. Crashed Pickdick Farm, Brede 10.20 a.m. Pilot Officer P. Olver baled out wounded landing at Westfield. Aircraft a write-off.
Major recovery by the Wealden Aviation Archaeological Group 1972. Complete Rolls-Royce Merlin engine, propeller hub, cockpit components and many other relics unearthed.

In August 1972, the Wealden Aviation Archaeological Group excavated the crash site of Spitfire P7309 which was shot down while being flown by Pilot Officer Olver of No. 603 Squadron. Two of the many items recovered were the throttle control and partial instrument panel.

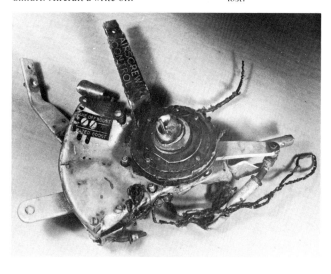

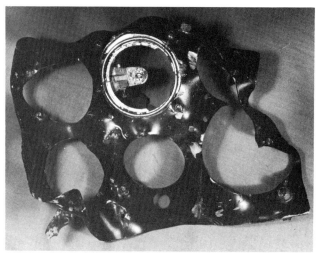

In 1938, Robert Holder *(above)* emigrated to New Zealand where he joined the Royal New Zealand Air Force. Returning to England in 1940, he was posted as a replacement to No. 151 Squadron at Digby where that unit was recovering from severe losses sustained in the battle and was gradually converting to night fighting. On October 26 at 8.40 p.m., 23-year-old Sergeant Bob Holder and Sergeant Douglas Stanley took off in their Hurricanes. Shortly after the two aircraft had become airborne, they were seen to dive into the ground and the subsequent inquiry stated that the possible cause was that the aircraft had collided. Both pilots were killed. Robert Holder was taken to Bidford-on-Avon for burial *(above right)* while Douglas Stanley, a New Zealander from Matamata, Auckland, went to the station churchyard. The burial ground for RAF Digby lies at nearby Scopwick *(right)*. It was here in December 1941 that an American pilot from Washington, DC, serving in the Royal Canadian Air Force was laid to rest. His name was John Gillespie Magee whose poem, found in his papers after his death with No. 412 Squadron and reproduced here in its original form, portrays like none other the unfettered joy of flight.

Saturday, October 26

29 SQUADRON, DIGBY

Blenheim L1375. Crashed on landing at base reason not stated 8.00 p.m. Pilot Officer J. D. Humphreys, Sergeant E. H. Bee, A/C W. C. Wilson unhurt. Aircraft repairable.

151 SQUADRON, DIGBY

Hurricane R4184. Night flying accident 8.40 p.m. Exact circumstances not recorded. Sergeant R. Holder killed. Aircraft a write-off.

Hurricane V7434. Night flying accident 8.40 p.m. Possible collision shortly after take-off. Sergeant D. O. Stanley seriously injured, died the following day. Aircraft a write-off.

HIGH FLIGHT

Oh! I have slipped the surly bonds of earth
　And danced the skies on laughter-silvered wings;
Sunward I've climbed, and joined the tumbling mirth
　Of sun-split clouds — and done a hundred things
You have not dreamed of — wheeled and soared and swung
　High in the sunlit silence. Hov'ring there
I've chased the shouting wind along, and flung
　My eager craft through footless halls of air.

Up, up the long, delirious, burning blue
　I've topped the wind-swept heights with easy grace
Where never lark, nor even eagle flew —
　And, while with silent lifting mind I've trod
The high, untrespassed sanctity of space,
　Put out my hand and touched the face of God.

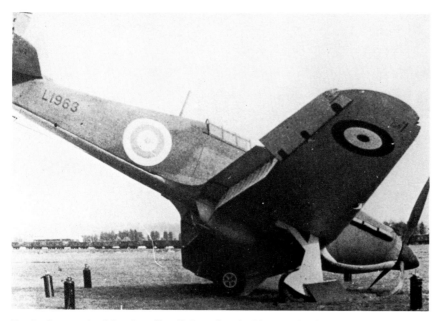

By the last week of October, No. 43 Squadron had been pulled back from the front line and were resting at Usworth. On the morning of the 27th, Sergeant Leonard Toogood, an RAFVR pilot with a total of 246 hours logged (51 on type), took off in Hurricane L1963 (seen *above* on an earlier prang soon after delivery) for high altitude aerobatic practice. Although it was seen in the company of other machines from the squadron, without any warning its nose dropped and it went into a power dive. Continuing its descent, it failed to pull out and smashed into the ground ten yards from Congburn Dene woods. Thirty-eight years passed . . . until the members of the North East Aircraft Museum arrived on the scene to excavate the crash site. The terrific force of the impact was immediately apparent but much of interest *(below)* was recovered including the pilot's parachute, wallet and maps. The final wreckage was found at a depth of fifteen feet.

222 SQUADRON, HORNCHURCH

Spitfire R6773. Crashed on Purleigh Barns Farm, Latchingden, 5.45 p.m. when engine caught fire during patrol. Sergeant P. O. Davis unhurt. Aircraft a write-off.

229 SQUADRON, NORTHOLT

Hurricane V6704. Shot down by Bf 109s off the French coast during attack on Heinkel He 59 11.30 a.m. Pilot Officer D. B. H. McHardy believed captured. Aircraft lost.

Hurricane W6669. Shot down by Bf 109s whilst attacking Heinkel He 59 moored off the French coast 11.30 a.m. Crashed in sea. Flying Officer G. M. Simpson missing. Aircraft lost.

234 SQUADRON, ST. EVAL

Spitfire X4355. Damaged by return fire from Ju 88 engaged over Lands End 3.15 p.m. Forced-landed near Porthleven. Pilot Officer E. B. Mortimer-Rose unhurt. Aircraft damaged but repairable.

302 SQUADRON, NORTHOLT

Hurricane V6735. Forced-landed near Sittingbourne out of fuel. Pilot Officer S. Kleczkowski slightly injured. Aircraft WX-M repairable.

308 SQUADRON, BAGINGTON

Hurricane V6536. Damaged in landing accident at base. Bounced on ridge in runway and lost a wheel. Pilot Officer B. Skibinski unhurt. Aircraft damaged but repairable.

421 FLIGHT, GRAVESEND

Hurricane II Z2345. Forced-landed through HT cables at South Darenth 4.55 p.m. Cause not stated. Sergeant F. S. Perkins unhurt. Aircraft LZ-H damaged but repairable.

602 SQUADRON, WESTHAMPNETT

Spitfire R6839. Failed to return from routine squadron patrol 12.30 p.m. Cause unknown. Sergeant D. W. Elcome missing. Aircraft lost.

604 SQUADRON, MIDDLE WALLOP

Blenheim L8373. Lost an airscrew during night patrol over Salisbury and crashed on landing due to undercarriage failure 1.20 a.m. Pilot Officer N. R. Wheatcroft, Sergeant Taylor unhurt. Aircraft damaged but repairable.

Sergeant Toogood was buried in Kingston Cemetery, St. Mary's Road, Portsmouth.

605 SQUADRON, CROYDON

Hurricane P3737. Damaged in combat with Bf 109s. Forced-landed at Town Row Green, Marks Cross 12.35 p.m. Flying Officer C. W. Passy unhurt. Aircraft a write-off.

Hurricane P2916. Shot down after inadvertent solo attack on Bf 109 formation. Crashed at Staplehurst near Cranbrook 3.45 p.m. Pilot Officer J. C. F. Hayter baled out unhurt. Aircraft UP-D a write-off.

Sunday, October 27

43 SQUADRON, USWORTH

Hurricane L1963. Crashed vertically from height during high-altitude aerobatics, cause unknown but probably oxygen failure. Fell at Congburn Dean, Edmondsley 10.25 a.m. Sgt. L. V. Toogood killed. Aircraft a write-off.

Major recovery by the Northumberland Aeronautical Collection in October 1978. Parts recovered were the tail wheel assembly, radio, radiator, pilot's seat, armour plate, main wheels and shattered remains of Rolls-Royce Merlin engine. Pilot's parachute recovered intact in excellent condition. Positive identification provided by pilot's wallet handed to the RAF.

66 SQUADRON, GRAVESEND

Spitfire II P7539. Crashed and burned out at Half Moon Lane, Hildenborough north-west of Tonbridge 8.30 a.m. Cause unknown but possible anoxia victim. Pilot Officer J. R. Mather killed. Aircraft a write-off.

Major recovery by Malcolm Petitt, a local enthusiast, revealed most major components and form part of his small private collection.

74 SQUADRON, BIGGIN HILL

Spitfire II P7368. Forced-landed with damage sustained in combat with Bf 109s over Maidstone 9.00 a.m. Squadron Leader A. G. Malan unhurt. Aircraft damaged but repairable.

Spitfire II P7526. Shot down in combat with Bf 109s over Maidstone 9.00 a.m. Crashed and exploded at Dundas Farm, Elmsted. Sergeant J. A. Scott killed. Aircraft a write-off.

John Scott, a pre-war Volunteer Reserve sergeant pilot with No. 74 Squadron at Biggin Hill, now buried at Alperton.

Spitfire II P7353. Hit by debris from Bf 109 during combat over Maidstone 9.05 a.m. Returned to base. Flying Officer W. H. Nelson unhurt. Aircraft repairable.

92 SQUADRON, BIGGIN HILL

Spitfire R6721. Forced-landed near Effingham during routine patrol 2.45 p.m. Cause not stated. Sergeant D. E. Kingaby unhurt. Aircraft a write-off.

145 SQUADRON, TANGMERE

Hurricane V7422. Forced-landed Hollington, near St. Leonards 12.20 p.m. having run out of fuel following combat with Bf 109s. Flying Officer D. S. G. Honor unhurt. Aircraft a write-off.

Hurricane N2494. Believed forced-landed Holmer Green, near Amersham 12.30 p.m. out of fuel following combat with Bf 109s. Sergeant D. B. Sykes unhurt. Aircraft a write-off.

Pilot Officer John Romney Mather, a Londoner from Blackheath serving with No. 66 Squadron, took off from Gravesend on a dawn patrol on October 27. Not long afterwards, his Spitfire crashed at Hildenborough. He was taken to St. Margaret's Churchyard at Ifield where a rather weathered memorial stone on the cemetery wall now records his passing (A. Saunders).

Hurricane P3167. Shot down by Bf 109 five miles south east of the Isle of Wight 5.15 p.m. Pilot Officer A. R. I. Jottard missing. Aircraft lost.

Hurricane V6888. Damaged in combat with Bf 109s east of the Isle of Wight 5.15 p.m. Ditched off shore at Bembridge. Sergeant J. K. Haire waded ashore unhurt. Aircraft a write-off.

Hurricane V7592. Shot down in combat with Bf 109s 5.20 p.m. Crashed in the Solent. Pilot Officer F. Weber baled out and rescued from sea by MTB. Aircraft lost.

222 SQUADRON, HORNCHURCH

Spitfire X4548. Ran out of fuel during combat with Bf 109s and flew through HT cables attempting forced-landing at Pattendens Farm, Battle Road, Hailsham 6.00 p.m. Crashed heavily. Pilot Officer E. F. Edsall seriously injured admitted to Hellingly Hospital. Aircraft a write-off.

Some small items including tip of red-painted spinner complete with 'de Haviland' badge discovered at crash site by the Wealden Aviation Archaeological Group in 1978.

603 SQUADRON, HORNCHURCH

Spitfire II P7439. Shot down in surprise attack by Bf 109s south of Maidstone 2.05 p.m. Crashed near Waltham. Flying Officer C. W. Goldsmith died 28.10.40. Aircraft a write-off.

Spitfire II P7365. Shot down by Bf 109s of III/JG27 in surprise attack south of Maidstone 2.05 p.m. Flew into a tree at Apple Tree Corner, Chartham Hatch. Pilot Officer R. B. Dewey killed. Aircraft a write-off.

Spitfire II P7286. Severely damaged in surprise attack by Bf 109s of III/JG27 and believed forced-landed Bethel Row, Throwley 2.10 p.m. Pilot Officer D. A. Maxwell unhurt. Aircraft damaged but repairable.

605 SQUADRON, CROYDON

Hurricane V7599. Hit in both wings by 20mm cannon during combat with Bf 109s. Forced-landed at Sewells Farm, Barcombe 9.40 a.m. Flying Officer A. Ingle suffered slight cuts to face. Aircraft UP-U a write-off.

609 SQUADRON, WARMWELL

Spitfire P9503. Oil system severely damaged by return fire from enemy aircraft engaged over Andover 11.50 a.m. Abandoned near Upavon. Pilot Officer P. A. Baillon baled out unhurt. Aircraft a write-off.

Monday, October 28

64 SQUADRON, COLTISHALL

Spitfire N3293. Forced-landed near Horsford during routine section patrol 11.20 a.m. cause not stated. Pilot Officer H. R. G. Poulton unhurt. Aircraft damaged but repairable.

307 SQUADRON, KIRTON-IN-LINDSEY

Defiant N1560. Undershot runway on landing from night patrol and crashed into a hayrick. Sergeant S. Grondowski unhurt. Aircraft a write-off.

616 SQUADRON, KIRTON-IN-LINDSEY

Spitfire   . Overshot runway landing into wind and overturned 1.13 p.m. Accident considered due to extreme negligence. Pilot Officer 'Nip' Hepple unhurt. Aircraft repairable.

Pilot Officer Alexis Rene Isidore Ghislain Jottard, a 28-year-old Belgian, held a commission as a fighter pilot in the Royal Belgian Air Force before the war. After his country capitulated in May 1940, he escaped through France, Algeria, Morocco and Gibraltar, arriving at Liverpool on July 16, 1940. He was posted as a replacement pilot to No. 145 Squadron at Drem, Scotland one month later. On October 10, 1940 the squadron moved south to Tangmere and seventeen days later, while patrolling over the Isle of Wight, Alexis Jottard was shot down by Bf 109s at 25,000 feet, crashing into the Channel. He was given a symbolic grave in Brussels although this is misleading as it should be marked 'Disparu' as are the other memorial graves.

Apart from some men wounded, No. 603 Squadron had not lost any pilots since Henry Matthews had been killed on October 7. On October 27 their lucky spell was broken with the deaths of two pilots in a surprise attack over Kent. Both were buried in the station churchyard at Hornchurch. Robert Dewey was killed instantly but South African Claude Goldsmith died the following day from his injuries. The inscription on his headstone *(below)* from John 15:13 is repeated on many Battle of Britain graves.

Sergeant Herbert 'Bert' Black from Ibstock, Leicestershire joined the RAFVR in 1937. This photograph was taken in Charnwood Forest in Leicestershire on the afternoon of the day war was declared. Classed as fighter pilot material he, nevertheless, was posted to No. 226 Squadron on Fairey Battles. He participated as an experienced pilot in the early Battle reconnaissance flights along the Franco-German border and later in the hazardous attacks on the German army columns pushing into Belgium and France. On his return to the UK he underwent fighter training and early in September was posted to No. 32 Squadron at Acklington to fly Hurricanes. He was then sent to No. 257 Squadron at

Debden on the 20th of the month and transferred to No. 46 Squadron at Stapleford Tawney in October to enable two Polish pilots to stay together. October 30 was planned as a happy reunion for Bert and his wife Gwen in the nearby village of Abridge but instead she received a telephone call that he was in Ashford Hospital having been shot down the previous day. What should have been a joyous occasion turned into a nightmare for Gwen Black when she arrived at Ashford to find her husband grievously burned. For eleven days and nights she kept a vigil by his bedside until November 9, when relief came with death. Bert was taken home for burial at St. Denys, Ibstock.

Tuesday, October 29

1 SQUADRON, WITTERING

Hurricane V7302. Wrecked in landing accident 12.50 p.m. Details unknown. Pilot Officer E. Cizek believed unhurt. Aircraft damaged but repairable.

Hurricane P3318. Hit in glycol system by return fire from Do 17 engaged 5.30 p.m. Forced-landed at Orton near Peterborough. Sergeant W. T. Page unhurt. Aircraft a write-off.

19 SQUADRON, DUXFORD

Spitfire II P7423. Believed 'picked-off' by Bf 109 whilst acting as 'weaver' during squadron patrol over south London 5.15 p.m. Crashed and burned out at Oak Lodge, London Road, Chelmsford. Sub-Lieutenant A. G. Blake killed. Aircraft a write-off.

Spitfire II P7379. Forced-landed Rochford out of fuel 5.05 p.m. Sergeant A. N. McGregor unhurt. Aircraft believed undamaged.

29 SQUADRON, DIGBY

Blenheim L1503. Hit tree on take-off. Sergeant A. J. A. Roberts unhurt. Aircraft believed damaged but repairable.

46 SQUADRON, STAPLEFORD

Hurricane   . Shot down in combat with Bf 109s and believed crashed in Hothfield Park near Ashford. Sergeant H. E. Black badly wounded and burned (died 9.11.40). Aircraft a write-off.

74 SQUADRON, BIGGIN HILL

Spitfire II P7385. Forced-landed during routine patrol cause not stated. 11.25 a.m. Sergeant H. J. Soars unhurt. Aircraft a write-off.

Of the nine Fleet Air Arm pilots killed during the Battle of Britain, only one, Sub-Lieutenant Arthur Blake, is buried in the United Kingdom. He was seconded from HMS Daedalus and killed flying with No. 19 Squadron at Duxford and now lies in the overgrown churchyard of St. Mary's, Langley Marish, Buckinghamshire.

92 SQUADRON, BIGGIN HILL

Spitfire . Collided with Sergeant Kingaby in taxi-ing accident at base 7.36 a.m. Sergeant H. Bowen-Morris unhurt. Aircraft repairable.

Spitfire . Collided with Sergeant Bowen-Morris in taxi-ing accident at base 7.36 a.m. Sergeant D. E. Kingaby unhurt. Aircraft repairable.

145 SQUADRON, TANGMERE

Hurricane P2720. Returned to base with damage sustained following fast dive during combat with Bf 109s over Portsmouth 3.15 p.m. Flying Officer P. W. Dunning-White unhurt. Aircraft damaged but repairable.

213 SQUADRON, TANGMERE

Hurricane V7622. Abandoned during squadron patrol 2.45 p.m. cause unknown. Believed crashed near base. Pilot Officer R. R. Hutley baled out but killed. Aircraft AK-N a write-off.

222 SQUADRON, HORNCHURCH

Spitfire P9318. Damaged in glycol system during destruction of Bf 109 of 3/ErpGr. 210 over Pluckley 1.45 p.m. Forced-landed at dummy aerodrome at Lenham. Sergeant J. H. H. Burgess unhurt. Aircraft ZD-P damaged but repairable.

232 SQUADRON, DREM

Hurricane V6848. Damaged in belly-landing at base due to undercarriage failure. Sergeant E. A. Redfern unhurt. Aircraft damaged but repairable.

249 SQUADRON, NORTH WEALD

Hurricane V7627. Damaged in bombing attack by Bf 109s of II(S)/LG2 during take-off from base 4.45 p.m. Pilot Officer K. T. Lofts unhurt. Aircraft damaged but repairable.

257 SQUADRON, NORTH WEALD

Hurricane V6852. Caught taking-off during low level bombing attack on base by Bf 109s of II(S)/LG2 4.40 p.m. Crashed and burned out. Sergeant A. G. Girdwood killed. Aircraft a write-off.

Hurricane P3893. Shot down in combat with Bf 109s and crashed at Bobbingworth near Matching 4.50 p.m. Pilot Officer F. Surma baled out unhurt. Aircraft a write-off.

Hurricane V6795. Damaged in combat with Bf 109s over Essex following low level attack on base. Landed safely 5.00 p.m. Flying Officer H. P. Blatchford unhurt. Aircraft damaged but repairable.

302 SQUADRON, NORTHOLT

Hurricane V6923. Forced-landed at White Waltham 3.30 p.m. following mid-air collision with Flight Lieutenant Thomson during routine patrol. Flight Lieutenant H. Czerny unhurt. Aircraft damaged but repairable.

Hurricane P3085. Collided with Flight Lieutenant Czerny during routine patrol over Brooklands 3.30 p.m. Abandoned over Chobham. F/Lt Thomson baled out slightly injured. Aircraft a write-off.

308 SQUADRON, BAGINGTON

Hurricane L2092. Overshot runway and hit a boundary wall in landing at Wittering. Flight Lieutenant Jasionowski unhurt. Aircraft damaged but repairable.

310 SQUADRON, DUXFORD

Hurricane P3707. Collided with Pilot Officer Fechtner whilst formating during 'wing' patrol 3.10 p.m. Forced-landed near base. Pilot Officer J. M. Maly slightly injured. Aircraft damaged but repairable.

Hurricane P3889. Crashed near base following collision with Pilot Officer Maly during 'wing' patrol 3.10 p.m. Pilot Officer E. Fechtner killed. Aircraft a write-off.

501 SQUADRON, KENLEY

Hurrican P3714. Forced-landed due to engine failure 3.05 p.m. Sergeant Michail unhurt. Aircraft repairable.

Hurricane V7595. Crashed near Leatherhead during routine patrol 2.15 p.m. Cause not stated. Sergeant P. O'Bryne believed unhurt. Aircraft a write-off.

602 SQUADRON, WESTHAMPNETT

Spitfire X4603. Wing tip damaged in combat with Bf 109s over Maidstone 1.30 p.m. Returned to base. Pilot Officer H. G. Niven unhurt. Aircraft repairable.

615 SQUADRON, HEATHROW

Hurricane V7383. Wrecked amongst trees forced-landing at Teston near West Malling due to engine failure following glycol leak 12.40 p.m. Adjutant H. G. Lafont unhurt. Aircraft a write-off.

Emil Fechtner, DFC, of No. 310 'Czech' Squadron at Duxford lies in his national plot at Brookwood.

Hurricane V6785. Shot down in combat with enemy aircraft 12.45 p.m. Pilot Officer N. D. Edmond seriously wounded. Aircraft damaged but repairable.

Alexander Girdwood, serving with No. 257 Squadron and killed during an attack on North Weald, was buried in his father's grave in Hawkhead Cemetery, Paisley, Scotland.

Pilot Officer Edridge was one of two pilots from No. 222 Squadron killed on October 30. Hilary Edridge was buried in Bath where his headstone is a prominent landmark in the Roman Catholic Cemetery *(right)* difficult to find off Prior Park Road.

Wednesday, October 30

1 SQUADRON, WITTERING

Hurricane P5187. Crashed on landing following air drill 10.30 a.m. Sergeant J. Dygryn believed unhurt. Aircraft a write-off.

23 SQUADRON, FORD

Blenheim L6721. Crashed at Orchard Way Road, South Berstead 8.30 p.m. having suffered R/T failure in deteriorating weather conditions following routine night patrol. Flight Lieutenant H. J. Woodward, Pilot Officer A. A. Atkinson, Sergeant H. T. Perry killed. Aircraft a write-off.

41 SQUADRON, HORNCHURCH

Spitfire II P7282. Crashed at New Barn Farm, Postling during combat over Ashford 4.02 p.m. Pilot Officer G. G. F. Draper slightly injured admitted to Willesborough Hospital. Aircraft a write-off.

Spitfire II P7375. Shot down in combat with Bf 109s over Ashford 4.10 p.m. Believed crashed on Church Farm, Stanford. Sergeant L. A. Garvey killed. Aircraft a write-off.

66 SQUADRON, WEST MALLING

Spitfire II P7446. Nosed over on landing at base 5.40 p.m. Sergeant W. J. Corbin unhurt. Aircraft *GULBUNGA* damaged but repairable.

Killed in the same combat just after mid-day was Pilot Officer Alfred Davies who was buried by his family in St. Mary Magdalene at Tamworth, Warwickshire.

Len Garvey from Birmingham was a member of the Birchfield Harriers which he joined in 1931. He was very prominent throughout the Midlands at the half-mile and mile distances and was a member of the team which won the Midland Junior Championship in 1934. He also ran in the Manchester to Blackpool relay in 1935 but he restricted his athletic activities on joining the Volunteer Reserve. He was shot down while serving with No. 46 Squadron and was buried in Birmingham's Witton Cemetery.

213 SQUADRON, TANGMERE

Hurricane P3641. Forced-landed near Amberley cause not stated. Pilot believed unhurt. Aircraft damaged but repairable.

219 SQUADRON, REDHILL

Beaufighter R2065. Hit trees trying to locate base in bad visibility. Crashed and exploded 150yds. south of Balcombe Place 8.10 p.m. Pilot Officer K. W. Worsdell, Sergeant E. C. Gardiner killed. Aircraft a write-off.

222 SQUADRON, HORNCHURCH

Spitfire N3119. Wing shot off during combat with Bf 109s. Crashed and burned out on Upper Wilting Farm, Crowhurst 12.11 p.m. Pilot Officer A. E. Davies killed. Aircraft a write-off.

Site excavated by the Wealden Aviation Archaeological Group 1979. Some engine components, manufacturer's labels and cockpit relics recovered.

Spitfire P9434. Engine and airscrew damaged in combat with Bf 109s over Dover 12.15 p.m. Returned to base. Pilot Officer J. M. V. Carpenter unhurt. Aircraft damaged but repairable.

Spitfire K9939. Severely damaged in combat with Bf 109s. Crashed in flames attempting to land at Longwood Farm, Ewhurst 12.15 p.m. Pilot Officer H. P. M. Edridge rescued from wreckage but died of injuries. Aircraft a write-off.

249 SQUADRON, NORTH WEALD

Hurricane V6561. Hit in wing root and fuselage by 20mm cannon during combat with Bf 109 south of Hawkinge 12.30 p.m. Returned to base. Flying Officer A. R. F. Thompson unhurt. Aircraft damaged but repairable.

Hurricane V7536. Failed to return from sporadic action with enemy fighters over the Channel 1.00 p.m. Pilot Officer W. H. Millington missing. Aircraft lost.

Hurricane V6685. Forced-landed out of fuel at Stoney Field, Blackford Farm, near Herstmonceux 1.20 p.m. following combat with Bf 109s over the Channel. Sergeant M. K. Macejowski unhurt but mistaken for enemy airman by local police. Aircraft undamaged.

253 SQUADRON, KENLEY

Hurricane V7301. Crash-landed at Southfleet following combat with Bf 109s 4.00 p.m. Sergeant P. J. Moore slightly injured. Aircraft damaged but repairable.

602 SQUADRON, WESTHAMPNETT

Spitfire X4269. Forced-landed on Mullbank Farm, Newchurch near Dymchurch damaged in surprise attack by Bf 109s over Dungeness 4.15 p.m. Pilot Officer D. H. Gage unhurt. Aircraft damaged but repairable.

Spitfire X4542. Crash-landed on foreshore at Greetstone near Lydd following surprise attack by Bf 109s over Dungeness 4.20 p.m. Sergeant W. B. Smith wounded. Aircraft a write-off.

Spitfire P9515. Slightly damaged in wing tip during surprise attack by Bf 109s over Dungeness 4.15 p.m. Returned to base. Pilot Officer A. McL. Lyall unhurt. Aircraft repairable.

Thursday, October 31

43 SQUADRON, USWORTH

Hurricane P3357. Forced-landed at Chirnside, Berwick due to engine failure 10.30 a.m. Sergeant B. Malinowski unhurt. Aircraft damaged but repairable.

601 SQUADRON, EXETER

Hurricane V6781. Damaged in heavy landing following formation flight 9.45 a.m. Sergeant Fearn unhurt. Aircraft damaged but repairable.

The only Beaufighter fatalities throughout the battle occurred on October 30 to No. 219 Squadron based at Redhill. The pilot, Kenneth Worsdell, from Bracknell, Berkshire, a prize cadet at Cranwell, was buried at Nutford, Surrey *(left)*. His crewman, Eric Gardiner, was taken to his home town of Pontefract, Yorkshire for burial.

The last airmen to be killed during the Battle of Britain crashed on the evening of October 30. Three men died in Blenheim L6721 — John Woodward, Allan Atkinson and Tom Perry (the airman we were able to get 'promoted' nearly forty years after the battle). If ever a picture told a story it is this one taken in Heckmondwike Cemetery in Yorkshire. On October 30, 1917, the Woodward's lost the head of the family when John, aged twenty-five, was killed on Paschendaele Ridge. Florence his wife, left alone with baby Herbert just one year old, must have especially mourned his loss when the anniversary of his death arrived each year. The years went by and her son, having obtained a degree, decided to follow his father into the forces by joining the RAF. He was awarded the DFC and was serving with No. 23 Squadron as a Blenheim pilot during the Battle of Britain when promoted to Acting Flight Lieutenant. October came and, as the battle was drawing to a close, he lost his life over West Sussex. The date was October 30. How terrible the news must have been to his mother already dreading this day. For seven more years she saw the 30th come and go — the sadness must have been appalling — and in 1948, almost as if she could not face it again, she died just seventeen days before the fateful day. (His rank is now officially recorded as Flying Officer.)

The Luftwaffe

Composition of the Luftwaffe

The Luftwaffe losses catalogued on the following pages follow official German nomenclature as found in the contemporary source material consulted. Presented in familiar diary form, each day includes all losses suffered by various ancillary units followed by those of the front-line 'operational' formations, the latter being simply presented in unit alphabetical order. This procedure, adopted throughout the period covered, does not reflect the tactical deployment of the units concerned within the various Luftflotten. Necessarily somewhat arbitrary, it does facilitate easy reference but it should be stressed that no conclusions can be formed from these records as to the Luftwaffe command organisation which varied from time to time throughout the battle.

NORMAL GESCHWADER ESTABLISHMENT

Geschwader Stab Schwarm
(Group HQ Staff Flight)

Stab I Gruppe	Stab II Gruppe	Stab III Gruppe
(I Wing HQ Staff)	*(II Wing HQ Staff)*	*(III Wing HQ Staff)*
1 Staffel *(Squadron)*	4 Staffel *(Squadron)*	7 Staffel *(Squadron)*
2 Staffel *(Squadron)*	5 Staffel *(Squadron)*	8 Staffel *(Squadron)*
3 Staffel *(Squadron)*	6 Staffel *(Squadron)*	9 Staffel *(Squadron)*

Normal Geschwader comprised three Gruppen as above. Any additional Gruppen constituted as follows:-

Stab IV Gruppe	Stab V Gruppe
(IV Wing HQ Staff)	*(V Wing HQ Staff)*
10 Staffel *(Squadron)*	13 Staffel *(Squadron)*
11 Staffel *(Squadron)*	14 Staffel *(Squadron)*
12 Staffel *(Squadron)*	15 Staffel *(Squadron)*

Note: Gruppen always indicated by Roman numbers — Staffeln by Arabic.

Examples: Stab KG2 = HQ Staff of Bomber Group 2   I/ZG26 = I Wing, long-range Fighter Group 26
Stab II/JG27 = HQ Staff of II Wing, Fighter Group 27   5/StG77 = No. 5 Squadron of Dive-bombing Group 77

The following explanatory notes are intended as a simple aid to readers unfamiliar with the various forms and style of unit designations employed by the Lutfwaffe during 1940.

Aufklaerungsverbaende *(Reconnaissance units)*
Generally deployed in Gruppe strength and operating in either a Fernaufklaerungs (long-range reconnaissance) role or Nah-Heeres-Aufklaerungs (close Army co-operation).

Examples: 3/Aufklaerungs Gruppe Ob.d.L. = No. 3 Staffel of the Luftwaffe High Command reconnaissance Gruppe.
3(F)/123 = No. 3 (long-range) Staffel of reconnaissance Gruppe 123.
4(H)/31 = No. 4 Staffel of Army reconnaissance Gruppe 31.

Ausbildungs Staffeln *(Training squadrons)*
Attached to various Jagd Geschwadern and Kampf Geschwadern in order to maintain an adequate level of replacements for losses suffered by their respective 'parent' units. They undertook basic operational training.

Example: Ausbildungs Staffel KG40.

Ergaenzungs Staffeln *(Replacement training squadrons)*
Organised along similar lines as the Ausbildungs Staffeln and attached to both Jagd Geschwadern and Kampf Geschwadern, these units provided a nucleus of replacement crews fully operationally trained.

Example: Ergaenzungs Staffel JG54.

Erprobungs Gruppe 210 *(Experimental test wing 210)*
Theoretically engaged on the operational evaluation of the still-experimental Messerschmitt Me 210, this specialist unit was actually deployed operationally as a single Gruppe flying Messerschmitt Bf 109s and Bf 110s. The daring, often brilliant precision attacks flown by this unit reflected the expertise of its aircrews who suffered some heavy casualties.

Jagdverbaende *(Fighter units)*
Messerschmitt Bf 109 equipped, these formations were normally deployed in Geschwader strength but often operated as independent Jagdgruppen for tactical purposes. During 1940, the first Nachtjagdgeschwadern (NJGs) were established as a night-fighter force in defence of Reich territory and for night intruder sorties over Britain.

Examples: 2/JG26 = No. 2 Staffel of Jagdgeschwader 26.
1/NJG2 = No. 1 Staffel of Nachtjagdgeschwader 2.

Kampfverbaende *(Bomber units)*
Conventional long-range bomber units generally deployed as a Geschwader but often single independent Gruppen operated. Some constituent elements specialised in low-level raids whilst others concentrated on purely night attacks.

Examples: 9/KG76 = No. 9 Staffel of Kampfgeschwader 76.
2/KGr.100 = No. 2 Staffel of independent Kampfgruppe 100.
I/KG.z.b.V.172 = First Gruppe of Kampf Geschwader 172 on special assignment (zur besondern Verwendung).

Kuestenfliegerverbaende *(Maritime Luftwaffe units)*
Largely engaged on coastal reconnaissance and mine-laying duties and deployed in Gruppe strength. Operated under Luftwaffe command but in close co-operation with the German Navy who provided most of the crews. Some formations later absorbed into Luftwaffe command structure and operated as conventional bombing units.

Examples: 1/196 = No. 1 Staffel of Kuestenfliegergruppe 196.
3/506 = No. 3 Staffel of Kuesten-fliegergruppe 506.

Lehr Geschwadern *(Instructional/operational development groups)*
Operationally deployed during 1940, these formations were originally conceived as operational development units, separate Gruppen within each Geschwader often having different functions and equipment. Absorbed into the Luftwaffe command structure they largely flew conventional attack missions.

Examples: V(Z)/LG1 = Fifth (Zerstoerer) Gruppe of Lehr Geschwader 1 (Bf 110s).
II(S)/LG2 = Second (Schlacht i.e. ground attack) Gruppe of Lehr Geschwader 2 (Bf 109s).
7(F)/LG2 = No. 7 (Fernaufklaerungs) Staffel of Lehr Geschwader 2 (Bf 110s).

SeenotflugKommando *(Air-sea rescue unit)*
Engaged on search and rescue missions and subject to tactical deployment in small complements of generally less than Staffel strength.

Stuka Geschwadern *(Dive-bombing groups)*
From the German 'Sturzkampf-flugzeug' i.e. dive-bombing aircraft. A generic term but synonymous with the Junkers Ju 87 with which these units were principally equipped during 1940.

Example: 6/StG77 = No. 6 Staffel of Stukageschwader 77.

Wettererkundungs Staffeln *(Weather reconnaissance squadrons)*
Ostensibly engaged on long-range weather reconnaissance and information gathering flights over enemy territory these units were often attached to regular reconnaissance formations and employed on armed incursion raids.

Zerstoerer Geschwadern *(Long-range fighter groups)*
'Destroyer' units, principally Bf 110 equipped during 1940, and engaged on bomber escort duties or long-range free-lance fighter missions.

Example: II/ZG26 = Second Gruppe of Zerstoerergeschwader 26.

Wednesday, July 10

'Gutted Griffin'. Shot down by Hurricanes of No. 145 Squadron on July 11 during an attack on Portsmouth, the burnt out cockpit and the port Jumo 211F engine of a 'Greif' Geschwader He 111 lie on the shingle of East Beach, Selsey.

Aufklarungs Gruppe Ob.d.L

Dornier Do 215. Crashed and burned out near Le Havre cause not stated. Lt. Rack, Lt. Blindow and Sonderfuhrer Stift (Lw. Kriegsberichter Kp.4) killed. One NCO wounded. Aircraft a write-off.

2(F)/11

Dornier Do 17P. Crash-landed at Cherbourg during routine domestic flight, cause not stated. No casualties. Aircraft 30% damaged.

4(F)/121

Dornier Do 17P. Severely damaged in fighter attack and belly-landed near Boulogne. Oblt. Somborn killed, two NCOs missing and one wounded. Aircraft 60% damaged.

2(F)/122

Junkers Ju 52 (5162). Crash-landed at Muenster-Loddenheide during routine domestic flight cause not stated. No casualties. Aircraft 35% damaged.

2/JG3

Messerschmitt Bf 109E-1. Crashed into the sea off Dieppe due to engine failure. Uffz. Sachse injured rescued by Seenotdienst. Aircraft lost.

I/JG27

Messerschmitt Bf 109E-1. Take-off accident at Mathieu aerodrome. Pilot unhurt. Aircraft 25% damaged.

Messerschmitt Bf 109E-4. Damaged in take-off accident at Mathieu. Pilot uninjured. Aircraft 30% damaged.

5/JG51

Messerschmitt Bf 109E-3. Shot down in combat with British fighters over the Thames Estuary. Uffz. Stocker killed. Aircraft lost.

East Beach in November 1979 belies the serenity of this wintry sunlit scene. Conflict still exists in the area only now it is between weekend chalet owners and the local council which wants them removed.

7/JG51

Messerschmitt Bf 109E-4. Hit in engine and cooling system in head-on attack by Hurricane over Dover 2.00 p.m. Crashed in flames on beach in France. Oberfw. Dau unhurt. Aircraft 25% damaged.

Messerschmitt Bf 109E-4. Forced-landed near Calais damaged in action with Pilot Officer St. John of No. 74 Squadron over the Channel 2.00 p.m. Uffz. Kull unhurt. Aircraft 30% damaged.

11/JG77

Messerschmitt Bf 109E-4. Severely damaged in take-off accident at Vaernes. Pilot unhurt. Aircraft 70% damaged.

I/KG2

Dornier Do 17Z. Shot down by British fighters and AA fire over the Channel off Dungeness. One NCO killed, one wounded, remainder missing. Aircraft lost.

Dornier Do 17Z. Forced-landed near Marquise severely damaged by RAF fighters over Dover. One NCO killed, two wounded. Aircraft 70% damaged.

Dornier Do 17Z. Damaged in fighter attack over English south coast. Returned to base. One NCO killed, one wounded. Aircraft repairable.

Dornier Do 17Z. Returned to base damaged in fighter attack over Dover. Two NCOs wounded. Aircraft repairable.

3/KG2

Dornier Do 17Z. Lost a wing in collision with Flying Officer Higgs of No. 111 Squadron and crashed near Dungeness Buoy 2.00 p.m. Hptmn. Krieger (St. Kap) and Oberfw. Thalman captured. Fw. Umkelmann, Fw. Osinsky missing. Aircraft U5+ FL lost.

II/KG3

Dornier Do 17Z. Failed to return from operational sortie exact circumstances unknown. Oblt. Bott and one NCO killed. Lt. Schroeder and one NCO missing. Aircraft lost.

III/KG51

Junkers Ju 88A. Damaged in accident at Memmingen aerodrome, cause not stated. No casualties. Aircraft 30% damaged.

III/KG53

Heinkel He 111H-2. Engaged by Green Section No. 242 Squadron over the North Sea fifteen miles off Lowestoft 8.20 a.m. Shot down by Sub-Lieutenant Gardner. Two NCOs killed. Lt. Kupfer and one NCO missing. Aircraft lost.

3/ZG2

Messerschmitt Bf 110C. Crashed due to undercarriage failure during forced-landing near Eltsch in deteriorating weather conditions on routine domestic flight. Uffz. Brannath and one NCO killed. Aircraft a write-off.

8/ZG26

Messerschmitt Bf 110-2. Shot down by RAF fighters and AA fire over Folkestone. Oblt. Siegmund captured and one NCO missing. Aircraft lost.

Messerschmitt Bf 110C-2. Believed brought down by AA fire whilst under attack by RAF fighters over Folkestone. Oberfw. Meyer captured wounded and Gefr. Rohde missing. Aircraft 3U+ GS lost.

Messerschmitt Bf 110C-4. Shot down in combat with RAF fighters over Folkestone. Lt. Kuhrke killed, one NCO missing. Aircraft lost.

III/ZG26

Messerschmitt Bf 110C-2. Returned to base slightly damaged by RAF fighters over the Channel. Crew unhurt. Aircraft repairable.

Messerschmitt Bf 110C. Severely damaged in combat with enemy fighters over the Channel but returned to base. One NCO baled out and missing. Aircraft 50% damaged.

Thursday, July 11

Seenotflugkdo. 1

Heinkel He 59. Shot down into the Channel by No. 217 Squadron Anson and abandoned by crew. Four NCOs discovered in dinghy near the Channel Islands and captured. Aircraft lost.

Wettererkundungs Staffel 26

Dornier Do 17. Failed to return from operational weather reconnaissance sortie. Believed crashed in sea, cause unknown. Reg. Rat Belger and three NCOs all missing. Aircraft lost.

In the smoking obscenity of this crater lie the mangled remains of two German airmen, one of whom was the nephew of the Luftwaffe chief, Hermann Goering. Their Bf 110 was shot down during an attack on Portland harbour and crashed on the Verne, high above the breakwater (censored in this photo) where once 200 sail could lie safely at anchor (Central Press).

2(F)/11

Dornier Do 17P. Failed to return from operational sortie circumstances not known. Three NCOs missing. Aircraft lost.

5/JG3

Messerschmitt Bf 109E-3. Damaged in taxiing accident at Baromosnil. Pilot unhurt. Aircraft 20% damaged.

I/KG1

Heinkel He 111. Failed to return from operational sortie. Lt. Wagner. Hptmn. Beloreus and three NCOs killed. Aircraft lost.

Heinkel He 111. Crashed and burned out near Bapaume following operational sortie. Oblt. Grunwald and three NCOs killed. Aircraft a write-off.

Heinkel He 111. Crash-landed at Montdidier due to engine failure following operational sortie. Crew unhurt. Aircraft damaged but repairable.

II/KG2

Dornier Do 17Z. Severely damaged by RAF fighters in action off Harwich and returned to base. Lt. Bornheim and two NCOs wounded. Aircraft 50% damaged.

I/KG3

Dornier Do 17Z. Returned to base with damage sustained in combat with RAF fighters. Lt. Fischer wounded. Aircraft damaged but repairable.

II/KG3

Dornier Do 17Z. Belly-landed at Schweinfurt during routine domestic flight, cause not stated. No casualties. Aircraft repairable.

The Verne Citadel, once the barracks of the Portland defence garrison, became a prison after WWII. The site of the crash (about ten feet from the top of the pinnacle of rock) was excavated and levelled by the labours of convicts and is now a soccer field for the inmates of the nearby Borstal.

I/KG51

Junkers Ju 88A. Failed to return from operational sortie. Crew of four NCOs missing. Aircraft lost.

Believed to be the aircraft investigated by the Devon Aircraft Research and Recovery Team at a depth of 150ft under water off Start Point, west of Dartmouth since a complete undercarriage leg accidentally recovered by a local trawler was added to their collection

Junkers Ju 88A. Crashed and burned out near Varnevil following engine failure. One NCO killed and one wounded. Aircraft a write-off.

I/KG55

Heinkel He 111H. Forced-landed on return to base following attack on Portsmouth 6.15 p.m. Severely damaged in attack by Pilot Officer Storrar of No. 145 Squadron over Selsey. Two NCOs wounded. Aircraft 80% damaged.

2/KG55

Heinkel He 111H. Shot down just off shore at Selsey Beach 6.15 p.m. by Pilot Officer Wakeham and Pilot Officer Lord Shuttleworth of No. 145 Squadron during attack on Portsmouth dockyard. Oblt. Schweinhagen, Oberfw. Slotosch and Fw. Steiner all captured wounded. Uffz. Mueller and Oberfw. Schlueter killed. Aircraft G1+LK lost.

Heinkel He 111H. Shot down into the Channel off Selsey by Squadron Leader Dutton of No. 145 Squadron during attack on Portsmouth 6.15 p.m. Fw. Aleith, Fw. Ruschewitz, Uffz. Maiereder, Uffz. Reindel and Uffz. Klein missing. Aircraft G1+HK lost.

II/LG1

Junkers Ju 88A. Failed to return from operational sortie circumstances unknown. Oblt. Vitende and one NCO killed. Two NCOs missing. Aircraft lost.

11/LG1

Junkers Ju 87B. Shot down in combat with RAF fighters over Dover. One NCO killed, one missing. Aircraft lost.

Junkers Ju 87B. Damaged by RAF fighter attack over the Channel off Dover. Forced-landed at St. Inglevert. Crew unhurt. Aircraft 10% damaged.

II(S)/LG2

Buecker Bue-131. Forced-landed near Obisfelde in deteriorating weather conditions during routine domestic flight. No casualties. Aircraft damaged but repairable.

III/StG2

Junkers Ju 87B. Failed to return from operational sortie and believed crashed in the Channel. Two NCOs missing. Aircraft lost.

II/StG77

Junkers Ju 87B. Crashed on landing at Flers believed due to undercarriage failure following routine domestic flight. Crew unhurt. Aircraft a write-off.

9/ZG76

Messerschmitt Bf 110C. Shot down by Green Section of No. 238 Squadron and forced-landed at Grange Heath near Lulworth 12.10 p.m. Harried by Wing Commander Dewar of No. 87 Squadron and Flying Officer Riddle of No. 601 Squadron. Oblt. Kadow (St. Kap) wounded and Gefr. Scholz both captured. Aircraft 2N+EP lost.

Messerschmitt Bf 110C. Shot down in combat over Portland and crashed on the Verne 12.00 p.m. Oblt. Goering and Uffz. Zimmermann missing. Aircraft lost.

Messerschmitt Bf 110C. Shot down by RAF fighters and crashed into the Channel off the Ney Breakwater 12.05 p.m. Gefr. Sorokoput killed. Lt. Schroder captured unhurt. Aircraft lost.

Messerschmitt Bf 110C. Crashed into the sea off Portland 12.00 p.m. following combat with RAF fighters. Lt. Graf zu Castell killed, one NCO missing. Aircraft lost.

Friday, July 12

2(H)/21

Henschel Hs 126. Crashed and burned out on take-off from St. Sabine, cause not stated. Two NCOs wounded. Aircraft a write-off.

II/JG2

Messerschmitt Bf 109E-3. Crash-landed at Husum during operational sortie. Pilot unhurt. Aircraft 30% damaged.

II/KG2

Dornier Do 17Z. Shot down during attack on convoy off Orfordness 9.30 a.m. by Hurricanes of No. 151 Squadron and Flying Officer Count Czernin of No. 17 Squadron. Crashed into the North Sea. Hptmn. Metchetzki (St. Kap), Oblt. Rowe and two NCOs missing. Aircraft lost.

Dornier Do 17Z. Crashed into the North Sea near convoy off Orfordness 9.30 a.m. following attack by Flying Officer Count Czernin and Flying Officer Hanson of No. 17 Squadron. Two NCOs missing. Fw. Baumeister and Gefr. Mehringer rescued seriously wounded. Aircraft lost.

9/KG26

Heinkel He 111H-3. Shot down by Yellow Section No. 603 Squadron (Pilot Officer Gilroy, Pilot Officer Caister and Sgt. Arber) in engagement over Aberdeen 1.10 p.m. Crashed and burned out near Lt. Huck. Uffz. Plischke. Uffz. Skokan. Uffz. Kerkhoff killed. Aircraft 1H+FT a write-off.

I/KG51

Junkers Ju 88A. Crash-landed at Villaroche following operational sortie, cause not stated. Four NCOs killed. Aircraft a write-off.

II/KG53

Heinkel He 111H-2. Shot down by Pilot Officer Bickerdyke of No. 85 Squadron in action over convoy ten miles east of Aldeburgh 8.40 a.m. Crashed in North Sea. Three NCOs killed, two missing. Aircraft lost.

8/KG53

Heinkel He 111H-2. Crashed in sea near convoy ten miles north-north-west of Aldeburgh Light 9.40 a.m. following attacks by Flying Officer Manger and Sergeant Griffiths of No. 17 Squadron. Gefr. Tonn killed. Uffz. Zittwitz and Gefr. Wagner drowned, Fw. Hartmann captured wounded together with Fw. Bolte. Aircraft A1+ES lost.

Heinkel He 111H-2. Shot down by Pilot Officer Pittmann and Sergeant Fopp of No. 17 Squadron over convoy off Orfordness 9.00 a.m. Crashed in sea four miles east-north-east of Shipwash Light. Oblt. von Brocke, Uffz. Weber and two NCOs killed, one missing. Aircraft lost.

Stab KG55

Heinkel He 111P. Shot down by 'B' Flight, No. 43 Squadron in action over Southampton Water and crash-landed at Hipley 4.30 p.m. Oblt. Kleinhans killed, Fw. Kalina, Oberfw. Knecht and Oberfw. Muller wounded and Fw. Mohn captured unhurt. Aircraft G1+FA lost.

III/StG1

Junkers Ju 87B. Forced-landed near Theville due to ruptured oil feed pipe. Crew unhurt. Aircraft 60% damaged.

Stab StG3

Heinkel He 111H. Forced-landed at Cherbourg following attack by Red Section No. 609 Squadron (Flight Lieutenant Howell, Flying Officer Edge and Pilot Officer Curchin) over Portland Bill 10.04 a.m. Three NCOs wounded. Aircraft 50% damaged.

III/StG 77

Junkers Ju 87B. Forced-landed near Breux due to engine failure on routine domestic flight. Crew unhurt. Aircraft 35% damaged.

Saturday, July 13

4(F)/14

Dornier Do 17M. Forced-landed near Osen following fighter attack. Crew unhurt. Aircraft repairable.

2(F)/123

Dornier Do 17P. Shot down by Red Section No. 238 Squadron (Flight Lieutenant Kennedy, Flying Officer Davis and Sergeant Parkinson) whilst engaged on reconnaissance mission. Crashed in sea off Chesil Beach 3.00 p.m. Lt. Weinbauer and Uffz. Peland killed. Oblt. Graf von Kesselstadt captured wounded. Aircraft 4U+DK lost.

3/906

Heinkel He 115. Failed to return from operational sortie over the Thames Estuary. Lt. Dr. Steinert and Oblt. zur See Hildebrand killed, one NCO wounded. Aircraft lost.

Erprobungs Gruppe 210

Messerschmitt Bf 110. Crash-landed at St. Omer damaged in combat with RAF fighters. Crew unhurt. Aircraft 45% damaged.

9/JG51

Messerschmitt Bf 109E. Shot down in combat with Spitfires over the Channel south of Dover 5.30 p.m. Lt. Lange killed. Aircraft lost.

Zerstorer Staffel/KG30

Junkers Ju 88C-2. Belly-landed at Schiphol aerodrome on routine domestic flight, cause not stated. Crew unhurt. Aircraft a write-off.

II/KG51

Junkers Ju 88A. Failed to return from operational sortie exact circumstances unknown. Oblt. Kaspar and three NCOs missing. Aircraft lost.

III/KG51

Junkers Ju 88A-1. Damaged in combat with RAF fighters, landed at Rouen. Crew unhurt. Aircraft 20% damaged.

I/KG54

Junkers Ju 88A. Damaged in forced-landing outside Paris due to adverse weather conditions during routine domestic flight. Crew unhurt. Aircraft 25% damaged.

II/KG76

Junkers Ju 88A-1. Crash-landed at Creil during domestic flight, cause not stated. Crew unhurt. Aircraft 30% damaged.

10/LG1

Messerschmitt Bf 110C. Returned to base slightly damaged following combat over the Channel south of Portland 3.20 p.m. One NCO wounded. Aircraft repairable.

14/LG1

Messerschmitt Bf 110C. Shot down in combat with RAF fighters over Portland 3.00 p.m. Lt. Eiseler and one NCO killed. Aircraft lost.

15/LG1

Messerschmitt Bf 110C. Returned to base severely damaged in fighter attack south of Portland 3.15 p.m. Uffz. Donath wounded. Aircraft 50% damaged.

Messerschmitt Bf 110C. Severely damaged in combat with RAF fighters off Portland 3.00 p.m. Returned to France. Lt. Krebitz wounded. Aircraft 60% damaged.

With one crew member dead and three others wounded, this KG55 Heinkel made a remarkably good crash-landing at Hipley, Hampshire on July 12. In the background is the Horse and Jockey public house on the far side of the Hambleton-Fareham road.

Some days later, RAF Technical Intelligence Officers clamber aboard the same aircraft, now camouflaged from prying German eyes.

ll/StG1

Junkers Ju 87B. Crash-landed on the beach at Cap Gris-Nez damaged in attack by Sergeant Cowsill of No. 56 Squadron 4.15 p.m. Crew unhurt. Aircraft damaged but repairable.

Junkers Ju 87B. Damaged in attack by Pilot Officer Brooker of No. 56 Squadron during engagement over the Channel off Calais 4.20 p.m. Forced-landed at Noorfontes. Crew unhurt. Aircraft 30% damaged.

Sunday, July 14

3(F)/121

Junkers Ju 88A. Crashed at Paimpol cause unknown during operational sortie. One NCO killed, Oblt. Specht and two NCOs wounded. Aircraft a write-off.

lll/JG2

Messerschmitt Bf 109E-1. Crash-landed at Rhein-Main aerodrome on internal domestic flight, cause not stated. Pilot unhurt. Aircraft 30% damaged.

8/JG3

Messerschmitt Bf 109E-1. Crashed near Boulogne after engagement with No. 610 Squadron off Dover 3.20 p.m. Severely damaged by Pilot Officer Litchfield. Pilot baled out wounded. Aircraft a write-off.

Messerschmitt Bf 109E-1. Damaged in attack by Pilot Officer Litchfield of No. 610 Squadron during combat over the Channel off Dover 3.20 p.m. Returned to Wissant. Pilot unhurt. Aircraft 40% damaged.

11/LG1

Junkers Ju 87B. Shot down by Yellow Section No. 615 Squadron (Flying Officer Gayner, Flying Officer Collard and Pilot Officer Hugo) in combat over the Channel off Dover 3.50 p.m. Oblt. Sonnberg killed, one NCO missing. Aircraft lost.

l/StG77

Messerschmitt Bf 108. Forced-landed at Trier due to engine failure on routine domestic flight. Pilot unhurt. Aircraft repairable.

Monday, July 15

1(F)/121

Junkers Ju 88A-1. Crashed and burned out on take-off from Stavanger. Crew of four NCOs wounded. Aircraft a write-off.

Kuesten Flieger Gruppe 806

Junkers Ju 88A. Damaged in taxi-ing accident at Utersen aerodrome. No crew casualties. Aircraft 40% damaged.

4/JG2

Messerschmitt Bf 109E-3. Crash-landed at Husum following operational sortie, cause not stated. Pilot unhurt. Aircraft 20% damaged.

l/JG26

Messerschmitt Bf 109E-4. Crash-landed at Boenninghardt during routine internal flight. Cause not stated. Pilot unhurt. Aircraft 40% damaged.

Messerschmitt Bf 109E-1. Damaged in crash-landing at Boenninghardt on domestic flight. Reason unknown. Pilot unhurt. Aircraft 35% damaged.

2/KG26

Heinkel He 111H-3. Shot down into the sea fifteen miles east of Peterhead 12.12 p.m. by Yellow Section No. 603 Squadron (Pilot Officer Morton and Pilot Officer Stewart-Clarke). Fw. Reinhardt killed. Oblt. Hollmann, Uffz. Walz, Obgefr. Probst and Obgefr. Prefzger captured. Aircraft 1H+EK lost.

Schul Staffel KG53

Heinkel He 111H-2. Extensively damaged in crash-landing following engine failure on domestic flight. Crew unhurt. Aircraft a write-off.

lll/KG55

Heinkel He 111P. Forced-landed near Beauville during routine domestic flight. Cause not known. Crew unhurt. Aircraft 25% damaged.

ll/LG1

Junkers Ju 88A. Failed to return from operational sortie. Two NCOs killed and two missing. Aircraft lost.

7/ZG2

Messerschmitt Bf 110C-5. Crashed and burned out at Wunsdorf on routine flight. Cause unknown. Oblt. Tiefenbrunner killed. Aircraft a write-off.

Tuesday, July 16

5(F)/122

Dornier Do 17P. Crashed on landing at Haute Fontaine due to undercarriage failure. Crew unhurt. Aircraft 40% damaged.

2/406

Dornier Do 18. Shot down into the sea on operational sortie. Crew rescued unhurt. Aircraft lost.

3/JG21

Messserschmitt Bf 109E-1. Crashed Antwerp on routine training flight. Cause unknown. Pilot killed. Aircraft a write-off.

l/JG27

Messerschmitt Bf 109E-4. Slightly damaged in forced-landing near Arras due to deteriorating weather during routine domestic flight. Pilot unhurt. Aircraft damaged but repairable.

Stab KG2

Dornier Do 17Z. Damaged in combat with enemy aircraft and crash-landed at St. Inglevert. No crew casualties. Aircraft damaged but repairable.

ll/KG3

Dornier Do 17Z. Crash-landed at St. Niklaas on routine domestic flight. No casualties. Aircraft 15% damaged.

9/KG26

Heinkel He 111H-3. Shot down during attack on British naval vessels twenty-five miles north-east of Frazerburgh 4.12 p.m. Uffz. Liedtke, Gefr. Heimbach killed, Oblt. Lorenz, Uffz. Beer captured. Aircraft 1H+KT lost.

3/KG30

Junkers Ju 88. Crashed Oslo-Fornebu on routine flight. Cause not stated. One NCO wounded. Aircraft 60% damaged.

6/KG54

Junkers Ju 88A. Shot down by Blue Section No. 601 Squadron (Flying Officer Rhodes-Moorhouse, Flying Officer Hubbard and Pilot Officer Grier) in combat over the Channel off St. Catherines Point 4.00 p.m. Gefr. Marb, Obgefr. Vetter killed. Fw. Fortmann and Gefr. Herbert captured. Aircraft B3+GP lost.

Wednesday, July 17

3(F)/123

Junkers Ju 88A. Crashed on take-off from Buc, cause not stated. Three NCOs seriously injured, one NCO only slight injuries. Aircraft a write-off.

Stab KG27

Heinkel He 111P. Failed to return from operational sortie. Three NCOs killed, Oberst. Georgi (Geschwader Kommodore), Oblt. Buss and one NCO missing. Aircraft lost.

l/KG27

Heinkel He 111P. Crashed and burned out at Luere-Vogesen whilst on routine flight, cause unknown. Oberarzt Dr. Zobel and four NCOs killed. Aircraft a write-off.

ll/KG27

Heinkel He 111P. Forced-landed at Le Blanc on operational sortie, cause not stated. Crew unhurt. Aircraft 35% damaged.

l/KG51

Junkers Ju 88A. Shot down in combat over the Channel. Oblt. Rechenberg and two NCOs killed, one NCO missing. Aircraft lost.

Thursday, July 18

Stuka Schul Staffel VIII Fliegerkorps

Junkers Ju 87B. Severely damaged when unable to pull out from practice dive-bombing attack at Lippstadt. Crew unhurt. Aircraft 60% damaged.

2/606

Junkers Ju 52. Forced-landed at Gabin-kirchen following fire in rear gunner's compartment during routine domestic flight. Three NCOs killed, Lt. zur See Stock and Lt. zur See Krenzien wounded. Aircraft repairable.

Erprobungs Gruppe 210

Messerschmitt Bf 110. Crashed near Antwerp from vertical dive, cause unknown. One NCO killed. Aircraft a write-off.

ll/JG2

Messerschmitt Bf 109E-3. Failed to return from operational sortie. Lt. Fuedick wounded. Aircraft lost.

I/KG3

Heinkel He 111H-2. Forced-landed near Lens due to engine failure on domestic flight. No crew casualties. Aircraft 20% damaged.

Stab II/KG3

Dornier Do 17Z. Crashed and burned out at Schweinfurt due to undercarriage failure. Crew unhurt. Aircraft a write-off.

I/KG30

Junkers Ju 88. Crash-landed at Aalborg following operational sortie. One NCO wounded. Aircraft 50% damaged.

I/KG54

Junkers Ju 88A. Failed to return from operational sortie. Two NCOs killed, Lt. Frisks and one NCO missing. Aircraft lost.

II/KG54

Junkers Ju 88. Crash-landed on Coulommiers aerodrome following operational sortie. No crew casualties. Aircraft 35% damaged.

II/LG1

Junkers Ju 88A. Failed to return from operational sortie. One NCO killed, Oblt. Pohl and two NCOs missing. Aircraft lost.

Junkers Ju 88A. Returned to base damaged following combat with RAF fighters. One NCO killed. Aircraft repairable.

Stab StG77

Dornier Do 17M. Failed to return from operational sortie, circumstances unknown. Oblt. Strecker and one NCO killed, one NCO missing. Aircraft lost.

Friday, July 19

4(F)/121

Dornier Do 17P. Engaged by Yellow Section No. 145 Squadron (Squadron Leader Peel and Pilot Officers Wakeham and Yule) over Croydon and shot down into the sea off Brighton 7.00 a.m. Also attacked by Green Section No. 257 Squadron (Flying Officer Mitchell, Pilot Officer Bon-Seigneur and Sergeant Hulbert). One NCO killed, Lt. Thiele and one NCO missing. Aircraft lost.

3(F)/123

Farman. Crash-landed at Toussus-Buc during routine domestic flight, cause not stated. Hptmn. Liebe-Piederit killed, one NCO wounded. Aircraft a write-off.

III/JG27

Messerschmitt Bf 109E. Damaged by Flight Lieutenant Simpson of No. 43 Squadron in combat off Selsey Bill 5.10 p.m. Returned to base. Lt. Graf von Kageneck wounded. Aircraft repairable.

9/JG51

Messerschmitt Bf 109E-4. Severely damaged in combat with No. 141 Squadron Defiants over Folkestone 12.45 p.m. and crashed on landing back at base. Fw. Heilmann critically wounded (died next day). Aircraft a write-off.

Messerschmitt Bf 109E-1. Forced-landed in France severely damaged in combat with Pilot Officer O'Meara of No. 64 Squadron over Folkestone 4.00 p.m. Uffz. Miesala wounded. Aircraft 60% damaged.

Messerschmitt Bf 109E-1. Damaged by Flying Officer Woodward of No. 64 Squadron during action over Folkestone 4.05 p.m. Returned to base. Pilot unhurt. Aircraft 40% damaged.

2/KG26

Heinkel He 111. Hit by AA fire during operational sortie over the Scottish coast. Returned to base. One NCO hit by shrapnel. Aircraft repairable.

I/KG40

Focke-Wulf Fw 200. Shot down by AA fire during mine-laying sortie. Crashed into the sea between Hartlepool and Sunderland 11.55 p.m. Hptmn. Stesszyn, Fw. Meier and Gefr. Zaunig drowned. Fw. Kulken and Fw. Nicolai captured. Aircraft F8+EH lost.

II/KG51

Junkers Ju 88A. Crash-landed at Orly airport following internal flight, cause not stated. No crew casualties. Aircraft 40% damaged.

III/KG55

Heinkel He 111P. Engaged by Red Section of No. 1 Squadron in sporadic engagement over Sussex 6.00 p.m. Eventually shot down into the Channel five miles off Shoreham by Red Section No. 145 Squadron (Squadron Leader Dutton, Flying Officer Ostowicz and Pilot Officer Newling). Uffz. Biskup, Fw. Maeder and Oblt. Westhaus killed. Fw. Kasten and Gefr. Mensel missing. Aircraft lost.

Saturday, July 20

1(F)/120

Dornier Do 17P. Shot down into the North Sea thirty miles east of Aberdeen 12.05 p.m. by Blue Section No. 603 Squadron (Flight Lieutenant Cunningham, Flying Officer Waterston, Pilot Officer Stapleton). One NCO killed, Lt. Heuer and two NCOs missing. Aircraft A6+HH lost.

4(F)/122

Junkers Ju 88. Engaged by Blue Section No. 56 Squadron (Flight Lieutenants Weaver and Gracie and Pilot Officer Page) during photo-recce mission. Crashed and burned out on Cockett Wick Farm, St. Osyth 5.50 a.m. Flg. von Haase baled out wounded and captured. Uffz. Hermsen, Oberfw. Prolss and Obergefr. Plock baled out unhurt and captured. Aircraft F6+BM a write-off.

5(F)/122

Dornier Do 17P. Slightly damaged in crash-landing at Rouen due to engine failure. Crew unhurt. Aircraft repairable.

Seenotflug kdo. 1

Heinkel He 59. Abandoned by crew twenty-five miles south of Selsey during attempts by Flying Officer Hubbard and Pilot Officers Doulton and Grier of No. 601 Squadron to escort inland 7.20 p.m. Four NCOs baled out and missing. Aircraft lost.

Seenotflug kdo. 4

Heinkel He 59. Shot down three miles off Cherbourg 3.15 p.m. by Pilot Officer Urwin-Mann of No. 238 Squadron. Four NCOs missing. Aircraft lost.

Stab I/JG27

Messerschmitt Bf 109E-1. Shot down by Flying Officer Cox and Sergeant Lacey of No. 501 Squadron 4.15 p.m. during search mission for earlier losses. Crashed in the Channel thirty miles north of Sark. Major Riegel (Gruppe Kommandeur) missing. Aircraft lost.

3/JG27

Messerschmitt Bf 109E-3. Ditched in the sea fifteen miles off Swanage 1.10 p.m. following attack by Flight Lieutenant Turner of No. 238 Squadron. Lt. Scherer missing. Aircraft lost.

Messerschmitt Bf 109E-4. Shot down by Flight Lieutenant Walch and Flying Officer Davis of No. 238 Squadron in combat over the Channel fifteen miles off Swanage 1.10 p.m. Oberfw. Beushausen killed. Aircraft lost.

1/JG51

Messerschmitt Bf 109E. Crashed at Audinghem following combat with RAF fighters. Oberfw. Sicking baled out but killed. Aircraft a write-off.

II/JG51

Messerschmitt Bf 109E-3. Shot down by Flight Lieutenant Olive of No. 65 Squadron in combat over the Channel off the French coast 6.30 p.m. Pilot rescued by Seenotdienst. Aircraft lost.

III/KG2

Dornier Do 17. Forced-landed at Zuyenkerke following fighter attack and extensively damaged. One NCO killed, Oblt. Davids wounded. Aircraft a write-off.

III/KG4

Junkers Ju 88A-1. Forced-landed at Zwischenahn during routine domestic flight. Cause not notified. No casualties. Aircraft 20% damaged.

Stabstaffel KG27

Heinkel He 111P. Crashed at Compiegne due to engine failure during non-operational sortie. Three NCOs severely injured, Oblt. Pommerening slightly hurt. Aircraft a write-off.

II/StG1

Junkers Ju 87B-1. Damaged by fighter attack on operations over the Channel. One NCO wounded. Aircraft 30% damaged.

Junkers Ju 87B. Forced-landed at Norrent-Fontes due to damage suffered in fighter attack during operations over the Channel. Crew unhurt. Aircraft 30% damaged.

Junkers Ju 87B. Returned to France damaged by fighters over the Channel. Crew unhurt. Aircraft 30% damaged.

Junkers Ju 87B. Crash-landed at St. Hilaire with damage sustained in fighter attack over the Channel. Crew unhurt. Aircraft 30% damaged.

Stab StG2

Dornier Do 17M. Severely damaged by enemy action and crashed near Theville following engine failure. One NCO killed. Lt. Schenkel and one NCO wounded. Aircraft a write-off.

Top: Visitor from Brussels. Airmen sift through the fire-gutted wreck of a Ju 88 of 4(F)/122 on Cockett Wick Farm, St. Osyth. The early morning 'snooper' was despatched on July 20 by the Hurricanes of 'Mouse' Weaver, 'Jumbo' Gracie and Geoff Page of No. 56 Squadron's Blue Section. *Above:* After examination, guards were posted to prevent unofficial inspection by the local populace. *Below:* A corner of England which has changed little in thirty-nine years — Cockett Wick Farm on September 15, 1979.

Sunday, July 21

1/406

Dornier Do 18. Failed to return from operational sortie and believed brought down in North Sea (PQ2697). One NCO killed. Lt. zur See Neumerkel and two NCOs missing. Aircraft lost.

1/606

Dornier Do 17. Shot down by RAF fighters off the coast of Scotland. Crashed in sea. Lt. zur See Geschke and three NCOs missing. Aircraft lost.

2/606

Dornier Do 18. Crashed, circumstances not stated, during routine ferry flight to Caen. Lt. zur See Sot killed and three NCOs wounded. Aircraft a write-off.

4(F)/14

Dornier Do 17M. Shot down by 'A' Flight of No. 238 Squadron during reconnaissance mission. Crashed on Nutford Farm, Blandford 3.00 p.m. Oblt. Thiel, Fw. Bohnen and Uffz. Werner all wounded POWs. Aircraft 5F+ OM a write-off.

Messerschmitt Bf 110C(2177). Forced-landed on Goodwood Home Farm at 10.25 a.m. following attacks by Red Section of No. 238 Squadron (Flight Lieutenant Turner, Flying Officer Davis and Pilot Officer Wigglesworth) during photo-reconnaissance mission. Oblt. Runde and Fw. Baden captured. Aircraft 5F+ CM lost.

Above: Dornier Do 17 of the Muenchhausen Staffel, 4(F)/14, burns itself out in a Dorset clover field after having been fired by its wounded crew. Attacked by Hurricanes of No. 238 Squadron, the aircraft crash-landed near Nutford Farm, about one mile to the north of Blandford, on July 21. *Below:* Thirty-nine years later and the lush verdure of 1940 has given way to this bare field.

1/JG26

Messerschmitt Bf 109E-4. Forced-landed near Emmerich due to engine failure. Pilot unhurt. Aircraft a write-off.

9/JG26

Messerschmitt Bf 109E-1. Forced-landed near Le Havre having lost bearings and run short of fuel during routine domestic flight. Pilot unhurt. Aircraft 40% damaged.

Messerschmitt Bf 109E-1. Involved in same flight as above and forced-landed near Le Havre. Pilot unhurt. Aircraft 40% damaged.

Messerschmitt Bf 109E-4. Involved in same flight as above. Forced-landed near Le Havre. Pilot unhurt. Aircraft 40% damaged.

Messerschmitt Bf 109E-4. Forced to land near Le Havre on same flight as those above. Pilot unhurt. Aircraft 40% damaged.

7/JG27

Messerschmitt Bf 109E-4. Involved in mid-air collision with Pilot Officer De Mancha of No. 43 Squadron during combat over the Isle of Wight 3.15 p.m. Crashed in sea. Lt. Kroker killed. Aircraft lost.

Left: One of the Dornier's wounded crew members receives first-aid before his removal to hospital. Cyril Davis and his sister Marion, son and daughter of Mr. Robert Davis (who owned Nutfield Farm in 1940), were among the first on the scene, Marion toting a .410 shotgun 'just in case'. For many years, the blood-stained helmet of one of the crew was in Cyril Davis's possession. *Right:* We visited the scene on October 29, 1979 where Mrs. Marion Palmer (nee Davis) explained the events of 1940. Now no longer owned by the family, Nutfield Farm has seen considerable change, viz. the removal of the chalk bank in the background.

III/JG77

Messerschmitt Bf 109E. Failed to return from sortie over the North Sea (PQ9589) circumstances of loss unknown. Oblt. Weber missing. Aircraft lost.

III/KG3

Dornier Do 17Z. Crashed near Duerzburg due to mid-air collision during routine domestic flight. Three NCOs killed. Aircraft a write-off.

II/KG51

Junkers Ju 88A. Crash-landed at Orly aerodrome following domestic flight. Cause not stated. Crew unhurt. Aircraft 40% damaged.

Schulstaffel KG53

Heinkel He 111H-2. Severely damaged in forced-landing at Elbing due to engine failure during routine flight. Crew unhurt. Aircraft 55% damaged.

I/KG54

Junkers Ju 88A. Crashed and caught fire on landing at Coulommiers following operational sortie. Four NCOs killed. Aircraft a write-off.

14/LG1

Messerschmitt Bf 110C. Severely damaged by Pilot Officer Considine of No. 238 Squadron in combat off Portland 3.50 p.m. Crash-landed at Theville. Fw. Wurgatsch killed. Aircraft a write-off.

I/StG2

Junkers Ju 87B. Destroyed by fire at Conde-sur-Ifa aerodrome. Cause not stated. No casualties. Aircraft a write-off.

Monday, July 22

4(F)/121

Dornier Do 17P. Intercepted by Blue Section No. 145 Squadron (Flight Lieutenant Boyd, Flying Officer Dunning-White, Pilot Officer Weir) during reconnaissance mission. Shot down into the sea twenty miles south of Selsey 7.40 a.m. Lt. Reichhardt and Fw. Rowe killed, Lt. Bormann slightly wounded rescued from dinghy by British MTB. Aircraft 7A+ DM lost.

III/JG52

Messerschmitt Bf 109E-3. Undercarriage collapsed on take-off from Jever on routine domestic flight. Oblt. Blume wounded. Aircraft a write-off.

2/KG30

Junkers Ju 88. Flew into the ground near Narvik during operational sortie. Cause unknown. Crew of four NCOs killed. Aircraft a write-off.

III/KG30

Junkers Ju 88A-1. Crashed at Aalborg due to engine failure. Crew unhurt. Aircraft a write-off.

II/KG53

Heinkel He 111H-2. Damaged in forced-landing at Sarton due to petrol failure, crew unhurt. Aircraft 35% damaged.

Stab StG1

Dornier Do 17M. Engine caught fire whilst taxi-ing at Quilly-le-Tesson aerodrome prior to take-off on operational sortie. Crew unhurt. Aircraft 30% damaged.

Stab StG77

Junkers Ju 87B. Crash-landed at Caen during routine flight. Cause not stated. Crew unhurt. Aircraft 60% damaged.

Tuesday, July 23

3(F)/122

Heinkel He 111H-2. Crash-landed at Zorge-Harz due to engine failure during routine flight. Lt. Scharper and two NCOs injured, one NCO killed. Aircraft a write-off.

4(F)/122

Junkers Ju 88. Failed to return from reconnaissance sortie over Dover. Lt. Forster and one NCO missing, two NCOs killed. Aircraft lost.

Kuestenflieger Gruppe 806

Junkers Ju 88A-1. Crashed at Uetersen on domestic flight. Cause unknown. Three NCOs killed. Aircraft a write-off.

Transportstaffel I Fliegerkorps

Buecker Bue 131. Crashed at Compiegne during aerobatic practice. Exact cause unknown. Two NCOs killed. Aircraft a write-off.

III/JG26

Messerschmitt Bf 109E. Slightly damaged on hitting trees during local flight. Pilot unhurt. Aircraft 10% damaged.

II/KG2

Dornier Do 17Z. Severely damaged in fighter attack off the North Foreland. Returned to base one NCO wounded. Aircraft 50% damaged.

Dornier Do 17Z. Returned to base damaged following attack by fighters over the North Foreland. One NCO wounded. Aircraft repairable.

'So the struck eagle, stretch'd upon the plain, No more through rolling clouds to soar again.' — Lord Byron. No better epitaph could have been written for Leutnaut Schauff whose Bf 109 crashed in Byron Avenue, Margate on July 24. *Below:* Byron Avenue, Margate on August 21, 1979 with the trees matured and no trace of the blazered civilian. The houses between the trees are Nos. 70 - 78. Nothing remains to indicate the point of impact.

Stabstaffel KG3

Dornier Do 17Z. Returned to base with two NCOs of crew wounded following operational sortie over the North Sea to Lowestoft. Aircraft repairable.

2/KG3

Dornier Do 17Z. Crashed into the sea off the Sussex coast following attack by AI-equipped Blenheim of FIU (Flying Officer Ashfield, Pilot Officer Morris and Sergeant Leyland) Lt. Kahlfuss and three NCOs wounded and rescued from the sea. Aircraft lost.

Wednesday, July 24

1(F)/123

Junkers Ju 88A. Crashed near Brest on operational mission due to technical fault. Exact cause unknown. Oblt. Muhlbauer and three NCOs killed. Aircraft a write-off.

Aufklarungs Staffel Ober Ost

Arado Ar 66. Crashed at Radom cause unknown, on domestic flight. Pilot and Scharfuhrer of SS Regiment 8 both killed. Aircraft a write-off.

Above: **The grim reaper! Forced-landed by its severely wounded pilot, Oberleutnant Bartels, in a field of early wheat at Northdown beside the Margate to Broadstairs railway line, this Bf 109E-1 of Stab III/JG26 missed a line of high-tension cables by only a few yards.** *Below:* **Another year and another crop but the yield was poorer on August 21, 1979.**

Erprobungs Gruppe 210

Messerschmitt Bf 110. Exploded and crashed into the sea off Harwich during attack on shipping. Believed victim of AA fire. Uffz. Hermann and one NCO killed. Aircraft lost.

II/JG26

Messerschmitt Bf 109E-1. Severely wounded in combat over the French coast and crashed on approach to Marquise-Ost aerodrome. Hptmn. Noack (Gruppen Kommandeur) killed. Aircraft a write-off.

Stab III/JG26

Messerschmitt Bf 109E-1(6296F). Forced-landed at Northdown, Margate 1.00 p.m. following attack by Spitfire. Oblt. Bartels (Geschwader TO) severely wounded and taken prisoner. Aircraft lost.

8/JG26

Messerschmitt Bf 109E-4. Shot down in combat over Margate 1.05 p.m. and crashed in Byron Avenue. Lt. Schauff baled out but parachute failed. Aircraft a write-off.

Stab III/JG52

Messerschmitt Bf 109E. Believed shot down into the sea by Flight Lieutenant Ellis of No. 610 Squadron during combat off Margate 11.35 a.m. Hptmn. von Houwald (Gruppen Kommandeur) killed. Aircraft lost.

7/JG52

Messerschmitt Bf 109E. Failed to return to base following combat with fighters over Margate. Crashed in the sea. Oblt. Fermer killed. Aircraft lost.

Messerschmitt Bf 109E. Shot down in combat over Margate and believed crashed in the Channel. Gefr. Frank killed. Aircraft lost.

8/JG52

Messerschmitt Bf 109E. Shot down by Pilot Officer Gray of No. 54 Squadron in combat off Margate 12.35 p.m. and crashed in sea eight miles off-shore. Oblt. Ehrlich (Staffel Kapitan) baled out but missing. Aircraft lost.

3/KG26

Heinkel He 111H-3. Port engine disabled following attacks by Red Section No. 603 Squadron (Flying Officer Read and Pilot Officers Gilroy and Haigh) off Aberdeen 7.30 a.m. Returned to base on one engine. Three NCOs wounded. Aircraft 25% damaged.

6/KG26

Heinkel He 111H-3. Crash-landed near Moen due to engine failure during routine domestic flight. Two NCOs killed. Aircraft a write-off.

1/KG27

Heinkel He 111P. Crash-landed near Muenster following engine failure on local flight. Lt. Stadel killed, three NCOs wounded. Aircraft a write-off.

1/KG40

Focke-Wulf Fw 200. Forced to ditch in the sea fifteen miles north-east of Belfast due to petrol failure during armed reconnaissance mission. Hptmn. Zenker, Uffz. Oeker and Gefr. Hohmann rescued from sea and POWs. Fw. Andreas and Uffz. Wagner both drowned. Aircraft F8+ BH lost.

III/KG54

RAF bombing attack on Bergen aerodrome night of July 23/24. Four NCOs killed, four more wounded. No aircraft loss.

3/LG1

Junkers Ju 88A. Brought down by Red Section of No. 92 Squadron (Flight Lieutenants Kingcombe and Paterson and Pilot Officer Bryson) during bombing attack on shipping in the Bristol Channel. Crashed on Martinhoe Common, near Lynton 7.40 a.m. Hauptmann von Maltitz, Fw. Pliefke and Uffz. Wachholz POWs. Fw. Weilmaier also captured but wounded. Aircraft L1+ DL a write-off.

1/StG2

Junkers Ju 87B. Damaged in crash-landing at Theville aerodrome cause not stated. Non-operational sortie. Crew unhurt. Aircraft 20% damaged.

1/StG77

Junkers Ju 87B. Collided with landing beacon at Caen aerodrome following routine domestic flight. Crew unhurt. Aircraft 15% damaged.

Thursday, July 25

Seenotflugkdo. 5

Heinkel He 59. Crashed on take-off from Norderney. Cause not stated. Crew unhurt. Aircraft lost.

Wettererkundungs Staffel 1

Heinkel He 111H-3. Shot down by Flying Officer Jones and Pilot Officer Lonsdale of No. 3 Squadron during weather reconnaissance mission. Crashed into the sea off Pentland Firth 8.30 a.m. Uffz. Bauck, Gefr. Muller and two NCOs killed. Reg. Rat Franken rescued from dinghy twelve miles off Rora Head by RN destroyer. Aircraft T5+ AL lost.

Above: **Edelweiss in the Cotswolds. A Ju 88 of 5/KG51 lies broken on the side of a Gloucestershire hill near Stroud on the afternoon of July 25. En route to bomb Gloster's factory at Hucclecote, it collided with a Miles Master of No. 5 FTS. Three crew members of the bomber parachuted to safety — and a POW camp. The upper surface and tip of the port wing show the point of impact in the collision (Daily Mirror).** *Below:* **Two of Mrs. Short's horses from Lower Weir Farm, Oakridge Lynch, wearily tackle the long steep slope of the field where the Junkers ended its days.**

17/Kampf Gruppe z.b.V.5

Heinkel He 46. Flew into a beacon at Bochum/Krs. Peine during routine domestic flight. Lt. Siegl mortally wounded (died later). Aircraft a write-off.

9/JG26

Messerschmitt Bf 109E-1. Shot down in combat over the Channel. Fw. Eberz killed. Aircraft lost.

Stab III/JG27

Messerschmitt Bf 109E-4. Stalled and crashed into the sea ten miles south of St. Catherine's Point during attack on Pilot Officer Goodman of No. 1 Squadron 3.20 p.m. Oblt. Kirstein killed. Aircraft lost.

5/JG51

Messerschmitt Bf 109E-1. Forced landed at St. Inveser with damage sustained in combat over the Channel. Uffz. Obst wounded. Aircraft a write-off.

III/JG52

Messerschmitt Bf 109E. Shot down into the sea off Dover 6.40 p.m. during combat with No. 610 Squadron Spitfires. Lt. Schmidt missing. Aircraft lost.

7/JG52

Messerschmitt Bf 109E. Shot down in combat with Spitfires of No. 610 Squadron 6.45 p.m. Crashed into the Channel off Dover. Oblt. Keidel (Staffel Kapitan) missing. Aircraft lost.

Messerschmitt Bf 109E. Crashed into the sea off Dover 6.40 p.m. during combat with No. 610 Squadron Spitfires. Oblt. Bielefeld (Staffel fuhrer) killed. Aircraft lost.

8/JG52

Messerschmitt Bf 109E. Brought down at Elvington Court near Deal following combat with No. 610 Squadron Spitfires 6.40 p.m. Uffz. Reiss captured. Aircraft 6+ a write-off.

6/KG1

Heinkel He 111. Returned to base slightly damaged by AA fire. One NCO wounded. Aircraft repairable.

Stab KG3

Dornier Do 17Z-3. Crash-landed at Antwerp during operational sortie. Cause not stated. Crew unhurt. Aircraft a write-off.

4/KG3

Dornier Do 17Z-3. Abandoned by crew due to petrol failure during operational sortie. Crashed at Combloux. Oblt. Schrader injured. Aircraft a write-off.

5/KG51

Junkers Ju 88A. Briefed to attack Glosters at Hucclecote. Collided with a Miles Master flown by Sergeant G. H. Bell of No. 5 FTS on approach to South Cerney aerodrome. Crashed at Oakridge, Gloucester 2.25 p.m. Uffz. Heine killed. Uffz. Dorner baled out wounded and captured together with Uffz. Hugelschafer and Gefr. Treue. Aircraft 9K+GN a write-off.

A Dornier 17M from Stab StG 1, despatched by pilots from No. 152 Squadron, comes to grief on July 25. Previously published as being located at Portisham, thanks to Peter Foote the location of this crash has been pin-pointed at East Fleet Farm, Fleet, Dorset (Central Press). The tower on the skyline is not Hardy's monument as others would have us believe but the chimney of the now-defunct Chickerall brick works!

III/KG53

Heinkel He 111H-3. Damaged in belly-landing at Kotwijk aerodrome following engine failure. Crew unhurt. Aircraft 40% damaged.

8/KG76

Dornier Do 17Z. Crashed on take-off from Cormeilles. Cause not stated. Crew unhurt. Aircraft 30% damaged.

II (Stuka)/LG1

Junkers Ju 87B. Returned to base damaged following interception by fighters over the Channel off Folkestone. One NCO wounded. Aircraft 15% damaged.

3/NJG1

Messerschmitt Bf 110. Crashed at Coesfeld during destruction of No. 3 Group Wellington. Exact circumstances not clear. Lt. Pack and one NCO killed. Aircraft a write-off.

Messerschmitt Bf 110C-4. Crash-landed near Guetersloh following collision with English parachute flare. One NCO wounded. Aircraft a write-off.

Stab StG 1

Dornier Do 17M. Shot down by Pilot Officer Holmes and Sergeant Wolton of No. 152 Squadron during photo-reconnaissance mission. Crashed and burned out at East Fleet Farm, Fleet, Dorset 12.00 p.m. Uffz. Lengenbrink killed, Fw. Grossmann wounded and captured with Fw. Erdmann. Aircraft A5+ EA a write-off.

II/StG1

Junkers Ju 87B. Shot down by fighters in combat over the Channel. Two NCOs killed. Aircraft lost.

Junkers Ju 87B. Shot down into the sea during combat with fighters over mid-Channel. Lt. Roden and one NCO killed. Aircraft lost.

III/StG1

Junkers Ju 87B. Shot down by fighters in combat over the Channel off Cherbourg. One NCO killed and one wounded. Aircraft a write-off.

Junkers Ju 87B. Returned to base with damage sustained in combat with fighters over the Channel. Crew unhurt. Aircraft 30% damaged.

Junkers Ju 87B. Slightly damaged in combat with enemy aircraft over mid-Channel. Returned safely to base. One NCO wounded. Aircraft repairable.

Friday, July 26

Aufklarungs Gruppe (H)/21

Henschel Hs 126. Damaged in taxi-ing accident at Lessey aerodrome. Crew unhurt. Aircraft repairable.

1/406

Dornier Do 18. Slightly damaged in engagement with RAF Sunderland. Returned safely to base. One NCO wounded. Aircraft repairable.

2/406

Dornier Do 18. Collided with another Do 18 during night take-off from Stavanger. Crew unhurt. Aircraft a write-off.

Dornier Do 18. Subject of collision mentioned above. One NCO injured. Aircraft a write-off.

I/JG27

Messerschmitt Bf 109E. Crash-landed at Plumetot aerodrome following routine local flight. Cause not stated. Pilot unhurt. Aircraft 50% damaged.

2/JG27

Messerschmitt Bf 109E-3. Shot down by Flight Lieutenant Walch of No. 238 Squadron in action twenty-five miles south of Portland 12.00 p.m. Crashed in the Channel. Fw. Boer missing. Aircraft lost.

1/KG4

Heinkel He 111H-4. Engaged in mine-laying sortie over the Bristol Channel and believed that engaged by Pilot Officer Cock of No. 87 Squadron over East Portishead Point. Crashed at Longfield Farm, Smeatharpe, near Honiton 0.55 a.m. following explosion in the aircraft. Oberfw. Kessler, Uffz. Fommer, Uffz. Hahnel and Gefr. Grabke killed. Uffz. Strickstrock baled out wounded POW. Aircraft a write-off.

I/KG55

Heinkel He 111P. Damaged in accident at Grandpre, cause not stated. No casualties. Aircraft 15% damaged.

3/KG76

Dornier Do 17Z. Failed to return from night attack on Rochford aerodrome. Believed crashed in sea circumstances unknown. Uffz. Hartz, Uffz. Bungardt, Oberfw. Ballowitz, and Fw. Kopisch all missing. Aircraft lost.

7/KG77

Junkers Ju 88 (3131). Crash-landed at Regensburg during domestic flight. Cause not stated. Crew unhurt. Aircraft 3Z+ AR 12% damaged.

Saturday, July 27

3(F)/121

Junkers Ju 88A. Damaged in fighter attack and belly-landed back at Chateaudun aerodrome. One NCO killed. Aircraft 10% damaged.

5(F)/122

Dornier Do 17P. Attacked by fighters over Haute Fontaine. Returned to base with slight damage. Crew unhurt. Aircraft repairable.

KG53

Heinkel He 111H-2. Suffered engine failure on routine domestic flight and forced-landed at Giebelstadt. Crew unhurt. Aircraft 15% damaged.

II/KG53

Heinkel He 111H-2. Failed to return from operational sortie. Exact fate unknown. One NCO killed and four missing. Aircraft lost.

II/KG54

Junkers Ju 88A. Forced-landed at St. Andre during non-operational sortie. Cause not stated. Crew unhurt. Aircraft 15% damaged.

III/KG55

Heinkel He 111P. Engine caught fire during operational sortie over Britain. Aircraft abandoned by crew crashed near Newbury 2 a.m. Fw. Metzner, Fw. Mankl, Uffz. Backer, Gefr. Morgenthal and Gefr. Ostheimer all captured. Aircraft G1+CS a write-off.

III/KG77

Junkers Ju 88A. Forced-landed at Regensburg on routine domestic flight. Cause not stated. Crew unhurt. Aircraft 20% damaged.

V/LG1

Messerschmitt Bf 110C. Accidentally hit the ground at Theville during local flying. Crew unhurt. Aircraft 10% damaged.

Erprobungs Gruppe 210

Messerschmitt Bf 110. Shot down from 2,000ft by AA fire during anti-shipping strike. Crashed into the sea off Harwich at over 400 mph. Oblt. Fallenbacher and one NCO killed. Aircraft lost.

I/StG 77

Junkers Ju 87B. Failed to return from operations over the Channel. Crashed in sea. One NCO killed and one missing. Aircraft lost.

5/NJG1

Dornier Do 17Z. Crashed near Krefeld cause unknown during routine local flight. Two NCOs killed. Aircraft a write-off.

Sunday, July 28

Seenotflugkdo. 1

Heinkel He 59. Landed on water to assist crippled He 59 (D-ASUC) of Seenotflugkdo 3 and severely damaged in attack by Flying Officer Ferriss of No. 111 Squadron 3.15 p.m. Lt. Wolke and one NCO wounded. Aircraft 60% damaged.

Seenotflugkdo. 3

Heinkel He 59. Shot down by RAF fighter during rescue mission. Landed on water ten miles west of Boulogne. Two NCOs killed. Lt. Sandgaard and two NCOs wounded. Aircraft D-ASUC a write-off.

Heinkel He 59. Shot down over the Channel by Sergeant Robinson of No. 111 Squadron 3.20 p.m. whilst engaged on search and rescue mission. Oblt. Chudziak and three NCOs missing. One wounded NCO rescued. Aircraft D-AROO lost.

Stab JG51

Messerschmitt Bf 109E-3. Severely damaged by Flight Lieutenant Webster of No. 41 Squadron in combat over the Channel off Dover 3.00 p.m. Belly-landed near the French coast. Major Molders (Geschwader Kommodore) wounded. Aircraft a write-off.

1/JG51

Messerschmitt Bf 109E-1. Believed badly damaged by Flight Lieutenant Webster of No. 41 Squadron in combat over Dover 2.50 p.m. Landed at Wissant. Pilot unhurt. Aircraft 20% damaged.

July 26 and RAF officers examine the remains of a Heinkel 111H of KG4, the 'General Wever' Geschwader, at Longfield Farm in Devon. The only crewman to survive landed at Middle Luxton Farm, half-a-mile away, where he was captured by Mr. B. J. Parsons. The site of the crash is now a corner of disused Smeatharpe aerodrome (constructed after the crash) from which the 439th Troop Carrier Group, Ninth USAAF, flew their paratroop-laden C47s to the drop zones of Normandy on June 6, 1944.

2/JG51

Messerschmitt Bf 109E-1. Believed shot down by Pilot Officer Bennions of No. 41 Squadron in combat off Dover 3.00 p.m. Crashed in sea. Gefr. Gebhardt missing. Aircraft lost.

III/JG53

Messerschmitt Bf 109E-1. Forced-landed at Lannion aerodrome due to engine failure during operational sortie. Oblt. Below wounded. Aircraft a write-off.

II/KG2

Dornier Do 17Z. Crashed at Bayreuth due to flying accident on routine local flight. One NCO killed, one Prufmeister wounded. Aircraft a write-off.

9/KG4

Junkers Ju 88A-1. Crashed at Theville during operational mission. Cause not stated. Four NCOs wounded (one died of injuries). Aircraft a write-off.

Junkers Ju 88A-1. Crashed on landing at Schiphol following operations. Cause not stated. Oblt. Podbielski and three NCOs injured. Aircraft a write-off.

Stab KG30

Junkers Ju 88. Flew into an excavator at Aalborg aerodrome during routine local flight. Exact circumstances not stated. Five NCOs slightly injured. Aircraft damaged extent not stated.

I/KG51

Junkers Ju 88A-1. Belly-landed at Laroche aerodrome following engine failure during operational sortie. Crew unhurt. Aircraft 40% damaged.

3/KG51

Junkers Ju 88A-1 (7036). Lost bearings and ran out of fuel during mission to bomb Crewe. Forced-landed at Buckholt Farm, Bexhill 5.00 a.m. Lt. Ruckdeschel, Oberfw. Bier, Uffz. Ohls and Uffz. Multhammer captured. Aircraft 9K + HL lost.

II/LG1

Junkers Ju 88A. Shot down into the sea off Plymouth 5.25 a.m. by Blue Section No. 234 Squadron (Flight Lieutenant Hughes and Pilot Officers Dewhurst and Horton). Lt. Pfanf and two NCOs missing, one NCO rescued from sea wounded. Aircraft lost.

3/NJG1

Messerschmitt Bf 110C. Hit by return fire from RAF bomber engaged during night sortie. Crashed at Ennigerloh. Crew of two NCOs killed. Aircraft a write-off.

Monday, July 29

I/JG27

Messerschmitt Bf 109E-1. Crashed on landing at Plumetot aerodrome due to undercarriage failure following routine domestic flight. Pilot unhurt. Aircraft 30% damaged.

II/JG27

Messerschmitt Bf 109E-3. Crash-landed on French coast following combat with RAF fighters. Oblt. Preiser (Gruppe TO) wounded. Aircraft 60% damaged.

I/JG51

Messerschmitt Bf 109E-4. Crashed and burned out at Wissant following combat with fighters over the Channel. Hptmn. Michele killed. Aircraft a write-off.

4/JG51

Messerschmitt Bf 109E-3. Forced-landed near Le Wast on dead engine following combat with fighters over the Channel. Pilot unhurt. Aircraft 50% damaged.

6/JG51

Messerschmitt Bf 109E-1. Crash-landed outside Calais following fighter action over the Channel. Fw. Hemmerling killed. Aircraft a write-off.

Stab KG2

Dornier Do 17Z. Landed back at St. Inglevert severely damaged in attacks from 'A' Flight No. 610 Squadron over the Channel off Dungeness 1.00 p.m. Lt. Hunger wounded. Aircraft 60% damaged.

III/KG4

Junkers Ju 88A-1. Belly-landed at Schiphol aerodrome following engine failure on domestic flight. Crew unhurt. Aircraft 50% damaged.

I/KG27

Heinkel He 111H. Ditched in the sea off Guernsey due to engine failure during operational sortie. Crew rescued from dinghy unhurt. Aircraft lost.

III/KG51

Junkers Ju 88A-1. Crashed at Nogent-le-Rothrou on operational mission. Cause unknown. Four NCOs killed. Aircraft a write-off.

I/KG53

Heinkel He 111H-2. Shot down into the North Sea off Lowestoft 2.45 p.m. by Blue Section No. 66 Squadron (Pilot Officers Oxspring, Pickering and Studd). Lt. Kliffken and two NCOs killed, two NCOs missing. Aircraft lost.

Heinkel He 111H-2. Shot down fourteen miles east of Hammonds Knoll by Spitfires of No. 66 Squadron and Hurricanes of No. 17 Squadron following interception 3.00 p.m. Crashed in North Sea. Lt. Schattka and four NCOs killed. Aircraft lost.

4/KG76

Junkers Ju 88A-1. Shot down into the Channel twenty miles south of Worthing 2.00 p.m. by No. 145 Squadron Hurricanes. Major Donaubauer and Uffz. Peters killed, Lt. Nier and Uffz. Cordes missing. Aircraft lost.

III/KG76

Dornier Do 17. Returned to base damaged following attack by Flying Officer Woods-Scawen of No. 85 Squadron over the Channel off Dover 3.05 p.m. Oberstlt. Genth (Gruppe Kommandeur) killed. Aircraft damaged extent not stated.

II/LG1

Junkers Ju 87B. Shot down by fighters in action over the Channel off Dover. Oblt. Kothe killed and one NCO missing. Aircraft lost.

Junkers Ju 87B. Shot down into the sea off Dover during combat with fighters. Lt. Furnwagner and one NCO missing. Aircraft lost.

II/StG1

Junkers Ju 87B. Returned to base damaged following engagement with fighters over the Channel. One NCO wounded. Aircraft 30% damaged.

Junkers Ju 87B. Crashed in the sea during combat with fighters. Crew rescued by Seenotdienst unhurt. Aircraft lost.

Junkers Ju 87B. Crash-landed at St. Inglevert with damage sustained in combat with fighters. One NCO wounded. Aircraft a write-off.

1/Erprobungs Gruppe 210

Messerschmitt Bf 110C-6. Returned to St. Omer damaged following attack by Flying Officer Blair of No. 151 Squadron over convoy off Orfordness 5.15 p.m. Lt. Beudel unhurt, gunner wounded. Aircraft S9+TH damaged extent not stated.

Tuesday, July 30

5/196

Arado Ar 196. Forced to ditch in Drontheim Fjord following engine failure on operational sortie. Lt. Muller killed, Lt. zur See Behrmann and one NCO missing. Aircraft lost.

2(F)/122

Junkers Ju 88. Ditched thirty miles off Happisburgh 9.00 a.m. due to engine failure during shipping reconnaissance of English east coast. Lt. Rabbow, Uffz. Kehres unhurt and took to dinghy with Uffz. Lemm and Gefr. Riemer both injured. Rescued by fishing vessel and landed at Gt. Yarmouth 3.8.1940. Aircraft F6+BK lost.

1/Erprobungs Gruppe 210

Messerschmitt Bf 110C. Shot down by Flight Lieutenant Hamilton and Sergeant Allard of No. 85 Squadron nineteen miles east of Harwich during attack on convoy 4.00 p.m. Lt. Herold and one NCO killed. Aircraft lost.

7/JG27

Messerschmitt Bf 109E-1. Crashed on landing at Caroubert aerodrome following operational sortie. Pilot unhurt. Aircraft 65% damaged.

6/KG4

Heinkel He 111P. Hit ground at Mark-Friedland during routine domestic flight. Exact cause unknown. Crew unhurt. Aircraft a write-off.

Heinkel He 111P. Crashed on take-off from Mark-Friedland on domestic flight. Lt. Ziegler slightly injured. Aircraft a write-off.

7/KG4

Junkers Ju 88A-1 (4102). Crashed and exploded outside Bury St. Edmunds 00.15 a.m. following mid-air fire. Cause unknown. Four NCOs killed. Aircraft 5J+ER a write-off.

8/KG26

Heinkel He 111H-4. Shot down twelve miles west of Aberdeen 12.05 p.m. by Sergeant Caister of No. 603 Squadron during interdiction sortie over the east coast. Four NCOs missing. Aircraft lost.

II/KG27

Heinkel He 111P. Failed to return from operations over the English mainland. Circumstances of loss unknown. Lt. Wiedenhoft and three NCOs missing. Aircraft lost.

II/KG51

Junkers Ju 88A-1. Forced-landed Fontainebleu following engine failure on routine domestic flight. Crew unhurt. Aircraft 30% damaged.

2/KG76

Dornier Do 17Z. Destroyed in accident at La Boessie aerodrome when bomb exploded prematurely. Four NCOs killed. Aircraft a write-off.

6/KG76

Junkers Ju 88A-1. Damaged in attacks by RAF fighters and returned to belly-land at Creil aerodrome. Crew unhurt. Aircraft 30% damaged.

Wednesday, July 31

Aufklarungs Gruppe Ob.d.L.

Dornier Do 215. Collided with a parked aircraft during take-off from Neufchateau aerodrome. Crew of four NCOs injured. Aircraft a write-off.

FH 104. Subject of collision mentioned above. No casualties. Aircraft a write-off.

JG2

Messerschmitt Bf 109. Crash-landed at Fecamp due to engine failure during operational sortie. Pilot injured. Aircraft a write-off.

9/KG4

Heinkel He 111P. Crashed at Pinnow during routine domestic flight. Exact cause unknown. Crew of four NCOs killed. Aircraft a write-off.

2/KG30

Junkers Ju 88A-1. Destroyed in attack on Aalborg aerodrome by RAF aircraft. Two NCOs killed and one wounded. Aircraft a write-off.

III/KG51

Junkers Ju 88A-1. Forced-landed at Orly airport in bad weather. Non-operational sortie. Crew unhurt. Aircraft 40% damaged.

1/KG55

Heinkel He 111. Shot down in combat with fighters. Crew baled out over Tours unhurt. Aircraft a write-off.

Heinkel He 111. Shot down in combat with fighters. Crew baled out unhurt. Aircraft a write-off.

II/ZG76

Messerschmitt Bf 110C. Crashed on take-off from Le Mans due to engine failure. Non-operational sortie. Crew unhurt. Aircraft 50% damaged.

Thursday, August 1

3/106

Heinkel He 115C. Crashed on landing at Schellingwoude following operational sortie. Cause not stated. Crew unhurt. Aircraft a write-off.

Heinkel He 115C. Landing accident at Schellingwoude after operational sortie. Cause not stated. Crew unhurt. Aircraft a write-off.

3/506

Heinkel He 115. Failed to return from operations. Crashed in sea circumstances unknown. Lt. zur See Richter and one NCO killed, one NCO missing. Aircraft lost.

Seenotzentrale Cherbourg

Heinkel He 59. Lost on mission over the English Channel circumstances unknown. No crew casualties recorded. Aircraft lost.

1/196

Arado Ar 196. Crashed on landing at Schellingwoude cause not stated. No crew casualties. Aircraft a write-off.

4 (H)/31

Henschel Hs 126. Failed to return from operational sortie. Exact cause of loss unknown. Two NCOs missing. Aircraft lost.

II/JG27

Messerschmitt Bf 109E-1. Bf 109E-3. Bf 109E-4. Aircraft damaged in RAF attack on Leeuwarden aerodrome. No aircrew casualties. Aircraft 50%, 10% and 40% damaged respectively.

3/KG4

Heinkel He 111H-4. Belly-landed at Soesterberg during operational mission. Cause not stated. No crew casualties. Aircraft 30% damaged.

9/KG4

Junkers Ju 88A-1. Shot down by RAF fighters during sortie over the English east coast. Crashed in North Sea. Oblt. Geisler. Oblt. Wagner and two NCOs missing. Aircraft lost.

Elham in the middle of the North Downs in Kent was in the centre of the battleground. *Above:* Here a Bf 109 has been hit by anti-aircraft fire directly over the village (Brenzett). *Below:* During the battle, a common sight in south-eastern England was the growing dumps of crashed aircraft. One was located in Elham itself beside the old main road now renamed 'The Row' (IWM).

The site of the dump was the back garden of Autumn Cottage.

KG30

Junkers Ju 88. Suffered engine failure on take-off and crash-landed near Stavanger-Sola aerodrome. Crew unhurt. Aircraft 40% damaged.

Junkers Ju 88. Overshot runway on landing at Stavanger-Sola following routine operational mission. Crew unhurt. Aircraft a write-off.

I/KG30

Junkers Ju 88A-1. Failed to return from operational sortie to Carlisle. Crashed in North Sea. Four NCOs missing. Aircraft lost.

3/KG30

Junkers Ju 88A-1. Crashed on landing at night on Aalborg aerodrome following routine domestic flight. Crew unhurt. Aircraft a write-off.

8/KG53

Heinkel He 111. Crashed near Giebelstadt on local flight. Flying accident, cause unknown. Lt. Altaker and Lt. Sedduig killed. Aircraft a write-off.

Stab II/KG76

Junkers Ju 88A-1. Returned to base with damage following attack by RAF fighters over the Channel. Fw. Kohl severely wounded died in hospital (17.8.40). Aircraft 15% damaged.

I/KG77

Junkers Ju 88. Crashed near Rothenburg during routine domestic flight. Cause unknown. Oblt. Roder and two NCOs killed. One NCO injured. Aircraft a write-off.

I/LG2

Messerschmitt Bf 109E. Crash-landed at Jever during local flying. Cause not stated. Pilot unhurt. Aircraft a write-off.

Friday, August 2

3/506

Heinkel He 115. Failed to return from mission over the Channel. Crashed in the sea cause unknown. Lt. zur See Starke and two NCOs missing. Aircraft lost.

Heinkel He 115. Missing following operational sortie. Circumstances of loss unknown. Oblt. zur See Ballier and one NCO killed. Lt. Ducoffre missing. Aircraft lost.

Seenotzentrale Boulogne

Heinkel He 59. Slipped its mooring buoy and damaged against the mole at Boulogne Harbour. No crew casualties. Aircraft 20% damaged.

3(F)/121

Junkers Ju 88A-1. Crashed at Dinard on operational sortie. Cause unknown. Oblt. Viefhues, Lt. Taubert and two NCOs killed. Aircraft a write-off.

2/JG3

Messerschmitt Bf 109E-4. Crash-landed at Poix due to engine failure during routine domestic flight. Pilot unhurt. Aircraft 40% damaged.

5/JG27

Messerschmitt Bf 109E-4. Crashed and burned out on landing at Leeuwarden cause not stated. Hptmn. von Ankum-Frank (Staffel Kapitan) killed. Aircraft a write-off.

8/KG2

Dornier Do 17Z. Crash-landed at Guines with damage following operational sortie. No crew casualties. Aircraft a write-off.

Dornier Do 17Z. Crashed on landing at Guines due to damage sustained during operations over the Channel. Crew unhurt. Aircraft 20% damaged.

I/KG51

Junkers Ju 88A-1. Crash-landed at Villaroche due to mechanical failure during routine domestic flight. Crew unhurt. Aircraft 30% damaged.

II/KG51

Junkers Ju 88A-1. Crash-landed at Orly aerodrome following operational sortie. Cause not stated. No crew casualties. Aircraft 30% damaged.

KG53

Heinkel He 111H-2. Forced-landed at Schwabisch-Hall during routine domestic flight. Cause not stated. Crew unhurt. Aircraft repairable.

II/KG55

Heinkel He 111. Forced-landed at Chartres damaged following action over England. No crew casualties. Aircraft 20% damaged.

5/NJG1

Dornier Do 17Z. Crash-landed at Schiphol aerodrome during operational sortie. Cause not stated. Crew unhurt. Aircraft 45% damaged.

I/StG2

Junkers Ju 87B-1. Crashed at Ernes aerodrome following engine failure on local flight. Two NCOs killed. Aircraft a write-off.

Stab staffel StG3

Dornier Do 17M. Crashed in flames at Dinan due to engine failure on routine domestic flight. Oblt. Kusko and two NCOs killed. Aircraft a write-off.

I/StG77

Junkers Ju 87B-1. Crashed near Bayeux due to engine failure on domestic flight. Crew unhurt. Aircraft 50% damaged.

Saturday, August 3

Seenotzentrale Boulogne

Heinkel He 59. Slipped its mooring buoy and collided with Boulogne harbour mole. No crew casualties. Aircraft 40% damaged.

3(F)14

Dornier Do 17P. Failed to return from operational reconnaissance mission, circumstances unknown. Oblt. Volkel, Oblt. Schafer killed and one NCO missing. Aircraft lost.

5/JG3

Messerschmitt Bf 109E-1. Crash-landed following engine failure during routine domestic flight over Aumale. Pilot unhurt. Aircraft a write-off.

III/JG27

Messerschmitt Bf 109E-1. Flying accident at Cherbourg. Crash-landed due to engine failure. Pilot unhurt. Aircraft 25% damaged.

6/JG51

Messerschmitt Bf 109E-1. Crashed at Desvres aerodrome due to engine failure on local flight. Pilot unhurt. Aircraft a write-off.

I/KG2

Dornier Do 17Z. Abandoned over Meloures during operational sortie. Cause not stated. Crew baled out unhurt. Aircraft a write-off.

II/KG4

Heinkel He 111P. Crash-landed at Mark Friedland during routine domestic flight. Cause not stated. Crew unhurt. Aircraft 80% damaged.

Heinkel He 111P. Crashed and burst into flames during emergency take-off practice at Mark Friedland aerodrome. Three NCOs killed, one wounded. Aircraft a write-off.

II/KG53

Heinkel He 111H-2. Damaged in forced-landing at Vendeville due to engine failure on operational mission. Lt. Bohmert and two NCOs wounded. Aircraft 80% damaged.

3/KG55

Heinkel He 111P. Failed to return from operational sortie over Bristol. Shot down by AA fire over English coast. Oberfw. Geissler killed. Uffz. Ohmann, Uffz. Weber, Uffz. Thieme and Uffz. Westphal all missing. Aircraft lost.

Sunday, August 4

2(F)/122

Heinkel He 111. Crash-landed at Wissel on routine domestic flight. Cause not stated. Oblt. Sommerich and one NCO injured. Aircraft 70% damaged.

7/KG1

Heinkel He 111H-2. Crash-landed at Rosieres during local flight, circumstances unknown. No crew casualties. Aircraft 35% damaged.

8/KG1

Heinkel He 111H-2. Damaged in forced-landing at Rosieres following engine failure. Flying accident. Crew unhurt. Aircraft 50% damaged.

9/KG1

Heinkel He 111H-2. Crash-landed at Rosieres during routine domestic flight, circumstances not stated. Crew unhurt. Aircraft 35% damaged.

7/KG3

Dornier Do 17Z. Damaged in taxi-ing accident at Altenburg. No crew casualties. Aircraft 40% damaged.

I/KG51

Junkers Ju 88A-1. Tyre burst on landing at Orly aerodrome following local flight. No crew casualties. Aircraft 40% damaged.

III/KG53

Heinkel He 111H-2. Forced-landed at Schwabisch-Hall due to engine failure. No crew casualties. Aircraft 40% damaged.

2/LG1

Heinkel He 111. Crash-landed following engine failure on routine domestic flight. Damaged landing near Beverloo. Crew of six NCOs injured. Aircraft a write-off.

IV/LG1

Junkers Ju 87B. Flew into the ground near Tramecourt during practice flight. Circumstances unknown. One NCO killed, one seriously injured died later. Aircraft a write-off.

Monday, August 5

Seenotflugkdo. Cherbourg

Heinkel He 59. Lost on operations over the Channel off Cherbourg. Believed crashed in sea. Two NCOs killed. Aircraft lost.

Kustenflieger Gruppe 606

Dornier Do 17Z. Crash-landed at Westerland on routine domestic flight. Cause not stated. Two NCOs injured. Aircraft 70% damaged.

1/196

Arado Ar 196. Crashed into the sea off Greenland during reconnaissance mission for the cruiser *Hipper*. No crew casualties notified. Aircraft lost.

3/Aufklaerungs Gruppe Ob.d.L.

Dornier Do 215. Forced-landed Berlin-Tempelhof aerodrome with damage caused by own flak during local flight. Crew unhurt. Aircraft 60% damaged.

The hunter that stayed on the hill. The tail unit of a KG4 Heinkel based at Soesterberg, near Utrecht in Holland, which struck the summit of Cairnsmore of Fleet, West Kirkcudbrightshire (2,331 feet above sea level), on August 8 while believed to be on a mine-laying operation to Belfast harbour. However, it seems that engine trouble forced the crew to jettison their load near Creetown in an attempt to clear the summit of the mountain (Associated Press).

5/JG3

Messerschmitt Bf 109E-1. Forced-landed at Orombon during routine domestic flight. Exact cause not stated. Pilot unhurt. Aircraft repairable.

I/JG27

Messerschmitt Bf 109E-1. Crashed on landing at Plumetot aerodrome due to undercarriage failure. Pilot unhurt. Aircraft 20% damaged.

1/JG51

Messerschmitt Bf 109E. Wrecked in collision on take-off from Pihen. Hptmn. Pitcairn injured. Aircraft a write-off.

Messerschmitt Bf 109E-4. Shot down by RAF fighters in combat over the Channel. Oberfw. Schmid killed. Aircraft lost.

8/JG51

Messerschmitt Bf 109E. Severely damaged in combat with RAF fighters over the Channel. Returned to base. Pilot unhurt. Aircraft 40% damaged.

I/JG54

Messerschmitt Bf 109E. Crash-landed at Bouin following combat with fighters over the Channel. Pilot unhurt. Aircraft 35% damaged.

Messerschmitt Bf 109E-4. Returned to base with slight damage sustained in action over the Channel. Oblt. Seiler wounded. Aircraft repairable.

3/JG54

Messerschmitt Bf 109E-3. Burst tyre on landing at Detmold following routine domestic flight. Pilot unhurt. Aircraft 60% damaged.

3/KG3

Dornier Do 17Z. Crash-landed at Le Culot aerodrome after operational sortie. Crew unhurt. Aircraft 15% damaged.

III/KG3

Dornier Do 17. Flew into the ground and exploded near Schweinfurth during routine domestic flight. Flying accident, cause unknown. Crew of four NCOs killed. Aircraft a write-off.

7/KG3

Dornier Do 17Z. Failed to return from operational sortie, cause unknown. Oblt. Ulrich and three NCOs missing. Aircraft a write-off.

9/KG3

Dornier Do 17Z. Flying accident exact circumstances unknown. Hit the ground near Meinberg during local flight. Four NCOs killed. Aircraft a write-off.

III/KG30

Junkers Ju 88A-1. Damaged in landing accident at Aalborg aerodrome due to under-carriage failure. No crew casualties. Aircraft 25% damaged.

III/KG51

Junkers Ju 88A. Belly-landed near Berka following engine failure on routine domestic flight. Crew unhurt. Aircraft 30% damaged.

2/KG100

Heinkel He 111. Crashed near Kothen on local flight, cause unknown. Two NCOs killed. Aircraft a write-off.

Although the crash site is very inaccessible necessitating a strenuous two-hour climb, it has been visited by numerous individuals and groups since the war. The tail section and wings, which were more or less intact up to 1971 when this photo was taken, have since been heavily 'souvenired'. The latest relic to go was the complete tail section removed by the North East Aircraft Museum with the help of a caterpillar tractor on November 10, 1979 (Warplane Wreck Recovery Group).

I/StG2

Junkers Ju 87B-2. Crashed on take-off from Conde, cause not stated. Crew unhurt. Aircraft repairable.

Transport Staffel I Flieger Korps

Junkers Ju 87. Damaged in crash-landing at Compiegne during routine local flight. Two NCOs wounded. Aircraft damage state not recorded.

Tuesday, August 6

Aufklarungs Gruppe (H)/21

Henschel Hs 126. Crashed on landing at Lessay aerodrome due to undercarriage failure following routine domestic flight. Pilot unhurt. Aircraft 60% damaged.

1/196

Arado Ar 196. Crashed at Schellingwoude on operational sortie. Exact circumstances not stated. One NCO killed. Lt. zur See Nowrat wounded. Aircraft a write-off.

2/Erprobungs Gruppe 210

Messerschmitt Bf 110. Crashed in sea off Denain during dive-bombing practice. Cause unknown. Lt. Prokop and one NCO killed. Aircraft a write-off.

Messerschmitt Bf 110. Crashed at Denain during routine maintenance test flight. Circumstances unknown. Uffz. Schulteis killed. Aircraft a write-off.

I/JG3

Messerschmitt Bf 109E. Crash-landed at St. Omer following operational sortie. Pilot unhurt. Aircraft 40% damaged.

II/JG53

Messerschmitt Bf 109E-4. Crashed on take-off from Dinan aerodrome. Pilot unhurt. Aircraft 50% damaged.

Messerschmitt Bf 109E-4. Crashed on take-off from Dinan on domestic flight. Pilot unhurt. Aircraft 40% damaged.

7/KG3

Dornier Do 17Z. Crash-landed at St. Trond on routine domestic flight. Cause not stated. No crew casualties. Aircraft 30% damaged.

KG53

Heinkel He 111H-2. Flying accident. Flew into the ground at Markheidenfeld due to engine failure. Four NCOs killed. Aircraft a write-off.

II/KG54

Junkers Ju 88. Damaged in taxi-ing accident at Erfurt-Bindersleben aerodrome. No crew casualties. Aircraft 40% damaged.

II/KG55

Heinkel He 111P. Forced-landed near Nancy following engine failure during routine domestic flight. No crew casualties. Aircraft 25% damaged.

II/LG2

Messerschmitt Bf 109E. Crashed at Dankmarshausen during local flight. Cause not stated. Pilot wounded. Aircraft a write-off.

3/ZG26

Messerschmitt Bf 110. Crashed at Yvrench on domestic flight, cause unknown. Pilot killed. Aircraft a write-off.

Wednesday, August 7

3/906

Heinkel He 115. Returned to base with slight damage following sortie over the English east coast. One NCO wounded. Aircraft 20% damaged.

5(H)/13

Henschel Hs 126B. Forced-landed at Lessay aerodrome during operational sortie. Cause not stated. Pilot unhurt. Aircraft 15% damaged.

3/Erprobungs Gruppe 210

Messerschmitt Bf 109E-4. Crashed into sea off Denain on local flight, circumstances unknown. Hptmn. Valesi killed. Aircraft a write-off.

4/JG3

Messerschmitt Bf 109E-1. Crashed on landing at Samer following routine domestic flight. Cause not stated. Pilot unhurt. Aircraft 45% damaged.

II/JG52

Messerschmitt Bf 109E-1. Crash-landed at Oldendorf due to engine failure. Pilot injured. Aircraft 60% damaged.

4/JG54

Messerschmitt Bf 109s. Damaged in RAF bombing attack on Haamstede aerodrome. No personnel casualties. One aircraft destroyed. One 70% damaged. Four more aircraft 30% damaged.

I/KG3

Dornier Do 17Z. Crashed on landing at Le Culot aerodrome following routine domestic flight. Cause not stated. Crew unhurt. Aircraft 75% damaged.

I/KG z.b.V.172

Junkers Ju 52 (5560). Crash-landed near Calais during operational sortie. No casualties reported. Aircraft repairable.

9/LG1

Junkers Ju 88A. Crashed at Chateaudun aerodrome following operations. Exact cause unknown. Lt. Harzog and three NCOs killed. Aircraft a write-off.

Thursday, August 8

I/JG3

Messerschmitt Bf 109E. Crashed on take-off from Colembert on operational sortie. Exact cause not stated. Pilot unhurt. Aircraft 30% damaged.

5/JG3

Messerschmitt Bf 109E-4. Crash-landed at Samer following operational flight. Circumstances not recorded. Pilot unhurt. Aircraft repairable.

8/JG26

Messerschmitt Bf 109E-4. Shot down in combat with RAF fighters over the Channel. Believed crashed in sea. Oblt. Oehm missing. Aircraft lost.

I/JG27

Messerschmitt Bf 109E-1. Shot down by RAF fighter during combat over the Isle of Wight. Abandoned aircraft crashed in the Channel. Pilot baled out and rescued by Seenotdienst. Aircraft lost.

Messerschmitt Bf 109E-3. Failed to return from operational sortie and combat over the Channel off the Isle of Wight. Shot down into the sea. Lt. Birkenbach killed. Aircraft lost.

Messerschmitt Bf 109E-3. Failed to return from combat with RAF fighters over the Isle of Wight. Shot down into the Channel. Lt. Bothfeld killed. Aircraft lost.

II/JG27

Messerschmitt Bf 109E-4. Shot down by fighters in action over the Isle of Wight. Ditched in Channel. Hptmn. Andres (Gruppe Kommandeur) rescued by Seenotdienst. Aircraft lost.

Messerschmitt Bf 109E-1. Shot down by RAF fighters in combat over the Channel off the Isle of Wight. Uffz. Uebe rescued. Aircraft a write-off.

Messerschmitt Bf 109E-4. Shot down into the sea during combat with RAF fighters. Oberfw. Krenzke rescued wounded. Aircraft lost.

Messerschmitt Bf 109E-4. Failed to return following action with RAF fighters over the Isle of Wight. Presumed crashed in the Channel. Uffz. Schulz missing. Aircraft lost.

Messerschmitt Bf 109E-2. Returned to base damaged following combat with enemy fighters. Pilot unhurt. Aircraft 60% damaged.

III/JG27

Messerschmitt Bf 109E-1. Returned to base damaged following action against RAF fighters. Gefr. Nittmann wounded. Aircraft 35% damaged.

Messerschmitt Bf 109E-4. Failed to return from operational sortie over the Channel. Believed shot down into the sea. Uffz. Girrbach missing. Aircraft lost.

II/JG51

Messerschmitt Bf 109E. Forced-landed at St. Omer-Wizernes following engine failure during operational sortie. Pilot unhurt. Aircraft 40% damaged.

8/JG51

Messerschmitt Bf 109E-4. Crash-landed at St. Omer due to engine failure on combat mission. Pilot unhurt. Aircraft 45% damaged.

9/JG51

Messerschmitt Bf 109E-1. Returned to base severely damaged by enemy action during sortie over the Channel off Dover. Pilot unhurt. Aircraft 60% damaged.

II/JG53

Messerschmitt Bf 109E-4. Crash-landed at Dinan aerodrome following combat mission. Exact cause not stated. Pilot unhurt. Aircraft 45% damaged.

III/JG54

Messerschmitt Bf 109E-4. Crashed on landing at Haamstede following operational sortie. Pilot unhurt. Aircraft 40% damaged.

I/KG4

Heinkel He 111H-4. Failed to return from operational sortie over Scotland. Crashed at Eastmans Cairn on the summit of Cairnsmore-of-Fleet, Kirkcudbrightshire and exploded on impact. Exact cause unknown. Lt. Zeiss, Uffz. Giebal, Uffz. von Toucheim and one NCO killed. Aircraft a write-off.
A well-known site visited by many groups and individuals over a period of years including the Dumfries and Galloway Aviation Group and Scotland West Aircraft Investigation Group. A memorial to all the aircrew who have died on the mountain is due to be unveiled on August 18, 1980.

9/KG4

Heinkel He 111P. Crashed at Fassberg on domestic flight. Three NCOs killed. Aircraft a write-off.

II/KG54

Junkers Ju 88A. Crashed and burned out at St. Andre following engine fire during local flight. One NCO killed, two injured. Aircraft a write-off.

I/KG77

Junkers Ju 88A. Crash-landed on Regensburg aerodrome during routine domestic flight. Cause not stated. Crew unhurt. Aircraft 25% damaged.

V/LG1

Messerschmitt Bf 110C. Returned to base damaged in combat with RAF fighters over the Channel. Two NCOs wounded. Aircraft 40% damaged.

Messerschmitt Bf 110C. Damaged in combat with fighters over the Channel. Returned to base. Crew unhurt. Aircraft 25% damaged.

Messerschmitt Bf 110C. Severely damaged in action against RAF fighters over the Channel. Crew unhurt. Aircraft 70% damaged.

Messerschmitt Bf 110C. Returned to base with severe damage sustained in combat with fighters over the Channel. Crew unhurt. Aircraft 70% damaged.

14(Z)/LG1

Messerschmitt Bf 110C. Shot down in combat with enemy fighters over the Channel. Crashed in the sea. Fw. Sturm and Fw. Brunner missing. Aircraft lost.

Messerschmitt Bf 110C. Severely damaged during combat with enemy fighters. Pilot wounded. Fw. Jentzsch killed. Aircraft 80% damaged.

II/StG1

Junkers Ju 87B. Damaged in combat with RAF fighters and returned to base. Oblt. Ostmann and one NCO wounded. Aircraft damaged but repairable.

III/StG1

Junkers Ju 87B. Returned to base damaged following combat with fighters over the Isle of Wight. Two NCOs wounded. Aircraft damage state not recorded.

9/StG1

Junkers Ju 87B. Failed to return following engagement with RAF fighters over the Channel. Believed crashed in the sea. Fw. Torngrind and Gefr. Bauer both missing. Aircraft lost.

Junkers Ju 87B. Missing following combat over the Channel off the Isle of Wight. Believed shot down into the sea by RAF fighters. Gefr. Walz and Gefr. Schutz both missing. Aircraft lost.

I/StG2

Junkers Ju 87B. Crashed on landing at Wuilly-le-Tessin aerodrome due to combat damage. One NCO wounded. Aircraft 40% damaged.

III/StG2

Junkers Ju 87B. Returned to base damaged following attack by RAF fighters. Two NCOs wounded. Aircraft damaged but repairable.

Stab I/StG3

Junkers Ju 87B. Failed to return from combat with enemy fighters over the Channel. Crashed in the sea. Oblt. Muller captured, Uffz. Krampfl killed. Aircraft lost.

I/StG3

Junkers Ju 87B. Crash-landed at Wuilly-le-Tessin aerodrome with combat damage following sortie over the Channel. One NCO wounded. Aircraft 45% damaged.

Junkers Ju 87B. Forced-landed at Theville with damage sustained in attack by RAF fighters over the Channel. One NCO wounded. Aircraft repairable.

2/StG3

Junkers Ju 87B. Failed to return from operations over the Channel. Crashed in sea. Fw. Zschweigert killed. Fw. Heinrich missing. Aircraft lost.

Junkers Ju 87B. Crashed into the Channel during engagement with RAF fighters. Uffz. Kleinhans and Uffz. Quante both killed. Aircraft lost.

Stab II/StG77

Junkers Ju 87B. Shot down into the sea by No. 145 Squadron Hurricanes during attack on convoy off Portsmouth. Hptmn. Plewig (Gruppe Kommandeur) rescued and captured. Fw. Schauer killed. Aircraft lost.

II/StG77

Junkers Ju 87B. Returned to base at Bourgy aerodrome with damage sustained in combat over the Channel with RAF fighters. Crew unhurt. Aircraft 25% damaged.

Junkers Ju 87B. Forced-landed at Cherbourg due to injuries received in combat over the Channel. Two NCOs wounded. Aircraft repairable.

Junkers Ju 87B. Forced-landed Deauville due to combat damage. Crew unhurt. Aircraft a write-off.

Junkers Ju 87B. Returned to Bourgy aerodrome damaged in fighter attack. Crew unhurt. Aircraft 70% damaged.

Junkers Ju 87B. Landed at Bourgy with damage sustained in attacks by RAF fighters during operations over the Channel. Crew unhurt. Aircraft 20% damaged.

4/StG77

Junkers Ju 87B. Failed to return from operational sortie over the Channel. Believed crashed in the sea. Hptmn. Schmack, Obergefr. Wuttke both missing. Aircraft lost.

Junkers Ju 87B. Shot down by Pilot Officer Parrott of No. 145 Squadron during operations over the Channel. Forced-landed at St. Lawrence, Isle of Wight 5.40 p.m. Uffz. Pittroff captured. Uffz. Schubert killed. Aircraft S2+ LM a write-off.

3/ZG26

Messerschmitt Bf 110. Collided with Bf 110 of same unit during operational sortie. Crashed near Conteville. Lt. Dziddek and one NCO wounded. Aircraft a write-off.

Messerschmitt Bf 110D. Subject of collision with Lt. Dziddek's aircraft and abandoned over Conteville. One NCO pilot baled out unhurt. One NCO killed. Aircraft a write-off.

Friday, August 9

3(F)/11

Dornier Do 17P. Destroyed accidentally at Oslo-Fornebu aerodrome. Exact circumstances not recorded. Lt. Hoh and Lt. Thiel wounded. Aircraft a write-off.

3(F)/123

Junkers Ju 88A. Returned to base damaged following attack by RAF fighters during operational reconnaissance sortie. One NCO killed. Aircraft 25% damaged.

I/JG53

Messerschmitt Bf 109E-1. Emergency forced-landing at Guernsey following engine failure during operational sortie. Collided with flak emplacement killing three men and injuring two others. Pilot severely injured. Aircraft a write-off.
Relics displayed at Forest Church Museum, Guernsey are captioned as being from a Heinkel He 111 which crash-landed there on this date. No such incident can be traced in the relevant contemporary Luftwaffe records and it is possible that the items displayed actually originated from this aircraft.

2/KG4

Heinkel He 111H-4. Shot down by AA fire during operations over Flamborough Head. Two NCOs killed, two missing. Aircraft lost.

7/KG26

Heinkel He 111H-3. Shot down in combat with RAF fighters during mission over the north-east coast of England. Crashed in the sea off Whitburn 11.52 a.m. Uffz. Denner, Fw. Haertel captured unhurt together with Uffz. Karkos and Uffz. Feinekat both wounded. All rescued by Naval patrol boat. Aircraft 1H+ ER lost.

III/KG51

Junkers Ju 88A (7052). Undercarriage collapsed on take-off from Montdesir aerodrome. No crew casualties. Aircraft 9K+ GS 75% damaged.

Junkers Ju 88A (5064). Crashed on take-off from Montdesir, exact cause not stated. Oberfw. Sonntag and crew unhurt. Aircraft 9K+ DD 50% damaged.

II/LG1

Junkers Ju 88A. Failed to return from operations over England, exact fate unknown. Briefed to attack Plymouth. Four NCOs missing. Aircraft lost.

III/ZG26

Arado Ar66. Damaged in crash-landing at St. Omer during local flight. Circumstances not recorded. Pilot injured. Aircraft 40% damaged.

7/ZG26

Messerschmitt Bf 110C-4. Crashed at Boblingen during routine domestic flight. Cause unknown. One NCO killed. Aircraft a write-off.

Saturday, August 10

2(H)/12

Henschel Hs 126B. Forced-landed at Trestel due to mechanical failure during operational sortie. Pilot unhurt. Aircraft 55% damaged.

Kustenflieger Gruppe 806

Junkers Ju 88A. Forced-landed at Brest-Sud aerodrome during routine domestic flight — cause not stated. No crew casualties. Aircraft 60% damaged.

5/JG2

Messerschmitt Bf 109E-4. Hit an obstruction shortly after take-off from Beaumont-le-Roger on local flight. Uffz. Graf Stollberg killed. Aircraft a write-off.

I/JG27

Messerschmitt Bf 109E-4. Damaged by bomb splinter during attack on Cherbourg aerodrome by RAF aircraft. No personnel losses. Aircraft 25% damaged.

Messerschmitt Bf 109E-4. Crash-landed at Cherbourg following routine domestic flight. Cause not stated. Aircraft 10% damaged.

III/KG4

Junkers Ju 88. Slightly damaged in RAF bombing raid on Schiphol aerodrome. No personnel losses. Aircraft repairable.

III/KG51

Junkers Ju 88A-1 (7071). Belly-landed at Beauvais aerodrome following operational sortie. Crew unhurt. Aircraft 9K+ JR 20% damaged.

Kampf Gruppe 126

Heinkel He 111. Damaged in RAF bombing attack on Schiphol aerodrome. No personnel losses. Aircraft 35% damaged.

Stab Staffel LG1

Junkers Ju 88A-1.Crash-landed at Godshorn following engine failure during routine domestic flight. Two NCOs wounded. Aircraft 70% damaged.

Sunday, August 11

1(F)/121

Junkers Ju 88A-1. Shot down by fighters during reconnaissance sortie and crash-landed on Newton Moor, Whitby 7.08 a.m. Lt. Meyer killed. Oblt. Marzusch, Fw. Hofft and Fw. Hacker captured. Aircraft 7A+ KH a write-off.

Seenotzentrale Cherbourg

Heinkel He 59. Shot down by Spitfires during rescue of three crew from RAF Blenheim brought down by Hptmn. Wiggers of I/JG51. One NCO wounded. Aircraft lost.

Heinkel He 59. Failed to return from search and rescue mission over the Channel. Believed crashed in the sea. Crew missing. Aircraft lost.

1/Erprobungs Gruppe 210

Messerschmitt Bf 110C-6. Shot down by RAF fighters during combat off Harwich. Crashed into the sea. Gefr. Weiss and Fw. Sturtz both killed. Aircraft lost.

Messerschmitt Bf 110C-6. Shot down into the sea off Harwich during combat with fighters. Lt. Bertram and one NCO killed. Aircraft lost.

I/JG2

Messerschmitt Bf 109E-4. Shot down in combat with RAF fighters. Pilot baled out wounded and rescued by Seenotdienst. Aircraft a write-off.

Messerschmitt Bf 109E-4. Failed to return from combat mission over the Channel. Exact fate unknown. Uffz. Bass killed. Aircraft a write-off.

II/JG2

Messerschmitt Bf 109E-4. Ditched in the Channel following combat with RAF fighters. Oblt. Rempel (Staffel Kapitan) killed. Aircraft lost.

Messerschmitt Bf 109E-4. Shot down in combat with RAF fighters over the Channel. Crashed in the sea. Uffz. Lange missing. Aircraft lost.

III/JG2

Messerschmitt Bf 109E-4. Failed to return from combat sortie and action with RAF fighters over the Channel. Oblt. Fricke killed. Aircraft lost.

Messerschmitt Bf 109E-3. Shot down in combat with RAF fighters and crashed in the Channel. Uffz. Toppler rescued unhurt by Seenotdienst. Aircraft lost.

Messerschmitt Bf 109E-1. Missing following operations over the Channel and combat with RAF fighters. Pilot believed rescued unhurt. Aircraft lost.

Messerschmitt Bf 109E. Crashed near Cherbourg following combat with RAF fighters over the Channel. Oblt. Steidle killed. Aircraft a write-off.

3/JG3

Messerschmitt Bf 109E-1. Shot down in combat with RAF fighters over Margate. Fw. Heise killed. Aircraft a write-off.

Messerschmitt Bf 109E-1. Failed to return from operational sortie over Margate and combat with RAF fighters. Fw. Hofelich killed. Aircraft lost.

III/JG26

Messerschmitt Bf 109E-1. Severely damaged in combat with enemy fighters over Calais. Pilot wounded. Aircraft 80% damaged.

I/JG27

Messerschmitt Bf 109E-1. Shot down in combat with RAF fighters over the Channel. Abandoned aircraft crashed in the sea. Pilot baled out unhurt and rescued by Seenotdienst. Aircraft lost.

The spinners glare like baleful eyes on the Jumos of this 'Totenkopf' Geschwader Ju 88. It was set upon by a Hurricane of No. 213 Squadron whereupon it lowered its undercarriage and landed on Portland Head, tearing down telephone wires on its approach. The undercarriage then collapsed slewing the aircraft round and it slid backwards to a halt. According to one eye witness we interviewed, as the pilot, Oberleutnant Wette, climbed down from the cockpit, a burst of machine gun fire from a defence post tore his legs off (Censored photograph from Central Press).

II/JG27

Messerschmitt Bf 109E-1. Failed to return from combat sortie over the Channel. Exact fate unknown. Uffz. Lackner missing. Aircraft lost.

Messerschmitt Bf 109E-1. Belly-landed at St. Mere Eglise aerodrome due to mechanical failure during routine domestic flight. Pilot unhurt. Aircraft repairable.

8/JG27

Messerschmitt Bf 109E-4. Failed to return from combat sortie over the Channel. Presumed crashed in sea. Uffz. Menz missing. Aircraft lost.

5/JG51

Messerschmitt Bf 109E-3. Missing following operations over the Channel. Exact fate uncertain. Fw. Walz missing. Aircraft lost.

I/JG54

Messerschmitt Bf 109E-4. Crashed on take-off from Campagne, cause not stated. Pilot unhurt. Aircraft 33% damaged.

6/JG54

Messerschmitt Bf 109E-3. Crashed at Haamstede due to engine failure whilst on operational sortie. Lt. Wagner injured. Aircraft a write-off.

3/KG2

Dornier Do 17. Crashed at St. Inglevert due to combat damage. Four NCOs wounded. Aircraft a write-off.

4/KG2

Dornier Do 17Z. Belly-landed at St. Omer with damage sustained in action over the Channel. Two NCOs wounded. Aircraft a write-off.

The boys stand in for the engines to show the exact position of the aircraft in relation to the cemetery in the background. St. George's church is just out of the wartime photo. The Portcrete factory on the left was known as the Bath and Portland Masonry works in 1940.

Dornier Do 17Z. Returned safely to base with one NCO crewman wounded following operations across the Channel. Aircraft repairable.

9/KG2

Dornier Do 17Z. Returned to base damaged following engagement with RAF fighters over the Channel between Ostend and Calais. One NCO wounded. Aircraft repairable.

Dornier Do 17Z. Damaged in attacks by RAF fighters over the Channel between Ostend and Calais. Returned to base with two NCOs wounded. Aircraft repairable.

Dornier Do 17Z. Attacked by RAF fighters off Calais and damaged. Returned to base with one NCO dead. Aircraft repairable.

9/KG4

Dornier Do 17Z. Severely damaged by repeated fighter attacks in operations over Channel off Folkestone. One NCO wounded. Aircraft a write-off.

Dornier Do 17Z. Returned to base with slight damage following action over the Channel. One NCO severely wounded later died. Aircraft repairable.

I/KG54

Junkers Ju 88A. Failed to return from operational sortie, circumstances unknown. One NCO killed, three missing. Aircraft a write-off.

Two days after it landed, Royal Air Force technicians, watched by the army guard and local civilians, began dismantling the Jumo engines. The port wing dive brakes hang extended inboard of the damaged wing tip. The wide sweep of Chesil Beach shimmers in the background under the August sun (Associated Press).

Junkers Ju 88A. Shot down by RAF fighters in combat over the Channel. Crashed in the sea. Crew rescued unhurt by Seenotdienst. Aircraft lost.

Junkers Ju 88A. Belly-landing at Evreux aerodrome due to damage suffered in combat with RAF fighters during sortie over the Channel. Crew unhurt. Aircraft 35% damaged.

Stab II/KG54

Junkers Ju 88A-1. Shot down by Flying Officer Strickland of No. 213 Squadron during sortie over Portland Harbour 10.40 a.m. Forced-landed at Blacknore Fort, Portland Head. Oblt. Wette badly wounded. Oberfw. Meier, Gefr. Gehre and Flgr. Kagenbaur captured unhurt. Aircraft B3+DC a write-off.

Junkers Ju 88A. Crashed in sea off Portland following fighter attack 10.50 a.m. Oblt. Schade killed. Fw. Basse and Fw. Bagus missing. Uffz. Klatte captured. Aircraft B3+CC lost.

Junkers Ju 88A. Missing following fighter attack over the Channel off Portland. Major Leonardi (Gruppe Kommandeur) and two NCOs killed. Oblt. Schott missing. Aircraft lost.

IV/LG1

Junkers Ju 87B. Shot down by fighters in action over the Thames Estuary. Believed crashed in the sea. Two NCOs missing. Aircraft lost.

II/StG1

Junkers Ju 87B. Shot down into the Thames Estuary during combat with RAF fighters. One NCO killed, one missing. Aircraft lost.

Stab ZG2

Messerschmitt Bf 110C-2. Shot down by fighters in combat over Cherbourg. Oblt. Hensel killed. Oblt. Schafer wounded. Aircraft a write-off.

Stab I/ZG2

Messerschmitt Bf 110C. Shot down over Portland during combat with enemy fighters. Crashed in the sea. Major Ott (Gruppe Kommandeur) and Fw. Zimehl both killed. Aircraft lost.

The boys have stood still but the editor has moved round to capture the present day view across Lyme Bay although low cloud merged the land and sea on October 30, 1979.

I/ZG2

Messerschmitt Bf 110D. Returned to base damaged following combat with RAF fighters off Portland. Crew unhurt. Aircraft 10% damaged.

Messerschmitt Bf 110C. Damaged in combat over the Channel off Portland. Returned safely to base. Crew unhurt. Aircraft 15% damaged.

Messerschmitt Bf 110C. Attacked by RAF fighters over the Channel off Portland and returned to base damaged. Crew unhurt. Aircraft 10% damaged.

1/ZG2

Messerschmitt Bf 110C. Shot down into the Channel by RAF fighters during operations over Portland. Lt. Jess and Gefr. Kossar both killed. Aircraft lost.

2/ZG2

Messerschmitt Bf 110C. Failed to return from operational sortie over Portland area. Presumed shot down into the Channel by RAF fighters. Fw. Teichert and Gefr. Kloss both missing. Aircraft a write-off.

'The devil in the cornfield'. Surrounded by the bounty of a rich harvest, the JG52 'Emil', Red 14 of Unteroffizier Zaunbrecher lies remarkably intact on Mays Farm, near Selmeston village, Sussex, where he was forced down after combat over Hastings on August 12. The buildings of Stonery Farm can just be seen on the right (Eastbourne Gazette).

Below: Stonery Farm still remains on the skyline on September 18, 1979. The main Lewes-Hastings railway line runs in the cutting across the middle distance.

3/ZG2

Messerschmitt Bf 110C-4. Missing following operations over Portland. Fw. Weis and Uffz. Schwarze both missing. Aircraft lost.

Messerschmitt Bf 110C. Forced-landed at Carquebut aerodrome with damaged suffered in combat over the Channel off Portland. Crew unhurt. Aircraft 20% damaged.

II/ZG2

Messerschmitt Bf 110D. Returned to base damaged by fighter attack. Crew unhurt. Aircraft 10% damaged.

4/ZG2

Messerschmitt Bf 110D. Failed to return following operations over the Channel to Portland and combat with RAF fighters. Uffz. Hoyer and Gefr. Dietz both missing. Aircraft lost.

1/ZG26

Messerschmitt Bf 110D. Shot down in combat with fighters over the Thames Estuary. Crashed in sea. Hptmn. Kogler and one NCO both rescued wounded. Aircraft a write-off.

Messerschmitt Bf 110. Failed to return from operational sortie over the Thames Estuary. Exact fate unknown. Fw. Puschnerus and one NCO missing. Aircraft lost.

2/ZG26

Messerschmitt Bf 110. Returned to base with damage caused by fighter attack during operations across the Channel. Crew unhurt. Aircraft 20% damaged.

Messerschmitt Bf 110C. Forced-landed at St. Omer with combat damage. Crew unhurt. Aircraft 70% damaged.

Monday, August 12

3/106

Heinkel He 115. Returned to base following loss of crewman who fell overboard on take-off from Schellingwoude. One NCO killed. Aircraft undamaged.

4(F)/121

Messerschmitt Bf 110C-4. Hit by own flak and set alight during operational reconnaissance sortie. Forced-landed near Barfleur. Crew unhurt, one NCO having baled out. Aircraft 30% damaged.

Erprobungs Gruppe 210

Messerschmitt Bf 110. Forced-landed near Calais following RAF fighter attack. One NCO wounded. Aircraft a write-off.

1/JG2

Messerschmitt Bf 109E-4. Overshot runway at advanced landing ground due to injuries suffered in combat with RAF fighters. Pilot wounded. Aircraft a write-off.

1/JG3

Messerschmitt Bf 109E-1. Forced-landed at Colombert during routine domestic flight. Cause not stated. Pilot unhurt. Aircraft 15% damaged.

III/JG3

Messerschmitt Bf 109E-4. Ditched in the Channel following combat with RAF fighters off Portland. Pilot rescued by Seenotdienst. Aircraft lost.

8/JG3

Messerschmitt Bf 109E-4. Crashed on the aerodrome at Bonninghardt due to brake failure. Pilot unhurt. Aircraft a write-off.

1/JG26

Messerschmitt Bf 109E-4. Shot down into the sea during combat with fighters over the Channel off Folkestone. Lt. Regenauer captured. Aircraft a write-off.

Messerschmitt Bf 109E-1. Shot down over Ashford by British fighters. Exploded over Standard Hill Farm, Elham 8.30 a.m. Oblt. Butterweck killed. Aircraft a write-off.

Site investigated by the Brenzett Aeronautical Museum and many small parts recovered.

2/JG52

Messerschmitt Bf 109E-1. Failed to return from operational sortie over Hastings. Uffz. Kern killed. Aircraft a write-off.

Messerschmitt Bf 109E-3. Missing following sortie over the Channel off Hastings and combat with RAF fighters. Lt. Gehlhaar missing. Aircraft lost.

Messerschmitt Bf 109E-1 (3367). Shot down by fighters in combat over Hastings. Forced-landed near Berwick railway crossing, east of Lewes. Uffz. Zaunbrecher captured. Aircraft 14+ a write-off.

Stab III/JG53

Messerschmitt Bf 109E-4. Failed to return from operational sortie over the Channel. Exact fate unknown. Hptmn. Harder (Gruppe Kommandeur) killed. Aircraft lost.

1/JG54

Messerschmitt Bf 109E. Crash-landed at Campagne following combat sortie. Cause not stated. Pilot wounded. Aircraft 25% damaged.

III/JG54

Messerschmitt Bf 109E. Crashed on landing at Guines-Sued following combat mission. Oblt. Schon wounded. Aircraft 60% damaged.

Messerschmitt Bf 109E-4. Forced-landed at Henmore near Margate 6.00 p.m. following combat with fighters. Oblt. Drehs captured. Aircraft a write off.

Messerschmitt Bf 109E-4. Failed to return from operational sortie over the Channel and combat with RAF fighters. Gefr. Stabner missing. Aircraft lost.

Messerschmitt Bf 109E-4. Returned to base damaged following combat with enemy fighters over the Channel. Lt. Eberle wounded. Aircraft 50% damaged.

Messerschmitt Bf 109E. Damaged in taxi-ing accident at Desvres aerodrome. Pilot unhurt. Aircraft repairable.

1/JG77

Messerschmitt Bf 109E-1. Forced-landed Esbjerg due to engine failure on routine domestic flight. Pilot unhurt. Aircraft 40% damaged.

Stab II/KG27

Heinkel He 111H-3. Shot down by night fighter following bombing attack on Bristol docks 00.20 a.m. Abandoned aircraft crashed at Sturminster Marshall, near Wimborne. Major Schlichting (Gruppe Kommandeur), Major Brehmer, Oberfw. Lohneng, Oberfw. Bendrich and Oberfw. Frey all baled out and captured. Aircraft 1G+ AC a write off.

Stab KG51

Junkers Ju 88A. Shot down by fighters and ground defences during attack on Ventnor RDF station. Crashed at Godshill Park, Isle of Wight 12.25 p.m. Oberst. Dr. Fisser (Geschwader Kommodore) killed. Oblt. Luderitz, Lt. Schad and Sonderfuhrer Nothelfer captured. Aircraft 9K+ AA a write-off.

1/KG51

Junkers Ju 88A-1. Missing following operational sortie over southern England. One NCO killed and three missing. Aircraft a write-off.

Junkers Ju 88A-1. Forced-landed at Le Havre with combat damage after sortie over southern England and attack by RAF fighters. Crew unhurt. Aircraft 30% damaged.

3/KG51

Junkers Ju 88A-1. Shot down by fighters over Portsmouth 1.00 p.m. Crashed near Godstone. Obgefr. Dickel killed. Obgefr. Hansmann, Gefr. Fahrenheim and Uffz. Zimmermann missing. Aircraft 9K+CL a write-off.

Junkers Ju 88A-1 (3134). Crashed at Horse Pasture Farm near Westbourne 12.15 p.m. following attack by fighters. Oblt. Graf, Uffz. Floeter and Gefr. Czepik killed. Gefr. Fleischmann baled out and captured. Aircraft 9K+ EL a write-off.

II/KG51

Junkers Ju 88A-1. Failed to return from operational sortie over southern England. Oblt. Schlegel and three NCOs missing. Aircraft a write-off.

Stab III/KG51

Junkers Ju 88A-1 (7073). Returned to base damaged in fighter attack during sortie over southern England. Lt. Schweisgut and Sonderfhr. Engel both wounded. Aircraft 9K+ ED 10% damaged.

III/KG51

Junkers Ju 88A-1. Failed to return from operational sortie over southern England. Three NCOs reported killed. Oblt. Noelker missing. Aircraft a write-off.

Junkers Ju 88A-1. Missing following attack by RAF fighters during operations over southern England. Lt. Seidel, Sonderfhr. Bigalke and one NCO killed. One NCO missing. Aircraft a write-off.

Junkers Ju 88A-1. Failed to return from mission over southern England. Believed shot down by fighters. Four NCOs missing. Aircraft a write-off.

Junkers Ju88 A-1. Missing following RAF fighter attack during operations over southern England. Lt. Hoechstetter and three NCOs missing. Aircraft a write-off.

8/KG51

Junkers Ju 88A-1 (5072). Failed to return from operations over southern England. Believed victim of RAF fighter attack and crashed Portsmouth docks 12.10 p.m. Oblt. Wildemuth, Oblt. Stark and Uffz. Rosch reported captured. Uffz. Droese killed. Aircraft 9K + FS a write-off.

Pedal control lever, parachute silk and shroud lines recovered from bottom of harbour now in the Kent Battle of Britain Museum believed to be from this aircraft. Pair of binoculars and propeller assembly recovered by the Wealden Avaition Archaeological Group.

9/KG51

Junkers Ju 88A-1 (5042). Forced-landed at Le Havre damaged by RAF fighters over southern England. One NCO wounded. Aircraft 9K + AT 30% damaged.

9/KG53

Heinkel He 111. Lost bearings on operational sortie and belly-landed and burst into flames at Alphen. Crew unhurt. Aircraft a write-off.

III/KG55

Heinkel He 111P. Both engines damaged in fighter attack during sortie to Bristol. Crashed and burned out on return to Rambervilliers. Uffz. Schmidt and Uffz. Held killed. Uffz. Bubel and Fw. Paulussen wounded. Aircraft a write-off.

Heinkel He 111P. Forced-landed at Villacoublay due to engine failure on non-operational sortie. Crew unhurt. Aircraft 25% damaged.

III/KG77

Junkers Ju 88A. Crash-landed at Illesheim aerodrome during routine local flight. Cause not stated. One NCO killed. Oblt. Pfeiffer and two NCOs injured. Aircraft a write-off.

I/LG1

Junkers Ju 88A-1. Crashed on take-off from Orleans-Bricy due to engine failure. Four NCOs seriously injured — one died later. Aircraft a write-off.

An enigmatic collection of relics dredged from the bottom of Portsmouth Harbour and now displayed in the Kent Battle of Britain Museum. Believed to be from the remains of Ju 88, No. 5072 of KG51, it contains a number of parachute shroud lines for when this aircraft was shot down on August 12 only three crew members are believed to have parachuted safely to captivity.

'O dark, dark, dark, amid the blaze of noon!' Samson Agonistes — John Milton

Coffined in the cockpit of their bomber lie three German airmen. The Ju 88 of 3/KG51 'Edelweiss' fell to the guns of RAF fighters fifteen minutes after noon on August 12, ending up in a field at Horse Pasture Farm on the Hampshire-Sussex border. The fourth crew member parachuted to safety. *Below:* Horse Pasture Farm on November 13, 1979. No plaque or marker hallows the spot where three men died in pursuit of a dream of conquest.

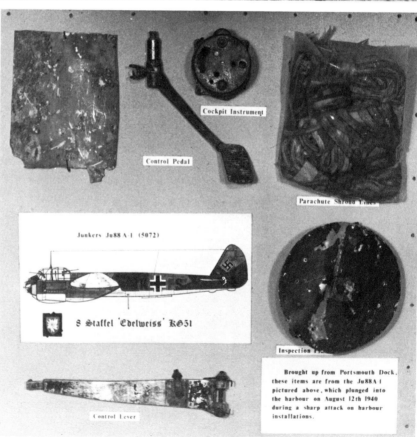

Cockpit Instrument

Control Pedal

Parachute Shroud Lines

Junkers Ju88 A-1 (5072)

8 Staffel 'Edelweiss' KG51

Inspection

Control Lever

Brought up from Portsmouth Dock, these items are from the Ju88A-1 pictured above, which plunged into the harbour on August 12th 1940 during a sharp attack on harbour installations.

III/LG1

Junkers Ju 88A-1. Flying accident at Chateaudun aerodrome. Crashed on take-off due to engine failure. Two NCOs injured. Aircraft 50% damaged.

II/StG2

Junkers Ju 87B. Forced-landed at Lannion aerodrome due to mechanical failure during operational sortie. Crew unhurt. Aircraft 40% damaged.

III/StG77

Junkers Ju 87B. Crashed on landing at Granville following routine domestic flight. Cause not stated. Crew unhurt. Aircraft repairable.

I/ZG2

Messerschmitt Bf 110D. Crashed on landing at St. Aubin following combat mission. Crew unhurt. Aircraft 35% damaged.

Messerschmitt Bf 110C-4. Returned to base damaged following engagement with RAF fighters. Crew unhurt. Aircraft 15% damaged.

Messerschmitt Bf 110C. Failed to return from sortie over the Channel. Exact fate uncertain, but believed crashed in sea. Oblt. Blume rescued. One NCO missing. Aircraft lost.

Above: Displaying three victory tallies on his rudder, Oberleutnant Paul Temme, adjutant of I/JG2 'Richthofen', missed a fourth and Shoreham aerodrome on August 13. Disabled by RAF fighters early in the morning of Adler Tag, he dropped his 'Emil' into a cornfield 'on the other side of the tracks' before surrendering. *Below:* The control tower and hangars of Shoreham Airport from New Salts Farm on September 11, 1979.

2/ZG2

Messerschmitt Bf 110D. Missing following operations over the Channel and combat with RAF fighters. Hptmn. Kulbel (Staffel Kapitan) and Uffz. Budig both killed. Aircraft a write-off.

II/ZG2

Messerschmitt Bf 110D. Returned to St. Aubin with combat damage following action over the Channel. Crew unhurt. Aircraft 20% damaged.

Messerschmitt Bf 110D. Damaged by RAF fighters in combat over the Channel. Returned to base, crew unhurt. Aircraft 40% damaged.

5/ZG2

Messerschmitt Bf 110C-2. Shot down in combat with RAF fighters south-east of Portland. Crashed in the sea. Uffz. Schuler and Obergefr. Evel both missing. Aircraft lost.

Messerschmitt Bf 110. Shot down by RAF fighters during engagement over the Channel off Portland. Uffz. Conrad killed and one NCO missing. Aircraft lost.

III/ZG26

Messerschmitt Bf 110C. Forced-landed at Calais following sortie over the Channel. Crew unhurt. Aircraft 45% damaged.

8/ZG76

Messerschmitt Bf 110C-2. Forced-landed at Caen aerodrome with damage sustained in combat with fighters over the Channel. Uffz. Petersen and one NCO wounded. Aircraft 35% damaged.

Messerschmitt Bf 110C-2. Shot down into the Channel during combat with fighters off Portland. Hptmn. Graf Hoyos (Staffel Kapitan) and Uffz. Krommes both killed. Aircraft lost.

Tuesday, August 13

Wettererkundungs Staffel 51

Heinkel He 111H-3. Crashed at Guyancourt due to instrument failure. One NCO killed. Lt. Stickel and one NCO wounded. Aircraft a write-off.

From Arras to Barham via Eastchurch. The crew of this 'Holzhammer' Dornier were lucky to finish up as POWs after their aircraft was intercepted by RAF fighters over the Thames Estuary on August 13. Broken in half, the crumpled remains of their bomber lie across the Canterbury-Folkestone railway line at Pherbec Bridge, Barham, Kent (Associated Press).

Police Constable 88 of the Kent County Constabulary mounts solitary guard at Barham. Note the Geschwader code U5 (Daily Mail).

3(F)/22

Dornier Do 17P. Crashed in the sea (PQ2970·15 West) during long-range reconnaissance sortie. Cause unknown. Lt. Pannhas killed. Two NCOs missing. Aircraft lost.

3(F)/122

Heinkel He 111. Returned to base damaged by enemy action during sortie over east coast of England. One NCO wounded. Aircraft repairable.

Kampfgruppe z.b.V.9

Junkers Ju 52 (6894). Hit an obstruction on take-off from Erbenheim aerodrome on routine domestic flight. Crew unhurt. Aircraft 70% damaged.

I/JG2

Messerschmitt Bf 109E-1. Forced-landed beside Shoreham aerodrome 7.10 a.m. damaged in combat with RAF fighters. Oblt. Temme (Gruppe Adjutant) captured unhurt. Aircraft lost.

Messerschmitt Bf 109E-4. Belly-landed at advanced landing ground near French coast due to damage sustained in combat with enemy fighters over the Channel. Pilot wounded. Aircraft 80% damaged.

5/JG26

Messerschmitt Bf 109E. Failed to return from combat with fighters over Folkestone. Crashed near Denton, Kent 4.15 p.m. Uffz. Wemhoner captured. Aircraft lost.

II/JG51

Messerschmitt Bf 109E. Returned to base damaged following engagement with RAF fighters. Pilot unhurt. Aircraft damaged but repairable.

9/JG51

Messerschmitt Bf 109E-1. Returned to base severely damaged by enemy fighters in combat over the Channel off Cap Gris-Nez. Uffz. Erdniss wounded. Aircraft 80% damaged.

Messerschmitt Bf 109E-1. Damaged in combat over Calais but returned safely to base. Pilot unhurt. Aircraft 80% damaged.

Messerschmitt Bf 109E-4. Severely damaged in action with British fighters over Coquelles. Returned to base, pilot unhurt. Aircraft 80% damaged.

II/JG53

Messerschmitt Bf 109E-1. Shot down by fighters in combat over the Channel off Weymouth. Oberfw. Trutwin killed. Aircraft lost.

Messerschmitt Bf 109E-1. Shot down by Flying Officer Nowierski of No. 609 Squadron and crashed in the sea off Weymouth 4.15 p.m. Lt. Pfannschmidt captured. Aircraft 9+ lost.

Messerschmitt Bf 109E-4. Crashed into Poole Harbour following attack by Pilot Officer Crook of No. 609 Squadron. Uffz. Hohenseldt captured. Aircraft lost.

Messerschmitt Bf 109E-4. Take-off collision at Guernsey aerodrome. Pilot unhurt. Aircraft 30% damaged.

Messerschmitt Bf 109E-4. Burst tyre on take-off from Dinan aerodrome. Pilot unhurt. Aircraft 60% damaged.

Messerschmitt Bf 109E. Returned to base with slight damage sustained in combat with RAF fighter over Dorchester. Oblt. Schulze wounded. Aircraft repairable.

Stab KG2

Dornier Do 17Z. Shot down in combat with enemy fighters over the Thames Estuary during attack on Eastchurch 8.30 a.m. Crashed at Barham. Oblt. Schlegel, Oblt. Oswald (Staffel Fuehrer) Oberfw. Babbe and Oberfw. Holz all captured. Aircraft U5+ KA a write off.
Officer's forage cap and Luftwaffe gravity knife confiscated from crew of this aircraft donated to the Kent Battle of Britain Museum.

Dornier Do 17Z. Returned to base damaged following action over the Thames Estuary. Two NCOs wounded. Aircraft 35% damaged.

7/KG2

Dornier Do 17Z. Crash-landed at Calais with battle damage. Crew unhurt. Aircraft 20% damaged.

Dornier Do 17Z. Shot down during attack on Eastchurch aerodrome and combat over the Thames Estuary. Three NCOs killed, Oblt. von Groben missing. Aircraft lost.

Dornier Do 17Z. Returned to base damaged in combat with RAF fighters over the Thames Estuary. Crew unhurt. Aircraft 45% damaged.

Dornier Do 17Z. Shot down by No. 111 Squadron during attack on Eastchurch aerodrome. Crashed at Birchington 7.30 a.m. Fw. Dannich, Fw. Schwertfeger, Obergefr. Nitzsche and Gefr. Beck all killed. Aircraft U5+ FR a write-off.

Dornier Do 17Z. Shot down by Hurricanes of No. 111 Squadron in combat over the Thames Estuary during mission to attack Eastchurch. Crashed on mudflats at Seasalter. Oberfw. Langer killed. Oblt. Muller, Oblt. Morch and Fw. Hansgen captured. Aircraft U5+ DS a write-off.
Intact Bramo Fafnir engine recovered from the beach by the Kent Battle of Britain Museum believed to be from this aircraft.

Dornier Do 17Z. Shot down by RAF fighters during attack on Eastchurch aerodrome 6.30 a.m. Forced-landed at Stodmarsh. Uffz. Vogel, Uffz. Arndt. Uffz. Mahringer and Gefr. Bahr all captured. Aircraft U5+ ER a write-off.

8/KG2

Dornier Do 17Z. Returned to base damaged following fighter attack during attack on Eastchurch. One NCO wounded. Aircraft 20% damaged.

Dornier Do 17Z. Hit by fighters during attack on Eastchurch. Returned to base with Lt. Gizinske and one NCO wounded. Aircraft repairable.

Dornier Do 17Z. Attacked by RAF fighters over the Thames Estuary during mission to bomb Eastchurch aerodrome. Returned to base with one NCO wounded. Aircraft 5% damaged.

August 21, 1979 and ex-PC 622J Wilf Nicoll of the Metropolitan Police guards the site. The scene of the crash was located in Greenhills Lane, Barham. The railway had been disused since the Beeching cuts and the tracks now no longer exist. The bridge was totally demolished some years ago, the only remains being a few brick outcrops amongst the dense undergrowth.

'... they will fall, one by one, an unpitied sacrifice in a contemptible struggle'. Edmund Burke, Irish statesman.

Dornier Do 17Z. Returned to base with one NCO wounded following action over the Thames Estuary. Aircraft repairable.

III/KG27

Heinkel He 111P. Shot down into the Channel north of Cherbourg by fighters. Three NCOs killed. Pilot rescued by Seenotdienst. Aircraft lost.

Stab I/KG54

Junkers Ju 88A-1. Crashed and exploded in Phillis Wood, Treyford 9.30 a.m. following attack by fighters during sortie to Farnborough. Oblt. Ostermann killed. Uffz. Rossler, Uffz. Seitz and Obergefr. Brieger captured. Aircraft B3+ DB a write-off.
Scattered surface wreckage collected by the Southern Area Wartime Aircraft Preservation Society.

I/KG54

Junkers Ju 88A-1. Shot down during sortie over southern England by RAF fighters. Oblt. Erdmann killed. Oblt. Meyer and two NCOs missing. Aircraft a write-off.

Junkers Ju 88A-1. Belly-landed at Evreux aerodrome due to battle damage. Crew unhurt. Aircraft 40% damaged.

Junkers Ju 88A-1. Forced-landed following fighter attacks over southern England. Crew unhurt. Aircraft damaged but repairable.

Junkers Ju 88A-1. Belly-landed back in France following fighter attack over the Channel. Crew unhurt. Aircraft damaged but repairable.

Junkers Ju 88A. Hit by fighter attack during sortie over Farnborough. Returned to base with one NCO wounded. Aircraft repairable.

Another Dornier of the 'Holzhammer' Geschwader which failed to return to its base at Cambrai after the Eastchurch raid on August 13. All four crew members were captured unhurt after a belly-landing at Paxton Farm, Stodmarsh, Kent.

Junkers Ju 88A-1. Returned to base damaged following fighter attack over southern England. One NCO wounded. Aircraft 5% damaged.
Junkers Ju 88A. Believed hit by AA fire over Guildford during sortie over southern England. Returned to base one NCO wounded. Aircraft repairable.

Stab II/KG54

Junkers Ju 88A-1. Shot down by RAF fighters over Odiham 6.30 a.m. Crashed and exploded in Swanbourne Lake, Arundel. Hptmn. Strauch and Fw. Bickel killed. Oblt. Rosse and Uffz. Scholz missing. Aircraft a write-off.

II/KG54

Junkers Ju 88A-1. Shot down by fighters during sortie over southern England. Two NCOs killed. Oblt. Freudebeul and one NCO missing. Aircraft a write-off.

Junkers Ju 88A-1. Belly-landed at Evreux aerodrome with damage sustained in fighter attack over southern England. Crew unhurt. Aircraft 40% damaged.

Junkers Ju 88A-1. Returned to France damaged by RAF fighter attacks. Belly-landed on Evreux aerodrome. Crew unhurt. Aircraft 40% damaged.

Junkers Ju 88A. Attacked by British fighters during sortie over southern England. Returned to base three NCOs wounded — one died later. Aircraft repairable.

Junkers Ju 88A-1. Damaged by fighters during operations over England but returned safely to base. One NCO wounded. Aircraft 5% damaged.

Junkers Ju 88A-1. Returned to base damaged and one NCO wounded in fighter attack over southern England. Aircraft 5% damaged.

I/KG77

Junkers Ju 88A-1. Crash-landed at Regensburg during local flight. Cause not stated. Crew unhurt. Aircraft 48% damaged.

Stab KGr.100

Heinkel He 111H-1. Forced-landed at Quimpes during operational sortie. Cause not stated. Crew unhurt. Aircraft 40% damaged.

I/LG1

Junkers Ju 88A-1. Forced-landed at Cherbourg aerodrome with damage from fighter attack. Crew unhurt. Aircraft 70% damaged.

II/LG1

Junkers Ju 88A-1. Tyre burst on take-off from Orleans-Bricy. Crew unhurt. Aircraft 50% damaged.

Junkers Ju 88A. Crashed and burned out at Orleans-Bricy aerodrome due to take-off accident. Four NCOs killed. Aircraft a write-off.

Looking north-west across the trees bordering the Great Stour river towards the A28 Canterbury-Margate road on August 21, 1979 with only the puttering of a tractor to disturb the rural scene.

III/LG1

Junkers Ju 88A-1. Failed to return from sortie over southern England. Briefed to attack Andover. One NCO killed, three missing. Aircraft a write-off.

8/LG1

Junkers Ju 88A-1. Shot down during attack on Andover. Lt. zur See Brinkbaeumer (of KustflGr. 806), Gefr. Roger and Gefr. Dietl killed. Hptmn. Scheuplein (Staffel-fuehrer) missing. Aircraft a write-off.

V/LG1

Messerschmitt Bf 110D. Forced-landed at Conde-sur-Ifa aerodrome damaged in attack by RAF fighters. Fw. Fleuer and one NCO wounded. Aircraft 50% damaged.

Messerschmitt Bf 110D. Damaged by RAF fighter attack. Forced-landed at Cherbourg aerodrome, crew unhurt. Aircraft a write-off.

Messerschmitt Bf 110. Returned to base with one NCO wounded following combat with RAF fighters. Aircraft repairable.

Messerschmitt Bf 110D. Belly-landed at Recquancourt aerodrome following fighter attack. Crew unhurt. Aircraft 60% damaged.

Messerschmitt Bf 110D. Returned to Recquancourt damaged in attack by RAF fighters over the Channel. Crew unhurt. Aircraft 10% damaged.

13/LG1

Messerschmitt Bf 110D. Shot down by fighters two miles west of Bournemouth and crashed into the Channel. Lt. Beck killed, Uffz. Hoyer missing. Aircraft lost.

Messerschmitt Bf 110D. Shot down in combat with fighters and crashed in the Channel two miles west of Bournemouth 11.50 a.m. Uffz. Lammel killed, Fw. Datz rescued by British and POW. Aircraft lost.

14/LG1

Messerschmitt Bf 110C-4. Believed shot down in combat with British fighters over the Channel west of Bournemouth. Lt. Werner and Gefr. Klemm missing. Aircraft lost.

15/LG1

Messerschmitt Bf 110D. Shot down over Lulworth during combat with enemy fighters 12.35 p.m. Uffz. Schuemichen and Obergefr. Giglhuber both baled out and captured. Aircraft L1+FZ lost.

Believed to be the aircraft recovered at Swalland Farm, Kimmeridge, Dorset in January 1960. Authorities assisted by celebrated enthusiasts Dennis Knight and Peter Foote.

Messerschmitt Bf 110D. Crashed in the sea west of Bournemouth during combat with enemy fighters. Oberfw. Wagner and Uffz. Heldt missing. Aircraft lost.

II (Schlacht)/LG2

Messerschmitt Bf 109E-7. Wing surface collapsed during dive-bombing practice over Rohrau weapons range. Oblt. Claus killed. Aircraft a write-off.

7/LG2

Messerschmitt Bf 110C-5. Belly-landed at Wissant following engine failure during operational sortie. Crew unhurt. Aircraft 40% damaged.

II/StG2

Junkers Ju 87B. Shot down into the Channel by RAF fighter. Crew picked up by German E-boat. Aircraft lost.

'How fast has brother followed brother
From sunshine to the sunless land.'   William Wordsworth.
A few pitiful pieces of twisted metal are all that remain of a Ju 88 of KG54, the 'Death's Head' Geschwader that crashed into Swanbourne Lake and exploded beneath the ancient walls of Arundel Castle. Two of its crew were carried with it one of whom had baled out, his parachute becoming entangled in the tail. The pilot, August Wilhelm Strauch, also baled out but was found the following day impaled through the stomach by a broken tree branch. He died in hospital (Daily Mirror).

Picnickers and lovers frequent the sunny banks of Swanbourne Lake on September 11, 1979 unaware of its connections with the distant summer of 1940. The site of the impact is in the foreground.

Junkers Ju 87B. Caught fire in mid-air during operational sortie. Cause unknown. Crashed near Guernsey. Two NCOs killed. Aircraft a write-off.

5/StG2

Junkers Ju 87B. Failed to return from operational sortie over the Channel. Crashed in the sea. Fw. Ott and Uffz. Gobel both killed. Aircraft lost.

Junkers Ju 87B. Shot down during mission over the Channel. Crashed and burned out at Rodden, Portisham. Fw. Lindenschmid and Gefr. Eisold both killed. Aircraft lost.

Junkers Ju 87B. Missing following operations over the Channel and combat with enemy fighters. Oberfw. Leesch missing. Fw. Schulz captured. Aircraft lost.

Junkers Ju 87B. Shot down by fighters in combat over the Channel. Oberfw. Haack, Uffz. Haselmayer both killed. Aircraft a write-off.

III/StG77

Junkers Ju 87B. Severely damaged in taxi-ing accident at Argentan. Crew unhurt. Aircraft 70% damaged.

Junkers Ju 87B. Taxied into flak emplacement at Tonneville aerodrome. Crew unhurt. Aircraft 50% damaged.

I/ZG2

Messerschmitt Bf 110C-4. Forced-landed at Le Havre with combat damage. Crew unhurt. Aircraft repairable.

Messerschmitt Bf 110C-4. Returned to base damaged in combat with RAF fighters. Uffz. Muller wounded. Aircraft repairable.

Messerschmitt Bf 110C-4. Attacked by RAF fighter in combat over the Channel. Returned to base with two NCOs wounded. Aircraft repairable.

I/ZG2

Messerschmitt Bf 110C-4. Shot down by fighters during escort sortie over Winchester. Crashed and burned out at North Baddesley 4.00 p.m. Uffz. Labusch killed. Lt. Munchmeyer captured. Aircraft a write-off.
Major recovery by Malcolm Petitt retrieved both engines and other components.

II/ZG2

Messerschmitt Bf 110. Returned to base with damage following fighter attack. One NCO wounded. Aircraft repairable.

I/ZG26

Messerschmitt Bf 110C-4. Forced-landed at Calais, damaged by enemy action during sortie over southern England. Crew unhurt. Aircraft 25% damaged.

Messerschmitt Bf 110C. Crashed at St. Omer on operational sortie. Exact cause not stated. Lt. Meisel and one NCO both unhurt. Aircraft a write-off.

2/ZG26

Messerschmitt Bf 110D. Damaged in forced-landing at Mollenbercel, cause not stated. Crew unhurt. Aircraft damaged but repairable.

3/ZG26

Messerschmitt Bf 110C-4. Damaged at St. Omer in crash of I/ZG26 aircraft. No personnel casualties. Aircraft 30% damaged.

Messerschmitt Bf 110C. Shot down by Flying Officer Weaver of No. 56 Squadron in combat over the Thames Estuary. Crashed at Warden Bay, Sheppey 4.05 p.m. Oblt. Fuchs and Uffz. Ebben both killed. Aircraft a write-off.
Site excavated by the Kent Battle of Britain Museum which unearthed an undercarriage leg, cannon firing mechanism, oxygen regulator, oxygen bottles, self-sealing fuel tank, first-aid kit, various makers' labels and perspex cockpit side panel bearing red-painted, angle of dive indicator. Relics from this machine also held by London Air Museum. Steve Vizard also has parts from the first-aid kit, cannon-firing bottles and other relics.

7/ZG26

Messerschmitt Bf 110. Forced-landed at Amsterdam during operational sortie, cause not stated. One NCO injured. Aircraft damaged but repairable.

8/ZG26

Messerschmitt Bf 110C. Crash-landed at Vlissingen following operational sortie. Crew unhurt. Aircraft a write-off.

8/ZG76

Messerschmitt Bf 110C. Failed to return from mission over the Channel off Portland. Uffz. Schindler killed and one NCO missing. Aircraft lost.

These relics from the crash site of a Bf 110C Zerstorer of 3/ZG26 'Horst Wessel' were found by Steve Vizard littering the surface of the ground at Warden Bay, Sheppey after a major recovery by the Kent Battle of Britain Museum.

9/ZG76

Messerschmitt Bf 110C. Missing following sortie over the Channel off Portland. Believed shot down into the sea. Uffz. Kuhlmann, Obergefr. Muller both missing. Aircraft a write-off.

Wednesday, August 14

2/Erprobungs Gruppe 210

Messerschmitt Bf 110D. Shot down by AA fire during attack on Manston. Crashed and burned out at Manston 12.10 p.m. Lt. Brinkmann and one NCO killed. Aircraft S9+ NK a write-off.

Messerschmitt Bf 110D. Collided with another aircraft from Erp.Gr. 210 crippled by flak and crashed at Manston 12.10 p.m. Uffz. Steding killed, Gefr. Schank baled out wounded and captured. Aircraft S9+ MK a write-off.

6/JG3

Messerschmitt Bf 109E-1. Failed to return from combat mission over Dover. Oberfw. Dabusga missing. Aircraft a write-off.

8/JG3

Messerschmitt Bf 109E. Shot down during operations over the Channel and crashed in the sea. Uffz. Flebbe killed. Aircraft a write-off.

1/JG26

Messerschmitt Bf 109E-1 (4827). Shot down by RAF fighters in combat over Dover. Crashed at Coldred 12.45 p.m. Uffz. Kemen wounded POW. Aircraft 8+ a write-off.
Complete tail section, top-decking from aft of cockpit still showing camouflage paint and machine gun trough from engine cowling recovered from nearby rubbish tip by the Kent Battle of Britain Museum.

4/JG52

Messerschmitt Bf 109E-1. Failed to return from combat sortie over the Canterbury area. Oberfw. Ruttinger missing. Aircraft a write-off.

Messerschmitt Bf 109E-1. Briefed for free-lance over the Canterbury area but failed to return to base. Oberfw. Weiss missing. Aircraft a write-off.

5/JG52

Messerschmitt Bf 109E-3. Missing following operations over Canterbury. Exact fate unknown. Oberfw. Potthast missing. Aircraft a write-off.

6/JG52

Messerschmitt Bf 109E-1. Take-off accident at Peuplingues. Pilot unhurt. Aircraft 60% damaged.

3/JG54

Messerschmitt Bf 109E-4. Damaged in taxiing accident at Campagne aerodrome. Pilot unhurt. Aircraft repairable.

I/KG27

Heinkel He 111P. Crash-landed at Villedieur following engine fire on operational sortie. Two NCOs injured. Aircraft a write-off.

Heinkel He 111P. Returned to base following RAF fighter attack. One NCO wounded. Aircraft repairable.

III/KG27

Heinkel He 111P. Failed to return from operational sortie north-east of Exeter. Shot down by fighters and crashed at Charterhouse near Cheddar 6.00 p.m. Oblt. Ohlenschlager, Fw. Jug, Uffz. Sulzbach, Uffz. Blumenthal and Gefr. Kupsch all captured. Aircraft 1G+ NT a write-off.

Heinkel He 111P. Missing following operations over south-west England and combat with enemy fighters. Hptmn. Riedel, Uffz. Witt and Gefr. Wolf missing. Uffz. Dolata killed. Aircraft a write-off.

Heinkel He 111P. Shot down by British fighters during sortie over south-west England. Crashed on Canns Farm near Puriton 6.05 p.m. Lt. Uhland, Uffz. Flick, Uffz. Krenn, Obergefr. Ramstetter and Gefr. Rother all baled out and captured. Aircraft 1G+ OT a write-off.

Site investigated by the South West Aircraft Recovery Group 1977 who report a modern cottage built over the exact point of impact. Radio dial and rudder activator unit presented to the group by the resident land owner currently held by the Pennine Aviation Museum.

8/KG27

Heinkel He 111P (2624). Failed to return from reconnaissance sortie north-east of Exeter and engagement with fighters. Crashed on Border House Farm near Chester 9.00 p.m. Oblt. Wiesemann, Fw. Rodder, Uffz. Schaum, Uffz. Ullmann and Uffz. Kochy all captured. Aircraft 1G+ FS a write-off.

Site excavated by the Warplane Wreck Investigation Group and some charred and shattered components from the starboard engine unearthed. Some relics subsequently presented to the surviving pilot who was contacted in Hagen, West Germany.

Heinkel He 111P. Shot down by fighters during weather-reconnaissance sortie north-east of Exeter. Fw. Knoblich and Uffz. Schrage killed. Fw. Dubral, Fw. Gietz both captured. Fw. Wiesemeier missing. Aircraft 1G+ CS a write-off.

III/KG53

Heinkel He 111H-4. Forced-landed at Bouillon following engine failure on local flight. No crew casualties. Aircraft 50% damaged.

Heinkel He 111H-4. Damaged in emergency forced-landing at Bouillon due to engine failure during routine domestic flight. No casualties. Aircraft 40% damaged.

II/KG54

Junkers Ju 88A-1. Flew into the ground near Wesel during local flight due to poor weather and deteriorating visibility. Oblt. Gerling and three NCOs killed. Aircraft a write-off.

Roaring out of the evening sky over Cheshire on August 14, this crippled Heinkel of 8/KG27, the 'Boelcke' Geschwader, crash-landed in a field outside Chester and slithered to a halt only feet away from Border House Farm. The crew attempted to set fire to their bomber and partially succeeded before their arrest by the farmer Mr. Anderton, a home guardsman, and his friend Mr. Jones, the butcher (shades of Dad's Army!). *Above:* Mr. Anderton (with .410 shotgun) and Mr. Jones, behind the leading edge of the Heinkel's port wing, proudly survey their extremely battered looking capture. The remains of the ventral gun cupola — 'Das Sterbebett' or death bed as it was known in certain Heinkel units — lie scattered in the foreground, wiped from beneath the fuselage with the 7.92mm MG15 still attached to its mount and a number of ammunition saddle drums. The square stone near the port wing-tip marks the border between the counties of Cheshire and Flint and gives the farm its name (Associated Press). *Below:* The border now separates Cheshire from the new county of Clwyd.

Left: **True to the traditions of his service, a young RAF aircraftman mounts unswerving guard over the gutted hulk despite the distraction of the comely, culotted Cheshire maiden probing the intestines of its port engine and who is obviously a technical** expert on Daimler-Benz aero engines (Daily Post). *Right:* **The Warplane Wreck Investigation Group examined the site and recovered pieces from the starboard engine and presented parts to the pilot who was traced now living in Hagen.**

Stab Staffel KG55

Heinkel He 111P (2898) Shot down at Eastdene 6.30 p.m. during operational sortie over England. Oberst. Stoeckl (Geschwader Kommodore), Oberst. Frank (Ch.d.St.Ig VIII), and Oblt. Brossler all killed. Fw. Grimmstein and Fw. Thiel captured wounded. Aircraft G1+ AA a write-off.

II/KG55

Heinkel He 111P. Crashed at Merzhausen aerodrome following loss of control due to failure of one engine. Lt. Wandfrei, Tr. Arzt Dr. Frhr. von Liebenstein and one NCO killed. Two NCOs injured. Aircraft a write-off.

2/KGr.100

Heinkel He 111H. Returned to base minus one crew member who baled out over Balcombe 4.30 a.m. following sortie over Cheltenham. Uffz. Dorner captured. Aircraft undamaged.

I/LG1

Junkers Ju 88A-1. Shot down following attack on Middle Wallop. Exploded on Plaitford Common, Romsey 6.00 p.m. Oblt. Heinrici, Gefr. Stark missing. Gefr. Ahrens killed. Gefr. Sauer captured. Aircraft a write-off.

Junkers Ju 88A-1. Failed to return from sortie over southern England and combat with enemy fighters. Lt. Stahl and two NCOs missing. One NCO killed. Aircraft a write-off.

10/LG1

Junkers Ju 87B. Shot down in combat with fighters over Folkestone. Oblt. Gramling and one NCO missing. Aircraft lost.

Junkers Ju 87B. Returned to base damaged following attack by RAF fighters over Folkestone. One NCO wounded. Aircraft 20% damaged.

2/ZG26

Messerschmitt Bf 110C-4. Forced-landed at St. Omer with combat damage. Crew unhurt. Aircraft 10% damaged.

Above: **Like a monument to its own dead, the starboard tailplane of a Heinkel 115 rears to the sky from a Scottish cornfield. Blinded by searchlights during an operational sortie along the east Scottish coast, the pilot of this twin-engined floatplane flew into high ground on the farm of Faldiehill, near the village of Arbirlot, Angus. With the disintegration that followed, it was strewn across two fields and lay undiscovered until a farm worker walking to work discovered the wreckage and the bodies of the crew. Only one out of the three was still alive — barely. After calling for aid at the farm, a gate was removed from a field and the living and the dead were reverently carried on it to a main road where transport conveyed them to hospital in Arbroath. There, the third man died. Detachments from the Fleet Air Arm at HMS 'Condor' and the Royal Air Force were present when they were buried with full military honours at Arbroath East Cemetery (Dundee Courier).** *Below:* **The fallow field of Faldiehill in November 1979 with the farm high on the left skyline. Mr. George Shepherd, editor of the Arbroath Herald, has the altimeter from this Heinkel on his desk.**

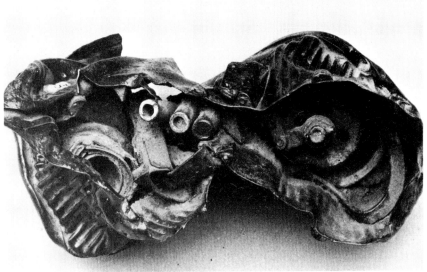

Left: **A smiling Hauptmann Rubensdoerffer pictured with his men of Erprobungs Gruppe 210 at Denain, France in the summer of 1940 (Tony Graves).** *Above:* **This battered saddle-drum magazine was all that Steve Vizard could find of Rubensdoerffer's Bf 110D which crashed at Bletchinglye Farm on August 15. (Note: Rubensdoerffer's crewman is now confirmed by Peter Cornwell as Obergefreiter Kretzer not Richard Ehekercher as stated on page 55 — Ed.)

Thursday, August 15

Seenotflugkdo. 4

Heinkel He 59. Shot down into the North Sea (PQ6997) by Lockhead Hudson during search and rescue mission. Lt. zur See Borner killed, one NCO wounded. Aircraft lost.

1/196

Arado Ar 196. Shot down by fighters during air-sea rescue mission over the Channel. Lt. zur See Schlenker killed, Hptmn. Wiegmink wounded. Aircraft lost.

1/506

Heinkel He 115C. Failed to return from operational sortie over Montrose. Dazzled by searchlights and flew into ground at Faldiehill, Panmure Estate, Arbroath 4.04 a.m. Oberfw. Hofert and Uffz. Schroers both killed. Lt. zur See Tonne wounded. Aircraft S4+ BH a write-off.

3(F)/31

Dornier Do 17P. Failed to return from long-range reconnaissance sortie. Cause of loss unknown. Oblt. Horn, Lt. Raasch and one NCO missing. Aircraft lost.

5(F)/122

Junkers Ju 88A-1. Missing following operational sortie over Rochester area. Exact circumstances unknown. Four NCOs killed. Aircraft a write-off.

Stab/Erprobungs Gruppe 210

Messerschmitt Bf 110D. Shot down by RAF fighters during attack on Croydon aerodrome 7.00 p.m. Crashed in flames on Bletchinglye Farm, Rotherfield. Hptmn. Rubensdoerffer (Gruppe Kommandeur) and Obergefr. Kretzer both killed. Aircraft S9+ AB a write-off.
This crash site is often confused with a later Dornier incident and of the various items recovered by groups from the area, it is believed that only Steve Vizard's are actually from S9 AB.

Messerschmitt Bf 110D (3374). Shot down by Sergeant Dymond of No. 111 Squadron and Sergeant Pearce of No. 32 Squadron during attack on Croydon. Crashed on Nutfield aerodrome 7.15 p.m. Oblt. Fiedeler (Gruppe Adjutant) killed. Uffz. Werner captured. Aircraft S9+ BB a write-off.

Messerschmitt Bf 110D (3339). Forced-landed on School Farm, Hooe 6.50 p.m. after attack by Hurricane during bombing of Croydon aerodrome. Lt. Koch (Gruppe TO) and Uffz. Kahl captured. Aircraft S9+ CB a write-off.

1/Erprobungs Gruppe 210

Messerschmitt Bf 110C-6. Shot down by Flight Lieutenant Connors and Sergeant Wallace of No. 111 Squadron during attack on Croydon 7.10 p.m. Crashed at Broadbridge Farm, Horley. Lt. Beudel and Obgefr. Jordan both killed. Aircraft S9+ TH a write-off.

2/Erprobungs Gruppe 210

Messerschmitt Bf 110C-6. Shot down by Squadron Leader Worrall and Flight Lieutenant Crossley of No. 32 Squadron and crashed at Ightham 7.00 p.m. Lt. Ortner baled out wounded, Obergefr. Lohmann killed. Aircraft a write-off.
Representative pieces in the Steve Vizard collection.

Messerschmitt Bf 110D (3341). Shot down during attack on Croydon. Crashed at Hawkhurst 7.10 p.m. Oblt. Habisch and Uffz. Elfner both captured. Aircraft S9+ CK a write-off.

3/Erprobungs Gruppe 210

Messerschmitt Bf 109E-4. Shot down at Frant 7.10 p.m. during escort mission for Bf 110s attacking Croydon. Lt. Marx (Staffel Kapitan) baled out and captured. Aircraft 3+ a write-off.
Site investigated by the London Air Museum and surface wreckage recovered. Relics also displayed in the Steve Vizard collection.

I/JG3

Messerschmitt Bf 109E-4. Landed at Colombert damaged following combat with RAF fighters. Pilot unhurt. Aircraft 25% damaged.

Stab I/JG51

Messerschmitt Bf 109E-4. Crashed at Pihen following combat with enemy fighters. Hptmn. Brustellin (Gruppe Kommandeur) wounded. Aircraft a write-off.

5/JG51

Messerschmitt Bf 109E-4. Crashed in sea off Margate during fighter combat 3.30 p.m. Fw. Stiegenberger rescued by lifeboat and captured. Aircraft 2+ lost.

6/JG51

Messerschmitt Bf 109E-3. Landed at Wissant with battle damage. Fw. Haase wounded. Aircraft 15% damaged.

II/JG53

Messerschmitt Bf 109E-1. Belly-landed at Dinan aerodrome during routine local flight following mechanical failure. Pilot unhurt. Aircraft 60% damaged.

2/JG54

Messerschmitt Bf 109E-4. Crashed at Courtrai following combat with RAF fighters. Fw. Schnaar killed. Aircraft a write-off.

Messerschmitt Bf 109E-4. Shot down in combat with enemy fighters over the Channel. Lt. Gerlach missing. Aircraft a write-off.

5/JG54

Messerschmitt Bf 109E. Shot down in combat with enemy aircraft over Dover and ditched in the Channel. Uffz. Hautkappe missing. Aircraft lost.

Above: 'You've had your chips mate!' This Junkers Ju 88 of Stab II/LG1 ended its days in a field of potatoes and rhubarb at The Jumps, West Tisted in Hampshire. Despite its mangled condition, the crew survived unhurt. Souvenir hunters have already cut the Swastika from the tail (Sport and General). *Below:* The aircraft came down on Oakleigh Farm where Fred Ings gave Oberleutnant Suin de Boutemard and his crew a cup of tea before they were taken into captivity.

9/JG54

Messerschmitt Bf 109E-4. Shot down during operational sortie over southern outskirts of London. Crashed Bullwood Farm, Hartley, Cranbrook 7.30 p.m. Uffz. Niedermaier killed. Aircraft a write-off.

Site investigated by the Kent Battle of Britain Museum and surface wreckage discovered.

1/JG77

Messerschmitt Bf 109E-1. Crashed during ferry flight from Jever. Cause unknown. Crashed at Wyk auf Foehr. Oblt Hauck killed. Aircraft a write-off.

Stab I/KG3

Dornier Do 17Z-3. Forced-landed at Wissant due to combat damage. Oberst. Frhr. von Wechmar (Gruppe Kommandeur) and Oblt. Koehnke wounded. Aircraft 60% damaged.

2/KG3

Dornier Do 17Z-2. Returned to base damaged following fighter attack over Dover. One NCO wounded. Aircraft repairable.

6/KG3

Dornier Do 17Z-2. Shot down during operations over the Thames Estuary. Crashed in the sea between Deal and Ramsgate 4.00 p.m. Lt. Walter, Fw. Schauer, Uffz. Kirchuebel and Uffz. Pieronczyk captured. Aircraft a write-off.

Dornier Do 17Z-2. Shot down one mile east of Reculver 3.30 p.m. during sortie over the Thames Estuary and combat with enemy fighters. Lt. Kringler, Uffz. Depenheuer and Gefr. Rohleder killed. Obergefr. Duda captured. Aircraft 5K+LP a write-off.

Dornier Do 17Z-2. Returned to base damaged by flak and fighter attack during operations over the Thames Estuary. One NCO wounded. Aircraft repairable.

Dornier Do 17Z-2. Hit by AA fire and attacked by fighters during sortie over the Thames Estuary. Returned to base two NCOs wounded. Aircraft repairable.

Dornier Do 17Z-3. Returned to base severely damaged following action over the Thames Estuary. Crew unhurt. Aircraft 60% damaged.

Dornier Do 17Z-2. Damaged in combat over the Thames Estuary. Returned to base one NCO wounded. Aircraft repairable.

1/KG26

Heinkel He 111H-4. Shot down into the sea off Cresswell Bay by fighters during sortie over Middlesbrough 2.00 p.m. Oblt. Koch, Uffz. Zimmermann, Gefr. Kulick, Gefr. Machglett, and Flgr. Henrichsen all captured. Aircraft a write-off.

8/KG26

Heinkel He 111H-4. Shot down by fighters on sortie to attack Dishforth. Oblt. von Lubke and two NCOs killed. One NCO missing. Aircraft a write-off.

Heinkel He 111H-4. Failed to return from operational sortie to attack Dishforth. Believed shot down into the sea by fighters. Oblt. Riedel and three NCOs missing. Aircraft a write-off.

Heinkel He 111H-4. Shot down during mission to attack Dishforth. Oblt. von Besser and four NCOs missing. Aircraft a write-off.

Heinkel He 111H-4. Briefed to attack Dishforth. Failed to return following fighter attack off English east coast. One NCO killed. Lt. Burk and three NCOs missing. Aircraft a write-off.

Heinkel He 111H-4. Shot down by fighters during sortie to attack Dishforth aerodrome. Crashed in sea thirty miles off Middlesbrough 2.00 p.m. Lt. Renner, Fw. Baldauf, Obergefr. Roessiger, Gefr. Lorenz and Uffz. Schumann captured. Aircraft 1H+FS a write-off.

9/KG26

Heinkel He 111H-4. Failed to return from operational sortie to attack Dishforth. Five NCOs killed. Aircraft a write-off.

Heinkel He 111. Shot down by fighters during mission to attack Dishforth. Crashed in North Sea. One NCO killed. Rest of crew rescued by German naval vessel, one NCO being wounded. Aircraft lost.

I/KG30

Junkers Ju 88C. Failed to return from sortie to bomb Driffield and interception by RAF fighters 1.30 p.m. Crew missing. Aircraft a write-off.

Junkers Ju 88C. Missing from combat sortie, cause not notified. Crew casualties not reported. Aircraft a write-off.

3/KG30

Junkers Ju 88A-5. Crashed near Bridlington 1.25 p.m. after being brought down during operational sortie over Flamborough Head. Uffz. von Lorentz, Uffz. Kenski, Obergefr. Trumann and Gefr. Goebel all captured. Aircraft 4D+KL a write-off.

II/KG30

Junkers Ju 88A-5. Belly-landed at Oldenburg aerodrome due to combat damage. Crew unhurt. Aircraft 40% damaged.

4/KG30

Junkers Ju 88A. Shot down during operational sortie to bomb Driffield. Crashed and burned out near Hunmanby 1.30 p.m. Fw. Pohl and Uffz. Kursch killed. Fw. Bihr and Uffz. Neumayer missing. Aircraft a write-off.

III/KG30

Junkers Ju 88C. Shot down during engagement with British fighters off English east coast. Four NCOs killed. Aircraft a write-off.

Junkers Ju 88C. Crash-landed in Holland with one NCO wounded following combat with RAF fighters over east coast of England. Aircraft damaged but repairable.

Junkers Ju 88C. Crashed on landing at Aalborg-West following operations over east coast of England and attack by RAF fighters. Crew unhurt. Aircraft 75% damaged.

7/KG30

Junkers Ju 88C. Shot down during sortie to attack aerodrome at Driffield. Forced-landed near Hornby 1.30 p.m. Fw. Henneske killed. Oblt. Bachmann, Uffz. Evers and Flgr. Walther all captured. Aircraft 4D+DR a write-off.

Junkers Ju 88C. Briefed to attack Driffield. Shot down by fighters. Lt. Riede killed. Uffz. Hartwich, Uffz. Panhuysen and Flgr. Ulbrich missing. Aircraft a write-off.

III/KG51

Junkers Ju 88A-1. Damaged in take-off accident at Etampes on routine domestic flight. Crew unhurt. Aircraft 15% damaged.

II/KG53

Heinkel He 111H-2. Ditched in the Channel following RAF fighter attack. Two NCOs killed and three wounded. Aircraft lost.

9 Erganzungs Staffel/KG54

Junkers Ju 88. Crash-landed at Fassberg aerodrome, cause not stated, on domestic flight. Crew unhurt. Aircraft a write-off.

2/KG55

Heinkel He 111H. Forced-landed at Carolles, near Granville due to engine failure. Uffz. Frey killed. Lt. Zobel and Fw. Marx injured. Aircraft G1+CK 70% damaged.

Stab KG76

Dornier Do17Z. Crashed on landing at Colonie, cause not stated. Non-operational mission. Crew unhurt. Aircraft 30% damaged.

Dornier Do 17Z. Returned to base damaged following attack by fighters over Redhill. Oblt. Lommatsch severely wounded (died 7.9.40) Fw. Winterhalder wounded. Aircraft repairable.

III/KG77

Junkers Ju 88A. Forced-landed on Regensburg aerodrome during routine domestic flight. Cause not stated. Crew unhurt. Aircraft repairable.

1/KGr100

Heinkel He 111H-1. Failed to return from operational sortie. Exact cause unknown. Lt. Lochbrunner and three NCOs missing. Aircraft a write-off.

3/KGr100

Heinkel He 111H-3. Forced-landed St. Brieux following operational sortie. Crew unhurt. Aircraft a write-off.

Heinkel He 111H-1. Crashed attempting landing at Bordeaux after operational sortie. Cause not stated. Crew unhurt. Aircraft a write-off.

1/KGr.z.b.V.172

Junkers Ju 52 (5121). Damaged in taxi-ing accident at Westerland. No personnel casualties. Aircraft 10% damaged.

I/LG1

Junkers Ju 88A-1. Shot down by RAF fighters in combat over the Channel. Crew rescued unhurt by Seenotdienst. Aircraft lost.

Stab II/LG1

Junkers Ju 88A. Shot down by Flight Lieutenant Hope and Sergeant Guy of No. 601 Squadron. Crash-landed at The Jumps, West Tisted 6.10 p.m. Oblt. Suin de Boutemard and Uffz. Weigang captured together with Oberfw. Grund and Fw. Luder who baled out. Aircraft L1+SC a write-off.

II/LG1

Junkers Ju 88A. Shot down by RAF fighters in engagement over southern England. Believed crashed at The Jumps, West Tisted 6.05 p.m. Four NCOs killed. Aircraft a write-off.
Site examined by the Southern Area Wartime Aircraft Preservation Society. Remains of both engines together with propeller blades, undercarriage and unexploded bomb found. Explosives rendered harmless by the authorities. Nothing found to establish identity.

Junkers Ju 88A. Crashed in Channel following engagement with fighters over southern England. Two NCOs wounded. Crew rescued by Seenotdienst. Aircraft lost.

Junkers Ju 88A-1. Shot down by RAF fighters during operations over the Channel. One NCO killed. Lt. zur See Nierlin (of Kusten Fl Gr. 806) and two NCOs missing. Aircraft lost.

4/LG1

Junkers Ju 88A. Shot down and crashed on Great Ham Farm, Earnley 6.30 p.m. during operations over south-east England. Uffz. Rimek killed. Uffz. Dieter, Uffz. Rezeppa and Gefr. Hohbom captured. Aircraft L1+FM a write-off.

Junkers Ju 88A. Shot down by No. 43 Squadron Hurricanes during operational sortie over south-east England. Crashed at Priors Leaze, Breach, Southbourne 6.30 p.m. Oblt. Moller (Kp.Ch.4.Fb.K.) and Gefr. Anders both killed. Oberfw. Richter, Fw. Dittmann both captured. Aircraft a write-off.

Junkers Ju 88A. Shot down by Flying Officer Clyde and Flying Officer Doulton of No. 601 Squadron. Crashed Twyford 6.00 p.m. Uffz. Poggensee, Uffz. Kusche, Uffz. Burkhardt and Uffz. Mueller captured. Aircraft L1+BM a write-off.

10/LG1

Junkers Ju 87B. Shot down by fighters during operations over the Channel near Folkestone 5.30 p.m. One NCO killed. Hptmn. Muenchenhagen baled out and captured wounded, Oberfw. Heyse killed. Aircraft lost.

Junkers Ju 87B. Harried by fighters and flew into HT cables at Morehall, Folkestone 5.30 p.m. Uffz. Weber and Uffz. Kraus killed. Aircraft a write-off.
Relics imbedded in attic timbers removed by Halstead War Museum.

14/LG1

Messerschmitt Bf 110C. Belly-landed at Cherbourg-West aerodrome with damage sustained in fighter attack. Fw. Jecke wounded. Aircraft 60% damaged.

The inherent dangers of aircraft archaeology are one of the reasons that the Air Force Board Secretariat issued new notes of guidance to groups in February 1980. This is Peter Dimond of the Southern Area Wartime Aircraft Preservation Society with the bomb unearthed in the crash site of the Ju 88 excavated at The Jumps, West Tisted. This site should not be confused with that of L1 + SC which came down five minutes later in the next field.

Above: **Unteroffizier Hermann Weber took his Stuka down to roof-top level in an effort to escape from pursuing fighters when his unit was intercepted near Folkestone on August 15. At More Hall his luck ran out when he flew full tilt into high-tension cables (seen in the background) which brought his aircraft crashing** down onto Nos. 82, 80 and 78 Shorncliffe Crescent. Both Weber and his gunner Franz Kraus died in the crash. *Below:* Thirty-nine years and one week later it is difficult to visualise the scene of destruction which existed in the surburban crescent in 1940. The missing fence posts are the only clue.

I/StG1

Junkers Ju 87B. Shot down in combat over the Channel. Crashed in sea. Crew of two NCOs baled out but missing. Aircraft lost.

II/StG2

Junkers Ju 87B. Failed to return from operational sortie over the Channel. Lt. von Rosen killed. One NCO missing. Aircraft a write-off.

Junkers Ju 87B. Missing following operations over the Channel. Two NCOs missing. Aircraft lost.

Junkers Ju 87B. Shot down by RAF fighters in combat over the Channel. Crashed in sea. Pilot rescued unhurt. One NCO missing. Aircraft lost.

Junkers Ju 87B. Returned to base with one NCO wounded following combat with RAF fighters over the Channel. Aircraft undamaged.

II/ZG2

Messerschmitt Bf 110C. Shot down by RAF fighters in combat over the Channel. One NCO killed. Aircraft a write-off.

Stab ZG76

Messerschmitt Bf 110C. Last seen in combat with RAF fighters. Presumed shot down into the sea. Oblt. Knop and Uffz. Neumayer missing. Aircraft lost.

Stab I/ZG76

Messerschmitt Bf 110D. Failed to return from sortie to east coast of England off Newcastle. Hptmn. Restemeyer (Gruppe Kommandeur) and Hptmn. Hartwich (W. Leitstelle 15) both missing. Aircraft lost.

Messerschmitt Bf 110D. Shot down by fighters during operations off east coast of England near Newcastle. Oblt. Loobes (Gruppe Adjutant) and Uffz. Brock both missing. Aircraft lost.

1/ZG76

Messerschmitt Bf 110D. Shot down by fighters over east coast and crashed at Streatlam, near Barnard Castle 1.36 p.m. Oblt. Kettling and Obergefr. Volk captured. Aircraft M8+ CH a write-off.

2/ZG76

Messerschmitt Bf 110D. Shot down in sea off east coast of England 1.00 p.m. Obgefr. Lenk killed. Fw. Ladwein captured. Aircraft M8+ EK a write-off.

Messerschmitt Bf 110D. Severely damaged by fighters during action over the North Sea off English east coast. Crash-landed at Esbjerg. Uffz. Geischecker killed. Uffz. Richter wounded. Aircraft a write-off.

3/ZG76

Messerschmitt Bf 110D. Shot down into the sea off the east coast of England during sortie to Northumberland coast. Lt. Koehler, Uffz. Oelsner both killed. Aircraft lost.

Messerschmitt Bf 110D. Returned to base one NCO wounded following attack by RAF fighters off English east coast. Aircraft repairable.

Messerschmitt Bf 110D. Failed to return from operational sortie to English east coast. Believed shot down into North Sea. Oberfw. Groening and Obergefr. Hahn both missing. Aircraft lost.

Messerschmitt Bf 110D. Returned to base damaged in fighter attack. One NCO wounded. Aircraft repairable.

Stab II/ZG76

Messerschmitt Bf 110C. Crashed at Broadlands near Romsey 5.55 p.m. during sortie over southern England and combat with RAF fighters. Uffz. Roehrich and Uffz. Neymayer both killed. Aircraft a write-off.

II/ZG76

Messerschmitt Bf 110C. Crash-landed Cherbourg-West due to combat damage. Lt. Hahn and one NCO wounded. Aircraft a write-off.

Messerschmitt Bf 110C. Shot down into the Channel by RAF fighters. Crew rescued unhurt. Aircraft lost.

Messerschmitt Bf 110C. Crashed on landing at Barneville following combat with fighters over southern England. One NCO wounded. Aircraft a write-off.

4/ZG76

Messerschmitt Bf 110C. Shot down into the Channel by RAF fighters. Oblt. Wien killed. Uffz. Diebold missing. Aircraft lost.

5/ZG76

Messerschmitt Bf 110C-4. Failed to return from operations over southern England and combat with RAF fighters. Oblt. Bremer and Uffz. Pauli missing. Aircraft a write-off.

6/ZG76

Messerschmitt Bf 110C. Shot down by Flying Officer Ostaszewski of No. 609 Squadron and Pilot Officer Zurakowski of No. 234 Squadron. Crashed and exploded at North Ashey Down, Isle of Wight 6.06 p.m. Fw. Birndorfer killed. Uffz. Guschewski captured. Aircraft M8+ BP a write-off.

Messerschmitt Bf 110C. Failed to return from operations over southern England. Believed shot down in Channel. Fw. Wagner and Uffz. Sporl both missing. Aircraft a write-off.

Stab III/ZG76

Messerschmitt Bf 110C. Shot down into Weymouth Bay 5.00 p.m. during operational sortie over the Channel. Hptmn. Dickore (Gruppe Kommandeur) killed. Uffz. Templin POW. Aircraft 2N+ BC lost.

7/ZG76

Messerschmitt Bf 110C. Shot down by fighters in combat over the Channel. Believed crashed in sea. Uffz. Kschamer and Uffz. Voigt missing. Aircraft lost.

Messerschmitt Bf 110C. Shot down into the Channel by RAF fighters. Uffz. Haas and Gefr. Hoffmann (of 8/ZG76) both missing. Aircraft lost.

9/ZG76

Messerschmitt Bf 110C. Crashed in the Channel following attack by RAF fighters during sortie to southern England. Lt. von Miakich killed. Uffz. Tschope missing. Aircraft lost.

Friday, August 16

2(F)/122

Junkers Ju 88A-1. Forced-landed at Lille, damaged in action. Two NCOs wounded. Aircraft 70% damaged.

Seenotflugkdo. 4

Dornier Do 24. Crashed attempting landing on heavy sea (PQ6997) during air-sea rescue mission. Crew unhurt. Aircraft lost.

II/JG2

Messerschmitt Bf 109E-4. Burst tyre on landing at Maneville following operational sortie. Pilot unhurt. Aircraft 40% damaged.

4/JG2

Messerschmitt Bf 109E-1. Abandoned during fighter operations over southern England. Crashed Turzes Farm, Burwash 5.00 p.m. Oblt. Mockel captured. Aircraft a write-off.
Local investigations by the Wealden Aviation Archaeological Group revealed one propeller blade in the village fire station now in the group's collection.

6/JG2

Messerschmitt Bf 109E-1. Failed to return from sortie over East Grinstead area. Fw. Hoehn missing. Aircraft a write-off.

4/JG3

Messerschmitt Bf 109E-4. Shot down in combat with fighters over the Channel off Wirrer au Bois. Hptmn. Mueller (Staffel Kapitan) wounded rescued from sea by German E-boat. Aircraft lost.

5/JG3

Messerschmittt Bf 109E-4. Shot down by fighters in combat over the Channel. Pilot rescued from sea by E-Boat. Aircraft lost.

7/JG3

Messerschmitt Bf 109E-4. Crashed on landing at Desvres following combat mission. Cause not stated. Pilot unhurt. Aircraft 40% damaged.

Stab II/JG26

Messerschmitt Bf 109E-4. Shot down in fighter combat over the Channel some six miles off Dover. Crashed in sea. Hptmn. Ebbighausen (Gruppe Kommandeur) missing. Aircraft lost.

6/JG27

Messerschmitt Bf 109E-1. Crashed at Cherbourg due to combat damage and possible pilot injury. Uffz. Wilbert killed. Aircraft a write-off.

III/JG27

Messerschmitt Bf 109E-4. Crashed following mid-air collision over the Isle of Wight. Oblt. Rosenboom killed. Aircraft a write-off.

Messerschmitt Bf 109E-4. Returned to base damaged following collision with Oblt. Rosenboom's aircraft during operational sortie over the Isle of Wight. Uffz. Ackmann unhurt. Aircraft 25% damaged.

4/JG51

Messerschmitt Bf 109E-3. Shot down during fighter operations over the Faversham area. Uffz. Buder captured. Aircraft a write-off.

Messerschmitt Bf 109E-1. Failed to return from operational sortie over south-east England. Pilot missing. Aircraft a write-off.

Stab JG53

Messerschmitt Bf 109E-4. Crashed on landing at Rennes from operational sortie due to undercarriage collapse. Pilot unhurt. Aircraft 35% damaged.

2/JG53

Messerschmitt Bf 109E-4. Shot down by fighters during sortie over the Isle of Wight. Fw. Hansen captured. Aircraft a write-off.

II/JG53

Messerschmitt Bf 109E-1. Shot down into the Channel during combat with RAF fighters. Pilot wounded rescued by Seenotdienst. Aircraft a write-off.

This 'Greif' Geschwader Heinkel alighted high on High Salvington near Worthing with two dead crewmen on August 16. On the skyline, visible through the haze, is the pimple top of Highdown Hill behind which lies the Channel. The nose of the bomber points directly at Goring-by-Sea (Worthing Gazette). *Below:* The sun beats down on the fields of High Salvington and the Channel waters are lost in haze behind Highdown Hill on September 11, 1979.

Messerschmitt Bf 109E-1. Crashed on landing at Guernsey following combat mission due to undercarriage failure. Pilot unhurt. Aircraft 50% damaged.

Messerschmitt Bf 109E-4. Shot down by fighters and crashed into the sea. Fw. Dinger rescued unhurt. Aircraft lost.

I/JG54

Messerschmitt Bf 109E-1. Forced-landed St. Inglevert following combat sortie. Uffz. Rimmel wounded. Aircraft a write-off.

3/JG54

Messerschmitt Bf 109E-4. Failed to return from operations over the Channel. Exact circumstances unknown. Fw. Knedler missing. Aircraft lost.

III/JG54

Messerschmitt Bf 109E. Returned to base damaged in combat with enemy fighters off Calais. Pilot wounded. Aircraft repairable.

7/JG54

Messerschmitt Bf 109E-4. Crashed during routine maintenance flight from Guines-Sued, cause unknown. Pilot wounded. Aircraft a write-off.

3/KG2

Dornier Do 17Z-2. Shot down by fighters east of Canterbury during sortie to attack Hornchurch aerodrome. Lt. Moellenbrok and Uffz. Hess both missing. Gefr. Reinicke and Gefr. Golob both killed. Aircraft a write-off.

Dornier Do 17Z-3. Failed to return from sortie to attack Hornchurch aerodrome and attack by British fighters over north Kent coast. One NCO killed. Oblt. Brandenburg and two NCOs missing. Aircraft a write-off.

Dornier Do 17Z-3. Crashed near Calais-Marck following action over Kent. Crew baled out, two NCOs wounded. Aircraft a write-off.

I/KG27

Heinkel He 111P. Shot down by fighters over the Isle of Wight and crashed in the Channel. Crew rescued, one NCO wounded. Aircraft lost.

II/KG51

Junkers Ju 88A-1. Forced-landed at Orly aerodrome due to mechanical failure during operational sortie. Crew unhurt. Aircraft 30% damaged.

III/KG51

Junkers Ju 88A-1. Belly-landed at Etampes aerodrome cause not stated. Crew unhurt. Aircraft 25% damaged.

II/KG54

Junkers Ju 88A-1. Crash-landed outside Strasbourg due to engine failure during routine domestic flight. Hptmn. Gehrke and one NCO injured. Aircraft a write-off.

II/KG55

Heinkel He 111P. Returned to base damaged in combat with RAF fighters over Feltham. Fw. Henze and Fw. Wurm both wounded. Aircraft repairable.

4/KG55

Heinkel He 111P. Shot down during operations over Feltham area. Crashed Upper Frithwold Farm, Northchapel, near Petworth. Hptmn. Sabler (Staffel Kapitan), Fw. Muller. Fw. Magerhans, Gefr. Szymanowski and Uffz. Schmidtke all killed. Aircraft G1+ LM a write-off.
Complete starboard wing bearing Balkankreuz and identity letter 'L' discovered in a wood on nearby Belchambers Farm by Wealden Aviation Archaeological Group in 1973. Crater caused by exploding aircraft excavated by them in 1979 but only minor fragments discovered.

6/KG55

Heinkel He 111P. Briefed to attack Heathrow aerodrome and shot down by RAF fighters. Crashed Anningtons Farm, Bramber 6.15 p.m. Oblt. Wieland, Fw. Lanstrof and Uffz. Appel baled out and captured. Uffz. Hattendorf and Uffz. Pulver both killed. Aircraft G1+ HP a write-off.

Heinkel He 111P. Returned to base damaged following sortie over west London. Crew unhurt. Aircraft 15% damaged.

III/KG55

Heinkel He 111P. Returned to base with one NCO wounded following combat sortie over Brighton. Aircraft repairable.

Heinkel He 111P. Forced-landed at Dreux due to engine trouble during operational sortie. Crew unhurt. Aircraft 80% damaged.

Heinkel He 111P. Crash-landed near Le Havre due to engine failure on combat sortie. Three NCOs wounded. Aircraft a write-off.

Above: Four dive-bombers of the 'Immelmann' Geschwader's 3rd Staffel fell to the guns of RAF fighters during the raid on Tangmere aerodrome on August 16. This Ju 87B T6+HL was the only one in which the crew survived, albeit seriously wounded. It crash-landed in fields near Selsey, before shedding its undercarriage on the B2145 and ending up in a hedge on the west side of the road just south of the junction to Church Norton. *Below:* One of the few 'after the battle' locations which has defied the changes of time. The twin cottages still stand as they did and the gap in the roadside hedge was still unfilled on November 13, 1979.

Another relic from the August 16 Tangmere raid is this 'Stuka' engine recovered by the Kent Battle of Britain Museum from Highpiece Field, Honor Farm at Pagham.

Oberleutnant Ernst Hollekamp *(left)* was the pilot of a Bf 110C of ZG2 (often mis-identified as a Heinkel) on an escort sortie with bombers engaged on raids during the early evening of August 16. Although these pictures were published during the war, thanks to research by Michael Ockenden, the background to his gruesome death on a rooftop in East-bourne can now be told. *Above:* The mangled remains of Hollekamp's Bf 110 fell in the grounds of Aldro School, Darley Road, Eastbourne. With its tail shot away after an attack by RAF fighters, it broke up in the air leaving a trail of wreckage strewn over three-quarters-of-a-mile (Fox Photos). *Below:* Aldro School on September 18, 1979 is now the East Sussex College of Higher Education and the grounds have dwindled considerably under the expansion of the county education authority's building programme. However, the rear wall of High Firs in the background peeping through the trees provides a mutual point of identification.

7/KG55

Heinkel He 111P (1582). Shot down during sortie to attack Great West aerodrome. Attacked by RAF fighters over Brighton area and forced-landed at High Salvington. Uffz. Weber and Gefr. Moorfeld killed. Lt. Theobald, Uffz. Hornbostel and Gefr. Glaser all captured. Aircraft G1+ FR a write-off.

7/KG76

Dornier Do 17Z-2. Crashed at Moatlands, Brenchley, Paddock Wood after being rammed by RAF fighter during operations over north Kent 1.00 p.m. Oberfw. Wachter and Fw. Klumb killed. Oberfw. Riedel and Oberfw. Brauer missing. Aircraft a write-off.
Site excavated by Steve Vizard who recovered a propeller blade, undercarriage leg, bomb rack, several minor components and assorted wreckage.

II/KG77

Junkers Ju 88. Flying accident during routine domestic flight. Flew into the Starnberger See, cause unknown. Three NCOs killed. Aircraft lost.

3/KGr126

Heinkel He 111H-4. Shot down by AA defences during sortie over Hull. Three NCOs killed. Oblt. Volkmar and one NCO missing. Aircraft a write-off.

III/LG1

Junkers Ju 88A-1. Forced-landed Chateaudun due to engine failure on operational sortie. Four NCOs wounded. Aircraft 80% damaged.

Junkers Ju 88A. Returned to base damaged by flak during operations over England. One NCO wounded. Aircraft repairable.

I/StG2

Junkers Ju 87B. Returned to base damaged following attack by RAF fighters. Crew unhurt. Aircraft 50% damaged.

Junkers Ju 87B. Damaged by fighter attack during operations over the Channel. Returned safely to base. Crew unhurt. Aircraft 10% damaged.

Junkers Ju 87B. Attacked by RAF fighters during sortie over the Channel. Returned to base with damage. Crew unhurt. Aircraft 10% damaged.

1/StG2

Junkers Ju 87B. Shot down by fighters north-west of Caen. Crashed in sea. Pilot rescued unhurt. Uffz. Neumann killed. Aircraft lost.

3/StG2

Junkers Ju 87B. Shot down during attack on Tangmere aerodrome 2.00 p.m. Crash-landed outside Selsey. Uffz. Koenig and Uffz. Schmid both captured badly wounded. Aircraft a write-off.

Junkers Ju 87B. Failed to return from mission to attack Tangmere aerodrome. Believed shot down in the Channel. Uffz. Bader and Uffz. Bohn missing. Aircraft a write-off.

Junkers Ju 87B. Shot down during attack on Tangmere. Believed that which crashed at Bowky Farm, South Mundham. Oberfw. Witt and Fw. Roecktaeschel both killed. Aircraft a write-off.

Junkers Ju 87B. Brought down by RAF fighters during sortie to attack Tangmere aerodrome. Believed that which crashed at Honar Farm, Pagham. Uffz. Linse and Obergefr. Messerschmitt both missing. Aircraft a write-off.

III/StG2

Junkers Ju 87B. Returned to base with combat damage. One NCO killed, another wounded. Aircraft repairable.

Junkers Ju 87B. Damaged in combat with RAF fighters. Returned safely to base. Hptmn. Bruecker and one NCO wounded. Aircraft repairable.

Junkers Ju 87B. Attacked by fighters during operational sortie and returned to base damaged. One NCO wounded. Aircraft repairable.

7/StG2

Junkers Ju 87B. Shot down off Selsey Bill by British fighters. Lt. Kuehn and Gefr. Wenzel both missing. Aircraft a write-off.

Junkers Ju 87B. Failed to return from operations over the Channel off Selsey Bill and combat with RAF fighters. Believed crashed in sea. Uffz. Liebing and Uffz. Wiartalla both missing. Aircraft lost.

Junkers Ju 87B. Shot down in combat with fighters off Selsey Bill and crashed into Poole harbour 1.00 p.m. Uffz. Voigt killed. Fw. Grafenhain captured. Aircraft a write-off.

Junkers Ju 87B. Missing following operational sortie over the Channel off Selsey. Uffz. Serwotka and Gefr. Wagner both missing. Aircraft lost.

I/StG3

Junkers Ju 87B. Returned to base damaged by flak. Oblt. Eppen and Lt. Heyder both wounded. Aircraft damage state not recorded.

I/StG77

Junkers Ju 87B. Forced-landed at Carentan due to engine failure during local flight. Crew unhurt. Aircraft 10% damaged.

Stab II/ZG2

Messerschmitt Bf 110D. Shot down by fighters over the Channel. Crashed near St. Aubin. Major Carl (Gruppe Kommandeur) and one NCO killed. Aircraft a write-off.

6/ZG2

Messerschmitt Bf 110C. Crashed into the grounds of Aldro School, Eastbourne 5.30 p.m. following fighter attack. Oblt. Hollekamp and Fw. Schurk both killed. Aircraft a write-off.

Pieces from this aircraft collected by the Wealden Aviation Archaeological Group and Hollekamp's D'ring in the hands of Mike Ockenden.

The body of Oberleutnant Ernst Hollekamp landed on the roof of Hillbrow in Gaudick Road, Eastbourne just over a quarter-of-a-mile from where his aircraft fell. The gable end of the roof has been forcibly moved outwards by the impact (S. Hall/A. Saunders). His gunner, Feldwebel Richard Schurk, baled out but landed in the sea. Local feelings were running high at the time and no attempt was made to save him.

Left: Sub-Officer P. G. Short of the Eastbourne Fire Brigade had the task of recovering the body. By mistake he caught hold of the D-ring on the German's parachute which sprang open on the roof (S. Hall/A. Saunders). *Right:* Peter Foote's photograph of Hillbrow today with nothing to indicate the former drama in a quiet suburban street.

Stab ZG26

Messerschmitt Bf 110C-2. Crash-landed at St. Omer following operational sortie. Crew unhurt. Aircraft 80% damaged.

2/ZG26

Messerschmitt Bf 110C. Failed to return from sortie over south-east England. Exact circumstances unknown. Uffz. Drenkhahn killed, one NCO missing. Aircraft a write-off.

5/ZG76

Messerschmitt Bf 110C. Failed to return from operations nineteen miles north of Brighton. Lt. Lemmer killed. Obergefr. Lewandowski missing. Aircraft a write-off.
Believed to be the machine which crashed at Shopwhyke House near Tangmere on this date. Excavated by the Wealden Aviation Archaeological Group, January 1978. Many pieces of shattered airframe recovered but nothing to establish identity beyond dispute.

Stab III/ZG76

Messerschmitt Bf 110C. Shot down during operational sortie over English south coast at Brighton 6.30 p.m. Lt. Marchfelder and Obergefr. Jentzsch both captured. Aircraft a write-off.

III/ZG76

Messerschmitt Bf 110C. Shot down into the Channel off Brighton by RAF fighters during sortie over English south coast. Crew rescued unhurt by Seenotflugdienst. Aircraft lost.

9/ZG76

Messerschmitt Bf 110C. Forced-landed at Lee Farm, Clapham 5.45 p.m. damaged by fighters. Oblt. Schlaffer (Staffel Kapitan) and Obergefr. Obser captured. Aircraft 2N+AP a write-off.

Saturday, August 17

1/196

Arado Ar 196. Reported destroyed at Boulogne by enemy vessel carrying Red Cross flag. No personnel losses. Aircraft a write-off.

1(F)/122

Heinkel He 111H-3. Lost bearings during transport flight and blundered into German flak zone. Shot down near Hattingen. One NCO killed, one wounded. Aircraft a write-off.

2/JG3

Messerschmitt Bf 109E. Crashed following loss of control during routine local flight. Uffz. Sachse killed. Aircraft a write-off.

3/JG3

Messerschmitt Bf 109E-1. Crashed at Le Touquet following operational sortie. Cause unknown. Pilot killed. Aircraft a write-off.

III/LG1

Junkers Ju 88A-1. Damaged in take-off accident at Chateaudun aerodrome. Burst tyre on take-off. Crew unhurt. Aircraft 15% damaged.

Above: An unwelcome visitor from Abbeville-Yvrench to the Officers' Mess at Shopwyke House on August 16 was this Messerschmitt Bf 110C which crashed into the grounds, narrowly missing the stately old mansion which was used by Westhampnett's squadrons. Both crew members who perished in the crash were believed to be from the 5th Staffel, II 'Haifisch' (Shark) Gruppe of ZG76 (S. Hall/A. Saunders). *Below:* Excavation by the Wealden Aviation Archaeological Group in January 1978 failed to positively identify the aircraft (Brenzett).

4/NJG1

Junkers Ju 88. Failed to return from mission over England. Shot down in sea off Spurn Head 3.00 a.m. Briefed to intrude over the Wash. Shot down by Pilot Office Rhodes and Sergeant Gregory in Blenheim night fighter from No. 29 Squadron. Oberfw. Zenkel, Fw. Schramm and Gefr. Roth all missing. Aircraft lost.

Sunday, August 18

6/JG2

Messerschmitt Bf 109E-4. Shot down by RAF fighters in combat over the Isle of Wight 2.40 p.m. Abandoned aircraft crashed at Tapnall Farm near Freshwater. Oblt. Moellerfriedrich baled out and captured. Aircraft a write-off.

Messerschmitt Bf 109E-1. Ditched in Channel off Cherbourg following action over the Isle of Wight at 2.40 p.m. Wounded pilot rescued by Seenotdienst. Aircraft lost.

2/JG3

Messerschmitt Bf 109E-4. Forced-landed at Leeds near Maidstone 1.50 p.m. damaged in combat with RAF fighters. Oblt. Tiedmann (Staffel Kapitan) captured unhurt. Aircraft 13+ a write-off.

II/JG3

Messerschmitt Bf 109E-1. Crashed on landing at Brombois following action over the Channel. Fw. Mueller unhurt. Aircraft 60% damaged.

6/JG3

Messerschmitt Bf 109E-4. Belly-landed at Boulogne with combat damage following sortie over southern England. Fw. Dobrick wounded. Aircraft 30% damaged.

Messerschmitt Bf 109E-4. Crash-landed at Marquise with severely wounded pilot following combat with RAF fighters. Uffz. Becker died of wounds. Aircraft a write-off.

III/JG3

Messerschmitt Bf 109E-4. Shot down by RAF fighters in combat over north Kent 1.40 p.m. Believed crashed near Bredhurst. Lt. von Fonderen killed. Aircraft a write-off.

8/JG3

Messerschmitt Bf 109E-4. Crashed and burned out at Brook Farm, Milebush, near Staplehurst 6.15 p.m. after combat with RAF fighters. Claimed by Squadron Leader Pemberton of No. 1 Squadron. Obergefr. Basell killed. Aircraft a write-off.

7/JG26

Messerschmitt Bf 109E-4. Shot down by Pilot Officer Eckford and Pilot Officer Pniak of No. 32 Squadron during combat over Canterbury area. Crashed at Kingston 5.30 p.m. Major Blume captured wounded. Aircraft a write-off.

Messerschmitt Bf 109E-1. Crashed inverted into a wood at Chilham 5.30 p.m. following combat with No. 32 Squadron Hurricanes over the Canterbury area. Shot down by Flight Lieutenant Brothers and Pilot Officer Wlasnowolski. Lt. Mueller-Duhe killed. Aircraft a write-off.

Component from undercarriage donated to the Kent Battle of Britain Museum

1/JG27

Messerschmitt Bf 109E-4. Shot down in combat with RAF fighters over the Channel off the Isle of Wight 2.30 p.m. Lt. Mitsdoerfer captured unhurt. Aircraft 6+ lost.

Messerschmitt Bf 109E-1. Failed to return from operations over the Channel and combat with fighters off the Isle of Wight. Crashed into the sea. Oblt. Trumpelmann killed. Aircraft lost.

2/JG27

Messerschmitt Bf 109E-4. Crashed into the Channel off the Isle of Wight during combat with British fighters 2.30 p.m. Fw. Sawallisch killed. Aircraft lost.

II/JG27

Messerschmitt Bf 109E-4. Shot down in combat with RAF fighters over the Channel 2.30 p.m. Crashed in sea off the Isle of Wight. Pilot rescued unhurt by Seenotdienst. Aircraft lost.

6/JG27

Messerschmitt Bf 109E-4. Damaged by fighter attack in combat over the Isle of Wight. Forced-landed outside Shanklin 2.35 p.m. Oblt. Neumann captured unhurt. Aircraft 6+ a write-off.

Messerschmitt Bf 109E-4. Crashed in sea off the Isle of Wight during fighter action 2.35 p.m. Uffz. Nolte killed. Aircraft lost.

I/JG51

Messerschmitt Bf 109E. Belly-landed at St. Inglevert following collision during operational sortie over the Channel. Oblt. Leppla unhurt. Aircraft 30% damaged.

5/JG51

Messerschmitt Bf 109E-3. Believed shot down by Flying Officer Witorzenc of No. 501 Squadron during combat over north Kent coast 5.35 p.m. Crashed in sea off Whitstable. Lt. Lessing killed. Aircraft lost.

Messerschmitt Bf 109E. Crashed in sea off Whitstable following combat with RAF fighters 5.35 p.m. Believed shot down by Pilot Officer Zenker of No. 501 Squadron. Hptmn. Tietzen (Staffel Kapitan) killed. Aircraft lost.

Stab JG53

Junkers Ju 52. Damaged in landing accident at Rennes involving He 111 of III/KG27. No personnel casualties. Aircraft 15% damaged.

II/JG54

Messerschmitt Bf 109E-3. Aircraft slightly damaged in RAF bombing attack on Vlissingen aerodrome at 10.00 p.m. No personnel casualties. Aircraft repairable.

Messerschmitt Bf 109E-3. Damaged in attack on Vlissingen aerodrome at 10.00 p.m. by Blenheim of No. 101 Squadron. No personnel losses. Aircraft 10% damaged.

7/JG54

Messerschmitt Bf 109E-4. Crashed on take-off from Guines-West on combat sortie. Cause not stated. Pilot unhurt. Aircraft 60% damaged.

1/KG1

Heinkel He 111H-3. Returned to base damaged by fighters during operations over Biggin Hill. One NCO killed, another wounded. Aircraft 20% damaged.

2/KG1

Heinkel He 111H-3. Shot down by No. 65 Squadron Spitfires and attacked by other British fighters following attack on Biggin Hill 1.30 p.m. Crash-landed at Snargate near Dymchurch. Uffz. Gericke killed. Lt. Ahrens, Oberfw. Katzmarski, Uffz. Schneider and Flgr. Natzke captured. Aircraft V4+ GK a write-off.

6/KG2

Dornier Do 17Z-3. Attacked by fighters over Whitstable 5.30 p.m. during sortie over the Thames Estuary. Returned to base. Hptmn. Lindemann wounded. Aircraft repairable.

6/KG4

Heinkel He 111P-4. Damaged landing at Eindhoven on burst tyre following operational sortie. No crew casualties. Aircraft 35% damaged.

III/KG4

Junkers Ju 88. Crashed on landing at Vlaardingen due to engine failure during operational sortie at night. Crew unhurt. Aircraft a write-off.

Junkers Ju 88A-1. Crash-landed near Rotterdam out of fuel during night operations. Crew unhurt. Aircraft 50% damaged.

II/KG27

Heinkel He 111P. Crashed at Laval due to engine failure following mission at night. Three NCOs wounded. Aircraft a write-off.

Heinkel He 111P (1408). Collided with Anson trainer piloted by Sergeant Hancock of No. 6 FTS during attack on Windrush aerodrome 11.50 p.m. Crashed and burned out at Blackbitch Farm, Aldsworth, Northleach. Oberfw. Dreher, Uffz. Schmidt, Uffz. Rave and Uffz. Lohrs all killed. Aircraft a write-off.

III/KG27

Heinkel He 111P. Landing accident at Rennes following night sortie. Collided with stationary Ju 52 of JG53. Crew unhurt. Aircraft 40% damaged.

III/KG51

Junkers Ju 88A-1. Forced-landed at Orly due to engine failure during non-operational sortie. Crew unhurt. Aircraft 10% damaged.

II/KG53

Heinkel He 111H-3. Shot down by Flying Officer Milne of No. 151 Squadron off the Essex coast 5.45 p.m. Crashed in sea. Major Tamm (Gruppe Kommandeur), Lt. Ludman and one NCO killed. Three NCOs missing. Aircraft lost.

Heinkel He 111H. Attacked by British fighters over Essex coast 5.45 p.m. Returned to base two NCOs wounded. Aircraft repairable.

III/KG53

Heinkel He 111. Briefed to attack North Weald. Shot down by Hurricanes in combat off the Essex coast 5.30 p.m. and crashed in sea. Lt. Woldmann, Uffz. Gropp and three NCOs missing. Aircraft lost.

7/KG53

Heinkel He 111H-2. Attacked by various British fighters during engagement over Essex 5.50 p.m. Forced-landed on sea off Ramsgate following further attack by Flight Lieutenant Hamilton of No. 85 Squadron. Oblt. Zipse, Uffz. Grasser, Gefr. Reinhardt, Gefr. Worch and Gefr. Mailander all captured after spending twenty-six hours in dinghy. Aircraft A1+ FR lost.

8/KG53

Heinkel He 111H-2. Shot down by Flying Officer Weaver of No. 56 Squadron during combat over Essex coast 5.35 p.m. Forced-landed Small Gains Farm, Foulness. Lt. Leber, Lt. Wester and two NCOs captured. Fw. Wild died of wounds. Aircraft A1+ FS a write-off.

1/KG76

Dornier Do 17Z (2504). Shot down by No. 32 Squadron Hurricanes over Kenley area 1.20 p.m. Crashed in Mill Lane, Hurst Green and burned out. Oblt. Stoldt. Fw. Gengel and Kriegsberichter Surk all killed. Oberfw. Lautersack and Fw. Beck captured. Aircraft F1+ 1H a write-off.

Fully inflated tail wheel donated to Halstead War Museum during investigation of site in 1970. Pieces from the engine in the Wealden group collection and many other components owned by Steve Vizard.

2/KG76

Dornier Do 17Z. Damaged by RAF fighters during operations over southern England. Returned to base Uffz. Dubensky wounded. Aircraft 20% damaged.

3/KG76

Dornier Do 17Z. Attacked by British fighters during combat mission and returned to base Fw. Schwarz wounded. Aircraft repairable.

5/KG76

Junkers Ju 88. Shot down by repeated RAF fighter attacks. Pilot Officer Wlasnowolski and Flight Lieutenant Brothers of No. 32 Squadron together with various other aircraft including No. 64 Squadron Spitfires all made attacks. Crashed into woods at Ide Hill 1.30 p.m. Oberfw. Eichhorn, Oberfw. Vetter, Fw. Geier and Gefr. Skuthan all killed. Aircraft a write-off.

Site investigated by Steve Vizard and various fragments of airframe and some minor components discovered. Complete tail fin from this machine in Dennis Knight's collection.

Junkers Ju 88. Landed at Creil with combat damage following sortie over southern England 1.30 p.m. Uffz. Zehetmair wounded. Aircraft 40% damaged.

Above: **This shredded, incinerated mass was once a German bomber containing four men. It became their crematorium on the night of August 18 but whether by an error of judgement or the wilful sacrifice of a British pilot will never be known. In carrying out a bombing raid on Windrush aerodrome near Aldsworth, Gloucestershire, this He 111 from KG27 collided with an unarmed Avro Anson twin-engined trainer from No. 6 Flying Training School upon which the Heinkel's gunners had opened fire. Witnesses stated that the Anson turned upon its German tormentor and rammed it. Whatever the cause, five men died that night including Sergeant Bruce Hancock, the twenty-six-year-old Anson pilot now buried in Hendon Cemetery, Middlesex (Grave 50061 in Section G5) (Gloucestershire Echo).**
Below: **Mr. Sandles, who as a young man was on fire watch duty during the weekend of August 18, points to the spot in the field where the Heinkel's crew met their deaths. He told us that Sergeant Hancock lay undiscovered until the following day and that he might have been saved had he been found earlier. He said that twelve trainee pilots were lost in similar attacks on Windrush. (Because Sergeant Hancock was from No. 6 FTS, not one of the accredited seventy-one Fighter Command squadrons in the Battle of Britain, his name does not appear on the list of British casualties.)**

6/KG76

Junkers Ju 88. Shot down by RAF fighters in engagement over southern England 1.40 p.m. Crashed at Aylesford near West Malling. Fw. Krebs and Sonderfuehrer Berchemeier both killed. Fw. Watermann and Uffz. Loeffler both captured. Aircraft F1+ GP a write-off.

Relics from this aircraft featured in Steve Vizard collection.

III/KG76

Dornier Do 17. Landed at Cormeilles damaged following fighter attack. Crew unhurt. Aircraft damaged but repairable.

8/KG76

Dornier Do 17Z. Shot down by Pilot Officers Stavert and Goodman and Flight Lieutenant Hillcoat of No. 1 Squadron over English south coast 1.40 p.m. following sortie over Kenley. Crashed in Channel. Lt. Leder, Uffz. Szybinski and Uffz. Disch killed. Uffz. Rudolf, Gefr. Ulbrich missing. Aircraft lost.

Dornier Do 17Z-2. Crashed on landing at Calais due to battle damage. Uffz. Wind-schild's crew unhurt. Aircraft 50% damaged.

9/KG76

Dornier Do 17Z-3. Forced-landed near Abbeville with damage following low-level raid on Kenley. Fw. Reichel unhurt. Uffz. Haas wounded. Aircraft F1+ CT 60% damaged.

Dornier Do 17Z-2. Forced-landed at Calais due to damage suffered during low-level attack on Kenley and engagement with RAF fighters. Fw. Stephani and another NCO both wounded. One NCO killed. Aircraft 50% damaged.

Dornier Do 17Z. Hit by ground fire over Kenley aerodrome 1.20 p.m. Pilot mortally wounded. Flown back to landing at Norrent-Fontes aerodrome by navigator Oberfw. Illg. Oblt Magin died of injuries. Aircraft repairable.

Dornier Do 17Z-2. Shot down by Kenley ground defences and attacks from Sergeants Dymond and Brown of No. 111 Squadron. Crashed and burned out at Leaves Green near Biggin Hill 1.30 p.m. Hptmn. Roth (Staffel-Kapitan), Hptmn. Peters. Oblt. Lamberty, Oberfw. Geier, Fw. Eberhard all captured. Aircraft F1+ DT a write-off.

Fragments collected from the surface of this crash site plus chunks of melted alloy in the Kent Battle of Britain Museum. Relics also held by the Halstead War Museum, the Warplane Wreck Investigation Group and Steve Vizard.

Dornier Do 17Z-2. Ditched in the Channel on return flight following attack on Kenley aerodrome 1.20 p.m. Hit by ground fire and attack from Sergeant Newton of No. 111 Squadron. Uffz. Unger and three NCOs rescued unhurt by Kriegsmarine. Aircraft lost.

Dornier Do 17Z-2. Hit by AA defences during low-level attack on Kenley aerodrome 1.20 p.m. and crashed in flames at Golf Road, Kenley. Oblt. Ahrends, Oberst. Dr. Sommer, Fw. Dietz, Fw. Greulich and Fw. Petersen all killed. Aircraft F1+ HT a write-off.

Dornier Do 17Z-2. Ditched in the Channel off Etampes on return flight following low-level attack on Kenley 1.20 p.m. Damaged by ground defences and No. 111 Squadron Hurricanes. Uffz. Schumacher and two NCOs rescued unhurt. One NCO missing. Aircraft lost.

A Sunday outing, August 18, 1940. The good people of Aylesford village, spiritually fortified after service in nearby St. Peter's, foregather in the orchard of Church Farm to witness the ghastly sifting of wreckage from a Ju 88 in which the lives of two German airmen from KG76 were crushed out (News Chronicle).

On August 23, 1979 the yawning gulf of a gravel pit lay behind Church Farm, Aylesford and armies, aircraft and apples have been swallowed up by time.

It seems that no book on the Battle of Britain is complete unless it includes a picture of the 'Leaves Green Dornier' and no archaeology group is satisfied unless they have a piece of it in their collection. Therefore, to satisfy tradition, here is the picture of the KG76 machine once again with the same spot today. This also gives us the opportunity to include a picture of the Swastika cut from the fin by pilots from nearby Biggin Hill (the extended runway runs behind the photographer) which was presented to No. 11 Group HQ at Uxbridge by the Station CO, Group Captain Richard Grice, and is now on display at the RAF Battle of Britain Museum at Hendon. Incredible as it may seem, the museum has only three relics on display which can be positively attributed to aircraft which fought in the battle.

Dornier Do 17Z. Returned to base, one NCO killed following low-level attack on Kenley aerodrome. Rest of crew including Uffz. Maassen unhurt. Aircraft repairable.

Dornier Do 17Z. Damaged by ground defences and fighter attack during low-level raid on Kenley. Returned to base one NCO killed. Oblt. Wittmann wounded. Fw. Raab unhurt. Aircraft repairable.

KGr100

Heinkel He 111H. Crash-landed at Dinard due to mechanical failure following sortie to attack Castle Bromwich. Crew unhurt. Aircraft a write-off.

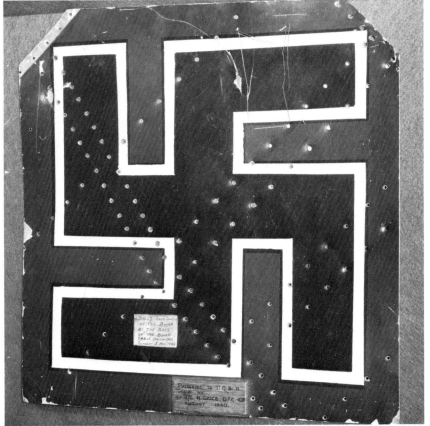

Above: **Mr. Turner-Smith** stands amid the shambles that was once his home 'Sunnycroft' in Golf Road, Kenley upon which Oberleutnant Ahrends's Do 17 crashed after it was hit by Kenley's AA defences during the low-level raid on August 18. Ahrends was the navigator and captain of the aircraft. Five men in the Dornier perished including an official war correspondent and Mr. Turner-Smith who was in the cottage at the time told reporters, 'I don't know why I am still alive' (Evening News). *Below:* Sunnycroft Farm, pictured on August 2, 1979, was rebuilt in 1947 and occupied once more by Mr. and Mrs. Turner-Smith. In 1951-52 it became the property of Mr. C. E. Jones who resided there for twenty-five years before selling to the present owners, Mr. and Mrs. Bennett. *Right:* This weathered piece of history was found by young Richard Bennett while digging in the garden in 1979.

1/LG2

Messerschmitt Bf 109E-3. Lost bearings during routine domestic flight and forced-landed at Liegescourt. Pilot injured. Aircraft 35% damaged.

Messerschmitt Bf 109E-4. Forced-landed at Liegescourt having lost bearings on local flight. Pilot injured. Aircraft 40% damaged.

7(F)/LG2

Messerschmitt Bf 110B. Shot down by No. 54 Squadron Spitfires during sortie over the Thames Estuary 11.30 a.m. Crashed in the sea. Oblt. Werdin and one NCO killed. Aircraft lost.

Stab I/StG77

Junkers Ju 87B-1. Shot down by RAF fighters over the Channel 2.30 p.m. Crashed in the sea off the French coast. Hptmn. Meisel (Gruppe Kommandeur) and Obergefr. Jakob both killed. Aircraft lost.

I/StG77

Junkers Ju 87B-1. Crashed attempting landing on beach north of Bayeux due to combat damage and possibly pilot injuries, following combat with fighters over the Channel 2.30 p.m. One NCO killed, Fw. Meyer-Bothling wounded. Aircraft a write-off.

Junkers Ju 87B-1. Crash-landed at Carentan following combat mission over the Channel. Oblt. Henze wounded. Aircraft 60% damaged.

Junkers Ju 87B-1. Returned to base damaged after combat with fighters 2.30 p.m. Oblt. Scheffel wounded, one NCO severely wounded (died later). Aircraft repairable.

Junkers Ju 87B-1. Damaged in fighter attack during sortie over the Channel 2.30 p.m. Returned to base Fw. Meier and Uffz. Maier both wounded. Aircraft repairable.

1/StG77

Junkers Ju 87B-1. Failed to return from sortie over the Channel. Attacked by RAF fighters six miles south-east of Portsmouth and presumed shot down in sea. Uffz. Weniger and Uffz. Mobes both missing. Aircraft lost.

2/StG77

Junkers Ju 87B-1. Shot down by British fighters during sortie over the Channel 2.30 p.m. Believed that which crashed at Chidham. Oblt. Sayler (Staffel-Kapitan) and Fw. Ziera both missing. Aircraft lost.

Shattered remains of Junkers Jumo 211 engine excavated from this site by Kent Battle of Britain Museum together with live 250kg bomb which was subsequently rendered harmless by RE Bomb Disposal Team from Chatham.

Junkers Ju 87B-1. Crashed into the Channel off the French coast following attack by fighters during sortie over Thorney Island 2.30 p.m. Oberfw. Neumeier and Uffz. Schmidtbauer both killed. Aircraft lost.

Junkers Ju 87B. Shot down by Pilot Officer Gray of No. 43 Squadron during attack on Thorney Island. Crashed at Spring Gardens, Cutmill, West Ashling 2.30 p.m. Uffz. Schmidt killed. Lt. Sinn baled out and captured. Aircraft a write-off.

Site excavated by the Wealden Aviation Archaeological Group in 1975 and some minor components and various fragments recovered.

For two years between 1977 and 1979, the Wealden Aviation Archaeological Group carried out a particularly hazardous recovery operation at Fishbourne Creek, Chichester (pictured *above* and indicated *below* on a map recovered from the mud) on the crash site of a Ju 87 which plummeted into the estuary on August 18. Adding to the natural difficulties, among the many relics found was a live bomb (S. Hall/A. Saunders).

Junkers Ju 87B-1 (5518). Shot down by Sergeant J. Hallowes of No. 43 Squadron during attack on Thorney Island 2.30 p.m. Crashed at Fishbourne Creek. Oblt. Wilhelm and Uffz. Worner both captured. Aircraft a write-off.

Major recovery under extremely difficult and hazardous conditions by the Wealden Aviation Archaeological Group during 1977-79. Site subject to tidal flooding and deep in estuary mud. Engine, propeller boss and blades excavated together with undercarriage legs and tail wheel oleo, tail section still bore traces of Swastika marking and showed evidence of numerous .303in bullet strikes. Cockpit canopy also found plus control column, first-aid kit, maps and gunner's tool kit in leather wallet. Many fragments found bearing legend '5518'. Live bomb towed out to sea by RN Bomb Disposal Team and blown up.

3/StG77

Junkers Ju 87B-1. Crashed 1½ miles east of Southbourne following fighter attack. Oblt. Schaffer and Uffz. Klotmann killed. Aircraft a write-off.

Junkers Ju 87B-1. Missing following combat sortie over the Channel 2.30 p.m. Crashed in sea. Oblt. Lehmann and Uffz. Winiarski missing. Aircraft lost.

Junkers Ju 87B-1. Shot down by Hurricanes over Thorney Island 2.30 p.m. Crashed at Whitehouse Farm, West Broyle, Chichester. Uffz. Kohl killed. Uffz. Dann missing. Aircraft a write-off.

Junkers Ju 87B-1. Shot down during attack on Thorney Island 2.30 p.m. Crashed in sea five miles south of Selsey Bill. Oberfw. Riegler and Gefr. Langwost both captured. Aircraft a write-off.

Junkers Ju 87B-1. Severely damaged in combat over the Channel off Portsmouth 2.30 p.m. Returned to French coast. Oblt Schmidt wounded. Uffz. Baersch severely wounded (died 2.10.40). Aircraft a write-off.

This was the last known Ju 87 'Stuka' (from the German Sturzkampfflugzeug) crash site in the British Isles which had not already been excavated (Evening Argus).

The dashboard clock *(left)* had stopped at 3.30 p.m. — one hour ahead of British Summertime. After July 1940, all the occupied countries were instructed by the Germans to follow Central European clock time, i.e. two hours ahead of Greenwich Mean Time. That from the gunner's compartment *(right)* indicates 3.12 p.m.

A valued find was the cleaning kit for the rear cockpit MG15 which was found complete in its leather wallet.

The 250kg bomb, uncovered at a depth of sixteen feet, was taken out to sea where it vented its destructive power harmlessly on the English Channel thirty-nine years after the battle (Evening Argus).

The last dive. With its 'Trumpets of Jericho' screaming, a Ju 87 plummets to destruction beyond the chimney pots of a children's home at West Broyle near Chichester. Shot down by Hurricanes on August 18, it was one of the eighteen aircraft of the Caen-based StG77 which were either lost or written off during the 'Massacre of the Stukas'.

II/StG77

Junkers Ju 87B-1. Failed to return from combat mission over the Channel. 2.30 p.m. Oblt. Sonntag missing. One NCO killed. Aircraft lost.

Junkers Ju 87B-1. Shot down by fighters over the Channel and crashed in sea. Oblt. Morenski missing. One NCO killed. Aircraft lost.

Junkers Ju 87B-1 (5167). Shot down by Sergeant Whall of No. 602 Squadron and forced-landed on Ham Manor Golf Course, Littlehampton, 2.30 p.m. Oberfw. Geiger killed. Oberfw. Schweinhardt captured. Aircraft S2+ UN a write-off.
Site investigated by the Wealden Aviation Archaeological Group. Swastika panel, first-aid kit, oil pressure gauge and 7.92mm ammunition belt from the aircraft known to be in a private collection.

Junkers Ju 87B-1. Crashed on landing at Barfleur with combat damage. Crew unhurt. Aircraft a write-off.

III/StG77

Junkers Ju 87B-1. Forced-landed at Caen with damage following sortie over the Channel 2.30 p.m. Crew unhurt. Aircraft 30% damaged.

Junkers Ju 87B-1. Crashed on landing at Argentan aerodrome following combat mission. Fw. Schulze and another NCO killed. Aircraft a write-off.

Junkers Ju 87B-1. Crashed on landing at Argentan due to combat damage following attack by fighters over the Channel 2.30 p.m. Crew unhurt. Aircraft 35% damaged.

Junkers Ju 87B-1. Shot down in flames by Sergeant Whall of No. 602 Squadron and crashed in the sea off Littlehampton 2.30 p.m. Uffz. Moll and Uffz. Schwemmer killed. Aircraft lost.

The Valkyrian immolation is complete. On August 18 the Stuka finally met its match in a sacrifice which was as vain as it was useless. With its crew mangled within the blazing wreckage-ringed crater, Harry Welch in cap and braces, a farm worker from nearby Whitehouse Farm, watches the pyre burning from a respectful distance (Daily Sketch).

Harry Welch who still remembers the incident clearly and describes lucidly some of the more gruesome aspects of the crash (including the dogs that feasted on the remains of the crew). He revisited the scene with us on November 13, 1979. This is the same place, the new housing estate being built about ten years previously.

WOODBINE CIGARETTE PACKETS TAKEN FROM A GERMAN PILOT WHO WAS WOUNDED AND TAKEN PRISONER AT CUTMILL, BOSHAM, SUSSEX ON AUGUST 18th, 1940, AFTER BALING OUT OF HIS Ju.87 "STUKA". HIS NAME WAS LTN.HANS SINN, AND IT IS ASSUMED THAT HE HAD OBTAINED THESE CIGARETTES FROM BRITISH PRISONERS, OR THAT THEY HAD BEEN FOUND BY HIM IN FRANCE AFTER THE DUNKIRK EVACUATION.

An unusual souvenir now owned by the Wealden group.

Above: **Another of the Stukas, this one from Geschwader 77, was landed intact on Ham Manor Golf Course (S. Hall/A. Saunders).** *Below:* **Naturally a specimen from the much-vaunted German terror weapon which had spearheaded the overthrow of the continent was a highly-prized trophy which led to souvenir hunting on a grand scale.**

Stab I/ZG26

Messerschmitt Bf 110C-4. Crashed on Dering Farm, Lydd 1.45 p.m. following attack by Squadron Leader MacDonell of No. 64 Squadron during engagement over southern counties. Oblt. Proske and Uffz. Mobius both captured. Aircraft U8+ BB a write-off.

Intact radio valve and various components including remains of charred parachute silk recovered at the time of the crash and donated to the Kent Battle of Britain Museum.

1/ZG26

Messerschmitt Bf 110C-2. Failed to return from operations over south coast of England. Believed crashed and exploded at Harbledown 1.40 p.m. Uffz. Mai and Uffz. Drenkhahn both missing. Aircraft a write-off.

2/ZG26

Messerschmitt Bf 110C-2. Ditched in the Channel off Dunkirk following sortie over English coast and combat with RAF fighters at 5.30 p.m. Hptmn. Kaminski (Staffel Kapitan) and Uffz. Strauch both rescued by Seenotdienst after four days in dinghy. Aircraft lost.

Messerschmitt Bf 110D/O. Crashed on landing at Hermelinghen following combat with fighters over south coast of England. Crew unhurt. Aircraft 40% damaged.

Messerschmitt Bf 110D/O. Crashed at Ypres following combat sortie over the Channel. Crew unhurt. Aircraft a write-off.

3/ZG26

Messerschmitt Bf 110C-4. Damaged in combat with enemy fighters over English south coast. Crashed on landing back at Clairmarais. Lt. Kopsell and crew unhurt. Aircraft U8+ BH 10% damaged.

Messerschmitt Bf 110D/O. Crashed at Le Nieppe following combat sortie. Crew unhurt. Aircraft a write-off.

Messerschmitt Bf 110C-4. Failed to return from operations over south coast of England. Believed crashed and burned out at Bonnington 1.40 p.m. following attack by Flying Officer Weaver of No. 56 Squadron. Oberfw. Stange and Uffz. Hesse both missing. Aircraft lost.

Messerschmitt Bf 110D/O. Shot down by fighters off French coast 1.40 p.m. Crashed in sea. Oblt. Kirchhof and Lt. Mader (of I/Ln.Rgt.32) both killed. Aircraft lost.

4/ZG26

Messerschmitt Bf 110C. Shot down by Pilot Officer Gray of No. 54 Squadron during sortie off English east coast 5.30 p.m. Crashed and burned out in Smith's Sandpits, Alton Park Road, Clacton. Hptmn. Luttke (Staffel Kapitan) and Uffz. Brillo both killed. Aircraft a write-off.

Messerschmitt Bf 110C. Shot down by ground fire following attack by RAF fighters off east coast 5.30 p.m. Crashed two miles east of Eastchurch. Uffz. Jackel killed, Uffz. Rutters captured. Aircraft 3U+ AM a write-off.

Messerschmitt Bf 110C. Shot down by No. 85 Squadron Hurricanes during operational sortie over English east coast 5.30 p.m. Ditched in sea off North Foreland. Uffz. Baar killed, Fw. Gierga rescued from sea and POW. Aircraft 3U+ CM lost.

Messerschmitt Bf 110C. Returned to Wizernes with damage following combat with fighters over the Thames Estuary 5.30 p.m. One NCO severely wounded died later. Aircraft 30% damaged.

6/ZG26

Messerschmitt Bf 110C (3060). Crashed and burned out at Pluckley 1.40 p.m. Shot down by Sergeant Robinson of No. 56 Squadron. Oberfw. Kiefel and Uffz. Hemmersbach both killed. Aircraft 3U+ IP a write-off.
Complete port rudder from this aircraft still bearing traces of painted Swastika marking and number '3060' displayed in the Kent Battle of Britain Museum.

Messerschmitt Bf 110C. Damaged in combat with No. 56 Squadron Hurricanes over southeast England and finally shot down in sea off Folkestone by Pilot Officer Goodman of No. 1 Squadron 1.45 p.m. Uffz. Wollin killed. Fw. Stange captured. Aircraft lost.

Messerschmitt Bf 110C. Forced-landed at Newchurch 1.35 p.m. following engagement with RAF fighters. Lt. Kastner and Uffz. Kaffenberger both captured. Aircraft 3U+ EP a write-off.

Messerschmitt Bf 110C. Crashed near Platts Heath, Lenham 1.40 p.m. following action involving No. 56 Squadron Hurricanes and final attack by Pilot Officer Mounsdon. Oblt. Hellmuth and Fw. Winter both killed. Aircraft a write-off.
Relics from this aircraft in the Steve Vizard Collection.

8/ZG26

Messerschmitt Bf 110C. Believed crashed near Godstone during combat with RAF fighters south of Kenley. Fw. Klare and Uffz. Brunger missing. Aircraft a write-off.

Messerschmitt Bf 110C. Crashed at Arques following combat mission. Crew unhurt. Aircraft 30% damaged.

Monday, August 19

Seenotflugkdo.2

Heinkel He 59. Crashed at Bergen, exact cause not stated. Lt. Jahnke and two NCOs killed. Lt. Brodman wounded. Aircraft a write-off.

4(F)/121

Junkers Ju 88A-1. Collided with an obstruction on landing at Conde-sur-Ifa aerodrome following long-range reconnaissance sortie. Lt. Durkow and three NCOs injured. Aircraft a write-off.

This port rudder from a Messerschmitt Bf 110 lay in a back garden at Pluckley until recovered by the Kent Battle of Britain Museum. It proved to be a unique find as it was identified as being from the Zerstorer Geschwader 26 aircraft of Oberfeldwebel Kiefel.

5/196

Arado Ar 196. Flew into the ground near Moldefjord in poor visibility. Lt. zur See Burk and one NCO killed. Aircraft a write-off.

Arado Ar 196. Collided with HT cables at Moldefjord during search mission for missing aircraft. Lt. zur See Hirschberg and one NCO killed. Aircraft a write-off.

4/JG3

Messerschmitt Bf 109E-1. Crash-landed at Brombois during routine domestic flight. Cause not stated. Pilot unhurt. Aircraft a write-off.

7/KG2

Dornier Do 17Z. Brought down in the sea off Yarmouth at 8.20 p.m. after bombing attack on Honington aerodrome. Lt. Hamb and three NCOs missing. Aircraft U5+ DR lost.

II/KG4

Heinkel He 111P-2. Crashed near Heringsdorf during searchlight co-operation flight. Oblt. Stiner and three NCOs killed. Aircraft a write-off.

III/KG27

Heinkel He 111P. Briefed to sortie over Liverpool and failed to return. Exact fate uncertain. Oblt. Siegel and two NCOs missing. One NCO killed. Aircraft a write-off.

I/KG51

Junkers Ju 88A-1. Crashed on landing at Caen following attack by fighters. Crew unhurt. Aircraft damaged but repairable.

III/KG51

Junkers Ju 88A-1 (7069). Failed to return from operational sortie over Little Rissington. Crashed in sea off Sussex coast. Fw. Haak, Fw. Moser, Fw. Schachtner and Uffz. Bachauer all killed. Aircraft 9K+ FR lost.

KGr.100

Heinkel He 111H-3. Crashed at Vertou due to petrol shortage. Lt. Zetzsche and one NCO injured. Aircraft a write-off.

Heinkel He 111H-2. Flying accident. Crashed at Crozon following mechanical failure. Crew unhurt. Aircraft a write-off.

Heinkel He.111H-2. Forced-landed near Les Sables due to petrol failure. Crew unhurt. Aircraft damaged but repairable.

Tuesday, August 20

Seenotflugkdo.3

Heinkel He 59. Propeller damaged on take-off from sea following rescue of ditched airman. Crew unhurt. Aircraft 50% damaged.

2/ErprobungsGruppe 210

Messerschmitt Bf 110D. Failed to return from operational sortie over English east coast at Aldeburgh. Exact cause unknown. Fw. Wohlfahrt and one NCO missing. Aircraft lost.

II/JG27

Messerschmitt Bf 109E-4. Crashed on landing at Carquebut following routine domestic flight. Pilot unhurt. Aircraft a write-off.

1/JG51

Messerschmitt Bf 109E-4. Shot down into the sea following fighter action. Fw. Maul rescued by He 59 of Seenotflugkdo.3. Aircraft lost.

I/JG53

Messerschmitt Bf 109E-1. Crashed on landing at Rennes following operational sortie. Pilot unhurt. Aircraft 35% damaged.

7/KG2

Dornier Do 17Z-3. Returned to base damaged by fighters during action off Aldeburgh. One NCO wounded. Aircraft 25% damaged.

9/KG2

Dornier D0 17Z-3. Failed to return from mission over England. Circumstances not recorded. Two NCOs missing and two more wounded. Aircraft a write-off.

9/KG3

Dornier Do 17Z-3. Shot down by fighters over Eastchurch. Crashed at Capel Hill Farm, Leysdown 4.15 p.m. Fw. Rudiger killed, three NCOs believed captured. Aircraft 5K+FT a write-off.
Site excavated by Steve Vizard, November 1979. Remains of shattered engines recovered together with assorted minor components and fuselage wreckage. An unexploded 250kg and five 50kg high explosive bombs also unearthed and detonated by EOD unit from RAF Wittering.

III/KG27

Heinkel He 111P. Crashed and burned out at Rennes on non-operational sortie. Crew of four all killed. Aircraft a write-off.

8/KG30

Junkers Ju 88A-1. Briefed to attack Thornaby aerodrome but shot down by fighters. Crashed at Patrington near Hull 7.10 p.m. One NCO killed, one severely wounded (died later), two others captured. Aircraft a write-off.

I/KG40

Focke-Wulf FW 200. Shot down by AA fire from cargo steamer during anti-shipping sortie over the Irish Sea. Oblt. Mollenhauser, Reg. Rat. Dr. Krueger and four NCOs all interned in Ireland. Aircraft lost.

III/KG77

Junkers Ju 88. Took fire during local domestic flight, cause unknown. Crashed at Obertraubling aerodrome. Crew unhurt. Aircraft 30% damaged.

Wednesday, August 21

KGr.806

Junkers Ju 88A-1. Failed to return from operational sortie. Cause unknown. Lt. zur See von Davidson and three NCOs missing. Aircraft lost.

Junkers Ju 88A-1. Failed to return from operational sortie. Cause unknown. Lt. zur See Miehr and two NCOs missing. One NCO killed. Aircraft lost.

6/JG54

Messerschmitt Bf 109E-1. Belly-landed at Vlissingen following operations over the Channel. Pilot unhurt. Aircraft 20% damaged.

III/JG54

Messerschmitt Bf 109E-4. Crashed on take-off from Guines-Sued aerodrome. Pilot unhurt. Aircraft a write-off.

2/KG2

Dornier Do 17Z-3. Shot down by No. 611 Squadron Spitfires during sortie over Norfolk 12.30 p.m. Crash-landed and burned out at Conifer Hill, Starston. Lt. Ermecke killed. Three NCOs baled out and captured. Aircraft a write-off.
Site investigated by the Norfolk and Suffolk Aviation Museum 1973. Scraps of badly-burned alloy, exploded 7.92mm ammunition and fragments of shattered perspex collected from the surface.

8/KG2

Dornier Do 17Z. Crashed into Gippeswyk Park, Ipswich 6.26 p.m. during sortie to attack North Weald. Lt. Kzienzyk and three NCOs captured. Aircraft U5+CS a write-off.

4/KG3

Dornier Do 17Z-3. Missing following operations over England. Exact cause unknown. Two NCOs killed and two missing. Aircraft a write-off.

6/KG3

Dornier Do17Z-2. Crashed in sea during operations over England. Two NCOs killed. Oblt. Matschosz missing. One NCO wounded. Aircraft a write-off.

Dornier Do 17Z-3. Failed to return from operational sortie over England. Crashed in the sea. Lt. Kruger and three NCOs all killed. Aircraft a write-off.

Dornier Do 17Z-3. Collided with left support aircraft seeking cloud cover after fighter attack during mission over southern England. Oblt. Schwarz (Staffel Kapitan) and three NCOs missing. Aircraft 5K+AP a write-off.

9/KG30

Junkers Ju 88A-1. Engines overheated during reconnaissance training flight over the North Sea. Crashed in sea forty miles east of Berwick 11.00 p.m. after aircraft caught fire. Crew of four NCOs captured. Aircraft 4D+LT lost.

II/KG53

Heinkel He 111H-2. Failed to return from operations over England. Cause of loss uncertain. Hptmn. Pfeiffer (Staffel Kapitan) and four NCOs all missing. Aircraft lost.

I/KG54

Junkers Ju 88A-1. Shot down by Squadron Leader O'Brien and Pilot Officer Doe of No. 234 Squadron in sortie over England. Crashed at Kings Sombourne 2.15 p.m. and burned out. Oblt. Birkenstock, Obergefr. Freude, Uffz. Schulze and Gefr. Becker believed captured. Aircraft a write-off.

II/KG54

Junkers Ju 88A-1. Shot down by No. 17 Squadron Hurricanes during attack on Brize Norton. Crashed on Marsh Farm, Earnley 4.15 p.m. Lt. Kiefer and three NCOs captured. Aircraft B3+BM a write-off.

Below left: **Manhandling the bombs uncovered by Steve Vizard at the Dornier crash site at Capel Hill Farm, Leysdown under the instruction of a bomb disposal officer from RAF Wittering.** *Right:* **The big bang of a 250kg bomb photographed from half-a-mile away (Steve Vizard).**

On Wednesday evening, August 21, a Dornier Do 17 from Kampfgeschwader 2 crashed in Gippeswyk Park at Ipswich *right*. The main part of the fuselage landed on the extreme southern corner *(above)* (East Anglian Daily Press). *Below:* It is thanks to research by John Le Mare that we were able to find the location now surrounded by a new housing estate built twenty-five years ago.

Thursday, August 22

Seenotflugkdo.3

Heinkel He 59. Damaged in heavy seas during storm at Boulogne harbour. No personnel casualties. Aircraft 50% damaged.

Heinkel He 59. Damaged during storm conditions at Boulogne harbour. No personnel casualties. Aircraft 50% damaged.

3(F)/121

Junkers Ju 88A-1. Shot down by No. 152 Squadron Spitfires during reconnaissance flight over the Bristol Channel. Crashed at Upcott Farm, Beaford, north of Okehampton 4.00 p.m. One NCO killed. Lt. Pfundtner, Lt. Baudler and one NCO captured. Aircraft 7A+ AL a write-off.

4/JG52

Messerschmitt Bf 109E-1. Crashed at Stade aerodrome having got into a flat spin during routine domestic flight. Uffz. Heilmeier killed. Aircraft a write-off.

1/KG2

Dornier Do 17Z. Crashed Escoudeuvres, cause not stated. Hptmn. von Winterfeldt and three NCOs killed. Aircraft a write-off.

7/KG30

Junkers Ju 88A-1. Crashed on landing at Aalborg-West following night operations. Crew unhurt. Aircraft 20% damaged.

8/KG30

Junkers Ju 88A-1. Missing following combat mission over southern England. Hptmn. Mainwald and two NCOs missing. One NCO wounded. Aircraft a write-off.

1/NJG 1

Messerschmitt Bf 110. Crashed on landing at Bonninghardt due to brake failure. Crew unhurt. Aircraft 60% damaged.

Friday, August 23

Wettererkundungs Staffel 1/Ob.d.L.

Heinkel He 111H-3. Shot down by fighters during sortie over the Orkneys. Three NCOs killed. Reg. Rat. a Kr. Knauf and one NCO both missing. Aircraft lost.

1/106

Junkers W34 Hi. Belly-landed at Mariensiel aerodrome during routine communications flight. Cause not stated. One NCO injured. Aircraft 50% damaged.

IV/KGr.z.b.V.1

Junkers Ju 52 (6324). Crashed at Dreux, Jersey due to mechanical failure. No crew casualties notified. Aircraft 1Z+ AA a write-off.

2/JG26

Messerschmitt Bf 109E-1. Crashed following collision over Boulogne. Uffz. Haferkorn killed. Aircraft a write-off.

II/JG26

Messerschmitt Bf 109E-1. Belly-landed at Marquise following operational sortie. Pilot unhurt. Aircraft 30% damaged.

Stab KG2

Dornier Do 17Z. Hit by ground fire during sortie to attack factories in Coventry. Crashed at Wickham Brook 9.20 a.m. Oblt. Hellingers (Staffel Kapitan), Oberfw. Wagner, Fw. Dietl and Uffz. Seidel captured. Aircraft U5+ EA a write-off.

Junkers Ju 88A-1. Landing accident at Aalborg-West following night operations over England. Crew unhurt. Aircraft 20% damaged.

I/KG27

Heinkel He 111P. Crashed at Avord aerodrome on routine domestic flight. Cause unknown. Lt. Ginzinger and three NCOs all killed. Aircraft a write-off.

Ausbildung Staffel KG40

Heinkel He 111H-4. Crashed near Reichenberg during training flight. Cause unknown. Oblt. Eschmann, Lt. zur See Meinhold and two NCOs all killed. Aircraft a write-off.

The running boar insignia and white '9' proclaim this Messerschmitt Bf 109E-1 as an aircraft from the 1st Staffel of JG52. Based at Coquelles, France, this particular specimen crash-landed in a field of stubble at Minster Road, Westgate on Sea after suffering engine failure on August 24.

I/KG55

Heinkel He 111P. Forced-landed near Le Havre damaged by AA fire during operations over Southampton. Gefr. Kaden killed, Lt. Weber wounded. Aircraft G1+DL 10% damaged.

Heinkel He 111H. Damaged by fighters during operational sortie over south coast of England. Forced-landed néar Le Havre. Oberfw. Heinze and Oberfw. Weis both wounded. Gefr. Kawlath baled out and missing. Aircraft G1+EK 25% damaged.

7/KG76

Dornier Do 17Z-2. Crash-landed at Cormeilles following combat mission. Crew unhurt. Aircraft a write-off.

III/LG1

Junkers Ju 88A-1. Failed to return from operational sortie over England. Hptmn. Schaumann (Staffel Kapitan) and three NCOs missing. Aircraft lost.

1/NJG1

Messerschmitt Bf 110. Crash-landed at Bonninghardt aerodrome. Oblt. Berger and one NCO both injured. Aircraft 50% damaged.

II/ZG76

Messerschmitt Bf 110C. Damaged in taxi-ing accident at Jersey aerodrome. Crew unhurt. Aircraft 40% damaged.

Saturday, August 24

1/196

Arado Ar 196. Damaged in harbour at Boulogne during heavy storm. No personnel casualties. Aircraft 20% damaged.

Arado Ar 196. Hit by bomb splinter whilst at dispersal in Boulogne harbour. No casualties. Aircraft 25% damaged.

2/506

Heinkel He 115. Damaged by heavy seas in storm whilst at moorings in Trondheim-See. No personnel casualties. Aircraft a write-off.

Heinkel He 115. Float and tail unit damaged during storm whilst moored in Trondheim-See. No casualties. Aircraft a write-off.

1(F)/122

Junkers Ju 88A-1. Shot down by own flak defences during sortie over Boulogne. Crew unhurt. Aircraft a write-off.

5(F)/122

Junkers Ju 88. Failed to return from reconnaissance sortie over the Channel. Lt. Hellermann, Lt. Hurck and one NCO missing. One NCO killed. Aircraft lost.

Aufklarungs Gruppe Ob.d.L.

Messerschmitt Bf 110. Believed shot down into the sea during operations over Sheerness. Lt. Hofer and two NCOs missing. Aircraft lost.

6/JG2

Messerschmitt Bf 109E-4. Crashed in sea off Shanklin 4.30 p.m. during fighter action over the Isle of Wight. Fw. Ebus killed. Aircraft lost.

Messerschmitt Bf 109E-1. Crash-landed near Le Havre with damage sustained in combat with RAF fighters over the Isle of Wight. Fw. Werner wounded. Aircraft a write-off.

I/JG3

Messerschmitt Bf 109E-3(1649). Severely damaged in attack by Bf 109 over Calais. Pilot unhurt. Aircraft a write-off.

The view north across the long fields of barley towards Westgate on Sea from the crash site on the west side of Minster Road on August 21, 1979.

Above: The weeping pelican of II/JG51 adorns the rear fuselage of this Bf 109E-4 which forced-landed in a stubble field at East Langdon, Kent after being brought down on August 24. As it landed, a police officer approached it with drawn revolver whereupon the pilot, Oberfeldwebel Beeck, raised his arms and said 'It's a fair cop' or the German equivalent thereof (Planet News). Below: One corner of Kent which seems timeless — passed by thousands of tourists each year as it lies right beside the main road from Dover to Deal. Even the washing still hangs on the line at the rear of the houses!

III/JG3

Messerschmitt Bf 109E-4. Forced-landed at Desvres damaged following fighter combat over the Channel. Pilot unhurt. Aircraft 25% damaged.

Messerschmitt Bf 109E-4. Crash-landed at Colombert following combat over southern England. Pilot unhurt. Aircraft a write-off.

7/JG3

Messerschmitt Bf 109E-4. Returned to base damaged following fighter action. Pilot unhurt. Aircraft 25% damaged.

9/JG3

Messerschmitt Bf 109E-1. Crashed and burned out on Broom Hill Farm, Camber 4.00 p.m. having been shot down during operations over southern England. Uffz. Kaiser captured. Aircraft 12+1 a write-off.

Messerschmitt Bf 109E-4. Crashed in sea off Herne Bay 4.10 p.m. during combat with RAF fighters. Lt. Achleitner baled out and rescued from sea by Herne Bay life-boat. Aircraft 8+1 lost.

III/JG26

Messerschmitt Bf 109E-4 (5020). Damaged in combat with RAF fighters. Crash-landed near Caffiers. Pilot unhurt. Aircraft a write-off.

7/JG26

Messerschmitt Bf 109E-4. Ditched in the Channel off Margate following action with enemy fighters. Wounded pilot rescued by Seenotflugkdo. Aircraft lost.

9/JG26

Messerschmitt Bf 109. Crash-landed at St. Inglevert following combat over the Channel. Pilot unhurt. Aircraft a write-off.

JG51

Messerschmitt Bf 109E-1. Ditched in the Channel due to engine failure during operational sortie. Pilot unhurt rescued by Seenotdienst. Aircraft lost.

1/JG51

Messerschmitt Bf 109E-4. Collided with RAF Spitfire during combat over the Channel and crashed in sea. Fw. Oglodek killed. Aircraft lost.

II/JG51

Messerschmitt Bf 109E-3. Engine damaged in combat over the Channel. Forced-landed Marquise. Pilot unhurt. Aircraft a write-off.

5/JG51

Messerschmitt Bf 109E-1. Shot down by Bf 109 during action involving RAF fighters over the Channel. Uffz. Delfs baled out wounded and rescued by Seenotdienst. Aircraft lost.

6/JG51

Messerschmitt Bf 109E-4 (5587). Forced-landed at East Langdon 12.55 p.m. due to engine failure following engagement with RAF fighters over Manston. Oberfw. Beeck captured unhurt. Aircraft 10+ a write-off.

8/JG51

Messerschmitt Bf 109E-4. Collided with Bf 109 flown by Uffz. Harheim during operations over the Channel off Ramsgate. Crashed in sea. Fw. Busch missing. Aircraft lost.

Messerschmitt Bf 109E-1. Crashed in sea off Ramsgate following collision with Fw. Busch. Uffz. Harheim missing. Aircraft lost.

9/JG51

Messerschmitt Bf 109E-1. Shot down in combat with fighters over the Channel. Uffz. Kroll killed. Aircraft lost.

1/JG52

Messerschmitt Bf 109E-1. Forced-landed at Minster Road, Westgate 3.45 p.m. following engine failure during operational sortie over the Thames Estuary. Fw. Bischoff captured unhurt. Aircraft 9+ a write-off.

II/JG53

Messerschmitt Bf 109E. Forced-landed at Dinan due to mechanical fault experienced during routine domestic flight. Pilot unhurt. Aircraft a write-off.

Stab JG54

Arado Ar 66 (6601). Communications aircraft destroyed in RAF bombing attack on Schiphol aerodrome. No personnel losses. Aircraft a write-off.

Stab III/KG4

Messerschmitt Bf 108 (1908). Damaged in bombing attack on Schiphol. No casualties. Aircraft 15% damaged.

Above: Three-quarters-of-an-hour after it crash-landed in a field at Clay Tye Hill, Bulphan, a Heinkel He III of 9/KG53 'Legion Condor' blew up scattering fragments far and wide. All of the crew, including two wounded members, escaped from the bomber before it was wrecked. Members of the local Home Guard and a youthful ARP messenger protect what remains (News Chronicle). *Below:* 'There must be a piece of it lying around somewhere', Wilf Nicoll muttered hopefully to the editor when they visited the scene of the Heinkel's demise on July 26, 1979.

Stab I/KG27

Heinkel He 111P. Forced-landed at Cherbourg with engine failure. Crew all unhurt. Aircraft a write-off.

I/KG51

Junkers Ju 88A-1. Crashed on landing at Villaroche aerodrome following operational sortie. Cause not stated. Crew unhurt. Aircraft 40% damaged.

III/KG51

Junkers Ju 88A-1. Shot down by RAF fighters during engagement over the Channel and crashed in the sea. One NCO killed, two missing. One NCO rescued unhurt. Aircraft lost.

III/KG53

Heinkel He 111H-2. Shot down by fighters following attack on Hornchurch. Crashed near Layer-de-la-Haye 4.00 p.m. Uffz. Kramer, Obergefr. Gleissner and Flgr. Salvino killed. Uffz. Schaffner baled out and captured unhurt. Major Ritzscherle baled out and missing — believed fell into Abberton Reservoir and drowned. Aircraft a write-off.

9/KG53

Heinkel He 111H-2. Shot down by fighters following attack on Hornchurch aerodrome. Crashed in sea thirteen miles off Brightlingsea 4.20 p.m. Hptmn. von Lonicer and Uffz. Pegatzki captured both wounded. Uffz. Dorn killed. Uffz. Schmidting and another NCO missing. Aircraft A1+ DT lost.

Heinkel He 111H-3. Shot down by Squadron Leader Kayll and Pilot Officer McClintock of No. 615 Squadron. Crashed and exploded at Clay Tye Hill, Bulphan 3.50 p.m. during attack on Hornchurch aerodrome. Lt. Luttigen, Uffz. Lackner and Fw. Fraas captured unhurt. Uffz. Platzer and Uffz. Hermans both wounded. Aircraft A1+ KT a write-off.

Heinkel He 111H-2. Shot down by fighters during attack on Hornchurch 4.00 p.m. Crashed in flames at Langford Grove Road, Langford. Oblt. Huhn, Fw. Jahger, Fw. Ultsch and Fw. Schmidt all killed. Gefr. Zaunick baled out wounded and captured. Aircraft A1+ BT a write-off.

Heinkel He 111H-2. Crash-landed near Great Wakering 4.15 p.m. following attack by Pilot Officer Ellacombe of No. 151 Squadron during sortie over Hornchurch aerodrome. Oblt. Winter, Fw. Engelhardt and Uffz. Wieck captured unhurt. Uffz. Schmidt and Gefr. Mauer both wounded. Aircraft A1+LT a write-off.

Stab II/KG76

Junkers Ju 88. Shot down (believed by AA fire) during combat with RAF fighters over Manston. Major Moricke (Gruppe Kommandeur) and Oblt. Schulte killed (washed ashore 6.9.40). Sonderfuehrer Wagner of Lw.Kr.Ber.Kp.4 also killed. One NCO missing. Aircraft lost.

Junkers Ju 88. Shot down in action over the Channel off Manston. Crashed in sea. Fw. Vetter, Fw. Flessner and Uffz. Meier missing, Fw. Meyer killed. Aircraft lost.

4/KG76

Junkers Ju 88. Crashed in sea off Manston following engagement by RAF fighters. Lt. Grell, Fw. Thomas and Uffz. Wetzker missing. Uffz. Henneberg killed. Aircraft lost.

Junkers Ju 88A. Returned to base severely damaged following operations over the Channel and combat with fighters over Manston. Oberfw. Jakobsmeier killed. Aircraft a write-off.

Attacked by fighters during a raid on Hornchurch aerodrome on August 24, this KG53 Heinkel crash-landed with two wounded crewmen near Samuels Corner, Landwick, Essex. Skimming low across a potato field, it crossed the main road bringing down power lines and striking a tree with its wing before slithering to a stop across another potato field. The spire of Great Wakering church lies in the background (Bill Gent).

Well guarded against the activities of souvenir hunters, the Heinkel awaits transportation to the nearest aircraft depot for breaking up (Bill Gent).

Evidence of the forced-landing is still visible four decades later. *Left:* The battered tree which caused the damage to the starboard wing and *above* the gap in the hedge where the bomber finally came to rest.

Junkers Ju 88A. Shot down into the Channel off Manston by RAF fighters. Uffz. Dubs, Uffz. Freimann and Uffz. Froba missing. Uffz. Kruell killed. Aircraft lost.

I/LG2

Messerschmitt Bf 109E-4. Returned to base damaged following combat over the Channel off Cap Gris-Nez. Pilot unhurt. Aircraft a write-off.

2/LG2

Messerschmitt Bf 109E-1. Shot down by Flying Officer Marston of No. 56 Squadron during engagement over the Thames Estuary and low-level chase over north Kent. Crashed on Mackledons Farm, Bobbing 4.00 p.m. Uffz. Moeller killed. Aircraft a write-off.
Site investigated by the Kent Battle of Britain Museum. Engine plate discovered just below turf and fragments of pilot's maps and parachute silk also recovered. Top section of elevator bearing splinter camouflage scheme also found.

Messerschmitt Bf 109E-4. Shot down by Pilot Officer Wicks of 56 Squadron during combat over the Thames Estuary 4.00 p.m. crashed at Canewdon. Uffz. Buschmeyer baled out and captured. Aircraft a write-off.
Site excavated by the London Air Museum. Intact Daimler-Benz DB 601 engine recovered with propeller boss and three blades and 20mm MGFF cannons.

5/ZG2

Messerschmitt Bf 110C-4. Crashed in sea off Cherbourg following combat over the Channel. Lt. Meyer killed. One NCO rescued by Seenotdienst. Aircraft lost.

8/ZG26

Messerschmitt Bf 110. Returned to base damaged in action over the Thames Estuary. One NCO wounded. Aircraft repairable.

Sunday, August 25

3/106

Heinkel He 115. Crashed on landing at Schellingwoude following routine domestic flight at night. Pilot unhurt. Aircraft a write-off.

III/JG2

Messerschmitt Bf 109E-1. Ditched in the Channel following combat with fighters. Wounded pilot rescued by Seenotdienst. Aircraft lost.

Messerschmitt Bf 109E-1. Crashed in sea following fighter combat over the Channel. Wounded pilot rescued by Seenotdienst. Aircraft lost.

Messerschmitt Bf 109E-1. Crashed on landing at base due to combat damage. Pilot unhurt. Aircraft damaged but repairable.

II/JG26

Messerschmitt Bf 109E (815). Crashed on landing at Blecqueneques after operational sortie. Pilot unhurt. Aircraft 20% damaged.

Stab II/JG27

Messerschmitt Bf 109E-4. Forced-landed near Colombieres following engine failure during local flight. Pilot unhurt. Aircraft 40% damaged.

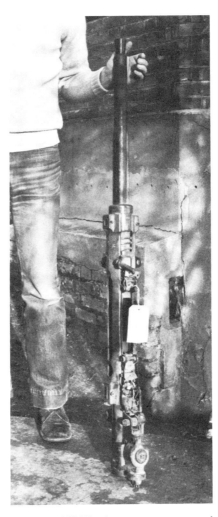

A 20mm MGFF wing cannon recovered from Unteroffizier Buschmeyer's 2/LG2 Messerschmitt Bf 109 at Canewdon.

1/JG53

Messerschmitt Bf 109E-1. Shot down by Pilot Officer Beamont of No. 87 Squadron during combat over Weymouth. Forced-landed and caught fire at Tatton House Farm, Buckland 5.30 p.m. Gefr. Broeker captured wounded. Aircraft a write-off.

5/JG53

Messerschmitt Bf 109E-4. Shot down in combat with RAF fighters and crashed in the sea off Weymouth 5.45 p.m. Oberfw. Baun rescued by Seenotdienst. Aircraft lost.

6/JG53

Messerschmitt Bf 109E-4. Failed to return from operations over the Channel and combat with fighters off Weymouth. Hptmn. Maculan missing. Aircraft lost.

Messerschmitt Bf 109E-4. Crashed in sea during fighter combat over the Channel off Weymouth. Fw. Seufert wounded and rescued by Seenotdienst. Aircraft lost.

Messerschmitt Bf 109E. Returned to base damaged following fighter action off Weymouth 5.30 p.m. Fw. Margstein wounded. Aircraft repairable.

1/JG54

Messerschmitt Bf 109E (6137). Damaged in fighter combat and forced-landed near Wissant. Pilot unhurt. Aircraft 15% damaged.

Messerschmitt Bf 109E-4. Shot down in combat over Dover by Pilot Officer Gray of No. 54 Squadron. Believed that which crashed at St. Nicholas at Wade 7.35 p.m.. Oblt. Held killed. Aircraft a write-off.
Site excavated by the Brenzett Aeronautical Museum and few minor components and fragments of airframe discovered. Bulk of aircraft penetrated 16ft of solid chalk.

3/KG4

Heinkel He 111H-4. Crashed on take-off from Zuidernes due to engine failure. Crew unhurt. Aircraft a write-off.

8/KG30

Junkers Ju 88A. Returned to base, one NCO wounded following fighter attack. Aircraft repairable.

II/KG51

Junkers Ju 88A-1. Crash-landed near Cherbourg following fighter attack during operational sortie over the Channel. Lt. Bender and Sonderfhr. Grosze (Lw.Kr.Ber.Kp.5) both wounded. Aircraft a write-off.

Junkers Ju 88A-1. Shot down by RAF fighters in combat over the Channel. One NCO killed, three others missing. Aircraft lost.

9/KG55

Heinkel He 111P. Shot down by night fighter during sortie to attack Harwell aerodrome. Crashed and exploded on the sea one mile off Hastings 1.30 a.m. Fw. Schmaderer rescued and captured. Gefr. Klesatschek killed. Lt. Jerusel, Fw. Neidel and Fw. Alt missing. Aircraft G1+ CT lost.

3/KG76

Dornier Do 17Z. Shot down into the Channel by RAF fighters. Crew all baled out and rescued from sea by Seenotdienst. Uffz. Eppelmann and Uffz. Liebmann both wounded. Aircraft lost.

V/LG1

Messerschmitt Bf 110C-2. Belly-landed at Roquancourt following combat with fighters. One NCO wounded. Aircraft a write-off.

Messerschmitt Bf 110C-1. Crash-landed at Barfleur with combat damage. Crew unhurt. Aircraft damaged but repairable.

13/LG1

Messerschmitt Bf 110C-2. Failed to return from operations over the Channel and engagement by RAF fighters. Oblt. Glienke and one NCO missing. Aircraft lost.

15/LG1

Messerschmitt Bf 110C-4. Presumed shot down in sea by British fighters during combat over the Channel. Uffz. Hamann and one NCO missing. Aircraft lost.

III/StG2

Junkers Ju 87B. Crashed on take-off at Ernes aerodrome due to engine failure. Crew unhurt. Aircraft a write-off.

I/StG77

Junkers Ju 87B. Crashed on landing at Maltot following routine domestic flight. Cause not stated. Crew unhurt. Aircraft 25% damaged.

I/ZG2

Messerschmitt Bf 110C-4. Returned to base damaged in fighter combat. Crew unhurt. Aircraft 20% damaged.

1/ZG2

Messerschmitt Bf 110C-4. Shot down by fighters during escort mission for Ju 88s of KG51. Crashed at Creech Barrow near Wareham 6.00 p.m. Oblt. Goetz and Uffz. Haupt both wounded baled out and captured. Aircraft a write-off.

Site investigated by the Wealden Aviation Archaeological Group in 1976 and numerous minor airframe and engine components recovered.

Messerschmitt Bf 110C-4. Crashed and exploded at Winfrith, East Chaldon, near Warmwell following attack by fighters during escort mission for KG51. Lt. Westphal and Obergefr. Brief killed. Aircraft 3M+ CH a write-off.

Messerschmitt Bf 110C-4. Crashed at Priory Farm, East Holme, near Wareham 6.00 p.m. Shot down by fighters whilst acting as escort to Ju 88s of KG51. Uffz. Becker and Obergefr. Wopzel both captured wounded. Aircraft 3M+ KH a write-off.

Crash site only twenty yards from the banks of the River Frome investigated by the Wealden Aviation Archaeological Group in 1979 and both Daimler-Benz DB 601 engines excavated together with both undercarriage legs, cockpit controls and instruments, oxygen bottles, armament and signal pistol bearing aircraft identity letter 'K' in paint and one leather gauntlet.

Messerschmitt Bf 110C-4. Failed to return from escort mission over Hampshire 6.00 p.m. Reputedly shot down in sea. Uffz. Horner and one NCO missing. Aircraft lost.

II/ZG2

Messerschmitt Bf 110C-4. Returned to base damaged in fighter combat over the Channel. Crew unhurt. Aircraft 25% damaged.

Messerschmitt Bf 110C-4. Severely damaged during fighter operations over the Channel. Returned to base, crew unhurt. Aircraft a write-off.

Messerschmitt Bf 110D/O. Returned to base with combat damage. Crew unhurt. Aircraft 20% damaged.

Monday, August 26

4 (F)/121

Junkers Ju 88A-1. Overshot runway on landing at Caen-Carpiquet and crashed into a dispersed Bf 110. Crew unhurt. Aircraft 20% damaged.

1/506

Heinkel He 115C (3253). Destroyed in RAF bombing of Tromso aerodrome. No personnel losses. Aircraft a write-off.

Heinkel He 115C (3247). Destroyed in RAF bombing attack on Tromso aerodrome. No casualties. Aircraft a write-off.

1/606

Dornier Do 17. Crashed during operations over St. George's Channel. Cause unknown. Lt. zur See Isedrick missing. Three NCOs killed. Aircraft lost.

The Wealden Aviation Archaeological Group has carried out two excavations near Wareham on Bf 110C-4s from 1/ZG2 lost on August 25. This is the group in action at Priory Farm at East Holme where a major recovery of parts was accomplished including the engines (S. Hall/ A. Saunders).

2/JG2

Messerschmitt Bf 109E-4 (5383). Shot down in combat with No. 43 Squadron fighters over Portsmouth. Crashed near Blendworth 5.25 p.m. Oblt. Griesebach baled out and captured. Aircraft a write-off.

First recovery mounted by the Southern Area Wartime Aircraft Preservation Society. Propeller boss excavated with steel hawser from original RAF salvage efforts still attached.

Neatly dug excavation by the Southern Area Wartime Preservation Society to investigate the wreckage of the JG2 Bf 109 at Blendworth (Peter Dimond).

7/JG2

Messerschmitt Bf 109E-4 (3702). Failed to return from operations over the Channel. Lt. Hoffmann killed. Aircraft a write-off.

3/JG3

Messerschmitt Bf 109E-4 (5132). Damaged in fighter combat over the Channel. Forced-landed near Calais. Pilot unhurt. Aircraft 20% damaged.

4/JG3

Messerschmitt Bf 109E-4 (5289). Shot down in combat over north Kent 12.30 p.m. by Flying Officer Marston of No. 56 Squadron. Crashed on Grays Farm, Reculver. Uffz. Finke killed. Aircraft a write-off.

Messerschmitt Bf 109E-1 (6221). Shot down during fighter sortie over the Canterbury area. Uffz. Muller missing. Aircraft a write-off.

5/JG3

Messerschmitt Bf 109E-1 (3317). Belly-landed at Ossendrecht following engine failure. Pilot unhurt. Aircraft repairable.

6/JG3

Messerschmitt Bf 109E-1 (3874). Shot down by RAF fighters during action over the Thames Estuary and crashed at Chislet Marshes near St. Nicholas at Wade. Uffz. Buchner killed. Aircraft a write-off.

Major recovery undertaken by the Brenzett Aeronautical Museum in 1975. Remains of wreckage excavated from between thirty and forty feet included the aircraft identity plate.

8/JG3

Messerschmitt Bf 109E-4. Damaged by fighters in combat over the Thames Estuary and crash-landed at Calais. Pilot unhurt. Aircraft 20% damaged.

9/JG27

Messerschmitt Bf 109E-1. Failed to return from operational sortie over the Channel. Believed crashed in sea. Uffz. Ackmann missing. Aircraft lost.

2/JG52

Messerschmitt Bf 109E-1. Shot down by fighters over Ramsgate 3.30 p.m. Uffz. Hartlieb killed. Aircraft a write-off.

Messerschmitt Bf 109E-4. Shot down during fighter action over Folkestone 3.30 p.m. Uffz. Bokel captured. Aircraft a write-off.

Messerschmitt Bf 109E-1. Crashed and burned out near Acol during combat with fighters over Ramsgate 3.15 p.m. Obergefr. Malecki captured. Aircraft 1+ a write-off.

Messerschmitt Bf 109E-1. Shot down in combat over Ramsgate 3.30 p.m. Forced-landed near Golf Club House at Sandwich. Fw. Bacher captured. Aircraft 2+ a write-off.

3/JG52

Messerschmitt Bf 109E-1. Shot down by No. 610 Squadron fighters during action over the Channel off Dover 11.55 a.m. Crashed in sea. Fw. Ziegler rescued by shore boat and captured. Aircraft lost.

1/JG53

Messerschmitt Bf 109E-4. Suffered engine failure during operational sortie over Portsmouth and crashed. Fw. Bezner killed. Aircraft a write-off.

II/JG53

Messerschmitt Bf 109E-4. Shot down into the Channel off Cherbourg during combat with fighters. Lt. Roos rescued unhurt by Seenotdienst. Aircraft lost.

5/JG53

Messerschmitt Bf 109E-4. Ditched in the Channel off Cherbourg during fighter combat. Lt. Berwanger believed rescued by Seenotdienst. Aircraft lost.

Messerschmitt Bf 109E-1. Shot down by RAF fighters during combat over the Channel off Cherbourg. Fw. Holdermann killed. Aircraft a write-off.

III/JG53

Messerschmitt Bf 109E-1. Crash-landed near Brest due to mechanical fault following operations over the Channel. Pilot unhurt. Aircraft a write-off.

II/JG54

Messerschmitt Bf 109E-1 (3639). Belly-landed on Beveland Island due to engine failure. Pilot unhurt. Aircraft 30% damaged.

1/KG2

Dornier Do 17Z. Attacked by fighters during sortie over Thames Estuary 3.00 p.m. Returned to base three NCOs wounded. Aircraft repairable.

2/KG2

Dornier Do 17Z-3. Severely damaged by fighter attacks over Hornchurch and forced-landed on Rochford aerodrome 3.30 p.m. Hptmn. Bose, Uffz. Schmidt, Uffz. Lunghard and Obergefr. Roeder captured. Aircraft U5+ LK a write-off.

Dornier Do 17Z-3. Attacked by fighters over Hornchurch and badly damaged. Crashed two miles south-west of Eastchurch 3.40 p.m. Major Gutzmann (Gruppe Kommandeur) Uffz. Buhr and Uffz. Schmolzer captured. Oblt. Hertel killed. Aircraft U5+ GK a write-off.

3/KG2

Dornier Do 17Z-2. Returned to base damaged following sortie over the Thames Estuary 3.30 p.m. Oblt. Buchholz (Staffel Kapitan) and Oblt. Konrad both wounded. Aircraft damaged but repairable.

4/KG2

Dornier Do 17Z (3445). Crashed and burned out near Namur during operational sortie. Cause unknown. Lt. Sachse killed. Three NCOs wounded. Aircraft U5+ MM a write-off.

7/KG2

Dornier Do 17Z-3. Engaged by fighters following attack on Debden aerodrome and brought down on Highams Farm, Thaxted 3.30 p.m. Oblt. Heidereich and Uffz. Panczack both killed. Fw. Hohenstadter and Uffz. Gussmann both baled out wounded and captured. Aircraft U5+ LR a write-off.

Dornier Do 17Z-3 (1207). Shot down by fighters following bombing of Debden. Crash-landed at Whitstead 3.40 p.m. Uffz. Knorky, Uffz. Schaffer, Uffz. Simon and Gefr. Schadt all captured. Aircraft a write-off.

Dornier Do 17Z-2. Crashed at Cole End, Wimbish 3.30 p.m. following attack on Debden aerodrome and combat with fighters. Lt. Krieger and Uffz. Illing both captured wounded. Uffz. Winter and Gefr. Schneider baled out and captured unhurt. Aircraft U5+ TR a write-off.

9/KG2

Dornier Do 17Z. Damaged in fighter attack over Colchester. Returned to base, one NCO wounded. Aircraft repairable.

2/KG3

Dornier Do 17Z (2541). Crash-landed near Tirlemont fuel exhausted following operational sortie across the Channel. One NCO killed. Lt. Wiesprzewski and another NCO wounded. Aircraft a write-off.

III/KG3

Dornier Do 17Z (3602). Crashed at Calais-Marck aerodrome following fighter attacks. One NCO wounded. Aircraft a write-off.

7/KG3

Dornier Do 172-Z (1160). Ditched on Goodwin Sands 1.40 p.m. following fighter attack. Gefr. Huhn killed. Uffz. Reinhard, Uffz. Ritzel missing. Fw. Essmert captured. Aircraft 5K+ AR lost.

Dornier Do 17Z (3329). Briefed to attack West Malling aerodrome but shot down by fighters over the Channel 1.40 p.m. Lt. Sachse killed and three NCOs wounded. Aircraft 5K+ GR a write-off.

Dornier Do 17Z-3 (2822) Fuel exhausted during sortie over the Channel to attack West Malling. Forced-landed St. Merville, two NCOs wounded. Aircraft damaged but repairable.

Dornier Do 17Z-3 (2646). Crashed into the sea at Foreness 12.55 p.m. during mission to bomb West Malling and engagement with RAF fighters. Lt. Eggert rescued severely wounded (died 28.8.40). Uffz. Ramm and Obergefr. Knochenmuss both drowned. Uffz. Haupt captured. Aircraft 5K+ ER a write-off.

8/KG4

Junkers Ju 88. Collided with another Ju 88 on take-off from Schiphol. Oblt. Meissner (Staffel Kapitan) and three NCOs killed. Aircraft a write-off.

Junkers Ju 88. Collided with Oblt. Meissner's aircraft on take-off from Schiphol. One NCO wounded. Aircraft a write-off.

6/KG30

Junkers Ju 88A-1 (3103). Failed to return from operational sortie, cause not known. One NCO killed, three others wounded. Aircraft lost.

III/KG53

Heinkel He 111H-2. Crashed into the ground near Brugge during combat sortie. Cause unknown. Lt. Weber and three NCOs killed. Aircraft a write-off.

I/KG55

Heinkel He 111P. Shot down by fighters during mission to bomb Portsmouth dockyard. Forced-landed on Helliers Farm, Wick 4.30 p.m. Fw. Schreck wounded, Oblt. Krenn, Uffz. Morrack, Uffz. Degen and Uffz. Schneiders all captured. Aircraft G1+ BB a write-off.
Prop blade and first-aid kit in the Wealden collection.

Heinkel He 111H (5370) Forced-landed at Le Havre following fighter attack during sortie to bomb Portsmouth docks. Uffz. Thaden wounded. Aircraft G1+ GL repairable.

Heinkel He 111H. Landed Dreux one NCO wounded following attack by fighters over Portsmouth. Aircraft repairable.

4/KG55

Heinkel He 111. Returned to base damaged following fighter attack over Portsmouth 4.30 p.m. Oblt. Herrfurth wounded. Aircraft G1+ AM repairable.

Heinkel He 111P. Attacked by fighters during sortie to bomb Portsmouth docks. Shot down by Sergeant Whall of No. 602 Squadron and landed on beach at East Wittering 4.30 p.m. Lt. Metzger captured wounded. Fw. Urhahn, Uffz. Schandner, Uffz. Paas and Flgr. Fessel all killed. Aircraft G1+ DM a write-off.
Site excavated by the Halstead War Museum in April 1971. Excavations revealed portions of lower gondola, port window section of airframe, a radiator and various fragments of shattered airframe and armour plate. Relics also held by the Kent Battle of Britain Museum. (See 'After the Battle' magazine No. 23)

Heinkel He 111P (2165). Crashed on North Brook Farm, Waterlooville at 4.45 p.m. following fighter attack during bombing sortie over Portsmouth docks. Oberfw. Hennecke baled out too low and killed. Lt. Walter, Uffz. Schufft, Flgr, Wimmer and Uffz. Marmer all captured. Aircraft G1+ GM a write-off.
Large panel from wing and tail wheel recovered from locality by the Wealden Aviation Archaeological Group in 1977.

5/KG55

Heinkel He 111P. Crashed in the Channel following attack by fighters during mission to bomb Portsmouth dockyard. Uffz. Steiger, Uffz. Losch and Gefr. Stratmann all wounded and rescued by Seenotdienst. Aircraft G1+GN lost.

I/KG77

Junkers Ju 88A-1. Crash-landed at Illesheim aerodrome due to engine malfunction during routine domestic flight. Crew unhurt. Aircraft 40% damaged.

I/LG1

Junkers Ju 88A-1 (3090). Damaged in landing accident at Orleans-Bricy aerodrome when tyre burst on landing. Crew unhurt. Aircraft 30% damaged.

II/ZG2

Messerschmitt Bf 110. Damaged in fighter combat and forced-landed at St. Pierre-Eglise. Crew unhurt. Aircraft a write-off.

4/ZG26

Messerschmitt Bf 110D/O. Shot down by fighters during bomber escort mission. Crashed and burst into flames at Great Tey 3.15 p.m. Oberfw. Rosler and Uffz. Heinrich killed. Aircraft 3U+CM a write-off.
Crash site excavated by the London Air Museum.

9/ZG26

Messerschmitt Bf 110C-4. Crashed and exploded on Crabtree Farm, Great Bentley 3.25 p.m. following fighter combat over Essex. Fw. Opper and Uffz. Nick both killed. Aircraft 2N+AK a write-off.
Major recovery by the London Air Museum revealed remains of shattered Daimler-Benz DB 601 engines, one propeller boss and part of propeller blade and a purse containing French and Belgian coins.

Messerschmitt Bf 110C-4 (3299). Failed to return from bomber escort sortie over Essex 3.30 p.m. Believed shot down by fighters and crashed in the Thames Estuary. Uffz. Reinhold killed and one NCO missing. Aircraft a write-off.

8/ZG76

Messerschmitt Bf 110C-4. Failed to return from combat sortie over England. Exact cause of loss unknown. Fw. Dahne and one NCO both killed. Aircraft a write-off.

Tuesday, August 27

3 (F)/10

Dornier Do 17P (3545). Shot down over Cap Gris-Nez, exact circumstances not stated. Crew casualties not recorded. Aircraft T1+BL a write-off.

4 (F)/14

Messerschmitt Bf 110C-5. Damaged in landing accident at Cherbourg. Ran over a bomb. Crew unhurt. Aircraft 15% damaged.

3 (F)/31

Dornier Do 17P. Shot down by Pilot Officer Considine and Flight Lieutenant Blake of No. 238 Squadron during photo-reconnaissance mission over Plymouth. Forced-landed Hurdwick Farm, Tavistock 10.30 a.m. Lt. Haffan, Fw. Klaushenke and Gefr. Schlesjel captured. Aircraft 5D+IL a write-off.
Minor component collected at the time of this crash donated to the Devon Aircraft Research and Recovery Team.

The Heinkel of KG55 which crashed on East Wittering beach on the afternoon of August 26. The controversy surrounding this aircraft (one publication speculated that the crew had been machine-gunned on the beach) was fully investigated in *After the Battle* magazine. The site was excavated by Peter Dimond of the SAWAPS group and Ken Anscombe of Halstead in 1971 (Features International).

Regrettably Ken Anscombe *(left)* of Halstead was one of only two wreck groups who refused to offer any information on their recoveries. He said he did not approve of our intention to publish details of crashes . . . and, that he was going to do his own book! We have attempted to include information from other sources on sites excavated by his private Halstead War Museum (and also the Robertsbridge Museum). This is a piece from the gondola which he did allow us to photograph for *After the Battle* magazine.

3/106

Heinkel He 115C (2782). Damaged in fighter attack during sortie over the North Sea (PQ4330). Lt. Arnim and two NCOs wounded. Aircraft 30% damaged.

Seenotflugkdo.2

Heinkel He 59 (935). Destroyed by enemy action in operations off Cherbourg harbour. Lt. zur See Mietlich and one NCO killed. Two NCOs missing. Aircraft a write-off.

6/JG3

Messerschmitt Bf 109E-4 (1471). Crashed on landing at Samer on burst tyre. Pilot unhurt. Aircraft a write-off.

I/JG52

Messerschmitt Bf 109E-1 (6215). Crashed on take-off from Calais-Marck. Pilot unhurt. Aircraft a write-off.

Stab III/KG1

Heinkel He 111H-2 (5376). Sortied to attack Coventry at night and believed shot down by AA fire. Crashed at Caterham 2.45 a.m. Major Fanelsa (Gruppe Kommandeur), Fw. Meyer and three NCOs baled out unhurt. Aircraft V4+ CD a write-off.

5/KG2

Dornier Do 17Z-2 (4188). Reported crashed near Slyne following interception by RAF night fighter. Three NCOs wounded. Aircraft a write-off.

6/KG2

Dornier Do 17Z-3 (2784). Belly-landed near St. Andre, fuel exhausted following operational sortie. Crew unhurt. Aircraft 35% damaged.

Above: 'Coo! It's a Ninekel'. On a Tuesday morning in August 1940, local families turn out to view Caterham's latest attraction. Like the tail flukes of a leviathan, the massive tailplanes of a KG1 'Hindenburg' Heinkel lie in the rear garden of No. 21 Manor Avenue, a bungalow occupied by a retired schoolmaster and his wife which was partly demolished when the flaming bulk of the bomber crashed upon it after suffering hits by accurate AA fire in the early hours. The crew, which included the Gruppe Kommandeur, baled out and were captured. *Below:* Looking across the rear gardens of the restored dwellings from Queens Park on an August evening thirty-nine years later.

Ausbildungs Staffel KG3

Dornier Do 17Z. Crash-landed at Schweinfurth following engine failure during local training flight. Two NCOs injured. Aircraft a write-off.

7/KG4

Junkers Ju 88A-5 (0284). Failed to return from operational sortie, cause unknown. Lt. Annis and two NCOs killed. Lt. zur See von Athens missing. Aircraft lost.

II/KG27

Heinkel He 111P. Damaged in landing accident at Bourges aerodrome after operational sortie. Crew unhurt. Aircraft 28% damaged.

6/KG30

Junkers Ju 88A-1 (4033). Crashed on landing at Aalborg following combat mission. Lt. Kieszner and three NCOs killed. Aircraft a write-off.

9/KG30

Junkers Ju 88A-1 (4076). Crashed, probably due to engine failure, shortly after take-off from Aalborg aerodrome on routine domestic flight. Crew unhurt. Aircraft 50% damaged.

Ausbildungs Staffel KG53

Heinkel He 111H-2 (5320). Damaged in taxiing accident at Giebelstadt. Crew unhurt. Aircraft AJ+JS 10% damaged.

II/KG55

Heinkel He 111P. Forced-landed at Chartres following operational sortie. Crew unhurt. Aircraft 35% damaged.

KGr.806

Junkers Ju 88A-1. Damaged on landing at Nantes from operations. Possible collision with another Ju 88. Crew unhurt. Aircraft 50% damaged.

Junkers Ju 88A-1. Believed damaged in collision with another Ju 88 which landed at Nantes. No casualties. Aircraft 10% damaged.

II/LG1

Junkers Ju 88A-1. Damaged in attack by RAF fighters during sortie over the Channel. Forced-landed back at Cherbourg. Crew unhurt. Aircraft 50% damaged.

V/LG1

Messerschmitt Bf 110C-2. Severely damaged in taxi-ing accident at Roquancourt. Non-operational loss. Crew unhurt. Aircraft a write-off.

Inspector W. H. Thompson, Winston Churchill's bodyguard: 'While at Dover Castle an Alert sounded and from the cliffside we could see the approach of the German bombers and the resulting clash when our fighters attacked. The battle went on over our heads for several moments. During the fighting, dodging and shooting, two German planes came down into the sea, perhaps half-a-mile from where we stood and watched. It thrilled us all to see the enemy in flames, hurtling down at terrific speed, to meet the rock-hard sea with a splash, a roar, a hiss and a fountain of exploding waters.

'Driving from Dover to Ramsgate, we saw a fighter plane shot down and Churchill immediately asked our driver to take us as close to the point where it would crash as we could get. We arrived at the spot. Churchill jumped out and proceeded on foot with me at his side. This was an unnecessary risk as the Germans did a great deal of strafing and always shot off whatever they still had aboard before scooting for home again. Firemen had arrived just before us. Flames were shooting up. We had not been able to determine whether it was a German fighter or one of our own.

' ''I hope to God it isn't a British plane!'' Churchill remarked. He walked right up to the blazing craft. To the relief of us all, we found it was a German and that the pilot had baled out.'

This incident occurred on Wednesday, August 28 and we established that Winston Churchill had visited the crash site of a Bf 109E-4 from Stab I/JG3 on Church Farm at Church Whitfield. The pilot, Leutnant Landry, came down over a mile away near the Duke of York's Royal Military School. Captain Horton was on hand to photograph the smoking fighter and the Prime Minister and Inspector Walter Thompson leaving the scene — see pages 716-717 (Imperial War Museum). We revisited the scene on May 21, 1980 but could find no trace of the wreckage.

Wednesday, August 28

Seenotflugkdo.3

Heinkel He 59 (1528). Shot down by fighters during rescue mission over the Channel (PQ1116). One NCO killed. Lt. zur See Sprenger and two NCOs rescued wounded. Aircraft lost.

Heinkel He 59 (1512). Engaged on air-sea rescue mission and shot down by RAF Spitfires. Crashed in sea at PQ1285. Four NCOs wounded. Aircraft lost.

KGr.z.b.V.108

Heinkel He 59 (1820). Damaged in collision with He 115 landing on sea at Stavanger-Sola. No personnel casualties. Aircraft BV+MH 55% damaged.

2/606

Dornier Do 17. Returned to base one NCO killed during operations over the English coast. Aircraft repairable.

I/JG2

Messerschmitt Bf 109E-1 (3337). Damaged in accident at Fecamp aerodrome. Exact circumstances not stated. Aircraft 20% damaged.

Stab I/JG3

Messerschmitt Bf 109E-4 (941). Shot down during combat with fighters over Dover and crashed at Church Farm, Church Whitfield 4.25 p.m. Lt. Landry baled out badly wounded and captured (died of injuries 23.9.40). Aircraft a write-off.
This incident was witnessed by Winston Churchill during a tour of inspection of Dover Castle and the crash site was visited by him shortly afterwards.

5/JG3

Messerschmitt Bf 109E-4 (6611). Shot down during combat with fighters over the Channel. Ditched in sea off Boulogne. Oberfw. Gotz wounded but rescued by Seenotdienst. Aircraft lost.

Messerschmitt Bf 109E-4 (1449). Crashed in the Channel off Boulogne during combat with fighters. Pilot rescued unhurt. Aircraft lost.

Messerschmitt Bf 109E-1 (5142). Believed ditched in the Channel following fighter action over Boulogne. Pilot wounded rescued by Seenotdienst. Aircraft lost.

Stab III/JG3

Messerschmitt Bf 109E-4 (5146). Shot down in combat with RAF fighters over Canterbury. Reported crashed following explosion over Kearsney 12.40 p.m. Oberfw. Trebing killed. Aircraft a write-off.
Site under investigation by the Brenzett Aeronautical Museum.

7/JG3

Messerschmitt Bf 109E-1 (3553). Shot down in combat over the Channel. Crashed in sea. Pilot rescued by Seenotdienst. Aircraft a write-off.

Stab JG26

Messerschmitt Bf 109E (2743). Shot down in combat with fighters over the Canterbury area. Crashed south of Chartham Downs 10.00 a.m. Hptmn. Beyer (Geschwader Adjutant) baled out and captured. Aircraft a write-off.

7/JG26

Messerschmitt Bf 109E (1353). Forced-landed at Goodnestone House Farm, Goodnestone 9.30 a.m. during combat over the Canterbury area. Fw. Straub captured. Aircraft 13+1 a write-off.

Stab JG27

Gotha Go 145 (1115). Failed to return from routine mail-delivery flight between Channel Islands and Strasbourg. Lost bearings and landed on Lewes Racecourse, Sussex. Pilot captured. Aircraft lost.

2/JG27

Messerschmitt Bf 109E-1 (3284). Crashed on landing at Peuplingues, cause not stated. Pilot unhurt. Aircraft 40% damaged.

Messerschmitt Bf 109E-4 (6234). Crash-landed at Peuplingues during routine domestic flight. Pilot unhurt. Aircraft 15% damaged.

III/JG27

Messerschmitt Bf 109E-4 (2782). Crash-landed at Cherbourg due to engine malfunction during local flight. Pilot unhurt. Aircraft 35% damaged.

Stab JG51

Messerschmitt Bf 109E-4 (5395). Shot down in combat with RAF fighters and crashed on South Barham Farm, Denton 9.10 a.m. Oblt. Kircheis (Geschwader Adjutant) baled out too low and broke a leg in heavy landing. Aircraft a write-off.
Major recovery by the Brenzett Aeronautical Museum in 1973 and complete remains of aircraft unearthed.

I/JG51

Messerschmitt Bf 109E-4 (1436). Severely damaged in combat over southern England and ditched in the Channel on return flight. Pilot rescued unhurt. Aircraft lost.

1/JG51

Messerschmitt Bf 109E-1 (6154). Crashed on landing at Pihen following combat sortie. Pilot unhurt. Aircraft 50% damaged.

III/JG51

Messerschmitt Bf 109E-4 (1984). Landed back at St. Omer-Clairmarais with combat damage. Oblt. Liegnitz wounded. Aircraft a write-off.

7/JG51

Messerschmitt Bf 109E-4 (1523). Crashed in Garden Wood, Poulton Farm, South Alkham 4.55 p.m. during combat with RAF fighters. Oberfw. Dau baled out and captured. Aircraft 14+ a write-off.
Site excavated by the Brenzett Aeronautical Museum in 1974. Daimler-Benz DB 601 engine recovered together with undercarriage, tail wheel and a pair of Luftwaffe flying boots from storage locker. Also investigated by Steve Vizard who recovered many items including a plate inscribed 'Bf 109'.

1/JG54

Messerschmitt Bf 109E-1 (6204). Shot down by Squadron Leader Denholm of No. 603 Squadron in engagement over Dungeness 7.15 p.m. Crashed at Copt Hill Farm, Capel. Fw. Schoettle baled out and captured. Aircraft 4+ a write-off.
Site excavated in 1976 by the Brenzett Aeronautical Museum which recovered all surviving major components and remains of shattered airframe.

II/JG54

Messerschmitt Bf 109E-4 (2759). Shot down in combat with fighters over the Channel between Dover and Calais. Crashed in sea. Uffz. Kleemann missing. Aircraft lost.

III/JG54

Messerschmitt Bf 109E-1 (3538). Damaged in landing accident at Soesterberg. Pilot unhurt. Aircraft 35% damaged.

Stab II/KG1

Heinkel He 111H-2 (5588). Damaged by enemy action during sortie over the Channel. Forced-landed at Calais one NCO wounded. Aircraft 50% damaged.

4/KG1

Heinkel He 111H-2 (5587). Crashed shortly after take-off from Montdidier believed due to premature explosion of bomb load. Lt. Beck died of wounds. One NCO injured. Aircraft a write-off.

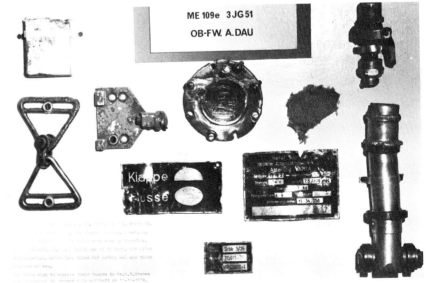

Oberfeldwebel Artur Dau's aircraft, claimed by Brenzett as shot down by Squadron Leader Peter Townsend, was excavated at Poulton Farm, near Church Hougham, Dover.

3/KG3

Dornier Do 17Z-2 (3378). Crashed and exploded at Muerringen during operational sortie. Exact cause unknown. Crew of four NCOs killed. Aircraft a write-off.

Dornier Do 17Z-3 (2807). Crashed near Marche on combat mission. Cause not stated. Oblt. Graf von Platen-Hallermund and one NCO killed. Two NCOs wounded. Aircraft a write-off.

4/KG3

Dornier Do 17Z-2 (3225). Shot down by fighters during operational sortie over England. Four NCOs wounded. Aircraft a write-off.

6/KG3

Dornier Do 17Z-3 (4251). Ditched in sea off Foreness Point 12.45 p.m. following RAF fighter attack. Lt. Krug, Gefr. Burghardt, Gefr. Gailer and Flgr. Brueckmann all captured wounded. Aircraft 5K+ LP a write-off.

Dornier Do 17Z (3411). Crashed at Mardyck with damage sustained in engagement with fighters. Crew unhurt. Aircraft 5K+ DP repairable.

3/KG53

Heinkel He 111H-2 (6878). Crashed near Vitry-en-Artois due to mechanical failure. Crew of five NCOs killed. Aircraft a write-off.

II/KG53

Heinkel He 111H-3 (5560). Forced-landed near Wesel due to radio breakdown and complete loss of bearings. Crew unhurt. Aircraft A1+ LM 50% damaged.

4/KG53

Heinkel He 111H-2 (5346). Crashed on take-off from Vendeville on operational sortie. Cause unknown. Lt. Simon and four NCOs killed. Aircraft a write-off.

5/KG53

Heinkel He 111H-2 (6815). Take-off accident at Vendeville, cause unknown. Hptmn. Neumann and three NCOs killed. One NCO wounded. Aircraft a write-off.

6/KG53

Heinkel He 111H-2 (2770). Crashed on take-off at Vendeville aerodrome. Crew of five NCOs all killed. Aircraft a write-off.

III/KG55

Heinkel He 111P (2692). Crashed at Villacoublay shortly after take-off to attack Liverpool. Cause not known. Lt. Muetzel, Lt. Scheithauer, Gefr. Schreiber, Oberfw. Brohr and Gefr. Bretthauer all killed. Aircraft G1+ BR a write-off.

Stab KGr.806

Junkers Ju 88A-1 (5075). Crashed on landing at Rennes due to undercarriage failure. Crew of four NCOs killed. Aircraft a write-off.

I/LG1

Junkers Ju 88A-1 (3124). Crashed at Massiac during operational sortie. Cause unknown. Three NCOs killed and one wounded. Aircraft a write-off.

3/Erprobungs Gruppe 210

Messerschmitt Bf 109E-4 (3741). Crash-landed at Koeln-Ostheim during routine domestic flight. Cause not stated. Pilot injured. Aircraft 15% damaged.

Messerschmitt Bf 109E (1208). Crashed on landing at Calais-Marck due to undercarriage failure following operational sortie. Pilot unhurt. Aircraft a write-off.

III/StG1

Junkers Ju 87B-1 (479). Believed damaged in collision with another Ju 87 at Deauville. Oblt. Kathe killed. Aircraft a write-off.

Junkers Ju 87B-1 (5236). Destroyed, believed by collision, in accident at Deauville. Lt. Muehltaler and one NCO killed. Aircraft a write-off.

Thursday, August 29

Transport Staffel FliegerKorps IV

Junkers Ju 52 (2904). Crashed and burned out at Loddenheide on landing from domestic flight. Crew of four NCOs injured. Aircraft NJ+ NR a write-off.

3/106

Heinkel He 115 (3263). Failed to return from operational sortie over the sea in PQ3376. Probably landed on the sea following engine failure. Lt. zur See Kinzel and Uffz. Brommen missing. Gefr. Hennigsen killed. Aircraft M2+ LL lost.

3/506

Heinkel He 115 (2771). Crashed on landing at Stavanger-Sola following operations over the North Sea. Oblt. zur See Raether killed. Aircraft S4+ DL a write-off.

Ditched Dornier. The starboard bullet-damaged rudder of a Dornier 17 of II/KG3 'Blitz-Geschwader' based at Antwerp-Deurne which came down in the sea off Foreness Point on August 28. Now on display at the RAF's Battle of Britain Museum at Hendon.

1/606

Dornier Do 17 (2878). Failed to return from operational sortie over the North Sea. Believed crashed in sea. Two NCOs killed. Lt. zur See Rees missing. Aircraft 7T+GH lost.

Dornier Do 17 (2838). Failed to return from mission over the North Sea. Crew all missing. Aircraft 7T+GL lost.

1 (H)/14

Henschel Hs 126B (4066). Damaged in crash-landing during local flight. Cause not recorded. Pilot unhurt. Aircraft 5H+BH 40% damaged.

2/JG3

Messerschmitt Bf 109E-4 (5338). Damaged in fighter combat over the south coast by Sergeant Booth of No. 85 Squadron and forced-landed near Pevensey 3.25 p.m. Oberfw. Lampskemper captured. Aircraft 8+ a write-off.

3/JG3

Messerschmitt Bf 109E-3 (1166). Failed to return from combat sortie over the Channel. Believed crashed in sea. Oblt. Floerke killed. Aircraft lost.

4/JG3

Messerschmitt Bf 109E-4 (5364). Shot down in combat with RAF fighters over Hastings 7.00 p.m. Uffz. Gericke killed. Aircraft a write-off.

Messerschmitt Bf 109E-1 (1134). Shot down in fighter combat and crashed on New Lodge Farm, Hooe 7.00 p.m. Oblt. Wipper died of wounds. Aircraft a write-off. *Site excavated by members of the Wealden Aviation Archaeological Group in 1973. Propeller boss and blade recovered together with various fragments of shattered Daimler-Benz DB 601 engine, airframe components and part of first-aid kit.*

III/JG3

Messerschmitt Bf 109E-1 (2615). Forced-landed at Colombert with battle damage. Pilot unhurt. Aircraft 45% damaged.

Messerschmitt Bf 109E-4 (964). Crashed on take-off from Desvres on operational sortie. Pilot unhurt. Aircraft a write-off.

Messerschmitt Bf 109E-1 (4031). Severely damaged in combat with fighters and forced to ditch in the Channel during return flight. Pilot rescued unhurt by Seenotkdo. Aircraft lost.

7/JG3

Messerschmitt Bf 109E-1 (6335). Believed shot down into the Channel during combat with RAF fighters. Uffz. Pfeifer missing. Aircraft lost.

I/JG26

Messerschmitt Bf 109E-1 (3634). Ditched in the Channel following combat with RAF fighters. Pilot rescued unhurt by Seenotkdo. Aircraft lost.

1/JG26

Messerschmitt Bf 109E-4 (1181). Shot down in combat with fighters over the Channel. Oberfw. Graf von Treuberg killed. Aircraft a write-off.

5/JG52

Messerschmitt Bf 109E-3 (1974). Crashed near Jever due to adverse weather conditions. Oberfw. Francke killed. Aircraft a write-off.

While on a night sortie over the Bristol Channel on August 29, this Heinkel He 111 of I/KG27 'Boelcke' based at Tours, was shot down by one of the few successful Spitfire 'cat's-eye' patrols. Before crashing, it jettisoned its bombs over fields at Woodfalls on the Wiltshire-Hampshire border and skimmed the roof tops at North Charford and Hatchet Green. It then struck an oak tree and high-tension cables which caused it to collide with a house in the village of Hale, four miles north-east of Fordingbridge, where it came to rest. The four crew members baled out with varying degrees of injury, one later dying in hospital. A seven-year-old evacuee was trapped when the ceiling fell on his bed, but was freed unhurt (Southern Evening Echo).

The house in Hale — once occupied by Mr. and Mrs. Dear, their son, an evacuee, John Alexander and one Heinkel — still stands in the quiet village bordering the New Forest (Henry Wills).

6/JG54

Messerschmitt Bf 109E-3 (1266). Crash-landed at Vlissingen following combat sortie. Pilot unhurt. Aircraft 10% damaged.

III/JG54

Messerschmitt Bf 109 (1547). Landed at Le Bortel due to engine trouble during operational sortie. Pilot unhurt. Aircraft 20% damaged.

II/KG2

Dornier Do 17Z-3 (2839). Engaged by night fighter during operations over the Channel. Crashed near Senlis-Persan. Two NCOs killed. Uffz. Mattusseck missing. Oblt. Kindler wounded. Aircraft U5+FP a write-off.

6/KG3

Dornier Do 17Z-3 (3480). Flew into a radio mast near Gent and crashed in flames. Lt. Zein and two NCOs killed. Aircraft 5K+FP a write-off.

3/KG27

Heinkel He 111H (3438). Shot down by Pilot Officer Wright of No. 92 Squadron during night operations over Bristol. Crashed at Hale 11.00 p.m. Oblt. Huenerbein, Uffz. Schlosser, Uffz. Siebers and Obergefr. Walpert all baled out and captured. Walpert later died of injuries. Aircraft 1G+EL a write-off.

I/KG40

Focke-Wulf FW 200C-2 (14). Slightly damaged in forced-landing at Bordeaux having exhausted fuel during operational sortie. Crew unhurt. Aircraft 10% damaged.

Above: ,On August 30, two Messerschmitt Bf 109s from JG54 'Gruenherz' collided during a combat south of Biggin Hill. Both pilots baled out and were captured. This is the surprisingly small crater of one with Layhams Farm in the background (Fox Photos). *Below:* Thirty-six years later, the Wealden group excavates the site (Peter Foote).

Ergaenzungs Staffel KG51

Junkers Ju 88A-1 (8018). Damaged in routine familiarisation flight. Cause not stated. Crew unhurt. Aircraft 40% damaged.

I/KG53

Heinkel He 111H-2 (2613). Crashed near Vitry-en-Artois due to mechanical fault during operational sortie. Two NCOs killed, another two injured. Aircraft A1+ FH a write-off.

III/KG55

Heinkel He 111P-2 (2858). Forced-landed at Sens fuel exhausted after operations over the Channel. Crew unhurt. Aircraft 30% damaged.

Heinkel He 111P (2151). Crashed at Versailles following combat sortie. Cause unknown. Crew of five NCOs killed. Aircraft a write-off.

5/KG77

Junkers Ju 88 (7090). Crashed into the Hornisgrinde following collision with another Ju 88 during routine domestic flight. Hptmn. Bus (Staffel Kapitan) and three NCOs all killed. Aircraft 3Z+ AN a write-off.

Junkers Ju 88 (4131). Collided with Hptmn. Bus's aircraft during local flight and crashed near the Hornisgrinde. Crew of four NCOs killed. Aircraft 3Z+ EN a write-off.

KGr.100

Heinkel He 111H-3 (6891). Ran out of fuel following combat mission and forced-landed at Chateaudun. Crew unhurt. Aircraft 40% damaged.

KGr.806

Junkers Ju 88A-1 (3116). Crashed at Vaernes during operational sortie. Cause unknown. Crew of four NCOs killed. Aircraft a write-off.

II/NJG1

Junkers Ju 88Z-2 (0256). Crashed at Elsdorf during air-firing practice. Cause unknown. Lt. Bregand and two NCOs killed. Aircraft a write-off.

Stab II/ZG26

Messerschmitt Bf 110C-2 (2121). Returned to base damaged following combat with RAF fighters over Hastings. Lt. Thuring wounded. Aircraft 3U+ CJ 25% damaged.

Friday, August 30

3/606

Dornier Do 17. Crashed and burned out at Bilbao due to undercarriage failure following operational sortie. Lt. zur See Hanschke and three NCOs killed. Aircraft a write-off.

3 (F)/22

Dornier Do 17P (1119). Failed to return from long-range reconnaissance mission over Scotland. Lt. von Seebeck, Uffz. Schobert and Fw. Aigner missing. Aircraft 4N+ AL a write-off.

4/Aufklaerungs Gruppe Ob.d.L.

Dornier Do 215 (0036). Missing from reconnaissance sortie over Norwich area. Oblt. Sonnleitner, Oberfw. Weise, Obgefr. Hofmann all killed. Fw. Neubauer missing. Aircraft G2+ JH a write-off.

Stuka-Ergaenzungs Staffel Flieger Korps VIII

Junkers Ju 87B (5345). Crashed near Lippstadt during practice dive-bombing attacks on ground targets. Oblt. Jaeger killed. Aircraft T6+ HZ a write-off.

II/JG2

Messerschmitt Bf 109E-4 (2753). Crashed near Dunkerque due to heavy damage sustained in combat over the Thames Estuary 5.00 p.m. Pilot unhurt. Aircraft a write-off.

4/JG2

Messerschmitt Bf 109E-4 (2765). Shot down during combat over the Thames Estuary and crashed in flames at Walderslade 4.55 p.m. Oberfw. Harbauer killed. Aircraft 1+ a write-off.
Site investigated by the Kent Battle of Britain Museum and various surface fragments collected including portions of pilot's seat harness.

8/JG2

Messerschmitt Bf 109E-4 (2782). Shot down in combat with fighters over Dungeness. Uffz. Reith captured. Aircraft lost.

II/JG3

Messerschmitt Bf 109E-1 (3350). Tail wheel collapsed on landing at Wierre-au-Bois following routine domestic flight. Pilot unhurt. Aircraft 15% damaged.

III/JG3

Messerschmitt Bf 109E-1 (6322). Damaged landing on burst tyre at Desvres following local flight. Pilot unhurt. Aircraft a write-off.

Left: **The RAF's 'Oliver Reed' — Squadron Leader John Ellis, DFC, of No. 610 Squadron spared a friendly glance for the photographer when he visited the site (Fox Photos).** *Right:* **Members of the Wealden Group couldn't resist the temptation to reconstruct the 1940 tableau — Steve Hall plays the star role (Peter Foote).**

I/JG26

Messerschmitt Bf 109E (5650). Forced to ditch in the Channel on return flight following combat with RAF fighters. Wounded pilot rescued by Seenotkdo. Aircraft lost.

II/JG26

Messerschmitt Bf 109E-4 (804). Severely damaged in combat over Folkestone and ditched in the Channel. Pilot rescued unhurt by Seenotkdo. Aircraft lost.

Messerschmitt Bf 109E-4 (6298). Crashed in sea due to damage suffered in combat with RAF fighters over Folkestone. Pilot rescued unhurt by Seenotkdo. Aircraft lost.

I/JG27

Messerschmitt Bf 109E-1 (6123). Shot down during fighter combat over the Thames Estuary 6.30 p.m. Crashed in sea. Oblt. Bertram baled out unhurt and rescued by Seenotdienst. Aircraft lost.

3/JG27

Messerschmitt Bf 109E-1 (3771). Forced-landed at Westwood Court, near Faversham damaged by Flying Officer Carbury of No. 603 Squadron during combat over London 4.45 p.m. Fw. Arnold captured. Aircraft 12+ a write-off.

Messerschmitt Bf 109E-1 (6270). Crashed at Park House, Westwell 6.50 p.m. following combat over Kent. Oblt. Axthelm captured. Aircraft 6+ a write-off.

Stab III/JG27

Messerschmitt Bf 109E-4 (1618). Crashed on landing at Guines following combat sortie. Pilot unhurt. Aircraft 40% damaged.

III/JG27

Messerschmitt Bf 109E-4 (1623). Shot down in combat over Dungeness and crashed in the sea. Fw. Lehmann killed. Aircraft lost.

Messerschmitt Bf 109E-1 (6330). Belly-landed at Dieppe due to mechanical failure following operational sortie. Pilot unhurt. Aircraft 30% damaged.

5/JG51

Messerschmitt Bf 109E-1 (6219). Damaged in taxi-ing accident at Jever aerodrome. Pilot unhurt. Aircraft 20% damaged.

2/JG52

Messerschmitt Bf 109E-1 (1973). Suffered engine failure during combat mission over Dover. Believed crashed in sea. Lt. Geller missing. Aircraft lost.

II/JG54

Messerschmitt Bf 109E-4 (6072). Broke up over Fickleshole Farm, Chelsham 11.55 a.m. following collision with Lt. Ziegler during engagement with RAF fighters. Oblt. Rath baled out wounded and captured. Aircraft 6+ a write-off.
Believed to be the aircraft recovered at Layhams Farm, Biggin Hill by the Wealden Aviation Archaeological Group in 1976. Complete Daimler-Benz DB 601 engine excavated together with propeller boss, armour plate, and various components. Nothing discovered to establish identity beyond dispute.

Messerschmitt Bf 109E-4 (1643). Collided with Oblt. Rath during combat with RAF fighters and crashed at Oxted 11.55 a.m. Lt. Ziegler captured. Aircraft 5+ a write-off.

10/KG1

Heinkel He 111H-2 (2720). Briefed to attack Farnborough and rammed by Hurricane flown by Pilot Officer Morris of No. 79 Squadron over Reigate 11.12 a.m. Crashed at Swires Farm, Capel and later exploded. Oberfw. Hornick, Fw. Stahlberg. Gefr. Heimel killed. Hptmn. Baess (Staffel Kapitan) severely wounded. Oblt. Foelisch captured. Aircraft V4+ BV a write-off.

Site investigated by the Air Historical Group 1976 and small surface fragments collected. Excavated by the Wealden Aviation Archaeological Group September 1979 and many fragments of shattered airframe and a few engine components recovered.

Heinkel He 111H-2 (5444). Shot down by Sergeant Allard of No. 85 Squadron in engagement over Surrey during mission to attack Farnborough. Crashed at Mannings Heath 11.30 a.m. Oblt. Waechter, Gefr. Maehlbeck both killed. Obergefr. Moenninghoff, Gefr. Struger captured wounded. Gefr. Hofer captured unhurt. Aircraft V4+ GV a write-off.

Heinkel He 111H-2 (5125). Became separated from formation and attacked by Spitfires over the English coast. Forced to land on the sea off Folkestone harassed by Sergeant Beardsley of No. 610 Squadron. Uffz. Burger, Gefr. Hildebrand, Gefr. Feierabend, Gefr. Roggemann and Gefr. Klappholz all rescued from the sea and landed at Dover. Aircraft V4+ MV lost.

Heinkel He 111H-2 (3305). Shot down by Pilot Officer Greenwood of No. 253 Squadron following attack on Farnborough aerodrome. Forced-landed at Haxted Farm, Lingfield 11.35 a.m. Gefr. Reis killed. Fw. Schnabel, Uffz. Paeslack both wounded and captured together with Uffz. Staerk and Gefr. Groth. Aircraft V4+ HV a write-off.

IV/KG1

Heinkel He 111H-2 (2750). Shot down by Pilot Officer Pegge of No. 610 Squadron during attack on Farnborough. Abandoned aircraft crashed at Roy Hill, Blackboys, Sussex 11.25 a.m. Oberfw. Rauschert and Flgr. Zinoegger killed. Oberfw. Riemann, Fw. Ester and Uffz. Stein captured wounded. Fw. Ester later died of injuries. Aircraft V4+ DW a write-off.

A 7.92mm MG15 machine gun from this aircraft in the Halstead War Museum

9/KG2

Dornier Do 17Z-3 (2868). Crashed near Brugge during operational sortie. Cause unknown. Lt. Wittmann and two NCOs killed. One NCO wounded. Aircraft U5+ FT a write-off.

III/KG27

Heinkel He 111P (1697). Crash-landed at Rennes following combat mission. Crew unhurt. Aircraft 30% damaged.

III/KG51

Junkers Ju 88A-1 (7076). Crashed on landing at Montdesir due to undercarriage collapse following routine domestic flight. Crew unhurt. Aircraft 9K+ DS 15% damaged.

3/KG53

Heinkel He 111H-2 (5532). Engaged by RAF fighters during attack on Radlett. Crashed in flames at Lifstan Way, Southend 5.15 p.m. Fw. von Kuehnheim, Uffz. Sam and Obergefr. Fischer killed. Lt. Roesler and Uffz. Gall baled out and captured. Aircraft A1+ JL a write-off.

Site investigated by the Essex Aviation Group but no relics discovered.

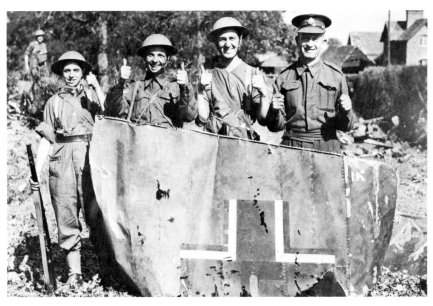

More fun and games by the Wealden Archaeological Group, this time at Swires Farm at Capel, south of Dorking. Pat Burgess, Brian Connolly, Andy Saunders and Steve Hall give the thumbs up on the spot where thirty-six years before army personnel stood with a section of wing from the He 111 that was rammed by Pilot Officer Morris of No. 79 Squadron (Paul Strudwick).

II/KG53

Heinkel He 111H-2 (2711). Briefed to attack Radlett and failed to return. Oberfw. Ostertrag, Uffz. Brock, Uffz. Franck killed. Fw. Beffert and Gefr. Schiedel missing. Aircraft A1+ JM lost.

Heinkel He 111H. Returned to base damaged and one NCO wounded following attack by fighters over Chelmsford 4.30 p.m. Aircraft repairable.

5/KG53

Heinkel He 111H-2 (3142). Severely damaged by fighters during engagement over Essex during attack on Radlett. Hit trees prior to forced-landing at Colne Engaine 4.30 p.m. Oberfw. Dietrich killed. Fw. Hummel, Fw. Steinberg, Fw. Fellner and Uffz. Hugenschuetz captured. Aircraft A1+ BN a write-off.

6/KG53

Heinkel He 111H-2 (2782). Severely damaged by fighters during attack on Radlett and crashed at Manston 4.35 p.m. during return flight. Fw. Eckert killed. Gefr. Koehler severely wounded (died 2.9.40). Gefr. Klapp. Gefr. Glueck and Fw. Stockl captured. Aircraft A1+ JP a write-off.

Heinkel He 111H-2 (6818). Ditched in sea off Sheppey 4.30 p.m. following attack by fighters. Uffz. Rascher, Uffz. Roempert, Uffz. Wagner, Uffz. Schall and Uffz. Fauerleber rescued unhurt. Aircraft A1+ GP lost.

7/KG53

Heinkel He 111H-2 (2624). Shot down in repeated attacks by Hurricanes during attack on Radlett. Crash-landed near The Rectory at Hunsdon 4.30 p.m. Gefr. Stilp severely wounded (died later). Gefr. Riess killed. Lt. Fischbach, Fw. Kusserow and Fw. Distler captured. Aircraft A1+ CR lost.

III/KG53

Heinkel He 111H. Forced-landed at St. Omer with damage sustained in fighter attack during sortie over Essex 4.30 p.m. One NCO killed. Aircraft repairable.

Ergaenzungs Staffel KG55

Heinkel He 111P (1629). Crashed and burned out near Chartres following flying accident during training flight. Lt. Konig, Uffz. Mueller, Gefr. Groh, Gefr. Raths and Gefr. Friedriski killed. Aircraft G1+KS a write-off.

Heinkel He 111P (1703). Collided with above aircraft during local training flight and crashed near Chartres. Crew of five NCOs all killed. Aircraft a write-off.

III/KG55

Heinkel He 111P (2813). Suffered engine failure during operational sortie and damaged in forced-landing at Nantes. Oblt. Nedden, Lt. Wronski and three NCOs all injured. Aircraft a write-off.

I/LG2

Messerschmitt Bf 109E-4 (2043). Shot down in combat over the Channel off Calais and crashed in sea. Hptmn. Mielke missing. Aircraft lost.

I/StG77

Junkers Ju 87B (355). Crashed on landing at Maltot following routine domestic flight. Cause not stated. Crew unhurt. Aircraft 20% damaged.

5/ZG2

Messerschmitt Bf 110 D/O (3315). Shot down by Hurricane during escort mission and exploded attempting forced-landing at Durrants Road, Ponders End 4.55 p.m. Hptmn. Schuldt and Uffz. Dyroff both killed. Aircraft A2+HK a write-off.

I/ZG26

Messerschmitt Bf 110C-4 (3582). Believed returned to base damaged following combat with fighters over the Channel. No crew casualties notified. Aircraft U8+CX a write-off.

3/ZG26

Messerschmitt Bf 110C-4 (3583). Damaged in fighter combat and crash-landed at Cap Gris-Nez. Crew unhurt. Aircraft U8+A1 a write-off.

II/ZG26

Messerschmitt Bf 110C. Returned to base damaged following combat over the Channel off Calais. One NCO wounded. Aircraft repairable.

5/ZG26

Messerschmitt Bf 110C-2 (3496). Shot down by RAF fighters during escort mission for He 111s of KG53. Forced-landed at Mill Hill Farm, Rettenden 4.30 p.m. Uffz. Franke and Uffz. Huebner captured. Aircraft 3U+KP a write-off.

4/ZG76

Messerschmitt Bf 110C (3257). Crashed at Enfield Sewage Farm, Wharf Road, Ponders End 4.55 p.m. during engagement with fighters. Hptmn. Wagner and Stabsfw. Schmidt both killed. Aircraft M8+BM a write-off.

Messerschmitt Bf 110C (3615). Shot down by RAF fighters during escort mission and crashed at Barley Beans Farm, Kimpton 4.30 p.m. Oberfw. Anthony killed. Uffz. Nordmeyer captured paralysed having suffered broken back. Aircraft M8+MM a write-off.

III/ZG76

Messerschmitt Bf 110C-2 (3235). Damaged in combat with RAF fighters and landed at Calais-Marck on one engine. Crew believed unhurt. Aircraft 2N+LM 30% damaged.

Saturday, August 31

Aufklaerungs Gruppe 21

Henschel Hs 126 (3246). Crash-landed near Illes due to engine failure during routine domestic flight. Pilot unhurt. Aircraft a write-off.

4/Aufklaerungs Gruppe Ob.d.L

Dornier Do 215 (0028). Failed to return from reconnaissance sortie over England. Uffz. Vogel and Fw. Maurer killed. Uffz. Goebbels and Uffz. Kamolz missing. Aircraft G2+LH lost.

II/JG2

Messerschmitt Bf 109E-1 (3510). Ditched in Channel due to severe damage suffered in fighter combat. Pilot rescued unhurt by Seenotkdo. Aircraft lost.

3/JG3

Messerschmitt Bf 109E-4 (5339). Shot down during combat with RAF fighters over the Thames Estuary and London. Crashed Whalebone Lane gunsite, Chadwell Heath 6.50 p.m. Oblt. Loidolt baled out and captured. Aircraft a write-off.

Severely damaged by a Hurricane during an escort mission on August 30, a Zerstorer of ZG2 attempted a forced-landing at Durrants Road, Enfield. In such a built-up area it was a desperate measure that was doomed to failure. The aircraft crashed into the greenhouses of Rochfords nursery garden at the rear of Nos. 16 to 22 Durrants Road killing both crewmen.

The little Edens of suburbia on October 13, 1979. Apple trees and runner beans now thrive prolifically over the site of the 1940 water-filled crater.

Above: Sudden death is rarely dignified particularly when it occurs in a sewage works. An airman removes ammunition from the wreckage of a ZG76 Messerschmitt which crashed after combat on August 30 at the Enfield Council sewage farm in Conduit Lane, about half-a-mile from the Durrants Road crash which occured at the same time. *Right and below:* Seventy-three-year-old Frank Dawson still vividly remembers the events of the day and on November 24, 1979 pointed out the damaged wall of the filter tank which was never repaired. He described how a dead crew member was catapulted from the German fighter, when it impacted into the ground, to land some distance away from the wreck close to the road and how a soldier passing on a bicycle seized the opportunity to rob the dead airman of his flying boots before pedalling furiously away.

Messerschmitt Bf 109E-4 (1503). Shot down by Sergeant Stokoe of No. 603 Squadron and crashed in garden between Anne Street and Robert Street, Plumstead during fighter action over south London 6.20 p.m. Lt. Binder killed. Aircraft a write-off.

Messerschmitt Bf 109E-4 (1082). Damaged in combat with Pilot Officer Berry of No. 603 Squadron over the Thames Estuary 6.45 p.m. Forced-landed on beach at Shoeburyness. Oblt. Rau captured. Aircraft 4+ a write-off.

4/JG3

Messerschmitt Bf 109E-1 (3175). Shot down in combat with RAF fighters over London 6.30 p.m. Lt. von Larisch killed. Aircraft a write-off.

Surface wreckage recovered from a site at West Kingsdown by the Kent Battle of Britain Museum said to be from this aircraft.

6/JG3

Messerschmitt Bf 109E-4 (1475). Shot down by Pilot Officer Millington of No. 79 Squadron during sortie over southern outskirts of London. Crashed on Lydd Ranges 6.30 p.m. Oblt. Westerhoff captured badly burned. Aircraft a write-off.

III/JG3

Messerschmitt Bf 109E-1 (3549). Crash-landed at Desvres following combat mission. Pilot unhurt. Aircraft 25% damaged.

Above: **A hell-hound from the Pas-de-Calais is brought to heel in an English field. The Messerschmitt Bf 109E-4 flown by Oberleutnant Fronhoefer of JG26 'Schlageter' lies useless in captivity at Ulcombe with the oast houses of Jubilee Hall Farm in the background. The aircraft was belly-landed after combat on August 31. It displays the gothic 'S' of JG26 and the 'Hollenhund' insignia of the 9th Staffel (Fox Photos).** *Below:* **Now sheep may safely graze free from the attentions of either hounds or low-flying aircraft in the meadow at Jubilee Hall Farm on August 23, 1979.**

I/JG26

Messerschmitt Bf 109E-1 (4806). Shot down by Flying Officer Carbury of No. 603 Squadron in combat over the Thames. Crashed in flames at Bridge Road, Rainham 12.45 p.m. Oblt. Hafer fell from aircraft and discovered with unopened parachute in the Ingrebourne Creek 2.9.40. Aircraft a write-off.

6/JG26

Messerschmitt Bf 109E-4 (5393). Shot down during fighter operations over the Canterbury area. Uffz. Heyer killed. Aircraft a write-off.

7/JG26

Messerschmitt Bf 109E-1 (6309). Shot down in combat believed broke up over Knatts Valley, Stansted 5.40 p.m. Uffz. Liebeck captured. Aircraft a write-off.

Large portion of parachute with Luftwaffe acceptance stamp in Steve Vizard collection attributed to this aircraft.

Messerschmitt Bf 109E-1 (3464). Crashed at Mill House Farm, Allington 6.30 p.m. following fighter action. Fw. Klar captured wounded. Aircraft a write-off.

9/JG26

Messerschmitt Bf 109E-4 (3712). Severely damaged in combat over southern England and crashed in the Channel during return flight. Oblt. Ebeling (Staffel Kapitan) baled out unhurt and rescued by Seenotkdo. Aircraft 3+ 1 lost.

Messerschmitt Bf 109E-4 (1184). Forced-landed on Jubilee Hill, Ulcombe 6.45 p.m. damaged in combat with Pilot Officer Gray of No. 54 Squadron. Oblt. Fronhoefer captured. Aircraft 10+ 1 a write-off.

3/JG27

Messerschmitt Bf 109E-1 (1486). Forced-landed at Peuplingues with combat damage. Pilot unhurt. Aircraft 35% damaged.

4/JG27

Messerschmitt Bf 109E-4 (1425). Damaged landing on burst tyre at Guines following combat sortie. Pilot unhurt. Aircraft 30% damaged.

3/JG51

Messerschmitt Bf 109E-4 (5355). Mid-air collision during patrol over Calais. Uffz. zur Lage baled out unhurt. Aircraft a write-off.

Messerschmitt Bf 109E-4 (4837). Collided with Uffz. zur Lage's aircraft during patrol over Calais. Oblt. Busch baled out unhurt. Aircraft a write-off.

Stab JG53

Messerschmitt Bf 109E-4 (5053). Forced-landed at Etaples, damaged following combat with RAF fighters. Pilot unhurt. Aircraft 40% damaged.

1/JG77

Messerschmitt Bf 109E-1 (6092). Shot down by Sergeant Taylor of No. 601 Squadron during operations over the Thames Estuary 1.20 p.m. Forced-landed Shornemead Fort, Gravesend. Fw. Kramer captured. Aircraft a write-off.
Cockpit clock taken from the wreck in 1940 donated to the Kent Battle of Britain Museum.

Messerschmitt Bf 109E-1 (4448). Crashed at Brook House Farm, Navestock 1.15 p.m. following combat with fighters. Lt. Petrenko captured wounded. Aircraft 4+ a write-off.

Messerschmitt Bf 109E-1 (4068). Shot down in combat over the Thames Estuary. Crashed between Walderslade and Boxley 1.20 p.m. Uffz. Keck baled out and captured. Aircraft 8+ a write-off.
Intact Daimler-Benz DB 601 engine recovered by the Kent Battle of Britain Museum which also acquired the maker's plate from the radio set of this machine. Site re-excavated in 1978 by Steve Vizard and complete pilot's armour, propeller boss and other components recovered.

Messerschmitt Bf 109E-1 (3652). Shot down by Flight Lieutenant Macdonald of No. 603 Squadron and crashed on Court Farm, Hunton 1.25 p.m. Fw. Evers severely wounded, died of injuries. Aircraft 9+ a write-off.

Messerschmitt Bf 109E-4 (5105). Shot down by Flight Lieutenant Robinson of No. 601 Squadron and crash-landed on Gates Farm, High Halden 1.00 p.m. Oblt. Ehrig captured. Aircraft 13+ a write-off.

2/JG77

Messerschmitt Bf 109E-1 (4076). Crashed Elham Park Wood 9.30 a.m. following combat with fighters. Oblt. Priebe baled out wounded and captured. Aircraft a write-off.
Site investigated by the Brenzett Aeronautical Museum and few parts and minor components recovered.

3/JG77

Messerschmitt Bf 109E-1 (5908). Crashed in the Channel following fighter combat over southern England. Pilot rescued unhurt by Seenotdienst. Aircraft lost.

Messerschmitt Bf 109E-1 (3642). Returned to base with battle damage. Pilot unhurt. Aircraft 35% damaged.

II/KG2

Dornier Do 17Z-3 (3483). Shot down by RAF fighters during attack on Duxford aerodrome. One NCO wounded. Aircraft U5+CN a write-off.

Stab III/KG2

Dornier Do 17Z-2 (3356). Slightly damaged by RAF fighters in combat over Colchester. Returned to base Major Fuchs (Gruppe Kommandeur) wounded. Aircraft U5+AD repairable.

III/KG2

Dornier Do 17Z. Returned to base damaged by RAF fighter attack during sortie over Colchester. One NCO wounded. Aircraft repairable.

Stab I/KG3

Junkers Ju 52 (1353). Belly-landed at St Inglevert following routine local communications flight. Cause not stated. Crew unhurt. Aircraft N3+AQ 15% damaged.

I/KG3

Dornier Do 17Z-2 (1178). Crashed on landing at St. Omer with combat damage. One NCO killed and three wounded. Aircraft 5K+KL a write-off.

Dornier Do 17Z-2 (3299). Belly-landed at Merville following operational sortie. Three NCOs wounded. Aircraft 5K+HL damaged but repairable.

II/KG3

Dornier Do 17Z-2 (3456). Damaged in fighter attack during sortie over Hornchurch. Returned to base. Lt. Schopper and four NCOs wounded. Aircraft 5K+BC 12% damaged.

Dornier Do 17Z-3 (3458). Returned to base slightly damaged in fighter attack during sortie over Hornchurch. One NCO wounded. Aircraft 5K+EM repairable.

4/KG3

Dornier Do 17Z-2 (3264). Shot down by fighters during attack on Hornchurch. Forced-landed on Eastwick Farm, Burnham-on-Crouch 1.25 p.m. Uffz. Bock mortally wounded (died 3.9.40). Oblt. Gahtz, Oberfw. Bulach and Gefr. Neumann all captured. Aircraft 5K+KM a write-off.

Dornier Do 17Z-3 (2669). Forced-landed at Princes Golf Club, Sandwich 1.40 p.m. following attack on Hornchurch and engagement with fighters. Also damaged by ground defences. Oberfw. Lange, Uffz. Krostopotsch, Fw. Berndt, and Fw. Wuensch all captured wounded. Aircraft 5K+LM a write-off.

Dornier Do 17Z. Returned to base damaged by AA fire during attack on Hornchurch 1.30 p.m. One NCO wounded another died of wounds. Aircraft repairable.

Dornier Do 17Z. Attacked by fighters during sortie over Hornchurch and returned to base damaged. One NCO wounded. Aircraft repairable.

5/KG3

Dornier Do 17Z-3 (3414). Shot down by fighters during bombing attack on Hornchurch. Crashed in sea near the South Goodwins 1.45 p.m. Fw. Nickel drowned. Uffz. Blasche captured together with Fw. Gutat and Uffz. Sonntag both being wounded. Aircraft 5K+GN lost.

7/KG27

Heinkel He 111P (1418). Crashed at Rennes aerodrome due to undercarriage failure following domestic flight. Crew unhurt. Aircraft 40% damaged.

II/KG51

Junkers Ju 88A-1 (6075). Crashed on landing at Orly following operational mission. Crew unhurt. Aircraft 30% damaged.

Junkers Ju 88A-1 (5028). Damaged at Villeneuve-Orly aerodrome circumstances not stated. Non-operational loss. Crew unhurt. Aircraft 30% damaged.

III/KG51

Junkers Ju 88A-1 (7051). Crash-landed at Etampes during routine domestic flight. Cause not reported. Crew unhurt. Aircraft repairable.

2/KG76

Dornier Do 17Z (3316). Briefed to attack Hornchurch aerodrome and engaged by fighters during return flight. Crashed at Newchurch 7.00 p.m. Lt. Klepmeier, Uffz. Bloss, Oberfw. Lang and Fw. Pfachler all captured wounded. Aircraft F1+BK a write-off.

KGr 806

Junkers Ju 88A-1 (4061). Crashed near Nantes during operational sortie cause unknown. Oblt. Janson, Fw. Erdmann, Fw. Duschelka and Obgefr. Mueller all killed. Aircraft a write-off.

2/Erprobungs Gruppe 210

Messerschmitt Bf 110D/O (3370). Damaged in fighter combat but returned to Calais-Marck. Crew unhurt. Aircraft S9+DK 30% damaged.

Messerschmitt Bf 110 D/0 (3568). Landed at Calais-Marck with combat damage. Crew unhurt. Aircraft S9+EK 25% damaged.

Messerschmitt Bf 110 D/O (3381). Severely damaged in combat with RAF fighters over southern outskirts of London 1.15 p.m. Forced-landed on Wrotham Hill. Uffz. Glaeske captured. Obgefr. Schweda killed. Aircraft S9+GK a write-off.

I/LG1

Junkers Ju 88A-1 (2113). Fuel system damaged by fighter attack. Forced-landed near Provinz. Crew unhurt. Aircraft a write-off.

III/LG1

Junkers Ju 88A-1 (2079). Crash-landed Chateaudun following combat sortie. Crew unhurt. Aircraft L1+AR 30% damaged.

14/LG1

Messerschmitt Bf 110. Shot down by fighters during sortie over the Thames Estuary 9.05 a.m. Crashed in sea off Foreness, Thanet. Lt. Eichholn rescued unhurt and captured. Uffz. Growe killed. Aircraft lost.

Messerschmitt Bf 110. Ditched in the sea near the Nore Light, Thames Estuary 9.10 a.m. following attack by fighters. Fw. Fritz and Obergefr. Doepfer both rescued and POWs. Aircraft L1+AK lost.

I/LG2

Messerschmitt Bf 109E-1 (4086). Crashed at Calais-Marck due to engine malfunction during local flight. Pilot unhurt. Aircraft a write-off.

Messerschmitt Bf 109E-4 (1399). Damaged on return from operational sortie. Exact circumstances not recorded. Pilot unhurt. Aircraft a write-off.

Above: **Burning itself out on Sandwich Flats, this Dornier 17Z of the 'Blitz' Geschwader, KG3, fell victim to fighters and ground fire on the last day of August before belly-landing with four wounded crew members aboard (Fox Photo).**

Below: **Pegwell Bay, with Ramsgate beyond, on August 21, 1979. After four decades of weathering and storms, the shingle beach has altered considerably since 1940. However, we were told that the remains of the Dornier are still visible at extreme low tides**

3/LG2

Messerschmitt Bf 109E-7 (5600). Shot down in combat with RAF fighters and crashed at Chathill Park Farm, Crowhurst 6.45 p.m. Oblt. von Perthes baled out landing at Hurst Green severely wounded (died of injuries). Aircraft a write-off.

I/ZG2

Messerschmitt Bf 110C-2 (3083). Crashed on landing at Granville following routine domestic flight. Crew unhurt. Aircraft 30% damaged.

Stab ZG26

Messerschmitt Bf 110 (3280). Damaged in fighter combat and belly-landed back at Wizernes crew unhurt. Aircraft U8+JH 15% damaged.

5/ZG26

Messerschmitt Bf 110. Returned to base slightly damaged following escort mission over Hornchurch and attack by fighters. One NCO wounded. Aircraft repairable.

6/ZG26

Messerschmitt Bf 110. Returned to base with combat damage and one NCO wounded. Aircraft repairable.

Stab III/ZG26

Messerschmitt Bf 110C-4 (2167). Damaged in fighter combat but returned to crash-land at Arques with one NCO wounded. Aircraft 3U+CD 38% damaged.

8/ZG26

Messerschmitt Bf 110D (3396). Crashed in the sea between Colne Point and Clacton 8.30 a.m. following attack by RAF fighters. Oblt. von Bergen and Uffz. Becker both captured. Aircraft 3U+HS lost.

6/ZG76

Messerschmitt Bf 110C (3603). Crash-landed at St. Inglevert with severe damage following fighter combat. Hptmn. Nacke and one NCO both wounded. Aircraft M8+KM a write-off.

Below left: **The Dornier crashed in a military training area with Princes Golf Club as the HQ. Here Oberfeldwebel Lange, the pilot, and another crewman are marched off to captivity (Fox Photos).** *Right:* **The changed facade came with the reconstruction of the building in 1948.**

Sunday, September 1

Six junior NCOs from RAF Cosford carry the remains of a former enemy to his last resting place in the German War Cemetery at Cannock Chase, Staffordshire on Tuesday, January 8, 1980. The officer pall-bearers are from RAF Shawbury.

1(F)/22

Messerschmitt Bf 110 (2206). Crash-landed at Ostende following long-range reconnaissance sortie. Cause not stated. Crew unhurt. Aircraft 4N+ CH 40% damaged.

1/106

Heinkel He 115 (2734). Damaged in landing at Nordeney following operational sortie. Exact circumstances not recorded. No crew casualties. Aircraft M2+ LH 20% damaged.

1/196

Arado Ar 196 (0059). Crashed on landing at Schellingwoude. Cause not stated. Crew unhurt. Aircraft T3+ EH a write-off.

I/JG2

Messerschmitt Bf 109E-4 (1968). Crashed at Conchez following collision with FW 58 during local flying. Pilot killed. Aircraft a write-off.

7/JG26

Messerschmitt Bf 109E-1 (3892). Crashed at Newbridge, Iden, near Rye 2.03 p.m. during free-lance fighter operations over southern England. Hptmn. Burschgens captured. Aircraft 11+ 1 a write-off.

I/JG52

Messerschmitt Bf 109E-4 (1902). Shot down in fighter combat and crashed on Capel Farm, Orlestone, Kent 10.30 a.m. Oberfw. Gerber killed. Aircraft a write-off.
Site investigated by the Historic Aircraft Archaeologists Group but nothing tangible discovered but many relics including maker's plate in the Steve Vizard collection.

Messerschmitt Bf 109E-4 (1510). Crashed and burned out at Coquelles during routine domestic flight. Cause unknown. Gefr. Gleser killed. Aircraft a write-off.

II/JG53

Messerschmitt Bf 109E-1 (6020). Crashed on take-off from Dinan aerodrome on domestic flight. Pilot unhurt. Aircraft 60% damaged.

III/JG53

Messerschmitt Bf 109E-4 (3237). Crash-landed near Boulogne due to engine failure following combat sortie over the Channel. Pilot unhurt. Aircraft a write-off.

Messerschmitt Bf 109E-4 (4020). Shot down in fighter combat over Thanet. Crashed, overturned and burst into flames south of Chilham, Kent 5.00 p.m. Oblt. Bauer killed. Aircraft a write-off.

Messerschmitt Bf 109E-4 (5087). Engaged on free-lance fighter operations over the Channel and shot down by Sergeant Goodman of No. 85 Squadron. Crashed at Strand Bridge, Winchelsea, near Rye 11.30 a.m. Lt. Strasser baled out and captured unhurt. Aircraft 10+ a write-off.
Site excavated by the Ashford and Tenterden Recovery Group in 1970. Complete Daimler-Benz DB 601 engine and variety of major components recovered now in the Brenzett Aeronautical Museum. First-aid kit, pilot's forage cap and maps donated to the Kent Battle of Britain Museum by a local resident.

Messerschmitt Bf 109E-4 (5155). Engine damaged during fighter combat over the south coast of England and forced-landed at Benylong. Pilot unhurt. Aircraft 50% damaged.

Oberleutnant Ekkehard Schelcher, a Gruppe Staff Officer of Jagd Geschwader 54 'Gruenherz' (Green Heart) based at Guines, six miles from Calais, missing from his unit on Monday, September 2, 1940. For thirty-seven years Schelcher lay buried with the wreckage of his 'Emil' not far from Chilham Castle. The spot was recognised by the German authorities as a registered war grave prior to the excavation (Patrick Smith Associates).

II/JG54

Messerschmitt Bf 109E-4 (1277). Crashed at Bonnington near Ashford, Kent following collision during fighter sortie over southern England 11.15 a.m. Oblt. Stangel captured. Aircraft a write-off.

Stab KG1

Heinkel He 111H. Returned to base with one NCO wounded following operational sortie over England. Aircraft repairable.

6/KG1

Heinkel He 111H-2 (2433). Severely damaged by fighter attack over Ashford. Returned to base with one NCO killed and another wounded. Aircraft V4+ GW 60% damaged.

III/KG27

Heinkel He 111H (1577). Crashed shortly after take-off from Rennes on combat sortie. Cause unknown. Oblt. Stoessel and three NCOs killed. Aircraft 1G+ GT a write-off.

Heinkel He 111P (2628). Crash-landed near Cherbourg due to petrol failure on operational sortie. No crew casualties. Aircraft 1G+ GS 60% damaged.

2/KG76

Dornier Do 17Z. Returned to base damaged by AA fire over Kenley aerodrome. Uffz. Schadhauser wounded. Aircraft repairable.

9/KG76

Dornier Do 17Z (3369). Shot down by Sergeant Allard of No. 85 Squadron during bombing sortie to Gravesend. Crashed at Dungeness Point, Kent 4.00 p.m. Gefr. Spiess killed. Uffz. Maasen baled out wounded and captured with Oberfw. Illg and Fw. Woehner. Aircraft F1+ AT a write-off.

Dornier Do 17Z. Returned to base damaged by AA fire over Tonbridge during sortie over southern England. Uffz. Hirsinger wounded. Aircraft repairable.

I/KG77

Junkers Ju 88A (2173). Engine caught fire during routine domestic flight. Crash-landed near Athies, Laon and burned out. No crew casualties. Aircraft 3Z+ CB a write-off.

1/KG100

Heinkel He 111H-3 (5687). Forced-landed due to petrol shortage at St. Briyoue during operational sortie. Crew unhurt. Aircraft 6N+ OH 30% damaged.

2/KG100

Heinkel He 111H-1 (5100). Crashed on landing at Vannes aerodrome following operational mission. Cause not stated. No crew casualties. Aircraft 6N+ MK 60% damaged.

III/LG1

Junkers Ju 88A-1 (7009). Crashed on landing at Chateaudun aerodrome and burned out following combat sortie. Oblt. Hirsch and one NCO killed. Two NCOs wounded. Aircraft L1+ FR a write-off.

14/LG1

Messerschmitt Bf 110. Shot down by fighters during sortie over Kent and forced-landed on Tarpot Farm, Bilsington, Ham Street near Ashford 2.00 p.m. Oberfw. Kobert and Fw. Meining captured unhurt. Aircraft L1+ OH a write-off.

3/NJG1

Messerschmitt Bf 110 (3510). Abandoned by crew over Lippborg during night operations due to petrol failure. Lt. Schmitz baled out and wounded. Aircraft G9+ BL a write-off.

I/ZG2

Focke-Wulf FW 58 (0089). Collided with Bf 109 of I/JG2 during routine domestic flight and crashed at Conchez. Oblt. Blume and two NCOs killed. Aircraft DB+ CR a write-off.

Monday, September 2

2(H)/32

Henschel Hs 126 (3033). Crashed on Konstanz aerodrome due to undercarriage failure. No crew casualties. Aircraft 20% damaged.

2(F)/122

Junkers Ju 88 (0276). Failed to return from long-range reconnaissance sortie and presumed crashed in sea. Oblt. Schmid, Fw. Jahnke, Obergefr. Rockstrol and Gefr. Kronberg missing. Aircraft F6+ DK lost.

1/KG.z.b.V.172

Junkers Ju 52 (6925). Crashed at Pritzwalk during parachute training flight. Cause unknown. Three NCOs killed. Aircraft N3+ CB a write-off.

3/406

Dornier Do 18 (0868). Shot down by fighters during operations over the North Sea (PQ8229). Lt. zur See Logier and one NCO killed. Two NCOs rescued by Seenotdienst. Aircraft K6+ DL lost.

1/806

Junkers Ju 88 (5069). Crashed on landing at Nantes in poor visibility. Crew unhurt. Aircraft M7+ HH 25% damaged.

Oberleutnant Schelcher's brother and his sister-in-law attended the funeral. Officially it was felt that as Hugh Beresford had been accorded a full military funeral with band only seven weeks previously, similar honours (minus the music) should be given to Schelcher. The land at Cannock Chase was given to the German War Graves Commission (Deutsche Kriegsgraberfursorge) in 1959 as they desired a location to carry out their general policy of concentrating their war dead in a central point in each theatre of war. Although many German graves can still be found scattered around the United Kingdom, 4,914 now lie re-interred in the sombre Soldatenfriedhof at Cannock.

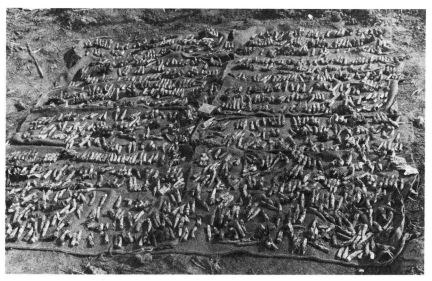

Junkers Ju 88 (5111). Engine caught fire during operational sortie and crashed at Pontivy. Hptmn. Schwengers killed. Three crew baled out unhurt. Aircraft M7+AH a write-off.

3/906

Heinkel He 115 (2218). Crashed on landing at IJmuiden following operational sortie. Cause not stated. Uffz. Bock killed. Lt. zur See Andersen wounded. Aircraft 8L+LL a write-off.

4/JG2

Messerschmitt Bf 109E-1 (6115). Shot down in combat with Hurricanes over southern Kent. Crashed at Cale Hill Park, Little Chart 1.13 p.m. Uffz. Glomb captured seriously wounded. Aircraft a write-off.

Messerschmitt Bf 109E-4 (1452). Forced-landed at West Hythe, south of Lympne Castle 1.30 p.m. Engine damaged in combat with Flight Lieutenant Reynell of No. 43 Squadron. Uffz. von Stein captured. Aircraft 12+ a write-off.

9/JG2

Messerschmitt Bf 109E. Shot down in combat over Kent and crashed on Streets Farm, Ulcombe near Maidstone 1.10 p.m. Lt. Kluge baled out severely wounded and died later. Aircraft a write-off.

Wreck excavated by the Kent Battle of Britain Museum which recovered Daimler-Benz DB 601 engine, cockpit armour, instruments including the clock showing exact time of impact, flap and trim controls, remains of control column, complete armament, and pilot's breast eagle. The original Imperial War Graves Commission marker was also donated by a local resident. Very pistol from this machine in Lashenden Air Warfare Museum.

Stab I/JG3

Messerschmitt Bf 109E-4 (1979). Crashed on take-off from Colombert on combat mission. Cause not stated. Pilot unhurt. Aircraft 33% damaged.

4/JG3

Messerschmitt Bf 109E-4 (5136). Damaged in landing accident at Wierre-au-Bois. Pilot unhurt. Aircraft repairable.

5/JG3

Messerschmitt Bf 109E-4 (1443). Crashed at Marquise following combat with RAF fighters over the Channel. Pilot unhurt. Aircraft a write-off.

Unconfirmed reports state that for many years a white cross marked the crash site of Oberleutnant Schelcher's Bf 109 behind Mountain Street, Chilham. Local wreck groups were refused permission, by the landowner and Ministry of Defence, to excavate the aircraft but authorisation was given to the Territorial Army as an exercise advantageous to squadron training. *Left:* Lance-Corporal Close with the engine uncovered by 590 Explosive Ordnance Disposal unit. *Right:* The risks of excavating war material were demonstrated during the operation which began on October 1, 1977. The following morning, some sixty 20mm cannon shells and 500 rounds of 7.92mm were recovered. They were laid out for photography but after three hours began fizzing, smoking and self-detonating. A live shell jammed in the breach of the 20mm cannon was successfully exploded without completely destroying the weapon.

6/JG3

Messerschmitt Bf 109E-4 (1469). Damaged in fighter combat and landed at Sangatte. Pilot unhurt. Aircraft 30% damaged.

9/JG3

Messerschmitt Bf 109E-1 (3609). Crashed on landing at Le Portel due to mechanical failure during combat sortie. Pilot unhurt. Aircraft a write-off.

1/JG51

Messerschmitt Bf 109E (4807). Shot down by Pilot Officer Gribble of No. 54 Squadron during combat over Kent. Crashed at Nethersole Park, Womenswold, east of Barham 8.00 a.m. Lt. Ruettowski killed. Aircraft a write-off.

Messerschmitt Bf 109E-1 (4850). Crashed in flames at Leeds Castle, near Maidstone 8.00 a.m. during combat with No. 54 Squadron Spitfires. Shot down by Squadron Leader Leathart. Lt. Thoerl baled out and captured unhurt. Aircraft a write-off.

Major recovery by London Air Museum. Complete Daimler-Benz DB 601 engine salvaged with propeller boss, undercarriage legs, cockpit controls, instruments and 7.92mm MG17 machine guns.

Messerschmitt Bf 109E-4 (3714). Crashed in the Channel during return flight after combat with Spitfires over southern England 8.00 a.m. Fw. Bar rescued unhurt by Seenotdienst. Aircraft lost.

8/JG51

Messerschmitt Bf 109E-4 (1632). Ditched in the Channel following combat sortie over southern England. Believed damaged by RAF fighters. Lt. Braun rescued unhurt by Seenotdienst. Aircraft lost.

I/JG52

Messerschmitt Bf 109E-4 (1261). Engaged on free-lance sortie over Eastchurch and shot down by Pilot Officer Ambrose of No. 46 Squadron. Belly-landed on Tile Lodge Farm, Hoath, near Westbere, Canterbury 5.40 p.m. Fw. Verlings captured unhurt. Aircraft 12+ a write-off.

Site investigated by the Historic Aircraft Archaeologist Group but nothing found.

I/JG53

Messerschmitt Bf 109E (6276). Failed to return from escort mission over the Channel and believed shot down by fighters into the sea. Lt. Riegel missing. Aircraft lost.

Messerschmitt Bf 109E-4 (3494). Forced-landed near Boulogne damaged in combat with RAF fighters. Uffz. Leschert wounded. Aircraft 50% damaged.

Messerschmitt Bf 109E (3584). Shot down in combat with RAF fighters during escort mission and forced-landed on the ranges, west of Hythe 8.17 a.m. Uffz. Karl captured unhurt. Aircraft 14+ a write-off.
Site now a gravel pit west of Palmarsh identified by Brenzett Aeronautical Museum.

Messerschmitt Bf 109E-4 (1167). Believed shot down in the Channel by RAF fighters during escort sortie. Oberfw. Kuehlmann missing. Aircraft lost.

Messerschmitt Bf 109E-4 (1569). Shot down by fighters in running battle over the Channel between Dover and Calais. Crashed in sea. Pilot rescued unhurt by Seenotdienst. Aircraft lost.

II/JG54

Messerschmitt Bf 109E-4 (1940). Crashed near Calais following collision during operational sortie. Oblt. Elsing killed. Aircraft a write-off.

Messerschmitt Bf 109E-1 (6225). Collided with Oblt. Elsing's aircraft during sortie over Calais. Crashed and destroyed. Uffz. Frauendorf killed. Aircraft a write-off.

Stab III/JG54

Messerschmitt Bf 109E-4 (1574). Shot down in combat with fighters and crashed at Chilham, near Canterbury, Kent 12.55 p.m. Oblt. Schelcher killed. Aircraft a write-off.
Site excavated by the Territorial Army Bomb Disposal Unit 1977 and remains of aircraft donated to the Kent Battle of Britain Museum. Large access panel and parachute D' ring in the Vizard collection. Remains of Oblt. Schelcher subsequently buried with full military honours at Cannock Chase German Military Cemetery.

Messerschmitt Bf 109E-4 (5292). Forced-landed at Audembert following combat with fighters over Canterbury 12.30 p.m. Pilot unhurt. Aircraft 60% damaged.

7/JG54

Messerschmitt Bf 109E-4 (1335). Crashed on landing at Guines-Sued following combat sortie. Pilot unhurt. Aircraft 50% damaged.

8/JG54

Messerschmitt Bf 109E-1 (3470). Crashed attempting forced-landing on Finns Farm, Kingsnorth near Ashford 4.45 p.m. following combat with fighters. Uffz. Elbers captured. Aircraft 2+ a write-off.

1/JG77

Messerschmitt Bf 109E-1 (3503). Crashed on take-off from Marquise-West on combat sortie. Cause not stated. Pilot unhurt. Aircraft 50% damaged.

3/JG77

Messerschmitt Bf 109E-1 (2695). Crash-landed near Wissant following operational sortie over the Channel. Pilot unhurt. Aircraft a write-off.

8/KG3

Dornier Do 17Z. Returned to base damaged following operational sortie over England. Hptmn. Delanda wounded. Aircraft repairable.

Above: **Leutnant Schipper was the sole occupant in this ZG2 Zerstorer when it crash-landed at Hougham, near Dover, on September 2. Gefreiter Schockenhoff, his gunner, baled out and landed unhurt about a mile away. Both crew members were made prisoners-of-war.** *Below:* **On September 13, 1979, Wilf Nicoll discusses the events of that far off day with George Norris who farms the land around St. Radegund's Abbey and still remembers the incident vividly.**

9/KG3

Dornier Do 17Z-2 (1187). Crashed on landing at St. Trond due to combat damage following operations over England. Sonderfuehrer Mai (Lw. Kr. Ber. Kp. (mot) 3.) killed. Three NCOs wounded. Aircraft 5K+ MT a write-off.

Dornier Do 17Z-2 (3269). Shot down by No. 249 Squadron Hurricanes during sortie over Chatham. Crashed on Rochford aerodrome 9.15 a.m. Uffz. Hilbrecht killed. Oblt. Rohr, Uffz. Seidel and Fw. Sprink all captured wounded. Aircraft 5K+ BT a write-off.

Dornier Do 17Z-3 (3390). Belly-landed at St. Omer following combat sortie. Crew unhurt. Aircraft 5K+ GT a write-off.

II/KG77

Junkers Ju 88A-1 (7097). Crashed and burned out at Untertuerkheim, near Stuttgart following engine failure during routine domestic flight. Four NCOs killed. Aircraft 3Z+ BN a write-off.

IV/LG1

Junkers Ju 87B-2 (5773). Forced-landed at Tramescourt following collision during operational sortie. Crew unhurt. Aircraft L1+ AV 20% damaged.

Junkers Ju 87B (5581). Abandoned by crew following collision over Tramescourt on combat mission. Crew baled out unhurt. Aircraft a write-off.

I/LG2

Messerschmitt Bf 109E (3579). Crash-landed at Calais following operational sortie possibly result of combat damage. Pilot unhurt. Aircraft 50% damaged.

I/ZG2

Messerschmitt Bf 110C-4 (3622). Crashed and burned out at Hougham near Dover 1.00 p.m. following fighter attack. Lt. Schipper and Gefr. Schockenhoff both captured unhurt. Aircraft 3M+ HK a write-off.

Messerschmitt Bf 110 D/O (3193). Returned to base damaged following combat with fighters over the Thames Estuary. Crew unhurt. Aircraft 25% damaged.

II/ZG2

Messerschmitt Bf 110 D/O (3197). Failed to return from operations over England and presumed shot down by fighters. Uffz. Deuker and Uffz. Krapp both missing. Aircraft lost.

Messerschmitt Bf 110 D/O (3269). Believed shot down by fighters during action over southern England. Exploded over Vensons Farm, Eastry, near Sandwich, Kent 12.45 p.m. Fw. Beil and Obergefr. Oehl killed. Aircraft A2+ KL lost.

2/ZG26

Messerschmitt Bf 110 D-1 (3309). Shot down by Sergeant Rolls of No. 72 Squadron during bomber escort sortie. Crash-landed in White Horse Wood, Birling, near Maidstone 8.10 a.m. Fw. Schuetz killed. Gefr. Stuewe captured wounded. Aircraft E8+ DK a write-off.

5/ZG26

Messerschmitt Bf 110C-4 (3536). Shot down by fighters during bomber escort sortie over the Thames Estuary. Crashed in sea off the Nore 9.00 a.m. Oberfw. Rochel and Uffz. Schoefler captured unhurt. Aircraft 3U+ GN lost.

Messerschmitt Bf 110C-4 (3045). Crash-landed at Wizernes due to engine failure following fighter combat over the Thames Estuary. Fw. Mueller and one NCO wounded. Aircraft 3U+ BN a write-off.

6/ZG26

Messerschmitt Bf 110. Returned to base with one NCO wounded following fighter combat over England. Aircraft repairable.

Messerschmitt Bf 110. Damaged in combat over England but returned safely to base with one NCO wounded. Aircraft repairable.

7/ZG26

Messerschmitt Bf 110C-4 (2191). Crash-landed at Arques following combat with enemy fighters. Fw. Dibowski wounded. Aircraft 3U+ BR 45% damaged.

4/ZG76

Messerschmitt Bf 110C (3226). Crashed and burned out on Frith Farm, Laindon Road, Billericay, Essex 4.40 p.m. following fighter combat. Oblt. Wrede and Uffz. Kukawka killed. Aircraft M8+ DM a write-off.

III/ZG76

Messerschmitt Bf 110C-4 (2095). Forced-landed near Calais damaged by RAF fighters. Crew unhurt. Aircraft 2N+ GM 50% damaged.

Tuesday, September 3

KG.z.b.v.106

Junkers Ju 52 (6923). Crashed near Sachau following mid-air collision during local flight. Lt. Engler and two NCOs killed. Aircraft KC+ CU a write-off.

KG.z.b.v.172

Junkers Ju 52 (5355). Collided with another Ju 52 during domestic flight over Sachau. Three NCOs killed. Aircraft N3+ FK a write-off.

Stab II/JG26

Messerschmitt Bf 109E-4 (0823). Failed to return from fighter sortie over Margate and presumed crashed in the Channel. Lt. Roch missing. Aircraft lost.

4/JG27

Messerschmitt Bf 109E-1 (6336). Severely damaged in landing collision at Fiennes aerodrome. Uffz. Morgenstern injured. Aircraft a write-off.

5/JG27

Messerschmitt Bf 109E-1 (2686). Believed damaged in combat over Ashford and collided on landing with Bf 109 of 4 Staffel at Fiennes. Oblt. Fluder wounded. Aircraft a write-off.

9/JG51

Messerschmitt Bf 109E-1 (6290). Shot down during combat with fighters over the Channel. Pilot wounded. Aircraft a write-off.

II/JG53

Messerschmitt Bf 109E-4 (1244). Crash-landed at Sempy following operations over the Channel. Pilot unhurt. Aircraft 55% damaged.

I/JG54

Arado Ar 66 (2234). Crash-landed near Lillers during routine domestic flight. Cause not stated. No crew casualties. Aircraft BA+ HQ 45% damaged.

5/KG2

Dornier Do 17Z-2 (3450). Shot down by fighters during bombing attack on North Weald. Crashed at Langenhoe near Pyefleet Creek 10.30 a.m. Lt. Schildt, Uffz. Swindek and Gefr. Niegisch killed. Fw. Kriegl captured unhurt. Aircraft U5+ AN a write-off.

Major recovery by the London Air Museum. Excavation revealed Bramo Fafnir engine, undercarriage oleo leg and tyre, radio operator's log book, a pocket handkerchief marked 'Niegisch', a number of documents, coins and wallets containing personal effects and money. Site originally located by a group of Colchester enthusiasts led by the late John Fisher who salvaged many interesting components.

5/KG26

Heinkel He 111H-3 (3252). Crashed at Maasbree near Venlo following mid-air collision during routine domestic flight. Oblt. Wanderer and two NCOs killed. Aircraft a write-off.

Heinkel He 111H-3 (3164). Collided with Oblt. Wanderer's He 111 during local flight over Venlo and crashed near Maasbree. Lt. Zobernig and two NCOs killed. Aircraft a write-off.

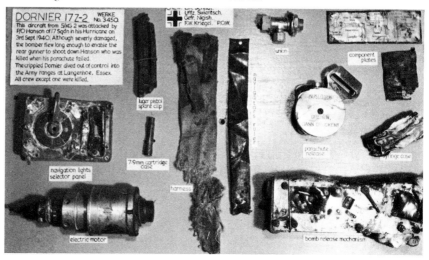

The London Air Museum unearthed these relics from one of the Dorniers (No. 3450) which was shot down during the bombing of North Weald on September 3.

Heinkel He 111H-3 (6825). Damaged in taxiing accident at Gilze-Rijen aerodrome. No crew casualties. Aircraft 1H+KN 20% damaged.

8/KG30

Junkers Ju 88A-1 (4016). Crashed at Mons-Soignies following engine fire during routine domestic flight. One NCO injured. Aircraft 4D+DS a write-off.

8/KG77

Junkers Ju 88A (5108). Crashed on landing at Laon due to burst tyre. Non operational sortie. No crew casualties. Aircraft 3Z+KS 55% damaged.

1/KG100

Heinkel He 111H-3 (6873). Belly-landed on Rennes aerodrome following technical failure during operational sortie. Crew unhurt. Aircraft 6N+BH 45% damaged.

3/KG100

Heinkel He 111H-2 (5455). Collided with another He 111 on the runway at Vannes. No crew casualties. Aircraft 6N+ML a write-off.

Heinkel He 111H-2 (5475). Damaged in collision on the runway at Vannes. Exact circumstances not recorded. Two NCOs injured. Aircraft 6N+AL 50% damaged.

I/LG2

Messerschmitt Bf 109E-7 (5572). Crashed on landing at Calais-Marck aerodrome following combat sortie. Cause not stated. Pilot unhurt. Aircraft 35% damaged.

4/LG2

Messerschmitt Bf 109E (6313). Forced-landed at Frevent during routine domestic flight having lost bearings. Pilot unhurt. Aircraft 15% damaged.

I/ZG2

Messerschmitt Bf 110C-4 (2146). Engine set alight by fighter attack during free-lance patrol. Abandoned over the Channel off Herne Bay 10.45 a.m. Oblt. Gottschalk and Uffz. Hoffmann both captured. Aircraft 3M+BK lost.

Messerschmitt Bf 110C-4 (2133). Collided with Fw. Wagenbrett's aircraft during bomber escort sortie. Crashed at Rye Hill, near Epping, Essex 10.50 a.m. Oblt. Mueller baled out and captured unhurt. Uffz. Korn killed. Aircraft 3M+HL a write-off.

Messerschmitt Bf 110C-4 (2065). Collided with Oblt. Mueller's aircraft during bomber escort sortie and crashed at Hobbs Cross, Harlow, Essex 10.50 a.m. Fw. Wagenbrett and Uffz. Schubert both killed. Aircraft 3M+EK a write-off.

Site excavated by the London Air Museum. Daimler-Benz DB 601 engine recovered together with propeller blades, both oleo legs, oxygen bottles, 20mm MGFF cannon and 7.92mm MG17 machine guns. Some relics also held by the Kent Battle of Britain Museum.

Messerschmitt Bf 110C-4 (3120). Shot down by fighters during escort sortie. Crashed at Edwins Hall, Stowmaries, Essex 11.00 a.m. Oblt. Messner and Obergefr. Santoni baled out and captured unhurt. Aircraft 3M+CB a write-off.

On the morning of September 3, Messerschmitt Bf 110 Zerstorers from ZG2 and ZG26 were intercepted over southern Essex by Hurricanes from Nos. 17 and 46 Squadrons. Altogether seven of their aircraft failed to return, the one *above*, the victim of a collision with another 110 north of Epping, crashing at Rye Hill (Fox Photos). *Below:* Today the landscape has been changed by the removal of hedges and trees.

Messerschmitt Bf 110C-4 (3113). Crashed at Pudsey Hall Farm, Canewdon near Rayleigh, Essex 11.18 a.m. following fighter combat. Oberfw. Winkler and Flgr. Weiler baled out and captured. Aircraft 3M + EL a write-off.

Major recovery by the London Air Museum. Marsh excavated to a depth of over 35 feet revealing both Daimler-Benz DB 601 engines, all six propeller blades, both undercarriage legs and tyres, tail wheel recovered still fully inflated, complete armament, armour plate, control column and cockpit instruments, first-aid kit, gunner's tool kit, both fins still bearing traces of Swastika markings. Some representative pieces donated to the Kent Battle of Britain Museum.

3/ZG26

Messerschmitt Bf 110C-4 (3294). Crash-landed at Fontend damaged in fighter combat. Pilot unhurt. Uffz. Klatt baled out over the Channel off Dover and killed. Aircraft U8+KL a write-off.

6/ZG26

Messerschmitt Bf 110D (3310). Shot down during fighter combat over the Wickford area. Crashed two miles south of Maldon, Essex 10.30 a.m. Lt. Manhard and Uffz. Drews both captured. Aircraft 3U+EP a write-off.

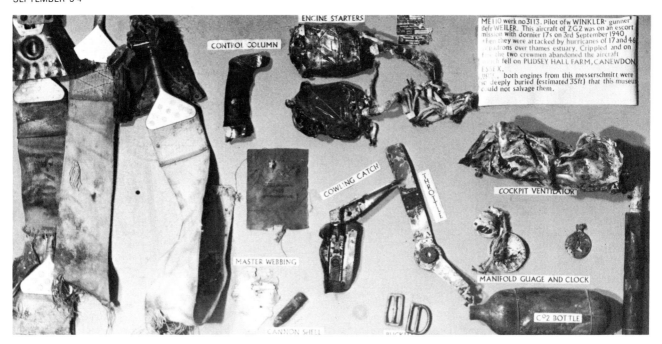

ME110 werk no.3113. Pilot ofw WINKLER· gunner gefr WEILER. This aircraft of ZG2 was on an escort mission with dornier 17s on 3rd September 1940 when they were attacked by hurricanes of 17 and 46 squadrons over thames estuary. Crippled and on fire the two crewmen abandoned the aircraft which fell on PUDSEY HALL FARM, CANEWDON ESSEX.
NB , both engines from this messerschmitt were so deeply buried (estimated 35ft) that this museum could not salvage them.

7/ZG26

Messerschmitt Bf 110C-2 (3225). Shot down by fighters during escort sortie over the Thames. Crash-landed at North Shoebury House, near Southend 10.38 a.m. Gefr. Uecker killed. Fw. Grau captured wounded. Aircraft 3U+KR a write-off.
Scattered fragments recovered from this site by the London Air Museum.

9/ZG26

Messerschmitt Bf 110C-2 (3578). Crashed on landing at Wissant following fighter combat over the Thames Estuary. Crew unhurt. Aircraft 3U+GT a write-off.

Wednesday, September 4

3(F)/Tannenburg

Messerschmitt Bf 110 (2175). Flying accident. Flew into the ground during routine domestic flight. Cause unknown. Oblt. Ellerlage killed. Aircraft TL+TI a write-off.

1(F)/123

Junkers Ju 88A (103). Engine caught fire during reconnaissance sortie. Crashed on landing at Brest-Sued aerodrome and burned out. Oblt. Krumbholz and two NCOs wounded. Aircraft 4U+MH a write-off.

5/196

Arado Ar 196 (0081). Forced-landed in the Skagerak following engine failure during operational sortie. No crew casualties. Aircraft 61+AL a write-off.

Erprobungs Gruppe 210

Messerschmitt Bf 110 D/O (3390). Shot down in the Channel off Littlehampton during combat with RAF fighters. Hptmn. von Boltenstern and Fw. Schneider both killed. Aircraft S9+AB lost.

JG2

Heinkel He 70 (1347). Forced-landed near Nuernberg due to engine failure on local communications flight. One NCO injured. Aircraft CF+BF 15% damaged.

The crash sites of three of the Zerstorers have been investigated by the London Air Museum. *Above:* These are some of the items recovered from 3113 at Pudsey Hall Farm, Canewdon, and *below* the engine from 2065 which crashed at Hobbs Cross, Harlow.

II/JG2

Messerschmitt Bf 109E-1 (2678). Failed to return from operational sortie. Exact fate unknown. Oblt. Muller missing. Aircraft lost.

I/JG26

Messerschmitt Bf 109E-1 (3884). Forced-landed at Audembert due to technical failure during combat sortie. Pilot unhurt. Aircraft 45% damaged.

II/JG26

Messerschmitt Bf 109E-4 (825). Crashed on landing at Marquise-Ost due to burst tyre following local flight. Pilot injured. Aircraft a write-off.

3/JG27

Messerschmitt Bf 109E-1 (6237). Crashed near Dunkirk following fighter action over the Channel. Fw. Harting wounded. Aircraft lost.

2/JG51

Messerschmitt Bf 109E-4 (2760). Crash-landed at Pihen aerodrome following fighter combat over the Channel. Pilot unhurt. Aircraft a write-off.

3/JG54

Messerschmitt Bf 109E-4 (5026). Shot down in combat with RAF fighters over the Channel off Dover. Crashed in sea. Oblt. Witt missing. Aircraft lost.

Messerschmitt Bf 109E-1 (4839). Crashed in the Channel off Calais during fighter combat. Pilot rescued unhurt by Seenotdienst. Aircraft lost.

I/JG77

Messerschmitt Bf 109E-4 (5807). Shot down by fighters in combat over the Channel. Pilot wounded. Aircraft a write-off.

4/KG26

Heinkel He 111H-4 (3287). Failed to return from bombing sortie over east coast of England and believed shot down in the sea. Uffz. Mahlmann, Oberfw. Suessmann, Fw. Ewerts, and Fw. Handwerker all missing. Aircraft 1H+AM lost.

5/KG26

Heinkel He 111H. Lost control and went into a spin during operational sortie but pilot regained control and returned safely to base. Uffz. Nowack baled out and killed. Aircraft undamaged.

I/KG51

Junkers Ju 88A-1 (2054). Forced-landed at Melun-Villaroche due to technical fault during routine domestic flight. Crew unhurt. Aircraft 25% damaged.

Junkers Ju 88A-1 (2057). Tyre burst on landing at Orly-Villeneuf aerodrome following local flight. No crew casualties. Aircraft 15% damaged.

I/LG1

Junkers Ju 88A-1 (4034). Belly-landed at Dinard aerodrome with battle damage. Crew unhurt. Aircraft L1+AK 40% damaged.

III/LG1

Junkers Ju 88A-1 (7004). Crash-landed at Chateaudun aerodrome following operational sortie over the Channel. No crew casualties. Aircraft L1+BR 60% damaged.

Above: **Possibly the first person on the scene of this Bf 110 crash of 3U + KR at North Shoebury on September 3 was Mrs. Lancaster from the local post office and general store who found one crewman killed and the other wounded in the neck and back.** *Bottom:* **New houses have altered the skyline but the field where the aircraft crashed is unchanged.**

14/LG1

Messerschmitt Bf 110 (3303). Shot down by fighters during free-lance sortie over southern England. Crashed and burned out at Waterloo Farm, West Horsley 1.45 p.m. Fw. Roehring killed. Uffz. Jackel captured wounded. Aircraft L1+BK a write-off.

Site excavated by the Air Historical Group 1977. Relics in London Air Museum also thought to be from this aircraft.

Messerschmitt Bf 110. Crashed at Upper Common, Netley, near Dorking, Surrey 1.45 p.m. following combat with fighters. Oblt. Junge and Uffz. Bremser both killed. Aircraft L1+FK a write-off.

Site investigated by the Air Historical Group and many small fragments discovered near the surface.

II/LG2

Messerschmitt Bf 109E-7 (5573). Crashed on landing at Calais-Marck following local flight. Cause not stated. Pilot unhurt. Aircraft 60% damaged.

Messerschmitt Bf 109E-7 (5564). Landing accident at Monchy-Breton after routine domestic flight. Pilot unhurt. Aircraft 50% damaged.

David Pack of the Air Historical Group with a prop blade from another Bf 110 L1 + BK which crashed at Waterloo Farm at West Horsley, Surrey, on September 4 — shot down by No. 253 Squadron Hurricanes.

7/NJG1

Messerschmitt Bf 110C-7 (1419). Crashed and burned out near Muenchen during local domestic flight. Cause unknown. Crew both killed. Aircraft a write-off.

Stab ZG2

Messerschmitt Bf 110C-4 (2116). Forced-landed at Mill Hill, Shoreham Downs, Sussex 2.00 p.m. damaged by fighters. Oblt. Schaefer and Uffz. Bendjus captured. Aircraft 3M+ AA a write-off.

I/ZG76

Messerschmitt Bf 110C-4 (3254). Shot down during escort sortie and crashed at High Salvington near Findon, Worthing 1.25 p.m. Oblt. Schiller and Fw. Winkler captured. Aircraft 2N+ BM a write-off.
Site investigated by the Wealden Aviation Archaeological Group in 1979 but only small surface fragments remained.

II/ZG76

Messerschmitt Bf 110C (3602). Forced-landed at Little Batts Farm, Brissenden, near Wadhurst, Sussex 1.35 p.m. damaged by fighters during escort duties. Oblt. Weber and Uffz. Michael captured. Aircraft M8+ AC a write-off.

Messerschmitt Bf 110C (3287). Severely damaged by fighters and ditched in the Channel seven miles off Pevensey Bay 1.45 p.m. during free-lance patrol. Oblt. Fr. Hartmann von Schlotheim and Uffz. Hommel both rescued from dinghy and captured. Aircraft M8+ 1M lost.

Messerschmitt Bf 110C (3229). Forced-landed at Boulogne following action with RAF fighters over London. Crew unhurt. Aircraft M8+ KN 40% damaged.

Messerschmitt Bf 110C (2089). Crashed at Cowden, near Tunbridge Wells, Kent 1.23 p.m. during fighter combat. Oblt. Piduhn and Gefr. Odene both killed. Aircraft M8+ CP a write-off.

The aircraft flown by one of the most publicised German 'aces', Oberleutnant Baron Franz von Werra — the 'one that got away' — came to grief in this field near Marden, Kent on September 5. A photographer from Fox Photos visited the site and brought back these pictures showing the removal of the armaments — the airman holds the reflector sight. The actual site of the forced-landing is now covered by a new orchard *opposite*.

III/ZG76

Messerschmitt Bf 110 C-4 (2104). Crashed and burned out at Coatwood Farm, Wisborough Green, Sussex 1.20 p.m. during fighter combat. Oblt. Raetsch and Gefr. Hempel both killed. Aircraft 2N+ KP a write-off.

Major recovery by the Wealden Aviation Archaeological Group at Toat Farm, Pulborough, Sussex in 1973 said to be this aircraft. Complete Daimler-Benz DB 601 engine excavated plus propeller boss and blade and one undercarriage leg.

Messerschmitt Bf 110C-4 (3101). Shot down by fighters during bomber escort sortie and forced-landed at Patching, near Angmering, Sussex 1.45 p.m. Lt. Muenich and Uffz. Kaeser captured unhurt. Aircraft 2N+ CN a write-off.

Messerschmitt Bf 110C-4 (3563). Shot down by fighters during bomber escort sortie. Forced-landed at Portway, Steyning, Sussex 1.35 p.m. Uffz. Schultis and Uffz. Bilbeck captured wounded. Aircraft 2N+ HM a write-off.

Messerschmitt Bf 110C-4 (3545). Shot down in combat with RAF fighters during operational sortie over England. Oberfw. Daun killed. Uffz. Mayer missing. Aircraft 2N+ AC a write-off.

Messerschmitt Bf 110C-1 (2837). Failed to return from operational sortie over the English coast and presumed shot down by fighters. Oblt. Florenz and Gefr. Herbert missing. Aircraft 2N+ DP lost. Possibly that which crashed at Church Farm, Washington, Pulborough, Sussex.
This site, now under a new road, was excavated in 1965 by a group of enthusiasts including Christopher Elliott, Peter Foote and Dennis Knight. Many components and manufacturer's labels were unearthed together with partial remains of crew but nothing to establish an identity beyond reasonable doubt. During later road development work, construction workers uncovered both Daimler-Benz DB 601 engines, propellers, undercarriage and a complete parachute, all of which are believed to have been scrapped.

Thursday, September 5

3(H)/12

Henschel Hs 126B (4153). Overshot runway and crashed on landing following routine domestic flight. Pilot unhurt. Aircraft a write-off.

3(F)/121

Junkers Ju 88A-1 (2124). Suffered engine failure on take-off from Chateaudun on routine local flight. Crashed and burned out. Lt. Zander and two NCOs wounded. Aircraft 7A+ BL 40% damaged.

3/406

Dornier Do 18 (0874). Forced-landed at Calais damaged following long-range sortie over the North Sea. Oblt. Dieterich and one NCO wounded. Aircraft K6+ KL state of damage not recorded.

8/JG2

Messerschmitt Bf 109E. Crashed at Detling, Kent 2.30 p.m. during fighter combat. Shot down by Pilot Officer Johnson of No. 46 Squadron. Oblt. Metz captured. Aircraft 2+ a write-off.

1/JG3

Messerschmitt Bf 109E-4 (1985). Damaged by RAF fighters during escort sortie and forced-landed on Handen Farm, Chapfall, near Aldington, Kent 10.10 a.m. Lt. Schnabel captured wounded. Aircraft 6+ a write-off.

Messerschmitt Bf 109E-1 (3612). Shot down by fighters during escort sortie over London. Oblt. Lammer missing. Aircraft lost.

2/JG3

Messerschmitt Bf 109E-4 (5342). Crashed into the Channel following combat with fighters. Lt. Klober killed. Aircraft lost.

Messerschmitt Bf 109E-1(3882). Forced-landed at Calais following fighter combat over the Channel. Pilot unhurt. Aircraft 50% damaged.

3/JG3

Messerschmitt Bf 109E-4 (750). Shot down during bomber escort mission and forced-landed near Wichling, Faversham, Kent 10.30 a.m. Uffz. Grabow captured unhurt. Aircraft 7+ a write-off.

Stab II/JG3

Messerschmitt Bf 109E-4 (1480). Shot down during diversionary fighter sweep over Kent and forced-landed at Winchet Hill, Love's Farm, Marden. Oblt. von Werra (Gruppe Adjutant) captured unhurt. Aircraft a write-off.

5/JG3

Messerschmitt Bf 109E-4 (1464). Crashed in the Channel during return flight following fighter combat over Kent. Pilot rescued unhurt. Aircraft lost.

5/JG27

Messerschmitt Bf 109E-1 (3627). Shot down in combat with fighters over Elham, Kent. Crashed near Appledore Station 4.15 p.m. Lt. Strobel killed. Aircraft a write-off.
Site excavated by the Brenzett Aeronautical Museum which recovered major components, remains of shattered airframe and maker's plate confirming aircraft identity beyond dispute. Armour plate from this aircraft donated to the Lashenden Air Warfare Museum. Site re-dug by Steve Vizard 1978 and makers' labels and oxygen apparatus uncovered.

1/JG52

Messerschmitt Bf 109E-4 (1949). Shot down in fighter combat over Ashford and crashed at Bethersden 10.30 a.m. Uffz. Kind killed. Aircraft a write-off.
Site investigated by the Kent Battle of Britain Museum and surface fragments recovered.

Stab JG53

Messerschmitt Bf 109E-1 (5375). Shot down during free-lance fighter sortie over the Channel. Forced-landed at Monkton, near Manston 3.45 p.m. Hptmn. Meyerweissflog captured unhurt. Aircraft a write-off.

II/JG53

Messerschmitt Bf 109E-1 (4053). Crash-landed at Sempy following operational sortie, cause not stated. Pilot unhurt. Aircraft 25% damaged.

Messerschmitt Bf 109E-1 (3429). Belly-landed at Sempy due to combat damage. Pilot unhurt. Aircraft 40% damaged.

7/JG53

Messerschmitt Bf 109E-1 (6064). Forced-landed at Wissant with combat damage following sortie over the Channel. Pilot unhurt. Aircraft a write-off.

Messerschmitt Bf 109E-1 (4017). Shot down in combat with fighters during sortie over the Thames Estuary to London. Lt. Deutsch missing. Aircraft lost.

Pilot:- LTN. STROBEL 5/J.G. 27
(GERMANY)

9/JG53

Messerschmitt Bf 109E-1(6252). Shot down in sea twelve miles off Hastings by RAF fighters 3.38 p.m. Fw. Ochsenkuehn captured unhurt. Aircraft lost.

I/JG54

Messerschmitt Bf 109E-4 (1096). Shot down by Flying Officer Haines of No. 19 Squadron in low-level combat over Kent. Crashed in Hardy Street, Maidstone 11.15 a.m. Uffz. Hotzelmann baled out and broke both legs in heavy landing. Aircraft 6+ a write-off.

Back garden excavation by the Kent Battle of Britain Museum which recovered many fragments of shattered DB 601 engine, portions of airframe and splinters of perspex. Complete propeller blade used as a bird table stand donated by a local resident. Cockpit clock taken in 1940 in the Vizard collection.

II/JG54

Messerschmitt Bf 109E-4 (1098). Shot down in combat over the Thames Estuary. Crashed in sea. Pilot rescued by Seenotdienst. Aircraft lost.

Steve Vizard's private Tonbridge Aircraft Museum is a storehouse of treasure from the Battle of Britain collected over a nine-year period. One souvenir taken in 1940 came from Messerschmitt 109 (1096) of JG54 which crashed at Hardy Street, Maidstone.

Messerschmitt Bf 109E-4 (5353). Shot down during fighter combat over the Thames Estuary off Southend. Uffz. Behse killed. Aircraft lost.

Stab III/JG54

Messerschmitt Bf 109E-4 (5291). Crashed and burned out at Bowers Gifford, near Pitsea, Essex 3.20 p.m. during combat with fighters. Shot down by Flight Lieutenant Bayne of No. 17 Squadron. Hptmn. Ultsch killed. Aircraft a write-off.

9/JG54

Messerschmitt Bf 109E-4 (5284). Shot down in combat over the Thames Estuary and believed crashed in sea. Fw. Dettler killed. Aircraft lost.

Stab I/KG1

Heinkel He 111H-3 (3324). Shot down by Blenheim night fighter of No. 25 Squadron during sortie to bomb Tilbury docks. Crashed at Rendlesham, Suffolk 01.00 a.m. Major Maier, Oblt. von Rittberg, Oberfw. Stockert and Uffz. Bendig all killed, Oblt. Biebrach baled out and captured unhurt. Aircraft V4+ AB a write-off.

6/KG2

Dornier Do 17Z (1134). Forced-landed near Calais damaged by fighters. Two NCOs wounded. Aircraft U5+ FP 20% damaged.

Dornier Do 17Z (2828). Damaged by fighters in sortie over the Channel and forced-landed near St. Omer with one NCO wounded. Aircraft U5+ KP 20% damaged.

6/KG4

Heinkel He 111P (3065). Hit by AA fire during night bombing sortie and crashed into Sunderland town 11.18 p.m. Oblt. Schraeder, Uffz. Reitz, Obergefr. Marten and Gefr. Wick all killed. Aircraft 5J+ JP a write-off.

Leutnant Strobel's Bf 109E-1 proved to be a worthwhile dig for the Ashford and Tenterden Recovery Group in 1971. This aircraft of 5/JG27 came down near Appledore Station in Kent on September 5, shot down by Sergeant Hurry of No. 43 Squadron. The Revi reflector sight, Walther signal pistol and control column displayed *(above)* in the Brenzett Aeronautical Museum on Romney Marsh are items highly sought after by aircraft archaeological groups. *Below:* Another relic from the same aircraft — the armour plate from behind the pilot's seat — can be seen at the Lashenden Air Warfare Museum at Headcorn aerodrome near Maidstone, Kent.

II/KG26

Heinkel He 111H-3 (3193). Damaged in collision prior to take-off at Gilze-Rijen aerodrome. No crew casualties. Aircraft 1H+CC 20% damaged.

Heinkel He 111H-3 (6896). Failed to return from sortie over English east coast. Uffz. Stenzel, Oberfw. Vetter, Fw. Wilde and Obergefr. Wart missing. Aircraft 1H+BC lost.

4/KG26

Heinkel He 111H-4 (5707). Shot down, believed by night fighter, and crashed near Amsterdam. Uffz. Heningsen and Fw. Hoeper killed. Lt. Katz baled out wounded. Aircraft 1H+JM a write-off.

Heinkel He 111H-4 (5703). Taxi-ing accident at Gilze-Rijen aerodrome. Exact circumstances not stated. Crew unhurt. Aircraft 1H+CM 20% damaged.

Heinkel He 111H-3 (3316). Damaged in taxi-ing accident at Gilze-Rijen. Possibly result of collision. Crew unhurt. Aircraft 1H+LM 20% damaged.

5/KG26

Heinkel He 111H-3 (3295). Belly-landed at Calais damaged following operational sortie over England. No crew casualties. Aircraft 1H+GN 50% damaged.

6/KG26

Heinkel He 111H-3 (6872). Collided with He 111 of Stab II/KG26 prior to take-off at Gilze-Rijen aerodrome. Crew unhurt. Aircraft 1H+CP 20% damaged.

Heinkel He 111H-4 (3318). Crashed and burned out on take-off from Gilze-Rijen aerodrome. Cause unknown. Lt. Baltes and three NCOs all killed. Aircraft 1H+FP a write-off.

Ausbildungs Staffel KG40

Heinkel He 111H-4 (3263). Forced-landed at Unterstedt on routine training flight. Cause not stated. Crew unhurt. Aircraft JZ+FL 30% damaged.

II/KG53

Heinkel He 111H-2 (3143). Belly-landed at Vendeville following combat with RAF fighters. One NCO wounded. Aircraft A1+CC 20% damaged.

III/KG53

Heinkel He 111H-2 (2632). Failed to return from bombing sortie over England. Crashed in the Channel off Herne Bay. Fw. Bohn killed. Uffz. Bolz, Uffz. Rosenberger, Uffz. Bickl and Gefr. Haack missing. Aircraft A1+GR lost.

Heinkel He 111H. Returned to base damaged by fighters with one NCO killed and another two wounded in sortie over England and combat with fighters. Aircraft repairable.

Heinkel He 111H-3 (3338). Hit by AA fire following bombing attack on oil tanks at Thameshaven and ditched in sea off the Nore 6.15 p.m. Fw. Anger, Uffz. Armbruster and Gefr. Novotny killed. Fw. Waier and Uffz. Lenger captured by naval patrol boat. Aircraft A1+CR lost.

Ausbildungs Staffel KG54

Junkers Ju 88A-1 (8025). Forced-landed at Lechfeld aerodrome with engine on fire due to ruptured fuel pipe during training flight. Crew unhurt. Aircraft 40% damaged.

II/KG54

Junkers Ju 88A-1 (4122). Written-off at St. Andre aerodrome, circumstances not reported. No crew casualties. Aircraft a write-off.

II/LG2

Messerschmitt Bf 109E-7 (2001). Crashed on landing at Calais-Marck following routine domestic flight. Cause not stated. Pilot unhurt. Aircraft 45% damaged.

Messerschmitt Bf 109E-7 (6315). Damaged in landing accident at Calais-Marck. Pilot unhurt. Aircraft 40% damaged.

Stab StG 1

Junkers Ju 87B (5447). Crashed at St. Pol during routine domestic flight. Cause unknown. Both crew killed. Aircraft A5+HA a write-off.

Friday, September 6

1/106

Heinkel He 115 (2730). Crashed during emergency take-off from Nordeney. Exact cause not stated. One NCO wounded. Aircraft M2+EH a write-off.

1/KGr.806

Junkers Ju 88A-1 (6043). Landed damaged at Nantes following operational sortie. Cause not recorded. No crew casualties. Aircraft M7+BH 40% damaged.

1/Erprobungs Gruppe 210

Messerschmitt Bf 110D/O (3373). Shot down during operations over Redhill aerodrome. Crashed south of Oxted, Surrey 9.15 a.m. Uffz. Rueger killed. Uffz. Ernst captured wounded. Aircraft S9+BH a write-off.

Stab/JG2

Messerschmitt Bf 109E-4 (5044). Shot down by fighters during advance fighter sweep over London. Crashed on Plumtree Farm, Headcorn near Maistone 9.00 a.m. Lt. Himmelheber baled out wounded and captured. Aircraft a write-off.
Site investigated by the London Air Museum and surface wreckage found including several minor components and spent 20mm cannon shells. Site re-examined by Steve Vizard in 1978 and further material recovered.

7/JG26

Messerschmitt Bf 109E-1 (3578). Briefed to sortie over Kenley area and failed to return. Believed shot down in the Channel by fighters. Gefr. Bieker killed. Aircraft lost.

Messerschmitt Bf 109E-4 (2781). Crashed at Hothfield, near Ashford, Kent 9.20 a.m. during fighter sweep over Kenley and combat with RAF fighters. Oblt. Christinnecke captured. Aircraft a write-off.

Messerschmitt Bf 109E-1 (3877). Shot down by fighters during fighter sortie over southern England to Kenley. Believed crashed in the Channel. Gefr. Holzapfel missing. Aircraft lost.

These fragments were all that could be found of the Bf 109E-4, No. 5044, which crashed at Plumtree Farm, Headcorn on September 6. Note that the caption details on the London Air Museum board are incorrect — the pilot was Leutnant Himmelheber of Stab/JG2.

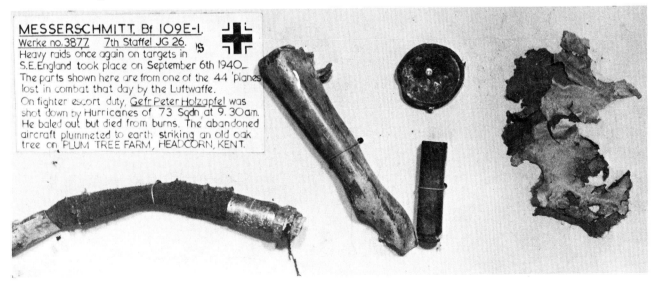

MESSERSCHMITT, Bf 109E-1
Werke no. 3877   7th Staffel JG 26.
Heavy raids once again on targets in S.E. England took place on September 6th 1940. The parts shown here are from one of the 44 planes lost in combat that day by the Luftwaffe.
On fighter escort duty, Gefr Peter Holzapfel was shot down by Hurricanes of 73 Sqdn at 9.30am. He baled out but died from burns. The abandoned aircraft plummeted to earth striking an old oak tree on PLUM TREE FARM, HEADCORN, KENT.

9/JG26

Messerschmitt Bf 109E (6033). Landed at Pihen with combat damage. Pilot wounded. Aircraft 30% damaged.

I/JG27

Messerschmitt Bf 109E-4 (5296). Belly-landed at Guines aerodrome due to engine failure during operational sortie. Pilot unhurt. Aircraft 25% damaged.

3/JG27

Messerschmitt Bf 109E-1 (3225). Crashed in the sea by the Nore boom 6.15 p.m. during fighter combat over the Thames Estuary. Oblt. Schueller captured unhurt. Aircraft 11+ lost.

5/JG27

Messerschmitt Bf 109E-4 (2762). Severely damaged in fighter attack during bomber escort mission and abandoned over Tonbridge, Kent 9.20 a.m. Crashed on Bank Farm, Tudeley. Fw. Braun baled out and captured unhurt. Aircraft 6+ a write-off.

Site investigated by Steve Vizard and many surface fragments found.

Messerschmitt Bf 109E-1 (3894). Returned badly damaged from bomber escort sortie over southern England and combat with fighters over Dungeness. Lt. Halbach wounded. Aircraft a write-off.

Stab III/JG27

Messerschmitt Bf 109E (1380). Shot down by Flight Lieutenant Ryder of No. 41 Squadron during bomber escort mission over Thameshaven. Crashed near Shoeburyness artillery range buoy 6.02 p.m. Hptmn. Schlichting (Gruppe Kommandeur) baled out and captured injured. Aircraft lost.

This impressive centrepiece to the Kent Battle of Britain Museum — a tailplane from a Bf 109E-4 — was found by Mike Llewellyn intact on the mudflats at Kingsnorth. There was competition with the London Air Museum to recover the remains of what proved to be a JG53 machine, No. 1129, shot down late on September 6 by Pilot Officer Bennions.

7/JG27

Messerschmitt Bf 109E (6318). Shot down in fighter combat and crashed at Blean, near Canterbury 6.45 p.m. Uffz. Nittmann captured unhurt. Aircraft 8+ a write-off.

3/JG52

Messerschmitt Bf 109E-4 (1138). Shot down by fighters during bomber escort over Kent. Crashed at Stone Street, near Sevenoaks 11.30 a.m. Oblt. Waller baled out over Seal and captured unhurt. Aircraft a write-off.

Site believed excavated by the Halstead War Museum and local enthusiast Ronald Gamage. Some relics in the Vizard Collection.

III/JG52

Messerschmitt Bf 109E-4 (5064). Crashed on landing at Coquelles following combat sortie. Cause unknown. Pilot unhurt. Aircraft a write-off.

I/JG53

Messerschmitt Bf 109E-4 (5347). Failed to return from sortie over the Channel off Hastings. Exact fate uncertain. Oblt. Gebhardt killed. Aircraft lost.

3/JG53

Messerschmitt Bf 109E-4 (1216). Shot down by fighters during bomber escort sortie over Tilbury. Reputedly crashed in England but location not traced. Oblt. Riegel missing. Aircraft a write-off.

II/JG53

Messerschmitt Bf 109E-4 (3751). Returned to base with combat damage. Oblt. Schulze-Blank wounded. Aircraft 35% damaged.

7/JG53

Messerschmitt Bf 109E-4 (1506). Shot down by fighters during free-lance fighter patrol over the Thames Estuary. Forced-landed on Vincents Farm outside Manston aerodrome 6.50 p.m. Uffz. Schulte captured. Aircraft 5+ I a write-off.

8/JG53

Messerschmitt Bf 109E-4 (1129). Shot down by Pilot Officer Bennions of No. 41 Squadron in combat over the Thames Estuary. Exploded over the mouth of the Medway 6.00 p.m. Uffz. Hempel killed. Aircraft a write-off.

Daimler-Benz DB 601 engine, propeller boss, one wing with undercarriage leg and radiator recovered from mud flats off Kingsnorth by the London Air Museum. Complete tail section, one wing, 7.92mm MG17 machine gun, set of engine exhaust stubs and an intact magazine of 20mm MGFF cannon ammunition recovered by the Kent Battle of Britain Museum.

2/KG26

Heinkel He 111H-3 (6902). Failed to return from bombing attack on London. Exact fate uncertain. Lt. Schachtebeck killed. Uffz. Fasz, Uffz. Jahme, Fw. Jessen and Gefr. Haslache missing. Aircraft 1H+ AK lost.

II/KG26

Heinkel He 111H-3 (5682). Returned to base damaged by AA fire following operations over the Channel. No crew casualties. Aircraft 1H+ NK 38% damaged.

4/KG26

Heinkel He 111H (6966). Crashed on landing at Gilze-Rijen aerodrome due to AA damage sustained during bombing mission over England. Crew unhurt. Aircraft 1H+FH a write-off.

Heinkel He 111H-5 (3516). Failed to return from sortie to Derby. Exact fate unknown. Uffz. Stut, Obergefr. Hubrig and Gefr. Schneider killed. Oblt. Kuckelt, Gefr. Kisling missing. Aircraft 1H+EM a write-off.

Heinkel He 111H-4 (3294). Shot down by own flak and crashed at Schiphol. Two NCOs killed. Oblt. Bischoff, Uffz. Kohlhepp and Obergefr. Gottschalk all wounded. Aircraft 1H+BM a write-off.

Heinkel He 111H-4 (5704). Crashed near Koeppern during operational sortie. Cause not stated. One NCO killed another wounded. Aircraft 1H+FM a write-off.

6/KG26

Heinkel He 111H-3 (3258). Failed to return from operational sortie to England. Exact fate unknown. Uffz. Bartels, Uffz. Schweizer, Oberfw. Staffeldt, Fw. Markuse and Gefr. Meier all killed. Aircraft 1H+HP lost.

9/KG26

Heinkel He 111H-3 (3173). Crashed into the town of Schwerin-Neumuehle during routine domestic flight. Cause unknown. (Civilian casualties: one woman and child killed, one child injured.) Crew of three NCOs killed. Aircraft 1H+LT a write-off.

III/KG27

Heinkel He 111P-2 (1532). Crashed at Rennes aerodrome due to mechanical failure during local flight. Crew unhurt. Aircraft 1K+LR 40% damaged.

I/KG30

Junkers Ju 88A-1. Crashed at Sorau on routine domestic flight due to mechanical failure. No crew casualties. Aircraft 4D+NF a write-off.

6/KG55

Heinkel He 111P-2 (1532). Shot down by own flak during operational sortie. Crashed on landing at Lisieux. Lt. Seeliger killed. Aircraft a write-off.

6/KG76

Junkers Ju 88A (3176). Shot down over the Channel off Littlestone by ground fire and fighter attack. Uffz. Haenel and Obergefr. Kohn killed. Oblt. Wagner and Uffz. Geyer missing. Aircraft F1+LP a write-off.

Junkers Ju 88A (8078). Forced-landed at Evreux due to battle damage following bombing sortie over the Channel. No crew casualties. Aircraft damage state not recorded.

Junkers Ju 88A (8104). Hit by AA fire and later attacked by fighters during raid on London. Forced-landed at Tanyards Farm, near Tonbridge 9.15 a.m. Lt. Kernbach, Uffz. Agel, Oberfw. Schumacher and Gefr. Riesel captured unhurt. Aircraft F1+HP a write-off.
Relics from this machine in the Steve Vizard Collection.

III/KG77

Junkers Ju 88A (3159). Crashed on landing at Cambrai following routine domestic flight. Crew unhurt. Aircraft 3Z+AD repairable.

II/LG2

Messerschmitt Bf 109E-7 (5567). Hit by AA fire during bomber escort sortie over Chatham. Forced-landed on Hawkinge aerodrome 6.14 p.m. Fw. Gottschalk captured unhurt. Aircraft +C a write-off.
Complete aircraft salvaged and evaluated by the Royal Aircraft Establishment at Farnborough in 1940. Items in Brenzett Aeronautical Museum said to be from this machine.

Messerschmitt Bf 109E-7 (3736). Crashed into the Channel off the Nore at 6.15 p.m. victim of AA fire during bomber escort sortie. Lt. Gueltgen captured. Aircraft +O lost.

Stab ZG26

Messerschmitt Bf 110C-4 (2145). Engine caught fire due to electrical fault during escort sortie over the Channel. Crashed in sea off Dover 9.20 a.m. Uffz. Roth killed. Oblt. Viertel baled out and captured. Aircraft 3U+CA lost.

I/ZG26

Messerschmitt Bf 110C-4 (2146). Shot down by fighters during combat sortie over Brooklands. Crashed at Cannons Hill Golf Course, near Coulsdon, Surrey 9.30 a.m. Uffz. Kiehn killed. Uffz. Neusz baled out and captured. Aircraft U8+CL a write-off.
Major recovery by the London Air Museum in 1976. Both Daimler-Benz DB 601 engines excavated together with propeller bosses, both undercarriage legs and tyres, tail wheel oleo, complete armament, cockpit instruments, first-aid kit, pilot's parachute and port tail fin still bearing traces of Swastika marking.

7/ZG26

Messerschmitt Bf 110D/O (3405). Failed to return from operational mission over England. Believed shot down by fighters. Gefr. Schumann killed. Fw. Kaufmann missing. Aircraft 3U+HR a write-off.

Saturday, September 7

Stab KG.z.b.V.2

Junkers Ju 52 (6517). Crashed at Johannisthal aerodrome following engine failure during routine domestic flight. One NCO wounded. Aircraft KD+GO a write-off.

SeenotflugKdo.3

Heinkel He 59 (0840). Crashed on landing in heavy sea (PQ1114) during air-sea rescue mission. Crew rescued unhurt by German naval vessel. Aircraft DA+WT lost.

4(F)/14

Messerschmitt Bf 110C-5 (2208). Failed to return from reconnaissance sortie over the Channel. Lt. Goedsche and Oblt. Russel both reported killed. Aircraft 5F+MM lost.

Messerschmitt Bf 110C-5 (2211). Crash-landed at Cherbourg damaged by fighters. Lt. Felix wounded. Aircraft 20% damaged.

1(F)/22

Messerschmitt Bf 110C (2207). Forced-landed near Vlissingen damaged following attack by fighters over the Channel. Two NCOs wounded. Aircraft 4N+DH 35% damaged.

1/106

Heinkel He 115 (2724). Shot down in North Sea (PQ6779) by Lockheed Hudson. One NCO wounded. Aircraft M2+FH a write-off.

1/JG2

Messerschmitt Bf 109E-4 (3909). Suffered engine failure during escort sortie to London. Forced-landed at St. Radegund's Abbey, near Dover 6.30 p.m. Oblt. Gotz captured unhurt. Aircraft 8+ a write-off.
Site investigated by the Brenzett Aeronautical Museum but no relics discovered.

5/JG2

Messerschmitt Bf 109E-1 (3320). Shot down by Flying Officer Scott of No. 41 Squadron during escort sortie. Crashed in the Channel off Folkestone 6.00 p.m. Uffz. Melchert captured. Aircraft 6+ lost.

Stab III/JG3

Messerschmitt Bf 109E-4 (5249). Shot down in combat over the Thames Estuary. Crashed in sea. Oblt. Goettmann killed. Aircraft lost.

8/JG3

Messerschmitt Bf 109E-1 (6271). Crashed in Channel following combat with RAF fighters. Pilot rescued unhurt by Seenotdienst. Aircraft lost.

4/JG26

Messerschmitt Bf 109E-4 (5385). Shot down by fighters during sortie to cover bombers returning from attack on London. Forced-landed on Sheerlands Farm, Pluckley, Kent 6.00 p.m. Oblt. Krug (Staffel Kapitan) captured unhurt. Aircraft 12+ a write-off.
'Tiger's-head' staffel insignia removed by troops in 1940 and donated to Kent Battle of Britain Museum by local landowner.

6/JG26

Messerschmitt Bf 109E-4 (0735). Crashed in the Channel off Shakespeare Cliff, Dover 7.00 p.m. Radiators damaged in fighter combat over London. Uffz. Braun captured unhurt. Aircraft lost.

1/JG27

Messerschmitt Bf 109E-4 (5390). Shot down by Flight Lieutenant Powell-Sheddon of No. 242 Squadron in combat over the Thames Estuary. Crashed Rainham Road, Hornchurch 5.30 p.m. Lt. Genske baled out and captured unhurt. Aircraft a write-off.

1/JG51

Messerschmitt Bf 109E-1 (4840). Shot down by fighters during escort sortie for bombers attacking London. Crashed at Bethersden near Ashford 5.45 p.m. Uffz. zur Lage baled out and captured. Aircraft 7+ a write-off.

2/JG51

Messerschmitt Bf 109E-1 (6342). Failed to return from bomber escort mission to London and believed shot down in the Channel. Oberfw. Stroehlein missing. Aircraft lost.

3/JG51

Messerschmitt Bf 109E-3 (5091). Shot down, believed by ground fire, during escort sortie over Kent. Crashed at Oad Street, Borden, near Sittingbourne 5.45 p.m. Gefr. Werner baled out and captured unhurt. Aircraft 9+ a write-off.
Site investigated by Kent Battle of Britain Museum but nothing tangible discovered.

Thirty-six years separate these two photographs *(above)* taken at the same spot on Cannons Hill Golf Course at Coulsdon. *Left:* All that was left after a Bf 110 of ZG26 smashed into the ground at 9.30 a.m. on September 6 (Tony Graves). *Opposite:* The crash site being investigated by the London Air Museum in 1976 (Brenzett). Both DB 601s were extracted together with extensive remains from the cockpit area which included Unteroffizier Kiehn's unused parachute, a first-aid kit with surgical instruments for emergency treatment on board (including a bone saw), seat harnesses, uniform buckles and the pilot's diary for 1940.

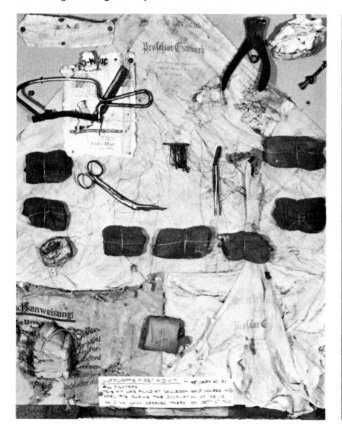

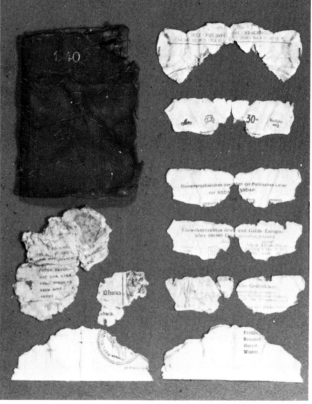

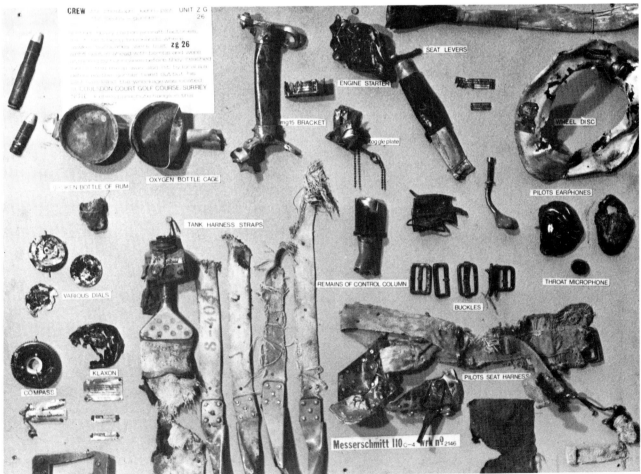

CREW ... UNIT Z G 26

zg 26

COULSDON COURT GOLF COURSE, SURREY

BROKEN BOTTLE OF RUM

OXYGEN BOTTLE CAGE

mg15 BRACKET

toggle plate

SEAT LEVERS

ENGINE STARTER

WHEEL DISC

PILOTS EARPHONES

VARIOUS DIALS

TANK HARNESS STRAPS

REMAINS OF CONTROL COLUMN

BUCKLES

THROAT MICROPHONE

KLAXON

COMPASS

PILOTS SEAT HARNESS

Messerschmitt 110 G-4 Wrk nº 2146

9/JG51

Messerschmitt Bf 109E-4 (4097). Shot down by fighters during bomber escort sortie to London. Crashed at Little Clacton, Essex 4.59 p.m. Uffz. Koch baled out and captured unhurt. Aircraft 11+ a write-off.

Messerschmitt Bf 109E-4 (2046). Crashed in the Channel following fighter combat over the south coast of England. Pilot rescued unhurt by Seenotdienst. Aircraft lost.

2/JG54

Messerschmitt Bf 109E (1153). Crashed on take-off from Guines on combat sortie. Pilot unhurt. Aircraft 60% damaged.

Stab I/JG77

Messerschmitt Bf 109E-4 (5129). Shot down over the Channel off Dungeness and crashed in sea. Pilot rescued unhurt by Seenotdienst. Aircraft lost.

1/JG77

Messerschmitt Bf 109E-4 (5811). Shot down during fighter-bomber sortie over England by Squadron Leader Johnstone of No. 602 Squadron. Crashed at Rolvenden, near Tenterden, Kent 5.45 p.m. Oberfw. Goltzsche captured. Aircraft 11+ a write-off.

3/Erprobungs Gruppe 210

Messerschmitt Bf 109E-4 (2021). Crashed in Channel during combat with fighters over Southampton. Pilot rescued unhurt by Seenotdienst. Aircraft lost.

3/KG1

Heinkel He 111 H-3 (8664). Crashed at Dieppe following operational sortie over the Channel. Probable cause battle damage. Three NCOs killed. One missing. Aircraft V4+ AT a write-off.

II/KG1

Heinkel He 111H. Returned to base damaged in fighter attack over London. Oberstlt. Koch (Gruppe Kommandeur) and one NCO wounded. Aircraft repairable.

4/KG1

Heinkel He 111H-2 (2745). Crashed at Bixschoote following bombing sortie over London. Hptmn. Neumann, Oblt. Brand and one NCO killed. Uffz. Goehn missing. Aircraft V4+ FU a write-off.

4/KG2

Dornier Do 17Z (2830). Shot down by fighters over London. Uffz. Christoph, Uffz. Greiner, Uffz. Treuer and Gefr. Pilz killed. Aircraft U5+ FM a write-off.

Stab KG3

Dornier Do 17Z-3 (2619). Shot down by AA fire during bombing attack on London. Hptmn. Otting (Staffel Kapitan) and Oberfw. Kleine both killed. Uffz. Voelkert and Fw. Hubert missing. Aircraft 5K+ DA a write-off.

5/KG3

Dornier Do 17Z (2840). Forced-landed at Calais due to combat damage. Lt. Leitner and one NCO wounded. Aircraft 5K+ FN 50% damaged.

III/KG3

Dornier Do 17Z. Returned to base three NCOs wounded by AA fire following sortie over London. Aircraft repairable.

Dornier Do 17Z. Hit by AA fire during bombing attack on London but returned to base with one NCO wounded. Aircraft repairable.

5/KG4

Heinkel He 111. Went into a spin due to technical fault and crashed near Clermont during operational sortie. Oblt. Wiegand and Uffz. Fellmann killed. Aircraft a write-off.

6/KG4

Heinkel He 111P-4 (3078). Shot down by AA fire during night bombing sortie over the Thames Estuary. Crashed in the Thames off Purfleet 10.40 p.m. Oblt. Klotz and Uffz. Wolf killed. Uffz. Klein and Gefr. Backmann captured unhurt. Uffz. Knoll missing. Aircraft 5J+ JP lost.

Site investigated by the Essex Historical Aircraft Society and small parts from one radiator recovered together with airframe components.

2/KG26

Heinkel He 111H-3 (6865). Damaged by AA fire and fighter attack over London but returned to base crew unhurt. Aircraft 1H+ DK 10% damaged.

3/KG26

Heinkel He 111H-3 (6937). Returned to base damaged by fighters and AA fire during sortie to bomb London. No crew casualties. Aircraft 1H+ FL 10% damaged.

Stab KG40

Heinkel He 111H-5 (3515). Failed to return from combat mission over England and presumed crashed in sea. Obstlt. Geiss (Geschwader Kommodore). Oblt. Schwengke missing. Fw. Czesny and Uffz. Lerique (both of 3/KGr.126) also missing. Aircraft 1T+ HH lost.

I/KG51

Junkers Ju 88A-1 (6076). Crashed at Melun-Villaroche aerodrome during routine domestic flight due to faulty servicing. Crew unhurt. Aircraft 50% damaged.

Stab III/KG51

Junkers Ju 88A (2617). Damaged in landing accident at Melun-Villaroche due to burst tyre. No crew casualties. Aircraft 9K+ CD 30% damaged.

I/KG53

Heinkel He 111H-3 (6912). Shot down by fighters during weather recce sortie over Anglia. Crashed in sea off Harwich 6.00 p.m. Oberfw. Mueller and Flgr. Honig missing. Oberfw. Winter, Oblt. Weber and Fw. Kempgen captured. Aircraft A1+ AB lost.

Heinkel He 111H. Returned to base damaged following bombing attack on London. No crew casualties. Aircraft damage state not recorded.

II/KG53

Heinkel He 111H-2 (2722). Belly-landed at Bruges due to combat damage following sortie over London. One NCO wounded. Aircraft A1+ AP 40% damaged.

Heinkel He 111H. Returned to base damaged by AA fire over London. Two NCOs wounded. Aircraft repairable.

Heinkel He 111H-2 (2777). Shot down by fighters during bombing sortie to Thameshaven and forced-landed on the Isle of Grain 5.30 p.m. Crew set fire to the aircraft. Obergefr. Neumann killed. Oblt. Breuer, Oberfw. Pitzkar, Gefr. Uhrich and Uffz. Bergmann captured. Aircraft A1+ DN a write-off.

II/KG54

Junkers Ju 88A-1 (6032). Failed to return from operations over England. Exact fate unknown. Oberfw. Schmitz, Oberfw. Brehmer, and Fw. Kalucza killed. Fw. Liebernecht missing. Aircraft B3+ AM lost.

Junkers Ju 88A-1 (4143). Crashed on landing at St. Andre due to undercarriage failure following routine domestic flight. Crew unhurt. Aircraft 40% damaged.

III/KG55

Heinkel He 111P (1731). Crashed and burned out at L'Aigle due to engine failure during operational sortie. Oblt. Wolf-Witte wounded. Aircraft a write-off.

Stab KG76

Dornier Do 17Z (2596). Crashed at Sundridge, west of Sevenoaks, Kent 6.00 p.m. following attack by fighters during photo-recce mission over London docks. Uffz. Rupprecht, Oberfw. Schneider and Oberfhr. Schneider killed. Fw. Rosche baled out and captured unhurt. Aircraft F1+ BA a write-off.

Crash site on a waterworks excavated by the Kent Battle of Britain Museum and one propeller blade and an oil pump, plus various fragments and a machine gun cleaning kit extricated under extremely difficult conditions. Oxygen mask donated by Sevenoaks resident bearing name 'ROSCHE' on leather trim. Maps in the Vizard collection.

This prop blade from the Dornier Do 17Z of Stab KG76, complete with bullet holes, was recovered by the Kent Battle of Britain Museum from Sundridge, Kent.

I/KGr.806

Junkers Ju 88A-1 (4094). Crashed at Nantes due to mechanical failure on operational sortie. Crew of four NCOs killed. Aircraft M7+ JK a write-off.

II/LG1

Junkers Ju 88A-1 (2044). Crashed on take-off from Orleans aerodrome due to engine failure. Crew unhurt. Aircraft L1+ EM 50% damaged.

Junkers Ju 88A-1 (7041). Crashed on landing on burst tyre at Orleans following routine domestic flight. No crew casualties. Aircraft L1+ AM 50% damaged.

1/LG2

Messerschmitt Bf 109E. Shot down by Sergeant Furst of No. 310 Squadron during fighter combat over Canterbury. Crashed at Little Stour River, Wickhambreux 5.35 p.m. Uffz. Goetting baled out and captured. Aircraft a write-off.

Site excavated by the Kent Battle of Britain Museum which recovered the control column, signal pistol, radio mast, Swastika marking from the tail, and complete belts of 7.92mm ammunition. Later re-excavated together with Southern Area Wartime Aircraft Preservation Society for the benefit of the surviving pilot who attended recovery operations. Propeller boss and blades, complete armour, armament, pilot's maps and compressed fuselage panels unearthed. First-aid kit in Steve Vizard Collection.

I/ZG2

Messerschmitt Bf 110C-4 (2216). Shot down by fighters during bomber escort sortie and crashed in flames at Old Tree Farm, Hoath, near Herne Bay, Kent 5.20 p.m. Lt. Kislinger killed. Uffz. Dahnke baled out and captured unhurt. Aircraft 3M+ LM a write-off.

Site excavated in November 1979 by the Historic Aircraft Archaeologist Group. Quantities of shattered airframe and several interesting components recovered. Pieces also in the Vizard collection.

Messerschmitt Bf 110C-4 (3117). Crashed at Eythorne, near Deal, Kent 5.50 p.m. following fighter attack during escort sortie. Fw. Jakob and Fw. Ottersbach both killed. Aircraft 3M+ FL a write-off.

Messerschmitt Bf 110C-4 (3246). Shot down by fighters during escort sortie over Thames-haven. Crashed at Noak Hill, Billericay, Essex 5.30 p.m. Oblt. Granz and Fw. Schutel baled out and captured unhurt. Aircraft EM+ BB a write-off.

Major recovery undertaken by No. 2393 (Billericay) Squadron ATC in the summer of 1971. Complete Daimler-Benz DB 601 engine excavated plus propeller boss with two blades attached, both undercarriage legs, cannon blast tubes, intact magazine of 7.92mm ammunition, two oil coolers, four compressed air bottles and several manufacturers' plates. Relics held by the Essex Aviation Group and the Historic Aircraft Museum, Southend. Pilot presented with propeller boss and one blade.

II/ZG2

Messerschmitt Bf 110D/O (3185). Crashed and burnt out at Swan Lane, Downham Hall, near Wickford, Essex 5.15 p.m. Lt. Abert and Uffz. Scharf killed. Aircraft A2+ BH a write-off.

Messerschmitt Bf 110D/O (3328). Shot down during escort mission and crashed on Bullers Farm, Little Burstead, Essex 5.30 p.m. Gefr. Hetz killed. Lt. Stix captured wounded. Aircraft A2+ JH a write-off.

Messerschmitt Bf 110D/O (3334). Shot down by fighters during combat over Ramsgate. Lt. Schonemann and Uffz. Meschede both killed. Aircraft A2+ NH a write-off.

Linked 7.92mm rounds from Unteroffizier Goetting's Bf 109E (1/LG2) displayed in the museum at Chilham Castle.

Messerschmitt Bf 110C-4 (3570). Ditched in the Channel five miles off Birchington, Thanet, Kent 6.00 p.m. following fighter attack. Uffz. Galla killed. Oblt. Brede captured unhurt. Aircraft A2+ ML lost.

In 1971 Pilot Officer Alick Grant wanted a project for the Air Training Corps cadets at Billericay and the search for and excavation of a local wartime crashed aircraft seemed ideal. He followed up a local story of a fighter or bomber being buried somewhere around the town and finally located the impact point off Noak Hill Road, Little Burstead. After the site was pin-pointed, many weeks were spent digging by hand, the wreckage first being identified as German, then as a Messerschmitt Bf 110, before a piece of metal numbered 3246 revealed it as a 1/ZG2 machine reported shot down over north London on September 7, 1940. The pilot, Oberleutnant Gerhard Granz, pictured *below left* in 1940, (not with 3246) was traced and invited to return to Billericay. Now a serving colonel in the post-war Luftwaffe, thirty-one years and ten days after he was shot down, he was presented with a propeller blade and hub as a souvenir from his aircraft by Flight Lieutenant Reg Ferriss, CO of No. 2393 Squadron, ATC (Peter Elgar).

3/123

Junkers Ju 88A. Shot down by fighters during photo-reconnaissance sortie to Liverpool. Crash-landed at Mallwyd, Machynlleth, Montgomeryshire 12.30 p.m. Lt. Boehle, Oblt. Kauter, Uffz. Leisler and Fw. Kobold all captured wounded. Aircraft 4U+ BL a write-off.

Sunday, September 8

1/106

Heinkel He 115 (2088). Shot down during operational sortie over the English coast. Crew rescued by Seenotdienst. Lt. zur See Molis wounded. Aircraft M2+ JH lost.

1/706

Arado Ar 196 (0095). Sunk at anchorage in Aalborg due to storm conditions. No personnel casualties. Aircraft CK+ FJ lost.

3/Erprobungs Gruppe 210

Messerschmitt Bf 109E-4 (1998). Crashed on take-off from Denain on routine local flight. Pilot unhurt. Aircraft 30% damaged.

I/JG53

Messerschmitt Bf 109E-4 (0867). Shot down in fighter combat and crashed at Seal near Sevenoaks 12.40 p.m. Uffz. Adelwart killed. Aircraft a write-off.

Site excavated by the Halstead War Museum and remains of shattered airframe unearthed together with one complete 20mm MGFF cannon. Some relics in the Kent Battle of Britain Museum and Brenzett Aeronautical Museum.

Messerschmitt Bf 109E-1 (3478). Collided with Oblt. Kuhnert's aircraft during sortie over the Channel. Oblt. Witmeier injured. Aircraft a write-off.

III/JG53

Messerschmitt Bf 109E-7 (1171). Crashed in the Channel following collision with Oblt. Witmeier during operational sortie. Oblt. Kuhnert (Staffel Kapitan) killed. Aircraft lost.

5/KG2

Dornier Do 17Z (2668). Shot down by AA fire during sortie to bomb London. Crashed near Farningham Road railway station, Kent 12.45 p.m. Oblt. Schneider, Uffz. Schumacher, Obergefr, Hoffmann and Flgr. Kohl all captured wounded. Aircraft U5+ BN a write-off.

Surface fragments from this aircraft or from 1130 recovered from general area of crash site by the Kent Battle of Britain Museum.

Dornier Do 17Z (1130). Hit by AA fire and exploded over Farningham Road railway station 12.45 p.m. Lt. Landenberger, Obergefr. Lotter and Flgr. Schuetze killed. Oberfw. Strobel captured wounded. Aircraft U5+ FN a write-off.

Dornier Do 17Z (3415). Exploded over Leeds, near Maidstone under attack from Sergeant Andrew of No. 46 Squadron 12.40 p.m. Oblt. Ziems, Uffz. Flisk, Uffz. Trost and Uffz. Selter all killed. Aircraft U5+ LN a write-off.

Surface fragments collected from strawberry plantation at Hollingbourne by the London Air Museum said to be from this aircraft.

III/KG2

Dornier Do 17Z (2785). Returned to base damaged by fighters following sortie over England. No crew casualties. Aircraft U5+ CP 35% damaged.

3/KG3

Dornier Do 17Z-2 (3426). Severely damaged in collision over Gent during routine domestic flight. Crew unhurt. Aircraft 5K+ GL a write-off.

Dornier Do 17Z-2 (3321). Crashed at Ertvelde north of Gent following mid-air collision. Hptmn. Kuekens (Staffel Kapitan) and two NCOs killed. Aircraft 5K+ CL a write-off.

Ergaenzungs Staffel KG4

Heinkel He 111P (2474). Damaged in landing accident at Fassberg aerodrome. Possible minor collision. No crew casualties. Aircraft 5J+ KU repairable.

Heinkel He 111P (2508). Believed involved in minor landing accident at Fassberg aerodrome. Crew unhurt. Aircraft 5J+ NU repairable.

II/KG27

Heinkel He 111P (2839). Crashed on take-off from Brest on combat mission. Cause not stated. Two NCOs killed, another wounded. Aircraft 1G+ NN a write-off.

Ausbildungs Staffel KG53

Heinkel He 111H-1 (5250). Crashed at Giebelstadt during night training flight. One NCO killed, another injured. Aircraft A1+ NR a write-off.

I/KG54

Junkers Ju 88A-1 (4032). Failed to return from operational sortie over England. Believed victim of ground defences. Hptmn. Brisch, Oberfw. Zingel, Fw. Ofschonka and Flgr. Kudina killed. Aircraft B3+ BK lost.

III/KG55

Heinkel He 111P-2 (3353). Crashed on landing at Villacoublay due to damage from AA fire during night raid on England. Lt. Richter and one NCO wounded. Aircraft 50% damaged.

Stab KGr.806

Junkers Ju 88A-1 (6136). Crashed at St. Clementin following operational sortie over England. Cause unknown, possibly damaged by AA fire. Four NCOs killed. Aircraft M7+ EA a write-off.

I/LG1

Junkers Ju 88A-1 (2122). Crashed and burned out at Orleans shortly after take-off on bombing mission. Major Kanus and three NCOs all killed. Aircraft L1+ BB a write-off.

II/LG1

Junkers Ju 88A-1 (2044). Crashed near Orleans due to engine failure during operational sortie. No crew casualties. Aircraft L1+ EM 60% damaged.

Junkers Ju 88A-1 (2102). Suffered engine failure during combat mission. Crashed near Orleans-Bricy aerodrome. Crew unhurt. Aircraft L1+ JM 60% damaged.

III/LG1

Junkers Ju 88A-1 (6060). Engine caught fire during operational sortie. Crashed and burned out near Chateaudun. Two NCOs killed, another wounded. Aircraft L1+ DS a write-off.

I/StG 77

Junkers Ju 87B-1 (0472). Damaged in taxi-ing accident at Maltot aerodrome. Non-operational sortie. Crew unhurt. Aircraft S2+ BL 20% damaged.

Junkers Ju 87B-2 (5589). Slightly damaged on landing at Maltot following routine domestic flight. Crew unhurt. Aircraft S2+ CB repairable.

Monday, September 9

Kurierstaffel 10

Junkers W 34 hau (1352). Suffered engine failure during routine domestic flight and forced-landed at Oldenburg. Crew unhurt. Aircraft GB+ NT 40% damaged.

1(H)/32

Henschel Hs 126A (2982). Damaged in minor taxi-ing accident at Rebstock aerodrome. No crew casualties. Aircraft V7+ LA 10% damaged.

Following the first massive daylight raid on London on September 7 (which continued with night bombing), there was little German activity over Britain the following day — thus there are few sites to investigate. This leading edge slat at Brenzett came from No. 0867 of JG53.

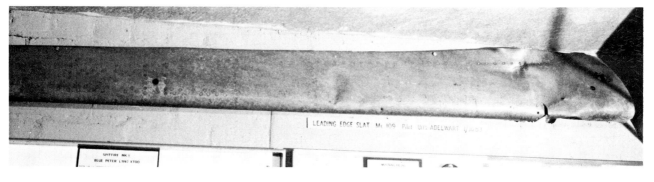

Remains of Unteroffizier Rauwolf's Bf 109E-1, down at Benenden on September 9, were recovered by Lashenden Air Warfare Museum. The pilot's seat armour, broken into four pieces, has been pieced together for the display.

Luftdienstkdo 64

Junkers W 34 (1377). Shot down by RAF bomber during operational sortie and crashed in the North Sea off Roevar Island. Crew rescued by Norwegian fishing boat — one NCO being wounded. Aircraft BB+ MG lost.

III/JG2

Messerschmitt Bf 109E-1 (2947). Forced-landed at Beaumont-le-Roger aerodrome following combat sortie. Pilot unhurt. Aircraft 30% damaged.

4/JG3

Messerschmitt Bf 109E (6138). Ditched in the Channel six miles off Newhaven 5.55 p.m. trying to reach French coast on damaged engine following attack by RAF fighters over Dover during bomber escort mission. Fw. Mueller rescued captured unhurt. Aircraft lost.

7/JG3

Messerschmitt Bf 109E-4 (5351). Shot down by fighters during operational sortie over the Channel. Believed crashed in sea. Fw. Bauer missing. Aircraft lost.

Messerschmitt Bf 109E-1 (6316). Forced-landed at Cooper's Field, Flimwell, near Hawkhurst, Kent 6.00 p.m. due to damaged engine following fighter combat. Uffz. Massmann captured unhurt. Aircraft 6+1 a write-off.
Relics in Malcolm Petitt's collection.

Stab I/JG27

Messerschmitt Bf 109E-4 (1394). Shot down by fighters during fighter sweep over Kent and forced-landed at Knowle Farm, Mayfield, Sussex 5.00 p.m. Oblt. Bode (Gruppe Adjutant) captured unhurt. Aircraft a write-off.

5/JG27

Messerschmitt Bf 109E-1 (3488). Shot down by fighters during escort sortie over England. Forced-landed on Charity Farm, Cootham, near Storrington, Sussex 5.50 p.m. Oblt. Daig captured unhurt. Aircraft 13+ a write-off.

6/JG27

Messerschmitt Bf 109E-1 (6280). Shot down during bomber escort mission and crashed on Mounts Farm, Benenden, Kent 6.15 p.m. Uffz. Rauwolf baled out and captured. Aircraft 7+ a write-off.
Major recovery by the Lashenden Air Warfare Museum which unearthed the Daimler-Benz DB 601 engine, fuel injection pump, radiator, main spar, undercarriage leg, complete cockpit armour, instruments, gunsight, control column, first-aid kit, pilot's maps and cap. Surviving pilot traced to Munich 1979.

7/JG27

Messerschmitt Bf 109E-4 (1617). Shot down in combat with fighters and crashed at Romans Gate Cottage, near Rudgwick, Sussex 6.00 p.m. Uffz. Born killed. Aircraft a write-off.
Crash site now under a main road. Visited by the Air Historical Group which acquired the radio from this aircraft from a local resident.

1/JG51

Messerschmitt Bf 109E-1 (3614). Forced-landed at Abbeville fuel exhausted following combat sortie over England. Pilot unhurt. Aircraft a write-off.

1/JG53

Messerschmitt Bf 109E-4 (1508). Crashed in flames on Cherry Tree Farm, near the Old Jail Inn, Jail Lane, Biggin Hill during combat with fighters 6.00 p.m. Fw. Honisch baled out and captured. Aircraft 5+ a write-off.
Relics from this aircraft donated to the Kent Battle of Britain Museum by an ex-airframe fitter based at Biggin Hill in 1940.

4/JG53

Messerschmitt Bf 109E-4 (0963). Shot down in combat with RAF fighters during sortie over the Channel. Oblt. Schulze-Blank (Staffel Kapitan) killed. Aircraft lost.

8/JG53

Messerschmitt Bf 109E (6139). Crashed and burned out at Sundown Farm, Ditcham, Hampshire 6.15 p.m. during combat with RAF fighters. Gefr. Becker killed. Aircraft a write-off.

1/JG54

Messerschmitt Bf 109E-1 (6103). Shot down in fighter combat over the Channel off south coast of England. Crashed in sea. Fw. Biber missing. Aircraft lost.

3/JG54

Messerschmitt Bf 109E-1 (3906). Crashed in the Channel during combat with RAF fighters. Pilot rescued unhurt by Seenotdienst. Aircraft a write-off.

I/JG77

Messerschmitt Bf 109E (4055). Forced-landed at Fecamp aerodrome fuel exhausted following combat sortie over the Channel. Pilot unhurt. Aircraft 30% damaged.

Messerschmitt Bf 109E-4 (3753). Ran short of fuel on return from combat sortie over England and forced-landed at Fecamp. Pilot unhurt. Aircraft 30% damaged.

3/KG1

Heinkel He 111H-3 (5713). Shot down by fighters following bombing attack on aerodrome near London. Landed at Sundridge, near Sevenoaks, Kent 6.00 p.m. Oblt. Kiunka, Uffz. Stumbaum, Uffz. Marck, Oberfw. Heidrich and Gefr. Reinecke all captured. Aircraft V4+ BL a write-off.
Parts recovered at the time in the Vizard collection.

4/KG1

Heinkel He 111H-2 (5460). Crashed at Mezieres during routine domestic flight due to mechanical failure. Crew unhurt. Aircraft V4+ GU 60% damaged.

6/KG1

Heinkel He 111H-2. Crash-landed due to engine failure following operational sortie over the Channel. No crew casualties. Aircraft damage state not recorded.

Heinkel He 111H-2 (2729). Forced-landed at Glisy damaged by AA fire during combat mission over England. Crew unhurt. Aircraft V4+ KW 35% damaged.

Ergaenzungs Staffel KG4

Heinkel He 111P-4 (2964). Crashed and burned out shortly after take-off from Sorau aerodrome on local training flight. One NCO killed. Aircraft VJ+ CL a write-off.

Stab KG30

Junkers Ju 88A-1 (0274). Shot down by No. 66 Squadron Spitfires during sortie to bomb London docks. Forced-landed in Church Field, Newells Farm, Nuthurst, near Horsham 6.00 p.m. Oblt. Heil, Uffz. Beck, Uff. Paustian and Fw. Fuss all captured. Aircraft 4D+ AA a write-off.

Stab II/KG30

Junkers Ju 88A-2 (5074). Forced-landed and burned out on Bannisters Farm, Toulver Lane, Barcombe, near Lewes 5.40 p.m. Shot down by fighters during bombing mission to London. Uffz. Deibler killed. Oblt. Golnisch, Uffz. Rolf and Uffz. Hamerla captured unhurt. Aircraft 4D+ KK a write-off.

Junkers Ju 88A-1 (8032). Failed to return from bombing sortie over England and believed shot down by fighters. Uffz. Stahl, Uffz. Fecht, Uffz. Hallert and Gefr. Goerth missing. Aircraft 4D+ FB lost.

It is not every cricket club that will allow their hallowed ground to be desecrated in the search of history. A 15/LG1 machine crashed at Worcester Park on September 9 and the London Air Museum pin-pointed the impact point on the Maori sports field *(above)*. Carefully excavated by hand, one remarkable find was the port tail fin complete with the Swastika emblem.

Stab III/KG30

Junkers Ju 88A (0333). Shot down by fighters over Sussex coast during sortie to bomb London docks. Forced-landed in sea off Pagham 5.50 p.m. Major Hackbarth (Gruppe Kommandeur) and Oberfw. Manger captured. Uffz. Sawallisch and Gefr. Petermann killed. Aircraft 4D+ AD a write-off.

8/KG30

Junkers Ju 88A-5 (3195). Shot down by fighters over southern England during bombing mission. Uffz. Hettinger and Obergefr. Baumgarten killed. Uffz. Vetter and Fw. Jung missing. Aircraft 4D+LS a write-off.

II/KG51

Junkers Ju 88A (0307). Crash-landed at Villeneuve-Orly aerodrome following combat mission over the Channel. Crew unhurt. Aircraft 30% damaged.

III/KG51

Junkers Ju 88A-1 (7063). Damaged in landing accident at Villaroche following routine domestic flight. Crew unhurt. Aircraft 15% damaged.

III/KG53

Heinkel He 111H-2 (2630). Crashed on Southfield Farm, near Alton, Hampshire 5.50 p.m. following collision with RAF fighter. Fw. Doering, Fw. Endorf and Fw. Wenninger killed. Oblt. Meinecke and Fw. Broderich captured having baled out. Aircraft A1+ZD a write-off.
Site excavated by the Southern Area Wartime Aircraft Preservation Society who recovered minor fragments from the airframe plus some shattered perspex and exploded 7.92mm machine gun ammunition.

Heinkel He 111H-2 (3306). Returned to base damaged by AA fire during bombing sortie over England. Two NCOs wounded. Aircraft A1+ AS 10% damaged.

Heinkel He 111H-2 (5548). Damaged by fighters during sortie over England and returned to base with one NCO killed and two wounded. Aircraft A1+ DS 22% damaged.

On the evening of September 9, German units en route for London were attacked and turned back. An escorting Bf 110 from III/ZG76 was hit by anti-aircraft fire and crashed *(above)* at Borden in Kent. The two crewmen baled out too low and were killed. Local legend has it that both were wearing dress shirts under their one-piece flying suits (Kent Messenger).

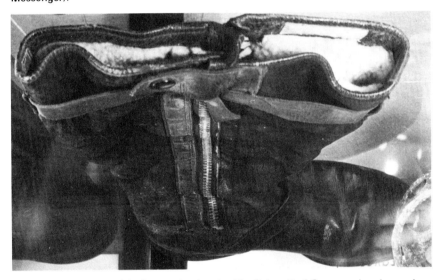

This flying boot was picked up at the time by Mr. Colenutt of Gravesend and was given to the Kent Battle of Britain Museum after it excavated the site.

Later the ubiquitous Steve Vizard recovered these items including a highly-prized Mercedes-Benz badge.

I/KG54

Junkers Ju 88A-1 (7086). Forced-landed near Paris due to battle damage following sortie over England. No crew casualties. Aircraft 40% damaged.

Ergaenzungs Staffel KG76

Dornier Do 17Z-3 (2560). Damaged in taxiing accident at Beaumont-le-Roger aerodrome. No crew casualties. Aircraft F1 + JH 30% damaged.

Stab LG1

Junkers Ju 88A-1 (5093). Crashed and burned out on take-off from Orleans-Bricy. Cause unknown. Four NCOs killed. Aircraft L1 + DA a write-off.

II/LG1

Junkers Ju 88A-1 (7078). Take-off accident at Orleans aerodrome. Crashed and burned out cause unknown but possibly collision. Four NCOs killed. Aircraft L1 + JP a write-off.

Junkers Ju 88A-1 (5106). Crash-landed at Orleans-Bricy aerodrome following operational sortie. Cause not stated. No crew casualties. Aircraft L1 + BM 40% damaged.

15/LG1

Messerschmitt Bf 110 (3298). Shot down by fighters during sortie over southern England. Crashed on Maori Sports Club, Old Malden Lane, Worcester Park, Surrey 6.00 p.m. Uffz. Pfafflhuber and Uffz. Kramp both killed. Aircraft L1 + DL a write-off.
Major recovery from under a cricket pitch by the London Air Museum. Remains of both Daimler-Benz DB 601 engines excavated together with both undercarriage legs, oxygen bottles, remains of a rubber dinghy, first-aid kit, a parachute and masses of compressed airframe including one tail fin still bearing traces of painted Swastika.

II/NJG 1

Messerschmitt Bf 110D (3136). Crashed near Ingelstadt on routine domestic flight due to mechanical failure. Both crew killed. Aircraft a write-off.

III/ZG76

Messerschmitt Bf110C (3207). Shot down over Croydon in combat with RAF fighters during escort sortie. Fw. Ostermuencher and Gefr. Zimmermann both killed. Aircraft 2N + EP a write-off.

Messerschmitt Bf 110C (2081). Returned to base severely damaged by RAF fighters following escort sortie over Croydon. Crash-landed at Quoeux aerodrome. Crew unhurt. Aircraft 2N + CP a write-off.

Messerschmitt Bf 110C (2137). Shot down by AA and crashed in flames at Borden, near Sittingbourne, Kent 6.00 p.m. Uffz. Bierling and Uffz. Kurella both killed. Aircraft 2N + FM a write-off.
Site excavated by Kent Battle of Britain Museum and remains of shattered Daimler-Benz DB 601 engines recovered together with large sections of compressed airframe, various components, propeller blade, oxygen bottles and aircrew forage cap and oxygen mask. Fragments recovered subsequently by Steve Vizard from a depth of eight feet.

Messerschmitt Bf 110C (3108). Ditched in sea five miles off Newhaven due to damage sustained in fighter attack over southern England 6.00 p.m. Fw. Koops captured unhurt. Uffz. Weiher killed. Aircraft 2N + EP lost.

Tuesday, September 10

Aufklaerungs Staffel Ob.d.L.

Heinkel He 116 (3058). Crashed on take-off from Vaerlose aerodrome following engine failure on routine domestic flight. Lt. Rading and one NCO injured. Aircraft D-ANYW a write-off.

III/KG z.b.V.1

Junkers Ju 52 (5589). Damaged in landing accident at Guines aerodrome. No crew casualties. Aircraft 1Z+ FU 35% damaged.

Seenotflugkdo 4

Focke-Wulf FW 58 (0002). Slightly damaged in minor taxi-ing accident at Wesermuende. Crew unhurt. Aircraft KP+ AB repairable.

2(H)/32

Henschel Hs 126B (3156). Forced-landed during routine domestic flight. Exact circumstances not recorded. Crew unhurt. Aircraft 45% damaged.

I/JG2

Messerschmitt Bf 109E-3. Crashed on take-off from Le Havre aerodrome on combat sortie. Cause not stated. Pilot unhurt. Aircraft 40% damaged.

II/KG4

Heinkel He 111Ps (2972, 2939, 2933, 2935, 3079, 3080, 2635 and 2637). Eight aircraft destroyed in RAF bombing attack on Eindhoven aerodrome. No personnel losses. Aircraft all write-offs.

Heinkel He 111Ps (2140 and 2792). Damaged in RAF bombing of Eindhoven aerodrome. No crew casualties. Aircraft 30% and 50% damaged respectively.

Heinkel He 111P-4 (2919). Crashed on landing at Soesterberg aerodrome after combat mission. Cause not stated. Crew unhurt. Aircraft 20% damaged.

Heinkel He 111P-4 (2869). Crashed at Eindhoven following operational sortie. Cause unknown but possibly battle damage. Lt. Arnold and two NCOs killed. One NCO wounded. Aircraft a write-off.

II/KG54

Junkers Ju 88A-1 (4146). Shot down by fighters during operations over southern England. Oblt. John, Uffz. Schauer, Uffz. Flamm and Gefr. Weiler all killed. Aircraft B3+ DP a write-off.

Junkers Ju 88A-1 (3093). Suffered engine failure on take-off from St. Andre on combat sortie. Crashed and burned out. Lt. Fischer and one NCO killed. Two NCOs wounded. Aircraft a write-off.

9/KG76

Dornier Do 17Z-3 (2778). Shot down by fighters during bombing mission to London and further damaged by ground-fire over Gatwick aerodrome. Crashed at West Hoathley, Sussex 6.10 p.m. Oblt. Domenik and Uffz. Strahlendorf killed. Uffz. Nuernberg and Gefr. Greza captured wounded. Aircraft F1+ ET a write-off.

Wednesday, September 11

Seenotsonderkdo Wesermuende

Focke-Wulf FW 58 (2033). Crashed on landing at Reims following routine domestic flight. Cause not stated. One NCO injured. Aircraft a write-off.

Fuhrungskette X Fliegerkorps

Heinkel He 111H-3 (3253). Suffered engine failure on return from operational sortie over the Moray Firth and damaged in landing accident. Hptmn. Kowalewski injured. Aircraft P4+ BA 30% damaged.

5/196

Arado Ar 196 (0067). Engaged on air-firing practice at Holtenau range and crashed following mid-air fire. Cause not stated. Crew unhurt. Aircraft 6W+ KN a write-off.

1/JG3

Messerschmitt Bf 109E-4 (5276). Collided with another Bf 109 during combat sortie over the Channel and crashed in the sea. Pilot rescued unhurt. Aircraft lost.

Messerschmitt Bf 109E-4 (5341). Returned to base damaged following mid-air collision over the Channel. Pilot unhurt. Aircraft 25% damaged.

The mark of the lion. In fine Wagnerian style, a Heinkel He 111H-3 of I/KG26 'Loewen' Geschwader burns itself out at Burmarsh, Kent on September 11 midst a forest of anti-invasion glider poles. A Spitfire triumphantly orbits the funereal smoke pillar while an injured crewman is carried off the field on a stretcher.

6/JG3

Messerschmitt Bf 109E-4 (5056). Crash-landed at Wierre-au-Bois aerodrome following operational sortie. Cause not stated. Pilot unhurt. Aircraft 45% damaged.

2/JG51

Messerschmitt Bf 109E-4 (1641). Shot down by Sergeant Higgins of No. 253 Squadron in combat over the Sussex coast. Crashed at Houndean Bottom, Lewes 3.30 p.m. Hptmn. Wiggers (Staffel Kapitan) killed. Aircraft a write-off.
Site investigated by the Wealden Aviation Archaeological Group 1978. Little evidence remains of crash site but tail panel bearing Swastika marking acquired from a local resident.

8/JG51

Messerschmitt Bf 109E-1 (6293). Shot down by Flight Lieutenant Edge of No. 253 Squadron during combat over the Tunbridge Wells area. Crashed and burned out on Foxhole Farm, Wadhurst 3.40 p.m. Fw. Siemer killed. Aircraft 9+ a write-off.
Spent rounds of 7.92mm ammunition and several fragments and minor components discovered on the site by Steve Vizard.

Stab KG1

Heinkel He 111H-3 (5606). Severely damaged by fighters during bombing sortie to London and forced-landed and burned out at Broomhill Farm, Camber 4.35 p.m. Lt. Behn, Uffz. Moeck, Uffz. Arndt, Fw. Sommer and Gefr. Maennich captured. Aircraft V4+ FA a write-off.

3/KG1

Heinkel He 111H-3 (3233). Shot down by fighters during sortie to bomb London docks. Forced-landed at Hildenborough, Kent 4.33 p.m. Uffz. Steinecke, Uffz. Hirsch, Uffz. Kramer, Gefr. Pfeiffer and Gefr. Puempel captured. Aircraft V4+ KL a write-off.

Above **The reason for the large numbers of troops in this well publicised photograph is that they were billeted in Burmarsh rectory just a few hundred yards from where the aircraft crashed. Here Feldwebel Heinz Friedrich (left), the Heinkel pilot, and a member of his crew, are escorted into captivity (Fox Photos).**

Bottom **Complete with maps and mushrooms (freshly picked), Wilf Nicoll is escorted from the field of battle by Gordon Ramsey on August 21, 1979.** *Centre* **The direction-finding loop aerial was removed as a souvenir at the time and is now displayed in the Brenzett Aeronautical Museum.**

Heinkel He 111H-3 (6852). Returned to base damaged by fighters during attack on London. One NCO killed and two wounded. Aircraft V4+ AL 60% damaged.

6/KG1

Heinkel He 111H-2 (2733). Forced-landed at Boisville with two NCOs wounded in fighter attack during bombing sortie over London. Aircraft V4+ BW 10% damaged.

Heinkel He 111H-2 (5364). Shot down by fighters during bombing attack on London. Forced-landed on Broomhill Farm, Camber, near Rye 3.15 p.m. Uffz. Hansen, Uffz. Markert, Uffz. Wildehopf, Uffz. Krall and Gefr. Wilhelm captured, Aircraft V4+ RW a write-off.

I/KG26

Heinkel He 111H-4 (6965). Forced-landed at Wevelgem with battle damage following bombing attack on England. No crew casualties. Aircraft 1H+ AB 15% damaged.

Heinkel He 111H-3 (5616). Landed at Wevelgem with damage from fighter attack over the Thames Estuary. One NCO wounded. Aircraft 1H+ BB 40% damaged.

Heinkel He 111H-3 (5680). Shot down by AA fire and fighters over London. Forced-landed and burned out at Burmarsh, Kent 4.00 p.m. Uffz. Hofmann, Uffz. Dreyer, Uffz. Stirnemann, Fw. Friedrich and Fw. George captured. Aircraft 1H+ CB a write-off.

1/KG26

Heinkel He 111H-4 (6962). Hit by AA fire during bombing attack on Woolwich Arsenal. Crashed at Cripps Corner, near Sedlecombe, Sussex 3.00 p.m. Uffz. Schang and Fw. Schaefer killed. Hptmn. Kuenstler (Staffel Kapitan), Uffz. Schmidt and Fw. Buettner captured. Aircraft 1H+AH a write-off.

Heinkel He 111H-4 (6977). Returned to base with one NCO wounded in fighter attack during bombing sortie to London. Aircraft 1H+EH 15% damaged.

Heinkel He 111H-4 (3214). Attacked by RAF fighters during mission over London but returned to base. Oblt. Lensch killed. Aircraft 1H+HH 40% damaged.

Heinkel He 111H-4 (6981). Severely damaged in fighter attack over London and abandoned by pilot. Bomb-aimer regained control and eventually forced-landed aircraft near Dieppe. Fw. Jabusch wounded baled out and captured. One NCO wounded. Aircraft 1H+KH a write-off.

2/KG26

Heinkel He 111H-3 (3215). Crashed in the Channel following fighter attacks during bombing sortie to London. Fw. Horn killed. Three NCOs rescued from sea by Seenot-flugkdo, one being wounded. Aircraft 1H+JK lost.

Heinkel He 111H-3 (5603). Returned to base damaged by fighters over London. No crew casualties. Aircraft 1H+FK 15% damaged.

3/KG26

Heinkel He 111H-3 (6854). Damaged in fighter attack during bombing raid on London. Returned to base, crew unhurt. Aircraft 1H+BL 25% damaged.

Heinkel He 111H-3 (3157). Briefed to bomb London docks. Shot down by fighters and crashed at Dormansland, near Lingfield, Surrey 4.00 p.m. Fw. Westfalen, Gefr. Zaehle and Uffz. Herms killed. Oblt. Abendhausen and Uffz. Hauswald baled out and captured. Aircraft 1H+ML a write-off.

II/KG26

Heinkel He 111H-3 (6856). Returned to base with one NCO wounded following RAF fighter attack. Aircraft 1H+AC 25% damaged.

Heinkel He 111H-5 (3545). Shot down by fighters during sortie over London. Uffz. Meusel killed. Lt. Wesemann, Fw. Giess and Fw. Gutacker missing. Aircraft 1H+BC a write-off.

4/KG26

Heinkel He 111H-5 (3540). Returned to base damaged following attack by fighters during bombing sortie over London. One NCO killed and two wounded. Aircraft 1H+CM 30% damaged.

5/KG26

Heinkel He 111H-3 (6903). Damaged by fighters over south coast of England during sortie to bomb London. Ditched in sea off Hastings 5.00 p.m. Oberfw. Kramer killed. Oblt. Bertram, Gefr. Schroeder and Gefr. Entrich rescued from sea by fishing boat and captured. Aircraft 1H+IN lost.

Heinkel He 111H-3 (6936). Crash-landed at Gilze-Rijen aerodrome following bombing sortie over England and engagement by RAF fighters. No crew casualties. Aircraft 1H+EN 40% damaged.

Heinkel He 111H-3 (3935). Damaged by fighters during sortie over London and returned to base crew unhurt. Aircraft 1H+FN 40% damaged.

II/KG54

Junkers Ju 88A-1 (6092). Crashed on landing at St. Andre aerodrome following routine domestic flight. Cause not stated. Crew unhurt. Aircraft 30% damaged.

Stab KG55

Heinkel He 111P (2683). Crashed and burned out at Villacoublay following operational sortie. Cause unknown but possible combat damage. Uffz. Lange, Fw. Eckert and Gefr. Wiedemann killed, Gefr. Koller wounded. Aircraft a write-off.

Recovered by Alan Fall and now displayed at Headcorn is this port main undercarriage oleo leg of a Messerschmitt Bf 110C, of 9/ZG26 from Barnes Cote, Harvel. Both crewmen were listed as missing from a sortie over England on September 11.

1/LG2

Messerschmitt Bf 109E-7 (2029). Shot down in fighter combat over southern outskirts of London. Crashed near Pilgrim's Way, Wrotham Hill 4.15 p.m. Uffz. Hechmaier killed. Aircraft a write-off.

Excavated by the London Air Museum which unearthed masses of shattered airframe components including the top of the control column and pieces bearing the legend '2029'. Relics also in the Steve Vizard Collection.

Messerschmitt Bf 109E-7 (5797). Crash-landed at Wissant following combat with fighters over south London. Pilot unhurt. Aircraft a write-off.

II/LG2

Messerschmitt Bf 109E-4 (2020). Crashed on landing at Calais-Marck after local flight. Cause not stated. Pilot unhurt. Aircraft 50% damaged.

2/StG77

Junkers Ju 87B-1 (5162). Crashed near Curfeuilles following collision during routine domestic flight. Two NCOs killed. Aircraft S2+PK a write-off.

Junkers Ju 87B-1 (5521). Involved in mid-air collision during local flight and crashed near Curfeuilles. One NCO killed. Aircraft S2+JK a write-off.

3/StG77

Junkers Ju 87B-2 (5739). Crashed at Curfeuilles following mid-air collision during routine domestic flight. Exact circumstances not recorded. One NCO killed and one injured. Aircraft S2+HL a write-off.

Junkers Ju 87B-2 (5630). Collided with another Ju 87 during local flight over Curfeuilles. No crew casualties. Aircraft S2+FL a write-off.

Junkers Ju 87B-1 (0472). Damaged in taxi-ing accident at Maltot aerodrome crew unhurt. Aircraft S2+BL 20% damaged.

1/ZG2

Messerschmitt Bf 110C-4 (3376). Failed to return from operational sortie over southern England. Exact fate unknown. Gefr. Kling and Gefr. Sossner both missing. Aircraft A2+MH lost.

Messerschmitt Bf 110C-4 (3623). Crash-landed at St. Aubin damaged by fighters in combat over southern England. Crew unhurt. Aircraft 50% damaged.

1/ZG26

Messerschmitt Bf 110C-4 (2190). Returned to base damaged following fighter combat over southern England. One NCO killed. Aircraft U8+KH 20% damaged.

2/ZG26

Messerschmitt Bf 110C-3 (1372). Developed engine trouble during bomber escort sortie over Kent and attacked by fighter prior to forced-landing on Cobham Farm, Charing 5.00 p.m. Fw. Brinkmann and Uffz. Krueshow captured. Aircraft U8+HL a write-off.

Stab II/ZG26

Messerschmitt Bf 110C-4 (3625). Shot down in combat with RAF fighters during escort sortie over southern England. Oblt. Henken and Fw. Radelmeier both killed. Aircraft 3U+HM a write-off.

4/ZG26

Messerschmitt Bf 110D-2 (3392). Failed to return from escort mission over the Thames Estuary and believed shot down by fighters and crashed in sea. Uffz. Kleiber killed. Oblt. Birkner missing. Aircraft 3U+DM a write-off.

6/ZG26

Messerschmitt Bf 110D-2 (3400). Shot down in combat with fighters over the Thames Estuary. Lt. Volk missing. Obergefr. Hofmann killed. Aircraft 3U+HP a write-off.

9/ZG26

Messerschmitt Bf 110C-4 (3231). Failed to return from combat sortie over the Thames Estuary. Shot down by fighters and crashed at Barnes Cote, Harvel, Kent. Oblt Junghans and Gefr. Eckert both missing. Aircraft 3U+ LT lost.

Site excavated by the Kent Battle of Britain Museum. Daimler-Benz Db 601 engine salvaged together wtih undercarriage leg complete with wheel and tyre, 20mm MGFF cannon and firing mechanism, ammunition drums, parachute buckles, crewman's pistol, cigarette case and Luftwaffe identity disc 60043/21' identified as belonging to Gefr. Paul Eckert. Relics also in Headcorn Museum from this aircraft but wrongly identified. Wound badge recovered on the surface in the Vizard collection.

II/ZG76

Messerschmitt Bf 110C (3285). Ditched in the Channel due to combat damage following sortie over southern England. Crew rescued unhurt by Seenotflugkdo. Aircraft M8+ KC lost.

Thursday, September 12

3(H)/14

Henschel Hs 126 (4204). Forced-landed at Malines following routine domestic flight. Cause not stated, no crew casualties. Aircraft 40% damaged.

4(F)/121

Dornier Do 17P (3530). Crashed on take-off from Boblingen aerodrome on local flight. Exact cause unknown but probably engine failure. Two NCOs killed. Aircraft a write-off.

1(F)/122

Junkers Ju 88A-1 (0318). Failed to return from long-range reconnaissance sortie over the Channel and believed shot down in sea by RAF fighters. Lt. Krautwurst, Fw. Bibers, Fw. Kaltenbach and Obergefr. Plaenge all missing. Aircraft F6+ NH lost.

6/JG27

Messerschmitt Bf 109E (3859). Damaged taxi-ing at Rennes prior to combat sortie. Pilot unhurt. Aircraft 30% damaged.

2/JG52

Messerschmitt Bf 109E-1 (3182). Crashed and burned out near Calais during local flight. Cause unknown. Pilot killed. Aircraft a write-off.

II/JG53

Arado Ar 68 (0362). Forced-landed at St. Malo aerodrome during local communications flight. Cause not recorded. One NCO injured. Aircraft DK+ QE 15% damaged.

II/KG4

Heinkel He 111P-4 (2924). Crashed on take-off from Eindhoven due to engine failure. No crew casualties. Aircraft 5J+ FN a write-off.

I/KG51

Junkers Ju 88A-1 (2089). Crashed near Melun-Villaroche during combat sortie. Cause unknown. Four NCOs killed. Aircraft a write-off.

Junkers Ju 88A-1 (4052). Returned to base damaged by fighter attack in sortie over southern England. Two NCOs wounded. Aircraft 40% damaged.

III/KG51

Junkers Ju 88A-1 (5053). Crashed at Rouen following bombing sortie over London. Cause not stated but probably battle damage. Two NCOs killed. Aircraft 9K+ DT 60% damaged.

I/KG54

Junkers Ju 88A-1 (6131). Damaged by fighters during sortie over England and returned safely to base. Crew unhurt. Aircraft 17% damaged.

II/LG1

Junkers Ju 88A-1 (2062). Crash-landed out of fuel at Romorantin following operational sortie. Hptmn. Ehrenfordt killed. Aircraft L1+ EM a write-off.

9/ZG26

Messerschmitt Bf 110 (3628). Damaged in forced-landing at Teutoburger-Wald during routine domestic flight. Circumstances not recorded. Crew unhurt. Aircraft 15% damaged.

II/ZG76

Messerschmitt Bf 110C (0361). Crashed during local flying over Cambrai. Cause not stated. Both NCOs of crew injured. Aircraft M8+ MN a write-off.

Friday, September 13

Seenotflugkdo 3

Heinkel He 59 (0932). Destroyed during RAF bombing attack on Boulogne. No personnel losses. Aircraft TV+ HM a write-off.

Kurierstaffel 110

Focke-Wulf FW 58C-2 (0251). Severely damaged in forced-landing at Etaples/le-Touquet during communications flight in deteriorating weather conditions. Two NCOs injured. Passenger Generalmajor Cantzler (Heer) also injured. Aircraft TD+ HK a write-off.

3/JG53

Messerschmitt Bf 109E-4 (6275). Overturned in landing accident at Neuville following routine domestic flight. Cause not stated. Pilot unhurt. Aircraft 30% damaged.

5/JG77

Messerschmitt Bf 109E (5262). Crashed on landing at Vaernes killing five civilian workmen. Pilot unhurt. Aircraft a write-off.

2/KG1

Heinkel He 111H-3 (5458). Crashed on landing at Montdidier aerodrome following operational sortie. Cause not stated but possible battle damage. Oblt. Eisenbrandt and one NCO killed. Two NCOs wounded. Aircraft V4+ OK a write-off.

8/KG27

Heinkel He 111P (2670). Collided with balloon cable following bombing attack on Ellesmere Port and crashed at 32 Stow Park Avenue, Newport, South Wales 3.30 a.m. Uffz. Bernd, Uffz. Okunek, Oberfw. Elster killed. Oblt. Wappler baled out and captured. Aircraft 1G+ DS a write-off.

III/KG55

Heinkel He 111P-2 (2910). Crashed at Etretat following operations over England. Possible result of combat damage. Lt. Rockenhauser, Fw. Neubacher, Uffz. Preuss, Fw. Link and Oberfw. Brannegger all killed. Aircraft a write-off.

III/LG1

Junkers Ju 88A-1 (6112). Severely damaged by fighters during combat over southern England. Returned to base one NCO wounded. Aircraft L1+ DD a write-off.

II/NJG 1

Junkers Ju 88C (0260). Damaged in landing accident at Lechfeld following routine domestic flight. Exact circumstances not recorded. No crew casualties. Aircraft 35% damaged.

Saturday, September 14

Seenotflugkdo 3

Heinkel He 59 (1513). Forced-landed near Boulogne during air-sea rescue mission. Cause not stated. Crew unhurt. Aircraft TV+ HO a write-off.

2(H)/12

Henschel Hs 126 (4255). Crashed on landing at Quimper due to foggy conditons. No crew casualties. Aircraft H1+ NK a write-off.

2(F)/22

Dornier Do 17P (3519). Crashed on landing at Stavanger-Sola due to burst tyre following operational reconnaissance sortie. No crew casualties. Aircraft 4N+ CK a write-off.

1/406

Dornier Do 18 (0875). Damaged at Thiestedt in stormy weather conditions. No personnel casualties. Aircraft K6+ KH 35% damaged.

3/KG4

Heinkel He 111H-4 (3294). Shot down by night fighter during sortie over London. Crashed at Newmans End, near Sheering, Essex 01.55 a.m. Uffz. Mueller-Wernscheid and Uffz. Toepfer killed. Oblt. Kell and Fw. Hobe baled out and captured unhurt. Aircraft 5J+ BL a write-off.

I/KG54

Junkers Ju 88A-1 (7083). Crashed on take-off from Evreux-Fauville on combat sortie due to engine failure. No crew casualties. Aircraft 30% damaged.

II/KG54

Junkers Ju 88A-1 (4092). Crashed on landing at St. Andre following operations over the Channel. Cause not stated but possibly combat damage. No crew casualties. Aircraft 30% damaged.

Stab KG55

Heinkel He 111H (5357). Shot down by fighters during operational sortie over southern England. Crashed in sea off south coast. Lt. Parey, Lt. Schlink, Obergefr. Petersen and Gefr. Wanger killed, Uffz. Geiger picked up by Seenotdienst wounded. Aircraft G1+ HA a write-off.

2/KGr.126

Heinkel He 111H-4 (5710). Shot down during operations over England. Oblt. Mesche, Lt. Viet, Uffz. Schraeder and Uffz. Schroeder missing. Aircraft 1T+ GK a write-off.

I/KGr.606

Dornier Do 17 (2687). Crashed on landing at Cherbourg-West following combat sortie. Exact circumstances unknown. Lt. zur See Sibeth and three NCOs all killed. Aircraft 7T+ FK a write-off.

Dornier Do 17Z (2815). Crash-landed back at Cherbourg-West aerodrome due to damage sustained in combat with fighters during sortie over England. No crew casualties. Aircraft 7T+ NH 50% damaged.

Dornier Do 17Z (1213). Damaged by fighters during sortie over England but returned to base, crew unhurt. Aircraft 7T+ BH 15% damaged.

Dornier Do 17Z (1216). Crash-landed at Cherbourg-West following operational sortie and combat with fighters over England. No crew casualties. Aircraft 7T+ FN a write-off.

Stab KGr.806

Junkers Ju 88A-1 (5071). Lost bearings and forced-landed near Caen out of fuel during operational sortie. Crew unhurt. Aircraft M7+ BA a write-off.

III/JG2

Focke-Wulf FW 58 (2984). Crashed at Le Havre during routine domestic flight due to mechanical failure. Lt. Schaefer and three NCOs all killed. Aircraft SE+ VK a write-off.

9/JG3

Messerschmitt Bf 109E-4 (0746). Damaged in fighter combat over the Channel and forced-landed back at Ambleteuse. Pilot unhurt. Aircraft 45% damaged.

Stab I/JG26

Messerschmitt Bf 109E-1 (5813). Shot down by Sergeant Dredge of No. 253 Squadron during combat over Kent. Exploded over Beacon Hill, Stone, near Teynham 4.00 p.m. Oblt. Daehne killed. Aircraft a write-off.

9/JG26

Messerschmitt Bf 109E-4 (1491). Crash-landed at St. Inglevert following fighter combat over southern England. Pilot unhurt. Aircraft 60% damaged.

1/JG77

Messerschmitt Bf 109E-1 (3854). Forced-landed and later burned out at Long Barn Farm, Boxley Hill, near Detling, Kent 4.30 p.m. during free-lance fighter sortie over England and combat with fighters. Fw. Ettler captured unhurt. Aircraft 4+ a write-off.
Part from fuselage owned by Steve Vizard.

6/LG2

Messerschmitt Bf 109E (2014). Shot down by No. 72 Squadron Spitfires during bomber escort sortie. Crashed at Tennant Wood, New Street Farm, Great Chart, near Ashford, Kent 6.35 p.m. Uffz. Blazejewski baled out and captured unhurt. Aircraft 1+ a write-off.

'September 15' crash sites are highly sought after by aviation wreck groups occuring on the day which is generally celebrated as the climax of the battle. One such aircraft, a Messerschmitt Bf 109E-4 from 3/JG3 'Udet' based at Colombert, was unearthed at Pluckley by the Brenzett group.

Sunday, September 15

Seenotflugkdo 3

Heinkel He 59 (1513). Crashed on landing in sea (PQ117) during air-sea rescue mission. Crew rescued unhurt. Aircraft lost.

Wettererkundungs Staffel 51

Heinkel He 111H-3 (6938). Failed to return from weather reconnaissance sortie over English coast and presumed shot down in sea by RAF fighters. Uffz. Baume, Uffz. Mueller, Oberfw. Schweitzer, Gefr. Mueller and Reg. Insp. Franzreb all missing. Aircraft 4T+ DH lost.

3/406

Dornier Do 18 (0810). Crashed on take-off from sea off the south coast of Ireland. Cause not stated. Crew all rescued unhurt. Aircraft K6+ FL lost.

Stab JG3

Messerschmitt Bf 109E-4 (5205). Shot down during free-lance fighter sweep over southern England. Crashed into outbuildings at Hanns Farm, Bilsington, Kent 12.15 p.m. Obstlt. Hasse von Wedel captured unhurt. Aircraft a write-off.
Petrol injection unit from this aircraft in Brenzett Aeronautical Museum.

I/JG3

Messerschmitt Bf 109E-4 (0945). Failed to return from combat sortie over the Channel and presumed shot down by fighters. Fw. Volmer missing. Aircraft lost.

Messerschmitt Bf 109E-4 (1563). Crashed in the Channel following combat with RAF fighters. Pilot rescued unhurt by Seenotdienst. Aircraft lost.

1/JG3

Messerschmitt Bf 109E (2685). Shot down by RAF fighters during free-lance fighter sweep over Kent. Crashed at St. Michaels, near Tenterden 3.00 p.m. Oberfw. Hessel baled out and captured. Aircraft a write-off.
Oxygen bottle and undercarriage leg in Vizard collection.

3/JG3

Messerschmitt Bf 109E-4 (1606). Crashed at Thorn Farm, Pluckley Brickworks, near Charing, Kent 2.00 p.m. during combat with fighters. Oblt. Reumschuessel (Staffel Kapitan) baled out and captured unhurt. Aircraft a write-off.
Major recovery by the Brenzett Aeronautical Museum. Most interesting items excavated included remains of pilot's flying helmet and oxygen mask and manufacturers' labels confirming identity as '1606'.

1/JG27

Messerschmitt Bf 109E-4 (6249). Forced-landed near Lille, fuel exhausted following combat sortie over southern England. Pilot unhurt. Aircraft 30% damaged.

Messerschmitt Bf 109E-4 (6232). Failed to return from operations over the southern counties and believed shot down in the Channel by RAF fighters. Oblt. Ahrens missing. Aircraft lost.

2/JG27

Messerschmitt Bf 109E-1 (6147). Attacked by fighters during escort sortie for bombers attacking London. Forced-landed at Homestead, Ifield, near Uckfield 12.30 p.m. Uffz. Walburger captured unhurt. Aircraft 5+ a write-off.

Messerschmitt Bf 109E-1 (3875). Crashed on landing at Guines-West aerodrome out of fuel and with combat damage. Gefr. Elles wounded. Aircraft a write-off.

7/JG51

Messerschmitt Bf 109E-4 (3266). Engine set alight in combat with fighters during bomber escort mission. Crashed at Nelson Park, St. Margaret's-at-Cliffe, near Dover 2.50 p.m. Lt. Bildau baled out and captured unhurt. Aircraft a write-off.
Site excavated by the Brenzett Aeronautical Museum and some minor components and fragments recovered.

9/JG51

Messerschmitt Bf 109E-4 (2803). Crashed and exploded in Longridge Orchard, Great Old Hay, Brenchley near Paddock Wood, Kent 2.20 p.m. following combat with RAF fighters. Fw. Klotz killed. Aircraft a write-off.

Site excavated by local enthusiast Malcolm Petitt of Tonbridge and also investigated by Steve Vizard who recovered some fragments from a depth of six feet.

Stab I/JG52

Messerschmitt Bf 109E-4 (3182). Lost control following collision with another Bf 109 during free-lance sortie over Kent. Believed crashed at Smarden. Lt. Bertel baled out and captured at Bounds End Farm, Staplehurst. Aircraft a write-off.

I/JG53

Messerschmitt Bf 109E-4 (6160). Shot down by fighters in combat over the English south coast. Uffz. Schersand killed. Aircraft a write-off.

1/JG53

Messerschmitt Bf 109E-4 (5197). Shot down by Flying Officer Lovell of No. 41 Squadron during combat over Canterbury and crashed at Adisham Court, near Bekesbourne 12.09 p.m. Fw. Tschoppe baled out badly burned and captured. Aircraft a write-off.

2/JG53

Messerschmitt Bf 109E. Crashed and burned out in Gore Wood, Aldington Court Farm, Bearstead, Kent 12.45 p.m. during combat with RAF fighters. Oblt. Schmidt killed. Aircraft a write-off.

Site investigated by Ron Gamage and later by the London Air Museum which salvaged the shattered remains of the Daimler-Benz DB 601 engine and a propeller boss together with remnants of airframe.

Right: This 7.92mm MG 17 was recovered by Malcolml Petitt from the crash site of Feldwebel Klotz's Bf 109 No. 2803 at Brenchley. It was surrendered to the Kent police who then passed it to the Imperial War Museum at Lambeth.

The Luftwaffe units taking part in 'Die Luftschlacht um England' lost sixty-one aircraft on September 15 of which thirteen are known to have been excavated by enthusiasts. Although Fighter Command only lost twenty-eight planes on this day (of which nine have been investigated), a direct comparison with the Luftwaffe losses is iniquitous as many more German aircraft were involved than British. Nevertheless, the figures still make an interesting comparison with the 1940 claim of 175-185 German aircraft destroyed for a loss of thirty RAF aircraft. Our 'puzzle corner' photo shows a Bf 109 from JG27 (identified by Peter Cornwell as No. 6147) which forced-landed at Ifield at 12.30 p.m. Portsmouth Carriers were contracted to collect crashed aircraft and they had over twenty on their premises at this stage of the battle. Our artist's sketch explains the photo — the Messerschmitt was kept at No. 161 Clapham Road for about a month and used as a collecting point for funds for an RAF charity (News Chronicle).

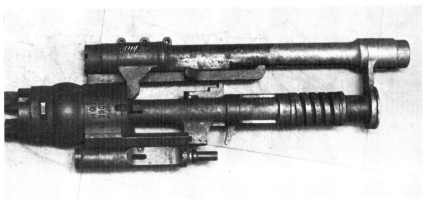

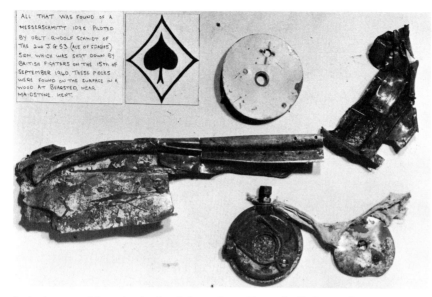

Pathetic memorials to the deaths of three pilots. *Above:* At 12.45 p.m., a Messerschmitt Bf 109E of the 53 'Pik As' Jagd Geschwader plunged into the heart of Gore Wood, Bearstead, burning itself and its pilot to ashes. All that remained on the surface of the ground over three decades later were a few blackened and twisted shards of metal (London Air Museum).

Then, at 2.20 p.m., a Bf 109 of 9/JG51 piloted by Feldwebel Fritz Klotz crashed and exploded in Longridge Orchard, Paddock Wood (Steve Vizard collection).

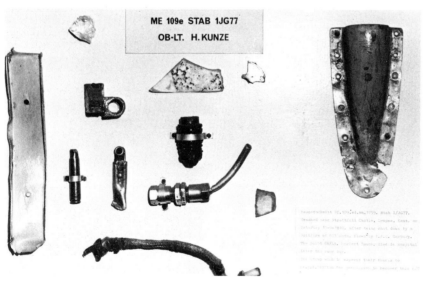

At 3.30 p.m. Oberleutnant Herbert Kunze, the Gruppe Adjutant of Stab I/JG77 was shot down at Stuttfall Castle, Lympne. He died of his injuries shortly afterwards (Brenzett Aeronautical Museum).

1/JG53

Messerschmitt Bf 109E-4 (5111). Forced-landed at Etaples with combat damage following sortie over southern England. Pilot unhurt. Aircraft 15% damaged.

3/JG53

Messerschmitt Bf 109E-4 (1590). Shot down in combat with fighters over southern outskirts of London. Crashed into Mullard Wood, Norheads Farm, Biggin Hill 12.00 p.m. Oblt. Haase (Staffel Kapitan) baled out but parachute failed. Aircraft a write-off.
Major recovery by local enthusiasts in 1969. Complete Daimler-Benz DB 601 engine excavated from beneath 15 feet of clay together with other relics now in the Halstead War Museum.

Messerschmitt Bf 109E-1 (3619). Severely damaged in fighter attack during bomber escort sortie over London. Forced-landed at Dymchurch Redoubt, Kent 12.42 p.m. Uffz. Feldmann captured unhurt. Aircraft 2+ a write-off.

Messerschmitt Bf 109E-4 (1345). Shot down in combat with fighters during sortie over southern England. Oberfw. Muller wounded. Aircraft a write-off.

III/JG53

Messerschmitt Bf 109E-4 (5251). Ditched in the Channel out of fuel following combat over southern England. Pilot rescued unhurt by Seenotdienst. Aircraft lost.

Messerschmitt Bf 109E-4 (1174). Crashed and burned out at Etaples following combat sortie. Pilot unhurt. Aircraft a write-off.

Stab I/JG77

Messerschmitt Bf 109E-4 (3759). Crashed into a dyke near Stuttfall Castle, Lympne, Kent 3.30 p.m. following combat with RAF fighters. Oblt. Kunze (Gruppe Adjutant) killed. Aircraft a write-off.
Representative pieces recovered by Brenzett Aeronautical Museum.

1/JG77

Messerschmitt Bf 109E-1 (4847). Engine damaged in combat with fighters and failed over the French coast causing forced-landing. Pilot unhurt. Aircraft 25% damaged.

3/JG77

Messerschmitt Bf 109E-4 (4802). Failed to return from fighter action over the Channel off Dungeness and believed shot down in sea by RAF fighters. Uffz. Meixner missing. Aircraft a write-off.

1/KG1

Heinkel He 111H-3 (3245). Crashed on landing at Le Houdrel damaged in fighter attack. Three NCOs wounded. Aircraft V4+ EH a write-off.

5/KG2

Dornier Do 17 Z-3 (2678). Shot down by No. 609 Squadron Spitfires following bombing of London docks. Forced-landed at Eighteen Pounder Farm, Westfield, near Hastings, Sussex 4.00 p.m. Oblt. Latz, Uffz. Reinisch and Fw. Hasse captured. Oberfw. Hafner baled out and missing. Aircraft U5+CN a write-off.
Incident investigated by the Wealden Aviation Archaeological Group 1977 and control column recovered in 1940 donated by a local resident.

Dornier Do 17Z-3 (2304). Shot down by AA fire and fighters during sortie to attack London area. Uffz. Boehmel and Uffz. Huber killed. Uffz. Moebius and Gefr. Birg missing. Aircraft U5+ HN a write-off.

Dornier Do 17Z-2 (1135). Returned to base damaged in fighter attack during sortie over London. Crew unhurt. Aircraft U5+ MN repairable.

7/KG2

Dornier Do 17Z (2539). Returned to base with combat damage following bombing sortie over London. Oblt. Schweitring killed. Aircraft U5+ ER repairable.

Dornier Do 17Z (1153). Damaged by fighters over London and returned to base with one NCO wounded. Aircraft U5+ KR repairable.

8/KG2

Dornier Do 17Z (3401). Crashed in the Channel following fighter attacks during bombing sortie over London. Gefr. Ertl killed. Fw. Duertmann missing. Two NCOs rescued from sea by Seenotdienst. Aircraft U5+ DS lost.

Dornier Do 17Z (2549). Shot down by fighters during bombing raid on London. Fw. Simon killed. Uffz. Hirsch, Uffz. Flemming and Gefr. Sandmann missing. Aircraft U5+ FS a write-off.

Dornier Do 17Z (4245). Brought down by fighters during raid on London. Oblt. Holleck-Weitmann killed. Uffz. Lindemeier missing. Uffz. Schweighardt wounded. Aircraft U5+ GS a write-off.

Dornier Do 17Z (3432). Returned to base one NCO wounded following fighter attack over London. Aircraft U5+ JS repairable.

Dornier Do 17Z (3440). Shot down by Pilot Officer Innes of No. 253 Squadron during sortie to bomb London docks. Crashed at The Chase, Chatham 3.05 p.m. Oblt. Kittmann, Uffz. Langer, Uffz. Stampfer and Kriegsberichter Koehler all baled out and captured unhurt. Aircraft U5+ PS a write-off.

9/KG2

Dornier Do 17Z (3405). Shot down by Pilot Officer Patullo of No. 46 Squadron during operational sortie to bomb London. Crashed in sea off Herne Bay 3.30 p.m. Uffz. Hoppe and Oberfhr. Staib killed. Gefr. Hoffmann and Gefr. Zierer captured. Aircraft U5+ FT a write-off.

Dornier Do 17Z (3230). Shot down by fighters during sortie to bomb London. Crashed near Cranbrook, Kent 5.00 p.m. Uffz. Lenz, Fw. Krummheuer and Fw. Glaser killed. Uffz. Sehrt captured wounded. Aircraft U5+ ET a write-off.

4/KG3

Dornier Do 17Z-3 (2879). Forced-landed at Calais with two NCOs wounded following bombing sortie over the Channel and combat with fighters. Aircraft 5K+ AM 40% damaged.

Dornier Do 17Z-2 (3457). Shot down by Squadron Leader Sample of No. 504 Squadron during sortie to bomb London docks. Crashed on Barnehurst Golf Course, near Dartford 2.45 p.m. Uffz. Burballa, Flgr. Bormann and Uffz. Hansburg killed. Lt. Michaelis captured. Aircraft 5K+ JM a write-off.
Wireless operator's code books and log book donated to the Kent Battle of Britain Museum together with manufacturer's plate from engine.

The hand grips from the control column of a Dornier Do 17Z-3 of the 'Holzhammer' Geschwader, KG2, based at Arras. The aircraft ended its days in a forced-landing at Eighteen Pounder Farm, Westfield at 4.00 p.m. This exhibit, removed from the aircraft in 1940, was donated to the Wealden Aviation Archaeological Group.

Dornier Do 17Z-3 (2881). Shot down by fighters during bombing sortie over the Thames Estuary. Crashed on the Isle of Grain 2.45 p.m. Uffz. Wien, Fw. von Goertz, Gefr. Schild and Gefr. Weymar all captured. Aircraft 5K+ CM a write-off.

Dornier Do 17Z-2 (3294). Crashed in flames in Gladstone Road, Laindon Hills, Billericay Essex 2.33 p.m. following fighter attack. Lt. Duemler, Uffz. Maskules and Fw. Vogel killed. Uffz. Friebel captured unhurt. Aircraft 5K+ DM a write-off.
Site excavated by No. 2243 (Basildon) Squadron ATC. Intact Bramo 323 engine complete with reduction gear and propeller boss donated to the Essex Aviation Group.

5/KG3

Dornier Do 17Z-2 (1176). Shot down by fighters during bombing sortie to London. Hptmn. Puettmann (Staffel Kapitan), Fw. Franke both killed. Oblt. Langenhain missing. Fw. Falke baled out and captured. Aircraft 5K+ DN lost.

Dornier Do 17Z-3 (3458). Brought down by AA fire and fighter attacks during raid on London. Oblt. Becker-Ross, Oberfw. Bruckner and Fw. Hansen killed. Fw. Brinkmann missing. Aircraft 5K+ GN a write-off.

Dornier Do 17Z-3 (2649). Returned to base with one NCO wounded in fighter attack over London. Aircraft 5K+ HN repairable.

Detail of a bullet-holed propellor blade in the Brenzett Museum recovered from Bourne Farm, Sandford Cross, the crash site of Heinkel He 111 of 3/KG53 shot down by fighters at 3.30 p.m.

Another Heinkel blade from the 'Legion Condor' Geschwader KG53 based at Lille-Nord, Belgium. This relic was recovered in 1940 and is now in the Lashenden Air Warfare Museum.

SEPTEMBER 15 — THE TRADITIONAL CLIMAX TO THE BATTLE AND ITS MOST FAMOUS CASUALTY

Sunday, September 15, 1940 — celebrated annually as Battle of Britain Day — was a climax to the aerial assault on Great Britain. Not for the number of Luftwaffe aircraft thought to have been shot down, but because a growing awareness in England that the threatened invasion had somehow been averted seemed vindicated in the violent combats witnessed over the southern counties and London itself on that day. Only three weeks previously, on August 20, in a speech to the House of Commons, the Prime Minister had immortalised 'The Few' as turning the tide of war, and this was to be the day when his rhetoric took on the hard edge of reality.

The morning dawned a little misty; but by eight o'clock the sky had cleared, with light cumulus at 2,000 to 3,000 feet. The cloud varied — in places it was enough to produce light local showers — and visibility was good for most of the day. The wind was from the west shifting to north-west as time went on.

By 10.50 a.m., the massing of Luftflotte 2 formations over Boulogne and the Pas-de-Calais, in full view of British RDF, confirmed a big raid was imminent and thus RAF fighters had been carefully deployed well in advance of the actual attack. Despite growing doubts amongst tactical commanders and Luftwaffe aircrews as to the real value of these continued daylight assaults, the day was to be a repeat of the first heavy attack on London on September 7. However, unlike earlier mass raids, the German bombers set direct course for London with no diversionary feints or secondary raids designed to confuse the British defences. So at 11.35 a.m. as the German formations, stepped-up from 15,000 - 26,000 feet, crossed the English coast at Dungeness they came under first attack from defending RAF squadrons

Three more British squadrons joined the fray over mid-Kent and the attackers were harried all the way as the battle raged over southern England and spread to the skies over Big Ben just as it was about to strike noon. Five minutes earlier, as the German bombers finally sighted the outskirts of their target, four more squadrons of RAF fighters had slammed into their flank; and these were closely followed by the Duxford Wing comprising five additional squadrons led by Squadron Leader Douglas Bader

In the melee that followed, bombs spilled down at random on London suburbs from Beckenham to Battersea hitting two bridges, an electricity sub-station and causing damage to many suburban homes. Two bombs fell in the grounds of Buckingham Palace, one damaging the Queen's private apartments though the Royal Family were not in residence at the time. Desperately trying to maintain some semblance of formation, the German bombers wheeled over central London and retired south pursued by RAF fighters.

Below, Londoners were starting to think of getting their scant Sunday dinner from the oven when the Luftwaffe arrived as an unwelcome guest; and no sooner were they putting away the dishes when, shortly after 2.00 p.m., the second wave came over. But by tea-time the last of the German stragglers had limped back to the Continent and the final alien speck had disappeared from the British radar screens. In the evening, on the wireless, the BBC gave its own sober imprimatur to what people had already begun to feel in their bones — that Jerry had got his come-uppance; the war was not yet lost.

If the British people could take heart from the events of that day, still justly celebrated each year, September 15 also held a moral for the German High Command. For if August 15 told them that air supremacy over England would not be easily wrested from the RAF, then September 15 suggested that it may not be gained at all! Had the British then been aware of the serious re-assessment of the air campaign against their island by the Luftwaffe High Command and of Hitler's postponement of Operation 'Seeloewe' which followed on September 17, their jubilation might have been even more enthusiastic; but, at the time, festivities centred upon the totally erroneous yet stimulating claim that up to 185 German aircraft had been destroyed.

Arguably, the most famous and certainly the most photographed German casualty of the entire Battle of Britain fell over London on this day. This was a Dornier Do 17Z of 1/KG76 which had taken off from its base at Nivelles just south of Beauvais at 10.05 a.m. with 27-year-old Oberleutnant Robert Zehbe at the controls. Picking up formation over Cap Gris-Nez and climbing to 15,000 feet, it set course with other aircraft from the 1st Staffel for landfall at Dungeness and thence direct to their target — central London.

Top: **The most photographed German crash in the battle.** *Left:* Mangled remains of the Dornier on the corner of Wilton Road and Terminus Place (Fox Photos). *Right:* Today the stone facade of Victoria Station still bears the scars of the forty-year-old battle which brought the war to the heart of London. The kiosk has disappeared and has been replaced with a prefabricated building for registered luggage. (Unteroffizier Hubel's grave at Cannock is No. 132 in Block 1 and Hans Goschenhofer's No. 333 in Block 5. Robert Zehbe now lies in Brookwood Military Cemetery — Plot 15, Row A, Grave 2.)

This aircraft and crew had taken part in the first heavy daylight raid on London on September 7 as well as some notable earlier attacks including the high-level raid on Kenley aerodrome on August 18. But on September 15 they were to be unlucky for, although they had avoided RAF fighters during their journey from the coast and had ploughed through some moderate AA fire emerging unscathed, one engine was still not developing full power and this had caused them to drop inexorably behind the main formation. Over the southern outskirts of the target area they were some 500 yards behind and at this point the aircraft came under the first concentrated attack by British fighters.

This was delivered by Flight Lieutenant J. Jefferies leading 'B' Flight of No. 310 (Czech) Squadron — part of the Duxford Wing — who fell on the German bombers over south London at 12.05 p.m. in the teeth of the British AA fire. In an accomplished attack which effectively sealed the fate of Zehbe's Dornier, Flight Lieutenant Jefferies set the port engine ablaze before pulling sharply away to one side to allow the three Hurricanes of his Green Section to follow his example. Led by Sergeant J. Hubacek, Sergeants R. Puda and J. Kaucky opened fire in turn on the hapless bomber, being joined by more RAF fighters from other units. These included Pilot Officers J. Curchin and A. K. Ogilvie of No. 609 Squadron, Ogilvie making his third attack on a German bomber that day, together with Pilot Officer P. T. Parsons of No. 504 Squadron. (The No. 609 Squadron account of this action was critical of Hurricane pilots who had hampered the Spitfires by delaying their attack when in a perfect position to do so. Whilst obviously referring to No. 310 Squadron's Green Section, this report is merely indicative of the understandable enthusiasm of pilots anxious to get to grips with any lame duck.)

During these withering attacks, two of the Dornier's crew were seen to vacate the stricken bomber. The wireless operator, Obergefreiter Ludwig Armbruster, and mechanic, Unteroffizier Leo Hammermeister, baled out at 3,000 feet over south London. Armbruster landed unhurt in Wells Park Road, Sydenham and he was taken prisoner, whilst the wounded Hammermeister came down two miles to the west in Dulwich. Meantime their aircraft, now burning fiercely, was under attack by no less than six British fighters as it wallowed towards Battersea.

A further attack was now made by Sergeant R. T. Holmes of No. 504 Squadron during which the Dornier's pilot, Oberleutnant Zehbe, baled out. Shortly afterwards his aircraft went into a vicious spin eventually breaking in half, shedding both wings outboard of the engines. As the rear fuselage containing the body of the young gunner, Unteroffizier Gustav Hubel, spiralled down over Fulham, the incongruous yet intact tail unit crashed onto a rooftop in the Vauxhall Bridge Road. The remainder of the wreck fell on the corner of Wilton Road in the forecourt of Victoria railway station where, predictably, it attracted a great deal of interest and attention. Naturally, the press maximised the propaganda potential of a crashed German aircraft shot down over central London and particularly on a day when bombs were dropped on Buckingham Palace and, in no time at all, both events became inextricably linked.

The hapless Zehbe came down at Kennington where he was fiercely attacked by a mob of frenzied civilians. Already badly wounded, he was eventually rescued by the authorities but not before his parachute and harness had been torn to shreds. He died of his injuries and was buried in Brookwood Military Cemetery. Gustav Hubel and the observer, Hans Goschenhofer, are both interred at Cannock Chase.

Sergeant Holmes, whose final attack on Zehbe's Dornier almost certainly contributed

to its eventual destruction, later stated that his wing struck something during his attack and that he was forced to bale out over Chelsea. Landing in Ebury Bridge Road, he was left in no doubt by excited onlookers that 'his' Dornier had crashed down the road near Victoria Station — a fact which he included in his official combat report.

The benefit of post-war research allows us to put the circumstances leading up to this celebrated crash into some better perspective, and the facts published here for the very first time recall a poignant drama enacted in full public view yet seemingly so well forgotten and confused with the passing years. As an incident during the engagements of that day it was one of many which prompted Churchill at the time to call September 15, 1940 ' one of the great days . . . the most brilliant and fruitful of any fought upon a large scale by the fighters of the Royal Air Force.'

PETER CORNWELL

The tail unit landed a few hundred yards away on this rooftop in Vauxhall Bridge Road (Fox Photos).

Dornier Do 17Z-2 (4200). Attacked by No. 605 Squadron Hurricanes during sortie to bomb London. Crashed at Widehurst Woods, Marden, Kent following collision with Pilot Officer Cooper-Slipper 4.30 p.m. Oberfw. Rilling killed. Oberfw. Howind, Oberfw. Hoebel and Fw. Zimmermann baled out and captured unhurt. Aircraft 5K+JN a write-off.
Site investigated by Lashenden Air Warfare Museum which collected a Luftwaffe pay book, Iron Cross and many small parts.

6/KG3

Dornier Do 17Z-2 (3470). Returned to base one NCO killed following raid on London and fighter attack over the target. Aircraft 5K+CP 50% damaged.

Dornier Do 17Z-3 (4237). Damaged by fighters during bombing raid on London and returned to base with one NCO wounded. Aircraft 5K+EM 15% damaged.

II/KG4

Heinkel He 111P-4 (3086). Forced-landed at Eindhoven damaged in fighter attack. No crew casualties. Aircraft 5J+HP 30% damaged.

I/KG26

Heinkel He 111H-4 (6985). Shot down by fighters during bombing attack on London. Forced-landed at Asplens Head, Foulness, Essex 3.00 p.m. Lt. Streubel, Fw. Schwarz, Fw. Marenbach, Fw. Potenberg and Gefr. Domes all captured. Aircraft 1H+1H a write-off.
Site within a restricted MoD area visited by the Essex Aviation Group 1971 when surface wreckage was still visible.

Heinkel He 111H-3 (5609). Damaged by AA fire and fighter attack in attack on London. Returned to base crew unhurt. Aircraft 1H+EL 20% damaged.

Heinkel He 111H-3 (5612). Returned to base damaged by AA fire and RAF fighters during bombing mission over London. No crew casualties. Aircraft 1H+GL 20% damaged.

On the shoulder of a hill above Castle Farm, Shoreham, Kent, this Dornier 17 of 8/KG76 forced-landed at 12.10 p.m. on September 15 after combat with Spitfires. Below the cockpit is the badge of the 8th Staffel — a red shield with three white Do 17 silhouettes superimposed on a grey vertical bomb (Central Press).

6/KG26

Heinkel He 111H-3 (6849). Crash-landed on return from bombing sortie over London and combat with fighters. Two NCOs wounded. Aircraft 1H+AP 50% damaged.

6/KG30

Junkers Ju 88A-1 (4020). Forced-landed at St. Malo damaged by fighters. One NCO wounded. Aircraft 4D+BH 40% damaged.

Junkers Ju 88A-1 (0101). Crashed following engine failure during local flight. No crew casualties. Aircraft 4D+KH 60% damaged.

I/KG51

Junkers Ju 88A-1 (7056). Crashed on landing at Melun-Villaroche aerodrome following combat sortie. Cause not stated but possibly battle damage. Two NCOs wounded. Aircraft a write-off.

Junkers Ju 88A-1 (3071). Failed to return from operational sortie over southern England and believed shot down by fighters. Lt. Richter, Uffz. Breuker, Uffz. Hirschfeld and Uffz. Schubert missing. Aircraft 9K+AH a write-off.

II/KG51

Junkers Ju 88A-1. Shot down by fighters during bombing sortie over the south coast of England. Oblt. de Vivanco and Uffz. Kupfernagel killed. Fw. Vogel and Gefr. Stelzner both missing. Aircraft 9K+KM a write-off.

Stab KG53

Heinkel He 111H-2 (3140). Shot down by fighters following bombing attack on Beckton gas works. Crashed near Tripcock Pier, Woolwich Arsenal 2.50 p.m. Fw. Benz, Fw. Schweiger, Uffz. Meier and Uffz. Geiger killed. Fw. Cionber missing. Aircraft A1+DA lost.

3/KG53

Heinkel He 111H-2 (5120). Forced-landed and set alight by crew at Horstead Hall, Essex 2.55 p.m. following fighter attack over London. Fw. Ortzki killed. Lt. Boeck, Uffz. Gerding, Uffz. Altmann and Obergefr. Kurzawski captured. Aircraft A1+EL a write-off.

Heinkel He 111H-2 (5481). Shot down by fighters during bombing mission to London 3.30 p.m. Crashed at Bourne Farm, Sandhurst. Uffz. Lehner and Uffz. Ruetig both killed. Oblt. Buechler, Gefr. Stamminger and Gefr. Richter baled out and captured. Aircraft A1+GL a write-off.
Propeller blade from this aircraft in the Brenzett Aeronautical Museum. Some items in Robertsbridge Aviation Museum also accredited to this machine.

Heinkel He 111H-2 (5494). Damaged by fighters during sortie over London and forced-landed at Boulogne with two NCOs wounded. Aircraft A1+JL 35% damaged.

II/KG53

Heinkel He 111H-3 (6843). Damaged by AA fire and attacked by fighters over Kent. Crashed on Burgess Farm, Frittenden, near Staplehurst 4.00 p.m. Fw. Grassl killed. Major Grube, Oblt. Schirning, Uffz. Schilling, Oberfw. Schmittborn and Fw. Nagel baled out and captured. Aircraft A1+GM a write-off.
Propeller blade recovered at the time donated to the Lashenden Air Warfare Museum.

Heinkel He 111H-2 (5718). Shot down by fighters during weather recce sortie over Kent. Forced-landed on Trafford Farm, Benenden 2.30 p.m. Fw. Mayer and Gefr. Hoffmann both killed. Lt. Baensch, Uffz. Bauer and Uffz. Buttler captured. Aircraft A1+LN a write-off.

The barley fields and orchards of Castle Farm on August 2, 1979 on the western slope above the valley of the Darent. The wooded mound of The Birches rises above the A225 Dartford-Sevenoaks road. The Dornier was extremely lucky not to collide with the high-tension cables that run almost directly above this spot.

Heinkel He 111H-1 (2771). Shot down by fighters during bombing attack on London docks. Forced-landed at West Malling aerodrome 3.00 p.m. Uffz. Lange and Gefr. Sailer both killed. Uffz. Zilling, Fw. Behrends and Fw. Lichtenhagen captured. Aircraft A1+AN a write-off.

III/KG53

Heinkel He 111H-3 (3340). Forced-landed at Armentieres damaged in fighter attack. Two NCOs wounded. Aircraft A1+BT 40% damaged.

III/KG55

Heinkel He 111P-2 (2815). Returned to base, Uffz. Schull killed and Gefr. Zornemann wounded in fighter attack during bombing sortie over Portland. Aircraft 25% damaged.

Heinkel He 111P-2 (1586). Shot down by fighters during running battle over the Channel. Crashed in sea. Uffz. Jansen, Uffz. Keil and Gefr. Konrad killed. Uffz. Rothen captured. Aircraft lost.

1/KG76

Dornier Do 17Z (2364). Crash-landed near Boulogne damaged by fighters over London. Uffz. Schaetzle killed. Uffz. Schmidt and Obergefr. Schwarz both wounded. Aircraft F1+EH 60% damaged.

Dornier Do 17Z (2361). Shot down by Sergeants Hubacek, Kaucky, Puda and Flight Lieutenant Jefferies of No. 310 Squadron together with Sergeant Holmes of No. 504 Squadron and Flying Officer Ogilvie of No. 609 Squadron in combat over London 11.50 a.m. Crashed in Victoria station yard. Oblt. Zehbe, Uffz. Goschenhofer and Uffz. Hubel killed. Uffz. Hammermeister and Obergefr. Armbruster captured. Aircraft F1+FH lost.

2/KG76

Dornier Do 17Z (2524). Crash-landed near Poix due to combat damage. Oblt. Florian wounded. Aircraft F1+JK 60% damaged.

3/KG76

Dornier Do 17Z (2651). Shot down by Sergeants Jefferys and Hurry of No. 46 Squadron, Pilot Officer Bodie and Flight Lieutenant Gillies of No. 66 Squadron and Pilot Officer Pollard and Flight Lieutenant Leather of No. 611 Squadron in combat over Kent 12.40 p.m. Crashed north of Sturry. Oberfw. Niebler, Fw. Wissmann and Uffz. Schatz killed. Oblt. Wilke and Uffz. Zremer captured. Aircraft F1+FL a write-off.

8/KG76

Dornier Do 17Z (2578). Shot down in sea off Herne Bay following sortie to bomb London 12.00 p.m. Uffz. Osenow and Fw. Keck killed. Uffz. Zahn and Uffz. Heitmann missing. Aircraft F1+BS lost.

Dornier Do 17Z (2555). Shot down by Pilot Officers Dundas and Tobin of No. 609 Squadron during sortie over Kent and forced-landed on Castle Farm, Shoreham 12.10 p.m. Fw. Schmid killed. Fw. Heitsch. Fw. Pfeiffer and Fw. Sauter captured. Aircraft F1+FS a write-off.

9/KG76

Dornier Do 17Z (2814). Target London docks. Shot down by Flight Sergeant Kominek of No. 310 Squadron and crashed near Red Lane Farm, Rotherfield, Sussex 12.15 p.m. Obergefr. Boehme, Gefr. Holdenried, Gefr. Kottutsch and Oberfhr. Wagner killed. Aircraft F1+AT a write-off.
Site investigated by the London Air Museum and many surface fragments recovered including parachute buckles, uniform buttons and chunks of melted alloy.

Dornier Do 17Z (3322). Shot down by Sergeant Tyrer of No. 46 Squadron and Pilot Officer Mortimer and Flight Lieutenant Brothers of No. 257 Squadron in combat over Kent. Forced-landed and burned out at Underriver, near Sevenoaks 12.30 p.m. Uffz. Malter killed. Oberfw. Streit, Fw. Raab and Fw. Teuffert captured. aircraft F1+DT a write-off.
Bullet-holed prop blade recovered at the time now owned by Steve Vizard together wtih other relics. Display board presented to Fw. Raab on his visit to the crash site in August 1979.

13/LG1

Messerschmitt Bf 110C-3. Shot down by fighters during bomber escort mission over the Thames Estuary. Crashed Hothfield Farm, Hothfield, near Ashford 4.00 p.m. Oblt. Mueller and Fw. Hoffmann killed. Aircraft a write-off.

Messerschmitt Bf 110C-3. Engaged on bomber escort sortie to London when intercepted by RAF fighters near target. Shot down in combat. Lt. Gorisch killed. Uffz. Gerick missing. Aircraft a write-off.

14/LG1

Messerschmitt Bf 110C-3. Failed to return from escort sortie over the Thames Estuary and believed shot down in combat with fighters. Lt. Adametz and Obergefr. Stief both missing. Aircraft lost.

1/LG2

Messerschmitt Bf 109E-7 (2061). Shot down by Sergeant Wojciechowski of No. 303 Squadron during escort mission over the Thames Estuary. Crashed in Hartlip Churchyard, near Rainham, Kent 3.00 p.m. Uffz. Streibing baled out and captured unhurt.
Parts recovered at the time in Vizard collection.

3/LG2

Messerschmitt Bf 109E-7 (2058). Forced-landed at Shellness Point, Isle of Sheppey 2.50 p.m. following attack by fighters during bomber escort sortie. Uffz. Klick captured unhurt. Aircraft 2+ a write-off.

Monday, September 16

The rear fuselage minus the empennage of a Junkers Ju 88A-1 of I/KG54 'Death's Head' Geschwader lies upside down in the front garden of No. 410 Tonbridge Road, Maidstone. The protuberances on the underside are the double dipole aerials of the Lorenz beam blind-landing system. Based at Evreux, the aircraft was shot down by a Defiant night fighter on September 17 (Fox Photos).

Seenotflugkdo.2

Heinkel He 59 (0529). Crashed on take-off from Boulogne harbour due to engine failure. One NCO killed. Major Klintzsch, Oblt. Dr. von Vogel and two NCOs injured. Aircraft DA+MG a write-off.

2(H)/32

Henschel Hs 126 (4109). Crash-landed near Cassel during routine domestic flight due to deteriorating weather conditions. No crew casualties. Aircraft a write-off.

4(F)/122

Junkers Ju 88 (0374). Failed to return from operational reconnaissance sortie over coast of England and believed shot down by fighters. Oblt. Starkloff, Hptmn. Luedke, Uffz. Pawletta and Oberarzt Dr. Guizetti all missing. Aircraft F6+HM lost.

3/506

Heinkel He 115C (3261). Suffered engine failure during operational sortie and ditched in North Sea off Berwick 1.00 a.m. Capsized aircraft brought into Eyemouth harbour. Hptmn. Kriependorf, Oblt. Lucas, Hptmn. Bergmann and Fw. Kalinowski rescued from dinghy by fishing boat and captured. Aircraft S4+CL a write-off.
Radio plate taken at the time now owned by Steve Vizard.

1/906

Heinkel He 115 (2754). Lost bearings in deteriorating weather conditions during sortie to Kinnairds Head and crashed near Aberdour 10.00 p.m. Hptmn. Kothe, Lt. zur See Aldus and Uffz. Meissner captured. Aircraft 8L+GH a write-off.

5/JG77

Messerschmitt Bf 109 (1539). Crashed on take-off from Vaernes on operational sortie. Pilot unhurt. (Two civilian workmen killed and three injured.) Aircraft a write-off.

I/KG27

Heinkel He 111P (2847). Damaged on take-off from Tours aerodrome on operational sortie. Cause not stated. No crew casualties. Aircraft 30% damaged.

III/KG51

Junkers Ju 88A-1 (7065). Take-off accident at Villeneuf. Exact circumstances not recorded. Crew unhurt. Aircraft 15% damaged.

On August 23, 1979, when we visited Maidstone to take this comparison photograph, a most surprising similarity was the chestnut paling fence. The new tiles on the porch roof and the absence of the sticky tape on the windows were all that had changed. Subsequent research unearthed two remarkable souvenirs taken by locals at the time. *Below:* This badly-torn flying boot, ripped from the foot of one of the crew (who were all killed), was displayed at the time by this portly gentleman for the photographer from Fox Photos. Forty years later we found the same old boot — in Steve Vizard's bedroom! *Opposite bottom:* This Rheinmetall-Borsig MG15 was retained by one of the firemen who had attended the crash. After his recent death it was discovered in his garden shed and donated to the Lashenden Air Warfare Museum.

Ergaenzungs-staffel KG53

Heinkel He 111P-2 (1578). Crashed on landing following routine training flight. Cause not stated. No crew casualties. Aircraft 45% damaged.

I/KG54

Junkers Ju 88A-1 (7087). Hit balloon cable during bombing sortie to Banbury and crashed in flames at Withybrook, near Coventry 11.06 p.m. Hptmn. Henke and Uffz. Rattay killed. Fw. Baur and Fw. Perleberg baled out wounded and both captured. Aircraft B3+ HH a write-off.

II/KG54

Junkers Ju 88A-1 (6050). Crashed and burned out near Evreux following combat sortie. Cause unknown. Lt. Weise and three NCOs all killed. Aircraft a write-off.

I/KG55

Heinkel He 111H (5370). Crash-landed at Dreux aerodrome following operations over the Channel. Exact cause not stated. No crew casualties. Aircraft 35% damaged.

4/KG76

Junkers Ju 88A-1 (3123). Abandoned by crew over Arlon following operations over England possibly due to combat damage. Crew baled out. Fw. Richter wounded. Aircraft F1+ BM a write-off.

KGr.806

Junkers Ju 88A-1 (7131). Forced-landed at Koeln-Ostheim due to mechanical failure during routine domestic flight. No crew casualties. Aircraft 25% damaged.

II/LG1

Junkers Ju 88A-1 (6135). Damaged in landing on burst tyre at Orleans aerodrome following local flight. Crew unhurt. Aircraft L1+ GP 40% damaged.

7(F)/LG2

Dornier Do 17P. Damaged in take-off accident at Karlsruhe aerodrome on local flight. No crew casualties. Aircraft 35% damaged.

3/NJG2

Junkers Ju 88C-2 (0190). Failed to return from night intruder sortie over eastern England and presumed shot down by defences. Fw. Pahn killed. Gefr. Reinisch and Gefr. Haberland missing. Aircraft R4+ AH lost.

Tuesday, September 17

Seenotflugkdo.3

Heinkel He 59 (1848). Damaged at moorings in Boulogne harbour due to storm. No personnel casualties. Aircraft NE+ TA 30% damaged.

Wettererkundungs Staffel 1

Heinkel He 111 (5175). Forced-landed near Lichtenfelde due to engine failure on routine domestic flight. Crew unhurt. Aircraft 35% damaged.

9/JG3

Messerschmitt Bf 109E-1 (3561). Belly-landed at Desvres aerodrome whilst on local flight. Cause not stated. Pilot unhurt. Aircraft 35% damaged.

7/JG26

Messerschmitt Bf 109E-1 (6294). Engaged on free-lance fighter sortie over Kent and suffered engine failure. Forced-landed on Broomhill Farm, Camber, near Rye 5.30 p.m. Uffz. Bock captured unhurt. Aircraft 2+ 1 a write-off.

6/JG27

Messerschmitt Bf 109E-1 (3544). Crashed on take-off from Crepon on routine domestic flight. Cause not stated. Pilot unhurt. Aircraft 60% damaged.

Stab II/JG53

Messerschmitt Bf 109E-4 (1313). Forced-landed at Wissant following combat with fighters over the Channel. Pilot unhurt. Aircraft 15% damaged.

Messerschmitt Bf 109E-4 (1644). Returned to base at Wissant damaged in fighter combat over the Channel. Pilot unhurt. Aircraft repairable.

9/JG53

Messerschmitt Bf 109E-4 (5141). Shot down in combat with fighters over the Thames Estuary and crashed in sea. Oblt. Stoll (Staffel Kapitan) missing. Aircraft lost.

Messerschmitt Bf 109E-4 (1228). Failed to return from combat sortie over the Thames Estuary and believed shot down by fighters into the sea. Oblt. Seliger missing. Aircraft lost.

Messerschmitt Bf 109E-1 (3177). Shot down in combat with fighters over north Kent. Crashed into Bishopden Wood, Dunkirk, near Faversham 4.00 p.m. Uffz. Langer killed. Aircraft a write-off.

Wreckage excavated by amateur enthusiasts and left scattered throughout woodland to the consternation of local authorities. Site cleared up' by members of the Kent Battle of Britain Museum who collected parachute release buckle, exploded 7.92mm ammunition and metal plate bearing legend 3177'. Subsequently re-excavated by the Wealden Aviation Archaeological Group which removed the Daimler-Benz DB 601 engine in February 1979. Site also investigated by the London Air Museum which recovered the propeller boss, an MG17 machine gun and various fragments and minor components. Some relics held by Halstead War Museum. Pilot's wrist watch and pieces of uniform reputed to be in Warplane Wreck Investigation Group collection.

8/KG4

Junkers Ju 88A-1 (2126). Shot down during operational sortie over southern England at night. Fw. Gebser and Obergefr. Krauss killed. Uffz. Borchardt and Uffz. Guldenberg both missing. Aircraft 5J+ BS a write-off.

7/KG30

Junkers Ju 88A-1 (0220). Forced-landed at Vlissingen damaged by RAF fighters during operational sortie over England. Three NCOs wounded. Aircraft 4D+ BR 40% damaged.

I/KG54

Junkers Ju 88A-1 (2152). Shot down by Sergeant Laurence and Sergeant Chard in Defiant night fighter of No. 141 Squadron and crashed in St. Andrews Close, Maidstone 11.45 p.m. Lt. Ganzlmayr, Uffz. Bauer, Uffz. Schloessler and Oberfw. Fachinger all killed. Aircraft B3+ OL a write-off.

Pistol and leather spent ammunition pouch from 7.92mm MG15 machine gun donated to the Kent Battle of Britain Museum. Pilot's badge together with documents and photographs also presented to them by the family of the late Rudolf Ganzlmayr. A 7.92mm MG15 machine gun `liberated' by local fireman now held by Lashenden Air Warfare Museum.

7/KG77

Junkers Ju 88 (5089). Crashed on take-off from Laon on operational sortie. Cause not stated but probably engine failure. Two NCOs killed. Lt. Zimmer and one NCO wounded. Aircraft 3Z+ CR a write-off.

II/LG1

Junkers Ju 88A-1 (3188). Shot down by fighter during sortie to bomb Speke factories. Crash-landed at Ladywell Barn, near Warminster, Wilts. 2.00 p.m. Lt. Heinrich killed. Major Cramer, Oberfw. Stuetzel and Fw. Schultz captured. Aircraft L1+ XC a write-off.

III/LG1

Junkers Ju 88A-1 (5012). Damaged by AA fire during sortie over England and forced-landed near Le Havre following engine failure. No crew casualties. Aircraft L1+ KT 10% damaged.

III/ZG76

Messerschmitt Bf 110C (3513). Crashed on landing at Laval due to mechanical failure. No crew casualties. Aircraft N2+ HN 60% damaged.

Wednesday, September 18

4/Aufklaerungs Gruppe Ob.d.L.

Dornier Do 215 (0038). Shot down by fighters during photo-reconnaissance sortie over Kent. Crashed at Collier Street, Yalding. Fw. Schuetz killed. Lt. Poser, Uffz. Linsner and Uffz. Wiesen baled out and captured. Aircraft G2+ KH a write-off.

Surface fragments in the Steve Vizard Collection.

3(F)/10

Dornier Do 17P (1063). Attacked by fighters during reconnaissance sortie over the Channel but returned to base crew unhurt. Aircraft T1+ EL 12% damaged.

Dornier Do 17P (1105). Damaged in fighter attack during sortie over the Channel and returned to base crew unhurt. Aircraft T1+ HL 30% damaged.

3(H)/32

Henschel Hs 126B (4202). Crashed on landing from routine domestic flight. Cause not stated. Crew unhurt. Aircraft 40% damaged.

3/JG3

Messerschmitt Bf 109E-1 (0897). Forced-landed near Calais following engine failure on operational sortie. Pilot injured. Aircraft 50% damaged.

1/JG27

Messerschmitt Bf 109E-4 (5388). Shot down in fighter combat over the Thames Estuary. Crashed into Squirrels Wood, Stockbury, near Sittingbourne. Oblt. Krafftschick missing. Aircraft a write-off.

Site excavated by London Air Museum which recovered remains of cockpit including many instruments and controls, control column, maps, pilot's watch together with various French and Belgian coins. Manufacturer's plate confirming identity as '5388' subsequently recovered from site by Steve Vizard.

Messerschmitt Bf 109E-7 (5574). Crashed on take-off from Cherbourg-West aerodrome on routine domestic flight. Gefr. Poppek killed. Aircraft a write-off.

2/JG27

Messerschmitt Bf 109E-1 (5366). Landed at Guines damaged following fighter combat over the Channel. Pilot unhurt. Aircraft 30% damaged.

9/JG27

Messerschmitt Bf 109E-1 (6327). Forced-landed near Harringe Court, Sellindge 1.15 p.m. due to damage received in combat with fighters during bomber escort sortie. Fw. Schulz captured severely wounded (died 12:12:40). Aircraft 7+ a write-off.

Messerschmitt Bf 109E-1 (2674). Shot down by fighters during escort mission over Kent and forced-landed on Willow Farm, Sandwich 1.10 p.m. Aircraft set alight by pilot Gefr. Gloeckner captured. Aircraft 1+ a write-off.

4/JG53

Messerschmitt Bf 109E-1 (4842). Shot down by Pilot Officer Oxspring of No. 66 Squadron during free-lance fighter sweep over Kent. Crashed at Guilton Ash near Sandwich 5.05 p.m. Lt. Bodendick baled out and captured severely wounded. Aircraft 10+ a write-off.

Site excavated by the Kent Battle of Britain Museum which recovered remains of shattered Daimler-Benz DB 601 engine, complete tail wheel, cockpit instruments and controls including control column, flap and trim controls and the aircraft main identity plate confirming '4842'.

1/JG54

Messerschmitt Bf 109E-1 (6220). Crashed in the Channel following combat with fighters. Pilot rescued unhurt by Seenotdienst. Aircraft lost.

9/JG54

Messerschmitt Bf 109E-4 (0972). Forced-landed at Guines-Sued due to engine failure during combat sortie. Pilot unhurt. Aircraft 20% damaged.

1/JG77

Messerschmitt Bf 109E-1 (2669). Shot down by fighters in combat over southern England. Gefr. Still killed. Aircraft a write-off.

1/KG30

Junkers Ju 88A-1 (8015). Crashed and burned out at Ludwigslust on take-off for routine domestic flight. Cause not stated. Two NCOs injured. Aircraft 4D+ JP a write-off.

Bomb-carrying Messerschmitt Bf 109s were an improvisation which appeared over England during the battle. The London Air Museum dug up such a machine, No. 5388, which had crashed in Squirrels Wood at Stockbury, Kent. The pilot, Oberleutnant Krafftschick, was listed as missing so that it was inevitable that personal effects would be found although the group did not report uncovering any human remains. They also recovered the bomb-fusing panel *(below left)*. The top of the control column *(below)* is now owned by Steve Vizard.

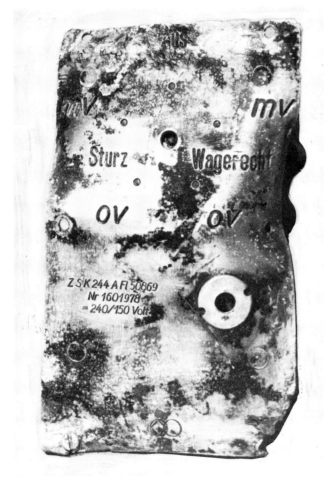

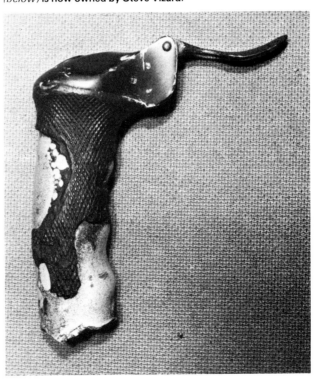

I/KG54

Junkers Ju 88A1 (4058). Crashed on landing at Schellingwoude aerodrome possibly due to combat damage. One NCO killed. Aircraft a write-off.

II/KG54

Junkers Ju 88A-1 (0226). Failed to return from operations over the Channel off the English south coast and believed shot down by fighters. Oblt. Winkler, Uffz. Pettau, Uffz. Schwenzfeier and Fw. Goedecke all missing. Aircraft B3+ CP lost.

Stab KG55

Heinkel He 111P (2503). Forced-landed at Evreux due to engine failure on combat mission. No crew casualties. Aircraft 30% damaged.

Stab III/KG77

Junkers Ju 88A-1 (3173). Shot down by fighters following bombing attack on London docks. Crashed and burned out at Eastry Mill, south of Sandwich, Kent 6.30 p.m. Major Kless (Gruppe Kommandeur) and Oblt. Lauth both killed. Uffz. Proebst and Fw. Himsel baled out and captured. Aircraft 3Z+ ED a write-off.

Site investigated by Steve Vizard and remains of shattered engine, airframe components and several manufacturers' labels recovered.

7/KG77

Junkers Ju 88A-1 (5098). Failed to return from bombing raid on London and presumed brought down by AA fire. Fw. Friedel, Fw. Nolte and Fw. Wursche all killed. Uffz. Stammnite missing. Aircraft 3Z+ KR lost.

8/KG77

Junkers Ju 88A-1 (3147). Shot down by fighters during sortie to bomb London docks. Crashed in sea off Southend 5.50 p.m. Uffz. Kuenkel, Uffz. Smorlatzky (of Lw.Kr.Ber. Komp.4) and Oberfw. Brendel killed. Uffz. Weidemueller baled out and captured badly injured. Aircraft 3Z+ AS lost.

Front cockpit canopy frame recovered from Southend beach and displayed in the Kent Battle of Britain Museum probably originated with this aircraft.

Junkers Ju 88A-1 (3142). Shot down by fighters during bombing sortie to London and combat over the Thames Estuary. Four NCOs missing. Aircraft 3Z+ BS a write-off.

Boys will be boys. September 18 proved a field day for these excited schoolboy souvenir hunters on Pitsea Marshes. After a low-level chase by Spitfires, this Ju 88 from the 'hard luck' Geschwader, KG77, crashed in flames at Pitsea. *Below:* Members of the Essex Aviation Group were equally excited when they excavated the wreck on October 6, 1979. The eventual hole measured some 60 feet by 40 feet with a maximum depth of 25 feet. Vast quantities of remains were uncovered including insulators and cable from an overhead power line carried into the ground by the aircraft (Essex Aviation Group).

Junkers Ju 88A-1 (5097). Target Tilbury docks. Shot down prior to reaching objective 5.00 p.m. and crashed at Mocketts Farm, Harty, Sheppey. Uffz. Eggert, Oberfw. Semerau, Fw. Damschen and Uffz. Treutmann killed. Aircraft 3Z+ ES a write-off.

Site excavated by the Kent Battle of Britain Museum and propeller boss unearthed together with quantities of minor components, parachute clips and buckles and Luftwaffe identity disc '65108/51' identified as belonging to Uffz. Hans Treutmann.

Junkers Ju 88A-1 (3162). Crashed in the sea off the Nore, Sheerness 5.30 p.m. following fighter attacks. Oblt. Fuchs killed. Gefr. Foelinger missing. Fw. Stier and Obergefr. Baumann captured. Aircraft 3Z+ FS lost.

Junkers Ju 88A-1 (5100). Crashed in sea off Sheerness 5.15 p.m. following fighter attacks during sortie to bomb Tilbury. Oblt. Weber and Fw. Kripmann both killed. Gefr. Neuweg missing. Fw. Goern captured wounded. Aircraft 3Z+ HS lost.

9/KG77

Junkers Ju 88A-1 (5104). Shot down by fighters during attack on Tilbury docks. Crashed at Cooling Court, Cooling, Kent 5.00 p.m. Uffz. Kurz and Gefr. Koehn both killed. Uffz. Glaeseker captured. Uffz. Burkart missing. Aircraft 3Z+ DT a write-off.

Site investigated by the Wealden Aviation Archaeological Group in 1979 and various 'souvenirs' including fuel pumps and elevator trim tab collected from a local farmer.

Junkers Ju 88A-1 (3168). Shot down by fighters during bombing attack on London and crashed in flames near Vange Creek, Pitsea Marshes, near Basildon, Essex 5.40 p.m. Fw. Wahl, Gefr. Buschbeck and Gefr. Lesker killed. Fw. Graf captured wounded. Aircraft 3Z+ FT a write-off.

Major recovery by the Essex Aviation Group, October 1979. Main wing spars, tail wheel, oxygen cylinders, propeller blades and assorted wreckage excavated. Bomb disposal team called in due to suspected presence of explosives.

Thursday, September 19

IV/KGz.b.V.1

Junkers Ju 52 (5516). Crashed on take-off at St. Denis on routine domestic flight due to engine failure. Two NCOs injured. Aircraft 1Z+ CX a write-off.

4(F)/121

Junkers Ju 88A-1 (0362). Forced-landed on Oakington aerodrome due to engine defect and presence of RAF fighters. Engaged on photo and weather reconnaissance sortie. Lt. Knab, Uffz. Zscheket, Uffz. Thoering and Obergefr. Bresch captured. Aircraft 7A+ FM a write-off.

5(F)/122

Junkers Ju 88A-6 (0400). Returned to base damaged in fighter attack during reconnaissance sortie over southern England. One NCO killed. Hptmn. Boehm (Staffel Kapitan) and Oblt. van Vleuten wounded. Aircraft F6+ ZA 50% damaged.

3/106

Heinkel He 115C (3259). Crashed on landing at Hofden following mine-laying sortie in British coastal waters. Hptmn. Kannengiesser (Staffel Kapitan), Oblt. Lohse and Obergefr. Kirchwehn killed. Aircraft M2+ CL a write-off.

7/KG2

Dornier Do 17Z (4242). Crash-landed near Cambrai due to combat damage. No crew casualties. Aircraft U5+ JR a write-off.

2/KG3

Dornier Do 17Z-2 (3429). Returned to base damaged and further damaged on landing following operational sortie over England. Oblt. Geissler wounded. Aircraft 5K+ LK 30% damaged.

6/KG3

Dornier Do 17Z-2 (2535). Crash-landed following engine failure during combat mission. Two NCOs injured. Aircraft 5K+ BP 50% damaged.

9/KG3

Dornier Do 17Z-3 (2647). Crashed on landing at St. Albert following routine domestic flight. Cause not stated. No crew casualties. Aircraft 5K+ GT 50% damaged.

4/KG4

Heinkel He 111P-4 (3087). Returned to base damaged following attack by RAF fighters during bombing sortie over southern England. Crew unhurt. Aircraft 5J+ DM 20% damaged.

9/KG4

Junkers Ju 88A-1 (5055). Damaged in landing accident at Schiphol aerodrome following combat sortie. No crew casualties. Aircraft 5J+ LT repairable.

III/KG27

Heinkel He 111P (1985). Belly-landed at Rennes due to combat damage. Crew unhurt. Aircraft 1G+ GT 25% damaged.

I/KG51

Junkers Ju 88A-1 (7058). Failed to return from operational sortie over the south coast of England. Exact fate unknown. Oberfw. Luckard and Uffz. Henker killed. Fw. Walter and Gefr. Roeder missing. Aircraft 9K+ DL lost.

II/KG51

Junkers Ju 88A-1 (3076). Forced-landed at Cherbourg-West aerodrome damaged by fighters. Crew unhurt. Aircraft 20% damaged.

Junkers Ju 88A-1 (7124). Damaged by fighters during operations over England and crash-landed at Orly aerodrome with one NCO wounded. Aircraft a write-off.

3/KG55

Heinkel He 111P-2 (2146). Shot down by AA fire during sortie to bomb Filton. Crashed at Thorley Wash, Spellbrook, near Bishops Stortford, Hertfordshire. 11.40 p.m. Uffz. Pohl, Uffz. Goliath and Fw. Alpers killed. Uffz. Gertz baled out and captured wounded. Aircraft G1+ GL a write-off.

1/KG77

Junkers Ju 88A-1 (6141). Shot down by fighters during bombing sortie over London. Gefr. Moeckel killed. Uffz. Kunz, Oberfw. Strahl and Fw. Winkelmann all missing. Aircraft 3Z+ CH a write-off.

Junkers Ju 88A-11 (2151). Shot down by fighters during armed reconnaissance sortie over England. Crashed at Culford Park, Hertfordshire 11.30 a.m. Uffz. Dorawa, Gefr. Schulz and Gefr. Scholz all killed. Uffz. Etzold captured wounded. Aircraft 3Z+ GH a write-off.

1/KGr.806

Junkers Ju 88A-1 (6100). Forced-landed at Caen-Carpiquet aerodrome due to damage from fighters. No crew casualties. Aircraft M7+ BL 20% damaged.

Junkers Ju 88A-1 (4065). Failed to return from operational sortie over England and believed shot down by fighters. Uffz. Dresen, Oberfw. Sowade, Uffz. Weigand and Gefr. Springfield all missing. Aircraft M7+ EH lost.

Friday, September 20

4(F)/121

Dornier Do 17P (1102). Attacked by fighters during reconnaissance sortie over England and crash-landed on return to Caen aerodrome. One NCO wounded. Aircraft 60% damaged.

1(F)/123

Junkers Ju 88A-1 (0379). Crash-landed near Pont de Briques following sortie over England and engagement by RAF fighters. One NCO killed. Oblt. Hoffmann, Lt. Rommel and one NCO wounded. Aircraft 4U+ EH a write-off.

1/706

Heinkel He 59 (2598). Hit a floating obstacle prior to take-off from Aalborg on operational mission. Crew unhurt. Aircraft 6T+ CK 25% damaged.

8/JG3

Messerschmitt Bf 109E-1 (1435). Crashed attempting forced-landing at Cap Gris-Nez following combat with fighters over the Channel. Pilot wounded. Aircraft a write-off.

9/JG27

Messerschmitt Bf 109E-4 (2789). Shot down by fighters during action over Kent and crashed at Ospringe 11.50 a.m. Uffz. Clauser killed. Aircraft a write-off.
Site investigated by Brenzett Aeronautical Museum and some minor fragments and components recovered. Reflector gunsight removed from the wreck in 1940 donated to them by a local resident. Signal pistol and other components in the London Air Museum.

5/JG53

Messerschmitt Bf 109E-1 (3427). Crashed on take-off from Dinan on combat sortie. Cause not stated. Pilot unhurt. Aircraft a write-off.

7/JG53

Messerschmitt Bf 109E-1 (5175). Returned to forced-landing at Boulogne following combat with RAF fighters over the Channel. Pilot unhurt. Aircraft repairable.

3/KG4

Junkers Ju 88 (1337). Forced-landed fuel exhausted following operations over England. No crew casualties. Aircraft 5J+ CT 30% damaged.

I/KG27

Heinkel He 111P (1683). Failed to return from bombing sortie over England. Exact fate unknown. Hptmn. Fellinger, Uffz. Spazier, Uffz. Nonnemann and Obergefr. Schwerb all missing. Aircraft 1G+ FP lost.

7/KG30

Junkers Ju 88A-1 (7048). Forced-landed at Melsbruck following operational sortie. Cause unknown. No crew casualties. Aircraft 4D+ MR 25% damaged.

9/KG30

Junkers Ju 88A-1 (4075). Crash-landed Melsbruck after combat sortie. Cause not stated. Crew unhurt. Aircraft 4D+ IT a write-off.

III/KG51

Junkers Ju 88A-1 (7092). Damaged in landing accident at Lille-Nord. Exact circumstances not recorded. Crew unhurt. Aircraft 9K+ MR 50% damaged.

4/KG54

Junkers Ju 88A-1 (4148). Lost control during bombing sortie over England at night. Crashed and exploded on Nos. 2 and 4 Richmond Avenue, Merton 00.20 a.m. Oberfw. Roerig. Fw. Fischer and Gefr. Neumann all killed. Fw. Schlake baled out slightly wounded and captured. Aircraft B3+ HM a write-off.
Site investigated by the Air Historical Group without result.

3/KGr.606

Dornier Do 17Z (1211). Severely damaged by AA fire during bombing attack on Liverpool but returned to base crew unhurt. Aircraft 7T+ ML a write-off.

Drama in a south London suburb. *Above:* Fireman and rescue teams carry out their grim task of searching the wreckage of two homes at Nos. 2 and 4 Richmond Avenue, Merton on the morning of September 20. At twenty minutes past midnight, a 'Totenkopf' Geschwader Ju 88 tumbled out of the sky, crashing and exploding on both houses, the inhabitants of which were mercifully tucked into their Anderson shelters. They survived but three crewmen from the bomber did not. After the rubble had been cleared, a static water supply tank was built on the site for use by Auxiliary Fire Service trailer pumps (**World Wide**). *Below:* In the early 1950s, two new houses were erected on the site — to the casual observer there is nothing to explain the new architecture.

Saturday, September 21

Kurierstaffel 2

Junkers W 34 (0498). Caught in deteriorating weather conditions during routine domestic flight and forced-landed near Roubaix following engine failure. Crew unhurt. Aircraft repairable.

Aufklaerungs Gruppe Ob.d.L.

Junkers Ju 88 (0246). Crashed on landing from reconnaissance mission over England. Cause not stated. No crew casualties. Aircraft K9+ 1H a write-off.

2/506

Heinkel He 115 (2765). Sunk at anchorage during storm at Trondheim harbour. No personnel losses. Aircraft S4+ LK a write-off.

5/KG2

Dornier Do 17Z-2 (3454). Crashed on landing at St. Leger following routine domestic flight. Cause not stated. No crew casualties. Aircraft U5+ FN a write-off.

1/KG40

Focke-Wulf FW 200C-1 (0023). Forced-landed at Brest out of fuel after operational sortie over the Atlantic. Crew unhurt. Aircraft F8+ EM 30% damaged.

5/KG40

Heinkel He 111P-4 (2868). Crashed and burned out due to engine failure on take-off on combat sortie. Lt. Diesel and one NCO killed. Two NCOs injured. Aircraft 5J+ EN a write-off.

3/KG77

Junkers Ju 88A-1 (2158). Flew into the ground near Laon during operational flight. Cause unknown. Oblt. Urban and three NCOs killed. Aircraft 3Z+ DS a write-off.

1/KGr.606

Dornier Do 17 (3497). Crash-landed at Sizun due to damage sustained in fighter attack. No crew casualties. Aircraft 7T+ LH a write-off.

3/KGr.606

Dornier Do 17 (3471). Damaged in combat with fighters over the Channel and crashed at Landerneau on return. Oblt. zur See von Krosigk and two NCOs killed. Aircraft 7T+ CL a write-off.

1/KGr.806

Junkers Ju 88A-1 (3079). Failed to return from operational sortie over Midlands and presumed brought down by ground fire. Lt. Grunwald, Fw. Baasch, Fw. Krueger and Fw. Strube all missing. Aircraft M7+ CH lost.

1/LG1

Junkers Ju 88A-1 (2088). Shot down by fighters during combat over southern England and forced-landed near Old Fishbourne, Bosham, Sussex 3.12 p.m. Oblt. Sodemann, Fw. Bergstrasser, Fw. Lorenz and Gefr. Bossert all captured. Aircraft L1+ AL a write-off.

5/LG2

Messerschmitt Bf 109E-4 (3716). Shot down by ground fire during sortie over Dover and crashed in the Channel. Pilot rescued unhurt by Seenotflugkdo. Aircraft lost.

6/LG2

Messerschmitt Bf 109E (5899). Forced-landed at Calais-Marck aerodrome during routine domestic flight. Cause not stated. Pilot unhurt. Aircraft 15% damaged.

2(F)/121

Dornier Do 215 (0023). Shot down by fighter during photo-reconnaissance mission over Liverpool. Crash-landed at Trawsfynydd, Merioneth, North Wales 4.55 p.m. Uffz. Pelzer killed. Lt. Book, Fw. Jensen and Fw. Kuehl captured wounded. Aircraft VB+ KK a write-off.

Sunday, September 22

2(F)/11

Messerschmitt Bf 110C-5 (2231). Forced-landed near Mardyck damaged by own flak during reconnaissance sortie. Crew unhurt. Aircraft MJ+ ZE 15% damaged.

4(F)/121

Junkers Ju 88A-1 (0352). Failed to return from weather-reconnaissance sortie over the Channel and shot down by fighters into the sea. Lt. Boettcher, Fw. Vater, Uffz. Mueller and Uffz. Rabe all took to dinghy and captured. Aircraft 7A+ AM lost.

2/506

Heinkel He 115s (3267, 1997). Two aircraft damaged at moorings in Trondheim harbour during a storm. No personnel losses. Aircraft S4+ FK and S4+ GK both 25% damaged.

3/906

Heinkel He 115B-1 (2412). Crashed at Schellingwoude during routine domestic flight. Caused by mechanical failure. Crew unhurt. Aircraft 8L+ EL a write-off.

3/JG27

Messerschmitt Bf 109E-1 (3381). Crashed on take-off from Guines-West on local flight. Cause not stated but probably suffered engine failure. Pilot unhurt. Aircraft 20% damaged.

8/JG53

Messerschmitt Bf 109E-1 (3519). Crashed on landing at Etaples following routine domestic flight. Cause not stated. Pilot injured. Aircraft a write-off.

7/KG2

Dornier Do 17Z-3 (2858). Crash-landed near Cambrai due to battle damage following sortie over the Channel. No crew casualties. Aircraft U5+ FR a write-off.

8/KG76

Dornier Do 17Z-2 (2809). Damaged in landing accident at Clermont aerodrome. Exact circumstances not recorded. No crew casualties. Aircraft F1+ HS repairable.

I/KGr.100

Heinkel He 111H-1 (5247). Crashed on take-off at Vannes due to technical fault. Three NCOs killed another wounded. Aircraft 6N+ MH a write-off.

I/LG1

Junkers Ju 88A-1 (3121). Crashed and burned out at Orleans-Bricy on take-off on operational sortie. Crew of four NCOs all killed. Aircraft L1+ JK a write-off.

IV/LG1

Junkers Ju 87B-1 (5586). Forced-landed near Hilversum due to engine failure on operational sortie. Crew unhurt. Aircraft L1+ LV 40% damaged.

Monday, September 23

Wettererkundungs Staffel 2

Heinkel He 111 (5396). Shot down by Blenheim during weather reconnaissance sortie over the Atlantic. Crashed in sea. Reg. Rat. Dr. Reinhardt and one NCO killed. Rest of crew believed rescued unhurt. Aircraft TG+ KA lost.

Seenotzentrale Boulogne

Heinkel He 59 (2596). Crashed in sea during routine domestic flight. Cause not stated but possible result of collision. Crew rescued from sea unhurt. Aircraft lost.

Heinkel He 59 (2792). Crashed in sea on local flight possibly following mid-air collision. Crew rescued unhurt. Aircraft lost.

4/JG2

Messerschmitt Bf 109E-4 (1969). Shot down by Flight Lieutenant Cosby and Sergeant Glen of No. 72 Squadron during bomber escort mission over southern England. Ditched in sea just off Folkestone pier 10.00 a.m. Uffz. Dilthey rescued injured. Aircraft 2+ lost.

Stab JG3

Messerschmitt Bf 109E-1. Shot down in combat with fighters over southern England. Oblt. Hopp killed. Aircraft a write-off.

3/JG3

Messerschmitt Bf 109E-1 (6367). Damaged in landing accident at St. Omer following routine domestic flight. Cause not stated. Pilot unhurt. Aircraft 15% damaged.

7/JG3

Messerschmitt Bf 109E-1 (6304). Shot down by RAF fighters during free-lance fighter sortie over Kent coast. Crashed in sea off Kingsdown south of Deal 10.22 a.m. Uffz. Elbing baled out and captured. Aircraft 3+ lost.

8/JG26

Messerschmitt Bf 109E-4 (5817). Shot down by Flight Lieutenant Kingcombe of No. 92 Squadron during free-lance fighter sweep over Kent. Crashed at Biddenden, near Tenterden 10.00 a.m. Oberfw. Grzymalla baled out and captured unhurt. Aircraft 9+ a write-off.

Messerschmitt Bf 109E-4 (3735). Radiator hit by Pilot Officer Drummond of No. 92 Squadron during combat over north Kent. Forced-landed in a pond near Grain Fort, Isle of Grain 9.55 a.m. Fw. Kuepper captured unhurt. Aircraft 4+ 1 a write-off.

Pristine control column removed from cockpit by a local resident in 1940 as a souvenir donated to the Kent Battle of Britain Museum during local enquiries.

Stab III/JG53

Messerschmitt Bf 109E-4 (5894). Shot down in combat with fighters over the Channel off Calais. Pilot unhurt. Aircraft a write-off.

9/JG53

Messerschmitt Bf 109E-1 (6279). Crashed in sea off Boulogne due to engine failure following combat with RAF fighters over the Channel. Pilot unhurt. Aircraft lost.

3/JG54

Messerschmitt Bf 109E-4 (1516). Shot down during combat with fighters and crashed at Barham, Kent 10.20 a.m. Oberfw. Knipp-scheer killed. Aircraft lost.

Ergaenzungs Staffel KG26

Heinkel He 111 (5391). Crashed and burned out at Luebeck-Blankenese on local training flight. Cause not recorded. Lt. Olerich and one NCO killed. Aircraft 1H+ BM a write-off.

I/KG51

Junkers Ju 88A-1 (2188). Forced-landed at Melun-Villaroche aerodrome following operational sortie. Cause not stated. No crew casualties. Aircraft 25% damaged.

II/KG54

Junkers Ju 88A-1 (7098). Crashed and burned out on take-off from St. Andre on combat sortie. Cause unknown but probably engine-failure. Three NCOs dead and one other wounded. Aircraft a write-off.

During a night bombing mission to London, this Heinkel from 6/KG26 was hit by anti-aircraft fire and set alight. Descending over Chobham, the aircraft broke up, the engines landing in the grounds of the Gordon Boys Home (renamed Gordon Boys School in 1952). The rear fuselage came down on the recreation ground where it burnt out. The

I/LG1

Junkers Ju 88A-1 (2084). Engine caught fire on take-off from Orleans-Bricy aerodrome. Landed safely crew unhurt. Aircraft 30% damaged.

3/LG2

Messerschmitt Bf 109E-7 (5803). Crashed at Calais-Marck following combat with fighters over the Channel. Pilot unhurt. Aircraft a write-off.

Messerschmitt Bf 109E-7 (2042). Forced-landed back at Calais-Marck due to combat damage following sortie over the Channel. Pilot unhurt. Aircraft 45% damaged.

Messerschmitt Bf 109E-7 (2057). Crashed on landing at Calais-Marck due to combat damage. Pilot unhurt. Aircraft a write-off.

Messerschmitt Bf 109E-7 (5094). Crashed in the Channel during combat with RAF fighters. Pilot rescued unhurt by Seenot-dienst. Aircraft lost.

3(F)/123

Junkers Ju 88A-1 (0130). Failed to return from operational reconnaissance sortie over England. Exact fate unknown. Personnel losses not recorded. Aircraft 4U+ CL lost.

Tuesday, September 24

2(H)/32

Henschel Hs 126B (3063). Forced-landed at Deulemont during operational sortie. Cause not stated. Crew unhurt. Aircraft 40% damaged.

Erprobungs Gruppe 210

Messerschmitt Bf 110D/O (3384). Shot down by AA fire during sortie over the English coast and crashed in the sea off Southampton Water. Lt. von der Horst and Obergefr. Ollers both missing. Aircraft S9+ HH lost.

I/JG2

Messerschmitt Bf 109E-4 (5269). Suffered engine failure during combat sortie and forced-landed at Theville. Pilot unhurt. Aircraft 35% damaged.

1/JG77

Messerschmitt Bf 109E-4 (1500). Damaged by ground fire during combat sortie and crashed on return to Wissant. Oblt. Kind wounded. Aircraft a write-off.

3/JG77

Messerschmitt Bf 109E-4 (5213). Crashed on landing at Marquise-West due to mechanical failure during operational sortie. Pilot unhurt. Aircraft a write-off.

8/KG1

Junkers Ju 88 (3206). Crashed on take-off from Hansdorf on operational sortie. Cause not stated. No crew casualties. Aircraft V4+ DT 35% damaged.

1/KG3

Dornier Do 17Z-3 (2633). Crashed at Antwerp due to combat damage. Three NCOs wounded. Aircraft 5K+ JH 60% damaged.

following day the wreckage was photographed by the press with army personnel and an ATS girl examining some burned and tattered parachute silk. All the crewmen had baled out and were captured. Although nothing marks the crash site today, these dogs obviously feel there is something worth sniffing (Keystone).

6/KG26

Heinkel He 111H-3 (3322). Shot down by AA fire during bombing mission to London. Crashed and burst into flames near Gordon Boys Home, West End, Chobham, Surrey 01.37 a.m. Uffz. Niemeyer, Gefr. Leibnitz, Gefr. Wenlich, Gefr. Jenreck baled out and captured. Aircraft 1H+ GP a write-off.
Surface fragments collected by the Air Historical Group.

I/KG54

Junkers Ju 88A-1 (4038). Damaged on take-off from Evreux-Fauville on combat sortie. Cause not stated. No crew casualties. Aircraft 35% damaged.

Junkers Ju 88A-1 (4099). Forced-landed Evreux-Fauville with damage caused by AA fire during sortie over England. Crew unhurt. Aircraft 35% damaged.

1/KG76

Dornier Do 17Z (1184). Forced-landed at Beauvais following operational sortie. Cause not stated. No crew casualties. Aircraft F1+ BH 30% damaged.

2/KG76

Dornier Do 17Z (3317). Forced-landed back at base damaged by fighters following bombing raid on London. Uffz. Curth wounded. Aircraft F1+ GK a write-off.

4/KG77

Junkers Ju 88A-1 (7120). Damaged by fighters during sortie over the Channel. Forced-landed at Couvron crew unhurt. Aircraft 3Z+ KM 30% damaged.

5/KG77

Junkers Ju 88A-1 (7107). Forced-landed at St. Armand with combat damage. No crew casualties. Aircraft 3Z+ FN 35% damaged.

6/KG77

Junkers Ju 88A-1 (7108). Crashed on landing near St. Omer due to damage sustained in combat with fighters over southern England. No crew casualties. Aircraft 3Z+ BP a write-off.

1/KGr.126

Heinkel He 111H-4 (6964). Failed to return from operational sortie over the Thames Estuary and believed shot down by fighters. Lt. zur See Drews, Uffz. Mellin, Gefr. Blau and Flgr. Saal missing. Aircraft 1T+ GH lost.

II/LG1

Junkers Ju 88A-1 (6126). Crashed on landing at Orleans-Bricy following routine domestic flight. Cause not stated. No crew casualties. Aircraft 35% damaged.

III/LG1

Junkers Ju 88A-1 (2076). Crashed and burned out on take-off from Caen on operational sortie. Cause unknown. Lt. Rintelen and three NCOs killed. Aircraft a write-off.

II/StG2

Junkers Ju 87B (5492). Crashed near Bangan due to engine failure on routine domestic flight. Crew unhurt. Aircraft a write-off.

II/ZG76

Messerschmitt Bf 110C-4 (2159). Returned to base damaged by AA fire during sortie over Southampton. Lt. Calame wounded. Aircraft 10% damaged.

Messerschmitt Bf 110C-2 (2638). Damaged by AA fire during sortie over Southampton and returned to base with one NCO wounded. Aircraft 10% damaged.

III/ZG76

Messerschmitt Bf 110C-4 (3534). Crashed in the Channel off Southampton due to flak damage. Uffz. Helwig and Uffz. Mirow both missing. Aircraft 2N+ DN lost.

Messerschmitt Bf 110C-4 (3251). Hit by AA fire during sortie over the Channel off Southampton and crashed in sea. Both NCOs rescued from sea unhurt by Seenotdienst. Aircraft lost.

Wednesday, September 25

1(F)/121

Heinkel He 111H-3 (2704). Crashed and burst into flames on landing at Stavanger-Sola aerodrome following routine domestic flight. Cause unknown. Oblt. Woelz and three NCOs killed. Aircraft 7A+ EH a write-off.

1/506

Heinkel He 115 (3265). Suffered engine failure during operational sortie and crashed in sea (PQ2843). Major Rentzsch, Lt. Bock and Oberfw. Schmidt missing. Aircraft S4+ AH lost.

3/JG27

Messerschmitt Bf 109E-1 (6061). Shot down in combat with fighters over the Channel and crashed in the sea. Pilot rescued unhurt by Seenotdienst. Aircraft lost.

7/JG27

Messerschmitt Bf 109E (5097). Forced-landed at Phillipi due to engine failure on combat sortie. Pilot unhurt. Aircraft repairable.

I/JG53

Messerschmitt Bf 109E (6981) Suffered engine failure during operational sortie and crash-landed near Cherbourg. Pilot injured. Aircraft a write-off.

4/KG1

Heinkel He 111H-2 (2639). Crashed on landing at Amiens following operations over the Channel. No crew casualties. Aircraft V4+ MU 50% damaged.

5/KG26

Heinkel He 111H-3 (5645). Crashed and burned out at Amiens-Glisy during bombing mission. Cause not stated. One NCO killed and three more wounded. Aircraft 1H+ AN a write-off.

III/KG51

Junkers Ju 88A-1 (4144). Crashed and burned out at Evreux aerodrome following bombing sortie over southern England. Lt. Meier, Fw. Eimers, Gefr. Herich and Gefr. Altmann all killed. Aircraft 9K+ FR a write-off.

7/KG53

Heinkel He 111H-2 (5307). Shot down during bombing sortie over England. No crew casualties notified. Aircraft A1+ HR a write-off.

1/KG55

Heinkel He 111H (6305). Shot down by fighters following bombing raid on Bristol Aero works and forced-landed on Westhill Farm, Studland, near Swanage 12.00 p.m. Uffz. Altrichter severely wounded and died. Hptmn. Koethke, Fw. Juerges, Gefr. Weisbach and Flgr. Mueller captured. Aircraft G1+ BH a write-off.

Above: **Shortly after it was damaged by accurate anti-aircraft fire over Portbury, the crew baled out of this KG55 Heinkel and it came to earth on Racecourse Farm. After decapitating an oak tree on the ridge above the farm, it pancaked into a field, breaking up as it slewed across the ground and through a hedge. Fires still smoulder amongst the wreckage from the massive disintegration of the aircraft.** *Below:* **The fields of Racecourse Farm broken up in readiness for winter sowing. In the slithering, rending crash, the bombs were torn loose and careered across two fields into the trees in the background lying undiscovered for several days. We could find no trace of remains around the hedgerows when we visited the farm on November 2, 1979.**

5/KG55

Heinkel He 111H (2126). Shot down by AA fire during bombing sortie to Bristol. Crashed on Racecourse Farm, Portbury, Somerset 11.50 a.m. Oblt. Weigel, Oberfw. Narres, Fw. Gerdsmeier and Gefr. Geib baled out and captured. Fw. Engel captured wounded. Aircraft G1+ DN a write-off.

A surface crash investigated by the South West Aircraft Recovery Group. Bomb winch handle recovered at the time of the crash by local landowner presented to their museum.

6/KG55

Heinkel He 111P (1579). Crash-landed at Caen damaged by fighters during bombing raid on Filton. Oblt. Kindor and Uffz. Turek wounded. Aircraft G1+ AP 50% damaged.

Heinkel He 111H (1525). Crashed at Church Farm, Woolverton near Frome 12.02 p.m. following fighter attack. Uffz. Mertz, Oberfw. Wittkamp, Oberfw. Kirchhoff and Gefr. Beck killed. Hptmn. Brandt (Staffel Kapitan) baled out and captured wounded. Aircraft G1+ EP a write-off.

7/KG55

Heinkel He 111P (2803). Shot down by fighters following bombing attack on Bristol and abandoned over Branksome Park, Poole following engine fire 12.08 p.m. Oblt. Scholz, Oblt. Broecker (Staffel Kapitan), Uffz. Hanft and Uffz. Weidner killed. Uffz. Schraps baled out and rescued wounded from Poole Harbour. Aircraft G1+ LR a write-off.

Left: **Crippled by an engine fire after combat over Dorset on the morning of September 25, a 'Griffon' Geschwader Heinkel 111 from Chartres was abandoned by its crew over Bournemouth. It crashed on 'Chatsworth' in Westminster Road on the Branksome Park estate (Bournemouth Daily Echo).**

Right: **On October 17, 1954, Peter Foote, local aviation historian, photographed 'Chatsworth' house still derelict. This is his picture looking north-east across Branksome Chine.** *Below:* **The site has now been developed and replaced by the luxury flats of Branksome Cliff.**

Messerschmitt Bf 110C (3263). Crashed in the Channel during combat with RAF fighters over Weymouth. Crew rescued unhurt by Seenotdienst. Aircraft lost.

Messerschmitt Bf 110C-4 (2194). Crashed on landing at Theville aerodrome following combat with fighters over the Channel. Crew both unhurt. Aircraft a write-off.

II/ZG76

Messerschmitt Bf 110C-2 (3111). Crashed at Wurzburg during routine domestic flight. Cause not stated. Lt. Pistor killed. Aircraft a write-off.

Thursday, September 26

Wettererkundungskette, Luftflotte 5

Heinkel He 111H-3 (6942). Damaged in landing accident at Vaernes following routine domestic flight. No crew casualties. Aircraft 1B+CH 45% damaged.

II/KG.z.b.V.1

Junkers Ju 52 (6937). Crashed near Willingen on local flight. Cause unknown. Two NCOs killed and four NCOs injured. Aircraft 1Z+DS a write-off.

4(F)/14

Messerschmitt Bf 110C-5 (2187). Shot down by fighter during reconnaissance mission over the Channel. Crashed in sea at Salt Mead Ledge, west of Cowes, Isle of Wight 5.40 p.m. Lt. Pank and Uffz. Schmidt killed. Aircraft 5F+CM lost.

I/KGr.100

Heinkel He 111H (2768). Forced-landed at Vannes following operational sortie. Cause not stated. No crew casualties. Aircraft 30% damaged.

7(F)/LG2

Messerschmitt Bf 110 (2185). Crash-landed and burned out at Beeneys Lane, two miles north of Hastings 11.30 a.m. following fighter engagement. Oblt. Weyergang and Fw. Nelson both killed. Aircraft L2+ER a write-off.
Site investigated by the Wealden Aviation Archaeological Group in 1974 and surface fragments discovered.

I/StG1

Junkers Ju 87R (5461). Crashed on take-off from Angers aerodrome on routine domestic flight following engine failure. Crew unhurt. Aircraft 50% damaged.

III/ZG26

Messerschmitt Bf 110C-4 (2130). Forced-landed at base with combat damage. Crew unhurt. Aircraft 20% damaged.

Messerschmitt Bf 110C-4 (3591). Shot down by fighters during escort sortie over Bristol. Crash-landed at Well Bottom, near Boyton, Wiltshire 11.30 a.m. Gefr. Schumacher killed. Fw. Scherer captured wounded. Aircraft 3U+GS a write-off.

5(F)/14

Dornier Do 17P (1092). Forced-landed near Bad Liebenwerder during routine domestic flight. Cause not stated. No crew casualties. Aircraft 10% damaged.

3/JG51

Messerschmitt Bf 109E-4 (5369). Shot down by RAF fighters during combat over the Channel off Dungeness. Crashed in sea. Fw. Meudner missing. Aircraft lost.

5/JG77

Messerschmitt Bf 109E-3 (0833). Engine caught fire on take-off from Fornebu on local flight. Cause unknown. Pilot unhurt. Aircraft 60% damaged.

Stab KG3

Dornier Do 17Z-3 (2591). Lost bearings whilst on operational sortie and forced-landed at Maastricht. Two NCOs injured. Aircraft 5K+FA a write-off.

I/KG27

Heinkel He 111H (6871). Forced-landed at Gijon in Spain during operational sortie. Exact circumstances not recorded. Later returned safely to base. Crew unhurt. Aircraft undamaged.

Heinkel He 111H (5406). Crashed near Tours due to mechanical failure on routine domestic flight. Two NCOs killed. Oblt. Fock injured. Aircraft a write-off.

I/KG54

Junkers Ju 88A-1 (6071). Damaged in landing accident at Evreux aerodrome during combat sortie. Circumstances not recorded. One NCO wounded. Aircraft 35% damaged.

2/KG55

Heinkel He 111H (5314). Failed to return from bombing sortie over the south coast of England. Shot down by fighters off the Isle of Wight. Oblt. Graf Schweinitz, Uffz. Widmann, Uffz. Schob, Gefr. Helfer and Gefr. Wastian all missing. Aircraft G1+BL lost.

3/KG55

Heinkel He 111P (3098). Forced-landed at Dreux following operational sortie over the Channel and attacked by fighters. Oblt. Karbe and Lt. Wilser injured. Aircraft 40% damaged.

KGr.100

Heinkel He 111H (5291). Damaged in landing accident at Vannes aerodrome following operational sortie. No crew casualties. Aircraft 30% damaged.

I/ZG26

Messerschmitt Bf 110C-4 (3028). Shot down by AA fire and fighters during escort sortie over Southampton. Forced-landed on Bleak Down, Newport, Isle of Wight 4.30 p.m. Fw. Rohde and Fw. Feder captured. Aircraft U8+HH a write-off.

7/ZG26

Messerschmitt Bf 110C-4 (3094). Crashed on Tapnall Farm, near Freshwater, Isle of Wight 4.30 p.m. following fighter attack, Lt. Konopka and Uffz. Eiberg both killed. Aircraft 3U+AR a write-off.

2/106

Dornier Do 18 (0881). Crashed in sea off Cornish coast during operational sortie over St. George's Channel. Cause unknown. Oblt. zur See Stelle, Oblt. Heuveldop, Uffz. Kahlfeld and Fw. Bresch all killed. Aircraft M2+EK lost.

Friday, September 27

3(F)/123

Junkers Ju 88A-1 (0393). Shot down by RAF fighter over Bristol during photo-recce mission to Liverpool. Ditched in sea at Porlock Bay, Somerset 9.45 a.m. Obergefr. Reuhl killed. Fw. Ackenhausen, Oblt. Rude and Oberfw. Riehle captured unhurt. Aircraft 4U+RL lost.

Stab Erprobungs Gruppe 210

Messerschmitt Bf 110D-3 (3378). Shot down by fighters during bombing sortie to Bristol. Crashed into trees at Bussey Stool Farm, Cranbourne Chase, near Shaftesbury 12.00 p.m. Hptmn. Lutz (Gruppe Kommandeur) and Uffz. Schoen killed. Aircraft S9+DH a write-off.

1/Erprobungs Gruppe 210

Messerschmitt Bf 110D-3 (3888). Shot down into the sea off coast of Dorset during operational sortie over south-west England. Lt. Schmidt and Fw. Richter both killed. Aircraft S9+JH a write-off. *BURIED IN BROOKWOOD MILITARY CEMETERY*

2/Erprobungs Gruppe 210

Messerschmitt Bf 110D/O (4270). Shot down by fighters following bombing attack on Filton. Forced-landed at The Beeches, Preston Hill, Iwerne Minster 12.00 p.m. Fw. Ebner and Gefr. Zwick both captured wounded. Aircraft S9+DU a write-off.

Messerschmitt Bf 110D/O (2248). Shot down during sortie over south-west England to Bristol. Crashed into the sea. Oblt. Roessiger (Staffel Kapitan) and Oberfw. Marx missing. Aircraft S9+GK a write-off.

6/JG3

Messerschmitt Bf 109E-4 (4141). Crashed in the Channel during combat with fighters. Pilot rescued unhurt by Seenotdienst. Aircraft lost.

III/JG3

Messerschmitt Bf 109E-4 (5340). Shot down in fighter combat over the Channel. Crashed in the sea. Oblt. Rech wounded and rescued by Seenotdienst. Aircraft lost.

8/JG3

Messerschmitt Bf 109E-1 (6197). Crash-landed at Coquelles with combat damage. Pilot unhurt. Aircraft a write-off..

Messerschmitt Bf 109E-4 (1283). Crashed at Wissant followed combat with RAF fighters over the Channel. Pilot unhurt. Aircraft a write-off.

9/JG3

Messerschmitt Bf 109E-1 (3217). Failed to return from combat with fighters over the Channel and presumed shot down into the sea. Uffz. Struwe missing. Aircraft lost.

3/JG27

Messerschmitt Bf 109E-1 (3369). Shot down in combat with fighters during escort sortie. Crashed at Mays Farm, Selmeston, near Lewes 9.45 a.m. Gefr. John baled out and captured unhurt. Aircraft 11+ a write-off.
Site excavated by the Wealden Aviation Archaeological Group in 1976. Only minor components and few fragments of shattered airframe recovered.

Messerschmitt Bf 109E-4 (5333). Crashed in the Channel during combat with fighters. Pilot rescued unhurt by Seenotdienst. Aircraft lost.

6/JG27

Messerschmitt Bf 109E-4 (1447). Exploded in mid-air over Aylesford, Kent 12.45 p.m. during combat with RAF fighters. Crashed on Hale Farm, Eccles. Uffz. Scheidt killed. Aircraft 5+ a write-off.

3/JG51

Messerschmitt Bf 109E-4 (5582). Crashed on landing at St. Inglevert following combat with RAF fighters over the Channel. Pilot unhurt. Aircraft a write-off.

Stab II/JG52

Messerschmitt Bf 109E-1 (3907). Crash-landed at Broad Street, near Hollingbourne, east of Maidstone 1.00 p.m. damaged by fighters during fighter operations over southern England. Oblt. Treiber captured wounded. Aircraft 8+ a write-off.

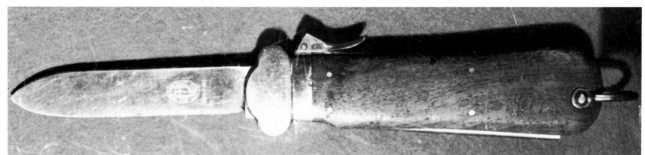

Guaranteed 'Rostfrei' is the makers claim for this Solingen steel knife which once belonged to Feldwebel Hoffman and now displayed at Brenzett. It was found at Brick House Farm, Tenterden where his Bf 109E crashed on September 27.

4/JG52

Messerschmitt Bf 109E-4 (5181). Shot down by fighters during free-lance sweep over Kent and crash-landed at Morrison House Farm, near St. Nicholas at Wade, Thanet 3.40 p.m. Fw. Bogasch captured. Aircraft 4+ a write-off.

Messerschmitt Bf 109E-1 (3442). Severely damaged by fighters in combat during free-lance sortie over Kent and crashed through HT cables at Northbourne Park, near Sandwich 3.50 p.m. Gefr. Bosch captured wounded. Aircraft 12+ a write-off.

Messerschmitt Bf 109E-1 (6245). Crashed at Petham, near Canterbury 3.00 p.m. following action with RAF fighters during free-lance fighter sweep over Kent. Lt. Geist captured. Aircraft 5+ a write-off.

5/JG52

Messerschmitt Bf 109E-1 (3431). Shot down during forward sweep over the Thames Estuary and crashed at Brick House Farm, High Halden, near Tenterden, Kent 12.50 p.m. Fw. Hoffmann baled out and captured. Aircraft 3+ a write-off.
Exact point of impact partly under a road and investigated by the Brenzett Aeronautical Museum without result. Pilot's gravity knife in their collection.

6/JG52

Messerschmitt Bf 109E-1 (6162). Shot down by fighters in combat over the Channel. Crashed in sea. Pilot wounded rescued by Seenotdienst. Aircraft lost.

Messerschmitt Bf 109E-4 (5152). Crashed on landing at Peuplingues aerodrome following fighter combat. Pilot unhurt. Aircraft a write-off.

II/JG53

Messerschmitt Bf 109E-4 (1168). Returned to base with combat damage. Pilot unhurt. Aircraft 10% damaged.

Messerschmitt Bf 109E-4 (1164). Damaged by RAF fighters in combat over the Channel. Returned safely to base. Pilot unhurt. Aircraft 15% damaged.

Messerschmitt Bf 109E-4 (1644). Returned to base damaged following fighter combat over the Channel. Pilot unhurt. Aircraft 15% damaged.

6/JG53

Messerschmitt Bf 109E-4. Crashed at Berck-sur-Mer following fighter combat. Pilot unhurt. Aircraft a write-off.

8/JG54

Messerschmitt Bf 109E (1538). Severely damaged in fighter combat over north Kent. Hit fence trying to land, somersaulted over main road and crashed in flames near Brenley House, Boughton, east of Faversham 12.05 p.m. Oblt. Schon killed. Aircraft a write-off.

8/KG2

Dornier Do 17Z (2871). Crashed at Remilly during routine domestic flight. Cause unknown. Lt. Landhorst and three NCOs all killed. Aircraft U5+ ES a write-off.

A rare find from the Ju 88 — fragments of a Luftwaffe code book which gave up their secrets thirty-six years too late!

The Air Historical Group excavation in progress on Folly Farm, South Holmwood on the Ju 88 of 2/KG77, No. 8095, which was shot down in flames on the morning of September 27. *Above:* The digger was at maximum reach but had only just exposed the rear of the port engine. *Below:* A further two days hand digging were necessary to free the engine from rock-hard clay at an overall depth of twenty feet (Air Historical Group).

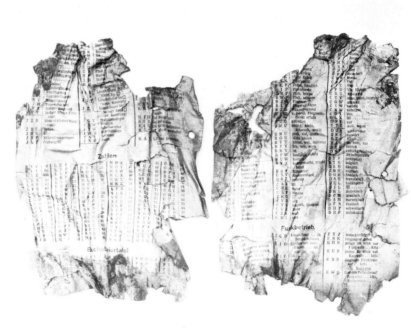

III/KG51

Junkers Ju 88A-1 (6153). Crashed at Oysonville near Etampes on combat sortie. Cause unknown but possible collision with 2174. Four NCOs all killed. Aircraft 9K+BR a write-off.

Junkers Ju 88A-5 (2174). Believed collided with 6153 during operational sortie. Crashed and burned out at Pussay near Etampes. Four NCOs killed. Aircraft GK+IR a write-off.

I/KG53

Heinkel He 111H-5 (3556). Forced-landed at Vitry-en-Artois following combat sortie. Cause not stated. No crew casualties. Aircraft A1+EH 25% damaged.

5/KG53

Heinkel He 111H-3 (3344). Forced-landed near Calais during combat mission. Cause not stated. One NCO wounded. Aircraft A1+DR 40% damaged.

I/KG54

Junkers Ju 88A-1 (4029). Damaged landing at Evreux aerodrome following operational sortie over the Channel. Cause not stated. No crew casualties. Aircraft 35% damaged.

Ergaenzungs Staffel KG55

Heinkel He 111P (1398). Damaged in taxi-ing accident at Landsberg prior to routine domestic flight. Crew unhurt. Aircraft 25% damaged.

1/KG77

Junkers Ju 88A-1 (8090). Hit by AA fire during approach to London. Crashed in the grounds of the Angas Home, Cudham, Kent 11.05 a.m. Gefr. Zabel baled out but parachute failed. Uffz. Kollmannsmager, Oberfw. Mueller and Oberfw. Mueller baled out and captured. Aircraft 3Z+DH a write-off.

Disabled by 'ack-ack' fire on its approach to London, this Ju 88A-1 of 1/KG77, abandoned by its crew, smashed through a flint wall and ended in tangled wreckage among the lettuces of a vegetable garden. The tower among the trees marks the main entrance to the Angas Home for Aged Seamen at Cudham, Kent (Fox Photos).

2/KG77

Junkers Ju 88A-1 (8095). Crashed in flames on Folly Farm, South Holmwood, near Dorking following fighter attack during bombing sortie to London 10.30 a.m. Uffz. Menningmann killed. Uffz. Schumann, Uffz. Tenholt and Uffz. Ackermann baled out and captured. Aircraft 3Z+HK a write-off.

Site excavated by the Air Historical Group and Southern Area Wartime Aircraft Preservation Society 1976.

Junkers Ju 88A-1 (2164). Ditched in sea off Lydd, Kent 9.40 a.m. following fighter attack. Uffz. Hertlein and Fw. Krebs killed. Uffz. Schmidt and Uffz. Sergocki captured unhurt. Aircraft 3Z+IK lost.

3/KG77

Junkers Ju 88A-1 (8109). Crashed in East Grinstead 9.30 a.m. following head-on attack by fighters. Uffz. Kasing, Uffz. Winkelmann and Fw. Precht all killed. Fw. Braeutigam captured wounded. Aircraft 3Z+BL a write-off.

Hidden behind a screen of trees and minus its tower which was demolished some years after the war when it became unsafe, the Angas Home is now administered by the Bromley Health Authority and houses twenty-eight sub-normal female patients plus attendant staff.

Junkers Ju 88A-1 (5103). Shot down during bombing sortie to London docks. Crashed and burned out in Hononton Park, near Horsmonden, Kent 3.30 p.m. Uffz. Merschen, Uffz. Damerius, Uffz. Hastrich killed. Uffz. Ludwig captured wounded. Aircraft 3Z+ CL a write-off.

Junkers Ju 88A-1 (8099). Forced-landed on Graveney Marshes, near Faversham, Kent 3.30 p.m. following fighter attack. Uffz. Ruhlandt, Uffz. Richter, Uffz. Richter and Gefr. Reiner all captured. Aircraft 3Z+ EL a write-off.

Stab II/KG77

Junkers Ju 88A-5 (0293). Brought down by ground defences and fighter attacks during bombing attack on London. Crashed in flames on Vexour Farm, Penshurst, near Tonbridge 3.30 p.m. Oblt. Lutze, Fw. Adler and Fw. Zeller killed. Uffz. Brodbeck captured. Aircraft 3Z+ DC a write-off.

Site excavated by the Halstead War Museum which recovered various components including both propeller bosses. Various relics also in the Steve Vizard collection.

4/KG77

Junkers Ju 88A-1 (4140). Failed to return from bombing mission to London. Believed shot down by fighters and crashed in sea. Uffz. Ganter, Fw. Noelp, Fw. Scheibner and Obergefr. Moettig all missing. Aircraft 3Z+ LM lost.

5/KG77

Junkers Ju 88A-1 (4117). Crashed in sea off Hastings 4.00 p.m. following attack by fighters. Oblt. Ziel, Fw. Niederer both killed. Uffz. Isensee missing. Gefr. Teichtmayer rescued by lifeboat and captured wounded. Aircraft 3Z+ DN lost.

Junkers Ju 88A-1 (7109). Brought down by ground defences and fighter attack during sortie over London. Gefr. Reinhardt and Gefr. Zott killed. Lt. Pflueger and Uffz. Groenke missing. Aircraft 3Z+ GN a write-off.

Junkers Ju 88A-1 (7112). Briefed to attack London and shot down by RAF fighters over target. Obergefr. Kuhn killed. Hptmn. Zetzsche (Staffel Kapitan), Fw. Marl and Gefr. Burkhardt missing. Aircraft 3Z+ HN a write-off.

6/KG77

Junkers Ju 88A-1 (4118). Shot down by fighters following bombing attack on London. Crashed at Sevenoaks, Kent 3.30 p.m. Oblt. Seif, Uffz. Gebhardt and Fw. Eichinger killed. Fw. Zinsmeister captured wounded. Aircraft 3Z+ DP a write-off.

III/LG1

Junkers Ju 88A-5 (4153). Shot down during mission over southern England. Fw. Soechting and Gefr. Lorenz both killed. Oblt. Strasser and Uffz. Forster missing. Aircraft L1+ BR a write-off.

The repaired section of the garden wall, through which the disintegrating German bomber exploded thirty-nine years before, is indicated by a member of staff on August 9, 1979.

9/ZG26

Messerschmitt Bf 110C-4 (3297). Collided with Pilot Officer Miller of No. 609 Squadron during fighter combat over Dorchester. Crashed on Dole Ash Farm, Piddletrenthide 11.45 a.m. Gefr. Lidtke killed. Gefr. Jackstedt baled out and captured. Aircraft 3U+ FT a write-off. LIDTKE WAS BURIED BESIDE THE HEDGEROW WHERE HE FELL. LATER BURIED IN BROOKWOOD MILITARY CEMETERY SURREY *

II/ZG76

Messerschmitt Bf 110D-3 (4215). Shot down during escort sortie over the Channel. Crashed in sea off Hastings 10.00 a.m. Oblt. von Eichborn rescued by fishing boat and captured badly burned. Uffz. Bartmus killed. Aircraft M8+ XE lost.

9/ZG76

Messerschmitt Bf 110D (3584). Damaged by fighters during sortie over southern England and crash-landed near Dieppe with one NCO wounded. Aircraft 2N+ DP a write-off.

CORPO AEREO ITALIANO

Fiat Br 20. Suffered engine failure during local familiarisation sortie and crashed near Spa in Belgium. No crew casualties. Aircraft damage state not recorded.

Fiat Br 20. Crashed on landing at Brussels-Evere aerodrome following local flight. Cause not stated. One crewman injured. Aircraft a write-off.

Saturday, September 28

2/406

Dornier Do 18 (0884). Shot down by RAF Blenheim whilst on patrol over the North Sea. Crew took to dinghy and rescued unhurt. Aircraft K6+ JK lost.

I/JG2

Messerschmitt Bf 109E-1 (6165). Crashed at Theville due to engine failure on combat mission. Pilot injured. Aircraft a write-off.

I/JG26

Messerschmitt Bf 109E-4 (3756). Shot down in combat with RAF fighters over the Channel. Pilot unhurt. Aircraft a write-off.

3/JG26

Messerschmitt Bf 109E-1 (6273). Shot down by fighters during combat over the Channel. Fw. Schuer killed. Aircraft lost.

5/KG2

Dornier Do 17Z (3355). Crashed at St. Leger on operational sortie. Cause not known. Oblt. Roch and three NCOs all killed. Aircraft U5+ AN a write-off.

8/KG4

Junkers Ju 88A-1 (4071). Hit by AA fire during night sortie over Beachy Head. Crashed in sea at 10.00 p.m. following engine failure. Lt. Langer, Obergefr. Kieg, and Oberfw. Camp killed. Gefr. Marschardt captured unhurt. Aircraft 5J+ GS lost.

I/KG26

Heinkel He 111H-4 (6977). Crashed near Douai following operations over the Channel. Cause unknown. Lt. Kose and three NCOs all killed. Aircraft 1H+ EH a write-off.

II/KG26

Heinkel He 111H-3 (5621). Crashed on return from combat mission. Cause unknown. Four NCOs killed. Aircraft a write-off.

5/KG26

Heinkel He 111H-3 (3190). Crashed at St. Germain following operational sortie. Cause unknown but possibly battle damage. Four NCOs killed. Aircraft 1H+ LN a write-off.

6/KG76

Junkers Ju 88A-1 (4162). Suffered engine failure during routine domestic flight and crashed at Le Lavissiere. One NCO killed. Oblt. Moelinnus and two NCOs injured. Aircraft F1+ HP a write-off.

KGr.806

Junkers Ju 88A-1 (5078). Crashed near Caen following operational sortie at night. Possibly damaged by AA fire over England. Lt. zur See Quedenau and one NCO both killed. Two NCOs wounded. Aircraft a write-off.

I/LG2

Messerschmitt Bf 109E-7 (4091). Crash-landed at Theville following engine failure on combat sortie. Pilot unhurt. Aircraft 35% damaged.

I/ZG2

Messerschmitt Bf 110. Ran out of fuel during routine domestic flight and crashed near Seilhac. Hptmn. Heinlein killed and one NCO injured. Aircraft a write-off.

Sunday, September 29

4 (F)/14

Dornier Do 17P (1096). Crashed on take-off from Plumetot aerodrome on long-range reconnaissance sortie. Cause unknown but probably engine failure. Lt. Breitenbach, Lt. von Nissen and one NCO killed. Aircraft a write-off.

2/JG26

Messerschmitt Bf 109E-4 (2767). Suffered engine failure whilst engaged on combat sortie and forced-landed at Cap Gris-Nez. Pilot unhurt. Aircraft 15% damaged.

4/JG54

Messerschmitt Bf 109E-4 (3185). Crash-landed at Berck-sur-Mer out of fuel following operations over the Channel. Pilot unhurt. Aircraft 50% damaged.

2/JG77

Messerschmitt Bf 109E-4 (3746). Shot down in fighter combat over southern England. Oblt. Leyerer killed. Aircraft a write-off.

3/KG1

Heinkel He 111H-3 (3336). Crashed at Montdidier during operational sortie. Cause unknown. Five NCOs all killed. Aircraft V4+ FL a write-off.

Heinkel He 111H-3 (3468). Forced-landed at Hendricourt due to engine failure during combat mission. No crew casualties. Aircraft V4+ EL 40% damaged.

5/KG1

Heinkel He 111H-2 (2714). Abandoned by crew over Dillingen during operational sortie. Cause not stated. Crew baled out unhurt. Aircraft V4+ AV a write-off.

Heinkel He 111H-2 (2736). Forced-landed at Marin whilst on combat mission. Cause not stated. No crew casualties. Aircraft 30% damaged.

Stab KG2

Messerschmitt Bf 108 (1924). Forced-landed near Fuerth due to engine failure during local communications flight. No crew casualties. Aircraft 15% damaged.

I/KG54

Junkers Ju 88A-1 (4051). Suffered engine failure during operational sortie and forced-landed at Lisieux. Crashed and burned out. One NCO killed. Aircraft a write-off.

III/KG55

Heinkel He 111P (2148). Forced-landed near Brest due to engine failure on combat mission. Crew unhurt. Aircraft 50% damaged.

Heinkel He 111P (2822). Shot down by fighters during bombing sortie over St. George's Channel. Fw. Birkholz, Uffz. Firchau and Gefr. Guenther killed. Oblt. Koehler and Fw. Lippert both missing. Aircraft G1+ DT a write-off.

Heinkel He 111P (2820). Crashed at St. Lo following bombing sortie over England. Believed damaged by AA fire. Uffz. Hernberg, Fw. Blessing, Obergefr. Nuscher, Gefr. Tasche and Uffz. Hemmerle all wounded. Aircraft G1+ BT a write-off.

Stab II/KG76

Junkers Ju 88A-1 (8088). Damaged during operations over England and forced-landed on return to Calais-Marck. No crew casualties. Aircraft F1+ EC 25% damaged.

Stab I/LG1

Junkers Ju 88A-5 (3135). Severely damaged during operations over England and abandoned by three of crew on return to France. Oberfw. Heinz remained in aircraft and killed in crash. Aircraft L1+ AB a write-off.

II/LG2

Messerschmitt Bf 109E-4F (5576). Forced-landed at Berck-sur-Mer aerodrome out of fuel following combat sortie over the Channel. Pilot unhurt. Aircraft 40% damaged.

Messerschmitt Bf 109E-4 (3719). Forced-landed at Monchy-Breton during routine domestic flight. Cause not stated. Pilot unhurt. Aircraft 40% damaged.

III/ZG26

Messerschmitt Bf 110C (3422). Crashed on St. Aubin aerodrome during local flight. Cause not stated. Crew unhurt. Aircraft a write-off.

Monday, September 30

1(F)/123

Junkers Ju 88A-1 (0385). Crashed in sea off Ventnor, Isle of Wight during reconnaissance sortie. Cause unknown. Uffz. Essemann, Uffz. Obermeier and Fw. Waak killed. Lt. Frenzel missing. Aircraft 4U+ MH lost.

I/JG2

Messerschmitt Bf 109E-4 (0847). Failed to return from operational sortie over south coast of England and believed shot down into the sea by RAF fighters. Fw. Hermes missing. Aircraft lost.

II/JG2

Messerschmitt Bf 109E-4 (5391). Returned to Calais-Marck damaged after combat with fighters over the Channel. Pilot unhurt. Aircraft repairable.

Messerschmitt Bf 109E-4 (3447). Failed to return from combat with fighters over the Channel and presumed shot down into the sea. Gefr. Schumacher missing. Aircraft lost.

5/JG2

Messerschmitt Bf 109E-4 (4861). Shot down in combat with fighters over south coast of England. Crashed at Sprakefield, Hundred Acres Farm, Sydling St. Nicholas, Dorset 5.00 p.m. Uffz. Gollinger baled out but killed. Aircraft a write-off.

III/JG2

Messerschmitt Bf 109E-4 (3338). Crashed on take-off from Octeville on combat sortie due to collision. Pilot killed. Aircraft a write-off.

Messerschmitt Bf 109E-4 (4831). Involved in collision shortly after take-off from Octeville. Crashed and burned out. Pilot killed. Aircraft a write-off.

Stab JG26

Messerschmitt Bf 109E-4 (5818). Crashed in flames at Hides Farm, Roundhurst, North Chapel, near Haslemere 4.40 p.m. during combat with fighters. Major Kienzle baled out and captured seriously wounded. Aircraft a write-off.

Minor components and fragments of airframe, radio mast, exhaust stub and 20mm MGFF magazine recovered by the Southern Area Wartime Aircraft Preservation Society. Also excavated by the Wealden Aviation Archaeological Group in 1976. Relics from this aircraft also held by the Kent Battle of Britain Museum.

3/JG26

Messerschmitt Bf 109E-1 (6346). Damaged in combat with fighters over southern England and forced-landed back at Audembert. Pilot unhurt. Aircraft 40% damaged.

4/JG26

Messerschmitt Bf 109E-4 (1190). Suffered engine failure during combat with fighters over the Sussex coast during bomber escort mission. Forced-landed at Eastdean, near Eastbourne 5.30 p.m. Uffz. Perez captured unhurt. Aircraft 4+ a write-off.

Complete airframe shipped to Canada for use in connection with 'Bundles for Britain' drive 1941. After touring Canada and the USA, it was eventually delivered to Arnprior Research Station, Ontario in 1945. Sold as scrap in 1957, it was eventually discovered in a junk yard in 1961 and acquired by three enthusiasts. Returned to the UK, this aircraft is currently under restoration at Hurn airport.

6/JG26

Messerschmitt Bf 109E-1 (2688). Forced-landed at Coquelles following combat with fighters over the Channel. Pilot unhurt. Aircraft 30% damaged.

7/JG26

Messerschmitt Bf 109E-4 (3645). Shot down in combat with fighters over the Channel. Gefr. Ziemens killed. Aircraft a write-off.

9/JG26

Messerschmitt Bf 109E-4 (3891). Crashed at Caffiers due to damage received in combat with fighters over southern England. Pilot wounded. Aircraft a write-off.

Messerschmitt Bf 109E-1 (4820). Shot down in combat with RAF fighters over the Thames Estuary. Gefr. Hornatschek killed. Aircraft a write-off.

Stab I/JG27

Messerschmitt Bf 109E-4 (1577). Crash-landed back at Marquise following combat sortie over southern England. Hptmn. Neumann unhurt. Aircraft a write-off.

1/JG27

Messerschmitt Bf 109E-1 (4878). Severely damaged in taxi-ing accident at Guines-West. Uffz. Neef wounded. Aircraft a write-off.

2/JG27

Messerschmitt Bf 109E-4 (2801). Crashed on landing at Guines-West due to combat damage. Lt. Kothmann wounded. Aircraft a write-off.

3/JG27

Messerschmitt Bf 109E-4 (3763). Crashed and burned out at Bell Lane, Nutley, near Haywards Heath 9.45 a.m. during combat sortie over southern England. Oblt. Bertram (Gruppe Adjutant) killed. Aircraft a write-off.

Small fragments of airframe excavated by the Wealden Aviation Archaeological Group in 1974. Surface fragments recovered by the Kent Battle of Britain Museum and also by the London Air Museum.

Messerschmitt Bf 109E-4 (3630). Shot down by fighters during combat over the Ashdown Forest 9.45 a.m. Crashed into Cinder Hill Pond, Horsted Keynes, near Haywards Heath. Uffz. Sander killed. Aircraft a write-off.
Site investigated by the London Air Museum and components recovered at time of crash donated by local landowner.

Left: **Messerschmitt Bf 109 No. 1190 was believed to have sustained a coolant leak following combat with Hurricanes over Beachy Head on the afternoon of September 30. It was being flown by Unteroffizier Horst Perez who had taken over the aircraft from its former pilot, Hauptmann Karl Ebbighausen, who went missing on August 16 in another aircraft (S. Hall/A. Saunders).** *Above:* **The aircraft came down at Eastdean, just to the south of the A259. A visit to the site in May 1980 indicated that the aircraft had spun completely round at the end of its run (Paul Strudwick). This Bf 109E-4 is one of the two German aircraft that flew in the battle and which still exist today — see chapter on The Survivors. The wing panel** *below* **from 1190 can be seen at Brenzett museum.**

4/JG27

Messerschmitt Bf 109E-1 (6306). Damaged by fighters during escort sortie over southern England and forced-landed at Pelsham House, Peasmarsh, Sussex 1.30 p.m. Uffz. Hammer captured. Aircraft 7+ a write-off.

6/JG27

Messerschmitt Bf 109E-1 (3859). Shot down by fighters during bomber escort sortie and crashed at Holmans Grove, Grayswood, near Haslemere 4.40 p.m. Lt. Schmidt baled out and captured. Aircraft 3+ a write-off.
Site investigated by the Wealden Aviation Archaeological Group in 1977. Few small pieces salvaged. Relics also held by the Southern Area Wartime Aircraft Preservation Society.

7/JG27

Messerschmitt Bf 109E-1 (4851). Overturned attempting forced-landing near Queen Anne's Gate, Windsor Great Park following combat with fighters during bomber escort sortie 5.00 p.m. Oblt. Fischer captured unhurt. Aircraft 9+ a write-off.

7/JG51

Messerschmitt Bf 109E-4 (1544). Crash-landed at Clairmarais aerodrome with combat damage following sortie over the Channel. Pilot unhurt. Aircraft 50% damaged.

Messerschmitt Bf 109E-1 (3391). Shot down in combat with fighters and crashed on Kennards Farm, Leigh, near Tonbridge 1.45 p.m. Flgr. Hubel killed. Aircraft a write-off.
Site excavated by the Halstead War Museum. Relics also held by the Kent Battle of Britain Museum and Steve Vizard.

Messerschmitt Bf 109E-1 (4856). Crashed and burned out at Nutfield, Surrey 1.45 p.m. following combat with RAF fighters. Uffz. Limpert killed. Aircraft a write-off.

9/JG51

Messerschmitt Bf 109E-4 (1331). Ditched in the Channel out of fuel following combat with fighters over southern England. Lt. Canier killed. Aircraft lost.

1/JG52

Messerschmitt Bf 109E-1 (1391). Shot down into the Channel off Newhaven during fighter combat 4.00 p.m. Lt. Kirchner captured. Aircraft lost.

3/JG52

Messerscmitt Bf 109E-4 (1262). Lost control during combat with RAF fighters during freelance sortie over Sussex 2.00 p.m. Abandoned aircraft crashed on Clayton Farm, Peasmarsh. Uffz. Wolff baled out and captured. Aircraft 14+ a write-off.

Site excavated by the Wealden Aviation Archaeological Group 1975. Propeller boss and remains of shattered Daimler-Benz DB 601 engine unearthed.

Messerschmitt Bf 109E-4 (3417). Shot down by fighters during bomber escort sortie over the Thames Estuary. Belly-landed outside Detling aerodrome 2.00 p.m. Gefr. Mummert captured unhurt. Aircraft 2+ a write-off.

First-aid kit and wing leading edge panel liberated' from this aircraft in 1940 donated to the Kent Battle of Britain Museum.

6/JG52

Messerschmitt Bf 109E-1 (3192). Shot down during sortie over southern England and crashed in flames near Kingswood Church, Dorking, Surrey 2.00 p.m. Gefr. Strasser baled out seriously wounded. Aircraft a write-off.

3/JG53

Messerschmitt Bf 109E-4 (1325). Forced-landed, fuel exhausted at Langley, near Eastbourne 2.05 p.m. following bomber escort sortie and combat with RAF fighters. Fw. Scholz captured unhurt. Aircraft 13+ a write-off.

Above: **Oberleutnant Karl Fischer of 7/JG27 was flying a bomber escort mission over London on September 30 when he tangled with RAF fighters — not two Anson trainers as has so often previously, yet erroneously, been described. In attempting a forced-landing near Queen Anne's Gate in Windsor Great Park, his Messerschmitt Bf 109E-1 overturned (Fox Photos).** *Below:* **Forty years later, a change of season reveals the houses along the north-western boundary of the park.**

II/JG53

Messerschmitt Bf 109E-1 (2693). Shot down in the Channel during combat with fighters. Pilot rescued unhurt by Seenotdienst. Aircraft lost.

Messerschmitt Bf 109E-1 (6384). Shot down into the Channel off Beachy Head during combat with fighters during bomber escort sortie 1.50 p.m. Uffz. Vogel captured unhurt. Aircraft 3+ lost.

7/JG53

Messerschmitt Bf 109E-1 (5175). Crash-landed near Strood, near Rochester, Kent 2.00 p.m. severely damaged in combat with fighters during escort sortie. Uffz. Poschenrieder captured seriously injured. Aircraft 12+1 a write-off.

7/JG54

Messerschmitt Bf 109E-1 (6050). Engine damaged by fighters during bomber escort sortie and forced-landed at Rock House Banks, near Normans Bay, Bexhill, Sussex 1.56 p.m. Uffz. Marcke captured. Aircraft 4+ a write-off.

9/JG54

Messerschmitt Bf 109E-4 (5116). Crashed and burned out on Dairy Farm, Golden Green, east of Tonbridge, Kent 1.45 p.m. following combat with fighters. Uffz. Braatz killed. Aircraft 6+ a write-off.

Surface fragments in Vizard collection.

4/KG2

Dornier Do 17Z-2 (3420). Forced-landed at Orleans following combat sortie over southern England. No crew casualties. Aircraft U5+ EM 15% damaged.

8/KG2

Dornier Do 17Z (2861). Crashed at Bertin-court following bombing sortie over England. Cause unknown but probably combat damage. Lt. Scheffel and three NCOs killed. Aircraft U5+ BS a write-off.

Stab III/KG3

Dornier Do 17Z-2 (3360). Crash-landed at St. Omer due to combat damage following bombing sortie over southern England. No crew casualties. Aircraft 5K+AD 50% damaged.

7/KG3

Dornier Do 17Z-3 (2822). Crash-landed near Boulogne with combat damage. Crew unhurt. Aircraft 5K+GR a write-off.

8/KG3

Dornier Do 17Z-3 (4227). Failed to return from bombing sortie over southern England and presumed shot down by fighters. Uffz. Schonn, Uffz. Schroff, Fw. Bauer, Fw. Salomo and Fw. Schierling all missing. Aircraft 5K+HR lost.

3/KG30

Junkers Ju 88A (0233). Crashed at Gilze-Rijen on return from combat sortie. Cause unknown but probably combat damage. Four NCOs killed. Aircraft 4D+DL a write-off.

II/KG30

Junkers Ju 88A-1 (0280). Damaged by fighters during bombing sortie over southern England and returned to Gilze-Rijen with two NCOs wounded. Aircraft 4D+FL 15% damaged.

Junkers Ju 88A-1 (6074). Forced-landed at Gilze-Rijen aerodrome due to combat damage. Crew unhurt. Aircraft 4D+AM 40% damaged.

Junkers Ju 88A-1 (0164). Returned to base damaged by fighters over southern England. No crew casualties. Aircraft 4D+GM repairable.

5/KG30

Junkers Ju 88A-1 (4030). Crash-landed at Lombartzyde with combat damage following bombing sortie to England. Crew unhurt. Aircraft 4D+GK 50% damaged.

III/KG30

Junkers Ju 88A-1 (3067). Failed to return from bombing sortie over England. Exact fate unknown. Oblt. Richter, Uffz. Fuchs and Fw. Laege missing. Aircraft 4D+BZ a write-off.

Junkers Ju 88A-1 (5062). Crashed and burned out near Kamenz during combat sortie. Exact cause unknown but possibly combat damage. Four NCOs killed. Aircraft 4D+AT a write-off.

I/KG51

Junkers Ju 88A-1 (2063). Shot down by fighters during bombing sortie to London. Crashed in sea three miles off Beachy Head 4.22 p.m. Fw. Paczinski, Gefr. Penka and Gefr. Roppert killed. Gefr. Durrschmidt missing. Aircraft 9K+DH lost.

In spite of the fearsome cockpit damage, Fischer was captured unhurt (Fox Photos).

Left: On October 3, Fischer's aircraft, looking decidedly the worse for wear, was put on display in Windsor's high street to help raise contributions for the Borough's Spitfire Fund (Topical Press). *Right:* Flower tubs mark the spot in Park Street today.

6/KG53

Heinkel He 111H-3 (3312). Crash-landed at Vendeville aerodrome following operational sortie over England. No crew casualties. Aircraft A1+ER 60% damaged.

I/KG54

Junkers Ju 88A-1 (7090). Crashed in the Channel on return flight from bombing mission over southern England due to combat damage. Crew rescued from sea by Seenot-dienst. Aircraft lost.

Stab KG55

Heinkel He 111P-2 (2836). Shot down by fighters and crashed in the Channel during bombing mission to Yeovil. Uffz. Barabas killed. Major Kuehl, Uffz. Steglich, Gefr. Feichtmair and Gefr. Becker rescued by Seenotdienst. Aircraft G1+JA lost.

I/KG55

Heinkel He 111P-2 (1616). Failed to return from bombing sortie over the Channel and presumed shot down by fighters into the sea. Oblt. Moessner, Uffz. Reiter, Uffz. Trenkmann, Gefr. Thuemel and Flgr. Geist all missing. Aircraft G1+AL lost.

II/KG55

Heinkel He 111P-2 (1545). Shot down by fighters into the Channel during bombing sortie to Yeovil. Uffz. Kuebler killed. Uffz. Eggert, Obergefr. Geyer, Gefr. Biedermann and Gefr. Roesel all missing. Aircraft G1+AM a write-off.

Heinkel He 111P-2 (2643). Shot down by fighters during bombing sortie over Yeovil. Obergefr. Schocke killed. Oberfw. Guttler, Gefr. Bauer, Gefr. Rudeck and Gefr. Strauss missing. Aircraft G1+CM a write-off.

Stab I/KG77

Junkers Ju 88A-1 (4050). Damaged in landing accident at Chamby aerodrome. Cause not stated. No crew casualties. Aircraft 3Z+DB 15% damaged.

2/KG77

Junkers Ju 88A-1 (2142). Damaged by AA fire and fighter attack during bombing sortie to London. Forced-landed on Gatwick Race Course 4.45 p.m. Uffz. Klasing killed. Oblt. Oeser, Gefr. Huelsmann and Fw. Goerke captured wounded. Aircraft 3Z+DK a write-off.

III/LG1

Junkers Ju 88A-1 (6061). Forced-landed at Illesheim during routine domestic flight. Cause not stated. Crew unhurt. Aircraft 20% damaged.

12/LG1

Junkers Ju 87B-1 (0217). Suffered engine failure during local flight and crashed near Antricourt. One NCO baled out too low and killed. Aircraft L1+JW a write-off.

II/ZG26

Messerschmitt Bf 110D/O. Returned to base severely damaged in fighter combat over the Channel. Two NCOs wounded. Aircraft a write-off.

Relics of a Bf 109E of 7/JG51 (3391) based at Wissant which crashed at Kennard's Farm at Leigh in Kent on the last day of September and now in Steve Vizard's collection. These include a fragment of the DB 601 engine containing the inlet and exhaust valves and the Henschel Flugzeugwerk engine badge.

'Cor, look at that!' A Junkers Ju 88 of 2/KG77 on public display at Primrose Hill, London on October 10, 1940 with its circle of appreciative, perennial schoolboys. KG77 re-entered the battle early in September 1940 and by the end of the month had suffered heavy casualties. This particular aircraft forced-landed on Gatwick Race Course on September 30 (Central Press).

Tuesday, October 1

The 'Buzzards' of Wissant. The fighter experten of No. 1 Staffel of Werner Moelders JG51 pose for a group photograph at their French base in 1940. Unteroffizier Garnith stands centre front (Lashenden Air Warfare Museum).

Reserve Luftflotten 3

Junkers Ju 88A-1 (7159). Crashed near Nancy following engine failure on routine domestic flight. One NCO killed, another injured. Aircraft a write-off.

Korpsfuehrungskette X Fliegerkorps

Heinkel He 111H-4 (3257). Returned to base severely damaged by AA fire following sortie over east coast of Scotland. Two NCOs wounded. Aircraft P4+ BA 50% damaged.

5/196

Arado Ar 196. Four aircraft destroyed by storm in Cherbourg harbour. No personnel losses. All four aircraft written-off.

4/JG26

Messerschmitt Bf 109E-1. Shot down in combat with RAF fighters over the Sussex coast 2.30 p.m. Dived vertically into Balmer Down, Falmer and exploded. Uffz. Bluder killed. Aircraft a write-off.
Site investigated by the Wealden Aviation Archaeological Group in 1973 and surface fragments discovered.

1/JG51

Messerschmitt Bf 109E-4 (5814). Shot down by Flying Officer Lovell of No. 41 Squadron in action over Ashford 4.50 p.m. Crashed at Chequers, Shadoxhurst. Uffz. Garnith baled out and captured. Aircraft 9+ a write-off.
Shattered Daimler-Benz DB 601 engine recovered by the Lashenden Air Warfare Museum which presented part to the pilot's widow traced in Munich. Site subsequently investigated by members of the Wealden Aviation Archaeological Group who discovered engine badge on surface.

1/KG2

Dornier Do 17Z (1177). Crashed at Mons-au-Chausee during routine domestic flight. Cause not stated. Two NCOs killed. Aircraft U5+ BH a write-off.

Above: The Bf 109 power plant was a Daimler Benz DB 601 12-cylinder, inverted V engine developing 1,150 h.p. This is the DB 601 from Unteroffizier Edward Garnith's aircraft shot down on the afternoon of October 1 and recovered by the Lashenden Air Warfare Museum from Shadoxhurst. *Below:* The Wealden group subsequently investigated the crash site and found this engine badge.

9/KG30

Junkers Ju 88A-1 (5343). Attacked by night fighter during operational sortie and crashed near Kloppenburg. Crew baled out unhurt. Aircraft 4K+ FZ a write-off.

II/KG51

Junkers Ju 88A-1 (3085). Crashed and burned out on take-off from Corbeil. Exact cause not stated. Oblt. Heinisch and three NCOs killed. Aircraft a write-off.

II/KG53

Heinkel He 111H-2 (5546). Believed shot down by AA fire during night sortie over England. Uffz. Wagner, Uffz. Konig, Gefr. Moehlenhoff, Gefr. Guenther and Gefr. Petroll all missing. Aircraft A1+ LN lost.

I/LG1

Junkers Ju 88A-1 (2154). Crashed on take-off from Chateaudun due to engine failure. Crew unhurt. Aircraft 20% damaged.

I/ZG26

Messerschmitt Bf 110D (4212). Shot down into the Channel during combat with fighters off Swanage. Lt. Scharnhost and one NCO both killed. Aircraft lost.

Wednesday, October 2

Seenotflugkdo. 4

Heinkel He 59 (1510). Forced-landed on sea in known minefield area (PQ8166-8241) during operational sortie. Cause unknown. Crew took to dinghy which triggered a mine. Lt. Barbinger killed. Oberfw. Niess, Fw. Horr and Gefr. Brandt missing. Aircraft NO+FU lost.

1/506

Heinkel He 115 (3266). Hit by AA fire and attacked by fighters during armed reconnaissance sortie. Landed on sea off Kinnairds Head 8.00 p.m. Oblt. Lenz, Uffz. Schweetke and Obergefr. Neuberg rescued from dinghy and all captured unhurt. Aircraft S4+AH lost.

3/906

Heinkel He 115 (2095). Crashed on landing at Schellingwoude following operational sortie. Cause not stated. Oblt. zur See Guenther killed. Aircraft 8L+DL lost.

3(H)/21

Henschel Hs 126B (4029). Crash-landed at Moerbecke during local flight, cause not stated. Crew unhurt. Aircraft a write-off.

6/JG27

Messerschmitt Bf 109E-1 (6351). Crashed on landing at Bonningues following combat sortie. Pilot unhurt. Aircraft 60% damaged.

Stab III/JG53

Messerschmitt Bf 109E-1 (6291). Crashed on Limpsfield Common, near Oxted 10.00 a.m. during combat with RAF fighters. Shot down by Pilot Officer Kendal of No. 66 Squadron. Oblt. Radlick (Staffel Kapitan) baled out but parachute failed. Aircraft a write-off.
Control column in the Vizard collection

Left: **Just a piece of rusted metal on a Lincolnshire beach . . . or was it? No doubt overlooked by many post-war visitors to Chapel St. Leonards, this is the centre-section of Heinkel No. 3554 of 1/KG53 which was ditched by its pilot on the beach on October 2, 1940. However, it can no longer be seen as the Royal Navy deemed it worthy of demolition in 1973 (Mike Hodgson).** *Right:* **Members of the Lincolnshire Aircraft Preservation Society recovered the Junkers Jumo engines in 1968 (T. Walsh).** *Below:* **This example, beautifully restored, is now displayed at the Lincolnshire Air Museum at Tattershall (C. H. Clover).**

8/JG53

Messerschmitt Bf 109E-4 (5901). Shot down by fighters in action over north Kent. Crash-landed at Addelsted Farm, East Peckham 10.15 a.m. Oblt. Fiel captured unhurt. Aircraft 7+1 a write-off.

Messerschmitt Bf 109E-4 (5374). Crashed at Sutherland Avenue, Biggin Hill during fighter combat over southern outskirts of London 10.00 a.m. Oblt. Stronk killed. Aircraft 4+1 a write-off.

Messerschmitt Bf 109E-1 (6370). Attacked by RAF fighters during bomber escort mission over London. Forced-landed on Forge Farm, near Goudhurst 10.00 a.m. Gefr. Zag captured. Aircraft 3+1 a write-off.

Stab KG2

Dornier Do 17Z (3423). Shot down by Hurricanes following bombing and strafing attack on Colchester. Forced-landed near Earl Soham 10.20 a.m. Oblt. Langer (Staffel Kapitan), Oblt. Eitze, Uffz. Deidel and Uffz. Bellmann captured unhurt. Aircraft U5+FA a write-off.

4/KG2

Dornier Do 17Z-3 (2659). Damaged by AA fire during operations over England. Returned to France and abandoned over Paris. Crew baled out unhurt. Aircraft U5+DM a write-off.

9/KG3

Dornier Do 17Z-2 (3270). Crashed at Le Culot following operational sortie. Cause unknown. Lt. Schulze and three NCOs killed. Aircraft 5K+CT a write-off.

8/KG4

Junkers Ju 88A-5 (8128). Lost bearings during general reconnaissance sortie and forced-landed at West Marsh Point, near Brightlingsea 6.10 a.m. when fuel run out. Uffz. Maierhofer, Obergefr. Preughaus, Obergefr. Hansmeier and Obergefr. Scholz all captured unhurt. Aircraft 5J+US a write-off.

9/KG4

Junkers Ju 88A-5 (6138). Crashed on landing at Schiphol aerodrome following operations over England. Cause not stated. Crew unhurt. Aircraft 40% damaged.

1/KG53

Heinkel He 111H-5 (3554). Shot down by Pilot Officer Smith of No. 151 Squadron during reconnaissance sortie and ditched in sea off Chapel St. Leonards 6.00 p.m. Oblt. Seidel, Oberfw. Ziller, Oberfw. Zickler, Oberfw. Weidner and Uffz. Kreuzer captured unhurt. Aircraft A1+CH a write-off.

Both engines recovered September 1967 by the Lincolnshire Aviation Society. One currently held by the Lincolnshire Air Museum, Tattershall, the other being displayed by Newark Air Museum. Remains of this wreck subsequently blown up by Royal Navy, March 1973.

Heinkel He 111H-3 (3334). Lost bearings during operational sortie and finally abandoned over Nancy. Crew baled out unhurt. Aircraft A1+DB a write-off.

6/KG53

Heinkel He 111H-2 (2635). Crashed on landing at Vendeville following operational sortie. Cause not stated. Crew unhurt. Aircraft A1+CP 10% damaged.

Ergaengzungs Staffel KG77

Dornier Do 17 (2427). Crashed in the Eifel mountains during routine training flight in deteriorating weather conditions and fog. Six NCOs all killed. Aircraft 3Z+FD a write-off.

1/KGr.126

Heinkel He 111H-4 (6948). Shot down by fighters during sortie over the Bristol Channel and crashed near Newquay. Lt. zur See Gruenewald and Uffz. Plenert killed. Lt. Schreyer, Uffz. Greeven and Gefr. Weger missing. Aircraft 1T+KH a write-off.

Hit by ground fire during a bombing attack on Hatfield aerodrome on October 3, this Junkers Ju 88 of I/KG77 staggered five miles from the target area before crash-landing in flames at Eastend Green Farm near Hertingfordbury. The crew of four were captured by farm hands (Planet News).

7(F)/LG2

Messerschmitt Bf 110C-5 (2263). Mid-air collision during domestic flight. Crashed near Brussels. Oblt. Eckert and one NCO killed. Aircraft L2+DR a write-off.

Messerschmitt Bf 110 (2188). Abandoned over Brussels following collision with Oblt. Eckert's aircraft. Crew baled out unhurt. Aircraft L2+FK a write-off.

Thursday, October 3

Kuestenflieger Gruppe 606

Dornier Do 17Z (3491). Believed brought down by AA fire during mission over England at night. Crashed in sea off Cornwall. Lt. zur See Schmidt and Obgefr. Dorfschmidt both killed. Fw. Wilm and Uffz. Seidenstahl missing. Aircraft 7T+EL a write-off.

Dornier Do 17Z (2530). Damaged in landing at Brest-Sued aerodrome after routine local flight. Cause not stated. Crew unhurt. Aircraft 20% damaged.

Wettererkundungs Staffel Ob.d.L.

Dornier Do 17Z-2 (2547). Attacked by fighters during weather reconnaissance sortie over the North Sea (PQ0070) and crashed on landing. Reg. Rat. a. Kr. Heinrich wounded. Aircraft T5+IU a write-off.

1(F)/122

Junkers Ju 88A-1 (0328). Failed to return from reconnaissance sortie over the east coast of England and believed shot down in sea by fighters. Oberfw. Spanke, Fw. Peters, Oberfw. Adler and Uffz. Webnitz missing. Aircraft F6+BH lost.

I/KG1

Heinkel He 111H (6923). Crashed on take-off from Montdidier. Cause not stated. Oblt. Goehler and three NCOs killed. Aircraft a write-off.

Heinkel He 111H (6824). Damaged in take-off accident at Montidier. Crew unhurt. Aircraft 60% damaged.

III/KG1

Junkers Ju 88A-1 (6107). Crashed on landing at Handorf aerodrome following routine domestic flight. Cause not stated. Crew unhurt. Aircraft V4+BT 20% damaged.

1/KG2

Dornier Do 17Z-2 (2579). Lost bearings during operational sortie and forced-landed when fuel exhausted. Crew unhurt. Aircraft U5+DH 40% damaged.

As Special Constable 103 attached to 'B' Division, Hertford Constabulary, John Mousley attended the scene of the crash in 1940 as a temporary guard until the army took over. Here on the exact spot on November 24, 1979 he describes events to Wilf Nicoll.

2/KG2

Dornier Do 17Z-3 (2638). Crashed near Marquise following mechanical failure. One NCO killed and two more injured. Aircraft U5+ AK a write-off.

5/KG30

Junkers Ju 88A-5 (4169). Failed to return from operational sortie over England. Exact circumstances unknown. Fw. Bunker killed. Uffz. Brandmueller, Gefr. Gerard and Gefr. Balt missing. Aircraft 4D+ FK lost.

7/KG30

Junkers Ju 88A-1 (7024). Both engines failed during operational sortie. Crashed in sea off Schouwen Island. Oblt. Bieger, Fw. Heilmeier, Gefr. Bauer and Gefr. Herndeck all killed. Aircraft 4D+ AR lost.

I/KG55

Heinkel He 111H (2749). Damaged by AA fire during sortie over England and crashed at Le Havre. Crew unhurt. Aircraft a write-off.

I/KG77

Junkers Ju 88A-1 (4136). Shot down by ground defences during bombing raid on de Havilland's factory adjoining Hatfield aerodrome. Crash-landed in flames on East-end Green Farm, north of Hertingfordbury and burned out 11.40 a.m. Oblt. Fiebig, Oberfw. Goebel, Fw. Ruthof and Uffz. Seifert all captured unhurt. Aircraft 3Z+ BB a write-off.

Friday, October 4

Seenotflugkdo. 4

Heinkel He 59 (2602). Forced-landed on sea during rescue mission and capsized when taken in tow. Crew taken off unhurt. Aircraft NE+ UX lost.

Kuestenflieger Gruppe 606

Dornier Do 17Z-3 (3617). Failed to return from operational sortie over England at night. Uffz. Fuchs killed. Lt. zur See Vollbrecht, Uffz. von Postel and Uffz. David missing. Aircraft 7T+ CH lost.

II/JG51

Messerschmitt Bf 109E-3 (991). Crashed on landing from routine domestic flight. Cause not stated. Pilot unhurt. Aircraft 15% damaged.

II/KG1

Heinkel He 111-2 (5586). Believed hit by AA fire during nuisance raid over southern England. Crashed at Mountfield, near Battle, Sussex 10.00 p.m. Uffz. Hildebrand, Uffz. Bauer and Gefr. Tschop killed. Gefr. Zuckriegel baled out and captured. Aircraft V4+ FW a write-off.

II/KG2

Dornier Do 17Z (4201). Crashed on landing at Bouly aerodrome following operations. Crew unhurt. Aircraft U5+ EP a write-off.

5/KG3

Dornier Do 17Z-2 (3343). Attacked by own fighters during domestic flight over the Dutch coast and crash-landed with three NCOs wounded. Aircraft 5K+ KN a write-off.

I/KG26

Heinkel He 111H-3 (5609). Shot down by fighters over the North Sea off Suffolk coast. Lt. Zingel, Uffz. Winter, Uffz. Reinelt and Uffz. Blasius all killed. Aircraft 1H+ EL a write-off.

I/KG51

Junkers Ju 88A-1 (6084). Damaged landing on burst tyre at Villaroche aerodrome. No crew casualties. Aircraft 30% damaged.

I/KG54

Junkers Ju 88A-1 (6101). Severely damaged in fighter attack during sortie across the Channel and crash-landed at Le Havre. Crew unhurt. Aircraft 50% damaged.

Stab KG76

Dornier DO 17Z (2610). Caught in deteriorating weather conditions and crashed at St. Pol when fuel exhausted. Crew unhurt. Aircraft a write-off.

II/KG76

Junkers Ju 88A-1 (6156). Shot down by AA fire during bombing sortie over London. Crashed and exploded at Meesons Lane, Belmont Castle, Grays, Essex 4.50 p.m. Oblt. Holzer, Uffz. Deiseroth, Fw. Kolb and Gefr. Graf all killed. Aircraft F1+ LP a write-off.
Site investigated by the Essex Historical Aircraft Society who recovered remains of shattered airframe, engine plate and a small pen knife.

4/KG76

Junkers Ju 88A-1 (8076). Damaged by ground fire during sortie over England. Crash-landed near Abbeville. Fw. Steindl wounded. Aircraft a write-off.

Junkers Ju 88A-1. Forced-landed Calais damaged by ground defences during sortie over England. Oberfw. Volke wounded. Aircraft a write-off.

III/KG76

Dornier Do 17Z (1136). Crashed attempting landing near Pontoise following night sortie over London. Oblt. Altenmueller, Oberfw. Zankl, Uffz. Schmelzle and Uffz. Hoffmann all killed. Aircraft a write-off.

Dornier Do 17Z (2887). Crashed on landing at Cormeilles in bad weather. Crew unhurt. Aircraft 50% damaged.

Dornier Do 17Z (2888). Crashed at Haudivilliers due to mechanical failure during routine domestic flight. Lt. Meister killed. Three NCOs wounded. Aircraft a write-off.

I/KG77

Junkers Ju 88A-1 (3160). Shot down into the sea off Southwold 10.10 a.m. by Squadron Leader Tuck of No. 257 Squadron during operational sortie over east coast of England. Uffz. Herold killed. Stabfw. Hartmann, Obergefr. Hackmann and Gefr. Einbrick missing. Aircraft 3Z+ HL lost.
Complete starboard undercarriage assembly and fully inflated tyre recovered from the beach at Easton Bavents by the Norfolk and Suffolk Aviation Museum.

1/KGr.100

Heinkel He 111H-3 (6831). Failed to return from operations over England at night. Believed brought down by AA fire. Uffz. Stock, Uffz. Krische, Fw. Tomuschat and Gefr. Perkel all missing. Aircraft 6N+ FH lost.

I/LG1

Junkers Ju 88A-1 (6113). Forced-landed at St. Valery-en-Caux with damage from AA fire sustained in sortie over England. Crew unhurt. Aircraft 40% damaged.

II/LG1

Junkers Ju 88A-1 (6165). Damaged during operations over England and forced-landed at Berck-sur-Mer with one NCO wounded. Aircraft L1+ EM 45% damaged.

Junkers Ju 88A-1 (6116). Shot down by fighters during action over the Channel off Dungeness. Crashed in sea. Gefr. Jahn and Gefr. Schoeffmann both killed. Uffz. Kross and Uffz. Kirchbaur missing. Aircraft L1+ EP lost.

Stab StG 3

Dornier Do 17Z (2832). Crashed on landing at Dinard following routine domestic flight. Cause not stated. No crew casualties. Aircraft 40% damaged.

For nearly forty years this starboard undercarriage leg, complete with inflated tyre, lay on the beach at Easton Bavents in Suffolk. It was recovered for display by members of the Norfolk and Suffolk Aviation Museum who identified it as coming from a Ju 88A-1, No. 3160, which had been shot down by Squadron Leader Stanford Tuck on October 4. The aircraft exploded over Southwold, the main part of the aircraft falling into the sea just off-shore (Bob Collis).

Saturday, October 5

4(H)/31

Henschel Hs 126 (3423). Attacked by RAF fighters during reconnaissance sortie over the Channel and crash-landed near Calais. Lt. Klaeden baled out and captured. One other NCO wounded. Aircraft 5D+ FM a write-off.

1/Erprobungs Gruppe 210

Messerschmitt Bf 110D/O (3382). Shot down in combat with fighters during sortie over south-east England. Oblt. Weimann (Gruppe Kommandeur) and Uffz. Huebner missing. Aircraft S9+ FH lost.

Messerschmitt Bf 110D-3 (3383). Crashed at Millbank Place near Ashford 11.30 a.m. during fighter combat over England. Fw. Duensnig and Fw. Keppitsch both killed. Aircraft S9+ GH a write-off.

Messerschmitt Bf 110D/O (3598). Forced-landed at Calais due to combat damage with one NCO wounded. Aircraft S9+ EH 15% damaged.

2/Erprobungs Gruppe 210

Messerschmitt Bf 110C-2 (4209). Forced-landed at Calais-Marck following fighter combat over southern England. One NCO wounded. Aircraft S9+ EK 40% damaged.

1/JG3

Messerschmitt Bf 109E-1 (4865). Shot down in combat with fighters and crashed and burned out at Runsell Farm, Bethersden 12.30 p.m. Fw. von Herwarth-Bittenfeld baled out wounded and badly burned and taken prisoner. Aircraft 2+ a write-off.
Tail wheel in Steve Vizard collection.

III/JG3

Messerschmitt Bf 109E-4 (3554). Crashed on landing at St. Inglevert following combat mission. Pilot unhurt. Aircraft 20% damaged.

9/JG3

Messerschmitt Bf 109E-4 (3876). Shot down by fighters during combat over the Channel. Crashed in sea. Pilot rescued by Seenotdienst. Aircraft lost.

5/JG26

Messerschmitt Bf 109E-4 (5384). Crashed on landing at Marquise-West following routine local flight. Cause not stated. Gefr. Muller killed. Aircraft a write-off.

Stab I/JG51

Messerschmitt Bf 109E-4 (4102). Damaged in combat with enemy fighters and forced-landed at Pihen aerodrome. Pilot unhurt. Aircraft 25% damaged.

3/JG51

Messerschmitt Bf 109E-4 (3502). Forced-landed at St. Omer due to engine failure during routine domestic flight. Pilot unhurt. Aircraft 30% damaged.

8/JG51

Messerschmitt Bf 109E-4 (3883). Ran out of fuel during operational sortie and forced-landed at Audembert. Pilot unhurt. Aircraft 30% damaged.

A complete German aircraft wheel and tyre found by Steve Vizard on Runsell Farm, Bethesden. It was there that Feldwebel von Herwarth-Bittenfeld was shot down on October 5, the tail wheel from his Bf 109 providing a handy acoutrement on the farmer's wheelbarrow!

1/JG53

Messerschmitt Bf 109E-4 (1804). Shot down by No. 501 Squadron Hurricanes during freelance mission over Kent and belly-landed near Frith Farm, west of Aldington 11.45 a.m. Uffz. Gehsla captured slightly wounded. Aircraft 10+ a write-off.

Messerschmitt Bf 109E-4 (1564). Crashed and burned out on Sheerlands Farm, Pluckley following combat with No. 501 Squadron Hurricanes 11.40 a.m. Lt. Zeis baled out and captured unhurt. Aircraft 3+ a write-off.

7/JG53

Messerschmitt Bf 109E-4 (5372). Severely damaged in combat over southern Kent and abandoned over the Channel during return flight. Crashed in sea off Cap Gris-Nez. Pilot baled out unhurt. Aircraft lost.

2/JG77

Messerschmitt Bf 109E-1 (4073). Shot down by fighters in combat over the Channel and crashed in sea. Pilot baled out wounded and rescued by Seenotdienst. Aircraft a write-off.

Ergaenzungs Staffel KG1

Heinkel He 111H-1 (2316). Forced-landed near Goldberg due to engine failure during routine domestic flight. Crew unhurt. Aircraft 30% damaged.

1/KG2

Dornier Do 17Z-2 (1212). Became lost during operational sortie and crashed near Krefeld with three NCOs injured. Aircraft U5+ GH a write-off.

2/KG3

Dornier Do 17Z-2 (2537). Crashed and burned out at Hamme. Cause unknown. Lt. Berghahn and three NCOs killed. Aircraft 5K+ AK a write-off.

1/KG26

Heinkel He 111H-3 (6933). Forced-landed at Amiens following operational sortie, crew unhurt. Aircraft 25% damaged.

7/KG30

Junkers Ju 88A-4 (4040). Damaged in landing at Eindhoven following combat sortie. Crew unharmed. Aircraft 4D+ ER 20% damaged.

4/KG30

Junkers Ju 88A-5 (8045). Crashed and exploded at Netherstead, near Colmworth 0.55 a.m. during night sortie over England. Cause unknown. Fw. Koschella, Fw. Wilhenig and Uffz. Bendarent all killed. Aircraft 4D+ HM a write-off.
Major recovery by the London Air Museum. Both Junkers Jumo engines excavated together with undercarriage legs and tyres, large section of compressed airframe, eight oxygen bottles, one parachute and a first-aid kit.

1/KG77

Junkers Ju 88A-1 (2160). Damaged by AA fire during operational sortie and forced-landed at Ligescourt. One NCO killed and another wounded. Aircraft 50% damaged.

KGr.806

Junkers Ju 88A-1 (7138). Forced-landed at Le Havre with combat damage. One NCO killed. Aircraft 50% damaged.

II/LG1

Junkers Ju 88A-1 (4134). Shot down in combat with RAF fighters during sortie over the Channel. Lt. Hoffmann, Gefr. Neuenberg, Gefr. Steiner and Uffz. Worbanger all killed. Aircraft L1+JN a write-off.

6/LG2

Messerschmitt Bf 109E-4 (3726). Engine damaged by fighter attack during free-lance fighter mission. Forced-landed on Pelsham Farm, Peasmarsh 11.30 a.m. Fw. Pankratz captured wounded. Aircraft a write-off.

Sunday, October 6

1(F)/123

Junkers Ju 88A-1 (383). Damaged landing on burst tyre at Buc aerodrome after operational sortie. No crew casualties. Aircraft 4U+KH 30% damaged.

3/KG1

Junkers Ju 88A-1 (3220). Crashed on take-off from Muenster-Handorf aerodrome on routine domestic flight. Cause not stated. Crew unhurt. Aircraft 45% damaged.

10/KG2

Dornier Do 17Z (2664). Crashed near Osnabruck due to mechanical failure during local flight. Lt. Obermayer and three NCOs wounded. Aircraft U5+AZ a write-off.

KG3

Dornier Do 17Z-3. Failed to return from operational sortie over England. Exact cause unknown. Four NCOs missing. Aircraft lost.

II/KG4

Heinkel He 111P-4 (2932). Damaged in landing accident at Soesterberg. Cause not stated. Crew unhurt. Aircraft 5J+FN 40% damaged.

5/KG4

Heinkel He 111P-4 (2970). Landing accident at Soesterberg. Cause not reported. Crew unhurt. Aircraft 5J+JN 20% damaged.

I/KG27

Heinkel He 111P (1520). Crashed and burned out at Tours following operational sortie. Oblt. Mahnke and four NCOs killed. Aircraft a write-off.

III/KG30

Junkers Ju 88A-1 (2111). Damaged in landing at Eindhoven following operational sortie. No crew casualties. Aircraft 4D+GR 30% damaged.

9/KG30

Junkers Ju 88A-1 (176). Failed to return from operations over England and believed shot down by AA fire. Gefr. Boebel killed. Oberfw. Ortlepp, Uffz. Roeder and Uffz. Holzmeier missing. Aircraft 4D+DT lost.

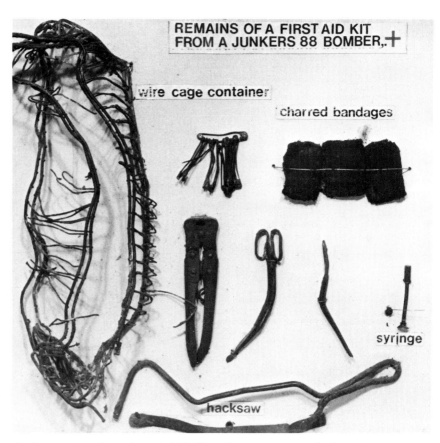

REMAINS OF A FIRST AID KIT FROM A JUNKERS 88 BOMBER.

wire cage container

charred bandages

syringe

hacksaw

The items on this display board held by Tony Graves once comprised the first-aid kit from a German bomber. They were recovered from the crash site of the Ju 88A-5 No. 8045 4D+HM, which came down at Nethertstead on October 5.

I/KG54

Junkers Ju 88A-1 (4079). Suffered engine failure during combat sortie and abandoned by crew. Crashed at Les Andelys. No crew casualties. Aircraft a write-off.

7/KG76

Dornier Do 17Z-3 (4221). Shot down by fighters during weather reconnaissance sortie over the Channel. Crashed attempting forced-landing near Mayfield, Sussex 11.05 a.m. Uffz. Wagner killed, Lt. Morr, Uffz. Mroszinsky and Fw. Pohl captured. Aircraft F1+FR a write-off.

II/NJG1

Messerschmitt Bf 110D/O (3174). Crashed at Koenen due to engine catching fire during routine domestic flight. Hptmn. Stillgried (Gruppe Kommandeur) and one NCO killed. Aircraft GO+CC a write-off.

10/NJG1

Messerschmitt Bf 109E-1 (3660). Crashed on take-off at Vlissingen aerodrome. Cause not stated. Pilot unhurt. Aircraft a write-off.

Monday, October 7

Flugbereitsschule Luftflotte 2

Junkers Ju 52 (5890). Damaged in taxi-ing accident at Evere. Crew unhurt. Aircraft 30% damaged.

1/196

Arado Ar 196A-2 (0069). Crashed at Schellingwoude during operational sortie. Cause not stated. Lt. Stelter and one NCO killed. Aircraft TB+BK a write-off.

4(F)/11

Dornier Do 17P (3527). Crashed on take-off at Le Bourget on routine domestic flight. Cause unknown. One NCO killed and two injured. Aircraft 6M+HM a write-off.

5(H)/14

Henschel Hs 126B-1 (4296). Crashed on landing at Vron aerodrome following local flight. Cause not stated. No crew casualties. Aircraft CZ+LK 40% damaged.

5/JG27

Messerschmitt Bf 109E-1 (3665). Shot down by No. 605 Squadron Hurricanes during escort sortie for 4/LG2 fighter-bombers. Forced-landed at Bedgebury Wood near Cranbrook 4.40 p.m. Uffz. Lederer captured wounded. Aircraft 10+ a write-off.

Messerschmitt Bf 109E-1 (3881). Shot down by Flight Lieutenant McKellar of No. 605 Squadron in combat over Sussex. Crashed and burned out on Mayfield Flats, Hadlow Down near Heathfield 5.30 p.m. Uffz. Lege killed. Aircraft a write-off. *Site investigated by the Wealden Aviation Archaeological Group in 1972 and some minor components excavated. Dubious panel in Robertsbridge Aviation Museum also attributed to this aircraft.*

9/JG27

Messerschmitt Bf 109E-4 (751). Shot down by RAF fighters during free-lance fighter sortie over London. Crashed and burned out at Oak Farm, Headcorn 2.00 p.m. Uffz. Bartsch baled out unhurt. Aircraft 13+ a write-off. *Site excavated by Steve Vizard in 1975 and remains of shattered airframe and many minor components found at a depth of 5-6 feet.*

On June 2, 1974, Alan Griggs was fishing off the Kent coast at Dymchurch when his net snagged an underwater obstruction. Not wanting to lose his nets, he buoyed the position and returned to Folkestone. Once back in harbour, Alan remembered that there was a local group of amateur divers run by Jess Henderson so he phoned to ask if they would be willing to try and free the net. Jess Henderson's first reaction was cautious and he asked for its position and the depth of the water. Alan answered that the net was buoyed in seven fathoms (42 feet) two miles off Hythe. Jess thought it was worth a try, so he said that his divers would make the attempt during the following weekend, weather permitting.

The divers met at Brewers Hill at Sandgate where the main road runs close to the beach, making access to the sea much easier. Two inflatable boats took six divers out to the approximate position and eventually the buoy was spotted and the presence of the net confirmed. It was Jess Henderson who was the first to spot the underwater obstruction — he found the net was hooked around the undercarriage legs of a small aircraft.

The divers then contacted the Brenzett Aeronautical Museum with the idea of recovering the aeroplane. Dave Buchanan, the museum's curator, was extremely interested and he suggested that one of his members might accompany the divers on their next visit to the wreck and Len Green, the museum's vice-president, agreed to go out on the following Sunday. The recovery of a connector plug proved the aircraft was German and, although there was much speculation as to the aircraft type, all the museum members were in favour of a Bf 109. However, before the aircraft could be beached, it had to be first dug out of the sand, the job being made more difficult when solid blue clay was discovered six inches down. Digging continued right throughout the summer weekends of 1974 and began again the following year, made much easier by the loan of a Coventry fire pump. The aircraft had now been uncovered down to the level of the cockpit, which was found to be unoccupied. Towards the end of the 1975 season, the divers tried to get a line down under the engine, with a view to anchoring it to the undercarriage to help take the lifting stresses. However the weather turned before this operation was completed and further diving in 1975 had to be abandoned. To add to the disappointment, the winter storms carried away the marker buoy.

Diving recommenced in April 1976 and, by May 9, the wreck had been relocated by drawing a weighted line between two inflatable boats. Now that most of the aircraft had been uncovered, it was possible to see that the whole aircraft was complete on the bed.

THE LARGEST GERMAN BATTLE OF BRITAIN RELIC RECOVERED FROM THE SEA BY THE BRENZETT GROUP

The only missing items seemed to be the tail and main wheels along with the undercarriage fairings and the cockpit canopy. In July, the divers finally managed to get a rope under the engine braced to the undercarriage. However, the first attempt to raise the aircraft was nearly a disaster. It had been planned to lift the aircraft by using oil drums attached with lifting clamps. But when the drums were filled with air the weight of the aircraft was too much and the clamps broke with the result that all nine drums rose to the surface and shot out of the water past the dinghys into the air.

During the weekend of July 10-11, the lifting clamps were replaced with a heavy chain and the divers then managed to fit twenty drums to the engine and the undercarriage. The drums were filled with air, using a portable compressor, although the air ran out before the drums were completely filled. However, enough buoyancy was obtained to pull the aircraft clear of the sand.

Next morning, the drums were successfully re-filled, and the aircraft was raised, unfortunately minus a third of the tail section which broke off and returned to the bottom. The aircraft was then towed towards the shore where it grounded about half-a-mile out. It was now possible to inspect the damage: about a third of the rear fuselage and tail were no longer attached and, worst still, both engine bearers had fractured, allowing the whole engine to tilt upwards.

It was originally planned to beach the aircraft on Saturday, July 24 but, as the aircraft now lay within the danger area of the Hythe ranges, the army agreed that the divers could raise the aircraft on the following day. Ready for the 10.45 a.m. high tide, fifteen drums were attached and the aircraft started to rise. Other divers went back to try and buoy the tail section but their air ran out before they could reach the spot. A large crowd of two to three hundred people had gathered on the beach to see the final beaching at the Redoubt. The aircraft was towed to shore until the propellor blades snagged on the sea bed when they unfortunately broke away from the engine. At this stage, nothing further could be done until the tide turned.

As the water went down the first things to be seen was the undercarriage, followed by the bomb rack and the undersurface of the wings. As more of the aircraft became visible, members of the museum staff realised that the crowd was slowly inching forwards following the tide out and that there would be a rush of souvenir hunters as soon as the aircraft was beached. Meanwhile, the propellor unit had been located and recovered by the divers. By 2.15 p.m. most of the wing surfaces were uncovered and the engine was found to be lying on the sand beside the leading edge of the wings.

At 3.30 p.m., the final lift commenced and, once the aircraft was suspended on the sea wall, the battle with souvenir hunters began and it took the museum team all their time and energy to keep the crowds back. When the aircraft had been loaded onto two lorries the crowds finally gave up and soon dispersed.

The next job was to clean the aircraft and treat it to check further corrosion and at the same time to try to establish its identity. The first clue was the engine number which put the date of its last flight as sometime after July 1940. The airframe number was then found on one of the wing spars and from this it was discovered that the aircraft had been made by a Messerschmitt sub-contractor — Arado. Cross-checking this number with German records indicated that the pilot on its last flight was a Leutnant Erich Meyer of 2/JG51 who ditched off Hythe on October 7, 1940. Contemporary records confirmed that Leutnant Meyer had survived the crash and became a prisoner-of-war and in April 1977, reports from Germany left the museum staff in no doubt that he was the pilot of the aircraft. Peter Cornwell credited Squadron Leader Hogan and Pilot Officer MacKenzie with a joint victory on Meyer's aircraft, both pilots being from No. 501 Squadron. However, Francis Mason specifically gave the claim of Meyer's aircraft to another No. 501 Squadron pilot — Flight Lieutenant Holden. Letters were despatched to the Ministry of Defence and to the Battle of Britain Fighter Association to try and discover if any of these pilots were still alive and, after analysing the combat reports of the three pilots concerned, it was finally established that Meyer was indeed shot down by Hogan and MacKenzie.

GORDON RAMSEY

Unteroffizier Heinrich Bley of 4/LG2 ditched his Bf 109E-4 during a fighter-bomber mission on October 7, escaping with a slight head injury. He was rescued by the Dungeness lifeboat, the 'Charles Cooper Henderson'. Willing helpers steady the lifeboat as it is winched over the shingle bank towards its shed.

In borrowed plimsolls and battledress trousers, Heinrich Bley takes his first steps on a long, long journey home. Escorted to captivity, he carries his Schwimmweste and summer issue flying helmet while the army officer carries his Walther signal pistol and is wearing his belt with holstered side-arm (Fox Photos).

Messerschmitt Bf 109E-1 (6131). Ditched in the Channel during return flight following fighter combat over southern England. Pilot rescued from sea by Seenotdienst. Aircraft lost.

2/JG51

Messerschmitt Bf 109E-4 (5805). Crash-landed at Calais following fighter combat. NCO pilot wounded. Aircraft 65% damaged.

Messerschmitt Bf 109E-4 (4853). Shot down by Squadron Leader Hogan and Flying Officer MacKenzie of No. 501 Squadron during escort mission for Bf 109 Jabos to London. Ditched in sea south of Sandgate 1.58 p.m. Lt. Meyer rescued unhurt and captured. Aircraft lost.
Epic recovery by the Brenzett Aeronautical Museum in 1976. Complete aircraft minus tail section recovered from the seabed and currently subject to careful restoration work. Plans to recover the missing tail section also under consideration.

Messerschmitt Bf 109E-4 (4103). Shot down by RAF fighters during free-lance fighter sweep over southern England. Forced-landed on Doleham Farm, Guestling 11.00 a.m. Oblt. Moelders (Staffel Kapitan) captured unhurt. Aircraft 1+ a write-off.

9/JG53

Messerschmitt Bf 109E-4 (1593). Severely damaged in combat with enemy fighters and abandoned over Boulogne. Pilot baled out unhurt. Aircraft a write-off.

Stab KG1

Heinkel He 111-3 (5646). Crashed on landing at Amiens due to undercarriage failure following routine domestic flight. No crew casualties. Aircraft V4+CA 40% damaged.

II/KG51

Junkers Ju 88A-1 (8064). Shot down by fighters during sortie to bomb Yeovil. Crashed and burned out at Sidling St. Nicholas, Dorset 4.20 p.m. Oblt. Heye, Lt. Bein, Oberfw. Konig and Oberfw. Krell captured unhurt. Aircraft 9K+SN a write-off.

The winch base of the original lifeboat station at Dungeness photographed on September 13, 1979. The road along which Heinrich Bley travelled to the PoW cage lies behind the parked white car. The present lifeboat station lies out of the picture about half-a-mile to the right having been moved twice since 1940.

4/LG2

Messerschmitt Bf 109E-4 (5391). Crashed in sea two miles off Greatstone following attack by fighters during fighter-bomber attack on London 2.00 p.m. Uffz. Bley captured wounded. Aircraft +A lost.
Aircraft located on the seabed by the Brenzett Aeronautical Museum and exact position plotted for possible future recovery venture.

Messerschmitt Bf 109E-4 (5566). Shot down during fighter-bomber sortie to London and crashed at Spa Golf Club, Tunbridge Wells 1.50 p.m. Uffz. Moerschel captured wounded. Aircraft +F a write-off.

5/LG2

Messerschmitt Bf 109E-4 (3717). Crash-landed at Calais-Marck with combat damage. Pilot unhurt. Aircraft 60% damaged.

Messerschmitt Bf 109E (2013). Crashed on landing at Calais-Marck following combat with fighters over the Channel. Pilot unhurt. Aircraft 50% damaged.

9/NJG1

Messerschmitt Bf 110D-1 (3308). Crashed on take-off from Stendal due to engine failure. Both crew unhurt. Aircraft G9+GT 80% damaged.

Stab StG3

Dornier Do 17Z-3 (2877). Belly-landed at St. Michel aerodrome during routine domestic flight, cause not stated. No crew casualties. Aircraft 40% damaged.

II/ZG26

Messerschmitt Bf 110D-2 (3416). Shot down by RAF fighters in action over Yeovil 4.20 p.m. Oberfw. Stahl and Uffz. Mauer missing. Aircraft 3U+HN a write-off.

Messerschmitt Bf 110E-1 (3427). Shot down by fighters during escort sortie to Yeovil and crashed in sea at Ringstead Bay, Dorset 5.00 p.m. Oberfw. Gensler and Uffz. Haefner baled out and captured unhurt. Aircraft 3U+FM lost.

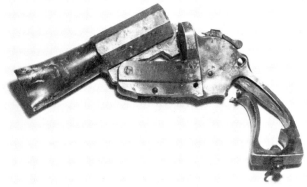

In August 1976, the Wealden group dug up the remains of a Messerschmitt Bf 110C-7 on Kingston Russell Dairy Farm at Long Bredy in Dorset. The aircraft from the 'Horst Wessel' Geschwader, ZG26, had crashed there after being shot down on October 7, 1940 while escorting a bombing raid to the Westland aircraft works at Yeovil. The remains of the two-man crew, missing at the time, were uncovered during the excavation and buried at Cannock Chase. *Above:* One of the parachute harnesses forcibly snapped on impact and a Walther signal pistol. *Below:* The tattered uniform of Unteroffizier Herbert Schilling, the wireless operator/air gunner (S. Hall/A. Saunders). (Werner Knittel was recovered by the Brenzett group — see October 28.)

Messerschmitt Bf 110C-7 (3418). Crashed at Kingston Russell Dairy Farm, Long Bredy, near Dorchester 5.00 p.m. during combat with RAF fighters. Oberfw. Herzog and Uffz. Schilling both killed. Aircraft 3U+JP a write-off.

This site was originally disturbed by unidentified amateurs and partial human remains recovered which were buried as unknown airmen at Cannock Chase. In August 1976, the Wealden Group carried out a major recovery, identified the remains of the crewmen who were buried at Cannock with full military honours.

III/ZG26

Messerschmitt Bf 110C-4 (3283). Shot down during combat over south-west England 4.20 p.m. on sortie to attack Yeovil. Crashed at Hart Hill, Stoborough, near Wareham. Lt. Sidow and Gefr. Repik both killed. Aircraft 3U+BT a write-off.

Messerschmitt Bf 110C-4 (3640). Shot down in sea off Weymouth by RAF fighters during combat over the Channel off south-west England 4.15 p.m. Oblt. Grisslich and Uffz. Obermayer captured. Aircraft 3U+GT a write-off.

Messerschmitt Bf 110E-1 (3421). Shot down by fighters during bomber escort sortie and crashed in sea at Weymouth Bay 5.15 p.m. Lt. Sommer and Uffz. Preuler captured wounded. Aircraft 3U+DD lost.

Messerschmitt Bf 110C-4 (3564). Forced-landed near Corfe Castle 5.00 p.m. after combat with fighters during escort mission for bombers attacking Yeovil. Obergefr. Bachmann killed. Gefr. Demmig captured. Aircraft 3U+JT a write-off.

Tuesday, October 8

Seenotflugkdo. 2

Heinkel He 59 (0534). Shot down by No. 235 Squadron Blenheims engaged over the Channel off Cherbourg 8.00 a.m. Crashed in sea. Lt. zur See Stelzner, Uffz. Hirschmann, Uffz. Fischer and Uffz. Wischer all missing. Aircraft TW+HH lost.

Heinkel He 59 (0541). Crashed in Channel following attack by No. 235 Squadron Blenheims off Cherbourg 8.00 a.m. Lt. zur See Schulz, Fw. Bridi, Obergefr. Kampf and Uffz. Stargnet all missing. Aircraft DA+MJ lost.

2(F)/22

Dornier Do 17 (3576). Crashed in sea off Rattray Head, Aberdeen 3.00 p.m. during reconnaissance sortie over England. Engine failure. Lt. von Eichstedt, Hptmn. Barth and Oberfw. Freund captured. Aircraft 4N+GK lost.

3(F)/121

Junkers Ju 88A-5 (0412). Shot down by fighters during operational sortie over the Midlands. Uffz. Bender and Gefr. Nikutta killed. Lt. Schedemund and Fw. Nippel missing. Aircraft 7A+JL a write-off.

4/JG3

Messerschmitt Bf 109E-4 (1656). Shot down by fighters during sortie over London. Severely damaged aircraft ditched in the Channel 1½ miles south-west of Abbotts Cliff 12.12 p.m. Oblt. Vogt (Staffel Kapitan) captured. Aircraft lost.

6/JG3

Messerschmitt Bf 109E-4 (1145). Damaged in take-off accident at Arques. Cause not stated. Pilot unhurt. Aircraft 20% damaged.

7/JG3

Messerschmitt Bf 109E-4 (1178). Crashed on landing at Desvres aerodrome following combat sortie. Pilot unhurt. Aircraft 40% damaged.

Ergaenzungs Staffel JG26

Messerschmitt Bf 109E-1 (3612). Crashed on landing at Domayle due to engine fire during routine training flight. Pilot unhurt. Aircraft a write-off.

8/JG51

Messerschmitt Bf 109E-4 (5282). Forced-landed at Ramecourt following engine failure during operational sortie. Pilot unhurt. Aircraft 30% damaged.

4/JG52

Messerschmitt Bf 109E-1 (3465). Shot down by RAF fighters during free-lance mission over the Thames Estuary. Crash-landed on Little Grange Farm, Woodham Mortimer, Essex 9.25 a.m. Fw. Boche captured wounded. Aircraft 2+ a write-off.

3/JG53

Messerschmitt Bf 109E-4 (0977). Damaged in landing accident at Etaples following routine domestic flight. Pilot unhurt. Aircraft 40% damaged.

4/JG53

Messerschmitt Bf 109E-1 (6200). Crashed on take-off from Berck-sur-Mer on operational sortie. Cause not stated. Pilot unhurt. Aircraft a write-off.

1/JG77

Messerschmitt Bf 109E-4 (0966). Rubber dinghy accidentally inflated in cockpit during free-lance sortie over Kent. Lost control and crash-landed near Vensons Farm, Eastry 7.45 a.m. Lt. Eschwerhaus captured unhurt. Aircraft 10+ a write-off.

3/KG4

Junkers Ju 88A (4125). Forced-landed at Schiphol aerodrome following operations over England. No crew casualties. Aircraft 5J+IR 30% damaged.

I/KG27

Heinkel He 111H-2 (5442). Crashed on landing at Tours following night sortie over England. Cause not stated. Crew unhurt. Aircraft 1G+CL a write-off.

III/KG27

Heinkel He 111P (1460). Crashed on take-off from Rennes due to engine failure. Four NCOs killed. Aircraft 1G+ER a write-off.

II/KG30

Junkers Ju 88A (4164). Flying accident due to mechanical failure during combat sortie. Crashed and burned out at Doerenberg. Hptmn. von Symonski (Gruppe Kommandeur) and three NCOs killed. Aircraft 4D+EP a write-off.

4/KG30

Junkers Ju 88A-1 (4067). Forced-landed at Gilze-Rijen following combat sortie. No crew casualties. Aircraft 4D+CM 20% damaged.

8/KG30

Junkers Ju 88A-1 (4081). Crashed on landing at Eindhoen following operational sortie. Crew unhurt. Aircraft 4D+AS 50% damaged.

Junkers Ju 88A-1 (5032). Landed damaged at Eindhoven aerodrome following combat sortie. No crew casualties. Aircraft 4D+HS 15% damaged.

I/KG40

Focke-Wulf FW 200C-2 (0022). Forced-landed at Brest damaged by AA fire from English naval vessel engaged during anti-shipping sortie. One NCO wounded. Aircraft F8+AK 20% damaged.

II/KG51

Junkers Ju 88A-1 (6115). Crashed and exploded at Toovies Farm, near Three Bridges, Sussex following attack by fighters 11.20 a.m. Lt. Doertlinger, Uffz. Semper, Gefr. Kohne and Gefr. Buttner all killed. Aircraft 9K+DM a write-off.

5/KG53

Heinkel He 111H-2 (2772). Crashed on landing at Oberweisenfeld aerodrome following routine domestic flight. Cause not stated. Crew unhurt. Aircraft A1+GN 35% damaged.

6/KG53

Heinkel He 111H-2 (2790). Forced-landed at Vendeville due to engine failure. One NCO wounded. Aircraft A1+KP 20% damaged.

Stab KG54

Junkers Ju 88A-1 (7093). Landing accident at Lechfeld aerodrome following local flight. Cause not stated. Crew unhurt. Aircraft VK+VU 35% damaged.

6/KG55

Heinkel He 111P-2 (1715). Hit by ground fire during incursion over Thorney Island and crashed and exploded at Stansted House, near Rowlands Castle 7.30 p.m. Lt. Flugge, Uffz. Ehrensberger, Uffz. Herber, Fw. Ens and Gefr. Pawlik all killed. Aircraft G1+MS a write-off.
Many large pieces of airframe found scattered throughout woodland here by Wealden Aviation Archaeological Group in 1976.

Heinkel He 111P-2 (1619). Returned to Villacoublay damaged by AA fire during sortie to bomb Eastleigh. Oberfw. Struckmeyer wounded. Aircraft damaged but repairable.

Heinkel He 111P-2 (2809). Damaged by fighters during attack on Thorney Island and landed damaged at Villacoublay. Uffz. Heinzl and Uffz. Bogner wounded. Aircraft repairable.

2/KGr.806

Junkers Ju 88A-1 (4068). Shot down by No. 312 Squadron Hurricanes during sortie to bomb Liverpool. Belly-landed near Bromborough Dock, Mersey 4.15 p.m. Oblt. Brueckmann, Uffz. Weth and Sonderfuehrer Lehmann captured. Lt. zur See Schlegel killed. Aircraft M7+DK a write-off.
Site investigated by the Warplane Wreck Investigation Group.

12/LG1

Junkers Ju 87B (5086). Mid-air collision over Marles during local flight. Crashed and burned out. Lt. Schlegel and one NCO killed. Aircraft L1+MW a write-off.

Junkers Ju 87B (0395). Crashed following collision with Lt. Schlegel's aircraft during routine domestic flight over Marles. Lt. Kuhn and one NCO injured. Aircraft L1+AW a write-off.

I/ZG26

Messerschmitt Bf 110C-3 (1373). Damaged in taxi-ing accident at Trecquile aerodrome. No crew casualties. Aircraft damaged but repairable.

Wednesday, October 9

Kuestenflieger Gruppe 606

Dornier Do 17Z-3 (2771). Failed to return from operational sortie over Crewe at night. Believed shot down by ground defences. Lt. zur See Harbou, Fw. Langer, Fw. Goehlisch and Obergefr. Ruebesam all killed. Aircraft 7T+HL a write-off.

4(H)/12

Fieseler Fi 156 (4281). Forced-landed at Blankenberge. Cause not stated. No personnel casualties. Aircraft 40% damaged.

3(F)/121

Junkers Ju 88A-5 (0433). Suffered engine failure during operational sortie and forced-landed at St. Brieux. No crew casualties. Aircraft 7A+ KL 40% damaged.

I/JG2

Messerschmitt Bf 109E-4 (4028). Damaged in forced-landing at Brecquebec having run out of fuel during routine domestic flight. Pilot unhurt. Aircraft 40% damaged.

4/JG3

Messerschmitt Bf 109E-4 (1463). Forced-landed at Arques due to engine failure. Pilot unhurt. Aircraft 35% damaged.

2/JG26

Messerschmitt Bf 109E-1 (6264). Crashed and burned out at Sangatte following combat sortie. Pilot wounded. Aircraft a write-off.

5/JG51

Messerschmitt Bf 109E-1 (3492). Crashed and burned out at Calais following combat sortie. Pilot killed. Aircraft a write-off.

7/JG54

Messerschmitt Bf 109E-4 (5327). Engaged by fighters during free-lance sortie over London and damaged. Forced-landed on Meridan Hunt Farm, west of Hawkinge 4.00 p.m. and set alight by pilot. Fw. Schweser captured. Aircraft 6+ a write-off.

9/JG54

Messerschmitt Bf 109E-4 (1573). Shot down in combat with enemy fighters over the Channel and crashed in sea. Lt. Eberle killed. Aircraft lost.

III/KG1

Junkers Ju 88A-5 (4230). Collided with Bf 110 of NJG1 whilst taxi-ing at Handorf. Crew unhurt. Aircraft V4+ KS 50% damaged.

III/KG27

Heinkel He 111P (1633). Crashed at Tours following operational sortie over the Channel and combat with fighters. Lt. Friele and two NCOs killed. One NCO wounded. Aircraft 1K+ CT a write-off.

Heinkel He 111P-2 (2116). Crashed on landing at Tours aerodrome following operational sortie over England at night. No crew casualties. Aircraft 30% damaged.

6/KG30

Junkers Ju 88A-5 (0311). Failed to return from operations over the coast of England and presumed crashed in sea. Four NCOs missing. Aircraft 4D+ EP lost.

I/KG51

Junkers Ju 88A-1 (4154). Crashed on landing at Villaroche due to undercarriage failure following combat sortie. No crew casualties. Aircraft 35% damaged.

Junkers Ju 88A-1 (6131). Crash-landed at Villaroche following operations over the Channel. One NCO killed. Lt. Haberl and another NCO wounded. Aircraft 45% damaged.

4/KG53

Heinkel He 111H-2 (5479). Forced-landed at Monteville following operational mission. Crew unhurt. Aircraft A1+ AM 25% damaged.

I/KG54

Junkers Ju 88A-1 (8039). Failed to return from night sortie over England and presumed victim of ground defences. Oberfw. Matzel, Uffz. Klinkmann, Gefr. Lockowandt and Gefr. Hasreiter all missing. Aircraft B3+ KH lost.

I/KG55

Heinkel He 111P-4 (2866). Engine failed during operations resulting in crash near St. Sabens. No crew casualties. Aircraft a write-off.

II/KG55

Heinkel He 111P-2 (2139). Damaged by AA fire during operations over England and forced-landed back at Chartres with one NCO wounded. Aircraft 40% damaged.

Stab NJG1

Messerschmitt Bf 110D/O(N) (3360). Collided with Ju 88 of III/KG1 whilst taxi-ing at Handorf aerodrome. Crew unhurt. Aircraft G9+ CA 45% damaged.

I/StG1

Junkers Ju 87R-1 (5291). Damaged in landing accident at Evrecy aerodrome. Exact cause not stated. Crew unhurt. Aircraft A5+ CL 15% damaged.

III/ZG76

Messerschmitt Bf 110D/O (3330). Damaged in taxi-ing accident at Laval. No crew casualties. Aircraft 2N+ EM 10% damaged.

Thursday, October 10

Kuestenflieger Gruppe 606

Dornier Do 17Z-3 (3618). Landed damaged at Brest following operational sortie over English coastal waters. Crew unhurt. Aircraft 7T+ KL 15% damaged.

Luftwaffen-Kontroll-Inspecktion

Junkers Ju 52. Crashed and destroyed during routine domestic flight. Exact circumstances unknown. Oberst. van Floten, Hptmn. Dr. Schweitzer, Major Augustini, Lt. Weiss, Uffz. Mauss, Uffz. Merten, Gefr. Thiel and Flgr. Stingl all killed. Aircraft a write-off.

6/JG27

Messerschmitt Bf 109E-1 (1312). Damaged in accident at Bonningues aerodrome. Not the result of an operational sortie. Pilot unhurt. Aircraft 15% damaged.

1/JG51

Messerschmitt Bf 109E-1 (6238). Damaged in take-off accident at Pihen. Exact cause unknown. Pilot unhurt. Aircraft a write-off.

III/JG52

Messerschmitt Bf 109E-1 (5200). Mid-air collision over Schonwalde aerodrome during local flying. Abandoned aircraft crashed and burned out. Pilot baled out unhurt. Aircraft a write-off.

Messerschmitt Bf 109E-3 (6333). Crashed near Schonwalde following mid-air collision. Pilot baled out unhurt. Aircraft a write-off.

4/JG53

Messerschmitt Bf 109E-1 (4143). Failed to return from combat sortie over the Channel and believed shot down into the sea. Oblt. Vogel (Staffel Kapitan) missing. Aircraft lost.

I/JG54

Messerschmitt Bf 109E (5238). Forced-landed at Groningen, fuel exhausted following combat sortie. Pilot unhurt. Aircraft repairable.

4/JG77

Messerschmitt Bf 109E (0839). Damaged due to storm at Stavanger-Sola aerodrome. No casualties. Aircraft 25% damaged.

1/KG2

Dornier Do 17Z (3442). Returned to base damaged following combat with RAF fighters over the Channel. Lt. Dilcher killed. Aircraft U5+ CH 10% damaged.

4/KG2

Dornier Do 17Z-2 (1201). Crashed at St. Leger following engine failure during operational sortie. No crew casualties. Aircraft a write-off.

7/KG3

Dornier Do 17Z (3293). Lost bearings during operational sortie and abandoned by crew over Borkum. Crashed and burned out. Crew baled out. one NCO injured. Aircraft 5K+ AR a write-off.

1/KG30

Junkers Ju 88A-1 (7020). Damaged in landing accident at Ludwiglust. No crew casualties. Aircraft 40% damaged.

Junkers Ju 88A-1 (8021) Damaged landing at Ludwiglust following routine domestic flight. Gefr. Suppick injured. Aircraft repairable.

Ergaengzungs Staffel KG51

Junkers Ju 88A-1 (5007). Crashed on take-off from Lechfeld on routine domestic flight. Cause not stated. Crew unhurt. Aircraft 9K+ FA 30% damaged.

8/KG51

Junkers Ju 88A-1 (0299). Shot down by AA fire during sortie to bomb West India Docks. Crashed into the River Roach at Horseshoe Corner 4.30 a.m. Uffz. Metschuldt, Uffz. Kafka, Uffz. Schragl and Fw. Wolff all baled out and captured unhurt. Aircraft 9K+ HS lost.

III/KG51

Junkers Ju 88A-1 (2104). Crashed on landing at Etampes-Montedesir aerodrome. Cause not stated. No crew casualties. Aircraft 25% damaged.

6/KG53

Heinkel He 111H-3 (5716). Returned to Holland and forced-landed at Holt with damage sustained in sortie over England. Crew unhurt. Aircraft A1+ FP 25% damaged.

II/KG55

Heinkel He 111P-2 (3132). Suffered engine failure during combat sortie and forced-landed at Chartres. No crew casualties. Aircraft 20% damaged.

III/LG1

Junkers Ju 88A-1 (6061). Crashed at Telgte due to engine failure during local flight. One NCO injured. Aircraft CF+ WD a write-off.

II/LG2

Messerschmitt Bf 109E-4 (3722). Damaged in combat with enemy fighters and crashed on landing at Breton. Pilot unhurt. Aircraft a write-off.

3/StG2

Junkers Ju 87B-2 (0513). Collided with another Ju 87 during local flight over Foret de Bretonne. Crashed and burned out. One NCO killed. Aircraft T6+ FL a write-off.

Junkers Ju 87B-2 (0557). Collided with another Ju 87 during domestic flight over Foret de Bretonne. Crashed and burned out. Oblt. Brucker and one NCO killed. Aircraft T6+ JL a write-off.

Friday, October 11

Kurierstaffel 110

Junkers W34Hi (0589). Crashed on take-off from Ypenburg on routine domestic flight. Cause not stated. No crew casualties. Aircraft 5D+ DV a write-off.

2/406

Dornier Do 18 (0848). Forced-landed on sea off Vardoen and capsized whilst under tow by steamship *Stralsund*. No personnel losses. Aircraft K6+ LK lost.

1/Kuestenflieger Gruppe 606

Dornier Do 17Z-3 (2772). Shot down by fighters during sortie to bomb Liverpool. Crashed in sea off Bardsey Island 7.15 p.m. Fw. Vetterl killed. Lt. zur See Krause, Uffz. Arpert and Gefr. Sundermann rescued by trawler and captured. Aircraft 7T+ EH lost.

Dornier Do 17Z-3 (2787). Attacked by fighters during bombing mission to Liverpool and set alight. Aircraft subsequently returned to Brest badly damaged. Uffz. Johannsen baled out over England and killed. Fw. Starf also baled out but captured. Aircraft 7T+ HH 45% damaged.

2/Kuestenflieger Gruppe 606

Dornier Do 17Z-3 (3475). Crashed in the Irish Sea, cause unknown, during mission to bomb Crewe. Lt. zur See Felber, Oblt. Richter and Gefr. Hoppmann killed. Uffz. Weber missing. Aircraft 7T+ EK a write-off.

4(H)/22

Henschel Hs 126 (0305). Damaged landing at St. Martin aerodrome following routine local flight. No crew casualties. Aircraft CH+ AM 10% damaged.

2(H)/32

Henschel Hs 126A (3042). Slightly damaged in flying accident at Roth due to mechanical failure during routine domestic flight. No crew casualties. Aircraft V7+ 2D damaged but repairable.

I(F)/121

Junkers Ju 88 (0414). Failed to return from long-range reconnaissance mission to Scotland. Exact fate unknown. Major Gerlach, Uffz. Koltermann, Uffz. Mehle and Gefr. Eha all missing. Aircraft 7A+ NH lost.

5/JG27

Messerschmitt Bf 109E-1 (6267). Shot down by RAF fighters in combat over the Channel. Crashed in sea. Uffz. Wiemann wounded and rescued by Seenotdienst. Aircraft lost.

1/JG51

Messerschmitt Bf 109E-4 (5357). Forced-landed at Sangatte following fighter combat over the Channel. Pilot unhurt. Aircraft 20% damaged.

4/JG53

Messerschmitt Bf 109E-4 (3751). Crashed on take-off from Berck-sur-Mer on operational sortie. Pilot unhurt. Aircraft a write-off.

6/JG53

Messerschmitt Bf 109E-1 (4832). Forced-landed at Berck-sur-Mer following routine domestic flight. Pilot unhurt. Aircraft 30% damaged.

1/JG77

Messerschmitt Bf 109E-4 (5109). Damaged in combat with RAF fighters in action over the Channel and crash-landed at Cap Gris-Nez. Pilot unhurt. Aircraft a write-off.

II/KG1

Heinkel He 111H-2 (2754). Crashed near Maarten due to mechanical failure on operational sortie. Uffz. Linke missing. Aircraft V4+ EW a write-off.

5/KG2

Dornier Do 17Z (2893). Crashed in the River Aisne having lost bearings whilst on routine navigational practice flight. Lt. Huebner, Obergefr. Zechner, Gefr. Schreiner and Flgr. Brueske all killed. Aircraft U5+ AN a write-off.

I/KG55

Heinkel He 111P-4 (2928). Forced to land at Dreux in bad weather and damaged. No crew casualties. Aircraft 40% damaged.

II/LG1

Junkers Ju 88A-5 (3187). Crashed on take-off from Orleans-Bricy aerodrome on operational sortie. No crew casualties. Aircraft L1+ YC 25% damaged.

Saturday, October 12

1/196

Arado Ar 196 (0088) Failed to return from operational sortie over the Channel. Believed shot down in sea. Hptmn. Thewaldt (Staffel Kapitan) killed. Uffz. Kottwitz missing. Aircraft 6W+ FN lost.

4(F)/14

Messerschmitt Bf 110C-5 (2243). Flew into ground, cause unknown, during operational sortie over Caen. Oblt. Doffek and one NCO killed. Aircraft 5F+ MM a write-off.

8/JG51

Messerschmitt Bf 109E-1 (3313). Crashed on take-off from Clairmarais aerodrome on routine domestic flight. Pilot unhurt. Aircraft a write-off.

1/JG52

Messerschmitt Bf 109E-3 (1966). Believed crashed at Beans Hill, Harrietsham 3.30 p.m. following combat with fighters during free-lance sortie over Kent. Oblt. Buesgen baled out wounded and captured. Aircraft 11+ a write-off.
Surface fragments in the Steve Vizard collection.

2/JG52

Messerschmitt Bf 109E (4132). Engaged in escort sortie for Bf 109 Jabos attacking London and shot down by fighters. Crashed on Chantry Farm, Hollingbourne, Kent 4.30 p.m. Oblt. Sauer baled out slightly wounded and captured. Aircraft a write-off.

3/JG52

Messerschmitt Bf 109E (5283). Abandoned following fighter attack during escort sortie for Bf 109 Jabos attacking Biggin Hill and London. Crashed at The Limes, Brabourne Down, near Ashford 4.30 p.m. Fw. Voss baled out unhurt. Aircraft 3+ a write-off.
Excavated by the Brenzett Aeronautical Museum.

His controls badly damaged in combat with RAF fighters, Siegfried Voss had no option but to abandon his JG52 Messerschmitt Bf 109E near Ashford on the afternoon of Saturday October 12. The aircraft crashed at Weeks Lane, West Brabourne — Voss being captured unhurt. These relics from the crash site are displayed in Brenzett's museum.

ME 109e 3JG52
FW. S. VOSS

4/JG52

Messerschmitt Bf 109E (5256). Shot down in fighter combat over the Thames Estuary and crashed in the sea off Sheerness. Uffz. Reichenbach killed. Aircraft lost.

Stab II/JG54

Messerschmitt Bf 109E-4 (4869). Shot down by Flight Lieutenant Tuck (flying with No. 92 Squadron) during action over Kent and forced-landed near Chapel Holding, Small Hythe, Tenterden 10.20 a.m. Lt. Malischewski captured unhurt. Aircraft a write-off.

7/JG54

Messerschmitt Bf 109E (5293). Failed to return from operational sortie over the Channel and presumed shot down in sea. Lt. Behrens missing. Aircraft lost.

II/JG77

Messerschmitt Bf 109E-1(3309). Crashed on landing at Stavanger-Sola after combat sortie. Cause not stated. Pilot killed. Aircraft a write-off.

To prevent its possible destruction by the Luftwaffe, soldiers camouflaged this Bf 109E-4 of JG54 'Gruenherz' with wheat straw from the recent harvesting. The pilot, Leutnant Malischewski, forced-landed his 'Emil' on October 12 (Fox Photos).

III/KG51

Junkers Ju 88A-1(7075). Crashed on take-off from Montdesir aerodrome on operational sortie. Cause not recorded. One NCO killed. Oblt. Simon and two NCOs injured. Aircraft 9K+DR a write-off.

II/LG1

Junkers Ju 88A-1 (3075). Attacked by RAF fighters during sortie over the Channel and crashed on landing on return to Orleans-Bricy aerodrome. No crew casualties. Aircraft L1+HN a write-off.

2/LG2

Messerschmitt Bf 109E-7 (5793). Failed to return from combat sortie over the Channel. Pilot killed. Aircraft a write-off.

Messerschmitt Bf 109E-4 (5563). Forced-landed at Calais-Marck following combat sortie due to engine failure. Pilot unhurt. Aircraft damaged but repairable.

Sunday, October 13

7/JG3

Messerschmitt Bf 109E-4 (0860). Shot down by RAF fighters in chase over Kent during escort sortie for Bf 109 Jabos attacking London. Forced-landed at Cuckold Coombe, Hastingleigh near Ashford 2.10 p.m. Gefr. Rungen captured unhurt. Aircraft 7+1 a write-off.

4/JG27

Messerschmitt Bf 109E-1 (6310). Crashed at Bonningues due to engine failure during combat sortie. Pilot unhurt. Aircraft a write-off.

Malischewski's landing place at Small Hythe, Kent visited on September 13, 1979. The field lies behind the old Tudor farmhouse in which Ellen Terry (Mrs. James Carew), the eminent Victorian actress, was born in 1848.

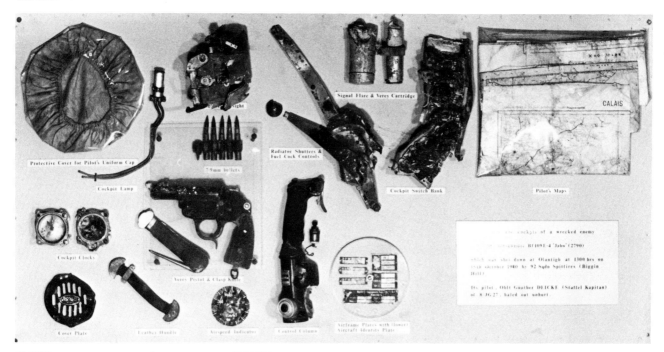

II/JG53

Messerschmitt Bf 109E-7 (5932). Suffered engine failure during operational sortie and crashed at St. Inglevert. Pilot unhurt. Aircraft a write-off.

7/JG54

Messerschmitt Bf 109E-4 (5066). Damaged on take-off from Guines-Sud on combat mission. Pilot unhurt. Aircraft 35% damaged.

II/KG54

Junkers Ju 88A-1 (5122). Take-off accident at St. Andre on operational sortie. Exact cause not stated. Crew unhurt. Aircraft B3+GN 20% damaged.

Stab KG76

Junkers W34Hi (2749). Hit ground near Rheinboellen in poor visibility during routine domestic flight. One NCO injured. Aircraft DA+ZX a write-off.

II/KG76

Junkers Ju 88A-1 (2136). Damaged in combat sortie and forced-landed back at Reims aerodrome. Fw. Waas and Uffz. Uhlig wounded. Aircraft F1+JM 30% damaged.

Stab KGr.126

Heinkel He 111H-4 (3265). Forced-landed at Witmundhafen damaged after operational sortie over England. No crew casualties. Aircraft 1T+CB 30% damaged.

2/KGr.126

Heinkel He 111H-4 (6978). Crashed on landing at Delmenhorst following routine domestic flight. Cause not stated. Crew unhurt. Aircraft 1T+DK a write-off.

Heinkel He 111H-4 (6983). Landing accident at Bremen following routine local flight. No crew casualties. Aircraft 1T+FK 30% damaged.

The 1970s were marked by frenzied competition and, sometimes, bitter rivalry between various archaeological groups which has largely given way to a more co-operative attitude. Many locations have been re-dug and many interesting items, missed during earlier investigations, have come to light. Oberleutnant Guenther Deicke crashed at Olantigh, Kent, on October 24. *Above:* The Kent Battle of Britain Museum and *below* the London Air Museum. Deicke himself finished the war in one piece!

III/LG1

Junkers Ju 88A-1 (7018). Suffered engine failure following operational sortie and crashed at Rouen. Crew unhurt. Aircraft L1+KT a write-off.

II/ZG26

Messerschmitt Bf 110D (3401). Forced-landed at Le Cateau during local domestic flight. Crew unhurt. Aircraft 25% damaged.

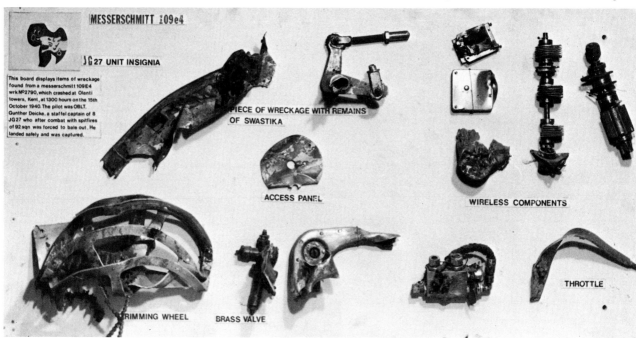

Monday, October 14

3/506

Heinkel He 115 (2677). Crashed on landing at Stavanger following mine-laying operations in English coastal waters. Crew unhurt. Aircraft S4+ LL a write-off.

4(F)/121

Junkers Ju 88A-1 (0314). Damaged in landing accident at Caen following routine domestic flight. No crew casualties. Aircraft 7A+ DM 40% damaged.

III/JG2

Messerschmitt Bf 109E-7 (0720). Believed crashed and burned out at Sway, Hants, during operations over the Channel. Exact cause uncertain. Obergefr. Lux missing. Aircraft 12+ lost.

4/JG3

Messerschmitt Bf 109E-4 (5359). Crashed on landing at Arques aerodrome after routine domestic flight. Cause not stated. Pilot unhurt. Aircraft 25% damaged.

Ergaenzungs Staffel JG52

Messerschmitt Bf 109E-1 (6147). Suffered engine failure during routine training flight and forced-landed near Grubbensort. Pilot unhurt. Aircraft 10% damaged.

9/KG2

Dornier Do 17Z (2556). Damaged in combat over the Channel and forced-landed back at Cambrai-Sued. No crew casualties. Aircraft U5+ BT 25% damaged.

2/KG3

Dornier Do 17Z-2. Crashed on take-off from Le Culot due to engine failure. Crew unhurt. Aircraft 5K+ FK 45% damaged.

Stab II/KG76

Focke-Wulf FW 44 (2672). Abandoned over Creil after engine failure during local flight. One NCO baled out and injured. Aircraft RG+ AW a write-off.

III/KG77

Junkers Ju 88A-1. Crashed on landing at Reims following night operational sortie. Exact cause not stated. No crew casualties. Aircraft 40% damaged.

I/NJG2

Dornier Do 17Z (2851). Returned to base severely damaged during night intruder sortie over England. Three NCOs wounded. Aircraft R4+ DK a write-off.

Tuesday, October 15

3(F)/123

Junkers Ju 88A-5 (0429). Damaged in landing accident at Buc aerodrome. Exact circumstances not stated. No crew casualties. Aircraft 4U+ CL 40% damaged.

I/JG2

Messerschmitt Bf 109E-4 (1588). Shot down by RAF fighters during free-lance fighter sortie over the Channel and forced-landed at Bowcombe Down, near Newport, Isle of Wight 12.45 p.m. Fw. Hellriegel captured unhurt. Aircraft 8+ a write-off.
Radio mast 'liberated' from this aircraft in 1940 and donated to the Kent Battle of Britain Museum together with other minor components.

II/JG2

Messerschmitt Bf 109E-1 (3279). Shot down during combat with RAF fighters over the English south coast and crashed at Everton, near Lymington, Hants. 1.30 p.m. Gefr. Pollach captured unhurt. Aircraft 10+ a write-off.

Messerschmitt Bf 109E-4 (1412). Crashed on landing at Beaumont-le-Roger following fighter action. Pilot wounded. Aircraft a write-off.

II/JG3

Messerschmitt Bf 109E-4 (6100). Crashed near Outreau due to engine failure on operational sortie. Pilot injured. Aircraft a write-off.

5/JG3

Messerschmitt Bf 109E-1 (3279). Forced-landed at Arques following combat sortie. Pilot unhurt. Aircraft 20% damaged.

Messerschmitt Bf 109E-1 (3251). Crashed on take-off from Arques on operational sortie. Cause not stated. Pilot unhurt. Aircraft 60% damaged.

8/JG3

Messerschmitt Bf 109E-4 (1294). Damaged by fighter attack during free-lance fighter sweep over Kent and forced-landed on Princes Golf Course, Sandwich 9.17 a.m. Oberfw. Bauer captured unhurt. Aircraft 7+ 1 a write-off.

Ergaenzungs Staffel JG26

Messerschmitt Bf 109E-1 (3910). Crashed on take-off from St. Omer on routine local training flight. Cause not stated. Pilot unhurt. Aircraft a write-off.

6/JG27

Messerschmitt Bf 109E-1 (3456). Damaged in combat with RAF fighters and ditched in the Channel off Cap Gris-Nez. Fw. Freis missing despite search by Seenotdienst. Aircraft lost.

8/JG27

Messerschmitt Bf 109E-4 (2790). Shot down by fighters in action over Kent and crashed at Trimworth Manor, Olantigh 1.00 p.m. Oblt. Deicke (Staffel Kapitan) baled out and captured unhurt. Aircraft a write-off.
Major recovery by the Kent Battle of Britain Museum. Remains of the Daimler-Benz DB 601 engine excavated together with both undercarriage legs, quantities of compressed airframe some still bearing the original painted Gruppe badge, cockpit instruments and controls including the control column, reflector gunsight, complete seat harness, signal pistol, pilot's maps and aircraft identity plate confirming '2790'. Some items also held by the London Air Museum.

4/JG51

Messerschmitt Bf 109E-1 (3535). Crashed on Owls Castle Farm, Lamberhurst 8.35 a.m. following combat with fighters during free-lance fighter sortie over Kent. Uffz. Hoehn baled out and captured unwounded. Aircraft 2+ a write-off.
Excavated by the Wealden Aviation Archaeological Group in 1974 and fragments of the shattered airframe recovered. Re-excavated by the same group in 1979 when remains of Daimler-Benz DB 601 engine were unearthed together with various pieces of airframe bearing number '3535' and propeller boss. Some pieces also in the Steve Vizard collection.

9/JG51

Messerschmitt Bf 109E-1 (6341). Crashed on landing at St. Omer following fighter combat. Pilot unhurt. Aircraft 25% damaged.

Ergaenzungs Staffel JG52

Messerschmitt Bf 109E-1 (3363). Forced-landed at Krefeld due to mechanical failure during routine local training flight. Pilot unhurt. Aircraft 50% damaged.

Stab JG53

Focke-Wulf FW 58C (2204). Crashed on take-off from Neuerberg on routine domestic flight. Cause not stated. No personnel casualties. Aircraft NF+ NV a write-off.

2/JG77

Messerschmitt Bf 109E-4 (1189). Crash-landed at Cap Gris-Nez following fighter combat over the Channel. Pilot unhurt. Aircraft a write-off.

II/KG26

Heinkel He 111H-3 (5637). Forced-landed at Beauvais with combat damage following operations over England. Three NCOs wounded. Aircraft 1H+ JL 20% damaged.

III/KG27

Heinkel He 111P (1734). Suffered engine failure on routine domestic flight and forced-landed at Rennes. No crew casualties. Aircraft 1G+ MS 20% damaged.

8/KG30

Junkers Ju 88A-5 (0271). Damaged in taxi-ing accident at Eindhoven. Crew unhurt. Aircraft 4D+ CS 20% damaged.

6/KG53

Heinkel He 111H-2 (6814). Damaged by fighters during operations over England and forced-landed at Arendonk. Crew unhurt. Aircraft 45% damaged.

4/KG55

Heinkel He 111P-2 (1542). Forced-landed near Cherbourg with one engine damaged following fighter attacks over the Channel. Lt. Hansen and Uffz. Reinhold wounded. Aircraft G1+ DM 40% damaged.

Ergaenzungs Staffel KG76

Dornier Do 17Z (3368). Crashed near Stuttgart due to mechanical failure during routine local flight. Four NCOs killed. Aircraft F1+ BR a write-off.

Above: **You could say that Leutnant Lenz's luck ran out on October 15, 1940! He was flying a Jabo mission when, according to contemporary newspaper reports, a bullet struck the bomb under his Messerschmitt Bf 109E-7. In the resultant explosion the cockpit and wing centre section were compressed to the thickness of eighteen inches, wreckage falling at Spruce Lawns, Elham. The engine, propeller and tail unit were scattered over a three mile area (Fox Photos).** *Below:* **Spruce Lawns photographed on August 21, 1979 still show the hut foundations of the chicken farm but little else.**

I/LG1

Junkers Ju 88A-1 (3138). Shot down by RAF fighters during operational sortie over the Channel. Believed crashed in sea. Fw. Doescher, Uffz. Weiske, Uffz. Osterried and Gefr. Annerl all missing. Aircraft L1+CK lost.

Stab I/LG2

Messerschmitt Bf 109E-7 (3734). Exploded over Spruce Lawns, Elham 9.20 a.m. during fighter-bomber sortie over England and engagement by RAF fighters. Lt. Lenz killed. Aircraft a write-off.

II/LG2

Messerschmitt Bf 109E-4 (5569). Crashed on landing at Calais-Marck after sortie over southern England and combat with RAF fighters. Pilot unhurt. Aircraft 25% damaged.

NJG1

Messerschmitt Bf 110D (3620). Shot down by return fire from RAF bomber engaged at night and crashed near Gardelegen. Lt. Mangersdorf and one NCO killed. Aircraft A9+FK a write-off.

4/NJG2

Messerschmitt Bf 110D (3812). Hit by return fire from RAF bomber intercepted during night sortie and abandoned by crew. One NCO wounded. Aircraft 2A+BL a write-off.

Wednesday, October 16

2/Kuestenflieger Gruppe 606

Dornier Do 17Z (2691). Crashed attempting forced-landing at Masbury Ring, near Wells during night bombing sortie to Liverpool. Oblt. zur See Blank, Fw. Faupel, Fw. Steppat and Obergefr. Schnacke all killed. Aircraft 7T+HK a write-off.

3/Kuestenflieger Gruppe 606

Dornier Do 17Z (2682). Crashed and exploded at Nantglyn, Denbighshire 7.25 p.m., cause unknown. Believed engaged on mission to bomb Crewe. Lt. zur See Havemann, Uffz. Soecknitz, Uffz. Hoelscher and Gefr. Faehrmann all killed. Aircraft 7T+LL a write-off.
Site investigated by the Warplane Wreck Investigation Group.

1(H)/21

Messerschmitt Bf 110E-1 (6300). Crashed at Bergen op Zoom, cause not stated, during routine domestic flight. Fw. Puelke and Fw. Wehner both injured. Aircraft 60% damaged.

3(F)/121

Junkers Ju 88A-5 (0390). Forced-landed at Brest due to mechanical fault during operational sortie. No crew casualties. Aircraft 7A+BL 30% damaged.

1(F)/122

Junkers Ju 88A-1 (5047). Forced-landed damaged at Vendeville following combat sortie. One NCO wounded. Aircraft F6+LH damaged.

6/KG2

Dornier Do 17Z-3 (3352). Damaged by enemy action during operational sortie and forced-landed at St. Leger with one NCO wounded. Aircraft U5+ CC 40% damaged.

6/KG3

Dornier Do 17Z (4252). Forced-landed at Antwerp following mechanical failure during local flight. No crew casualties. Aircraft 30% damaged.

II/KG26

He 111H-3 (3310). Failed to return from night operational sortie over England and presumed brought down by ground defences. Oblt. Sommer, Uffz. Braeutigan, Uffz. Kaublau and Gefr. Felleger all missing. Aircraft 1H+ DN a write-off.

Stab II/KG30

Junkers Ju 88A-5 (0317). Crashed with full bomb load near Bishop Stortford Church 7.50 p.m. and exploded. Hptmn. Hass (Gruppe Kommandeur), Fw. Suhr, Fw. Kessels and Kriegsberichter Penfold all killed. Aircraft 4D+ DM a write-off.

9/KG30

Junkers Ju 88A-1 (0170). Crashed on landing at Eindhoven following combat sortie. Crew unhurt. Aircraft 4D+ KT a write-off.

1/KG53

Junkers Ju 52 (5323). Damaged in landing accident at Antwerp, cause not stated. Non-operational sortie. No crew casualties. Aircraft 30% damaged.

Ergaenzungs Staffel KG54

Heinkel He 111P (2486). Crashed on landing at Augsburg following routine local training flight. Cause not stated. Crew unhurt. Aircraft a write-off.

II/KG55

Heinkel He 111P-2 (2840). Damaged in taxi-ing accident at Chartres. Crew unhurt. Aircraft GL+ SN 15% damaged.

I/KG76

Dornier Do 17Z (3448). Crashed attempting landing near Nivillers following night sortie in bad weather. Fw. Ott, Uffz. Beer, Uffz. Schneider and Oberfw. Schneidereit all killed. Aircraft F1+ FH a write-off.

I/KG77

Junkers Ju 88A-1 (2149). Crashed near Beauvais following mechanical failure on operational sortie. Crew unhurt. Aircraft 3Z+ HH a write-off.

Junkers Ju 88 (2162). Suffered engine failure during combat sortie and crashed near Sevres. Oblt. Krauss, Uffz. Klinger, Uffz. Joern and Obergefr. Sonntag injured. Aircraft a write-off.

II/KG77

Junkers Ju 88A-1 (7094). Crashed at Neufchatel following operational sortie over the Channel. Oblt. Berbecker and three NCOs killed. Aircraft 3Z+ AP a write-off.

III/KG77

Junkers Ju 88A-1 (5139). Crashed and burned out at Amiens on return from combat mission over England. Oblt. Reiss and three NCOs killed. Aircraft 3Z+ DT a write-off.

2/KGr.126

Heinkel He 111H-4 (6955). Shot down by No. 264 Squadron Defiant night fighter and crashed on Creaseys Farm, Hutton 2.00 a.m. Lt. Newald and Gefr. Granetz baled out and captured. Uffz. Glaser and Gefr. Tordik killed. Aircraft 1T+ BB lost.

Major recovery by the Essex Aviation Group July 1978 with assistance from the East Anglian Drainage Authority. Intact Junkers Jumo 211F engine excavated together with propeller boss and blades, seat armour, cockpit instruments and controls, magazines of 7.9mm MG15 ammunition and navigator's flight bag containing navigation aids and instruments.

Details of this aircraft quoted above are based on original contemporary Luftwaffe records. Documentary evidence and the excavation of this machine indicates actual Werk Nummer 5709 and codes 1T+ LK.

Heinkel He 111H-5 (3510). Blundered into balloon barrage and crashed on foreshore at Shotley, Essex 10.20 p.m. during mine-laying sortie. Oblt. zur See Stender, Fw. Guenther, Uffz. Martin and Obergefr. Irrgang all killed. Aircraft IT+ JU lost.

7/NJG1

Messerschmitt Bf 110C (2634). Crash-landed near Mecheln due to mechanical fault during operations. Crew unhurt. Aircraft G9+ FR a write-off.

I/NJG3

Messerschmitt Bf 110 (3302). Crashed attempting forced-landing at Perleberg during routine domestic flight in deteriorating weather conditions. Oblt. Zobel and one NCO both injured. Aircraft L1+ AK a write-off.

Thursday, October 17

III/Luft. Lande Geschwader 1

Henschel Hs 126 (4359). Reported to have crashed during routine domestic flight. Exact circumstances not recorded. Obergefr. Odenwald and Gefr. Bienecke both injured. Aircraft a write-off.

3(H)/14

Henschel 126B (3116). Damaged landing at Keerbergen aerodrome following local flight. No crew casualties. Aircraft 25% damaged.

2(H)/21

Henschel Hs 126B (3331). Crashed on Bergen aerodrome, cause unknown, during local flying. Lt. Ruttkowski injured. One NCO killed. Aircraft P2+ HK a write-off.

1/KG z.b.V.101

Junkers Ju 52 (6379). Damaged in landing accident at Buc aerodrome. Cause not stated. Crew unhurt. Aircraft damaged but repairable.

III/JG2

Messerschmitt Bf 109E-7 (1445). Crashed near Lorient during routine domestic flight cause not stated. Pilot unhurt. Aircraft a write-off.

Ergaenzungs Staffel JG3

Messerschmitt Bf 109E-1 (3900). Crashed on take-off at Wizernes on local training flight. Exact cause not recorded. Pilot unhurt. Aircraft 12% damaged.

4/JG3

Messerschmitt Bf 109E-1 (4830). Crashed on landing at Arques following operations over the Channel. Pilot unhurt. Aircraft 10% damaged.

I/JG27

Messerschmitt Bf 109E. Crashed at Dollern during routine domestic flight. Cause unknown. Gefr. Wels killed. Aircraft a write-off.

4/JG27

Messerschmitt Bf 109E-4. Crashed on take-off from Bonningues on combat sortie. Cause not stated. Pilot unhurt. Aircraft a write-off.

Ergaenzungs Staffel JG52

Messerschmitt Bf 109E-1 (3023). Slightly damaged in taxi-ing accident at Krefeld. Pilot unhurt. Aircraft repairable.

Stab I/JG53

Messerschmitt Bf 109E-7 (4138). Shot down in combat with RAF fighters over the Channel and crashed in sea. Hptmn. Mayer (Gruppe Kommandeur) killed. Aircraft lost.

3/JG53

Messerschmitt Bf 109E-4 (1106). Severely damaged by Pilot Officer Draper of No. 74 Squadron in combat over the Thames Estuary and belly-landed at Manston 3.45 p.m. Oblt. Rupp captured unhurt. Aircraft 1+ a write-off.

8/JG53

Messerschmitt Bf 109E-7 (5923). Shot down in combat with fighters over the Channel and crashed in sea off French coast. Pilot rescued unhurt. Aircraft lost.

I/JG77

Messerschmitt Bf 109E-4 (2050). Ditched in the Channel off Cap Gris-Nez following combat with British fighters. Pilot rescued unhurt by Seenotflugkdo. Aircraft lost.

I/KG1

Heinkel He 111H-2 (5563). Damaged by AA fire during bombing mission over England and forced-landed near Crecy. No crew casualties. Aircraft a write-off.

II/KG1

Heinkel He 111H-2 (2728). Damaged by AA fire and crashed at Mons due to engine failure following combat mission. No crew casualties. Aircraft a write-off.

Stab KG2

Dornier Do 17Z (3379). Crashed and burned out at Eroillers on return from operational sortie. Exact cause unknown but believed result of combat damage. Four NCOs killed. Aircraft a write-off.

Above: **At 2.00 a.m. on October 16, a Heinkel He 111 of 2/KGr.126 was despatched by a Defiant night fighter, crashing at Creaseys Farm near Brentwood. Daylight revealed the horror of the scene with the early air permeated with the stench of high-** octane petrol, burning rubber and scorched metal. *Below:* **On July 23, 1978 some aircraft wreckage was discovered by Anglian Land Drainage workmen while laying drains at Hutton and the Essex Aviation Group excavated the site the following week.**

Kurt Newald — then and now. Oberleutnant Newald was one of the two survivors from the crash, landing by parachute some 200 yards from the burning aeroplane. He returned to the spot on September 7, 1979 and explained that, 'we saw no chance to travel unrecognised in our uniforms through south-east England to catch a Channel ferry so we decided to surrender!'

1/KG27

Heinkel He 111H (5564). Fuel exhausted during combat mission and crashed at Ecommoy. Oblt. Sickmann killed. Oberfw. Eilms, Fw. Gebhardt and Uffz. Jannsen wounded. Aircraft a write-off.

1/KG55

Heinkel He 111P-4 (2867). Crashed on landing at Dreux following operational sortie. No crew casualties. Aircraft a write-off.

1/LG1

Junkers Ju 88A-1 (2095). Ran out of fuel following combat sortie and stalled during attempted forced-landing near Le Havre. Crashed and burned out. Oblt. Paeckel killed. Aircraft a write-off.

ll/LG2

Messerschmitt Bf 109E (5569). Damaged in landing accident at Breton aerodrome. Exact cause not stated. Pilot unhurt. Aircraft 20% damaged.

1/NJG2

Junkers Ju 88C-2 (0251). Crashed on landing at Gilze-Rijen following operational sortie. Crew unhurt. Aircraft R4+ EL 20% damaged.

4/NJG2

Messerschmitt Bf 110D (3385). Crashed and burned out at Capelle following combat sortie. Oblt. Zimmermann and one NCO killed. Aircraft 3M+ AH a write-off.

lll/ZG76

Messerschmitt Bf 110D-2 (3391). Forced-landed at St. Aubin due to damage sustained in combat. Crew unhurt. Aircraft 20% damaged.

The dig provided a good illustration of the dubious accuracy of some Luftwaffe records. The German quartermaster-general's records state that Oberleutnant Newald's aircraft was No. 6955 yet evidence to the contrary was suggested by a number discovered on the engine casing — 5709. Obviously engines could have been switched in the heat of the battle but it does indicate the care which must be taken in attempting to identify relics or crash sites.

Friday, October 18

5(F)/122

Junkers Ju 88A-5 (0409). Crash-landed near Laon during operational sortie. Cause not stated. No crew casualties. Aircraft 50% damaged.

1/JG2

Messerschmitt Bf 109E (0748). Crashed and burned out at St. Brieuc during routine domestic flight. Cause unknown. Fhr. Siebold killed. Aircraft a write-off.

lll/JG2

Messerschmitt Bf 109E-4 (5348). Crashed at Grandcamp during operational sortie. Oblt. Falting killed. Aircraft a write-off.

ll/JG53

Messerschmitt Bf 109E-4 (1343). Crashed in flames near Morleaux during routine operational sortie. Cause unknown. Pilot killed. Aircraft a write-off.

Ergaenzungs Staffel KG1

Heinkel He 111H-1. Suffered engine failure during routine training flight and crash-landed at Muenster. Uffz. Goetzel injured, rest of crew unhurt. Aircraft a write-off.

Stab KG2

Dornier Do 17Z-3 (2674). Crashed at Kalkar during combat sortie. Cause of crash unknown. Lt. Steudel, Fw. Brey, Obergefr. Lintz and Obergefr. Grabner all killed. Aircraft a write-off.

8/KG2

Dornier Do 17Z-3 (2876). Forced-landed near St. Romain during operational sortie. Cause not stated. No crew casualties. Aircraft 40% damaged.

Stab ll/KG4

Heinkel He 111P-4 (3081). Crashed on landing at Eindhoven following combat mission. Crew unhurt. Aircraft 15% damaged.

II/KG51

Junkers Ju 88A-1 (7160). Failed to return from bombing attack on London area. Four NCOs killed. Aircraft 9K+EC a write-off.

I/KG54

Junkers Ju 88A-1 (4062). Crashed at Vierville in bad weather following operational sortie. Flg. Feldmann injured, rest of crew unhurt. Aircraft a write-off.

Junkers Ju 88A-1 (6152). Returned to Vierville and crashed on landing in bad weather after combat sortie. Crew unhurt. Aircraft a write-off.

Junkers Ju 88A-1 (7095). Caught in deteriorating weather conditions on return from operational sortie and crashed on landing at Evreux. Uffz. Streitz and Uffz. Meissner both injured. Aircraft 45% damaged.

Junkers Ju 88A-1 (7152). Crashed on landing at Caen in poor weather conditions following operational sortie. Four NCOs killed. Aircraft a write-off.

II/KG54

Junkers Ju 88A-1 (7064). Crashed on landing at Orleans-Bricy following operational sortie. Crew unhurt. Aircraft a write-off.

Junkers Ju 88A-1 (6098). Abandoned over Bagnoles on return from operational mission due to poor weather conditions. Crew baled out unhurt. Aircraft a write-off.

I/KG55

Heinkel He 111P-4 (3105). Crashed on landing at Evreux following combat sortie. No crew casualties. Aircraft 60% damaged.

II/KG76

Junkers Ju 88A-1 (8070). Attacked by fighters during operations over England and crashed at Calais. Crew unhurt. Aircraft 60% damaged.

KGr.806

Junkers Ju 88A-1 (7121). Crashed at Fauville on return from operational sortie in bad weather conditions. Fw. Kunert injured, rest of crew unhurt. Aircraft a write-off.

Junkers Ju 88A-1 (7133). Damaged in landing accident at Evreux aerodrome. Exact circumstances not stated. Crew unhurt. Aircraft 20% damaged.

III/LG1

Junkers Ju 88A-1 (8050). Failed to return from sortie to bomb London area. Believed shot down by fighters. Four NCOs missing. Aircraft LI+NT lost.

Junkers Ju 88A-5 (3177). Crashed at Fecamp following operational sortie over England. Gefr. Kulin wounded, rest of crew unhurt. Aircraft a write-off.

Junkers Ju 88A-5 (2207). Suffered engine failure during operational sortie and forced-landed at Granville. No crew casualties. Aircraft 30% damaged.

III/NJG1

Messerschmitt Bf 110C (0973). Crashed on landing at Stendal following combat sortie. Cause not stated. Crew unhurt. Aircraft 60% damaged.

A mid-air explosion during combat over Woolwich on October 20 destroyed this Messerschmitt Bf 109E of 6/JG52 from Peuplingues. Oberfeldwebel Friedemann fell to his death from the shattered cockpit, his parachute unopened. His machine minus the tail section fell at Wickham Street, Welling, Kent among the temporary wooden housing for bombed-out Londoners (Evening News).

The modernisation carried out in recent years at Wickham Street presented difficulties of comparison on July 26, 1979 but enquiries among local senior residents enabled us to locate the general area of the crash.

II/ZG2

Messerschmitt Bf 110. Landing accident at The Hague following routine domestic flight. Cause not stated. Crew unhurt. Aircraft 30% damaged.

Saturday, October 19

Kuestenflieger Gruppe 606

Dornier Do 17Z (1210). Crashed on landing at Brest following operational sortie, cause not recorded. No crew casualties. Aircraft 30% damaged.

8/KG2

Dornier Do 17Z-2 (1153). Crashed at Cambrai during routine domestic flight. Cause not stated. Crew unhurt. Aircraft a write-off.

II/KG4

Heinkel He 111P-4 (2923). Crashed on landing at Soesterberg after operations over England. Crew unhurt. Aircraft 30% damaged.

7/KG4

Junkers Ju 88A-1 (5128). Crashed on landing at Schiphol due to undercarriage failure. Oblt. Herrmann (Staffel Kapitan) and Oberfw. Stiefelhagen wounded. Aircraft a write-off.

9/KG30

Junkers Ju 88A-1 (7160). Undercarriage collapsed on landing at Eindhoven following combat sortie. No crew casualties. Aircraft a write-off.

III/KG77

Junkers Ju 88A-1 (5102). Expended fuel during operational sortie and crashed at Cansau. Crew unhurt. Aircraft a write-off.

I/StG 3

Junkers Ju 87B-1 (0237). Damaged in taxi-ing accident at Bary aerodrome. Crew unhurt. Aircraft damaged but repairable.

8/StG77

Junkers Ju 87B (5617). Crashed at Occagnes due to mid-air collision during routine domestic flight. Two NCOs killed. Aircraft a write-off.

Junkers Ju 87B (5628). Collided with another Ju 87B during local flying and crashed near Occagnes. Both crew killed. Aircraft a write-off.

Sunday, October 20

Kuestenflieger Gruppe 806

Junkers Ju 88A-1 (5068). Crashed on landing at Caen following routine domestic flight. Cause not stated. No crew casualties. Aircraft 10% damaged.

Junkers Ju 88A-1 (7129). Crash-landed at Caen aerodrome due to engine failure on operational sortie. No crew casualties. Aircraft 40% damaged.

4(F)/121

Junkers Ju 88A-5 (0415). Crash-landed at Caen aerodrome following long-range reconnaissance sortie. Uffz. Rickshausen killed. Uffz. Sauslikat wounded. Aircraft a write-off.

III/JG2

Junkers W 34 (778). Crash-landed near Tours during routine domestic flight. Cause not stated. No crew casualties. Aircraft 20% damaged.

7/JG27

Messerschmitt Bf 109E-1 (6350). Crashed on landing at Guines-West after local flight. Pilot unhurt. Aircraft 50% damaged.

5/JG52

Messerschmitt Bf 109E-7 (5930). Engaged on fighter escort mission for Bf 109 Jabos of 3/LG2 attacking London. Intercepted by Spitfires and shot down over West Malling. Crashed in Mereworth Wood 2.15 p.m. Fw. Bielmaier baled out and captured unhurt. Aircraft 4+ a write-off.
Major recovery organised by the late Alan Fall of the Air-Britain Excavation Committee 1973. Intact Daimler-Benz DB 601N engine amongst the many items unearthed now displayed in the Lashenden Air Warfare Museum. Pieces in the Vizard collection.

6/JG52

Messerschmitt Bf 109E-4 (2780). Attacked by RAF fighters during escort sortie over London and exploded over Woolwich 1.45 p.m. Oberfw. Friedemann fell from aircraft with unopened parachute. Aircraft 1+ a write-off.

Stab JG53

Messerschmitt Bf 109E-1 (4112). Crashed on landing at St. Inglevert following fighter combat. Pilot unhurt. Aircraft repairable.

9/JG54

Messerschmitt Bf 109E-4 (1525). Shot down by Flight Lieutenant McKellar of No. 605 Squadron during free-lance fighter operations over southern England. Forced-landed at North Fording House, near New Romney 10.20 a.m. Fw. Joburg captured slightly wounded. Aircraft 6+ a write-off.

3/JG77

Messerschmitt Bf 109E (4007). Crashed at Foxhunt Green, Chervey Farm, Waldron, near Uckfield 2.38 p.m. following fighter combat during free-lance mission. Fw. Wilhelm baled out and captured unhurt. Aircraft 11+ a write-off.
Site partially excavated by the Halstead War Museum and later completely cleared by the Wealden Aviation Archaeological Group in 1973. Manufacturers badge from the engine presented to the surviving pilot by London aviation artist Geoffrey Stevens.

1/KG27

Heinkel He 111P (2452). Suffered engine failure during operational sortie and forced-landed at Tours. Crew unhurt. Aircraft 50% damaged.

Ergaenzungs Staffel KG51

Heinkel He 111H (1726). Mid-air fire during local training flight causing crash near Lechfeld. Fw. Appelbeck and Uffz. Reisache both killed. Fw. Kirchberger wounded. Aircraft a write-off.

Ergaenzungs Staffel KG54

Junkers Ju 88A-1 (2055). Damaged in taxi-ing accident at Lechfeld aerodrome. Crew unhurt. Aircraft 40% damaged.

III/KG55

Heinkel He 111P-2 (2806). Taxi-ing accident at Villacoublay. Crew unhurt. Aircraft 25% damaged.

II/KG76

Junkers Ju 88A-5 (6124). Crashed on landing at Cormeissel following combat sortie over the Channel. No crew casualties. Aircraft 60% damaged.

III/KG77

Junkers Ju 88A-1 (3152). Engine caught fire during operational sortie and aircraft eventually crashed and burned out at Abbeville. Gefr. Hollstein killed, rest of crew escaped unhurt. Aircraft a write-off.

1/KGr.100

Heinkel He 111H-2 (2726). Crashed on take-off from Vannes on combat sortie. Cause unknown. Four NCOs killed. Aircraft a write-off.

3/LG2

Messerschmitt Bf 109E (5804). Crash-landed at Calais following fighter-bomber sortie over London and combat with RAF fighters 2.00 p.m. Pilot unhurt. Aircraft a write-off.

Messerschmitt Bf 109E (2059). Shot down by Flying Officer Mungo-Park of No. 74 Squadron during fighter-bomber attack on London. Crashed on Chapel Farm, Lenham Heath 2.00 p.m. Uffz. Mairl baled out but parachute caught fire. Aircraft a write-off.
Major recovery by the London Air Museum. Complete Daimler-Benz DB 601 engine excavated with propeller boss, two 20mm MGFF cannon and remains of shattered airframe.

Messerschmitt Bf 109E-1 (5598). Returned to base damaged following fighter-bomber attack on London and interception by RAF fighters 2.00 p.m. Pilot unhurt. Aircraft 20% damaged.

7(F)/LG2

Messerschmitt Bf 110C-5 (2228). Shot down by No. 92 Squadron Spitfires during photo-recce sortie over Thames Estuary. Forced-landed and burned out at Bockingfold, Horsmonden 12.50 p.m. Oblt. Lemmerich captured. Uffz. Ebeling killed. Aircraft L2+MR a write-off.

3/NJG2

Junkers Ju 88C-2 (0278). Crashed on landing at Eindhoven following operational sortie at night. Cause not stated. Fw. Schlicht injured. Aircraft 60% damaged.

Monday, October 21

Seenotflugkdo 1

Junkers W 34 Hi (1400). Damaged in collision with Arado Ar 66 at Buc aerodrome. No crew casualties. Aircraft repairable.

2(H)/14

Buecker Bu 131. Crashed on take-off from Hastenrath on routine domestic flight. Cause not stated. Crew unhurt but one civilian killed. Aircraft 40% damaged.

3(F)/123

Junkers Ju 88A-1 (0403). Crashed on take-off from Brest on long-range reconnaissance sortie. Cause unknown. Oberfw. Hening killed. Oblt. Jasper, Uffz. Ruschenberg and Uffz. Bachmann injured. Aircraft a write-off.

Erprobungs Gruppe 210

Messerschmitt Bf 110 (3367). Crashed on landing at St. Leger following local flight. Cause not stated. Uffz. Hesse and Uffz. Staeler both injured. Aircraft a write-off.

A Junkers Ju 88A-5 of 1/KG51 'Edelweiss' acquired the dubious honour of being the hundredth victim to fall to the guns of No. 609 Squadron. The machine, No. 8116, crashed and burned out at Manor Farm Field, Black Bush, killing the entire crew. The successful RAF pilots, Flight Lieutenant Frank Howell, DFC, and Pilot Officer Sidney Hill, admire their trophy from the wreck. This prize hung in the squadron's crew room at Biggin Hill and, although we tried to trace its present whereabouts, it is believed to have gone missing when the unit moved to Germany some years later. Being an auxiliary squadron, the unit has now disbanded.

Stab JG1

Focke-Wulf FW 58 (2670). Forced-landed near Charleville due to petrol failure during routine domestic flight. No casualties. Aircraft 20% damaged.

II/KG1

Heinkel He 111H-2 (5467). Damaged in landing accident at Rosieres following operational sortie. Cause not stated. Crew unhurt. Aircraft 20% damaged.

III/KG1

Junkers Ju 88A-1 (2212). Landing accident at Bapaume due to battle damage. No crew casualties. Aircraft 30% damaged.

I/KG51

Junkers Ju 88A-5 (8116). Shot down by No. 609 Squadron Spitfires during bombing sortie over England. Crashed and burned out at Manor Farm Field, Black Bush, Milford on Sea 1.47 p.m. Oblt. Fabian, Uffz. Wilhelm, Uffz. Scholz and Gefr. Stadelbauer all killed. Aircraft 9K+BH a write-off.

Stab KG53

Heinkel He 111H-3 (3160). Crashed on landing at Vendeville with damage sustained in operations over England. Crew unhurt. Aircraft a write-off.

3/KG53

Heinkel He 111H-5 (3758). Forced-landed at Hesdin during combat mission due to petrol shortage. No crew casualties. Aircraft 25% damaged.

III/KG55

Heinkel He 111H-2 (2663). Crashed in flames at Villacoublay after mid-air fire during operational sortie. Crew baled out unhurt. Aircraft a write-off.

III/KG76

Dornier Do 17Z (3397). Failed to return from operational sortie over southern England and presumed shot down by fighters. Fw. Stoesser killed. Lt. Wildhagen, Fw. Lieschl and Fw. Blaschke missing. Aircraft F1+LS a write-off.

KGr.806

Junkers Ju 88A-1 (4172). Crash-landed at Caen aerodrome following combat sortie. Exact cause not stated. No crew casualties. Aircraft 50% damaged.

8/NJG1

Messerschmitt Bf 110D (3143). Crashed on take-off from Stendal on night operations. Cause unknown but possibly engine failure. Oblt. Walther (Staffel Kapitan) and Uffz. Hoffmann both killed. Aircraft a write-off.

On the night of October 21/22, a Dornier 17Z-3 from Kuestenflieger Gruppe 606 took off from Lanveoc-Poulmic at 11.45 p.m. en route for Liverpool. The aircraft ran into bad weather near Shrewsbury which reputedly damaged the aircraft and the captain decided to turn back. Flying south, a severe electrical storm upset their instruments so much that, although they had in fact reached France, the compass indicated they were travelling north. Turning about, the Dornier flew back to England where, with no aerodromes in sight and running short of fuel, the crew decided to bale out landing on Salisbury Plain. It was only when they saw notices in English that they realised they were not in France. The unmanned bomber flew on autopilot an unbelievable 130 miles before making a perfect belly-landing on the tidal mud at Shotley Gate, Suffolk.

Tuesday, October 22

Kuestenflieger Gruppe 606

Dornier Do 17Z-3 (2783). Briefed to attack Liverpool and flew into magnetic storms over England. Belly-landed at Ness Point, Shotley, Essex 01.04 a.m. Lt. Stirnar, Lt. zur See Wuerdemann, Uffz. Schornisch and Uffz. Kuttner baled out over Salisbury Plain and captured unhurt. Aircraft 7T+AH lost.

2/JG26

Messerschmitt Bf 109E-4 (1124). Shot down by Flying Officer Coke of No. 257 Squadron in combat over the Channel 4.30 p.m. Broke up in mid-air, bulk of aircraft crashed in the sea off Littlestone Golf Links. Uffz. Arp killed. Aircraft 10+ lost.

5/JG27

Messerschmitt Bf 109E-1 (6285). Damaged in taxi-ing accident at Bonningues. Pilot unhurt. Aircraft 40% damaged.

7/JG27

Messerschmitt Bf 109E-4 (5581). Ditched in the Channel following combat with RAF fighters. Pilot rescued from sea unhurt. Aircraft lost.

1/JG51

Messerschmitt Bf 109E-1 (5362). Crashed on landing at Pihen following routine domestic flight. Pilot unhurt. Aircraft 60% damaged.

3/JG51

Messerschmitt Bf 109E-1 (4822). Severely damaged in attacks by Squadron Leader Malan and Flying Officer Mungo-Park of No. 74 Squadron during escort mission for Bf 109 Jabos attacking London. Crashed in the Channel four miles east of Hastings 2.30 p.m. Fhr. Mueller baled out and captured unhurt. Aircraft 10+ lost.

6/JG51

Messerschmitt Bf 109E-1 (0686). Damaged in landing accident at Mardyck following combat sortie. Pilot unhurt. Aircraft 10% damaged.

Ergaenzungs Staffel JG52

Messerschmitt Bf 109E-1 (3187). Crashed on landing at Krefeld following local training flight. Cause not stated. Pilot unhurt. Aircraft 40% damaged.

KG27

Junkers Ju 52 (1339). Crashed on landing at Avord following routine domestic flight. Cause not notified. Fw. Beck killed. Lt. Neuziel injured. Rest of crew unhurt. Aircraft a write-off.

1/KG27

Heinkel He 111H (5443). Crashed into barracks at Tours aerodrome on return from night operations over England. Lt. Wilhelm, Uffz. Bautz, Uffz. Jenau and Uffz. Forster all killed. (Thirteen ground-crew killed and eleven more injured.) Aircraft a write-off.

III/KG27

Heinkel He 111P (2626). Caught fire in mid-air during operational sortie and crashed in flames at Rennes. Major Fr. von Sternburg (Gruppe Kommandeur) Lt. Jansen, Fw. Kramwinkel and Uffz. Schmidt all killed. Aircraft a write-off.

Heinkel He 111P (1392). Crashed at Tours aerodrome following mid-air fire. Oblt. Walther, Uffz. Taussmann, Uffz. Moosbauer and Fhr. Schmiedfelden killed. Aircraft a write-off.

8/KG30

Junkers Ju 88A-5 (2180). Crashed attempting forced-landing at Eindhoven in bad visibility. No crew casualties. Aircraft 60% damaged.

I/KG40

Focke-Wulf FW 200 (0024). Failed to return from weather reconnaissance sortie over the Irish Sea. Presumed lost at sea, cause unknown. Oblt. Schuldt, Fw. Berghaus, Fw. Gruber, Fw. Ploeger, Gefr. Gressle and Meteorologe Dr. Sturm all missing. Aircraft F8+OK lost.

2/KG53

Heinkel He 111H-5 (3571). Crashed on landing at Vitry-en-Artois following combat sortie. Cause not stated. Oblt. Mueller and three NCOs killed. Oberfw. Kraft injured. Aircraft a write-off.

I/KG54

Junkers Ju 88A-1 (7158). Damaged landing at Evreux, cause not recorded. No crew casualties. Aircraft 10% damaged.

II/KG77

Junkers Ju 88A-1 (0301). Crashed on take-off from Rheims on operational sortie. Cause not stated. No crew casualties. Aircraft a write-off.

Junkers Ju 88A-5 (0327). Damaged in landing accident at Reims aerodrome following operations over England. Crew unhurt. Aircraft 30% damaged.

KGr.806

Junkers Ju 88A-1 (7130). Crashed and burned out at Caen during operational sortie. Cause unknown. Oblt. zur See Reischle and three NCOs killed. Aircraft a write-off.

Wednesday, October 23

1(F)/120

Heinkel He 111H-2 (5280). Forced-landed at Groix during reconnaissance sortie. Cause not stated. No crew casualties. Aircraft 30% damaged.

2/JG77

Messerschmitt Bf 109E-1 (5011). Damaged landing at Oslo-Fornebu following local flight. Pilot unhurt. Aircraft 10% damaged.

The spot where the Dornier landed is now marked by the wreck of a derelict barge. The location is just below the famous Royal Navy station HMS Ganges, closed in 1976 on the recommendation in the 1971-73 report of the Defence Lands Committee and still available for sale at £500,000.

9/KG3

Dornier Do 17Z-2 (3362). Abandoned over Esneux when fuel exhausted following operations over the Channel. Crew baled out unhurt. Aircraft a write-off.

KG27

Junkers Ju 52 (5054). Crashed on landing at Avord aerodrome following routine domestic flight. Cause not stated. Gefr. Wunderlich injured, rest of crew unhurt. Aircraft 60% damaged.

II/KG77

Junkers Ju 88A-1 (3158). Crashed near Laon on operational sortie, cause not stated. Fw. Kretschmer and Uffz. Meyer both wounded. Aircraft a write-off.

III/KG77

Junkers Ju 88A-1 (3151). Crashed at Neuilly Hospital following operations over the Channel. Exact circumstances not recorded. Fw. Kissel killed. Two NCOs wounded. Aircraft a write-off.

Junkers Ju 88A-1 (5107). Failed to return from raid on London and presumed shot down by ground defences. Lt. Spaar and three NCOs all missing. Aircraft 3Z+ HT lost.

Above: **Attacked by RAF fighters on October 24 during a photo-reconnaissance mission to the Midlands, this Dornier Do 215 L2 + KS broke up before crashing at Eaton Socon near St. Neots. Although the crew baled out three were found dead. The wreckage fell in several pieces in fields on the western side of the old Great North Road. This is the rear fuselage and tailplane — bullet-holed and blistered and charred by fire (Biggleswade Chronicle).** *Below:* **Today the new A1 trunk route bypasses Eaton Socon and bisects the crash site.**

Thursday, October 24

2(F)/22

Heinkel He 111H-2 (5306). Damaged in taxiing accident at Luebeck. No crew casualties. Aircraft 35% damaged.

1(H)/41

Henschel Hs 126 (4130). Ditched in the sea off French coast during local flight. Cause not stated. Crew rescued unhurt by fishing boat. Aircraft C2+ DH lost.

3/Aufklaerungs Gruppe Ob.d.L.

Dornier Do 215 (0060). Shot down by fighters during photo-reconnaissance sortie to Coventry and Birmingham. Crashed near the Crown Inn, Eaton Socon 12.35 p.m. Lt. Meyer, Uffz. Hoffmann and Uffz. Broening baled out but killed. Gefr. Dorr baled out and captured wounded. Aircraft L2+ KS a write-off.

8/JG27

Messerschmitt Bf 109E-4 (3703). Damaged in landing accident at Guines-West following combat sortie. Pilot unhurt. Aircraft 35% damaged.

Messerschmitt Bf 109E-4 (1558). Suffered engine failure during combat mission and crashed off Cap Gris-Nez. Uffz. Linke missing. Aircraft 2+ lost.

Ergaenzungs Staffel JG54

Messerschmitt Bf 109E-1 (6071). Crashed on take-off from Bergen on local training flight. Cause unknown. Fw. Brixel killed. Aircraft a write-off.

4/JG77

Messerschmitt Bf 109E (0820). Forced-landed in Sweden, cause unknown, during routine domestic flight. Overturned on landing. Uffz. Froba interned. Aircraft 3+ a write-off.

III/KG1

Junkers Ju 88A-5 (3221). Crashed Bapaume-Grevillers during routine domestic flight. Cause not stated. No crew casualties. Aircraft a write-off.

1/KG2

Dornier Do 17Z (2591). Crashed in flames at Le Clouse during operational sortie. Cause unknown. Uffz. Meyer, Uffz. Schermann, Obergefr. Welf and Gefr. Faust all killed. Aircraft a write-off.

Dornier Do 17Z (3444). Crashed at St. Court following combat mission. Cause unknown. Fw. Dillger, Obergefr. Kunze, Obergefr. Fuerst and Gefr. Maas all killed. Aircraft a write-off.

9/KG2

Dornier Do 17Z-2 (2863). Severely damaged in fighter attack during sortie over England and returned to base. Gefr. Schinz killed. Fw. Bohnhof, and Gefr. Elbert wounded. Aircraft a write-off.

5/KG30

Junkers Ju 88A-5 (0265). Engine failure caused crash-landing at Gilze-Rijen aerodrome during operational mission. Oblt. Baumbach, Uffz. Menz, Fw. Thies and Fw. Kohler all injured. Aircraft a write-off.

II/KG51

Junkers Ju 88A-1 (3171). Damaged in landing accident at Orly aerodrome following combat sortie. No crew casualties. Aircraft 20% damaged.

Ergaenzungs Staffel KG55

Heinkel He 111H-2 (5330). Crashed in flames at Camens during local training flight. Cause unknown. Oblt. Wamser and four NCOs killed. Aircraft a write-off.

II/KG55

Heinkel He 111P-4 (3100). Crashed at Halberstadt during routine domestic flight. Cause unknown. Oberfw. Jesuiter and Fw. Gaas both killed. Aircraft a write-off.

IV/LG1

Junkers Ju 87 (5200). Damaged landing at Courtrai following routine local flight. Cause unknown. Crew unhurt. Aircraft 30% damaged.

Friday, October 25

1/KG z.b.V.108

Junkers Ju 52 (6945). Crashed at Hommelvik on routine domestic flight. Cause not recorded. No crew casualties. Aircraft a write-off.

3(F)/11

Dornier Do 17P (4073). Crash-landed at Zutkerque following reconnaissance sortie. Exact cause not recorded. Crew unhurt. Aircraft 30% damaged.

3(H)/12

Henschel Hs 126B (3439). Crashed on landing at Denain from routine domestic flight. Cause not stated. Crew unhurt. Aircraft 60% damaged.

4(F)/14

Dornier Do 17P (4158). Crashed and burned out at Plumetot following long-range reconnaissance sortie. Lt. Hoecker and two NCOs killed. Aircraft a write-off.

2(F)/122

Messerschmitt Bf 110C-5 (2257). Shot down by fighters during bomber escort sortie and crashed in sea off Yarmouth 3.00 p.m. Gefr. Gneist killed. Lt. Wacker picked up by HMS Widgeon and landed at Harwich. Aircraft S6+MC lost.

3/Erprobungs Gruppe 210

Messerschmitt Bf 109E-4 (3765). Damaged in landing accident at Calais-Marck aerodrome following combat mission. Pilot unhurt. Aircraft 20% damaged.

II/JG2

Messerschmitt Bf 109E-4 (4860). Crashed at Montdemarsan during combat sortie. Cause not notified. Pilot unhurt. Aircraft a write-off.

Ergaenzungs Staffel JG3

Messerschmitt Bf 109E-3 (0946). Crashed on take-off from St. Omer on local training flight. Gefr. Schuck injured. Aircraft a write-off.

2/JG26

Messerschmitt Bf 109E (3631). Forced-landed at Boulogne following combat over the Channel. Pilot unhurt. Aircraft 20% damaged.

II/JG26

Messerschmitt Bf 109E-1 (3601). Damaged in combat over the Channel and forced-landed at Marquise-Ost. Pilot unhurt. Aircraft 40% damaged.

5/JG26

Messerschmitt Bf 109E-4 (3724). Shot down by No. 501 Squadron Hurricanes in combat over southern England. Crashed at Church Street Farm, near Ticehurst Road Station, Sussex 12.00 p.m. Oblt. Eichstaedt baled out but parachute failed. Aircraft 12+ a write-off.

8/JG26

Messerschmitt Bf 109E-4 (5815). Engaged by No. 92 Squadron Spitfires during free-lance fighter operations over Kent 1.30 p.m. Shot down by Flying Officer Villa and crashed on Congelow Farm, Yalding. Fw. Gaertner baled out and captured slightly wounded. Aircraft 7+1 a write-off.

Site excavated by local enthusiast, Alfred Batt of Maidstone. Elevator mass balance, 7.92mm MG17 ammunition and fabric from rudder bearing victory tabs in Kent Battle of Britain Museum. Several relics also in the Steve Vizard collection.

Some of the items obtained by Steve Vizard from a 'Schlageter' Messerschmitt Bf 109E of 8/JG26 which succumbed to the attentions of RAF fighters on October 25. The aircraft crashed near Yalding, Kent, Feldwebel Josef Gaertner baling out slightly wounded.

Messerschmitt Bf 109E-4 (5795). Engaged on free-lance fighter sweep and shot down by Pilot Officer Sherrington of No. 92 Squadron. Crashed at Riverhill House, south of Sevenoaks 1.40 p.m. Lt. Ripke fell five miles away with unopened parachute. Aircraft 2+1 a write-off.

Tail wheel from this aircraft used for several years on a local resident's wheelbarrow until acquired by the Halstead War Museum in 1963. Site impossible to excavate but investigated by Steve Vizard and several fragments collected from hilltop.

At 3.00 p.m. on October 25, a Messerschmitt Bf 109E piloted by Hauptmann Asmus of Stab/JG51, broke up in combat over Marden, Kent scattering fragments like confetti and creating an unintentional bonanza for aircraft preservation groups many years after the event. The reflector gunsight can now be seen in the Kent Battle of Britain Museum and the side panel and bucket seat, found stored in a barn, at the Lashenden Museum.

Stab JG51

Messerschmitt Bf 109E-4 (3737). Exploded over Millbush Inn, Marden, Kent during engagement with RAF fighters 3.00 p.m. Hptmn. Asmus baled out and captured wounded. Aircraft a write-off.

Complete cockpit side incorporating the pilot's bucket seat acquired by the Lashenden Air Warfare Museum. Reflector gunsight from this aircraft in Kent Battle of Britain Museum.

6/JG51

Messerschmitt Bf 109E-4 (5724). Returned to Mardyck damaged following combat sortie over the Channel. Pilot unhurt. Aircraft 10% damaged.

7/JG51

Messerschmitt Bf 109E-1 (6281). Shot down by RAF fighters during free-lance fighter operations and crashed on Lidham Hill Farm, Guestling, Sussex 3.30 p.m. Fw. Koslowski baled out and badly burned. Aircraft a write-off.

Site excavated by the Brenzett Aeronautical Museum and the Wealden Aviation Archaeological Group in August 1975. Propeller boss recovered together with blades, undercarriage leg, reflector gunsight and cockpit clock. Bulk of this aircraft sunk over 35ft in mud at the bottom of a dyke.

Messerschmitt Bf 109E-1 (3548). Brought down in combat with No. 501 Squadron Hurricanes during escort mission for Bf 109 fighter-bombers attacking London. Forced-landed at Stonewall Farm, Hunton, Kent 12.00 p.m. Fw. Birg captured unhurt. Aircraft 4+ a write-off.

9/JG51

Messerschmitt Bf 109E-4 (4098). Returned to base damaged by AA fire during combat sortie over Dover. Pilot unhurt. Aircraft 30% damaged.

Messerschmitt Bf 109E-4 (4099). Damaged by AA fire during operations over Dover but returned safely to base. Pilot unhurt. Aircraft 50% damaged.

Messerschmitt Bf 109E-4 (4100). Shot down during fighter combat over the Channel off Dover. Crashed in sea. Pilot rescued unhurt. Aircraft lost.

6/JG53

Messerschmitt Bf 109E-4 (1080). Failed to return from combat sortie over the Channel and engagement by RAF fighters. Uffz. Schulz missing. Aircraft 2+ lost.

5/JG54

Messerschmitt Bf 109E-4 (1988). Damaged by fighters during escort mission for Bf 109 Jabos attacking London. Engine temperature resulted in forced-landing at Broom Hill, near Lydd, Kent 9.30 a.m. Oblt. Schypek captured unhurt. Aircraft 7+ a write-off.

Messerschmitt Bf 109E-4 (5178). Attacked by fighters during fighter-bomber escort sortie. Eluded by flying into cloud over coast and became disorientated. Crash-landed west of Galloways, Dungeness 1.55 p.m. Lt. Wagner captured unhurt. Aircraft 2+ a write-off.

3/JG77

Messerschmitt Bf 109E-4 (5104). Radiator damaged in combat with RAF fighters and forced-landed on downs at Harveys Cross, Telscombe, north of Saltdean, Sussex 1.30 p.m. Gefr. Raisinger captured unhurt. Aircraft 13+ a write-off.

Messerschmitt Bf 109E-1 (5812). Forced-landed at St. Andeyelle following combat sortie over southern England. Pilot unhurt. Aircraft 25% damaged.

Above: The crater in a water-filled ditch on Brede marshes made by the Bf 109 evacuated by Feldwebel Willi Koslowski when shot down on the afternoon of October 25. By coincidence, two groups, Brenzett and Wealden, planned to excavate the site at Guestling and, as the ditch forms the boundary between two farms, each had approached a different landowner for permission to dig. Ultimately they agreed to join forces on a combined operation in August 1975 *(below)*. *Right:* This nice Revi reflector gunsight went to the Wealden collection (S. Hall/ A Saunders).

II/KG1

Heinkel He 111H-2 (5325). Crashed near Arras due to petrol failure during combat mission. Uffz. Siefert injured. Aircraft a write-off.

II/KG54

Junkers Ju 88A-1 (6095). Damaged in landing accident at Dreux aerodrome following operational sortie. No crew casualties. Aircraft 35% damaged.

III/KG55

Heinkel He 111P-2 (1528). Suffered engine failure during combat sortie and forced-landed at Villacoublay. Crew unhurt. Aircraft 30% damaged.

II/KG76

Junkers Ju 88A-1 (3081). Damaged in taxi-ing accident at Cormeilles. Exact circumstances not recorded. Crew unhurt. Aircraft 15% damaged.

III/KG76

Dornier Do 17Z (2882). Crashed in flames at Cormeilles aerodrome following operational sortie. Cause unknown, possible result of combat damage. Oberfw. Jaeckel, Oberfw. Sachs, Oberfw. Faller and Fw. Rumpel all killed. Aircraft a write-off.

I/KG77

Junkers Ju 88A-1 (2140). Crashed on landing at Reims following combat mission. No crew casualties. Aircraft 40% damaged.

II/KG77

Junkers Ju 88A-1 (4135). Failed to return from mission to bomb London at night and presumed shot down by ground defences. Oberfw. Hoehn, Fw. Muller, Fw. Carnet and Gefr. Tschentke all missing. Aircraft 3Z+ES lost.

III/KG77

Junkers Ju 88A-1 (6140). Failed to return from night bombing attack on London. Believed brought down by AA fire. Uffz. Hekers, Uffz. Pirschan, Obergefr. Hoffmann and Obergefr. Gurnkranz all killed. Aircraft 3Z+KT lost.

Ergaeanzungs Kette KGr.100

Heinkel He 111H-2 (5469). Crashed and burned out at Luneburg during take-off on local training flight. Lt. Nachtmann and two NCOs killed. Aircraft a write-off.

1/KGr.126

Heinkel He 111H-4 (3228). Crashed and burned out at Nantes during operational sortie. Cause unknown. Uffz. Reith, Obergefr. Loewe, Gefr. Kirchner and Oberfhr. Mayer all killed. Aircraft a write-off.

8/KGr.806

Junkers Ju 88A-5 (4185). Crashed on take-off from Caen on operational mission. Cause unknown. Oblt. Neumann, Oblt. zur See Metzner and two NCOs killed. Aircraft a write-off.

II/LG2

Messerschmitt Bf 109E-4 (3718). Damaged in taxi-ing accident at Calais-Marck aerodrome. Pilot unhurt. Aircraft 40% damaged.

II/ZG26

Messerschmitt Bf 110C-7 (3630). Crashed at St. Aubin following routine domestic flight. Cause not stated. Crew unhurt. Aircraft a write-off.

Saturday, October 26

Seenotflugkdo. 3

Heinkel He 59 (1984). Shot down by Sergeant O'Manney of No. 229 Squadron whilst engaged on air-sea rescue mission over the Channel off Boulogne 11.00 a.m. Lt. Wilke, Uffz. Backmaier and Gefr. Michels killed. Aircraft lost.

2(F)/123

Junkers Ju 88A-1 (0348). Returned to base damaged by AA fire during long-range reconnaissance sortie over England. Uffz. Gruenmueller and Fw. Fischer both wounded. Aircraft repairable.

1/506

He 115B (1889). Shot down by RAF Hampden during patrol over North Sea and forced-landed on sea. Lt. zur See Kemper, Uffz. Grotefeld and Obergefr. Forster took to dinghy and landed near Yarmouth next day. Aircraft S4+AH lost.

8/JG27

Messerschmitt Bf 109E (1132). Forced-landed at Guines-West following routine local flight. Pilot unhurt. Aircraft 20% damaged.

Ergaenzungs Staffel JG52

Messerschmitt Bf 109E (3474). Crashed on take-off from Krefeld on local training flight. Pilot unhurt. Aircraft 35% damaged.

1/JG53

Messerschmitt Bf 109E-7 (5929). Believed shot down in the Channel off Littlestone during combat with RAF fighters. Oberfw. Strack killed. Aircraft 6+ lost.

4/JG53

Messerschmitt Bf 109E-1 (6180). Shot down during combat with RAF fighters over the Channel and crashed in sea. Pilot rescued unhurt by Seenotdienst. Aircraft lost.

6/JG53

Messerschmitt Bf 109E (3429). Returned to base damaged following combat with No. 92 Squadron Spitfires over Tonbridge 10.30 a.m. Pilot unhurt. Aircraft 20% damaged.

Messerschmitt Bf 109E-4 (1099). Severely damaged in combat over Tonbridge 10.30 a.m. but returned safely to base. Pilot unhurt. Aircraft 40% damaged.

Like some primeval thing emerging into the light of day. The engine of a German fighter plane leaves its grave nearly a quarter of a century after it buried itself on October 26, 1940. This DB 601 from a 6/JG53 Bf 109 is now in the private Halstead War Museum (Gordon Anckorn).

Messerschmitt Bf 109E-1 (6391). Shot down by Sergeant Fokes of No. 92 Squadron during combat over Tunbridge Wells. Crashed at Chalket Farm, Pembury 10.30 a.m. Uffz. Geiswinkler killed. Aircraft 8+ a write-off.

Site excavated by the Halstead War Museum and complete Daimler-Benz DB 601 engine recovered together with many major components, controls and remains of crumpled airframe. Some minor components also held by Kent Battle of Britain Museum.

II/JG77

Messerschmitt Bf 109E (6090). Believed damaged in collision at Herdla. Exact circumstances not recorded. Lt. Arnoldy injured. Aircraft repairable.

Messerschmitt Bf 109E (6202). Damaged (believed result of minor collision) at Herdla. Uffz. Niemeyer injured. Aircraft repairable.

III/KG1

Junkers Ju 88A-5. Abandoned by crew over Rosieres due to fuel shortage during operational sortie. No crew casualties. Aircraft a write-off.

Shot down on a free-lance mission over south-east London on October 27, this Bf 109E-7 of JG3 'Udet' crashed into a beet field at Wickham Court Farm, east of Croydon. Leutnant Wilhelm Busch the Signals Officer of I/JG3 baled out landing near the New Addington Estate where he was reputedly set upon by a group of incensed housewives (Central Press).

I/KG26

Heinkel He 111H-3 (6854). Hit by ground defences during bombing attack on Lossiemouth aerodrome and exploded in mid-air 6.30 p.m. Oblt. Imholz, Uffz. Radloff, Uffz. Weniger and Fw. Bastian all killed. Aircraft 1H+ BL a write-off.

Site identified by the Scotland West Aircraft Investigation Group.

Heinkel He 111H-3 (3319). Damaged by AA fire during night bombing sortie over Scotland and returned to base. Uffz. Kruger wounded. Aircraft 20% damaged.

Heinkel He 111H-3 (6937). Returned to base damaged by AA fire during night bombing sortie over Scotland. Fw. Jessen wounded. Aircraft 20% damaged.

2/KG53

Heinkel He 111H-5 (3637). Failed to return from sortie to bomb London at night and believed brought down by AA fire. Lt. Hanau, Lt. Cichi and three NCOs all missing. Aircraft A1+ KL lost.

Stab KG55

Heinkel He 111P-2 (2653). Crashed on landing from combat mission over London and burned out at Versailles. Cause unknown, but probably battle damage. Oblt. Eitner, Lt. Oberhofer, Gefr. Schweikert, Uffz. Kruemmel and Uffz. Kemlitz all killed. Aircraft a write-off.

Thankfully on August 2, 1979 we found the New Addington housewives friendlier. With Wickham Court Farm in the background, Mr. Bristow, who was the first person on the scene in 1940, relates the tale of the women's action.

A unique and disciplined recovery undertaken by the Air Historical Group was that of a Messerschmitt Bf 109E-4 of 2/JG52 which crashed at East Park, Newchapel, near East Grinstead on October 27. The crash site was under a tarmac road and permission was granted to dig a limited area only. Working under the most confined conditions the group recovered parts of the engine and a huge hoard of badly corroded 7.92mm rounds — all of which were reburied when the hole was filled in (Air Historical Group).

Heinkel He 111P-2 (2666). Crashed on landing at Villacoublay following operational sortie. Cause not stated. No crew casualties. Aircraft a write-off.

II/KG55

Heinkel He 111P-2 (3354). Crashed on landing at Cormeilles aerodrome following operational sortie. No crew casualties. Aircraft 25% damaged.

II/KG76

Junkers Ju 88A-5 (6159) Crash-landed at Creil following operations over England. Cause not stated. No crew casualties. Aircraft 50% damaged.

II/KG77

Junkers Ju 88A-1 (7111). Suffered engine failure during operational sortie and forced-landed at Soissons. Crew unhurt. Aircraft 50% damaged.

I/NJG1

Messerschmitt Bf 110C-2 (3599). Damaged in collision with Bf 110 of II/NJG1 at Schiphol aerodrome. Crew unhurt. Aircraft 35% damaged.

II/NJG1

Messerschmitt Bf 110C-2 (3538). Collided with Bf 110 of I/NJG1 at Schiphol aerodrome and damaged. Crew unhurt. Aircraft 35% damaged.

Sunday, October 27

Flugbereitschaft Luftgau kdo. Belg./Nordfr.

Henschel Hs 126 (5279). Crashed on landing at Calais-Marck following routine domestic flight. Cause not stated. No crew casualties. Aircraft 20% damaged.

3(H)/32

Fieseler Fi 156 (0689). Damaged in forced-landing near Amiens during local flight. Cause not recorded. Crew unhurt. Aircraft 35% damaged.

3(F)/121

Junkers Ju 88A-5 (0452). Suffered engine failure during operational sortie and damaged in forced-landing at Morlaix aerodrome. No crew casualties. Aircraft 20% damaged.

Stab I/JG3

Messerschmitt Bf 109E-7 (4124). Shot down by RAF fighters during free-lance fighter operations over Kent. Crashed on Fisher Farm, West Wickham 12.00 p.m. Lt. Busch (Gruppe Nachr. Offz.) baled out and captured wounded. Aircraft a write-off.

6/JG27

Messerschmitt Bf 109E-4 (1329). Crashed on take-off from Denain on routine domestic flight. Cause not stated. Pilot unhurt. Aircraft a write-off.

8/JG27

Messerschmitt Bf 109E. Forced-landed Cap Gris-Nez with combat damage following fighter operations over southern England 9.00 a.m. Pilot unhurt. Aircraft 20% damaged.

Messerschmitt Bf 109E-4 (1603). Shot down in combat with RAF fighters during free-lance sortie over Kent. Crashed near Hooks Wood, Lenham 9.00 a.m. Oblt. Pointer (Staffel Kapitan) baled out and captured unhurt. Aircraft 10+ a write-off.
Site excavated by local enthusiasts, John Rawlings and Alf Batt, who recovered many components and fragments of airframe together with various manufacturers' labels, one confirming identity as '1603'. Some relics also in the Vizard collection.

9/JG27

Messerschmitt Bf 109E-1 (4818). Forced-landed at Calais with combat damage. Gefr. Busenkeil wounded. Aircraft 40% damaged.

2/JG52

Messerschmitt Bf 109E-4 (1268). Shot down by Flight Lieutenant McKellar of No. 605 Squadron during fighter combat over Surrey. Crashed at East Park, near Newchapel, East Grinstead 8.30 a.m. Gefr. Bott baled out unhurt. Aircraft 5+ a write-off.
Remains of shattered Daimler-Benz DB 601 engine and airframe components recovered from under a tarmac drive by the Air Historical Group.

3/JG52

Messerschmitt Bf 109E-4 (2798). Shot down in combat with No. 74 Squadron Spitfires during escort mission for Bf 109 Jabos attacking London 9.40 a.m. Crashed at Upstreet, near Canterbury. Oblt. Steinhilper baled out slightly wounded. Aircraft 2+ a write-off.
Pilot's wrist compass and piece of Swastika marking from the tail of this machine donated to the Kent Battle of Britain Museum by a local resident.

Messerschmitt Bf 109E-4 (3525). Forced-landed at Penshurst landing-ground 9.15 a.m. following combat over Kent with No. 74 Squadron Spitfires. Fw. Schieverhofer captured unhurt. Aircraft 4+ a write-off.
Radio frequencies card 'liberated' from the cockpit of this aircraft in 1940 donated to Brenzett Aeronautical Museum by a local resident.

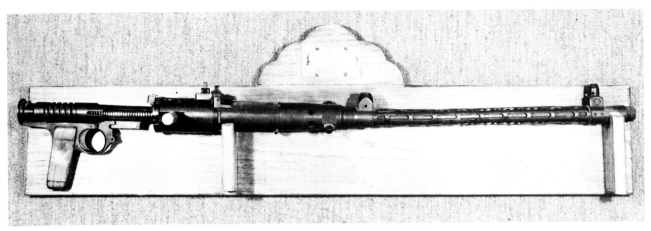

2/JG53

Messerschmitt Bf 109E-1 (1504). Damaged in taxi-ing accident at Etaples aerodrome. Pilot unhurt. Aircraft 25% damaged.

4/JG53

Messerschmitt Bf 109E-4 (5243). Failed to return from combat sortie over England and presumed shot down by fighters. Uffz. Schlitt missing. Aircraft 5+ lost.

7/JG54

Messerschmitt Bf 109E-1 (3576). Engine severely damaged by RAF fighters in action over Kent during free-lance sweep to London. Belly-landed on beach near Lydd water tower 9.40 a.m. Uffz. Zimmermann captured unhurt. Aircraft 13+ a write-off.

5/JG77

Messerschmitt Bf 109E (3590). Forced-landed at Hitra on routine domestic flight. Exact cause not stated. Pilot unhurt. Aircraft 20% damaged.

Messerschmitt Bf 109E (1407). In formation with Bf 109 above and also forced-landed on Hitra cause unknown. Possible loss of bearings during local flight and shortage of fuel. Pilot unhurt. Aircraft 20% damaged.

I/KG1

Heinkel He 111H-2 (5541). Suffered engine failure during sortie to bomb Horsham St. Faith aerodrome and ditched in sea off Clacton 11.30 a.m. Uffz. Behres, Uffz. Heinhold, Gefr. Roesenberg, Gefr. Hartleib, and Fw. Saumsiegel captured unhurt. Aircraft V4+ HW lost.

III/KG1

Junkers Ju 88A-5 (2194). Crashed on landing at Greville aerodrome following routine domestic flight. Cause not stated. No crew casualties. Aircraft a write-off.

3/KG2

Dornier Do 17Z-2 (3443). Returned to base with battle damage following operations over England. Uffz. Rutkowski wounded. Aircraft repairable.

7/KG3

Dornier Do 17Z. Returned to base damaged in fighter attack during mission over England. Fw. Passler killed. Aircraft repairable.

MG15 from the Ju 88A-5 of 7/KG4 shot down by the defences of Driffield aerodrome on October 27 and retained by them as a trophy.

9/KG3

Dornier Do 17Z. Attacked by fighters during sortie over England but returned safely to base. Fw. Heese wounded. Aircraft repairable.

7/KG4

Junkers Ju 88A (6129). Shot down by ground fire during attack on Driffield aerodrome 6.00 p.m. Belly-landed on Richmond Farm, Duggleby, Yorkshire. Oblt. Podbielski (Staffel Kapitan), Uffz. Heier, Uffz. Jidrowski captured unhurt. Uffz. Pionteck killed. Aircraft 5J+ ER a write-off.

8/KG4

Junkers Ju 88A-1 (6048). Failed to return from bombing mission over England and presumed shot down by AA fire. Oblt. Marlwitz, Oberfw. Ehrbach, Uffz. Schmitz and Gefr. Herold all missing. Aircraft 5J+ HS a write-off.

II/KG26

Heinkel He 111H-3 (3326). Temporary loss of control during operational sortie. Landed with severe damage. Oblt. Kuene, Uffz. Lehmann baled out and landed injured. Aircraft a write-off.

5/KG53

Heinkel He 111H-2 (5500). Crash-landed at Vendeville aerodrome during operational sortie. Cause not stated. No crew casualties. Aircraft a write-off.

Ergaenzungs Staffel KG54

Junkers Ju 88A-1 (3099). Crashed on landing near Berleberg during local training flight. Cause not stated. No crew casualties. Aircraft a write-off.

III/KG76

Dornier Do 17Z (1150). Briefed to attack Stradishall aerodrome and failed to return. Believed shot down by RAF fighters. Uffz. Ebeling, Uffz. Fritz, Uffz. Karl, and Obergefr. Wuelpern all killed. Uffz. Johannes missing. Aircraft F1+ HR lost.

III/LG1

Junkers Ju 88A-1 (6150). Crashed on landing at Manneville following combat sortie. Cause unknown. Crew unhurt. Aircraft 50% damaged.

3/NJG2

Junkers Ju 88A-1 (6144). Crashed on take-off from Gilze-Rijen aerodrome on night operations. Cause not stated. Crew unhurt. Aircraft 60% damaged.

Ergaenzungs Staffel ZG26

Messerschmitt Bf 110C-4 (3625). Damaged in taxi-ing accident at Guyancourt. Crew unhurt. Aircraft 20% damaged.

A fragment of tail fin from the Bf 109E-4 of 3/JG52 from Coquelles which was shot down at Upstreet on October 27, 1940 and donated to Chilham Castle together with the pilot's wrist compass.

Monday, October 28

Seenotflukdo. 1

Dornier Do 27 (0075). Crashed at Nordwyk following engine failure on routine local flight. Lt. Scheel killed. Lt. zur See Unterhorst and Uffz. Kruse both injured. Aircraft a write-off.

Kuestenflieger Gruppe 606

Dornier Do 17Z (3437). Crashed on landing at Brest following operational sortie. Cause not stated. No crew casualties. Aircraft 40% damaged.

2(F)/123

Messerschmitt Bf 110C-5 (2241). Crashed on take-off from Saarbruecken on routine domestic flight. Cause not stated. Hptmn. Dechand and Major Obernitz both injured. Aircraft 60% damaged.

Ergaenzungs Staffel KG1

Heinkel He 111H-2 (2788). Crashed at Nordhausen during domestic flight due to engine failure. No crew casualties. Aircraft a write-off.

1/KG3

Dornier Do 17Z-2 (2544). Suffered engine failure during night operations over Kent and crash-landed at Boughton Malherbe, near Maidstone 1.00 a.m. Fw. Vosshagen captured badly wounded. Fw. Schreiber, Fw. Nitsche and Uffz. Hausdorf killed. Aircraft 5K+CH a write-off.

8/KG3

Dornier Do 17Z. Attacked by fighters during sortie over the Channel and returned to base with Gefr. Buettner and Flgr. Ziebursch both wounded. Aircraft repairable.

I/KG51

Junkers Ju 88A-1 (5112). Landing accident at Villaroche aerodrome after operations over the Channel. Collided with another Ju 88. Crew unhurt. Aircraft 20% damaged.

Junkers Ju 88A-1 (5125). Collided with Ju 88 above on landing at Villaroche following combat sortie. Crew unhurt. Aircraft 25% damaged.

III/KG51

Junkers Ju 88A-1 (8040). Briefed to attack London and failed to return from mission. Exact fate unknown. Gefr. Koenig killed. Uffz. Kramer, Gefr. Hauff and Gefr. Zimmermann missing. Aircraft 9K+MT lost.

I/KG53

Heinkel He 111H-2 (3536). Suffered engine failure during routine domestic flight and forced-landed at Oppy/Arras aerodrome. No crew casualties. Aircraft 30% damaged.

II/KG76

Junkers Ju 88A-5 (8078). Crashed on landing following operational sortie. Exact circumstances not recorded. Crew unhurt. Aircraft a write-off.

I/KG77

Junkers Ju 88A-1 (2146). Crashed and burned out at St. Dizier during routine domestic flight. Cause unknown. Lt. Wagner and two NCOs killed. Obergefr. Schmitt injured. Aircraft a write-off.

Ergaenzungs Kette KG100

Heinkel He 111H-1 (2420). Crashed and burned out near Luneburg during local flight. Cause unknown. Three NCOs killed. Aircraft a write-off.

7/NJG1

Messerschmitt Bf 110D (3356). Crashed in flames at Rendburg during night operational sortie. Cause not known. Uffz. Bertram and Oberfw. Lorenz both killed. Aircraft a write-off.

4/ZG26

Messerschmitt Bf 110C/D (3429). Crash-landed at Jever following mechanical failure during combat sortie. Hptmn. Hoppe wounded. Aircraft a write-off.

5/JG27

Messerschmitt Bf 109E-8 (4906). Shot down by Pilot Officer Gilroy of No. 603 Squadron in combat over north Kent. Crashed near Pinewood Garage, London Road, Maidstone 2.00 p.m. Uffz. Gonschorrek baled out slightly wounded. Aircraft 2+ a write-off.
Pieces picked up at the time now owned by Ron Gamage.

Stab II/JG51

Messerschmitt Bf 109E-4 (5095). Shot down by RAF fighters during combat over south coast. Crashed at Fielding Land, Dymchurch 5.10 p.m. Lt. Knittel (Gruppe Adjutant) killed. Aircraft a write-off.
Major recovery by the Brenzett Aeronautical Museum in 1973. Excavations revealed all major components, cockpit controls and instruments and remains of the pilot who was buried with full military honours following statutory inquest.

4/JG51

Messerschmitt Bf 109E-4 (1420). Shot down in combat with RAF fighters over south coast 2.00 p.m. Believed crashed in sea. Fw. Dieter-John killed. Aircraft 10+ lost.

1/JG53

Messerschmitt Bf 109E-8 (6395). Crash-landed at Boulogne following fighter combat over the Channel. Pilot unhurt. Aircraft a write-off.

4/JG53

Messerschmitt Bf 109E-4 (1531). Shot down during combat with RAF fighters and crashed at North Common, Chailey, near Haywards Heath 5.00 p.m. Fw. Berg baled out and captured unhurt. Aircraft 3+ a write-off.
Site excavated by the Wealden Aviation Archaeological Group in 1973. Remains of shattered Daimler-Benz DB 601 engine and propeller boss salvaged.

Tuesday, October 29

3(F)/31

Dornier Do 17P (3553). Damaged in landing accident at Orleans following routine domestic flight. Cause not stated. No crew casualties. Aircraft 50% damaged.

5(F)/122

Junkers Ju 88A-1 (0364). Damaged in minor taxi-ing accident at Haute-Fontaine. No personnel losses. Aircraft repairable.

1/196

Arado Ar 196 (0063). Missing from sortie over North Sea (PQ8259) and presumed crashed in sea, cause unknown. Oberfw. Eich and Fw. Stamp both missing. Aircraft lost.

3/506

Heinkel He 115C (2762). Crashed on Jan Mayen Island during operational sortie. Circumstances not recorded. Crew unhurt. Aircraft a write-off.

Heinkel He 115C (2788). Crashed during operational sortie. Cause not stated. Crew unhurt. Aircraft a write-off.

Ergaenzungs Staffel JG2

Messerschmitt Bf 109E-1 (3273). Crashed and burned out near Octeville during routine training flight. Cause not stated. Pilot baled out unhurt. Aircraft a write-off.

Messerschmitt Bf 109E-4 (1451). Crashed at Manneville and burned out on local training flight. Gefr. Dietrich killed. Aircraft a write-off.

I/JG2

Messerschmitt Bf 109E-1 (4063). Damaged by AA fire during operations over the Channel and crash-landed at Cherbourg. Uffz. Bader wounded. Aircraft a write-off.

III/JG2

Messerschmitt Bf 109E-4 (3657). Shot down by AA fire during sortie over the Isle of Wight. Crashed in sea. Oblt. Wolf (Gruppe Adjutant) killed. Aircraft lost.

5/JG3

Messerschmitt Bf 109E-1 (4873). Crashed at Arques during routine local flight. Cause unknown. Oberfw. Goetz killed. Aircraft a write-off.

9/JG3

Messerschmitt Bf 109E (5341). Crashed in the Channel following combat with RAF fighters. Pilot rescued unhurt by Seenotdienst. Aircraft lost.

Messerschmitt Bf 109E-4 (5153). Forced-landed near Wootton Cross Roads, Shepherdswell, Kent 5.15 p.m. following fighter combat. Oblt. Troha (Staffel Kapitan) captured unhurt. Aircraft 5+1 a write-off.

8/JG26

Messerschmitt Bf 109E-4 (5794). Shot down by Pilot Officer Kumiega and Sergeant Hogg of No. 17 Squadron during free-lance fighter operations over England. Crashed at Marsh House Farm, Tillingham, Essex 5.00 p.m. Fw. Jaeckel baled out and captured unhurt. Aircraft 1+ a write-off.
Site investigated by London Air Museum.

Stab I/JG51

Messerschmitt Bf 109E-4 (5334). Shot down by fighters in combat over southern England. Believed crashed in the Channel. Oblt. Terry (Gruppe Adjutant) missing. Aircraft 2+ lost.

For over three decades this was the grave of Leutnant Werner Knittel. Shot down by RAF fighters on October 28, 1940, his Messerschmitt became his coffin burying him twenty-four feet down in soft ground at Burmarsh, Kent. The excavation of his aircraft and remains by the Brenzett group in September 1973 received international coverage by the news media and, for a short space of time, Werner Knittel was a celebrity acquiring greater fame thirty-three years after his death than he ever did during his thirty-nine years of life. He was buried with the other German war dead at Cannock Chase, Staffordshire — this was his original headstone (but see page 679). Personal effects are on display at the Brenzett Aeronautical Museum (Brenzett).

3/JG51

Messerschmitt Bf 109E-1 (4816). Shot down in running battle with RAF fighters during free-lance sortie over Dover. Crashed at the Gate Inn, west of Elham 5.00 p.m. Fw. Bubenhofer baled out and captured unhurt. Aircraft 13+ a write-off.

Site excavated by the Brenzett Aeronautical Museum.

4/JG51

Messerschmitt Bf 109E-4 (5370). Shot down by Flying Officer Nelson of No. 74 Squadron in combat over Kent and flew into the ground at Dodds Farm, Langton, Tunbridge Wells 5.20 p.m. Lt. Tornow killed. Aircraft 9+ a write-off.

Messerschmitt Bf 109E-1 (4828). Crashed in flames and exploded on Plummers Plain, Horsham, Sussex following combat with Pilot Officer Marsland of No. 253 Squadron. Uffz. Lenz died of injuries. Aircraft 5+ a write-off.

5/JG51

Messerschmitt Bf 109E-4 (1397). Failed to return from free-lance fighter operations over southern England and combat with enemy fighters. Fhr. Brunk missing. Aircraft 2+ lost.

6/JG52

Messerschmitt Bf 109E-7 (5933). Crashed in the Channel following combat with RAF fighters. Pilot rescued unhurt by Seenot-dienst. Aircraft lost.

I/KG1

Heinkel He 111H-3 (3296). Failed to return from bombing sortie to attack West Raynham and presumed brought down by ground defences. Oblt. Suss and two NCOs missing. Gefr. Overkaping killed. Aircraft V4+ DH lost.

III/KG1

Junkers Ju 88A-5 (2210). Crash-landed at Bapaume following combat sortie. No crew casualties. Aircraft 60% damaged.

WERNER KNITTEL
LT.
*8.7.01 + 28.10.40

EIN UNBEKANNTER
DEUTSCHER SOLDAT

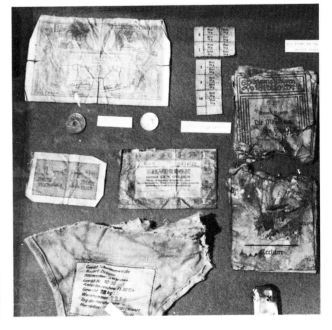

8/KG4

Junkers Ju 88A-1 (5014). Failed to return from operational sortie over England. Exact fate unknown. Oblt. zur See Schubert and three NCOs missing. Aircraft 5J+ US lost.

9/KG53

Heinkel He 111H-2 (5536). Abandoned by crew due to loss of bearings following bombing attack on Gravesend aerodrome. Crashed in River Crouch, near Parkstone Quay, Essex 1.07 a.m. Uffz. Sigger, Uffz. Klitscher, Uffz. Luedecke, Oberfw. Penzel and Oberfw. Metzger all baled out and captured unhurt. Aircraft A1+ LT lost.

II/KG77

Junkers Ju 88A-1 (6127). Crashed and burned out at Reims during routine domestic flight. Cause unknown. Oberfw. Gehring and three NCOs all killed. Aircraft 3Z+ JP a write-off.

I/LG1

Junkers Ju 88A-1 (2082). Suffered engine failure during routine local flight and crashed at Orleans-Bricy. Fw. Heyden and three NCOs killed. Aircraft a write-off.

3/LG2

Messerschmitt Bf 109E-7 (2032). Forced-landed at Wissant with combat damage following sortie over the Channel. Pilot unhurt. Aircraft 25% damaged.

4/LG2

Messerschmitt Bf 109E-4 (5593). Shot down by fighters following low-level attack on North Weald and forced-landed at Wick, near Langenhoe, Essex 5.10 p.m. Oberfw. Harmeling captured slightly wounded. Aircraft + N a write-off.

Messerschmitt Bf 109E-4 (5562). Crashed at Goldhanger, Essex 5.00 p.m. following low-level bombing attack on North Weald and running battle with RAF fighters. Fw. Rank killed. Aircraft + B a write-off.
Site investigated by Essex Aviation Research and Recovery Group 1974. Pieces of shattered Daimler-Benz DB 601 engine and propeller boss now in London Air Museum.

5/LG2

Messerschmitt Bf 109E-4 (4145). Abandoned over Langenhoe following low-level bombing of North Weald and combat with RAF fighters 5.00 p.m. Oblt. von Schenk baled out with severe head injuries and died refusing medical help. Aircraft + S a write-off.

III/ZG76

Messerschmitt Bf 110D-3 (4218). Crashed on landing at Denain aerodrome following routine domestic flight. Cause unknown. Fw. Hocheder and Obergefr. Sengbusch both killed. Aircraft a write-off.

2/Erprobungs Gruppe 210

Messerschmitt Bf 110D (3655). Crashed and burned out at St. Ingelevert due to engine failure following combat sortie. Uffz. Buettner and Fw. Troeppel both killed. Aircraft a write-off.

3/Erprobungs Gruppe 210

Messerschmitt Bf 109E-4 (2024). Shot down by Sergeant Burgess of No. 222 Squadron in running battle over Kent. Crashed on Sheerlands Farm, Pluckley 2.30 p.m. Oblt. Hintze (Staffel Kapitan) baled out and captured wounded. Aircraft 6+ a write-off.
Joint recovery by the Kent Battle of Britain Museum and the London Air Museum, April 1976. Complete Daimler-Benz DB 601 engine and propeller boss recovered and retained by the latter. Armament, various fragments and components together with aircraft identity plate confirming '2024' in the Kent Battle of Britain Museum.

Wednesday, October 30

3(F)/10

Dornier Do 17P. Damaged by AA fire during reconnaissance sortie over Dover. Returned safely to base. Oberfw. Baucks wounded. Aircraft repairable.

3(H)/14

Henschel Hs 126 (4008). Crashed at St. Pierre during operational sortie. Cause unknown. Oblt. Obenhuber and Fw. Hartmann both killed. Aircraft a write-off.

4(H)/23

Henschel Hs 126 (3293). Collided with stationary vehicle at Schiphol following routine local flight. Cause not stated. Crew unhurt. Aircraft 45% damaged.

III/JG2

Messerschmitt Bf 109E-4 (4854). Damaged by shrapnel during RAF bombing attack on Le Havre aerodrome. No personnel loss. Aircraft 10% damaged.

4/JG3

Messerschmitt Bf 109E-4 (1126). Forced-landed at Wissant damaged following fighter combat over the Channel. Pilot unhurt. Aircraft 30% damaged.

6/JG3

Messerschmitt Bf 109E-4 (6360). Shot down in fighter combat over Kent 4.15 p.m. Crashed in flames at Leylands, near Meopham. Uffz. Fahrian baled out slightly wounded. Aircraft 9+ a write-off.
Site investigated and dug by several groups including the Halstead War Museum and Kent Battle of Britain Museum but only small pieces recovered.

Messerschmitt Bf 109E-4 (1474). Crash-landed in hop field on Court Lodge Farm, East Farleigh, Kent during combat with RAF fighters. Gefr. Schuller captured wounded. Aircraft 1+ a write-off.

Ergaenzungs Staffel JG26

Messerschmitt Bf 109E-4 (1137). Crashed on take-off from St. Omer on routine local training flight. Pilot unhurt. Aircraft 20% damaged.

7/JG26

Messerschmitt Bf 109E-4 (5242). Exploded over Brook Farm, Marden during fighter action over Kent 12.00 p.m. Uffz. Toepfer killed. Aircraft 8+ a write-off.
Few fragments recovered by Lashenden Air Warfare Museum.

8/JG26

Messerschmitt Bf 109E-4 (5912). Shot down into the Channel during combat with RAF fighters. Pilot rescued unhurt. Aircraft lost.

3/JG53

Messerschmitt Bf 109E-1 (3475). Crashed near Luxembourg during routine domestic flight. Cause not stated. Pilot unhurt. Aircraft 30% damaged.

1/JG77

Messerschmitt Bf 109E-1 (3250). Crashed on landing at Marquise following combat with RAF fighters over the Channel. Pilot unhurt. Aircraft 55% damaged.

2/JG77

Messerschmitt Bf 109E-4 (2053). Forced-landed at Cap Gris-Nez damaged in fighter action over the Channel. Pilot unhurt. Aircraft 35% damaged.

2/KG3

Dornier Do 17Z-3 (2617). Abandoned by crew when fuel exhausted after operational sortie over the Channel. Crashed at Herenthal. Crew baled out unhurt. Aircraft a write-off.

3/KG4

Heinkel He 111H-4. Damaged in landing accident at Soesterberg. Exact circumstances not recorded. Crew unhurt. Aircraft 50% damaged.

Stab III/LG1

Junkers Ju 88A-5 (2199). Crashed out of fuel near Orleans. Crew baled out unhurt. Aircraft a write-off.

8/LG1

Junkers Ju 88A-1 (5008). Shot down by fighters during armed incursion raid and belly-landed at Priggs Yard, Middle Fen, Stuntney, Ely, Cambridgeshire 2.50 p.m. Uffz. Arndt., Uffz. Broehner, Obergefr. Flieger and Gefr. Kellner captured. Aircraft L1+ GS a write-off.

I/StG1

Junkers Ju 87R-1 (5541) Damaged in collision with stationary Do 215 at Brest aerodrome. Crew unhurt. Aircraft 20% damaged.

Thursday, October 31

4(H)/21

Henschel Hs 126B (3436). Crashed on landing at Theville following routine domestic flight. Cause not stated. Crew unhurt. Aircraft 20% damaged.

I/KG z.b.V.172

Junkers Ju 52 (6429). Crashed at Mlawa during routine domestic flight. Cause not stated. No crew casualties. Aircraft a write-off.

Ergaenzungs Staffel KG51

Junkers Ju 88A-1 (2116). Crash-landed on Lechfeld aerodrome following local flight. Cause not stated. Crew unhurt. Aircraft 20% damaged.

III/KG76

Dornier Do 17Z (2886). Abandoned by crew when fuel exhausted following operational sortie over England. Crashed near Sedan. Crew baled out unhurt. Aircraft a write-off.

Dornier Do 17Z (2367). Crashed at Compiegne out of fuel following combat sortie. Crew baled out unhurt. Aircraft a write-off.

I/KG77

Junkers Ju 88A-1 (2144). Crashed on take-off from Laon on operational sortie. Cause not stated. No crew casualties. Aircraft 25% damaged.

Above: Following a low-level bombing raid on North Weald on October 29 by the Messerschmitt Bf 109s of II(Schlacht)/LG2, a running fight developed between the raiders and RAF fighters. Hans Joachim Rank, a 25-year-old pilot crashed into a field beside the Goldhanger Road at Maldon. Haemorrhaging badly from a gunshot wound in the right thigh, he was conveyed to a house at No. 32A Spital Road, Maldon and then to St. Peter's Hospital but, despite medical attention, he died from his injuries and shock. *Below:* This part of Essex has changed little during the passage of thirty-nine years. Charity Farm stands in the background: a fine comparison to end this account and taken on a fitting day — September 15, 1979.

The Balance Sheet

A direct comparison of the losses suffered by both sides in the Battle of Britain is iniquitous because of the different composition of the forces involved. Whereas the Luftwaffe committed their entire air force in the west to the attack on England, the opposing British forces are generally reckoned to be the units which made up RAF Fighter Command alone. Although the seventy-one RAF units taking part were specifically named in 1960, no precise definition has ever been given by the German authorities of the Luftwaffe units involved. Nevertheless, a statistical summary of the losses in men and machines will no doubt be of interest and the Editor is indebted to Mrs. Marjorie Foreman for many hours spent meticulously compiling and correlating the following totals extracted from the chapters on *The Aircraft Losses.* While the RAF totals of personnel killed have been cross-checked with the individual graves and memorials given in the chapter on *The Casualties,* and can therefore be accepted as being one hundred per cent accurate, no such claim can be made for the Luftwaffe casualties. German records are far from complete and there is no central memorial commemorating missing aircrews similar to the one at Runnymede. Some of the German airmen who died still remain in their original place of burial in the UK whilst others have been concentrated in the German War Cemetery at Cannock Chase. (This move seems to have resulted in some confusion as at least one airman to our knowledge who was definitely missing in 1940 and whose remains have never been found now has a grave at Lichfield.) German airmen were also buried in Belgium, France, Holland, Denmark and Norway (since moved to larger area cemeteries) while the bodies of others were brought home to the Fatherland after the war. Whilst nothing is impossible, had we attempted to visit all these graves to check the details and to cross-check the thousands of German casualties in the battle, this book would have been vastly more expensive than it is and, anyway, we have got to leave something for a future German 'Johannes Holloway'! Many of the crews who were wounded but got back to the Continent may have died later so it would be fair to say that the total German

losses in personnel are certainly higher than those stated here.

As far as RAF self-inflicted losses are concerned, these were mainly suffered by Blenheim crews as this aircraft could be — and often was — mistaken for the Junkers 88. Pilot Officer D. N. Woodger and Sergeant D. L. Wright were killed on August 24, Pilot Officer D. W. Hogg on September 3 and Sergeants O. K. Sly, R. E. Stevens and AC2 A. Jackson on October 13 in attacks by friendly fighters. Sergeant R. D. Baker was reputedly shot down by a Spitfire on August 11 and anti-aircraft fire caused the deaths of Flight Lieutenant S. D. P. Connors, Flying Officer R. Hope and Sergeant F. E. R. Shepherd. (Peter Cornwell comments that there are almost certainly others where the exact cause of the loss is unrecorded.)

As a matter of interest, we have included the claims and losses announced in 1940 (set in italic type) but every listing we have consulted differs. Even on the most famous day of September 15 the claims of the number of German aircraft shot down vary from 175 (Daily Express), 183 (reported to the Prime Minister on the evening of September 15) and 185 (the Official History of the Second World War). In general, German losses were at the time greatly exaggerated but, in fairness to the Air Ministry, British losses were always honestly stated as reference to the tables below will show. This accuracy is quite remarkable bearing in mind missing pilots could have come down on the Continent or in the Channel and become PoWs without the immediate knowledge of the British authorities. No separate daily totals were issued for July as the battle was deemed at the time to have commenced on August 1. Also no figures were given for the losses of German aircrew.

Although, therefore, an overall comparison of British and German losses is unfair, a more reasonable one could possibly be provided by comparing German fighter aircraft losses with those of Fighter Command. We have therefore included a breakdown of all Bf 109 and Bf 110 losses, both in crew and aircraft, which may provide an interesting comparison of respective fighter losses in the Battle of Britain.

July

	ROYAL AIR FORCE		LUFTWAFFE		Bf 109 & 110	
	Aircrew	Aircraft	Aircrew	Aircraft	Aircrew	Aircraft
10	2	3	29	11	8	6
11	3	6	41	17	5	4
12	4	5	28	9	-	-
13	5	6	11	6	3	2
14	1	1	3	3	-	1
15	-	2	6	5	1	1
16	1	1	4	4	1	1
17	1	1	15	4	-	-
18	8	5	16	6	1	2
19	11	10	13	5	1	1
20	7	9	18	12	4	5
21	2	2	19	12	3	5
22	1	2	6	4	-	1
23	-	2	10	5	-	-
24	3	5	23	15	8	8
25	7	9	19	19	7	9
26	1	1	9	5	1	1
27	2	2	12	5	2	1
28	1	6	14	11	3	4
29	3	6	25	11	2	2
30	-	1	21	9	2	1
31	5	7	6	7	-	1
	68	92	348	185	52	56

August

	ROYAL AIR FORCE		LUFTWAFFE		Bf 109 & 110	
	Aircrew	Aircraft	Aircrew	Aircraft	Aircrew	Aircraft
1	5 *1*	4 *1*	19	13 *2*	-	1
2	1 -	3 -	16	7 -	1	1
3	- -	- -	11	6 -	-	2
4	1 -	1 -	2	2 -	-	-
5	1 *1*	2 *1*	17	8 *4*	1	2
6	1 -	6 -	9	6 *1*	4	4
7	- -	4 -	5	3 -	1	1
8	20 *13*	21 *16*	30	24 *60*	9	12
9	1 -	3 -	13	6 *1*	1	2
10	- -	- -	1	1 -	1	1
11	25 *24*	28 *26*	48	38 *60*	27	25
12	11 *12*	18 *13*	52	32 *62*	14	17
13	4 *3*	15 *13*	66	39 *78*	16	18
14	4 *5*	9 *7*	35	20 *31*	8	8
15	11 *17*	35 *34*	128	76 *180*	40	35
16	11 *8*	24 *22*	55	44 *75*	14	22
17	- -	2 -	6	5 *1*	2	2
18	10 *10*	33 *22*	97	67 *153*	28	32
19	4 *1*	5 *3*	23	11 *6*	-	1
20	1 *1*	2 *2*	11	8 *7*	2	3
21	- -	4 *1*	29	13 *13*	-	1
22	2 *2*	4 *5*	9	4 *10*	1	1
23	- -	1 -	20	8 *4*	1	1
24	10 *7*	20 *19*	46	41 *50*	10	24
25	13 *10*	18 *13*	18	22 *55*	10	15
26	7 *4*	29 *15*	46	43 *47*	16	21
27	4 -	7 -	12	11 *5*	-	3
28	10 *7*	14 *14*	46	32 *28*	3	15
29	1 *2*	10 *9*	45	24 *11*	6	10
30	9 *15*	24 *25*	57	40 *63*	9	21
31	9 *11*	38 *37*	21	39 *94*	8	29
	176 *154*	384 *298*	993	693 *1101*	233	330

September

	ROYAL AIR FORCE		LUFTWAFFE		Bf 109 & 110	
	Aircrew	Aircraft	Aircrew	Aircraft	Aircrew	Aircraft
1	6 *6*	13 *15*	15	16 *29*	4	10
2	4 *8*	14 *20*	30	35 *65*	15	25
3	6 *7*	14 *15*	21	20 *25*	6	13
4	12 *5*	17 *17*	23	25 *64*	18	22
5	8 *11*	20 *20*	37	28 *39*	8	18
6	7 *7*	20 *19*	36	33 *46*	10	21
7	16 *13*	25 *22*	52	41 *103*	13	24
8	2 *2*	5 *3*	29	16 *11*	2	3
9	6 *7*	17 *13*	38	30 *52*	14	19
10	- -	3 -	11	13 *2*	-	-
11	18 *17*	29 *24*	35	29 *93*	14	12
12	1 -	1 -	14	7 *3*	1	2
13	3 -	3 -	10	7 *2*	-	1
14	4 *3*	13 *9*	19	13 *18*	1	3
15	16 *11*	29 *25*	93	61 *185*	14	26
16	- -	1 -	14	10 *7*	-	1
17	3 *1*	6 *3*	14	8 *12*	3	4
18	3 *3*	12 *12*	36	20 *48*	4	7
19	- -	- -	22	10 *5*	-	-
20	5 *4*	8 *7*	9	8 *6*	1	3
21	1 -	1 -	14	11 *2*	-	1
22	- -	1 -	7	6 *1*	-	1
23	2 *3*	11 *11*	14	17 *12*	2	11
24	2 *2*	6 *4*	12	11 *9*	4	5
25	5 *1*	6 *4*	25	16 *26*	4	7
26	3 *3*	8 *8*	18	9 *34*	5	4
27	20 *17*	28 *34*	82	57 *133*	30	38
28	10 *7*	17 *7*	24	12 *6*	2	4
29	2 *2*	6 *4*	16	9 *10*	1	2
30	8 *10*	21 *22*	59	47 *49*	13	32
	173 *150*	355 *318*	829	625 *1097*	189	319

October

	ROYAL AIR FORCE		LUFTWAFFE		Bf 109 & 110	
	Aircrew	Aircraft	Aircrew	Aircraft	Aircrew	Aircraft
1	6 *3*	7 *3*	16	9 *5*	3	3
2	- *1*	2 *1*	24	18 *12*	4	6
3	3 -	1 -	21	9 *1*	-	-
4	1 *1*	1 *1*	32	15 *3*	-	-
5	2 *2*	7 *9*	18	15 *23*	5	10
6	2 -	2 -	16	8 *2*	2	2
7	9 *6*	17 *16*	11	19 *28*	8	16
8	8 *2*	8 *2*	32	17 *8*	-	5
9	5 -	3 *1*	18	9 *4*	2	4
10	6 *3*	8 *5*	13	12 *5*	1	5
11	4 *3*	9 *9*	17	10 *9*	-	3
12	5 *4*	11 *10*	7	13 *12*	6	10
13	3 -	4 *2*	-	6 *2*	-	3
14	1 -	1 -	1	4 -	1	1
15	6 *6*	15 *15*	12	16 *18*	4	13
16	2 -	3 -	34	15 *6*	-	2
17	5 *3*	5 *3*	11	16 *4*	3	8
18	5 -	6 -	19	14 -	3	3
19	2 -	1 -	4	6 *2*	-	-
20	5 -	5 *3*	11	11 *8*	3	7
21	2 -	2 -	10	7 *4*	2	2
22	4 *4*	6 *6*	28	12 *3*	1	3
23	1 -	1 -	5	4 -	-	-
24	3 -	3 -	21	12 *3*	3	3
25	6 *3*	14 *10*	30	24 *17*	3	15
26	4 *2*	8 *2*	19	10 *6*	2	3
27	6 *4*	14 *8*	11	16 *13*	1	8
28	- -	1 -	18	14 *6*	4	7
29	5 *2*	12 *7*	30	28 *33*	13	20
30	9 *4*	9 *5*	3	8 *9*	1	4
31	- -	- -	-	2 -	-	-
	120 *53*	186 *118*	492	379 *246*	75	166

The Survivors
BY GORDON RILEY

In any conflict of the magnitude of the Battle of Britain it is surprising to find any survivors at all, particularly when one recalls that the aircraft which fought would have been particularly early models of their respective types and that natural wastage would have taken its toll of them once the battle itself was over. Thus it is that comparatively few aircraft remain from this period and of these only one is still in airworthy condition.

When compiling this list it was necessary to decide on certain parameters with which to frame the types and examples to be included and it was decided to list only front-line combat aircraft, it seeming pointless to include a Magister for example, even if it was flying during the battle period. Of these front-line types, I have chosen to list *all* those which were in existence during the battle, even if they were undergoing major servicing at the time and did not actually *fight;* after all some probably could have been made airworthy if the need had arisen.

There are a number of aircraft, particularly in the Royal Air Force Battle of Britain Museum at Hendon, that are of the correct *type* but were built too late to fight, this being true of the Junkers Ju 87, Junkers Ju 88, Messerschmitt Bf 110 and Heinkel He 111. These have therefore been excluded. Similarly there are a number of non-combat types still in existence which did fly during the period under review, e.g. the Lysander at Hendon which operated with No. 225 Squadron on coastal and photo-reconnaissance missions, but it is felt that these are not really eligible for inclusion as they did not engage in actual *combat* with the enemy. Also there are some aeroplanes which masquerade as battle veterans, the so-called 'Blenheim' at Hendon being a Canadian-built Fairchild Bolingbroke!

Obviously there will be those who think that a particular type which is worthy of inclusion has been omitted but, on balance, I feel that the list as it stands is representative of the true combatants of the Battle of Britain.

Flying Officer James Nicolson flew K9942 on fifty-five occasions between July 22, 1939 and May 6, 1940 totalling 53¾ hours.

SUPERMARINE SPITFIRE Mk I K9942
Royal Air Force Museum, Hendon

Delivered to No. 72 Squadron, RAF Church Fenton, April 24, 1939, joining 'A' Flight of that unit. Subsequent bases included Leconfield (October 1939), Drem, Church Fenton, Acklington (on March 2, 1940) and Gravesend (on June 1, 1940). The aircraft suffered Category B damage (beyond repair on site) on June 5, 1940 when it returned to Gravesend following a patrol over Dungeness at 20,000ft and landed with the wheels up. The aircraft was transferred to No. 4 Maintenance Unit (MU) Ruislip, with effect from June 21, 1940 and the damage was repaired there by General Aircraft Limited. K9942 was then dispatched to No. 6 MU at Brize Norton before joining No. 57 Operational Training Unit (OTU) at Hawarden on August 17, 1940.

K9942 served with this unit until February 6, 1942 when it was once again declared Category B. Repairs were commenced one week later on February 13 and the aircraft was awaiting collection by September 10, being delivered to No. 33 MU at Lyneham thirteen days later. By April 10, 1943 it was on charge with No. 53 OTU at Kirton-in-Lindsey where it suffered Category B damage for a third time on October 22. Following repairs it was again issued to No. 33 MU on March 3, 1944 and moved to No. 82 MU at Lichfield on May 15. By August 28 it had been allocated for museum purposes and passed to No. 52 MU at Cardiff.

It moved to No. 58 MU at Newark in September 1951 and later appeared in static displays on Horse Guards Parade, Whitehall, during various Battle of Britain Week celebrations before passing to No. 71 MU at Bicester which used it as a travelling exhibit before refurbishing it in its original No. 72 Squadron markings and codes which it bears today. It was finally installed in the Royal Air Force Museum, Hendon on November 9, 1971.

SUPERMARINE SPITFIRE Mk I P9306
Museum of Science & Industry, Chicago, Illinois, USA

Taken on strength by the RAF on January 20, 1940, the operational life of this aircraft began on July 9 with its transfer to No. 74 'Tiger' Squadron based at Hornchurch. From the first day of the Battle of Britain it was in action and during an interception on July 10, flying from the forward aerodrome at Manston, Pilot Officer P. C. F. Stevenson destroyed one Messerschmitt Bf 109E, damaging another and, on a later sortie the same day, damaged two Bf 110s.

During its service life with the squadron, it flew patrols and interceptions from both Hornchurch and Manston, on July 20 flying five separate sorties from the forward 'drome. Among the many pilots who flew her one became a legend within the service, Flight Lieutenant Adolph Gysbert 'Sailor' Malan;

SUPERMARINE SPITFIRE Mk I P9444
Science Museum, South Kensington

This Spitfire was delivered to the Royal Aircraft Establishment at Farnborough, Hampshire, on April 5, 1940 but by May 23, 1940 it was on charge with No. 6 MU at Brize Norton from where it was delivered to No. 72 Squadron on June 4. It was badly damaged in a crash-landing on July 3 and was taken to No. 1 Civilian Repair Unit (CRU) for rectification on July 12. The work seems to have taken some considerable time as it was not re-issued to No. 45 MU, Kinloss until March 14, 1941. It was transferred to No. 58 OTU on July 4 but it was soon involved in further damage, which was repaired on site between August 19-23, 1941, re-entering service with the same unit. Further damage was done to the aircraft on December 17 when it was declared Category Ac (beyond local repair). It was, however, repaired on site and was back in service by December 20. On May 5, 1942 it suffered once more and this time was declared Category B but the work was done and the aircraft ready for collection by June 13. It was taken to No. 8 MU, Little Rissington, by June 18 and was issued to No. 61 OTU on August 5.

P9444 managed to escape further misfortune until January 30, 1943 when another accident caused it to be declared

Although P9306 was withdrawn from active service in 1941, it is now displayed with C and C1 pattern roundels of the 1942-47 period.

Category B once again. Air Service Training and others like Pilot Officers D. G. Cobden and P. C. B. St. John flew the aircraft fairly regularly. On August 11 Sergeant T. B. Kirk destroyed a Bf 110 off Clacton while flying P9306. Only three weeks before he had flown practice flights on the same aircraft as a replacement pilot!

With the various movements of the squadron, P9306 flew from a number of bases: Wittering, Kirton-in-Lindsey, Coltishall, Duxford and Martlesham. While at Kirton it was flown by Pilot Officer B. V. Draper on August 29 during the filming of a documentary on the activities of an RAF fighter squadron for the *March of Time* series promoted by the editors of *Life* and *Time* magazines.

From September 17, 1940 until July 17,

1941, the aircraft was out of service with various maintenance units. It went to No. 54 MU, Cambridge on the 17th and was transferred to No. 4 MU twelve days later. On December 7 it went to No. 45 MU before being re-issued to No. 131 Squadron in July 1941. In October it transferred to No. 52 OTU and had an uneventful career for the next fifteen months before Category B damage necessitated repairs at Westland's and No. 33 MU before moving to No. 61 OTU on May 4, 1943. It suffered one accident on September 23 and was repaired on site. From January to August 1944, P9306 spent time in various MUs before being allocated to the Chicago museum for exhibition purposes. The aircraft was shipped via New York the following month and went on permanent display in 1944.

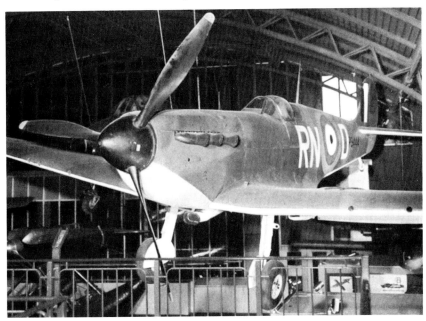

P9444 was non-operational during the accepted period of the Battle of Britain undergoing repairs to an accident suffered on July 3.

709

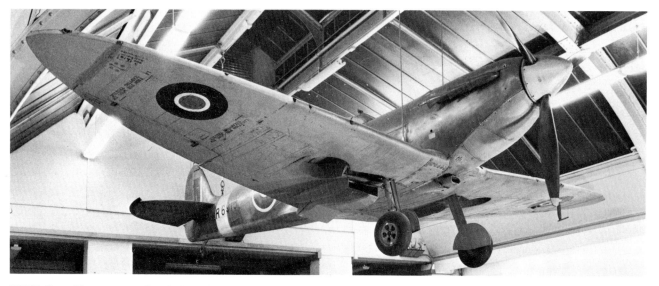

R6915 flew fifty-seven sorties during the battle with thirteen different pilots. One Bf 109, two Bf 110s and one He 111 are credited to Pilot Officer Noel Agazarian and one Bf 110 to Flying Officer John Dundas. Six other aircraft are claimed as damaged.

Limited took it away for repair at Hamble on February 7 and it was complete by March 29, arriving at No. 12 MU Kirkbride on March 31 where it was stored until issued to No. 53 OTU on May 12. Another Category B accident soon followed and Scottish Aviation took it in for repair between November 14, 1943 and February 18, 1944. It then passed through a chain of MUs, Nos. 39, 82 and 52, before being allocated for display purposes on August 28, 1949. It made its first public appearance on Horse Guards Parade in 1949 and then moved to No. 58 MU at Newark in 1951, being allocated to the Science Museum and moved to their store at Sydenham on December 16, 1954. It was restored in No. 72 Squadron markings in 1961 and put on display in the new aviation hall in 1963.

SUPERMARINE SPITFIRE Mk I R6915
Imperial War Museum, South Lambeth

Built at Southampton by Vickers-Supermarine, R6915 was delivered to No. 6 MU Little Rissington on July 11, 1940 and was passed on to 'B' Flight Blue Section of No. 609 Squadron coded PR-U ten days later. Following presumed operational damage, the aircraft was delivered to No. 1 Civilian Repair Unit on October 14 and then to No. 12 MU at Kirkbride on December 12. On January 21, 1941 it went to No. 602 Squadron until it joined No. 61 OTU on July 6 and as from July 22 it was officially on charge with No. 43 Group. One week later, on July 29, R6915 was with General Aircraft Limited at Hanworth and records show that on October 2 it was on charge with No. 45 MU, Kinloss and then with No. 5 MU at Kemble! By April 2, 1942 it was in the hands of No. 1 CRU once again and was awaiting collection from that unit on April 15 being delivered to No. 6 MU on April 28 before passing back to No. 61 OTU on June 21. The aircraft survived another ten months without further mishap before becoming involved in a flying accident on April 20, 1943. Repairs are thought to have been effected on site and on June 13 it joined No. 57 OTU receiving further damage as a result of a flying accident on September 21. The damage was repaired by December 10 and fifteen days later it was delivered to No. 39 MU at Colerne. Leaving that unit for a few weeks in the early part of 1944, it was back at Colerne by February 24.

R6915 then moved to Lichfield with No. 82 MU on May 10, 1944 and thence to Cardiff with No. 52 MU on August 25. It was handed over to the Imperial War Museum on August 26, 1946 and struck off charge on June 21, 1947. (Note the 1942-47 pattern roundels.)

SUPERMARINE SPITFIRE Mk I X4590
Royal Air Force Battle of Britain Museum, Hendon

Taken on official charge on September 22, 1940, X4590 was delivered to No. 609 Squadron at Warmwell on October 8. While being flown by Pilot Officer S. J. Hill of that unit, it had a half share in shooting down a Junkers Ju 88 on October 21, the aircraft being mainly involved with flying interceptor patrols at that time. Four days later it suffered damage while being flown by Pilot Officer Hill. On February 24, 1941 the aircraft was transferred to No. 66 Squadron at Exeter from where it carried out interception and convoy patrols before being moved to No. 57 OTU on April 7, 1941 and then on to No. 303 Squadron at Speke on July 18. On July 24, the aircraft was posted, on paper at least, to No. 43 Group Disposal Account as surplus to requirements and was dispatched to Scottish Aviation Limited on July 30 for repairs which were complete by October 31 when it was delivered to No. 37 MU, Burtonwood.

After some time in store the aircraft was allocated on February 14, 1942, to No. 53 OTU but suffered further damage only two days later. Repairs were effected locally and it was back on strength by August 8. Another accident on or about March 9, 1943 put it in the shop once again but it was restored to its unit on April 19. The life at the OTU was obviously a hard one as another mishap on October 4 was recorded as Category B 'Repair in Workshops' and it was not ready for collection again until February 18, 1944 by which time a Mk I Spitfire was an antique indeed. It was sent to No. 3 MU, Milton on March 20 and then to No. 82 MU, Lichfield on May 16 before being allocated to No. 52 MU, Cardiff on August 28, 1944 for museum purposes. At some later and unknown date it was allocated to the Exhibition Flight at Bicester and eventually handed over to the RAF Museum, being displayed at the Cosford Aerospace Museum prior to its installation in the Battle of Britain Museum in 1978.

SUPERMARINE SPITFIRE Mk II P7350
Royal Air Force Battle of Britain Memorial Flight, RAF Coningsby

This aircraft was ordered by the Air Ministry from the Nuffield Organisation against Contract No. 981687/39 dated April 12, 1938 and was built at the Castle Bromwich 'shadow factory' with fuselage number CBAF 14, indicating that it was the fourteenth of the 11,939 Spitfires which were eventually built there. It was test flown in August 1940 and taken on Air Ministry charge on August 13, being delivered to No. 6 MU at Brize Norton on August 17 against Allotment Number 11190.

In November 1978, the Battle of Britain Museum was opened beside the RAF Museum at Hendon. Of the fourteen aircraft on display, only Spitfire X4590 (in the foreground *below*) and Messerschmitt Bf 109E-3/B *(overleaf)* can claim to have seen action during the period of the battle. The other exhibits (especially four of the German aircraft) while of the correct type, were constructed later in the war. The Hurricane P2617 in the second pen is included in this chapter as a survivor but was undergoing repairs from May 29 to November 21, 1940. The blast pen is a slightly-reduced scale representation of the real thing as a full sized E-pen could not be fitted into the layout. The bell, dated 1940, came from RAF Biggin Hill.

It was delivered to No. 266 (Rhodesia) Squadron at Wittering on September 6 and issued with code letters UO-T, the unit later moving to Hornchurch, but on October 17 it was transferred to No. 603 (City of Edinburgh) Squadron of the Auxiliary Air Force and the codes were changed to XT- . Whilst in service with this unit it suffered a Category B flying accident on October 31 and was sent to No. 1 CRU at Cowley for repairs which were complete by November 15 when it was transferred to No. 37 MU at Burtonwood for storage.

Its next operational unit was No. 616 'County of South Yorkshire' Squadron, another Auxiliary Air Force squadron, to which it was issued on March 18, 1941 but less than a month was to pass before it was transferred to No. 64 Squadron on April 10. August 5 saw the aircraft transferred to Scottish Aviation at Prestwick for overhaul and repair and it was eventually sent to No. 37 MU once again on January 29, 1942.

On April 27, P7350 was issued to the Central Gunnery School at RAF Sutton Bridge where it passed an uneventful ten months before suffering another Category B flying accident on February 4, 1943 necessitating its transfer to Air Service Training for repair. The repairs were completed by March 20 and three days later it arrived at No. 6 MU Brize Norton. On March 31 it was issued to No. 57 OTU with which unit it passed the next twelve months before falling foul of yet another Category B flying accident on April 22, 1944. Air Service Training Limited collected it for repairs on April 30 and these were complete and the aircraft awaiting collection on July 13. Eleven days later it was transferred to No. 39 MU at Colerne for storage.

It was noted 'on charge' at Colerne in the Air Ministry Home Census of Aircraft on March 21, 1946 and the following year was transferred to non-effective stock prior to its sale to Messrs John Dale Limited, a firm of scrap merchants. When the company received the log books they realised the historical importance of this particular Spitfire and presented it to RAF Colerne as a museum piece.

The aircraft remained at Colerne until 1967 as part of what eventually became a very extensive aircraft museum which was finally disbanded as a result of defence spending cuts when the base was closed in the mid-1970s. However, in 1967, Spitfire Productions Limited were looking for suitable aircraft to use in the film Battle of Britain and P7350 was delivered to RAF Henlow by road. Late in the year it was surveyed by John Simpson of Simpsons Aeroservices Limited and the

airframe, engine and propeller were all found to be in excellent condition. As a result of the inspection, an overhaul was commenced in April 1968 and on May 20, 1968 it flew from Henlow to Duxford in the hands of Squadron Leader M. A. Vickers — its first sortie for over twenty-four years.

Bearing the civil registration G-AWIJ, P7350 was issued with a Restricted Category Certificate of Airworthiness and flown at Duxford, Debden, Hawkinge, Sywell and Panshanger as well as other film location airfields. On August 11, 1968, Flight Lieutenant R. B. Lloyd took it to the south of France (Duxford-Deauville-Nantes-Bordeaux-Montpelier and return) for filming purposes due to the atrocious English summer weather.

On September 24, the Rolls-Royce Merlin XII No. 12313, which had been fitted since at least 1944, was found to have metal in the oil filters and was declared unfit for flying purposes. A Merlin 35, No. 204573/A.510174, was installed at Duxford and the Spit flown to Bovingdon for the final film rundown.

In October 1968 it was allocated to the RAF Battle of Britain Memorial Flight and flown from Bovingdon to Coltishall by Squadron Leader Mills. On April 28, 1969 it was dispatched to No. 5 MU Kemble for stripping and respray, returning to Coltishall on June 12 in the hands of Squadron Leader Stuart Paul, bearing the post-Battle of Britain codes ZH-T of No. 266 Squadron. It has since appeared in a variety of colours and codes, reflecting the policy of the Memorial Flight of repainting the aircraft after each major overhaul. Its three-blade propeller has now also given way to a four-blader.

HAWKER HURRICANE Mk I L1592
Science Museum, South Kensington

Built in 1938, this particular Hurricane is one of the first batch of fifty production aircraft ordered for the Royal Air Force and was initially delivered to No. 56 Squadron. Its second and final unit was No. 615 'County of Surrey' Squadron with which it received the code letters KW-Z which it still bears today. It had a very short service life as, on August 18, in the height of the Battle of Britain, it was attacked by a Bf 109 and crash-landed at Croydon. As far as is known it never flew again (although it appeared as a static US-N in the film Angels One Five in 1952) and it was eventually allocated to the Science Museum, being refurbished by Hawkers before being placed on display in the enlarged aviation gallery in 1963.

HAWKER HURRICANE Mk I P2617
Royal Air Force Battle of Britain Museum, Hendon

Built under contract by the Gloster Aircraft Company, this Hurricane was delivered to No. 20 MU at Aston Down on January 19, 1940 and moved to No. 6 MU at Brize Norton on February 24. According to the official records it was allocated to both No. 615 Squadron *and* to No. 1 Repair & Salvage Unit on April 14 but the next day it was with No. 607 Squadron flying in the Battle of France, rapidly suffering Category B damage in a flying accident and was dispatched to No. 4 MU Ruislip for repair on May 29. P2617 missed the Battle of Britain as it was undergoing repairs and was not issued to No. 1 (Canadian) Squadron until November 21.

It is believed to have moved from that unit back to Glosters but was issued to No. 15 MU at Wroughton on March 29, 1941 and then on to Kemble with No. 5 MU on May 4. No. 9 Flying Training School (FTS) took the aircraft on charge on July 31, 1941. It passed to No. 9 SFTS on December 6, No. 8 FTS from January 10, 1942 and then back to No. 9 SFTS on March 9. It was with this unit on May 9 that it suffered a Category Ac flying accident and a team from Hawkers arrived five days later to effect repairs which enabled it to return to flying duties from May 23. The aircraft suffered two more accidents and was retired from flying duties on August 21 the following year with its delivery to No. 22 MU at Silloth. It moved to No. 52 MU, Cardiff on August 6, 1944 and then on to No. 76 MU Wroughton for 'museum storage'.

In 1952, it appeared in *Angels One Five* coded US-B. The aircraft was taken on charge by No. 71 MU, Bicester in the early 1960s and used as a travelling exhibit until honourably retired to the Royal Air Force Museum, Hendon in 1972 where it graced the Sydney Camm Hall until it moved to the new Battle of Britain Museum in 1978.

MESSERSCHMITT Bf 109E-3 1190
Privately owned, Bournemouth, Dorset

This Messerschmitt was built at Leipzig in 1939 by Erla Maschinenwerk and was operated by the 4th Staffel of Jagdgeschwader 26 (4/JG26) based at Marquise-Ost. The aircraft carried a white figure 4 with black outline and had previously carried the double-chevron insignia of a Gruppen Kommandeur — believed to have been Hauptmann Karl Ebbighausen of II/JG26. Five of Ebbighausen's victory markings appeared on

Hurricane L1592 before its installation in the Aviation Gallery at the Science Museum.

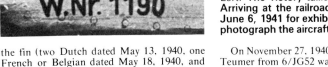

the fin (two Dutch dated May 13, 1940, one French or Belgian dated May 18, 1940, and two RAF dated May 25 and June 14, 1940).

The aircraft was being flown by Unter-offizier Horst Perez on September 30, 1940 when it was attacked by Hurricanes over Beachy Head, later belly-landing in a field at Eastdean, Sussex with only superficial damage. It was taken to the Royal Aircraft Establishment and was later dispatched to the United States and Canada where it was used for exhibition purposes in connection with the 'Bundles for Britain' campaign. It arrived by sea in Nova Scotia early in 1941 and the following June is known to have been exhibited in the New York area.

At the end of hostilities it was delivered to the Arnprior Research Establishment in Ontario and in November 1966 it returned to the UK for restoration at Hurn Airport near Bournemouth.

MESSERSCHMITT Bf 109E-3/B 4101
Royal Air Force Battle of Britain Museum, Hendon

The E sub-type of the Bf 109 was nicknamed 'Emil' by the Luftwaffe and entered service in December 1938. Deliveries of the E-3 variant began in the summer of 1940.

This Bf 109E-3/B, a fighter-bomber version, was built by the Erla Maschinenwerk at Leipzig and was first used by the 6th Staffel of Jadgeschwader 52 (6/JG52). It later went to the 2nd Staffel of Jagdgeschwader 51 (2/JG51) based at Wissant and evidently saw operational use during the Battle of Britain. Its conversion to the fighter-bomber con-figuration is believed to have been undertaken in the field.

On November 27, 1940, Leutnant Wolfgang Teumer from 6/JG52 was flying 4101 over the Thames estuary when he was attacked by three Spitfires. He jettisoned his 250kg (550lb) bomb into the water, but one of the Spitfires scored hits on the Messerschmitt, damaging the radiator and cooling system. Teumer was obliged to make a wheels-up landing at RAF Manston and was made prisoner.

His aircraft was repaired and made air-worthy by using serviceable components from other captured Bf 109s. In RAF markings, and with the British serial number DG200, it

was extensively flown for evaluation purposes, notably at the Royal Aircraft Establishment, Farnborough; by Rolls-Royce at Hucknall; at Hatfield and at the Aircraft and Armament Experimental Establishment, Boscombe Down. It was transported to No. 1426 Enemy Aircraft Flight at Duxford in 1942 for further flight testing.

The aircraft is now exhibited in what is believed to be a close approximation to its original colour scheme apart from the badge of I/JG51, which was not originally worn but appeared on other aircraft of the Gruppe.

The only one of Manston's six 'kills' which has survived is the Bf 109 which landed on November 27, 1940. *Above:* **Pictured as DG200 when allocated to the Director General Research and Development at Rolls-Royce at Hucknall in 1941 and** *below* **as it is today on display at Hendon (Rolls-Royce and S. G. Richards).**

The Battle of Britain Memorial Flight

On September 15, 1945, three hundred RAF fighters led an impressive ninety-minute fly-past over London. Led by Group Captain Douglas Bader, aircraft from twenty-five squadrons of Fighter and Coastal Command took part including Spitfires, Mustangs, Typhoons, Tempests, Beaufighters, Mosquitos and Meteors. On the same day, some ninety Royal Air Force aerodromes were opened to the public for the first time since the Empire Air Day in 1939. The list of stations comprised twenty-one from Flying Training Command, seventeen from Transport Command, sixteen from Bomber Command, twelve from Fighter Command, eleven from Technical Training Command, ten from Coastal Command and three from Maintenance Command. Thereafter, both the fly-past, led by the immortal Spitfire and Hurricane, and the Battle of Britain open days became annual events

By 1947 the number of stations open on Battle of Britain Day had slightly fallen to seventy-five but still catering for the public in every corner of the country. However, by 1963 and the post war run down of the service, the number had dropped to fifteen. The following year it was down to twelve, in 1971 it was seven, in 1974 three and in 1978 only two airfields, Abingdon and St. Athan, held official Battle of Britain Open Days.

The participation of the traditional Spitfire and Hurricane in the London fly-past was stopped amid much protest in 1959 after the Spitfire forced-landed on a cricket pitch and the fly-past itself was discontinued after the one on September 17, 1961.

Today the Royal Air Force's Battle of Britain Memorial Flight remains as the only aerial tribute to the battle. The Flight was first formed at Biggin Hill in 1957

Left: On September 15, 1945 the first of the 'Battle of Britain' Day anniversary fly-pasts took place over London. Outside No. 1 hangar at North Weald, twelve Spitfires piloted by veterans of the battle prepare to take off for the occasion led by Group Captain

Douglas Bader (Radio Times). *Right:* Where yesterday's heroes waited to commemorate their fallen brethren in an aerial tribute, the long nosed Spitfires have been replaced by a long-nosed saloon car. The hangar is now used for industrial storage.

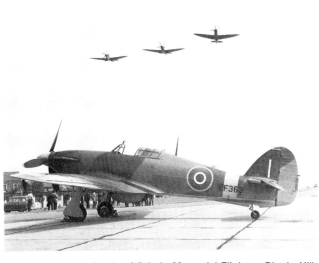

Formation of the Battle of Britain Memorial Flight at Biggin Hill. On July 11, 1957, the three airworthy Spitfires then remaining in the Royal Air Force were flown to Biggin to join the sole Hurricane on the Flight (Keystone).

The saluting base for the annual Battle of Britain fly pasts over London was the Royal Air Force Memorial on Victoria Embankment. Air Chief-Marshal Lord Dowding is pictured at the poorly attended service on September 15, 1958 (Popperfoto).

SL574 comes to grief on September 20, 1959 (Press Association).

and provided the aircraft for the annual London fly-past until the 1959 crash. Thereafter its flying activities have been limited to air displays or special events and all flying is carried out under increasingly severe restrictions. The Memorial Flight has seen several changes of station during its twenty-three years of existence, being based at North Weald, Martlesham Heath, Coltishall and, currently, at RAF Coningsby.

Today the unit has only one genuine Battle of Britain vintage aeroplane and it is the only flying example in the world of all the aircraft which fought in the battle. For forty years the sound of the Merlin has thrilled and excited and is synonymous with 1940. When you next hear *this* particular aircraft — Spitfire P7350 — the last living memorial, spare a thought for all those who fought and died for us in the Battle for Britain.

'The gratitude of every home in our Island, in our
Empire, and indeed throughout the world, except in the
abodes of the guilty, goes out to the British airmen who,
undaunted by odds, unwearied in their constant
challenge and mortal danger, are turning the tide of
world war by their prowess and by their devotion.
Never in the field of human conflict was so much owed
by so many to so few.'

Winston Churchill, House of Commons, August 20, 1940.

Addenda

With the long production period of a book of this size and complexity, it was inevitable that additional information would come to light after pages were passed for press.

PAGE 55. Hauptmann Walter Rubensdoerffer's crewman has now been established as Obergefreiter Kretzer — see page 571 of aircraft losses for August 15. Peter Cornwell suggests that the Feldwebel Richard Ehekercher, frequently referred to as crewman, was brought about by some misinterpretation or corruption of details available at the time of the crash.

PAGE 172. The German unit carrying out the attack on North Weald on October 29 was not 3/Erprobungs Gruppe 210 as stated but 4/LG2. Several previously published sources state the former but reference to page 704 of Peter Cornwell's aircraft losses for October 29 confirms 4/LG2. Note therefore that Otto Hintze of 3/Erprobungs Gruppe 210 did not lead this raid but a sortie over Kent during which he was shot down at Sheerlands Farm, Pluckley.

PAGE 255. The following reply has been received from the historian at the Naval Historical Branch of the Ministry of Defence concerning the codes allocated to Royal Navy squadrons, in particular Nos. 804 and 808:
'The form of side letter codes employed by the Royal Navy for its aircraft during the 1939-44 period of the Second World War was related to the ship, the squadrons allocated to that ship and the aircraft within the squadron. By the spring of 1940, few front-line aircraft wore the initial letter indicating the carrier ('A' for ARK ROYAL, 'L' for ILLUSTRIOUS, etc) and all that then appeared was the numeral indicating the squadron (1-9) and the individual letter for the aircraft. I believe, but am unable to substantiate, that 804 and 808 were both "5"'s, the former black and the latter red, with a different range of letters for each (with 21 aircraft and 24 usable letters this was possible), and codes would appear as "5-A" or "5-D", etc.'
Also please note that the losses in aircrew suffered by No. 604 Squadron should read 3.

PAGE 259. RAF Casualties on August 13 should read 4 — totals are correct.

PAGE 275. The following spelling correction has been received from the Etat-Major de la Force Aerienne of Belgium in Brussels: van den Hove d'ERTSENRYCK should be spelt ERTSENRIJCK. His full Christian names were Albert Emmanuel Alix Dieudonne Jean Ghislain. This pilot's name also appears several times in *The Aircraft Losses*.

PAGE 308. The Tangmere Memorial Museum is now hoped to open sometime in 1981 with the new title of the Tangmere Museum of Military Aviation at Goodwood.

PAGE 397. The grave of the unknown airman in All Saints Churchyard at Staplehurst, the headstone of which is cryptically dated September 1940 (see illustration), is now believed to be that of Flight Lieutenant F. W. Rushmer of No. 603 Squadron reported missing on September 5. The entry in the burial register states that fragmentary remains were buried on September 11 of an airman killed due to enemy action on September 5. Body recovered in the parish of Smarden.

PAGE 430. The BBC TV Programme on the recovery of Flight Lieutenant Hugh Beresford's aircraft is now simply to be titled 'Missing' and the one-hour documentary will be televised in September 1980.

PAGE 553. In the entry under Saturday, August 3 for III/JG27 the pilot has now been named as Fhr. Kargel who was injured in the crash landing at Cherbourg.

PAGE 716. Winston Churchill first spoke the words which have now become synonymous with the Battle of Britain in a review of the progress of the war to the House of Commons in the afternoon of Tuesday, August 20, 1940. We have reproduced the text as given in Hansard for there was no sound recording made at the time. On May 13, 1945, in a broadcast on the Home Service of the BBC at 9.00 p.m., The Right Hon. Winston Churchill included the following in his description of the previous five years conflict: 'In July, August and September 1940, forty or fifty squadrons of British fighter aircraft in the Battle of Britain broke the teeth of the German air fleet at odds of seven or eight to one. May I repeat again the words I used at that momentous hour: "Never in the field of human conflict was so much owed by so many to so few." With the omission of the beginning of the second sentence, this is the version available on several sound recordings today.

LIST OF V.C. WON BY AIRMEN.

32 AIRMEN AWARDED V.C. FOR AERIAL OPS., DURING 1939-45; 4 WENT TO MEN OF THE MARITIME AIR STRUGGLE.

Addenda

F/O LLOYD ALLAN TRIGG. VC. DFC RNZAF 200 SQN. (POSTUMOUS) SUNK U-468. COMMANDED BY OBERLEUTANT ZUR SEE CLEMENS SCHAMONG. VC 2 NOV 43.

FLTLT DAVID ERNEST HORNELL VC RCAF 162 SQN (POSTUMOUS) SUNK U-1225. VC 24 JUL 44.

F/O KENNETH CAMPBELL (SCOT) VC 22 SQN (POSTUMOUS). TORPEDOD THE "GNEISENAU" IN BREST HARBOUR. VC 13 MAR 42.

FLTLT JOHN ALEXANDER CRUICKSHANK (SCOT) VC 210 SQN. SUNK U-347. VC 21 SEP 44

F/O DE GARLAND & SGT T GRAY VC's (BOTH POSTUMOUS) 12 SQN. FLYING "BATTLE" A/C ON AN ATTACK ON THE BRIDGE AT VELDWEZELT 14 MAY 40